Gabrielle Kremer – Eduard Pollhammer – Julia Kopf – Franziska Beutler (Hrsg.)

# ZEIT(EN) DES UMBRUCHS

Akten des 17. Internationalen Kolloquiums zum provinzialrömischen Kunstschaffen
Wien – Carnuntum, 16.–21. Mai 2022

Veröffentlichungen aus den Landessammlungen Niederösterreich
Nr. 7

Gabrielle Kremer – Eduard Pollhammer – Julia Kopf – Franziska Beutler (Hrsg.)

# ZEIT(EN) DES UMBRUCHS

Akten des 17. Internationalen Kolloquiums
zum provinzialrömischen Kunstschaffen
Wien – Carnuntum, 16.–21. Mai 2022

Österreichisches Archäologisches Institut
Sonderschriften Band 64

**Herausgeber**
Österreichisches Archäologisches Institut
Reihenherausgabe: Sabine Ladstätter, Martin Steskal, Alice Waldner, Barbara Beck-Brandt
Dominikanerbastei 16
A-1010 Wien
<www.oeaw.ac.at/oeai/>

Das Österreichische Archäologische Institut ist eine Forschungseinrichtung der
Österreichischen Akademie der Wissenschaften

Veröffentlichungen aus den Landessammlungen
Niederösterreich, Nr. 7
Herausgegeben von Armin Laussegger

Gedruckt mit Unterstützung des Landes Niederösterreich

Eigentümer & Verleger
Verlag Holzhausen GmbH
Traungasse 14–16
A-1030 Wien
<https://shop.verlagholzhausen.at/collections/archaeologia>

**HOLZHAUSEN**
— *Der Verlag* —

Lektorat und Redaktion: Barbara Beck-Brandt, Franziska Beutler, Julia Kopf, Gabrielle Kremer, Wien
Englisches Lektorat: Sarah Homan-Cormack, Wien
Satz und Layout: Andrea Sulzgruber, Wien

Alle Rechte vorbehalten
1. Auflage 2024
Verlagsort: Wien – Printed in Austria

Die verwendete Papiersorte ist aus chlorfrei gebleichtem Zellstoff hergestellt, frei von säurebildenden Bestandteilen und alterungsbeständig.
ISSN 1998-8931
ISBN 978-3-903207-86-8

Copyright © 2024
Verlag Holzhausen GmbH

Bibliografische Information der Österreichischen Nationalbibliothek und der Deutschen Nationalbibliothek: Die ÖNB und die DNB verzeichnen diese Publikation in den Nationalbibliografien; detaillierte bibliografische Daten sind im Internet abrufbar. Für die Österreichische Bibliothek: <https://onb.ac.at>, für die Deutsche Bibliothek: <http://dnb.dnb.de>.
Alle Rechte, insbesondere das Recht der Vervielfältigung und Verbreitung sowie der Übersetzung, sind dem Verlag vorbehalten. Kein Teil des Werks darf in irgendeiner Form (durch Fotokopie, Mikrofilm oder ein anderes Verfahren) ohne schriftliche Genehmigung des Verlags reproduziert oder unter Verwendung elektronischer Systeme gespeichert, verarbeitet, vervielfältigt oder verbreitet werden.

# INHALT

Vorwort ................................................................................................................ 9

*Isabel Rodà de Llanza*
Keynote lecture: Roman sculpture as a multidisciplinary research focus ...................... 11

**Methoden der Forschung**

*Erich Draganits – Beatrix Moshammer – Gabrielle Kremer – Andreas Rohatsch – Michael Doneus*
Die Steinbruchlandschaft von Bad Deutsch-Altenburg (Ostösterreich). Eine Rohstoffquelle seit der Römerzeit ................................................................................................ 31

*Roland Dreesen – Eric Goemaere – Gabrielle Kremer*
Provenance analysis of the natural stones in funerary monuments from the western part of the *civitas Treverorum* ........................................................................................... 43

*Anique Hamelink – Nicolas Delferrière – Ursula Rothe*
Polychromie auf Porträtgrabsteinen: *clavi* auf gallischer Kleidung? ........................... 51

*Sophie Insulander*
Prokonnesian marble in the architecture of imperial *Ephesos*. Attempting an archaeological evaluation ...................................................................................... 63

*Stephan Karl – Paul Bayer – Kerstin Bauer*
The Roman stone monuments of Seggau Castle revisited. On the potential of the spatial recording and analysis of ancient stone monuments ....................................... 71

*Veselka Katsarova – Vasiliki Anevlavi – Sabine Ladstätter – Walter Prochaska*
Roman sculptures from Kasnakovo, Bulgaria. Archaeological and archaeometric investigations ...................................................................................................... 89

*Gabrielle Kremer – Robert Linke – Georg Plattner – Eduard Pollhammer – Marina Brzakovic – Robert Krickl – Nirvana Silnović*
Colours revealed: First results on a polychrome Mithras relief from *Carnuntum* ........... 101

*Sébastien Laratte – Véronique Brunet-Gaston – Christophe Gaston – Régis Bontrond – Céline Schneider – Gilles Fronteau – Patrick Huard*
L'Arc de Mars à Reims: modèle 3D et SIG ............................................................. 111

*Alexandra S. Rodler-Rørbo – Barbara Tober*
Colourful walls of *Noricum*. Mineral pigment characterization for provenance evaluation ........................................................................................................... 123

## Zeiten des Umbruchs: Denkmäler der fortgeschrittenen Kaiserzeit und Spätantike

*Cristina-Georgeta Alexandrescu*
Late Roman funerary monuments from *Scythia* ..................................................... 133

*Stefan Ardeleanu*
Ritualized funerary *mensae* of the western late antique world. Typology and use
spectrum between micro-regional and global trends .................................................. 145

*Luca Bianchi*
Un'ultima testimonianza di arte romana di stato a *Mursa* ........................................ 163

*Lorenzo Cigaina*
Zirkus und *spectacula* im spätantiken *Aquileia*. Stadtrömische Einflüsse und
provinziale Rückflüsse am Befund einiger Steindenkmäler ...................................... 175

*Montserrat Claveria*
The sarcophagus of Covarrubias (Burgos, Spain). Images of eternity between
paganism and Christianity ........................................................................................ 189

*Maria-Pia Darblade-Audoin*
Les hermès de Welschbillig. Style et technique au IVe siècle dans le Nord des Gaules .... 199

*Nicolas Delferrière – Anne-Laure Edme*
Le sarcophage romain de Mantoche conservé au musée Baron Martin de Gray
(Haute-Saône, France). Un exemple atypique en Gaule du Centre-Est ....................... 211

*Anne-Laure Edme*
»Time of change«: Le traitement des monuments païens à l'heure de l'essor du
christianisme ............................................................................................................ 221

*Nadežda Gavrilović Vitas*
Late antique mythological statuary in the Roman Central Balkans. Its function and
meaning .................................................................................................................... 235

*Stylianos E. Katakis*
The twilight of the Asklepios cult in Epidauros. The evidence of the building activity,
inscriptions, and sculptures ...................................................................................... 249

*Panagiotis Konstantinidis*
Religious syncretism in late Roman *Achaea*. Reconsidering the identity of
»Isthmia IS 445« ....................................................................................................... 263

*Aleksandra Nikoloska*
Statuary collections from the late antique residences in *Stobi* ................................. 277

## Neue Funde und Forschungen

*Jeanine Abdul Massih – Frédéric Alpi – Zeina Fani Alpi*
*Cyrrhus*, place militaire de l'armée romaine en Syrie du Nord. Indices archéologiques,
épigraphiques et iconographiques ............................................................................. 291

*Lucia Carmen Ardeț – Adrian Ardeț*
Statue group of Liber Pater accompanied by Pan and panther from Roman *Dacia* ......... 301

*Georgia Aristodemou*
A Polyphemus group in Crete? An old find reconsidered ............................................. 309

*Fabian Auer*
Ad limbum diducti – Entrückungsdarstellungen in der Sepulkralkunst der Donauprovinzen. Überlegungen zu Bildchiffren und deren Ursprung ...................................... 323

*Domagoj Bužanić*
Examples of Roman ornamental waterspouts from Croatia ......................................... 335

*Fulvia Ciliberto – Paola Ventura*
Nuove sculture funerarie da *Aquileia* ........................................................................ 343

*Chloé Damay*
Preliminary research on output from one or more limestone sculpture workshops
in *Thugga* (Tunisia) ................................................................................................. 355

*Zdravko Dimitrov*
New stone monuments from *Colonia Ulpia Traiana Ratiaria* ...................................... 363

*Michael Eisenberg – Arleta Kowalewska*
The Flowers Mausoleum at Hippos of the Decapolis. A first glance into one of
the finest Roman provincial architectural decorations in basalt .................................... 371

*Carlos Fabião – Trinidad Nogales – Nova Barrero – Amílcar Guerra – Joaquim
Carvalho – José María Murciano – Rafael Sabio – Catarina Viegas – Sofia Borges –
Ricardo Laria Machado – Daniel Moreno – João Aires – Sandro Barradas*
Anfiteatro de *Ammaia* (*Lusitania*). Nuevo ejemplo de modelo provincial .................. 387

*Sabrina Geiermann – Hannelore Rose*
Das Römergrab Weiden. Aspekte seiner Präsentation vom 19. bis in das 21. Jahrhundert ... 405

*Emmanouela Gounari*
Roman portraits from *Philippi* .................................................................................. 415

*Jochen Griesbach*
»Über Geld spricht man nicht!«? Unterschiede in der Zurschaustellung von Reichtum und Status in römischen Grabdenkmälern Italiens und der Nordwestprovinzen ....... 427

*Tibor Grüll – Nándor Agócs – János Jusztinger – Ernő Szabó*
The iconographic motif of book-scrolls on funerary reliefs in *Noricum* ...................... 445

*Craig A. Harvey*
A marble statue fragment of Victoria/Nike from Humayma, Jordan (Nabataean
*Hawara*, Roman *Hauarra*) ...................................................................................... 457

*Melissa Kays*
Monuments of Aurelia Paulina and her portrayal of social change in Roman
Asia Minor ................................................................................................................. 469

*Ute Kelp – Anja Klöckner*
Das Große Weinschiff aus Neumagen. Neue Überlegungen zu Rekonstruktion
und Bedeutung ........................................................................................................ 483

*Martin Kemkes*
Neue Statuenfragmente aus dem Westkastell von Öhringen am Obergermanischen
Limes ..................................................................................................................... 499

*Pierre-Antoine Lamy – Christine Louvion,* avec la collaboration de *Marie-Laure Florent-Michel* et *Charlie Mairel*
Sous l'œil de Junon. Nouveau regard sur le programme décoratif du second forum
de *Bagacum* (Bavay, Nord) .................................................................................... 517

*Katja Lembke*
Stone monuments of Roman Egypt as monuments of state ................................... 535

*Ana Zora Maspoli – Örni Akeret – Cornelia Alder – Debora Brunner – Sabine Deschler-Erb – Claudia Gerling – Natalie Schmocker – Ulrich Stockinger*
*Hic sitae sunt.* Interdisziplinäre Auswertung der frühkaiserzeitlichen Gräber der
Maxsimila Cassia und Heuprosinis im Gräberfeld Brugg/Remigersteig in *Vindonissa* .... 547

*Sorin Nemeti*
The Danubian Riders. Art, myth and ritual of a regional cult ................................ 559

*Christine Ruppert – Gabrielle Kremer – Andrea Binsfeld*
Grabbauten des 1. Jahrhunderts in der westlichen *civitas Treverorum* ................. 571

*Mirjana Sanader*
Eine Skulptur des Apollo Kitharodos aus Dalmatien ............................................. 581

*Alfred Schäfer*
Zwei Gebälkblöcke mit römischem Opferzug ........................................................ 589

*Astrid Schmölzer*
Goddesses of *Germania inferior*. Investigations into the iconography of the
Rhineland Matronae ............................................................................................... 601

*Kathrin Schuchter*
Die Enthauptung Medusas auf norischen und pannonischen Grabreliefs. Überlegungen
zu Musterbüchern, Werkstätten und Bildschemata ................................................ 613

*Nedjma Serradj-Remili – Leila Benchernine*
Stèles inédites de la Numidie et de la Maurétanie Césarienne et nouvelle lecture ......... 621

*Nirvana Silnović*
A new lion statuette from the Mithraeum in Jajce .................................................. 637

*Katarina Šmid*
The curious bust, found in the third Poetovian Mithraeum in *Poetovio, Pannonia
superior* ................................................................................................................. 647

*Jakob Unterhinninghofen*
Grabaltäre mit Meerwesendekor aus dem Treverergebiet. Untersuchungen zu
Chronologie, Typologie und Ikonografie .............................................................. 659

# VORWORT

Das 17. Internationale Kolloquium zum Provinzialrömischen Kunstschaffen in Wien und Carnuntum vom 16. bis 21. Mai 2022 war für viele Teilnehmerinnen und Teilnehmer die erste größere Fachtagung in physischer Präsenz seit rund zwei Jahren. Die Pause während der Pandemie hat nicht nur zur Verschiebung der Veranstaltung um ein Jahr, sondern auch zu Umbrüchen in vielen Bereichen unseres Arbeitsumfeldes geführt. Zu den Nutzen dieser Entwicklung zählen unter anderem die verbesserten Möglichkeiten digitaler Kommunikation. Während der Tagung ist jedoch der Mehrwert persönlichen Austauschs und direkter Erfahrung stark ins Bewusstsein gerückt – eine Bereicherung, die aus unserer Sicht wesentlich zum Gelingen beigetragen und unsere Entscheidung, die Veranstaltung nicht hybrid durchzuführen, im Nachhinein legitimiert hat. Die – unfreiwillige – Aktualität des Titels »Zeit(en) des Umbruchs« soll jedoch nicht die ursprüngliche Intention der Tagung verschleiern.

Zum einen wollten wir die Diskussionen über das provinzialrömische Kunstschaffen um den Aspekt der technisch-naturwissenschaftlichen Methoden erweitern, die gerade für die Forschungen zu antiken Steindenkmälern in den letzten Jahren zunehmend an Bedeutung gewonnen haben. Ziel war es nicht, die traditionellen Methoden der Stilkritik, Ikonografie und interdisziplinären geisteswissenschaftlichen Ansätze zu verdrängen oder zu ersetzen, sondern vielmehr das Forum für komplementäre Möglichkeiten der Analyse zu öffnen. Die Kombination der Methoden und die gegenseitige Befruchtung der Forschungsansätze sollten im Mittelpunkt der Diskussionen stehen. In vielen Beiträgen wird sichtbar, welche neuen Fragestellungen und umfangreichen Perspektiven sich für die Provinzialrömische Archäologie und Kunstgeschichte dadurch ergeben. Die Entwicklung der Methoden selbst und deren Diskussion bleibt selbstverständlich weiterhin den speziell darauf ausgerichteten Fachtagungen – etwa zu den Gesteinsmaterialien oder zur Polychromie römischer Steindenkmäler – vorbehalten.

Zum anderen verweist der Titel der Tagung auf den zweiten thematischen Schwerpunkt, der auf die spätrömische und spätantike Epoche gelegt wurde, und dem manche Beiträge gefolgt sind. In dieser Zeitspanne machen sich vielfältige Umbrüche auf unterschiedlichen Ebenen bemerkbar, die inhaltliche, symbolische und formale Aspekte, aber auch den Umgang mit Steindenkmälern und deren Verwendung ganz allgemein betreffen. Hier kam es wesentlich auf die Berücksichtigung der gesellschaftlichen und archäologischen Kontexte an, die notwendig sind, um die Aussagekraft der Steindenkmäler in ihrer gesamten Bandbreite zu erschließen.

Die überwiegende Anzahl der Beiträge gilt Neufunden und aktuellen Forschungsthemen. Die große Zahl der Anmeldungen erforderte auch für diese Tagung eine Auswahl und eine Beschränkung der Themen. Um trotzdem möglichst vielen Kolleginnen und Kollegen die Teilnahme zu ermöglichen, wurden einige Präsentationen als Kurzvorträge gehalten. Die darauf beruhenden Beiträge in diesem Band fallen etwas kürzer aus als die der Langvorträge. Die Konzentration auf Steindenkmäler der römischen Provinzen und der nördlichen Randzone Italiens in ihren unterschiedlichen Erscheinungsformen als Bestandteile von architektonischen und skulpturalen Ensembles oder als Inschriftenträger wurde dabei konsequent beibehalten. Die Erweiterung der zu Beginn der Tagungsreihe auf die Donau- und die Nordwestprovinzen beschränkten räumlichen Abgrenzung verstanden wir hingegen als bereichernd und folgen damit der in Köln (2001) und Mérida (2009) initiierten Entwicklung der CRPA-Kolloquien.

Unser Dank gilt in erster Linie den Teilnehmerinnen und Teilnehmern der Tagung, die durch ihre Präsentationen und Diskussionen deren Inhalt und Qualität bestimmt haben. Den Autoren und Autorinnen ist es zu verdanken, dass die Ergebnisse vorgelegt und langfristig genutzt werden können. Für das sehr gelungene, spontan gehaltene abschließende Resümee ist Jochen Griesbach im Speziellen zu danken.

Die Austragung der Veranstaltung wurde durch das reibungslose Zusammenspiel dreier Institutionen möglich, die das Forschungsgeschehen auf dem Gebiet der provinzialrömischen Archäologie in Wien und Carnuntum wesentlich bestimmen: das Österreichische Archäologische Institut der Österreichischen Akademie der Wissenschaften, die Historisch-Kulturwissenschaftliche Fakultät der Universität Wien und die Landessammlungen Niederösterreich – Archäologischer

Die Teilnehmerinnen und Teilnehmer des Kolloquiums zu Besuch in der »Römerstadt Carnuntum«

Park Carnuntum. Dem Organisationskomitee gehörten als maßgebliche Vertreter Andreas Pülz und Gabrielle Kremer (ÖAW/ÖAI), Eduard Pollhammer und Bernadette Malkiel (Landessammlungen NÖ – Archäologischer Park Carnuntum), Günther Schörner und Julia Kopf (Institut für Klassische Archäologie der Universität Wien) sowie Fritz Mitthof und Franziska Beutler (Institut für Alte Geschichte und Altertumskunde, Papyrologie und Epigraphik der Universität Wien) an. Als Kooperationspartner konnten wir die Gesellschaft der Freunde Carnuntums, die Römerstadt Carnuntum, das Wien Museum, das Kunsthistorische Museum Wien und das Bundesdenkmalamt gewinnen. Den Verantwortlichen sowie den Mitarbeitern und Mitarbeiterinnen, allen voran Christa Farka, Markus Wachter, Michaela Kronberger, Georg Plattner und Eva Steigberger gilt unser aufrichtiger Dank. Sie ermöglichten uns vielfache Einblicke in die reichhaltigen Bestände ihrer Sammlungen und Grabungsstätten und sorgten für fachkundige Führungen sowie für gastfreundliche Bewirtung. Den reibungslosen Ablauf der Tagung gewährleisteten zudem Ida Muharemovic (ÖAI) und Michaela Löffler-Leutgeb, Norbert Braunecker, Marina Brzakovic, Jasmine Cencic, Tanja Koch, Eva Pimpel, Fahira Sapaj und Anna-Maria Stieberitz (LSNÖ/APC) sowie Olivér Borcsányi, Felix Michler, Tomás Sobihard und Elisabeth Todt (Universität Wien). Fachkundige Führungen durch das römische Wien boten Kristina Adler-Wölfl und Sophie Insulander. Die abschließende Exkursion am 21. Mai 2022 führte uns nach Bruckneudorf, ins Burgenländische Landesmuseum Eisenstadt, ins Stadtmuseum Mannersdorf und nach Leithaprodersdorf. Für Führungen danken wir Heinz Zabehlicky, Eva Steigberger, Heribert Schutzbier und Robert Krickl, der Gemeinde Leithaprodersdorf für die burgenländische Gastfreundschaft.

Die Aufnahme des Tagungsbandes in die Reihe der Sonderschriften des ÖAI ermöglichten Sabine Ladstätter und Barbara Beck-Brandt. Armin Laussegger ist zu verdanken, dass der Tagungsband auch in die Reihe der Veröffentlichungen aus den Landessammlungen Niederösterreich aufgenommen wurde. Das Sprachlektorat Englisch lag in den bewährten Händen von Sarah Homan-Cormack, Satz und Layout verdanken wir Andrea Sulzgruber.

Nicht zuletzt sei dem wissenschaftlichen Komitee der CRPA-Tagungen für die wohlwollende Unterstützung gedankt, besonders denjenigen Mitgliedern, die sich wiederholt für den Austragungsort Carnuntum eingesetzt haben. Dass das langjährige Vorhaben im Jahr 2022 trotz aller Erschwernisse schließlich an den Tagungsorten Wien und Carnuntum erfolgreich realisiert werden konnte, verdanken wir der kooperativen Bereitschaft aller Beteiligten.

*Gabrielle Kremer – Eduard Pollhammer – Julia Kopf – Franziska Beutler*
*Wien, im September 2023*

Isabel Rodà de Llanza[1]

# KEYNOTE LECTURE:

# ROMAN SCULPTURE AS A MULTIDISCIPLINARY RESEARCH FOCUS

It is a great honour for me, and also for Spanish Roman sculpture research, that I am able to be here today to address you[2]. I am aware, and I would like to acknowledge publicly, that I owe this opportunity to the kindness of Gabrielle Kremer. She has persistently advocated in previous Colloquia on Roman Provincial Art, so that finally, in 2022, the seventeenth colloquium is being held in Vienna and *Carnuntum*, at a time of transition and change in which there is a great need to reflect on our current hectic world. All this has been made possible by the efficient work of the Austrian Academy of Sciences and the Austrian Archaeological Institute (OeAI) – Department of Classics, as well as the personal interest of Gabrielle Kremer, who has bravely overcome both personal difficulties and those caused by the coronavirus. Despite the sorrows, here we are, ready to start our working sessions and with a hospitable welcome that we all deeply appreciate.

The long road that has brought us here began in 1989, when Manfred Hainzmann and Erwin Pochmarski's initiative first took shape, with an initial meeting held in Graz[3]. The last three meetings have taken place in Dijon (2015)[4], Graz (2017)[5] and Tübingen[6]. From the outset, our colloquia have been involved in the »Corpus Signorum Imperii Romani« (CSIR).

The first of our colloquia was held in the areas of the Rhine-Danube Limes. The seventh, held in Cologne 2001 and edited by Peter Noelke, included a section dedicated to *Hispania* with three contributions by Walter Trillmich, Angelika Franz with Fiona A. Greenland and Markus Trunk[7]. However, the title was so broad that by 2007 the tenth colloquium was held in Arles and Aix-en-Provence, focusing on regional sculpture workshops[8]. In that meeting, it was proposed that the 2009 meeting be held in Spain. The National Museum of Roman Art and the Catalan Institute of Classical Archaeology set to work and arranged for Mérida to host the eleventh colloquium, with a focus on the relationship between the centre and the provinces, following the usual biennial intervals[9]. The Vienna meeting was initially scheduled for last year, but prudence warranted postponing it until now. We are all glad that it is now possible and, furthermore, face to face, since on so many other occasions we have been relegated to online meetings, which are much less lively.

---

[1] UAB-ICAC, research group ArPA. Work was carried out within investigation project, »Sulcato marmore ferro (SULMARE). Canteras, talleres, artesanos y comitentes de las producciones artísticas en piedra en la Hispania Tarraconensis« (PID2019-106967GB-I00).
[2] The lecture style of the keynote speech, held on 16 May 2022, has been largely retained here.
[3] The list of the first twelve colloquia with the corresponding edition of the Proceedings can be seen in Alexandrescu 2015, 9 n. 3.
[4] Lefebvre 2017.
[5] Porod – Scherrer 2019.
[6] Lipps 2021.
[7] Noelke 2003.
[8] Gaggadis-Robin et al. 2009.
[9] Nogales – Rodà 2011.

I have been asked by the organisers to focus on the value of interdisciplinary research on Roman stone monuments, in accordance with the guiding theme of this conference. To this end, allow me to take stock of the relevant studies on Roman sculpture in Spain and neighbouring France, as examples of countries in which constant and intensive research work has been undertaken in recent years. In France, the CSIR series did not materialise, as it was decided to publish the »Nouvel Espérandieu« under the direction of Henri Lavagne. Since 2003, seven volumes have been published with the support of the Académie des Inscriptions et Belles-Lettres[10].

Likewise, the »Rencontres« were held, the first of which concerned Roman sculpture in the West and dealt with the controversial portrait from Arles attributed to Julius Caesar[11]. There followed a second with commendable regularity and the publication of the minutes[12]. The third meeting took place in November 2019 at the Musée Départemental Arles Antique, organized by Guillaume Biard, Vassiliki Gaggadis-Robin and Nicolas de Larquier. Vassiliki Gaggadis-Robin, chère amie, has constantly watched over all of this.

In Spain, the »Reuniones sobre Escultura Romana en Hispania« (Meetings on Roman Sculpture in Hispania) began in 1992. The first was held in Mérida and the ninth in Yecla[13]. As *Hispania* includes both present-day Spain and Portugal, the meetings have been convened in both Spanish and Portuguese venues, with the involvement of numerous institutions. The tenth colloquium was held in late October 2022 in Faro and Mértola, in the beautiful Algarve and Alentejo regions.

This joint effort has also been crystallised in the publication of numerous monographs and the publication of ten volumes of the CSIR Spain since 2001[14]. It includes all types of sculptures in stone, except for architectural decoration, and also large-format bronzes. Small bronzes have not been included in these volumes.

The current director is Professor José Miguel Noguera from the University of Murcia who works with an advisory committee of specialists in Archaeology and History of Art from the various autonomous regions of Spain, in an excellent collaborative environment. The next director will be Professor Montserrat Claveria from the Autonomous University of Barcelona.

We are in Vienna and it is necessary to acknowledge the great job done by Austrian researchers on the edition of the corresponding CSIR volumes at the Austrian Academy of Sciences. The first volumes of this series have been published here, and among the various volumes on *Carnumtum*, I would like to highlight the supplement 1, edited in 2012 by our kind hostess, Gabrielle Kremer, with interdisciplinary contributions by Christian Gugl, Christian Uhlir and Michael Unterwurzacher[15]. Recent volumes have been published by Erwin Pochmarski, one of the initiators of the CRPA Colloquia[16].

I have spoken at length, albeit in synthesis, in order to reach the current point at which we find ourselves in the study of Roman sculpture. Fortunately, we can state that it is in relatively good health. I would also like to point out that doctoral theses devoted by young researchers to this subject are frequent, which is always a source of satisfaction. In my opinion, a challenge for the future that I see facing future generations that are a little younger than mine is to create a major database of Roman sculpture on the same level as, for example, that being built in the field of epigraphy.

The study of each individual piece has now been superseded and, therefore, stylistic analysis has become an important element, although only one of several. We have to recognise that many

---

[10] Terrer et al. 2003; Darblade-Audoin 2006; Moitrieux 2010; Lemoine 2013; Moitrieux – Tronche 2017; Corré – Gaggadis-Robin 2018; Moitrieux et al. 2022.
[11] Gaggadis-Robin – Picard 2016.
[12] Gaggadis-Robin – de Larquier 2019.
[13] Nogales 1993; Massó – Sada 1996; León – Nogales 2000; Nogales – Gonçalves 2004; Noguera – Conde 2008; Abascal – Cebrián 2010; Acuña et al. 2013; Márquez – Ojeda 2018; Noguera – Ruiz 2020.
[14] Claveria 2001; Garriguet 2001; Baena – Beltrán 2002; Vidal 2005; Beltrán et al. 2006; Noguera 2012; Merchán 2015; Moreno 2016; López 2017; Beltrán – Loza 2020. For Portugal, Souza 1990.
[15] Kremer 2012.
[16] Pochmarski 2021.

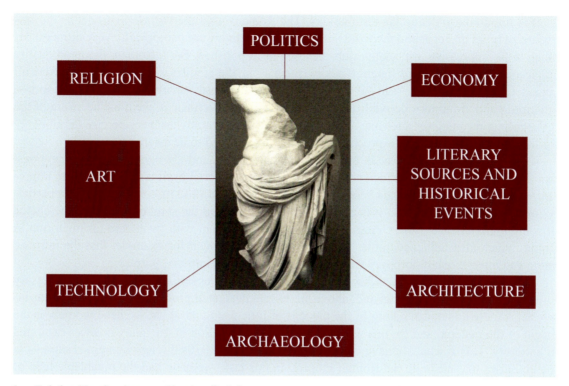

1   Relationship of sculptures with other disciplines

disciplines of the sciences of antiquity need to collaborate for the study of sculpture. Taking all aspects into account allows a better interpretation of a particular production or sculptural ensemble (fig. 1). The most precise information possible is necessary regarding the place of discovery, the raw material and the circulation of models, techniques, manufacturing processes, style and iconography, as well as programmes, symbolism, and the like. Architecture helps us to understand the relationship with the framework into which the sculpture should be inserted. Religion and politics are also important, as sculpture was an important element in the propaganda of emperors and elites, as was the desire for self-representation among the members of the various strata of society. Furthermore, we must not fail to take into account economic factors, by not only gauging the cost of sculptural productions, but also the channels through which they were traded. Finally, we should look at the relationship that can be established with the historical moment and the events with which a certain sculptural production can be interwoven. In cases where the context of the find is known, it should be kept in mind and the pertinent data consulted. If possible, the archaeologists who excavated the site should be consulted to better place the sculptural remains in their environment and chronological framework, thus contributing an important element to the landscape for which the piece was conceived and created.

Once again, teamwork is important, especially when we enter the field of other disciplines in what we understand globally as »the sciences«, although archaeology and the humanities also belong to this category.

Today we cannot fully understand or study a sculpture if we do not ask ourselves the questions I have just outlined. It is essential to determine the material from which the piece was sculpted. In an ideal situation we would be able to carry out archaeometric analyses; however we must recognise that this is often not possible, given the difficulty in obtaining permission to extract samples. In spite of everything, wherever possible we should attempt to go beyond generically classifying the type of stone, i.e. limestone, sandstone, marble, granite, porphyry, etc., to ascertain its extraction point. This can be undertaken macroscopically and formulated as a possibility or hypothesis. Analytical verification is essential, above all, in the case of white marbles. Coloured marbles are easier to identify with the naked eye if one is familiar with the lithotypes.

It is important to define the terminology. The Romans used the term *lapis* to define the less exclusive types of stone, and the word *marmor* for types that were geologically very different but much more impressive, especially after they had been polished. For a Roman, the good quality cretaceous limestones, the different types of true marble, the granites and the porphyries were all considered to be *marmora*. As in our modern languages the words »marble«, »marbre«, »marmo«, »mármol« and »Marmor« derive from the Latin *marmor*; nevertheless, we must be aware of the difference in meaning for a Roman and for us. Geologists naturally use very precise terminology for the various stones, and this precision is something we need to be aware of.

It is very encouraging to see in our colloquia, and Vienna and *Carnuntum* are no exceptions, that the concern for investigating and identifying the raw material itself is becoming more important, and that greater attention is being paid to the processes prior to its configuration as a partially- or fully-finished sculpture. It is also possible to understand the symbolic value of the choice of some materials over others. Augustus himself selected them with great care for his forum in Rome, which also influenced other provinces. It is well known, for example, that the intrinsic value and intense red of porphyry was meant to represent the imperial purple.

Thus we enter the field of archaeometry. Geology is now essential for us, and it is necessary to work closely with geologists and, above all, to find dedicated professionals who share our interests. A mere geological dating of the piece is of little use to us. What we need to know is the origin of the material and for this we need a reference collection of the many quarries exploited in antiquity. This is what we have been doing since the late 1970s through numerous surveys in the countries that made up the Roman Empire. In this task, we have had the invaluable help of Professor Aureli Àlvarez, who poured all his efforts into determining the origins of the pieces we submitted for analysis at the Laboratory for the Study of Ancient Stone Materials of the Autonomous University of Barcelona (LEMLA). Continuous growth and development has also led to an expansion of this area in the Catalan Institute of Classical Archaeology with the establishment of the Archaeometric Studies Unit (UEA), directed by Anna Gutiérrez Garcia-Moreno and the incorporation of Pilar Lapuente, Professor of Geology at the University of Zaragoza. This line of research has developed alongside another one oriented towards artistic productions, with which sculpture and analytics have always gone hand in hand within our group ArPA (Archaeometry and Artistic Productions).

Throughout Spain, especially since the early 2000s, archaeometric studies and the determination of stone materials have proliferated. A very important part of this has been the surveying and excavation of ancient quarries to specify the origin of the different *marmora*. Here I would like to highlight the decisive studies of Jean-Claude Bessac in the 1980s[17]. As both an archaeologist and a sculptor, he contributed new perspectives by studying the working techniques of the stonemasons and sculptors and providing very useful information on the tools they used. A highly commendable work was the monograph on the Bois de Lens quarries that supplied a white limestone of extraordinary quality for the buildings of *Nemausus*[18].

Let's briefly review the bibliography published in Spain in the last twenty years: The proceedings of two congresses deal extensively with Hispanic *marmora*[19], followed by the catalogue of an exhibition, which presents the 16 main types exploited on the Iberian Peninsula[20], including marble from Estremoz (Portugal) and Almadén de la Plata (Sevilla), both from the Osa Morena anticline and widely used for sculptural productions. New studies are constantly widening its distribution radius outside of *Baetica*. For example, at the Dijon Colloquium we presented a very battered head from the Julio-Claudian period found in Zaragoza, perhaps attributable to the emperor Tiberius. We will return to this later.

---

[17] Bessac 1987.
[18] Bessac 1996.
[19] Nogales – Beltrán 2008; García-Entero 2012.
[20] Àlvarez et al. 2009.

2   The Roman villa of *Sagrera* (Barcelona), Broccatello shaft and capital (MUHBA, photos J. Casanovas)

Another favourite topic of research in Spain, parallel to that being undertaken in other countries, has been the detection of quarries, as we see in one volume which deals with chronology, techniques and work organisation[21].

The following two volumes are very recent contributions. The first, the product of a three-year competitive research project, looks at the *marmora* of *Baetica*, effectively intertwining archaeological research and archaeometry[22]. The second focuses on the materials, workshops and production in the quarries themselves, a very important aspect for detecting partially finished pieces and their marketing, as well as the finishing process carried out at the place of reception[23].

The hard cretaceous limestones were not very suitable for sculptural work. They include the showy Broccatello or La Cinta jaspi from the quarries of *Dertosa*, today Tortosa, near the mouth of the river Ebro[24]. We can appreciate this on a plaque we will also see later, as well as on other architectural elements (fig. 2)[25].

We have no evidence of any sculptural use of marmor from *Tarraco*, the so-called Santa Tecla stone, which was widely used for epigraphy[26]. We do have a few examples of sculptures in the hard cretaceous limestone from *Emporiae*, as well as bas-reliefs carved from the *marmor Saetabitanum*, known today as Buixcarró, quarried in the territory of the ancient *Saetabis*, present-day Xàtiva[27].

In contrast, the cheaper soft limestones and sandstones had to be covered with stucco and a final layer of paint that constituted the true epidermis of the sculptures. This fragile layer has only very occasionally been preserved until today.

---

[21] Gutiérrez Garcia-M. – Rouillard 2018.
[22] Beltrán et al. 2018.
[23] Vinci et al. 2020.
[24] Gutiérrez Garcia-M. 2009, 229–245.
[25] Rodà – Alcubierre 2020.
[26] Àlvarez et al. 2009b.
[27] Cebrián 2012; Soler 2019, 250–252 n. 34–35.

3   Examples of reuse in the cathedral of Barcelona (photos J. M. Puche)

We recognise the importance of polychromy, an important international line of study, which will also be dealt with in major sessions in this Colloquium[28]. A champion of polychrome sculptures in Spain is Professor Trinidad Nogales, the current director of the National Museum of Roman Art in Mérida[29].

Likewise, careful attention should be paid to *spolia* (fig. 3) and the reuse of materials from antiquity in later constructions[30]. Beyond their strictly economic value, they contribute a profound symbolism by, for example, integrating pagan productions in Christian contexts. This makes up somewhat for the loss of a large number of works, either due to *damnationes* of various kinds or to the reduction of marble in ovens, in order to turn it into good quality lime.

ASMOSIA (Association for the Study of Marmora and Other Stones in Antiquity) was set up to deal specifically with the stone resources used in antiquity. On the subject of marble itself, an authentic ›bombshell‹ was dropped in the ninth edition of ASMOSIA held in Tarragona in 2009[31]. This was the identification of the Göktepe quarries of fine-grained white marble, which radically changed the evaluation and expansion of the *Aphrodisias* workshops, as we will see later. Likewise, the objective evidence presented on the so-called Greco scritto, which was believed to have been extracted entirely from present-day Algeria, made it very clear that it could also have come from quarries near *Ephesos*. These cases serve as examples of how much has been done, how much remains to be done and the surprises we may still have to come.

Consequently, it is necessary to continue tracking down and surveying hitherto unknown quarry areas, as is planned for the sessions of this Colloquium. In Spain, for example, this has been undertaken in present-day Galicia, with results that have exceeded expectations[32]. In the French

---

[28]   See also Liverani 2004; Brinkmann 2008; Brinkmann – Bendala 2010. The 11th International Round Table on Polychromy in Ancient Sculpture and Architecture, organized by the Musei Capitolini and Museo Nazionale Romano, was held in Rome from 9 to 12 September 2022.

[29]   Nogales 2010; Merchán et al. 2020a.

[30]   Mateos – Morán 2020; Beltrán de Heredia – Rodà 2020.

[31]   Gutiérrez Garcia-M. et al. 2012.

[32]   Gutiérrez Garcia-M. et al. 2016 and 2018; González Soutelo et al. 2014.

Pyrenees, Pilar Lapuente Mercadal has detected the existence of an extraction area of fine-grained white marble in Louvie-Soubiron, which will have to be differentiated from the Lunense marbles[33].

With all this, Spanish research has become fully integrated in the line, which incisively marked the work of such scholars as John B. Ward Perkins, Marc Waelkens, Norman Herz and Luc Moens who, in 1992, published these volumes – the first a compilation – that have become absolute reference works for all of us[34]. Around the same time, the symposium held in 1988 and published in 1990 was also very significant for ancient sculpture[35].

Italian research has made a fundamental contribution to Roman *marmora* studies. The long bibliography produced by professors Patrizio Pensabene[36], also a great specialist in sculpture, and Lorenzo Lazzarini, founder of the review »Marmora«, from the field of geology, provide an essential background for our studies[37]. Finally, I wish to highlight how the countries that were once part of the Roman Empire are producing global monographs that deal with the use of *marmora*. As an example, we can cite the volume that covers Roman *Dacia*[38].

I have perhaps spoken enough about these issues, although we should never lose sight of the fact that, before it became a sculpture, a block of marble would have been extracted with a precise technique and skill from a quarry, the quality of which, as well as the faults in the stone itself, would have conditioned the final result. Michelangelo himself was well aware of this when he travelled to the Carrara quarries to see the block of marble he was to sculpt. In a well-known anecdote, he exclaimed »There's my David, I just have to remove what's left over ... «.

A major boost to Spanish research and its dissemination on an international level was the ninth edition of ASMOSIA held in Tarragona in 2009[39]. The front cover of the minutes shows the plaque from the latrines of the Roman villa of Els Munts in the *Tarraco ager*. Made of Broccatello, it bears the engraved silhouette of a dolphin and illustrates the unsuitability for sculpture of hard limestones, no matter how attractive they were. The highly prized Broccatello – its name evokes the appearance of brocade made of gold threads on a purple background – was used above all for small cornices, slabs and cladding *crustae*, as well as for plain column shafts and certain capitals, as we have seen in *Barcino* (fig. 2)[40].

Let add me that the thirteenth edition of ASMOSIA, also delayed by the pandemic, took place here in Vienna in September 2022. It was organised by Sabine Ladstätter and Walter Prochaska under the auspices of the Austrian Archaeological Institute at the Austrian Academy of Sciences. The city of Vienna, in addition to its many merits and attractions, was for us the capital of Roman stone studies throughout 2022.

For the research into stone raw materials, it is necessary to deal with the subject by beginning with a macroscopic autopsy, to better interpret the sculptures we intend to study. Without knowing what they are made of, we will be unable to present solid conclusions regarding the technique, elaboration, finishes, models, whether the workshops were local or not, the price, and commercialisation, not forgetting the challenges of conservation in its current state (fig. 4).

I will now provide examples with cases in which archaeometry and interdisciplinarity have allowed a much more accurate joint analysis of the artefact.

At the Dijon Colloquium, organised and edited by Sabine Lefebvre, together with Trinidad Nogales and Pilar Lapuente[41], we presented a Julio-Claudian portrait from Zaragoza, ancient

---

[33] Lapuente et al. 2021a.
[34] Ward-Perkins 1992; Waelkens et al. 1992.
[35] Marble Papers 1990.
[36] E.g. Pensabene 1998; Pensabene 2013.
[37] E.g. Lazzarini 2007.
[38] Müller et al. 2012.
[39] Gutiérrez Garcia-M. et al. 2012.
[40] Rodà – Alcubierre 2020.
[41] Nogales et al. 2017.

4 Sculptures, sarcophagi, half-worked capitals at the foot of the Proconnesus marble quarries 2018 (photos I. Rodà)

*Caesar Augusta* on the river Ebro, the ancient *Hiberum*. The analysis, using petrography, cathodoluminescence and isotopes, gave us a pleasant surprise. The isotopic values projected in the corresponding diagram for fine-medium grained marbles (<2 mm) led to a double possibility for their origin: either the Estremoz Anticline in Portugal, or *Docimium*, near Afyon in Turkey. The petrographic and cathodomicrofacies comparison with quarry samples from our database is similar to some quarry samples from the Pardais area (southern end of the Estremoz Anticline), ruling out the Turkish origin. In conclusion, the overall result of the analytical study of the marble sample points to a Hispanic origin: the quarries of the Estremoz Anticline located in the present-day Alto Alentejo region of Portugal, a marble area that supplied a large amount of material for the capital of *Lusitania*, *Augusta Emerita*. At the moment, the portrait from Zaragoza constitutes the easternmost testimony of the sculptural use of this marble that, until a few years ago, was considered limited to all intents and purposes to the area of Mérida.

The determination of the raw materials is essential to clarify the distribution radius of the sculptural productions. Here are two more cases:

In Oviedo Cathedral the sarcophagus of the child Ithacius is preserved. It was believed to have been made in an Aquitanian workshop, but subsequent analysis has revealed that it is once again an example of the use of marble from Estremoz, with a new point of attention on the diffusion of the so-called local marbles, which, as we see, are not so local[42].

Another interesting case is that of the late-period sarcophagi (around AD 400) from the *Tarraco* necropolis. Their similarity, both visual and macroscopic, to those of Carthage is such that it led us to believe they may have been sculpted in *Tarraco* itself, following Carthaginian models. However, when viewed under a microscope, the thin sections attest their differences: the micritic limestone from Tarragona does not correspond to the bioesparite, the so-called kadel, from Carthage[43]. Therefore, the *Tarraco* sarcophagi were imported directly and fully finished from Carthage. They would have crossed the Mediterranean in ships that would also have brought the African pottery that reached our shores in large quantities.

---

[42] Vidal – García-Entero 2015; Vidal et al. 2016.
[43] Rodà 1990.

A current international line of research focuses on alabaster, to which Simon J. Barker and Simona Perna devote their studies[44]. Recently, several researchers in *Baetica* have been studying calcitic alabasters[45]. The exploitation zones in the south of the Iberian Peninsula are being traced and locally extracted materials identified. Also of considerable importance are the studies undertaken on the theatres of Cádiz (*Gades*) and Cartagena (*Carthago Nova*). In the *scaenae frons* of the latter, there was a mass use of red travertine from the Hispanic quarries of Mula (Murcia)[46]. On the other hand, for the Cádiz theatre, the Theatrum Balbi, the majestic marble decoration reveals a very early use of imported marble for a Hispanic building, in the early Augustan period according to the archaeological data[47]. This opulence was due to the main protagonists, namely Balbus the Younger and perhaps Agrippa, who provided precious imported marbles[48], such as Alabaster Fiorito for the ornamentation. These materials were used at the same time for the decorative programmes of Rome promoted by Augustus. Balbus inaugurated his theatre in Rome in 13 BC[49]. We know that four onyx columns were placed in it, as they were described by Pliny[50].

5   Statue traditionally believed to be of the god Asclepius, from the Greek town of *Emporion* on the northern Spanish Mediterranean coast, present-day Catalonia (MAC-Empúries, photo I. Rodà)

The *Gades* theatre would even surpass the Theatrum Balbi of Rome in its splendour and in a somewhat earlier chronology. Cádiz's theatre is the earliest Hispanic example of architectural magnificence in imported marble, parallel to the theatrical building undertaken by Agrippa and Balbus in Rome and Italy.

Although Hispania had marble sculptures prior to the arrival of the Romans, they were all fully finished and made from foreign and imported materials[51]. This can be seen in the Phoenician sarcophagi of Cádiz in Parian marble from the Sidon workshops, as well as in the base of an ideal statue in marble, also from Paros, of which the feet have been recently discovered. It was found at the spectacular site of Turuñuelo in Extremadura, which was destroyed at the end of the 5th or the beginning of the 4th century BC[52]. Likewise, the Emporitan sculpture (fig. 5), traditionally considered to be of the god Asclepius, from the end of the 2nd century BC, is an imported piece of unique typology, the torso of which was carved in Greek Paros marble and the rest of the body with its clothing in Pentelic marble. It is the only Greek sculpture found in the western part of the Greek world contemporary to the famous Venus de Milo, with the advantage that ours has arms.

---

[44] Barker – Perna 2018 and in press.
[45] Loza – Beltrán 2018; Ontiveros 2018.
[46] Soler 2005 and 2012.
[47] Bernal – Arévalo 2011, 269–272; Bernal et al. 2014.
[48] Rodà et al. 2011; Ventura – Borrego 2011; Ventura et al. 2021; Àlvarez et al., in press.
[49] Manacorda 2011.
[50] Plin. nat. 36, 60. Platner – Ashby 1929, 513.
[51] Rodà 2020.
[52] Rodà 2020; Lapuente et al. 2020.

6   Metropolitan models in the forum of *Augusta Emerita* (left); Aeneas, Ascanius and Anchises group (right) (MNAR Merida, photos I. Rodà)

In a parallel chronology, between the 5th and the 1st century BC, the great Iberian sculpture, which in its last phase was already Roman, used only local limestones. In the initial centuries of its existence it manifested the strong influence of the Greek models.

Although marble sculptures were imported during the Roman Republic, it was under Augustus and Agrippa that imported marble spread on a large scale. At the same time, the exploitation of marble quarries began all over *Hispania*. We have evidence of this in the sculptures and also the inscriptions that sometimes provide us with important dates to situate the beginning of the use of local marble.

The portraits of Mérida residents show this very clearly. Professor Trinidad Nogales has studied them with great enthusiasm and care, having baptised them as the first generation of Mérida residents[53]. The extraordinary quarries of high quality marble at Estremoz allowed the large-scale ›marbleisation‹ of Mérida as the capital of *Lusitania*. This closely followed the models of the *urbs*, to such an extent that the sculptural finds of Mérida have shown Rome the statuary groups lost to the Forum of Augustus in Rome. These include, for example, the group of Aeneas, Ascanius and Anchises, which Walter Trillmich so masterfully restored (fig. 6) and which is now virtually on display at its original location[54].

The provinces have a lot to show the centre of power. For example, a copy of the Merida group is exhibited the Museo dei Fori Imperiali, as is another of the grand statues from the Córdoba Tienda Collection representing Aeneas or Romulus, for which the best quality Carrara marble was used[55]. The *Baetis* (today Guadalquivir) had better navigability conditions than the *Anas* (today Guadiana).

---

[53] Nogales 1997, 134–138.
[54] Merchán et al. 2020b.
[55] Rodríguez Oliva 2009, 128–129.

7    The imperial worship area of *Tarraco*: model of the Museu Bíblic (Tarragona) and *clipeus* in MNAT (photos S. Grimau and R. Cornadó)

Huge amounts of imported marble arrived along the entire Mediterranean coast of *Hispania* and the *Baetis* Valley, especially Lunense marble. In *Tarraco* (fig. 7), capital of the largest province in the Roman Empire, *Hispania Citerior*, there are not only free-standing sculptures made of Carrara marble, among them some of early chronology, but also unworked blocks destined to build and decorate the porticoes of the Flavian-era imperial worship area, following the models of the Forum of Augustus in Rome. The workshop waste excavated in abundance in the upper part of the town proves that the artisans worked *in situ*. The programme was unitary and the differences in execution are due to the hands of the various craftspersons who worked on the ornamentation and not to the fact that they were made in successive phases. A very interesting proposal has been made regarding this grand architectural programme, as well as that of the *Carthago Nova* theatre: the overall cost for each of them has been calculated at more than 330,000 sesterces. According to Patrizio Pensabene and Ricardo Mar[56], the marble used in the porticoes of the *Tarraco* worship area reached a volume of 705.82 m$^3$ = 26,962.3 p$^3$ and was equivalent to 134,811 HS. Together with the costs of the cladding surface, the total market costs of the marble used in the porticoes has been calculated to HS 330,762.

Naturally, the waterways favoured the marble trade, although even in this aspect Rome practiced the »e pur si muove«. In a town in the interior of Spain, *Segobriga* in Cuenca, a magnificent iconographic programme was carried out that concentrated on the forum basilica. This has been well studied by José Miguel Noguera as part of the CSIR[57]. For life-size or slightly larger statues, all kinds of imported Pentelic, Thassos and Luni-Carrara white marbles were used. Overland transport (probably from the port of *Carthago Nova*) was expensive, but the people of *Segobriga* could afford it, since their wealth came from the exploitation and sale of *lapis specularis* in the Augustan era and for much of the 1st century AD.

The aforementioned, recently identified marble of Göktepe was particularly abundant in the decoration of large late-period villas. As examples, we may mention the portrait of emperor Hadrian from the villa of Los Torrejones (Yecla, Murcia)[58] (fig. 8), the Portuguese villa of Quinta das Longas (Elvas)[59], which has been well interpreted by Trinidad Nogales, and the villa of Valdetorres de Jarama (Madrid)[60], the excellent artisanship of which used both white and blackish varieties

---

[56] Mar – Pensabene 2009, 377.
[57] Noguera 2012.
[58] Noguera – Ruiz 2018.
[59] Nogales et al. 2004; Lapuente et al. 2021b.
[60] Castellano 2004; Fernández Ochoa et al. 2022, 163–164. 367–368.

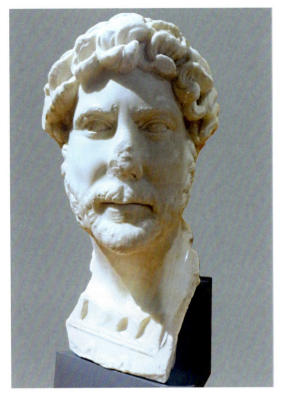 

8   Emperor Hadrian (Göktepe marble) from the villa of Los Torrejones, Yecla, Murcia (left) and funerary sculptures from *Barcino* carved in local sandstone, MUHBA (photos I. Rodà)

for the sculptures. Ongoing studies on the Iberian Peninsula, as well as in various parts of the Empire, will no doubt identify new assemblages.

Also very important will be the studies questioning the distribution networks of the various marbles. The impact of imperially owned *marmora* can be noted to a greater or lesser degree in all the domains of the Empire, depending on the geographical conditions of the different towns and their territories. However, we can sometimes distinguish the limits of its expansion when similar marbles were available nearby. For example, when studying the sculptures of the Augusteum in the Dalmatian town of *Narona* (Vid, Croatia), to which Emilio Marin has dedicated so many years of his professional life, we were able to determine that Greek marble predominated in this Adriatic coastal town and that, in the case of fine-grained whites, only Pentelic was used and not Carrara[61].

We see how official sculpture, with well-defined models and types, led to the standardisation of the productions and programmes in the most diverse areas of the Empire, for example in the iconography of the *Segobriga* forum and the *Narona* Augusteum. However, on the level of local productions, which usually used local stone, the panorama is much wider and the varied traditions of the different areas are reflected.

Therefore, in conclusion, it only remains to discuss local stone, which sometimes had a notable distribution radius, as we can see, for example, with the Broccatello from *Dertosa*. When it comes to sandstones, their use and distribution was much more restricted, but they do offer an excellent window onto the study of local workshops and the expansion and success of their models.

A good example is that of *Barcino* (Barcelona), a colony founded in 19 BC, after the Cantabrian wars had ended[62]. As a small town, a *parvum oppidum* according to Pomponius Mela, it was

---

[61]   Marin – Rodà 2004, 167–174. 371–373.
[62]   Rodà – Beltrán de Heredia 2021.

very active thanks to its control of a fertile agricultural territory and the movement provided by its seaport at the mouth of the river *Rubricatum* (Llobregat). It also had an excellent sandstone extracted from the quarries of Montjuïc that served both for building and sculptural ornamentation. It was used, for example, on the Augustan-period forum temple, the capitals of which reveal the use of a technique from the Triumviral period with the typical triangular cavities.

This sandstone was also used in the private sphere, where it was worked following Italic models (fig. 8). This is not surprising as, judging by the onomastics of the many preserved inscriptions, the first generation of *Barcino*'s residents came from the Italian peninsula[63]. In the funerary monuments, we can clearly see how the local workshops adopted and profusely used the Italic models, which we also see in the neighbouring town of *Baetulo* (Badalona) with productions from the *Barcino* workshop[64].

However, we must bear in mind that these models did not always arrive by a direct route, but rather via the grand capital of the neighbouring province of *Narbonensis*. *Narbo*, in addition to having a local stone not very different macroscopically from that of *Barcino*, also extensively adapted the models generated in Italy. Did the models applied in *Barcino* come in part from *Narbo*[65]? Thanks to the spectacular remodelling undertaken as part of the inauguration of the new Narbonne Museum and the project initiated by a Spanish-French team, these questions are again under discussion.

But therein lies the servitude and grandeur of our discipline that offers new readings, proposals and lines of research, always in an atmosphere of collaboration and interdisciplinarity, as we have been able to verify in all the editions of the »Roman Provincial Art Colloquia« and will witness throughout this most recent Colloquium, the seventeenth, here in Vienna. *Ago vobis gratias maximas*.

## BIBLIOGRAPHY

| | |
|---|---|
| Abascal – Cebrián 2010 | J. M. Abascal – R. Cebrián (eds.), Escultura romana en Hispania VI. Homenaje a Eva Koppel (Segobriga 2008) |
| Acuña et al. 2013 | F. Acuña – R. Casal – S. González Soutelo (eds.), Escultura romana en Hispania VII. Homenaje al Prof. Alberto Balil (Santiago de Compostela 2011) |
| Alexandrescu 2015 | C.-G. Alexandrescu (ed.), Cult and Votive Monuments in the Roman Provinces. Proceedings of the 13th International Colloquium on Roman Provincial Art in Bucharest, Alba Iulia, Constanţa 27.05.–03.06.2013 (Cluj-Napoca 2015) |
| Àlvarez et al. 2009a | A. Àlvarez et al., Marbles and Stones of Hispania = Marbres i pedres d'Hispania = Mármoles y piedras de Hispania. Exhibition catalogue (Tarragona 2009) |
| Àlvarez et al. 2009b | A. Àlvarez et al., El *marmor* de Tarraco. Explotació, utilització i comercialització de la pedra de Santa Tecla en època romana = Tarraco Marmor. The Quarrying, Use and Trade of Santa Tecla Stone in Roman Times (Tarragona 2009) |
| Àlvarez et al., in press | A. Àlvarez – A. Gutiérrez Garcia-M. – I. Rodà, Mármoles importados para la ornamentación del teatro. Análisis petrológico de siete elementos arquitectónicos in El *Theatrum Balbi* de Gades II (Cádiz, in press) |
| Baena – Beltrán 2002 | L. Baena – J. Beltrán, Las esculturas romanas de la provincia de Jaén, CSIR España I 2 (Murcia 2002) |
| Barker – Perna 2018 | S. Barker – S. Perna, Alabaster. Quarrying and Trade in the Roman World: Evidence from Pompeii and Herculaneum, in: D. Matetić Poljak – K. Marasović (eds.), Interdisciplinary Studies on Ancient Stone. Proceedings of the XIth ASMOSIA Conference Split 18.–22.05.2015 (Split 2018) 45–64 |

---

[63] Rodà 2011.
[64] Claveria – Rodà 2015; Rodà 2009.
[65] Rodà 2000.

| | |
|---|---|
| Barker – Perna, in press | S. Barker – S. Perna, ›Alabaster‹: an interdisciplinary study of the sources and uses of calcite-alabaster across archaeological contexts. Proceedings of an international workshop held at the Norwegian Institute in Rome, 09.–10.05.2019 (in press) |
| Beltrán – Loza 2020 | J. Beltrán – M. L. Loza, Provincia de Cádiz (Hispania Vlterior Baetica), CSIR España I 8 (Cádiz 2020) |
| Beltrán et al. 2006 | J. Beltrán – M. A. García García – P. Rodríguez Oliva, Los sarcófagos romanos de Andalucía, CSIR España I 3 (Murcia 2006) |
| Beltrán et al. 2018 | J. Beltrán – M. L. Loza – E. Ontiveros (coord.), Marmora Baeticae. Usos de materiales pétreos en la Bética romana. Estudios arqueológicos y análisis arqueométricos, SPAL. Monografías Arqueología 27 (Sevilla 2018) |
| Beltrán de Heredia – Rodà 2020 | J. Beltrán de Heredia – I. Rodà, Spolia y reutilización. Elementos de la Antigüedad clásica y tardía en la Catedral de Barcelona, in: J. Beltrán de Heredia (ed.), La basílica de la Santa Creu i Santa Eulàlia: la Catedral abans de la Catedral. IV Jornades de les basíliques històriques de Barcelona 2019, Studia Historica Tarraconensia 10 (Barcelona 2020) 37–71 |
| Bernal – Arévalo 2011 | D. Bernal – A. Arévalo (eds.), El *Theatrum Balbi* de Gades, UCA (Cádiz 2011) |
| Bernal et al. 2014 | D. Bernal et al., Del *Theatrum Balbi* de Gades. Recientes excavaciones arqueológicas (2010–2012), in: J. M. Álvarez Martínez – T. Nogales – I. Rodà (eds.), Actas del XVIII Congreso internacional de Arqueología Clásica: centro y periferia en el mundo clásico Mérida 13.–17.05.2013, I (Mérida 2014) 847–851 |
| Bessac 1987 | J.-Cl. Bessac, L'outillage traditionnel du tailleur de pierre de l'antiquité à nos jours, RANarb Suppl. 14 (Paris 1987) |
| Bessac 1996 | J.-Cl. Bessac, La pierre en Gaule Narbonnaise et les carrières du Bois des Lens (Nîmes). Histoire, archéologie, ethnographie, et techniques, JRA Suppl. 16 (Ann Arbor 1996) |
| Brinkmann 2008 | V. Brinkmann (ed.), Bunte Götter. Die Farbigkeit antiker Skulptur. Ausstellungskatalog Liebighaus Skulpturensammlung (Frankfurt am Main 2008) |
| Brinkmann – Bendala 2010 | V. Brinkmann – M. Bendala (eds.), El color de los dioses. El colorido de la estatuaria antigua. Exhibition Museo Arqueológico Regional, Alcalá de Henares (Madrid 2010) |
| Castellano 2004 | A. Castellano, Tritó o gegant/Tritón o gigante, Nióbide/Nióbide, Esculapi/Esculapio, in: I. Rodà (dir.), Aqua romana (Barcelona 2004) 271–273 |
| Cebrián 2012 | R. Cebrián, Las canteras de Buixcarró y el uso del marnor Saetabitanum = The Buixcarró quarries and the use of marmor Saetabitanum, in: García-Entero 2012, 155–168 |
| Claveria 2001 | M. Claveria, Los sarcófagos romanos de Cataluña, CSIR España I 1 (Murcia 2001) |
| Claveria – Rodà 2015 | M. Claveria – I. Rodà, Esculturas e inscripciones del entorno funerario de *Barcino*, in: S. Augusta-Boularot – E. Rosso (eds.), Signa et tituli. Monuments et espaces de représentation en Gaule Méridionale sous le regard croisé de la sculpture et de l'épigraphie (Arles 2015) 175–189 |
| Corré – Gaggadis-Robin 2018 | X. Corré – V. Gaggadis-Robin, Marseille et ses environs, Nouvel Espérandieu 6 (Paris 2018) |
| Darblade-Audoin 2006 | M.-P. Darblade-Audoin, Lyon, Nouvel Espérandieu 2 (Paris 2006) |
| Fernández Ochoa et al. 2022 | C. Fernández Ochoa – M. Zarzalejos – J. Salido (eds.), Tempus Romae. Exhibition Museo Arqueológico Regional, Alcalá de Henares (Madrid 2022) |
| Gaggadis-Robin et al. 2009 | V. Gaggadis-Robin – A. Hermary – M. Reddé – C. Sintes (eds.), Les ateliers de sculpture régionaux: techniques, styles et iconographie. Actes du X$^e$ Colloque International sur l'Art Provincial Romain, Arles et Aix-en-Provence 21.–23.05.2007 (Arles 2009) |
| Gaggadis-Robin – de Larquier 2019 | V. Gaggadis-Robin – N. de Larquier (eds.), La sculpture romaine et ses remplois. Actes des II$^{es}$ Rencontres autour de la sculpture romaine (Bordeaux 2019) |
| Gaggadis-Robin – Picard 2016 | V. Gaggadis-Robin – P. Picard (eds.), La sculpture romaine en Occident. Nouveaux regards. Actes des Rencontres autour de la sculpture romaine 2012 (Arles 2016) |
| García-Entero 2012 | V. García-Entero (ed.), El *marmor* en Hispania. Explotación, uso y difusión en época romana (Madrid 2012) |
| Garriguet 2001 | J. A. Garriguet, La imagen del poder imperial en Hispania. Tipos estatuarios, CSIR II 1 (Murcia 2001) |
| González Soutelo et al. 2014 | S. González Soutelo et al., El mármol de O Incio: proyecto de caracterización y estudio de la explotación y uso de un *marmor* local en la Galicia romana, in: J. M. Álvarez |

| | Martínez – T. Nogales – I. Rodà (eds.), Actas del XVIII Congreso internacional de Arqueología Clásica: centro y periferia en el mundo clásico Mérida 13.–17.05.2013, I (Mérida 2014) 323–326 |
|---|---|
| Gutiérrez Garcia-M. 2009 | A. Gutiérrez Garcia-M., Roman Quarries in the northeast of Hispania (modern Catalonia), Documenta 10 (Tarragona 2009) |
| Gutiérrez Garcia-M. – Rouillard 2018 | A. Gutiérrez Garcia-M. – P. Rouillard (eds.), Lapidum natura restat. Canteras antiguas de la península Ibérica en su contexto (cronología, técnicas y organización de la explotación) = Carrières antiques de la péninsule Ibérique dans leur contexte (chronologie, techniques et organisation de l'exploitation), Documenta 31 (Tarragona 2018) |
| Gutiérrez Garcia-M. et al. 2012 | A. Gutiérrez Garcia-M. – P. Lapuente – I. Rodà (eds.), Interdisciplinary Studies on Ancient Stone. Proceedings of the IX[th] ASMOSIA Conference Tarragona 2009, Documenta 23 (Tarragona 2012) |
| Gutiérrez Garcia-M. et al. 2016 | A. Gutiérrez Garcia-M. et al., The marble of O Incio (Galicia, Spain): quarries and first archaeometric characterisation of a material used since Roman times, ArchéoSciences. Revue d'Archéometrie 40, 2016, 103–117 |
| Gutiérrez Garcia-M. et al. 2018 | A. Gutiérrez Garcia-M. et al., New data on Spanish marbles: the case of Gallaecia (NW of Spain), in: D. Matetić Poljak – K. Marasović (eds.), Interdisciplinary Studies on Ancient Stone. Proceedings of the XI[th] ASMOSIA Conference Split 18.–22.05.2015 (Split 2018) 401–411 |
| Kremer 2012 | G. Kremer, Götterdarstellungen, Kult- und Weihedenkmäler aus Carnuntum. Mit Beiträgen von C. Gugl, C. Uhlir, M. Unterwurzacher, CSIR Carnuntum Suppl. 1 (Wien 2012) |
| Lapuente et al. 2020 | P. Lapuente et al., Addressing the controversial origin of the marble source used in the Phoenician anthropoid sarcophagi of Gadir (Cadiz, Spain), Archaeometry 2020, DOI: 10.1111/arcm.12623 |
| Lapuente et al. 2021a | P. Lapuente et al., Louvie-Soubiron Marble: Heritage Stone in the French Pyrenean Ossau Valley. First Evidence of the Roman Trans-Pyrenean Use, Geoheritage 13/1, 2021, DOI: 10.1007/s12371-021-00534-2 |
| Lapuente et al. 2021b | M. P. Lapuente – T. Nogales – A. Carvalho, Mineralogical Insights to Identify Göktepe Marble in the Sculptural Program of Quinta Das Longas Villa (Lusitania), Minerals 11, 2021, DOI: 10.3390/min11111194 |
| Lazzarini 2007 | L. Lazzarini, Poikiloi lithoi, versiculores maculae: i marmi colorati della Grecia antica (Pisa 2007) |
| Lefebvre 2017 | S. Lefebvre (dir.), Iconographie du quotidien dans l'art provincial romain: modèles régionaux. Actes du XIVème Congrès International d'Art Provincial Romain Dijon 01.–06.06.2015 (Dijon 2017) |
| Lemoine 2013 | Y. Lemoine, Fréjus, Nouvel Espérandieu 4 (Paris 2013) |
| León – Nogales 2000 | P. León – T. Nogales (coord.), Actas de la III Reunión sobre escultura romana en Hispania Córdoba 1997 (Madrid 2000) |
| Lipps 2021 | J. Lipps (ed.), People Abboard. Proceedings of the XVI[th] International Colloquium on Roman Provincial Art Tübingen 09.–13.04.2019, Tübinger Archäologische Forschungen 31 (Tübingen 2021) |
| Liverani 2004 | P. Liverani (ed.), I colori del bianco. Policromia nella scultura antica (Rome 2004) |
| López 2017 | I. López, Osuna (Provincia de Sevilla, Hispania Vlterior Baetica), CSIR España I 7 (Sevilla 2017) |
| Loza – Beltrán 2018 | M. L. Loza – J. Beltrán, El uso de los travertinos calcíticos en las *provinciae Tarraconensis et Baetica*. Una aproximación general, in: Beltrán et al. 2018, 137–149 |
| Manacorda 2011 | D. Manacorda, El complejo de Balbo en Roma, in: Bernal – Arévalo 2011, 387–407 |
| Mar – Pensabene 2009 | R. Mar – P. Pensabene, Financiación de la edilicia pública y cálculo de los costes del material lapídeo: El caso del foro superior de Tárraco, in: J. López – O. Martin (eds.), Tarraco: Construcció i arquitectura d'una capital provincial romana. Actes del Congrés Internacional en homenatge a Theodor Hauschild, Tarragona 2009, Butlletí Arqueològic 31, 2009, 345–409 |
| Marble Papers 1990 | Marble. Art Historical and Scientific Perspectives on Ancient Sculpture 1990. Papers delivered at a symposium organized by the Departments of Antiquities and Antiquities Conservation held at the J. Paul Getty Museum 1988 (Malibu 1990) |

| | |
|---|---|
| Marin – Rodà 2004 | E. Marin – I. Rodà (eds.), Divo Augusto, La descoberta d'un temple romà a Croàcia = El descubrimiento de un templo romano en Croacia (Split 2004) |
| Márquez – Ojeda 2018 | C. Márquez – D. Ojeda (eds.), Escultura romana en Hispania VIII. Homenaje a Luis Baena del Alcázar, Córdoba 2016 (Cordoba 2018) |
| Massó – Sada 1996 | J. Massó – P. Sada (eds.), Actes II Reunió sobre escultura romana a Hispània = Actas II Reunión sobre escultura romana en Hispania, Tarragona 1995 (Tarragona 1996) |
| Mateos – Morán 2020 | P. Mateos – C. J. Morán (eds.), Exemplum et Spolia I. La reutilización arquitectónica en la transformaciñon del paisaje urbano de las ciudades históricas, Mérida 2019, MYTRA 7 (Mérida 2020) |
| Merchán 2015 | M. J. Merchán, Écija (Provincia de Sevilla, Hispania Vlterior Baetica), CSIR España I 5 (Tarragona 2015) |
| Merchán et al. 2020a | M. J. Merchán et al., La digilitazión tridimensional y su aplicación en el estudio de la escultura romana, in: Noguera – Ruiz 2020, 445–457 |
| Merchán et al. 2020b | M. J. Merchán – T. Nogales – P. Merchán, Técnicas de documentación de la policromía en la estatuaria antigua. Augusta Emerita como ejemplo, in: A. Fernández Díaz – G. Castillo (coord.), La pintura romana en Hispania: del estudio de campo a su puesta en valor (Murcia 2020) 331–337 |
| Moitrieux 2010 | G. Moitrieux (with the collaboration of J.-N. Castorio), Toul et la cité des Leuques, Nouvel Espérandieu 3 (Paris 2010) |
| Moitrieux – Tronche 2017 | G. Moitrieux – P. Tronche, Saintes: la cite des Santons et Angoulême, Nouvel Espérandieu 5 (Paris 2017) |
| Moitrieux et al. 2022 | G. Moitrieux et al., Metz et la cité des Médiomatriques I–II, Nouvel Espérandieu 7 (Paris 2022) |
| Moreno 2016 | A. S. Moreno, Pollentia (Islas Baleares, Hispania Citerior), CSIR España I 6 (Granada 2016) |
| Müller at al. 2012 | H. W. Müller – B. Schwaighofer – I. Piso – M. Benea, Der Marmor im römischen Dakien (Cluj-Napoca 2012) |
| Noelke 2003 | P. Noelke (with F. Naumann-Steckner – B. Schneider), Romanisation und Resistenz in Plastik, Architektur und Inschriften der Provinzen des Imperium Romanum. Neue Funde und Forschungen. Akten des VII. Internationalen Colloquiums über Probleme des Provinzialrömischen Kunstschaffens Köln 02.–06.05.2001 (Mainz/Rhine 2003) |
| Nogales 1993 | T. Nogales (coord.), Actas de la I Reunión sobre Escultura romana en Hispania, Mérida 1992 (Madrid 1993) |
| Nogales 1997 | T. Nogales, El retrato privado en Augusta Emerita I–II (Badajoz 1997) |
| Nogales 2010 | T. Nogales, El color de Roma: Escultura y policromía en *Augusta Emerita*, in: Brinkmann – Bendala 2010, 241–251 |
| Nogales – Beltràn 2008 | T. Nogales – J. Beltràn (eds.), *Marmora Hispana:* explotación y uso de los materiales pétreos en la Hispania romana (Rome 2008) |
| Nogales – Gonçalves 2004 | T. Nogales – L. J. Gonçalves (coord.), Actas de la IV Reunión sobre escultura romana en Hispania = IV Reuniao sobre escultura romana na Hispania, Lisboa 2002 (Madrid 2004) |
| Nogales – Rodà 2011 | T. Nogales – I. Rodà (eds.), Roma y las provincias: modelo y difusión. XI Coloquio Internacional de Arte Romano Provincial, Mérida 2009 (Rome 2011) |
| Nogales et al. 2004 | T. Nogales – A. Carvalho – M. J. Almeida, El programa decorativo de la Quinta das Longas (Elvas, Portugal): un modelo excepcional de las *uillae* de la Lusitania, in: Nogales – Gonçalves 2004, 103–156 |
| Nogales et al. 2017 | T. Nogales – P. Lapuente – I. Rodà, Dos nuevos retratos de Caesar Augusta (Zaragoza), in: Lefebvre 2017, 271–280 |
| Noguera 2012 | J. M. Noguera, Segobriga (Provincia de Cuenca, Hispania Citerior), CSIR España I 4 (Tarragona 2012) |
| Noguera – Conde 2008 | J. M. Noguera – E. Conde (eds.), Escultura romana en Hispania V. Actas de la reunión internacional Murcia 09.–11.11.2005 (Murcia 2008) |
| Noguera – Ruiz 2018 | J. M. Noguera – L. Ruiz, El retrato de Adriano de la villa de Los Torrejones (Yecla, Murcia) y su contexto arqueológico, in: Márquez – Ojeda 2018, 299–317 |

| | |
|---|---|
| Noguera – Ruiz 2020 | J. M. Noguera – L. Ruiz (eds.), Escultura romana en Hispania IX. Reunión sobre escultura romana en Hispania Yecla 2019, Yakka 22 (Murcia 2020) |
| Ontiveros 2018 | E. Ontiveros, Apéndice. Caracterización arqueométrica de los traverinos calcíticos de Mijas (Málaga), in: Beltrán et al. 2018, 150–155 |
| Pensabene 1998 | P. Pensabene (ed.), Marmi antichi II. Cave e tecnica di lavorazione, provenienze e distribuzione (Rome 1998) |
| Pensabene 2013 | P. Pensabene, I marmi nella Roma antica (Rome 2013) |
| Platner – Ashby 1929 | S. B. Platner – T. Ashby, A Topographical Dictionary of Ancient Rome (London 1929) (digitized edition, Cambridge 2015, DOI: 10.1017/CBO9781316219706) |
| Pochmarski 2021 | E. Pochmarski, Die Grabbaureliefs des Stadtgebietes von Flavia Solva I, CSIR Österreich IV 4 (Vienna 2021) |
| Porod – Scherrer 2019 | B. Porod – P. Scherrer (eds.), Der Stifter und sein Monument. Gesellschaft – Ikonographie – Chronologie. Akten des 15. Internationalen Kolloqiums zum Provinzialrömischen Kunstschaften Graz 14.–20.06.2017 (Graz 2019) |
| Rodà 1990 | I. Rodà, Sarcofagi della bottega di Cartagine a Tarraco, in: A. Mastino (ed.), L'Africa Romana. Atti del VII Convegno di Studio Sassari 15.–17.12.1989 (Sassari 2019) 727–736 |
| Rodà 2000 | I. Rodà, La escultura del sur de la Narbonense y en norte de Hispania: paralelos y contactos, in: León – Nogales 2000, 173–196 |
| Rodà 2009 | I. Rodà, Los talleres de la ciudad de Barcino (Barcelona), in: Gaggadis-Robin et al. 2009, 513–529 |
| Rodà 2011 | I. Rodà, *Imago mortis*: el componente itálico en el mundo funerario de *Tarraco* y *Barcino,* in: J. Andreu – D. Espinosa – S. Pastor (coord.), Mors omnibus instat. Aspectos arqueológicos, epigráficos y rituales de la muerte en el Occidente romano (Madrid 2011) 233–254 |
| Rodà 2020 | I. Rodà, Los primeros usos del mármol en la escultura de Hispania, in: Noguera – Ruiz 2020, 101–120 |
| Rodà – Alcubierre 2020 | I. Rodà – D. Alcubierre, El ›broccatello‹ o jaspi de la Cinta a *Barcino*, in: X. Aquilué et al. (eds.), Estudis sobre ceràmica i arqueologia de l'arquitectura. Homenatge al Dr. Alberto López Mullor (Barcelona 2020) 445–453 |
| Rodà – Beltrán de Heredia 2021 | I. Rodà – J. Beltrán de Heredia, *Barcino*, in: T. Nogales (ed.), Ciudades romanas de Hispania = Cities of Roman Hispania (Rome 2021) 315–336 |
| Rodà el al. 2011 | I. Rodà et al., Anexo: Informe del análisis de un conjunto de muestras procedentes del Teatro Romano de Cádiz, in: Bernal – Arévalo 2011, 222–226. 254–256 |
| Rodríguez Oliva 2009 | P. Rodríguez Oliva, La escultura ideal, in: P. León (coord.), Arte romano de la Bética. Escultura (Sevilla 2009) 41–151 |
| Soler 2005 | B. Soler, El travertino rojo de Mula (Murcia). Definición de un mármol local, Verdolay 9, 2005, 141–164 |
| Soler 2012 | B. Soler, Planificación, producción y costo del programa marmóreo del teatro romano de Cartagena, in: García-Entero 2012, 193–228 |
| Soler 2019 | B. Soler, Lastra con decoración vegetal, Lastra con decoración geométrica, in: J. M. Noguera (ed.), Villae. Vida y producción rural en el sureste de Hispania (Murcia 2019) 250–252 |
| Souza 1990 | V. de Souza, CSIR Portugal (Coimbra 1990) |
| Terrer et al. 2003 | D. Terrer et al., Vienne (Isère), Nouvel Espérandieu 1 (Paris 2003) |
| Ventura – Borrego 2011 | A. Ventura – J. de D. Borrego, *Notae lapicidinarum Lunensium, damnatio memoriae* y *graffito* maldiciente en una inscripción del teatro romano de *Gades,* in: Bernal –Arévalo 2011, 227–253 |
| Ventura et al. 2021 | A. Ventura – J. de D. Borrego – F. J. Alarcón, M. Agrippa ¿propietario de canteras de mármol en Carrara? Nueva *nota lapicidinarum Lunensium* hallada en el teatro romano de *Gades*, AEspA 94, 2021, DOI: 10.3989/aespa.094.021.05 |
| Vidal 2005 | S. Vidal, La escultura hispana figurada de la antigüedad tardía (ss. IV–VII), CSIR España II 2 (Murcia 2005) |
| Vidal – García-Entero 2015 | S. Vidal – V. García-Entero, The use of Estremoz marble in late antique sculpture of Hispania: new data from petrographic and cathodoluminiscence analyses, in: P. Pensa- |

| | |
|---|---|
| | bene – E. Gasparini (eds.), ASMOSIA X. Proceedings of the 10th International Conference Rome 21.–26.05.2012, I (Rome 2015) 413–420 |
| Vidal et al. 2016 | S. Vidal – V. García-Entero – A. Gutiérrez Garcia-M., La utilización del mármol de Estremoz en la escultura hispánica de la antigüedad tardía: los sarcófagos, digitAR 3, 2016, 119–128, DOI: 10.14195/2182-844X_3_14 |
| Vinci et al. 2020 | S. Vinci – A. Ottati – D. Gorostidi (eds.), La cava e il monumento. Materiali, officine, sistema di costruzione e produzione nei cantieri edilizi di età imperiale (Rome 2020) |
| Waelkens et al. 1992 | M. Waelkens – N. Herz – L. Moens, Ancient Stones: quarrying, trade and provenance. Interdisciplinary Studies on Stones and Stone Technology in Europe and Near East from the Prehistoric to the Early Christian Period (Leuven 1992) |
| Ward-Perkins 1992 | H. Dodge – B. Ward-Perkins (eds.), Marble in Antiquity. Collected papers of J. B. Ward-Perkins, Archaeological Monographs of the British School at Rome 6 (London 1992) |

*Isabel Rodà de Llanza, Catedràtica Honorària d'Arqueologia, Departament de Ciències de l'Antiguitat i Edat Mitjana, Universitat Autònoma de Barcelona and second member of ICAC, Villarroel 191, 08036 Barcelona, Spain.*
*[e] isabel.roda@uab.cat*

**METHODEN DER FORSCHUNG**

Erich Draganits – Beatrix Moshammer – Gabrielle Kremer – Andreas Rohatsch – Michael Doneus

# DIE STEINBRUCHLANDSCHAFT VON BAD DEUTSCH-ALTENBURG (OSTÖSTERREICH)

## EINE ROHSTOFFQUELLE SEIT DER RÖMERZEIT

**Abstract**

In order to gain information about Roman quarries in the hinterland of *Carnuntum* and *Vindobona*, quarries in Miocene sedimentary rocks in the southernVienna Basin, Leitha Mountains, Rust Hills and Hundsheim Mountains were documented using high-resolution airborne laser scanning data and aerial photographs. In total, 658 quarries, possible quarries and shallow quarries were interpreted in the remote sensing data. In addition, historical maps, historical photographs, paintings, documents and graffiti on quarry walls were used to obtain age determinations in this diachronic dataset. As an example for the whole study area, the region around Bad Deutsch-Altenburg, which is perfectly suited for this purpose due to its proximity to *Carnuntum* and the excellent source situation, is presented in more detail.

## EINLEITUNG

Die Lage am Südufer der Donau an der Porta Hungarica, am Ostrand des Wiener Beckens, und die vorhandenen geologischen Möglichkeiten zur Steingewinnung waren ohne Zweifel gewichtige Gründe für die Übernahme und den Ausbau des keltischen Siedlungsstandortes an der Stelle des späteren *Carnuntum* durch die Römer. Bereits die keltische Wurzel des Ortsnamens *karn (Fels) scheint auf die »steinreiche« Umgebung des in vielerlei Hinsicht günstigen Siedlungsgebietes hinzuweisen[1]. Der im Lauf des 1. Jahrhunderts n. Chr. zum Aufbau der Infrastruktur und in der Folge zum schrittweisen Ausbau der militärischen Anlagen sowie der Metropole anfallende Bedarf an Baumaterial war enorm. Die frühesten militärischen Grabstelen der *legio XV Apollinaris* aus *Carnuntum*[2] belegen, dass bereits vor dem systematischen (partiellen) Ausbau der Militärlager in Stein ab flavischer Zeit lokale und regionale Steinbrüche in Betrieb gewesen sein müssen. Das Vorhandensein und vor allem die Nähe zu geeigneten Abbaugebieten dürfte daher seit dem Beginn der römischen Präsenz[3] sowohl unter ökonomischen als auch unter strategischen Gesichtspunkten eine wichtige Rolle gespielt haben[4]. Deren Prospektion, Erschließung und Abbau erfolgte wohl bis zu ihrer Verlegung um 114 n. Chr. durch die *legio XV Apollinaris*. Eine

---

[1] s. z. B. Urban 2006, 175; Anreiter u. a. 2000 leiten das Toponym von *(s)kar-n- (< *(s)kar- »rough, hard«) ab und schreiben: »may belong to easternmost fringe of Eastern Alpine I[ndo]E[uropean]«; Falileyev 2010, 13 stellt den Ortsnamen *Carnuntum* zum keltischen Stamm carno- »peak, tumulus, cairn« und vergleicht ihn mit mittelirisch carn/walisisch carn (für die beiden letzten Literaturhinweise danken wir Andreas Hofeneder).

[2] Mosser 2003; Weber-Hiden 2017; Kremer u. a. 2021. – Als Beispiel sei die Porträtstele des Rufus Lucilius (40–44 n. Chr.) genannt, die aus Corallinaceenkalkarenit der Hundsheimer Berge gefertigt ist: Archäologisches Museum Carnuntinum (AMC) Inv. CAR-S-932; CIL III 13484; Mosser 2003, Nr. 109; lupa 12.

[3] Die erste literarische Quelle bei Velleius Paterculus 2, 109, 5 (Erwähnung von *Carnuntum* für das Jahr 6 n. Chr.). Zum historischen Hintergrund s. Kovács 2014, 23–57 bes. 42–43.

[4] Vgl. Vitr., arch. 1, 2, 8: *Haec ita observabitur, si primum architectus ea non quaeret quae non poterunt inveniri aut parari nisi magno* (Sie [= die zweckmäßige Einteilung der Baukosten] wird so beobachtet, wenn erstens der Architekt keine Baumaterialien anfordert, die nicht [in der Nähe] gefunden werden oder nur teuer beschafft werden können) (Übers. C. Fensterbusch [Hrsg.] ⁴[Darmstadt 1964]; cf. <https://penelope.uchicago.edu/Thayer/E/Roman/Texts/Vitruvius/1*.html> [29.03.2023].

1 Bauinschrift der *legio XV Apollinaris*, *centuria* des C. Aconius (AMC Inv. CAR-S-1253) aus Corallinaceen-Kalkarenit der Hundsheimer Berge (Landessammlungen Niederösterreich, Archäologischer Park Carnuntum, Foto N. Gail)

Bauinschrift dieser Legion, ein sog. Zenturienstein, wurde 1893 im »Steinbruch am sogenannten ›Quadenwall‹«[5], dem heute abgetragenen Teil des Kirchenbergs von Bad Deutsch-Altenburg gefunden (Abb. 1)[6].

Aus dem antiken Siedlungsgebiet von *Carnuntum* ist heute eine für die Nordwestprovinzen außergewöhnlich hohe Anzahl an Steinmonumenten – Skulpturen, Grab- und Votivdenkmäler, Architekturteile – überliefert[7]. Durchschnittlich sind fast 10 % dieser Objekte aus Marmor gefertigt, einem Material, das nach *Carnuntum* importiert werden musste, wobei der Anteil je nach Fundgattung (Skulptur, Architektur) stark variiert[8]. Die Provenienz der Gesteine für die übrigen 90 % der Monumente war Untersuchungsgegenstand eines Forschungsprojektes an der Österreichischen Akademie der Wissenschaften[9]. Ziel dieses Projektes war es, lokale und regionale antike Steinbrüche oder Abbaugebiete im Wiener Becken und im Leithagebirge zu identifizieren und mit dem Bestand an römerzeitlichen Monumenten zu vergleichen. Auf diese Weise sollten unter anderem Informationen zu Fragen der Bildhauerwerkstätten, der Transportrouten oder der ökonomischen und siedlungshistorischen Entwicklung im Hinterland der Legionsstandorte *Carnuntum* und *Vindobona* gewonnen werden.

Eine Teilstudie im Rahmen des CarVin-Projektes konzentrierte sich auf die Auswertung von hochauflösenden Luftaufnahmen, detaillierten Geländemodellen aus Airborne Laser Scanning (ALS) Höhendaten, Textquellen, historischen Karten sowie historischen Bildern und Fotos und deren Integration und Analyse in einem geografischen Informationssystem (GIS)[10]. Ziel dieses Artikels ist es, das Potenzial dieser integrierenden Herangehensweise anhand der Ergebnisse für den Bereich um Bad Deutsch-Altenburg, der nur weniger als 1 % der gesamten untersuchten Fläche ausmacht, exemplarisch aufzuzeigen.

---

[5] Bormann 1893, 220.
[6] CIL III 13479; Mosser 2003, Nr. 232; lupa 10429 (mit irriger Fundortangabe).
[7] Allein im Archäologischen Museum Carnuntinum in Bad Deutsch-Altenburg werden an die 3000 Monumente und Einzelteile verwahrt. Die epigrafischen Datenbanken EDCS und EDH führen aus dem Carnuntiner Territorium derzeit 2295 bzw. 1717 Inschriften an (Abruf 20.01.2023). In der Bilddatenbank »Ubi erat lupa« sind unter dem Fundort »Carnuntum« derzeit 1142 Objekte zu finden (Abruf 20.01.2023). – s. auch Krüger 1970; Krüger 1972; Krüger 1976; Kremer 2012; Beszédes 2020.
[8] Kremer 2012, 421–430 (mit weiterer Literatur).
[9] FWF P 26368-G21: »Steindenkmäler und Steingewinnung im Raum Carnuntum – Vindobona. Interdisziplinäre Auswertung einer archäologischen Fundgattung« (Projekt CarVin). Zuletzt Kremer u. a. 2021 (mit Literatur).
[10] Für ausführliche Quellenangaben, Methoden, Daten, Auswertungen und Diskussionen wird auf die ausführliche Publikation dieser Teilstudie verwiesen: Draganits u. a. 2023.

## GEOLOGISCHER ÜBERBLICK

Das Untersuchungsgebiet in Ostösterreich befindet sich in einem geodynamisch sehr komplexen Grenzgebiet zwischen den Ostalpen, den Westlichen Karpaten und dem Pannonischen Becken. Dieses Gebiet ist charakterisiert und geformt durch die noch immer andauernde Kollision von Europa, Afrika und dazwischen befindlichen Mikrokontinenten, aus der eine Krustenverdickung resultiert[11], und überprägt durch laterale Extrusion[12] und Extension durch die Entstehung des Pannonischen Beckens[13].

In dem Projekt wurden archäologische Steinartefakte (Bausteine, Skulpturen etc.) aus Kalkrotalgen [coralline Algen]-dominierten (Schutt-)Kalken bis Kalkbrekzien und -konglomeraten, Lumachellen, Kalksandsteinen, Quarzsandsteinen und Oolithen untersucht, die in diesem Gebiet während des mittleren und späten Miozäns (Langhium, Serravallium und Tortonium, i.e. Badenium, Sarmatium und frühes Pannonium der zentralen Paratethys; etwa vor 16–10 Millionen Jahren) abgelagert worden waren[14]. Lithostratigrafisch stammen diese Sedimente hauptsächlich aus der Leitha-Formation und Leithakalk-Äquivalenten der Studienka-Formation, Holic Formation und Skalica Formation[15]. Die Sedimente aus dem Langhium und Serravallium wurden im Meer abgelagert[16]; die Sedimente aus dem unteren Tortonium werden meist als Sedimente eines Süßwassersees interpretiert[17]. Die geologische Situation der Hainburger Berge ist von Godfrid Wessely zusammengefasst[18].

## VERWENDETE FERNERKUNDUNGSDATEN UND DEREN INTERPRETATION

Aus Airborne Laser Scanning (ALS) erzeugte digitale Geländemodelle (DGM) mit 1 × 1 m Auflösung und <10 cm vertikaler Genauigkeit standen für das gesamte >950 km² große Untersuchungsgebiet zur Verfügung. Die ALS-Daten von Niederösterreich wurden in den Jahren 2006–2010 gemessen, jene im Burgenland im Jahr 2010. Zusätzlich wurden Orthofotos mit einer Auflösung von 0,2 m von Befliegungen in den Jahren 2010–2013 verwendet. Sämtliche Daten wurden systematisch nach Spuren von Steinbrüchen untersucht und die Ergebnisse in einer GIS-basierten räumlichen Datenbank gespeichert. Im gesamten Untersuchungsgebiet wurden in den Fernerkundungsdaten 479 Steinbrüche, 108 mögliche Steinbrüche und 71 seichte Steinbrüche in den miozänen Gesteinen interpretiert[19]. Die unterschiedlichen Typen von Steinbrüchen wurden basierend auf den Beobachtungen und Erfahrungen während der Interpretation der Fernerkundungsdaten definiert: (i) Steinbrüche sind Vertiefungen im Gestein, >4 m tief und besitzen mindestens eine sehr steile Abbauwand; (ii) mögliche Steinbrüche sind ähnlich wie Steinbrüche, aber unsicherer; (iii) seichte Steinbrüche sind <4 m tief, haben meist undeutliche und oft unregelmäßige Ränder, Abraum wurde fast nie wahrgenommen; (iv) inaktive Steinbrüche sind ein Typ, der nur in den historischen Karten klassifiziert wurde, beispielsweise, wenn ein Steinbruch explizit als »alt« gekennzeichnet wurde.

## FALLBEISPIEL: STEINBRUCHLANDSCHAFT BAD DEUTSCH-ALTENBURG

Die Region von Bad Deutsch-Altenburg, am Westrand der Hundsheimer Berge gelegen, wurde als Beispiel unserer geoarchäologischen Kartierung von Steinbrüchen ausgewählt wegen ihrer

---

[11] Cavazza u. a. 2004; Schuster u. a. 2019.
[12] Ratschbacher u. a. 1991a; 1991b; Schuster u. a. 2019.
[13] Horváth u. a. 2006.
[14] Piller u. a. 2007.
[15] Pivko u. a. 2017; Harzhauser u. a. 2020.
[16] Piller – Harzhauser 2005; Wiedl u. a. 2012; Wiedl u. a. 2013; Wiedl u. a. 2014.
[17] z. B. Harzhauser u. a. 2003.
[18] Wessely 2006, 183–187. s. auch Wessely 1961.
[19] Draganits u. a. 2023.

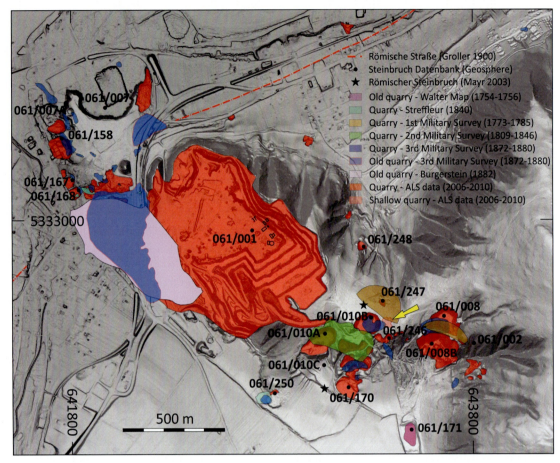

2  Die in den ALS-Daten und historischen Karten interpretierten Steinbrüche im Raum Bad Deutsch-Altenburg und Pfaffenberg auf einer Visualisierung des digitalen ALS-Geländemodells (1 × 1 m): (i) Höhenwerte in Graustufen, Prozent Clip Streckung; (ii) 50 % transparente Hangneigungskarte, Azimuth 315° mit 45° Beleuchtungswinkel, Minimum-Maximum-Streckung; (iii) 50 % transparente Hangneigungskarte mit Standardabweichung Streckung. Sterne kennzeichnen die in Mayr 2003, Abb. 8 als römische Steinbrüche bezeichneten Areale. Der seichte Steinbruch am Sattel zwischen Pfaffenberg und Hundsheimer Berg ist mit einem gelben Pfeil gekennzeichnet (Karte E. Draganits)

Nähe zu *Carnuntum* und der relativ guten Quellenlage in Form von zahlreichen relevanten Studien über Geologie[20], Archäologie[21] und Geschichte von Steinbrüchen[22], historischen Karten[23], detaillierten Katasterkarten[24] sowie historischen Fotos und Grafiken[25]. Ohne diese außergewöhnlich große Menge an detaillierten Daten wäre die Interpretation der Fernerkundungsdaten sehr schwierig gewesen. Der Nachteil dieses Gebietes sind auf jeden Fall die intensiven Steinbruchaktivitäten, vor allem ab dem 19. Jahrhundert, die verständlicherweise eine Vielzahl der älteren Spuren vernichtet haben[26].

Abbildung 2 zeigt die Interpretation der Steinbruchlandschaft von Bad Deutsch-Altenburg, basierend auf ALS-basierten Geländemodellen, Orthofotos, geologischen Karten und histori-

---

[20] Burgerstein 1882; Karrer 1900; Wessely 1961; Fuchs u. a. 1985; Wessely 2006; Pivko 2012; Mayr 2003.
[21] Tragau 1897; Kandler 2000; Thür 2000.
[22] Lachmayer 1999; Farka 2000; Geng-Sesztak u. a. 2000.
[23] Maynzeck 1717; Walter 1754–1756; Erste, Zweite und Dritte Landesaufnahme; Streffleur c. 1840; s. z. B. <https://maps.arcanum.com/de> (29.03.2023); <https://maps.hungaricana.hu/en> (08.04.2023).
[24] Henner 1819.
[25] Farka 2000; Geng-Sesztak u. a. 2000; Springer – Sacken 2000.
[26] Lachmayer 1999; Farka 2000; Geng-Sesztak u. a. 2000.

schen Karten[27]. Trotz seiner kleinen Fläche spiegelt dieses Gebiet die diachrone Entwicklung der Steinbrüche im Untersuchungsgebiet sehr gut wider. Während in der Ersten Landesaufnahme (1773–1781) und der Zweiten Landesaufnahme (1809–1818) nur sehr wenige Steinbrüche eingezeichnet sind, kommt es in der Dritten Landesaufnahme (1872–1873) zu einem dramatischen Anstieg der kartierten Steinbrüche. Insgesamt zeigt die Interpretation dieses Bereiches mehr als 70 Steinbrüche in den ALS-Daten und historischen Karten. Bis auf wenige Ausnahmen sind alle in den ALS-Daten kartierten Steinbrüche auch in den historischen Karten zu finden. In einer petrografischen Diplomarbeit[28] werden zwei »römische Steinbrüche« im Bereich des Pfaffenberges eingezeichnet, ohne jedoch Gründe für diese zeitliche Einordnung anzugeben. Da keine Koordinaten von den Steinbrüchen in der Diplomarbeit vorhanden sind, wurde ihre Lage aus Abbildung 8[29] rekonstruiert und in Abbildung 2 eingezeichnet. Die beiden Punkte könnten möglicherweise auf jeweils etwa 100 m östlich davon gelegene Steinbruchareale hinweisen (Abb. 2).

Von speziellem Interesse sind zwei Gebiete nördlich und nordwestlich vom Pfaffenberg, die durch ihre unregelmäßige, raue, ›unnatürliche‹ Darstellung des Terrains auffallen, mit zahlreichen unregelmäßigen kleinen Hügeln und Vertiefungen, sowohl in der Karte von Josef Streffleur[30] (Abb. 3) als auch in der Dritten Landesaufnahme (1872–1873). Diese Gebiete wurden als ehemalige Steinbrüche interpretiert[31], und bezeichnenderweise scheinen beide Gebiete weder in historischen Karten als Steinbrüche[32] noch in historischen Berichten auf[33].

Der Bereich nördlich des Pfaffenberges ist durch Straßenbau und Bahnbau fast komplett zerstört und wurde nicht näher untersucht. Das Gebiet nordwestlich des Pfaffenberges, das in der Dritten Landesaufnahme die besprochene auffällige Topografie zeigt, befindet sich heute im Bereich des Bahnhofs von Bad Deutsch-Altenburg, der Hainburgerstraße und nordöstlich der Neustiftgasse (Abb. 2). Auch Maximilian Groller[34] zeichnet in seinem Lageplan in diesem Bereich unregelmäßige Vertiefungen ein. Laut der geologischen Karte kommen dort Sedimente aus dem Badenium und Sarmatium vor[35]. Wenn es sich bei dieser Fläche wirklich um einen ehemaligen Steinbruch handelt[36], so muss er älter als die Karte von János Kováts aus dem Jahr 1717[37] und als die extrem detaillierte Karte von Constantin J. Walter (1754–1756) sein. Es finden sich auch keine schriftlichen Hinweise auf Steinbruchaktivitäten in diesem Areal[38].

Könnte es sich also um römische Steinbrüche handeln? Die betreffende Fläche befindet sich rund 1,5 km nordöstlich des Legionslagers *Carnuntum* auf ähnlicher Seehöhe und direkt neben der römischen Straße von *Carnuntum* entlang der Donau nach Osten (Abb. 2). Leo Burgerstein führte 1882[39] die ersten detaillierten geologischen Studien in Bad Deutsch-Altenburg durch und verfasste eine geologische Karte im Maßstab 1 : 12 500 (Abb. 4 oben). Er zeichnete auch eine Landschaftsskizze von Bad Deutsch-Altenburg mit Blick nach Osten in Richtung Pfaffenberg, die den Bereich des möglichen Steinbruchs sehr gut darstellt (Abb. 4 unten). Er liefert dazu die folgende Beschreibung: »Von der westlichen kleineren Leithaconglomeratmasse am Südwest-Abhange des Pfaffenberges … zieht sich gegen den Ort zu zerlapptes, sanfthügeliges Terrain,

---

[27] Draganits u. a. 2023.
[28] Mayr 2003.
[29] Mayr 2003, Abb. 8.
[30] Streffleur c. 1840. Die Karte von Streffleur, im Maßstab 1 : 1728, ist auch die detaillierteste Darstellung der ehemaligen Wallanlage im Norden des Kirchenberges von Bad Deutsch-Altenburg (s. Neugebauer-Maresch 1980), die ebenfalls dem Steinabbau zum Opfer fiel.
[31] Draganits u. a. 2023.
[32] z. B. Anonymous c. 1828; Streffleur c. 1840; Burgerstein 1882.
[33] z. B. Geng-Sesztak u. a. 2000.
[34] Groller 1900, Taf. I Lageplan B.
[35] Fuchs u. a. 1985.
[36] Draganits u. a. 2023.
[37] Kováts 1717.
[38] Geng-Sesztak u. a. 2000.
[39] Burgerstein 1882.

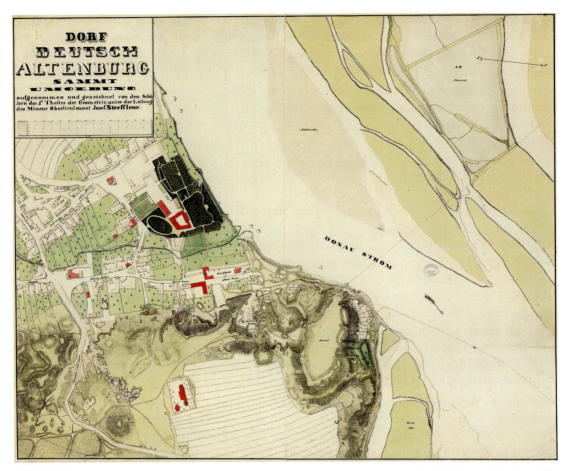

3 Detaillierte topografische Karte von Josef Streffleur, ca. 1840. Sie zeigt in großem Detail (M. 1 : 1728) die auffällig hügelige Topografie des Bereiches südlich der Straße nach Hainburg, die als Überreste eines römischen Steinbruches interpretiert werden. Sie bildet auch zahlreiche, kleinere Steinbrüche ab, die offensichtlich in der Zeit der Kartenerstellung deutlich frischer erhalten waren. Die Karte enthält auch den Hütelberg – sogar mit den Mundlöchern der Grabungsstollen – und die detaillierteste Darstellung der durch Steinabbau zerstörten, ehemaligen Wallanlage im Norden des Kirchenberges (Országos Széchényi Könyvtár, TK 2074)

welches aus einer Anhäufung von losen Nulliporenstücken oder Schutt von Nulliporenkalk besteht und auf der Karte für sich ausgeschieden ist; man sieht dieses Material an dem Chausseeeinschnitt, welcher die Hügelreihe durchschneidet, gut aufgeschlossen; nach dem Einblick, den man bei Anlage der Chaussee bekam, sind es möglicherweise die (dann colossalen) Massen von Abraum aus altrömischen Steinbrüchen.«[40]

Im Saal XIII des 1889 eröffneten Naturhistorischen Museums Wien hängt ein Gemälde von Robert Russ, das den erwähnten Bereich mit Blickrichtung Norden zeigt, mit der Pfarrkirche und dem Hütelberg im Hintergrund. Der Vordergrund zeigt gelbliche, relativ weiche, horizontal geschichtete Sedimentgesteine, die offensichtlich auf unterschiedlichen Niveaus abgebaut wurden. In dem Zusammenhang ist die Bemerkung von Carl Tragau über die Ausgrabung eines der Befestigungstürme an der Ostseite des römischen Legionslagers wichtig: »Zur Verwendung kam das beste Gestein der Umgegend, Leithakalk aus den Brüchen des Hundsheimer-, Pfaffen- und Kirchenberges. Tatsächlich fanden sich zwischen Deutsch-Altenburg und dem Fuße des Pfaffenberges (…) zahlreiche Abfälle von Steinzurichtung, welche mit dem im Lager und im Castell am Stein verwendeten Material übereinstimmen.«[41]

---

[40] Burgerstein 1882, 111–112.
[41] Tragau 1897, 195.

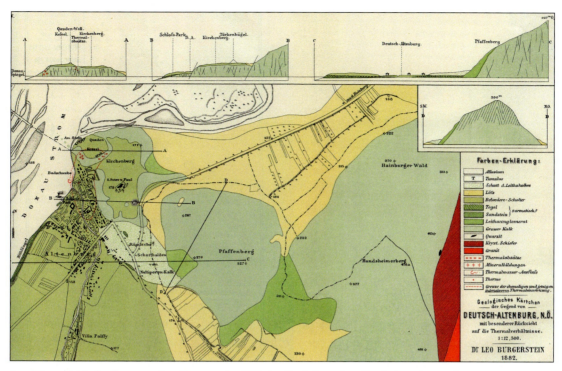

4   Die geologische Karte von Leo Burgerstein, 1882, ist die früheste Detailaufnahme der Geologie im Bereich von Bad Deutsch-Altenburg. Von speziellem Interesse ist jene Fläche, die er im Bereich Bahnhof, Hainburger Straße und nordöstlich der Neustiftgasse, abgrenzt und mit »Römische? Schutthalden von Nulliporen-Kalk« kennzeichnet (aus: Burgerstein 1882, Taf. 1)

Felix Karrer, der sich bereits sehr früh mit den neogenen Sedimenten des Wiener Beckens beschäftigt hat und die Baustein-Sammlung des Naturhistorischen Museums Wien gründete, beprobte Steine während der damaligen Ausgrabungen in *Carnuntum*. Er schreibt: »Vom Nulliporenkalk [Corallinaceae] vom römischen Steinbruch südlich der Bahnstation Deutsch-Altenburg liegen vor: Muster eines Werksteines aus den Bauten ›am Stein‹, ferner Proben vom Amphitheater, vom Nemeseum usw. Sehr häufig findet sich dieser Nulliporenkalk als roher Bruchstein im Nemeseum verwendet.«[42]

Da das besprochene Gebiet nordwestlich des Pfaffenberges, im Bereich des heutigen Bahnhofs, das nächst gelegene (1,5 km) und ein sehr leicht zugängliches Vorkommen (direkt an der römischen Straße von *Carnuntum* nach *Gerulata*) von neogenen Kalksandsteinen (*sensu lato*) für *Carnuntum* ist, wäre es überraschend, wenn es für die Steinversorgung nicht genützt worden wäre. Das Gebiet ist insgesamt bis zu 700 m lang und 300 m breit, hat eine Fläche von etwa 18 ha und zählt damit zu den größten interpretierten Steinbrüchen des gesamten Untersuchungsgebietes.

Die anhand der ALS-basierten Geländemodelle kartierten ›seichten Steinbrüche‹ sind von speziellem Interesse, da sie in den historischen Karten kaum aufscheinen und auch in der Abbaue-Datenbank der GeoSphere Austria kaum zu finden sind[43]. Ein schönes Beispiel für diesen Steinbruchtyp ist jener am Sattel zwischen dem Pfaffenberg und dem Hundsheimer Berg (Abb. 2). Er ist von nur sehr geringer Tiefe (Abb. 5), zeigt in den ALS-Daten eine sehr unregelmäßige Form und scheint weder in den historischen Karten noch in der Abbaue-Datenbank der GeoSphere Austria auf. Der seichte Steinbruch liegt auf fast gleicher Seehöhe und nur 700 m südöstlich des Pfaffenberg-Plateaus, auf dem spätestens ab der Mitte des 1. Jahrhunderts n. Chr. ein römischer Kultplatz existierte[44]. Die militärische Präsenz ist dort durch den frühesten datierten Votivaltar aus

---

[42] Karrer 1900, 4; Draganits u. a. 2023, Abb. 13 zeigt eine Gesteinsprobe aus dem Bereich der Hainburgerstraße 29.
[43] s. Draganits u. a. 2023, Abb. 3.
[44] Zuletzt Jobst 2021.

5 Geländefoto (20. März 2015) des seichten Steinbruchs am Sattel zwischen dem Pfaffenberg und dem Hundsheimer Berg zeigt die geringe Tiefe des Steinbruchs und die relativ geradlinige Begrenzung in diesem Bereich; Barbara Hodits als Maßstab (Foto E. Draganits)

*Carnuntum*, die Weihung eines Soldaten der *legio XV Apollinaris* an Victoria[45], bezeugt. Das Heiligtum wurde 1985 durch Steinbruchabbau komplett zerstört[46]. Der erwähnte seichte Steinbruch bietet sich als eine nahe liegende, praktische Gesteinsquelle für Bauten in diesem Heiligtum an. Ob das wirklich der Fall war, kann nur ein Vergleich der dort vorkommenden Gesteine mit den im Heiligtum verwendeten zeigen.

## CONCLUSIO

Die vorliegende Kartierung von Steinbrüchen in Fernerkundungsdaten zeigt nachdrücklich das Potenzial detaillierter ALS-Daten in der (geo-)archäologischen Prospektion. Insgesamt konnten in den ALS-basierten Geländemodellen 479 Steinbrüche, 108 mögliche Steinbrüche und 71 seichte Steinbrüche in Sedimentgesteinen aus dem Miozän kartiert werden, von denen 343, vorwiegend kleine oder am Rande größerer Steinbrüche gelegene, in der existierenden Steinbruchdatenbank der GeoSphere Austria nicht aufscheinen[47]. Mithilfe historischer Karten, historischer Bilder und Dokumente konnten chronologische Informationen in dem diachronen Datensatz[48] ergänzt werden.

Die Integration und Interpretation aller verfügbaren Daten in einer GIS-Umgebung war eine wichtige Voraussetzung für die erfolgreiche Abwicklung dieses Forschungsvorhabens. Die dadurch gegebene Möglichkeit, alle interpretierten Steinbrüche in ihrer Fläche und nicht nur als Punkt zu dokumentieren, ermöglichte erstmals eine Quantifizierung ihrer Entwicklung, Ausdehnung und Verteilung[49].

Archäologische Prospektion beschäftigt sich vorwiegend mit der Interpretation der Erdoberfläche und ihrer Materialien, die aus einer Kombination von geologischen und anthropogenen Formationsprozessen resultieren. Deshalb benötigt jede archäologische Prospektion zumindest teilweise geoarchäologische Expertise.

---

[45] Piso 2003, 17 Nr. 1; Mosser 2003, 266–267 Nr. 201 Taf. 27; Kremer 2012, 313–316 Abb. 9.
[46] Thür 2000.
[47] Draganits u. a. 2023.
[48] Draganits u. a. 2023.
[49] Draganits u. a. 2023

## DANKSAGUNG

Wir danken Franz Humer für seine Unterstützung und das Interesse an unseren Forschungen. Dank geht auch an das Amt der Burgenländischen Landesregierung, Servicestelle Geodaten, und das Amt der Niederösterreichischen Landesregierung, Abteilung Hydrologie und Geoinformation, für den Zugang zu hochauflösenden Geländedaten und Luftbildern. Die Geosphere Austria ermöglichte die Verwendung ihrer GIS-Abbaue-Datenbank und ihres Abbauearchivs.

## BIBLIOGRAFIE

| | |
|---|---|
| Anonymous c. 1828 | Anonymous, Deutsch-Altenburg in Nied. Östrch im J. 1828. C. 1:4,000, Széchényi-National Library, TK 346. (1828), <https://maps.hungaricana.hu/en/OSZKTerkeptar/345> (29.03.2023) |
| Anreiter u. a. 2000 | P. Anreiter – U. Roider – M. Haslinger, The names of the eastern Alpine region mentioned in Ptolemy, in: D. N. Parsons – P. Sims-Williams (Hrsg.), Ptolemy: Towards a linguistic atlas of the earliest Celtic place-names of Europe. Papers from a workshop, sponsored by the British Academy, in the Department of Welsh, University of Wales, Aberystwyth, 11.–12.04.1999 (Aberystwyth 2000) 113–142 |
| Beszédes 2020 | J. Beszédes, Római kori sírkövek Carnuntumból és városi territoriumáról (Budapest 2020) |
| Burgerstein 1882 | L. Burgerstein, Geologische Studie über die Therme von Deutsch-Altenburg an der Donau, Denkschriften der kaiserlichen Akademie der Wissenschaften, mathematisch-naturwissenschaftliche Klasse 45/2, 1882, 107–122, <https://www.zobodat.at/pdf/DAKW_45_2_0107-0122.pdf> (29.03.2023) |
| Cavazza u. a. 2004 | W. Cavazza – F. Roure – W. Spakman – G. M. Stampfli – P. A. Ziegler (Hrsg.), The TRANSMED Atlas. The Mediterranean Region from Crust to Mantle (Berlin 2004), DOI: 10.1007/978-3-642-18919-7 |
| Draganits u. a. 2023 | E. Draganits – B. Moshammer – G. Kremer – M. Doneus, Geoarchaeological remote sensing prospection of Miocene limestone stone quarries in the hinterland of Roman Carnuntum and Vindobona (Vienna Basin, Austria), Austrian Journal of Earth Sciences 116, 2023, 39–83, DOI: 10.17738/ajes.2023.0003 |
| Falileyev 2010 | A. Falileyev, Dictionary of Continental Celtic Place-Names (Aberystwyth 2010) |
| Farka 2000 | C. Farka (Hrsg.), Der Kirchenberg. Archäologie und Geschichte im Bereich der Marienkirche von Bad Deutsch-Altenburg, Niederösterreich (Bad Deutsch-Altenburg 2000) |
| Fuchs u. a. 1985 | W. Fuchs – G. Wessely – R. Grill, 61 Hainburg an der Donau – 62 Pressburg. Geologische Karte der Republik Österreich 1:50.000 (Wien 1985), <https://opac.geologie.ac.at/wwwopacx/wwwopac.ashx?command=getcontent&server=images&value=GK0061_000_A.pdf> (29.03.2023) |
| Geng-Sesztak u. a. 2000 | G. Geng-Sesztak – W. Krems – H. Lachmayer (Hrsg.), Bad Deutsch-Altenburg – Bild einer Gegend (Wien 2000) |
| Groller 1900 | M. Groller, Topographie der Umgebung von Carnuntum, RLÖ 1 (Wien 1900) 11–18 |
| Harzhauser u. a. 2003 | M. Harzhauser – G. Daxner-Höck – W. E. Piller, An integrated stratigraphy of the Pannonian (Late Miocene) in the Vienna Basin, Austrian Journal of Earth Sciences 95–96, 2003, 6–19, <https://www.ajes.at/images/AJES/archive/Band%2095-96/harzhauser_daxner-hoeck_piller_ajes_v95_96.pdf> (29.03.2023) |
| Harzhauser u. a. 2020 | M. Harzhauser – M. Kranner – O. Mandic – P. Strauss – W. Siedl – W. E. Piller, Miocene lithostratigraphy of the northern and central Vienna Basin (Austria), Austrian Journal of Earth Sciences 113/2, 2020, 169–199, DOI: 10.17738/ajes.2020.0011 |
| Henner 1819 | H. Henner, Gemeinde Deutschaltenburg in N:ÖsterreichV:U:W:W. Franziszeischer Kataster, 1:2800 (Wien 1819) |
| Horváth u. a. 2006 | F. Horváth – G. Bada – P. Szafián – G. Tari – A. Ádám – S. Cloetingh, Formation and deformation of the Pannonian basin: Constraints from observational data, in: D. G. Gee – R. A. Stephenson (Hrsg.), European lithosphere dynamics, Geological Society London Memoirs 32, 2006, 191–206, DOI: 10.1144/GSL.MEM.2006.032.01.11 |

| | |
|---|---|
| Jobst 2021 | W. Jobst, Das Heiligtum des Jupiter Optimus Maximus auf dem Pfaffenberg/Carnuntum III. Ausgrabungen und Funde im Spannungsfeld der Interessen, RLÖ 41 (Wien 2021) |
| Kandler 2000 | H. Kandler, Der Kirchenberg von Bad Deutsch-Altenburg und seine archäologischen Denkmäler, in: Farka 2000, 13–38 |
| Karrer 1900 | F. Karrer, Aus Carnuntum, Monatsblätter des Wissenschaftlichen Club in Wien 22,1, 1900, 2–6 |
| Kovács 2014 | P. Kovács, A history of Pannonia during the principate (Bonn 2014) |
| Kováts 1717 | J. Kováts, Mappa continens dominia inter Posonium et Neostadium vel integra vel partes Leitae fluvio ... Magyar Nemzeti Levéltár (1717) S 16 – No. 5, <https://maps.hungaricana.hu/en/MOLTerkeptar/7404/> (29.03.2023) |
| Kremer 2012 | G. Kremer, Götterdarstellungen, Kult- und Weihedenkmäler aus Carnuntum. Mit Beiträgen von C. Gugl, C. Uhlir, M. Unterwurzacher, CSIR Österreich, Carnuntum Suppl. 1 (Wien 2012) |
| Kremer u. a. 2021 | G. Kremer – S. Insulander – E. Draganits – M. Kronberger – B. Moshammer – M. Mosser – A. Rohatsch, Stone Supply for Carnuntum and Vindobona – Provenance Analysis in a Historico-Economical Context, in: D. van Limbergen – D. Taelman (Hrsg.), The Exploitation of Raw Materials in the Roman World: A Closer Look at Producer-Resource Dynamics. Proceedings 19th International Congress of Classical Archaeology Cologne/Bonn 22.–26.05.2018 (Heidelberg, 2021) 47–62, DOI: 10.11588/propylaeum.706 |
| Krüger 1970 | M.-L. Krüger, Die Reliefs des Stadtgebietes von Carnuntum. I. Teil: Die figürlichen Reliefs, CSIR Österreich I 3 (Wien 1970) |
| Krüger 1972 | M.-L. Krüger, Die Reliefs des Stadtgebietes von Carnuntum. II. Teil: Die dekorativen Reliefs (militärische Ausrüstungsgegenstände, tierische oder vegetabile Ornamente), CSIR Österreich I 4 (Wien 1972) |
| Krüger 1976 | M.-L. Krüger, Die Rundskulpturen des Stadtgebietes von Carnuntum, CSIR Österreich I 2 (Wien 1967) |
| Lachmayer 1999 | H. Lachmayer (Hrsg.), Steinbruch (Wien 1999) |
| Maynzeck 1717 | J. H. Maynzeck, Mappa continens dominia inter Posonium et Neostadium, vel integra vel partes Leita fluvio adiacentes, cursum Leita in hoc tracta et partem Danubii. 160 × 35 cm. Magyar Nemzeti Levéltár (Budapest 1717) S 70 – No. 30, <https://maps.hungaricana.hu/hu/MOLTerkeptar/11032> (08.04.2023) |
| Mayr 2003 | N. Mayr, Zur Petrologie und ausgewählten technologischen Eigenschaften der Inschriftentafeln des römischen Tempelbezirkes auf dem Pfaffenberg (Diplomarbeit Universität Wien 2003) |
| Mosser 2003 | M. Mosser, Die Steindenkmäler der legio XV Apollinaris, WAS 5 (Wien 2003) |
| Neugebauer-Maresch 1980 | C. Neugebauer-Maresch, Zur verschwundenen Befestigungsanlage »Am Stein«, Bad Deutsch-Altenburg, NÖ, MUAG 30, 1980, 37–57 |
| Piller – Harzhauser 2005 | W. E. Piller – M. Harzhauser, The myth of the brackish Sarmatian Sea, Terra Nova 17, 2005, 450–455, DOI: 10.1111/j.1365-3121.2005.00632.x |
| Piller u. a. 2007 | W. E. Piller – M. Harzhauser – O. Mandic, Miocene Central Paratethys stratigraphy – current status and future directions, Stratigraphy 4/2–3, 2007, 151–168 |
| Piso 2003 | I. Piso, Das Heiligtum des Jupiter Optimus Maximus auf dem Pfaffenberg/Carnuntum I. Die Inschriften (Hrsg. W. Jobst), RLÖ 41 Sonderbd. 1 (Wien 2003) |
| Pivko 2012 | D. Pivko, Miocene limestone as dressed stone for Carnuntum Roman town and surrounding settlements in Upper Pannonia (Austria, Slovakia, Hungary), in: A. Gutiérrez Garcia-Moreno – P. Pilar Lapuente Mercadal – I. Rodà de Llanza (Hrsg.), Interdisciplinary studies on ancient stone. Proceedings of the IX[th] ASMOSIA Conference in Tarragona 2009 (Tarragona 2012) 480–486 |
| Pivko u. a. 2017 | D. Pivko – N. Hudáčková – J. Hrabovský – I. Sládek – A. Ruman, Palaeoecology and sedimentology of the Miocene marine and terrestrial deposits in the »Medieval Quarry« on Devínska Kobyla Hill (Vienna Basin), Geological Quarterly 61/3, 2017, 549–568, <https://gq.pgi.gov.pl/article/view/25578> (29.03.2023) |
| Ratschbacher u. a. 1991a | L. Ratschbacher – O. Merle – P. Davy – P. Cobbold, Lateral extrusion in the Eastern Alps I: boundary conditions and experiments scaled for gravity, Tectonics 10, 1991, 245–256, DOI: 10.1029/90TC02622 |

| | |
|---|---|
| Ratschbacher u. a. 1991b | L. Ratschbacher – W. Frisch – H.-G. Linzer – O. Merle, Lateral extrusion in the Eastern Alps II: structural analysis, Tectonics 10, 1991, 257–271, DOI: 10.1029/90TC02623 |
| Schuster u. a. 2019 | R. Schuster – A. Daurer – H.-G. Krenmayr – M. Linner – G. W. Mandl – G. Pestal – J. M. Reitner, Rocky Austria. The geology of Austria – brief and colourful (Wien 2019) |
| Springer – Sacken 2000 | K. Springer – K. Sacken (Hrsg.), Bad Deutsch-Altenburg: Fotos – Bilder – Karten. Eine Dokumentation (inkl. 8 CD-ROMs) (Bad Deutsch-Altenburg 2000) |
| Streffleur c. 1840 | J. Streffleur, Dorf Deutsch Altenburg sammt Umgebung. 1:1,728, 58,5×72,5 cm, Országos Széchényi Könyvtár, Budapest, TK 2074 (c. 1840), <https://maps.hungaricana.hu/en/OSZKTerkeptar/2073> (29.03.2023) |
| Thür 2000 | H. Thür, Der Tempelbezirk auf dem Pfaffenberg, in: Geng-Sesztak u. a. 2000, 315–325 |
| Tragau 1897 | C. Tragau, Die Befestigungsanlagen von Carnuntum, AEM 20, 1897, 173–203 |
| Urban 2006 | O. Urban, Boier und Daker im Raum Carnuntum, in: F. Humer (Hrsg.), Legionsadler und Druidenstab. Vom Legionslager zur Donaumetropole, Katalog des NÖ Landesmuseums N.F. 462 (Bad Deutsch-Altenburg 2006) 172–177 |
| Walter 1754–1756 | C. I. Walter, Aufnahmskarte der wirklichen Grenzen zwischen dem Königreich Ungarn u. dem Erzherzoghtum Österreich unter der Ens … 1:13,700, HM Hadtörténeti Intézet és Múzeum, B IX c 1402 (1754–1756), <https://maps.hungaricana.hu/en/HTI-Terkeptar/2925> (29.03.2023) |
| Weber-Hiden 2017 | I. Weber-Hiden, Die ältesten Inschriften aus Carnuntum, in: P. Kovács (Hrsg.), Tiberius in Illyricum. Contributions to the history of the Danubian provinces under Tiberius' reign (14–37 AD) (Budapest 2017) |
| Wessely 1961 | G. Wessely, Geologie der Hainburger Berge, Jahrbuch der Geologischen Bundesanstalt 104, 1961, 273–349, <https://www.zobodat.at/pdf/JbGeolReichsanst_104_0273-0349.pdf> |
| Wessely 2006 | G. Wessely, Hainburger Berge, in: G. Wessely (Hrsg.) Niederösterreich. Geologie der Österreichischen Bundesländer (Wien 2006) 183–187 |
| Wiedl u. a. 2012 | T. Wiedl – M. Harzhauser – W. E. Piller, Facies and synsedimentary tectonics on a Badenian carbonate platform in the southern Vienna Basin (Austria, Central Paratethys), Facies 58, 2012, 523–548, DOI: 10.1007/s10347-011-0290-0 |
| Wiedl u. a. 2013 | T. Wiedl – M. Harzhauser – A. Kroh – S. Ćorić – W. E. Piller, Ecospace variability along a carbonate platform at the northern boundary of the Miocene reef belt (Upper Langhian, Austria), Palaeogeography Palaeoclimatology Palaeoecology 370, 2013, 232–246, DOI: 10.1016/j.palaeo.2012.12.015 |
| Wiedl u. a. 2014 | T. Wiedl – M. Harzhauser – A. Kroh – S. Ćorić – W. E. Piller, From biologically to hydrodynamically controlled carbonate production by tectonically induced palaeogeographic rearrangement (Middle Miocene, Pannonian Basin, Facies 60, 2014, 865–881, DOI: 10.1007/s10347-014-0408-2 |

*Erich Draganits, Institut für Geologie, Universität Wien, Josef-Holaubek-Platz 2, 1090 Wien, Österreich.*
*[e] erich.draganits@univie.ac.at*

*Beatrix Moshammer, Geological Survey Austria, Geosphere Austria, Neulinggasse 38, 1030 Wien, Österreich.*

*Gabrielle Kremer, Österreichisches Archäologisches Institut, Österreichische Akademie der Wissenschaften, Dominikanerbastei 16, 1010 Wien, Österreich.*
*[e] gabrielle.kremer@oeaw.ac.at*

*Andreas Rohatsch, Institut für Geotechnik, TU Wien, Karlsplatz 13, 1040 Wien, Österreich.*
*[e] andreas.rohatsch@tuwien.ac.at*

*Michael Doneus, Institut für Urgeschichte und Historische Archäologie, Universität Wien, Franz-Klein-Gasse 1, 1190 Wien, Österreich; Human Evolution & Archaeological Sciences (HEAS), University of Viennna, Universitätsring 1, 1010 Vienna, Austria.*
*[e] michael.doneus@univie.ac.at*

Roland Dreesen – Eric Goemaere – Gabrielle Kremer

# PROVENANCE ANALYSIS OF THE NATURAL STONES IN FUNERARY MONUMENTS FROM THE WESTERN PART OF THE *CIVITAS TREVERORUM*

**Abstract**

Within the framework of current research projects on the funerary monuments from *civitas Treverorum*, petrographic analyses were undertaken for the first time. The determinations from a representative selection of architectural blocks and sculptures resulted in a first overview of the stone types employed in antiquity for monumental tombs in this region. Three different types of limestone and four types of sandstone are briefly presented and assigned to their respective quarrying areas known to date.

## INTRODUCTION

Treveran funerary monuments are the subject of two current research projects conducted by the Austrian Academy of Sciences in collaboration with the University of Luxembourg (western part of the *civitas*) and the University of Frankfurt, in cooperation with the Rheinisches Landesmuseum Trier (eastern part of the *civitas*)[1]. This particular region within the Roman province of *Gallia Belgica* is famous for the quantity and the richness of its funerary monuments, among them very well-known ones such as those of Neumagen and Arlon (fig. 1). Since the *civitas Treverorum* is located on the French-German linguistic border and since it has a share in four modern states, comprehensive material studies for this formerly contiguous area are in some respects still a research desideratum today. Furthermore, important recent discoveries, such as the mausoleum of Bertrange[2] or the Roman monuments found on the Titelberg[3], have added new insights, triggering a more profound analysis of the whole assembly of known monuments in this region. Recent studies have investigated the Treveran monuments under various aspects, including the reconstruction of their architectural structure[4], the development of a characteristic regional architectural[5] and sculptural ornamentation, the meaning and the effect of the pictorial decoration[6], or the archaeological and socio-historical contextualization of the monuments[7].

The exact origin and provenance of the stone materials employed has only occasionally been addressed in earlier studies. Wilhelm von Massow, for example, distinguished between the funeral monuments from Neumagen made of sandstone and others made of limestone, linking this criterion also to the chronology of the monuments[8]. Researchers were aware that materials of diverse provenances were used for the elaborate funerary monuments: they pointed out the differences in quality between the available local stones and the stones imported from further afield, such as the limestones of the Norroy quarries[9]. More recently, the use of local or regional stone material has

---

[1] Mahler 2017; Kremer – Ruppert 2019; Binsfeld et al. 2020.
[2] Kremer 2009.
[3] Metzler et al. 2016; Kremer 2019.
[4] Numrich 1997; Ruppert 2018; Ruppert 2020.
[5] Kremer, in prep.
[6] Klöckner – Stark 2018.
[7] Scholz 2018; Krier 2020.
[8] von Massow 1932, 28, referring to Hettner; see Hettner 1903.
[9] E.g. Mertens 1958, 24 for the monuments from Buzenol, or Mertens 1967, 25 for Arlon.

1   Collection of blocks from funerary monuments in the Museum of Arlon (photo G. Kremer)

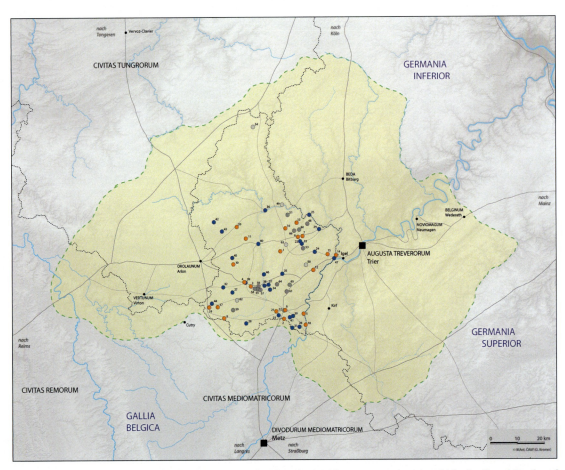

2   Map of the *civitas Treverorum* showing the finding locations of funerary monuments within the Grand Duchy of Luxembourg (© OeAI-OeAW, G. Kremer/J. Krier/S. Mühling)

become an increasingly important issue[10]. The topic is closely linked to the history of the transport routes and to the work processes in the ancient quarries and workshops. It can also play a role in the identification of the owners and their position in the sociohistorical context.

## AIMS, MATERIALS AND ANALYTICAL METHODS

This study aims at accurately identifying the various rock types used and their geological-geographical provenances, as well as locating some of the ancient quarries, thereby obtaining new data on the organization of the workshops, on their chronology and on their economic relationships. This will obviously contribute to a better understanding of the usage of decorative stones in northern Gaul, where the Treveran territory still represents a ›white spot‹ on the general distribution map[11]. The inventory of Roman funerary monuments in the western part of the *civitas Treverorum* includes several thousand specimens (complete blocks and fragments) although so far, no single tombstone has been conserved entirely. The distribution map for the Grand Duchy of Luxembourg (fig. 2) shows a concentration of monuments in its southern part, along the Roman roads connecting Trier (*Augusta Treverorum*) and Reims (*Durocortorum*), as well as Trier and Metz (*Divodurum*) and also along the Moselle valley. Blue dots correspond to assemblies of fragmented funerary monuments, orange dots represent sites of monument foundations preserved *in situ*, whereas grey dots refer to architectural elements of funerary monuments that are only known from the literature.

In the course of the above-mentioned research projects, petrographic analyses were carried out on a selection of objects that can be considered representative of the funeral architecture of the Treveran region[12]. Besides macroscopic investigations (by hand lens), microscopic analysis and thin section petrography have been applied in order to properly identify the origin and the provenance of the different rock types. Additionally, both SEM- and semi-quantitative geochemical analyses (EDS and X-ray diffraction) have been carried out by the laboratories of the Belgian Geological Survey in Brussels. All these analytical tools enabled the identification of the exact lithological nature of the various inventoried rock types (major components, fabrics, cements, weathering phenomena and patinas) in order to differentiate them correctly. Furthermore, a comparative petrographical analysis with samples taken from geological samples and/or collections allowed their most probable provenance areas to be pinpointed. The investigated study material comes from different sources: 1. the authorized sampling of non-sculpted parts of archaeological objects[13], 2. the *in situ* sampling of geological reference materials, 3. reference collections of decorative stones stored at the RBINS in Brussels and 4. a thin section collection made from samples previously collected in the active Rumelange quarry[14].

## GEOLOGY OF THE WESTERN PART OF THE *CIVITAS TREVERORUM*

From a geological point of view, the *civitas Treverorum* is divided into three different parts. Its southern part (Éislek and the southern part of the Belgian Ardennes) corresponds to the Givonne-Eifel anticlinorium and the Neufchâteau synclinorium, that are composed of a several thousand metres thick sequence of Early Devonian quartzites, sandstones, conglomerates and phyllites. In antiquity, these rock types were only used occasionally as millstones, whetstones and roof slates. The central and south-western parts of the *civitas* on the other hand consist of Mesozoic terranes

---

[10] See among others Stribrny 1987; Stoll 1992; Panhuysen 1996; Noelke 2006; Giljohann – Wenzel 2015; Coquelet et al. 2018.
[11] Boulanger – Moulis 2018.
[12] Kremer et al. 2022.
[13] We would like to thank the museum directors Michel Polfer, Elodie Richard and Marcus Reuter and their numerous staff members, especially Muriel Prieur, Franziska Dövener and Christine Ruppert, for their support.
[14] Boulvain et al. 2017.

composed of several plurimetric series of Triassic and Jurassic rocks, forming cuestas that border the Paris Basin. During Roman times, several types of sandstones and limestones from these sedimentary series were used for construction purposes. Finally, the south-eastern part of the *civitas*, located south of Trier, corresponds mainly to Early Devonian formations of the Rheinisches Schiefergebirge that are chiefly composed of shales and quartzitic sandstones.

## CHARACTERISTIC LITHIC MATERIALS OF THE TREVERAN FUNERARY MONUMENTS

So far, seven different rock types have been identified, comprising three types of limestone (belonging to the group of the »Pierres blanches« or white limestones) and four types of sandstone.

The most common limestone type observed in the funerary monuments of the *civitas* is the Norroy Stone (»Lothringer Kalk«, fig. 3, 1–2), a badly sorted pseudo-oolitic limestone (cortoidal grainstone) of Middle Bajocian (Middle Jurassic) age, belonging to the Calcaires à Polypiers Supérieurs Formation. The Roman origin of the (still visible) quarries in Norroy-lès-Pont-à-Mousson (Meurthe-et-Moselle department, Grand Est region, France) along the Moselle is proven by the discovery of several stelae dedicated by legionaries to Jupiter and Hercules Saxanus (god of the quarry workers) as well as by the presence of numerous semi-finished architectonic elements in the immediate surroundings (columns and shafts)[15]. However, different facies of the Norroy limestone have also been observed in the monuments studied, mainly based on differences in grain size and porosity. Based on the geographical distribution of the mineralogically characterised architectural elements and funeral sculptures throughout the northern Roman provinces, and the location of antique quarries of Norroy-lès-Pont-à-Mousson, and by assuming that heavy loads were transported by the Romans by flat-bottomed boats on rivers, the main means of transport route was the river Moselle.

A frequently occurring rock type that has remained unnoticed until now in the western part of the *civitas Treverorum* is a bioclastic grainstone of Bajocian age: it is much whiter than the Norroy stone and represents a peri-reefal facies that is characteristic of the lower part of the Audun-le-Tiche Formation which caps the Bajocian cuesta. This is the so-called Audun-le-Tiche Stone (fig. 3, 3–4) that crops out to the south of the Titelberg (bare plateau, southwest of Pétange in the extreme southwest of Luxembourg)[16], as well as along the French-Luxembourgian border between the towns of Audun-le-Tiche (Moselle department, Grand Est region, France) and Rumelange/Differdange (Grand Duchy of Luxembourg). It is mainly composed of large bioclasts derived from reefal build-ups, including various skeletal parts of corals, bryozoans, echinoderms, sponges, bivalves, etc.

The Jaumont Stone (fig. 4) is a yellow to orange Upper-Bajocian oolitic limestone, chiefly composed of ooids, cortoids and bioclasts, displaying an important mouldic porosity. This rock type has been quarried in the Moselle valley, in the Jaumont region (e.g. near Montois-la-Montagne, Moselle department, Grand Est region, France) and is frequently found in funerary monuments of the Virton area (Province of Luxembourg, Belgium), Torgny (Rouvroy, Province of Luxembourg, Belgium), Montmédy (Meuse department, Grand Est region, France) and along the Chiers valley[17]. This stone has different modern names such as »Pierre de Soleil« in France due to its golden colour or »Pierre de France« in Belgium (as part of the Longwy Formation). The name »Jaumont« refers to and is an abbreviation of the »Montagne Jaune« (yellow hill). The Jaumont Stone is still used today, as can be admired in numerous buildings of the French and Belgian Lorraine area (e.g. the Roman Catholic church of the Saint-Stephen cathedral in Metz, France).

Within the sandstone group, the fine- to medium-grained red litharenitic sandstones of the Lower Triassic Buntsandstein were already previously known as source materials for the manu-

---

[15] Coquelet et al. 2013; Laffite 2018.
[16] Muller 2015.
[17] Mailland 2001.

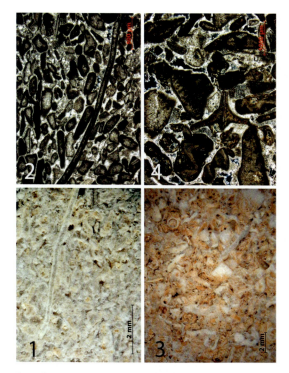
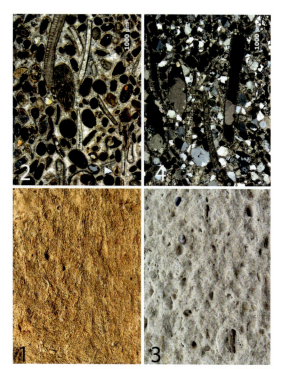

3  1) Macroscopical view of Norroy stone showing characteristic elongated cortoids; 2) micrograph of a thin section showing a cortoidal grainstone microfacies (PPL); 3) macroscopical view of the stone of Audun-le-Tiche showing coarse skeletal debris (bioclasts); 4) micrograph of a thin section showing a coarse bioclastic grainstone microfacies (XPL) (pictures R. Dreesen)

4  1) Macroscopical view (L 5 cm) of the Jaumont limestone showing a characteristic oolitic facies (mouldic porosity) with dispersed shell debris; 2) micrograph of a thin section showing an oolitic grainstone facies (XPL); 3) macroscopic view of the surface of a building stone made of the Altwies Stone (tribunes of Dalheim theatre): coarse, pale-grey to beige quartzarenitic sandstone showing mouldic porosity, dispersed black and white pebbles and mollusk shells; Size of pebbles 1 cm; 4) micrograph of a thin section in the Altwies Stone: coarse-grained quartzarenite with a calcite cement and large bioclasts composed of mollusk shells (recrystallized) showing partial dissolution (XPL) (pictures R. Dreesen)

facturing of funerary monuments, the most prominent among them being the so-called Igeler Säule near Trier[18].

Three other sandstone types have now been identified among the monuments of the area under investigation.

In the north-eastern tip of the Paris Basin (the »Luxembourg-Trier Gulf«) the Lower Liassic, otherwise formed by blueish-grey limestone and claystone alternations (»Blue Liassic«) also called the »Lorraine facies«, shows lenticular insertions of arenaceous sediments referred to as the Luxembourg Sandstone(s) Formation. Due to a bimodal distribution of the calcium carbonate content, the Luxembourg Sandstone appears in the outcrop as an alternation of yellowish ochre, poorly cemented sandstones (10–20 % carbonate) and grey to whitish, cement-rich sandy limestones (30–60 % carbonate). But some extreme facies with less than 1 % or even up to 90 % of carbonate occur as well. The fine- to medium-grained yellowish Luxembourg Sandstone is thus a calcareous sandstone (a sandstone with a calcite cement). It is of Hettangian/Sinemurian age and contains shells of bivalves and moulds of gastropods, brachiopods and ammonites. Calcareous ooids can be present as well. It crops out over a large area in the Belgian Lorraine area (Virton, Orval, Florenville) and in Gutland (Luxembourg city, Müllertal). This lithostratigraphical unit includes, from the south-east to the north-west, the Hettange, Ernzen, Metzert, Virton, Orval or Florenville sandstones, that represent local facies or denominations of the Luxembourg Sandstone.

---

[18] A general overview in Bedon 1984, 43–52; Heckenbenner 2018.

The Luxembourg Sandstone Formation provides different building materials in Luxembourg, where over 150 old quarries are known and 11 extraction sites are still active today. The only and best-known location of a former Roman quarry of Luxembourg sandstone is in Hersberg, near Bech (Luxembourg)[19]. Besides its use as building sands or granulates, its whitish carbonate-rich sandy limestone facies was especially appreciated as a building stone and a free stone for several centuries, and exported beyond the borders of Luxembourg[20].

The Altwies Stone (fig. 5) was unknown so far as a building or decorative stone and is recognized here as a source material for the first time: it is a white, coarse to gravely calcareous quartzarenitic sandstone containing numerous fossil shells (large bivalves and gastropods). It forms the basal beds (channel lags) of Sinemurian sandstones and calcareous sandstones in the south-east of the Grand Duchy of Luxembourg. It crops out in the area of Altwies (near Mondorf-les-Bains) where antique quarry faces have also recently been discovered. Most conspicuous is its use as a major construction stone in the Roman theatre of Dalheim[21].

The fourth sandstone type is a white and quite pure, micaceous and porous quartzarenitic sandstone. It can be assigned to the Muschelkalk (Mid-Triassic) and crops out along the Lorraine-Luxembourg border (near Ellange, Mondorf-les-Bains).

In contrast with the adjacent *civitates*, calcareous tufas (called »travertins« or »cron« in the Lorraine area) were not identified as local building stones nor as ornamental stones in the funerary monuments of the *civitas Treverorum*. Furthermore and peculiarly no »white French limestones« – other than the Norroy limestone – which are generally frequently used as ornamental stones in the *civitates Nerviorum* and *Tungrorum* and which were imported through the fluvial network of the Meuse river basin – including the beige Lutetian limestone from the Reims and Paris area, the Euville crinoidal limestone, the pseudo-oolitic peloidal limestone of Chémery (Verdun area), the orange-yellow calcarenite of Dom-le-Mesnil, the white chalky limestone of Lézennes (Picardy), the white chalky limestone of Avesnes (Avesnes-le-Sec), the pale-yellow calcarenitic Caen limestone, the yellow oolitic limestone of Marquise (Pas-de-Calais) … – have been reported in the *civitas Treverorum* so far[22].

5  Tribunes of the Roman theatre of Dalheim, made in quartzarenitic sandstone of Altwies (photo R. Dreesen)

---

[19] Paulke 2015.
[20] Colbach 2005; Wies – Wertz 2004.
[21] Henrich 2015.
[22] Coquelet et al. 2020.

# BIBLIOGRAPHY

| | |
|---|---|
| Bedon 1984 | R. Bedon, Les carrières et les carriers de la Gaule Romaine (Paris 1984) |
| Binsfeld et al. 2020 | A. Binsfeld – A. Klöckner – G. Kremer – M. Reuter – M. Scholz (eds.), Stadt – Land – Fluss. Grabdenkmäler der Treverer in lokaler und überregionaler Perspektive. Akten der Internationalen Konferenz in Neumagen und Trier 25.–27.10.2018, TrZ Beih. 37 (Trier 2020) |
| Boulanger – Moulis 2018 | K. Boulanger – C. Moulis (eds.), La pierre dans l'antiquité et au Moyen Âge en Lorraine. De l'extraction à la mise en œuvre (Nancy 2018) |
| Boulvain et al. 2017 | F. Boulvain – L. Belanger – R. Colbach – S. Dechamps – D. Delsate – D. Deligny – P. Ghysel – J. Michel – S. Philippo – B. Ramlot, New sedimentological data from Triassic to Jurassic boreholes (Bonnert, Haebicht, Grouft, Grund, Consdorf) and sections (Tontelange, Differdange, Rumelange) from southern Belgium and Luxembourg. Professional Paper – Service Géologique de Belgique 319, 2017, 43 |
| Colbach 2005 | R. Colbach, Overview of the geology of the Luxembourg Sandstone(s), Ferrantia 44, 155–160 |
| Coquelet et al. 2013 | C. Coquelet – G. Cremers – R. Dreesen – E. Goemaere, Les »pierres blanches« dans les monuments publics et funéraires de la cité des Tongres, Signa 2, 2013, 29–34 |
| Coquelet et al. 2018 | C. Coquelet – G. Creemers – R. Dreesen – É. Goemaere (eds.), Roman ornamental stones in North-Western Europe. Proceedings of the international conference in Tongeren 20.–22.04.2016 (Namur 2018) |
| Coquelet et al. 2020 | C. Coquelet – É. Goemaere – R. Dreesen – G. Creemers, Les pierres belges, l'originalité des décors marmoréens en cité des Tongres et dans les régions voisines, Aquitania 36, 2020, 235–260 |
| Giljohann – Wenzel 2015 | R. Giljohann – S. Wenzel, Verwendung und Verbreitung von Lothringer Kalkstein zwischen Andernach und Mayen in römischer Zeit, Berichte zur Archäologie in Rheinhessen und Umgebung 8, 2015, 19–39 |
| Heckenbenner 2018 | D. Heckenbenner, Les carrières gallo-romaines de la Croix Guillaume Saint-Quirin, in: Boulanger – Moulis 2018, 191–213 |
| Henrich 2015 | P. Henrich, Das gallorömische Theater von Dalheim »Hossegronn«, Luxembourg, Dossiers d'archéologie du Musée national d'histoire et d'art 15 (Luxembourg 2015) |
| Hettner 1903 | F. Hettner, Illustrierter Führer durch das Provinzialmuseum in Trier (Trier 1903) |
| Klöckner – Stark 2018 | A. Klöckner – M. Stark, Picture and ornament – funerary monuments from Trier seen as media ensembles, in: Coquelet et al. 2018, 275–284 |
| Kremer 2009 | G. Kremer, Das frühkaiserzeitliche Mausoleum von Bartringen, Dossiers d'archéologie du Musée national d'histoire et d'art 12 (Luxembourg 2009) |
| Kremer 2019 | G. Kremer, Monuments votifs ou monuments funéraires? Les fragments de sculptures du Titelberg, in: V. Gaggadis-Robin – N. de Larquier (eds.), La sculpture et ses remplois. Actes des IIes rencontres autour de la sculpture romaine, Arles 28.–29.10.2016 (Bordeaux 2019) 271–280 |
| Kremer, in prep. | G. Kremer, Monuments funéraires de la *civitas Treverorum* occidentale: le décor architectural, in: Actes du colloque »Le décor d'architecture dans les cités du Centre-Est: une école régionale?«, Sens 14.–15.10.2021, in prep. |
| Kremer et al. 2022 | G. Kremer – R. Dreesen – E. Goemaere, Les monuments funéraires gallo-romains et l'emploi de la pierre dans la région occidentale de la Civitas Treverorum, in: M. Piavaux – C. Moulis – M. Macaux – L. Verslype (éds.), Pierre à pierre II. Économie de la pierre dans la vallée de la Meuse et dans les régions limitrophes (Ier siècle avant J.-C. – VIIIe siècle). Actes du colloque international Namur/Dinant 06.–08.12.2018, Études et Documents, Archéologie 45 (Namur 2022) 149–161 |
| Kremer – Ruppert 2019 | G. Kremer – C. Ruppert, Les monuments funéraires de la *civitas Treverorum* (partie occidentale), Annales de l'Institut archéologique du Luxembourg – Arlon 148, 2017 (2019) 29–41 |
| Krier 2020 | J. Krier, Die einheimische Führungsschicht in den Grabdenkmälern und Grabinschriften des Trevergebietes: das 1. Jh. n.Chr. – und danach?, in: Binsfeld et al. 2020, 37–49 |
| Laffite 2018 | J.-D. Laffite, Les carrières antiques des côtes de Moselle: Norroy-lès-Pont-à-Mousson, Montauville, Maidières et Jezainville, in: Boulanger – Moulis 2018, 248–279 |

| | |
|---|---|
| Mahler 2017 | K.-U. Mahler, Römerzeitliche Grabdenkmäler im Trevererraum. Internationaler Workshop im Rheinischen Landesmuseum Trier 2017, mit Beiträgen von A. Binsfeld, K. Deppmeyer, S. Faust, A. Klöckner, G. Kremer, H. Müller, T. Reich, M. Reuter, C. Ruppert, M. Scholz, M. Stark, M. Tabaczek, Y. Schmuhl, FuAusgrTrier 49, 2017, 43–55 |
| Mailland 2001 | C. Mailland, La Pierre de Jaumont. 2000 ans de carrières (Metz 2001) |
| Mertens 1958 | J. Mertens, Sculptures Romaines de Buzenol, Le Pays gaumais 19, 1958, 17–124 |
| Mertens 1967 | J. R. Mertens, Nouvelles sculptures romaines d'Arlon, Archaeologia Belgica 103, 1967, 147–160 |
| Metzler et al. 2016 | J. Metzler – C. Gaeng – P. Méniel – M.-P. Darblade-Audoin – N. Gaspar – L. Homan – G. Kremer – N. Metzler-Zens, L'espace public du Titelberg, Dossiers d'archéologie du Centre national de recherche archéologique 17 (Luxembourg 2016) |
| Muller 2015 | J.-M. Muller, Patrimoine historique et culturel en forêt, in: Mutations. Mémoires et perspectives du Bassin Minier (Esch/Alzette 2015) 117–125 |
| Noelke 2006 | P. Noelke, Bildhauerwerkstätten im römischen Germanien. Möglichkeiten und Grenzen ihres Nachweises, BJb 206, 2006, 87–144 |
| Numrich 1997 | B. Numrich, Die Achitektur der römischen Grabdenkmäler aus Neumagen (Trier 1997) |
| Panhuysen 1996 | T. S. M. Panhuysen, Romeins Maastricht en zijn beelden, CSIR Nederland. Germania inferior (Maastricht 1996) |
| Paulke 2015 | Ein römischer Steinbruch bei Hersberg, Gemeinde Bech (Luxembourg). Archaeologia luxemburgensis 2, 2015, 114–123 |
| Ruppert 2018 | C. Ruppert, Tombeaux monumentaux d'Arlon/*Orolaunum vicus*, Signa 7, 2018, 179–183 |
| Ruppert 2020 | C. Ruppert, Die frühkaiserzeitliche Grabarchitektur aus *Orolaunum vicus*/Arlon. Rekonstruktion und Kontextualisierung der Grabbauten einer lokalen Elite (unpubl. Diss. University of Luxembourg, Luxembourg 2020) |
| Scholz 2018 | M. Scholz, Zur Repräsentation munizipaler Magistrate und Würdenträger in Monumentinschriften in Augusta Treverorum/Trier und in anderen *civitas*-Metropolen Ostgalliens, in: Coquelet et al. 2018, 49–59 |
| Stoll 1992 | O. Stoll, Die Skulpturenausstattung römischer Militärlager an Rhein und Donau (St. Katharinen 1992) 58–65 |
| Stribrny 1987 | C. Stribrny, Die Herkunft der römischen Werksteine aus Mainz und Umgebung. Vergleichende petrographische und geochemische Untersuchungen an skulpierten Kalksteinen, CSIR D II 8, Germania superior (Mainz 1987) |
| von Massow 1932 | W. von Massow, Die Grabmäler von Neumagen (Berlin 1932) |
| Wies – Wertz 2004 | P. Wies – P. Wertz, Les carrières de Grès d'Ernzen (Larochette). Guide d'excursion Geologica Belgica du 30.09.2004 (2004), non publié |

*Roland Dreesen, Department of Archaeology, Historical Archaeology Research Group, Ghent University – Campus Ufo, St.-Pietersnieuwstraat 35, 9000 Ghent; Gallo-Roman Museum, Kielenstraat 15, 3700 Tongeren, Belgium.*
*[e] roland.dreesen@telenet.be*

*Éric Goemaere, Geological Survey of Belgium, Operational Direction Earth & History of Life, Royal Belgian Institute of Natural Sciences, 13 Jennerstreet, 1000 Brussels, Belgium.*
*[e] egoemaere@naturalsciences.be*

*Gabrielle Kremer, Austrian Archaeological Institute, Austrian Academy of Sciences, Dominikanerbastei 16, 1010 Vienna, Austria.*
*[e] gabrielle.kremer@oeaw.ac.at*

Anique Hamelink – Nicolas Delferrière – Ursula Rothe

# POLYCHROMIE AUF PORTRÄTGRABSTEINEN: *CLAVI* AUF GALLISCHER KLEIDUNG?

**Abstract**
Gravestone depictions give us a unique insight into the cultural and social identities of ordinary people in the Roman provinces, especially where they have survived in large numbers, such as in Gaul and the Danube provinces. With most of the original paintwork missing, however, the image these have provided to scholars has been mostly effectively black-and-white. In eastern France, however, close inspection and enhanced research practices have led to the discovery of considerable quantities of paintwork remains on stone monuments. These are starting to call into question prevailing ideas about the nature of some of the clothing styles depicted, such as the so-called Gallic tunic. Most recent research has interpreted this garment as entirely indigenous in character, but the discovery of so-called *clavi*, a Roman form of decoration that consists of two straight bands reaching from the shoulders to the hem of the tunic, suggests that the clothing worn by provincial Gauls on their gravestones might have been influenced by Roman styles more than previously thought.

2012 publizierte eine der Autorinnen der vorliegenden Studie eine detaillierte Analyse der weiblichen Version des sog. gallischen Ensembles[1], eine Zusammenstellung von Kleidungsstücken, die den häufigsten Kleidungsstil auf römischen Grabsteinen in Gallien darstellt und schließlich im gesamten römischen Nordwesten getragen wurde[2]. Während die männliche Version davon – ein wadenlanges Kleidungsstück mit Ärmeln und ohne Gürtel (die sog. gallische Tunika) und ein kreisförmiger Umhang mit integrierter Kapuze (der sog. gallische Umhang) – aus der vorrömischen männlichen gallischen Kleidung stammte[3], entwickelte sich die weibliche Version, bestehend aus einer ähnlichen, aber knöchellangen Tunika, einem rechteckigen Umhang und einer runden Haube[4], Ende des 1. Jahrhunderts n. Chr. Bis dahin war die weibliche Kleidung durch unterschiedliche stammesbezogene Kleidungsstücke gekennzeichnet, die in der Eisenzeit in den keltischen Teilen Europas getragen wurden (oft als »Menimane-Ensemble« nach einem Stein aus Mainz bezeichnet) und aus einer langärmeligen Untertunika, einer schlauchförmigen, ärmellosen Übertunika, an den Schultern mit Fibeln festgesteckt, einer weichen, runden Haube und einem großen rechteckigen Umhang bestand[5]. Die gallische Kleidung für Frauen war eine neugeschaffene weibliche Version der männlichen Kleidung aus der Eisenzeit, die eine Verschiebung von einer stammesbasierten zu einer breiteren regionalen Identität bedeutete, wahrscheinlich als Folge der Urbanisierung und des verstärkten Handels im Nordwesten in der Römerzeit[6].

Das allgegenwärtigste Element des gallischen Ensembles für Männer und Frauen war die charakteristische Tunika. In ihrer Form hatte sie einen entschieden ›unrömischen‹ Charakter, da

---

[1] Rothe 2012a.
[2] Böhme 1985, 425–430; Wild 1968; 1985; Rothe 2009, 36–37. 45–46; 2012a.
[3] Rothe 2009, 31–34; 2012a, 240; s. auch Wild 1985; Böhme 1985; Boppert 1992; Roche-Bernard 1993; Noelke 1998. Vgl. Langlois 1959; Kolb 1973; Andrikopoulou-Strack 1986; Freigang 1997 (gallischer Umhang als römische *paenula*).
[4] Wild 1985; Böhme 1985, 430–436; Rothe 2009, 34–36. 42–43. 45.
[5] Böhme 1985, 425–430; Wild 1968; 1985. Der Begriff und seine Definition stammen von Wild, dessen Kleidertypologie für die Region bis heute weitestgehend gilt.
[6] Rothe 2012a. Vgl. die gegenteilige Situation in den Donauprovinzen: Rothe 2012b.

sie ohne Gürtel getragen wurde[7] und normalerweise Ärmel hatte, wobei der Körper der Tunika manchmal so breit war, dass nur sog. Endärmel entstanden[8]. Die Tatsache, dass die männliche Version der Tunika bis zur Mitte der Wade reichte, war ebenfalls ›unrömisch‹: römische Männertuniken reichten bis längstens unter das Knie[9]. Die weibliche gallische Kleidung war eine Innovation der Römerzeit, wurde aber auch in der Studie von 2012 als »keineswegs römische oder ›romanisierte‹ Kleidung«[10] beschrieben. Obwohl die Möglichkeit angesprochen wurde, dass sowohl lokale als auch römische Stoffe für gallische Gewänder verwendet und Klassen- und Statusunterschiede in der Qualität der Stoffe zum Ausdruck gebracht worden sein könnten, bedeutete das Fehlen der ursprünglichen Bemalung der Denkmäler, dass Informationen über Farben, Stoffstile und mögliche dekorative Elemente unbekannt blieben[11]. Es wurde vorgeschlagen, dass Stoffe mit mehrfarbigem Karomuster hergestellt worden waren, die bei den Galliern angeblich beliebt waren[12], oder einfarbig gewesen waren[13].

Das oben Genannte muss jedoch nun im Lichte neuer Beweise, unter anderem erhaltene Bemalungen auf mehreren Grabdenkmälern aus Ostgallien, neu bewertet werden[14].

## POLYCHROMIE AUF OSTGALLISCHEN GRABSTEINEN

Obwohl sich Studien zur Polychromie der griechisch-römischen Skulptur in den letzten zwanzig Jahren rasant entwickelt haben[15], konzentrierte sich ein Großteil davon auf Griechenland und Rom. Die Arbeit an Pigmentresten in den römischen Provinzen, und insbesondere in Gallien, hinkte hinterher, und das obwohl bereits im 19. und frühen 20. Jahrhundert bemalte Überreste auf vielen Steinen beobachtet worden waren[16]. Sie geben uns einen Einblick in die Vielfalt an Informationen, die mit dem Wegfall der Farbdekoration verlorengegangen sind.

Unter den kürzlich in Ostgallien (Frankreich) gesammelten und erstmals von Nicolas Delferrière und Anne-Laure Edme publizierten Monumenten mit Farbresten[17] sind mehrere Baublöcke und komplette Grabdenkmäler, die besonders gut erhaltene Reste konservieren und für die Erforschung altgallischer Kleidung von besonderem Interesse sind:

1. Das 1834 bei Arbeiten an der Stadtkaserne (Couvent des Ursulines) von Langres (*Andemantunnum*, Hauptstadt der *civitas* der Lingoni; Haute-Marne) entdeckte Kalksteinmonument mit der Bezeichnung »Divixta-Stele« ist 1,62 m hoch, 0,70 m breit und 0,47 m tief (Abb. 1) und derzeit im Guy Baillet Museum in Langres ausgestellt (Inv. 845.18)[18]. Die Stele hat eine flache Spitze und einen dreieckigen Giebel mit Akroteria auf der Hauptfläche. Es überragt eine Kartusche, die auf jeder Seite mit einer Pelta verziert ist und die folgende Inschrift trägt:

---

[7] Außer von Dienern und Arbeitern, z. B. Avituspfeiler, Neumagen (Espérandieu 1915, 5145. 5222; Rothe 2009, Kat. T60 Taf. 11). Gürtellosigkeit als abstoßend in römischer Kultur: Lee 2015, 135–136; Olson 2017, 144.

[8] Variationen entstanden auch zwischen diesen zwei Möglichkeiten (Rothe 2012a, 5). Für Muster und weitere Abbildungen s. Wild 1985.

[9] z. B. Arbeiterszenen in Ostia und Rom (Zimmer 1982), aber auch Quint. inst. 11, 3, 138.

[10] Rothe 2012a, 7. s. auch Wild 1985, 413. Vgl. Freigang 1997, 306–307.

[11] Rothe 2009, 57; 2012a, 241.

[12] Diod. 5, 31, 1; Plin. nat. 8, 196; 35, 150; Wild 1970, 53–54; 1985, 408–409; 1964 für *scutulatus* (kariert).

[13] Schoppa 1960, 143; Wild 1970, 79–81.

[14] s. zu diesem Thema auch unsere Überlegungen in Rothe u. a. 2023.

[15] z. B. Brinkmann – Wünsche 2004; Bankel – Liverani 2004; Jockey 2013; Jockey 2014; Liverani – Santamaria 2014; Bracci u. a. 2018; Jockey 2018; Bourgeois 2019; Mulliez 2019.

[16] Thiollet 1847–1859; Julliot 1898; Blanchet 1918–1924; Grenier 1904; von Massow 1932. Weiteres: Delferrière – Edme 2018a, 269; 2018b, 7–8; 2019a, 94–96.

[17] Delferrière – Edme 2018a; 2018b; 2019a; 2019b.

[18] Luquet 1838, 303–305, Kat. 16; Péchin d'Autebois 1847a; 1847b, Kat. 24; Péchine 1847–1860, Kat. 4; Brocard 1873, Kat. 45; Brocard 1886, Kat. 45; Royer 1902, Kat. 45; Espérandieu 1911, Nr. 3280; Royer 1931, Kat. 45; Decorse 2000, Nr. 8; Joly 2001, 133.

*D(iis) M(anibus) / Divixtae / Scottus mar(itus) / p(onendum) c(urauit)*[19]
»Den Göttern der Verstorbenen. Für Divixta ließ ihr Ehemann Scottus (dieses Denkmal) errichten.«

Unter einer gewölbten Nische, die von zwei Säulen mit Kapitellen eingerahmt wird, befindet sich die Darstellung einer stehenden Frau. Sie ist mit zwei Tuniken bekleidet, von denen die zuunterst getragene Fransen hat; die obere ist eine gallische Tunika mit Endärmeln. Die Frau trägt auch einen Schal, der über den Oberkörper drapiert ist und bis zur Mitte der Wade reicht. In ihrer linken Hand hält sie einen Obstkorb, und ihre rechte Hand ruht auf dem oberen Teil dieses Korbes.

Die Originalfarbe dieser Stele ist sehr gut erhalten. Neben dem grünen Nischenhintergrund und den roten Haaren wurden gemalte Details hinzugefügt, ohne vorher in den Stein gemeißelt worden zu sein. Besonders sichtbar ist dies im Gesicht des Verstorbenen: Die Augenbrauen, Pupillen und das Relief der Augenlider sind durch rote Pinselstriche markiert[20]. Die Kleidung ist ebenfalls bemalt: Der Schal ist gelb und in regelmäßigen Abständen mit zwei braunschwarzen Linien durchzogen; auch der Fransenrand der Tunika weist gelbe Farbreste auf. Am wichtigsten für die aktuelle Studie ist ein roter Streifen, der vertikal vom rechten Knie bis zur Höhe des Knöchels über die äußere Tunika verläuft (Abb. 2). Das Ende des Schals bedeckt

1  Die Divixta-Stele aus Langres im Guy Baillet Museum (Foto N. Delferrière)

2  Detail der Divixta-Stele mit roter Linie am Saum der gallischen Tunika (Foto N. Delferrière)

---

[19] CIL XIII 5759; Mowat 1890, Kat. 45; Drioux 1934, Kat. 330; Guyard 1961, Kat. 76; Le Bohec 2003, Kat. 454.
[20] Delferrière – Edme 2018a, 277–278 Abb. 12; 2018b, 20–21 Abb. 14; 2019a, 104–105 Abb. 13; Delferrière 2020, 179–180 Abb. 4.

3   Grabstele aus der Umgebung von Beaune im Musée des Beaux-Arts de Beaune (Foto N. Delferrière)

5   Detail der Grabstele aus der nordöstlichen Mauer von Langres mit dünner, roter Linie auf der unteren Partie der Tunika (Foto A.-L. Edme)

4   Grabstele aus der nordöstlichen Mauer von Langres, jetzt im Depot des Guy Baillet de Langres Museum (Foto A.-L. Edme)

den oberen Teil dieses Streifens, was von den Restauratoren zunächst als der einzig übriggebliebene Teil einer allumfassenden Streifendekoration interpretiert wurde[21]. Es sind aber vermutlich die Überreste zweier vertikaler roter Linien, die parallel von der Schulter bis zum Saum verlaufen. Gemäß der Epigrafik und Typologie der Stele wurde eine Datierung in das 2. Jahrhundert n. Chr. vorgeschlagen[22].

2. Eine weitere Stele aus Ostgallien ist mit Resten von Bemalungen erhalten, die uns erlauben, das Aussehen der dargestellten Kleidung besser zu verstehen (Abb. 3). Die Stele aus Kalkstein wurde vor 1910 in der

---

[21] Delferrière – Edme 2019a, 104 Abb. 13.
[22] Edme 2018, Kat. Ling-297.

Nähe von Beaune (Gebiet der Aedui; Côte-d'Or) entdeckt und wird heute im Musée des Beaux-Arts de Beaune (Inv. 44.795) aufbewahrt[23]. Sie ist an der Spitze abgebrochen, 1,10 m hoch, 0,45 m breit und 0,10 m tief. In einer geschwungenen Nische ist die Verstorbene stehend dargestellt. Sie trägt eine gallische Tunika mit Endärmeln. In ihrer rechten, zur Brust geführten Hand hält sie einen Becher und in der linken Hand einen Krug. Ihr Haar besteht aus feinen Locken, die zu ihrem Hinterkopf geführt sind. Spuren roter Farbe sind noch in den Konturlinien um die Gesichtszüge, in den Haaren und in zwei vertikalen Streifen an jeder Seite der Tunika sichtbar, die nur von den Hüften bis zum Saum erhalten sind[24]. Der Stil der Stele und die Darstellung der Verstorbenen lassen auf eine Datierung an das Ende des 2. Jahrhunderts n. Chr. schließen[25].

3. Die dritte hier interessierende Stele wurde zu einem unbekannten Zeitpunkt vor 1911 in der nordöstlichen Stadtmauer von Langres entdeckt (Abb. 4). Sie besteht aus Lingon-Kalkstein und ist 1,36 m hoch, 0,67 m breit und 0,32 m tief. Sie befindet sich derzeit im Depot des Museums Guy Baillet de Langres (Inv. 845.17)[26]. In einer flachen Nische steht ein (wahrscheinlich bärtiger) Mann. Er wendet den Kopf nach links und trägt eine gallische Tunika mit Endärmeln, die bis unter die Knie reicht. Seine Frisur ist buschig und besteht aus großen gewellten Strähnen, die ihm bis in den Nacken fallen. In der rechten Hand hält er einen scheinbar diagonal verlaufenden Riemen (einer Tasche [?]) und in der linken Hand den Henkel eines mit Früchten gefüllten Weidenkorbes. Auf dem Stein sind noch zahlreiche

6 Grabstele aus Dijon im Musée Archéologique de Dijon (Foto A.-L. Edme)

Farbspuren sichtbar: Teile des Nischenhintergrunds sind hellrot bemalt, eine große dunkelrote Linie umgibt den Körper der Figur, und am unteren Teil der Tunika befinden sich die Überreste eines dünnen, roten Streifendekors; an der oberen linken Schulter sind auch makroskopisch nur schwierig auszumachende Spuren von Polychromie zu erkennen (Abb. 5). Die Datierung dieses Grabdenkmals ist nicht leicht zu bestimmen, wird aber zwischen dem 1. und 3. Jahrhundert n. Chr. angenommen[27].

---

[23] Espérandieu 1910, Kat. 2103; Imbert 1970, Kat. 18; Thévenot 1971, Kat. 44; Provost u. a. 2009, 21–22. 51; Lamy 2015, Kat. 21.195; Edme 2018, Kat. Éd-346; Delferrière – Edme 2018b, 9–10 Kat. 1.

[24] Delferrière – Edme 2018b, 9–10 Kat. 1; 2019a, 99. 105.

[25] Lamy 2015, Kat. 21.195; Menec 2015, Kat. 239; Edme 2018, Kat. Éd-346.

[26] Royer 1902, Kat. 188; Espérandieu 1911, Kat. 3279; Royer 1931, Kat. 188; Guyard 1961, Kat. 188; Decorse 2000, Kat. 10; Menec 2015, Kat. 225; Edme 2018, Kat. Ling-337; Delferrière – Edme 2019a, 98.

[27] Edme 2018, Kat. Ling-337.

4. Eine weitere Stele eines Lingonen aus feinem oolithischen Kalkstein (Asnières-Stein), von der nur noch der rechte Teil erhalten ist, wurde vor 1911 in Dijon entdeckt (Abb. 6). Sie ist 1,47 m hoch, 0,52 m breit und 0,40 m tief. Vermutlich wurde sie für die Wiederverwendung im spätantiken *castrum* zugeschnitten. Die Stele wird heute im Archäologischen Museum von Dijon aufbewahrt (Inv. Arb. 165)[28]. Sie zeigt zwei stehende männliche Figuren. Die linke ist fast vollständig weggebrochen, die rechte hat hingegen eine struppige Frisur und trägt eine wadenlange gallische Tunika mit Endärmeln. Sie streckt der anderen Person ihre rechte Hand entgegen. Bei den letzten Restaurierungsarbeiten wurden umfangreiche Reste der Farbe freigelegt[29]. Das Haar der erhaltenen Figur wurde orange/rot bemalt, und die Details der Kleidung und Schuhe wurden

7  Detail der Grabstele aus Dijon mit roten Streifen an den Schultern (Foto A.-L. Edme)

mit roten Linien gemalt: die Riemen der Sandalen, der Ausschnitt, die Armausschnitte und die Nähte an den Seiten der Tunika. Zwei dünne Zierbänder verlaufen an der Tunika von den Schultern bis zur Taille, wo sie hinter einem Arm und Stofffalten verschwinden (Abb. 7). Es ist wahrscheinlich, dass sich diese Linien bis zum Saum fortgesetzt haben, aber die Farbe ist in diesem Bereich verblasst. Auf den ersten Blick deuten diese Linien an den Schultern auf Nähte von eingesetzten Ärmeln hin, aber aufgrund der Weite der Tunika beginnen die Ärmel auf halber Höhe des Oberarms[30]. Daher dürften diese Linien dekorative Bänder wiedergeben. Darüber hinaus sind scheinbar Verstärkungsvorrichtungen als rote Kreuze an Stellen der Tunika dargestellt, an denen ein Reißen des Stoffes verhindert werden sollte: am unteren Rand der Seitennähte und der Öffnung der Armausschnitte[31]. Die Datierung auch dieses Grabdenkmals ist nicht leicht zu bestimmen, dürfte aber zwischen dem 1. und 3. Jahrhundert n. Chr. liegen[32].

## INTERPRETATION

Aus den oben dargelegten Beweisen geht hervor, dass die weiten, nicht gegürteten Tuniken, die üblicherweise in der gallischen Region getragen wurden und als modisches Identitätsmerkmal dienten, manchmal mit zwei vertikalen Streifen verziert sein konnten, anscheinend am häufigsten in einer rötlichen Farbe. Deutlich wird auch, dass ein solcher Schmuck eine verblüffende Ähnlichkeit mit der typisch römischen Tunikadekoration hat: den sog. *clavi*.

*Clavi* bestanden im Allgemeinen aus zwei parallelen, einfarbigen Bändern in verschiedenen Breiten, die von den Schultern bis zum Saum der römischen Tunika liefen. Sie wurden normalerweise in den Stoff eingewebt, einige der aufwendigeren *clavi* der Spätantike waren angenäht. Rot

---

[28] Espérandieu 1911, Kat. 3479; Deyts 1976, Kat. 232; Edme 2018, Kat. Ling-148.
[29] Desroches – Sawatzky 2015.
[30] Sowohl römische als auch gallische Tuniken wurden normalerweise auf dem Webstuhl ohne nachträgliches Hinzufügen von Ärmeln in T-Form gewebt, aber gallische Tuniken scheinen auf beide Arten hergestellt worden zu sein. Für in Form gewebte Tuniken s. Granger-Taylor 1982; 2007. Für eine ausführlichere Diskussion über Tunikaärmel, s. Pausch 2003, 84–86.
[31] Diese Details zeigen, dass die Tunika aus einem großen Tuch gefertigt war, das in der Mitte für den Ausschnitt durchbohrt wurde; die Enden wurden zusammengenäht, um die Ärmel zu bilden (Delferrière – Edme 2018a, 275–276 Abb. 7; 2018b, 20. 22 Abb. 15; 2019a, 97. 105 Abb. 14).
[32] Edme 2018, Kat. Ling-148.

und Violett waren beliebte Farben, aber sowohl textile als auch bildliche Beweise zeugen von einer breiten Palette möglicher Farbtöne, einschließlich Blau, Grün und Rosa, zumindest für spätere Perioden[33]. In Rom wurden *clavi* traditionell von Männern auf ihren Tuniken getragen. Bestimmte Arten purpurner *clavi* waren das gesetzliche Vorrecht der beiden Stände des römischen Adels: der *angustus clavus* (schmaler Streifen) für die *equites* und der *latus clavus* (breiter Streifen) für die Senatoren.

In der Kaiserzeit konnten *clavi* sowohl als Statusmarker als auch als allgemeine Tunikadekorationen verwendet werden, und das in einer Vielzahl von Breiten. Der *latus clavus* wurde sogar von einfachen Leuten verwendet, anscheinend ohne Angst vor rechtlichen Konsequenzen[34]. *Clavi* wurden schließlich auch von Frauen getragen, obwohl es mangels schriftlicher Beweise und Bemalungen auf Statuen und Reliefs schwer festzustellen ist, wann dies begann. Zu den frühesten Darstellungen römischer Frauen in Tuniken mit *clavi* gehören einige wenige pompejanische Fresken[35]. Es ist unwahrscheinlich, dass es bis in die Spätantike eine Mehrheitsmode für Frauen war, als *clavi* zur Hauptdekoration zeitgenössischer Tuniken wie der *dalmatica* und der *tunica manicata* wurden[36]. *Clavi* als Tunikaschmuck finden sich auch in anderen Teilen des Römischen Reiches. So sind sie beispielsweise in Grabporträts für Männer und Frauen in Ägypten und Syrien belegt, obwohl hier möglicherweise ein früherer griechischer Einfluss im Spiel ist[37].

Im Gegensatz zum Mittelmeerraum scheinen solche Zierbänder in der vorrömischen Kleidung Nord- und Westeuropas gefehlt zu haben. Textilfragmente deuten darauf hin, dass Streifen, Karo-, Fischgräten- und Rautenmuster sowie einfarbige Stoffe üblich waren, mit oder ohne Hinzufügen von dekorativen (brettgewebten) Bordüren. Farbstreifen erscheinen als allgemeines Gesamtmuster in bronze- und eisenzeitlichen Stoffen, nicht aber nur als zwei Bänder[38]. Das Vorhandensein von *clavi* auf gallischen Tuniken in der galloromischen Grabkunst stellt daher ein Fremdelement auf einem ansonsten einheimischen Kleidungsstück dar.

Gelegentlich treten *clavi* auch in anderen Teilen der nördlichen Provinzen in der figurativen Kunst auf. Mehrere Reliefs aus der Römerzeit, etwa aus Pannonien, haben erhaltene Malereien, die die Verwendung von *clavi* auf Tuniken zeigen, darunter mindestens ein Stück in der Obhut des Bundesdenkmalamtes in Wien[39] und eine sog. Diener-Szene, die jetzt im Schloss Tata in Ungarn untergebracht ist[40]. Letztere zeigt die untere Hälfte von drei Figuren, von denen zwei Tuniken mit Resten gemalter *clavi* tragen. Eine ist eine kurze, weiße Tunika mit rotorangen *clavi*, die andere ist eine längere, orangegelbe Tunika mit dunkelroten *clavi*. Diese stehen jedoch außerhalb des Bereiches der gallischen Tunika und können nur bedingt als römische Gewänder bezeichnet werden. Sie könnten auch spätrömische Gewänder darstellen, auf denen *clavi* im gesamten Reich allgegenwärtig waren. Leider erweisen sich textfreie Reliefdenkmäler aus Pannonien wie dieses als kaum datierbar[41].

---

[33] Pausch 2003, 112; Bender-Jørgensen 2011, 76. 79.

[34] z. B. Hor. sat. 1, 5, 35: *scriba* mit *latus clavus*; Plin. nat. 33, 29: Herold mit *latus clavus*; Opferdienerstatuette im Palazzo dei Conservatori in Rom (Pausch 2003, 261 Abb. 86); *fullo* auf einer Freske in Pompeii (Gell 2010, 2 Taf. 51).

[35] z. B. *fullonica*-Szene aus dem Haus des Veranius Hypsaeus (Museo Archeologico Nazionale; Coarelli 2002, 136), möglicherweise auch die erste Szene in der Villa der Mysterien (Sauron 1998). s. auch Ov. am. 3, 269: *Pallida purpureis spargat sua corpora virgis*.

[36] z. B. Pausch 2003, 118–124.

[37] Die frühsten Beispiele sind: ein *loculus*-Porträt einer Frau aus Palmyra (Landesmuseum Mainz; Pausch 2003, 236 Abb. 13); eine Tunika in der Abegg-Stiftung in Riggisberg (Inv. 4219), Datum: 50–232 n. Chr. (Schrenk – Knaller 2004, 158); Tunika A (MC 1100) vom Mons Claudianus, Datum 100–120 n. Chr. (Jørgensen 2018, 17 Abb. 3); zwei frühe Mumienporträts, Datum 55–70 n. Chr. (British Museum Inv. EA74713 und EA74716).

[38] Grömer 2012, 41; 2016a, 40. 171–198; 2016b; Wild 2002, 11. 18. 21.

[39] Inv. W 9565.

[40] lupa 5924. Diese ›Diener‹ sind haufig auf norischen und pannonischen Stelen abgebildet, aber es ist bisher nicht klar, was sie repräsentieren. s. Walde 2001; Pochmarksi 2003.

[41] s. auch Dalmatien, z. B. eine Frauentunika aus Livno in Bosnien-Hercegovina: lupa 29997.

Die oben beschriebenen, neu veröffentlichten Bemalungen auf ostgallischen Steinen[42] zeigen, dass *clavi* als Schmuck auf einem nachweislich einheimischen Kleidungsstück, der gallischen Tunika, im römischen Nordwesten verwendet wurden, und zwar lange vor der Allgegenwart von *clavi* in spätantiker Kleidung. Dies führt dazu, andere Funde neu zu bewerten, von denen man sonst angenommen hätte, dass sie römische Tuniken darstellen, wie etwa eine wollene Kindertunika im Musée de Berry, die zwei grüne – jedoch interessanterweise aufgemalte – *clavi* aufweist[43]. Auch können Mosaikbilder aus Gallien, die in Alltagsszenen Menschen mit *clavus*-verzierten Tuniken zeigen, nun zumindest als gallische und nicht als römische Tuniken angesehen werden[44].

Das neue Bild, das wir jetzt von der gallischen Tunika gewinnen, ist umso interessanter, als die *Tres Galliae* als Region, obwohl reich an römischer figurativer Kunst – insbesondere an Grabdenkmälern –, besonders resistent gegen römische Kleidungsstile gewesen zu sein scheinen. Sehr wenige Darstellungen, meist nur die der sehr Reichen, zeigen Männer oder Frauen in römischer Kleidung wie Toga oder *tunica* und *palla*. Die überwiegende Mehrheit bildet sowohl Männer als auch Frauen im lokalen gallischen Ensemble mit der charakteristischen Tunika ab[45]. Die oben vorgelegten Belege verdeutlichen, dass die typische gallische Tunika jedoch manchmal mit einem charakteristischen römischen Schmuckelement, nämlich den *clavi*, verziert war[46]. Anhand der noch spärlichen Belege ist es schwierig festzustellen, welche Menschen genau in Gallien *clavi* trugen und warum. Die hier präsentierten Beweise zeigen, dass das Geschlecht kein bestimmender Faktor war, denn *clavi* schmücken die gallischen Tuniken von Männern und Frauen. Wir dürfen jedoch nicht davon ausgehen, dass alle gallischen Tuniken diese Dekoration aufwiesen. Andere, aus Platzgründen hier nicht weiter diskutierte Objekte, wie die neuen Fresken in Maasbracht[47] und die Tunika aus Les Martres-de-Veyre[48], zeigen sowohl mit *clavi* verzierte als auch schlichte gallische Tuniken.

Es ist wahrscheinlich, dass die Entscheidung, *clavi* zu tragen, eher eine Frage des persönlichen Geschmacks war als eine des Status, und vielleicht eine bewusste Anspielung auf die römische Mode darstellte. Wenn wir noch mehr Grabporträts mit erhaltener Bemalung hätten, würden wir eine noch bessere Kenntnis dieses Kleiderstückes bekommen, wie auch von den Menschen, die sich für *clavi* entschieden haben. So eröffnet die Entdeckung der *clavi* neue Möglichkeiten, um herauszufinden, wie sich die Gallorömer verstanden und wie sie dies auf ihren Grabsteinen zum Ausdruck brachten. Erfreulicherweise wird nun immer mehr Zeit auf die Entdeckung von Bemalung an römischen Provinzdenkmälern verwendet[49]. Angesichts der rasanten Entwicklung der Pigmenterkennungstechnologie ist zu hoffen, dass weitere Entdeckungen gemacht und mehr Informationen aus diesem wertvollen Material gewonnen werden können.

---

[42] s. auch eine neu entdeckte Dekoration auf der Tunika von Grab A/E aus Les-Martres-de-Veyre (Breniquet u. a. 2017; Lorente 2020) und neue Wandmalereifragmente aus der Villa in Maasbracht (NL), die auch *clavi* auf gallischen Tuniken bezeugen (Swinkels 2019, 97–99). s. nun auch Rothe – Hamelink – Delferriere 2023, 551–554.

[43] Ferdière 1984, annexe 3 (A. Michelet), 264–266; Roche-Bernard 1993, 8–9.

[44] z. B. der sog. rustikale Kalender aus Saint-Romain-en-Gal (Musée des antiquités nationales in Saint-Germain-en-Laye: Balmelle – Darmon 2017, 188–190 Abb. 239).

[45] s. z. B. Wild 1985; Freigang 1997; Rothe 2009 und Espérandieu's Corpus der gallischen Reliefskulptur (Espérandieu 1910; 1911).

[46] Für eine Rekonstruktion des Aussehens der gallischen Tunika mit *clavi* s. Rothe u. a. 2023, 551–553.

[47] Swinkels 2019, 97–99.

[48] Audollent 1923; Fournier 1956; Desrosiers – Lorquin 1998, 60; Lorente u.a. 2020.

[49] s. z. B. Arbeit des österreichischen Bundesdenkmalamtes: <https://www.carnuntum.at/de/aktuelles-in-und-ueber-carnuntum/aktuelles-aus-der-wissenschaft/roemische-steindenkmaeler-von-carnuntum> (04.05.2023).

# BIBLIOGRAFIE

| | |
|---|---|
| Andrikopoulou-Strack 1986 | J.-N. Andrikopoulou-Strack, Grabbauten des 1. Jahrhunderts n. Chr. im Rheingebiet. Untersuchungen zu Chronologie und Typologie, BJb Beih. 43 (Bonn 1986) |
| Audollent 1923 | A. Audollent, Les tombes Gallo-Romaines à inhumation des Martres-de-Veyre (Puy-de-Dôme), Mémoires présentés à l'Académie des Sciences et Belles-Lettres 13, 1923, 275–328 |
| Balmelle – Darmon 2017 | C. Balmelle – J.-P. Darmon, La mosaïque dans les Gaules romaines (Paris 2017) |
| Bankel – Liverani 2004 | H. Bankel – P. Liverani (Hrsg.), I colori del Bianco. Policromia nella scultura antica (Rom 2014) |
| Bender-Jørgensen 2011 | L. Bender-Jørgensen, Clavi and non-clavi: definitions of various bands on Roman textiles, in: C. Alfaro – J.-P. Brun – Ph. Borgard – R. Bierobon Benoit (Hrsg.), *Purpureae Vestes* III. Textiles y tintes en la ciudad antigua. Actas del III Symposium Internacional sobre Textiles y Tintes del Mediterráneo en el mundo antiguo, Neapel 13.–15.11.2008, Collection du Centre Jean Bérard 36 (Valencia 2011) 75–81 |
| Blanchet 1918–1924 | A. Blanchet, La polychromie des bas-reliefs de la Gaule romaine, Bulletin de la Société archéologique de Sens 33, 1918–1924, 1–22 |
| Böhme 1985 | A. Böhme, Tracht- und Bestattungssitten in den germanischen Provinzen und der Belgica, in: ANRW II 12, 3 (Berlin 1985) 423–455 |
| Boppert 1992 | W. Boppert, CSIR Deutschland II 6, Germania Superior: Zivile Grabsteine aus Mainz und Umgebung (Mainz 1992) |
| Bourgeois 2019 | B. Bourgeois (Hrsg.), Les couleurs de l'antique. Actes de la 8e table ronde sur la polychromie de la sculpture et de l'architecture antique, Technè 48 (Paris 2019) |
| Bracci u. a. 2018 | S. Bracci – G. Giachi – P. Liverani – P. Pallechi – F. Paolluci (Hrsg.), Polychromy in Ancient Sculpture and Architecture. Acts from the latest international conference dedicated to stone and its colours (Livorno 2018) |
| Breniquet u. a. 2017 | C. Breniquet – M. Bèche-Wittmann – C. Bouilloc – C. Gaumat, The Gallo-roman Textile Collection from Les Martres-deVeyre, France, Archaeological Textiles Review 59, 2017, 71–81 |
| Brinkmann – Wünsche 2004 | V. Brinkmann – R. Wünsche (Hrsg.), Bunte Götter – Die Farbigkeit antiker Skulptur, Staatliche Antikensammlungen und Glyptothek (München 2004) |
| Brocard 1873 | H. Brocard, Catalogue du Musée de Langres fondé et administré par la Société Historique et Archéologique de Langres (Langres 1873) |
| Brocard 1886 | H. Brocard, Catalogue du Musée de Langres fondé et administré par la Société Historique et Archéologique de Langres (Langres 1886) |
| Decorse 2000 | S. Decorse, Les stèles funéraires du musée de Langres et leurs divers aspects socioculturels (Dijon 2000) |
| Delferrière 2020 | N. Delferrière, L'emploi de la couleur sur les monuments funéraires de Gaule romaine. Méthodologie d'étude et premiers résultats à partir des collections de l'Est, in: A. Binsfeld – A. Klöckner – G. Kremer – M. Reuter – M. Scholz (Hrsg.), Stadt – Land – Fluss. Grabdenkmäler der Treverer in lokaler und überregionaler Perspektive. Akten der Internationalen Konferenz in Neumagen und Trier 25.–27.10.2018, TrZ Beih. 37 (Trier 2020) 175–186 |
| Delferrière – Edme 2018a | N. Delferrière – A.-L. Edme, La polychromie des stèles de la nécropole des *Bolards* (Nuits-Saint-Georges, Côte-d'Or), RAE 67, 2018, 267–286 |
| Delferrière – Edme 2018b | N. Delferrière – A.-L. Edme, La polychromie des stèles funéraires du musée des Beaux-Arts de Beaune, Recueil des travaux de la Société d'Histoire et d'Archéologie de Beaune 36, 2018, 7–27 |
| Delferrière – Edme 2019a | N. Delferrière – A.-L. Edme, Polychromie et monuments funéraires. L'exemple de la Gaule de l'Est, in: B. Porod – P. Scherrer (Hrsg.), Der Stifter und sein Monument: Gesellschaft, Ikonographie, Chronologie. Akten des 15. Internationalen Kolloquiums zum Provinzialrömischen Kunstschaffen Graz 14.–20.06.2017 (Graz 2019) 94–111 |
| Delferrière – Edme 2019b | N. Delferrière – A.-L. Edme, Parlando di … »barbari«. L'antichità a colori. Il caso della Gallia dell'Est, Archeologia Viva 198, 2019, 54–60 |
| Desroches – Sawatzky 2015 | E. Desroches – F. Sawatzky, Fragment de stèle à deux personnages, Musée archéologique de Dijon (unveröffentlichter Restaurationsbericht 2015) |

| | |
|---|---|
| Desrosiers – Lorquin 1998 | S. Desrosiers – A. Lorquin, Gallo-Roman Period Archaeological Textiles found in France, in: L. Bender Jørgensen – C. Rinaldo (Hrsg.), Textiles in European Archaeology. Report from the 6$^{th}$ NESAT Symposium in Borås 07.–11.05.1996 (Göteborg 1998) 53–72 |
| Deyts 1976 | S. Deyts, Musée archéologique de Dijon: sculptures gallo-romaines mythologiques et religieuses (Paris 1976) |
| Drioux 1934 | G. Drioux, Les Lingons. Textes et inscriptions antiques (Paris 1934) |
| Edme 2018 | A.-L. Edme, Les différents modes d'évocation des défunts chez les Éduens, les Lingons et les Séquanes au Haut-Empire (I$^{er}$–III$^e$ siècles): de l'épigraphie à la représentation figurée (Diss. Universität Dijon 2018) |
| Espérandieu 1910 | É. Espérandieu, Recueil général des bas-reliefs, statues et bustes de la Gaule romaine III: Lyonnaise, première partie (Paris 1910) |
| Espérandieu 1911 | É. Espérandieu, Recueil général des bas-reliefs, statues et bustes de la Gaule romaine IV: Lyonnaise, deuxième partie (Paris 1911) |
| Espérandieu 1915 | É. Espérandieu, Recueil général des bas-reliefs, statues et bustes de la Gaule romaine VI: Belgique deuxième partie (Paris 1915) |
| Ferdière 1984 | A. Ferdière, Le travail du textile en Région Centre de l'Age du Fer au Haut Moyen-Age, RACFr 23/2, 1984, 209–275 |
| Fournier 1956 | P.-F. Fournier, Patron d'une robe de femme et d'un bas gallo-romain trouvés aux Martres-de-Veyre, Bulletin Historique et Scientifique de l'Auvergne 76, 1956, 202–203 |
| Freigang 1997 | Y. Freigang, Die Grabmäler der gallo-römischen Kultur im Moselland. Studien zur Selbstdarstellung einer Gesellschaft, JbRGZM 44, 1997, 277–440 |
| Gell 2010 | W. Gell, *Pompeiana*: The Topography, Edifices, and Ornaments of Pompeii (Nachdr. Cambridge 2010) |
| Granger-Taylor 1982 | H. Granger-Taylor, Weaving Clothes to Shape in the Ancient World: the Tunic and Toga of the Arringatore, Textile History 13/1, 1982, 3–25 |
| Granger-Taylor 2007 | H. Granger-Taylor, Weaving Clothes to Shape in the Ancient World. 25 years on. Corrections and Further Details with Particular Reference to the Cloaks from Lahun, Archaeological Textiles Newsletter 45, 2007, 26–35 |
| Grenier 1904 | A. Grenier, La polychromie des sculptures de Neumagen, RA 3, 1904, 245–262 |
| Grömer 2012 | K. Grömer, Austria: Bronze and Iron Ages, in: M. Gleba – U. Mannering (Hrsg.), Textiles and textile production in Europe from prehistory to AD 400 (Oxford 2012) 27–64 |
| Grömer 2016a | K. Grömer, The Art of Prehistoric Textile Making. The Development of Craft Traditions and Clothing in Central Europe, Veröffentlichungen der Prähistorischen Abteilung (VPA) 5, NHM (Wien 2016) |
| Grömer 2016b | K. Grömer, Colour, pattern and glamour: Textiles in Central Europe 2000–400 BC, in: J. Ortiz – C. Alfaro – L. Turell – M. J. Martínez (Hrsg.), Textiles, basketry and dyes in the ancient mediterranean world. Proceedings of the V$^{th}$ International Symposium on textiles and dyes in the ancient mediterranean world, Montserrat 09.–12.03.2014 (Valencia 2016) 37–44 |
| Guyard 1961 | M. Guyard, Les inscriptions gallo-romaines de Langres (Diss. Universität Dijon 1961) |
| Imbert 1970 | G. Imbert, Catalogue commenté des objets gallo-romains du musée de Beaune (Diss. Universität Dijon 1970) |
| Jockey 2013 | P. Jockey, Le mythe de la Grèce blanche. Histoire d'un rêve occidental (Paris 2013) |
| Jockey 2014 | P. Jockey, Les couleurs et les ors retrouvés de la sculpture antique, RA 58/2, 2014, 355–370 |
| Jockey 2018 | P. Jockey, Les arts de la couleur en Grèce ancienne … et ailleurs. Approches interdisciplinaires. Actes du colloque international tenu à Athènes, 23.–25.04.2009, BCH 56 (Paris 2018) |
| Joly 2001 | M. Joly, Langres, Carte archéologique de la Gaule 52/2 (Paris 2001) |
| Jørgensen 2018 | L. B. Jørgensen, Textiles from Mons Claudianus, 'Abu Sha'Ar and Other Roman Sites in the Eastern Desert, in: J.-P. Brun – T. Faucher – B. Redon – S. Sidebotham (Hrsg.), The Eastern Desert of Egypt during the Greco-Roman Period: Archaeological Reports (Paris 2018), <https://books.openedition.org/cdf/5234#illustrations> (30.03.2023) |

| | |
|---|---|
| Julliot 1898 | G. Julliot, Inscriptions et monuments du musée gallo-romain de Sens: descriptions et interprétations (Sens 1898) |
| Kolb 1973 | F. Kolb, Römische Mäntel: *paenula*, *lacerna*, μανδύη, RM 80, 1973, 69–167 |
| Lamy 2015 | P.-A. Lamy, De la carrière à l'abandon: la sculpture sur pierre chez les Éduens, I$^{er}$–IV$^e$ siècles ap. J.-C. (Diss. Universität Dijon 2015) |
| Langlois 1959 | S. Langlois, Le vêtement gallo-romain d'après les scènes figurées sur des reliefs du Musée archéologique de Dijon, Mémoires de la Commission des Antiquités du Département de la Côte-d'Or 25, 1959, 195–208 |
| Le Bohec 2003 | Y. Le Bohec, Inscriptions de la cité des Lingons. Inscriptions sur pierre, Archéologie et histoire de l'art 17 (Paris 2003) |
| Lee 2015 | M. M. Lee, Body, dress, and identity in ancient Greece (Cambridge 2015) |
| Liverani – Santamaria 2014 | P. Liverani – U. Santamaria (Hrsg.), Diversamente bianco. La policromia della scultura romana (Rom 2014) |
| Lorente u. a. 2020 | P. Lorente – F. Medard – C. Breniquet, A New Approach to the Study of the Exceptional Textile Collection from the Gallo-Roman Site of Les Martres de Veyre, in: M. Bustamante-Álvarez – E. H. Sánchez López – J. Jiménez Ávila (Hrsg.), Redefining Ancient Textile Handcraft. Structures, Tools and Production Processes. Proceedings of the VII$^{th}$ International Symposium on Textiles and Dyes in the Ancient Mediterranean World, Granada 02.–04.10.2019 (Granada 2020) 171–186 |
| lupa | F. und O. Harl, <lupa.at> (Bilddatenbank zu antiken Steindenkmälern) |
| Luquet 1838 | J.-F.-O. Luquet, Antiquités romaines. Notes sur diverses découvertes archéologiques faites à Langres et aux environs, Annuaire ecclésiastique et historique du diocèse de Langres 1878, 253–576 |
| Menec 2015 | F. Menec, Langres-*Andemantunnum* (Haute-Marne, Champagne-Ardenne). Étude urbanistique de la capitale de cité des Lingons (Diss. Universität Paris 2015) |
| Mowat 1890 | R. Mowat, Inscriptions de la cité des Lingons conservées à Dijon et à Langres, RA 3$^e$ série XVI, 1890, 1–74 |
| Mulliez 2019 | M. Mulliez (Hrsg.), Restituer les couleurs. Le rôle de la restitution dans les recherches sur la polychromie en sculpture, architecture et peinture murale/Reconstruction of Polychromy, Archeovision 8 (Bordeaux 2019) |
| Noelke 1998 | P. Noelke, Grabreliefs mit Mahldarstellungen in den germanisch-gallischen Provinzen – soziale und religiöse Aspekte, in: P. Fasold – T. Fischer – H. von Hesberg – M. Witteyer (Hrsg.), Bestattungssitte und kulturelle Identität Grabanlagen und Grabbeigaben der frühen römischen Kaiserzeit in Italien und den Nordwest-Provinzen. Kolloquium Xanten 16.–18.02.1995 (Bonn 1998) 399–418 |
| Olson 2017 | K. Olson, Masculinity and dress in Roman antiquity (Abingdon 2017) |
| Pausch 2003 | M. Pausch, Die römische Tunika (Augsburg 2003) |
| Péchin d'Autebois 1847a | M.-Fr.-E. Péchin d'Autebois, État des diverses collections composant le musée fondé par la Société historique et archéologique de Langres, Mémoires de la Société Historique et Archéologique de Langres I/1, 1847, X–XX |
| Péchin d'Autebois 1847b | M.-Fr.-E. Péchin d'Autebois, Catalogue provisoire du musée fondé par la société historique et archéologique de Langres (Langres 1847) |
| Péchiné 1847–1860 | P. Péchiné, Notices sur les costumes des Gaulois en général et des Lingons en particulier. À propos de quelques monuments de l'ère gallo-romaine, Mémoires de la Société Historique et Archéologique de Langres I, 1847–1860, 59–64 |
| Pochmarski 2003 | E. Pochmarski, Zur Typologie und Chronologie der sog. norischen Mädchen, Anodos 3, 2003, 181–193 |
| Provost u. a. 2009 | M. Provost – R. Joly – M. Mangin – R. Goguey – G. Chouquer (Hrsg.), La Côte d'Or, d'Allerey à Normier, Carte archéologique de la Gaule 21/2 (Paris 2009) |
| Roche-Bernard 1993 | G. Roche-Bernard, Costumes et textiles en Gaule romaine (Paris 1993) |
| Rothe 2009 | U. Rothe, Dress and Cultural Identity in the Rhine-Moselle Region of the Roman Empire, BARIntSer 2038 (Oxford 2009) |
| Rothe 2012a | U. Rothe, The ›Third Way‹: Treveran women's dress and the ›Gallic Ensemble‹, AJA 116/2, 2012, 235–252 |

| | |
|---|---|
| Rothe 2012b | U. Rothe, Dress in the middle Danube provinces: the garments, their origins and their distribution, ÖJh 81, 2012, 137–231 |
| Rothe u. a. 2023 | U. Rothe – A. Hamelink – N. Delfièrre, Roman Clavus Decoration on Gallic Dress. A Reevaluation Based on New Discoveries, AJA 127/4, 2023, 545–562 |
| Royer 1902 | C. Royer, Catalogue du Musée de Langres fondé et administré par la Société Historique et Archéologique de Langres (Langres 1902) |
| Royer 1931 | C. Royer, Catalogue du Musée de Langres fondé et administré par la Société Historique et Archéologique de Langres (Langres 1931) |
| Sauron 1998 | G. Sauron, La grande fresque de la Villa des Mystères à Pompéi. Mémoire d'une dévote de Dionysos (Paris 1998) |
| Schoppa 1960 | H. Schoppa, Farbspuren auf den Grabfiguren von Ingelheim, Landkreis Bingen, Germania 38, 1960, 143 |
| Schrenk – Knaller 2004 | S. Schrenk – R. Knaller, Textilien des Mittelmeerraumes aus spätantiker bis frühislamischer Zeit 4 (Riggisberg 2004) |
| Swinkels 2019 | L. J. F. Swinkels, The wall painting fragments, in: W. K. Vos – C. Bakels – T. A. Goossens (Hrsg.), The Roman Villa at Maasbracht. The archaeology and history of a Roman settlement on the banks of the river Meuse (Province of Limburg, The Netherlands) (Leiden 2019) 83–127 |
| Thévenot 1971 | É. Thévenot, Le Beaunois gallo-romain, Collection Latomus 113 (Brüssel 1971) |
| Thiollet 1847–1859 | F. Thiollet, Album Thiollet, unveröffentlicht (Sens 1847–1859) |
| von Massow 1932 | W. von Massow, Die Grabmäler von Neumagen (Berlin 1932) |
| Walde 2001 | E. Walde, Die Dienerinnen auf den römischen Grabreliefs in der Provinz Noricum, in: T. A. S. M. Panhuysen (Hrsg.), Maastrichter Akten des 5. internationalen Kolloquiums über das provinzialrömische Kunstschaffen (Maastricht 2001) 235–243 |
| Wild 1964 | J. P. Wild, The *Caracallus*, Latomus, 23, 3, 1964, 532–536 |
| Wild 1968 | J. P. Wild, Clothing in the north-west provinces of the Roman Empire, BJb 168, 1968, 166–240 |
| Wild 1970 | J. P. Wild, Textile Manufacture in the Northern Roman Provinces (Cambridge 1970) |
| Wild 1985 | J. P. Wild, The clothing of Britannia, Gallia Belgica and Germania Inferior, in: ANRW II 12, 3 (Berlin 1985) 362–422 |
| Wild 2002 | J. P. Wild, The textile industries of Roman Britain, Britannia 33, 2002, 1–42 |
| Zimmer 1982 | G. Zimmer, Römische Berufsdarstellungen (Berlin 1982) |

*Anique Hamelink, Universiteit van Amsterdam, Eduard van Beinumstraat 37, 2324 KM Leiden, Niederlande.*
*[e]anique.hamelink@gmail.com*

*Nicolas Delferrière, Université Clermont-Auvergne, départment d'histoire de l'art et d'archéologie, 63001 Clermont-Fd Cedex, Frankreich.*
*[e] nicolas.delferriere@hotmail.fr*

*Ursula Rothe, Open University, Walton Hall, Milton Keynes MK7 6AA, Vereinigtes Königreich.*
*[e] ursula.rothe@open.ac.uk*

Sophie Insulander

# PROKONNESIAN MARBLE IN THE ARCHITECTURE OF IMPERIAL *EPHESOS*

## ATTEMPTING AN ARCHAEOLOGICAL EVALUATION

**Abstract**

This paper aims to examine the use of Prokonnesian marble in *Ephesos* against the background of local stone exploitation. As provenance analyses have shown, this marble was used for the construction of seven important buildings in Roman imperial *Ephesos*: four big bath-gymnasia, the neocorate Temple of Hadrian (Olympieion), the so-called Serapeion and the tomb of a local benefactor. These observations are intriguing when considering the numerous white marble quarries situated in *Ephesos*' territory, whose use for local architecture is well-attested. At the same time, the city's port facilitated the import and transshipment of various stones. The quarries on *Prokonnesos* experienced a huge upsurge in the 2nd century AD, quickly becoming one of the dominant import marbles of the Roman Empire. By examining the way Prokonnesian marble was used in these buildings, it is possible to recognise patterns of use and gain a better understanding of the possible reasons for importing this marble to *Ephesos*.

## INTRODUCTION

Over the last 15 years, under the leadership of Sabine Ladstätter and Walter Prochaska, the Austrian Archaeological Institute (OeAI) has been conducting extensive provenance and quarry studies[1]. As part of this research focus, almost all known buildings in *Ephesos* have been sampled and submitted to provenance analysis using petrographic and geochemical methods such as isotope analysis, trace element analysis, the examination of fluid inclusions and EPR[2]. These studies, conducted by Walter Prochaska[3] and Natalia Toma[4], have significantly improved the state of research on marble distribution in imperial *Ephesos*, thus allowing for the in-depth investigation of specific aspects. In a recently completed master's thesis written at the University of Vienna, the author tried to examine the usage patterns of Prokonnesian marble in the imperial architecture of *Ephesos*[5].

One important result of these provenance analyses was that white marble imported from the island of *Prokonnesos* (modern-day Marmara) was used for the construction of seven prominent buildings in imperial *Ephesos* (fig. 1). These comprise the four major bath-gymnasia of *Ephesos* as well as the so-called Serapeion and the neocorate Temple of Hadrian, also known as the Olympieion. The seventh relevant building, the monumental monopteros tomb of local benefactor

---

[1] <https://www.oeaw.ac.at/en/oeai/research/historical-archaeology/object-itineraries/provenance-studies-white-marbles> (06.11.2022).
[2] The analysis methods used by Walter Prochaska comprise petrography, isotope analysis, trace element analysis and fluid inclusion (FI) analysis, while the samples taken by Natalia Toma were investigated using petrographic examination, isotope analysis (performed by Nils Andersen, Kiel University) and EPR (performed by Donato Attanasio, National Research Council [CNR], Rome).
[3] See Prochaska – Grillo 2010; Kerschner – Prochaska 2011, 132–144; Prochaska – Grillo 2012; Prochaska 2013; Anevlavi et al. 2020.
[4] Toma 2020, 377–397. 422–429.
[5] The author would like to thank Sabine Ladstätter for supervising the thesis, and Walter Prochaska for the possibility to examine the results of his research from an archaeological viewpoint.

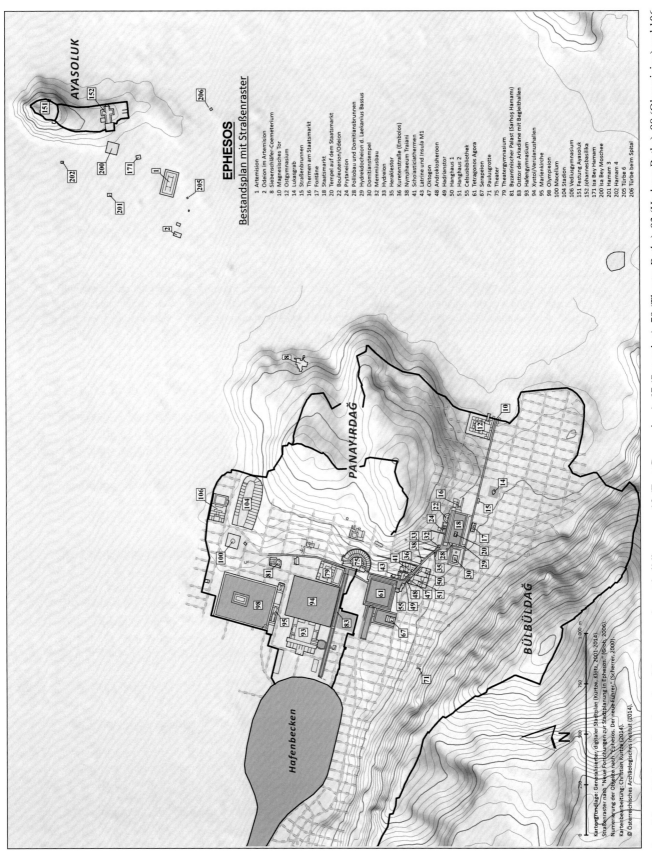

1 Map of *Ephesos* showing six of the seven relevant buildings: nos. 12 (East Gymnasium), 67 (Serapeion), 79 (Theatre Baths), 93 (Harbour Baths), 98 (Olympieion) and 106 (Vedius Gymnasium) (OeAI-OeAW, C. Kurtze)

T. Flavius Damianus, was located 2.7 km south-east of *Ephesos* next to the road to *Magnesia* on the Maeander (near the modern-day village of Acarlar).

The evidence of Prokonnesian marble being used for these constructions is intriguing when considering the existence of several high-quality white marble quarries situated in *Ephesos*' territory whose important role for the local architecture is well-attested by the geological analyses[6]. Thus, the main aim of the thesis was to examine the patterns of use for Prokonnesian marble in these buildings and the factors that could have led to the decision to use it.

## GROUP 1: THE BATH-GYMNASIUM COMPLEXES

The state of archaeological research, the number of samples taken, and the methods used for analysis vary from building to building. This makes it difficult to reliably determine the marble distribution, particularly in the case of the bath-gymnasia. However, it is possible to recognize some general patterns of use.

The examined buildings can be separated into two groups, with marked differences in the way Prokonnesian marble was used for their construction. The first group consists of the four large bath-gymnasium complexes, namely the Harbour Baths/Harbour Gymnasium, the Theatre Baths, the Vedius Gymnasium, and the East Gymnasium. In these buildings, bases and capitals in Prokonnesian marble (fig. 2) were repeatedly combined with polychrome column shafts made of Dokimeian Pavonazzetto marble, granite from the Troad or Egypt or regionally imported breccias[7]. This type of combination of coloured stones and white marble is typical of luxurious bath buildings across the Roman Empire and served to emphasise the valuable architectural elements made in polychrome stone and thus highlight their prestige[8].

2   Corinthian capital of the ›Ephesos type‹ from the Harbour Baths, Prokonnesian marble (photo W. Prochaska)

Another important observation is that in at least three of these bath-gymnasia, local marble was used next to Prokonnesian marble for elements of the rising architecture, namely bases, capitals and parts of the entablature (fig. 3)[9]. This contrasts with the pattern of marble distribution in the Olympieion and Serapeion, in which all rising architectural components were obtained from one source. Further sampling would be necessary to better understand the extent of local white marble use in relation to the use of Prokonnesian marble in the bath-gymnasia and the reasoning behind it.

## GROUP 2: THE TEMPLES AND THE DAMIANUS TOMB

The second group comprises the two monumental temple complexes (Serapeion and Olympieion) and, as far as can be inferred from preliminary analyses, the grave monument of T. Flavius Damianus.

---

[6] Prochaska – Grillo 2012, 585; Russell 2013, 146–147. For the separation of these quarries into groups, see Yavuz et al. 2011, 224; Prochaska 2016a, 341–342; Anevlavi et al. 2020, 17.
[7] Plattner 2016, 698; Anevlavi et al. 2020, 13; Toma 2020, 379–390. 423–428; Walter Prochaska, personal communication.
[8] Toma 2020, 142.
[9] Toma 2020, 423–428; Prochaska 2016b, 33; Walter Prochaska, personal communication.

3   Architrave block of the palaestra of the Vedius Gymnasium with a part of the building inscription, local (Ephesos II) marble (AT-OeAI-99-00229803 [photo A-W-OAI-EVG-00919])

4   Column bases and column shaft fragment in the pronaos of the Serapeion, Prokonnesian marble (AT-OeAI-99-00124264 [photo A-W-OAI-DIA-123791])

5   Column drum fragment from the Olympieion, Prokonnesian marble (photo W. Prochaska)

The Serapeion makes for an excellent case study, since it was the most extensively sampled building, and its building history has recently been studied in detail[10]. Additionally, in the case of the temples the sampling was not limited to elements of the rising architecture, but also included less representative components such as steps, door thresholds and parts of the pavement, thus enhancing our understanding of marble distribution within the buildings.

A closer examination of these buildings reveals a very different situation from the bath-gymnasia. As the most important result, it is apparent that for both the Serapeion and the Olympieion, the entire rising architecture was made of Prokonnesian marble[11]. Unlike in the bath-gymnasium complexes, white marble was preferred for the columns, which was also the case for the tomb of T. Flavius Damianus. The column shafts of the Serapeion were exceptional as they were monolithic and measured 12 m in height[12] (fig. 4). The even taller columns of the Olympieion, on the other hand, were composed of drums (fig. 5). The decision to import all rising architectural parts from one quarrying source indicates that the temples' components were ordered from *Prokonnesos* in a singular, large contract[13].

The examination of several floor slabs and door thresholds from the Serapeion and the Olympieion showed that local stones as well as marble from *Prokonnesos* and other sources were used[14]. For some of these elements, which were subjected to significant wear, the use of local marble may be seen in the context of repair and replacement. The paving slabs made of imported marble could have been acquired for the construction projects independently of the order for the Prokonnesian rising architecture, as the framework for the trade in wall and floor revetment was different from the trade in monumental architectural elements[15]. Alternatively, their use in the temple could have been secondary: This was the case for several steps of the staircase leading up to the Serapeion temple, which were made of marble from *Dokimeion*-Altıntaş and taken from a building of the Trajanic period[16].

## QUESTIONS OF CHRONOLOGY

The quarries of *Prokonnesos* reached trans-regional importance from the Flavian period onward, exporting marble to Rome and several provinces for major construction projects[17]. This development was greatly facilitated by their location next to a natural harbour. One of the research questions of the thesis dealt with the starting date of Prokonnesian marble imports to *Ephesos*.

For this question, the Harbour Baths are both the most relevant and simultaneously the most problematic building, problematic due to only having been partially excavated at the end of the 19th and in the early 20th century. The palaestra, which is generally but not unanimously dated to the Domitianic period, would be the earliest structure in all the buildings examined in the thesis, while the bath building was constructed in the Hadrianic period[18]. Three sampled architectural elements which can be assigned to the first construction phase[19] were found to be made of Ephesian marble, while three objects for which a Hadrianic dating has convincingly been suggested[20] were made from Prokonnesian marble.

---

[10] See Schulz 2017; Schulz 2019. The detailed publication of these new results is currently in preparation.
[11] Prochaska 2013, 44; Plattner 2016, 698.
[12] Schulz 2019, 46.
[13] Schulz 2017, 361; Toma 2020, 410.
[14] Walter Prochaska, personal communication.
[15] Russell 2013, 134; Toma 2020, 202.
[16] Taeuber 2013a, 43; Taeuber 2013b, 40; Prochaska 2013, 44; Taeuber 2014.
[17] Bruno et al. 2002, 291–297; Attanasio et al. 2008, 747; Russell 2013, 147–148.
[18] Plattner 2016, 698.
[19] See Strocka 1988, 295; Baier 2006, 68–75.
[20] See Strocka 1988, 302; Plattner 2003, 126; Baier 2006, 75–80. 120–126.

Therefore, the use of Prokonnesian marble in the Harbour Baths can be clearly detected only for the Hadrianic period[21]. The other imperial-era buildings which used Prokonnesian marble can be dated between the Hadrianic period and the late 2nd century AD. When seen in the context of other sampled buildings in *Ephesos*, it becomes clear that up until the 2nd century, local marble was the predominant building material in the city[22]. From the Hadrianic period onward, this pattern changed and marble from *Prokonnesos* was imported for several prestigious construction projects, where it was partially used next to local material, and partially used exclusively. What could have prompted this change?

## POSSIBLE REASONS FOR THE IMPORT OF PROKONNESIAN MARBLE TO *EPHESOS*

While no definite explanation can be given for this development, an attempt in examining possible causes was made. For the temples, one factor could have been their monumentality. Georg Plattner has suggested that perhaps by the 2nd century AD, the local Ephesian quarries could not produce blocks or cylinders of a sufficient size for these building projects[23]. In this context, the location of the construction sites near the harbour could also have played a role: It is possible that shipping the massive components from the quarries of *Prokonnesos* to the harbour of *Ephesos* was less expensive than having them transported by land from the surroundings of the city[24].

Another possible factor is the relationship between quarries, clients, and contractors, which influenced the acquisition of building materials[25]. We can only speculate about this since epigraphic references to these contractors or marble traders are lacking for the Ephesian buildings. The combination of polychrome stones and Prokonnesian marble in the bath-gymnasia could have been imported together as part of one order for construction material[26], possibly influenced by contractors' connections to specific quarries. This aspect is particularly interesting when considering Dokimeian Pavonazzetto marble, for which *Ephesos* might have played an important role as transshipment harbour[27].

In any case, Prokonnesian marble was a high-quality material, steadily gaining in popularity and perfectly suited for construction purposes, as is clearly attested to by its use in high-prestige buildings in various parts of the Roman Empire. Its use for seven high-profile buildings over the course of a century shows that the material fulfilled the requirements placed on it and successfully complemented the existing local marbles.

## BIBLIOGRAPHY

| | |
|---|---|
| Anevlavi et al. 2020 | V. Anevlavi – D. Bielefeld – S. Ladstätter – W. Prochaska – C. Samitz, Marble for the Dead. The Quarry of Ab-u Hayat, Ephesos, and Its Products, ÖJh 89, 2020, 11–60 |
| Attanasio et al. 2008 | D. Attanasio – M. Brilli – M. Bruno, The Properties and Identification of Marble from Proconnesos (Marmara Island, Turkey). A New Database Including Isotopic, EPR and Petrographic Data, Archaeometry 50/5, 2008, 747–774, DOI: 10.1111/j.1475-4754.2007.00364 |
| Baier 2006 | C. Baier, Kaiserzeitliche Konsolengeisa in Kleinasien. Untersuchungen zur Bauornamentik von flavischer bis in severische Zeit am Beispiel Ephesos (Diploma thesis University of Vienna 2006) |

---

[21] Cf. Plattner 2016, 698.
[22] Anevlavi et al. 2020, 13.
[23] Plattner 2016, 699.
[24] Plattner 2016, 699.
[25] See Russell 2013, 202–207.
[26] Cf. Toma 2020, 410.
[27] Russell 2011, 150; Toma 2020, 103.

| | |
|---|---|
| Bruno et al. 2002 | M. Bruno – S. Cancelliere – C. Gorgoni – L. Lazzarini – P. Pallante – P. Pensabene, Provenance and Distribution of White Marbles in Temples and Public Buildings of Imperial Rome, in: J. J. Herrmann, Jr. – N. Herz – R. Newman (eds.), ASMOSIA 5. Interdisciplinary Studies on Ancient Stone. Proceedings of the Fifth International Conference of the Association for the Study of Marble and Other Stones in Antiquity, Museum of Fine Arts, Boston, 1998 (London 2002) 289–300 |
| Kerschner – Prochaska 2011 | M. Kerschner – W. Prochaska, Die Tempel und Altäre der Artemis in Ephesos und ihre Baumaterialien, ÖJh 80, 2011, 73–154 |
| Plattner 2003 | G. A. Plattner, Ephesische Kapitelle des 1. und 2. Jhs. n. Chr. Form und Funktion kaiserzeitlicher Architekturdekoration in Kleinasien (Ph.D. diss. University of Vienna 2003) |
| Plattner 2016 | G. A. Plattner, The Quarries of Ephesos and Their Use in the Ephesian Architecture, in: T. Ismaelli – G. Scardozzi (eds.), Ancient Quarries and Building Sites in Asia Minor. Research on Hierapolis in Phrygia and Other Cities in South-Western Anatolia: Archaeology, Archaeometry, Conservation, Bibliotheca archaeologica 45 (Bari 2016) 693–700 |
| Prochaska 2013 | W. Prochaska, Geologie, Wissenschaftlicher Jahresbericht des Österreichischen Archäologischen Instituts 2013 (2014) 43–44, <http://www.oeaw.ac.at/fileadmin/Institute/OEAI/PDF/Kommunikation/OeAI_Jahresbericht_2013.pdf> (07.09.2023) |
| Prochaska 2016a | W. Prochaska, Marmore des Mausoleums, in: P. Ruggendorfer, Das Mausoleum von Belevi. Archäologische Untersuchungen zu Chronologie, Ausstattung und Stiftung. Mit Beiträgen von G. Forstenpointner, A. Galik, F. Kanz, M. Pfisterer, W. Prochaska, M. Schätzschock, H. Taeuber, M. Trapichler, G. E. Weissengruber, FiE 6, 2 (Wien 2016) 337–346 |
| Prochaska 2016b | W. Prochaska, Marmorsurvey, Wissenschaftlicher Jahresbericht des Österreichischen Archäologischen Instituts 2016 (2017) 33, <http://www.oeaw.ac.at/fileadmin/Institute/OEAI/PDF/Kommunikation/OeAI_Jahresbericht_2016.pdf> (07.09.2023) |
| Prochaska – Grillo 2010 | W. Prochaska – S. M. Grillo, A New Method for the Determination of the Provenance of White Marbles by Chemical Analysis of Inclusion Fluids: the Marbles of the Mausoleum of Belevi/Turkey, Archaeometry 52/1, 2010, 59–82, DOI:10.1111/j.1475-4754.2009.00470.x |
| Prochaska – Grillo 2012 | W. Prochaska – S. M. Grillo, The Marble Quarries of the Metropolis of Ephesos and Some Examples of the Use for Marbles in Ephesian Architecture and Sculpturing, in: A. Gutiérrez Garcia-Moreno – P. Lapuente – I. Rodà (eds.), Interdisciplinary Studies on Ancient Stone. Proceedings of the IX ASMOSIA Conference Tarragona 2009 (Tarragona 2012) 584–591 |
| Russell 2011 | B. Russell, *Lapis transmarinus*. Stone-Carrying Ships and the Maritime Distribution of Stone in the Roman Empire, in: D. Robinson – A. Wilson (eds.), Maritime Archaeology and Ancient Trade in the Mediterranean. Proceedings of the 2008 OCMA Conference Madrid (Oxford 2011) 139–155 |
| Russell 2013 | B. Russell, The Economics of the Roman Stone Trade, Oxford Studies on the Roman Economy (Oxford 2013) |
| Schulz 2017 | T. Schulz, Eine antike Großbaustelle. Ausführung und Bauablauf des Serapis-Tempels in Ephesos, in: D. Kurapkat – U. Wulf-Rheidt (eds.), Werkspuren. Materialverarbeitung und handwerkliches Wissen im antiken Bauwesen. Internationales Kolloquium in Berlin vom 13.–16. Mai 2015, DiskAB 12 (Regensburg 2017) 359–372 |
| Schulz 2019 | T. Schulz, The So-called Serapeion in Ephesos: First Results of the Building Research, in: D. Schowalter – S. Ladstätter – S. Friesen – C. Thomas (eds.), Religion in Ephesos Reconsidered. Archaeology of Spaces, Structures, and Objects, Novum Testamentum, Suppl. 177 (Boston 2019) 41–61 |
| Strocka 1988 | V. M. Strocka, Wechselwirkungen der stadtrömischen und kleinasiatischen Architektur unter Trajan und Hadrian, IstMitt 38, 1988, 291–307 |
| Taeuber 2013a | H. Taeuber, Epigrafik, Wissenschaftlicher Jahresbericht des Österreichischen Archäologischen Instituts 2012 (2013) 43, <http://www.oeaw.ac.at/fileadmin/Institute/OEAI/PDF/Kommunikation/OeAI_Jahresbericht_2012.pdf> (30.05.2023) |
| Taeuber 2013b | H. Taeuber, Epigrafik, Wissenschaftlicher Jahresbericht des Österreichischen Archäologischen Instituts 2013 (2014) 39–44, <http://www.oeaw.ac.at/fileadmin/Institute/OEAI/PDF/Kommunikation/OeAI_Jahresbericht_2013.pdf> (30.05.2023) |

| | |
|---|---|
| Taeuber 2014 | H. Taeuber, Epigrafik, Wissenschaftlicher Jahresbericht des Österreichischen Archäologischen Instituts 2014 (2014) 54, <http://www.oeaw.ac.at/fileadmin/Institute/OEAI/PDF/Kommunikation/OeAI_Jahresbericht_2014.pdf> (30. 05. 2023) |
| Toma 2020 | N. Toma, Marmor – Maße – Monumente. Vorfertigung, Standardisierung und Massenproduktion marmorner Bauteile in der römischen Kaiserzeit, Philippika 121 (Wiesbaden 2020) |
| Yavuz et al. 2011 | A. B. Yavuz – M. Bruno – D. Attanasio, An Updated, Multi-Method Database of Ephesos Marbles, Including White, Greco Scritto and Bigio Varieties, Archaeometry 53/2, 2011, 215–240, DOI: 10.111/j.1475-4754.2010.00542.x |

*Sophie Insulander, Wien Museum, Karlsplatz 8, 1040 Vienna, Austria.*
*[e] sophie.insulander@wienmuseum.at*

Stephan Karl – Paul Bayer – Kerstin Bauer

# THE ROMAN STONE MONUMENTS OF SEGGAU CASTLE REVISITED

## ON THE POTENTIAL OF THE SPATIAL RECORDING AND ANALYSIS OF ANCIENT STONE MONUMENTS

**Abstract**

In 2019–2021, the so-called Römersteinwand in Seggau Castle in Styria/Austria was renovated. It was built as a lapidarium in 1831 from the *spoliae* derived from a late antique tower and contains more than 100 relief and inscription stones, mostly made of local marble. The removal of the plaster covering the edges allowed an extensive examination of the stones. In addition to the conventional documentation, the stones were also recorded in 3D using Structure-from-Motion in order to obtain a uniform and comprehensive database for stylistic, technical and quantitative evaluations. The intensive study of the stones, furthermore, led to new discoveries beyond the information gained by removing the plaster, including new adaptations of fragments, revised readings of inscriptions and also an architectural reconstruction attempt. The quantitative analysis of the stone dimensions reveals a strong tendency to standardisation of formats based on the *pes Romanus* in integers.

## INTRODUCTION

The south-eastern part of the Roman province *Noricum* is characterised by a rich legacy of stone monuments, mostly from the sepulchral sphere, for which primarily a local white marble from the eastern Alps was preferred[1], but also less precious stones like limestone were used. This production started already in the late 1st century BC, flourished in the 2nd century AD, boomed during the Severan era and declined from the mid 3rd century onwards[2]. This artistic craftsmanship mirrors, after all, periods of economic prosperity of the Roman settlements in south-eastern *Noricum*. Research on these Roman stone monuments has long been a specific focus within provincial Roman archaeology; they were evaluated intensively in epigraphical, iconographical, typological and chronological terms.

The analysis of Roman stone monuments, especially by visual comparison, is mainly based on personal physical observations and descriptive or photographic documentation, such as those published by the »Corpus Signorum Imperii Romani« (CSIR) or in other printed media. Within publication activities, the image database of ancient stone monuments »Ubi Erat Lupa« (<http://lupa.at>) is a milestone towards digital Cultural Heritage and applications of new digital technologies. The open accessible database, on the one hand, improves the quality of data for scientific research by continuously expanding and bringing it up to date. On the other hand, it shares this data for educational purposes and with the wider public. Additionally, the web-based database is not restricted to ancient or modern borders.

Advances in digital technologies have led to an increasing creation of 3D cultural heritage models, e.g. of excavated remains of buildings, but also of single finds in the course of archaeological fieldwork. However, computational analysis of this 3D data of archaeological finds is still

---

[1] Djurić 2019.
[2] See e.g. Piccottini 1994, 5–6; Kremer 2001, 17–18; Hudeczek 2008, 7; Pochmarski 2016. For a chronological distribution of stones from Styria see Marko 2021, 100 fig. 3.

in its infancy. Nevertheless, there are sporadic and occasional approaches using methods of geometric analysis from computer science for tackling specific problems in archaeological research. With respect to ancient stone monuments this wide field in archaeology can be roughly divided into four groups as follows (giving some selected references):

1. Architecture: Sapirstein and Psota 2018 used 3D models for the analysis and estimation of the original dimension of the not completely preserved column drums of the Hera Temple at Olympia. For this, a modified ICP algorithm, which calculates an ›inside‹ parameter for fitting fragments with partly lost original surfaces compared to an idealised model, was developed. A penetration free alignment of matching blocks was also addressed by Thuswaldner et al. 2009 for the digital anastylosis of the Octagon in *Ephesos*. Additionally, the authors integrated constraints into the matching process by extracting features like straight edges (e.g. of the cornice profile) or clipping/clamping holes.

2. Sculpture: 3D shape comparison is able to quantify similarity and to ensure traceability. Such an approach was proposed by Zhang et al. 2013 for classical sculptures and Roman copies, by Lu et al. 2013 for portrait sculptures of Augustus or by Langner 2021 for emperors of the Julio-Claudian dynasty. Furthermore, Hölscher et al. 2020 investigated the head's asymmetries using geodesic distances and Thiessen polygons, exemplified on an archaic Greek marble head of a bearded man, the so-called Sabouroff head.

3. Inscriptions/bas-reliefs: Shape perception enhancement is an important factor in the field of epigraphy. Sapirstein 2019 presented a hybrid approach by combining advantages of 2D and 3D analytical techniques. Transformed and projected in 2.5D raster, the segmentation algorithm restores the original (uninscribed) plane of the inscription and classifies incisions and breaks. Finally, a displacement map was generated and visualised by different modes. Elevation raster maps generated from the 3D geometry was also proposed by Monna et al. 2018 for the documentation of carved stones in bas-relief, in this case of the deer stones from Mongolia. These raster maps were treated by common algorithms developed for geomorphological studies like sky-view factor or positive openness[3].

4. Tool marks: Studying working traces (tool marks) on stone monuments can be strongly improved by using 3D data and non-photorealistic visualisation techniques. Already early on, Levoy et al. 2000 used accessibility shading to visualise chisel marks on sculptures by Michelangelo. 3D models and subsequent transverse and longitudinal sections were used by Trefný et al. 2022 for the classification of different working traces regarding the sculptor's tools and applied working techniques.

This paper presents and discusses results of a systematic application of 3D technologies on a large and diverse complex of Roman stone monuments, with the find context Seggau.

## THE FIND CONTEXT SEGGAU

The Roman stone monuments from Seggau Castle near Leibnitz in Styria/Austria represent one of the most important contexts of this find category in the north-western provinces. In terms of marble objects, it includes more than two thirds of the known total of stone monuments from the nearby *municipium* of *Flavia Solva* and its surrounding area[4]. The stones preserved in Seggau or removed from there in modern times can mainly be assigned to sepulchral architecture; only a small proportion represent honorary monuments and votive altars.

The reason for this unusually high concentration of stone monuments from the Roman period at Seggau Castle is related to the fact that in Late Antiquity a mighty tower with a side length of

---

[3] Kokalj – Hesse 2017, 22–24.

[4] *Flavia Solva* and its surrounding area include the cadastral communities of Seggauberg, Leibnitz, Altenmarkt, Wagna, Kaindorf an der Sulm, Leitring and Grottenhofen. Restricted to marble, 217 monuments are recorded in the database »Ubi Erat Lupa«, of which 158 originate from Seggau (148 were found in the Old Tower).

15 m and a wall thickness of 3.8 m was built on this hilltop. For its construction, the stone buildings and monuments along the necropolis roads and in the public spaces of *Flavia Solva*, which were apparently abandoned and no longer maintained, were extensively demolished[5]. As is usually the case in quarries, the blocks were cut into suitable ashlars or other formats on the spot. Extensive demolition layers along the *Flavia Solva* cemetery road (Spitalsgelände and Altenmarkt cemeteries), which have been archaeologically excavated and can be dated to Late Antiquity, such as layers of marble chippings and mortar, rubble layers with cuttings and the use of cut-off frame and cornice parts in wells testify to this large-scale stone recycling[6].

This tower, mentioned in a document from 1219 as *turris antiqua*, already existed when the archbishops of Salzburg built Leibnitz Castle close to the south of the *turris* in the 1130s, thereby occupying a deeper position on this hill. With the foundation of the diocese of Seckau, its own castle, Seggau Castle, arose around the Old Tower. Whether the tower ever served as a residential tower for the prime bishops is not clear, but already about 120 years later it was described as ruinous (*turris desolata*). However, the written sources report for the year 1341 that the *turris antiqua* was raised and extended to a fortified watch-tower. Overall, however, it was not fully integrated into the castle. In the course of the combination of the Archiepiscopal castle Leibnitz and the Episcopal castle Seggau, realised after 1594, an attempt was made to demolish the tower, but this was not successful due to its massiveness. It was eventually used as a bell tower and more or less left to its fate. Ultimately, it had to be demolished in two campaigns in 1815/1816 and between 1826 and 1831 due to its acute danger of collapse[7].

In the masonry of the tower, numerous Roman stone monuments with their reliefs and inscriptions came to light again. A representative and considered selection of a total of 108 stones[8], mostly marble, was visibly built in in 1831 at the ground floor level of a new corridor in front of the mediaeval wing of the building originally adjacent to the tower. This museum-like arrangement built partly on the site of the Old Tower is the present so-called Römersteinwand (fig. 1).

Since the construction of this corridor, the built in stone monuments as well as the walls have been subject to various changes, which have affected not only the appearance but also the substance of the stones. In 2016, the Episcopal Estate Administration of Seggau Castle and the Austrian Federal Monuments Office decided to carry out a complete restoration of the »Römersteinwand«, which, in addition to conservation measures on the stones, included a complete renewal of the plastering according to monument preservation guidelines in a close approximation to the aesthetic and design concept of the first plastering in 1831. After extensive preliminary work, this complete restoration was finally carried out in 2019 and, after a break in 2020 due to the COVID-19 pandemic, resumed in 2021[9]. After the removal of the plaster, the appearance of the »Römersteinwand« largely resembled its condition as a shell construction in 1831. This restoration project offered the rare opportunity to closely examine and document the wall surfaces including the foundation zone as well as the individual stones in an unplastered state.

---

[5] For the Old Tower see Karl – Wrolli 2011; Karl 2013.

[6] Karl 2013, 281–286; Lamm 2016, 187–197. A publication about a late antique well within the cemetery »Spitalsgelände« consisting of some hundreds of *spoliae*, excavated in 1981/1982 but published only in short notes (Fuchs 1983), is currently in process by the first two authors. For the phenomenon of large-scale recycling see Kremer – Kitz 2018, 362–365.

[7] Karl 2013, 173. 176–177. A small remnant of this late antique tower, namely its eastern corner including the foundation zone, has survived in the mediaeval masonry of the so-called Seckauer Haus in the Upper Castle, which was formerly attached to it; see Karl – Wrolli 2011, 65–73. 82–85; specifically on the building technique, see Karl 2013, 210–227.

[8] For the stone monuments of Seggau Castle from the Roman period, see Hainzmann – Pochmarski 1994. For the number, which has changed up to the present day, see Karl 2018, 14 tab. 1.

[9] Bayer et al. 2020.

1   The so-called Römersteinwand of the Seggau Castle after the restorations 2019–2021 (© K. Bauer [Archaeogon, Bayer & Karl GesbR])

## METHODS AND WORKFLOW

In both restoration campaigns, only a short period of a few weeks was available to document the Roman stone monuments incorporated in the wall, both those normally visible and those that were fully plastered, mostly undecorated ashlars. The aim was to document both the walls and the individual stones as well as possible, both photographically and three-dimensionally.

First of all, the stones were carefully cleaned from recent plaster, wall paint and dirt. The cleaning of the gaps between the stones was of particular importance in order to document and measure the full dimensions of the otherwise concealed edges and to obtain as much information as possible from the sides turned into the wall.

### Photographic documentation

The first step in the documentation was a conventional photographic acquisition of the stones: frontal photos were taken of all of them, while only angled photos were possible for the details that appeared in the spandrels of the wall. The pictures were taken in the dark with artificial lighting from an angle in order to reveal as much detail as possible. The stones on the outer façade were photographed in 2019 by Ortolf and Friederike Harl, the stones in the corridor in 2021 by the authors of this article. The photos are available in the database »Ubi Erat Lupa«.

### 3D documentation and data processing

In order to capture as much information as possible, all stones were documented in 3D with Structure-from-Motion (SfM) using Agisoft Metashape[10]. A series of typically 30–100 photos from dif-

---

[10]   For taking the photos, a Nikon D7000 was used in 2019 and 2020 and a Nikon Z 5 in 2021.

ferent angles was taken from each stone for the 3D reconstruction, the models were georeferenced and thereby also scaled with tachymetric measurements of targets glued onto the wall next to the stones. Inside the corridor fewer targets were used and larger portions of the wall were documented at once due to the lack of suitable space for the measuring instrument; however, this should not affect the quality of the result. Finally, this work resulted in 3D models of 156 stones – counting only the built in stones (per fragment) within the »Römersteinwand« – created from 9477 photos.

The processing of the created 3D models involved several steps (fig. 2). Firstly, the georeferenced and therefore already scaled models were clipped to an adequate area showing also the surrounding masonry. This data can be used for conservation purposes. Secondly, the models were virtually cut out of the surrounding wall. At this stage, the files were cleaned (outliers, erroneous vertices etc.) and manually orientated in GigaMesh, which was also used to measure the dimensions of the stones and to create textureless grey orthographic renderings. In some cases, adjoining fragments were assembled in CloudCompare. Thirdly, the stones were reconstructed based on the 3D model and observations made on site. The reconstruction primarily serves to deal with the stone object in more detail; it is limited to the essentials and is exclusively predictive based on existing information on the stone itself. For some, the measurements taken by Kaspar Harb before the construction of the wall and corridor could be taken into account[11]. Finally, traces of reuse were mapped on the stones, such as the lifting holes and reworkings from Late Antiquity associated with the construction of the Old Tower, but there are also later traces, particularly from the construction of the »Römersteinwand« in 1831.

In addition to the stones, the entire exterior wall, the corridor behind it and the adjacent staircase to the south were recorded by a terrestrial laser scanner in 2019[12]. The laser scan served to measure the »Römersteinwand« affected by the restoration together with the adjacent building parts as a whole in a larger frame in order to obtain a 3D documentation for historical building research as well as a fusion with the SfM models (fig. 3). However, the architectural history and the current presentation of the stone monuments will be published elsewhere[13].

Comparing the two applied acquisition techniques (Laser and SfM) requires some discussion of the accuracy and precision achieved. As is known, the marble translucency and its heterogeneous granular structure produce a significant bias and increased noise in the measurements by optical scanners, such as laser or, to a lesser extent, structured light scanners. The light penetrates and encounters a number of crystalline domains, resulting in a wide scattering but also in a bias in the depth measurement. This effect is called subsurface scattering and can only be avoided if the surface is covered with a matt coating. The effect of error was quantified and evaluated on Carrara marbles with a grain size below 1 mm[14], but to the best of our knowledge never on coarse-grained marbles from the eastern Alps. For these we have to assume a much stronger bias. SfM is therefore the better choice for marbles, as here the geometric data is calculated from the pixels of the photos taken. SfM has undergone a development in recent years that now makes this documentation method equal in accuracy and precision to laser scanning techniques. The resolution of the SfM models from Seggau is below 0.5 mm for all stones.

**Potential of 3D data and geometric analysis**

The basic requirement for working with 3D data of stone monuments is high data quality: the entire process chain must be coordinated with the desired result. Both the data acquisition (in the

---

[11] For the edition of Kaspar Harb's handwritten manuscript of 1837, see Karl – Wrolli 2011, 155–234.
[12] We would like to thank Boris Stummer and Josef Schauer from the Department of Hydrology and Geoinformation at the Office of the Provincial Government of Lower Austrian for the laser scan, and Eduard Pollhammer (Department of Art and Culture, Archaeological Park Carnuntum) for the mediation.
[13] The construction of the »Römersteinwand« and its changes till today are the focus of a separate paper by the first two authors for the »Fundberichte aus Österreich« (FÖ).
[14] Godin et al. 2001; Garcia-Fernandez 2016.

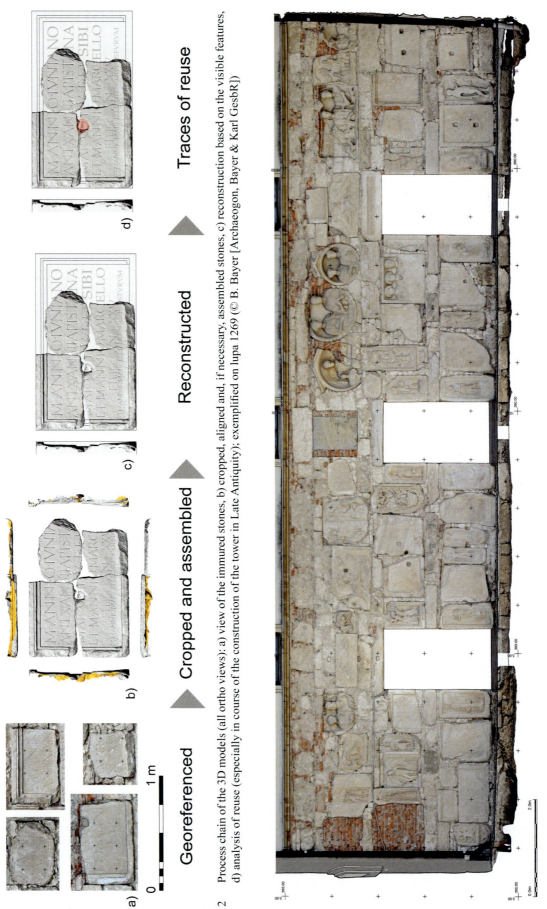

2   Process chain of the 3D models (all ortho views): a) view of the immured stones, b) cropped, aligned and, if necessary, assembled stones, c) reconstruction based on the visible features, d) analysis of reuse (especially in course of the construction of the tower in Late Antiquity); exemplified on lupa 1269 (© B. Bayer [Archaeogon, Bayer & Karl GesbR])

3   Orthoview of the exterior wall of the »Römersteinwand«; SfM models from the wall and the foundation zone, fused partly with Laserscan data from adjacent buildings (© S. Karl [Archaeogon, Bayer & Karl GesbR])

case of SfM camera, lighting, scaling, photographic knowledge) and the data processing (software, parameters, data handling) have to function perfectly from a technical point of view in order to achieve good results. A certain technical know-how is therefore essential. The impact of these new technologies can mainly be grouped into following categories:

### Uniform representation

»Classical archaeology is at its core a visual discipline«, Martin Langner once stated[15]. As a scientific discipline, archaeology needs appropriate documentation for the comprehensibility of the results. Compared to photographs, 3D models of stone monuments have the great advantage that the stone surfaces can be represented uniformly without texture and with consistent virtual lighting. The true-to-scale models can be oriented very precisely, and the renderings of the 3D data are orthographic. These uniform representations are a great help in recognising similarities, finding matching fragments, positioning of interrelated components (cf. figs. 4. 5. 7) or discussing questions concerning the workshops[16].

### Enhancement of visibility

Different filtering techniques make it possible to highlight certain properties of the surface and thus increase the visibility of certain traits. Some of these methods have been borrowed from geography, others have been developed specifically for archaeological questions[17]. Especially for the re-reading of poorly preserved inscriptions, such visualisations are very helpful, ideally using several methods in parallel to extract as much information as possible from the stones (cf. fig. 8). An autopsy of the inscriptions remains indispensable to verify the results. Methods used on the Seggau stones include curvature visualisation, ambient occlusion, height maps and distance calculations to a smoothed surface (an idealised uninscribed surface).

### Intersections and reassembly

Besides the complex filtering procedures, section lines can be extracted from 3D models at arbitrary positions. Applications are, for example, the systematic investigation of the shapes of profiled frames or other architectural details, but also – especially in the context of Seggau – the lifting holes and other modifications from the reuse of the stones. Another significant advantage of 3D models over photos is the possibility of virtually assembling matching fragments and visualising them without distortion (cf. figs. 2. 5)[18]. Possible matches can already be recognised from the renderings and preliminarily arranging, while the final visualisations and measurements are created from the merged 3D models. Particularly in the case of immured stones or stones stored at different places, the matching of fragments can be excellently checked and represented virtually.

## RESULTS AND DISCUSSION

The proposed workflow turned out to be very efficient, especially in the process toward more thoughtful interpretative tasks based on the acquired 3D data. 156 stones – counting only the stones (per fragment) built into the »Römersteinwand« – were recorded in the main phase, resulting after the matching process in 148 highly accurate 3D models. Due to the fast acquisition

---

[15] Langner 2021, 379: »Die Klassische Archäologie ist im Kern eine visuelle Disziplin.«
[16] Cf. e.g. Pochmarski 2007, 93 figs. 1 and 2 with the renderings of 3D models concerning the similarity in regard to lupa 1238 and lupa 1317.
[17] For geometric analysis in the field of Cultural Heritage see the survey by Pintus et al. 2016.
[18] With the exception of lupa 1269, all new matchings were achieved by working with the renderings or 3D models.

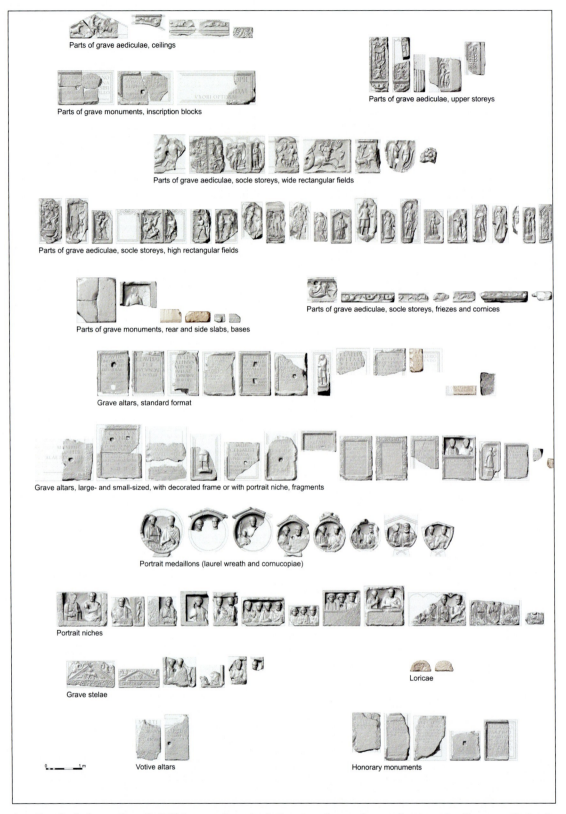

4 Typological grouping of all 115 stones from the find context Seggau immured or stored at Seggau and already integrated into the database »Ubi Erat Lupa«, mostly visualised by their front view; marble in grey, limestone in sepia (© S. Karl [Archaeogon, Bayer & Karl GesbR])

method the prime work on the »Römersteinwand« was extended to all Roman stone monuments built into or stored at Seggau Castle. The database of 3D models comprises a total of 183 objects, whereby fragments belonging together are counted as one piece. By far the largest part of these other stones are directly related to the demolition material of the Old Tower, but there are also other objects such as two *loricae* of local limestone which were incorporated in a wall on the ground floor of the so-called Vizedomhaus dated to the 13th or 14th century.

Several new observations could be made regarding these stones that have been known and intensively researched since 1831, partly due to the removal of the covering plaster, partly due to the uniform and well-comparable renderings of the 3D models and, above all, due to close observation. In the course of a successful cooperation with Ortolf and Friederike Harl, all new results including the newly measured dimensions of the stones as well as photos and renderings can be found in the database »Ubi Erat Lupa«, improving and enlarging the set of stone monuments at Seggau to 115 objects[19]. Within this section, only the new findings on four selected monuments will be shown in detail. Additionally, the following list briefly summarises the most significant new observations:

Tab. 1  The most significant new discoveries and observations made during the restoration campaigns 2019 and 2021

| lupa number | Short description |
| --- | --- |
| lupa 1268 | Two crouching lions could be documented on the pediment. |
| lupa 1319 | A plant *candelabra* is on the left side of the portrait niche and identifies it as part of a grave stele. |
| lupa 1320 | A *librarius* on the right side of the portrait niche identifies it as part of a grave stele, cf. lupa 1220. |
| lupa 1321 | The presence of an inscription on the front side turned into the wall confirms that the stone with an already known servant relief is a grave altar: ---] / [---]ns / / - / - / - [---]r / [--- . |
| lupa 1325 | A framed field could be observed on the left side. |
| lupa 1260, 1329 | The medallions are formed by two cornucopiae, cf. lupa 1204. |
| lupa 1330 | The left side has a framed field, the right side is flat for connecting to an adjacent stone. |
| lupa 1331 | The framed inscription field could be documented on the right side of the visible relief. |
| lupa 1285 | The left side also bears a relief. |
| lupa 4840, 5107, 5147 | These honorary monuments have framed fields on the sides. |
| lupa 1259 (+ 5751) | Matching fragments of a pediment with Ganymede sitting on a rock, offering a cup to an eagle; behind the rock is a dog on a leash and behind the eagle a bow (cf. lupa 13331). |
| lupa 33202 | One of three fragments of fluted pilasters built into the walls fits with the already known fragment S-31 (Karl – Wrolli 2011, 73 no. S 31). |

## DIMENSIONS AND STANDARDISATION

Epigraphic sources, but also depictions on stone monuments (e.g. lupa 14590) prove that the Roman foot (*pes Romanus*, p.R.) was considered as a unit of measurement within the imperial marble trade[20]. A major advantage of 3D models is that accurate values for height, width and depth can be extracted using the bounding box function. By converting all completely preserved or securely reconstructed dimensions within the set of Seggau stones to the Roman measurement system and evaluating their discrete distribution according to intervals of 1 *unica* (= $^1/_{12}$ p.R. = 2.47 cm) peaks at positions 29.6 ± 1.85 cm (~ 1 p.R.), 59.2 ± 1.85 cm (~ 2 p.R.), 88.8 ± 1.85 cm (~ 3 p.R.) and 118.4 ± 1.85 cm (~ 4 p.R.) are clearly standing out (diagram 1). Stones that cannot

---

[19] lupa 33200–33211 were newly added to the database. All new results from the total of 183 stones affected by this BDA project from 2019–2021 will be part of a detailed and more comprehensive publication by the three authors, intended for the »Fundberichte aus Österreich« (FÖ).

[20] Toma 2020, 35–37.

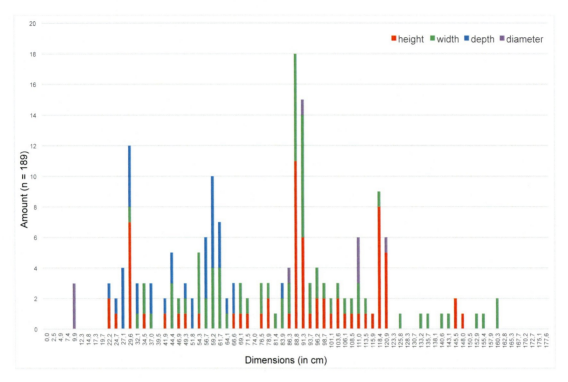

Diagram 1   Sequence of completely preserved or securely reconstructed dimensions according to height, width, depth and diameter (in case of portrait medaillons); the representation is limited to 177.6 cm (~ 6 p.R.)

be oriented are excluded from this conversion. Within the 183 stones only two stones are larger than 177.6 cm (~ 6 p.R.): lupa 1322 with a width of 195 cm and lupa 1264 with a width of 207.9 cm. Also in the Roman marble quarries in the eastern Alps the measurement of 1 p.R. and its multiple can most often be deduced, both on the quarry faces and the raw products[21].

The typological assignment of the stones could be strongly improved by the scaled models and the visual enhancement based on the uniform and normalised renderings (fig. 4). Such classification reveals certain formats and implies a certain kind of standardisation within the production process. Ortolf Harl has already pointed out the urge to standardise the measurements of Roman burial structures[22]. Standardisation is particularly evident in the grave altars, where groups of different sizes can be seen. The most extensive group, the so-called grave altars of the standard format, has heights between 114 and 121 cm, widths between 85 and 93 cm and depths between 57 and 62 cm which correspond approximately to 4, 3 and 2 p.R. Groups of different size formats can also be seen in the portrait medallions.

## Grave inscription of Marcus Annius Iunianus and his family (lupa 1269)

The grave inscription of Marcus Annius Iunianus and his family (cf. fig. 3) has recently been published[23]. In addition to the already known three fitting fragments, a fourth one could be identified, which completes the reading. The reconstruction of the text allows a good estimation of the original dimensions of the stone, 155 × 91 cm. Another stone from Seggau (lupa 1285) has almost the same dimensions. These two blocks have a profiled frame on three sides, while the lower frame is simple square-shaped. With this special frame design, but also in the dimensions,

---

[21]   Karl – Bayer 2021, 70. 99–102.
[22]   Harl 1997, 189 n. 13.
[23]   Karl – Bayer 2020.

5   Portrait niches lupa 1336 (left) and lupa 1337 with the joining satyr relief lupa 1281 (right). Although very similar in style and dimensions, the portrait niches do not belong together. Hardly visible is the carved-off satyr relief next to the woman (© S. Karl [Archaeogon, Bayer & Karl GesbR])

the two Seggau blocks correspond to the inscription block in the base level of the Priscianus tomb in Šempeter v Savinjski dolini (lupa 11198), so that it is likely that they once belonged to such grave monument types.

## Portrait niches (lupa 1336. 1337+1281)

Since Erna Diez' guide to the stone monuments of Seggau Castle, it has been assumed that two fragments of portrait niches, one with a woman with a melon hairstyle (lupa 1336), the other with a bearded man (lupa 1337), could belong together (fig. 5)[24]. The break in the middle, however, does not allow any clear conclusions about whether the two belong together, even without the covering by the plaster. Previous supporting arguments include the very similar heights of the stones and the similarities of the portraits and garments.

In the carved-off relief to the left of the woman, the visualisations of the 3D data helped to identify a figure rushing to the right in a framed field, holding an object in the lowered right hand and with the left hand raised above the head. It is obviously a satyr in a very similar posture to those in the centre fields of the two three-figure reliefs from Hartberg (lupa 6070) and Bad Waltersdorf (lupa 6069) or like the one on a relief also walled in Seggau (lupa 1281). For the second portrait niche lupa 1337, the adjoining side field on the right could be identified in the relief stone lupa 1281, representing a satyr in a similar dancing pose as the one next to the woman. A drawing by Kaspar Harb from 1828[25], when this stone had not yet been walled in, shows the course of the fracture on the left, which corresponds to the fracture on the portrait niche. The matching is also confirmed by the same bedding surface's plane which slightly slopes backwards. In contrast to the side reliefs, both portrait niches are not framed and open at the top. This and the raw, partly still bossed joint surface on the side of the broken-off satyr relief speak for a use in the masonry structure of grave buildings.

Despite all the similarities, the fact that the woman is looking down to the right and the man is looking forward speaks against the two portraits belonging together. Such a difference cannot be observed in any of the other grave portraits in *Solva* and is also not to be expected, since the mar-

---

[24] Diez 1959, 58 nos. 115. 116; Hainzmann – Pochmarski 1994, 254–257 nos. 95. 96; Pochmarski 2011, 67–68 nos. 34. 35 pl. 20, 2–3.
[25] Karl – Wrolli 2011, 167 no. 18 pl. 48.

6 The corner block (lupa 5914) with the cleaning of the stables of Augias (Labour VI) on the front side and the newly discovered killing of the Stymphalian birds on the right side (Labour V) (© P. Bayer [Archaeogon, Bayer & Karl GesbR])

ried couples immortalised in stone either look forward in parallel or are turned slightly towards each other so that their gazes cross, possibly at the viewpoint of a visitor to the grave. Also, the height of the satyr on lupa 1281 is higher than on lupa 1336. In all probability, we are dealing with two very similar portrait niches with adjoining satyr reliefs, likely resulting in the existence of two almost identical tomb buildings.

**Heracles relief blocks (lupa 1322. 5913. 5914)**

Among the few mythological reliefs in Seggau, three blocks with scenes of the labours of Heracles are particularly noteworthy. Gabrielle Kremer and Erwin Pochmarski have recently dealt with their undisputed affiliation as parts of the socle storey of a funerary aedicula[26]. New insights have now been gained through the removal of the plaster.

Contrary to previous assumptions, it turned out that the protruding field with the taming of Diomedes' horses (lupa 1322) is not the left side field of a three-part block, but the central field. To the left of this central field is the remnant of a field receding as on the right, with the remains of a Noric-Pannonian volute ornament. The block with the cleaning of the Augean stables (lupa 5914) could now be clearly identified as a corner block. In addition, another labour of Heracles was revealed on the side in the right-hand gap (fig. 6). A figure is depicted in a standing position to the right, holding his right arm strongly bent and raised above his chest. A quiver with arrows can be seen above the right shoulder; to the left of the body, below the elbow, remains of the lion's skin hanging down from the back are recognisable. This is clearly a depiction of the killing of the Stymphalian birds. In 2003, during the creation of a new entrance in the room behind the corridor of the »Römersteinwand«[27], the block with the theft of the apples of the Hesperides (lupa 5913) was removed from the wall, revealing that it must be the left rear corner block of the socle and confirming that the reliefs covered only three sides of the socle.

With this new data a reconstruction is proposed for the »Heracles aedicula«. Assuming symmetry within the three sides of the socle storey, the corner fields on the left and right side must have the same width (62 cm) as the one with the Hesperidean episode (Labour XII) on the left rear corner. The field with the cleaning of the stables of Augeas (VI), however, is narrower (58 cm), which is why this most likely belongs to the front side and forms the right corner field with the

---

[26] Kremer 2001, 214–215 no. 136 fig. 127; Kremer 2014, 74 fig. 30–32; Pochmarski 2021, 38–41 no. 28–30 pl. 20–22.
[27] Karl – Wrolli 2011, 64–65. 111 no. Harb-Nr. 33 pl. 25.

field depicting the killing of the Stymphalian birds (V) on the right side. The clockwise sequence of the preserved labours of Heracles (VIII and VII) on the triptych lupa 1322 and its wider fields (each 65 cm) suggest that lupa 1322 forms the centre of the front. This results in a reconstructed width of the socle storey of 3.11 m, while the depth cannot be reconstructed with certainty due to the missing middle blocks of the secondary sides. The height of the blocks and the closed front (without the otherwise usual grave inscription) indicate a two-tiered socle, with the Labours of Heracles on the lower tier.

If the secondary sides of the socle also had five fields as the quinquepartite front side, the total number of fields would be 15, in which not only a complete *dodekathlos* – in clockwise reading – but also non-canonical labours[28] or other scenes may have been depicted. The order of the preserved scenes corresponds to that given by Diodorus and the »Tabula Albana«[29]. The canonical order of Diodorus recurs only rarely, for example on Roman Asiatic columnar sarcophagi from the second half of the 2$^{nd}$ century AD[30]. However, a composition with 15 fields requires a socle on a square ground, which is quite unusual in comparison to other preserved grave aediculae in the south-eastern part of Noricum[31]. Taking into account the aspect ratio of the aedicula socle of the Spectatii tomb in Šempeter v Savinjski dolini (lupa 13256), a depth of the socle storey of the Heracles aedicula with a front width of 3.11 m would be 2.45 m. A similar result can be reached by considering the width of a single field which corresponds to approximately 2 Roman feet (p.R.). By inserting middle blocks on the left and right side with a width of two fields (ca. 118 cm; 4 p.R.) the socle depth reaches 2.43 m (fig. 7). On these middle blocks further Heraclean labours could be displayed – divided by a frame or not –, but it remains speculative which labours, in which order and if they are replaced or supplemented with other scenes. Only the first labour, the slaying of the Nemean lion, can be assumed as displayed on the right rear corner block.

**Votive altar for Jupiter Optimus Maximus (lupa 5148)**

Two votive altars are built into the »Römersteinwand«, one for Mars (lupa 5108), the other for Jupiter (lupa 5148). Both show typical traces of their reuse in an ashlar masonry structure[32], in our case the Old Tower. For this purpose, the cornices above the shaft with the inscription and any protruding profiled bases were carved off. In relation to the scope of our paper the one for Jupiter deserves more attention. The altar is complete in width and height, only parts of the top are broken off. The shaft slightly tapers towards the top. On the top above the carved-off cornice the remnant of the right lateral acroteria is preserved. A lifting hole for a forceps (the opposite hole has to be assumed on the not visible right side of the altar) was deepened into the inscription field, damaging the inscription in the middle left area.

The altar dedicated to Jupiter Optimus Maximus was erected and consecrated by two cult commissioners as well as by the *civitas* (of the Solvensians [?])[33]. Below this, two persons are listed in each of eleven lines. The twelfth and last line was filled with only one name. The listed donors, all of them men, have both Latin and foreign names.

On the basis of the 3D visualisations (fig. 8) in combination with close observation, it was now possible to correct letters of the previous readings, especially in the marginal areas of the stone as well as in more abraded places within the inscription field, and to recognise new ligatures that change the reading of some names. The different way in which the names were shortened in the

---

[28] Cf. the reliefs with Heracles and Alcestis in Piber (lupa 1393) and Ptuj (lupa 4216). The relief from Piber has an estimated width of ca. 107 cm.
[29] Diod. 4, 8–27; IG XIV 1293. For Heracles Dodekathlos see RE Suppl. III (1918) 1020–1028 s. v. Herakles (Otto Gruppe).
[30] LIMC V (1990) 5–16; 11 no. 1730–1731 s. v. Herakles (John Boardman).
[31] Cf. Kremer 2001, 377–378.
[32] Cf. e.g. the stone monuments from the late antique bridge head fortification at Bölcske: Beszédes et al. 2003.
[33] For the most recent work see Hainzmann 2016.

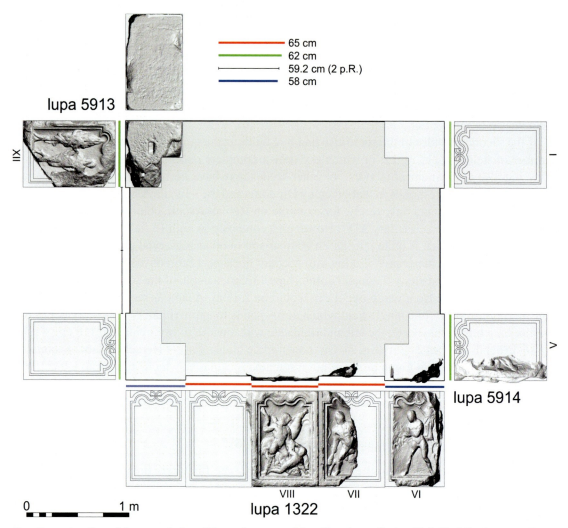

7 Reconstruction of the ground plan of the socle storey of the »Heracles aedicula« (© S. Karl [Archaeogon, Bayer & Karl GesbR])

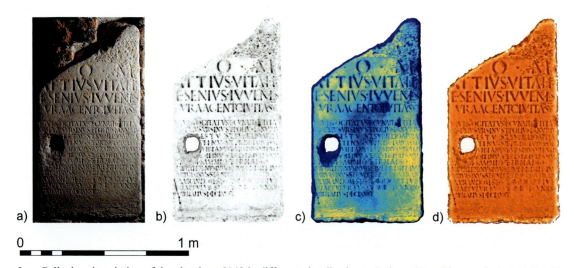

8 Collegium inscription of the altar lupa 5148 in different visualisations: a) photo, b) ambient occlusion, c) height map, d) depth map to an idealised uninscribed plane (© P. Bayer [Archaeogon, Bayer & Karl GesbR])

two columns is notable. While the left column is shortened by means of ligatures, in the right column the final letters of the names are not written out.

The newly discovered numbering at the beginning of each of the twelve name lines from *unus* to *duodecim* (tab. 2) is far not documented by any other example on Noric *collegium* inscriptions. These were previously overlooked or read as part of the names, yet could now be recognised with the help of the renderings from the 3D models. This discovery can now also explain the shift of the dividing *ET* column from the central axis to the right; both name columns have the same width.

The meaning of the numbering remains unknown at this point. However, it could be an indication of a pairwise distribution of men to tasks within this group. The division into twelve sections could refer on the one hand to the number of months, and on the other hand to the mythological sphere, for example the number of Olympian gods or the Heraclean labours[34].

Tab. 2    The new reading of the *collegium* inscription (lupa 5148)

*[I(ovi)] O(ptimo) M(aximo)*
*Attius Vital(is)*
*e·t Senius Iuvenis*
*[c]ura(m) agent(es) civitasq(ue)*

| I | Iul(---) Cogitatus | e·t | Cunaito Titia[n](---) |
|---|---|---|---|
| [II | ---]inius Ursinus | e·t | Polius Ianuriu(s) |
| [III | ---]estus | e·t | Surillio Appia[n](---) |
| [IIII | ---]tinus | e·t | Priscianus Sab[-](---) |
| [V | ---] Vibianus | e·t | Ursinus Vitalis |
| [VI | ---] Aqilinus | e·t | Ceser(---) Iulianu[s] |
| VI[I | ---]n Sammio | e·t | Ermadio |
| VIII | V·alen·tinus Ia·nu·a·ri·s | e·t | Iul(ius) Primitiv(---) |
| VIIII | U·rsinus Secund(---) | e·t | Triclo Veran(---) |
| X | Uran·i(---) Dom·estic[---] | e·t | Aur(---) Martius |
| XI | Appul(---) Ursus | e·t | Aur(---) Secun·din[---] |
| XII | Malius Decian·us | e·t | *(vacat)* |

## CONCLUSION

Finally, we would like to summarise the added value of 3D documentation of Roman stone monuments. Especially in the case of a large-scale and unwieldy group of materials such as building stones, which usually have to be visited and documented on site, the advantages of uniformly displayable 3D data become apparent, without, however, denying the relevance of conventional photographic documentation.

Many findings, such as the newly discovered fitting fragments in four cases, are the result of an interaction between a detailed autopsy and the 3D model, which changes and expands the previous visual perception. The scaled and uniformly displayable 3D models increase the comprehensibility of the results and allow further investigations and visualisations that are not feasible using photos or the originals. The models offer a broad field for the development of computer-aided methods for the analysis of geometric features such as letter shapes, frame profiling, garment folds, anatomic details and the like.

---

[34] A publication of the new findings concerning the inscriptions of the »Römersteinwand« is in planning together with Manfred Hainzmann.

The benefit of these methods is comparable to the revolution in landscape archaeology through LiDAR data and its analytical methods, which enable a completely new way of seeing and discovering.

## BIBLIOGRAPHY

| | |
|---|---|
| Bayer et al. 2020 | P. Bayer – J. Fürnholzer – B. Hebert – S. Karl – J. Nimmrichter – M. Yasar, Die Römersteinwand von Schloss Seggau, BDA wiederhergestellt 56 (Vienna 2020) |
| Beszédes et al. 2003 | J. Beszédes – Zs. Mráv – E. Tóth, Die Steindenkmäler von Bölcske – Inschriften und Skulpturen – Katalog, in: Á. Szabó – E. Tóth (eds.), Bölcske. Römische Inschriften und Funde, Libelli Archaeologici Ser. Nov. 2 (Budapest 2003) 103–218 |
| Diez 1959 | E. Diez, Flavia Solva. Die römischen Steindenkmäler auf Schloß Seggau bei Leibnitz ²(Vienna 1959) |
| Djurić 2019 | B. Djurić, The Logistics behind Ancient Art. The Case of Noricum and Pannoniae. Festvortrag, in: B. Porod – P. Scherrer (eds.), Der Stifter und sein Monument. Gesellschaft – Ikonographie – Chronologie. Akten des 15. Internationalen Kolloquiums zum Provinzialrömischen Kunstschaffen Graz 14.–20.06.2017 (Graz 2019) 8–30 |
| Fuchs 1983 | G. Fuchs, Ein spätantiker Brunnen aus Flavia Solva, PAR 33, 1983, 7–9 |
| Garcia-Fernandez 2016 | J. Garcia-Fernandez, An Assessment of Errors and Their Reduction in Terrestrial Laser Scanner Measurements in Marmorean Surfaces, 3D Research 7, 2016, Article 77, DOI: 10.1007/s13319-015-0077-0 (29.03.2023) |
| Godin et al. 2001 | G. Godin – M. Rioux – J.-A. Beraldin – M. Levoy – L. Cournoyer – F. Blais, An assessment of laser range measurement on marble surfaces, 5th Conference on Optical 3D Measurement Techniques Vienna 01.–04.10.2001 (Vienna 2001) 49–56, <https://graphics.stanford.edu/papers/marble-assessment/> (29.03.2023) |
| Hainzmann 2016 | M. Hainzmann, CVRA(M) • AGENT(ES) • CIVITASQ(VE) adnotationes ad CIL III, 5319 (Noricum, Flavia Solva), Antichità Altoadriatiche 85, 2017, 347–360 |
| Hainzmann – Pochmarski 1994 | M. Hainzmann – E. Pochmarski, Die römerzeitlichen Inschriften und Reliefs von Schloß Seggau bei Leibnitz, Die römerzeitlichen Steindenkmäler der Steiermark 1 (Graz 1994) |
| Harl 1997 | O. Harl, Norikum oder Oberpannonien? Die Grabädikula eines Kaiserpriesters aus Bad Waltersdorf/Steiermark, in: G. Erath – M. Lehner – G. Schwarz (eds.), Komos. Festschrift Thuri Lorenz (Vienna 1997) 185–202 |
| Hölscher et al. 2020 | T. Hölscher – S. Krömker – H. Mara, Der Kopf Sabouroff in Berlin: Zwischen archäologischer Beobachtung und geometrischer Vermessung, in: A. Delivorrias – E. Vikela – A. Zarkadas – N. Kaltsas – I. Trianti (eds.), ΣΠΟΝΔΗ. Αφιέρωμα στη μνήμη του Γιώργου Δεσπίνη (Athens 2020) 125–138 |
| Hudeczek 2008 | E. Hudeczek, Die Rundskulpturen des Stadtgebietes von Flavia Solva, CSIR Österreich IV 1 (Vienna 2008) |
| Karl 2013 | S. Karl, Turris antiqua in castro Leybentz. Zur frühesten Baugeschichte der Burgenanlage Leibnitz/Seggau im Kontext der spätantiken Ostflanke der Provinz Noricum mediterraneum (Diss. Karl-Franzens-University Graz 2013) |
| Karl 2018 | S. Karl, Visualisierung historischer Erscheinungsbilder der Römersteinwand im Schloss Seggau, Sprechende Steine 32, 2018, 7–15 |
| Karl – Bayer 2020 | S. Karl – P. Bayer, Die Annii. Eine epigraphische Familienzusammenführung an der Seggauer Römersteinwand, in: E. Steigberger (ed.), Von den Alpen bis ans Meer. Festschrift Bernhard Hebert, Forschungen zur geschichtlichen Landeskunde der Steiermark 86 (Vienna 2020) 101–104 |
| Karl – Bayer 2021 | S. Karl – P. Bayer, Schrämspuren, in: S. Karl, Das römerzeitlich genutzte Marmorsteinbruchrevier Spitzelofen/Kärnten – Montanarchäologische Forschungen. Mit Beiträgen von P. Bayer, M. Grabner, M. Hainzmann, R. Haubner, A. G. Heiss, K. Layr, D. Modl, W. Prochaska, S. Strobl, B. Toškan, E. Wächter, M. Weißl und S. Wiesinger, FÖ Beiheft 1 (Vienna 2021) 67–75 |
| Karl – Wrolli 2011 | S. Karl – G. Wrolli, Der Alte Turm im Schloss Seggau zu Leibnitz. Historische Untersuchungen zum ältesten Bauteil der Burgenanlage Leibnitz in der Steiermark, Forschungen zur geschichtlichen Landeskunde der Steiermark 55 (Graz 2011) |

| | |
|---|---|
| Kokalj – Hesse 2017 | Ž. Kokalj – R. Hesse, Airborne laser scanning raster data visualization. A Guide to Good Practice (Ljubljana 2017), DOI: 10.3986/9789612549848 (05.05.2023) |
| Kremer 2001 | G. Kremer, Antike Grabbauten in Noricum. Katalog und Auswertung von Werkstücken als Beitrag zur Rekonstruktion und Typologie, SoSchrÖAI 26 (Vienna 2001), <https://e-book.fwf.ac.at/view/o:183> (29.03.2023) |
| Kremer 2014 | G. Kremer, Wiederverwendete Teile von Grabanlagen aus Carnuntum. Zu ausgewählten Neufunden aus dem Bereich südlich der Zivilstadt, CarnuntumJb 2014, 67–78 |
| Kremer – Kitz 2018 | G. Kremer – I. Kitz, Reuse of Roman ornamental stones in the hinterland of Carnuntum, in: C. Coquelet – G. Creemers – R. Dreesen – É. Goemaere (eds.), Roman ornamental stones in north-western Europe: natural resources, manufacturing, supply, life & afterlife, Études et Documents Archéologie 38 (Namur 2018) 361–372 |
| Langner 2021 | M. Langner, Das Gesicht hinter dem Marmor. Computergestützte Maßvergleiche an römischen Kaiserporträts, in: J. Lang – C. Marcks-Jacobs (eds.), Arbeit am Bildnis. Porträts als Zugang zu antiken Gesellschaften. Festschrift Dietrich Boschung (Regensburg 2021) 377–384 |
| Levoy et al. 2000 | M. Levoy – K. Pulli – B. Curless – S. Rusinkiewicz – D. Koller – L. Pereira – M. Ginzton – S. Anderson – J. Davis – J. Ginsberg – J. Shade – D. Fulk, The Digital Michelangelo Project: 3D Scanning of Large Statues, in: J. R. Brown – K. Akeley (eds.), SIGGRAPH, 00. Proceedings of the 27$^{th}$ annual conference on Computer graphics and interactive techniques (New York 2000) 131–144, DOI: 10.1145/344779.344849 (29.03.2023) |
| Lu et al. 2013 | M. Lu – Y. Zhang – B. Zheng – T. Masuda – S. Ono – T. Oishi – K. Sengoku-Haga – K. Ikeuchi, Portrait Sculptures of Augustus: Categorization via Local Shape Comparison, in: Proceedings of the 2013 Digital Heritage International Congress (DigitalHeritage) Marseille 28.10.–01.11.2013, Vol. 1 (IEEE Xplore) 661–664, <https://ieeexplore.ieee.org/document/6743812> (29.03.2023) |
| Marko 2021 | P. Marko, Good Times, Bad Times? An Overview of Findings on the 3$^{rd}$ Century in the Territory of Flavia Solva/Wagna, in: M. Auer – C. Hinker (eds.), Roman Settlements and the ›Crisis‹ of the 3$^{rd}$ Century AD, Ager Aguntinus 4 (Wiesbaden 2021) 93–105 |
| Monna et al. 2018 | F. Monna – Y. Esin – J. Magail – L. Granjon – N. Navarro – J. Wilczek – L. Saligny – S. Couettee – A. Dumontet – C. Chateau, Documenting carved stones by 3D modelling – Example of Mongolian deer stones, Journal of Cultural Heritage 34, 2018, 116–128, DOI: 10.1016/j.culher.2018.04.021 (29.03.2023) |
| Piccottini 1994 | G. Piccottini, Grabstelen, Reiter- und Soldatendarstellungen sowie dekorative Reliefs des Stadtgebietes von Virunum und Nachträge zu CSIR Österreich II 1–4, CSIR Österreich II 5 (Vienna 1994) |
| Pintus et al. 2016 | R. Pintus – K. Pal – Y. Yang – T. Weyrich – E. Gobbetti – H. Rushmeier, A Survey of Geometric Analysis in Cultural Heritage, Computer Graphics Forum 35, 2016, 4–31, DOI: 10.1111/cgf.12668 (29.03.2023) |
| Pochmarski 2007 | E. Pochmarski, Werkstätten von Porträtreliefs aus Flavia Solva, RÖ 30, 2007, 91–105 |
| Pochmarski 2011 | E. Pochmarski, Die Porträtmedaillons und Porträtnischen des Stadtgebietes von Flavia Solva, CSIR Österreich IV 2 (Vienna 2011) |
| Pochmarski 2016 | E. Pochmarski, Die typologischen, ikonographischen und chronologischen Probleme der Grabstelen und Grabaltäre im Territorium von Flavia Solva, in: F. Humer – G. Kremer – E. Pollhammer – A. Pülz (eds.), Akten der 3. Österreichischen Römersteintagung in Carnuntum 02.–03.10.2014 (Vienna 2016) 143–161 |
| Pochmarski 2021 | E. Pochmarski, Die Grabbaureliefs (erster Teil) des Stadtgebietes von Flavia Solva, CSIR Österreich IV 4 (Vienna 2021) |
| Sapirstein 2019 | P. Sapirstein, Segmentation, Reconstruction, and Visualization of Ancient Inscriptions in 2.5D, Journal on Computing and Cultural Heritage 12/2, 2019, Article 15, <https://dl.acm.org/doi/10.1145/3286977> (29.03.2023) |
| Sapirstein – Psota 2018 | P. Sapirstein – E. Psota, Pattern Matching and the Analysis of Damaged Ancient Objects: The Case of the Column Drum, Journal on Computing and Cultural Heritage 9/3, 2018, Article 13, <https://dl.acm.org/doi/10.1145/2901297> (29.03.2023) |
| Thuswaldner et al. 2009 | B. Thuswaldner – S. Flöry – R. Kalasek – M. Hofer – Q. Huang – H. Thür, Digital Anastylosis of the Octagon in Ephesos, Journal on Computing and Cultural Heritage 2/1, 2009, Article 1, <https://dl.acm.org/doi/10.1145/1551676.1551677> (29.03.2023) |

| | |
|---|---|
| Toma 2020 | N. Toma, Marmor – Maße – Monumente: Vorfertigung, Standardisierung und Massenproduktion marmorner Bauteile in der römischen Kaiserzeit, Philippika 121 (Wiesbaden 2020) |
| Trefný et al. 2022 | M. Trefný – D. Mischka – M. Cihla – A. G. Posluschny – F. R. Václavík – W. Ney – C. Mischka, Sculpting the Glauberg ›prince‹. A traceological research of the Celtic sculpture and related fragments from the Glauberg (Hesse, Germany), PLoS One 17, 2022, e0271353, DOI: 10.1371/journal.pone.0271353 (29.03.2023) |

*Stephan Karl, Dr.-Emperger-Weg 14, 8052 Graz, Austria.*
*[e] stephan.karl@chello.at*

*Paul Bayer, Rosenhaingasse 5, 8010 Graz, Austria.*
*[e] paulbayer@gmx.net*

*Kerstin Bauer, Rosenhaingasse 5, 8010 Graz, Austria.*
*[e] ke.bauer@edu.uni-graz.at*

Veselka Katsarova – Vasiliki Anevlavi – Sabine Ladstätter – Walter Prochaska

# ROMAN SCULPTURES FROM KASNAKOVO, BULGARIA

## ARCHAEOLOGICAL AND ARCHAEOMETRIC INVESTIGATIONS

**Abstract**
The site known as the Sanctuary of the Nymphs and Aphrodite, near the village of Kasnakovo, South-East Bulgaria is a large architectural complex dating to the Roman period. It covers an area of about 15 acres and has several buildings with rich architectural decoration. The nature of the finds discovered at the site provides a reason to believe that the sanctuary was private and was part of the villa of a wealthy family of Thracian origin. Among the destruction layers in two of the buildings many fragments of marble statues have been found. Only in three cases is it possible to identify the sculptural images – a male foot in a sandal, the head of a young satyr, and a statue of Isis. Archaeometric investigations of the artefacts have revealed the use of imported marbles from Attica and Thasos for statuary purposes. The archaeometric analysis strengthens the archaeological research and supplies supplementary information on the marble preferred for statuary displayed in the Roman villa near Kasnakovo.

## THE PROJECT

In 2018–2019, 28 white marble and limestone artefacts (architectural elements and sculptures) from the so-called Sanctuary of the Nymphs and Aphrodite near the village of Kasnakovo (Dimitrovgrad Municipality, South-East Bulgaria) were investigated, as part of the project »Provenance Matters: A multi-proxy Approach for the Determination of White Marbles in the Roman East« funded by the Innovation Fund OeAW (Project No. OeAW4009)[1]. The interesting results achieved allowed the research to be expanded into a new project: »Fingerprinting White Marbles: Quarries and Cities of Roman Thrace, 1st–3rd centuries AD«, between the National Archaeological Institute with Museum of the Bulgarian Academy of Sciences and the Austrian Archaeological Institute of the Austrian Academy of Sciences. This article focuses on the archaeological context, the iconography and the marble provenance of the sculptures discovered during the 2013–2017 excavation campaigns in Kasnakovo.

## THE ARCHAEOLOGICAL SITE

In antiquity, the archaeological site near Kasnakovo fell within the boundaries of the city territory of *Augusta Traiana* (fig. 1) – one of the newly founded cities in the Roman province of Thrace[2]. One of the most important roads in the Roman Empire, the *Via Diagonalis*, passed along the left bank of the Maritsa river (*Hebros*) and provided the settlements of the city territory of *Augusta Traiana* with direct access to the North Aegean coast.

The site is situated on a low hill in the northern region of the Eastern Rhodope Mountains (fig. 2). The Banska river, a right tributary of the Maritsa river, flows to the west of the hill which is artificially terraced, with five relatively flat and wide terraces, oriented east-west. The largest, and lowest terrace, is oriented north-south. At its southern end there are karst rocks from which

---

[1] Anevlavi et al. 2019, 52–55.
[2] Kamisheva 2012, 29–32; Boteva 1992, 25–30.

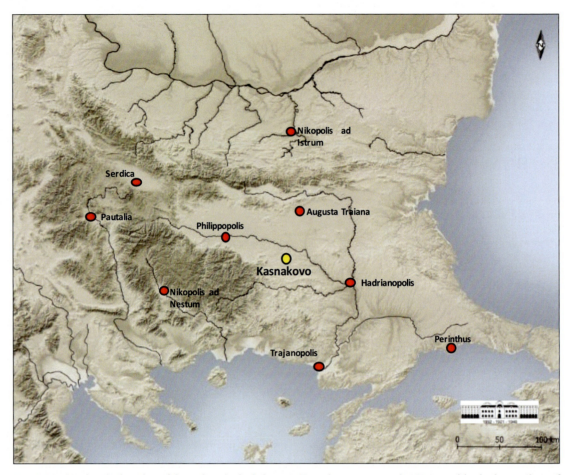

1  Map showing the location of the archaeological site near Kasnakovo, compared to Roman cities in the province of Thrace (© National Institute of Archaeology with Museum – BAS)

cold water springs. Since the end of the 19th century, the archaeological site near Kasnakovo has been known as the Sanctuary of the Nymphs and Aphrodite due to a Greek inscription (IGBulg. III/2, 1714) carved on the stone arch that stands above the spring. The inscription contains an explicit statement of the dedication of the fountain to the Nymphs and Aphrodite by a romanized married couple, where the husband is of undisputed Thracian origin[3]. Around the middle of the 2nd century, the Thracian Titus Flavius Beitukent Esbeneios and his wife Claudia Montana contributed to the building of the nymphaeum with three small pools. The Flavian Romanization of the dedicator and the mention of the name of the emperor's tribe Quirina, have been highlighted by some scholars as evidence that this is in fact the heir of an aristocratic Thracian family of *strategoi*, incorporated in the administration of the province during the reign of Vespasian (69–79 AD)[4]. Almost all known inscriptions of *strategoi* in Thrace from the Roman era have been found in sanctuaries and are associated with their foundation[5]. It seems that it was the *strategoi* and their descendants who introduced a new type of deity worship into the Thracian lands by setting up inscriptions, erecting altars and dedicating statues and reliefs with Greek iconography[6]. At the same

---

[3]  Venedikov 1950, 114; Aladzhov 1962, 9; Aladzhov 1997, 108.
[4]  Tatsheva 2007, 41.
[5]  Šarankov 2015, 73 n. 38.
[6]  Šarankov 2015, 74.

2   Aerial view from the east of the Sanctuary of the Nymphs and Aphrodite (© E. Mihov)

time, the members of this social group are considered with confidence to be the owners of some of the largest villa estates in Thrace since the second half of the 1st century AD[7].

After almost 40 years of interruption the archaeological investigations at the site were resumed in 2007. Archaeological observations, surveys, excavations and geophysical surveys produced considerable amounts of new data which expand what is known about the chronology, character, and functions of the site[8]. Until now, archaeological excavations have been carried out in the area of five different buildings with residential, religious and hygienic purposes. Ongoing investigations have shown that over an area of about 15 acres a large architectural complex was developed, including buildings of various layouts and functions (fig. 3). The type of the finds discovered at the site suggests that the sanctuary was private and that it belonged to the villa of a wealthy family of Thracian origin.

## ARCHAEOLOGICAL CONTEXT OF THE SCULPTURES

Archaeological excavations in two buildings of the complex near Kasnakovo have uncovered remarkable monuments of Roman sculpture. One of these buildings is located on the uppermost terrace east of the nymphaeum (fig. 3, 5), while the second one is slightly to the north of the nymphaeum (fig. 3, 7).

The building on the highest terrace has a rectangular plan with two rooms[9]. Its dimensions are 11 × 8.50 m (fig. 4 a). There is certain evidence of polychrome mosaics already destroyed in antiquity, decorating the floor of the larger room. The layout of the building very closely resembles two popular types of Greco-Roman temples – the tetrastyle prostyle and the temple *ad antes*. The finds discovered during the excavations include coins, small bronze jewellery, hobnails and four lead frames of votive mirrors. These finds reveal that the building was used between the second half of the 2nd and the end of the late 3rd/early 4th century AD.

---

[7]   Dinčev 1997, 11 n. 22; Kabakčieva 2007, 233–244.
[8]   Kacarova 2013, 485–497; Kacarova 2017, 568–583; Kacarova 2018, 35-42; Kacarova 2020, 271–284.
[9]   Kacarova 2017, 572–573 fig. 4 a. b.

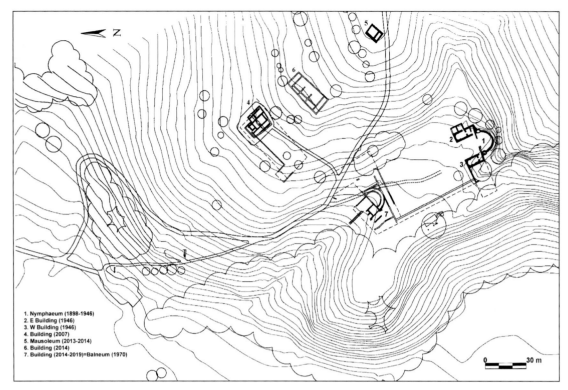

3   Plan of the architectural complex from the Roman era with all buildings recorded to date (© Atelier 3)

Among the debris of the building, fragments of at least two life-size marble statues were also found. The small size of most fragments only allows a hypothetical and cautious reconstruction of the statues from which they originated. One of the larger marble pieces is a part of a left elbow, probably from a female statue (fig. 4 b). It is 0.24 m high and 0.08 m in width, broken at both ends and with a heavily worn surface with barely visible traces of drapery. The condition of the fragment does not allow a more specific identification of the image.

Two other larger pieces belong to a male statue – a part of the leg above the knee (preserved dimensions: 0.17 m high and 0.10 × 0.12 m wide, fig. 4 c) and a right foot wearing a sandal, with part of a plinth (preserved dimensions: 0.26 × 0.28 m wide; 0.18 m high, fig. 4 d). The sandal is made of leather straps that cross over the top of the foot and tie at the ankle. The best parallel for such a model is a *caliga* of a bronze statue of a cavalryman from the 1st or the 2nd century AD[10], now in the Archaeological Museum of Bologna (Italy). The heel of the *caliga* has a spike that was apparently used as a spur by the rider. Unfortunately, this part is not preserved on the Kasnakovo sculpture.

The presence of two life-size sculptures – of a man in military attire and a draped woman – in the small building on the highest terrace makes it possible to identify the structure as the family mausoleum of the owners of the villa. An additional argument for this interpretation is the complete absence of finds of votive reliefs, which are the most widespread dedicatory monuments found in large quantities in Thracian sanctuaries and temples of the Roman era.

Two impressive monuments of Roman sculpture were discovered during excavations of the largest building in the architectural complex, which is probably the residence of the owners[11]. Its surface area, estimated through geophysical survey, exceeds 2,700 m². Archaeological excava-

---

[10] <https://followinghadrian.com/2013/12/12/artefact-of-the-week-bronze-caliga-from-an-over-life-size-statue-of-a-roman-legionary> (19.10.2022).

[11] Kacarova 2020, 271–284.

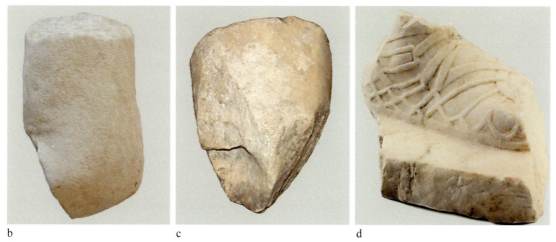

4  a) The mausoleum (© H. Popov); b) Left elbow of a marble female sculpture (© V. Katsarova); c) Fragment of a leg from a male sculpture (© V. Katsarova); d) Sandalled foot from a male sculpture (© K. Georgiev)

tions in the western half of the building cover an area of 1,000 m² (fig. 5 a). Its architectural plan includes a semi-circular courtyard surrounded by a covered portico with a colonnade, a large central room with mosaics and wall-paintings, living rooms, a swimming pool and a bathroom with hypocaust[12].

A marble statue of Isis was discovered in the destruction layer from the first half of the 4th century on the floor in the central room, near its southern wall. The dimensions of the room are considerable – 12.70 (N/S) × 7.20 m (E/W). Its floor was decorated with mosaics in *opus tessellatum*, of which only about 25 m² have been preserved. The interior is designed with niches decorated with frescoes.

The statue of Isis is 0.78 m high including the plinth (fig. 5 b). Her arms and head are missing, but nevertheless the identification is undeniable. She wears her characteristic linen *himation*

---

[12] Aladzhov 1997, 109 fig. 54; Kacarova – Petkova 2020, 993–997.

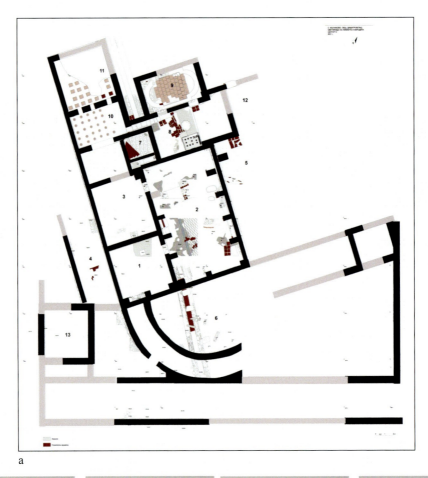

5 a) Excavated area of the residential building (© V. Katsarova, K. Petkova); b) Statue of Isis – front (© R. Stoyčev); c) Statue of Isis – left (© R. Stoyčev); d) Statue of Isis – right (© R. Stoyčev); e) Statue of Isis – back (© R. Stoyčev)

draped over the shoulders and tied between the breasts in the emblematic Isis knot. The body is presented in a relaxed position, with the left supporting leg and the right leg slightly bent at the knee. The left hand was lowered along the body, and the right was raised in front, as can be seen from the place of its fracture (fig. 5 c. d). The drapery of the *himation* is designed with wide, shallow folds, which on the back are graphically depicted (fig. 5 e). The carving of the shoulders and back make it clear that the head of the figure was not veiled. On her left shoulder is a break mark, probably of a descending curl. The hairstyle of Isis, which is extremely important for dating the sculpture, is uncertain. The statue from Kasnakovo is a small-scale copy of the most popular Greco-Roman image of the Egyptian goddess Isis in the Mediterranean[13]. The origin of this iconography in the 3rd–1st centuries BC is associated with the Ptolemaic dynasty and the cult of the deified Arsinoe II, and portraits of Ptolemaic queens and princesses[14]. A colossal female statue, with the same iconography, known as Madame Lucretia, is thought to have been placed in the Temple of Isis in Rome on the *Campus Martius* around the beginning of the 3rd century AD[15].

Almost all well-known statues of Isis in Greco-Roman iconography displayed in the world's museums have had missing arms or hands added in the modern era. It is generally accepted that the goddess originally holds a *sistrum* in one hand and a *situla* with water from the river Nile in the other. A large number of female images on gravestones from Attica, Greece between the 1st century BC and the beginning of the 4th century AD with similar iconography are interpreted as devotees rather than priestesses[16]. The earliest evidence of the penetration of the cult of Isis into Thrace is from Perinth and dates from the third quarter of the 3rd century BC[17]. Sanctuaries of the goddess from the 2nd to 1st centuries BC are certainly attested in *Thasos*, *Maroneia*, *Perinthus*, *Dionysopolis* and *Mesambria*. At the end of the 2nd and especially in the first half of the 3rd century AD images of Isis and Serapis appear on the reverse of coins of a number of Thracian cities – *Pautalia*, *Serdica*, *Philippopolis*, *Hadrianopolis*, *Deultum* and others[18]. However, there are very few finds showing the spread of the cult of Isis in the inland region of Thrace. The archaeological finds related to its distribution date from the time of the Flavians to the end of the 3rd century[19].

According to the features of its iconography the temple statue of Isis from Kasnakovo corresponds to the widespread depictions of Isis and her devotees, such as the sculpture of Isis from *Stobi* (North Macedonia) dated to the 2nd century AD[20], the statue of Isis from *Aenona* (Croatia) dated to the first half of the 1st century AD[21] or her devotee Alexandra on an Attic gravestone dated to the 2nd century AD[22]. Despite the fact that the statue was discovered in a context dating to the first half of the 4th century, it was created not later than the end of the 2nd to the beginning of the 3rd century.

Around the middle of the 4th century, dwellings for new inhabitants of the site were built in the courtyards and part of the premises of the residential building. These new structures were made of non-durable materials, and the finds related to them are ceramic vessels, animal bones, querns, tools and small jewellery. These dwellings were inhabited until the end of the 4th to the beginning of the 5th century AD.

A marble head (height 0.24 m) from a life-size statue of a satyr was found in one of these dwellings, dug into the space of the semi-circular courtyard (fig. 6 a). The prolonged burial of the sculpture in soil with a high content of organic materials has caused damage to its surface. A young satyr with thick hair and short flaming locks is presented (fig. 6 b. d). Neither goat ear is covered with hair. Above the forehead there are two short horns, of which the left one is broken off (fig. 6 c). The forehead is low, with protrusions. The eyes are almond-shaped, with pronounced upper eyelids; pupils and lacrimal ducts are carved with a drill. The mouth is slightly open, and the cheekbones are strongly emphasized by deep folds on both sides of the nose. The chin is short and rounded, and the face is broad overall, with quite a flat profile.

Statues of satyrs, either alone or as companions of Dionysus, were extremely popular decorations in the private buildings and gardens of the wealthy during the Roman era. One of the most

---

[13] Tran tam Tinh 1990a, 761–796; Tran tam Tinh 1990b, 501–526.
[14] Bricault – Versluys 2014, 9–12.
[15] Ensoli 1998, 421–423.
[16] Walters 1988; Walters 2000, 87–89.
[17] Bricault 2007, 246.
[18] Thram Tan Tin 1998, 172–195.
[19] Tačeva 1982, 74; Bricault 2007, 266; Popova 2016, 244.
[20] Bitrakova-Grozdanova 2015, 45 f.
[21] Karković Takalić – Mudronja 2020, 113–117.
[22] Walters 1988, pl. 24 a. b.

b  c  d

6  a) The late antique dwelling and findspot of the head of a satyr (© R. Stoyčev); b) Head of a satyr – ¾ profile (© R. Stoyčev); c) Head of a satyr – full face (© R. Stoyčev); d) Head of a satyr – back (© R. Stoyčev)

frequently reproduced images is the so-called Resting Satyr, attributed to Praxiteles[23]. Since we only have the head of the figure, it is difficult to determine what the statue looked like – resting, pouring wine, dancing, or in any other activity. The style of his hairdo, the way the eyes, nose and mouth are shaped, and the slightly detached facial expression of the Kasnakovo satyr allow it to be dated to the end of the Antonine era, or more precisely to the last quarter of the 2$^{nd}$ century[24]. A head of a satyr similar in style, found in *Heracleia Lyncestis* (North Macedonia) is dated to the Severan period[25].

## ARCHAEOMETRIC INVESTIGATIONS

Five marble sculptures from Kasnakovo were the subject of archaeometric research – PM-BG-017 (satyr head), PM-BG-018 (Isis statue), PM-BG-025 (fragment of a leg), PM-BG-063 (fragment

---

[23] Ridgwey 1997, 266.
[24] Petkova 2018, 47.
[25] Sokolovska 1987, 188–189 pl. 66, 1.

of a left elbow) and PM-BG-024 (foot with sandal). The main tasks of the investigations were to answer questions about the origin of the marble, specifics of the marble trade in Thrace and possible contacts with other regions.

The analytical methods applied to the samples from statues included petrographic investigations, chemical analysis with a large range of elements (variables: Mn, Mg, Fe, Sr, Y, V, Cd, La, Ce, Yb, U), isotopic analysis ($\delta 18O$ ‰, $\delta 13C$ ‰) as well as fluid inclusion analysis (crush-leach method, variables: Li/Na, Cl/Na, K/Na, Br/Na, I/Na). Statistical treatment for each sample was applied. All samples were compared with the large database of quarry samples built up by Walter Prochaska from the University of Leoben and the OeAI/OeAW, which covers the most important marble quarries in Asia Minor, Greece, Italy, and Bulgaria. For the finds from Kasnakovo, the local quarries were taken into consideration, in combination with the important sub-regional and supra-regional ancient quarries, such as Penteli, Thasos, and *Prokonnesos*.

The results showed that the marbles of the sculptures originated from different locations. The material of the three statues PM-BG-018 (Isis statue), PM-BG-025 (fragment of a leg) and PM-BG-024 (foot with sandal) originate from the Penteli quarry in Attica, Greece. The marble is characterized by a fine grain size, white colour and a slight schistosity of the structure. The observed traces of mica and chlorite are also strong indications for Pentelic marble (fig. 7).

The artefact PM-BG-063 (fragment of a left elbow) can originate from Cape Vathy at Thasos Island in Northern Greece with its white colour, medium to coarse grained, prominent dolomitic marble. The petrographic characteristics in combination with the chemical analysis have proven the Thasian provenance (fig. 8).

The marble of the last statue PM-BG-017, the satyr's head, is of local provenance. The artefact was compared with the database of the local Bulgarian quarries and the conclusion is that the marble originates from the quarries of present-day Asenovgrad, south of ancient *Philippopolis*.

Archaeometric research has shown that the sculptures were made of the high-quality marbles from Thasos and Penteli, famous in the ancient world, in combination with local sources from inland Thrace. Future investigations at the area of Asenovgrad in combination with analysis of sculptures from major Roman cities (such as *Philippopolis*, *Augusta Traiana*, etc.) will reveal the possibility of local sculpture workshops in the area.

## CONCLUSIONS

Roman sculptures from Kasnakovo provide some new guidelines for the analysis and cultural-historical interpretations of the archaeological site. Particularly interesting are questions related to the statue of Isis. Until now, such a monument had not been discovered in this part of the Roman province of Thrace, and more precisely the city territory of *Augusta Traiana*. Only two bronze applications for a cosmetic box with an image of Isis-Aphrodite were found in the grave of a woman buried in the second half of the 2nd to the beginning of the 3rd century AD in the necropolis of the owners of the villa near Chatalka[26]. It seems that the cult of Isis was not generally widespread in the Thracian community, but found followers among certain individuals and families. This suggests that the appearance of the statue of Isis in Kasnakovo is less indicative of the worshipping of her cult than for the remarkably high level of Hellenization and Romanization of the owners of the villa. As members of the Thracian elite, this family had not only the financial means, but also the spiritual desire to have a statue of Isis. According to the data on the origin of the marble for the statue, it was probably made in Greece and brought finished to Kasnakovo. The active integration of the Thracian aristocracy within Roman provincial administration and political structure is documented epigraphically and by archaeological finds from the period of the early Julio-Claudian and Flavian dynasties. The incorporation of these lands within the global economic network of the Roman Empire led to the adoption of a new way of life. The owner of

---

[26] Buyukliev 1994, 205–211.

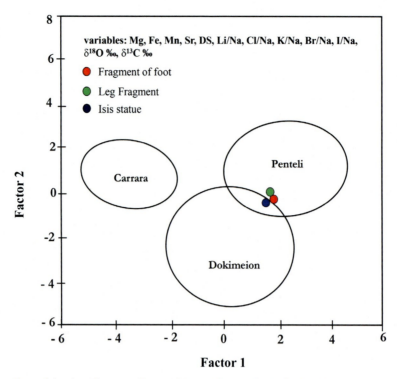

7   The multivariate diagram of the calcitic marble samples indicating the provenance of the Pentelic quarry (© V. Anevlavi, W. Prochaska)

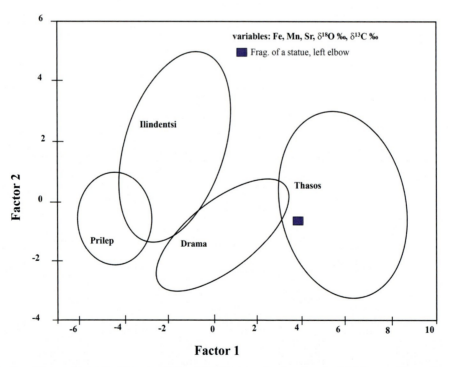

8   The multivariate diagram of the dolomitic sample showing the Thasian marble as the source of origin of the sculpture (© V. Anevlavi, W. Prochaska)

the villa at Kasnakovo, Titus Flavius Beitukent and his successors were influenced by Roman fashion. They invested heavily in the marble decoration of their villa and in the design of a beautiful garden with a nymphaeum. In general, the decoration of private houses, villas and gardens in the Thracian lands reveals the personal preferences of the owners[27]. Here we find a reflection of fashionable trends in Roman imperial times, according to which gardens are frequently decorated with statues of Aphrodite, Dionysus and his entourage, and Egyptian themes.

## BIBLIOGRAPHY

| | |
|---|---|
| Aladzhov 1962 | D. Aladzhov, Svetilište na nimfite i Afrodita kraij s. Kasnakovo (Haskovo 1962) |
| Aladzhov 1997 | D. Aladzhov, Selišta, pametnici, nahodki ot Haskovskija kraij (Haskovo 1997) |
| Anevlavi et al. 2019 | V. Anevlavi – C. Cenati – V. Katsarova – W. Prochaska – S. Ladstätter, Marble Provenance Analysis: The case study of Kasnakovo, Bulgaria, Metalla Sonderheft 9, 2019, 52–55 |
| Bitrakova-Grozdanova 2015 | V. Bitrakova-Grozdanova, Les cultes orientaux dans la Haute Macédonie, leur surive et leur adoption au temps romain, in: A. Nikoloska – S. Müskens (eds.), Romanising oriental gods? Religious transformations in the Balkan Provinces in the Roman period. New finds and novel perspectives. Symposium Skopje 18.–21.09.2013 (Skopje 2015) 35–71 |
| Boteva 1992 | D. Boteva, Augusta Traiana and its Territory, IndexQuad 20, 1992, 25–30 |
| Bricault 2007 | L. Bricault, La diffusion isiaque en Mésie Inférieure et en Thrace: politique, commerce et religion, in: L. Bricault – M. J. Versluys (eds.), Nile into Tiber: Egypt in the Roman World. Proceedings of the III[rd] International Conference of Isis Studies, Leiden 11.–14.05.2005 (Leiden 2007) 245–266 |
| Bricault – Versluys 2014 | L. Bricault – M. J. Versluys, Isis and Empires, in: L. Bricault – M. J. Versluys (eds.), Power, politics and the cult of Isis. Proceedings of the V[th] International Conference of Isis studies, Boulogne-sur-Mer 13.–15.10.2011 (Leiden 2014) 3–35 |
| Buyukliev 1994 | H. Buyukliev, Kăm problema za razprostranenieto na iztočnite kultove v administrativnata teritoria na Avgusta Traiana, Marica-Iztok, Arheologičeski proučvania 2 (Sofia 1994) 205–211 |
| Dinčev 1997 | V. Dinčev, Rimskite vili v dnešnata bălgarska teritoria (Sofia 1997) |
| Ensoli 1998 | S. Ensoli, L'Iseo e Serapeo del Campo Marzio con Domiziano, Adriano e i Severi, l'assetto monumentale e il culto legato con l'ideologia e la politica imperiali, in: N. Bonacasa – N. C. Naro – E. C. Portale – A. Tullio (eds.), L'Egitto in Italia dall'Antichità al Medioevo: riassunti. Atti del III Congresso Internationale Italo-Egiziano, Roma – Pompei 13.–19.11.1995 (Rome 1998) 407–438 |
| IGBulg. III/2 | G. Mihailov, Inscriptiones graecae in Bulgaria repertae III (Sofia 1964) |
| Kabakčieva 2007 | G. Kabakčieva, Văznikvane na vilni stopanstva v Trakija i za osnovatelite na antičnite vili Čatalka i Armira, Izvestia na Starozagorskija istoričeski muzeij II (Stara Zagora 2007) 233–244 |
| Kacarova 2013 | V. Kacarova, Novi danni za selištnoto obitavane prez antičnostta kraij Izvora na nimfite i Afrodita pri s. Kasnakovo, obština Dimitrovgrad, in: K. Rabadziev – H. Popov – M. Damyanov – V. Katsarova (eds.), Sbornik v pamet na akad. D. P. Dimitrov (Sofia 2013) 485–497 |
| Kacarova 2017 | V. Kacarova, Nova sgrada ot arhitekturnija kompleks Svetilište na nimfite i Afrodita pri s. Kasnakovo, obština Dimitrovgrad, in: H. Popov – Y. Cvetkova (eds.) ΚΡΑΤΙΣΤΟΣ. Sbornik v čest na professor Petăr Delev (Sofia 2017) 568–583 |
| Kacarova 2018 | V. Kacarova, Svetilište na nimfite i Afrodita pri s. Kasnakovo – 10 godini novi arheologičeski proučvanija (2007–2017), in: Muzeijni letopisi – 90 godini organizirano muzeijno delo v grad Haskovo (Haskovo 2018) 35–42 |
| Kacarova 2020 | V. Kacarova, Svetilište na nimfite i Afrodita pri s. Kasnakovo – novi arheologičeski proučvanija na t. nar. Teatăr prez 2014-2015 g., in: B. Bozhkova – E. Genčeva (eds.), In |

---

[27] Koleva 2017, 66–89.

|  |  |
|---|---|
|  | memoriam Ivani Venedikov. Po slučaij 100-godišninata ot rozhdenieto mu, GodMuzSof 14 (Sofia 2020) 271–284 |
| Kacarova – Petkova 2020 | V. Kacarova – K. Petkova, Archeologičeski proučvanija na obekt Svetilište na nimfite i Afrodita, s. Kasnakovo, obština Dimitrovgrad, in: Archeologičeski otkritija i razkopki prez 2019 g., II (Sofia 2020) 993–997 |
| Kamisheva 2012 | M. Kamisheva, Augusta Traiana, in: R. Ivanov (ed.), Tabula Imperii Romani, K 35/2 Philippopolis (Sofia 2012) 29–32 |
| Karković Takalić – Mudronja 2020 | P. Karković Takalić – D. Mudronja, Arhivski podaci, mineraloško-petrografska i ikonografska analiza kipa Izide iz Enone, VjesAMuzZagreb 43, 2020/3, 93–121 |
| Koleva 2017 | M. Koleva, Rimska idealna skulptura ot Bălgarija (Sofia 2017) |
| Petkova 2018 | K. Petkova, Mramorna glava na satir ot Svetilišteto na nimfite i Afrodita pri s. Kasnakovo, in: Muzeijni letopisi – 90 godini organizirano muzeijno delo v grad Haskovo (Haskovo 2018) 43–49 |
| Popova 2016 | V. Popova, Kultăt kăm Izida i Sarapis v rimskata plastika ot Bălgaria. Addendum, in: Studia Classica Serdicensia V. Monuments and texts in Antiquity and beyond. Essays for the centenary of Georgi Mihailov (1915–1991) (Sofia 2016) 208–250 |
| Ridgwey 1997 | B. Ridgwey, Fourth-Century Styles in Greek Sculpture (London 1997) |
| Šarankov 2015 | N. Šarankov, Novi danni za trakijskite stratezi, ArchaeologijaSof 56/1–2, 2015, 62–78 |
| Sokolovska 1987 | V. Sokolovska, Antička skulptura vo SR Makedonija (Skopje 1987) |
| Tačeva 1982 | M. Tačeva. Istorija na iztočnite kultove v Dolna Mizija i Trakija prez V v. pr. n. e. – IV v. ot n. e. (Sofia 1982) |
| Tatsheva 2007 | M. Tatsheva. Der thrakische Adel und die Verwaltung der Provinz Thracia, in: Thracia 17. In honorem annorum LX Cirili Yordanov (Sofia 2007) 33–47 |
| Tran tam Tinh 1990a | V. Tran tam Tinh, Isis, in: LIMC V 1 (Zurich 1990) 761–796 |
| Tran tam Tinh 1990b | V. Tran tam Tinh, Isis, in: LIMC V 2 (Zurich 1990) 501–526 |
| Tran tam Tinh 1998 | V. Tran tam Tinh, Serapis et Isis en Thrace et en Mésie Inferieure: problèmes iconographiques, in: Pulpudeva suppl. 6, Semaines Philippopolitaines de l'histoire et de la culture Thrace, Plovdiv 10.–12.10.1986 (Sofia 1998) 172–195 |
| Venedikov 1950 | I. Venedikov, Razkopkite pri s. Kasnakovo prez 1945 i 1946 g., BIBulg 20, 1950, 105–115 |
| Walters 1988 | E. J. Walters, Attic grave reliefs that represent women in the dress of Isis, Hesperia Suppl. 22 (Athens 1988) |
| Walters 2000 | E. J. Walters, Athenian Isis grave reliefs, in: L. Bricault (ed.), De Memphis à Rome. Actes du Ier Colloque international sur les études isiaques, Poitiers 08.–10.04.1999 (Leiden 2000) 61–89 |

*Veselka Katsarova, National Archaeological Institute of with Museum, Bulgarian Academy of Science, Saborna Str. 2, 1000 Sofia, Bulgaria.*
*[e] vesi_kazarova@yahoo.com*

*Vasiliki Anevlavi, Austrian Archaeological Institute, Austrian Academy of Sciences, Dominikanerbastei 16, 1010 Vienna, Austria.*
*[e] vasiliki.anevlavi@oeaw.ac.at*

*Sabine Ladstätter, Austrian Archaeological Institute, Austrian Academy of Sciences, Dominikanerbastei 16, 1010 Vienna, Austria.*
*[e] sabine.ladstaetter@oeaw.ac.at*

*Walter Prochaska, Austrian Archaeological Institute, Austrian Academy of Sciences, Dominikanerbastei 16, 1010 Vienna, Austria.*
*[e] walter.prochaska@oeaw.ac.at*

Gabrielle Kremer – Robert Linke – Georg Plattner –
Eduard Pollhammer – Marina Brzakovic – Robert Krickl –
Nirvana Silnović

# COLOURS REVEALED: FIRST RESULTS ON A POLYCHROME MITHRAS RELIEF FROM *CARNUNTUM*

**Abstract**

The PolychroMon project funded by the Austrian Academy of Sciences/Heritage Science Austria 2020 is conducting comprehensive research on the polychromy of Roman stone monuments from the Danubian provinces. For exemplifying aims and applied methods, this paper provides first results of the investigation of a Mithraic tauroctony relief from *Carnuntum*, which shows several painted elements not rendered by carving. Especially highlighted is the occurrence and distribution of the pigment Egyptian blue, which was *inter alia* used to enhance the plasticity of the figures by pictorial shadowing. Preliminary remarks on the meaning of colour indicate good conformity with known Mithraic reliefs – however, this research is still at a preliminary stage within this project.

## INTRODUCTION

The rapidly expanding research on the polychromy of ancient stone monuments resulted in a growing awareness of the importance of colour for our understanding of sculptural and architectural monuments of Classical Antiquity[1]. Coupled with the development of refined multidisciplinary research methodologies, it provided an impetus for a number of case studies carried out across the Mediterranean region[2]. However, despite the growing interest in the topic, our knowledge of polychromy in the Roman period remains very limited[3]. Especially studies of the sculptural and architectural polychromy in the Roman provinces are still sporadic[4]. The aim of the PolychroMon project[5] is, therefore, to fill in this lacuna by conducting a first comprehensive survey of the polychromy of Roman stone monuments from the Danube provinces.

The multidisciplinary team includes individual members from the Austrian Academy of Sciences, the State collections of Lower Austria, the Kunsthistorisches Museum Vienna, and the Federal Monuments Authority Austria. The project is primarily focusing on the votive, funeral and architectural stone artefacts from *Carnuntum*, the Vienna Basin and the Leitha Mountains, the majority of which are preserved in the collections of the institutions involved. Most of the artefacts selected for the examination are made of local or regional stone[6], with occasional usage of Alpine or imported marble (from Greece, Asia Minor and Italy)[7].

---

[1] E.g. Brinkmann – Wünsche 2003; Bradley 2009a, 427–457; Østergaard 2018. Most recently Østergaard – Schwartz 2022, 29–31.
[2] Østergaard 2017, 159–166.
[3] E.g. Liverani – Santamaria 2014; Østergaard et al. 2014, 52.
[4] E.g. Østergaard 2018; Kopczynski et al. 2017, 139–154; Delferrière – Edme 2018/2019; Campbell 2020; Lipps – Berthold 2021; Neri et al. 2022.
[5] »Colours revealed – Polychromie römerzeitlicher Monumente der Donauprovinzen (PolychroMon)«. Funded by Austrian Academy of Sciences/Heritage Science Austria, 2021–2025. Cooperation between Austrian Archaeological Institute (OeAI)/Austrian Academy of Sciences (OeAW), Landessammlungen Niederösterreich, Kunsthistorisches Museum Vienna (KHM) and Bundesdenkmalamt (BDA). Project leaders: G. Kremer, R. Linke, G. Plattner, E. Pollhammer <https://www.oeaw.ac.at/oeai/forschung/altertumswissenschaften/antike-religion/polychromon> (25.03.2023). – Kremer et al., 2022; Kremer et al. 2023a; Kremer et al. 2023b; Plattner et al., in prep.
[6] The lithotypes found in the stone artefacts from the Vienna Basin and the Leitha region were analyzed as a part of the »CarVin project«, see e.g. Kremer et al. 2021.
[7] Kremer et al. 2018, 557–565; C. Uhlir – M. Unterwurzacher in: Kremer 2012, 421–430.

1    Tauroctony relief from the area of the auxiliary fort at Petronell-*Carnuntum*, Archäologisches Museum Carnuntinum inv. CAR-S-99 (AMC, photo N. Gail)

The primary data obtained during the project will be used to examine a number of concerns about the polychromy of Roman stone artefacts from a multidisciplinary perspective. Apart from detecting the original appearance of the monuments as far as possible, an analysis of the raw materials, the paint stratigraphy and the underlying manufacturing processes will be carried out. Important information about the prior (documented and undocumented) conservation and restoration of monuments and relevant storage circumstances will be considered as well when interpreting the analytical data.

A special research focus is placed on the objects of the Mithras cult from the region under investigation and the semantics of their polychromy[8]. The provincial capital *Carnuntum* was one of the earliest centres of the cult in the western provinces and the rich material evidence of sacral and votive monuments, both from the city and its hinterland, makes it a particularly well-suited case-study regarding the significance of colour in religious and ritual context[9]. A painted tauroctony relief from *Carnuntum*[10] (fig. 1) will serve as an example to briefly present different methods applied within this project.

## PAINTED RELIEF WITH BULL-KILLING SCENE FROM *CARNUNTUM*

A painted relief with bull-killing scene (66 × 100 × 15 cm) was found in the area of the auxiliary fort in Petronell-*Carnuntum* in 1932[11]. The limestone relief was broken into seven fragments, which are now mounted on a plate. The upper right corner with the bull's head and the bust of Luna are missing and the relief has suffered several other damages. It depicts the well-known

---

[8]  Kremer 2012, e.g. 330–337. 382–386 cat. 74–87. 189–202. 350–370. 706–708. 734; Kremer 2021, 419. On colours in the Mithras cult see Magrini et al. 2019, 2160–2170.
[9]  Humer – Kremer 2011; Kremer 2012.
[10] Archäologisches Museum Carnuntinum (AMC), inv. CAR-S-99.
[11] Kremer 2012, 105 no. 191 pl. 54 (with literature); lupa 13683.

scene of Mithras killing the bull, set inside a rectangular field with a smooth border running along its edges. In the background, traces of light blue, dark blue, yellow and brown-red colour are still observable with the naked eye. Mithras is wearing a Phrygian cap with traces of red colour (and a yellow tip [?]), while his long and curly hair is painted yellow. Several traces of colour are visible on his clothes as well: yellow on the tunic, light red with a dark red border on the fluttering cloak, green with some red on the trousers, and dark red on his shoes.

The bull's tail ends in a large tripartite yellow ear, while additional details of the structure of the wheat ears are rendered with delicate paint strokes. Besides the two main protagonists, the scene involves the animal companions – a dog, a serpent, and a scorpion (traces of red and yellow) at their usual places. A green plant with red-yellow fruit is painted below the bull's testicles. To the left of Mithras' head, a yellow star-shaped ornament is painted on the background. In the upper left corner, a bust of Sol is preserved with yellow hair, a painted crown of rays (red) and with some traces of red colour on his cloak. His mouth and nostrils bear traces of red colour, while eye rims and eyebrows are painted black.

## INVESTIGATION OF PIGMENTS

One of the main goals of the project is to determine the materials used for colouring the stone objects as well as to localize minute traces of pigments, often not visible to the naked eye. As a representative example of the procedure and its possible outcomes, the following section provides the preliminary results of the detection of Egyptian blue – a widely used blue pigment in antiquity[12] – in the previously described tauroctony relief.

After the autopsy, which is a basic investigation and documentation of visible colour remains, possible pigment traces no longer visible to the naked eye were first examined using non-invasive techniques. As a first step, comprehensive multispectral imaging (MSI) was performed on the tauroctony relief. This method provides information on the distribution and materiality of the pigments by applying several different techniques. For example, figure 2 shows the recording of visible reflected light (VIS) and visible induced infrared luminescence radiation (VIL)[13], performed with a customized ILCE-7R camera sensitive to the spectral range of ~350–1000 nm wavelength, equipped with a SEL50M28 lens

2 Multispectral images of the tauroctony relief CAR-S-99; visible reflected light (top) and visible induced infrared luminescence (bottom) – the intense white areas in the latter indicate the presence of Egyptian blue pigment (OeAI-OeAW, photo R. Krickl)

---

[12] Eastaugh 2004.
[13] Dyer et al. 2013.

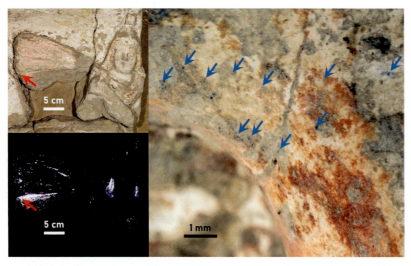

3 Macro photography (right) showing red and blue pigment particles on the cloak – the area indicated with a red arrow in a visible reflected (top left) and visible induced infrared luminescence image (bottom left) (OeAI-OeAW, photo R. Krickl)

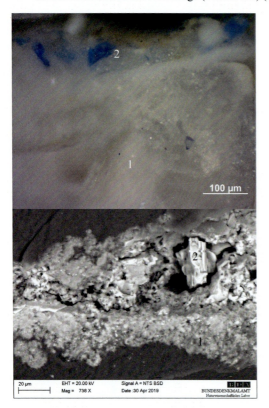

4 Investigations on cross-sections of sample material from an area below the bull's body by LM (upper image) and SEM/EDX (lower image) give evidence for the presence of Egyptian blue (BDA, photos R. Linke)

(fig. 2). As camera filters, Hoya Y1U-VIR (VIS) and Schott RG850 (VIL) were used respectively. In both cases, the sample was irradiated with two custom-made 100 W COB LED light sources with ~5500 K white light broad band emission filtered with Hoya Y1UVIR filters, oriented ~45° on both sides to the optical axis. For white balance and colour calibration, a Zenith Lite™ Diffuse Reflectance Target and X-Rite ColorChecker® were included in each image. Thus, the results obtained highlight the distribution of the Egyptian blue pigment which appears bright white in VIL images due to its very intense emission behaviour[14]. The detection limit of this technique is very low, enabling the localization of even dust-size particles that are not visible to the naked eye.

As a second step, the previously detected areas of high VIL signal were investigated by macro photography, performed with an ILCE-6400 camera with SEL30M35 lens and white balanced with the help of WhiBal® G7 grey card. The detection of submillimetre-sized blue grains localized at these specific regions provided further support for the interpretation of the Egyptian blue pigment (fig. 3). Final confirmation was achieved using invasive methods. Micro-sampling was performed in selected areas for cross-section analyses using light (LM) and scanning electron microscopy (SEM) with energy-dispersive X-ray spectroscopy (EDX) (fig. 4)[15]. For that purpose, the samples were embedded in epoxy resin and investigations were carried out on polished cross-sections by means of optical light microscopy (Zeiss Axio Scope.A1) and SEM/EDX (Zeiss EVO MA15, coupled with a Bruker Xflash 630M). The result of this investigation has shown that the optical properties, crystal morphology and chemical

---

[14] Accorsi et al. 2009.
[15] Sample 243/19. This analysis was part of a preliminary project, carried out by the Austrian Academy of Sciences, the Federal Monuments Authority Austria and the Archaeological Museum Carnuntinum in 2019/2020 (CaFarb).

composition of the samples are in agreement with the values of (synthetic) cuprorivaite, the blue colouring phase of Egyptian blue. Concerning the paint stratigraphy, the blue pigment was applied using the lime binding on top of a limewash ground layer with a sintered surface (fig. 4).

Potentially useful methods for further investigations of pigments found on the tauroctony relief include portable systems for X-ray fluorescence spectroscopy for chemical analysis, hyperspectral imaging, fibre optics reflectance and Raman spectroscopy for spectral fingerprinting, which are all planned to be performed. The results will help to further discriminate between pigment phases and provide substantiated identification.

## INTERPRETATION

Due to the limited scope of this paper, the following section will focus on the role of the Egyptian blue pigment on the tauroctony relief from *Carnuntum*. As is clearly visible on the multispectral images, Egyptian blue was used for accentuating the contours of Mithras and the bull (fig. 2). The contours allowed the carved figures to stand out more prominently from the background, which enhanced their overall visibility. There seems to be a prevalent localization of the detected remnants mainly on the lower (right) parts of protruding features of the sculpture. It cannot be ruled out that this is an analytical artefact due to inhomogeneous abrasion and insular preservation. Perhaps, however, the emphasis on the shadows on the right side was also intended to create the impression of an incidence of light from the upper left, the position of Sol.

Another area with a particularly strong presence of Egyptian blue is the inner side of the Phrygian cap, where blue was used to produce the shadowing effect. Egyptian blue is further noticed along the folds of Mithras' billowing cloak. Here, as well as in the inner section of the upper part of the Phrygian cap, the blue coincides with the application of red ochre pigment (fig. 3). The purple colour thus achieved was used to accentuate the folds on Mithras' cap and cloak, which would hence appear more voluminous and would contribute to the dramatic effect of the fluttering cloak.

Finally, a vertical stripe of Egyptian blue below Mithras' left knee seems to coincide with the application of red pigment as well. Purple was in this case used to paint the *dorsuale*, a decorative ritual ribbon placed over the bull's back. These woollen ribbons were of either scarlet or white colour and are encountered in numerous depictions of ancient sacrifices[16]. They were used as a visual sign of the sacrificial status of the animal[17].

A good comparative example is found on the tauroctony relief from the Mithraeum under Santo Stefano Rotondo[18]. Here, four vertical lines were painted on the bull's back, directly below the Mithras' knee, in red and yellow ochres. On the relief from *Carnuntum*, traces of four analogous lines can still be observed even with the naked eye, with a similar usage of purple and yellow hues.

As this brief survey has shown, colour was used extensively not just to paint the surface of the relief but also to create various colouristic effects: to enhance the plasticity of the figures, to indicate deep shadows or to express voluminosity. Furthermore, colour was used to add elements not rendered by carving, like the plant below the bull's testicles, the ray crown of the god Sol or the star next to Mithras' head. Paint layers applied on top of each other served to depict delicate structures on monochrome surfaces, as for example on the grain-bearing tip of the bull's tail (fig. 5). In addition, pigment mixtures could also be detected in various places, which will be investigated in a further step. The colour palette includes calcium carbonate white, yellow ochre, red ochre, red lead, green earth and carbon black. The investigations carried out so far reveal that

---

[16] Scheid 2007, 264. See e.g. on the Jupiter Dolichenus relief from *Carnuntum*, AMC inv. CAR-S-90; Kremer 2012, 99–100 cat. 183.
[17] Weddle 2012, 149.
[18] Museo Nazionale Romano inv. 205837. Magrini et al. 2019, 2164 fig. 3 a.

5   Detail of the upper left corner of the relief with the bust of Sol and the bull's tail (AMC, photo N. Gail)

the majority of painting was applied on a white limewash as grounding and that lime was used as binding material.

## ON THE MEANING OF COLOURS

While it is not possible to discuss the potential meaning of each colour here, some preliminary remarks can be made.

As previously mentioned, particular attention within the PolychroMon project is given to the study of the use of colour in the cult of Mithras. In order to understand the function of its polychromy, it is necessary to mention the original viewing context and purpose of the monument. Although the relief was not found *in situ*, a great number of Mithraea with preserved sculptural installations give an idea of specific viewing conditions present in Mithraic temples. A cult image – relief, sculpture, wall painting or mosaic – depicting Mithras sacrificing the heavenly bull, is usually found mounted on the rear wall of the Mithraeum, as a focal point of each temple. Mithraea were ideally subterranean cave-like structures or, when conditions did not allow for an underground location, they tried to emulate otherwise the dark ambience of the cave. Sources of light were limited, restricted to the small ceiling openings or, more often, to the flickering light of the lamps and various lighting effects[19].

Considering the dark ambience of the temple, cult images had to be visually impactful in order to fulfil their purpose. This means that all the protagonists of the tauroctony scene had to

---

[19]   Clauss 2000, 120–130.

be visible and recognizable to the ritual participants. Besides lighting, colour was an important tool to achieve this. But how could the selection of colours be correlated to the meaning of the tauroctony scene?

The tauroctony scene is, as mentioned earlier, a sacrificial scene. Two main protagonists of this dramatic event are Mithras and the sacrificial bull, whom the invincible and omnipotent god (as he is usually called in dedicatory inscriptions) sacrifices. While the bull is painted white, Mithras wears dark red clothes: a Phrygian cap, a cloak and shoes, all of them bearing traces of red colour, while traces of yellow are visible on his tunic and green on the trousers (probably used to indicate embroidered decoration as seen on the fresco painting in the Mithraeum at Santa Maria Capua Vetere[20]).

The pure white colour of the bull is in compliance with the rules of Roman animal sacrifice, according to which white animals were sacrificed to the gods above (celestial or earth gods), while those below or associated with night received animals with dark hides[21].

Red colour traditionally had cultic significance, especially for Dionysus, Priapus, Pan and, above all, Jupiter[22]. The red associated with these deities was none other than purple, the most important and most expensive colour in antiquity[23]. As it was highly exclusive, purple was a marker of high social status and was associated with imperial authority and divine power[24]. Since the production of purple pigments from shellfish was extremely expensive, other red colourants and paint mixtures were used to imitate the costly purple[25]. Red colour used for Mithras' clothes was thus a suitable choice for this deity. In the tauroctony scene, he is depicted victoriously straddling the already slumped bull. Purple was traditionally worn by victorious generals in triumphal processions and was associated with peace and prosperity[26]. By sacrificing the bull, Mithras created the universe and all living things, and secured the beneficent cosmic order and agrarian prosperity (note the tuft of ears at the end of the bull's tail and the plant with fruit below the bull's testicles)[27]. As a creator and ruler of the universe, his red clothes, with their long history as regal and as a symbol of dominance and rulership, would immediately bring such connotations to the minds of the ritual participants. Similarly, the yellow hair of Sol would have been associated with the deity as well as with bright solar light, emanating from the god in the form of a radiate crown (fig. 5).

Although there is much more that can be said about the meaning of colours in the cult of Mithras, it would require taking into account a larger amount of monuments and space. Such a comprehensive study is one of the goals of the PolychroMon project, while this brief study is intended to illustrate the main methodological points and research questions pursued.

## BIBLIOGRAPHY

| | |
|---|---|
| Accorsi et al. 2009 | G. Accorsi – G. Verri – M. Bolognesi – N. Armaroli – C. Clementi – C. Miliani – A. Romani, The exceptional near-infrared luminescence properties of cuprorivaite (Egyptian blue), ChemComm *23*, 3392–3394, DOI: 10.1039/B902563D (25.03.2023) |
| Bradley 2009a | M. Bradley, The importance of colour on ancient marble sculpture, Art History 32, 2009, 427–457, DOI: 10.1111/j.1467-8365.2009.00666.x (30.03.2023) |
| Bradley 2009b | M. Bradley, Colour and Meaning in Ancient Rome (Cambridge 2009) |
| Brinkmann – Wünsche 2003 | V. Brinkmann – R. Wünsche (eds.), Bunte Götter. Die Farbigkeit antiker Skulptur (Munich 2003) |

---

[20] Vermaseren 1971, pl. 3.
[21] Scheid 2007, 264; Verg. georg. 2, 146.
[22] Henke 2020, 581–586.
[23] Eastaugh et al. 2004, 373; Bradley 2009b, 189. 209.
[24] Reinhold 1970, 48–61; Bradley 2009b, 209.
[25] Brøns – Sargent 2018, 488–489.
[26] Isid. orig. 18, 2, 5–6; Verg. Aen. 4, 262–263.
[27] Gordon 2017, 93–130.

| | |
|---|---|
| Brøns – Sargent 2018 | C. Brøns – M. L. Sargent, Pigments and dyes: the use of colourants for the depiction of garments on Egyptian mummy portraits in the Ny Carlsberg Glyptotek, in: M. S. Busana – M. Gleba – F. Mei – A. R. Tricomi (eds.), Textiles and Dyes in the Mediterranean Economy and Society. Proceedings of the VI[th] International Symposium on Textiles and Dyes in the Ancient Mediterranean World, Padova – Este – Altino 17.–20.10.2016 (Zaragoza 2018) 481–490 |
| Campbell 2020 | L. Campbell, Polychromy on the Antonine Wall distance sculptures: Non-destructive identification of pigments on Roman reliefs, Britannia 51, 2020, 68–113 |
| Clauss 2000 | M. Clauss, The Roman Cult of Mithras: The God and his Mysteries (Edinburgh 2000) |
| Delferrière – Edme 2018/2019 | N. Delferrière – A.-L. Edme, La polychromie des stèles de la nécropole des Bolards (Nuits-Saint-Georges, Côte-d'Or), RAE 67, 2018/2019, 267–286, <http://journals.openedition.org/rae/10874> (25.03.2023) |
| Dyer et al. 2013 | J. Dyer – G. Verri – J. Cupitt, Multispectral Imaging in Reflectance and Photo-induced Luminescence Modes: A User Manual (London 2013) |
| Eastaugh et al. 2004 | N. Eastaugh – V. Walsh – T. Chaplin – R. Siddall, The Pigment Compendium. A Dictionary of Historical Pigments (Amsterdam 2004) |
| Gordon 2017 | R. L. Gordon, Cosmic Order, Nature, and Personal Well-Being in the Roman Cult of Mithras, in: A. Hintze – A. Williams (eds.), Holy Wealth: Accounting for This World and The Next in Religious Belief and Practice. Festschrift John R. Hinnells (Wiesbaden 2017) 93–130 |
| Henke 2020 | F. Henke, Die Farbigkeit der antiken Skulptur. Die griechischen und lateinischen Schriftquellen zur Polychromie (Wiesbaden 2020) |
| Humer – Kremer 2011 | F. Humer – G. Kremer (eds.), Götterbilder – Menschenbilder. Religion und Kulte in Carnuntum, Katalog des NÖ Landesmuseums NF 498 (St. Pölten 2011) |
| Kopczynski et al. 2017 | N. Kopczynski – L. de Viguerie – E. Neri – N. Nasr – P. Walter – F. Bejaoui – F. Baratte, Polychromy in Africa Proconsularis: investigating Roman statues using X-ray fluorescence spectroscopy, Antiquity 9, 2017, 139–154, DOI: 10.15184/aqy.2016.250 (30.03.2023) |
| Kremer 2012 | G. Kremer, Götterdarstellungen, Kult- und Weihedenkmäler aus Carnuntum. Mit Beiträgen von C. Gugl, C. Uhlir, M. Unterwurzacher, CSIR Österreich, Carnuntum Suppl. 1 (Vienna 2012) |
| Kremer 2021 | G. Kremer, Carnuntum, Capital of Pannonia Superior: Votive Monuments and Sacral Topography, in: M. Rajčeva – M. Steskal (eds.), Roman Provincial Capitals under Transition. Proceedings of the International Conference Plovdiv 04.–07.11.2019, SoSchrÖAI (Vienna 2021) 407–422 |
| Kremer et al. 2018 | G. Kremer – I. Kitz – B. Moshammer – M. Heinrich – E. Draganits, Stone Monuments from Carnuntum and Surrounding Areas (Austria) – Petrological Characterization and Quarry Location in a Historical Context, in: D. Matetić Poljak – K. Marasović (eds.), ASMOSIA XI. Interdisciplinary Studies of Ancient Stone. Proceedings of the 11th International Conference of ASMOSIA Split, 19.–22.05.2015 (Split 2018) 557–565 |
| Kremer et al. 2021 | G. Kremer – S. Insulander – E. Draganits – M. Kronberger – B. Moshammer – M. Mosser – A. Rohatsch, Stone Supply for Carnuntum and Vindobona – Provenance Analysis in a Historico-Economical Context, in: D. van Limbergen – D. Taelman (eds.), The Exploitation of Raw Materials in the Roman World: A Closer Look at Producer-Resource Dynamics, Panel 4.4. Proceedings of the 19th International Congress of Classical Archaeology Cologne/Bonn, 22.–26.05.2018 (Heidelberg 2021) 47–62, DOI: 10.11588/propylaeum.706 (25.03.2023) |
| Kremer et al. 2022 | G. Kremer – R. Linke – G. Plattner – E. Pollhammer – R. Krickl – N. Silnović – V. Pitthard, Ein Löwenaufsatz mit polychromer Farbfassung aus Carnuntum, CarnuntumJb 2022 (2023) 43–54 |
| Kremer et al. 2023a | G. Kremer – R. Linke – G. Plattner – E. Pollhammer – M. Brzakovic – R. Krickl – N. Silnovic – V. Pitthard, Minerva in colours: First results on a polychrome Roman sculpture from Carnuntum (Pannonia), Heritage 6/7, 2023, 5213–5241, DOI: 10.3390/heritage6070277 (03.11.2023) |
| Kremer et al. 2023b | G. Kremer – R. Linke – G. Plattner – E. Pollhammer – R. Krickl – N. Silnović, Forschungen zur Polychromie römerzeitlicher Denkmäler in den Donauprovinzen, Acta Carnuntina 13/2, 2023, 4–19 |

| | |
|---|---|
| Lipps – Berthold 2021 | J. Lipps – C. Berthold, Zur Polychromie der Mannheimer Römersteine, in: J. Lipps – S. Ardeleanu – J. Osnabrügge – C. Witschel (eds.), Die römischen Steindenkmäler in den Reiss-Engelhorn-Museen Mannheim (Ubstadt-Weiher 2021) |
| Liverani – Santamaria 2014 | P. Liverani – U. Santamaria (eds.), Diversamente bianco: la policromia della scultura romana (Rome 2014) |
| lupa | F. und O. Harl, <lupa.at> (Bilddatenbank zu antiken Steindenkmälern) |
| Magrini et al. 2019 | D. Magrini – S. Bracci – G. Bartolozzi – R. Iannaccone – S. Lenzi – P. Liverani, Revealing Mithras' Color with the ICVBC Mobile Lab in the Museum, Heritage 2, 2019, 2160–2170, DOI: 10.3390/heritage2030130 (30.03.2023) |
| Neri et al. 2022 | E. Neri – M. Alfeld – N. Nasr – L. de Viguerie – P. Walter, Unveiling the paint stratigraphy and techniques of Roman African polychrome statues, Archaeological and Anthropological Sciences 14, 2022, 1–11, DOI: 10.1007/s12520-022-01586-3 (30.03.2023) |
| Østergaard 2017 | J. S. Østergaard, Colour shifts. On methodologies in research on the polychromy of Greek and Roman sculpture, ProcDanInstAth 8, 2017, 149–176 |
| Østergaard 2018 | J. S. Østergaard, Polychromy, sculptural, Greek and Roman, in: The Oxford Classical Dictionary, DOI: 10.1093/acrefore/9780199381135.013.8118 (05.10.2022) |
| Østergaard – Schwartz 2022 | J. S. Østergaard – A. Schwartz, A late archaic/early classical Greek relief with two hoplites (Ny Carlsberg Glyptothek IN 2787), JdI 137, 2022, 1–37 |
| Østergaard et al. 2014 | J. S. Østergaard – M. L. Sargent – R. H. Therkildsen, The polychromy of Roman ›ideal‹ marble sculpture of the $2^{nd}$ century CE, in: P. Liverani – U. Santamaria (eds.), Diversamente bianco. La policromia della scultura romana (Rome 2014) 51–69 |
| Platter et al., in prep. | G. Plattner – G. Kremer – R. Linke – E. Pollhammer – R. Krickl – V. Pitthard, Farbigkeit römischer Architektur in Carnuntum und im Wiener Becken – eine Spurensuche, in: Akten der Tagung »Colour Schemes and Surface Finish of the Roman Architectural Orders« Mainz 07.–09.11.2022 Mainz, in preparation |
| Reinhold 1970 | M. Reinhold, History of Purple as a Status Symbol in Antiquity (Brussels 1970) |
| Scheid 2007 | J. Scheid, Sacrifices for Gods and Ancestors, in: J. Rüpke (ed.), A Companion to Roman Religion (Oxford 2007) 263–271 |
| Vermaseren 1971 | M. J. Vermaseren, Mithriaca I. The Mithraeum at S. Maria Capua Vetere (Leiden 1971) |
| Weddle 2012 | C. Weddle, The Sensory Experience of Blood Sacrifice in the Roman Imperial Cult, in: J. Day (ed.), Making Senses of the Past. Toward a Sensory Archaeology (Carbondale 2012) 137–158 |

*Gabrielle Kremer, Austrian Archaeological Institute, Austrian Academy of Sciences, Dominikanerbastei 16, 1010 Vienna, Austria.*
*[e] gabrielle.kremer@oeaw.ac.at*

*Robert Linke, Federal Monuments Authority Austria, Arsenal, Objekt 15, Tor 4, 1030 Vienna, Austria.*
*[e] robert.linke@bda.gv.at*

*Georg Plattner, Kunsthistorisches Museum Vienna, Burgring 5, 1010 Vienna, Austria.*
*[e] georg.plattner@khm.at*

*Eduard Pollhammer, Office of the Lower Austrian Federal Government, Department of Art and Culture, Archaeological Park Carnuntum, Badgasse 42, 2405 Bad Deutsch-Altenburg, Austria.*
*[e] eduard.pollhammer@noel.gv.at*

*Marina Brzakovic, Office of the Lower Austrian Federal Government, Department of Art and Culture, Archaeological Park Carnuntum, Badgasse 42, 2405 Bad Deutsch-Altenburg, Austria.*
*[e] marina.brzakovic@noel.gv.at*

*Robert Krickl, Austrian Archaeological Institute, Austrian Academy of Sciences, Dominikanerbastei 16, 1010 Vienna, Austria.*
*[e] robert.krickl@oeaw.ac.at*

*Nirvana Silnović, Austrian Archaeological Institute, Austrian Academy of Sciences, Dominikanerbastei 16, 1010 Vienna, Austria.*
*[e] nirvana.silnovic@oeaw.ac.at*

Sébastien Laratte –
Véronique Brunet-Gaston (coordination) –
Christophe Gaston – Régis Bontrond – Céline Schneider –
Gilles Fronteau – Patrick Huard

# L'ARC DE MARS À REIMS: MODÈLE 3D ET SIG

**Abstract**

As part of a restoration project for the »Porte de Mars« in Reims, an archaeological intervention in several phases took place. The first phase consisted of an excavation at the foot of the building, covering its entire perimeter. The second phase was linked to the dismantling of the concrete roofing installed in the 19th century; this enabled the upper part of the building to be examined and the construction method used in the inner part of the piers to be determined. The last stage will allow the archaeological, architectural, stylistic and geological study of the building to be resumed, in particular to specify the method of construction of the monument and the stones used, to analyse its decoration and to highlight the various restorations already carried out. It also permits all the data acquired to be synthesised, first in a 3D model, and subsequently in a GIS containing all the information about the monument.

## INTRODUCTION

La »Porte de Mars« est l'un des monuments antiques les plus emblématiques de Reims (Marne), dans le nord-est de la France (fig. 1). Ce monument a été l'un des premiers à être labellisé monument historique dans le pays[1]. Construit dans le premier quart du IIIe siècle[2], cet arc monumental est le plus grand arc conservé en élévation dans le monde antique. C'est un arc à trois travées, de 32,25 m de long, 6,45 m de large et 12 m de haut aujourd'hui[3]. L'architrave et le pilier nord-ouest ont été entièrement restitués par l'architecte Narcisse Brunette au XIXe siècle[4]. La préservation de l'édifice est principalement due à son intégration dans les fortifications successives de la ville entre l'Antiquité et le XIXe siècle. Aujourd'hui, il est situé dans le centre-ville de Reims où il a retrouvé son isolement d'origine. À partir de 2016, le lancement d'une campagne de restauration de la Porte de Mars a nécessité une étude pluridisciplinaire associant l'archéologie, l'archéologie du bâti, les sciences de la terre et les restaurateurs.

Ainsi, plusieurs phases d'intervention archéologique ont eu lieu: la première a consisté en une fouille au pied du monument, sur tout son pourtour[5]. La deuxième phase s'est déroulée sous la forme d'un suivi de travaux de démontage de la couverture en ciment installée au XIXe siècle[6], afin d'observer le lit d'attente sommital des blocs et de préciser le mode de construction de la partie interne des piles. Pendant deux ans (entre 2016 et 2018), l'arc a été entouré d'échafaudages qui recouvraient l'ensemble du bâtiment et permettaient d'accéder aux parties supérieures de l'édifice (fig. 2). La description des blocs a pu être faite aisément grâce à l'exceptionnelle accessibilité aux parties hautes de ce dispositif d'échafaudage. Lors de la phase d'étude architecturale, une nacelle a dû être mise en œuvre.

---

[1] Anonyme 1993.
[2] Brunet-Gaston et al. 2020.
[3] Lefèvre et al. 1985.
[4] Reims Histoire-Archéologie 1986.
[5] Bontrond et al. 2015.
[6] Bontrond – Panouillot 2017.

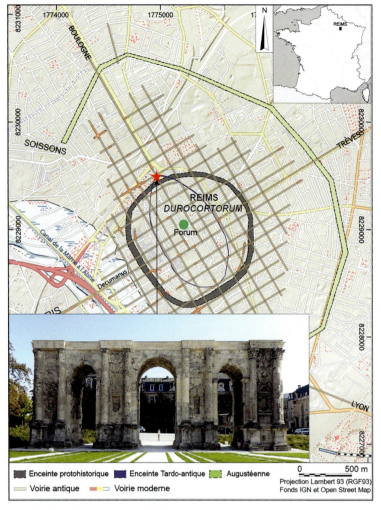

1 Carte de localisation de l'édifice et vue de la façade nord de la Porte de Mars (S. Laratte)

Le démontage de la structure métallique adossée à la maçonnerie a ensuite permis d'entamer le processus de modélisation 3D de l'édifice par photogrammétrie. Cette phase a commencé assez rapidement après la description de ses matériaux de construction. La construction étant isolée de toute autre construction, il était d'autant plus facile de produire un modèle numérique exhaustif. La dernière étape, qui consiste en la préparation de la publication (à sa juste valeur) de l'édifice, doit permettre de reprendre l'étude archéologique, architecturale, stylistique et géologique du bâti, afin notamment de préciser le mode constructif du monument, d'analyser son décor et de mettre en évidence les différentes restaurations déjà effectuées. Pour ce faire, il est rapidement apparu nécessaire de construire un support numérique utilisable par les différents acteurs de la chaîne de restauration, transdisciplinaire, impliquant une interopérabilité avec les outils spécifiques des conservateurs ou pouvant être utilisé pour la diffusion des connaissances scientifiques vers le grand public.

## LE BUT DE LA RECHERCHE PLURIDISCIPLINAIRE

Le développement, depuis le début des années 2000, des thèmes de recherche tirant parti d'outils informatiques de gestion de l'information spatialisée et l'augmentation constante des performances de traitement des ordinateurs et des capacités logicielles ont permis le développement d'études intégrées de bâtiment ou de sites à fortes valeurs patrimoniales[7]. Différents outils de traitement des données spatiales et de modélisation tridimensionnelle ont vu le jour. Il s'agit soit d'outils paramétriques comme le BIM (Building Information Modeling), soit d'outils sémantiques comme le SIG (Système d'Information Géographique). Ces outils nécessitent des niveaux d'expertise très différents: si les SIG – d'usages généralisés et disponibles gratuitement – peuvent être utilisés après une courte formation, les BIM sont généralement coûteux et très complexes, ce qui limite leur accessibilité au grand public. Notre choix de support s'est donc rapidement porté sur l'utilisation d'une plateforme SIG, utilisée depuis longtemps par de nombreux acteurs du domaine

---

[7] Canuti et al. 2004; Dore 2012; Historic England 2017; Bitelli et al. 2019; Granier et al. 2019.

afin d'intégrer des jeux de données résultant de l'étude d'un monument entier.

Le travail décrit ici a été réalisé dans le cadre d'une approche pluridisciplinaire intégrant un relevé photogrammétrique rapproché, une caractérisation des matériaux de construction et la description de leurs altérations. Enfin, la compilation des données collectées (géométriques, descriptives et analytiques) a été réalisée au sein d'une plateforme SIG, dont la conception logique était orientée pour constituer un support permettant de combiner les jeux de données issus de ces approches descriptives. L'intégration de ce travail dans le contexte plus large de la grande campagne de restauration de la Porte de Mars a mis à l'épreuve cette solution en facilitant son utilisation par des publics non spécialistes (fig. 3).

2  a) Échafaudages autour de l'arc, b) description géologique des blocs, c) relevés architecturaux (S. Laratte et V. Brunet-Gaston)

## LA RÉALISATION DU SUPPORT NUMÉRIQUE

En l'absence de support géométriquement fiable pour décrire le monument (relevé architectural, dessins …), il a fallu en construire un nouveau, les anciens relevés étant surinterprétés et les dimensions partiellement erronées. Il s'agit d'enregistrer des jeux de données spatiales (photographies, topographie, etc.) et de les transférer dans un support d'enregistrement numérique global. Afin de proposer des rendus en deux dimensions de la porte, il a été nécessaire de passer au préalable par l'acquisition d'un modèle tridimensionnel géométriquement fiable du monument (maquette 3D). Cette modélisation photogrammétrique a été réalisée par la société AGP, qui a produit un tel modèle par photogrammétrie aéroportée obtenue par drone. La société s'est chargée de réaliser les traitements permettant la réalisation de la maquette, puis l'extraction des divers rendus des façades grâce à l'extraction de photographies orthorectifiées. La résolution du modèle laissait à désirer par endroit, car de grands écarts de luminosité rendaient illisibles certaines niches; l'intérêt de cette méthode est qu'une couverture photographique détaillée a pu être rajoutée à ce premier document. Le marquage géographique des clichés et les points de contrôle relevés par Patrick Huard (topographe INRAP) ont permis d'une part la réalisation de la maquette numérique et d'autre part sa mise à l'échelle et la fiabilité géométrique des supports dérivés. La technique photogrammétrique consiste à effectuer des mesures automatisées par ordinateur dans une scène, en utilisant le décalage de parallaxe obtenu entre des images successives acquises selon des points de vue différents.

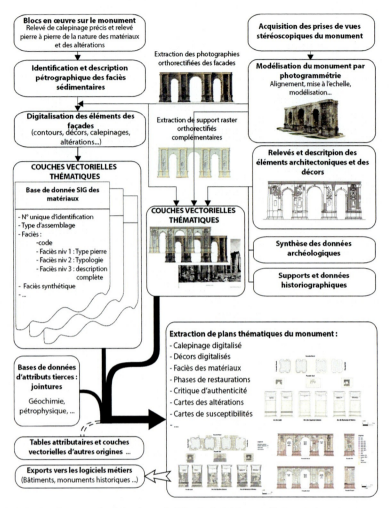

3   Synthèse méthodologique de l'étude du bâtiment (S. Laratte)

Correctement spatialisées, les maquettes 3D obtenues sont orientées conformément à leur modèle et les mesures qui y sont réalisées sont représentatives. Ces propriétés permettent alors l'extraction à partir de ce modèle 3D de rendus orthorectifiés ou ›développés‹ (traités géométriquement pour être utilisés à la manière d'une carte). Pour des voûtes, par exemple, cette méthode permet de compiler sur un même document un ensemble de structures issues de façades géométriquement opposées ou orthogonales (fig. 4).

Toutes les façades du monument sont extraites sous la forme de photographies orthorectifiées, dont l'échelle est doublement contrôlée. Le calage géographique de l'image finale est alors très bon avec une erreur inhérente à la méthode de quelques millimètres à l'échelle du monument. À ce stade, toutes les façades ainsi que les déroulés des intrados de voûtes sont extraits depuis le logiciel de modélisation photogrammétrique. Il en résulte un ensemble de photographies, à l'échelle, exemptes de déformations géométriques liées à la prise de vue et possédant des coordonnées spatiales en chacun de leurs points. QGIS a été choisi pour sa capacité à manipuler tous les types de données appelés à être utilisés dans l'étude, pour sa (très) relative facilité d'utilisation et surtout pour son interopérabilité. Cette dernière qualité est indispensable au vu de la diversité des compétences appelées à travailler transversalement et à la finalité du travail utilisé dans le cadre du projet de restauration par de nombreux corps de métiers.

Les données générées grâce à la modélisation photogrammétrique sont ensuite injectées dans un système de logiciel capable d'intégrer des données spatialisées de différentes natures et de croiser les unes avec les autres. Le logiciel QGis[8] combine des fonctionnalités de dessin assisté par ordinateur (DAO) avec une base de données spatiale et permet de travailler et d'exporter la plupart des fichiers SIG et DAO standard. Cette combinaison permet donc de hiérarchiser différemment les informations en fonction de leur origine, mais aussi en fonction de leur typologie géométrique. Ces solutions logiciels utilisées classiquement pour traiter des données cartographiques sont en effet capables de manipuler des fichiers de nature distincte (cartes, plans, photographies…) et des informations digitalisées ou calculées (sous formes vectorielles). Au-delà de la simple fonction de dessin assisté par ordinateur du logiciel, chaque couche intègre une base

---

[8]   QGIS Development Team 2018.

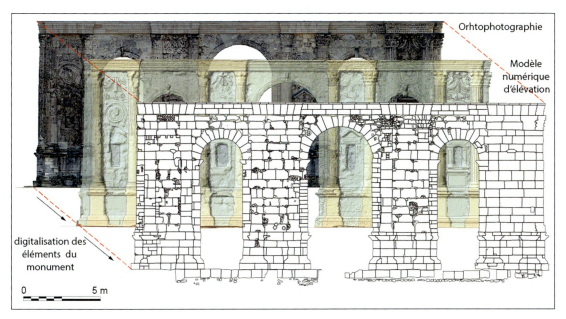

4   Orthophotographies, modèle numérique et digitalisation du monument (S. Laratte et al.)

de données relationnelle enrichissant chaque entité graphique avec une grande quantité d'informations. Les données sont donc structurées de manière très classique pour ce type de système, selon leur nature et selon leurs capacités à être mises en relation les unes avec les autres. La combinaison des informations contenues dans chaque couche et des couches entre elles permet de générer des ensembles de ›cartes‹ du monument, avec un focus spécifique au questionnement de l'utilisateur. L'intégration de toutes les informations collectées a été réalisée dans un environnement SIG.

## ÉTUDE DE CAS: L'ALTÉRATION DES PIERRES

L'étude des matériaux de construction a été réalisée lors d'une enquête de terrain par une équipe de l'université de Reims. Elle est incluse dans la thèse de doctorat portant sur les matériaux de construction antique de la ville de Sébastien Laratte[9]. Le travail sur les géomatériaux s'est donc déroulé en deux phases: la première phase a consisté en un relevé du calepinage réalisé sur le dessin de l'enveloppe du bâtiment. La seconde phase a consisté à l'association d'une identification systématique de la nature de chaque élément selon les canons de la sédimentologie de faciès (nature de la roche, texture, faciès, présence de macro- ou de microfossiles, origine …). Les caractérisations de chacun de ces éléments ont été réalisées sur la base d'une classification hiérarchisée à trois niveaux de complexité croissante, initialement conçue et utilisée pour la description des outils de macro-outillages de mouture en contexte archéologique[10]. Le recours à cette classification, outre sa diffusion antérieure, permettait d'exploiter avantageusement sa capacité intrinsèque à être synthétique, tout en permettant une grande précision de description. La présence d'échafaudages a permis d'identifier pierre par pierre toute la surface des façades, même dans les parties supérieures du bâtiment habituellement inaccessibles. Après le démontage de l'échafaudage, et afin de compléter la documentation de l'état actuel du monument, un diagnostic associé à une cartographie des altérations des pierres (fig. 5) a été réalisé sur la base des définitions du »glossaire illustré sur les formes d'altération de la pierre« de l'ICOMOS[11].

---

[9]  Laratte 2022.
[10] Boyer – Fronteau 2011; Buchsenschutz et al. 2020.
[11] Anson-Cartwright et al. 2008.

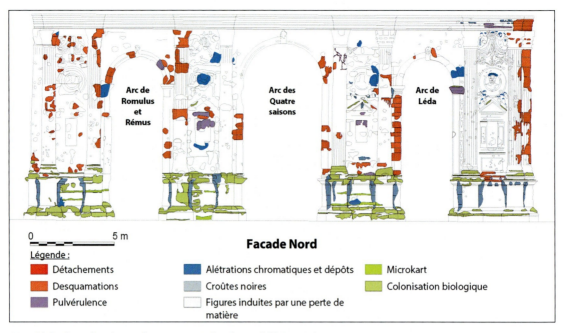

5   Altérations des pierres du monument, façade nord (S. Laratte)

Au laboratoire, chaque élément est digitalisé d'après l'orthophotographie, comparé au relevé *in situ*. Les descriptions sont intégrées dans la base de données associée à chaque élément. La base de données des géomatériaux, conçue pour offrir une lecture à plusieurs niveaux interrogeables indépendamment ou conjointement par l'intermédiaire de requêtes spécifiques, offre la possibilité d'être étendue avec des bases de données préexistantes grâce aux fonctionnalités de jointure entre tables attributaires de l'outil SIG. Cet appariement de données permet d'associer aux pierres du monument des données attributaires spécifiques à une typologie d'objet en particulier. Cette fonctionnalité permet plus spécifiquement de représenter des données spécifiques comme des résultats analytiques de composition (c.-à-d. géochimie) ou de caractérisation des propriétés des pierres (porosité, capillarité, etc.). La partie purement orientée vers la géologie comprend donc des critères d'identification des roches, comme la nature lithologique (calcaire, grès, pierre meulière …), puis le faciès synthétique (calcaires à *Ditrupa*, calcaire à Milioles …) et la description complète de la roche (fig. 6). Elle contient également des informations relatives à l'origine proposée pour chaque matériau en accord avec la vaste base documentaire sur les géomatériaux de construction de Reims et de sa région.

Pour les matériaux de construction, cette approche permet une documentation très précise du monument jusqu'aux plus petits composants. La structuration en couche distincte propre aux SIG autorise par ailleurs le croisement de plusieurs couches les unes avec les autres en fonction de leurs relations spatiales et attributaires avec notamment la possibilité d'interroger les altérations de la pierre en fonction du faciès des matériaux (ou d'autres attributs).

Cependant, il faut signaler quelques défauts, principalement liés à l'utilisation de supports orthorectifiés. Il est par exemple très difficile de s'intéresser aux murs situés dans le plan orthogonal au plan de l'orthophotographie (murs latéraux des dés de colonnes), à moins d'avoir recours à une multitude de supports spécifiquement générés et développant toutes les ›faces‹ appartenant aux façades du monument. De plus, alors que dans le document initial, la résolution estimée suffisante par le prestataire s'est également parfois révélée insuffisante, elle s'est révélée dans les faits trop faible pour permettre une lecture précise des éléments de décor des façades. La présence sur ces parois de croûtes minérales ou d'encrassement liées à la pollution urbaine a par ailleurs rendu ce besoin de précision impératif pour autoriser leur lecture.

Des points de vigilance se sont aussi dégagés au fur et à mesure de l'avancée du travail et en particulier lorsqu'il s'agissait de s'intéresser à des éléments communs à plusieurs façades (dans la couche matériaux ces éléments sont liés, constituant deux éléments graphiques pour une seule

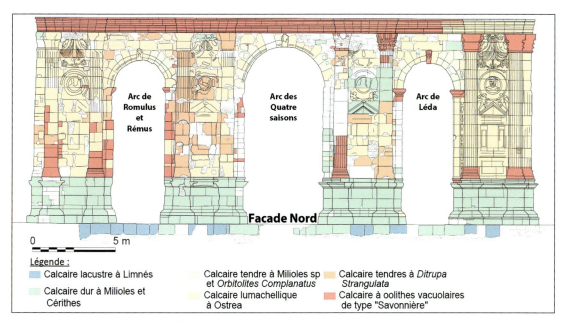

6   Faciès des pierres, exemple de la façade nord (S. Laratte)

entrée sur la base de données attributaire). L'attention portée à ces éléments en spécifique a été particulièrement utile afin de ne pas surestimer artificiellement les résultats de quantifications des usages des matériaux. Ce point permet de contrôler également la qualité des relevés, puisqu'un même élément devait impérativement posséder des caractéristiques identiques, quelle que soit la face du bloc envisagée.

Les documents de base et en particulier les orthophotos sont dérivés directement de la modélisation 3D. Cette étape de calcul peut introduire des artefacts et des aberrations qui, même mineurs, imposent des limites aux raisonnements géométriques.

L'exploitation des cartes thématiques de caractérisation pétrophysique des blocs montre une rationalisation de l'utilisation des pierres d'époque romaine en fonction de leurs capacités intrinsèques de transfert de l'eau. Les pierres les moins capillaires (correspondant par ailleurs à celles de plus grande densité apparente) constituaient l'ensemble des sous-sols de l'édifice. Puis les pierres utilisées dans les élévations ont été sélectionnées parmi les pierres moins denses, plus aptes à la sculpture, mais aussi au transfert de l'eau. L'ablation de la partie supérieure originale du bâtiment n'a pas permis de tirer des conclusions sur les matériaux d'origine de ces parties. Cependant, la présence de pierres calcaires à forte capillarité/faible capacité d'évaporation pour les chapiteaux des colonnes et les arcs semble être la règle pour les éléments conservés. Ensuite, les pierres utilisées dans les élévations ont été choisies parmi des pierres moins denses et beaucoup plus aptes au transfert de l'eau. Cette dernière caractéristique est secondaire puisque, de par leur position, elles ne sont, dans leur disposition originale, pas ou peu exposées aux intempéries et isolées de l'humidité du sol par les éléments du socle.

## ÉTUDE DE CAS: LES PHASES DE RESTAURATION DU MONUMENT

L'identification des matériaux de construction, qui s'est faite dans un premier temps par description directe des blocs en place, a permis d'illustrer la grande diversité des matériaux présents dans la construction. Les matériaux d'origine étaient de gros blocs calcaires quadrangulaires provenant des gisements de calcaire lutétien situés à 25 à 35 km au nord-est de la ville[12]. C'est donc un ensemble de cinq calcaires du lutétien moyen qui a été mis en œuvre au cours de la construction de

---

[12]   Fronteau et al. 2011; Fronteau et al. 2014; Laratte 2022.

7  Synthèse des phases de restauration du monument (S. Laratte et al.)

l'édifice, tandis qu'un panel beaucoup plus large de matériaux a été nécessaire aux restaurations et reconstructions réalisées sur le monument. Ces derniers, principalement issus d'affleurements proches de la ville (moins de 10 km), recouvrent l'ensemble du spectre des matériaux utilisés dans la construction de la ville au cours de son histoire. Les restaurations effectuées entre le début du XIXe siècle et les années 1920 ont en revanche été réalisées avec des matériaux beaucoup plus hétérogènes, comme on peut l'observer dans la cathédrale médiévale de Reims[13]. L'utilisation d'outils de géotraitement SIG, notamment des outils de comptage et de classification, ainsi que les fonctions de croisement de données, a donné accès à la quantification de ces matériaux. Cette projection a donc permis de déterminer que, à l'échelle du monument, les matériaux originels n'occupaient plus que 55 % des façades visibles. Cependant, dans les faits, il existe une grande hétérogénéité entre les différentes façades (entre 8 et 70 % des maçonneries d'origine). C'est en croisant les faciès décrits avec les études de matériaux menées sur des monuments contemporains dans la ville[14] et les sources historiographiques[15] que l'origine antique ou non des éléments de construction a été déterminé ainsi que les éventuels remplois de matériaux antiques dans des restaurations modernes. Seuls les éléments antiques ont été dessinés, après contrôle sur place, dans une nacelle (cf. fig. 2).

La mise en parallèle de la couche géomatériaux et de celle des neuf grandes phases de travaux de restauration réalisées depuis le XVIIIe siècle[16] permet de déduire quels blocs sont antiques. Il faut impérativement associer ces études avec l'analyse du calepinage et du projet architectural. En effet, certains blocs peuvent avoir un matériau antique, mais des traces d'outils modernes montrent une mise en œuvre récente. Des blocs antiques peuvent également avoir été remployés ou déplacés lors des restaurations (fig. 7). La discrimination de ces éléments permet donc de proposer d'une part une critique d'authenticité et d'autre part une carte des phases de restauration. Cette dernière permet également de déterminer des ›associations de matériaux‹ qui caractérisent des associations de faciès de restauration spécifiques à chacune des périodes de travaux sur le monument. Ces associations de faciès placent en parallèle les matériaux de construction et leurs modalités de mise en œuvre.

## LES MISES AU NET DES RELEVÉS ET LES INTERPRÉTATIONS DANS LE CADRE D'UNE ÉTUDE ARCHITECTURALE ET ICONOGRAPHIQUE

La phase finale de l'intégration de toutes les informations pluridisciplinaires collectées a été réalisée dans un même environnement SIG. À titre d'exemple, dans un dessin (fig. 8), où les données de QGis ont été réimportées dans Illustrator en vue de la publication: on peut voir un détail de l'élévation de la façade ouest de l'arche centrale; un personnage en pied, portant un manteau sur son bras droit, et un homme barbu, vraisemblablement agenouillé sur la droite.

C'est la capacité d'interopérabilité de la solution logiciel utilisée pour documenter et maintenir les données issues de l'étude de ce monument qui est ici mise à profit. Cet aspect en particulier permet d'extraire et de valoriser aisément les relevés, tout en conservant une forte contextualisation. La possibilité offerte d'exporter les données vers d'autres formats, souvent utilisés comme une norme dans certains corps de métiers, assure donc un bon potentiel de diffusion des informations produites et maintenues dans les bases de données spatialisées.

Nous ne pouvons hélas présenter plus sans déflorer la future publication de cet édifice majeure du monde antique.

---

[13] Turmel 2014; Turmel et al. 2014.
[14] Turmel 2014.
[15] Fronteau et al. 2011; Fronteau et al. 2014; Fronteau et al., à paraître.
[16] Eugène Architecte du Patrimoine 2018; Brunet-Gaston et al. 2020.

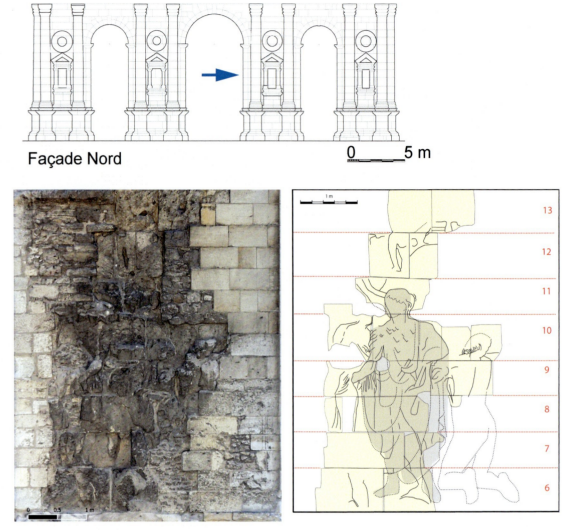

8  Planche pour la publication du panneau ouest de l'arche axiale (V. Brunet-Gaston)

## CONCLUSION

En conclusion, le processus mis en œuvre dans ce travail concerne la gestion et la représentation des données 3D à l'aide d'un outil logiciel fondamentalement dédié au traitement de données 2D. Cette méthode a servi de base fiable pour la création de cartographies thématiques enrichies de données pluridisciplinaires (historiques, archéologiques, architecturales et géologiques). Les jeux de données collectés au cours de cette étude ont été croisés en fonction des besoins des utilisateurs, afin de construire des cartes spécifiques permettant de répondre aux problématiques initiales de l'étude (nature des matériaux, authenticité, phases de restauration, décors et stylistiques …). L'avantage de cet outil réside dans sa relative facilité d'utilisation, en plus de son ouverture, car il est basé sur une architecture de logiciel libre. Cette ouverture repose à la fois sur les données qui gardent un caractère ouvert et éditable, mais aussi sur le logiciel, qui utilise des formats de données interopérables avec la plupart des solutions logiciels spécifiques aux métiers du bâtiment et de la restauration. Ce type de documentation constitue une base d'archive où peuvent être intégrées des informations relatives au monument (graphiques et numériques) et peut donc présenter une base de données patrimoniale dédiée à l'édifice. L'utilisation de la photogrammétrie comme support original permet également d'effectuer des acquisitions complémentaires sur certaines parties du bâtiment ou d'augmenter significativement la résolution sur ces zones, sans avoir à effectuer toutes les étapes de modélisation. De plus, elle ouvre la possibilité de documenter d'éventuelles modifications des façades du bâtiment consécutives à des travaux de restauration ou d'éventuelles dégradations.

Enfin, la géométrie très simple de la Porte de Mars se prête bien à l'utilisation de l'outil présenté, car elle ne comporte que de grandes façades avec de grandes baies couvertes par des voûtes. Le développement de telles surfaces sur les plans est alors aisé. Dans le cas d'un monument plus complexe, comme une église aux multiples murs courbes, un développement géométriquement fiable serait probablement beaucoup plus laborieux, tant du point de vue de l'acquisition photogrammétrique que de la construction du support SIG.

## BIBLIOGRAPHIE

Anonyme 1993 — Anonyme, Notice no°PA00078825, base Mérimée, ministère français de la Culture, 1993, <http://www2.culture.gouv.fr/public/mistral/merimee_fr?ACTION=CHERCHER&FIELD_1=REF&VALUE_1=PA00078825> (01.11.2021)

Anson-Cartwright et al. 2008 — T. Anson-Cartwright – V. Vergès-Belmin – E. Bourguignon – P. Bromblet – J. Cassar – A. E. Charola – E. De Witte – J. Delgado-Rodrigues – V. Fassina – B. Fitzner – L. Fortier – Others, Illustrated glossary on stone deterioration: Glossaire illustré sur les formes d'altération de la pierre, éd. par International Scientific Committee for Stone, Monuments and Sites 15 (Paris 2008)

Bitelli et al. 2019 — G. Bitelli – G. Gatta – A.-M. Guccini – A. Zaffagnini, GIS and Geomatics for archive documentation of an architectural project: The case of the big Arc of entrance to the Vittorio Emanuele II Gallery of Milan, by Giuseppe Mengoni (1877), Journal of Cultural Heritage 38, 2019, 204–212, DOI: 10.1016/j.culher.2019.01.002

Bontrond et al. 2015 — R. Bontrond – M. Guiot – A. Troublard – S. Vitzikam, Reims »Boulevard Désaubeau« Marne, Grand-Est (Alsace – Champagne-Ardennes – Lorraine) (Rapport de fouille SRA Champagne-Ardenne 2015)

Bontrond – Panouillot 2017 — R. Bontrond – B. Panouillot, Reims »Boulevard Désaubeau«, Marne, Grand Est (Alsace – Champagne-Ardenne – Lorraine) (rapport de fouille), Service archéologique, Reims Métropole, Grand Reims, décembre 2018

Boyer – Fronteau 2011 — F. Boyer – G. Fronteau, Les géomatériaux meuliers: de l'identification des sources géologiques à la définition de catégories de gisements, dans: O. Buchsenschutz – L. Jacottey – F. Jodry – J.-L. Blanchard (éds.), Evolution typologique et technique des meules du Néolithique à l'an mille, Rencontres Archéologiques de l'Archéosite Gaulois Rieux-Volvestre 2009 (Bordeaux 2011) 121–135

Brunet-Gaston et al. 2020 — V. Brunet-Gaston – R. Bontrond – C. Gaston – P. Huard – S. Laratte – G. Fronteau, L'arc monumental dit »la Porte de Mars« (Reims) (rapport de recherche), Service Archéologique du Grand Reims 2020

Buchsenschutz et al. 2020 — O. Buchsenschutz – G. Fronteau – S. Lepareux-Couturier (éds.), Les meules du Néolithique à l'époque médiévale: technique, culture, diffusion, RAE Suppl. (Dijon 2020), <http://books.openedition.org/artehis/2965> (09.09.2020)

Canuti et al. 2004 — P. Canuti – N. Casagli – R. Fanti – A. Iotti – E. Pecchioni – A. P. Santo, Rock weathering and failure of the »Tomba della Sirena« in the Etruscan necropolis of Sovana (Italy), Journal of Cultural Heritage 5/3, 2004, 323–330, DOI: 10.1016/j.culher.2003.11.001

Dore 2012 — C. Dore, Integration of HBIM and 3D GIS for Digital Heritage Modelling, 2012, <https://arrow.tudublin.ie/beschreccon/71/> (28.10.2022)

Fronteau et al. 2011 — G. Fronteau – A. Turmel – C. Thomachot-Schneider – J.-P. Deroin, Building material supply strategy in »Chalky Champagne« area (France): combined use of local raw materials and importations from surrounding regions, Geophysical Resaerch Abstracts 13, EGU General Assembly 2011 (Vienne 2011)

Fronteau et al. 2014 — G. Fronteau – A. Turmel – C. Pichard – B. Decrock – A. Devos – O. Lejeune – D. Ménival – L. Chalumeau – A. Combaud, Les approvisionnements en pierre de construction à Reims: des choix marqués par de fortes contraintes géologiques, géographiques et socio-économiques, dans: J. Lorenz – F. Blary – J.-P. Gély (dir.), Construire la ville. Histoire urbaine de la pierre à bâtir (Paris 2014) 235–250

| | |
|---|---|
| Fronteau et al., à paraitre | G. Fronteau – S. Laratte – A. Devos – C. Pichard, L'emploi antique des géomatériaux à Reims/Durocortorum, Gallia 79/1, 2023, à paraitre |
| Granier et al. 2019 | X. Granier – M. Chayani – V. Abergel – P. Benistant – L. Bergerot et al., Les recommandations du Consortium 3D SHS (rapport technique) CNRS; SHS (2019), <https://hal.archives-ouvertes.fr/hal-01683842> (23.03.2020) |
| Historic England 2017 | Historic England, Photogrammetric Applications for Cultural Heritage. Guidance for Good Practice (Swindon 2017), <https://historicengland.org.uk/images-books/publications/photogrammetric-applications-for-cultural-heritage/heag066-photogrammetric-applications-cultural-heritage/> (07.10.2020) |
| Laratte 2022 | S. Laratte, Les ressources en pierre de construction dans le bâti antique de Reims et leur utilisation, application à l'étude de la Porte de Mars (Thèse en préparation Université de Reims Champagne Ardenne 2022), <https://www.theses.fr/s223096> (19.09.2022) |
| Lefèvre et al. 1985 | F. Lefèvre – R. Legros – M. Ardhuin, La Porte Mars de Reims (Reims 1985), <https://www.bm-reims.fr/PATRIMOINE/doc/SYRACUSE/416674/la-porte-mars-de-reims> (07.02.2019) |
| QGIS Development Team 2018 | QGIS Development Team, Qgis3.14 QGIS Geographic Information System. Open Source Geospatial Foundation Project, <http://qgis.osgeo.or; http://qgis.osgeo.or.> (05.05.2023) |
| Reims Histoire-Archéologie 1986 | R. Neiss, Les arcs antiques de Reims, Reims histoire archéologie 1 (Reims 1986) |
| Turmel et al. 2014 | A. Turmel – G. Fronteau – C. Thomachot-Schneider – C. Moreau – L. Chalumeau – V. Barbin, Stone uses in Reims Cathedral: provenance, physical properties and restoration phases, Geological Society, London, Special Publications 391, 2014, 17–30 |
| Turmel 2014 | A. Turmel, Répartition et utilisation des pierres et géomatériaux de construction dans le bâti du Pays rémois – analyse spatiale et propriétés pétrophysiques (Thèse de doctorat Université de Reims Champagne Ardenne 2014), DOI: 10.1144/sp391.7 |
| Eugène Architecte du Patrimoine 2018 | Colletif, »La Porte de Mars« de Reims, Notice technique, Eugène Architecte du Patrimoine, Paris 2018 |

*Véronique Brunet-Gaston, INRAP, IRAA, 10 rue lavoisier, 25000 Besançon, France.*
*[e] veronique.brunet-gaston@inrap.fr*

*Sébastien Laratte, GEGENAA, 2, Esplanade Roland Garros, 51100 Reims, France.*
*[e] sebastien.laratte@univ-reims.com*

*Christophe Gaston, INRAP, 10 rue lavoisier, 25000 Besançon, France.*
*[e] christophe.gaston@inrap.fr*

*Régis Bontrond, SAGR, Rue du Val Claire, 51100 Reims, France.*
*[e] Regis.BONTROND@grandreims.fr*

*Céline Schneider, GEGENAA, 2, Esplanade Roland Garros, 51100 Reims, France.*
*[e] celine.schneider@univ-reims.fr*

*Gilles Fronteau, GEGENAA, 2, Esplanade Roland Garros, 51100 Reims, France.*
*[e] gilles.fronteau@univ-reims.fr*

*Patrick Huard, INRAP, 28 rue Robert Fulton, 51100 Reims, France.*
*[e] patrick.huard@inrap.fr*

Alexandra S. Rodler-Rørbo – Barbara Tober

# COLORFUL WALLS OF *NORICUM*

## MINERAL PIGMENT CHARACTERIZATION FOR PROVENANCE EVALUATION

**Abstract**

This work uses portable energy dispersive X-ray fluorescence spectroscopy (pXRF) and powder X-ray Diffraction (PXRD) for characterizing mineral pigments of 1st to 3rd century AD. Roman wall paintings from several sites of the peripheral province *Noricum*. The pigments red and yellow ochre, green earth, Egyptian blue, and cinnabar were widely used, and two of the analyzed wall painting fragments were painted with red lead. This work was part of a larger investigation into trade of pigments and exploitation of local resources after *Noricum* became part of the Roman Empire. This work contributes to better understanding ancient networks of colorant production and trade and how they changed over time.

## INTRODUCTION

Most of today's Austria was part of the celtic *Regnum Noricum*, which maintained trade relations with the Roman Empire since the 2nd century BC and became part of the Roman Empire in ca. 15 BC. As trade flourished, the area was quickly romanized and this is reflected by, e.g., surviving wall paintings of high proficiency in painting and plastering technique and utilizing precious and rare pigments[1].

Mineral pigments have been used in various contexts and for a wide range of decorative purposes. The pigments that were typically used in Roman contexts include the naturally occurring red and yellow ochre, green earth, and cinnabar as well as the human-made orange pigment minium, a lead oxide that was produced by heating the mineral hydrocerussite, and Egyptian blue, that was produced by fusing calcite, quartz, and a copper compound at high temperatures[2]. While the use of cinnabar in wall paintings is usually difficult to evaluate through visual examination alone[3], Egyptian blue is easily recognized and was widely used for Roman wall paintings. In *Noricum*, this included large-scale applications and smaller surfaces, and it was often combined with a range of other pigments[4].

The geochemical provenance analysis of ancient mineral pigments recently added to the discussion of colorant trade networks[5]. Material choice might hint at local customs or enable discussing cultural, economic, or political changes[6]. A pre-selection of suitable samples by pXRF is important for pigment provenance analysis; specific element compositions, albeit semi-quantitative, and specific element ratios can support this.

Here, wall painting fragments from several Roman sites in Austria were investigated using pXRF and for selected samples using PXRD analysis. The aim was to chemically and mineralogically characterize the ancient color palette in the peripheral province *Noricum* and to select suitable samples for pigment provenance research.

---

[1] Kenner – Praschniker 1947; Kenner 1950; Gostenčnik 2001; Dörfler 2009; Tober 2014; Tober 2017.
[2] E.g. Pradell et al. 2006; Grifa et al. 2016.
[3] E.g. Tober 2013.
[4] E.g. Béarat et al. 1997; Tober 2015; Linke et al. 2017.
[5] E.g. Rodler et al. 2017.
[6] E.g. Curley et al. 2020; D'Imporzano et al. 2021.

## MATERIALS AND METHODS

### Roman sites and analyzed wall painting fragments

A total of 661 wall painting fragments with blue, red, yellow, green, and orange paint were analyzed for the Roman sites that are briefly described below. An overview of pigments is listed in table 1. Several publications focus on wall painting fragments (see below), however, traces of paint were also documented for reliefs, portraits and funerary structures from *Noricum*[7].

In the mid-1st century BC, a Roman forum was founded in the Celtic *Regnum Noricum* on the hill Magdalensberg in Carinthia, Austria (close to *Virunum*, fig. 1). This was the political, administrative, and economic center of *Noricum*. Colorful wall decorations, resembling the styles known from *Pompeii*, were described by, e.g., H. Kenner[8] and K. Gostenčnik[9].

*Virunum* was in today's Zollfeld valley on the foot of the hill Magdalensberg. *Noricum* was elevated to a Roman province under the emperor Claudius in the mid-1st century AD and *Virunum* served as the capital and seat of the provincial governor (*procurator Augusti provinciae Norici*) until the second half of the 2nd century AD. A wide range of wall paintings has been described from this site[10]; all analyzed fragments have been consolidated during previous conservation work.

*Teurnia* was established in the mid-1st century AD near Lake Millstatt in western Carinthia. The first living units of Roman terrace houses were most likely finalized in AD 66. Another major building phase was between AD 141–161. The buildings were probably abandoned after a fire and latest by the 3rd century AD (Severan coins ca. AD 193–235[11]; cf. Aurelian coins ca. AD 270–275[12]).

*Iuvavum* (today's Salzburg) was founded in the 1st century AD and had its apogee in the mid-2nd to 3rd centuries AD. Most wall painting fragments were excavated in the city centre of Salzburg in 1999–2001. The Roman structures were found underneath significant urban development of the first and second inner courtyard and the middle wing of the »Neue Residenz« and are dated to the 2nd–3rd centuries AD. These structures were interpreted as workshops as well as prestigious houses with wall paintings (up to six layers)[13].

*Flavia Solva* (today's Wagna) was founded in south-eastern Styria in AD 70, connected settlements of the Early Imperial period within and beyond the south-eastern Alps and was important for culturally and economically integrating *Noricum* into the Roman Empire[14]. *Flavia Solva* was part of a far-reaching trade network and various commodities were locally produced[15]. This site flourished in the 2nd century and again in the mid-3rd century AD until it was abandoned in the early 5th century[16]. However, the forum has not been located and there was no water transportation system or canalization.

*Lauriacum* (today's Enns) – situated southwest of the mouth of the river Enns – was located at trading routes along the Danube, to the Barbaricum in the north and to the Adriatic harbour *Aquileia*. In the late 2nd century AD, the *legio II Italica* established the only legionary fortress of the Danube Limes in *Noricum*. A monumental building inscription of this fortress is dated to AD 200–202. In addition to the *praefectus legionis*, the »Notitia Dignitatum« mentions a *praefectus classis Lauriacensis*, commander of a part of the Danube fleet[17]. In the first half of the 2nd century AD,

---

[7] E.g. Kremer 2001, 125. 164. 374.
[8] Kenner 1950.
[9] Gostenčnik 2001.
[10] E.g. Kenner – Praschniker 1947; Dörfler 2009.
[11] Gugl 2000.
[12] Glaser 2002.
[13] Kovacsovics 2001; Kovacsovics 2003; Tober 2014.
[14] Hinker 2010.
[15] Radbauer 2010; Glöckner 2010; Gostenčnik 2010.
[16] Csapláros – Sosztarits 2010.
[17] Ubl 1997; Ubl 2006a; Ubl 2006b.

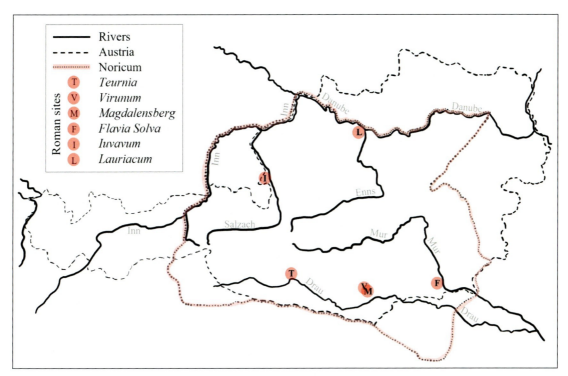

1  Map of Roman *Noricum* and present-day Austria (red and black dotline, resp.); the sites of this study are marked with red points (clockwise: *Lauriacum*, *Flavia Solva*, *Virunum*, Magdalensberg, *Teurnia*, *Iuvavum*) (A. S. Rodler-Rørbo)

the civilian settlement flourished, however, it is not certain if it was raised to a *municipium*. A specialist portrait workshop was located in *Lauriacum*[18].

## Semi-quantitative element analysis by pXRF

The paint layers of wall fragments were investigated with a pXRF spectrometer (Olympus InnovX Delta Premium 6000 with a Rh anode, 8-40 keV, Si-drift detector, 4W X-ray tube, current of 5-200 µA). This instrument was routinely calibrated with the supplied »Cal Check (standardization) Coupon« (316 stainless steel alloy) and a default element analysis at both 10 and 40 keV was used for a total of 120 s. The integrated Compton Normalization algorithm allows achieving low Limits of Detection and an accuracy of 2–3 %.

## Phase characterization by PXRD

Selected samples of blue and red paint with high Cu and Hg concentrations, respectively, were collected with a scalpel and ground to fine powders. Powder aliquots were placed on low-background holders suitable for very small samples (<50 mg) for analysis by PXRD using a D8-Advance Eco system (Bruker), equipped with a theta-theta goniometer, sample spinner, and LynxEye XE-T position-sensitive detector. CuKα radiation was used at 40 kV and 25 mA, using a primary Ni-filter, a fixed divergence slit (0.6°), and 2.3° primary and secondary soller slits. Measurements were performed from 5–75 °2θ, at increments of ca. 0.01°2θ. Naturally occurring quartz in the samples was used as an internal standard for calibrating the diffraction angles. The software EVA (Bruker) was used to match the analyzed patterns to known mineral phases for relative quantification by Rietveld refinement with TOPAS V4.0 (Bruker).

---

[18] Kremer 2001, 334, and references therein.

Table 1    Analyzed Roman wall painting fragments

| Site | Egyptian blue | Green earth | Yellow ochre | Red ochre | Cinnabar | Red lead |
|---|---|---|---|---|---|---|
| Magdalensberg | 28 | | 1 | 3 | 31 | 1 |
| *Virunum* | 13 | | | 3 | 3 | |
| *Teurnia* | 216 | 2 | 8 | 30 | 11 | |
| *Iuvavum* | 56 | 10 | 11 | 27 | 8 | |
| *Flavia Solva* | 93 | 7 | 17 | 27 | 50 | 1 |
| *Lauriacum* | 4 | 9 | 5 | 6 | 2 | |

Table 2    List of element concentrations for pigment characterization by pXRF

| | n | Fe (%) | Hg (%) | S (%) | Pb (%) | K (%) | Si (%) | Cu (%) |
|---|---|---|---|---|---|---|---|---|
| Egyptian blue | 411 | ~1.2 | ~0.02 | ~0.3 | ~0.1 | ~0.3 | ~11.3 | ~2.95 |
| | | (nd–6.8) | (nd–1.5) | (0.01–4.1) | (0.01–15.0) | (0.01–2.9) | (1.0–22.0) | (0.5–7.9) |
| Green earth | 28 | ~3.4 | ~0.01 | ~0.3 | ~0.03 | ~1.1 | ~6.3 | ~0.07 |
| | | (0.16–8.0) | (nd–0.07) | (0.01–2.5) | (0.01–0.2) | (0.1–2.4) | (1.4–12.8) | (0.01–0.6) |
| Yellow ochre | 42 | ~5.0 | – | ~0.3 | ~0.02 | ~0.2 | ~4.6 | ~0.01 |
| | | (0.6–12.9) | (nd–0.01) | (0.02–1.7) | (0.01–0.2) | (0.04–0.7) | (1.6–9.2) | (0.01–0.03) |
| Red ochre | 96 | ~5.3 | ~0.03 | ~0.4 | ~0.09 | ~0.1 | ~3.1 | ~0.01 |
| | | (0.5–18.6) | (nd–0.5) | (0.01–2.5) | (0.01–1.9) | (0.01–1.0) | (0.7–8.7) | (0.01–0.1) |
| Cinnabar | 105 | ~1.3 | ~5.9 | ~6.7 | ~0.9 | ~0.07 | ~2.7 | ~0.07 |
| | | (nd–7.7) | (1.1–21.3) | (1.4–12.4) | (0.01–9.7) | (0.01–0.3) | (1.4–8.8) | (nd–0.7) |
| Red lead | 2 | ~1.3 | – | ~8.4 | ~6.5 | – | ~2.7 | ~0.01 |
| | | (0.3, 2.2) | (nd–1.9) | (6.9, 9.8) | (5.7, 7.3) | (nd–0.05) | (2.5, 3.1) | (0.01, 0.01) |

Notes: Average element concentrations and ranges (in brackets); n = number of analyses, here: number of wall painting fragments; nd = not detected

Table 3    Pigment powders analyzed by PXRD

| | *Flavia Solva* | | | | *Teurnia* | | | | | | | | | *Virunum* | *Iuvavum* |
|---|---|---|---|---|---|---|---|---|---|---|---|---|---|---|---|
| Sample ID | FLS-052 | FLS-094 | FLS-111 | FLS-207 | TEU-060 | TEU-184 | TEU-222 | TEU-074 | TEU-075 | TEU-076 | TEU-077 | TEU-089 | TEU-093 | VIR-007 | IUV-001 |
| | Blue | Blue | Blue | Red | Blue | Blue | Blue | Red | Red | Red | Red | Red | Red | Blue | Red |
| GOF | 2.75 | 1.34 | 3.32 | | 2.61 | 1.29 | 1.79 | | | | | | | 1.65 | |
| Phases (%) | | | | | | | | | | | | | | | |
| Quartz | | | | 9.64 | | | | 2.51 | 0.30 | 3.67 | | 0.88 | 2.55 | | 4.21 |
| α-Quartz | 13.20 | 8.67 | 22.43 | | 14.50 | 15.59 | 24.70 | | | | | | | 6.25 | |
| Calcite | 41.30 | 41.73 | 46.54 | 32.26 | 49.10 | 46.58 | 21.80 | 51.81 | 57.97 | 32.88 | 40.39 | 58.08 | 30.73 | 57.56 | 60.64 |
| Cuprorivaite | 34.80 | 26.33 | 23.58 | | 27.50 | 23.21 | 31.78 | | | | | | | 20.62 | |
| Albite | 3.00 | 8.03 | 4.47 | | 1.60 | 5.93 | 6.46 | | | | | | | | |
| Aragonite | 4.40 | 15.24 | 1.80 | | | 6.78 | 4.64 | | | | | | | 15.57 | |
| Cristobalite | | | 1.18 | | 2.85 | | | | | | | | | | |
| Muscovite | | | | 2.29 | | 1.92 | | | | | | | | | |
| Microcline | | | | | 4.40 | | 6.56 | | | | | | | | |
| Wollastonite | | | | | | | 4.04 | | | | | | | | |
| Feldspar | 3.30 | | | | | | | | | | | | | | |
| Cinnabar | | | | 51.70 | | | | 42.56 | 39.26 | 61.42 | 59.61 | 38.72 | 64.52 | | 32.56 |
| Dolomite | | | | 3.18 | | | | 3.11 | 2.56 | 1.70 | | 2.31 | 2.20 | | 1.47 |
| Hematite | | | | 0.36 | | | | | | 0.32 | | | | | 0.27 |
| Kaolinite | | | | 0.56 | | | | | | | | | | | 0.84 |

Notes: GOF = goodness of fit; empty = phase not detected

## RESULTS

Wall painting fragments with red and yellow ochre had characteristically high iron concentrations (Fe ~5 %), while green earth was relatively high in potassium (K ~1 %), and cinnabar in mercury (Hg ~6 %) and sulfur (S ~7 %) (tab. 2). However, Hg concentrations of cinnabar samples ranged from 1–21 % while their Fe concentrations were often in the range of red ochre. Similar to this, wall paintings with Egyptian blue had a wide range of Cu concentrations (up to 8 %), with an average of ~3 % and frequently paired with high Fe concentrations comparable to ochre. Most fragments with Egyptian blue paint were from *Teurnia*, while the number of fragments with cinnabar was relatively high for *Flavia Solva* and Magdalensberg (tab. 1). Two red samples were identified as minium due to relatively high Pb concentrations (~7 %): one from *Flavia Solva* and one from Magdalensberg. Of the samples screened by pXRF, a few were also analyzed by PXRD (tab. 3). This selection included blue paint, where the main phases were cuprorivaite (~20–35 %), followed by calcite (~22–58 %), the low temperature/low pressure modifications of $SiO_2$ (α-quartz ~6–25 %), and relics of high temperature modifications of $SiO_2$ (e.g. cristobalite) and wollastonite ($CaSiO_3$). One blue sample included feldspar. The analyzed red paint layers had cinnabar (~32–65 %) and calcite (~30–60 %) as the two main phases. Minor contributions of quartz and dolomite were detected in most samples, in some also muscovite, hematite, and kaolinite.

## DISCUSSION

The quantity of objects that can be analyzed by pXRF and the speed at which the semi-quantitative elemental composition is available is a tremendous advantage when screening hundreds of boxes of wall painting fragments for subsequent element and isotope analysis for pigment provenance research. While a visual examination is the first approach for a fast evaluation, pXRF analysis has proven very useful[19], specifically in order to separate various reds into the pigments red ochre, cinnabar and red lead. Relatively high Fe, Hg and S, or Pb concentrations, respectively, are thus key for seeing more than just another red hue. Moreover, ratios such as Fe : Pb or Fe : Hg can hint at pigment mixtures[20] of red ochre and red lead or red ochre and cinnabar, respectively. When deciding which samples to select for further analysis, least mixed samples would enable a more straightforward provenance interpretation[21]. A recent example of a quantitative pigment mixture evaluation by pXRF[22] is promising. However, this still must be tested further and, as pointed out by the vast literature on pXRF[23], the results are semi-quantitative and cannot be easily used to discuss element concentrations between samples, sites, or periods.

Of the wall painting fragments that were selected for further analysis, several were also analyzed by pXRD, in order to confirm the pigment type characterization by pXRF. Even though the pigment composition varied between the different samples, all samples initially selected as Egyptian blue and cinnabar paint were confirmed by pXRD (tab. 3). All Egyptian blue samples had the calcium-copper phyllosilicate cuprorivaite as the main phase, which is the naturally occurring mineral counterpart to the human-made mineral commonly referred to as Egyptian blue. Also, calcite was identified, which was perhaps part of the mixture for preparing the paint and/or the binder. Furthermore, the low temperature/low pressure modification of $SiO_2$ (α-quartz) as well as other relics of high temperature modifications of $SiO_2$ (such as cristobalite) and wollastonite ($CaSiO_3$) were identified, consistent with recent Egyptian blue experiments of T. Pradell et al.[24]. While the cinnabar paint samples contained quartz and dolomite as well as muscovite, hematite,

---

[19] Beeston – Becker 2013.
[20] Fontana et al. 2014.
[21] Rodler et al. 2021.
[22] Fontana et al. 2014.
[23] E.g. Vandenabeele – Donais 2016.
[24] Pradell et al. 2006.

and kaolinite, the main phases were calcite and cinnabar. This also hints at mixing during paint preparation, calcite-rich layers underneath the cinnabar paint and/or as component of the binder. Even though cinnabar samples with high Fe concentrations were not selected for PXRD analysis, hematite was detected in traces for some of the analyzed samples.

This work is part of a larger investigation that sought to reveal cultural changes in *Noricum* after it became part of the Roman Empire, by analyzing mineral pigment processing and material provenance. As A. N. Curley et al.[25] recently highlighted, introducing new materials as paint eventually led to using locally available resources. Hence, while this work builds on the vast literature on archaeological and art historical aspects of Roman wall paintings in *Noricum*[26], this work used fast elemental analysis by pXRF and mineralogical characterization of a few fragments to select suitable samples for pigment provenance research. The aim was to test where resources came from, what trade contacts might have existed and how they changed over time. Such questions can be addressed by differences in the mineralogy and elemental composition of pigments, and through variation in isotope ratios of certain elements. For example, the presence of feldspar for one of the Egyptian blue samples might hint at a specific composition of the starting material such as beach sand[27]. However, feldspar is contained in many silicate sands and this sample was found in *Flavia Solva,* which was part of a far-reaching trade network and where a wide range of commodities were imported as well as locally produced[28]. It is possible that either finished pigments or resources for making Egyptian blue were imported from elsewhere. Following the results of this work, trace element and Pb-isotope analysis can then potentially exclude least likely copper sources and possibly hint at material recycling. Moreover, element and isotope data of Egyptian blue samples and locally available sands might enable testing a local provenance hypothesis further. In combination, this can elucidate the origin and exploitation of resources, production processes, and trade contacts that existed in the period during which materials such as pigments were manufactured.

## CONCLUSIONS

The elemental evaluation by pXRF of Roman wall paintings is a useful step in selecting suitable samples for further analysis. The pigments red and yellow ochre, green earth, and Egyptian blue were widely used as paint and for decorative patterns. Cinnabar was also used as paint, sometimes mixed with red ochre, and two wall painting fragments had red lead as paint. The use of Egyptian blue and cinnabar were also confirmed by PXRD for a few selected samples. This approach was useful for a fast and reliable sample evaluation for further geochemical analysis of pigment processing and material provenance. The aim was to investigate changes in trade and production of pigments over time that were used for wall paintings in *Noricum*.

## ACKNOWLEDGEMENTS

A. Rodler-Rørbo is grateful for the support of F. Glaser, H. Dolenz and D. Ebner-Baur, Landesmuseum Kärnten, R. Harreither, Museum Lauriacum, H. Wendling and U. Hampel, Salzburg Museum, B. Porod, Universalmuseum Joanneum, C. Lengauer, University of Vienna, and S. Ladstätter and P. Fragnoli of the Austrian Archaeological Institute of the Austrian Academy of Sciences. The project that generated the data for this work has received funding from the European Union's Horizon 2020 research and innovation programme under the Marie Skłodowska-Curie grant agreement No 845075.

---

[25] Curley et al. 2020.
[26] E.g. Dörfler 2009; Tober 2014; Tober 2017.
[27] Dariz – Schmid 2021.
[28] Radbauer 2010; Glöckner 2010; Gostenčnik 2010.

# BIBLIOGRAPHY

Béarat et al. 1997     H. Béarat – M. Fuchs – M.Maggetti, in: H. Béarat – M. Fuchs – M. Maggetti – D. Paunier (eds.), Roman wall painting. Materials, techniques, analysis and conservation. Proceedings of the international workshop Fribourg 07.–09.03.1996 (Fribourg 1997)

Beeston – Becker 2013     R. F. Beeston – H. Becker, Investigation of ancient Roman pigments by portable X-ray fluorescence spectroscopy and polarized light microscopy, ACS Symposium Series 1147, 2013, 19–41, DOI: 10.1021/bk-2013-1147.ch002

Csapláros – Sosztarits 2010     A. Csapláros – O. Sosztarits, Colonia Claudia Savaria – Die Topografie der ältesten Stadt von Pannonien, in: Porod 2010, 72–79

Curley et al. 2020     A. N. Curley – A. M. Thibodeau – E. Kaplan – E. Howe – E. Pearlstein – J. Levinson, Isotopic composition of lead white pigments on qeros: implications for the chronology and production of Andean ritual drinking vessels during the colonial era, Heritage Science 8, 2020, DOI: 10.1186/s40494-020-00408-w

D'Imporzano et al. 2021     P. D'Imporzano – K. Keune – J. M. Koornneef – E. Hermens – P. Noble – A. L. S. Vandivere – G. R. Davies, Time-dependent variation of lead isotopes of lead white in $17^{th}$ century Dutch paintings, Science Advances 7, 2021, DOI: 10.1126/sciadv.abi5905

Dariz – Schmid 2021     P. Dariz – T. Schmid, Trace compounds in Early Medieval Egyptian blue carry information on provenance, manufacture, application, and ageing, Scientific reports 11, 2021, DOI: 10.1038/s41598-021-90759-6

Dörfler 2009     I. Dörfler, Die römischen Wandmalereien der Wohnterrassen von Teurnia, RÖ 32, 2009, 17–77

Fontana et al. 2014     D. Fontana – M. F. Alberghina – R. Barraco – S. Basile – L. Tranchina – M. Brai – A. Gueli – S. O. Troja, Historical pigments characterisation by quantitative X-ray Fluorescence, Journal of Cultural Heritage 15/3, 2014, 266–274, DOI: 10.1016/j.culher.2013.07.001

Glaser 2002     F. Glaser, Teurnia, in: M. Šašel Kos – P. Scherrer (eds.), The autonomous towns of Noricum and Pannonia, Situla 40 (Ljubljana 2002) 135–147

Glöckner 2010     G. Glöckner, Glas in Flavia Solva, in: Porod 2010, 48–55

Gostenčnik 2001     K. Gostenčnik, Frühtiberische Wandmalereien vom »Plateaubau« auf dem Magdalensberg, Rudolfinum. Jahrbuch des Landesmuseums für Kärnten 2001 (2002) 175–178

Gostenčnik 2010     K. Gostenčnik, Antikes Wirtschaftsleben in Flavia Solva, in: Porod 2010, 56–65

Grifa et al. 2016     C. Grifa – L. Cavassa – A. De Bonis – C. Germinario – V. Guarino – F. Izzo – I. Kakoulli – A. Langella – M. Mercurio – V. Morra, Beyond Vetruvius: new insights in the technology of Egyptian blue and green frits, Journal of the American Ceramic Society 99, 2016, 3467–3475, DOI: 10.1111/jace.14370

Gugl 2000     C. Gugl, Archäologische Forschungen in Teurnia. Die Ausgrabungen in den Wohnterrassen 1971–1978. Die latènezeitlichen Funde vom Holzer Berg, SoSchrÖAI 33 (Vienna 2000)

Hinker 2010     C. Hinker, Solva vor den Flaviern. Zur Gründung von Flavia Solva, in: Porod 2010, 8–15

Kenner 1950     H. Kenner, Die antike römische Wandmalerei in Kärnten, Carinthia 140, 1950, 150–171

Kenner – Praschniker 1947     H. Kenner – C. Praschniker, Der Bäderbezirk von Virunum (Vienna 1947)

Kremer 2001     G. Kremer, Antike Grabbauten in Noricum. Katalog und Auswertung von Werkstücken als Beitrag zur Rekonstruktion und Typologie, SoSchrÖAI 36 (Vienna 2001)

Kovacsovics 2001     K. Kovacsovics, FÖ 40, 2001, 672 s. v. Bundesdenkmalamt 2002

Kovacsovics 2003     W. K. Kovacsovics, Die archäologischen Untersuchungen in ersten Innenhof der Neuen Residenz, in: E. Marx – P. Laub (eds.), Die Neue Residenz in Salzburg. Vom »Palazzo Nuovo« zum Salzburg Museum, JSM 47–48, 2003, 113–132

Linke et al. 2017     R. Linke – F. Pintér – M. Santner – A. Sagmeister – V. Pitthard – M. Griesser – S. Barfuss, Werktechnik der Wand- und Deckenmalereien aus dem »Haus der Medusa« – Materialwissenschaftliche Untersuchungen, in: M. Santner (ed.), Das Haus der Medusa – Römische Wandmalereien in Enns, Fokus Denkmal 8 (Vienna 2017) 187–207

Porod 2010     B. Porod (ed.), Flavia Solva. Ein Lesebuch (Graz 2010)

| | |
|---|---|
| Pradell et al. 2006 | T. Pradell – N. Salvado – G. D. Hatton – M. S. Tite, Physical processes involved in production of the ancient pigment, Egyptian blue, Journal of the American Ceramic Society 89, 2006, 1426–1432, DOI: 10.1111/j.1551-2916.2005.00904.x |
| Radbauer 2010 | S. Radbauer, Die römerzeitliche Keramik von Flavia Solva, in: Porod 2010, 40–47 |
| Rodler et al. 2017 | A. S. Rodler – G. Artioli – S. Klein – P. Fink-Jensen – C. Brøns, Provenancing ancient pigments: lead isotope analyses of the copper compound of Egyptian blue pigments from ancient Mediterranean artefacts, JASREP 16, 2017, 1–18, DOI: 10.1016/j.jasrep.2017.09.008 |
| Rodler et al. 2021 | A. S. Rodler – S. M. Matthys – C. Brøns – G. Artioli – C. Snoeck – V. Debaille – S. Goderis, Investigating the provenance of Egyptian blue pigments in ancient Roman polychromy, Archaeometry Workshop XVIII/2, 97–122, <http://www.ace.hu/am/2021_2/2021_2_tartalom.html> (10.04.2023) |
| Tober 2013 | B. Tober, Pompeji im Salzkammergut? Römische Wandmalereien aus dem »Museum Hallstatt«, in: R. Breitwieser – M. Frass – G. Nightingale (eds.), Calamus. Festschrift Herbert Graßl, Philippika 57 (Wiesbaden 2013) 569–580 |
| Tober 2014 | B. Tober, Wand- und Deckenmalereien im Territorium Iuvavum – die dekorative Raumausstattung als Ausdruck römischer Lebensform (Problematik und Perspektiven), in: R. Kastler – W. Kovacsovics – F. Lang – P. Laub (eds.), Das Territorium von Iuvavum. Bestandsaufnahme und Forschungsstrategien, Colloquium Iuvavum 15.–17.03.2012 (Salzburg 2014) 319–336 |
| Tober 2015 | B. Tober, Die römischen Wand- und Deckenmalereien aus Saalfelden/Wiesersberg, ASalzb (Salzburg 2015) |
| Tober 2017 | B. Tober, Archäologische Analyse der Wand- und Deckenmalereien aus dem »Haus der Medusa«. Die Bedeutung für die Wandmalereiproduktion in Norikum, in: M. Santner, Das Haus der Medusa – Römische Wandmalereien in Enns, Fokus Denkmal 8 (Vienna 2017) 145–186 |
| Ubl 1997 | H. Ubl, Raum X Wandmalerei und Kat. Nr. XII/1 Deckenfresko, in: H. Ubl (ed.), Katalog zur Schausammlung »Römerzeit« des Museums Lauriacum – Enns II. Katalog der Ausstellung, FiL 12/2 = Sonderband I 2 (Enns 1997) 315–319. 334–337 |
| Ubl 2006a | H. Ubl, Lauriacum und die Legio II Italica, in: G. Winkler (ed.), Schausammlung »Römerzeit« im Museum Lauriacum Enns I. Textband, FiL 12/1 = Sonderband I 1 (Enns 2006) 37–56 |
| Ubl 2006b | H. Ubl, Lauriacum – die zivilen Siedlungsräume, in: G. Winkler (ed.), Schausammlung »Römerzeit« im Museum Lauriacum Enns I. Textband, FiL 12/1 = Sonderband I 1 (Enns 2006) 57–83 |
| Vandenabeele – Donais 2016 | P. Vandenabeele – M. K. Donais, Mobile spectroscopic instrumentation in archaeometry research, Applied Spectroscopy 70, 2016, 27–41, DOI: 10.1177/000370281561106 |

*Alexandra Rodler-Rørbo, Austrian Archaeological Institute of the Austrian Academy of Sciences, Dominikanerbastei 16, 1010 Vienna, Austria.*
*[e] alexandra.rodler-rorbo@oeaw.ac.at*

*Barbara Tober, Classical Archaeology, Paris Lodron University Salzburg, Residenzplatz 1, 5020 Salzburg, Austria.*
*[e] barbara.tober@plus.ac.at*

# ZEITEN DES UMBRUCHS:
## DENKMÄLER DER FORTGESCHRITTENEN KAISERZEIT UND SPÄTANTIKE

Cristina-Georgeta Alexandrescu

# LATE ROMAN FUNERARY MONUMENTS FROM *SCYTHIA*

**Abstract**

The epigraphic evidence from *Scythia* has been a steady focus of research, although little attention was given to the material, shape and especially the provenance of monuments. Like the majority of the epigraphic finds from the region, the late Roman funerary monuments have been found reused as building material or even for epitaphs. This proves the economic value that the slabs of marble and limestone retained in different historical periods, as well as the careful handling of materials, showing an awareness of their worth and characteristics. One particular aim of this paper is to shed light on the transition from the funerary monuments dated to the $2^{nd}$ and $3^{rd}$ centuries, to the epitaphs identified as Christian through text and/or decoration. The state of research makes the task difficult and sets limits to the discussion and its possible conclusions, as, especially for the northern area of the province, the finds are isolated. The metropolis of the region, the former Greek colony *Tomis*, provides a complex information basis for both the late Roman and Early Christian periods and presents a special case study, which can only be briefly outlined here.

## POLITICAL, ADMINISTRATIVE AND ECONOMIC FRAMEWORK

The territory between the Danube and the Black Sea, known today as Dobruja, was a geopolitical unit since antiquity. As of the $1^{st}$ century BC it was part of the province of *Moesia*, later *Moesia inferior*. The invasions of the Goths, Carps and other peoples in the forties and at the beginning of the fifties of the $3^{rd}$ century AD also had devastating effects there. The wars in the $3^{rd}$ century brought social life to a relative standstill. Numerous destruction horizons can be traced back to the middle of the $3^{rd}$ century, with their interpretation, however, not always linked to a particular historical event. It is therefore not surprising that, from the middle and second half of the $3^{rd}$ century, very few funerary monuments and other artistic evidence have survived[1]. The small number of monuments thus reflects the general decline quite well.

Only after the victories of Gallienus over the Heruli and of Claudius over the Goths at *Naissus* in 269, was emperor Aurelian able to switch to a consolidation policy. This context is when the abandonment of the province of *Dacia* occurred, with the province being reformed anew south of the Danube, as *Dacia ripensis*.

A fundamental administrative reform took place at the beginning of the late Empire, when some of the territories of *Moesia inferior* were divided into three new provinces, namely, *Scythia*[2], *Moesia secunda* (eastern Lower Moesia) and *Moesia prima* (western Lower Moesia). The far-reaching reforms of Diocletian and his successor changed the economic, social and cultural conditions in the Roman Empire. There was continuity in structure and density of settlement in the province of *Scythia* on the one hand, and in some cases, even a further development. On the other hand, the rich production of funerary stelae before the mid-$3^{rd}$ century was carried out in very few cases. This is probably due to the fundamental change in burial customs and ideas of the afterlife accompanying the introduction of Christianity, and to some extent to the reduced availability of private financial means as well. While the first factor still needs further investigation due to the state of research, the second is obvious.

---

[1] See, for an overview, e.g. Conrad 2004, 5–11; Zahariade 2006, 343–361; Oppermann 2010, 211.
[2] In the literature and common use the area is called *Scythia minor*, which is not the correct/official name of the province.

Starting with the reign of Constantine, but especially during the rule of Anastasius and Justinian, intensive activity took place, consisting of repairs, rebuilding or simple new fortification in the main centres of *Scythia*. Besides those along the Danube and on the Black Sea shores, remarkable works were erected in the inland centres at *Tropaeum Traiani*, *Ulmetum* and *Ibida*. This is of great relevance for our discussion here, as in many of those sites – but interestingly not in all of them – old local available slabs and blocks, in the form of former votive and funerary monuments of various shapes as well as architectural elements, were reused as building materials. Most of the funerary monuments of interest here were found in this form, meaning that *in situ* finds in the region of interest up until now are rare.

## FUNERARY MONUMENTS OF THE 2ND TO THE 3RD CENTURY AD

The studies dedicated to the funerary monuments in *Moesia inferior* pointed out the preference for stelae, especially along the Danube and in the territory of the military centres, with fewer occurrences of funerary altars, columns and sarcophagi, which are present in the Greek cities on the Black Sea shores and in the northern part of the province, in centres like *Noviodunum* and *Troesmis*[3]. Funerary buildings have not yet been properly investigated, given the scarce evidence but also the poor state of documentation of available finds. For the 2nd to 3rd centuries, a significant observation was the widespread activity and influence on the local production carried out by sculptors from Asia Minor, an area from where significant marble imports were made through the main harbour, *Tomis*. The established workshops adapted to the requests of the local and regional market, making use successfully of locally available lithic materials suitable for sculpture, particularly along the Danube and in the north of the province.

While the eastern part of the territory shows influences of Greek traditions combined with Roman ones, the centres along the Limes (Danube) use a simpler iconography, introduced in the Early Roman period through the military centres, established and also taken over by the civilians. Popular themes, well incorporated into the local traditions, were the funerary banquet and the heroized deceased as rider[4]. Customized depictions reflecting the profession of the deceased or special iconographic compositions are rare. Portraits seem to have been an exception, with their main occurrence in the eastern centres of the province, such as *Histria*, *Tomis* and *Kallatis*. Towards the second half of the 3rd century funerary monuments for individuals became rare, the usual form being a stela/inscription mentioning the entire family. One such example is the stela erected by Claudia Cocceia (fig. 1), wife of Aur. Ditusanus, *stator tribuni*, fallen *in barbarico*, while she was alive, and for her daughter[5]. The degree of importance given to either the depiction or the epitaph underwent a slow transformation from the end of the 2nd century, when the epitaph was more relevant, until the end of the succeeding century when it took over the entire monument.

Elites and members of the military, who had the necessary financial means, are certainly best represented in the evidence. Found in the form of reused building materials, and against the background of an undeveloped state of systematic research as far as settlements and necropoleis are concerned, the funerary monuments and especially the epigraphic material are only a partial source, particularly for the second half of the 3rd century and the 4th century.

---

[3] Conrad 2004; Alexandrescu-Vianu 2007; Alexandrescu-Vianu 2008/2009.
[4] E.g. ISM IV 177 (*Sacidava*).
[5] ISM IV 187 (from *Sacidava*): *D(is) M(anibus) / Aurel(ius) Ditus/anus stra/tor trib(uni) vix(it) / an(nos) XLVIII et Cl(audia) / Coc(ceia) coniu(n)x / memoria(m) / posuit viro / suo qui di/(sperdit)us(?) est / in barbarico / et Aure(lia) Ael(ia) fil(ia) eius et her(es)*.

## DATING CRITERIA

The find context, as already mentioned usually a secondary one, offers an extensive *terminus ante quem*. Reliable dating criteria are provided by inscriptions, yet less from the manner in which they are carved. Portraits or stylistic hints are rare. References to military units, ranks or even historical events (e.g. the battle of Chalcedon[6]) can ensure a *terminus post quem* for the monument or at least for the inscription. Indirect evidence for dating individual monuments would certainly be the find context and possible grave inventory, including in an ideal case coins.

The quality of the craftsmanship of the monuments is quite varied, and therefore it is difficult to propose a precise chronological framework for sculpture without further evidence from epigraphic and/or archaeological data. The schematic, notch-like, shallow carving in local stone, but also in marble, is by far not a late Roman characteristic, as this style was previously evident on both votive and funerary sculpture throughout the territory[7]. This point is relevant when trying to ascertain characteristic elements as well as changes in behaviour, rites and rituals over a certain period and in a particular region, as is the case here. There is still no evidence in this region for the existence of special funerary areas, family tombs, special necropoleis of soldiers or, later, of Christians in the environs of a particular centre in the province[8]. Analogies with other provinces are certainly possible, and the conclusions cannot theoretically be far from reality, but this does not mean that the actual local situation can be highlighted or that comparative analyses at an interprovincial level are possible at the moment.

The tall stelae used especially along the Danube in military centres such as *Sacidava*, *Capidava*, *Troesmis*, or *Halmyris*, find a late Christian echo in one of the stelae reused as building material in the fortification of *Ulmetum* (2.25 × 0.50 × 0.22 m)[9]. So far, this is the largest Christian stela from the region under

1   Stela of Aur. Ditusanus, from *Sacidava* (after ISM IV 187)

---

[6] IGLR 206 (see below and fig. 4).
[7] *Histria*: Alexandrescu-Vianu 2000, cat. 177; *Tomis*: ISM VI 2, 294; *Halmyris*: Zahariade – Alexandrescu 2011, cat. 20.
[8] See e.g. Achim 2015.
[9] IGLR 210, dated to the 5$^{th}$ c. AD.

2   Stela of Aurelia Sambatis, from *Tomis*, initial and present state of conservation (1: after IGLR 17; 2: photo C.-G. Alexandrescu)

analysis. The epitaph refers to two young people, a boy and a girl, mourned by their apparently quite wealthy families. A cross was carved on the lower part of the monument[10].

## CHARACTERISTICS OF THE LATE ROMAN FUNERARY MONUMENTS – TRADITION AND CHANGE

At the end of the 3rd century and at the beginning of the 4th century AD the design of the stelae was more simple, and the slabs employed were smaller; the register (or registers), featuring a scene or scenes related to the heroization of the deceased and/or to the funerary banquet, was elimi-

---

[10] It must be mentioned, however, that this monument is known only from the illustration published by V. Pârvan (Pârvan 1912, pl. 4), and it is therefore impossible to prove if the slab was reused more than once, or if there was a different depiction than the one interpreted. See also Barnea 1979, 120–121 pl. 42.

nated. The carved family portrait (husband and wife; parents and children) became increasingly schematic until the depiction disappeared completely. However, some decorative motifs from the previous period were preserved: vegetal motifs, ivy and vine framing the border of the individual fields, with or without the kantharos in the lower part of the monument[11], and pseudo-architectural features such as pediment or columns (fig. 2, 1–2)[12].

For the smaller examples, the recollection of the earlier layout of the stelae can be postulated, while for the tall stelae, it remains unclear if an older semi-finished stela, still available on site, was re-used[13].

On simple stelae, with or without a profiled frame of the field of inscription, and with or without vegetal ornaments, the epitaphs indicate that the deceased belonged to the Christian community. Some examples from *Tomis*, such as the stela for Aurelia Ianuaria and Aurelia Domna[14], dated to the 4th century, may be mentioned here. The epitaph states that the deceased »gives her soul to God«, and entrusts the children to their grandparents »until they will reunite on the Elysian fields«.

Dove, fish, palm, rosette or crown with a rosette in the middle, and the vine are elements considered to be (more or less hidden) indicators of the (Christian) religion of the deceased. These, however, are far from exclusively Christian motifs, and may also be common non-Christian funerary symbols[15]. Thus, the fragmentarily preserved epitaph[16] bearing the depiction of a bird (dove [?]), dated to the 3rd century, is not necessarily Christian.

In addition to the simpler monuments, there are examples with elaborate iconography, dated to the 3rd–4th century. Above the epitaph, one or two relief fields can depict the traditional funerary banquet, executed in a rudimentary or even misunderstood fashion, such as that on the stela for Flavius Tatianus (fig. 3) found in Rasova[17]. The rider is also featured, both motifs being sometimes com-

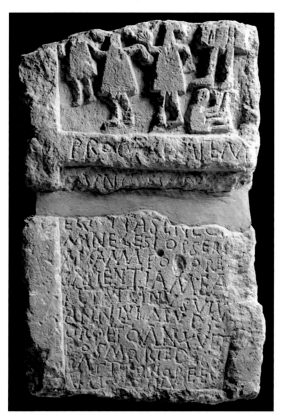

3 Stela of Fl. Tatianus, from Rasova (photo C.-G. Alexandrescu)

---

[11] IGLR 209 (*Ulmetum*).
[12] ISM VI 2, 367 (*Tomis*); 373 (*Tomis*).
[13] IGLR 270 (*Aegyssus*); 236 (*Troesmis*); ISM IV 197 (*Sacidava*).
[14] ISM VI 2, 527: *Aur(elia) Ianuaria Ian(uari) an(norum) iu/ncta pari Fla(vio) Mart[i]no / et amplius vixi menses V dies [---] pr/o com(m)oda fuit spir[it]um D/eo rede[re et] Aur(elia) Domna so/ror Ian[uari] an[n(orum)] [---] III iuncta pa/ri vixit menses X d(iem) I fatum co/<m=N>plevit durus pro carita/te coniugi(!) et sorori(!) ip[si] / vivite parentes et n<o=E>str/is provid[ete fili]is estote / memores iterum [El]ysiis co/[fu]turi ave vale viator.* The monument is best illustrated in Barnea 1979, 54–55 pl. 9.
[15] In some cases the interpretation of the depiction cannot be verified, as the monument is lost or not visible (in the case of *spolia* documented but not removed from the wall). One example is a stela in the episcopal basilica from *Histria*, on which the publication of the excavations (Suceveanu 2007, 150–151) documented the schematic depiction of a fish instead of a *hereda distinguens* at the end of the epitaph, thereby concluding that the stela is one of the earliest evidence of Christians in *Histria* and the surrounding region.
[16] ISM VI 2, 499 (*Tomis*).
[17] ISM IV 215: *Pro caritatem(!) // [f]unc su[m] / [---] /egi vita(m) sene(!) cr[i]/mine ges(s)i opserv/avi(!) fama(m) podore(!) / sapientia mea / Fl(avius) Tatianus vix(it) / ann(os) LXI m(enses) V d(ies) se[x] / (h)or(as) VI(?) et*

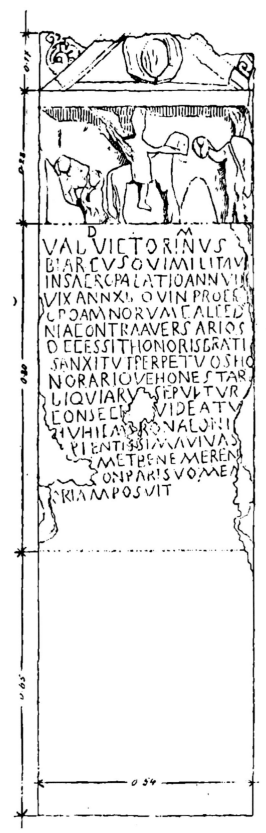

bined in one field. The best example is the cenotaph of Valerius Victorinus *biarchus*, who fell in the battle of Chalcedon (324) in Licinius' army; furthermore, this is also one of the most closely dated monuments (fig. 4, 1–2), given the details mentioned in the epitaph[18].

The epitaphs mentioning the entire family have been discussed already. Special cases are the stelae of individuals, especially children,

4  Stela of Val. Victorinus, from *Ulmetum*, initial and present state of conservation (1: after Pârvan 1912, fig. 25; 2: photo C.-G. Alexandrescu)

*q(ui) m(issus) an(nis) XV et / pos(t) morte(m) deco/ra(vi)stis (h)onore et (?) / tu(?) Cl(audia) [---] co(n)iux*. This stela was set up 15 years after the death of the husband.

[18] IGLR 206 (from *Ulmetum*): *D(is) M(anibus) / Val(erius) Victorinus / biarc(h)us qui militavi[t] / in sacro palatio ann(os) VII [---] / vix(it) ann(os) XL qui [i]n proe[li]/o Roamnorum(!) Calc(h)ed[o]/nia contra a(d)versarios / decessit honoris grati[a] / sanxit ut perpetuo se ho/norari sive honestare / liquiaru[m] sepultur[a] / consecr[ar]i videatu[r] / hu<h>ic Ma[t]rona coni[ux] / pientissima viva s[e] / [sibi] et bene meren/[ti] conpari suo mem/oriam posuit.*

which again feature the extended presentation of the family members. A less well-known monument, the stela of the 3-year old Ulpia Aurelia Valeria, found in *Tomis* and kept in the British Museum exemplifies this[19]. The scene of the funerary banquet, as well as the lines of the epitaph, are misplaced within the layout of the large slab (2.13 m high and 0.91 m wide).

In the epigraphic habit, the transition towards Christian epitaphs is also evident, with the use of introductory and final formulas (in Latin), of epigrams (in Greek), with some expressions or hints which point towards the new religion.

A modest but detailed limestone stela dating to the late 3rd century and commemorating the 6-year old boy Λιλλας[20], in *Tomis*, is a further example of the recollection of the earlier tradition of large funerary altars in this city. Above the inscription field, the parents and the child are depicted as individual busts (fig. 5), while in the pediment a bird pecking on a grape is depicted (?). The customary depiction of the entire family is also featured on the small stela of Aurelia Sambatis (fig. 2, 2)[21]. The reduced dimensions of the slabs of these two examples are also indicative of the gradual transition towards the later small marble stelae, after the marble supply had been restarted in the same city for the architectural program of a particularly Christian character.

5   Stela of the boy Λιλλας, from *Tomis* (after ISM VI 2, 384)

One outstanding example of customized stelae in the region is that of the soldier Flavius Ursus[22], who died at the age of only 20 years, dated to late 3rd century (fig. 6). The detailed rendering of the harness and the portrait are remarkable, as are the depiction of the scroll which Ursus holds. The stela is carved on a hard sandstone slab (preserved height 1.16 m) formerly used as a threshold element. The epitaph mentions significant details of the life of Ursus, but makes no reference to other family members.

A couple of decades later, the Latin epitaph of the Christian soldier Terentius (fig. 7), who had already served for 5 years but who died at only 20[23], was also erected in *Tomis*. Worth noting in

---

[19] ISM VI 2, 465 (dated 271–330 AD): *D(is) M(anibus) / Ulpiae Aureliae Va/leriae virgini dextra/t(a)e annis III mensibus / VIIII d(iebus) XVII filiae Aure/li Herculani v(iri) e(gregii) du/cenari(i) qui vixit annis / XIII(?) mens(ibus) VIII d(iebus) XVI / nepotiae pientissi/m(a)e Ulp(ius) Valerius Au/relianus v(ir) e(gregius) cente/narius et Titinia / Mansueta stola/ta femina viator / resiste et lege nihil ul/tra crudelius h(oc?) m(onumento?) c(ernere?) p(otes?).*
[20] ISM VI 2, 384 (*Tomis*).
[21] ISM VI 2, 367 (from *Tomis*): *D(is) M(anibus) / Aur(elia) Sambatis / (h)abens ius li/berorum vixi/t ann(os) XXV m(enses) V / d(ies) XII anima re/dedit cui gem/ens Victorinu/s maritus / ave vale viat(or).*
[22] ISM VI 2, 529 (from *Tomis*): *Fl(avius) Ursus fil(ius) Q(uinti) Mestri / q(uon)d(am) d(e) eq(uitibus) n<u=O>(meri) II cataf(ractariorum) no/tus ab iure an(norum) II fact/us an(norum) XVI pro<ba=VI>tus / mil(es) of(ficialis) Ladici pr(a)ef(ecti) st/ip(endiorum) IIII vixit an(nos) XX et / s<e=IN>mestr(i)um [e]t cui / Gemenia Matrona m/[ater].*
[23] ISM VI 2, 545 (from *Tomis*): *In h<o=U>c tumul<o=U>/{m} est positus / Terentius / filius Gaio/n(a)e annor(um) vigin/ti <q=C>(u)inque mil/itans inter sa/gittar(io)s iunio/res.*

6   Stela of Fl. Ursus, from *Tomis* (photos C.-G. Alexandrescu)

this case is the basic shape of the stela and its overall layout with separated registers, similar to the stela of Λιλλας, but here employed in a new, adapted manner.

The individual histories are remembered through epitaphs, which still make use of elaborated formulas or even epigrams, until the epitaph mentions only a name and bears a relevant sign, the cross, i.e. »the cross of death and resurrection«, as stated in a bilingual inscription from the area of *Tropaeum Traiani*[24]. The large cross takes over the space while the text is reduced to essentials. The work process is interesting, as it apparently began with the inscription and not with the depiction, as pointed out in the case of two epitaphs from *Tomis* dated to the first half of the 6th century[25].

## CASES OF REUSE

Half-finished funerary stelae of the 2nd to the 3rd century AD seem to have been used decades later due to the difficult supply of slabs from quarries. One example is the tall stela from Dunavăț, near *Halmyris* (preserved height 1.80 m)[26]. Further fragmentarily preserved monuments, bearing similar epitaphs, were found in the area of *Noviodunum*, *Troesmis* and *Aegyssus*[27]. They have in common the large dimensions, the layout and schematic decoration, as well as the lengthy epitaphs, in some cases mentioning many children who died at an early age[28].

Of further interest is a marble stela from *Tomis*[29]: this was summarily prepared in that the first line with the *D(is) M(anibus)* dedication was carved, but due to errors in the placement of the decoration and inscription it was probably considered at first a reject (fig. 8, 2). It was, however, pre-

---

[24]   ISM IV 80.
[25]   ISM VI 2, 551 and 546.
[26]   IGLR 168: *Artemidora / coniu(n)x cum fili/o suo et filia sua / Viventia patri eo/rum titulum posu/erunt // D(is) M(anibus) / memoria Ne/potiani prin/cipalis vixit / annis XXXVII Vic/tor fil(ius) vix(it) an(nis) II / Iuli(a)na filia v(ixit) an(nis) III / Heraclius fra(ter) / vixit an(nis) III Vita/lis frat(er) vix(it) an/nis V / valete lecto/res*.
[27]   ISM V 250 (Niculițel); IGLR 270 (*Aegyssus*); 236 (*Troesmis*); ISM IV 197 (*Sacidava*). The dating of the epitaphs is aided by the reference to *legio I Iovia* and *legio II Herculia*.
[28]   On the demographic situation of this region in late Roman times, see Mihailescu-Bîrliba 2009.
[29]   ISM VI 2, 496 (dated to the 3rd c.) and the Christian epitaph ISM VI 2, 554 = IGLR 48 (dated to the 6[rd] c.).

served in stock due to the value of the material. Subsequently it was reused at least twice – at first in the 3rd century (a funerary epigram), and then in the 6th century (fig. 8, 1) – as a funerary inscription, before being reused as building material (or possibly as an object of furniture, for example a table).

A further extreme example, this time a limestone slab, was documented by Vasile Pârvan in the fortification at *Ulmetum*[30]. In this case the slab was reused three times, beginning in the second half of the 2nd century.

A very old find from *Tomis*, in one of the vaulted funerary chambers, dated based on the reported numismatic finds to the reign of Constantine the Great, is of particular interest. Several fragments of limestone reliefs from this tomb were recognized to have been initially the door to the chamber[31]. Although it is not possible to make a detailed presentation and analysis of this find, it should be mentioned here as it is unique in many ways: it is the only preserved specially designed door (1.28 × 0.76 m) and it carries depictions of mythological subjects (Isis-Aphrodite in a Nilotic landscape, Herakles). In general, mythological subjects were not depicted on funerary monuments in the region. Therefore, the question arises whether the door and the funerary chamber are to be dated after AD 313, or if they are of earlier date and were later reused. The reuse may concern either the funerary chamber or only the relief itself, in which case it might have had a different meaning for the Christian users of the funerary building. Christian funerary practice allowed for such later reuse, visiting and interventions, as were for instance well documented in the case of the famous hypogeum from *Tomis*[32].

7   Stela of Terentius, from *Tomis* (after ISM VI 2, 545)

## CHRISTIAN ELEMENTS AND TRANSITION TOWARDS CHRISTIAN FUNERARY MONUMENTS

Based on the scant available evidence, we can conclude that the late Roman funerary monuments from *Scythia* seem to make use of the same main iconographic motifs and design schemas as in the previous periods, with great and even increased importance given to epitaphs. Individual

---

[30] IGLR 208: *Valeates(!) / vos qui supe/ris setis(!) et co/letes(!) manes t[u]/res(!) quia vos / ad nos veni/turi(!) setis(!) / Aur(elius) Sisinius pa/ganus vixit / annis super / LXX / et superis de s/[uo et] conug[i ---]*. For the find context and reuse, see Pârvan 1913, 332–338 no. 3.
[31] Bordenache 1968 (with literature).
[32] Barbet – Bucovală 1996.

8   Marble stela from *Tomis*, with multiple reuses
    (1: after ISM VI 2, 496; 2: after ISM VI 2, 554)

examples testify to the possibility of having customized stelae including a depiction, especially in the centre of the province, *Tomis*[33].

The Christian elements, mainly the cross, gradually appear on large slabs and will become the main motif on the commonly used small marble slabs. The mostly unworked sides and reverse of some of the slabs raise the question of how and where the inscriptions were displayed.

The majority of Christian funerary inscriptions from *Scythia* are small in scale (less than or about 1.00 m high), have a simpler layout and display a preference, when available, for the cross as the only decorative motif.

The change in rite as well as in the shape and iconography of funerary monuments, from the late 4th century up to the 6th century, can be best observed in the metropolis, *Tomis*, as the main commercial, political and religious centre of the province. This city preserves the most numerous Christian evidence[34] as well as the highest production of Christian funerary slabs, both in marble and in local limestone. Additional Christian funerary monuments, such as sarcophagi and especially the vaulted funerary chambers are again attested at *Tomis*. The cross and the palm were also used to decorate one of the funerary chambers with wall painting, uncovered at Cernavodă, ancient *Axiopolis*[35]. In other sites within the province (such as *Noviodunum*, *Ulmetum*, *Troesmis*) there is evidence of early churches, but no epigraphic or archaeological evidence of Christian

---

[33] ISM VI 2, 539 and 540.
[34] Netzhammer 1918; Oppermann 2010.
[35] Oppermann 2010, 232 and pl. 95 (with literature).

character. This certainly is only a reflection of the state of current archaeological research. Thus in the near future, *Tomis* is expected to be systematically approached as a case study[36], in order to obtain eloquent insights into the history of *Scythia* in the Late Roman period, and into its early Christian communities.

## ACKNOWLEDGEMENT

The present research and the participation at the conference in Vienna were possible with the financial support of the project PN-III-P4-ID-PCE-2020-1031.

## BIBLIOGRAPHY

| | |
|---|---|
| Achim 2015 | I. Achim, Churches and graves of the Early Byzantine period in Scythia Minor and Moesia Secunda: the development of a Christian topography at the periphery of the Roman Empire, in: J. Rasmus Brandt – M. Prusac – H. Roland (eds.), Death and Changing Rituals: Function and Meaning in Ancient Funerary Practices, Studies in funerary archaeology 7 (Oxford 2015) 287–342 |
| Achim – Cliante 2017 | I. Achim – L. Cliante, Anciennes recherches, nouvelles considérations sur la crypte repérée dans le périmètre de la rue Karl Marx à Constanţa, MCA (serie nouă) 13, 2017, 73–88 |
| Alexandrescu-Vianu 2000 | M. Alexandrescu-Vianu, Histria 9. La sculpture en pierre et en terre cuite (Bucharest 2000) |
| Alexandrescu-Vianu 2007 | M. Alexandrescu-Vianu, Ateliere sculpturale în Dobrogea romană (I), StCercIstorV 58/1–2, 2007, 55–60 |
| Alexandrescu-Vianu 2008/2009 | M. Alexandrescu Vianu, Atelierele de sculptură din Moesia Inferior. 2. Relaţiile cu Bithynia, StCercIstorV 59/60, 2008/2009, 53–80 |
| Barbet – Bucovală 1996 | A. Barbet – M. Bucovală, L'hypogée paléochrétien des Orants à Costanţa (Roumanie), l'ancienne Tomis, MEFRA 108/1, 1996, 105–158 |
| Bărbulescu – Buzoianu 2012 | M. Bărbulescu – L. Buzoianu, Tomis. Comentariu istoric şi arheologic (Constanţa 2012) |
| Barnea 1979 | I. Barnea, Christian Art in Romania I (Bucharest 1979) |
| Bordenache 1968 | G. Bordenache, Un documento tardo di sincretismo pagano, StCl 10, 1968, 177–183 |
| Conrad 2004 | S. Conrad, Die Grabstelen aus Moesia inferior. Untersuchungen zu Chronologie, Typologie und Ikonografie (Leipzig 2004) |
| IGLR | E. Popescu, Inscripţiile greceşti şi latine din secolele IV–XIII descoperite în România (Bucharest 1976) |
| ISM IV | E. Popescu, Inscriptions de Scythie mineure, IV. Tropaeum – Durostorum – Axiopolis (Bucharest 2015) |
| ISM V | E. Doruţiu-Boilă, Inscripţiile din Scythia Minor, V. Capidava. Troesmis. Noviodunum (Bucharest 1985) |
| ISM VI 2 | A. Avram – M. Bărbulescu – L. Buzoianu, Inscriptions grecques et latines de Scythie Mineure VI, suppl. fasc. 2. Tomis et son territoire (Bucharest 2018) |
| Mihailescu-Bîrliba 2009 | L. Mihailescu-Bîrliba, Speranţa de viaţă, mortalitatea, stuctura de vârstă şi fertilitatea în Scythia Minor (sfârşitul secolului al III-lea–secolul al VI-lea), in: L. Mihailescu-Bîrliba (ed.), Structuri etno-demografice la Dunărea de Jos (Iaşi 2009) 101–123 |
| Netzhammer 1918 | R. Netzhammer, Die christlichen Altertümer der Dobrudscha (Bucharest 1918) |
| Oppermann 2010 | M. Oppermann, Das frühe Christentum an der Westküste des Schwarzen Meeres und im anschließenden Binnenland: historische und archäologische Zeugnisse, ZAKSSchriften 19 (Langenweissbach 2010) |
| Pârvan 1912 | V. Pârvan, Cetatea Ulmetum I. Descoperirile primei campanii de săpături din vara anului 1911 (Bucharest 1912) |

---

[36] For partial syntheses on *Tomis* see e.g. Oppermann 2010; Bărbulescu – Buzoianu 2012; Achim – Cliante 2017.

| | |
|---|---|
| Pârvan 1913 | V. Pârvan, Cetatea Ulmetum II 2. Descoperirile campaniei a doua și a treia de săpături din anii 1912 și 1913 (Bucharest 1913) |
| Suceveanu 2007 | A. Suceveanu, Histria 13. La basilique épiscopale (Bucharest 2007) |
| Zahariade 2006 | M. Zahariade (ed.), Scythia Minor: a history of a later Roman province (284–681), Pontic provinces of the later Roman Empire I (Amsterdam 2006) |
| Zahariade – Alexandrescu 2011 | M. Zahariade – C.-G. Alexandrescu, Halmyris 2. Greek and Latin Inscriptions, Signa and Instrumenta from Halmyris found between 1981 and 2010, BARIntSer 2261 (Oxford 2011) |

*Cristina-Georgeta Alexandrescu, Institutul de Arheologie »Vasile Pârvan«, str. Henri Coandă nr. 11,*
*010667 Bucharest 1, Romania.*
*[e] cgetalexandrescu@gmail.com*

Stefan Ardeleanu

# RITUALIZED FUNERARY *MENSAE* OF THE WESTERN LATE ANTIQUE WORLD

## TYPOLOGY AND USE SPECTRUM BETWEEN MICRO-REGIONAL AND GLOBAL TRENDS

**Abstract**

This paper offers a first typological overview of late antique funerary *mensae* and discusses their function in commemorative funerary rituals on the basis of technical/decorative observations. In addition to the well-known sigma-shaped *mensae*, there was a much broader spectrum of ritualized tomb covers in Late Antiquity. Many of these slabs have holes, feed pipes, socket frames, gutters, spouts, libation tubes, feeding troughs, traces of burning and oil/resin, or residues in catch basins, which strikingly point to post-mortem practices. The slab's ritual function has rarely been recognized as such due to the focus on inscription texts and failure to examine their lateral and reverse sides. These funerary monuments and their underlying commemorative practices were popular throughout Late Antiquity and regionally even into the Early Middle Ages. They were common only in the West – in the Hispanic, North African, Italic, Illyrian, Gallic, Rhine, and Danubian provinces –, indicating an overarching *koine* of commemorative practices shared not only by the elites, but also the lower social strata. Despite these transregional commonalities, locally very different technical and decorative designs emerged.

## PROBLEMATIZING AND DEFINING COMMEMORATIVE RITUALS IN LATE ANTIQUE FUNERARY CONTEXTS

When the council held at *Bracara Augusta* in AD 572 explicitly prohibited the consumption of food and drinks (*prandia*) at tombs[1], the late antique Church looked back on a centuries-long struggle against these *convivia*, *epula* or *refrigeria*[2]. As in the period before the rise of Christianity, commemoration of the dead at tombs apparently continued to be materialized by extensive alcohol consumption and excessive feasting[3]. The heaviest critic of the meals in honor of the dead came in the 4th century AD in the person of Augustine, who periodically attacked the *convivia* and the excesses (*ebrietates*) at tombs[4]. The early Church tried to stop or at least to reinterpret these ›pagan‹ rites into eucharistic practices and charitable almsgiving for the poor. With a series of council decisions, the *ecclesia* was successful in doing so. At least, this is how it is seen by the majority of research to this day[5].

That this old dogma represents a distorted view is proven by an enormous quantity of literary, epigraphic, archaeological and iconographic sources. In order to contextualize this evidence, it is necessary to recall some fundamental changes in the funerary matrix of the ancient world during the 3rd to 4th centuries. In addition to the new trend of celebrating the death days (*dies natales*) of

---

[1] Vives 1963, 7–8. 102 (Braga II, Kanon 68–69); Barral i Altet 1978, 52. I thank Anna Sitz and Mark Ohlrogge for worthful comments and proofreading of this paper.
[2] E.g. Tert. spect. 12, 4; 13; Tert. De corona 3, 3; 10, 21; Cypr. ep. 67; Ambr. de Hel. 17, 62.
[3] Dunbabin 2003; Braune 2008.
[4] August. epist. ad Aurel. 13 (22), 3; conf. 6, 2, 2; 29, 9; epist. 22, 1, 3; 22, 6; serm. 48, 361; Enarratio in Psalmum 12, 15; cf. Kotila 1992.
[5] Kotila 1992, 62: »The traditional cult of the dead was strictly forbidden to Christians in the days of Cyprian, and for this reason was apparently exceptional and rare«; Mateos Cruz 1999, 137: »rito eucarístico que sustituye al rito funerario practicado por los familiares«; Jensen 2008; Dresken-Weiland 2010, 197–198.

the martyrs, commemoration of the ›ordinary dead‹ in intra- and extra-urban burial grounds registered a growing importance in the processes of social negotiation of late antique communities. In some regions, more than a dozen feast days honoring the dead were fixed in the urban annual calendars[6]. Recent analyses have shown how commemoration at the tomb slowly passed into the hands of whole communities and how clerics in particular were responsible for controlling *memoria* and occupying prestigious positions in these new mortuary spaces[7]. From the entire Empire, enormous burial halls and ›funerary churches‹ are known, some with several thousand burials[8]. These new hierarchized burial spaces of collective *memoria* ›absorbed‹ the public spaces of the old city nuclei, such as fora or spectacle arenas. Commemoration of the deceased at the grave became a central fixed point of everyday life.

In what archaeologically tangible forms was this new increase in the importance of commemorating the dead materialized? In my project[9], I examine funerary commemoration rites through an investigation of any form of materially preserved practices that can be attributed to the posthumous commemoration of the dead. In contrast to the traditional preference of scholarship for explicit funeral-related rites, I am interested in the actions that can be traced archaeologically after the closure of graves. The recognition of rites for commemorating the dead is not always easy to accomplish archaeologically because critical finds from post-funeral contexts, such as fragmented objects from circulation levels or layers abutting or overlying graves, have too often been neglected or destroyed in excavations[10]. Further, it is highly difficult to recognize circulation levels in necropoleis[11] and to differentiate between burial-accompanying finds (e.g. those encountered in grave pit fills) and post-depositional residues or material from sequential burial activities, due to frequent tomb re-use, tomb robbing and inaccurate excavation. Finally, problems related to the history of research must be taken into account. Although there is a long debate on late antique funerary commemoration, it has so far been conducted very inconsistently or without an overall view of all available sources. The scholarly discourse remains strongly dominated by the aforementioned late antique written sources, which unanimously verbalize the ecclesiastical polemic against the holding of funerary ceremonies at graves[12]. There are, however, promising developments that allow a series of new insights in commemorative rituals at tombs. The materiality of tomb markers allows conclusions about their ritual use: libation holes/tubes, flooding installations or storage devices for food or drink. Residue analyses, e.g. in libation tubes or on grave covers[13], as well as botanical and faunal analyses, are slowly becoming established in burial excavation practices, with spectacular results concerning the high diversity of rituals and substances used[14]. Further, diachronic analysis of ceramics and glass scattered around tombs, as well as find assemblages from accessible catacombs, mausolea or hypogea attesting long-term ritual frequentation are extremely informative about drinking and dining customs performed in such spaces[15]. In particular, one group of grave markers, so-called funerary *mensae*, are the focus of this contribution and serve as indisputable evidence of an ancient, pagan habit of convivial commemoration of the dead that was handed down well into Late Antiquity and even deep into the Middle Ages.

---

[6] Volp 2002, 225–227.

[7] Yasin 2009; Ardeleanu 2018; several contributions in Ardeleanu – Cubas Díaz 2023.

[8] Neyses 1999; Ardeleanu 2023.

[9] This book project with the preliminary title »Ritus, Kultobjekt und Bild im Grabraum: Kommemorative Bestattungsrituale in den spätantiken Westprovinzen« is realized in the framework of the Center for Advanced Studies »RomanIslam« at the University of Hamburg, which is funded by the German Research Foundation (DFG).

[10] Navarro 1988, 28; Felle et al. 1994; Giuntella 1999; Marinone 2000; Spera 2005; Ripoll – Molist 2012; Pearce 2015, 450. 463–465; several contributions in Ardeleanu – Cubas Díaz 2023.

[11] Ripoll – Molist 2012, 26.

[12] Février 1990; Kotila 1992; Volp 2002, 234–239; Dunbabin 2003, 175–187; Dresken-Weiland 2010, 181–212; Zimmermann 2012.

[13] Spera 2005, 31–32; De Santis 2008, 4547–4548; Acampora 2013, 405–419; De Santis 2015, 207–208.

[14] Deschler-Erb et al. 2021; Pearce 2015.

[15] Giuntella et al. 1985; Bonacasa Carra 1996; Giuntella 1999; Spera 2005; De Santis 2008; Acampora 2013; De Santis 2015; Sterrett-Krause 2017.

## MATERIALIZING COMMEMORATION AT THE TOMB: LATE ANTIQUE FUNERARY *MENSAE* – GENERAL CHARACTERISTICS AND PREDECESSORS

Funerary *mensae*, in contrast to relic *mensae*, are grave markers above one or more burials with slightly raised surfaces (*klinai, lecti*) for the practicing of the funerary banquet (fig. 1). In scholarly literature, the term *mensa*, although known from late antique epitaphs, usually indicates the whole banquet monument. This is somewhat misleading, for *mensa* actually only means the table inserted within the monument. Food and drinks were served on this inset table, while the participants of the commemorative meals could lay in different configurations around this table. On several commemorative days a year, such as the *novemdialis, parentalia* or *feralia*, people gathered here to recline and dine with the deceased. Banquet representations in the Roman catacombs and painted graves from the 4th to the 5th century in the Balkan peninsula can be considered as a sort of ›instructions for use‹ for the arrangement of reclining and banqueting[16]. The paintings from the walk-in *cubicula* of Rome's catacombs, which were designed for posthumous use by several tomb visitors, prove complex sequences of ritual practices. As Jane Tulloch has shown, they not only call upon the descendants in imagery and writing to hold *convivia* but also signal social hierarchies during the banquet[17]. Individually portrayed family members are depicted camped on the *lecti*, and in some cases dignified women are stylized as presiding over the banquets, where the classical ideal number of seven banqueteers is often repeated[18]. Banqueters communicate with each other and standardized, inscribed drinking toasts added to the paintings encourage the participants to mix and consume various drinks.

Funerary *mensae* are not an innovation of Late Antiquity but developed already in the Imperial period. In *Ostia*, Carmona or *Pompeii*, *triclinia* and *biclinia* of the 1st to the 3rd century were built in front of and within mausolea, which were then revisited for communal meals[19]. A characteristic feature of these structures is the plastered and inclined reclining surface. In North Africa and southern Spain numerous stone *mensae* of the Imperial period were attached to funerary stelae, some of them depicting almost a menu in relief of what was to be eaten at the graves: fish, cakes, eggs, and chicken[20]. These *mensae* with an undoubtedly pagan tradition of the *convivium funebre* must be kept in mind as predecessors when discussing the late antique *mensae*, which later developed innovative and independent features. In what follows, I tackle such questions as how these monuments actually functioned in ritual use, to which social commemorative structures they were committed, and which supra-regional commonalities or special local forms occurred. My contribution is conceived as a first typology (fig. 1) of late antique funerary *mensae* with corresponding distribution maps. Late antique funerary *mensae* can be divided into six or seven types on the basis of their form, size, technique, materiality, the position of the table, reclining arrangement and ritual use.

## TYPE 1A: SIGMA-SHAPED *MENSA* MONUMENTS

Because of technical, material and ritual commonalities, type 1 is to be separated into two subtypes according to their shape. The best known type is 1a with a semicircular shape and waterproof plaster cover, built over one or several graves (fig. 1, 1a)[21]. The sigma-shaped monuments, similar to domestic *stibadia*[22], allowed for a radial arrangement of 5–12 banqueters lying around the table. The actual *mensa*, which itself was positioned as a sigma-shaped or rectangular slab on

---

[16] Jastrzebowska 1979; Valeva 2001; Dunbabin 2003, 175–187; Jastrzebowska 2021.
[17] Tulloch 2006.
[18] Jastrzebowska 2021.
[19] Braune 2008.
[20] Février 1964; Jensen 2008.
[21] Nussbaum 1961; Chalkia 1991.
[22] Morvillez 2019.

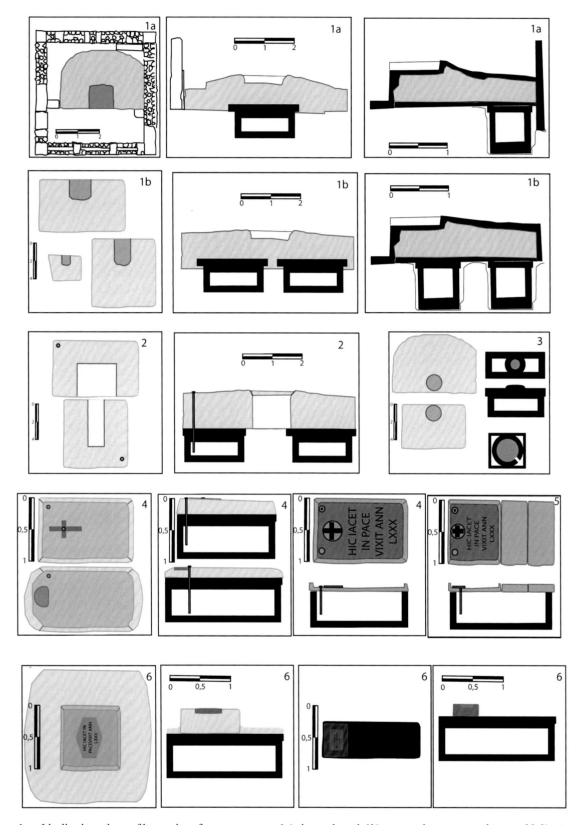

1 Idealized typology of late antique funerary *mensae*. 1a) sigma-shaped, 1b) rectangular, square and trapezoid, 2) *triclinia*, 3) circular tables, 4) individual *mensae*, 5) small tomb covers, 6) *mensa* tables (drawing S. Ardeleanu)

the straight side of the monuments (fig. 2)[23], often accommodated an epitaph, and was mostly lower in relation to the couches. Sigma-*mensae* were thus explicitly designed for use by several commemorators and not by individuals. Such *mensae* are known almost unanimously from urban contexts and are mainly to be attributed to elite grave owners. Many of them derive from delimited *areae*, probable burial sites of wealthy families[24]. There are vividly painted 4th century examples from *Emerita*[25], local representatives with elaborate mosaic epitaphs and painted couches from *Bulla Regia*[26] or mosaiced tables from *Tipasa*[27]. Technically almost identical examples with entirely plastered surfaces of the 4th to the 6th century are attested

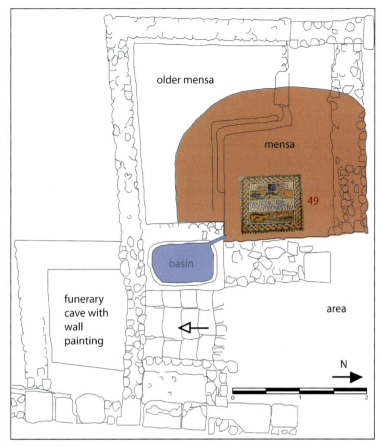

2   Sigma-shaped funerary *mensa* with mosaic table of the early 4th century from *Tipasa* (reconstruction S. Ardeleanu after Bouchenaki 1973, fig. 6)

from *Tipasa*[28], *Troia*[29], *Carthago Nova*[30] or *Tarraco*[31]. The *mensae* from *Carthago Nova* are clearly associated to slightly earlier Mauretanian counterparts with their mosaiced tables. They point not only to the well-attested connectivity of these two regions, but also to a sort of funerary *koine* working on both sides of the Alboran sea (fig. 3).

Most likely, also other examples of sigma-shaped tables in stone from *Pannonia*[32] to *Mauretania*[33], from the Adriatic area[34] to *Africa Proconsularis*[35] and from *Tarraco*[36] to Trier[37], also be-

---

[23]   E.g. in *Tipasa*: Bouchenaki 1975, figs. 6 (area 1, first *mensa*). 10 (area 3 *mensa* 8). 38. 129–132. 213–215.
[24]   *Tipasa*, Matarès: Bouchenaki 1975; *Tarraco*: Del Amo 1979.
[25]   Méndez Grande 2005; Picado Pérez 2006–2008, 254–255 fig. 50–54; Sánchez Hidalgo et al. 2009–2011, fig. 33–36.
[26]   Chaouali et al. 2018, fig. 11.
[27]   Ardeleanu 2018, figs. 1. 3. 8.
[28]   Bouchenaki 1975; Ardeleanu 2018, 493–494; Ardeleanu 2023.
[29]   De Almeida et al. 1982.
[30]   Barral i Altet 1978, 62–64.
[31]   Del Amo 1979.
[32]   *Savaria*: CIL III 4218; Duval 1985, 442.
[33]   *Satafis*: Février 1964, 165. 167; cf. Ardeleanu 2023, 140.
[34]   *Dyrrachium*: Shkodra-Rrugia 2017, fig. 9, 2; *Aquileia*: CIL V 8986a.
[35]   *Mactaris*: CIL VIII 23575; *Theveste*: Ardeleanu 2023, 127 fig. 10.
[36]   Barral i Altet 1978, 57–58 fig. 11.
[37]   CIL XIII 3882; Neyses 1999, 439–440; Gauthier 1975, cat. 169. Neyses 1999, 440 implausibly restores wall epitaphs, for which no *in situ* parallels are known.

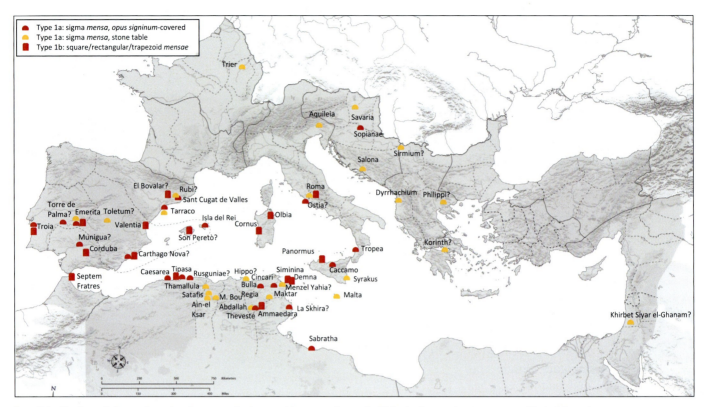

3   Distribution of sigma-shaped and rectangular/trapezoid *mensae* (types 1a/b) in the late antique *oecumene* (S. Ardeleanu)

longed to this type. Based on the sigma shape of the preserved stone tables and *in situ* contexts[38], it is plausible to assume that these stone slabs were embedded in larger, sigmoidal or rectangular *mensa* monuments. From *Mauretania Sitifensis,* perforated tables for the pouring of liquids are known[39]. Some sigma-shaped stone tables present lowered surfaces and carefully cut frames, which on the one hand makes their integration into higher reclining platforms favorable, and on the other hand shows that they were intended to hold liquids within their framed surface[40]. This specifically ritual-associated feature is also the main reason for the highly sophisticated (and expensive) plastering of the waterproof *opus signinum*-covered sigma-*mensae*[41]. As the *signinum*-surface is attested frequently in closed funerary spaces (catacombs, churches, mausolea, burial halls) the commonly accepted explanation of protection against rain water is not satisfactory[42]. This waterproofing may moreover be associated with the rite of *refrigerium*, i.e. the ›refreshment‹ after the burdens of earthly life, a recurring topic of late antique texts[43]. Funerary inscriptions of the 3rd to the 4th century refer to the *refrigerium* as a place of paradise-like status for the soul in a sphere next to God. At the same time, the *refrigerium* was still a convivial ritual celebrated in honor of the dead practiced at or over graves. I suggest that the *refrigerium* was also performed as a flooding ritual, as evidenced by the materiality of the lowered and framed stone, by the mosaiced or plastered tables, and by water-installations (channels, cisterns, basins) installed next to or within the *mensae*, which clearly attest the ritual ›washing‹ of not only the tables, but also of

---

[38] Lancel 1956, 329–331; Ardeleanu 2023, fig. 10.
[39] AE 1972, 771.
[40] Barral i Altet 1978, 57–58 figs. 9. 11. 14; cf. *Mactaris*: CIL VIII 23575; Prévot 1984, XII 8.
[41] Cf. libation depictions in Rome's catacombs: Jastrzebowska 1979, fig. 12.
[42] Neyses 1999, 416.
[43] Dresken-Weiland 2010, 181–183.

the couches[44]. Further, some epitaphs explicitly name the cover slabs as *mensa cum titulum* [*!*] *refrigerationis*, which in this case cannot point to the *refrigerium* as an intermediate place near God[45]. One famous *mensa* mosaic from *Tipasa* not only refers to a realistic meal with its (floodable) maritime scene, but also in its inscription specifically calls the users to a *convivium* in *pax et concordia* (fig. 2)[46].

## TYPE 1B: *MENSA* MONUMENTS WITH RECTANGULAR OR TRAPEZOID SHAPE

A radial pattern of reclining should also be reconstructed in the case of square, rectangular, and trapezoid *mensae* grouped around a (mostly sigmoid) table on the lateral side. This is why I refer to these *mensae* as type 1b, represented by examples from *Cornus*[47], *Tipasa*[48] and *Carthago Nova*[49] (figs. 1, 1b; 3). Burnt remains were found on the surface of one such rectangular *mensa* from *Tarraco*, possibly indicating the burning of herbs or fragrances or even the preparation of individual dishes on the *mensa* itself. Due to their stratigraphic position above the *mensa*, the numerous oyster shells, domestic animal bones, glass fragments, and pottery found in the ashes may indeed point to residues of *convivia* practiced here[50]. As with the sigma-*mensae*, waterproofing of both the couches and the tables is a key characteristic. In *Emerita*, they had colorful paintings and painted epitaphs[51].

While most *mensae* were designed for commemorating only one person buried under the *mensa*, large *mensae* over several sarcophagi are also attested for type 1. This points to reclining surfaces for large groups of convivial participants. In *Emerita*[52], *Tipasa* and *Theveste*[53], substantial *mensae* 4–8 m in diameter or width are attested. They appear clustered in open necropoleis and not enclosed by burial precinct walls, which emphasizes their ›collective‹ character. Also in *Troia*[54], in *Carthago Nova*[55] or in *Sabratha*[56] veritable *mensa* batteries were erected, partly in rows or opposite to each other. Although some had mosaic framing, their arrangement, size and the complete absence of epitaphs suggest simultaneous celebrations by larger less wealthy groups, who could not afford family burial grounds for private commemoration or the particularly prestigious burials within churches.

Yet, numerous *mensae* were built in churches and their annexes, such as in *Troia*[57], on the Isla del Rei[58] or in *Tipasa*[59]. Here, *mensae* were placed directly next to bishop's tombs, in the main and side naves, and in church annexes. Furthermore, some *mensa* epitaphs belong to clerics, who apparently did not renounce this form of popular commemoration[60].

---

[44] *Tarraco*: Del Amo 1979, 141 (tombs 1386, 1379, 1590, 180); Barral i Altet 1987, 62; *Tipasa*: Bouchenaki 1975, figs. 6. 10. 11. 29. 136. 214. 220–223; Ardeleanu 2023, 140 with more examples.
[45] *Auzia*: CIL VIII 20780; Février 1964, 153.
[46] Bouchenaki 1975, 16–17; Février 1990, 358–359; Ardeleanu 2018, 475 fig. 1.
[47] Giuntella et al. 1985, fig. 14–17 tab. 4; Giuntella 1999, fig. 38.
[48] Bouchenaki 1975, figs. 6 (area 2, *mensa* 3). 10 (area 3, *mensa* 2). 29. 133–136. 206; Ardeleanu 2018, no. 69 figs. 3. 7.
[49] Barral i Altet 1978, 62–64 fig. 13.
[50] Barral i Altet 1978, 60–62 (tomb 685).
[51] AE 2019, 801.
[52] Picado Pérez 2006–2008, fig. 52.
[53] Kadra 1989, pl. 10; Ardeleanu 2018, 493–494; Ardeleanu 2023, 142 fig. 18.
[54] De Almeida et al. 1982, 259–261.
[55] Barral i Altet 1987, 62–64 fig. 13.
[56] Giuntella et al. 1985, 50 fig. 54.
[57] De Almeida et al. 1982.
[58] Rita Larrucea 2020, 303.
[59] Ardeleanu 2018, 488 no. 63.
[60] Ardeleanu 2018, 481 no. 67.

## TYPE 2: *TRICLINIUM*-SHAPED *MENSA* MONUMENTS

This type of funerary *mensae* is marked by a square or rectangular shape with tables situated in such a central position of the couch that radial reclining becomes impossible (fig. 1, 2). Instead, the relatively narrow couches are grouped in a U-shape around the table allowing for parallel reclining along the table. In the event that the couches present adequate width and depth, such as in *Tarraco*[61], in *Sanisera*[62] and in *Tipasa*[63], a diagonal reclining arrangement in a classical *triclinium* scheme for up to a dozen diners is plausible. These *triclinia* are part of the above-mentioned funerary banquet tradition of the Roman West (fig. 4). Technically, they hardly differ from type 1a/b, except for the lack of any examples with elaborate mosaic or painted decoration.

## TYPE 3: *PISCINAE (?)* – CIRCULAR *MENSA* TABLES

Across the Western world, *mensae* with circular tables are known in differing materials, such as rock-cut on Malta[64], *signinum*-plastered at *Tipasa*[65], painted in *Emerita*[66], as stone discs from the northern Adriatic zone[67] and as marble slabs from *Pannonia*[68] and Crete[69] (figs. 1, 3; 4). Although only a few have been found *in situ*, a similar half-radial reclining practice around circular tables, as in the case of the sigmoid *mensae*, is suggested by contextual finds. However, circular funerary *mensa* tables, such as examples from *Salona* or *Aquileia*, were also inlaid in rectangular or square tomb covers[70]. They might have been used as tables for liquid-based rituals. Reclining on these monuments was impossible, at least if they were not part of larger adjacent couches. Striking characteristics of these *mensae* are their lowered surface with high frames, drainage spouts and circular channels for liquid regulation[71]. These features allowed for controlled liquid storing (perhaps during the *refrigerium*) and fittingly, several epitaphs denominate the monuments themselves as *piscinae*[72]. This supports the idea of a close union between the dead and those left behind. The ritualized *mensae* and *piscinae* with their inscribed epitaphs became a sort of placeholders for the deceased, who metaphorically took part in the ritualized unity and *concordia* of the family.

## TYPE 4: *LECTI (?)* – SOCLE-*MENSAE* WITH SINGLE RECLINING OPTION

Probably the most widespread type of funerary *mensae* was an above-ground structure in rectangular, oval or elliptical shape (figs. 1, 4; 5). They imitated the dimensions of the tomb beneath and took over several ritual-associated characteristics, such as waterproofed plastering and inserted marble tables for vessel/food storage, libation holes as well as sophisticated framing for the collection of liquids. With these features it is most likely that they developed from the grave marker type of *cupae* (fr. *caissons*; it. *cassoni*), well-distributed throughout the Italic, Hispanic

---

[61] Del Amo 1979, 45–48 fig. 1.
[62] Rita Larrucea 2020, 302–304 fig. 4.
[63] Bouchenaki 1975, figs. 6 (area 1 *mensa* 2). 10 (area 3 *mensa* 11). 18 (u-shaped *mensa* in southern area). 107. 220–222; Ardeleanu 2018, fig. 7 (NW-zone).
[64] Buhagiar 2007, figs. 34 b; 35 b; 42 b (L-shaped couch); 43 a; 78 c; Jensen 2008, 127 figs. 4. 13.
[65] Bouchenaki 1975, figs. 11 (caveau 2, *mensa* 5). 18 (northern area, possibly martyr tomb, discussion in Ardeleanu 2018, 480–481). 250–252.
[66] Sánchez Hidalgo et al. 2009–2011, fig. 34.
[67] *Iader*: Duval 1985, 445–446; *Salona*: Duval 1984, figs. 9. 10. 12. 19. 20; Duval 1985, 445; Marin et al. 2010, cat. 81–88. 474; *Aquileia*: Duval 1985, fig. 4, 1.
[68] *Sirmium*: Duval 1984, figs. 1. 2. 4–6; Duval 1985, 443–444 fig. 1; Popović 2022, 151–157.
[69] Chalkia 1991, 74 Typ E Gr. 21. 22 fig. 68 denies any commemorative use, although one *mensa* was found *in situ* covering a tomb.
[70] Duval 1985, 445–454 figs. 9. 10; Marin et al. 2010, cat. 82. 86 (?). 88; cf. *Theveste*: AE 1995, 1747.
[71] Duval 1985, 445 figs. 9. 10; Marin et al. 2010, cat. 80 (?). 81. 82 (?). 747.
[72] Marin et al. 2010, cat. 81– 83. 747 (even transcribed in Greek).

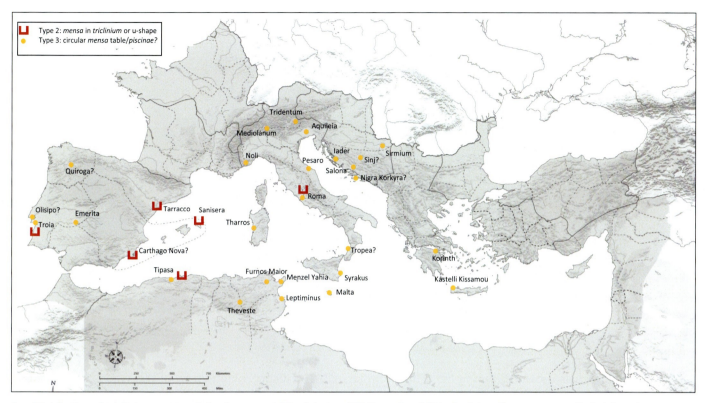

4    Distribution of *triclinia-mensae* and circular *mensa* tables (*piscinae* [?]) (types 2 and 3) in the late antique *oecumene* (S. Ardeleanu)

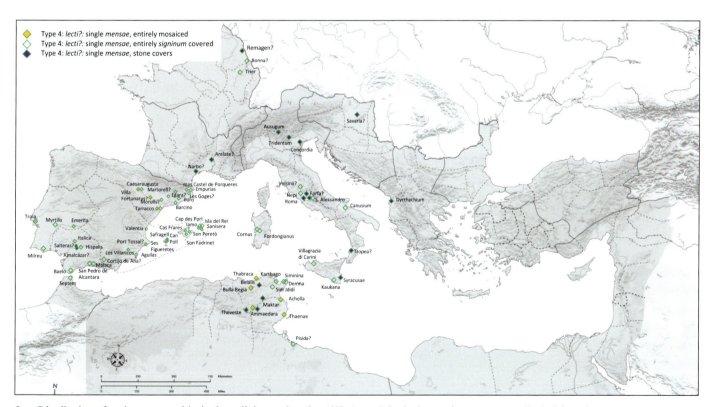

5    Distribution of socle-*mensae* with single reclining option (*lecti* [?]) (type 4) in the late antique *oecumene* (S. Ardeleanu)

6   5th century-tomb cover for bishop Hilarius from *Arelate* with libation hole (FAN.1992.2567, Musée départemental Arles antique, © Rémi Bénali)

and African provinces during the 1st to 3rd centuries[73]. The distinctive criterium of this type is a more or less human-sized platform, which in contrast to the ›collective‹ *mensa*-types 1a, 1b and 2 allowed only individual reclining above the tomb. Stone specimens are attested in dense clusters in the northern Adriatic region[74] and in central *Africa Proconsularis*, where extensive local series of the 3rd to the 7th century are known (fig. 5)[75]. Single *mensae* inserted into church floors come from *Belalis Maior*[76] and *Mactaris*[77], where epitaphs mention *castimoniales* and libation holes and cavities for meals structure the elaborate *carmina*. Which substances were libated in each specific case is largely unknown. In Rome, however, a few analyses have been carried out on libation tubes documented *in situ* piercing Late Antique sarcophagi[78]. These have shown that in addition to wine and water, fragrant oils and resins were libated. Besides the ›nourishment‹ of the deceased, the substances may also have played an important role in reducing odor, which could quickly become a hygienic problem for commemorators, especially in closed burial spaces such as mausolea or densely occupied funerary churches[79]. Some holes in *Theveste*[80], *Hippo Regius*[81] or *Syracusae*[82] were very carefully perforated and had collection basins or stepped surfaces for the insertion of sieve-like bowls in metal or clay, in order to facilitate the libation process and to filter libated substances. In *Arelate*, such a tomb cover with complex libation features commemorated a bishop (fig. 6)[83].

---

[73] Stirling 2007.
[74] *Salona*, Grado, *Concordia*: Duval 1985, figs. 13. 16–18. 20.
[75] *Mactaris*: AE 1993, 1727; Prévot 1984, cat. II 4 (with cavities carved before inscription); X, 26; X, 46; *Theveste*: AE 1968, 641; AE 1974, 707; AE 1995, 1748 [?]. 1751. 1752. 1756; two anepigraphic single *mensae* with floodable Christograms: Lancel 1956, 324; at least 4 further examples in: Kadra 1989; Ardeleanu 2023, fig. 18.
[76] AE 1974, 694. 696 (*episcopus*).
[77] Prévot 1984, cat. II 4.
[78] Spera 2005, 31–32; De Santis 2008, 4547–4548; Acampora 2013, 405–419; De Santis 2015, 207–208.
[79] Cf. Reifarth 2013.
[80] AE 1968, 641; Giuntella et al. 1985, 55–56 figs. 55. 56.
[81] Ardeleanu 2023, no. 136.
[82] Sgarlata 2003, 40 figs. 14. 15.
[83] CIL XII 949.

7 Group of single *mensae* (type 4) and *mensa* tables (type 6) with *signinum* covers within a late antique necropolis of *Hispalis* (Del Carmen Barragán 2010, fig. 60)

Along the southern Iberian Peninsula, single *mensae* with *signinum* surfaces were extremely widespread and used well into the Middle Ages[84]. Only in this zone, specific regional features of décor such as moulded or carved crosses above the *mensae* developed. Common characteristics of this group are their slightly declining lateral sides, inset semicircular or rectangular marble tables, drainage channels, plastered frames for water regulation and receptacles for food storage. Technically almost identical examples of the 4th to the 6th century are known from *Hispalis*[85], *Troia*, *Emerita* (painted)[86], *Malaca*, from *Tarraconnensis* and the Balearics[87]. In *Hispalis*, the individual character of these *mensae* becomes evident through their anepigraphic appearance and their mostly isolated placement within an open necropolis with monumental tombs (fig. 7). However, a few *mensae* were uncovered within a walled area, others in a *triclinium*-arrangement, which again suggests their use in family burial grounds or collective festivities[88].

This type of *mensa* was ideally suited for use in varied funerary spaces. Regional examples entirely covered with mosaics were found in mausolea, churches, and areae of northern and central *Africa Proconsularis*[89], *Byzacena*[90], Porto Torres[91] and Zaragoza[92]. In *Canusium*[93], Matarò[94], Son Peretò (Mallorca)[95], *Syracusae*[96] and Trier[97] such single *mensae* of the 5th to the 7th century are attested in hypogea, areae, catacombs, burial halls or annex rooms of churches, sometimes in *triclinium*-arrangement[98]. Further examples are known from rural villae or rural churches of the 5th to the 7th century[99]. In *Myrtilis*, dozens of such platforms sprout from a church floor with waterproof plastered surfaces[100]. This ensemble made a standard liturgical use almost impossible.

---

[84] Navarro 1988; Del Amo 1979, 141–143; Burch et al. 1999; Gurt Esparraguera – Ribera i Lacomba 2005; Riera Rullan 2009; Ripoll – Molist 2012, 19; González Fernández et al. 2022, 18 fig. 6.
[85] Del Carmen Barragán Valencia 2010, figs. 38. 60. 85. 86. 89. 92. 98. 100. 102. 103. 105. 115. 121. 127. 127. 132. 142. 149. 151. 154. 169. 188 (with spout). 198. 211. 212. 215.
[86] Picado Pérez 2006–2008, 255 fig. 54.
[87] Navarro 1988; Riera Rullan 2009.
[88] Del Carmen Barragán Valencia 2010, fig. 18 (nos. 3. 4. 5).
[89] *Bulla Regia*: Chaouali et al. 2018, 194–195; *Thabraca/Clupea*: Duval 1976, 29–30 fig. 11; Ardeleanu 2023, fig. 14; *Ammaedara*: Baratte 2011, figs. 169. 171.
[90] *Acholla*: Duval 1976, 30. 93; *Thaenae*: Ardeleanu 2023, 139 fig. 15.
[91] Duval 1976, 73–75; Giuntella et al. 1985, fig. 43.
[92] Galve Izquierdo et al. 2005, figs. 3. 9.
[93] De Santis 2020.
[94] Navarro 1988, 30.
[95] Riera Rullan 2009, 107–109 figs. 48–51. 54. 60.
[96] Sgarlata 2003, 38.
[97] Neyses 1999, 425–429.
[98] In Zaragossa (Galve Izquierdo et al. 2005, figs. 3. 9), Son Peretò (Riera Rullan 2009, fig. 60) and Trier (Neyses 1999, 425), their *triclinium*-arrangement in rooms with typical offset doorways has not yet been observed by scholarship so far.
[99] Los Villaricos: González Fernández et al. 2022, 18 fig. 6; Mas Castell: Burch et al. 1999.
[100] Macias 1993.

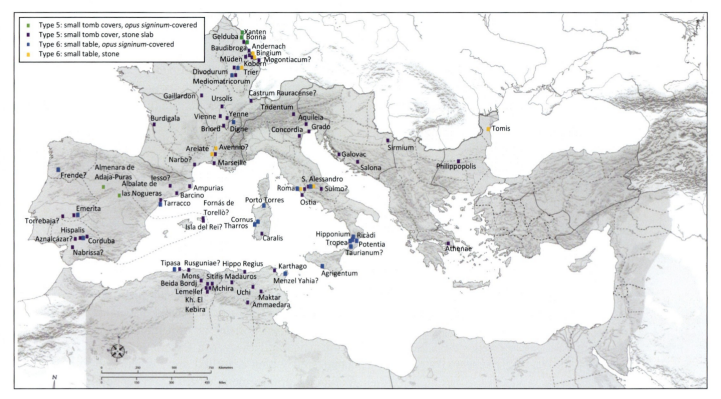

8 Distribution of small tomb covers with flooding/offering option and of *mensa* tables (types 5 and 6) in the late antique *oecumene* (S. Ardeleanu)

However, several banqueters were able to lie around the platforms in a commemorative manner, whereby the place on the *mensa* itself might have become a position of honor within the banquet.

## TYPE 5: SMALL TOMB COVERS WITH FLOODING/OFFERING OPTION

Type 5 is marked by small-format grave covers at the circulation level of their original context (framing, libation holes, food cavities) as our aforementioned types. Their constitutive characteristic is that reclining on the slabs themselves was impossible due to their small shape. Theoretically, several of these slabs might have belonged to monuments of our types 1–4 or 6, but *in situ* examples attest their use as an independent type. An important series is known from *Mactaris*, where numerous epitaphs call these slabs *mensae*[101]. Although most of their find contexts are lost, such *mensae* from central and western *Africa Proconsularis* and *Sitifensis* bear reliefs and carved features explicitly referring to ritual practice (figs. 1, 5; 8)[102]. While bowls, *urcei* and *paterae* invited viewers to pour/drink wine, plates and circular depressions motivated users to deposit food on the small covers. Two larger micro-regional series of the 5th to the 6th century made of framed rectangular slabs with epitaphs come from western *Dalmatia* to *Pannonia*[103] and from the Middle-Rhine region[104]. The *mensae* from *Salona*, likely placed horizontally over sarcophagi in churches, only rarely exceeded a length or width of 1 m. Interestingly, they were used mainly for prestigious

---

[101] Prévot 1984, 161–163 nos. II 5; III 13; X 17. 26. 33. 29. 48, 55, 68; XI 4. 10; XI 12. 14. 30; XII 1. 8. 12. 20. 26–28. 40. 46. 48. 49. 53. 59; Ardeleanu 2023, fig. 17.
[102] Ardeleanu 2023, no. 131.
[103] *Savaria*: CIL III 4185 (?); *Sirmium*: Popović 2022, 158–161.
[104] *Baudobriga*: CIL XIII 7558; Boppert 1971, 134 (with cavity [?]); *Bingium*: CIL XIII 7527; Kobern-Gondorf: CIL XIII 7644; *Mogontiacum*: ILCV 1543.

episcopal tombs, whose epitaphs were engraved on the upper rim of the floodable slabs[105]. In all cases, reclining around the small socles was possible only on a lower surface, similar to the final type discussed here.

## TYPE 6: SMALL TABLES WITH LOWER RECLINING SURFACE

A special type of ritualized grave markers is the small *mensa* table of mostly rectangular form above one or more tombs. Such tables show striking similarities to the aforementioned types in their technical and decorative design (plastering, painting, inserted epitaphs). They are characterized by their pedestal-like shape, usually developing some 0.20–1 m above walking level (fig. 1, 6). It was not possible to recline on them due to their small size. The most widespread variant is a *signinum*-plastered socle, found in both open necropoleis and churches throughout the West (fig. 8). Two main clusters of this plastered type from the 4th to the 6th century emerged in southern Calabria[106] and Trier/environs[107], while tables in stone appear as far east as *Tomis*[108]. The socles were used for holding food and vessels, while banqueteers reclined on the floor around the socle. *In situ* examples of the late 4th and 5th centuries in *Emerita*[109], *Hispalis* (fig. 7)[110] and Trier (fig. 9)[111] show that the *signinum* covered both the floodable socles and the lower reclining surfaces, the latter being inclined downwards from the socle for convenience reasons. In the areas around Tropea[112] and Trier[113], epitaphs were inserted as trapezoid, square and triangular marble slabs into the socles. In some cases, only the geometric slabs have survived, but my recent autopsy demonstrated that they preserve traces of mortar/plaster on their rear and lateral sides, proving that they formerly belonged to this type. The best-documented series comes from Trier, with several *in situ* finds within the huge burial hall at St. Maximinus (fig. 9). Two examples of the second half of the 4th century one of which painted red, were documented in the entrance of an apsidal burial annex giving way to the huge hall[114]. The lower *signinum* surface might have filled the entire floor of the annex, enabling up to 18 (familial [?]) banqueteers to recline in *triclinium*-arrangement around the two socles. In smaller burial buildings in Bonn and Xanten, similar *signinum*-socles without epitaphs, but with inserted clay bowls for libation/meal storage were found alongside plastered seating benches and single *mensae*[115]. In St. Maximinus, *tituli* of the 7th to the 8th century are still embedded in their socle

9 Funerary *mensa* table for a certain Urbicia in an apsidal annex of the burial hall of St. Maximinus in Trier (S. Ardeleanu, with permission of S. Schu, Museum am Dom, Trier)

---

[105] Marin et al. 2010, 262–276 cat. 72–78. 80.
[106] Buonocuore 1987, 12–54.
[107] Neyses 1999; Schmidt 2000, 259 fig. 8; 270–271 fig. 16.
[108] Popescu 1976, 73 nos. 27. 37.
[109] Mateos Cruz 1999, 138 with unplausible interpretation as *lectus triclinaris*.
[110] Del Carmen Barragán Valencia 2010, 82–83 figs. 60. 89.
[111] Neyses 1999.
[112] Buonocuore 1987, 12–54.
[113] Several cases in: Neyses 1999; surely belonging to this type: Gauthier 1975, cat. 11; Merten 2018, cat. 17. 25. 29; Ardeleanu 2021, 347–350 no. 43; cf. Metz: Gauthier 1975, cat. 247.
[114] Neyses 1999, 414–418.
[115] Schmidt 2000, 259 fig. 8; 270–271 fig. 16.

or preserved their geometric shape[116]. These Medieval examples provide spectacular evidence for the continuity of *refrigeria* and *convivia* in St. Maximinus at a time when the burial hall was transformed into a veritable church with clear eucharistic function[117].

Another 4th to 6th-century variant of the Moselle/Lower Rhine-tables were rectangular or square stone cists with inset epitaphs. A few *in situ* finds over tombs prove a similar use as their *signinum* relatives[118]. Analogous to other *mensa* types, they bore cavities and libation holes[119], such as an incised monogram with a central hole piercing an example from Kobern[120]. Stone cists with insertable rectangular and geometric epitaphs are common in Trier[121] and its area[122]. Often, either the cist or the epitaph inlays have survived only. Over a timespan of 200 years of extensive epigraphic research at Trier, this group has never been recognized as ritualized monuments[123]. Several ›normed‹ groups with square and rectangular format and almost identical sizes suggest specialized workshops producing these monuments, while imported and colorful marbles for the epitaphs, some of them mentioning high officials, point to wealthy commissioners. The popularity of the cists in an elite-milieu is further supported by gypsum-burials documented under some of these markers[124]. Even *presbyteri, castimoniales* and *subdiaconi* used such monuments[125]. Besides their material features, epigraphic evidence too supports the idea of the practicing of ritual commemoration at/on them. From a total of 30 mentions of deposition dates on Trier's late antique epitaphs, not fewer than seven appear on socles, in which a ritual use is probable either by context or by materiality[126]. This is not a coincidence. For proper commemoration it was essential to fix recurring feasting days and the associated rites permanently and precisely. Where, if not at the grave marker itself, to which bereaved were supposed to return regularly, would this have made more sense? Through this process of physical inscription and the various functions of the tables, the socles literally became the center of the cult.

A last variant of the isolated table is represented by both *signinum* and stone socles from Rome's 3rd to 4th-century catacombs. They were rarely built over tombs and never bear individual epitaphs[127], but were built as cylindrical, polygonal and rectangular pedestals or hewn into the rock. Some occupy corners, back walls and entrances of *cubicula*, others the ends of corridors. Their clear connection to burials cannot be denied, as is shown by their physical proximity to floor-*formae*, wall-*loculi* and to *cubicula* easily accessible to larger groups of visitors. Therefore, they are interpreted today as part of commemorative *convivia* and not, as long assumed, as *mensae oleorum*, in which liquids libated over saint remains, would have been collected.

## CONCLUSION

As indissoluble components of burial and commemoration of the dead, collective dining and drinking are still today among the most important practices of coping with grief and human loss in this world. Convivial gathering provides solace; it promotes cohesion and *concordia* between the deceased and the bereaved even beyond the traumatic experience of death. And it instills a sense of belonging, not only to families but also to larger communities. As my distribution maps show,

---

[116] Merten 2018, cat. 17. 25.
[117] Weber 2006.
[118] Neyses 1999, 414.
[119] Gauthier 1975, cat. 75. 109 (?). 184; Merten 2018, cat. 12.
[120] CIL XIII 7639.
[121] Gauthier 1975, cat. 12. 35. 62. 69. 119 (?). 144; Merten 2018, cat. 19. 21.
[122] ILCV 3570. 3570 (*Antunnacum*); CIL XIII 7560 (*Baudibroga*).
[123] Gose 1958: »Fassung«, »Grabinschrift«; Gauthier 1975, 20: »D'autres étaient encastrées dans une dalle«; Neyses 1999: »Sockel«, »Grabsteine«, »Steinfassungen«.
[124] Reifarth 2013.
[125] Gauthier 1975, cat. 109. 142A; Merten 2018, cat. 28.
[126] Gauthier 1975, cat. 109. 142A. 153; Merten 2018, cat. 17. 25. 28. 30.
[127] Chalkia 1991, 75; Marinone 2000, 76–77; Chalkia 2018.

funerary *mensae* were common only in the Western *oecumene*, if one excludes isolated cases from the Balkan peninsula, the Aegean and the Near East. Whether this can be explained by different commemorative practices, or by variable success of the Church against them, is difficult to say. In my view, regional preferences will have played an important role, for, with the exception of libation devices, no predecessors of ritualized *mensae* are found in the East even for imperial times. On the other hand, clear clusters emerge in the *Sitifensis, Caesariensis, Proconsularis, Lusitania,* the Moselle and Middle Rhine area, along the Hispanic south coast and in the northern Adriatic zone. It is precisely in North Africa, in Italy, on the Iberian Peninsula and in *Dalmatia* that the predecessor types of *cupae, triclinia, biclinia, mensa* tables and libation covers are attested in high numbers. Both in technical and decorative design, the analogies are striking, and only in the first three macro-regions, the entire typological spectrum is represented. The monuments' overall distribution, which includes the islands of Sicily, Sardinia, the Balearics and Malta as important intermediaries[128], attests to the existence of a highly entangled western *koine* of funerary commemoration apparently shared by elite and middle classes of the Long Late Antiquity. However, the use of cheap material, spoliation processes and the frequency of *mensae* without epitaphs suggests that lower classes valued these rites and monuments, too[129]. Surprisingly, *mensae* appear almost exclusively in urban contexts, which underscores their importance for the transformed public function of late antique burials and the highly representative, sociohierarchical character in the commemoration of the dead of urban communities.

Despite these ›global‹ similarities, striking localisms are ubiquitous, such as the vivid paintings on the Emeritan *mensae*, the mosaiced *mensae* in *Africa Proconsularis* or the plastered crosses in *Tarraconensis*. It is crucial that global (i.e. the typological basic forms, ritual devices) and local elements (i.e. decoration, materiality) merge at the same time on the very same monuments. Therefore, it seems appropriate to me to speak of ›glocal‹ monuments in such cases, since both levels are well-represented. This also bears the advantage that we do not have to serve the problematic methodological opposition between ›pagan‹ and ›Christian‹, emphasized too often by previous research.

It can be stated that the total number of late antique *mensae* far exceeds that of their Imperial period predecessors. They peaked certainly in Late Antiquity and obviously translated without difficulty into Christian contexts. From the 4th to the 8th century, the construction and ritual use of *mensae* in churches was constantly practiced, partly by clerics themselves. These contexts are most densely distributed on the Iberian Peninsula, in Italy and in North Africa, from where we also hear the loudest clerical criticism. As with so many sets of laws, an accumulated polemic against this ›incorrect behavior‹ is rather to be read as a confirmation of the perpetuated rituals. Texts, epigraphic material and archaeological observations complement each other. The multiple functionalities of the *mensae*, the perforated tables, the plate reliefs, the carved bowls, the banquet-alluding tomb paintings and mosaics strikingly invited the users to perform ritual acts at the monuments, which are then so vividly described in the metatexts.

## BIBLIOGRAPHY

| | |
|---|---|
| Acampora 2013 | L. Acampora, Libagioni e riti funerari. A proposito di un'inedita lastra della catacomba di Pretestato, in: F. Bisconti – M. Braconi (eds.), Incisioni figurate della tarda antichità. Convegno Roma 22.–23.03.2012 (Vatican 2013) 405–419 |
| Ardeleanu 2018 | S. Ardeleanu, Directing the Faithful, Structuring the Sacred Space. Funerary Epigraphy in its Archaeological Context in Late-Antique Tipasa, JRA 31, 2018, 475–501 |
| Ardeleanu 2021 | S. Ardeleanu, Grabmonumente, in: J. Lipps – S. Ardeleanu – J. Osnabrügge – C. Witschel (eds.), Die römischen Steindenkmäler in den Reiss-Engelhorn-Museen Mannheim (Mannheim 2021) 212–351 |

---

[128] Martorelli et al. 2015.
[129] Similarly Morvillez 2019, 218 for domestic *stibadia*.

| | |
|---|---|
| Ardeleanu 2023 | S. Ardeleanu, Materializing Death in Late Antique North Africa. An Overview on Microregional Epitaphic Habits and Funerary Rituals, in: Ardeleanu – Cubas Díaz 2023, 108–157 |
| Ardeleanu – Cubas Diaz 2023 | S. Ardeleanu – J. Cubas Díaz (eds.), Funerary Landscapes of the Late Antique *Oecumene*. Contextualizing Epigraphic and Archeological Evidence of Mortuary Practices. Conference Heidelberg 30.05.–01.06.2019 (Heidelberg 2023) |
| Baratte 2011 | F. Baratte, L'area orientale, in: F. Baratte – F. Bejaoui (eds.), Recherches archéologiques à Haidra 4 (Rome 2011) 147–182 |
| Barral i Altet 1978 | X. Barral i Altet, Mensae et repas funéraire dans les nécropoles d'époque chrétienne de la péninsule Ibérique, in: IX congresso di archeologia cristiana, Rome 21.–27.09.1975 (Vatican 1978) 49–69 |
| Bonacasa Carra 1996 | R. Bonacasa Carra, Agrigento. La necropoli paleocristiana *sub divo* (Rome 1996) |
| Boppert 1971 | W. Boppert, Die frühchristlichen Inschriften des Mittelrheingebietes (Mainz 1971) |
| Bouchenaki 1975 | M. Bouchenaki, Fouilles de la nécropole occidentale de Tipasa (Matarès) (Algier 1975) |
| Braune 2008 | S. Braune, *Convivium funebre*. Gestaltung und Funktion römischer Grabtriklinien als Räume für sepulkrale Bankettfeiern (Hildesheim 2008) |
| Buhagiar 2007 | M. Buhagiar, The Christianisation of Malta. Catacombs, Cult Centres and Churches in Malta to 1530 (Oxford 2007) |
| Buonocore 1987 | M. Buonocore, Inscriptiones Christianae Italiae septimo saeculo antiquiores 5 (Bari 1987) |
| Burch et al. 1999 | J. Burch – J. M. Nolla – J. Sagreda – D. Vivó i Sureda, Els temples i els cementeris antics i altmedievals de mas Castell de Porqueres (Banyoles 1999) |
| Chalkia 1991 | E. Chalkia, Le mense paleocristiane. Tipologia e funzioni delle mense secondarie nel culto paleocristiano (Vatican 1991) |
| Chalkia 2018 | E. Chalkia, Le mense delle catacombe di Roma, RACr 94, 2018, 331–349 |
| Chaouali et al. 2018 | M. Chaouali – C. Fenwick – D. Booms, Bulla Regia I. A New Church and Christian Cemetery, LibSt 49, 2018, 187–197 |
| De Almeida et al. 1982 | F. De Almeida – J. Paixão – A. C. Paixão, Cementerio paleocristiano o romano tardio de Troia, in: II Reunió d'Arqueologia paleocristiana Hispànica, Montserrat 02.–05.11.1978 (Barcelona 1982) 259–263 |
| De Santis 2008 | P. De Santis, s. v. riti funerari, in: Nuovo dizionario patristico e di antichità Cristiane III (2008) 4531–4554 |
| De Santis 2015 | P. De Santis, Riti e pratiche funerarie nel processo di costruzione di una memoria identitaria: esempi da Sardegna e Sicilia, in: Martorelli et al. 2015, 203–220 |
| De Santis 2020 | P. De Santis, L'ipogeo H nel complesso catacombale di Canosa di Puglia alla luce delle recenti indagini, RArCr 96, 2020, 91–115 |
| Del Amo 1979 | M. Del Amo, Las mensae funerarias de la Necrópolis Romano-Cristiana de Tarragona y otras formas relacionadas con ellas, in: E. Soler Álvarez (ed.), Recull Andreu Aleu i Teixido (Tarragona 1979) 39–56 |
| Del Carmen Barragán Valencia 2010 | M. del Carmen Barragán Valencia, La necrópolis tardoantigua de Carretera de Carmona (Híspalis) (Sevilla 2010) |
| Deschler-Erb et al. 2021 | S. Deschler-Erb – U. Albarella – S. Valenzuela Lamas – G. Rasbach (eds.), Roman Animals in Ritual and Funerary Contexts. Conference Basel 01.–04.02.2018 (Wiesbaden 2021) |
| Dresken-Weiland 2010 | J. Dresken-Weiland, Bild, Grab und Wort. Untersuchungen zu Jenseitsvorstellungen von Christen des 3. und 4. Jhs. (Regensburg 2010) |
| Dunbabin 2003 | K. Dunbabin, The Roman Banquet. Images of Conviviality (Cambridge 2003) |
| Duval 1976 | N. Duval, La mosaïque funéraire dans l'art paléochrétien (Ravenna 1976) |
| Duval 1984 | N. Duval, Mensae funéraires de Sirmium et de Salone, VjesDal 77, 1984, 187–226 |
| Duval 1985 | N. Duval, Piscinae et mensae funéraires. De Salone à Aquilée, in: Aquileia, la Dalmazia e l'Illirico. Atti della XIV Settimana di Studi Aquileiesi 23.–29.04.1983 (Udine 1985) 437–462 |
| Felle et al. 1994 | A. Felle – M. Del Moro – D. Nuzzo, Elementi di »corredo-arredo« delle tombe del cimitero di S. Ippolito sulla Via Tiburtina, RACr 70, 1994, 89–158 |

| | |
|---|---|
| Février 1964 | P.-A. Février, Remarques sur les inscriptions funéraires datées de Maurétanie césarienne orientale, MEFRA 76, 1964, 105–172 |
| Février 1990 | P.-A. Février, Kult und Geselligkeit. Überlegungen zum Totenmahl, in: J. Martin – B. Quint (eds.), Christentum und antike Gesellschaft (Darmstadt 1990) 358–390 |
| Galve Izquierdo et al. 2005 | P. Galve Izquierdo – A. Blanco Morte – J. Cebolla Berlanga, Edificio de culto paleocristiano en Zaragoza, in: Gurt Esparraguera – Ribera i Lacomba 2005, 483–498 |
| Gauthier 1975 | N. Gauthier, Recueil des inscriptions chrétiennes de la Gaule antérieures à la renaissance carolingienne. Première Belgique (Paris 1975) |
| Giuntella 1999 | A. Giuntella, Cornus I 1. L'Area cimiteriale orientale (Oristano 1999) |
| Giuntella et al. 1985 | A. Giuntella – G. Borghetti – D. Stiaffini, Mensae e riti funerari in Sardegna. La testimonianza di Cornus (Tarent 1985) |
| González Fernández et al. 2022 | R. González Fernández – F. Fernández Matallana – J. Zapata Parra – J. Martínez García – M. Martínez Sánchez, El sarcófago de la necrópolis tardorromana de Los Villaricos, Pyrenae 51, 2022, 7–41 |
| Gose 1958 | E. Gose, Katalog der frühchristlichen Inschriften in Trier (Berlin 1958) |
| Gurt Esparraguera – Ribera i Lacomba 2005 | J. Gurt Esparraguera – A. Ribera i Lacomba (eds.), VI Reunió d'Arqueologia Cristiana Hispànica, Valencia 08.–10.05.2003 (Valencia 2005) |
| Jastrzebowska 1979 | E. Jastrzebowska, Les scènes de banquet dans les peintures et sculptures chrétiennes de IIIᵉ et IVᵉ s., Recherches augustiniennes 14, 1979, 4–90 |
| Jastrzebowska 2021 | E. Jastrzebowska, Origine del numero di sette convitati cristiani nelle catacombe romane, in: C. Dell'Osso – P. Pergola (eds.), *Titvlvm nostrvm perlege*. Miscellanea in onore di Danilo Mazzoleni (Vatican 2021) 612–624 |
| Jensen 2008 | R. Jensen, Dining with the Dead. From the Mensa to the Altar in Christian Late Antiquity, in: L. Brink – O. Green – D. Green (eds.), Commemorating the Dead. Texts and Artifacts in Context (Berlin 2008) 107–143 |
| Kadra 1989 | K. Kadra, Nécropoles tardives de l'antique Théveste: mosaïques funéraires et mensae, in: A. Mastino (ed.), L'Africa Romana IV (Sassari 1989) 265–282 |
| Kotila 1992 | H. Kotila, *Memoria mortuorum*. Commemoration of the Departed in Augustine (Rome 1992) |
| Lancel 1956 | S. Lancel, Une nécropole chrétienne à Tébessa, LibycaBServAnt 4, 1956, 320–331 |
| Macias 1993 | S. Macias, Un espaço funerário, in: C. Torres – S. Macías (eds.), Museu de Mértola. Basílica paleocristã (Mértola 1993) 30–62 |
| Marin et al. 2010 | E. Marin – J.-P. Caillet – N. Duval – D. Feissel – N. Gauthier – F. Prévot, Salona 4. Inscriptions de Salone chrétienne (Paris 2010) |
| Marinone 2000 | M. Marinone, I riti funerari, in: L. Pani Ermini (ed.), *Christiana loca*. Lo spazio cristiano nella Roma del primo millenio (Rome 2000) 71–80 |
| Martorelli et al. 2015 | R. Martorelli – A. Piras – P. G. Spanu (eds.), Isole e terraferma nel primo cristianesimo. 11. Congresso nazionale di archeologia cristiana, Sant'Antioco 23.–27.09.2014 (Cagliari 2015) |
| Mateos Cruz 1999 | P. Mateos Cruz, La basílica de Santa Eulalia de Mérida (Madrid 1999) |
| Méndez Grande 2005 | G. Méndez Grande, *Mensae* funeraria en Augusta Emerita, in: Gurt Esparraguera – Ribera i Lacomba 2005, 475–482 |
| Merten 2018 | H. Merten, Die frühchristlichen Inschriften aus St. Maximin bei Trier (Trier 2018) |
| Morvillez 2019 | E. Morvillez, À propos du fonctionnement des installations de banquet en sigma, AntTard 27, 2019, 193–221 |
| Navarro 1988 | R. Navarro, Necrópolis y formas de enterramiento de época cristiana en las Baleares, in: Les Illes Balears en temps cristians fins als àrabs, Maó 31.10.–04.11.1984 (Ciutadella 1988) 25–40 |
| Neyses 1999 | A. Neyses, Lage und Gestaltung von Grabinschriften im spätantiken Coemeterial-Großbau von St. Maximin in Trier, JbRGZM 46, 1999, 413–446 |
| Nussbaum 1961 | O. Nussbaum, Zum Problem der runden und sigmaförmigen Altarplatten, JbAC 4, 1961, 18–43 |
| Pearce 2015 | J. Pearce, Beyond the Grave. Excavating the Dead in the Late Roman Provinces, in: L. Lavan – M. Mulryan (eds.), Field Methods and Post-Excavation Techniques in Late Antique Archaeology (Leiden 2015) 441–482 |

| | |
|---|---|
| Picado Pérez 2006–2008 | Y. Picado Pérez, La evolución de Augusta Emerita a Mãrida: nuevos datos para el análisis de las áreas extramuros, Memoria 12, 2006–2008, 225–270 |
| Popescu 1976 | E. Popescu, Inscriptiones intra fines Dacoromaniae repertae Graecae et Latinae anno CCLXXXIV recentiores = Inscripţiile greceşti şi latine din secole IV–XIII descoperite în România, Inscripţiile antice din Dacia şi Scythia minor, Academia de Ştiinţe Sociale şi Politice a Republicii Socialiste România (Bucharest 1976) |
| Popović 2022 | I. Popović, Les *mensae* funéraires, in: I. Popović – M. Vasić – J. Guyon – D. Moreau (eds.), La basilique Saint-Irénée de Sirmium et sa nécropole (Turnhout 2022) 151–161 |
| Prévot 1984 | F. Prévot, Recherches archéologiques Franco-Tunisiennes à Mactar 5. Les inscriptions chrétiennes (Rome 1984) |
| Reifarth 2013 | N. Reifarth, Zur Ausstattung spätantiker Elitegräber aus St. Maximin in Trier (Rahden 2013) |
| Riera Rullán 2009 | M. Riera Rullán, Enterramientos de la Antigüedad Tardía en las islas de Cabrera y Mallorca, in: J. López Quiroga – A. Martínez Tejera (eds.), Morir en el Mediterráneo Medieval. Congreso Madrid 17.–18.12.2007 (Oxford 2009) 99–149 |
| Ripoll – Molist 2012 | G. Ripoll – N. Molist, L'arqueologia funerària a Catalunya de l'Antiguitat tardana al món medieval, in: G. Ripoll – N. Molist (eds.), Arqueologia funerària al nord-est peninsular (Barcelona 2012) 12–32 |
| Rita Larrucea 2020 | M. Rita Larrucea, Un fragment de mensa romana am pròtoma de lleó trobat a Sanitja, in: J. Hernández-Gasch (ed.), VIII Jornades d'arqueología de le Illes Balears, Alcúdia 11.–13.10. 2018 (Alcúdia 2020) 299–308 |
| Sánchez Hidalgo et al. 2009–2011 | F. Sánchez Hidalgo – S. Sanabria Murillo – R. Rosa, Evolución de un área extramuros al noreste de Augusta Emerita, Mérida, excavaciones arqueológicas 13, 2009–2011, 425–483 |
| Schmidt 2000 | W. Schmidt, Spätantike Gräberfelder in den Nordprovinzen des römischen Reiches und das Aufkommen christlichen Bestattungsbrauchtums, SaalbJb 50, 2000, 213–441 |
| Sgarlata 2003 | M. Sgarlata, S. Giovanni a Siracusa. Catacombe di Roma e d'Italia (Vatican 2003) |
| Shkodra-Rrugia 2017 | B. Shkodra-Rrugia, Hapësirat funerale dhe qyteti në Dyrrachium gjatë periudhës romake të vonë deri në mesjetën e hershme), Illiria 41, 2017, 289–334 |
| Spera 2005 | L. Spera, Riti funerari e ›culto dei morti‹ nella tarda antichità. Un quadro archeologico dai cimiteri paleocristiani di Roma, Augustinianum 45, 2005, 5–34 |
| Sterrett-Krause 2017 | A. Sterrett-Krause, Drinking with the Dead? Glass from Roman and Christian Burial Areas at Leptiminus, JGS 59, 2017, 47–82 |
| Stirling 2007 | L. Stirling, The Koine of the Cupula in Roman North Africa and the Transition from Cremation to Inhumation, in: D. Stone – L. Stirling (eds.), Mortuary Landscapes of North Africa (Toronto 2007) 110–137 |
| Tulloch 2006 | J. Tulloch, Women Leaders in Family Funerary Banquet, in: C. Osiek – M. MacDonald (eds.), A Woman's Place. House Churches in Earliest Christianity (Minneapolis 2006) 164–193 |
| Valeva 2001 | J. Valeva, La peinture funéraire dans les provinces orientales de l'Empire romain dans l'Antiquité Tardive, Hortus Artium Medievalium 7, 2001, 167–208 |
| Weber 2006 | W. Weber, Vom Coemeterialbau zur Klosterkirche. Die Entwicklung des frühchristlichen Gräberfeldes im Bereich von St. Maximin in Trier, RömQSchr 101, 2006, 240–259 |
| Vives 1963 | J. Vives, Concilios visigóticos e hispano-romanos, España Cristiana (Barcelona 1963) |
| Volp 2002 | U. Volp, Tod und Ritual in den christlichen Gemeinden der Antike (Leiden 2002) |
| Yasin 2009 | A. Yasin, Saints and Church Spaces in the Late Antique Mediterranean. Architecture, Cult, and Community (Cambridge 2009) |
| Zimmermann 2012 | N. Zimmermann, Zur Deutung spätantiker Mahlszenen. Totenmahl im Bild, in: G. Danek – I. Hellerschmidt (eds.), Rituale. Identitätsstiftende Handlungskomplexe (Vienna 2012) 171–185 |

*Stefan Ardeleanu, Research Assistant at the »RomanIslam – Center for Comparative Empire and Transcultural Studies«, Universität Hamburg, Edmund-Siemers-Allee 1, 20146 Hamburg, Germany.*
*[e] st.ardeleanu@gmail.com*

Luca Bianchi

# UN'ULTIMA TESTIMONIANZA DI ARTE ROMANA DI STATO A *MURSA*

**Abstract**
A relief from *Mursa*, belonging to a lost triumphal monument, shows an emperor crowned by Victoria between two dismounted knights in the common scheme of the Dioscuri. They are characterized as patrons of Sarmatian cavalry units, as can be deduced from the headgear they wear instead of the usual *pileus*: a »Spangenhelm« and a closed casque of Iranian tradition. The types, as well as the portrait of a helmeted emperor, point to a date in the 4th century. Despite its clumsiness, the work is a significant, and somewhat unexpected example of Roman state art still produced in eastern *Pannonia* at this late date. The inscription is missing, but a link with the battle of *Mursa* (351) may be suggested on the basis of other evidence.

Mi è gradito esporre in questa sede alcune considerazioni su un problematico rilievo di *Mursa* in cui mi sono imbattuto nel preparare la sezione a me affidata dello »Handbuch der Archäologie« sui monumenti di stato romani a cura di Tonio Hölscher (fig. 1)[1]. È un pezzo sul quale merita soffermarsi, per poco che attiri la sua grossolana fattura, come documento di un'arte ufficiale ancora coltivata in Pannonia nella fase di declino della scultura locale che inizia più o meno con la metà del III secolo, quando l'attività edilizia si contrae, i monumenti ufficiali scompaiono, almeno nella fascia limitanea e sub-limitanea orientale, e quelli funerari si rarefanno e scadono nettamente di qualità. Si aggiungono, come ulteriore motivo d'interesse, eccezionali peculiarità iconografiche.

Il pezzo fu rimesso in luce da uno sterro per lavori di costruzione nel complesso della Facoltà di Medicina di Osijek[2]. Non si conosce il contesto e non si hanno reperti associati. Trattasi di un blocco decorato su una sola faccia con una composizione che comprende una coppia di cavalieri appiedati e il gruppo centrale di un armato del tipo »Marte Ultore« incoronato da una Vittoria. Il primo editore lo classificò come monumento votivo ai Cabiri, trascurando il tema dell'incoronazione e dando eccessivo peso a una scritta incisa in un angolo: *ier(o)i*, epiclesi usata per un gran numero di divinità, e di cui vedremo che si può tentare una diversa spiegazione. I punti deboli di questa lettura sono già stati rilevati, senza però proporne altre[3]. A mio parere il contesto iconografico indica la pertinenza a un monumento onorario (e di qualche pretesa, a giudicare dalle dimensioni del pezzo conservato: 1,15 × 0,40 × 0,33 m), che doveva completarsi con altri elementi, fra i quali una base con un testo epigrafico più esteso. I particolari interni delle figure sono in gran parte cancellati dalla corrosione di un calcare molto friabile, ma qualche dettaglio significativo si distingue.

Il gruppo centrale ripropone il topos celebrativo dell'incoronazione di un imperatore da parte di Vittoria, che qui reca una seconda corona nella mano abbassata. L'incoronato calza un elmo sul quale ne è posata una terza, come distintivo imperiale; indossa una corazza con spallacci, striata verticalmente, tunica con maniche lunghe e *bracae* fino al ginocchio. Nella corazza è riconoscibile un raro tipo a liste verticali, di probabile matrice ellenistica. È documentato in Italia da fregi

---

[1] Capitoli su Pannonie (con Gabrielle Kremer), Dacie e Mesie. Il volume è attualmente in preparazione.
[2] Bulat 1997, 26. Ringrazio Ivo Vukmanić, conservatore del lapidario del Museo Archeologico di Osijek, per il consenso alla mia richiesta di pubblicazione e per informazioni.
[3] Turković 2006, 14–15; breve scheda descrittiva in lupa 5267 (l'incoronato è definito erroneamente Giove).

1   *Mursa*: rilievo con un imperatore incoronato dalla Vittoria e Dioscuri; Arheološki Muzej Osijek (O. Harl, lupa 5267)

con panoplie non posteriori agl'inizi del principato[4], ma ritorna ancora in rilievi provinciali di media età imperiale, indosso a Marte o come componente di trofeo[5]. A dispetto delle sproporzioni e dell'incertezza del disegno, la Vittoria è corretta nella presentazione iconografica, forse perché l'esecutore aveva ancora presente una delle tante redazioni di un tema che in *Pannonia* ritorna con straordinaria frequenza e varietà tipologica nell'apparato figurativo di edifici pubblici e monumenti onorari e votivi[6]: si distinguono i contorni del *sakkos* e di un chitone con *kolpos*, che serba tracce della fitta pieghettatura, e nella disposizione delle ali permane una veduta obliqua.

La presentazione dell'imperatore elmato non è accolta dall'arte monumentale, anche se già dalla metà del III secolo le monete rompono con la tradizione di mostrarlo senza protezione del capo; ma non è questa, come vedremo, l'unica eccezione nelle province dell'Illirico. Ricordiamo brevemente che i ritratti monetali di Gallieno e Postumo sono i primi che mostrano imperatori con elmi laureati, annunziando il valore semantico assunto dall'elmo come emblema di potere nel secolo successivo: si tratta infatti di elmi attici o corinzi, non più in uso da lungo tempo e tradizionalmente associati a figure divine, adatti perciò a distinguere l'imperatore come capo supremo dell'esercito[7]. Le immagini d'imperatori elmati s'intensificano progressivamente nella tarda antichità. Dopo la battaglia di ponte Milvio Costantino affianca ai modelli desueti (in seguito da lui abbandonati) un casco composto del tipo genericamente detto ad arco, affermatosi nella seconda metà del III secolo[8]. Tralasciando i sottotipi, ricordo che si caratterizza per una cresta longitudinale che congiunge due semicalotte orlate da una fascia piatta, di raccordo col

---

[4] Polito 1998, 47. 158. 169 fig. 108.

[5] V. l'epigrafe di costruzione del castro di *Bremenium* (High Rochester, Northumberland), con figure laterali di Marte ed Ercole: RIB 1284 (II sec.); anche un'edicola votiva di Marte da Custom Scrubs, Gloucestershire (III sec., elemento di datazione il cinturone con fibbia circolare): Toynbee 1963, n. 63, ma la corazza è ibrida, forse perché il modello è stato frainteso. Inoltre il trofeo riprodotto su una stele di legionario da *Calcedonia*, di datazione discussa, comunque non anteriore all'età di Caracalla (anche qui sono riprodotti cinturoni con fibbia ad anello): Bianchi 2017, 207 (con altra bibliografia).

[6] Mráv 2012, 251–278. Il fenomeno è messo generalmente in relazione con le visite di Settimio Severo e le sue provvidenze a favore della provincia (in particolare per le molte epigrafi di fondazione con figure laterali di Vittorie), ma il tema ricorre anche prima. Tra le province danubiano-balcaniche la Pannonia è quella che ha restituito il maggior numero di monumenti figurati con temi istituzionali romani, per lo più di carattere militare. L'argomento, che non è stato ancora oggetto di uno studio complessivo, sarà trattato nel cit. volume dello »Handbuch«.

[7] Avverto che la tesi è dibattuta: discussione in Facchinetti 2005, 747–748.

[8] Approfondita trattazione dell'argomento: Facchinetti 2005, 749–752.

paranuca (se presente), paragnatidi con aperture per le orecchie e paranaso, non riprodotto sulle monete⁹. Rimane controversa la cronologia del celebre medaglione attribuito di solito alla zecca di *Ticinum* (questione estranea al nostro argomento nella quale non si entra), dove Costantino calza il fastoso ›elmo persiano‹ con la costa mediana sormontata da un cimiero di piume, il coppo impreziosito di gemme e un cerchio frontale con il cristogramma, punto focale del dibattito sulla complessa tematica di queste emissioni (fig. 2)¹⁰.

L'esecutore del rilievo di *Mursa* ha delineato un casco schematico, non però inclassificabile, più allungato degli elmi a calotta e al quale ha volutamente conferito una forma ovoide (troncata dalla corona), abbozzando inoltre paragnatidi aperte, forse allo scopo di lasciare interamente visibile il volto dell'imperatore, anche se

2  Cosiddetto medaglione di *Ticinum*, diritto: Costantino; Staatliche Münzsammlung München (Max Hirmer, Bildarchiv Foto Marburg)

intenti ritrattistici sono da escludere. Per questo secondo particolare e per la sagoma, non ricollegabile a nessuna delle fogge riprodotte dagl'incisori, ricorda l'elmo molto stilizzato, ma di più accurato rendimento, del busto raffigurato sulla corazza del trofeo pertinente alla porta principale della cinta muraria di Tropaeum Traiani, portata a compimento durante il regno congiunto di Costantino e Licinio (figg. 3. 4). L'epigrafe di costruzione lo data fra il 314/315 (anno dell'entrata in carica del prefetto del pretorio Petronius Annianus) e il marzo del 316, prima della nomina dei cesari che non sono menzionati¹¹.

Mi si passerà una digressione su questo notevole trofeo tardoantico, che all'astratta trasfigurazione del tema unisce una sua riacquistata pregnanza come proclamazione di vittoria universale e sicurezza dei confini, dichiarate nel testo epigrafico, perché non ha attirato l'attenzione che merita. La parte conservata comprende una corazza del tipo a corsetto, tornato in auge con la tetrarchia, e un tronco d'albero da cui si dipartono due rami a forcella, ai quali sono applicati gli schinieri. Il tronco è un volume cilindrico, con tre nodosità cuoriformi distribuite come vertici di un triangolo. Pterigi in due strati sono disposti in modo non funzionale, con alternanza decorativa, allungando i sottostanti negli spazi di risulta fra gli esterni; i dettagli sono in parte veristici (*cingulum* adorno di falere e placchette, fibbia con doppio ardiglione), in parte convenzionali (l'ornato a girali del fo-

---

⁹ La definizione si estende a due tipi differenti, a loro volta raggruppati in sottotipi, ed entrambi riconoscibili sulle emissioni costantiniane (e.g. RIC VII, Lyon 102; *Ticinum* 25, 82 ecc.; Trier 209; Siscia 55, 82, 101): elmi *Intercisa* ed elmi Berkasovo, da parata o di alti ufficiali, composti di due o più piastre ricoperte di lamina d'argento dorato e adorne di pietre semipreziose e paste vitree: v. James 1986, 109–113 (con altra bibliografia). Sugli elmi tardoantichi, origine e tipologie, vi è un'abbondante letteratura: per gli elmi ad arco e riproduzioni monetali cito ancora Facchinetti (v. n. 8); un corpus fu pubblicato da Klumbach 1973. Sui modelli materiali e culturali dei caschi-diadema, dei quali si è riconosciuto il prototipo negli elmi ad arco, rimando alla ricerca collegiale Lusuardi Siena et al. 2002, nata dallo studio della stessa sulla corona ferrea (Lusuardi Siena 1998, 173–253), che ha concluso per un'insegna di potere gotica originariamente affine a un casco.

¹⁰ Ai tre esemplari noti se ne è aggiunto un quarto, comparso nel 2018 sul mercato numismatico. L'ultimo riesame, che dedica particolare attenzione ai motivi equestri e all'*adlocutio* sul rovescio, data il medaglione al 321 (quinquennali dei cesari): Lenski 2018, 258–295; la letteratura è discussa pp. 265–274. Per i vicennali di Costantino optano Carlà – Castello 2010, 87 (dubbi anche sull'associazione alla zecca di *Ticinum*, 263, sottoscritta invece da Lenski).

¹¹ Margineanu Cârstoiu – Barnea 1979, 145, 9.8; lupa 21340. È discusso se i due imperatori abbiano condotto insieme una spedizione contro i goti sul basso Danubio: così Suceveanu – Barnea 1991, 129–130; Mirković 2012, 13–14; *contra*: Porena 2003, 312–314 e n. 277.

3  Tropaeum Traiani: trofeo costantiniano; Adamclisi Muzeul (O. Harl, lupa 21340-2)

4  Tropaeum Traiani: trofeo costantiniano, part.: busto imperiale (O. Harl, lupa 21340-6)

dero della spada e del balteo, gli schinieri); simbolica la spada con un'impraticabile elsa ad aquila bicipite, allusiva ai due imperatori. Sulla corazza, due incassi destinati a una cornice di bronzo bordano un riquadro dove risalta in altorilievo, su un disegno a fasce di denti di lupo, un busto galeato dal volto imberbe, geometrizzato nell'ovale della sagoma e nei lineamenti, gli occhi sbarrati con grandi pupille rotonde; indossa *trabea consularis* orlata da liste (in origine forse evidenziate a colore) e calza un elmo ogivale con apice a globetto, dal quale si dipartono due bande sinuose simmetriche di un cimiero stilizzato. Secondo me vuol ritrarre Costantino, sull'esempio di Traiano, che si era fatto rappresentare come incarnazione della *virtus*, cavaliere vittorioso in battaglia, sulla corazza del proprio trofeo e di cui Costantino si era prefisso l'imitazione[12]. La Scizia Minore era parte dei domini di Licinio, ma sia l'aspetto del monumento che il testo dell'iscrizione collegiale dedicata dai due prefetti del pretorio furono certamente concordati; Costantino riaffermava così il rango preminente che il collega gli aveva riconosciuto dopo la vittoria su Massenzio.

La sagoma del casco lo avvicina allo »Spangenhelm«, l'elmo composto a spicchi radiali confluenti verso una piastra con apice, tenuti da listelli ribaditi e da una fascia intorno al giro del cranio (fig. 8). Nella redazione di Tropaeum Traiani i dettagli del coppo non sono annotati (ma è omissione ricorrente), mentre è rilevata la fascia, sotto un largo solco per l'inserto di una corona; paragnatidi disgiunte come nel rilievo di *Mursa*, ma di linee più sicure, incorniciano il volto con volute decorative. Ovviamente la combinazione di elmo e *trabea consularis* è inverosimile ed esalta l'occasione con simboli di potere: la costruzione delle mura della città di fondazione traianea[13], nel quadro di eventi di ben più ampia portata ai quali l'iscrizione accenna con toni panegiristici, evocando il precedente dell'azione di Traiano sul basso Danubio durante le guerre daciche. Parla di nuova sicurezza dei confini e di vittoria universale (*edomitis ubique barbarum gentium*

---

[12]  Sull'*imitatio Traiani*, che sostituirà l'*imitatio Alexandri*: Zecchini 1993, 130–132; Bleckmann 2012, 204–205. 214 (per Costantino). Per una rilettura del trofeo di Traiano, da ultimo: Bianchi 2011, 9–60; v. anche Barnea – Lohmann 2021, 59–80 (con breve storia degli studi).

[13]  Per la controversia sullo stato giuridico dei *Tropaeenses Traianenses* v. Matei-Popescu 2014, 205–223.

5   Gilău (Cluj): stele funeraria con Dioscuri (?), Stagioni e ritratto; Cluj Napoca, Muzeul Național de Istorie a Transilvaniei (Singer, DAI-Rom 703599)

*populis*) per merito della *virtus* e della *providentia* dei due augusti. La scelta di un elmo di tipo diverso da quelli dei coni non dipende forse solo dalla facilità con cui è possibile riprodurlo chiaramente in veduta frontale, osservazione valevole se mai per il rilievo di *Mursa*; più probabilmente è stato preferito un modello che in questa zona era già familiare. Lo »Spangenhelm« è ritenuto uno sviluppo di V secolo, ma soprassedendo sulla questione, anticipiamo che proprio a Tropaeum Traiani si segnalano, in area danubiana, le attestazioni più precoci di una forma ripetutamente rappresentata fin dal I secolo d. C. dall'iconografia sarmatica delle tombe dipinte di Panticapeo e dei rilievi funerari della Crimea[14].

I due cavalieri del rilievo in esame ricalcano lo schema ordinario dei Dioscuri che trattengono per le redini i cavalli, qui bardati con gualdrappe; ma non ripetono il tipo ordinario del giovane nudo con clamide, noto anche in Pannonia dove ritorna come tema funerario, sebbene non dei più comuni[15]. Sulla figura di sinistra si seguono ancora, parzialmente, i contorni e le pieghe di un chitone con *kolpos*: erano quindi vestiti alla greca, rieccheggiando lontani modelli attici non peraltro sconosciuti nelle province del settore, occasionalmente ripresi anche in *Dacia* (fig. 5)[16]. Del tutto singolari sono invece i copricapi che sostituiscono il *pileus*. Uno è uno »Spangenhelm« ogivale, di linee più precise e un po' più dettagliato di quello dell'imperatore, con l'apice e i segmenti radiali definiti lungo i contorni; dietro il profilo quasi del tutto abraso, rivolto verso il gruppo centrale, resta il lungo paranuca di cui gli elmi di questo tipo possono essere o no dotati[17]. L'altro è un casco emisferico sormontato da un'ala (da immaginarne due, una sola definita nella veduta di profilo) che copriva integralmente il volto di cui non sono definiti i lineamenti; ma non perché il lavoro non sia stato ultimato, come qualcuno si è chiesto: fra testa e collo è infatti ben distinguibile la prosecuzione di un contorno ininterrotto. Si trattava dunque di un elmo a secchio, affine a quello che completa l'armamento esotico di uno dei due *sagittarii* presentati con tutta probabilità come traci nel rilievo gladiatorio del Museo Bardini di Firenze, da collocare per stile, impianto compositivo ed elementi di costume all'inizio della serie dei rilievi repubblicani con scene di *munus*, intorno alla metà del I secolo a. C. (fig. 6)[18]. Le due redazioni non sono identiche: il casco dell'arciere poggia in modo più stabile (e verosimile) sulle spalle; non ha il profilo curvilineo di quello schizzato dall'artigiano di *Mursa*, che lo avvicina alle bigonce del tardo medioevo, ed è orlato da una cerchiatura con bulloni; il coppo è conico, sormontato da un apice. In ogni modo la sommarietà dell'altra riproduzione non consente di ridefinire con certezza le caratteristiche strutturali. Il *cli-*

---

[14] Esempio ben noto, il rilievo del cavaliere catafratto Tryphon da Tanais (III sec.): v. ora Balty 2018, 37; altra bibliografia: Coulston 2013, 473.

[15] Migotti 2005, 277–275 (sarcofago di *Siscia*, con Dioscuri presentati come patroni degli *augustali*); altre redazioni su lastre pertinenti a edicole si raccolgono nella zona di *Aquincum*: Erdély 1974, n. 94, 95; lupa 3189.

[16] Nemeti – Nemeti 2014, 244 (con altra bibliografia).

[17] La gronda applicata di listelli o squame, documentata archeologicamente, è ignorata dalle raffigurazioni romane, qualche esempio ne offre l'arte sasanide: Coulston 2013, 473; sui ritrovamenti Negin 2015, 538.

[18] Faedo 1986, n. 11; Flecker 2015, A 35 (con altra bibliografia); Bianchi 2021, 41.

6  Firenze, Museo Bardini: rilievo gladiatorio (foto museo)

7  Taq-i Bustan, grande iwan: statua equestre, part. (Ivan Vdovin, foto Alamy C5KTPM)

*banarius* del famoso graffito di Dura Europo offre un riscontro più vicino nel tempo al rilievo di *Mursa*, mostrando inoltre maggiori analogie con la redazione della lastra Bardini: ritroviamo un coppo conico, benché più allungato e segnato da tratti incisi, a indicazione degli spicchi dello »Spangenhelm«; ma sul viso ricade un camaglio[19]. Per la metà del IV secolo si ha notizia di *clibanarii* dell'esercito romano recanti elmi con maschera (da non confondere con la maschera fisionomica degli elmi di cavalleria ›sportivi‹, non usati in battaglia)[20]; ma per ritrovare un casco a secchio bisogna molto scendere nel tempo, fino alla statua di cavaliere vittorioso scolpita ad altorilievo nel registro inferiore del grande iwan di Taq-i Bustan, che un minuzioso riesame del complesso ha assegnato a un rifacimento finale voluto dall'ultimo sovrano sasanide Yazdgard III (fig. 7)[21]. Nell'equipaggiamento è stata riscontrata qualche novità rispetto alla tradizione sasanide, in particolare la faretra appesa di lato, introdotta sull'esempio degli arcieri delle confederazioni turche della Transcaucasia nord-orientale sottomesse da Khusrow II nel 568/569. L'elmo non è stato preso in considerazione, ma è evidente che non si riallaccia ai copricapi dei sovrani sasanidi, a parte un possibile richiamo al ›corimbo‹ nella forma del cimiero. Per alcuni dettagli (rivetti alla base del coppo, indicazione delle sopracciglia)[22] lo si è incluso ultimamente in una serie di caschi

---

[19] Da ultimo: Fowlkes Childs – Seymour 2019, n. 134.
[20] James 1986, 120 n. 44.
[21] Mode 2006, 393–413, specialmente 400–401, e sull'interpretazione dell'immagine del cavaliere 461–462. Sul grande iwan, in particolare sulla scena di caccia, v. anche Compareti 2016, 71–93.
[22] Estremamente corrose, non visibili nella foto di cui dispongo: v. Kubik 2016, 81–82 fig. 4.

crestati emisferici che continuerebbero una tradizione iranica presasanide[23]. Si esita a postulare un prototipo comune per esemplari documentati da riproduzioni sporadiche e cronologicamente così distanziate come quelle dei monumenti di *Mursa* e Taq-i Bustan e del rilievo fiorentino, sebbene l'area di diffusione rimanga circoscritta all'Iran e a regioni limitrofe o esposte a influenze iraniche come la Tracia; il che vale anche per la raffigurazione di *Mursa*, se rappresenta un'arma difensiva importata da truppe sarmatiche nella Transdanubia. Nondimeno, qualche indizio di continuità s'intravede: per il cimiero ad ali non si danno riscontri (prescindendo da elmi alati di varia epoca e provenienza, improponibili come termini di paragone); applicate al casco di una figura divina, le ali possono essere un ricordo di un simbolo sacrale ricorrente delle corone dei sovrani sasanidi, di cui manterrebbero la funzione semantica[24]. Per giunta, nel rilievo gladiatorio di Firenze ritroviamo curiosamente la stessa combinazione di elmi ›barbarici‹ appaiati in quello pannonico: l'avversario dell'arciere col casco chiuso calza infatti un elmo ogivale con lungo paranuca, coincidenza fortuita ma indicativa dell'origine che si attribuiva a quei pezzi di armamento; concorrono alla caratterizzazione tracia della classe dei *sagittarii*[25], con altre notazioni di costume delle quali la più significativa è un inedito *subligaculum* di pelliccia. Nell'immaginario romano le popolazioni balcaniche hanno oscillato a lungo fra oriente e settentrione, e l'indumento di pelliccia evoca il barbaro nordico.

Per quanto riguarda gli elmi compositi, la relazione fra le due serie tipologiche – i crestati ad arco e gli »Spangenhelme« – non riesce del tutto chiara, ma si tende ormai a escludere che i secondi siano un diretto sviluppo dei primi. Gli esemplari altomedievali non sembrano dirette imitazioni di modelli sasanidi, e la tesi prevalente è che il tipo sia un portato di ausiliari levantini o sarmati, tanto più che la sua comparsa precede i contatti con l'impero persiano[26]. Le metope del trofeo di Adamclisi, dove notoriamente la rappresentazione dell'armamento delle unità dell'esercito romano non è ancora uniformata in funzione della riconoscibilità come sulla Colonna Traiana, cui risale la definitiva caratterizzazione del legionario in corazza segmentata, tendenzialmente confermano che le guerre contro sarmati e traco-daci abbiano favorito mutue influenze e imitazioni: vi figurano infatti legionari con tuniche squamate o lunghe cotte di maglia, e occasionalmente con »Spangenhelme«[27]. Ma è sullo scorcio del III secolo che gli elmi compositi si affermano a scapito di quelli a blocco unico, più pesanti ma più solidi, nella misura in cui contengono costi e tempi di fabbricazione[28]. Viene spesso citata la scena di *adlocutio* dell'arco di Galerio (fig. 8), come prima raffigurazione di truppe scelte dell'esercito romano equipaggiate al modo dei *cataphractarii* sarmati, e con »Spangenhelme« provvisti di paranuca e paranaso[29]. Sulla Colonna Traiana elmi simili completano l'armamento dei sarmati rossolani (sc. XXXI. XXXVII) e integrano i trofei a lato della Vittoria che scrive sullo scudo, nella composizione simbolica di cesura tra i due capitoli della narrazione (LXXVIII) (fig. 9); compaiono anche fra le componenti sarmatiche della congerie d'armi sullo zoccolo[30]. Fra le unità dell'esercito romano li portano solo gli ausiliari siriaci (LXX. CIX. CXV).

L'identificazione della coppia di cavalieri del rilievo di *Mursa* è scontata, malgrado l'assenza di attributi specifici. Si tratta dei Dioscuri, non di attendenti che fiancheggiano l'imperatore nella formula di attenzione tripartita dei rilievi ›storici‹ (peraltro mai accompagnati da cavalli), tant'è

---

[23] Kubik 2016, 81–82.
[24] Su figure simboliche e insegne di potere nei rilievi rupestri sasanidi: Rostami et al. 2015, 48–62; corone: 56–57.
[25] Raramente raffigurati, ricompaiono solo sui bicchieri di Aco: Flecker 2015, 64; l'equipaggiamento varia, ma su una delle matrici Aco è delineato un elmo conico orientaleggiante: Lodi 2017, 133 figg. 11–13.
[26] In particolare James 1986, 107–134; anche Robinson 1975, 85; Negin 2015, 238.
[27] Fulger – Damato 2018, 180 elencano sette esempi, ma in qualche caso la conservazione è troppo compromessa; si riconoscono negli elmi senza visiera e con liste radiali delle metope 17, 18, 19 (non rubricata dai due AA. cit.), 22, 31.
[28] Su contesto storico e incidenza delle condizioni materiali nel processo produttivo: James 1986, 132–134.
[29] Laubscher 1975, 47–48.
[30] Accurato riesame: Stefan 2015, tavv. 60–63.

8  Salonicco, arco di Galerio: *adlocutio* (Hermann Wagner, D-DAI-ATH-Thessaloniki 223)

vero che almeno uno conserva tracce di una veste greca: trascrizione pedissequa di un modello, forse; ma è anche possibile che l'esecutore abbia lasciato ai cavalieri l'antico costume come segno di venerabilità, aggiornando solo quel dettaglio che visualizzava uno stretto legame con una determinata formazione militare: appunto gli elmi. In effetti, se anche i Dioscuri non sono in completo assetto di guerra, la militarizzazione attualizzata da elmi di foggia contemporanea evidenzia la loro tradizionale funzione di protettori delle unità di cavalleria, e più in generale, il loro valore di *exempla* da imitare nella solidarietà fra commilitoni. Questo aspetto, sommato alle competenze di divinità salvifiche e psicopompe, spiega le ricorrenti raffigurazioni della coppia sui pezzi di armamento da parata, indossati per festività nelle quali trovava posto anche la memoria dei caduti[31]. Il monumento di *Mursa* celebrava quindi una vittoria imperiale (o in nome dell'imperatore, cui è regola attribuire ogni successo militare), forse conseguita con l'apporto decisivo di truppe di cavalleria, se prestando alle loro divinità tutelari pezzi di armamento contemporaneo, le avvicinava ostensibilmente ai combattenti, quasi che fossero intervenuti in loro aiuto.

Il termine cronologico fissato dai dati antiquari si accorda con le caratteristiche di fattura: figure piatte e dettagli incisi, contorni incerti. *Mursa* ha restituito numerose sculture di vario genere e qualità, sia in marmo che in pietra locale, distribuite per la maggior parte fra II secolo e III. Tra le prime si annoverano stele affini per tipologia e caratteristiche formali a quelle in marmo della Pannonia occidentale, indicative di contatti e passaggi di officine con le accresciute ambizioni dei notabili, quando *Mursa* viene promossa a municipio in età adrianea; fenomeno che si osserva anche a *Viminacium*[32]. I lavori in calcare sono mediamente di livello inferiore, ma denotano una certa pratica, che nel nostro caso evidentemente si è persa. La più tarda epigrafe di fondazione, o rifondazione di un edificio in onore di un imperatore nomina Costanzo Cloro e Costantino[33]; Giuliano l'Apostata è ricordato da un miliario per la riparazione di una strada[34]. Con i Costantinidi *Mursa* fu teatro di un evento di capitale importanza: la sanguinosa battaglia fra gli eserciti di Costanzo II e Magnenzio, preceduta da un fallito tentativo di espugnazione da parte dell'usurpatore. Secondo la tendenziosa testimonianza antiariana di Sulpicio Severo (Chron. 2, 38, 5, 7), Costanzo trascorse la giornata in preghiera nella Basilica dei Martiri fuori città, insieme al vescovo ariano Valente, che con uno strattagemma riuscì a comunicargli per primo la notizia della vittoria affermando che gli era stata annunziata da un angelo, per accrescere il suo ascendente su di lui: andava quindi attribuita all'efficacia delle preghiere, non al valore dell'esercito. È poco credibile, però, che l'imperatore non abbia avuto parte attiva negli accaniti combattimenti, ai quali diedero

---

[31] E.g. Petculescu 2003, n. 335 (con altra bibliografia); Toynbee 1963, n. 104. Il campionario delle immagini utilizzate per la decorazione, accanto a soggetti militari e figure divine di facile collocazione nel quadro di valori dell'esercito (Marte e Vittoria, busti di Minerva o Virtus, Giove o aquila) comprende delfini e altri temi desunti dall'iconografia funeraria: in generale Garbsch 1978.

[32] Sulle stele in marmo di *Viminacium*: Pilipović 2011, 593–612; stele di *Mursa* tipologicamente e stilisticamente affini: e.g. lupa 3084. 4290. Sulle caratteristiche dei lavori in marmo e in calcare di *Mursa* e altri centri pannonici dell'attuale Croazia: Buzov 2015, 955–967; sarcofagi: Pochmarski 2019, 247–260.

[33] Dalle vicinanze (Beli Manastir): lupa 26290.

[34] CIL III 10648; lupa 26319 (con bibliografia).

9    Colonna Traiana: sc XVIII (part.), Vittoria e trofeo sarmatico (DAI Rom 1249511)

una decisiva svolta le manovre congiunte della sua cavalleria catafratta e degli arcieri corazzati a cavallo[35]. Nel rilievo figurano divinità pagane, ed era Magnenzio il filopagano, ma queste non sarebbero difficoltà ostative, considerato che i temi di vittoria hanno avuto ancora lunga vita nell'impero cristiano. Personaggi mitici molto popolari come i Dioscuri potevano conservare, agli occhi dei soldati di cavalleria, l'accezione di figure esemplari, per quanto la loro presenza su un monumento ufficiale strida con l'interpretazione della vittoria che Valente avrebbe dato all'imperatore; ma forse solo apparentemente: si può anche intenderla come una strumentalizzazione del concetto che la vittoria è sempre ottenuta col sostegno di Dio, concetto giudaico introdotto nel mondo romano da Costantino e che sarà visualizzato dal tema della *dextera dei*[36]. D'altro canto, nel panegirico pronunziato in occasione dei quinquennali dei cesari, Nazario si dilunga su un prodigio che non quadra con la versione cristiana della vittoria del Milvio, ma dovette pur avere una certa risonanza, se ancora lo storico bizantino Zonara riporta prodigi simili avvenuti durante le battaglie di Costantino: l'apparizione in Gallia di una schiera di cavalieri, che inviati in suo aiuto dal cielo, chiedevano informazioni sulla via da prendere per unirsi alla sua armata[37]. Nazario descrive il loro aspetto, splendido e terribile, e li paragona ai Dioscuri (*duo cum equis*), venuti in soccorso dei romani nella battaglia del Lago Regillo. Alla luce di questo passo forse si comprende perché l'epiclesi *ier(o)i* sia stata incisa accanto a uno dei cavalieri del rilievo di *Mursa* senza accompagnarla a un nome; l'uso eccezionale del greco avvalora la supposizione che il monumento sia stato un'iniziativa di unità militari di provenienza orientale, ma approvata in alto o dallo stesso Costanzo, che a *Mursa* si trattenne ancora per un anno dopo la battaglia (se la commemorazione si riferisce a questo evento).

Certo è che nelle scelte figurative è ancora percepibile quel particolare attaccamento degli imperatori alle truppe di cavalleria che riaffiora a più riprese dalla tematica equestre dei *coni*, in

---

[35]   Bleckmann 1999, 63; sulla battaglia di *Mursa* v. ora Drinkwater 2022, 28–68.
[36]   Sulla sostituzione del simbolo ai temi narrativi nella pittura trionfale, ridicolizzata da Eunapio: Killerich 2015, 75.
[37]   Pan. Lat. 4 (10) 15, 4–6. L'episodio mitico è discusso trattando del medaglione costantiniano di *Ticinum* da Lenski 2018, 280–281. Sulle varianti cristianizzate di Zon. 13, 1, 27 e il rapporto di Costantino con i Dioscuri: Bleckmann 2012, 214–216.

sincronia con l'importanza della cavalleria pesante fra III secolo e IV[38]; lo stesso medaglione costantiniano di *Ticinum* ne offre un esempio, con la citazione dell'iconografia dei Dioscuri (anticipata da Claudio Gotico, di cui Costantino si proclamò discendente)[39] nell'autopresentazione dell'imperatore che trattiene il cavallo per le redini (fig. 2), e sul rovescio, l'*adlocutio* alla quale presenziano anche cavalieri: il collegio dei cesari, secondo l'ultima lettura, in ogni caso un'innovazione rispetto alle precedenti versioni del tema[40].

Naturalmente, in mancanza d'indicazioni epigrafiche, considerazioni sull'occasione della dedica rimangono congetturali, ma ricorderei che Ammiano Marcellino (21, 16. 15), in un ritratto morale molto negativo di Costanzo II, denuncia la superbia di questo imperatore, che volle innalzare archi trionfali nelle Pannonie e nelle Gallie in ricordo non di vittorie contro nemici esterni, bensì di una strage nelle province (*ex clade provinciarum*), violando la consuetudine di non celebrare col trionfo e con l'arco i successi nelle guerre civili. Il precedente della vittoria sul ›tiranno‹ Massenzio conseguita *iustis armis*, come recita l'iscrizione dell'arco di Costantino a Roma, legittimava probabilmente agli occhi del figlio la sua iniziativa. In effetti, le province nominate dallo storico indicano che gli archi commemoravano le vittorie su Magnenzio, e Ammiano Marcellino precisa che furono eretti con gran dispendio di mezzi. Se non erano soltanto le dimensioni, ma anche un apparato scultoreo di pregio a richiedere tanto dispendio, doveva trattarsi di lavori importati, perché lo scadimento della produzione plastica locale in questa fase è generale. L'ipotesi ricorrente che uno degli archi pannonici di Costanzo sia lo »Heidentor« di *Carnuntum*, spogliato dell'originario arredo plastico in marmo, solleva però svariate difficoltà[41].

Sull'aspetto del monumento di *Mursa* nulla ovviamente si può dire, se non che il formato, e forse anche la tematica del blocco superstite, col suo accento sul ruolo dell'esercito come strumento della *virtus* di un imperatore vittorioso, sembrano appropriati allo zoccolo di un modesto trofeo. In ogni caso, è proprio per l'eccezionalità di un monumento di vittoria pannonico in questa fase che si è tentati di metterlo in relazione con una battaglia le cui conseguenze andarono molto al di là dell'ambito locale: spianò a Costanzo la strada per l'occidente, e dopo la seconda sconfitta di Magnenzio in *Gallia* e il suo suicidio, la dinastia di Costantino riprese il controllo esclusivo del potere imperiale.

## BIBLIOGRAFIA

| | |
|---|---|
| Balty 2018 | J.-C. Balty, Cippes, autels funéraires et stèles militaires d'Apamée: typologie des monuments, modèles iconographiques et ateliers, Syria 95, 2018, 15–63 |
| Barnea – Lohmann 2021 | A. Barnea – P. Lohmann, Ein Monument am Rande des Imperiums. Architektur und Bildprogramm des Tropaeum Traiani, in: P. Lohmann (ed.), Archäologie und Politik. Die zwei Geschichten des Tropaeum Traiani zwischen Heidelberg und Adamklissi. Begleitband zur Pop-up-Ausstellung (Heidelberg 2021) 54–81 |
| Bastien 1994 | P. Bastien, Le buste monétaire des empereurs romains III (Wetteren 1994) |
| Bianchi 2011 | L. Bianchi, Il trofeo di Adamclisi nel quadro dell'arte di stato romana, RIA 61, 2011, 9–61 |
| Bianchi 2017 | L. Bianchi, La figura del militare: mutamenti d'immagine, in: S. Lefebvre (ed.), Iconographie du quotidien dans l'art provincial romain: modèles régionaux. Actes du XIVème Congrès international d'art provincial romain Dijon 01.–06.06.2015 (Digione 2017) 99–215 |
| Bianchi 2021 | L. Bianchi, Due rilievi gladiatorii di Dyrrachium, RdA 45, 2021, 31–46 |
| Bleckmann 1999 | B. Bleckmann, Die Schlacht von Mursa und die zeitgenössische Deutung eines spätantiken Bürgerkriegs, in: H. Brandt (ed.), Gedeutete Realität. Krisen, Wirklichkeiten, Interpretationen (3.–6. Jh. n. Chr.) (Stoccarda 1999) 47–101 |

---

[38] Sull'argomento: Bleckmann 2012, 215–216.
[39] Bastien 1994, tav. 112, 7.
[40] Lenski 2018, 282–286.
[41] Discussione in De Maria 1995, 307. Sul monumento: Jobst 2001 (con attribuzione a Costanzo); sui ritrovamenti monetali che orienterebbero verso la metà del IV sec.: Găzdac 2000, 215–257, particolarmente 222.

| | |
|---|---|
| Bleckmann 2012 | B. Bleckmann, Costantino dopo la battaglia sul Ponte Milvio: note sul medaglione di *Ticinum*, in: E. Covolo – G. Spameni Gasparro (ed.), Costantino il Grande alle radici dell'Europa. Atti del Congresso Internazionale di Studio in occasione del 1700° anniversario della Battaglia di Ponte Milvio e della conversione di Costantino (Città del Vaticano 2012) 195–220 |
| Bulat 1997 | M. Bulat, Spomenici kulta Kabira iz Osijeka, OsjZbor 22/23, 1997, 21–32 |
| Buzov 2015 | M. Buzov, Roman sculpture in Pannonia between imports and local products, in: P. Pensabene – E. Gasparini (ed.), Interdisciplinary Studies on Ancient Stones: Asmosia X. Proceedings of the 10th International Conference of ASMOSIA, Association for the Study of Marble & Other Stones in Antiquity, Roma 21.–26.05.2012 (Roma 2015) 955–967 |
| Carlà – Castello 2010 | F. Carlà – M. G. Castello, Questioni tardoantiche. Storia e mito della ›svolta costantiniana‹ (Roma 2010) |
| Compareti 2016 | M. Compareti, Observations on the Rock Reliefs at Taq-i Bustan: A Late Sasanian Monument along the ›Silk Road‹, The Silk Road 14, 2016, 71–83 |
| Coulston 2013 | J. C. N. Coulston, Late Roman Equipment Culture, in: A. Sarantis – N. Christie (ed.), War and Warfare in Late Antiquity (Leida 2013) 463–492 |
| De Maria 1995 | S. De Maria, Cassio Dione, Ammiano Marcellino e gli archi trionfali della Pannonia. Architettura e temi dell'ideologia imperiale, in: G. Hajnóczi (ed.), La Pannonia e l'impero romano. Atti del convegno internazionale, Accademia d'Ungheria e l'Istituto austriaco di cultura, Roma 13.–16.01.1994 (Milano 1995) 299–312 |
| Drinkwater 2022 | J. F Drinkwater, The Battle of Mursa, 351: Causes, Courses and Consequences, Journal of Late Antiquity 15/1, 2022, 28–68 |
| Erdély 1974 | G. Erdély, A római kőfaragás és kőszobrászat Magyarországon (Budapest 1974) |
| Facchinetti 2005 | G. Facchinetti, Monete e insegne del potere: la raffigurazione degli elmi fra IV e VI secolo d. C., in: C. Alfaro – C. Marcos – P. Otero (ed.), XIII Congreso internacional de Numismática. Actas – Proceedings – Actes 1 (Madrid 2005) 747–758 |
| Faedo 1986 | L. Faedo, Rilievo con munus gladiatorio, in: E. Neri Lusanna – L. Faedo (ed.), Il museo Bardini a Firenze II. Le sculture (Milano 1986) n. 17, 194 |
| Flecker 2015 | M. Flecker, Römische Gladiatorenbilder. Studien zu den Gladiatorenreliefs der späten Republik und der Kaiserzeit aus Italien, Studien zur antiken Stadt 15 (Wiesbaden 2015) |
| Fowlkes Childs – Seymour 2019 | B. Fowlkes Childs – M. Seymour, The World between Empires. Art and Identity in the Ancient Middle East (New York 2019) |
| Fulger – Damato 2018 | A. C. Fulger – R. Damato, Iconografia militare sulle metope di Adamclisi, in: M. Popescu – I. Achim – F. Matei-Popescu (ed.), La Dacie et l'empire romain. Mélanges d'épigraphie et d'archéologie offerts à Constantin C. Petolescu (Bucarest 2018) 175–194 |
| Garbsch 1978 | J. Garbsch, Römische Paraderüstungen, MünchBeitrVFG 30 (Monaco di Bavaria 1978) |
| Găzdac 2000 | C. Găzdac, Coin Finds and the Heidentor Monument from Carnuntum, CarnuntumJb 2000, 215–257 |
| James 1986 | S. James, Evidence from Dura Europos for the Origins of Late Roman Helmets, Syria 63, 1986, 107–134 |
| Jobst 2001 | W. Jobst, Das Heidentor von Carnuntum. Ein spätantikes Triumphalmonument am Donaulimes (Vienna 2001) |
| Killerich 2015 | B. Killerich, Visual Dynamics: Reflections on Late Antique Images (Bergen 2015) |
| Klumbach 1973 | H. Klumbach (ed.), Spätrömische Gardehelme, MünchBeitrVFG 15 (Monaco di Bavaria 1973) |
| Kubik 2016 | A. L. Kubik, Introduction to studies on late Sasanian protective armour. The Yarish-Mardy helmet, Historia i Świat 5, 2016, 77–105 |
| Laubscher 1975 | H. P. Laubscher, Der Reliefschmuck des Galeriusbogens in Thessaloniki, AF 1 (Berlino 1975) |
| Lenski 2018 | N. Lenski, The Date of the Ticinum Medallion, NumAntCl 47, 2018, 251–295 |
| Lodi 2017 | G. Lodi, Terra sigillata da Ariano Ferrarese. I manufatti trasportabili e la circolazione delle idee, in: M. Flecker (ed.), Neue Bilderwelten. Zur Ikonographie und Hermeneutik Italischer Sigillata, Tübinger Archäologische Forschungen 23 (Rahden/Westf. 2017) 113–134 |
| lupa | F. Harl – O. Harl, <lupa.at> (Bilddatenbank zu antiken Steindenkmälern) |

| | |
|---|---|
| Lusuardi Siena 1998 | S. Lusuardi Siena, L'identità materiale e storica della corona: un enigma in via di soluzione?, in: G. Buccellati (ed.), La corona ferrea nell'Europa degli imperi II. Alla scoperta del prezioso oggetto (Milano 1998) 173–252 |
| Lusuardi Siena et al. 2002 | S. Lusuardi Siena – C. Perassi – G. Facchinetti, Gli elmi tardoantichi (IV–VI sec.) alla luce delle fonti letterarie, numismatiche e archeologiche: alcune considerazioni, in: M. Buora (ed.), Miles Romanus dal Po al Danubio nel tardoantico. Atti del convegno internazionale Pordenone - Concordia Sagittaria 17.–19.03.2000 (Pordenone 2002) 21–62 |
| Mărgineanu Cărstoiu – Barnea 1979 | M. Mărgineanu Cărstoiu – A. Barnea, Piese de arhitectură din cetatea Tropaeum Traiani, in: I. Barnea – A. Barnea (ed.), Tropaeum Traiani I. Cetatea (Bucarest 1979) 129–177 |
| Matei-Popescu 2014 | F. Matei-Popescu, Tropaeum Traiani, in: I. Piso – R. Varga (ed.), Trajan und seine Städte (Cluj-Napoca 2014) 205–223 |
| Migotti 2005 | B. Migotti, The Iconography of the Dioscuri on a Sarcophagus from Siscia, HistriaAnt 13, 2005, 277–285 |
| Mirković 2012 | M. Mirković, Co-Regency: Constantine and Licinius and the Political Division of the Balkans, ZborRadBeograd 49, 2012, 7–18 |
| Mode 2006 | M. Mode, Art and Ideology at Taq-i Bustan: The Armoured Equestrian, in: M. Mode – J. Tubach (ed.), Arms and Armour as Indicators of Cultural Transfer. The Steppes and the Ancient World from the Hellenistic Time to the Early Middle Ages (Wiesbaden 2006) 394–413 |
| Mráv 2012 | Z. Mráv, Building Munificence of Septimius Severus in the Cities of the Pannonian Provinces: Epigraphic Evidence, in: B. Migotti (ed.), The archaeology of Roman southern Pannonia. The state of research and selected problems in the Croatian part of the Roman province of Pannonia, BARIntSer 2393 (Oxford 2012) 251–278 |
| Negin 2015 | A. E. Negin, A Bearded Face-Mask Helmet from the Collection of the National Museum in Belgrad, AKorrBl 45/4, 2015, 535–547 |
| Nemeti – Nemeti 2014 | I. Nemeti – S. Nemeti, *Heros Equitans* in the Funerary Iconography of *Dacia Porolissensis*. Models and Workshops, Dacia 58, 2014, 241–255 |
| Petculescu 2003 | L. Petculescu, Antique Bronzes in Romania. Exhibition Catalogue (Bucarest 2003) |
| Pilipović 2011 | S. Pilipović, Un gruppo di stele funerarie provenienti da Viminacium (Moesia Superiore), Classica et Christiana 6/2, 2011, 593–612 |
| Pochmarski 2019 | E. Pochmarski, Beobachtungen zu den Sarkophagen aus Mursa und Cibalae, Prilozi povijesti umjetnosti Dalmaciji 44, 2019, 247–260 |
| Polito 1998 | E. Polito, Fulgentibus armis. Introduzione allo studio dei fregi d'armi antichi (Roma 1998) |
| Porena 2003 | P. Porena, Le origini della prefettura del pretorio tardoantica (Roma 2003) |
| Robinson 1975 | H. Russell Robinson, The Armour of Imperial Rome (Londra 1975) |
| Rostami et al. 2015 | H. Rostami – S. R. Mousavi Haji – Z. Vasegh Abbasi, A New Insight into Symbolic Figures and Special Badges in the Sassanian Rock Reliefs, International Journal of Archaeology 3/6, 2015, 48–62 |
| Stefan 2015 | A. S. Stefan, La Colonne Trajane (Parigi 2015) |
| Suceveanu – Barnea 1991 | A. Suceveanu – A. Barnea, La Dobroudja romaine (Bucarest 1991) |
| Toynbee 1963 | J. M. C. Toynbee, Art in Roman Britain (Londra 1963) |
| Turković 2006 | T. Turković, Ikonografska interpretacija sarkofaga s Kabirima iz Arheološkog Muzej u Splitu, Peristil 49, 2006, 5–18 |
| Zecchini 1993 | C. Zecchini, Ricerche di storiografia latina tardoantica (Roma 1993) |

*Luca Bianchi, (ex) Università di Roma I La Sapienza, Piazza Stefano Jacini 5, 00191 Roma, Italia.*
*[e] luca.bianchi3@gmail.com*

Lorenzo Cigaina

# ZIRKUS UND *SPECTACULA* IM SPÄTANTIKEN *AQUILEIA*

## STADTRÖMISCHE EINFLÜSSE UND PROVINZIALE RÜCKFLÜSSE AM BEFUND EINIGER STEINDENKMÄLER

**Abstract**
Iconographic sources about circus life, games, and rituals in late Roman *Aquileia* are scant (e.g. gems, clay lamps, etc.). Some stone monuments, however, still deserve a reappraisal in this regard: 1) an armed youth incised on a slab representing a *venator*; 2) a consular office-bearer on a sarcophagus acroterion, who might be conventionally portrayed as giving the starting signal for chariot races; 3) the relief of the »Magistrate's Procession«, which is likely connected with the Dioscuri cult; 4) one of the twin gods shown on a relief tondo belonging to a series which depicts several gods alongside a probable local river; 5) an unpublished relief fragment of a cultic throne (*solisternium*), which can be added to a group of five slabs possibly pertaining to a Tetrarchic imperial cult hall. On the whole, *Aquileia* as a provincial capital took over modes of imperial and senatorial representation from Rome, while also remaining receptive to new stylistic impulses from the eastern Empire.

Einige teilweise schon bekannte Steindenkmäler von *Aquileia* lassen neue Kenntnisse zum dortigen Zirkus, dessen Darbietungen sowie dem damit verbundenen Kaiserpalast zu. Eine kleine methodische Präzisierung sei hier gleich am Anfang vorausgeschickt: Wie in Rom, so wurden auch in *Aquileia* und anderswo Tierhetzen (*venationes*) sowohl im Amphitheater als auch im Zirkus abgehalten, sodass der Austragungsort einer Darstellung ohne klärende Hinweise nicht bestimmt werden kann. Dementsprechend muss ebenso der ursprüngliche Standort eines Steindenkmals offenbleiben, wenn sich dieser nicht eindeutig auf einen der beiden öffentlichen Bauten zurückführen lässt.

An der nördlichen Adriaküste gelegen, nahm *Aquileia* eine strategische Stellung am Drehpunkt zwischen Seerouten und Landwegen zu den Balkanprovinzen ein[1]. Nach Jahrzehnten wirtschaftlicher Stagnation und militärischer Spannungen im 3. Jahrhundert gewann es im Zuge der Provinzialisierung Italiens durch Diokletian eine zentrale Rolle als Hauptstadt der *Venetia et Histria* zurück. Zuerst hielten sich die Tetrarchen, dann Konstantin und seine Nachfolger abermals im Kaiserpalast auf (vgl. Paneg. 6, 6, 2: 307 n. Chr.), den die archäologischen Forschungen in der Ortschaft Marignane oder eher zwischen Zirkus und Forum lokalisieren[2]. Dabei sei die in der Spätantike häufige Assoziation von Zirkus und Palast noch einmal aufgegriffen. 294 n. Chr. wurde eine eigenständige Prägestätte in *Aquileia* eröffnet, wofür ein *procurator monetae* (Not. dign. occ. 11, 40) zuständig war[3]. Das Wirken des *praepositus thesaurorum per Italiam* (Not. dign. occ. 11, 27), eine Art Finanzminister für Italien, bestätigt die finanzielle Relevanz der Stadt. Eine kaiserliche Textilwerkstätte unter der Verantwortung des *procurator gynaecii Aquileiensis* deckte den Bedarf des Kaiserhofes und der Armee[4]. Unter Letzterer diente ein ausgewähltes berittenes Korps – der *sacer comitatus* – als kaiserliche Leibgarde[5]. Den Nachschubdienst für die Donauarmee versah

---

[1] Häufig zitierte Stellen hierzu: Strab. 5, 1, 8; Herodian 8, 2, 3.
[2] Tiussi u. a. 2013, 75–77 mit älterer Literatur (G. Mian); Tiussi – Villa 2017.
[3] Paolucci – Zub 2000; Tiussi u. a. 2013, 82–84 (G. Gorini).
[4] Not. dign. occ. 11, 49; dazu Maiuro 2012, 340.
[5] Vgl. die Grabstelen tetrarchisch-konstantinischer Zeit mit Darstellung von »stehenden Soldaten« der untermösischen Legionen *XI Claudia* und *I Italica* (Cigaina 2012/2013 mit Literatur).

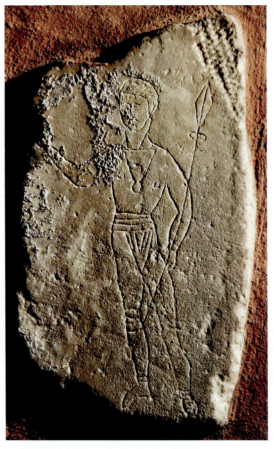

1  Triest, Museo d'Antichità J. J. Winckelmann, Marmorplatte aus Aquileia mit Ritzzeichnung eines *venator* (lupa 16037, Foto O. Harl/© Trieste – Civico Museo d'Antichità J. J. Winckelmann)

nunmehr *Aquileia* durch den Transport von Proviant, Munition und Truppen in verstärktem Maß, nicht zuletzt mithilfe der hier neu angelegten Militärflotte[6]. Im Rahmen des urbanen Aufstiegs war wahrscheinlich noch in tetrarchischer Zeit der Zirkus (ca. 470 × 95 m) an der Nordwestecke der Stadt erbaut worden und blieb wohl bis zur Zerstörung von *Aquileia* durch Attila 452 in Gebrauch[7]. Auch das Amphitheater lag – ebenso wie das Theater – am westlichen Stadtrand, wobei der Eindruck eines Stadtviertels für *spectacula* im Westen von *Aquileia* entsteht. Das Amphitheater wurde bereits um die Mitte des 1. Jahrhunderts n. Chr. errichtet und ununterbrochen bis zu seiner Aufgabe in der zweiten Hälfte des 4. Jahrhunderts verwendet[8]. Dessen spätantike Nutzungsphase deckt somit nur einen Teil des hier betrachteten Zeitraums vom Ende des 3. bis zur Mitte des 5. Jahrhunderts, während der Zirkus nicht zuletzt aufgrund seiner wahrscheinlichen Nähe zum Kaiserpalast das wichtigste Szenario für die öffentlichen Spiele und die Auftritte des Kaisers sowie der Hochmagistrate war. Dieser großen Bedeutung wird der Befund figürlicher Steindenkmäler und Artefakte in Bezug auf das Zirkusleben nicht gerecht, denn neben den wenigen Gegenständen der Kleinkunst – quasi ›Merchandising-Waren‹, z. B. Öllampen, Terra-Sigillata-Schalen, Gemmen[9] – lassen sich nur vereinzelte Inschriften anführen, wie etwa die Grabtafel des Wagenlenkers Urbicus aus der zweiten Hälfte des 4. Jahrhunderts[10]. Diesen Forschungsstand möchte die vorliegende Neuauswertung einiger Einzelstücke sowie Ensembles von Reliefs, die nun um ein unpubliziertes Fragment bereichert werden können, in manchen Punkten konkretisieren.

1) Ein erstes Bildzeugnis liefert eine Marmorplatte mit Ritzzeichnung eines frontal stehenden Mannes mit Speer in der gesenkten linken Hand und mit erhobener Rechter, die einen Gegenstand gehalten haben könnte oder leer im Begrüßungsgestus (*salutatio*) emporgestreckt war (Abb. 1)[11]. Wegen einer Bruchlinie an dieser Stelle muss diese Frage unbeantwortet bleiben. Jedenfalls

---

[6]  Not. dign. occ. 42, 4: *praefectus classis Venetum, Aquileiae*.

[7]  Humphrey 1986, 621–625; Basso 2004, 327. 334; Tiussi u. a. 2013, 77–81 mit Literatur (L. Villa). 425 n. Chr. wurde der Usurpator Johannes im aquileiesischen Zirkus hingerichtet (Prok. BV 1, 3, 9; vgl. Philostorgius 12, 13).

[8]  Basso 2004, 325–326; vgl. 328–331 Abb. 5 zum Stadtviertel; Basso 2018 (Ergebnisse der Grabungskampagnen 2015–2017). Mit seinen Ausmaßen (148 × 112 m, für ca. 21 000 Zuschauer) war es nach der Arena von Verona das zweitgrößte der *Venetia et Histria*.

[9]  Vgl. Tiussi u. a. 2013, Kat. 41–46. 90: darunter sind die früh-/mittelkaiserzeitlichen Objekte als Importstücke anzusehen – z. B. Kat. 42; Novello u. a. 2019, Kat. 73: Gemmen des 2.–3. Jhs. mit Darstellung des Circus Maximus in Rom – oder mit einer möglichen früheren, in vergänglichem Material angelegten Pferderennbahn in Verbindung zu setzen.

[10]  InscrAq 2929 = Vergone 2007, Nr. 30 = Tiussi u. a. 2013, Kat. 40 = EDR078685 (C. Zaccaria 2015); lupa 23544: bemerkenswert ist die auf Rom bezogene Onomastik des Wagenlenkers Urbicus mit dem Beinamen Romulus.

[11]  InscrAq 2928; lupa 16037. Triest, Museo d'Antichità J. J. Winckelmann, Orto Lapidario, eingemauert. H 43,5 cm; B 25,5 cm, rundum abgebrochen.

scheinen das in Profilansicht wiedergegebene rechte Bein sowie der Kopf in Dreiviertelansicht nach links, der Richtung des Gestus – und damit des Kommunikationsaktes, sei es Jubel oder Begrüßung – zu folgen. Der Mann ist nur mit einem Lendenschurz (*subligaculum*) und mit weichen, geschlossenen Schuhen bekleidet, die durch eine enge Schnürung bis über den Knöchel reichen. Außerdem trägt er ein Armband am linken Handgelenk und einen Knieschutz am rechten Knie sowie ein langes Halsband mit ovalem Anhänger (*bulla*). Im Allgemeinen lassen sich die Ritztechnik ebenso wie der fließende Linienverlauf mit den zahlreichen frühchristlichen Grabplatten von *Aquileia* vergleichen, die in das 4.–5. Jahrhundert datieren[12].

Gedeutet wurde die bislang sehr knapp besprochene Figur von Giovanni Brusin – worin ihm wiederum Cecilia Ricci folgt – als kaiserliche Leibwache (*protector*)[13]. Ähnliche Kettenanhänger werden von der Leibgarde beispielsweise am Theodosius-Obelisk in Konstantinopel (hier jedoch herzförmig) und auf dem Missorium desselben Kaisers in Madrid getragen, was für Brusins Benennung plädieren könnte[14]. Die Haartrachten und die Kleidung unterscheiden sich allerdings offensichtlich. Mehrere präzise Parallelen findet hingegen der aquileiesische Lanzenträger im Kolosseum in Rom, wo auf zwei Marmorplatten der Auskleidung der Sitzstufen gleichartige Figuren eingeritzt sind. Bei dem einen Vergleichsstück hält der Junge mit Lanze in der linken Hand und mit *bulla* einen Palmwedel als Siegeszeichen in der vorgestreckten Rechten,

2  Rom, Kolosseum, Marmorplatte mit Ritzzeichnung eines *venator* mit Lanze in der linken Hand und mit *bulla* (nach La Regina 2001, 20 Abb. 5; © Ministero della Cultura – Parco archeologico del Colosseo)

was eine mögliche Ergänzung für die Platte aus *Aquileia* nahelegen könnte (Abb. 2)[15]. Bei dem anderen Beispiel verdeutlicht die Szene einer Tierhatz mit Molossern und Bären die Betätigung derartiger Speerträger als *venatores* oder *bestiarii* im Rahmen von Amphitheater- oder Zirkusspielen[16]. Ob die aquileiesische Darstellung, die merkwürdige Ähnlichkeiten mit den stadtrömischen aufweist, ebenso als Verkleidungsplatte einer Sitzstufe im lokalen Amphitheater oder im Zirkus oder eher als Grabplatte mit zu restituierender Inschrift zu bestimmen ist, lässt sich nicht

---

[12] Vgl. z. B. die Marmorplatte mit Darstellung eines stehenden *ex protectore* mit Lanze: AE 1991, 772 = InscrAq 2913 = Vergone 2007, Nr. 139 = Piussi 2008, Kat. III.45 = EDR078684 (M. A. Novillo Lopez 2015); lupa 23558 (352 n. Chr.).

[13] InscrAq 2928; Ricci 2014, 251 Anm. 89.

[14] Henrich 2022, 80 bzw. 247 Abb. 2; 292 Kat. 7 (388 n. Chr.; dazu Piussi 2008, 66. 71 Abb. 8; 83 Abb. 2 Kat. III.40); vgl. auch einige Hermen aus der Villa von Welschbillig, Henrich 2022, 174. 298 Kat. 59 (2. Hälfte 4. Jh.) sowie das Missorium des Constantius II. aus Kerch. Bei diesen Soldaten hängt aber die *bulla* an einem Torques.

[15] Sabbatini Tumolesi 1988, 91–92 Abb. 1; La Regina 2001, 20. 23 Abb. 5 Kat. 42, mit der Akklamation *[felici]ter* (CIL VI 32261c = Orlandi 2005, 528 Kat. 25: 4.–5. Jh.); Langner 2001, 49–50. 160 Abb. 928. Rom, Kolosseum: Cipollino; H 113; B 52; T 15 cm.

[16] La Regina 2001, 223–224 Abb. 1 Kat. 39; Langner 2001, 55. 160 Abb. 1119.

3   Grado, Marmorrelief (wahrscheinlicher Sarkophagakroter): a) Vorderansicht: Magistrat mit Adlerszepter, b) linke Profilansicht, konstantinisch, 306–337 n. Chr. (a: lupa 14755, Foto O. Harl; b: Foto L. Cigaina/© Friuli Venezia Giulia – Soprintendenza per i Beni Archeologici)

eruieren. Auf einen Grabkontext könnten vielleicht die im Trauerausdruck gesenkten Mundwinkel hindeuten.

2) Das zweite Zeugnis, das hier betrachtet werden soll, ist ein Relieffragment aus prokonnesischem Marmor in Grado, der Hafenstadt von *Aquileia* (Abb. 3 a–b)[17]. Wohl als Halbfigur ist hier ein Hochmagistrat frühkonstantinischer Zeit dargestellt. Sichere Anhaltspunkte für eine solche Datierung liefert die zeitgenössische Porträtkunst, wie bereits Paola Lopreato dargelegt hat. Beispielsweise finden sowohl der durch Spitzmeißel gepunktete Bart tetrarchischer Reminiszenz als auch die Stirnfranse mit gleichmäßigen Sichellocken genaue Entsprechungen am Konstantinsbogen, der 315 n. Chr. vollendet wurde[18]. Das gleichsam expressionistische Stilmittel des frontalen Auges trotz der Dreiviertelansicht begegnet uns in denselben Jahren auf dem mittleren Mosaikmedaillon der aquileiesischen Südbasilika, deren Chronologie durch die Inschrift des Bischofs Theodorus in den Jahren 313 bis ca. 320 n. Chr. fest verankert ist[19].

Nach Lopreatos Einschätzung könnte das Bruchstück als selbstständiges Grab- oder Ehrendenkmal in Gestalt einer Stele angesehen oder einem größeren Denkmal zugeordnet werden. Um diese typologische Unbestimmtheit zu beheben, könnte man etwa die Viertelkreisform beider Nebenseiten heranziehen, die wohl auf den Mittelakroter der Längsseite eines Sarkophagdeckels zu beziehen ist, wozu im Übrigen der in *Aquileia* gebräuchliche Marmor aus *Prokonnesos* passen würde. Denn auf Wunsch von Auftraggebern hohen Standes war eine Platzierung des Bildnisses des Grabherren in der Mitte der Deckellangseite möglich – statt wie sonst üblich in den Eckakroteren. Der Sarkophagdeckel der Aurelia Agrippina in den Vatikanischen Museen bietet ein gutes Beispiel aus der zweiten Hälfte des 3. Jahrhunderts n. Chr.[20], während uns der Sarkophag des Fl. Iulius Catervius in Tolentino aus dem späten 4. Jahrhundert wahrscheinlich die ursprüngliche Grundgliederung des Deckels aus *Aquileia* mit rechteckigem Mittelakroter vor Augen führt[21].

---

[17]   Lopreato 1987; Lopreato 1989, 16 Abb. 11; Lopreato 1991, 191–192 Abb. 76; Piussi 2008, 143 Abb. 15 Kat. IV.2 (P. Casari); Tiussi u. a. 2013, 209 Kat. 14 (G. Mian); lupa 14755. 1970 bei Bauarbeiten am Fundament des Glockenturms des Doms in Grado gefunden, im dortigen Lapidarium aufbewahrt; H 23,5; B 38; T 22 cm.

[18]   Gepunkteter Bart: L'Orange 1939, 80–102 Taf. 14–17. 22 b–c. e (Oratio- und Liberalitas-Friese); 168 Taf. 43 (Konstantinkopf im Eberjagd-Medaillon); Sichellocken: 169 Taf. 45 c–d (Liciniuskopf im Medaillon des Opfers an Hercules).

[19]   Piussi 2008, 144 Abb. 6 (P. Casari).

[20]   Köhler 1998, 332–333, 33* Nr. 49a; EDR133802 (S. Meloni 2013). Vgl. auch den etwa zeitgenössischen Sarkophag in der Albanagruft in Trier (Unruh 2017, 54–55 Abb. 48).

[21]   Dresken-Weiland 1998, Kat. 148 Taf. 56, 1 (spätes 4. Jh.); vgl. Kat. 151 Taf. 62, 1 (Mantova, Ende 4. Jh.): beides ist einer stadtrömischen Werkstatt zugewiesen.

Der in *toga contabulata* porträtierte Mann hält in der linken Hand ein Adlerszepter (*scipio*), das ihn als amtierenden oder als ehemaligen Konsul (*consularis*) auszeichnet[22]. Es könnte sich wohl um einen Statthalter (*corrector*) der Provinz *Venetia et Histria* handeln, der in der Hauptstadt *Aquileia* residierte[23], aber auch um einen höheren Amtsträger wie etwa den *praefectus praetorio* für Italien und *Illyricum*, der durch den Codex Theodosianus häufig in *Aquileia* nachgewiesen ist[24], ohne dass man selbstverständlich andere aus *Aquileia* gebürtige *consulares* ausschließen könnte.

Die frappierende Ähnlichkeit mit den stadtrömischen Spielgeberdarstellungen, wie etwa auf den späteren Konsular-Diptychen des Boethius 487 oder des Magnus 518 n. Chr., legt die Ergänzung des weißen Leinentuches (*mappa*), das als Startzeichen der Pferderennen abgeworfen wurde, in der rechten, gesenkten Hand nahe[25]. Die ikonografische Assoziation dieses Attributs mit dem *scipio* ist schon älter, wofür zunächst Münzbildnisse des Kaisers Tacitus Zeugnis geben[26]. Die *mappa* ist des Weiteren regelmäßig bei Magistratsdarstellungen in spätantiken Zirkusszenen, wie beispielsweise auf dem konstantinischen Mosaik der Villa in Piazza Armerina, vorhanden, wodurch auf den einzig zulässigen Zusammenhang für das Tragen von Triumphinsignien wie dem Adlerszepter durch nichtkaiserliche Würdenträger hingewiesen wird[27]. Auch im Relief von Grado dürfte daher diese Bildkonvention befolgt worden sein.

3) Es bietet sich nun die Möglichkeit, die bekannte Marmorplatte aus einem Sarkophagdeckel mit der Reliefdarstellung der »Pompa del Magistrato« (Prozession des Magistrates) erneut zu betrachten (Abb. 4; ca. 360–370 n. Chr.). Zuletzt hat Katharina Zanier mit Vorsicht vorgeschlagen, die Szene mit dem stadtrömischen Ritual der *lavatio Matris Deum* am 27. März zu identifizieren, wobei der heilige Stein der Göttin Kybele von ihrem Tempel auf dem Palatin bis zum Zusammenfluss von Almone (*Almo*) und Tiber mit einem Festzug mitgetragen und dort im Wasser gereinigt wurde[28]. Nach den literarischen Zeugnissen sei aber der kleine Stein, wohl ins Kultbild der Kybele eingelassen, auf einem Wagen (*carpentum*)[29] – nicht in einem Schrein auf einem Traggestell

---

[22] Für die Spätantike vgl. Prud. 10, 148–150.

[23] z. B. L. Nonius Verus (wohl aus *Mutina* gebürtig), ehemaliger *consul suffectus*, *corrector Venetiae et Histriae* nach 317 n. Chr. und Patron Aquileias (CIL XI 831; s. dazu Lopreato 1987, 170; Panciera 1987, 85–86. 92 Nr. 8; 94 Nr. 10).

[24] Bernier, im Druck: so 337, 379 und 386 n. Chr.

[25] Lopreato 1987, 169 Abb. 5 (Boethius); s. Delbrueck 1929, 61–63 Kat. 7. 22; vgl. Kat. 9–12. 17. 19–21; Volbach 1976, 29 Kat. 6. 23–24 Taf. 3. 10; Rollé Ditzler 2019, 349 Abb. 117 (Boethius); vgl. 344–353 Abb. 114–116. Wie Delbrueck anmerkt, könnte der traditionelle Adler – statt der auf Diptychen üblichen Kaiserbüste – auf das Amt eines *consul suffectus* hinweisen, was der Laufbahn des erwähnten L. Nonius Verus entsprechen würde (s. o. Anm. 23).

[26] RIC V Tacitus 120 (276 n. Chr.). Diese Ikonografie ist während der Tetrarchie und in konstantinischer Zeit sehr verbreitet; vgl. zudem die *solidi* des Julian Apostata im Konsulgewand (RIC VIII Antioch 204–206: 361–363 n. Chr.) und den Kontorniat des Petronius Maximus als Konsuls 433 n. Chr. (RIC X Valentinian III 2179; Rollé Ditzler 2019, 347–348 Abb. 116 a).

[27] Piazza Armerina: Carandini u. a. 1982, 338 Taf. 57; Humphrey 1986, 145. 226 Abb. 66. 112–113; Grosser 2021, 265–266 Kat. M28 (Zweiapsidensaal Nr. 3 in der Therme: Palaestra [?]). Vgl. auch den Magistrat – wohl den *C(a)ecilianus* der davorliegenden Inschrift – auf dem Mosaik mit Zirkusdarstellung der Villa in Gerona (Spanien): Humphrey 1986, 147–148. 239–241 Abb. 69. 120 (Mitte–spätes 4. Jh.); Rodà 2005, 218–221 (Anfang 4. Jh.); Marchet 2008, 300–303 Abb. 6; Grosser 2021, 262–263 Kat. M22 Taf. 10, 1; s. außerdem Humphrey 1986, 145–147 Abb. 67 (spätantikes Relief im Vatikan); 148. 234–235 Abb. 70. 118 (Mosaik aus Italica, Ende 3.–4. Jh.). – Zum repräsentativen Wert der Zirkusdarstellungen für die Senatsaristokratie s. Gabelmann 1980; Engemann 2008, 53–65; Marchet 2008; Wagner 2021, 248–264. 290–304.

[28] Rebaudo – Zanier 2012/2013, 277–285 Abb. 12–20 mit Literatur; so auch Wrede 2001, 84–85 Taf. 21, 3 (stadtrömischer Sarkophag); Latham 2016, 216–217 Anm. 175 Abb. 84. Dazu s. Scrinari 1972, Kat. 614; Schäfer 1989, 424 Kat. S 35; Di Filippo Balestrazzi 2005, 93–94. 112–116 Abb. 15–16; Reinsberg 2006, 191 Kat. 2 Taf. 102, 5; La Rocca – Tortorella 2008, 152 Kat. I 3.6; Madigan 2013, 50–53 Abb. 24; lupa 20678. H 0,35; B 0,72; T 0,11 m. – Der an der rechten Bruchlinie erhaltene Flügel samt einem Reliefrest an der unteren Reliefecke dürfte eher einem inschriftentragenden Eros (Wrede) als einer am Festzug teilnehmenden Victoria (Di Filippo Balestrazzi, Zanier, Madigan, Latham) angehört haben. – Zum *lapis sacer*: Vollmer 2014, 226–231.

[29] Prud. 10, 154–160; vgl. Amm. 23, 3, 7; zum kleinen Format (durch Menschenhand mühelos tragbar): Arnob. nat. 7, 49. – Vgl. die Münzdarstellungen des konischen Steins (*betylos*) des Sonnengottes Elagabal aus Emesa auf einer

4 *Aquileia*, fragmentarisches Marmorrelief aus einem Sarkophagdeckel: Kultprozession eines Magistrates wohl anlässlich eines Dioskurenfestes, 360–370 n. Chr. (nach Forlati Tamaro 1980, Abb. 31; © Friuli Venezia Giulia – Soprintendenza per i Beni Archeologici)

5 *Delos*, Wandmalerei an einem Hausaltar: Kultszene, späthellenistisch (nach Bulard 1926, Taf. 3, 1)

(*ferculum*) – getragen worden, und die Senatoren seien barfuß mitgegangen, während hier der Magistrat senatorisches Schuhwerk (*calcei senatorii*) trägt und bequem auf einem Sesselwagen gefahren wird. Nach der expliziten Aussage des Arnobius (7, 49 f.) weise außerdem der schwärzliche Kybele-Stein – ein eisenhaltiger Meteorit – eine raue Oberfläche mit Vorsprüngen auf, während das aquileiesische Kultobjekt als polierte konische Masse erscheint.

Eine ähnliche Form zeigen dagegen die sieben Eier in gesenkter Position, die auf der *spina* des Zirkus bei den Wagenrennen als Rundenzähler dienten[30]. Durch Tertullian und weitere Quellen wird der Zusammenhang dieser *ova* mit dem Ei überliefert, aus dem die Dioskuren gebo-

---

Quadriga: RIC IV Elagabalus 61c–d. 62. 64–65. 143b. d; 144. 195b. d; 196A. a. d; 197; Latham 2016, 130–132 Abb. 39–40. Die Annahme von Di Filippo Balestrazzi, dass es sich beim aquileiesischen Relief um diesen Stein handle, hält nicht stand, da unter anderem dessen offizieller Kult auf die Regierungszeit des Elagabal beschränkt war.

[30] z. B. Grosser 2021, 281–282 Kat. Sr12 Taf. 17, 2 (Sarkophag des späten 3. Jhs. n. Chr.).

ren wurden³¹. Eine Kultstätte der Zwillingsgötter befand sich nicht nur auf der *spina* des Circus Maximus, sondern auch im Circus Flaminius (woher die Statuen der Dioskuren auf dem Kapitol kommen) sowie im Hippodrom von Konstantinopel³². Der Gegenstand in *Aquileia* lässt sich am besten mit der Dioskurenkappe (*pileus*) vergleichen, die von den literarischen Quellen als die Hälfte des Dioskuren-Eis gedeutet wird³³. Sie findet sich als Weihegabe oder stellvertretendes anikonisches Kultbild aus Stein oder Silber beispielsweise auf *Delos* wieder³⁴. In einigen Fällen weist die Aufstellung der geweihten Kappe auf einem Steintisch oder in einem Silbertempelchen eindeutig auf deren Verehrung hin, die im Übrigen in Wandmalereien mit Kultszenen auf derselben Insel explizit dargestellt wird (Abb. 5)³⁵.

Das aquileiesische Relief dürfte daher wahrscheinlich einen *pileus* als Kultsymbol (*exuviae*) der Dioskuren wiedergeben, das im Rahmen einer *pompa* mitgetragen wurde. Dabei könnte wohl der *natalis Castoris et Pollucis* am 8. April gemeint sein, der nach dem Zeugnis des Chronografen des Filocalus noch 354 n. Chr. mit Wagenrennen im Zirkus feierlich begangen wurde³⁶. Die konventionelle Säulenarchitektur mit verkröpftem Gebälk im Hintergrund könnte dann das Forum Romanum mit dem Castortempel andeuten, das vom Aufzug auf dem Weg zum Circus Maximus gerade verlassen wird.

4) Auf das Viertel des Zirkus und des Kaiserpalasts nimmt auch das nächste zu betrachtende Ensemble von etwa zwölf Relieftondi aus prokonnesischem Marmor mit Götterbüsten Bezug, deren Fundorte sich an der Nordwestecke der Stadt konzentrieren³⁷. Anhand stilistischer Merkmale datieren sie wohl in die erste Hälfte des 4. Jahrhunderts n. Chr. Im Lichte des vorher Gesagten verwundert nicht, darunter wieder einen Dioskur – und nicht wie meistens behauptet Attis oder Mithras – anzutreffen (Abb. 6 a)³⁸. Denn die kugelförmige, glatte Kappe (*pileus*) mit mittlerem Dübelloch für den Einsatz eines Metallsternes sowie die aufgeworfene Stirnfrisur (Anastolé) nach dem berühmten Vorbild der hellenistischen Statue Alexanders des Großen als Dioskur legen diese Benennung nahe.

Die normalerweise als Jupiter benannte Büste bedarf wohl auch einer Neuinterpretation, da an der Brust sowie auf der drapierten, linken Schulter ein stabförmiges Attribut angelehnt war, das später gründlich abgemeißelt wurde (Abb. 6 b)³⁹: dessen dünne, sich verjüngende Form könnte zu

---

[31] Tert. spect. 8, 3; vgl. Isid. orig. 18, 29, 1; dazu Quinn-Schoffield 1967; Humphrey 1986, 260–262.

[32] Circus Maximus: Marcattili 2009, 191–198; Marroni 2019, I 82–83. – Circus Flaminius: Nista 1994, 78 (E. La Rocca). 123–128 (P. L. Tucci). 153. 160–170 (C. Parisi Presicce); Marroni 2019, I 75–80; Gartrell 2021, 64–73. – Konstantinopel: Zos. 2, 31, 1 (Ausbauphase Konstantins I.); hierzu Bassett 1991, 90.

[33] Lykophr. 506–507; Lukian. 26, 1. Sextus Empiricus (math. 9, 37) deutet die zwei *pilei* auf die himmlischen Hemisphären; dazu Nista 1994, 73 (E. La Rocca).

[34] LIMC III (1986) 588 Nr. 247–249 Taf. 476 s. v. Dioskouroi (A. Hermary).

[35] Vgl. die Inventarlisten ID 1417 A I 161: τράπεζα λιθίνη ἐφ' ἧς πῖλοι λίθινοι δύο (ein Steintisch, woraufzwei Steinkappen); ID 1442 B 43: πῖλον ἀργυροῦ(ν) ἔχοντα ἐφ' ἑαυτοῦ ζωιδ[άρι]ον ἀργυροῦν ἐν ναιδίωι ἀργυρῶι (Silberpilos mit einer Silberstatuette darauf, innerhalb einer Silberkapelle). Wandmalereien: Bulard 1926, 66–67 Taf. 3, 1 (hier Abb. 5); 68 Taf. 3, 2d (als Omphalos bezeichnet); vgl. 101–102 Abb. 30. – Im sepulkralen Bereich ist die Form einiger Grabaltar- und Urnenbedeckungen (u. a. aus der nahen Concordia) vergleichbar: Di Filippo Balestrazzi 2012, Kat. 106–108 (mit Parallelen besonders aus der Ägäis und Mittelitalien, zuweilen als Omphalos benannt).

[36] Divjak–Wischmeyer 2014, 208. 221–222. 224. 262–263; vgl. 217–218. Falsch überliefert ist hier das Datum des 7. April. – Mehrfach belegt ist der Dioskurenkult in der Spätantike, besonders in Rom: Nista 1994, 98 (B. Poulsen). 212 (G. L. Gregori); Marroni 2019, II 157–159; im Bezug auf die *pompa circensis* vgl. den Sarkophagdeckel mit *tensa* der Dioskuren: Wrede 2001, 82. 97 Taf. 18, 2; Latham 2016, 215–216 Abb. 82 (4. Jh. n. Chr.). In den Provinzen vgl. das Ledamosaik in Trier mit Kultszene und Dioskuren-Ei, 350–400 n. Chr. (Unruh 2017, 83–84 Abb. 82); das Tricliniummosaik der Villa in Noheda (Cuenca, 4. Jh. n. Chr.) mit Dioskurenbild auf der römerartigen *spina* des olympischen Hippodroms (Valero Tévar 2013, 316 Abb. 13; dazu 310–311 Abb. 6: Dioskurenstatuette aus demselben Raum; zu Olympia vgl. Paus. 5, 15, 3 f.).

[37] Scrinari 1972, Kat. 606–613 (antoninisch); Mian 2004, 470–494 Abb. 26–33; Tiussi u. a. 2013, 76–79 Abb. 2–11; 226–231 Kat. 34–39 mit Literatur (G. Mian). Innendurchmesser 66–74 cm.

[38] Mian 2004, 479–480 Abb. 26 b Nr. 8; Tiussi u. a. 2013, Kat. 38 (G. Mian: Attis oder Mithras); lupa 13982 (Dioskur).

[39] Mian 2004, 471 Abb. 26 a Nr. 1; Tiussi u. a. 2013, Kat. 34 (G. Mian).

6   Aquileia, Medaillons mit Reliefbüsten von Göttern: a) Dioskur, b) lokaler Flussgott (?), 300–350 n. Chr. (a: lupa 13982, Foto O. Harl; b: aus Tiussi u. a. 2013, 227 Kat. 34; © Friuli Venezia Giulia – Soprintendenza per i Beni Archeologici)

7   Aquileia, Sockelreliefs aus Kalkstein: a–e) Handelsschiff, verwundete Tigerin, Panzer, Quadriga, Tiara mit *harpé*, f) dazugehöriges neues Fragment mit zeichnerischer Rekonstruktion: gemmenbesetzter Thron mit Medusa-Appliken, um 300 n. Chr. (a–e: lupa 14309–14313; f: lupa 18805; Foto O. Harl; Zeichnung J. Windmaißer/© Friuli Venezia Giulia – Soprintendenza per i Beni Archeologici)

einem Schilfzweig bestens passen, der häufig mit Oceanus oder insbesondere mit Flussgöttern – unter anderem mit dem Fluss *Natiso* in *Aquileia* – assoziiert wird[40].

Durch diese Umbenennungen würde allerdings die kanonische Zahl der zwölf Götter überschritten, da man der Vollständigkeit halber einen zweiten Dioskur und Jupiter selbst voraussetzen sollte. Von der vermuteten Existenz zweier Göttergruppen unterschiedlicher Größe und Qualität abgesehen, möchte man hier den Hauptfundort von fünf zusammenhängenden Medaillons an der Stelle des heutigen Friedhofs hervorheben, wo in der Spätantike gerade die *carceres*

---

[40]   z. B. LIMC VIII (1997) 25–27 Nr. 7. 12. 21a–c. 23 s. v. Tiber, Tiberinus (R. Mambella); 907–915 Nr. 1. 98 s. v. Oceanus (H. A. Cahn); Reinsberg 2006, Kat. 80 Taf. 114. – *Aquileia*: Scrinari 1972, Kat. 556 (*Aesontius*/Isonzo). 557 (*Natiso*/Natissa); Di Filippo Balestrazzi 2005, 110–112 Abb. 13–14; lupa 13958. 13959.

des Zirkus gestanden haben müssen, d. h. ein nachweislich beliebter Aufstellungsort heidnischer Götterbilder⁴¹.

5) Das fünfte und letzte Steindenkmal setzt sich aus den bekannten ›Metopen‹ mit zeichenhaften Reliefdarstellungen zusammen, die üblicherweise um die Mitte des 2. Jahrhunderts n. Chr. datiert werden (Abb. 7 a–e)⁴². Der Reihe nach erkennt man ein Handelsschiff, eine durch zwei Speere erstochene Tigerin⁴³, einen Panzer mit Gorgoneion, eine Quadriga, eine mit Edelsteinen besetzte phrygische Mütze samt einem Schwert mit Hacken (*harpé* oder *ensis hamatus*). Dieser Gruppe wurde kürzlich ein neues Bruchstück in der Museumsausstellung beigefügt, dessen genauer Fundort in *Aquileia* wie für die anderen Reliefs unbekannt ist (Abb. 7 f)⁴⁴. Erhalten ist dabei die obere rechte Ecke der Platte mit der partiellen Darstellung eines Throns⁴⁵: sichtbar sind dessen mit Gemmen besetztes Vorderbein, die gepolsterte, unten mit Zickzackmuster gekennzeichnete Zarge, das Querholz und eine Applike in Gestalt eines Gorgoneion an der oberen Eckverbindung. Die Proportionierung des Gegenstandes fordert eine Rekonstruktion auf zwei aneinander anstoßenden Platten, wie es sonst bei dem Schiffs- bzw. dem Quadriga-Relief derselben Serie der Fall war. Der so resultierende Leerplatz auf der linken Platte könnte wohl ein weiteres Machtattribut aufgenommen haben, das in der hier vorgelegten Zeichnung versuchsweise als ein Szepter nach der Vorlage der »Insignien des Maxentius« ergänzt worden ist⁴⁶.

Die Dekoration mit Reihen von großen Edelsteinen wurde während der Tetrarchie aus dem persischen Raum für Prunkkleider und Throne übernommen⁴⁷. Engere Parallelen findet der aquileiesische Thron in zwei Porphyrstatuen sitzender Tetrarchen aus *Alexandria* und Šarkamen in Serbien (Abb. 8), von denen er eine vereinfachte Version darstellt⁴⁸. Nun legt der massive, klobige Stil der anderen Reliefs ebenfalls eine tetrarchische Datierung nahe.

Das Bild des leeren Throns lässt sich der bekannten Ikonografie der *lectisternia* oder hier besser *solisternia* zuordnen, wobei die Götter durch ihren Sitz und die jeweils auf diese gelegten Attribute (*exuviae*) an öffentlichen Orten, besonders im Theater und im Zirkus, vergegenwärtigt werden⁴⁹. Dabei wird der Kaiserkult eng in den Rahmen der olympischen Götter verwoben, indem die divinisierten Kaiser gleichsam in den göttlichen Kreis aufgenommen werden.

Unter dem aquileiesischen Thron ist ein bogenförmiger Gegenstand fragmentarisch erhalten, bei dem es sich um den Henkel eines Gefäßes, etwa eines Kantharos oder einer Kanne handeln könnte; eine Amphore ist zum Beispiel auf kaiserzeitlichen Münzen von *Nikomedia* in Bezug auf das Festmahl der *lectisternia* unter der Kline dargestellt⁵⁰. Da weitere Attribute jedoch normalerweise auf oder neben dem Thron platziert werden und auch angesichts des kantigen Profils des

---

⁴¹ Fundkarte von Heinrich Maionica (1893) Nr. 43 (Mian 2004, 471 Abb. 12). – Vgl. das Zirkusmosaik von der Piazza Armerina, wobei die zwölf Statuen den zwölf Startboxen entsprechen (Carandini u. a. 1982, 338 Taf. 57), und das Mosaik von Gerona (s. o. Anm. 27).

⁴² Scrinari 1972, Nr. 596a–e; Vermaseren 1978, 93 Nr. 224 Taf. 88; Steuernagel 2004, 239; De Franzoni 2009 mit Literatur; lupa 14309–14313 (spätantik). Durchschnittliche Maße (ganz): H 130; B 89; T 20 cm.

⁴³ Meist wird sie als Löwin angesprochen. Von beiden Speeren ist jeweils ein Schaftstumpf auf dem Rücken des Tieres sowie die Spitze vor dessen Brust bzw. unter der linken Zitze erhalten.

⁴⁴ lupa 18805: H 68; B 43; T 23 cm.

⁴⁵ Dass es sich um eine *sella curulis* handeln könnte (lupa 18805), muss anhand des zahlreichen Vergleichsmaterials ausscheiden: vgl. Wanscher 1980, 121–190; Schäfer 1989.

⁴⁶ Henrich 2022, Kat. 1.

⁴⁷ Alföldy 1970, 8. 141. 244. – Vgl. in der Reliefgruppe die Gemmen der Tiara und des Pferdegeschirrs.

⁴⁸ Alexandria: LSA-1003; Rollé Ditzler 2019, 248–249 Taf. 67–68. – Šarkamen: LSA-1118; Popović u. a. 2018, 73–74 Abb. 28 Kat. 27. – Zudem können der im tetrarchischen Kaiserkultsaal in Luxor gemalte Thronschemel sowie die Throne Konstantins I. (326–330 n. Chr.) bzw. Valentinians und Valens' (364–367 n. Chr.) auf Goldmedaillons (RIC VII 577 Nr. 44 Taf. 18; RIC IX 116 Nr. 1) herangezogen werden: Deckers 1983, 269. 642 f. Kat. 226 Abb. 102–104.

⁴⁹ Alföldy 1970, 159. 252–257; La Rocca 2007; Madigan 2013, 83–101; Vollmer 2014, 33–38. 43–107. 119–156. 225–281; vgl. bes. Taf. 29 (flavische Münzen). 34–35 (Marmorthrone in Aschaffenburg).

⁵⁰ RPC VI 3473 (235–238 n. Chr.); Vollmer 2014, Taf. 7, 4 (238–244 n. Chr.). – Man könnte auch an ein loses Doppelband (*taenia* o. Ä.) denken (z. B. Popović u. a. 2018, Kat. 22; Henrich 2022, 36 Kat. 28: Tympanon aus Felix Romuliana, Anfang 4. Jh.).

8   Šarkamen (Serbien), Rekonstruktion der porphyrischen Thronstatue eines Tetrarchen, Anfang 4. Jh. n. Chr. (nach Popović u. a. 2018, 74 Abb. 28; Zeichnung A. Kapuran/© Gangemi Editore)

krummen Elements sowie dessen scheinbarer Zusammenfügung mit dem Thronfuß, sind hier wahrscheinlicher zwei gegenläufige Doppelvoluten als charakteristisches Muster – und zugleich als Querverbindung – zahlreicher Throne seit der spätklassischen Epoche bis in die Kaiserzeit zu rekonstruieren[51].

In Bezug auf den mit dem Thronmotiv häufig verknüpften Kaiserkult könnte man den Tetrarchen Maximianus Herculius als Kultempfänger vermuten, denn er residierte zeitweise in *Aquileia* und wurde nach seinem Tod 310 als *divus* noch unter Konstantin verehrt[52].

Der ursprüngliche Baukontext der aquileiesischen ›Metopen‹ kann annähernd bestimmt werden: Die glatte Sockelzone der Reliefplatten weist nämlich auf eine Aufstellung im unteren Wandbereich eines Innenraums hin, wobei die Reliefs durch leichten Vorsprung gegenüber dem Hintergrund mit schmucklosen Steinplatten abgewechselt haben dürften[53]. Die Vorlage für eine solche Bautypologie bieten einige Marmor- oder Kaisersäle des griechischen Ostens, am treffendsten die frühkaiserzeitliche Ausstattung des Heroon des Diodoros Pasparos in *Pergamon*, wobei im unteren Wandbereich vergleichbare Reliefs mit symbolhaften Darstellungen angebracht waren (Abb. 9)[54].

Sowohl in *Pergamon* als auch in *Aquileia* umschreiben die Bilder zeichenhaft die Betätigungsfelder des Geehrten, seine Tugenden sowie seine Religiosität[55]: die verletzte Tigerin – ein Bildtopos – dürfte sich somit auf die von ihm gestifteten Tierhetzen beziehen[56]; die

---

[51] Alföldy 1970, 244–245 Abb. 2. 11 Taf. 14, 6; 16, 1. 2; hervorzuheben ist der Vergleich mit einem Silberlöffel der Eusebii aus der Nähe von *Aquileia* (mit seitlichen Einzelvoluten allerdings): Abb. 12; Piussi 2008, 366. 372–373 Kat. VIII 5 (Mitte 4. Jh.). Vgl. die Voluten unter der Thronsitzfläche bereits auf apulischen rotfigurigen Vasen (4. Jh. v. Chr.): Trendall – Cambitoglou 1978–1982, II Taf. 163, 4; 175, 2; 176, 1; 194; 206, 6; 324; 333, 1; 360, 2; bes. 461 Kat. 17/23 Taf. 164, 1 (durchbrochene Voluten); vgl. I 415 Kat. 16/4 Taf. 146, 4. Für kaiserzeitliche Parallelen s. auch Vollmer 2014, Kat. 4. 5.2 (Aschaffenburg). 25–26. 28–29 Taf. 4, 10; 30, 1–4; 33–34.

[52] Clauss 1999, 189–193. 202–203. 519. – Zu den Aufenthalten Maximians und seines Sohnes Maxentius in *Aquileia* s. Cigaina 2012/2013, 303. 306. Anhand der Angleichung beider Kaiser an Hercules könnte man eventuell eine Keule im linken Reliefteil ergänzen: vgl. D.C. 72, 17, 4 (Diphros des Commodus-Hercules); Vollmer 2014, 482 Kat. 7.11 Taf. 27, 3 (Thronrelief in Biella).

[53] Die Anathyrose mit einem 6–7 cm breiten, polierten Randstreifen lässt diese Rekonstruktion zu.

[54] Radt 1999, 136–137. 248–254 (nach 17 n. Chr.; bis zur 2. Hälfte des 3. Jhs. im Betrieb): darunter sind auch zwei Brustpanzerreliefs (Abb. 200 d). Für die unterschiedlich breiten Vorsprünge des Sockels vgl. den Marmorsaal des Vediusgymnasiums in *Ephesos* (Mitte 2. Jh. n. Chr.): Steskal – La Torre 2008, 19–23. 295–296 Taf. 60–65. 68. 114–117.

[55] In diese Richtung weist schon Steuernagel 2004, 239.

[56] Zum Topos: Wrede 2001, 79; zum Bildthema: Tiussi u. a. 2013, 171 Abb. 3 (»Casa delle Bestie Ferite« in *Aquileia*, 2. Hälfte 4. Jh.).

9  *Pergamon*, Heroon des Diodoros Pasparos: Ecke des Marmorsaals, 1. Jh. n. Chr. (nach Radt 1999, Abb. 199; Dia E. Steiner 1974/© DAI Istanbul, Pergamon-Fotoarchiv)

Quadriga auf Wagenrennen oder, falls sie von Apollo/Sol gelenkt worden wäre, auf das weitere Umfeld des Zirkus und der *pompa circensis*[57], alternativ auf eine Kaiserapotheose[58]; das Schiff könnte auf die Verbesserung des Seehandels und insbesondere der *annona* verweisen, welche ein Motiv der Panegyrik ist und im lokalen Kontext auf die neugebauten tetrarchischen Kornmagazine (*horrea*) am Flusshafen anspielen könnte[59]; der Panzer dürfte dann die Sieghaftigkeit im Krieg evozieren; der Thron versinnbildlicht, wie gesagt, eine göttliche Präsenz, vielleicht ebenjene des Kaisers Maximianus[60]; schließlich sind die Tiara und die *harpé*, die schon lange als Bildchiffren der Mater Magna gegolten haben, jetzt nach näherer Überprüfung der Bildkombination eher mit Mithras in Zusammenhang zu bringen[61]. Dafür spricht auch die Gemmenverzierung der Tiara mit Halbmond- und Sternmustern, die der astralen Symbolik zahlreicher Mithrasdarstellungen entsprechen[62]. Bezüglich der hier angenommenen Verehrung eines Tetrarchen kann man die enge Verbindung des Kaiserkollegiums zu Mithras heranziehen, wie sie etwa durch den von ihnen 308 n. Chr. in *Carnuntum* geweihten Altar bezeugt ist, wobei der iranische Gott als Beschützer der tetrarchischen Staatsordnung (*fautor imperii sui*) angerufen wird[63]. Wenn man abschließend die militärisch angehauchten Bildmotive – Rüstungsteile, *venationes*, Mithraskult – sowie den groben Stil der Reliefs in Erwägung zieht, scheint es nicht ganz abwegig, das Ensemble als Teil

---

[57] Vgl. das Relief aus Pozzuoli in Wrede 2001, 81 Taf. 20, 2 (um 300 n. Chr.); La Rocca – Tortorella 2008, 153 Kat. I 3.7 (330–350 n. Chr.).

[58] Vgl. RIC VI, Treveri 809; Paneg. 6, 14, 3 (307 n. Chr.): Himmelfahrt des *divus* Constantius I.; RIC VIII, Treveri 44. 68. Lugdunum 12. Arelate 42 usw.: *divus* Constantinus.

[59] Vgl. Paneg. 3, 15, 4 (auf Maximian, 291 n. Chr.); 11, 14, 2. 5–6 (auf Julian, 362 n. Chr.); dazu Mause 1994, 174 mit Anm. 53; *horrea* in *Aquileia*: Tiussi u. a. 2013, 95–96 Abb. 2–3.

[60] Beiläufig angemerkt, bietet dieses Relief eine der letzten Darstellungen des heidnischen *solisternium*, bevor es im späten 4. Jh. auf den Thron Christi (*Hetoimasia*) umgedeutet wurde: vgl. den Sarkophag in Frascati und das Relief in Berlin (Alföldy 1970, 256–257; La Rocca 2007, 104 Abb. 28; Vollmer 2014, 357–405 Kat. 12–13 Taf. 56, 1–2). Frappierende Ähnlichkeiten weist das Thronbild auf dem Elfenbeinkästchen aus Samagher (Pula) im Einflussbereich von *Aquileia* auf (Vollmer 2014, 402–403 Kat. 35 Taf. 58, 1: um 420 n. Chr.).

[61] De Franzoni 2009, 22–28 (jedoch mit Deutung auf einen Mithraspriester).

[62] Vgl. das gleiche kreuzförmige Sternmuster am Relief vom Mithräum des Circus Maximus in Rom: Vermaseren 1956, I Nr. 435–436 Abb. 122 = EDR073200 (A. Carapellucci 2015: 3. Jh.).

[63] CIL III 4413 = ILS 659 = Vermaseren 1960, II Nr. 1697–1698 Abb. 438–439 = EDH, HD023078 (J. Osnabrügge 2017); CSIR Österreich I 3, Nr. 176; CSIR Österreich Carnuntum Suppl. 1, Nr. 351 Taf. 106–107; lupa 4951. – Zur besonderen Frömmigkeit Maximians s. Paneg. 3, 6, 1 f.

der Skulpturenausstattung eines Kaisersaales der in *Aquileia* stationierten Truppen *comitatenses* anzusehen.

Insgesamt betrachtet, zeugen die besprochenen Denkmäler von der erfolgten ›Dekapitalisierung‹ Roms, d. h. von dessen Verlust der Rolle als Hauptstadt des Reiches zugunsten provinzialer Residenzstädte wie *Aquileia*. In Absenz des Kaisers werden die traditionellen Kaiserinsignien und der Repräsentanzapparat in verstärktem Maße von Senatoren in Anspruch genommen, die sich als Hüter der paganen Tradition verstehen. Der Zirkus wird zu einem primären Raum des metropolitanen Lebens: vor dem versammelten Volk treten hier Kaiser und zunehmend Senatoren auf, stiften Tierhatzen und Wagenrennen sowie weiterhin die Pflege der heidnischen Kulte im Rahmen der *pompa circensis*. Als noch maßgebendes Zentrum scheint Rom diese Tendenzen auf die spätantike Provinzhauptstadt *Aquileia* ausgestrahlt zu haben. Daneben dringen auf italischen Boden neue energische, massive Ausdrucksformen von den östlichen und balkanischen Provinzen ein, wobei sich die herausragende, quasi göttergleiche Machtstellung der Kaiser in der etwas naiven, jedoch effektvollen Bildsprache der Tetrarchie behaupten kann.

## BIBLIOGRAFIE

| | |
|---|---|
| Alföldy 1970 | A. Alföldy, Die monarchische Repräsentation im römischen Kaiserreiche ²(Darmstadt 1970) |
| Bassett 1991 | S. G. Bassett, Antiquities in the hippodrome of Constantinople, DOP 45, 1991, 87–96 |
| Basso 2004 | P. Basso, Topografia degli spazi ludici di Aquileia, Antichità Altoadriatiche 59, 2004, 317–337 |
| Basso 2018 | P. Basso, L'anfiteatro di Aquileia. Ricerche d'archivio e nuove indagini di scavo (Quingentole 2018) |
| Bernier, im Druck | A. Bernier, *Dat(a) Med(iolano)*. Imperial sojours and administrative reforms in fourth-century Milan, in: M. Löx – F. Wöller (Hrsg.), Milan. Imperial capital and Christian metropolis (3rd–6th century AD), im Druck |
| Bulard 1926 | M. Bulard, Description des revêtements peints a sujets religieux, Délos 9 (Paris 1926) |
| Carandini u. a. 1982 | A. Carandini – A. Ricci – M. De Vos, Filosofiana. The villa of Piazza Armerina: the image of a Roman aristocrat at the time of Constantine (Palermo 1982) |
| Cigaina 2012/2013 | L. Cigaina, Le stele aquileiesi con »stehende Soldaten« e il problema del reimpiego, AquilNost 83/84, 2012/2013, 299–316 |
| Clauss 1999 | M. Clauss, Kaiser und Gott. Herrscherkult im römischen Reich (Stuttgart 1999) |
| De Franzoni 2009 | A. De Franzoni, Considerazioni su un rilievo »metroaco« del Museo Archeologico Nazionale di Aquileia: una rilettura iconografica, AquilNost 80, 2009, 13–40 |
| Deckers 1983 | J. Deckers, Constantin und Christus. Das Bildprogramm in Kaiserkulträumen und Kirchen, in: H. Beck – P. C. Bol (Hrsg.), Spätantike und frühes Christentum. Ausstellungskatalog Frankfurt am Main (Frankfurt am Main 1983) 267–283 |
| Delbrueck 1929 | R. Delbrueck, Die Consulardiptychen und verwandte Denkmäler (Berlin 1929) |
| Di Filippo Balestrazzi 2005 | E. Di Filippo Balestrazzi, Il rilievo storico, Antichità Altoadriatiche 61, 2005, 93–123 |
| Di Filippo Balestrazzi 2012 | E. Di Filippo Balestrazzi, Sculture romane del Museo Nazionale Concordiese di Portogruaro (Rom 2012) |
| Divjak – Wischmeyer 2014 | J. Divjak – W. Wischmeyer (Hrsg.), Das Kalenderhandbuch von 354. Der Chronograph des Filocalus I (Wien 2014) |
| Dresken-Weiland 1998 | J. Dresken-Weiland, Repertorium der christlich-antiken Sarkophage, II. Italien mit einem Nachtrag Rom und Ostia, Dalmatien, Museen der Welt (Mainz am Rhein 1998) |
| Engemann 2008 | J. Engemann, Die Spiele spätantiker Senatoren und Consuln, ihre Diptychen und ihre Geschenke, in: G. Bühl – A. Cutler – A. Effenberger (Hrsg.), Spätantike und byzantinische Elfenbeinbildwerke im Diskurs (Wiesbaden 2008) 53–96 |
| Forlati Tamaro 1980 | B. Forlati Tamaro (Hrsg.), Da Aquileia a Venezia: una mediazione tra l'Europa e l'Oriente dal II secolo a.C. al VI secolo d.C. (Mailand 1980) |
| Gabelmann 1980 | H. Gabelmann, Circusspiele in der spätantiken Repräsentationskunst, AW 11/4, 1980, 25–38 |

| | |
|---|---|
| Gartrell 2021 | A. Gartrell, The cult of Castor and Pollux in ancient Rome. Myth, ritual, and society (Cambridge 2021) |
| Grosser 2021 | F. C. Grosser, Darstellungen von Wagenlenkern in der römischen Kaiserzeit und frühen Spätantike (Wiesbaden 2021) |
| Henrich 2022 | P. Henrich (Hrsg.), Der Untergang des römischen Reiches. Ausstellungskatalog Trier (Darmstadt 2022) |
| Humphrey 1986 | J. H. Humphrey, Roman circuses: arenas for chariot racing (Berkeley 1986) |
| ID | Inscriptions de Délos (Paris 1926–) |
| InscrAq | J. B. Brusin, Inscriptiones Aquileiae I–III (Udine 1991–1993) |
| Köhler 1998 | J. Köhler, Bildkatalog der Skulpturen des Vatikanischen Museums, II. Museo Pio Clementino – Cortile Ottagono (Berlin 1998) |
| L'Orange 1939 | H. P. L'Orange, Der spätantike Bildschmuck des Konstantinbogens (Berlin 1939) |
| La Regina 2001 | A. La Regina (Hrsg.), Sangue e arena. Ausstellungskatalog Rom (Mailand 2001) |
| La Rocca 2007 | E. La Rocca, I troni dei nuovi dei, in: T. Nogales – J. González (Hrsg.), Culto imperial: política y poder. Actas del Congreso Internacional Mérida 18.–20.05.2006 (Rom 2007) 75–104 |
| La Rocca – Tortorella 2008 | E. La Rocca – S. Tortorella (Hrsg.), Trionfi romani. Ausstellungskatalog Rom (Mailand 2008) |
| Langner 2001 | M. Langner, Antike Graffitizeichnungen: Motive, Gestaltung und Bedeutung (Wiesbaden 2001) |
| Latham 2016 | J. A. Latham, Performance, memory, and processions in ancient Rome. The pompa circensis from the Late Republic to Late Antiquity (New York 2016) |
| Lopreato 1987 | P. Lopreato, Grado. La stele con ritratto di un magistrato tardo-antico, Antichità Altoadriatiche 30, 1987, 165–171 |
| Lopreato 1989 | P. Lopreato, Il lapidario di Grado (Mariano del Friuli 1989) |
| Lopreato 1991 | P. Lopreato, Grado. Lapidario del Duomo. Stele con ritratto di magistrato, in: La tutela dei beni culturali e ambientali nel Friuli – Venezia Giulia (1986–1987), Relazioni 8 (Triest 1991) 191–192 |
| LSA | Last Statues of Antiquity, <http://laststatues.classics.ox.ac.uk> (01.12.2022) |
| lupa | F. und O. Harl, <lupa.at> (Bilddatenbank zu antiken Steindenkmälern) (29.11.2022) |
| Madigan 2013 | B. Madigan, The ceremonial sculptures of the Roman gods (Leiden 2013) |
| Maiuro 2012 | M. Maiuro, Res Caesaris. Ricerche sulla proprietà imperiale nel Principato (Bari 2012) |
| Marcattili 2009 | F. Marcattili, Circo Massimo: architetture, funzioni, culti, ideologia (Rom 2009) |
| Marchet 2008 | G. Marchet, Mittere mappam (Mart. 12.28.9): du signal de départ à la théologie impériale (I$^{er}$ a.C.–VII$^e$ p.C.), in: J. Nelis-Clément – J.-M. Roddaz (Hrsg.), Le cirque romain et son image (Bordeaux 2008) 291–317 |
| Marroni 2019 | E. Marroni, Il culto dei Dioscuri in Italia. Parte I. Testimonianze – Parte II. Caratteri e significati (Pisa 2019) |
| Mause 1994 | M. Mause, Die Darstellung des Kaisers in der lateinischen Panegyrik (Stuttgart 1994) |
| Mian 2004 | G. Mian, I programmi decorativi dell'edilizia pubblica aquileiese. Alcuni esempi, Antichità Altoadriatiche 59, 2004, 425–509 |
| Nista 1994 | L. Nista (Hrsg.), Castores: l'immagine dei Dioscuri a Roma (Rom 1994) |
| Novello u. a. 2019 | M. Novello – G. Plattner – C. Tiussi (Hrsg.), Magnifici ritorni. Tesori aquileiesi dal Kunsthistorisches Museum di Vienna. Ausstellungskatalog Aquileia (Rom 2019) |
| Orlandi 2005 | S. Orlandi, Epigrafia anfiteatrale dell'Occidente romano, VI. Roma. Anfiteatri e strutture annesse con una nuova edizione e commento delle iscrizioni del Colosseo (Rom 2005) |
| Panciera 1987 | S. Panciera, I patroni di Aquileia fra la città e Roma, Antichità Altoadriatiche 30, 1987, 77–95 |
| Paolucci – Zub 2000 | R. Paolucci – A. Zub, La monetazione di Aquileia romana (Padua 2000) |
| Piussi 2008 | S. Piussi (Hrsg.), Cromazio di Aquileia 388–408: al crocevia di genti e religioni. Ausstellungskatalog Udine (Cinisello Balsamo 2008) |

| | |
|---|---|
| Popović u. a. 2018 | I. Popović – C. Tiussi – M. Verzár (Hrsg.), Treasures and emperors: the splendour of Roman Serbia. Ausstellungskatalog Aquileia (Rom 2018) |
| Quinn-Schoffield 1967 | W. K. Quinn-Schoffield, Castor and Pollux in the Roman Circus, Latomus 26, 1967, 450–453 |
| Radt 1999 | W. Radt, Pergamon. Geschichte und Bauten einer antiken Metropole (Darmstadt 1999) |
| Rebaudo – Zanier 2012/2013 | L. Rebaudo – K. Zanier, Pezzi difficili. Due sculture aquileiesi del IV secolo d.C., AquilNost 83/84, 2012/2013, 273–288 |
| Reinsberg 2006 | C. Reinsberg, Die Sarkophage mit Darstellungen aus dem Menschenleben. Vita Romana, ASR 1, 3 (Berlin 2006) |
| Ricci 2014 | C. Ricci, Protendere per protegere. Considerazioni sul carattere della presenza militare ad Aquileia tra Massimino e Costantino, Antichità Altoadriatiche 78, 2014, 239–254 |
| Rodà 2005 | I. Rodà, Els mosaics de Bell-lloc, in: Girona a l'abast X. Girona romana (Girona 2005) 214–223 |
| Rollé Ditzler 2019 | I. Rollé Ditzler, Der Senat und seine Kaiser im spätantiken Rom. Eine kulturhistorische Annährung (Wiesbaden 2019) |
| Sabbatini Tumolesi 1988 | P. Sabbatini Tumolesi, Gli spettacoli anfiteatrali alla luce di alcune testimonianze epigrafiche, in: A. M. Reggiani (Hrsg.), Anfiteatro Flavio. Immagine testimonianze spettacoli (Rom 1988) 91–99 |
| Schäfer 1989 | T. Schäfer, Imperii insignia: sella curulis und fasces. Zur Repräsentation römischer Magistrate (Mainz 1989) |
| Scrinari 1972 | V. S. M. Scrinari, Museo Archeologico di Aquileia. Catalogo delle sculture romane (Rom 1972) |
| Steskal – La Torre 2008 | M. Steskal – M. La Torre (Hrsg.), Das Vediusgymnasium in Ephesos. Archäologie und Baubefund I–II, FiE 14, 1 (Wien 2008) |
| Tiussi u. a. 2013 | C. Tiussi – L. Villa – M. Novello (Hrsg.), Costantino e Teodoro. Aquileia nel IV secolo. Ausstellungskatalog Aquileia (Mailand 2013) |
| Tiussi – Villa 2017 | C. Tiussi – L. Villa, Aquileia in età tetrarchica e constantiniana: trasformazioni urbanistiche e monumentali bel settore occidentale, AquilNost 88, 2017, 91–147 |
| Trendall – Cambitoglou 1978–1982 | A. D. Trendall – A. Cambitoglou, The red-figured vases of Apulia I–II (Oxford 1978–1982) |
| Unruh 2017 | F. Unruh, Trier. Biographie einer römischen Stadt: von Augusta Treverorum zu Trier, AW Sonderheft 3.17 (Darmstadt 2017) |
| Valero Tévar 2013 | M. Á. Valero Tévar, The late-antique villa at Noheda (Villar de Domingo García) near Cuenca and its mosaics, JRA 26, 2013, 307–330 |
| Vergone 2007 | G. Vergone, Le epigrafi lapidarie del Museo Paleocristiano di Monastero (Aquileia) (Triest 2007) |
| Vermaseren 1956–1960 | M. J. Vermaseren, Corpus inscriptionum et monumentorum religionis Mithriacae I–II (Hagae Comitis 1956–1960) |
| Vermaseren 1978 | M. J. Vermaseren, Corpus cultus Cybelae Attidisque (CCCA) IV. Italia – aliae provinciae (Leiden 1978) |
| Volbach 1976 | W. F. Volbach, Elfenbeinarbeiten der Spätantike und des frühen Mittelalters ³(Mainz am Rhein 1976) |
| Vollmer 2014 | C. Vollmer, Im Anfang war der Thron. Studien zum leeren Thron in der griechischen, römischen und frühchristlichen Ikonographie (Rahden/Westf. 2014) |
| Wagner 2021 | H. Wagner, Das spätantike Rom und die stadtrömische Senatsaristokratie (395–455 n. Chr.): eine althistorisch-archäologische Untersuchung (Berlin 2021) |
| Wanscher 1980 | O. Wanscher, Sella curulis. The folding stool: an ancient symbol of dignity (Kopenhagen 1980) |
| Wrede 2001 | H. Wrede, Senatorische Sarkophage Roms: der Beitrag des Senatorenstandes zur römischen Kunst der hohen und späten Kaiserzeit (Mainz am Rhein 2001) |

*Lorenzo Cigaina, Universität Regensburg, Institut für Klassische Archäologie, Universitätsstraße 31, 93053 Regensburg, Deutschland.*
*[e] lorenzo.cigaina@ur.de*

Montserrat Claveria

# THE SARCOPHAGUS OF COVARRUBIAS (BURGOS, SPAIN)

## IMAGES OF ETERNITY BETWEEN PAGANISM AND CHRISTIANITY[1]

**Abstract**

The sarcophagus preserved in the Collegiate Church of Covarrubias was used as the tomb of the Countess Sancha of Navarre, who died in 959. Since the 18th century, several authors have dealt with this piece from the point of view of the reuse of ancient sculptures in later historical periods, which has allowed us to discern that it is a sarcophagus used in Hispanic territory as early as antiquity. Scattered publications delayed its chronology from the beginning to the end of the 4th century and doubted its production in the Metropolis. This article analyses its iconography in detail and, with the help of the observation of its technical elaboration, confirms its late chronology and its manufacture in a workshop in Rome. The opulence of their portraits and the neutral, non-Christian message conveyed by the combination of their images reveal that their owners belonged to a pagan provincial elite hostile to the Christian beliefs about the afterlife prevalent at the time.

## THE SARCOPHAGUS AND ITS REUSE AFTER ANTIQUITY

In the collegiate church of San Cosme y Damián in Covarrubias, a small town near Burgos, there is a Roman sarcophagus[2] (fig. 1) that has traditionally been identified with the tomb of Countess Sancha de Navarra, who died in the year 960. It is assumed that this sarcophagus was placed in the neighbouring monastery of San Pedro de Arlanza, together with the tomb of her husband, Count Fernán González, and there both burials were long honored for containing the remains of the mythical founder of the kingdom of Castile and his wife. In 1841, because of the dilapidated state of San Pedro de Arlanza due to the processes of entailment that began in Spain at the end of the 17th century, the two sarcophagi were transferred to the collegiate church of Covarrubias, where they can still be found.

The place where the sarcophagus was found is unknown and there are currently no documentary sources that provide details that prove the aforementioned historical journey, constituting one of the most debated aspects in the historiography of this sarcophagus[3]. However, there is no doubt that this sepulcher was object of the type of reuse typical of the north of the Iberian Peninsula in the Middle Ages, which was the prestigious burials of high nobles and ecclesiastics, as can be deduced from the tradition of historical memory to which this sarcophagus has been subjected, and from the still-preserved remains of this reuse, such as the mediaeval style of the mismatched lid that covers it and the lion-shaped pedestals that enhance it (fig. 2). These data are important in the context of this study because in the Spanish Middle Ages this type of reuse was practiced with Roman sarcophagi found or preserved since ancient times in the territory of the peninsula, unlike

---

[1] Study carried out within the framework of the State Research Agency project HAR2017-84907-P »El sarcófago romano en la Península Ibérica. Art-queología, arqueometría y conservación/restauración«.

[2] It is a 58 cm high, 193 cm long and 94 cm wide sarcophagus chest preserved in the presbytery of the church. We would like to thank Archbishopric of Burgos Heritage Delegate D. J. Álvarez Quevedo for the permission to proceed to the study of this piece and D. J. M. Valderrama Carranza for facilitating our access and the observation of the piece in the Collegiate Church of San Cosme y San Damián in Covarrubias.

[3] Among the extensive literature published on the subject, we highlight the following: García y Bellido 1949, 278–280. 276 pl. 230–231 (with prior literature); Bovini 1954, 29–31 no. 4 fig. 7; Moralejo 1984, 189–191 fig. 3 and specially Moráis Morán 2012, 717–733 which updates this discussion.

1　Sarcophagus of Covarrubias in the presbytery of the Collegiate Church of San Cosme and San Damián, Covarrubias (Burgos, Spain) (photo author)

in modern times when humanist trends encouraged the inflow of sarcophagi from Italy[4]. For these reasons, we can deduce that the Covarrubias sarcophagus must have come from a funerary context in Roman *Hispania*.

## EXPRESSING CONVICTIONS/READING MESSAGES

It is a fine-grained, compact, non-translucent white marble sarcophagus of very good quality, for which permission to take a sample and carry out a petrological analysis has not been obtained. Nonetheless, there is no doubt that it is an imported piece, whose structure, style, and iconography fully coincide with those produced in the workshops of the city of Rome[5]. It shows no relationship with the sarcophagi manufactured in the territory of the Hispanic peninsula, which generally display a rough, inexperienced carving and a simpler iconography[6]. The interest of this metropolitan sarcophagus in this colloquium on provincial Roman art lies in its imagery. Our aim is to reach a complex understanding of its representations, which will provide us with information on the iden-

---

[4]　Moralejo 1984, 188–192; Moráis Morán 2012, 721–726; Bauer 2020, 57–66; Claveria 2022, 185–187.

[5]　See in this respect Koch – Sichtermann 1982, 310, where there is doubt as to its Roman or local origin, although later publications confirm that it was produced in a workshop in Rome: Schroeder 1993, 418; Brandenburg 2002, 32; Claveria 2004, 276–277.

[6]　On the characteristics of this local production see Claveria 1996, 193–212; Vidal 2005, *passim*; Claveria 2020, 151–166; Claveria, in press; Vidal, in press.

2  Front of the Covarrubias sarcophagus with the lion-shaped feet and the cover because of its reuse (photo author)

tity of the deceased and insights into the values, beliefs and desires of a well-settled provincial society amidst a crucial period for the expansion of Christian ideology in a pagan world.

The sarcophagus must be dated to the last quarter of the 4th century, based on the style of its relief and the hairstyles displayed in its portraits[7] and an ostensible stylistic homogeneity in its figures, showing that they all belong to the time of production of the chest and that it has not been subjected to subsequent reworking, all the figures therefore being part of the original conception of its ornamentation, and arranged on the front of the sarcophagus. Its right side was made over in modern times to carve the inscription dedicated to Doña Sancha[8], the slight depression of its surface indicating the absence of reliefs in its original state.

Seen through the eyes of the observer, the front is organized into three image fields, dominated by a large, strigillated panel with the portraits of the deceased arranged in the centre. This central section is flanked by two panels with pastoral images that occupy the space at either end of the front. The dominant visual focus is the busts of the deceased highlighted by the central *clipeus* which, faithful to the predominant formula from the 3rd century onwards, reproduced a double circular listel that frames the couple[9] (fig. 3). In the tradition of a widespread practice regarding clipped images alluding to marital *concordia*[10], the man is on the right of the observer and the woman on the left, placed slightly behind him with her body shortened, gently clasping her husband's arm and looking at him tenderly.

This composition was so widespread in pagan sarcophagi with *clipeus* that the busts were often already prepared on the products that were kept in stock in the workshop waiting to be

---

[7] García y Bellido 1949, 231 and Schroeder 1993, 418 dated it to the beginning of the 4th c., but later stylistic and technical considerations indicate a later chronology: see Brandenburg 2002, 32; Beltrán – Cortés 2007, 477. About the portraits of this time see too Studer-Karlen 2012, 219–222.
[8] García y Bellido 1949, 278–279; Moráis Morán 2012, 720.
[9] Huskinson 2015, 118.
[10] Birk 2013, 125. 143. 153; Huskinson 2015, 118–119. 137.

3   Detail of the *clipeata* couple in the centre of the front of the Covarrubias sarcophagus (photo author)

4   Detail of the images in the centre of the front of the Covarrubias sarcophagus (photo author)

personalized according to the taste of the client post-purchase[11]. In this case, however, there is a clear uniformity between the portraits and the rest of the motifs in the relief, both stylistically and technically, which has been noted as evidence that the portraits were made at the same time as the rest of the figures and as a procedure characteristic of Roman sarcophagi produced from the last decades of the 4th century onwards, which is a further indication of the late chronology of this box[12]. As was customary, the heads were individualized with vague portrait features[13] and the bodies with identifying attire. The husband is wearing the *contabulata* toga, an item of clothing particularly used for sarcophagi from the end of Severus' rule as a sign of the wearer's participation in public life. This sign of prestige is underlined by the *volumen* clasped in his hands[14]. His wife is distinguished by the rich jewelry adorning her neckline, a symbol of family wealth and high status, especially on 4th-century sarcophagi[15]. Her respectable dress and tender demeanor complement her husband's public role, harking to his good qualities in the private realm[16].

In summary, the reasons for depicting the couple in the ways described above respond to a codified language conveying the patrimonial well-being, wealth and dignity of the family. Their attire and hairstyles are very much in keeping with the fashions of the time, indicative of the elitist and informed nature of those who used or commissioned the sarcophagus.

The strigillated panel that circumscribes the couple in the *clipeus* does not have a merely decorative function (fig. 2). In her monograph on strigillated sarcophagi, Janet Huskinson indicated that these panels helped to enhance the relationship between the portraits and the other depictions on the sarcophagus in which the deceased were placed, creating a wide diversity of physically and symbolically significant frames[17]. As an architectural framework, it harks to the ›Tomb‹ that

---

[11]  Huskinson 2015, 51. 53–56. 118; Liverani et al. 2010, 34–35.
[12]  Van Dael 1999, 402.
[13]  Concerning the schematization of portraits on late Roman sarcophagi see Studer-Karlen 2012, 13–18.
[14]  Brandenburg 2002, 32; Cadario 2011, 212–213. 215; Huskinson 2015, 118–120. 125.
[15]  Cf. Brandenburg 2002, 32; Olson 2008, 97; Studer-Karlen 2012, 14; Birk 2013, 141–142. 153; Huskinson 2015, 41–43.
[16]  Regarding the depiction of the traditional concept of marriage on sarcophagi with portraits of spouses in *clipeus* see Birk 2013, 153–155. 156; Huskinson 2015, 137.
[17]  Huskinson 2015, 117.

contains the body or bodies of the deceased, to the space of the Manes[18]. However, at the same time, the visual, undulating, repetitive neutrality of its grooves favors the singularization of the rest of the image fields on the front, while simultaneously promoting different relationships between them in the observer's mind.

Among these satellite images with respect to the protagonists in the centre is the figure depicted under the *clipeus*[19] (fig. 4), who is kneeling on his right leg and holding the ends of a billowing cloak. This iconography corresponds to the representative scheme of the kneeling Ouranos-Caelus, of which only a few images have been documented, including a bronze statuette in the Kunsthistorisches Museum, Vienna[20]. Another more widespread type only reproduces the bust of this allegorical character, appearing as a privileged and passive spectator in various mythological sarcophagi from the 2nd and 3rd centuries[21]. However, this motif cannot be found documented among the set of images that tended to be chosen to occupy the lower central space under the *clipeus* on the fronts of pagan sarcophagi, such as theatrical masks and cornucopiae full of fruit[22]. The reason for this choice is that this image, while rare, was more suitable to express the beliefs and desires of the couple depicted there regarding the afterlife.

The primordial god Ouranos was relegated to the role of the personification of heaven in the Greco-Roman iconographic tradition. Stripped of myth, this character symbolizes the firmament on Prima Porta Augustus's breastplate[23], and his positioning under the gods in the mythical and divine funerary scenes of the 2nd and 3rd centuries AD has been interpreted as an image of heaven that represents the residence of the gods or the deified emperors[24]. In the Dodekatheoi on the north side of the Arch of Galerius in Thessalonica (AD 297), Caelus assimilated to Kosmos is depicted alongside Aeternitas, under the imperial thrones, both acting as allegories of the universality and eternity of the Empire[25]. To this effect, it is reasonable to think that the image of Ouranos-Caelus was placed under the *clipeus* of this sarcophagus as an allusion to the couple's afterlife in the kingdom of Caelus.

The messages communicated through the reliefs that make up this central field of images are enriched by the bucolic scenes on the panels located at both ends of the front of the sarcophagus (fig. 5). They relate to the beliefs of whoever commissioned the sarcophagus about the nature of the aforementioned kingdom of Caelus, or in other words of the desired superterrestrial setting. These idyllic images, which became hugely popular on the fronts of the sarcophagi with continuous friezes during the last third of the 3rd century[26], evoke a paradisiacal natural environment where peace, prosperity and spiritual contemplation reign[27]. Based on the iconographic canons created for the rural scenes depicted on the sides of the mythological sarcophagi of Endymion[28] and founded on the discourses of wealth and abundance sung by Virgil, bucolic panels prolifer-

---

[18] Platt 2017, 363–377; Claveria 2019, 438 no. 26–27.
[19] Regarding the format and rank of the figures that occupy this place in strigillated sarcophagi see Huskinson 2015, 99–100.
[20] Tran Tam Tinh 1994, 134 type D no. 15.
[21] Tran Tam Tinh 1994, 133 type C no. 7–10. 136; Koch-Sichtermann 1982, pls. 197 (Paris Trial). 213 (Phaeton) or 216 (Prometheus).
[22] Among these images, we find another representation similar to the kneeling Caelus, but with an obviously supporting function, and so different from the one expressed on this frontal. We are referring to the figure of Atlas, king and bearer of the heavens, who already supported the inscription with the deceased's data on some 2nd c. urns, and also on contemporary sarcophagi, and who from the 3rd c. held a *clipeus* as a presumed incarnation of the king of the west, resting place of the deceased according to some pagan funerary beliefs (see Arce – Balmaseda 1986, 15 pl. 48–49).
[23] Tram Tam Tinh 1994, 133 no. 4.
[24] Tram Tam Tinh 1994, 136.
[25] Tram Tam Tinh 1994, 135–136 no. 6.
[26] Himmelmann 1980, 28; Koch-Sichtermann 1982, 118–119; Brandenburg 2002, 32–33.
[27] Studer-Karlen, 2012, 75; Huskinson 2015, 96–97.
[28] Schumacher 1977, 27–28; Himmelmann 1980, 125.

5    Detail of the panels at the ends of the front of the Covarrubias sarcophagus (photo author)

ated on early 4th-century strigillated sarcophagi, where they were stripped of all mythological meaning[29]. They expressed not only the enjoyment of a *vita felix* in the afterlife, but also a way of life on earth based on the cultural exercise of the spirit[30], in a peaceful environment that strengthens the harmony of marriage and lasting love, concepts also intelligible on the portraits featured on this sarcophagus.

These images, which still focus on the privileged lifestyle of the tomb's owner and his hope for a peaceful and happy afterlife, devoid of clear references to the eternal paradise of Christian beliefs, contrast with the iconography of two other coeval sarcophagi which also include the image of Caelus: In the sarcophagus of Iunius Bassus, deceased in the year AD 359[31], and in a Theodosian sarcophagus in Saint Peter's at the Vatican[32], the image of Ouranos-Caelus is placed under the feet of the triumphant Christ, symbolizing in both Christ's absolute dominion over the cosmos[33]. The portraits of the deceased have disappeared, and all the image fields of both sarcophagi depict scenes from the life of Christ. Both examples are evidence that in those »times of transition and changes«, the spread of Christian ideology in society meant the overcoming of the images and notions blended in representations like those on the Covarrubias sarcophagus.

## FINAL CONSIDERATIONS: THE COVARRUBIAS SARCOPHAGUS IN ITS GEOGRAPHICAL AND TEMPORAL COORDINATES

The Covarrubias sarcophagus was imported in the first quarter of the 4th century after being commissioned from a workshop in the city of Rome to serve as a tomb in an unknown place, but most likely in the north central-western area of the Iberian Peninsula (fig. 6).

---

[29]    Huskinson 2015, 196–198; Studer-Karlen 2012, 74–76.
[30]    Klauser 1960, 125–129; Provoost 1978, 407–408; Cambi 1994, 40; Koch 2000, 17. 22.
[31]    Rep I 279–283 no. 680 pl. 104; Koch 2000, 284 pl. 64 fig. 43.
[32]    Rep I 274–277 no. 677 pl. 106; Koch 2000, 303 pl. 65.
[33]    Tram Tam Tinh 1994, 134 nos. 11–12. 136.

6  Map of the Iberian Peninsula showing the area in which the Covarrubias sarcophagus may have been used in antiquity (photo author)

The lack of archaeological context prevents us from knowing how many deceased it accommodated; however, its depth of 94 cm, some 30 cm more than an average sarcophagus, speaks of the intention of its use for the burial of more than one individual. The lack of an inscription deprives us of information about the person who commissioned it, be it the husband, his wife or a relative or acquaintance very close to the family.

As we have seen, the depictions of this sarcophagus are manifestly rooted in pagan iconographic models and conceptions, for example, the iconography of Caelus and the pastoral scenes, and the centrality and honorific meaning of his portraits[34]. However, the nature of the chosen images and how they are placed on the strigillated structure of the front side reveal cultural and social issues that hark to the changing and plural ideology of the last decades of the 3rd century and the first decades of the 4th century: This ideology translated into a symbolic language that imposed itself on mythological imagery, relegating it in favor of allegorical representations, which the

---

[34] Fejfer 2008, 128–129; Claveria 2019, 437–439.

patrons of the period combined, complemented and syncretized according to the beliefs and messages they wished to convey[35]. To this effect, the strigillated sarcophagi provided the ideal compositional framework to depict these concepts on the tombs of these clients, which is why this type of sarcophagus became so popular[36]. For the most part, these allegories appeal to the cultivation of personal spirituality, philanthropic cooperation and unearthly reward in a paradise of abundance and happiness. These ideas fueled the spread of Christianity among urban elites and Christian themes began to be combined with these symbols, eventually coming to dominate depictions on sarcophagi a quarter of a century later. However, the Covarrubias sarcophagus dates from the last third of the 4th century, when Christian iconography prevailed in the art of sarcophagi.

Through the preserved sarcophagi, we can observe in *Hispania* an active spread of Christianity already in pre- and proto-Constantinian period, especially in the eastern area of the peninsula, which was commercially very dynamic due to the flow of the Mediterranean. Just over a hundred decorated sarcophagi have survived from the 4th century, more than 90 of which show Christian scenes. Another 15 pieces contain more generic symbolic representations, mostly belonging to the first quarter of this century, and the latest example being the Covarrubias box, which dates to the end of this century. Although its cover has not been preserved and, therefore, we do not know what motifs were chosen to complete the decoration of the sepulcher, the iconography of its front, more related to the neutral language of sarcophagi from the end of the 3rd and first decades of the 4th century than to the more widespread Christian themes at the time, corroborates the assumption of Hugo Brandenburg[37], according to whom this type of representation on sarcophagi from the second half of the 4th century reveals that their patrons, including the owners of the Covarrubias example, belonged to a pagan upper class anchored in a ›nostalgic traditionalism‹ far removed from the most widespread beliefs of the time[38].

## BIBLIOGRAPHY

| | |
|---|---|
| Arce – Balmaseda 1986 | LIMC III 1–2 (1986) 12–16 s. v. Atlas (Late Hellenistic and Roman) (J. Arce – L. J. Balmaseda) |
| Bauer 2020 | D. Bauer, Sarcophagi and the Emergence of Romanesque Sculpture in Northern Spain, Ikon 13, 2020, 57–66 |
| Beltrán – Cortés 2007 | M. C. Beltrán Martínez – V. Cortés Alonso, Cronología de los sarcófagos de los leones y de Covarrubias a base del tocado femenino, in: J. M. Abascal Palazón – J. M. Noguera Celdrán – F. J. Navarro (eds.), Crónica del IV Congreso Arqueológico del Sudeste Español, Murcia (Murcia 2007) 469–478 |
| Birk 2013 | S. Birk, Depicting the dead (Aarhus 2013) |
| Bovini 1954 | G. Bovini, I sarcofagi paleocristiani della Spagna. Collezione Amici delle Catacombe 22 (Vatican City 1954) |
| Brandenburg 2002 | H. Brandenburg, Das Ende der antiken Sarkophagkunst in Rom. Pagane und christliche Sarkophage im 4. Jahrhundert, in: G. Koch (ed.), Akten des Symposiums »Frühchristliche Sarkophage« Marburg 30.06.–04.07.1999 (Marburg 2002) 19–39 |

---

[35] See as example the sarcophagus from the end of the 3rd c. of Baebia Hertofile Rep I 325–326 no. 778 pl. 124; Koch 2000, pl. 19.

[36] Cf. Meinecke 2020, 673.

[37] Brandenburg 2002, 32–38; Brandenburg 2004, 12–13.

[38] Other similar examples are the well-known vintage sarcophagus from the Vigna Buonfigliuoli near the Cimitero di Pretestato (Rep I 26–28 no. 29 pl. 10; Brandenburg 2002, 32–33), another from the Catacomba di Pretestato 353 CE (Rep I 72 no. 87 pl. 26) or two others from the Cimitero di San Sebastiano (Rep I 138 no. 238 pl. 53 and Rep I 138–139 no. 239 pl. 53). In the 2nd half of the 4th c., several Roman sarcophagi display honorific portraits of the deceased in *clipeus* or shells placed in the centre of the frontal, such as an example preserved in the Musée de l'Arles Antique 325 CE (Studes-Karlen 2012, 15 fig. 3) or the well-known Lot's sarcophagus (Rep I 116–119 pl. 45; Koch 2002, pl. 63), but most combine these portraits with Old and New Testament scenes or theological images, which is why Brandenburg 2002 and 2004 noted that these late sarcophagi with neutral scenes catered to an affluent clientele with tastes and beliefs of the past.

| | |
|---|---|
| Brandenburg 2004 | H. Brandenburg, Osservazioni sulla fine della produzione e dell'uso dei sarcofagi a rilievi nella tarda antichità nonché sulla loro decorazione, in F. Bisconti – H. Brandenburg (eds.), Sarcofagi tardoantichi, paleocristiani e altomedievali. Atti della giornata tematica dei Seminari di Archeologia Cristiana Roma 08.05.2002 (Vatican City 2004) 1–34 |
| Cadario 2011 | M. Cadario, Il linguaggio dei corpi nel ritratto romano, in: E. La Rocca – C. Parisi Presicce – A. Lo Monaco (eds.), Ritratti. Le tante facce del potere (Rome 2011) 209–221 |
| Cambi 1994 | N. Cambi, The Good Shepherd Sarcophagus and its group (Split 1994) |
| Claveria 1996 | M. Claveria, Nuevos datos en torno a la producción de sarcófagos en Tarraco, in: J. Massó – P. Sada (eds.), Actas de la II Reunión sobre Escultura Romana en Hispania Tarragona 30.–31.03.1995 (Tarragona 1996) 193–212 |
| Claveria 2004 | M. Claveria, El sarcófago romano en la Tarraconense, in: T. Nogales Basarrate – L. G. Gonçalves (eds.), Actas de la II Reunión sobre Escultura Romana en Hispania Lisboa 07.–09.02.2002 (Madrid 2004) 273–306 |
| Claveria 2019 | M. Claveria, La representación del/la difunto/a en los sarcófagos de la provincia tarraconense de los siglos III al V, in: J. López Vilar (ed.), Tarraco Biennal 4t Congrés Internacional d'Arqueologia i Món Antic – VII Reunió d'Arqueologia Cristiana Hispànica Tarragona 21.–24.11.2018 (Tarragona 2019) 435–443 |
| Claveria 2020 | M. Claveria, El sarcófago romano en Hispania. Estado de la investigación y nuevos fragmentos, in: J. M. Noguera Celdrán – L. Ruiz Molina (eds.), Escultura Romana en Hispania IX (Yecla 2020) 151–166 |
| Claveria 2022 | M. Claveria, El sarcófago romano en la cultura artística del Renacimiento español, in: B. Cacciotti (ed.), Roma e la Spagna in dialogo. Interpretare, disegnare, collezionare l'antichità classica nel Rinascimento (Madrid 2022) 185–195 |
| Claveria, in press | M. Claveria, Roman sarcophagi in the Iberian Peninsula. Methodology and results, in: M. Claveria – M. Trunk (eds.), Conditoria Provinciarum. El sarcófago romano en las provincias, in press |
| Fejfer 2008 | J. Fejfer, Roman portraits in context (Berlin 2008) |
| García y Bellido 1949 | A. García y Bellido, Esculturas romanas de España y Portugal (Madrid 1949) |
| Himmelmann 1980 | N. Himmelmann, Über Hirten-Genre in der antiken Kunst (Opladen 1980) |
| Huskinson 2015 | J. Huskinson, Roman strigillated sarcophagi (Oxford 2015) |
| Klauser 1960 | T. Klauser, Studien zur Entstehungsgeschichte der christlichen Kunst III, JbAChr 3, 1960, 112–133 |
| Koch 2000 | G. Koch, Frühchristliche Sarkophage, HdArch (Munich 2000) |
| Koch – Sichtermann 1982 | G. Koch – H. Sichtermann, Römische Sarkophage, HdArch (Munich 1982) |
| Liverani et al. 2010 | P. Liverani – G. Spinola – P. Zander, The Vatican Necropoles: Rome's City of the Dead (Turnhout 2010) |
| Meinecke 2020 | K. Meinecke, What can be done with the ubiquitous strigillated sarcophagi (review J. Huskinson), JRA 33, 2020, 668–670 |
| Moráis Morán 2012 | J. A. Moráis Morán, La »construcción« del pasado a través de la memoria de los muertos: Los sarcófagos de Fernán González y doña Sancha, in: Actas del CEHA XVII Congreso Nacional de Historia del Arte, Barcelona 22.–26.09.2008 (Barcelona 2012) 717–733 |
| Moralejo 1984 | S. Moralejo, La reutilización e influencia de los sarcófagos antiguos en la España medieval, in: B. Andreae – S. Settis (eds.), Colloquio sul reimpiego dei sarcofagi romani nel medioevo, Pisa 05.–12.09.1982, Marburger Winckelmannprogram 1983 (Marburg 1984) 187–203 |
| Olson 2008 | K. Olson, Dress and the Roman Woman. Self-Presentation and Society (Milton Park 2008) |
| Platt 2017 | V. Platt, Framing the Dead on Roman Sarcophagi, in: J. Elsner – J. Huskinson – M. Squire (eds.), The frame in Greek and Roman art. A cultural history (Cambridge 2017) 353–381 |
| Provoost 1978 | A. Provoost, Il significato delle scene pastorali del terzo secolo d.C., in: U. M Fasola (ed.), Atti del IX Congresso Internazionale di archeologia cristiana, Roma 21.–27.09.1975 (Vatican City 1978) 407–408 |

| | |
|---|---|
| Rep I | F. W. Deichmann, Repertorium der christlich-antiken Sarkophage. Rom und Ostia I (Wiesbaden 1967) |
| Schroeder 1993 | S. F. Schroeder, Tafeln 222a. 223, in: W. Trillmich – T. Hauschild – M. Blech – H. G. Niemeyer – A. Nünnerich-Asmus – U. Kreilinger (eds.), Hispania Antiqua. Denkmäler der Römerzeit (Mainz on the Rhein 1993) 418 |
| Schumacher 1977 | W. N. Schumacher, Hirt und »Guter Hirt«. Studien zum Hirtenbild in der Römischen Kunst von 2. bis zum Anfang des 4. Jhs. unter besonderer Berücksichtigung der Mosaiken in der Südhalle von Aquileja, RömQSchr Suppl. 34 (Freiburg 1977) |
| Studer-Karlen 2012 | M. Studer-Karlen, Verstorbenendarstellungen auf frühchristlichen Sarkophagen (Turnhout 2012) |
| Tram Tam Tinh 1994 | LIMC VII 1–2 (1994) 132–136 s. v. Ouranus-Caelus (V. Tram Tam Tinh) |
| Van Dael 1999 | P. Van Dael – M. Immerzeel, Der sarcofaagindustrie rond 400. Het estelijke Middellandse-Zeegebied (doctoral thesis), Leiden, 1996: one or more sarcophagi workhops in the fourth and fifth centuries? (review), AntTard 7, 1999, 401–403 |
| Vidal 2005 | S. Vidal, La escultura hispànica figurada de la Antigüedad Tardía (siglos IV–VII) (Murcia 2005) |
| Vidal, in press | S. Vidal, Early Christian sarcophagi from Hispania: current status and future perspectives, in: M. Claveria – M. Trunk (eds.), Conditoria Provinciarum. El sarcófago romano en las provincias, in press |

*Montserrat Claveria, Universitat Autònoma de Barcelona – Institut Català d'Arqueologia Clàssica, Departament d'Art i de Musicologia, Edifici B – Campus UAB, 08193 Bellaterra (Cerdanyola del Vallès) Barcelona, Spain.*
*[e] montserrat.claveria@uab.cat*

Maria-Pia Darblade-Audoin

# LES HERMÈS DE WELSCHBILLIG

## STYLE ET TECHNIQUE AU IV[E] SIÈCLE DANS LE NORD DES GAULES

**Abstract**
The herms of Welschbillig remain one of the most important assemblages of portraits from Late Antiquity. Between 337 and 395, Trier had maintained its status of principal imperial residence in the West. The sumptuous villa of Welschbillig was built in the Valentinian period, within the boundary lines of the »Langmauerbezirk«, and therefore can be considered as belonging to the imperial estate. It was probably abandoned at the time of the successive transfers of the imperial court from Trier to northern Italy. The collection of herms had a short-lived use, while in Gaul and Spain, the vast majority of the statues found in late antique villas were heirloom pieces. They are characterized by a great homogeneity of technique, carved in limestone from Lorraine (Gaul) in about 375. Among the 70 herms there are divinities, Satyrs, *putti*, Hellenistic sovereigns, Roman emperors, Greek authors and philosophers. The progress made in Roman sculpture studies allows us to re-examine these pieces of sculpture. The preliminary investigation of style and technique will focus on 63 herms.

L'ouverture, cette année, du Colloque International d'Art Provincial Romain[1] vers la période de l'Antiquité tardive nous donne l'opportunité d'aborder la sculpture de cette période avec beaucoup de curiosité. La sculpture de l'Antiquité tardive a été souvent considérée comme une forme malhabile et déformée du grand art romain impérial. O combien de vieux catalogues et anciens ouvrages sur les sculptures romaines ont classé bien souvent des documents inachevés ou d'une qualité esthétique médiocre comme datant de l'Antiquité tardive. Il n'est pas question ici de tenter d'établir la sculpture de cette période en tant qu'ouvrage de bon goût, entreprise qui serait hors de sujet, mais de regarder plus précisément la technique utilisée par les sculpteurs dans le dernier tiers du IVe siècle, à travers ce groupe homogène formé par les hermès de la villa de Welschbillig. Cette collection constitue encore aujourd'hui l'un des plus grands regroupements de portraits de l'Antiquité tardive. Aux représentations d'auteurs grecs et de philosophes s'ajoutent celles de divinités, putti, souverains grecs et romains. L'ouvrage de Henning Wrede publié en 1972[2] demeure toujours le travail de base sur cet ensemble, aussi aborderons-nous ce sujet avec une grande modestie. Toutefois, les travaux effectués dans l'étude de la sculpture romaine depuis cinquante ans et les nouvelles découvertes autorisent à questionner à nouveau ces documents sculptés. Le projet collectif »Last Statues of Antiquity« dirigé par Roland R. R. Smith et Brian Ward-Perkins, qui rassemble dans une même base de données[3] les statues de l'Antiquité tardive[4], est maintenant un outil fondamental. Aussi avant d'entreprendre toute étude iconographique, il nous a semblé nécessaire de regarder de plus près l'aspect technique de ce groupe d'œuvres si particulier.

---

[1] Dont je remercie très sincèrement tous les organisateurs. Mes remerciements vont également au Landesmuseum de Trèves, S. Faust et K. Deppmayer.
[2] Wrede 1972.
[3] LSA, University of Oxford: <http://laststatues.classics.ox.ac.uk/> (05.04.2023).
[4] Sont recensés dans cette base les hermès de Welschbillig suivants: Socrates (inv. 19131) = LSA 2638; Vespasien (inv. G 16d) = LSA 2637; Ménandre (inv. 19123) = LSA 2640; Polydeuces (inv. 18876) = LSA 2639; »Germain« (inv. 18865) = LSA 1075.

## UN PROJET ICONOGRAPHIQUE CONSTRUIT

La vaste et somptueuse villa de Welschbillig, célèbre pour son jardin orné d'un bassin[5] entouré de mosaïques, son nymphée et sa vaste salle cruciforme avec ses pièces de réception a été bâtie *ex nihilo* à la période valentinienne[6], à moins d'une vingtaine de kilomètres au nord de Trèves, à l'intérieur de l'espace délimité par les »longs murs«, le »Langmauerbezirk«. Depuis le début du IVe siècle, Trèves était devenu le cœur politique et intellectuel de la partie occidentale de l'empire. Trèves était à la fois capitale de la préfecture du prétoire des Gaules, du diocèse des Gaules et de la province de Belgique I, et une résidence impériale. Au IVe siècle, et en particulier dans sa deuxième moitié, la présence impériale a été attestée à maintes reprises d'après les sources littéraires et juridiques[7]. La présence d'une élite proche des instances impériales, d'aristocrates et de sénateurs a favorisé l'installation ou la réfection de nombreuses villas dans l'arrière-pays trévire[8]. Evoquées par le poète Ausone, qui séjourna à Trèves entre 369 et 383[9], les villas du pays trévire offrent toutefois une réalité archéologique plus complexe et plus variée, leur taille étant plus modeste que dans d'autres régions de Gaule (comme l'Aquitaine, par exemple). Cependant, la villa de Welschbillig appartient au petit groupe de villas proches de Trèves (avec Konz, Newel, Oberweis et Echternach) dont la *pars urbana* est supérieure à 2000 m$^2$ [10]. Ces villas construites à neuf ou réaménagées vers le milieu du IVe siècle seraient le reflet d'une période de stabilité économique et politique sous et à partir de l'empereur Julien[11]. Mais Welschbillig figure aussi parmi les rares villas qui étaient occupées jusqu'à la fin de l'époque valentinienne, en conservant leur caractère résidentiel (comme Konz, Echternach, Wasserbillig), tandis que le départ de la cour impériale vers l'Italie dans les années 380 amorce un déclin des domaines ruraux[12].

Il est admis aujourd'hui de manière plutôt assurée que Welschbillig a appartenu au domaine impérial. La période de sa construction à l'époque de Valentinien et sa présence dans l'espace du »Langmauerbezirk« en sont les indices essentiels[13]. Le mur de clôture de 72 km de long enserre un espace de 220 km$^2$ entre Trèves et Bitburg à partir de la villa de Welschbillig[14]. Les interprétations de cette construction comme limites d'un domaine de chasse ou d'élevage de chevaux[15] sont abandonnées au profit de l'interprétation supposant l'existence d'un vaste domaine impérial, gérant plusieurs dizaines d'établissements ruraux. Cette hypothèse avait déjà été émise par Wrede[16]. La participation de *primani*, soldats appartenant aux *comitatenses* (ou aux *pseudocomitatenses*)[17], à la construction du mur ainsi que la présence de nombreuses pièces d'équipement militaire mises au jour dans les établissements ruraux et sanctuaires situés sur ce domaine permettent de supposer que le propriétaire n'était autre que l'empereur lui-même[18]. L'installation des ateliers de céramique de Speicher-Herforst sur le domaine vient conforter l'hypothèse[19].

---

[5] Wrede 1972, 16: bassin: 58,30 × 17,80 m.
[6] Wrede 1972, 28 (2[ième] moitié du IVe s.) et 29 fig. 7: restitution de la villa; Van Ossel 1992, n. 71; Balmelle – Van Ossel 2001, 536–557.
[7] Années: 314–316, 325, 327, 331, 337, 339, 345, 352 (?), 356, 364–381, 385, 389–390. D'après M. Kasprzyk in: Fort et al. 2021b, 100 tableau fig. 15.
[8] Roux 2021, 215.
[9] Auson. Mos. 283–338.
[10] Van Ossel 1992.
[11] Balmelle – Van Ossel 2001, 536–537.
[12] Roux 2021, 217.
[13] Gilles 1984, 288–290; Gilles 1985, 15.
[14] Wrede 1972, 7 plan fig. 1.
[15] Heinen 1985, 290.
[16] Wrede 1972, 28; à la suite de Koethe 1935.
[17] CIL XIII 4139 = AE 2009, 913; CIL XIII 4140 = AE 2009, 913.
[18] Gilles 1999; Van Ossel 2021, 202–203 fig. 4.
[19] Bienert 2012.

1 Pilier, inv. 18871 (RLM Trier, photo Th. Zühmer)

Les hermès de Welschbillig ont été sculptés dans une pierre calcaire à grains fins: la pierre de Norroy[20]. Cette pierre de Norroy est extraite dès l'Antiquité des carrières de Norroy-lès-Pont à Mousson, en Meurthe-et-Moselle (France). Les Romains l'exportaient vers Metz, Strasbourg, Nimègue ou Mayence par exemple. Quelques inscriptions dédiées à Hercule Saxanus, l'Hercule des carrières, y ont été laissées par des centurions chargés de travailler la pierre ou de superviser le travail au Ier siècle apr. J.-C[21].

Somme toute, les cent hermès de Welschbillig eurent une durée de vie assez courte, compte tenu de la date de construction de la villa et de son abandon. Seulement soixante-dix ont été mis au jour dans les fouilles. Ici, les documents sculptés sont contemporains de l'édifice, ce qui sous-entend l'intervention rapide d'un atelier. Cette constatation contraste avec les normes relevées dans le reste de l'empire où sur l'ensemble des statues découvertes dans les villas de l'Antiquité tardive, les pièces héritées ou acquises d'époques antérieures, par exemple en Gaule et en Espagne, sont plus nombreuses que les statues et portraits contemporains[22]. Le ralentissement de l'activité des sculpteurs pendant l'Antiquité tardive est un fait acquis, mais nous sommes toujours soumis aux contingences de l'archéologie et, comme le fait justement remarquer Christian Witschel, le petit nombre des portraits ou bases de statues mis au jour à Trèves n'est sûrement pas représentatif de ce que fut la parure de la capitale impériale en cette période tardive[23]. Aussi, bien que situé dans un registre bien particulier, le témoignage des sculptures de Welschbillig n'en est-il que plus précieux dans le nord des Gaules.

Les 100 piliers formant cet ensemble entouraient un lac ornemental de 60 m de long. Pilier et hermès sont sculptés dans un même bloc[24]. La hauteur totale est importante: 120 cm. Les piliers étaient raccordés entre eux par une balustrade[25] (fig. 1).

Les premières galeries de portraits de philosophes ou poètes anciens apparaissent vers les années 50 av. J.-C.[26]. Les collections réunies autour d'un point d'eau évoquent la galerie d'hermès du bassin de la »Villa dei Papiri« à *Herculaneum*, par exemple[27]. Mais la présence d'une balustrade reliant ces hermès est plus rare, les exemples se situant pour une grande majorité d'entre eux dans la période du Bas-Empire. On citera l'exemple précoce des hermès doubles du »Hanghaus 1« d'Ephèse, également installés près d'un bassin et reliés par une balustrade de

---

[20] Ce résultat est issu de l'étude pétrographique réalisée récemment (sans échantillon) par Roland Dreesen et Eric Goemaere (Institut Royal des Sciences Naturelles de Belgique) dans le cadre d'un projet de l'Académie autrichienne des Sciences de Vienne.
[21] CIL XIII 4623. 4624. 4625.
[22] Stirling 2007, 308.
[23] Witschel 2005; Witschel 2016, 75: Trèves: statues et bases: LSA 584. 1076. 2402. 2407. 2610.
[24] Wrede 1972, fig. 11: schéma de la taille des piliers.
[25] Wrede 1972, 37 fig. 12: plan de la balustrade et emplacement des piliers.
[26] Lorenz 1965; Wrede 1985, 78; Neudecker 1988, 65–66.
[27] Neudecker 1988, 105–114.

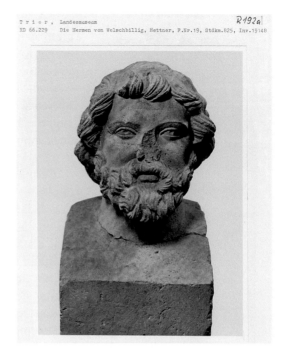

2  Antonin le Pieux (?), inv. 19147 (RLM Trier, photo Th. Zühmer)

3  Marc-Aurèle (?), inv. 19148 (RLM Trier, photo Th. Zühmer)

80 cm de hauteur et datés de l'époque antonine ou sévérienne[28]. Les 17 hermès mis au jour dans l'orchestra du théâtre de Pergé ont vraisemblablement été installés avec leur balustrade lors de la construction d'un bassin à l'époque de l'empereur Tacite, vers 275–276 apr. J.-C[29]. Une balustrade d'hermès doubles entourait la loge d'honneur de l'amphithéâtre de Salone vers 305–313 apr. J.-C.[30]. Le Nymphée de Trajan à Ephèse fut également enrichi d'une balustrade d'hermès simples représentant des planètes (Saturne, Sol, Luna, Mars, Mercure, Jupiter, Vénus) et reliés par une balustrade[31]. L'ensemble est daté vers 300–315 apr. J.-C.[32] ou de la deuxième moitié du IV$^e$ siècle[33]. Un autre exemple de balustrade ›cosmique‹ avait été érigé au Serapeum de Carthage. Il subsiste trois piliers, conservés au Louvre, portant les hermès simples de Sol, Mercure et Mars, datés du III$^e$ ou du IV$^e$ siècle[34].

## HERMÈS SIMPLES ET DUPLICATION DES MODÈLES

La promenade organisée autour du bassin permettait de flâner, dans un esprit inspiré du Gymnase, parmi les hermès simples de personnages célèbres dans le registre philosophique et littéraire aussi bien que de divinités ou de bons empereurs et souverains. La confortable et conséquente hauteur des piliers ainsi que leur orientation donnaient le loisir au promeneur d'admirer et d'apprécier chaque détail d'un visage dans un grand confort visuel. Toutefois, une particularité remarquable de cette collection est la duplication de certains modèles. Plusieurs exemples de ›doubles‹ sont attestés. Il ne s'agit pas bien évidemment de copies parfaites, mais de portraits d'une très grande ressemblance due à des éléments communs, comme on peut le voir sur certains portraits d'hermès concrètement doubles (portraits adossés). On donnera simplement l'exemple d'un hermès double d'Ephèse représentant un jeune homme, daté de la fin du IV$^e$ siècle apr. J.-C.[35]. Un des

---

[28] Hanslmayer 2016, 127 pls. 56–60; 74 a (restitution L. Bier).
[29] Hanslmayer 2016, 143–145.
[30] Hanslmayer 2016, 145.
[31] Hanslmayer 2016, 128–134 pls. 61–67; 74 b (restitution U. Quatember).
[32] Hanslmayer 2016, 134.
[33] Wrede 1972, 125, datation reprise par E. Rathmayr in: Auinger – Rathmayr 2007, 251.
[34] Laporte – Bricault 2020, 80–82 no. S27–29 figs. 95 a–b; 97 a–b; 98 a–b.
[35] Hanslmayr 2016, 155 no. A. 26 pl. 30.

exemples les plus remarquables à Welschbillig est le portrait attribué par Wrede à Antonin le Pieux (inv. 19147; fig. 2)³⁶ et son ›double‹ (inv. 19148), qu'il attribue à Marc-Aurèle (fig. 3)³⁷. Leur présence peut être comprise comme celle de véritables icônes politiques et intellectuelles du passé. Mais l'identification est sujet à discussion. On peut compléter cette liste avec deux jeunes femmes ou adolescents (inv. 19138. 19139), deux jeunes hommes (inv. 19145. 19146), Polydeuces (inv. 18876. 18877), Ménandre (inv. 19123. 19124), les putti (inv. G 16c. G 16g), Vespasien (inv. G 16d. G 16c bis), Philippe de Macédoine (?) (inv. 19129. 19130) et d'autres exemples (19150. 19152. 19125. 19126. 19133. 19132. 19137. 19144).

## L'ASPECT GÉNÉRAL

L'atelier de sculpteurs qui a élaboré le groupe sculpté de Welschbillig a proposé une grande

4   Faune, inv. 18873 (RLM Trier, photo Th. Zühmer)

variété de personnages, essentiellement masculins. Même si l'on a pu constater la présence de ›doubles‹, les personnages offrent une grande diversité iconographique. Toutefois, on peut relever des caractères communs à la conception de tous ces hermès. La régularité et la forme des piliers va avoir une incidence sur l'aspect général des bustes. Cet aspect est indéniablement celui de sculptures massives. La profondeur des bustes est ajustée à celle des piliers. De profil, l'épaisseur des cous se prolonge pour aller parfois chez certains sujets presque jusqu'à l'aplomb de l'arrière du pilier. Le résultat donne une physionomie alourdie aux silhouettes. On remarque un aspect massif semblable sur les hermès du Serapeum de Carthage cités plus haut.

Indépendamment de la diversité des représentations, les visages sont rendus de face et rarement tournés (sauf inv. 18868. 18870. 19125. 19127. 19133. 19138. 19139. G 13). La forme des visages est rectangulaire, massive, les fronts sont plats, les pommettes larges. Les oreilles sont en général épaisses et larges, les pavillons bien visibles de face.

Peu de visages ont des rides, toutefois particulièrement atténuées (inv. G 12. G 15. G 16f. 19117. 19118. 19129. 19130. 19132. 19133). Les visages montrant une expression sont également rares. Le Faune souriant (inv. 18873; fig. 4), le Faune enfant (inv. 18875) et les putti (inv. G 16c. G 16g) ont une expression joyeuse et rieuse. L'expression volontaire de Vespasien³⁸, avec ses sourcils froncés et quelques rides sur le front (inv. G 16d. G 16c bis), appartient à un autre registre. La froideur générale des expressions sur tout le reste du groupe s'accommode avec le sérieux donné aux visages de philosophes.

Les sourcils sont fins, ils suivent par un très discret bourrelet parfois à peine visible la ligne de l'arcade sourcilière. Le traitement des sourcils est identique sur tout le groupe, à l'exception d'un personnage avec des sourcils épais (inv. 19118).

Les nez sont droits, petits, courts aux narines de faible largeur. Les bouches sont courtes et dépassent rarement la largeur des narines.

Les mentons et les mâchoires sont forts, les ovales pleins, ils rattrapent la massivité des cous. Quelques mentons sont parfois proéminents (par exemple un Faune enfant, inv. 18875).

---

[36] Wrede 1972, no. 21 pls. 18, 2; 19, 2.
[37] Wrede 1972, no. 19 pls. 20, 1. 3. 4.
[38] Wrede 1972, no. 92 pls. 15, 3; 16, 1.

## LE TRAITEMENT DES YEUX

Sur les 63 hermès accessibles pour cette étude, trois sont trop mutilés et n'ont plus d'yeux (inv. 04-306. 18879. 19128). Sur le reste du groupe, les yeux sont réguliers et dessinés en amande. Les paupières inférieures et supérieures sont épaisses. Seul le traitement de la pupille et de l'iris change. On relève sept groupes pour le traitement de cette partie, dont un groupe avec le globe lisse et six groupes pour les iris et pupilles marqués.

Groupe 1. – Globe lisse: inv. 18873 (Faune); inv. G16d (Vespasien).

Groupe 2. – Une seule cuvette est creusée régulièrement pour marquer iris et pupille, au centre du globe: inv. 18871. 19123 (Ménandre). 19122. 19136.

Groupe 3. – La pupille est creusée au trépan et forme un trou rond régulier, l'iris est cernée profondément par un trait, le tout au centre du globe: inv. 19129 (Philippe de Macédoine [?]); inv. 19130. 19131 (Socrate); inv. G 16i. 19121. 19118. 19133. 19117. 19134. 18876 (Polydeuces); inv. 18877. G 13. 19146. G 16k (bis). 19138. 19140. 19145.

Groupe 4. – La pupille est creusée au trépan par des coups irréguliers (effet de pupille parfois carrée) et l'iris est cerné profondément par un trait, le tout au centre du globe: inv. 19132. 19137. 18878. G 16k (Vénus). 18880. 19119. G 16c bis. 19120. 19125. 18869 (Mars); inv. 18874. 19144. 19147 (Antonin le Pieux [?]); inv. 18868. 19148. 19139. 18872.

Groupe 5. – Une seule cuvette est creusée pour représenter la pupille et l'iris, située en haut du globe: inv. 19150. 18870. 19135. 18866. G 16l. 18865 (»Germain«).

Groupe 6. – Un trou marque la pupille, l'iris est cerné, le tout placé vers le haut du globe: inv. G 16c. G 16g (putto); inv. G 12. 19127 (enfant); inv. 19151. 19149. 18875 (Faune jeune); inv. 19152. 19141. G 14.

Groupe 7. – L'iris est creusé en lunule ce qui fait ressortir la pupille, le tout placé vers le haut du globe: inv. 19126. G 15. G. 16f. 19124. 19142. G 16b.

Le traitement des globes oculaires offre une grande diversité qui sous-entend de multiples interventions et d'habitudes prises par certains sculpteurs, si l'on tient à l'aspect technique. La forme des yeux associée à celle des sourcils sur cette collection découle de la recherche d'une forme de classicisme. Seuls deux hermès n'ont pas d'yeux marqués, mais des globes lisses. On peut penser que les globes lisses sur l'hermès du Faune sont une interprétation logique sur une sculpture idéale, technique que l'on retrouve bien souvent sur les copies romaines de sculptures idéales où la pupille était peinte. Toutefois, la seconde sculpture avec des globes lisses est un portrait supposé de Vespasien (inv. G 16d). Au contraire, une Vénus (inv. G 16k)[39], qui est sans conteste une sculpture idéale inspirée ici de l'art classique grec, possède des pupilles marquées (groupe 4). Même si tous les hermès de Welschbillig ne nous sont pas parvenus, les documents portant des globes lisses font figure d'exception. Pour ces deux cas de Welschbillig, on peut sous-entendre une référence au passé, une volonté de respecter les modèles originaux. Ce peut être aussi une façon pour le sculpteur de se distinguer. Il existe cependant quelques portraits de l'Antiquité tardive avec des yeux non marqués[40]. Les différentes manières de traiter iris et pupilles ont-elles une incidence sur l'iconographie? Sur toutes les paires d'œuvres (ou duos) relevés, seuls les paires inv. 19147/19148; 19137/19144; 19129/19130; 18876/18877; 19146/19145; G 16c/G 16g ont des yeux qui appartiennent à un même groupe (parmi les groupes 3, 4 et 6).

Les groupes 3 et 4 forment les ensembles les plus nombreux, et associés au groupe 2, on y voit iris (et pupilles) au centre du globe oculaire. Au contraire, les groupes 5, 6 et 7 amènent l'iris vers le haut du globe. Le rendu de l'iris de ces trois derniers groupes, qui intensifie le regard, rappelle celui des portraits sous la Tétrarchie (exemples de Chiragan)[41]. Mais on le retrouve aussi sur certains portraits de philosophes ou sur un portrait d'Alexandre en médaillon à *Aphrodisias*, datés

---

[39] Wrede 1972, no. 89 pl. 44, 3–4.
[40] Ménandre *Aphrodisias*, Lenaghan 2018, 461 fig. 2; tête féminine Corinthe, inv. S-2474 (LSA 76); tête féminine Corinthe S-896 (LSA 77); homme Corinthe, inv. S-1199 (LSA 71); homme Athènes (LSA 120), par exemple.
[41] Balty 2008, figs. 1–7. 25. 47 par exemple.

par Smith du début du V<sup>e</sup> siècle[42]. Les détails des yeux classés par groupe pourraient aussi se comprendre comme une sorte de signature de chaque sculpteur, si l'on considère ici le contexte de l'entreprise, qui demandait rapidité et efficience.

Sur le portrait en marbre attribué à l'empereur Gratien, mis au jour en 1898 tout près de la basilique de Trèves, on peut voir malgré les épaufrures de la surface ses yeux marqués (fig. 5)[43]. L'iris est cerné et la pupille était marquée au trépan. L'iris est large et occupe toute la hauteur du globe. Mais le regard est droit. Ses larges yeux en amande sont surmontés de sourcils fins. La couronne fait supposer que le portrait date de l'année 375, date de la mort de Valentinien I, moment où Gratien va gouverner la partie occidentale de l'empire (avec son demi-frère Valentinien II). Le portrait, sans préciser son identification, est daté plus largement par Christian Witschel de la fin du IV<sup>e</sup> siècle ou du début du V<sup>e</sup> siècle apr. J.-C.[44]. Le visage est surmonté d'une coiffure courte à frange peignée d'arrière en avant et traitée avec des mèches particulièrement fines. Sur les tempes, les pattes s'épaississent pour former un indice capillaire proéminent le long des maxillaires et passer sous le menton en mourant. Cette partie, qui attire l'attention et caractérise le portrait, contraste par son traitement en boucles épaisses avec une utilisation modérée du trépan.

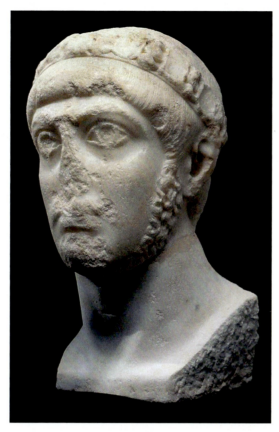

5  Gratien (?), inv. 1898-306 (RLM Trier, photo Th. Zühmer)

## BARBES ET CHEVELURES

Comme le souligne Smith à propos de la série des portraits de philosophes d'*Aphrodisias* de l'Antiquité tardive, il est utile aussi de considérer le contexte historique et d'estimer le contexte culturel pour tenter des datations[45]. Le projet iconographique de Welschbillig apparait au premier regard construit, cohérent et réfléchi, non seulement par son ampleur mais par son contenu. La part la plus importante est donnée aux représentations de philosophes anciens, de poètes et intellectuels du passé et probablement du présent. Ces nouveaux portraits d'importants intellectuels anciens et contemporains étaient érigés dans l'Antiquité tardive avec les mêmes fonctions qu'ils avaient à la fin de la République et au début de l'Empire. Ils appartenaient à l'univers d'une élite éduquée et cultivée. Au IV<sup>e</sup> et au V<sup>e</sup> siècles, certains philosophes faisaient même l'objet d'une véritable vénération. Les élites cultivées de Trèves n'ont sûrement pas échappé à cet environnement intellectuel bouillonnant du IV<sup>e</sup> siècle. Ce n'est pas un hasard si le nombre le plus important de portraits de philosophes se retrouvent dans les grands centres intellectuels (au IV<sup>e</sup> s. Athènes, Alexandrie, Apamée, Pergame, Ephèse, Sardes, et au V<sup>e</sup> s. Athènes, Alexandrie et *Aphrodisias*)[46]. A Trèves, Valentinien I appelle Ausone à la cour en 364 pour devenir le précepteur de Gratien,

---

[42]  Smith 1991, 147 fig. 2–3.
[43]  Rheinisches Landesmuseum Trier inv. 1898-306 (Fundstücke, Stuttgart 2009, fiche 68 p. 146–147, S. Faust, vers 375 [LSA 584]).
[44]  Witschel 2016, 76 fig. 5.5.
[45]  Smith 1991, 157.
[46]  Smith 1991, 157.

6   »Germain«, inv. 18865 (RLM Trier, photo Th. Zühmer)

7   Jeune homme, inv. 19121 (RLM Trier, photo Th. Zühmer)

alors âgé de cinq ans. Il ne repartira à Bordeaux qu'à la mort de Gratien, assassiné à *Lugdunum* le 25 août 383. Ammien Marcellin précisait que Gratien préférait les études aux exercices militaires, mais il parlait là d'un enfant de sept ans[47]. Le concepteur du programme de Welschbillig a eu probablement l'ambition de rivaliser avec les grands centres de pensée de l'Orient. Toutefois, si l'on peut constater par les sources l'environnement intellectuellement riche de Trèves, on ne peut pas être assuré de la véritable identité de l'auteur de ce projet. Le fait que Welschbillig soit dans le domaine impérial resserre le champ d'hypothèses autour de Valentinien et de son fils et leur entourage proche. Karl-Josef Gilles soutenait l'hypothèse que le domaine (incluant la villa), propriété de l'empereur, avait été géré par un *praefectus laetorum*[48].

Les barbes et les chevelures de la collection forment un assemblage de caractères anciens et contemporains. Les bases techniques font appel à tout le vocabulaire romain en matière de traitement des mèches. Les pattes volumineuses remarquées sur le portrait de Gratien (?) décrit plus haut vont se retrouver sur quelques exemplaires d'hermès. Par exemple, sur le portrait dit du »Germain«[49], nommé ainsi par Wrede afin de souligner sa contemporanéité: on peut voir ces pattes épaisses, qui descendent assez bas (fig. 6). Les cheveux du »Germain«, avec ses mèches très fines peignées d'arrière en avant, qui forment une grosse frange en bourrelet et sont coupées droit dans la nuque, rappellent dans une certaine mesure la coiffure du portrait impérial. Cette coiffure va se reproduire sur les hermès de personnages contemporains (inv. 18874. G 16b. G 16k) ainsi que sur une représentation de Mars[50] (bien que mutilée). Mars jeune imberbe est casqué. La forme de son casque est d'un type attique du IV$^e$ siècle av. J.-C.[51]. Le casque porté par l'hermès de Mars du Nymphée de Trajan a Ephèse a une forme identique à celui de Welschbillig[52], qui donc fait référence à l'iconographie traditionnelle de la Grèce classique. Les représentations des hermès de Vénus à

---

[47] Amm. 2, 27, 6, 9 (Gratian).
[48] Gilles 1999, 258.
[49] Wrede 1972, no. 82 pl. 33, 1–2 (LSA 1075).
[50] Wrede 1972, no. 83 pl. 44, 1–2.
[51] Grace à l'étude de Pena – Ojeda 2020, portant sur les hermès de petite taille représentant Alexandre casqué dans le monde romain, on peut garder ici l'hypothèse d'un casque de Mars.
[52] Hanslmayer 2016, 129–130 no. D 2 C pl. 63.

8   Socrate, inv. 19131 (RLM Trier, photo Th. Zühmer)   9   Philosophe, inv. 19150 (RL M Trier, photo Th. Zühmer)

Welschbillig et du Nymphée de Trajan à Ephèse font aussi référence à la Grèce classique[53]. Le casque de l'hermès de Mars du Serapeum de Carthage, cité plus haut, est assez proche[54].

Toute une panoplie de ciseaux et de trépans de diverses tailles a participé à l'élaboration de la représentation des chevelures et des barbes faisant référence à toutes les époques de la Grèce et de Rome.

Une série représente des hommes jeunes imberbes, à la coiffure courte et peu épaisse. Les mèches très fines sont peignées d'arrière en avant, sans utilisation du trépan, et coupées parfois sur la frange par de discrètes fourchettes (inv. G 16i. 19119. 19120. 19121. 19122. 19141. 19142) (fig. 7). Il est intéressant de constater que le marquage des iris et pupilles de cette série de coiffure identique se répartit sur cinq groupes différents. Ces visages jeunes et leur type de coiffure évoquent les élèves brillants et les disciples des philosophes représentés à leur côté, on citera l'exemple d'*Aphrodisias*[55]. A Welschbillig, Polydeuces, le disciple d'Hérode Atticus a été reconnu, sa coiffure étant caractéristique des jeunes de la période antonine (inv. 18876)[56].

Le poète Ménandre est identifiable grâce à la forme de son visage, son grand front et la découpe particulière de sa chevelure avec un début de calvitie (inv. 19123)[57]. Il est un des intellectuels les plus représentés dans l'Antiquité tardive[58].

Socrates est le philosophe le plus représenté[59] dans l'Antiquité tardive[60]. Le portrait de Welschbillig (inv. 19131; fig. 8)[61] se distingue des autres versions de l'Antiquité tardive par le traitement

---

[53] Wrede 1972, 81 pl. 44, 3–4; Ephèse: Hanslmayer 2016, 131 no. D 2 F pls. 66. 67 e–h.
[54] L'hypothèse de la représentation des planètes à Welschbillig pourra être proposée, peut-être une représentation de Luna dans un hermès féminin jeune portant un collier avec un croissant de lune, inv. 19140, qui s'ajoutera à Mars et Vénus.
[55] Smith 1991, 154–155, jeune pupille, no. 9 fig. 10, daté du début du Ve s.
[56] Wrede 1972, no. 80 pl. 12, 1 (LSA 2639).
[57] Wrede 1972, no. 35 pl. 10, 1–2 (LSA 2640); Lenaghan 2016, 262 fig. 21, 2; Lenaghan 2018.
[58] Fittschen 1991.
[59] Catoni – Giuilani 2020.
[60] Lenaghan 2016, 261 fig. 21, 1.
[61] Wrede 1972, no. 9 pl. 1, 1–3 (LSA 2638).

10   Philosophe, inv. 19134 (RLM Trier, photo Th. Zühmer)

11   Philosophe, inv. 19132 (RLM Trier, photo Th. Zühmer)

particulier de sa chevelure et de sa barbe en mèches très longues détaillées au trépan. La chevelure mi-longue se recourbe sur un côté et forme une anglaise sur le côté gauche. Un autre philosophe porte une barbe longue où le trépan est utilisé avec davantage de modération (inv. 19150; fig. 9). Un troisième exemple de philosophe est remarquable par l'utilisation du trépan dans la barbe volumineuse aux mèches très longues et dans la chevelure formée de boucles en coques. Le contraste fort sur cette œuvre en fait une véritable construction visuelle (inv. 19134; fig. 10)[62].

Le portrait d'un homme d'âge mûr (inv. 19132; fig. 11) portant une calvitie et des mèches courtes sur les côtés ainsi qu'une barbe courte et bouclée rappelle les portraits stylisés d'intellectuels de la fin de la période antonine et de la période sévérienne[63].

12   Jeune femme, inv. 18872 (RLM Trier, photo Th. Zühmer)

La collection de Welschbillig se distingue également par la présence de quelques hermès féminins, dont la représentation de femmes jeunes aux cheveux longs traités en mèches fines tombant sur les épaules, avec une utilisation très discrète du trépan. La coiffure est agrémentée d'une épaisse frange (inv. 19136. 19135. 19140. 18872; fig. 12). Cette coiffure à frange peut être comprise comme celle de personnages contem-

---

[62]   Wrede 1972, no. 22 pl. 46, 2.
[63]   Zanker 1995, 214–215 fig. 121–122.

porains. Remarquons toutefois que la frange avec les cheveux longs a déjà été utilisée (rarement) dans les périodes précédentes, par exemple dans la représentation de Thalassa, couchée au pied du char d'Artémis sur un relief du monument des Parthes à Ephèse (IIe s. apr. J.-C.)[64].

## CONCLUSION

L'intérêt de ce groupe de sculptures est remarquable par le nombre qui nous est parvenu et par le fait que ces sculptures ne sont ni réutilisées ni retravaillées. Elles reflètent l'art du portrait de la deuxième moitié du IVe siècle au temps de Valentinien et Gratien dans le nord des Gaules, près de la capitale impériale et très probablement sur un domaine impérial. Ces hermès en pierre de Norroy ont un aspect massif inhérent à la structure même des piliers avec lesquels ils font corps et qui leur donne un caractère de sculpture provinciale, un peu raide et guindé. Toutefois, dans les choix du traitement de certaines parties du visage commun à tout le groupe et dans l'atténuation de certains caractères, on peut voir la recherche d'une forme de classicisme, plus proche de ce qui deviendra l'idéal esthétique de la »renaissance théodosienne«[65] avec des visages rajeunis, sans fortes marques de l'âge, à l'expression souvent figée[66]. La grande diversité du traitement du marquage de la pupille et de l'iris montre un éventail de techniques différentes utilisées au sein d'un même atelier, sur un même site et dans une période de fabrication que l'on suppose être courte. Cette diversité, dans le groupe étudié, n'a pas d'incidence sur l'iconographie. La remarquable diversité des techniques utilisées pareillement dans le traitement des chevelures et barbes se met là au service de l'iconographie mais les références aux modèles anciens montrent une grande flexibilité. Mais malgré cette diversité de techniques, les hermès de Welschbillig sont aisément reconnaissables parmi les autres séries d'hermès de l'Antiquité tardive. En cela leur style peut s'entendre comme celui d'un groupe particulier.

## BIBLIOGRAPHIE

| | |
|---|---|
| Auinger – Rathmayer 2007 | J. Auinger – E. Rathmayer, Zur spätantiken Statuenausstatung der Thermen und Nymphäen in Ephesos, dans: F. A. Bauer – C. Witschel (éds.), Statuen in der Spätantike (Wiesbaden 2007) 237–269 |
| Balmelle – Van Ossel 2001 | C. Balmelle – P. Van Ossel, De Trèves à Bordeaux: la marque des élites dans les campagnes de la Gaule romaine aux IVe et Ve siècles, dans: P. Ouzoulias – C. Pellecuer – C. Raynaud – P. Van Ossel – P. Garmy (éds.), Les campagnes de la Gaule à la fin de l'Antiquité. Actes du colloque de Montpellier 11.–14.03.1998 (Antibes 2001) 533–552 |
| Balty 2008 | J.-C. Balty, Sculptures antiques de Chiragan (Martres-Tolosane). Les portraits romains I 5. La Tétrarchie. Musée des Antiques de Toulouse (Toulouse 2008) |
| Bergmann – Kovacs 2016 | M. Bergmann – M. Kovacs, Portraits styles, in: Smith – Ward-Perkins 2016, 280–294 |
| Bienert 2012 | B. Bienert, Eifelkeramik – Dependance Speicher/Herforst (Eifelkreis Bitburg-Prüm): Zum gegenwärtigen Forschungsstand zu den römischen Großtöpfereien in der Südeifel, dans: M. Grünewald – S. Wenzel (éds.), Römische Landnutzung in der Eifel: neue Ausgrabungen und Forschungen. Tagung in Mayen 03.–06.11.2011 (Mayence 2012) 343–356 |
| Catoni – Giuliani 2021 | M. L. Catoni – L. Giuliani, Der verurteilte Philosoph, die Satyrn und das Hässliche: das frühe Sokrates-Porträt im Kontext, JdI 136, 2021, 152–197 |
| Fittschen 1991 | K. Fittschen, Zur Rekonstruktion griechischer Dichterstatuen 1. Die Statue des Menander, AM 106, 1991, 243–279 |
| Fort et al. 2021a | B. Fort – A. Hostein – S. Janniard – M. Kasprzyk (éds.), La présence de l'Etat dans l'Est de la Gaule durant l'Antiquité tardive (250–450 ap. J.-C.). Actes du colloque international Dijon 08.–10.11.2012, RAE Suppl. 52 (Dijon 2021) |

---

[64] Meyer 2006, 129–130 fig. 3.
[65] Hannestad 1994, 141–142.
[66] Bergmann – Kovacs 2016, 285–286.

| | |
|---|---|
| Fort et al. 2021b | B. Fort – A. Hostein – S. Janniard – M. Kasprzyk, La présence de l'état dans l'est du diocèse des Gaules au IV$^e$ s.: au miroir des sources matérielles et écrites, dans: Fort et al. 2021a, 81–132 |
| Gilles 1984 | K.-J. Gilles, Langmauer, dans: Trier, Kaiserresidenz und Bischofssitz: die Stadt in spätantiker und frühchristlicher Zeit. Katalog Rheinisches Landesmuseum Trier (Mayence 1984) 288–290 |
| Gilles 1985 | K.-J. Gilles, Die Langmauer bei Trier, dans: Carte Archéologique du Grand-Duché de Luxembourg, feuille 14 (Luxembourg 1985) 6–16 |
| Gilles 1999 | K.-J. Gilles, Neuere Untersuchungen an der Langmauer bei Trier, dans: F. R. Hermann – K. Bittel – U. Fischer – H. Ament (éds.), Festschrift Günter Smolla (Wiesbaden 1999) 254–258 |
| Hannestad 1994 | N. Hannestad, Tradition in late antique sculpture. Conservation, modernization (Aarhus 1994) |
| Hanslmayer 2016 | R. Hanslmayer, Die Skulpturen von Ephesos. Die Hermen, FiE 10, 2 (Vienne 2016) |
| Heinen 1985 | H. Heinen, 2000 Jahre Trier I. Trier und das Trevererland in römischer Zeit (Trèves 1985) |
| Koethe 1935 | H. Koethe, Der spätrömische Mauerring von Bitburg, TrZ 10, 1935, 1–5 |
| Laporte – Bricault 2020 | J.-P. Laporte – L. Bricault, Le Serapeum de Carthage, Supplément à la Bibliotheca Isiaca I (Bordeaux 2020) |
| Lenaghan 2016 | J. Lenaghan, Cultural heroes, dans: Smith – Ward-Perkins 2016, 259–266 |
| Lenaghan 2018 | J. Lenaghan, Two portraits from Aphrodisias: late-antique re-visualizations of traditionnal culture-heroes ?, JRA 31, 2018, 458–473 |
| Lorenz 1965 | T. Lorenz, Galerien von griechischen Philosophen- und Dichterbildnissen bei den Römern (Mayence 1965) |
| Meyer 2006 | M. Meyer, Der Kaiser, Apollon-Helios und die Stadt. Zur Interpretation der Reliefs mit Wagenfahrt, dans: W. Seipel (éd.), Das Partherdenkmal von Ephesos. Akten des Kolloquiums Wien 25.–28.04.2003, Schriften des Kunsthistorischen Museums 10 (Vienne 2006) 129–141 |
| Neudecker 1988 | R. Neudecker, Die Skulpturenausstattung römischer Villen in Italien (Mayence 1988) |
| Pena – Ojeda 2020 | A. Pena – D. Ojeda, Miniature Herms representing Alexander the Great, Hesperia 89, 2020, 83–124 |
| Roux 2021 | M. Roux, Les impacts de la présence et du départ des bureaux impériaux et préfectoraux à Trèves (IV$^e$–V$^e$ siècle de N.E.), dans: Fort et al. 2021a, 201–221 |
| Smith 1991 | R. R. R. Smith, Late roman Philosophers, in: Aphrodisias Papers 2. The theatre, a sculptor's workshop, philosophers, and coin-types, dans: R. R. R. Smith – K. T. Erim (éds.), JRA Suppl. 2 (Ann Arbor 1991) 144–158 |
| Smith – Ward-Perkins 2016 | R. R. R. Smith – B. Ward-Perkins (éds.), The last statues of antiquity (Oxford 2016) |
| Stirling 2007 | L. M. Stirling, Statuary Collecting and Display in the Late Antique Villas of Gaul and Spain: A Comparative Study, dans: F. A. Bauer – C. Witschel (éds.), Statuen in der Spätantike (Wiesbaden 2007) 307–321 |
| Van Ossel 1992 | P. Van Ossel, Etablissements ruraux de l'Antiquité tardive dans le Nord de la Gaule, CNRS, Gallia Suppl. 51 (Paris 1992) |
| Van Ossel 2021 | P. Van Ossel, L'emprise de l'état romain tardif sur l'économie du diocèse des Gaules: que nous apprennent les sources archéologiques?, dans: Fort et al. 2021a, 197–209 |
| Witschel 2005 | C. Witschel, Trier und das spätantike Städtewesen im Westen des römischen Reiches, TrZ 67/68, 2005, 223–272 |
| Witschel 2016 | C. Witschel, Hispania, Gallia and Raetia, dans: Smith – Ward-Perkins 2016, 69–79 |
| Wrede 1972 | H. Wrede, Die spätantike Hermengalerie von Welschbillig: Untersuchungen zur Kunsttradition im 4. Jahrhundert n. Chr. und zur allgemeinen Bedeutung des antiken Hermenmals (Berlin 1972) |
| Wrede 1985 | H. Wrede, Die antike Herme (Mayence 1985) |
| Zanker 1995 | P. Zanker, Die Maske des Sokrates: das Bild des Intellektuellen in der antiken Kunst (Munich 1995) |

*Maria-Pia Darblade-Audoin, Institut Català d'Arqueologia Clàssica (ICAC), Pl. Rovellat s/n, 43003 Tarragona, Espagne.*
*[e] mdarblade@icac.cat; maria-pia.darblade-audoin@wanadoo.fr*

Nicolas Delferrière – Anne-Laure Edme

# LE SARCOPHAGE ROMAIN DE MANTOCHE CONSERVÉ AU MUSÉE BARON MARTIN DE GRAY (HAUTE-SAÔNE, FRANCE)

## UN EXEMPLE ATYPIQUE EN GAULE DU CENTRE-EST

**Abstract**
A Roman sarcophagus, well preserved overall, was unearthed during sand extraction work in Mantoche (Haute-Saône, France) in 1846. Both the coffin and its lid are preserved: the lid is decorated with acroteria in the form of theatrical masks at the corners and in the centre, with a mutilated bust, probably of the deceased, on the main side. This sarcophagus has been the subject of representations in the 19th century and a few brief mentions, but is often neglected in more recent archaeological literature because of its location in a small museum in the Burgundy-Franche-Comté region (Museum Baron Martin of Gray). The quality of the sculptural decoration of the masks and the presence of the bust of the deceased directly on the lid of the sarcophagus raise questions about local funerary production and constitute a particularly atypical example. The aim of this paper is to present this piece, to place it in the context of funerary production in Central-Eastern Gaul, and to examine comparisons on a wider scale.

## INTRODUCTION

Le sarcophage romain de Mantoche[1] (Haute-Saône; fig. 1), en raison de son iconographie et de sa préservation assez remarquable, est intéressant à plus d'un titre, ce qui rend inexplicable le relatif silence de la littérature archéologique à son sujet. Il a notamment échappé à l'inventaire systématique et exhaustif du »Recueil général des bas-reliefs, statues et bustes de la Gaule romaine« d'Émile Espérandieu! Seule Hélène Walter a su lui accorder une notice relativement bien documentée dans »La sculpture funéraire gallo-romaine en Franche-Comté«[2], qu'elle publia en 1974. Certes, ce sarcophage est conservé dans le musée d'une petite ville, Gray, d'un département peu peuplé, la Haute-Saône, au sein de la région Bourgogne–Franche-Comté, mais il trône néanmoins au centre de la salle consacrée aux antiquités gallo-romaines, en véritable pièce maîtresse[3]. Ce paradoxe nous a donc conduits à nous intéresser particulièrement à ce sarcophage et à sa place au sein des productions funéraires romaines du territoire lingon[4], et plus largement du centre-est des Gaules[5].

1  Localisation de Mantoche (Haute-Saône, France) (DAO: N. Delferrière, 2022)

---

[1]  Nous tenons à remercier l'ensemble de l'équipe du musée Baron Martin de Gray, et en particulier Mme Brigitte Olivier, sa responsable, pour son accueil et l'intérêt porté à notre étude.
[2]  Walter 1974, 129–130 no. 164.
[3]  Inv. 2009.0.679.
[4]  La commune de Mantoche se situe aux confins des cités lingonne et séquane, mais si l'on considère la Saône comme frontière, Mantoche appartient bien au territoire lingon (Nouvel 2016).
[5]  Nous remercions notre amie Marie-Anaïs Janin pour sa relecture épigraphique impeccable des exemples d'autres sarcophages cités.

## LA DÉCOUVERTE DU SARCOPHAGE

Le sarcophage romain de Mantoche a été découvert au tout début du mois de juillet 1846 sur le flanc d'une colline située à 500 m au sud du village, au lieu-dit »Sur la Perrière«[6]. C'est en effet à l'occasion de travaux dans une sablière, préalables à la construction d'un canal, qu'un ouvrier du village vit apparaître le sarcophage, à proximité immédiate d'une statue moderne de la Vierge, symbole cocasse s'il en est. Charles Dodelier, architecte et conservateur du musée de Vesoul, membre de la Commission d'archéologie de la Haute-Saône[7], en fut très rapidement averti afin de l'étudier[8]. Entre-temps, peu après sa découverte, le 10 juillet 1846, le sarcophage fut exposé dans le hall d'entrée de l'Hôtel de ville de Gray[9], puis transféré dans les collections du musée municipal, à une période inconnue, mais forcément après 1903, date de création de l'actuel musée Baron Martin dans le château qui domine la ville. Bien plus tard, entre 1964 et 1974, il fut installé au cœur de la salle archéologique au niveau inférieur du musée; une inscription peinte en rouge sur l'un des petits côtés de la cuve du sarcophage rapporte le lieu et la date de la découverte.

## LE CONTEXTE ARCHÉOLOGIQUE

Si l'on en croit les témoignages du milieu du XIXe siècle, au moment de la découverte, le sarcophage fut retrouvé dans un secteur, une colline, particulièrement riche en vestiges archéologiques romains dont certains avaient déjà été observés dès 1837, à tel point que »les voyageurs apercevaient depuis la route ses monuments imposants«[10]. Le mobilier et les blocs architecturaux mis au jour témoignent de l'existence d'une nécropole qui paraissait importante[11]: »des vases de différentes formes et d'une belle conservation, lacrymatoires, urnes, verres, agrafes et instruments de bronze, les fragments d'un flambeau dont la flamme renversée était l'emblème de la nuit éternelle, une tête colossale de pleureur, les débris d'une frise dont les rinceaux supportent une cigogne poursuivant un serpent à travers le feuillage, des socles aux larges moulures, des corniches sculptées avec richesse, la partie supérieure d'une jambe, qui annonce une statue de deux mètres et demi de hauteur«[12]. Ainsi, à côté du sarcophage qui fait l'objet de notre étude, un mausolée particulièrement imposant et richement décoré devait également avoir existé: les fragments de flambeaux[13] en ronde-bosse ainsi qu'un masque tragique colossal en calcaire en témoignent[14]. De plus, à l'endroit même où le sarcophage avait été découvert, de nouvelles fouilles furent réalisées par M. Virot, notaire, en 1898. Plusieurs inhumations ont été mises au jour présentant des squelettes accompagnés de plusieurs verreries et céramiques[15]. Il s'agit donc là d'un espace funéraire qui participait à la dynamique d'occupation du territoire de Mantoche, constitué d'une agglomé-

---

[6] La Presse Grayloise du 25 juillet 1846 (archives); Clerc 1847, 141–142; Dodelier 1847; Longchamps 1860, 47; Mouton 1878, 11. 123; Gasser 1898, 91; Gasser 1900, 236; Gasser 1901, 238–241; Martet 1956, 14.

[7] Thévenin 2006, 23.

[8] Clerc 1847, 141–142; Dodelier 1847; Marnotte 1847, 97–102.

[9] Walter 1974, 129 no. 164.

[10] La Presse Grayloise du 25 juillet 1846 (archives); Clerc 1847, 141; Poly 1897, 81. Le reste du territoire de la commune de Mantoche est extrêmement riche en vestiges romains et fait l'objet de plusieurs études depuis de nombreuses années. Un *aureus* de Didia Clara découvert en 1822, mais sans contexte précis, et aujourd'hui conservé au sein du médailler de la Bibliothèque municipale de Besançon a notamment fait l'objet d'une étude très récente par Florent Potier (Potier 2022).

[11] Walter 1974, 129–131, no. 164–166.

[12] Clerc 1847, 141.

[13] La Presse Grayloise du 25 juillet 1846 (archive); Clerc 1847, 141; Marnotte 1847, 101; Mouton 1878, 124; Gasser 1901, 204; Walter 1974, 130 no. 165.

[14] La Presse Grayloise du 25 juillet 1846 (archive); Clerc 1847, 141; Marnotte 1847, 101; Mouton 1878, 124; Gasser 1901, 204; Walter 1974, 131 no. 166; Bonvalot 1994, 119; Joan 2016, 227.

[15] Gasser 1898, 91.

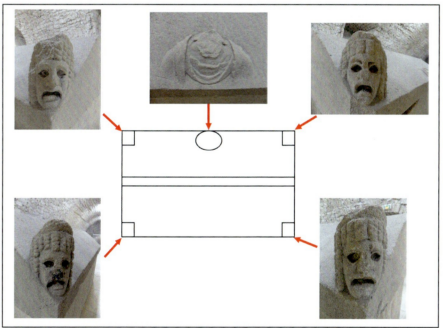

2   Le sarcophage romain de Mantoche au musée Baron Martin de Gray; vue générale et détails (clichés N. Delferrière, 2022; DAO: A.-L. Edme, 2022)

ration secondaire avec un port[16] et d'une grande villa à mosaïques[17], la »Villa des Maizières«[18], découverte dès le XIXᵉ siècle.

Si l'on peut se réjouir d'une relative bonne conservation du sarcophage, les autres éléments découverts ont malheureusement été perdus, dispersés dans des collections privées, voire détruits. Le sarcophage contenait d'ailleurs lui-même un autre sarcophage en plomb, dont nous n'avons plus aucune trace. Des offrandes (céramiques, verroteries, dont des urnes placées à chaque angle du sarcophage, et un fer de lance), présentes au moment de l'ouverture du couvercle, accompagnaient les trois défunts, qui reposaient dans le sarcophage. La trace de ce mobilier est difficile à retrouver, mais il n'est pas impossible qu'il soit actuellement conservé au sein de l'ancienne collection Drioton, issue déjà de celle du notaire Virot, et située au musée archéologique de Dijon[19].

## LA DESCRIPTION DU SARCOPHAGE

Le sarcophage est complet (fig. 2), cuve et couvercle sont intacts, exception faite de la tête du défunt sculptée en ronde-bosse sur l'un des grands côtés du couvercle. L'ensemble a été taillé dans un bloc monolithe de calcaire à entroques dont la provenance est sans doute à chercher du côté des affleurements situés le long du Doubs, à 2–3 km de Besançon[20]. Tous les éléments sont traités en très haut relief, voire en ronde-bosse.

La cuve est quadrangulaire et mesure 2,28 m de longueur, 0,83 m de largeur et 0,75 m de hauteur; les parois sont épaisses de 0,09 m. L'extérieur a été poli, mais des traces d'outils sont toujours visibles à l'intérieur de la cuve. Aucune épitaphe n'a été gravée sur le sarcophage, mais une inscription peinte récente, relative à la découverte (*cf. supra*), est encore visible sur un petit côté de la cuve.

Le couvercle prend la forme d'un toit à double pente avec un faîte central. Haut de 0,43 m, il est légèrement plus long et large que la cuve (2,35 × 0,95 m; largeur du faîte: 0,05 m). Chaque angle est orné d'un masque de théâtre tragique figuré avec une bouche ouverte largement pendante, haut de 0,22 m et large de 0,21 m. Les chevelures sont traitées en six à huit épaisses boucles descendant le long des joues et six plus courtes sur le front. Sur le haut des têtes ceintes d'un diadème, les mèches sont raides et tirées vers l'arrière. Les yeux et les bouches sont très profondément creusés, ce qui accentue l'expression rude et pathétique des masques. La figuration du défunt, placée au centre d'un long côté du couvercle, est assez originale, car elle mêle haut relief au niveau des épaules et ronde-bosse pour le cou et la tête. Le buste est large à sa base de 0,40 m et est conservé sur une hauteur de 0,23 m. Bien que la tête soit manquante, le buste paraît être plutôt masculin: le défunt est, en effet, vêtu de deux tuniques superposées et d'une écharpe lâchement enroulée autour des épaules. L'ensemble des éléments structurels et décoratifs tend à indiquer une production locale datable de l'Antiquité tardive, probablement autour du IVᵉ siècle, d'après l'avis d'Hélène Walter, qui n'explicite cependant pas les critères qui l'ont conduit à une telle datation[21].

---

[16] Labre – Demesy 1986, 99–106; Petit – Mangin 1994, 119; Faure-Brac 2002, 320; Venault – Nouvel 2014, 224–228.

[17] Plusieurs écoinçons ornés de chevaux marins sont conservés au musée Baron Martin de Gray (Faure-Brac 2002, 325 fig. 382).

[18] Gasser 1900; Labre – Demesy 1986, 99–106; Faure-Brac 2002, 320–327; Venault – Nouvel 2014, 224–228.

[19] Les recherches que nous avons initiées n'ont pour l'instant pas eu l'effet escompté. La »Carte archéologique de la Gaule« évoque aussi des objets déposés au musée de Gray après leur découverte, mais qui étaient perdus au moment de la rédaction de l'ouvrage en 2002 (Faure-Brac 2002, 329). Lors de notre venue au musée Baron Martin en 2022, il nous a été stipulé que des objets de Mantoche avaient été retrouvés dans les réserves, l'enquête est en cours.

[20] Debrand-Passard et al. 1984.

[21] Walter 1974, 170.

## COMPARAISONS STYLISTIQUES ET FORMELLES

Comme l'a très justement démontré Jean-Claude Béal »pour les sarcophages de calcaire produits en Gaule romaine, le type de couvercle à acrotères corniers et médians est le plus courant à Arles, à Vienne, à Lyon (…). Le modèle a été très largement diffusé dans les provinces septentrionales de l'empire: on le trouve à Rouen[22] (Seine-Maritime), à Mantoche (Haute-Saône) comme sur les couvercles à fronton de Cologne[23]«[24].

Si des couvercles à portraits en buste sont connus – notamment pour le IIIe siècle – cette mise en valeur caractéristique du relief ne semble pas à notre connaissance avoir été expérimentée ailleurs. Les quelques couvercles à portraits connus, notamment à Arles, figurent le ou les défunts en bustes-portraits dans des acrotères corniers ou médians. C'est le cas de deux couvercles découverts respectivement aux Alyscamps en 1588[25] (fig. 3) et dans le quartier de la Trinquetaille au XVIIIe siècle[26], qui sont tous deux datés du IIIe siècle. Un autre couvercle arlésien[27], découvert en 1639 et aujourd'hui disparu, est connu par trois dessins produits au XVIIe et au XIXe siècles: les angles sont ornés de masques tragiques et le défunt figure en buste dans un acrotère central (fig. 4). Deux exemples issus des collections germaniques peuvent être rapprochés des exemples de Narbonnaise: découverts à Cologne, ils présentent sur le couvercle les portraits des défunts nommés par les épitaphes (fig. 5). Si le premier[28] est daté plutôt précisément, entre 231 et 270 apr. J.-C., le second[29] est de la seconde moitié du IIe siècle. Un couvercle de sarcophage, exposé au Römisches Museum d'Augsburg[30], possède des acrotères corniers ornés de masques de théâtre, une défunte allongée sur des coussins et accompagnée d'un paon sous un fronton placé au centre d'un long côté, et un portrait sous une niche cintrée au niveau du petit côté gauche. La coiffure de la défunte date cette production de la période sévérienne.

Plusieurs arguments tendent en effet à placer ce monument dans le courant du IVe siècle, bien que l'absence de la tête figurée en ronde-bosse nous prive de données importantes. Pour Hélène Walter, la datation du sarcophage est du IVe siècle, mais sans qu'elle explicite ses critères[31]. Bien plus tôt, Édouard Clerc[32] indiquait que le style du sarcophage appartenait plutôt aux premières années du IVe siècle. Lydie Joan[33], à l'instar de Nathalie Bonvalot, reprend également une datation du IVe siècle. Tout d'abord, si les sarcophages sont employés très tôt dans les provinces méridionales, leur utilisation en Gaule Belgique et dans les Germanies est bien moins développée et n'apparait que dans le courant du IIIe siècle. Les figurations des masques tragiques et du buste sont de bonne facture, bien que de production régionale. Les vêtements du défunt comme les coiffures des masques sont cohérents avec les figurations de défunts datées des IIe, IIIe et même IVe siècles, bien que ces dernières soient beaucoup moins nombreuses.

Localement et même régionalement, peu de sarcophages de pierre ont été mis au jour. Seuls quatre sarcophages antiques sont mentionnés parmi les découvertes faites anciennement à Besançon[34] et aucun autre dans le territoire séquane. Un sarcophage fut découvert en 1694 dans la nécro-

---

[22] Lequoy – Guillot 2004, no. 520 p. 222–223.
[23] Espérandieu 1922, 6437. 6488.
[24] Béal 2013, 224.
[25] Ms 240, 189; CIL XII 912; Espérandieu 1922, 192; Gaggadis-Robin 2005, 194–195.
[26] Ms NAF 4367, 14–17; Ms 903, 36; Gaggadis-Robin 2005, 196–197.
[27] Ms 903, 34; Ms 567, 26; Rothé – Heijmans 2008, 612. Le sarcophage a été mis au jour lors d'un abaissement du niveau de Rhône causé par une forte sécheresse. Dans un manuscrit conservé à Arles par l'avocat J. Raybaud et aujourd'hui non localisé, F. de Rebattu indique avoir creusé autour de deux de ces sarcophages – dont celui-ci – le 8 février 1661 (Constans 1920, 296). Le sarcophage comprenait en outre une épitaphe: CIL XII 853 (= CLE 553).
[28] Espérandieu 1922, 6437; pour l'épitaphe: CIL XIII 8352 (= ILS 7538 = AE 1904, 23 = RSK 325).
[29] Espérandieu 1922, 6488; pour l'épitaphe: CIL XIII 8426 (= RSK 364).
[30] Augsburg, Römisches Museum, no. 397.
[31] Walter 1974, 170.
[32] Clerc 1847, 142
[33] Joan 2016, 229.
[34] Lerat 1964, 140–141; Joan 2016, 227.

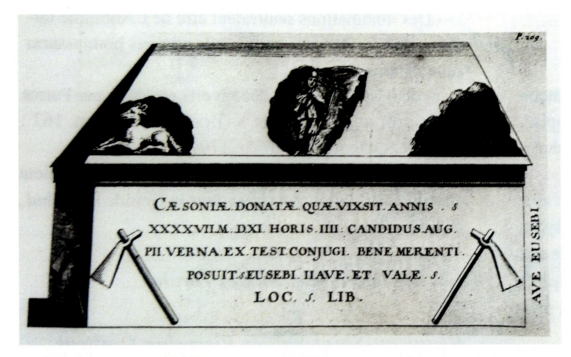

3   Le sarcophage romain de Saint-Ferjeux à Besançon (dessin du XIXe s. extrait de Lerat 1964, 138 fig. 46, d'après F.-I. Dunod de Charnage) et le couvercle d'un sarcophage romain découvert aux Alyscamps à Arles (cliché V. Gaggadis-Robin)

pole de Saint-Ferjeux à Besançon, à proximité du lieu où deux autres sarcophages fragmentaires ont été mis au jour en 1627[35] et 1823[36]. Quant au territoire lingon, il n'a livré à ce jour que deux cuves de sarcophages antiques, respectivement à Dijon[37] et Griselles[38]. Parallèlement à ces arguments, nous ne pouvons que regretter l'absence d'une inscription gravée qui nous aurait fourni de nombreuses informations précieuses. Cette absence peut résulter de deux possibilités, soit la présence d'une inscription uniquement peinte et aujourd'hui disparue, soit le dépôt du sarcophage au sein d'un mausolée familial, lui-même pourvu d'une inscription, l'un n'excluant pas l'autre. En effet, les vestiges d'un monument funéraire de ce type ont été identifiés à proximité du lieu

---

[35]   CIL XIII 5391.

[36]   Le sarcophage dit »de Virginia«, aujourd'hui exposé au Musée des beaux-arts et d'archéologie de Besançon (inv. D.896.3.1), s'il ne comporte pas de décor, est cependant remarquable pour son épitaphe: CIL XIII 5383 (= CLE, 455 = AE 1999, 1125).

[37]   Sans décor, il possède néanmoins une épitaphe: ILTG 409 (= AE 1954, 195 = ILingons 74): *D(is) M(anibus)/ Flaviae Billiccissioni*.

[38]   Probablement sans décor à l'origine, une scène biblique fut ajoutée à une date postérieure, peut-être lors de son remploi; une épitaphe, antique, demeure: CIL XIII 5658 (= ILingons, 320): *Moniment/um Sabinei, / {i} Sabinia/ni, an(norum) LXVI.*

Ms 567

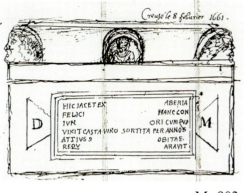
Ms 903

Ms 903

4   Plusieurs dessins d'un même sarcophage romain d'Arles trouvé en 1639, extraits de plusieurs manuscrits (Aa. Vv., voir Ms 903, 34 et 34bis; Ms 567, 26)

de découverte du sarcophage, bien que les données primaires liées à cette découverte ne nous permettent pas d'affiner le degré de proximité entre ces localisations[39]. Lors de sa mise au jour en 1846, le sarcophage contenait un cercueil de plomb renfermant trois squelettes (deux adultes et un enfant) et un ensemble d'objets en verre. Du fait de l'ancienneté de la découverte, nous manquons de certaines informations qui auraient été précieuses pour l'interprétation du monument. De plus, tout le contenu du sarcophage ayant été perdu, il n'est plus possible d'étudier le mobilier ni les squelettes. Ainsi, il n'est pas possible de dire si les individus inhumés dans la cuve étaient les destinataires originels du sarcophage. La taille du monument et la présence d'une seule figuration de défunt tendraient à indiquer une réouverture postérieure, l'inhumation primaire n'ayant pas été prévue pour être multiple (un seul défunt figuré et un sarcophage taillé pour un seul individu). Une fracture est visible sur le bord de la cuve et résulte d'un pillage ancien. Du mobilier précieux ayant été découvert au XIXe siècle, il est possible que ce soit le dépôt funéraire du premier occupant qui ait été pillé avant le remploi du sarcophage, peut-être à l'époque mérovingienne.

Il est difficile de dire si la cassure de la tête figurée du sarcophage de Mantoche est due à une volonté spécifique de détruire l'image du défunt primaire ou si cela ne résulte que de la fragilité structurelle de cet élément saillant. La bonne conservation des quatre masques acrotères pourrait indiquer une plus forte probabilité de la première hypothèse, bien que trois des nez soient brisés et qu'un éclat soit visible sur l'un des masques.

En raison du nombre de vestiges funéraires découverts à proximité et de la présence d'une villa de grandes dimensions dans les parages, on peut légitimement se questionner sur la nature de cette nécropole et du contexte dans lequel s'inscrit ce sarcophage. Comme nous l'avons dit, un

---

[39]   Tous ces vestiges ont été mis au jour en même temps, soit en 1846, mais qu'en était-il de la position exacte du sarcophage? Tout proche des fondations du mausolée? Enterré parmi les sépultures à inhumation plus tardives?

CIL XIII 8352

CIL XIII 8426

5  Deux sarcophages romains découverts à Cologne: Espérandieu 1922, 6437 = CIL XIII 8352 et Espérandieu 1922, 6488 = CIL XIII 8426 (clichés © RGM Köln)

mausolée au moins a été identifié, grâce aux blocs et à un masque tragique de grande taille mis au jour à proximité du sarcophage. Il s'agit, sans nul doute, d'un acrotère comme le mausolée de Faverolles nous en a livré des exemplaires de très grande qualité[40]. La présence de la »Villa des Maizières« non loin de là interroge aussi sur l'existence d'une nécropole privée, donc familiale. Le sarcophage pourrait ainsi appartenir à l'un des membres de la maison et, pourquoi pas, à l'un des propriétaires successifs de la villa, mais nous sommes conscients que ce type d'hypothèse a ses limites en l'absence d'un contexte archéologique clair et d'un apparat épigraphique apportant un nom aux multiples défunts retrouvés à Mantoche, et en particulier pour ceux sarcophage décoré.

## ARCHIVES

La Presse Grayloise du 25 juillet 1846

| | |
|---|---|
| Ms 240 | L. Romyeu (de), Histoire des antiquités d'Arles ou plusieurs écrits et épitaphes antiques trouvés là mesmes et en autres lieux (1574), médiathèque d'Arles |
| Ms 567 | Père Etienne Dumont, Descriptions des anciens monuments d'Arles (1789, imprimé en 1808), médiathèque d'Arles |
| Ms 903 (545) | F. de Rebattu, Antiquités d'Arles, recueil de quelques monuments et pièces de l'antiquité qui sont dans la ville d'Arles ou dehors ez environs d'icelle, commencé le 1er avril 1655, bibliothèque Méjanes, Aix en Provence |

---

[40] Février 1993 et toute la bibliographie qui y est mentionnée.

| | |
|---|---|
| Ms NAF 4367 | F. de Rebattu, Antiquités de la ville d'Arles, 1655, par M. Rebattu, écuyer, conseiller du roy au siège sénéchal de cette ville, Bibliothèque Nationale de France, département des manuscrits, Paris |

## BIBLIOGRAPHIE

| | |
|---|---|
| Béal 2013 | J.-Cl. Béal, Les sarcophages antiques de pierre dans la cité des Ségusiaves, RAE 62, 2013, 211–230 |
| Bonvalot 1994 | N. Bonvalot, avec la collaboration de M. Demésy – P. Nowicki, Mantoche (Haute-Saône), dans: J.-P. Petit – M. Mangin (éds.), Atlas des agglomérations secondaires de la Gaule Belgique et des Germanies (Paris 1994) 118–119 |
| CLE | F. Bücheler, Carmina Latina Epigraphica I–II (Lipsiae 1895–1897) |
| Clerc 1847 | É. Clerc, La Franche-Comté à l'époque romaine représentée par ses ruines (Besançon 1847) |
| Constans 1920 | L.-A. Constans, Notes sur quelques inscriptions d'Arles, REA 22/4, 1920, 291–297 |
| Debrand-Passard et al. 1984 | S. Debrand-Passard – S. Courbouleix – M.-J. Lienhardt, Synthèse géologique du sud-est de la France I. Stratigraphie et paléogéographie, Mémoires du BRGM 125 (Orléans, 1984) |
| Dodelier 1847 | Ch. Dodelier, Un sarcophage gallo-romain à Mantoche (Vesoul 1847) |
| Espérandieu 1922 | É. Espérandieu, Recueil général des bas-reliefs, statues et bustes de la Gaule romaine, Gaule Germanique (deuxième partie) VIII (Paris 1922) |
| Faure-Brac 2002 | O. Faure-Brac, La Haute-Saône, Carte archéologique de la Gaule 70, Académie des Inscriptions et Belles-Lettres (Paris 2002) |
| Février 1993 | S. Février, Le mausolée gallo-romain de Faverolles (Haute-Marne), dans: A. Ferdière (éd.), Monde des vivants, monde des morts en Gaule rurale. Actes du colloque ARCHEA/AGER à Orléans, 07.–09.02.1992, RACFr Suppl. 6 (Tours 1993) 93–98 |
| Gaggadis-Robin 2005 | V. Gaggadis-Robin, Les sarcophages païens du musée d'Arles antique (Arles 2005) |
| Gasser 1898 | A. Gasser, Antiquités romaines de Mantoche, Bulletin de la Société Grayloise d'Émulation 1, 1898, 89–94 |
| Gasser 1900 | A. Gasser, La mosaïque et les ruines gallo-romaines de Mantoche, Bulletin de la Société Grayloise d'Émulation 3, 1900, 236–245 |
| Gasser 1901 | A. Gasser, Recherches archéologiques sur le territoire de Mantoche, Bulletin de la Société Grayloise d'Émulation 4, 1901, 165–284 |
| Ilingons | Y. Le Bohec, Inscriptions de la cité des Lingons. Inscriptions sur pierre (Paris 2003) |
| Joan 2016 | L. Joan, Bilan sur les nécropoles du Bas-Empire en Franche-Comté, dans: N. Arachard-Comparot – M. Kasprzyk, avec la collaboration de B. Fort (éds.), L'Antiquité tardive dans l'Est de la Gaule II. Sépultures, nécropoles et pratiques funéraires en Gaule de l'Est, RAE Suppl. 41 (Dijon 2016) 225–237 |
| Labre – Demesy 1986 | S. Labre – M. Demesy, Mantoche (Haute-Saône), dans: M. Mangin – B. Jacquet – J.-P. Jacquet (éds.), Les agglomérations secondaires de Franche-Comté (Paris 1986) 99–106 |
| Lequoy – Guillot 2004 | M.-C. Lequoy – B. Guillot, avec la collaboration de J. Le Maho, Rouen, Carte archéologique de la Gaule 76-2. Rouen (Paris 2004) |
| Lerat 1964 | L. Lerat, Besançon antique des origines à la fin du IV$^e$ siècle (Paris 1964) |
| Longchamps 1860 | Ch. Longchamps, Découvertes et observations archéologiques faites dans la Haute-Saône de 1842 à 1860, Mémoires de la Commission Archéologique de la Haute-Saône II (Vesoul 1860) |
| Marnotte 1847 | P. Marnotte, Mémoire sur divers objets d'antiquité trouvés à Mantoche, près de Gray, Actes de l'Académie de Besançon, séance du 28 janvier 1847, 97–102 |
| Martet 1956 | J. Martet, La Haute-Saône à travers l'histoire (Vesoul 1956) |
| Mouton 1878 | Abbé Mouton, Histoire d'Autrey, de sa seigneurie, de ses environs (Gray 1878) |
| Nouvel 2016 | P. Nouvel, Entre ville et campagne, formes de l'occupation et élites gallo-romaines dans le Centre-est de la Gaule. Apport de 20 années de prospections et de fouilles archéologiques, Habilitation à diriger des recherches, Université de Bourgogne-Franche-Comté (Besançon 2016) |

| | |
|---|---|
| Petit – Mangin 1994 | J.-P. Petit – M. Mangin, Atlas des agglomérations secondaires de la Gaule Belgique et des Germanies (Paris 1994) |
| Poly 1897 | F. Poly, La Haute-Saône sous la domination des Romains. 1ère partie: les voies romaines, Bulletin de la Société d'agriculture, lettres, sciences et arts de la Haute-Saône 28, 3e série, 1897, 1–138 |
| Potier 2022 | F. Potier, Un *aureus* de Didia Clara découvert à Mantoche (Haute-Saône) en 1822, BNumParis 77/6, 2022, 213–219 |
| Rothé – Heijmans 2008 | M.-P. Rothé – M. Heijmans, Arles, Crau, Camargue, Carte archéologique de la Gaule 13-5 (Paris 2008) |
| RSK | B. Galsterer – H. Galsterer, Die römischen Steininschriften aus Köln (Cologne 1975) |
| Thévenin 2006 | A. Thévenin, Le XIXe s. et les débuts de la recherche archéologique en Haute-Saône, dans: L. Baray (éd.), Artisanats, sociétés et civilisations. Hommage à Jean-Paul Thévenot. Actes du colloque organisé par l'UMR 5594, Dijon, et le Centre de Recherche et d'Étude du Patrimoine (CEREP), Sens 02.–03.04.2003, RAE Suppl. 24, 2006, 11–29 |
| Venault – Nouvel 2014 | St. Venault – P. Nouvel, Projet collectif de recherche, Agglomérations antiques de Bourgogne, Franche-Comté et Champagne méridionale, inventaire archéologique, cartographie et analyses spatiales, rapport d'activité 2014 (Besançon 2014) |
| Walter 1974 | H. Walter, La sculpture funéraire gallo-romaine en Franche-Comté, Annales littéraires de l'Université de Besançon 176 (Paris 1974) |

*Nicolas Delferrière, enseignant contractuel en histoire de l'art et archéologie antique, département d'histoire de l'art et d'archéologie, Université Clermont-Auvergne, Site Gergovia, 29, bd Gergovia, TAS 20406, 63001 Clermont-Fd Cedex 1, France.*
*[e] nicolas.delferriere@hotmail.fr*

*Anne-Laure Edme, responsable de recherches archéologiques à l'Inrap Grand-Est (Châlons-en-Champagne), chercheuse associée à l'UMR 6298 ARTEHIS, 15 rue de Valmy, 51000 Châlons-en-Champagne, France.*
*[e] anne-laure.edme@inrap.fr*

Anne-Laure Edme

## »TIME OF CHANGE«: LE TRAITEMENT DES MONUMENTS PAÏENS À L'HEURE DE L'ESSOR DU CHRISTIANISME

**Abstract**
Although ancient *spolia* have been the subject of much research for more than a century, especially on the occasion of the colloquium organized in Arles in 2016, their variety is such that it is now possible to envisage new studies. Indeed, the nature of these sculptures, their period of employment and the form they take are very varied. Valuable testimonies show that the reuse of ancient sculptures with a cult and funerary significance occurred early on, probably from the moment when Christianity superseded paganism. *Castra* and *necropoleis* are exceptional conservators of reused sculptures. Archives and museum collections are also rich in clues regarding this phenomenon. Although only a few of the contexts can be dated with certainty to Late Antiquity, they are of considerable interest. To what extent did the change in rites and beliefs affect the shape of funeral monuments? What treatment was then inflicted on pagan monuments?

## INTRODUCTION

Il n'existe pas de récit unique de la fin du »paganisme«. C'est un processus complexe qui voit divers cultes évoluer dans des directions différentes selon les régions et les populations. Ainsi, entre la déclaration de Constantin en 313 faisant du christianisme une religion autorisée et l'édit de Théodose en 380 déclarant le christianisme religion d'Etat, la société romaine a été profondément remaniée tout en conservant plusieurs éléments culturels et institutionnels issus de son passé païen. De plus, de nombreuses recherches ont démontré l'importance des facteurs régionaux et des politiques locales dans la compréhension de l'évolution des cultes non chrétiens, notamment dans l'Est de l'Empire[1].

Dès le début du IVe siècle s'est amorcé un processus de déconsécration des monuments et des objets – c'est-à-dire de conversion d'un élément païen en objet chrétien[2]. La Maison Carrée de Nîmes en est un parfait exemple, puisque ce temple dédié à la famille impériale est entre autres devenu une église, sauvant ce monument de la destruction. Ce phénomène de déconsécration a également parfois été complété par une exécration, soit la réduction à un usage non religieux d'un objet ou d'un monument[3], entraînant une perte du caractère sacré. Le bûchage de certains reliefs et l'apposition de croix sur des sculptures de divinités ou de membres de la famille impériale sont parmi les moyens classiquement employés pour exécrer ces images[4]. Ces différents phénomènes expliquent la différence de traitement qu'ont pu subir les monuments du Haut Empire à partir du IVe siècle, allant d'une conservation quasi parfaite à une totale disparition[5]. Ce type de destruction

---

[1] Notamment Testard 1988; Boglioni 2008; Creissen 2014.
[2] Le Goff 1977a, 223–235.
[3] Boglioni 2008, 75–76.
[4] Le XVIe livre du Code Théodosien présente divers textes traitant de l'interdiction des cultes païens, certains réclamant la purification des idoles païennes par l'imposition d'un signe chrétien. Ce fait est attesté par l'archéologie, puisque plusieurs têtes de divinités ou de membres de la famille impériale ont ainsi subi une retouche durant l'Antiquité tardive. Cette retaille a consisté en l'apposition d'une croix chrétienne sur le visage sculpté (tête de déesse, Musée archéologique de Vathi à Samos; tête d'Aphrodite d'après Praxitèle, Musée archéologique national d'Athènes; statues d'Auguste et de Livie, Musée d'Ephèse à Selçuk; buste de Germanicus, British Museum). Voir Dierkens 2008; Creissen 2014, 280; Brown 2016.
[5] Le remploi de blocs architecturés comme d'éléments statuaires en simple matériaux de construction est bien documenté (Davoine 2018). Retaille et insertion dans les *castra* pour certains, alors que d'autres étaient destinés à

d'objets ou de lieux de culte païens est décrit notamment par Sulpice Sévère dans la biographie de Martin de Tours: »Il [Martin] retourna donc au village et, tandis que les foules païennes le regardaient, sans bouger, démolir jusqu'aux fondations cet édifice impie, il réduisit en poussière tous les autels et les statues«[6]. De nombreux lieux de culte chrétiens ont ainsi été bâtis sur les vestiges de temples païens détruits pour faire place nette[7], bien que les témoignages archéologiques d'une telle pratique en Gaule soient très rares[8]. Certaines de ces destructions dénotent une réelle volonté de démontrer la »victoire d'une religion sur une autre, désormais totalement soumise«[9]. La montée en puissance des communautés chrétiennes, puis l'adoption du christianisme comme religion unique ont entraîné tout un ensemble de transformations au sein de la société romaine, y compris dans les domaines privés[10]. Toutes les régions de l'Empire ont été touchées, à des degrés différents, par ces phénomènes tant religieux que culturels.

Il est particulièrement intéressant d'observer le traitement spécifique apporté aux monuments de l'*Urbs*. En effet, les textes et inscriptions démontrent une réelle volonté de préservation des édifices païens dans le temps, bien que leurs activités initiales aient cessé[11]. On ne dénote donc pas d'acharnement religieux contre les monuments de Rome, les destructions sporadiques étant dues à des incendies ou des actes de remplois[12]. La conversion des temples païens de Rome en édifices à vocation chrétienne n'est attestée qu'à partir de 609, au moment de la transformation du Panthéon en l'église Sancta Maria ad Martyres. L'appropriation de l'espace sacré païen a tout d'abord été économique, mesurée et progressive avant d'être purement culturelle – en lien avec le respect dû au patrimoine historique commun[13]. C'est bien par la pratique du remploi opportuniste des pierres des édifices anciens que le paganisme en tant que religion a finalement disparu.

L'art funéraire a ainsi subi des transformations importantes au cours du IVe siècle, que ce soit en terme de formes, de modèles ou de mises en œuvre. Si dans un premier temps les chrétiens ont refusé les images, tant par volonté de se démarquer que par manque de finances, ils se sont progressivement mis à en employer, en premier lieu en contexte funéraire. Les thèmes et modèles iconographiques gréco-romains se sont vus réarrangés afin de correspondre aux nouvelles croyances, ce qui a permis la création de nouveaux langages iconographiques. Les symboles païens ont été réinterprétés pour correspondre au paradigme chrétien[14]. C'est de cette manière que la figure de l'Hermès Criophore a servi d'inspiration à l'image du Bon Pasteur et que le Christ barbu ressemble fortement à un philosophe grec. Les scènes païennes étant plus considérées comme culturelles que cultuelles, leur réinterprétation a permis d'exprimer de nouvelles croyances tout en s'inscrivant dans la continuité de la culture gréco-romaine. La même observation peut être faite

---

nourrir les nombreux fours à chaux nécessaires aux travaux permanents des villes. Ainsi entre 2007 et 2014, une quarantaine de statues de divinités ont été mises au jour dans le Rhône à Arles: destinés à un four à chaux, ces éléments et le chariot qui les contenait auraient été emportés par une crue soudaine du fleuve, sauvant ainsi ces sculptures de la destruction (Long 2016, 35–37).

[6] Sulp. Sev. 14, 6.
[7] Creissen 2014, 280. L'idée d'une purification de l'espace est d'ailleurs évoquée par Eusèbe de Césarée lorsqu'il narre la destruction par Constantin d'un sanctuaire à Aphrodite à Jérusalem pour y installer le complexe du Saint-Sépulcre (Eus. Caes. Const. 3, 25–30).
[8] Creissen 2014, 282–286.
[9] Ceissen 2014, 280. Thomas Creissen parle même de »remplois de relégation« pour évoquer les éléments lapidaires pris aux temples païens et remployés de manière parfois humiliante dans les espaces chrétiens. Les pierres du Marneion de Gaza ont ainsi été récupérées en 402 lors de la destruction du temple et installées pour paver le sol de la cour d'accès à l'église »afin que les hommes mais aussi les chiens et les cochons puissent les piétiner« (Caillet 1996, 195–196).
[10] Ratti 2012.
[11] Amiri 2015, 112–114.
[12] En 458, l'empereur Majorien rappelle au préfet de Rome la nécessité de préserver les monuments païens récupérés par des particuliers pour bâtir à moindre coût de nouveaux édifices (Novell. Maior. 4).
[13] Amiri 2015, 115–116: »Le souci patrimonial de l'*Urbs* païenne constitue une constante de la politique impériale depuis Constantin, sans cesse réaffirmée, en dépit du zèle chrétien de la plupart des dirigeants impériaux.«
[14] Testard 1988, 143.

pour les figures d'Orphée, Ulysse et Sol qui sont associés au Christ. Même chose encore dans le domaine architectural, les premières églises reprenant le plan des basiliques romaines. Le choix de ce type de bâtiment résulte encore une fois d'une volonté forte de se démarquer des païens et de leurs temples. De plus, la »Maison de Dieu« étant ouverte à tous, contrairement aux temples païens réservés aux prêtres, le modèle de la basilique était plus adapté à l'accueil d'un grand nombre de fidèles.

Si de nouveaux monuments funéraires sont créés ou réinventés selon ces nouveaux modèles, comme les catacombes ou les sarcophages, on peut aussi observer en Gaule une réutilisation des monuments du Haut Empire. Cette nouvelle vie donnée à des tombeaux préexistants va alors prendre des formes diverses qui résultent de deux principaux types d'action: une conservation en l'état ou une modification totale ou partielle. Notons que si ces réutilisations ont été enclenchées durant l'Antiquité tardive, elles ont connu un certain succès durant toute la période médiévale, avec un renouveau lors du siècle des Lumières et même une persistance jusqu'au XXe siècle[15]. Tous les exemples qui vont être présentés ici proviennent des territoires de l'Est de la Gaule, principalement des cités des Eduens, des Séquanes et des Lingons (fig. 1).

## DE LA CONSERVATION DE L'OBJET ...

La première de ces actions consiste donc à conserver le monument dans son état d'origine. L'emploi qui peut ensuite en être fait est variable mais il a pu être observé que les remplois de ce type restent globalement cantonnés à l'enceinte des nécropoles et des cimetières.

La nécropole de Pont l'Evêque à Autun (Saône-et-Loire) a fait l'objet d'une fouille préventive en 2004[16]. A cette occasion, plus de 450 tombes à inhumation et à incinération ont été mises au jour, ainsi que près de 200 stèles dont 79 étaient complètes. Datées des IIe et IIIe siècles, ces stèles ont été découvertes en position secondaire. Si la majorité a été rejetée dans des fossés et des fosses dépotoirs, un certain nombre a été déposé à l'intérieur des fosses d'inhumation, à plat au-dessus du cercueil de bois aujourd'hui disparu[17] (fig. 2). La question d'un acte rituel ou symbolique se pose ici, ces stèles ayant pu avoir une fonction apotropaïque aux yeux des récupérateurs. De nombreuses hypothèses ont été émises quant à cette réutilisation spécifique des monuments funéraires du Haut Empire. Ainsi, l'acte rituel pourrait être lié à une confusion des figurations de défunts avec des images saintes, qui auraient alors été conservées comme des idoles protégeant l'âme des défunts chrétiens. La réouverture de la tombe dans l'optique d'une nouvelle inhumation d'un membre de la famille peut aussi avoir entraîné la dépose du monument du défunt primaire sur le cercueil de son descendant. De même, il est envisagé que ces monuments aient, au IVe siècle, été considérés comme de simples éléments architecturaux constitutifs de la tombe. Comme nous le verrons avec d'autres exemples, l'emploi de stèles comme couvercles ou encadrement de sarcophages est attesté sur plusieurs sites gallo-romains. Enfin, le dépôt de très nombreuses stèles dans des fosses dépotoirs peut résulter d'un phénomène de rejet, peut-être consécutif au changement de forme des tombeaux ou au refus plus catégorique de conservation des monuments païens. Le site de Pont-l'Evêque offre donc un très bon aperçu de certains traitements non destructeurs subis par les monuments païens au cours du IVe siècle.

Les fouilles menées depuis 2008 à Luxeuil-les-Bains (Haute-Saône) ont permis la mise au jour d'un ensemble de vestiges tant antiques que médiévaux (un quartier d'habitation romain occupé du Ier au IIIe siècle, une nécropole païenne du IVe siècle, une basilique funéraire paléochrétienne des Ve et VIe siècles, devenue monastique à l'époque mérovingienne et agrandie en 670 pour devenir la »Crypte de Saint-Valbert«)[18]. Ont notamment été découverts les vestiges médiévaux

---

[15] Edme 2019.
[16] Venault et al. 2009.
[17] Venault et al. 2009, 134–136.
[18] Bully et al. 2009; Bully 2010.

1   Carte de localisation des monuments évoqués (© A.-L. Edme d'après Fichtl 2004)

de l'église funéraire Saint-Martin de l'abbaye de Luxeuil, l'un des principaux monastères européens entre le VIIe et le Xe siècle. Ce sont environ 350 sépultures, dont 150 sarcophages de pierre, qui ont été mises au jour sur ce site archéologique de première importance. Le site se démarque également par le très grand nombre de sarcophages mérovingiens et leur très bon état de conservation. C'est au sein de cet ensemble qu'a été découverte une stèle funéraire antique en position de remploi, couchée sur une cuve de sarcophage pour en former le couvercle[19] (fig. 3 a). Si à Autun les stèles étaient couchées face décorée vers le haut, le soin a été pris à Luxeuil de placer la face sculptée vers l'intérieur de la cuve, comme si les personnages figurés regardaient le défunt. Le possible acte rituel observé à Autun se retrouve ici dans un contexte plus tardif d'un siècle puisque la stèle est associée à un sarcophage mérovingien.

---

[19]   Edme 2019, 109.

2  Autun, Pont-l'Evêque, stèles funéraires en position secondaire (tiré de Venault 2008, 212–214)

Les découvertes du XIXe siècle recensent à Beaune (Côte-d'Or) la mise au jour d'un sarcophage de plomb entouré par six stèles et un muret[20]. Comme le montre le dessin produit en 1819[21], les stèles étaient enterrées verticalement autour du sarcophage, faces sculptées tournées à nouveau vers le défunt (fig. 3 b). Nous avons ici un autre exemple d'une possible fonction apotropaïque accordée à ces monuments funéraires du Haut Empire.

Un autre type de remploi de monument antique par une population chrétienne est visible dans l'église Saint-Pierre de Moirans (Isère)[22]. Construite au XIIe siècle, elle possède deux remplois de sarcophages du IIe siècle. Le premier est localisé dans le chœur de l'église, au sein d'un ensemble de sarcophages mérovingiens et carolingiens. Intact mais apparemment privé de son couvercle, c'est ici sa fonction initiale qui a perduré. L'épitaphe originelle n'a été ni bûchée ni même modifiée pour correspondre aux nouveaux occupants du tombeau[23] (fig. 4 a). Seule modification notable, l'ajout d'une cloison faite de blocs calcaires délimitant un caisson où les réductions de plusieurs individus ont été découverts. Nous reviendrons un peu plus loin sur le second sarcophage.

Le hameau de Sens, dépendant de la commune de Sennecy-le-Grand (Saône-et-Loire), conserve ce qui est peut-être le plus ancien lieu de culte chrétien en élévation en France. En effet, la chapelle Saint-Médard est datée du IVe siècle et conserve dans ses murs un sarcophage

---

[20] Provost 2009, 54–55.
[21] Charlot 1991, 68; Edme 2019, 106.
[22] Diverrez et al. 2012; Depierre et al. 2016.
[23] Ces deux sarcophages et leur inscription ont fait l'objet d'une étude de notre part, à paraître.

3  Stèles remployées à Luxueil-les-Bains (© S. Bully) et Beaune (tiré de Charlot 1991)

du IIIe siècle. Il est positionné dans le mur extérieur sud, au niveau du décroché formé par la jonction du chœur hémisphérique avec la nef quadrangulaire. C'est l'angle du sarcophage qui forme ce décroché à la base du mur (fig. 5). Le couvercle est quant à lui posé à quelques mètres de la chapelle et associé à une autre cuve – fragmentaire et de dimensions différentes[24]. Cet assemblage forme une petite fontaine que la tradition veut miraculeuse. Le remploi de ce sarcophage est difficile à dater mais sa position actuelle semble très ancienne – peut-être dès la construction de la chapelle au IVe siècle. Seule certitude, le remploi est antérieur au XIXe siècle, puisque Marcel Canat a vu le sarcophage à son emplacement actuel dans le mur extérieur vers 1855 et ne l'a pas indiqué comme récemment accompli[25]. L'usage de remployer des blocs antiques comme pierres à bâtir est particulièrement bien documenté, puisqu'il s'agit de l'une des réutilisations les plus couramment observées en Gaule romaine[26].

## … À SA TRANSFORMATION

Le second sarcophage antique mis au jour dans l'église de Moirans (Isère) est un très bon exemple de modification d'un monument païen au sein d'un édifice chrétien (fig. 4 b). Bien que plus tardif, car daté du Moyen âge classique, ce remploi reprend les codes introduits lors de l'érection des *castra* au cours de l'Antiquité tardive. Le sarcophage a été partiellement retaillé au niveau des petits côtés, puis comblé de blocaille et de mortier afin de servir de base à l'un des piliers de la nef. L'inscription a été laissée lisible puisque non altérée et tournée vers la nef[27]. Seules les deux

---

[24] Edme 2019, 110–111.
[25] Canat 1857, 254.
[26] Le colloque organisé à Arles en 2016 traitait de cette problématique et a permis de réunir de nombreux travaux portant sur cette thématique. Voir Gaggadis-Robin – Larquier 2016.
[27] Rémy 2004, 343.

dernières lignes, cachées par le pavage, sont restées inédites jusqu'aux fouilles menées dès 2002. Notre étude à paraître des sarcophages de Moirans restitue l'inscription complète et en fournit une interprétation approfondie.

Comme nous l'avons rappelé, les très nombreux *castra* construits durant l'Antiquité tardive ont conservé des blocs antiques remployés jusqu'à leur démontage quasi-systématique à partir du XIXe siècle. Les collections muséales de Dijon (Côte-d'Or), Langres (Haute-Marne), Sens (Yonne) – pour ne citer que celles-là – sont composées en grande partie de blocs issus de ces démantèlements. Il s'agit à la fois de fragments de décor, d'architecture et d'inscriptions. Tous ou presque ont subi une retaille visant à éliminer

4   Deux sarcophages en remploi dans l'église de Moirans (© A.-L. Edme)

les parties les plus saillantes des reliefs. De plus, les blocs les plus grands ont été fractionnés afin d'être plus facilement insérés dans les murailles. La conservation en l'état de certains murs de remparts antiques permet une bonne compréhension des techniques mises en place pour ces remplois. Malgré les importantes modifications apportées à ces blocs sculptés et inscrits, il est intéressant de noter que les récupérateurs ont souvent fait le choix d'exposer les faces sculptées aux yeux des passants[28]. Cette pratique pourrait être liée à une volonté de mise en évidence de la richesse culturelle de l'Empire à un moment de grands bouleversements politiques.

Un sarcophage en marbre blanc, trouvé anciennement dans l'une des nécropoles d'Autun (Saône-et-Loire), atteste par son décor de deux emplois successifs. Le premier usage est datable du IIe siècle par son décor évoquant une scène de sacrifice. Ce sarcophage a ensuite été réutilisé à la fin du IVe siècle pour une défunte chrétienne. Une inscription a été ajoutée sur une des faces de la cuve, qui a conservé sa fonction originelle[29]. Il est intéressant de mettre cette découverte en lien avec les fouilles menées par l'équipe de Carole Fossurier en 2020 dans la nécropole paléochrétienne de Saint-Pierre l'Etrier, d'où provient ce fragment[30]. En effet, plusieurs sarcophages chrétiens, en pierre et en plomb, y ont été mis au jour. Cette nécropole, active entre le IIIe et le Ve siècle, est restée longtemps dans les mémoires, car plusieurs mausolées étaient encore visibles au XVIIIe siècle – dont certains renfermaient des sarcophages de marbre. La nécropole accueillait

---

[28] Edme 2019, 105–106.
[29] CIL XIII 2718: *Eufronia Euf[r(oni)] / filia et m[at(er)] / naufragio [e]/necta nat[a] / pri(die) Kal(endas) No[v(embre)] / percepit / III Id(us) April(es) / decessit pri(die) Kal(endas) Mai(as).*
[30] Labaune 2020. Le rapport de fouille est à paraître.

5   Le sarcophage de Sens, commune de Sennecey-le-Grand (© A.-L. Edme; dessin tiré de Canat 1857, pl. 10)

ainsi des sépultures chrétiennes parmi les plus anciennes de la moitié nord de la Gaule; en provient d'ailleurs l'une des premières mentions du Christ en Gaule, avec l'inscription de Pectorius, datée du IVe siècle et mise au jour en 1839[31].

La petite église de Griselles (Côte-d'Or) conserve dans sa crypte un témoignage rare de réutilisation d'un sarcophage antique datable de l'époque paléochrétienne. Les études menées suite à deux campagnes de fouilles dans la crypte[32] ont conclu à la réutilisation à des fins chrétiennes au VIe siècle d'un mausolée antique et de son sarcophage, eux-mêmes datables de la seconde moitié du IIe siècle. Le site est connu comme étant un lieu de pèlerinage organisé autour de la tombe du saint ermite Valentin et visité de manière continue, depuis sa création à la fin du VIe siècle jusqu'au XIXe siècle. Le développement du culte des saints au plus près de leur lieu d'inhumation est attesté dès la fin du IVe siècle, et se caractérise bien souvent par un fort élan bâtisseur au profit de basiliques suburbaines dédiées à des martyrs ou des religieux considérés comme des modèles de sainteté. A Griselles, les trois éléments constitutifs du tombeau sont issus de remplois: la cuve

---

[31] Garrucci 1856, 32–47.
[32] Sapin – Deflou-Leca 2001.

6   Le sarcophage de Sabinus à Griselles (© A.-L. Edme)

portant l'épitaphe de Sabinus provient du mausolée originel du IIe siècle; le couvercle était initialement associé à une autre cuve antique et le ›sur-couvercle‹ médiéval provient certainement d'un aménagement postérieur du tombeau (fig. 6). De nombreuses traces de retailles sont d'ailleurs visibles sur les différents composants du sépulcre. La partie supérieure de la cuve a été tronquée, ce qui est attesté par la disparition des premières lignes de l'épitaphe, le couvercle ayant quant à lui été retaillé pour correspondre aux dimensions de la cuve. Les calcaires constitutifs de ces deux éléments sont différents, ce qui pourrait démontrer qu'ils ne fonctionnaient pas ensemble à l'origine. Le couvercle a subi deux retailles successives: la première visant à l'adapter à la taille de la cuve, qui est plus petite, la seconde pour l'installation, probablement au XVe siècle, du ›sur-couvercle‹ du XIIe/XIII[e] siècle. Outre la mise en scène du tombeau ainsi créé, il est intéressant de noter la pérennité de la fonction funéraire des différents monuments qui le composent. Ces derniers ont été spécifiquement choisis pour recréer le tombeau originel du saint et l'embellir.

Les collections muséales de Langres (Haute-Marne) et Avallon (Yonne) possèdent chacune une stèle romaine recreusée pour en faire un sarcophage. Si le fragment d'Avallon est très lacunaire et ne présente plus qu'une partie du décor latéral végétalisé, la stèle de Langres nous est parvenue complète (fig. 7 a). Tout le cadre architecturé du monument a été conservé et seule la partie centrale, où figurait la représentation du défunt, a subi une retaille[33]. La stèle a été profondément évidée à l'époque mérovingienne pour être transformée en cuve de sarcophage. Le même traitement a dû être appliqué à la stèle d'Avallon avant sa destruction dans un troisième temps.

Un exemple assez similaire provient d'une découverte fortuite faite à Tanay (fig. 7 b), près de Mirebeau-sur-Bèze (Côte-d'Or)[34]. Là aussi, nous sommes en présence d'une stèle dont le cœur a été creusé dans un second temps pour devenir un sarcophage. Le creusement n'est pas aussi profond qu'à Langres en raison de la faible épaisseur de la stèle. Contrairement aux exemples précédents, seul l'espace nécessaire à l'installation d'un corps a été aménagé, ce qui a permis une relative conservation du décor original. Ce monument était dédié à un couple, le côté extérieur des têtes étant encore visible. L'inscription a quant à elle été gravée sur la face latérale gauche

---

[33] Royer 1931, 72. Mise au jour au grand séminaire de Langres, la stèle est aujourd'hui conservée au musée d'art et d'histoire Guy Baillet (inv. R2006.1.97).
[34] Edme 2019, 109.

et permet de dater la stèle du IIe siècle. Il est intéressant de constater que ce monument a subi une seconde retouche – comme à Avallon – puisqu'il a été fracturé en neuf fragments. Il n'est malheureusement pas possible de caractériser ce geste, qui pourrait être dû à une réouverture de la tombe mérovingienne, peut-être en lien avec une action de pillage.

Le phénomène de remploi des blocs païens antiques, amorcé dès le IVe siècle, s'est poursuivi au fil des siècles, parfois assorti d'une retaille fonctionnelle ou cultuelle – comme à Saint-Pierre-de-Varennes en Saône-et-Loire (fig. 8). Le tympan de l'église présente deux stèles funéraires qui ont subi une retouche afin que les personnages figurés s'adaptent aux saints dédicataires du lieu: Marie (en position d'orant) et Saint Pierre (tenant une clé). Les traitements infligés aux monuments païens sont nombreux

7   Les stèles retaillées de Langres et Tanay (© A.-L. Edme)

et variés et il n'est pas rare de rencontrer des blocs insérés anciennement dans des murs, que ce soit au sein des églises, des châteaux ou des demeures privées[35]. Si c'est bien souvent pour une raison esthétique ou fonctionnelle, quelques exemples dénotent une volonté divergente. Les exemples de Gaule romaine tendent à démontrer un changement progressif des mœurs religieuses – sans réel conflit. Les monuments païens sont plus volontiers réutilisés que détruits, probablement pour des raisons économiques, et il n'est pas rare de voir des chrétiens se faire inhumer dans ou avec une stèle funéraire païenne[36]. L'appropriation et la transformation des monuments païens s'est le plus souvent fait sans heurts ni violence, sur un laps de temps plus ou moins long. »A charge pour la culture partagée par chacun de se constituer en un lieu de passage d'un monde à l'autre«[37].

Les études portant sur les rapports entre la culture cléricale et la culture folklorique à l'époque mérovingienne[38] ont démontré qu'au moins trois lignes de conduites distinctes peuvent partiellement être perçues dans le traitement des monuments: la destruction, l'oblitération et la dénatu-

---

[35]   Edme 2019.
[36]   A noter que les travaux de Nicole Belayche concluent à la difficulté de tracer une évolution linéaire du *ratio* entre païens et chrétiens, notamment en raison des rapports de force très variables à l'échelle locale (Belayche 2009, 193). Rome est à ce titre le symbole de cette divergence de traitement local des vestiges païens au sein de la nouvelle culture romaine chrétienne.
[37]   Amiri 2015, 116.
[38]   Le Goff 1977a; Le Goff 1977b.

ration. En effet, le refus de la culture folklorique passe bien souvent par l'une de ces catégories, mais il est à noter qu'elles sont souvent complémentaires et même associées à des phénomènes plus tempérés[39]. Si la pratique de nourrir les fours à chaux avec des fragments de monuments anciens est bien attestée, il est presque impossible de connaître la nature de ces monuments et de voir dans cette action une volonté religieuse plutôt qu'opportuniste. La même observation peut être faite pour les *spolia* et les remplois divers qui permettent une économie de la pierre en circuit fermé. Bien que des textes anciens évoquent les nombreuses destructions de monuments païens par les chrétiens, il est important de rappeler que beaucoup de ces récits sont hagiographiques et recèlent donc une part non négligeable d'exagérations et d'inventions[40]. Les traces archéologiques de fondations d'églises sur des vestiges de temples sont ainsi très rares, les structures romaines étant souvent multiples et non pas purement religieuses. La réappropriation d'un même lieu peut avoir des motifs divers et il a été démontré que beaucoup de ces sites avaient connu une période d'abandon avant d'être réoccupés par un monument chrétien[41]. Il s'agit dont bien d'un phénomène polymorphe et complexe qui a évolué différemment en fonction des contextes et des lieux.

8   Le tympan de l'église de Saint-Pierre-de-Varennes (© A.-L. Edme)

En revanche, les exemples que nous avons évoqués attestent d'une certaine oblitération – soit une superposition d'éléments chrétiens à des prédécesseurs païens – ainsi que d'une dénaturation – c'est-à-dire un changement radical de signification et d'utilisation[42]. Comme l'a parfaitement démontré Pietro Boglioni, »dans la réalité des situations concrètes, [ces catégories] se présentent à nous comme entremêlées dans une variété de synthèses originales, qui comportaient à la fois destruction de certains éléments de la culture païenne antérieure, ›récupération orientée‹[43] d'autres, et dénaturation proprement dite, dans un processus original qu'on pourrait appeler

---

[39] Boglioni 2008, 77.
[40] Creissen 2014, 287. C'est notamment le cas du récit que Sulpice Sévère fait des campagnes de destruction de saint Martin.
[41] Creissen 2014, 284–287.
[42] Boglioni 2008, 75–76.
[43] Une lettre de Grégoire le Grand à Augustin, en mission en Angleterre et retranscrite par Bède le Vénérable, présente les verbes *inmutare* et *commutare,* soit deux termes signifiant »transformer« (Bed. Ven. 1, 30).

de ›récupération re-sémantisante‹«[44]. De même, bien que l'idée d'une politique agressive des chrétiens envers les païens ait été véhiculée depuis très longtemps, les études historiques et archéologiques – dans la lignée desquelles cette analyse s'inscrit – tendent au contraire à démontrer une lente et progressive transformation de la société passant à la fois par une acceptation d'une nouvelle religion et l'incorporation d'éléments païens et folkloriques au sein de celle-ci[45].

## BIBLIOGRAPHIE

| | |
|---|---|
| Amiri 2015 | B. Amiri, Temples et cultes païens dans la Rome chrétienne: modalités d'appropriation et de transformation, dans: S. Ratti (éd.), Une Antiquité tardive noire ou heureuse? Actes du colloque de Besançon 12.–13.11.2014, ISTA 1332 (Besançon 2015) 105–117 |
| Bed. Ven. | Bède le Vénérable, Histoire ecclésiastique du peuple anglais (Paris 1999) |
| Belayche 2009 | N. Belayche, *Ritus* et *cultus* ou *superstitio*? Comment les lois du Code Théodosien (IX & XVI) de Constantin à Théodose parlent des pratiques religieuses traditionnelles, dans: S. Crogiez-Pétrequin – P. Jaillette (éds.), Traduire le Code théodosien (Rome 2009) 191–208 |
| Boglioni 2008 | P. Boglioni, Du paganisme au christianisme: la mémoire des lieux et des temps, Archives de sciences sociales des religions 144 (Paris 2008) 75–92 |
| Brown 2016 | A. R. Brown, Crosses, Noses, walls, and wells: Christianity and the fate of sculpture in late antique Corinth, dans: T. M. Kristensen – L. Stirling (éds.), The afterlife of Greek and Roman sculpture: late antique responses and practices (Ann Arbor 2016) 150–176 |
| Bully et al. 2009 | S. Bully – L. Fiocchi – A. Baradat – M. Čaušević-Bully – A. Bully – M. Dupuis – D. Vuillermoz, L'église Saint-Martin de Luxeuil-les-Bains (Haute-Saône). Première campagne, Bucema 13 (Auxerre 2009) 33–38 |
| Bully 2010 | S. Bully, L'église Saint-Martin de Luxeuil-les-Bains (Haute-Saône). Deuxième campagne, Bucema 14 (Auxerre 2010) 39–43 |
| Caillet 1996 | J.-P. Caillet, La transformation en église d'édifices publics et de temples à la fin de l'Antiquité, dans: C. Leppeley (éd.), La fin de la cité antique et le début de la cité médiévale: de la fin du IIIe siècle à l'avènement de Charlemagne. Actes du colloque de Paris-X-Nanterre 01.–03.04.1993, Edipuglia (Bari 1996) 191–211 |
| Canat 1857 | J.-P. Caillet, La transformation en église d'édifices publics et de temples à la fin de l'Antiquité, dans: C. Leppeley (éd.), La fin de la cité antique et le début de la cité médiévale: de la fin du IIIe siècle à l'avènement de Charlemagne. Actes du colloque de Paris-X-Nanterre 01.–03.04.1993, Edipuglia (Bari 1996) 191–211 |
| Charlot 1991 | M. Charlot, La station gallo-romaine des Maladières à Beaune (Côte-d'Or), Société d'histoire et d'archéologie de Beaune 72 (Beaune 1991) 63–72 |
| Creissen 2014 | T. Creissen, La christianisation des lieux de culte païens: »assassinat«, simple récupération ou mythe historiographique?, dans: W. Van Andringa (éd.), La fin des dieux, Gallia 71/1, 2014, 279–287 |
| Davoine 2018 | Ch. Davoine, Encadrer le remploi. Destruction des édifices et réutilisation des matériaux dans les textes juridiques romains (Ier–IIIe siècle ap. J.-C.), Ædificare, Revue internationale d'histoire de la construction 2/4, 2018, 255–276 |
| Depierre et al. 2016 | G. Depierre – D. Bouquin – A. Badin de Montjoye, Ancienne église Saint-Pierre à Moirans, Rapport de fouille programmée 2011–2015 (Grenoble 2016) |
| Dierkens 2008 | A. Dierkens, *Aedes inlicitis rebus vacuas ne quis conetur evertere* (Cod. Theod. XVI, X, 18). Réflexions sur l'espace sacré en Gaule pendant l'Antiquité tardive et le Haut Moyen Âge, dans: A. Morelli – A. Dierkens (éds.), Topographie du sacré. L'emprise religieuse sur l'espace, Problèmes d'histoire des religions 18 (Bruxelles 2008) 71–89 |
| Diverrez et al. 2012 | F. Diverrez – M. Poulmarc'h – A. Schmitt, Nouvelles données sur les inhumations *ad sanctos* à l'époque moderne en milieu rural: le cas de l'église Saint-Pierre de Moirans |

---

[44] Boglioni 2008, 77.

[45] »On a cherché (›inventé‹ au sens archéologique du terme) des temples à détruire, des pratiques païennes à combattre, afin de pouvoir renouveler l'actualité du triomphe du christianisme, bien avant que la question ne devienne un dossier historiographique« (Sotinel 2004, 53).

| | |
|---|---|
| | (Isère), Bulletins et Mémoires de la Société d'anthropologie de Paris 24 (Paris 2012) 167–178 |
| Edme 2019 | A.-L. Edme, La seconde vie des sculptures antiques: le phénomène du remploi des monuments funéraires dans l'Est de la Gaule (cités des Eduens, des Lingons et des Séquanes), dans: Gaggadis-Robin – Larquier 2016, 105–120 |
| Eus. Caes. Const. | Eusèbe de Césarée, Vie de Constantin, trad. J.-P. Migne (Paris 1857) 909–1230 |
| Fichtl 2004 | S. Fichtl, Les peuples gaulois (Paris 2004) |
| Gaggadis-Robin – Larquier 2016 | V. Gaggadis-Robin – N. Larquier (de), La sculpture et ses remplois. Actes des IIe rencontres autour de la sculpture romaine 28.–29.10.2016 (Bordeaux 2019) |
| Garrucci 1856 | R. Garrucci, Nouvel examen de l'inscription grecque d'Autun, Mélanges d'épigraphie ancienne 1 (Paris 1856) |
| Labaune 2020 | Y. Labaune, Nécropole paléochrétienne de Saint-Pierre l'Etrier: projet de construction d'une maison individuelle – Autun, extra-muros, Saint-Pantaléon, hameau de Saint-Pierre l'Etrier, ruelle Saint-Pierre (Saône-et-Loire). Rapport de diagnostic archéologique, Service archéologique de la ville d'Autun (Autun 2020) |
| Le Goff 1977a | J. Le Goff, Culture cléricale et traditions folkloriques dans la civilisation mérovingienne, dans: J. Le Goff (éd.), Pour un autre Moyen Age (Paris 1977) 223–235 |
| Le Goff 1977b | J. Le Goff, Culture cléricale et culture folklorique au Moyen Age: Saint Marcel et le dragon, dans: Le Goff 1977a, 236–279 |
| Long 2016 | L. Long, Contextes d'identification et d'étude archéologique du César d'Arles, dans: V. Gaggadis-Robin – P. Picard (éds.), La sculpture romaine en Occident. Nouveaux regards. Actes des Rencontres autour de la sculpture romaine 09.–25.06.2012, Bibliothèque d'Archéologie Méditerranéenne et Africaine 20 (Arles 2016) 25–38 |
| Provost 2009 | M. Provost (éd.), La Côte d'Or, d'Allerey à Normier, Carte archéologique de la Gaule 21, 2 (Paris 2009) |
| Ratti 2012 | S. Ratti, Polémiques entre païens et chrétiens (Paris 2012) |
| Rémy 2004 | B. Rémy (éd.), Inscriptions latines de Narbonnaise V 2: Vienne, CNRS éditions (Paris 2004) |
| Royer 1931 | J. Royer, Catalogue du Musée de Langres, fondé et administré par la Société historique et archéologique (Langres 1931) |
| Sapin – Deflou-Leca 2001 | Ch. Sapin – N. Deflou-Leca, Saint-Valentin de Griselles: du culte érémitique à la fondation monastique, Mémoires de la Commission des Antiquités de la Côte-d'Or 39 (Dijon 2001) 75–126 |
| Sotinel 2004 | C. Sotinel, La disparition des lieux de culte païens en Occident. Enjeux et méthode, dans: M. Narcy – E. Rebillard (éds.), Hellénisme et christianisme (Villeneuve-d'Ascq 2004) 35–60 |
| Sul. Mart. | Sulpice Sévère, Vie de saint Martin, trad. J. Fontaine, I (Paris 1967) |
| Testard 1988 | M. Testard, Observations sur le passage du paganisme au christianisme dans le monde antique, BAssBudé 2 (Paris 1988) 140–161 |
| Venault 2008 | S. Venault, Autun – Saint-Pantaléon (Saône-et-Loire), Pont-l'Evêque, rapport de fouilles archéologiques, Inrap (Dijon 2008) |
| Venault et al. 2009 | S. Venault – S. Deyts – Y. Le Bohec – Y. Labaune (éds.), Les stèles funéraires de la nécropole de Pont-l'Évêque: Contextes de découverte et étude du corpus, BAParis (Paris 2009) 129–204 |

*Anne-Laure Edme, Responsable de recherches archéologiques, Inrap, UMR 6298 ARTEHIS, 15 rue de Valmy, 51000 Châlons-en-Champagne, France.*
*[e] anne-laure.edme@inrap.fr*

Nadežda Gavrilović Vitas

# LATE ANTIQUE MYTHOLOGICAL STATUARY IN THE ROMAN CENTRAL BALKANS

## ITS FUNCTION AND MEANING

**Abstract**
The period of Late Antiquity in the Roman Central Balkans, with the decline of paganism and the rise of Christianity, inevitably brought different views with regard to the mythological sculpture which adorned not only palatial complexes, *thermae* and important public buildings, but also private homes of prominent and wealthy citizens. Because of the symbolism that mythological sculptures carried, most of them were destroyed partially or completely in the 3rd and 4th centuries by the Christians or in some cases even pagans. Many statues were also broken, burnt or demolished in barbarian attacks to which the territory of the Roman Central Balkans was exposed, particularly by Hunnish troops from 441 onwards when many urban centres such as *Singidunum*, *Viminacium*, and *Naissus* were burnt and destroyed with the majority of the population killed. As in other Roman provinces, in the Roman Central Balkans as well mythological sculptures were mainly discovered in a decapitated and damaged state, with nude sculptures and statues suffering damage particularly in the areas of the face and genitalia. Although certainly some of the mythological statues were destroyed in barbarian attacks, destructions, wars, and fires, nonetheless damage to the majority of them can presumably be attributed to the Christians who demolished pagan imagery in their belief that they were expelling demons from them. In this manner, they were deprived of any symbolic meaning, and no longer represented any danger to the sacred order of Christianity.

The period of Late Antiquity in the Roman provinces of the Central Balkans is characterized by certain changes regarding statuary in general, with particular emphasis on mythological sculptures and statues due to their symbolism from the 3rd through the 4th and 5th centuries, when paganism was in decline and the burgeoning Christianity was becoming stronger and stronger. The appearance of stone sculpture in the territory of the Central Roman provinces is not so early – the first portraits, honorary, mythological and cult statues appear from the beginning of the 2nd century and coincide with the formation of the earliest Roman urban settlements which first gained the status of *municipia* and, later, colonies[1]. The earliest finds of stone sculptures produced in the provincial workshops are dated later, to the second half of the 2nd century. Sculptures known so far from the end of the 3rd century show that after the period of the so-called Military Emperors, the renewal of the work of provincial sculptors and workshops in centres like *Singidunum*, *Viminacium*, *Ulpiana* and numerous centres on the Limes coincided with the reign of Diocletian and lasted until the end of the 4th century[2].

The group of mythological and cult sculpture represents the most numerous group of statuary from the Central Balkans, including over 500 representations of deities and heroes mostly copying Greek sculpture of the Classical or Hellenistic period, particularly great art works from the Late Hellenistic epoch from the 2nd and 1st centuries BC. However, from the corpus of mythological statuary known thus far, it can be observed that the prevailing themes belonged to Greek and Eastern mythology and religions, while motives typical for Roman themes such as images of Janus, Romulus and Remus, Sabine women, etc. are not known. In contrast, statues of local

---

[1] Tomović 1993, 12.
[2] Tomović 1993, 32.

mythological deities and heroes, such as for instance the Thracian horseman or Dea Dardanica, are well known from the period of Late Antiquity[3]. Grouping the finds of mythological late antique statuary showed that in spite of its abundance, it was concentrated either in urban centres such as *Singidunum* or *Viminacium*, Limes fortifications or imperial complexes such as *Mediana* in *Naissus* and *Felix Romuliana*/Gamzigrad. This conclusion implies that mythological statues, of which some were at the same time cult statues as well, not only constituted part of the public scenery placed in open spaces, but were also part of the sanctuaries, shrines and private *lararia*. Unfortunately, only a small number of mythological sculptures and statues were found in their original context, which due to their damaged condition can be ascribed mainly to Christian or barbarian destruction. Thus, unfortunately, we cannot know where certain statues, such as Hercules with Telephos or Fortuna from *Viminacium*, were originally placed in Late Antiquity and later, or which functions they had in that period – whether they retained their cultic function or were purely part of the decoration of the building where they were placed. However, on certain statues, as in the cases of Aphrodite Sosandra, Hermes/Mercury and Hygieia from *Mediana, Naissus*[4], we can observe traces of modification which suggest a transformation of mythological or cult statues into portrait presentations. These changes, which encompassed re-carving, removing and adapting certain details of the statues, were directed towards the new function of the statues – transforming the cult statues into portrait statues, incorporating them into new locations such as civic spaces, baths, domestic contexts, etc. in which they were reused. This occurrence was typical particularly in the cities which developed extensively in the 3rd and the 4th century, for example antique *Naissus*, today's Niš, birth city of the emperor Constantine the Great.

With 32 marble and porphyry statues and many statuary fragments discovered so far, the well-known late antique suburb of *Naissus, Mediana* represents an excellent example of the aforementioned phenomenon. *Mediana* belonged to the imperial domain of emperor Constantine the Great, and underwent three building phases from the end of the 3rd century to the attack of the Huns in AD 441. The settlement comprises 20 objects identified to date, with the peristyle villa including *thermae* and monumental gate as the central and best studied building at *Mediana*, covering some 6,000 m². The mythological statues were unearthed at different locations and buildings at *Mediana* over almost one hundred years, from the first archaeological excavations in 1932, with the most important discovery from the archaeological campaign in 1972, when in one of the rooms of the peristyle villa, *cubiculum* w-4, a group of fragmented and mostly decapitated marble and porphyry statues were discovered, probably deliberately hidden from danger[5]. The group find of sculptures encompassed porphyry statues of Aesculapius and Hygieia (figs. 1. 2), marble statues of Aesculapius alone and the god with Telesphoros, marble statues of Hygieia, Aphrodite Sosandra/Europa/Helotia, a marble torso of Hermes/Mercury, Hercules with Telephos, Dea Dardania, a fragmented statuary composition of Drunken Dionysus with a Satyr, five fragments of sculptural compositions relating to the cult of Dionysus, and statuary fragments from the twelve labours of Hercules.

New finds from the following decades of archaeological research showed that some of the statues were destroyed in antiquity not only in the villa, but also outside the villa – in 2002 several sculptural fragments were discovered in trench 25A located at the north edge of the foundation wall of the »Gate-Arch«[6]. Among them was a marble fragment of a deity's head, identified as

---

[3] On the ›Thracian Rider‹ see Gavrilović Vitas, in press. On Dea Dardanica with previous bibliography cf. Vasić et al. 2016, 53. 94 fig. 16; 103. 104.

[4] The marble sculpture of Aphrodite Sosandra from *Mediana*, dating to the 2nd c., was modeled after the famous bronze statue of Aphrodite Sosandra by the sculptor Kalamis in 465 BC. The marble sculpture of Hermes/Mercury, dating to the end of the 2nd or the beginning of the 3rd c., represents a standing nude young man, with a draped himation over his left shoulder, while a marble sculpture of Hygieia, dating to the 1st half of the 3rd c., belongs to the iconographic type of the goddess standing, dressed in a long, pleated *chiton*, with presumably a *patera* in her left hand (the attribute is missing), Vasić et al. 2016, 87 figs. 5; 88 figs. 6. 7.

[5] Јовановић 1975, 57–66.

[6] M. Vasić thinks that the sculptural fragments were presumably thrown in a medieval burial pit in the Middle Ages (suggested by the fragments of medieval pottery discovered around the sculptural fragments), Vasić 2017,

1  Porphyry statue of Aesculapius from *Mediana* (photo Institute of Archaeology Belgrade)

2  Porphyry statue of Hygieia from *Mediana* (photo Institute of Archaeology Belgrade)

Aesculapius and dated from the middle of the 2nd to the first decade of the 3rd century. Besides these, other mythological statues were discovered in different locations and buildings at *Mediana*, such as a torso of Magna Mater (?), a head of a satyr, a head of a maenad and a head of Diana. Additionally, fragments of different marble and porphyry statues or statuary compositions were also discovered in different parts of the peristyle villa – in its garden and around it, probably discarded and scattered away from where they were originally placed[7]. Some of the statues were demolished and their fragments were found in completely different parts of the villa, as in the case of the statue of Venus with a dolphin, where the statue's head was found in the villa's northern part (in the north-western room w-1), while the statue's base with carved feet and a fragmented figure of a dolphin was excavated in trench 24A near the foundations of the gate, in the southern part of the villa[8]. Since some of the statues were covered with the debris layer of the collapsed roof

---

205–210 fig. 1–4. FTIR analysis of $CO_2$-3 groups was done on the Venus' head and on the base of the sculpture with carved feet and a fragmented figure of a dolphin, which showed that the fragments were carved from the same single marble block: Crnoglavac et al. 2013, 73–78.

[7] Vasić 2018, 92; Vasić – Gavrilović 2012, 137–149.

[8] Vasić – Gavrilović 2012, 139. 147; Crnoglavac et al. 2013, 73–78.

constructions of *stibadium* B, it is clear that they were damaged in the period following the villa's devastation and burning, either during the villa's destruction or perhaps by newly settled inhabitants in the fourth quarter of the 4th century[9]. A close resemblance to the find of a bronze fence with two rows of *cancelli* and herms with the heads of Aesculapius and Luna discovered at *Mediana* during the archaeological campaign in 2000 suggests itself: the parts of the fence were carefully deposited and buried in a rectangular pit, presumably, like the statues from room w-4 of the peristyle villa, hidden from some danger[10]. Although not fully preserved – because when reconstructed heads of Sol and Hygieia from two preserved herms were obviously missing, along with two more heads of unknown deities (presumably Diana and Dionysus [?]) –, the bronze fence was probably removed from its original place into the peristyle villa, presumably at the apsis entrance of the *stibadium* B, and buried in the ground before the *stibadium* B roof construction collapsed[11]. It was hidden with great care, either because of the symbolism of the deities represented on herms or because the fence was made of bronze and therefore was regarded as valuable. Judging by the way in which the fence was carefully deposited in the ground, it seems that it was considered as more precious than the marble statues which were decapitated and smashed into pieces before the villa's destruction in the 5th century (proved by archaeological stratigraphy)[12]. It seems that the nude sculptures which adorned different buildings at *Mediana* were perceived as particularly offensive and were therefore subjected to damage. This can be observed for example in the sculptural composition of the Drunken Dionysus with a Satyr, which was almost completely destroyed, similarly to nude statues from other provinces[13].

Analyzing the corpus of *Mediana*'s statues discovered so far, we can conclude that they are of different styles and were modelled in different periods. Some statues, such as the marble statue of Aesculapius with Telesphoros with the Greek inscription on its base, represent mediocre provincial work from the middle of the 4th century, while other statues, for example Aphrodite Sosandra or Hermes/Mercury, represent skilfully modelled works of art. Only two statues (Aphrodite Sosandra, maenad) are from the 2nd century, two statues (Hermes/Mercury and satyr with a panther) date to the beginning of the 3rd century, while most of the statuary belongs to the second half of the 3rd century and the period up to the 4th century. Besides two porphyry statues of Aesculapius and Hygieia with dedications in Greek by a certain Roimetalkes[14], it is certain that there were more porphyry statues, some of them representing the same deities (Aesculapius, Hygieia), to judge from the porphyry statuary fragments discovered in almost every archaeological campaign at *Mediana*.

---

[9] Vasić – Gavrilović 2012, 139.

[10] During the archaeological excavations in 2000, a bronze railing, consisting of *cancelli* (only three *cancelli* have been found) and herms with busts of the deities Aesculapius and Luna between them, was discovered north-west of the *thermae* of the peristyle villa. The parts of the fence allow it to be disassambled and reassembled. The fence consisted of two segments with a passage between them, with herms with heads of male deities on the left side of the fence and and herms with heads of goddesses on the fence's right side – the heads of Hygieia and Sol are missing, as are the heads of another divine pair (possibly Venus or Diana and Dionysus [?]): Vasić 2004, 79–85.

[11] Vasić 2018, 98.

[12] The newly installed people after AD 378, who inhabited only several rooms in the peristyle villa, cleaned the villa of rubble and sculptures, however they did not destroy the sculptures but deposited them in rooms (room w-4) or pits: Vasić 2018, 92.

[13] Sauer 2003, 31–32. The marble sculptural composition of the Drunken Dionysus with a Satyr was discovered in 1932 in the area of the *thermae* (north-western part of the peristyle villa) at *Mediana*. Only a base of rectangular shape with two pairs of feet – one placed on a ram's head – and fragments of a tree and a rock as well as the paws of a four-legged animal, probably a panther, are preserved. However, the reconstruction of the sculptural composition showed that it represented a nude standing drunken Dionysus, leaning on a naked satyr. The sculpture from *Mediana* is analogous to the Ludovisi Dionysus from the last decades of the 2nd c., which represents the standing naked Dionysus leaning with his left hand on the right arm of the smaller figure of a naked satyr, while behind the wine god is a tree and near his right leg a panther. The sculpture from *Mediana* is dated to the 2nd half of the 2nd c.: Gavrilović 2017, 193–203.

[14] Vasić et al. 2016, 84–85 figs. 1. 2, with previous literature.

The last fragmented sculptural find from the archaeological excavations at *Mediana*, in the area of the *thermae* in 2019, is again related to the iatric cults – this time to Hygieia, who was most probably represented by the white marble statue to which belongs a hand holding a *patera* with an egg in it[15].

What can we presume about the function of all the statues known so far from *Mediana*? As already mentioned, no building at *Mediana* is older than the end of the 3rd century, therefore statues dated to the period before the 3rd century were brought to the villa, to the *thermae* and to other buildings at *Mediana*. Since the second building phase of the villa, from AD 330 to 334 when Constantine visited Niš for the last time, represents the phase when the villa was reconstructed and lavishly decorated with more than 1,000 $m^2$ of mosaics, monumental marble columns, architectural sculpture, fresco painting, etc., it can be presumed that the majority of the statues arrived then. As in other imperial domains, they reflect the class and taste of the owner. Certainly, decorating the villa with sculptures presumably continued during Constans' reign, who also spent time in Niš, and possibly at *Mediana*, between AD 338 and 340. In that context, it can be presumed that the statuary collection from *Mediana* was formed from the 4th century onwards as a collection of sculptures and statues from different periods. The choice of mythological figures corresponds with the one known from late antique villas in the centres of the neighbouring provinces, such as *Sirmium* (Palace of Theodosius), but also from villas in more distant provinces such as the villa at Chiragan in south-western Gaul, the villa at Montmaurin, the Panaya Domus in Corinth, or the Villa Valdetorres de Jarama in Spain near Madrid, since the most frequent deities represented are Aesculapius, Hercules, Dionysus, Venus, and Diana[16]. As previously mentioned, two porphyry statues of Aesculapius and Hygieia discovered in room w-4 of the peristyle villa at *Mediana* contain votive inscriptions from a certain Roimetalkes, *vir perfectissimus*, and his wife Philippa[17], while on the marble statue of Aesculapius with Telesphoros is a votive inscription, also in Greek, dedicated by the god's priest[18]. Assuming that Roimetalkes was governor of Egypt during Constantine the Great's reign, he could have brought the porphyry statues from Egypt with him to *Naissus*[19]. All three cult statues were brought to *Mediana* presumably from some sanctuary of iatric deities, perhaps located in Thrace. The porphyry statues were modelled in Egypt most probably in the tetrarchic period. An interesting detail shows the attempt to erase Roimetalkes' name from the Hygieia porphyry statue, which implies the *damnatio memoriae* of an important imperial official and presumably the intention to reuse a cult statue as a purely decorative one. The hypothesis of a short-lived sanctuary of Aesculapius and Hygieia during Julian Apostata's reign at *Mediana* should be mentioned, which would be corroborated by the numerous statues and fragments of statues of the mentioned deities and the proximity of Niš spa near *Mediana* with its thermal springs[20]. However, no evidence confirming this hypothesis has been found so far, as for example votive offerings to deities in the shape of body parts, such as are usually discovered in Asklepieia throughout the Roman Empire. Thus, we can conclude that in Late Antiquity, the mythological statues which decorated *Mediana*'s buildings were not cult statues, but part of the domain's decoration and an expression of the *paideia*, the education and the taste of the owner[21].

The second imperial domain with mythological statues from Late Antiquity is *Felix Romuliana*, where fortifications, two temples, palaces and public buildings were built after the victory of Galerius over the Sarmatians, the Quadi and the Bastarni on the Danube, probably in AD 297[22].

---

[15] Documentation of the Institute of Archaeology Belgrade.
[16] Videbech 2015, 452. 474 n. 21; Stirling 2005, 30. 37. 179.
[17] Vasić et al. 2016, 84–85 figs. 1. 2.
[18] The inscription in Greek is placed on the base of the sculptural group of Aesculapius with Telesphoros and is translated as: »To the Saviour Aesculapius, Sim … priest«, Vasić et al. 2016, 86 fig. 3.
[19] Petrović 1994, 89.
[20] Vasić 2018, 93.
[21] Videbech 2015, 454.
[22] Srejović 2011a, 47.

3   Marble relief of Sleeping Ariadne (photo Institute of Archaeology in Belgrade)

After the emperor's death in Serdica in 311, *Felix Romuliana* was transformed into a fortified settlement which existed as such until the end of the 6th and the beginning of the 7th century[23]. Undisputable analogies can be drawn between the collections of mythological statues from *Mediana* and *Romuliana*, concerning the choice of deities such as Dionysus, Hercules, Aesculapius, Venus and others. The difference lies, however, in their different function – the mythological statues from *Romuliana* were part of Galerius' ideology and served to underline his connection with the divine father Jupiter, and the analogy between the emperor on the one hand and semi-gods such as Hercules, Dionysus and Aesculapius on the other hand, who also had a mortal mother and a divine father[24]. Galerius' identification with saviour deities, who after their victorious campaigns withdrew to Olympus, was also important for emphasizing a close connection between the emperor and Hercules and Dionysus on monuments in Thessaloniki, such as in the scene of sacrifice on Galerius' triumphal arch and on the small arch at the entrance to the octagon of the imperial palace. The fact that the heads of Jupiter's and Hercules' colossal statues, the decapitated statue of Aesculapius, six fragmented statues of Athena or Muses, Apollo's torso, presumably Dionysus' head, fragments of other porphyry and marble mythological statues and the damaged marble relief of Sleeping Ariadne (fig. 3) were all mainly found scattered in and around the palace and the *thermae*, suggests a similar destruction of the statues that were placed in the palace and the *thermae*, in the large temple dedicated to Jupiter and the Emperor (perhaps Hercules too) and in the small temple dedicated to Galerius' mother and the mountain deities (perhaps Magna Mater)[25]. Most of the statues were damaged probably during the 4th century, while some of them were discovered used as *spoliae* in commercial buildings from the 6th century, such as the representation of Sleeping Ariadne[26].

The heads of over life-size sculptures of Jupiter and Hercules (fig. 4) were discovered in the area around the large temple[27], where their statues were most probably placed. Near the head of

---

[23] Archaeological excavations refering to the period from the last quarter of the 4th to the beginning of the 7th c. show the existence of two phases – phase I (last quarter of the 4th–middle of the 5th c.) and phase II (middle of the 5th–beginning of the 7th c.). All the structures and buildings, as archaeological material from both phases show barbarization of the population, ruralization of the settlement and economy, emphasized military-defensive aspects and Christianization: Petković 2011, 189–199.

[24] Srejović 2011b, 159–166.

[25] More about the large and the small temple in *Felix Romuliana* and the statuary discovered in them in Čanak-Medić – Stojković-Pavelka 2011, 77–85; Живић 2015, 408–465.

[26] During the archaeological excavations in the *thermae* in 1993, a large part of the sculpture of the Sleeping Ariadne was discovered, while four years later in the same area three more fragments of the same sculpture (torso, lower part of Ariadne's body and a part of left shoulder and arm) were found. All the fragments were discovered in secondary use, as *spoliae* in the building from the 6th c.: Лаловић 2001, 139–143; Живић 2015, 488.

[27] Colossal marble heads of Jupiter and Hercules were discovered during the archaeological excavations led in 1978, 1986 and 1987, in the eastern and south-eastern areas of the palace of *Romuliana* known as areas of the large

4   Marble head of Hercules from *Felix Romuliana* (photo Institute of Archaeology Belgrade)

Jupiter, a male right hand holding an eagle with outspread wings was also found[28], which suggests that Jupiter was represented enthroned with an eagle on his hand, analogous to the statue of Zeus from *Milasa* in *Caria* in Asia Minor[29]. A head of Hercules was also discovered in the area of the large temple, presumably belonging to the representation of the hero resting, copying the iconographic type of Hercules Farnese. Other fragmented statues of Apollo or Dionysus, a satyr and a female holding a torch were all also discovered in the area of the large temple, while in the north-western part of the palace in *Romuliana*, a marble statue of Aesculapius was brought to light, representing the god standing and slightly leaning on his staff around which a snake is entwined[30]. The back of the statue is summarily modelled, implying that the statue was placed with its back towards the wall, probably in one of the palace's niches, similarly to the statues of Athena which were also found in different parts of the palace (discovered in the area of the large temple, in the southern part of the fortification's western gate or in the north-western part of the palace)[31]. A fragmented porphyry statue of Victoria was a part of the larger than life-size sculptural composition of Galerius or perhaps of the emperors Galerius and Severus or Licinius represented together – as they are shown on coins from AD 293 minted in *Cyzicus* and *Antiochia*[32], or on the pilaster from *Romuliana*[33]. The porphyry statue of Galerius crowned by Victoria was discovered in a rubble layer in the area of the *thermae*, where

---

temple, Срејовић – Цермановић-Кузмановић 1987, 118. 120 nos. 50. 51; Tomović 1993, 102 no. 122 fig. 20, 1. 2; 105–106 no. 135 fig. 17, 3; Живић 2015, 408 no. 1 pl. 31, 1; 410 no. 3 pl. 32, 1.

[28] A fragmented male right hand of white marble holding an eagle (parts of the bird are clearly presented in its claws and wide-spread wings) was also discovered in archaeological excavations in 1987 in the south-eastern area of the palace of *Romuliana* in the sector of the large temple, Живић 2015, 410 no. 2 pl. 31, 2.

[29] Живић 2015, 408.

[30] Živić 2011, 125–127.

[31] So far, there are seven fragmented marble statues of Athena known from the locality of *Romuliana* (one statue is of dubious identification, because it could also represent a Muse); these were all found in archaeological excavations in 1963, 1969, 1974, 1978, 1981 and 1992: Живић 2015, 415–423 no. 7–13.

[32] Fragments of porphyry statues from *Romuliana* were discovered in different locations in the locality, thus one part of the wings of Victoria were excavated in 1971 in one of the palace's rooms, while the other part of the goddess' wings as well as the parts of her feet were found in the area of the large temple in 1972 and 1975. Judging from the preserved fingers of the goddess' right hand on Galerius' crown, her statue was presented crowning him on his left side above him (or above him and Severus or Licinius), Поповић 2017, 79.

[33] A limestone pilaster (height 2.16 m) was discovered on the facade of the eastern gate of the later fortification in the archaeological excavations of 1986. On its front side, five medallions are presented and in the first, third and fifth medallion, tetrarchs are shown in hierarchical order – the tetrarch shown on the left side of the medallion is of a higher place than the one shown on the right side. In the first medallion, Diocletian and Maximian Herculius are shown, in the third medallion Galerius and Maximius Daia and in the fifth medallion Constantius Chlorus and Flavius Valerius Severus (Severus II): Живић 2015, 471.

it was brought from another place, most probably the palace or perhaps the tholos structure with columns[34]. Although Dionysus' bride Ariadne was not a divinity, the marble representation influenced by the Hellenistic representations of Ariadne and dated to the second half of the 3rd century was subjected to severe damage, particularly in the area of her face and breasts, which implies that her nudity was obviously deemed offensive by the persons who damaged it[35]. Judging from the summarily modelled back of the relief, it can be presumed that it was probably placed in a niche either in the *thermae* or in the palace[36]. The motif of Sleeping Ariadne is frequently encountered in late antique villae and was very popular, along with other Dionysiac motifs, in the 3rd and the 4th centuries[37].

All the sculptures mentioned here were modelled in the second half of the 3rd or in the beginning of the 4th century, copying mostly Greek classical art works from the 4th century BC. Marble analysis showed that the majority was made of the fine-grained marbles from the Pentelic quarries near Athens and the imperial quarries of Afyon/*Docimium* in Asia Minor[38], by artists from large artistic centres, presumably Thessaloniki. Some of them, however, like the Sleeping Ariadne or the sculptural group representing the hunt of the wild boar were modelled from the white marble exploited in the vicinity of Plovdiv (*Philippopolis*) in *Thracia*[39]. It is clear that some of the sculptures, like those of Jupiter and Hercules, had a cultic meaning and function, as they were placed and discovered in the large temple area, while others such as the statues of Aesculapius, Apollo, Dionysus, Athena, Satyr and the Sleeping Ariadne relief decorated rooms of the palace or the *thermae* and were chosen by Galerius because of the symbolism they bore, however most probably without any cultic meaning. Some of the statues, like those of Dionysus or Apollo, or the relief of the Sleeping Ariadne were smashed into pieces and discovered in a seriously fragmented state, which could have been caused by Christians who saw a sexual connotation in the nudity of pagan statuary, thus judging them offensive, vulgar and potentially dangerous because of their »demonic powers«[40]. Unlike at *Mediana*, no group of sculptures in *Romuliana* was discovered hidden or buried. This occurrence was not rare in the provinces of the Central Balkans, in the context of mythological and cult statuary and votive reliefs. The example of the important local Sanctuary of Zeus and Hera Soudeipteinoi from the Belava mountain near Pirot (*Turres*) demonstrates violence towards numerous votive reliefs displaying images of the divine pair because of their symbolism. They were discovered smashed into pieces probably during the first half of the 4th century, in the period of the strengthening of Christianity in the area mentioned, supported by the activism of Nicetas of *Remesiana*, bishop and ardent missionary of Christianity[41].

Similar damage can also be observed on a group of cultic marble statues and votive reliefs discovered by chance during agricultural work in 1934 in the locality of *Timacum Minus*, today's Ravna near Knjaževac, in the Roman settlement area between the *castellum* and the road which

---

[34] The fragments of a monumental porphyry sculpture of Galerius were discovered in the *thermae* in secondary use as *spolia*, most probably brought from the palace where the sculpture could have been originally placed as a symbol of Galerius' triumph over Persia in AD 298 or, less likely, the sculpture stood in the tholos building with columns turned towards the sacral complex on Magura, Поповић 2017, 81.

[35] The sculptural relief of white marble represented the Sleeping Ariadne nude, en face with wavy long hair and her eyes closed, lying on the bed with a cloth covering the lower part of her naked body. Her right arm is bent at the elbow and raised above her head, while she is leaning on her left hand on the bed. Particular damage was done in the area of Ariadne's forehead, lips, chin and breasts: Лаловић 2001, 239–240.

[36] Лаловић 2001, 239; Живић 2015, 487–488 no. 1 pl. 85, 1.

[37] Stirling 2005, 54; Videbech 2015, 453. The relief of the Sleeping Ariadne from *Romuliana* bears striking iconographic and stylistic similarities with the statuette of the Sleeping Ariadne from the villa at Chiragan.

[38] Prochaska – Živić 2018, 301.

[39] Живић 2015, 466.

[40] Jacobs 2010, 278. Writing about a young girl who saw a statue of nude Venus in the *thermae*, bishop Quodvultdeus describes her as »being possessed by a demon«, who was later exorcised as the statue was destroyed: Kristensen 2013, 224.

[41] Gavrilović Vitas – Dana 2022, 181–216.

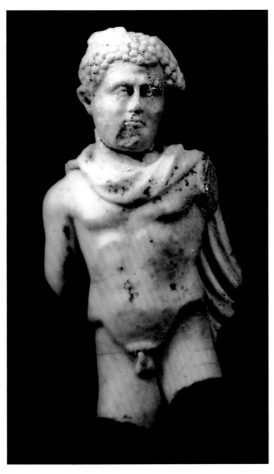

5   Marble statue of Dionysus from *Timacum Minus* (photo Petković, Gavrilović Vitas, Miladinović Radmilović, Ilijić 2016)

led to the north[42]. Two marble heads of a male deity, in earlier literature identified as the god Serapis but in our opinion more probably representing Jupiter Dolichenus, dated to the 3rd century, and of a goddess, presumably Isis (or perhaps Tyche [?]), dated to the end of the 3rd or beginning of the 4th century, unfortunately disappeared during the Second World War. They were discovered together with a dozen fragmented marble statues and votive reliefs, such as the statues of Venus, Dionysus (fig. 5), Jupiter Dolichenus on a bull, fragmented Dionysiac scenes, etc.[43]. There are no details about the exact state in which the statues and reliefs were found – but since they were discovered all together gathered in one place, we can presume that they could have been buried by their worshippers after their abuse by Christians, as was done with cult images in other parts of the Roman Empire, as late antique sources testify by reporting pagans' hope for the return of the true gods and the restoration of ancient cults[44]. As for the demolishing of cult images from *Timacum Minus*, their damaged state speaks for itself. All the statues were discovered decapitated, the nude Venus statues suffered damage in the area of their faces and genitals, while the rest of them were smashed into pieces, implying their destruction presumably at the end of the 4th or in the 5th century. The meaning of this kind of violation is quite clear – due to the symbolism that mythological statues and reliefs carried and their veneration, they represented a threat to the diffusion and acceptance of Christianity in eastern parts of the Central Balkans territory, not only because of their appearance, but because of their placement in pagan temples, which were still visited by the worshippers of the deities represented. Votive inscriptions from *Timacum Minus* further suggest the existence of temples of Jupiter, Mars, Diana, a sanctuary dedicated to the Thracian horseman and a Mithraeum[45], which were all perceived as a threat to the Christians. Based on the funerary practices and votive monuments of the 4th century from *Timacum Minus* and its vicinity, it can be presumed that in these parts of the Central Balkans, even after the imperial edicts against pagans and pagan temples in the 4th century, venerators of pagan deities still practiced their religion in their private *lararia* inside their homes.

Besides the group finds mentioned here, a hidden lot of marble statues of Jupiter Dolichenus was discovered in the Limes locality of Egeta, Brza Palanka. A *sacrarium* from a Dolichenus sanctuary of oval shape was discovered accidently during agricultural work in 1962, in the area between the civilian settlement and the late antique necropolis in Egeta, with most of the cult

---

[42] IMS III/2, 42.
[43] Petrović – Jovanović 1997, 60–65 no. 4–19.
[44] Hiding and burying of cult sculptures, statues and votive reliefs was also one of the pagan responses to Christian destruction of pagan mythological objects, sometimes in the hope of a revival of paganism: Kristensen 2013, 32.
[45] IMS III/2, 42–43.

6   Marble statuary composition of Jupiter Dolichenus and Juno Dolichena from Brza Palanka, Egeta (photo N. Borić, Institute of Archaeology Belgrade)

7   Marble Mithraic votive icon from Mramor (photo National Museum Niš)

objects aligned near the interior wall of the Sacrarium and a few of them placed in the centre of the room[46]. Altogether six marble statues of Jupiter Dolichenus, a Mithraic votive relief, a bronze *tabula ansata* with a collective dedication to the god from the *cohors I Cretum*, a holder for a triangular plate, two bronze lamps, bronze coins of Geta and silver coins of Elagabalus were found. Seventeen years after the discovery of Dolichenus' Sacrarium, in 1979, a gilded triangular votive plate with the representation of Jupiter Dolichenus and the Castores was bought by the Historical Museum in Belgrade from an agricultural worker living in Egeta, who had ploughed it up near the Sacrarium, so it can be presumed that it was a part of a whole with a bronze holder for a *signum* discovered in the Sacrarium in 1962. The names of the dedicants from the bases of the statues, such as Pompeus Isauricus and Kastor, imply dedicators of eastern origin. Although the *cohors I Cretum* was stationed in Egeta, soldiers there were not the only venerators of Jupiter Dolichenus. Members of the civilian administration, merchants, slaves and freedmen also worshipped the god. All statues of Dolichenus, along with a Mithraic votive icon, were discovered in a fragmented state, with the figure of the god decapitated or destroyed completely. The figures of the deities are only partially preserved in a statuary composition of Jupiter Dolichenus with Juno Dolichena (fig. 6). We cannot be certain about the life span of the Dolicheneum in Egeta, but judging by a coin of Elagabalus found in the Sacrarium, it existed until AD 222. However, it was not destroyed in a fire, as Istvan Toth suggested, listing it with other Limes' *dolichena* attacked by Maximinus Thrax due to their wealth: no traces of fire were attested in the structure nor were there traces of calcification on the sculptures of Jupiter Dolichenus and Juno Dolichena, to which Toth refers as the consequence of the high temperature (fire)[47]. Iconographic details on the gilded votive plate

---

[46] The excavated structure of oval shape was 3.5 m long and 3.8 m wide, oriented in north-south direction, with the entrance on the northern side. It was built from stones and pebbles, with occasional fragments of bricks and *tegulae,* with interior walls painted in a yellowish colour. In the middle of the room, a large stone block in the shape of an irregular parallelepiped was found, with four oval symmetrically positioned holes in one half of its upper side, Gavrilović Vitas 2020, 206–207.

[47] For an elaboration of the subject of the Sacrarium of the Dolicheneum in Egeta not being destroyed in the fire during Maximinus Thrax' attacks on Dolichenus sanctuaries along the Limes, see Gavrilović Vitas 2021, 113.

(like the images of the *labrys*, the bulls driving the *bigae* and the figures of the Castores) are identical to the same motifs known from votive stelae of local gods from *Syria* and Asia Minor. This implies a significant oriental influence in the iconographic details of the objects from the Sacrarium in Egeta, and their modelling presumably in an eastern workshop or in one of the larger military centres with Syrian priests, who were well acquainted with the theology and practices of the cult, for example *Locus Felicis*/Mauer an der Url or Komlod.

Rare mythological sculptures from the 3rd century, which were presumably used as part of the decoration of public spaces or buildings in Late Antiquity, were discovered undamaged – for example the statue of Hercules with Telephos from *Singidunum* (fig. 7)[48], found in the centre of today's Belgrade near the entrance to the Roman camp. Similarly, figures of *genii* of spring and winter[49], which were used as funerary sculptures in Late Antiquity, somehow escaped greater damage and survived the turbulent period of barbarian attacks and Christian wrath towards mythological statues in the Central Balkans.

Other mythological statues were not so fortunate, as can be seen for instance in the examples of the heads of the goddesses Fortuna and Venus from *Viminacium*, and also from other urban and Limes centres. Bearing harmful symbolism for Christians, the mythological statues were either severely damaged, as we saw on previous examples, or were

8   Marble sculpture of Hercules with Telephos from *Singidunum* (Gavrilović 2014, cat. 23 fig. 18)

marked with crosses and halos, presumably during the 5th century, in a wish either to expel the demons from them or to purify them so that they could be reused. Particularly targeted were the statues of deities such as Aphrodite/Venus, Hercules, Dionysus and Aesculapius, but in the Roman Central Balkans, mythological statues with crosses are not yet known. However, on a few votive icons with representations of the so-called Danubian Riders or Mithras (e.g. the Mithraic votive icon from Mramor, fig. 7), we can observe crosses and halos around the deities' heads[50]. These markings are analogous to the marking of mythological statues with crosses in other Roman provinces. It is difficult to establish, however, in the case of the finds from the Central Balkans, whether the crosses and halos were signs of purifying the representation, its baptism and acceptance of its image into a Christian meaning, or a sign of exorcism and desecration of the images' former function.[51]

Resuming the analysis and interpretation of mythological statuary from the Roman provinces of the Central Balkans in the period of Late Antiquity, we can conclude that the interest of the

---

[48] Gavrilović 2014, 31 cat. 23 fig. 18.
[49] Срејовић – Цермановић-Кузмановић 1987, 168–170 nos. 74. 75.
[50] Гавриловић Витас 2017, 191–206; Gavrilović Vitas, in press.
[51] Kristensen 2013, 127; Kristensen – Stirling 2019, 21.

local elite in statuary decor remained strong mainly in urban and domestic environments. Some of the statues maintained their cultic function for a short period of time, until they were destroyed or buried in undamaged or partially damaged state. Other statues, due to the lack of materials, continued to be used with an artistic and decorative function in public places, fora, buildings, and theatres. The owners of late antique villas and domains kept their inherited sculptural collections, adding new ones to them in appreciation of mythological statuary that copied the Classical style. However, the existing archaeological context implies intentional damage of mythological statues, and the smashing of their faces and genitals in particular, with the goal of defacing the images and thus destroying potential powers and the »demonic spirit of the deities« (at least based on Christian belief). Political changes in the 4th and later 5th centuries and edicts from Constantine to Theodosius contained in the Codex Theodosianus against pagans, pagan temples, sacrifice, ritual practices etc., had similar consequences for the mythological statuary in the Central Balkans as in other parts of the Roman Empire, in their changed appreciation and use; some of these objects were used for a certain period of time as purely works of art without any cultic meaning. Unfortunately, numerous statues were discarded, reused or destroyed, with the exception of those that survived by being hidden away and buried, such as the group of porphyry and marble statues from *Mediana* or the statues from *Timacum Minus*, presumably in the pagan hope of preserving them from destruction and oblivion, for better times.

## BIBLIOGRAPHY

| | |
|---|---|
| Čanak-Medić – Stojković-Pavelka 2011 | M. Čanak-Medić – B. Stojković-Pavelka, Architecture and spatial structure of the imperial palace, in: I. Popović (ed.), Romuliana – Gamzigrad, Monographs of Institute of Archaeology, Belgrade 49 (Belgrade 2011) 49–106 |
| Crnoglavac et al. 2013 | V. Crnoglavac – D. Išljamović – B. Todorović, Performed of Fourier tansformed infrared (FTIR) spectroscopy in identification of sculptural fragments from Mediana (Примена Fourier-ове трансформационе инфрацрвене спектроскопије у идентификацији фрагмената скулптуре са Медијане), Зборник Народног Музеја у Нишу 22 (Niš 2013) 73–78 |
| Gavrilović 2014 | N. Gavrilović, The Cults of Hercules and Mercury in Upper Moesia from the first to the fourth century (Belgrade 2014) |
| Gavrilović 2017 | N. Gavrilović, The marble group depicting Drunken Dionysus with Satyr from Mediana, in: M. B. Vujović (ed.), Ante portam auream. Studia in honorem professoris Aleksandar Jovanović (Belgrade 2017) 193–203 |
| Гавриловић Витас 2017 | Н. Гавриловић Витас, Вотивне иконе бога Митре из античке збирке Народног музеја у Нишу, Зборник Народног музеја, XXIII-1, Археологија (Belgrade 2017) 191–206 |
| Gavrilović Vitas 2020 | N. Gavrilović Vitas, Dolicheneum and Dolichenus' cult objects from the locality Brza Palanka – Egeta. Contribution to the study of the cult of Iuppiter Dolichenus, in: I. Radman-Livaja – T. Bilić (eds.), Monumenta Marmore Aereque Perenniora, a volume dedicated to Ante Rencić-Miočević (Zagreb 2020) 204–223 |
| Gavrilović Vitas 2021 | N. Gavrilović Vitas, Ex Asia et Syria. Oriental Religions in the Roman Central Balkans, Archaeopress Roman Archaeology 78 (Oxford 2021) |
| Gavrilović Vitas, in press | N. Gavrilović Vitas, Rider Monuments in the Territory of the Central Balkans' Roman Provinces: The Issues of the Iconography and Context of the Monuments (in press) |
| Gavrilović Vitas – Dana 2022 | N. Gavrilović Vitas – D. Dana, Zeus and Hera *Souideptenoi*. The Sanctuary at Belava Mountain near Turres/Pirot, Starinar 72, 2022, 181–216 |
| IMS | Inscriptions de la Mésie Superieure I–VI (Belgrade 1976–1995) |
| Jacobs 2010 | I. Jacobs, Production to Destruction? Pagan and Mythological Statuary in Asia Minor, AJA 114/2, 267–303 |
| Јовановић 1975 | A. Јовановић, Неки аспекти проблема скупног налаза скулптура са Медијане код Ниша (Certains aspects du problème de la trouvaille collective de sculptures à Mediana près de Naissus), Старинар 24/25, 1973/1974, 57–66 |
| Kristensen 2013 | T. M. Kristensen, Making and Breaking the Gods. Christian Responses to Pagan Sculpture in Late Antiquity (Aarhus 2013) |

| | |
|---|---|
| Kristensen – Stirling 2019 | T. M. Kristensen – L. Stirling, The Lives and Alternatives of Greek and Roman Sculpture: From Use to Refuse, in: T. M. Kristensen – L. Stirling (eds.), The Afterlife of Greek and Roman Sculpture (Ann Arbor 2019) |
| Лаловић 2001 | А. Лаловић, Скулптура Аријадне из Ромулијане, Vestigatio Vetustatis. Александрини Цермановић-Кузмановић од пријатеља, сарадника и ученика, Универзитет у Београду, Филозофски факултет, Центар за археолошка истраживања, књ. 20 (Belgrade 2001) 239–243 |
| Petković 2011 | S. Petković, Romuliana in the time after the palace, in: I. Popović (ed.), Felix Romuliana – Gamzigrad, Monographs of Institute of Archaeology, Belgrade 49 (Belgrade 2011) 167–200 |
| Petrović 1994 | P. Petrović, Mediana, Residence of Roman Emperors (Belgrade 1994) |
| Petrović – Jovanović 1997 | P. Petrović – S. Jovanović, Културно благо Књажевачког краја. Археологија (The Cultural Heritage of Knjaževac Region. Archaeology) (Belgrade 1997) |
| Поповић 2017 | И. Поповић, *ПОРФИР* – моћ царева и достојанство богова/PORPHYRY – Power of Emperors and Dignity of Gods (Belgrade 2017) |
| Prochaska – Živić 2018 | W. Prochaska – M. Živić, The Marbles of the Sculptures of Felix Romuliana in Serbia, in: D. Matetić Poljak – K. Marasović (eds.), Asmosia XI, Interdisciplinary Studies of Ancient Stone. Proceedings of the Eleventh International Conference of ASMOSIA, Split 18.–22.05.2015 (Split 2018) 301–311 |
| Sauer 2003 | E. Sauer, The Archaeology of Religious Hatred in the Roman and early Medieval world (London 2003) |
| Srejović 2011a | D. Srejović, Imperial Palace, in: I. Popović (ed.), Felix Romuliana – Gamzigrad, Monographs of Institute of Archaeology, Belgrade 49 (Belgrade 2011) 43–49 |
| Srejović 2011b | D. Srejović, Diva Romula, Divus Galerius, in: I. Popović (ed.), Felix Romuliana – Gamzigrad, Monographs of Institute of Archaeology, Belgrade 49 (Belgrade 2011) 159–166 |
| Срејовић – Цермановић-Кузмановић 1987 | Д. Срејовић – А. Цермановић-Кузмановић, Римска скулптура у Србији (Roman Sculpture in Serbia) (Belgrade 1987) |
| Stirling 2005 | L. M. Stirling, The Learned Collector. Mythological Statuettes and Classical Taste in Late Antique Gaul (Ann Arbor, MI 2005) |
| Tomović 1993 | M. Tomović, Roman Sculpture in Upper Moesia (Belgrade 1993) |
| Vasić 2004 | M. Vasić, Bronze Railing from Mediana, Starinar 53/54, 2003/2004, 79–109 |
| Vasić 2017 | M. Vasić, Fragment of a Statue of Asclepius from Mediana, in: M. B. Vujović (ed.), Ante portam auream. Studia in honorem professoris Aleksandar Jovanović (Belgrade 2017) 205–210 |
| Vasić 2018 | M. Vasić, Sculptures and »the sanctuary of Aesculapius« in Mediana, Starinar 68, 2018, 89–109 |
| Vasić – Gavrilović 2012 | M. Vasić, N. Gavrilović, Venus or Diana from Mediana, Starinar 62, 2012, 137–149 |
| Vasić et al. 2016 | M. Vasić – G. Milošević – N. Gavrilović Vitas – V. Crnoglavac, Constantine's villa at Mediana (Niš 2016) |
| Videbech 2015 | C. Videbech, Private Collections of Sculpture in Late Antiquity. An Overview of the Form, Function and Tradition, in: J. Fejfer – M. Moltesen – A. Rathje (eds.), Tradition. Transmission of Culture in the Ancient World, Acta Hyperborea 14 (Copenhagen 2015) 451–479 |
| Živić 2011 | M. Živić, Artistic achievements in the imperial palace, in: I. Popović (ed.), Felix Romuliana – Gamzigrad, Monographs of Institute of Archaeology, Belgrade 49 (Belgrade 2011) 107–140 |
| Живић 2015 | М. Живић, Камена пластика на територији провинције Dacia Ripensis у раздобљу III–IV века (Stone Sculpture in the territory of the province of Dacia Ripensis in the 3$^{rd}$–4$^{th}$ century AD, unpublished PhD), Докторска дисертација одбрањена на Филозофском факултету Универзитета у Београду (Belgrade 2015) |

*Nadežda Gavrilović Vitas, Institute of Archaeology, Knez Mihailova 35, 11 000 Belgrade, Serbia.*
*[e] nadia011@yahoo.com; ngavrilo@ai.ac.rs*

Stylianos E. Katakis

# THE TWILIGHT OF THE ASKLEPIOS CULT IN EPIDAUROS

## THE EVIDENCE OF THE BUILDING ACTIVITY, INSCRIPTIONS, AND SCULPTURES[1]

**Abstract**
Building activity in the Sanctuary of Apollo Maleatas and Asklepios at Epidauros did not cease during Late Antiquity. A perimetric stoa built around the central area of the sanctuary and the numbering and marking with symbols of a great number of altars testify to the reorganization of the cult in the 4th century AD. The preliminary results of the ongoing »post-excavations« in the so-called Building K, where more than 35 statues and votive statuettes of gods were found in 1886, reveal a rearrangement of the edifice for a rather mystical cult. In the city of Epidauros, the study of the last phase of the theatre dated to the 4th or 5th century AD has also provided strong evidence for the existence of a pagan, mystical cult. The statuette of the young Asklepios holding a scroll, dated to the late 4th century, draws upon the iconography of Christ. These data agree with the written sources that Epidauros was still not fully Christianized at the end of the 5th century, although a Christian basilica had been erected just outside the sanctuary in the early 5th century.

Even though our knowledge of the early phases of the Sanctuary of Apollo Maleatas and Asklepios in Epidauros has increased considerably in the last decades[2], its final phase, the period from about the middle of the 3rd century AD onwards (until the full Christianization of the area), remains rather obscure. The archaeological evidence remains insufficient, due to the poor documentation during the excavations at the end of the 19th century; therefore, a more careful study and reappraisal of all available data can prove fruitful (fig. 1).

The 2nd century AD constitutes the second most prosperous period for the Sanctuary of Apollo Maleatas and Asklepios. Hadrian was the only Roman emperor who visited Epidauros; the year of his visit, AD 124/125, became the first year of a new era that would remain valid at least until the late 4th century[3]. Nevertheless, although the Epidaurians honoured him as »saviour« and »builder«, no building activity in the sanctuary can be attributed to Hadrian[4]. Around AD 160, the Roman senator S. Iulius Maior Antoninus Pythodorus, who originated from Nysa in Asia Minor, financed the restoration of many old buildings and the construction of several new ones, transforming the landscape of the sanctuary, as evidenced by the description of Pausanias (2, 27, 6–7) a few years

---

[1] The subject is too extensive to be fully analyzed in a conference paper, therefore I will refer to the most important points and new observations, 20 years after the publication of the sculptures of the Roman period (Katakis 2002). I would like to thank the organizers for their kind invitation to participate in the conference, as well as the National Archaeological Museum at Athens (henceforth NAM; Dr A.V. Karapanagiotou, Dr D. Ignatiadou) and the Ephorate of Antiquities of Argolis (Dr A. Papadimitriou) as well as Prof. Em. V. Lambrinoudakis (director of the excavations since 1974), and Dr J. Mavrommatidis (architect, restorer of many Epidaurian monuments) for providing me with photos and the permission to publish them. I am also indebted to Dr P. Konstantinidis for correcting and improving my initial English text.
[2] Due to research of V. Lambrinoudakis: cf. Lambinoudakis 2002; Lambrinoudakis 2013; Lambrinoudakis 2018.
[3] Cf. Katakis 2002, 389–400 n. 561–562.
[4] IG IV² 606 v. 8–9: ἡ πόλις τὸν ἑαυτῆς σωτῆρα καὶ οἰκιστήν (AD 124/125); Melfi 2007, 195 n. 503 (the base is located opposite Building E (fig. 1 n. 4) and not near the Stoa of Kotys; initially, in the 3rd c. BC, it belonged to a statue of Antigonos Doson [IG IV² 589]). It is thought that Hadrian reorganized the cult, see Melfi 2007, 83–90. On the relations between Hadrian and the sanctuary: Melfi 2010a, 331–334 fig. 3.

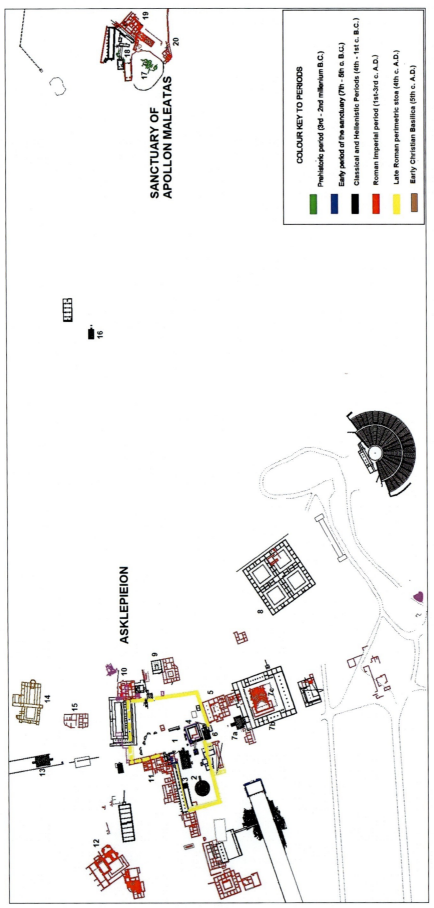

1 Plan of the Sanctuary of Apollon and Asklepios at Epidauros: 1) Temple of Asklepios and altar, 2) Tholos, 3) Stoa of the Dormitory, 4) Building E, 5) Building Φ, 6) Temple of Artemis, 7a) Propylon of the Hestiatorion/Temple of Hygieia, 7b) Hestiatorion, 7c) Odeion, 8) Katagogion (Hostel), 9) Building Π, 10) Northeastern Baths, 11) Building K, 12) Northwestern Baths, 13) Propylaia, 14) Basilica, 15) House of the Partridge, 16) Temple of Aphrodite on the way to the Apollon sanctuary, 17) Prehistoric settlement, 18) Core of the Apollon sanctuary (temple, altar, stoa), 19) Skana, 20) Bath (© EphAArg; V. Kazolias, elaborated by the author)

later⁵. In about AD 200, the Odeion (fig. 1 no. 7c)⁶ was built in the courtyard of the monumental early Hellenistic Hestiatorion or Banquet Hall (fig. 1 no. 7b), which was partially destroyed in the 1st century BC. Probably at the same time, its propylon was turned into a temple of Hygieia (fig. 1 no. 7a), as evidenced by the existence of an inscribed altar in front of its ramp⁷.

What happened next? The last phase of the sanctuary from about the middle of the 3rd century until the Christianization of the area remains somewhat obscure. Unfortunately, the so-called great excavations conducted from 1881 up to 1928 (i.e., up to the death of their director, P. Kavvadias) did not provide sufficient documentation for this period. Although we know that building activity in the sanctuary did not cease, the exact dating of the monuments proves unattainable, as a large part of the remains were dismantled during the excavations in order to reach earlier layers, which contemporary opinion deemed to be more important⁸. The main reason for their demolition was that many sculptures, inscriptions, and architectural members of Classical period buildings were embedded in them⁹. In addition, there is no information about possible invasions of the Heruli in the area of Epidauros in AD 267 or of the Goths in AD 395¹⁰.

Today we are sure about the late antique phases mainly in the bath complexes around the core of the sanctuary. More specifically, at the Northeastern Baths (fig. 1 no. 10), the initial *alvei* were divided into smaller individual ones, a modification that can be dated to the late 4th century or even the early 5th century¹¹, while the great northwestern double bath complex (fig. 1 no. 12) was extensively remodelled also in the 4th century¹². A recently partially excavated smaller bathhouse, east of the Northeastern Baths (fig. 1 no. 10), was built in the late 4th century and was in use with some modifications till the 6th century¹³, evidence that people continued to visit the area of the sanctuary¹⁴.

---

5   Katakis 2002, 325. 518–519 n. 1672–1673; Melfi 2007, 99–101. 121–123; Melfi 2010a, 334–339.
6   Katakis 2002, 508 n. 1558 (2nd c.); Aslanidis 2003; Melfi 2007, 124–125. 137; Melfi 2010a, 335; Melfi 2010b, 319–321 (2nd half of the 2nd c., associated with the building activity sponsored by Antoninus, in AD 160–180, remodelled in early 3rd c.); Vitti 2016, 171–174 fig. 3,100–102.
7   Kavvadias 1900, 148–149 with plan; Katakis 2002, 224. 413 n. 730–731; Melfi 2007, 112–113.
8   There are no traces, for example, of the ruins documented by Defrasse – Lechat 1895, pl. 11 (just behind the temples of Asklepios and Artemis) and fig. on p. 49, or even by Kavvadias 1899, 104 pl. 3 (right) at the eastern part of the Dormitory Stoa. The travellers of the 17th–19th c. AD paid no attention to the ruins of the later periods because they were interested only in the Classical period (Defrasse – Lechat 1895, 6–13). In 1764/1766, Chandler wrote: »il ne reste … que des tas de pierres, des morceaux de murailles en brique …« (Defrasse – Lechat 1895, 9–10). Kavvadias dated most of these structures to the late Roman and again the Frankish period, but he gave no sufficient evidence (Kavvadias 1900, 24. 128 n. 1; 131).
9   E.g. according to Kavvadias 1885, 44–52 pl. 1–2, the early Hellenistic statuettes of Nikai from the acroteria of the Temple of Artemis NAM 159–161 (Reinhardt 2018, 126–133. 374–375 fig. 99–107), the late classical relief of the seated Asklepios NAM 173 (Holtzmann 1984, 873 no. 62*), as well as the group of the youths NAM 301 and 302 (Katakis 2002, 107–108 n. 115a–b pl. 120–121) were found embedded in the later walls built on Building E (fig. 1 no. 4).
10  Cf. Avraméa 1997, 53–60; Jacobs 2014.
11  Ginouvès 1955, 141–146 fig. 7–10; Lambrinoudakis 1999, 53 (S. Petrounakos), where damage due to earthquakes is mentioned, which led to repairs and the modification of the *alvei*; Trümper 2014, 222 fig. 6; Vitti 2016, 186–192 no. 3.3.3 fig. 3, 118–123.
12  It is about two buildings, excavated in 1921–1922 (Katakis 2002, 305 with n. 1538), of which only the northern and larger one has been thoroughly studied by Bilis 2007 (this study is unfortunately ignored by Melfi 2007, 113–115 fig. 19, who maintains the old identification of the complex as the Iseion; Trümper 2014, 222, and Vitti 2016, 174–186 no. 3.3.2 fig. 3, 103–116. The smaller southeastern thermal building is lavishly decorated with mosaics, the unpublished designs of which are kept in the Archive of the Archaeological Society at Athens.
13  The excavator mentions also that coins and ceramics of the 11th–13th c. were found above the destruction level. Lambrinoudakis 2002, 224, suggests that the bath may have continued operating into Christian times; Petrounakos 2003.
14  It is worth noting that a female head found here probably belongs to a figure from the pediments of the early 4th c. BC Asklepios Temple (Petrounakos 2003, 66–67 fig. 29–30; Mostratos 2013, 314–315 no. 360a). Therefore, the temple must already have been damaged when the head was re-used here.

The most impressive late antique building project in the Asklepieion is a stoa built around the central area of the sanctuary (the »sacred esplanade« with the great altar and the row of exedras in the middle, 100 × 80 m, and the smaller area of the temple, the Tholos, and the Stoa of the Enkoimeterion/Dormitory Hall [fig. 1 nos. 1–3]), using architectural elements of older buildings. In the foundations or retaining walls of the western part of this enclosure, west, and south of the Tholos, elements of the partially destroyed Hestiatorion were used, maybe in about AD 200, when the Odeion was erected and the propylon was turned into the Temple of Hygieia. For the construction of the colonnade and the rest of the stoa, the dismantling of the so-called Katagogion (i.e. hostel), the largest building in the sanctuary, dating to the Early Hellenistic period, furnished 144 Doric columns and hundreds of blocks (fig. 1 no. 8)[15].

The date of this extraordinary building programme is not clear. A few recent excavation trenches have confirmed a dating to the 4th century. 30 years ago, I tentatively attributed it to an initiative of the emperor Julian (AD 361–363), as, owing to his theology, Asklepios was equated to Jesus and was believed to be incarnated in Epidauros[16]. Although this attribution seems logical and was repeated in subsequent scholarship[17], it is not certain, and so far there is no need to suggest that the aforementioned building programme was sponsored by an imperial bequest[18]. A dating to the first half of the 4th century is also possible, as part of the same programme of regularisation and renovation of the cult, which also comprised the marking and numbering of altars in the sanctuary, discussed below. The fact that blocks removed from the stylobate of the stoa were re-used in the early Christian basilica in the first half of the 5th century (fig. 1 no. 14) suggests that at that time the stoa was at least partially damaged, probably due to an earthquake[19]. As it seems, this ambitious project turned out to be short-lived.

Inscriptions are the most important source of information on the history of the sanctuary after Pausanias' visit, although their number is now considerably reduced[20]. Examples dated with certainty to the Late Roman period provide us with valuable information about the cult, as well as their dedicants[21].

At the end of the 3rd/beginning of the 4th century, three inscriptions with paeans to all gods, Apollo, Asklepios, Hygieia, Athena, and Pan were inscribed on limestone blocks of the Hestiatorion re-used in the Odeion[22]. It is worth noting that their formulation presents some affinities to Christian practices[23].

Some time after AD 306 and before AD 355, a major project was undertaken in the sanctuary, namely the reorganisation of the cult, which included the marking of over 200 altars with symbols and alphabetic numerals, like the altar of the hero Epidauros of the 3rd century BC (fig. 2)[24]. Such extensive use of symbols finds no direct parallel in the Greek world. Although I believe that the marking of the altars could have been contemporary to the building of the perimetric stoa, there is no evidence that these two projects were somehow linked; the marking of the altars could have been the initiative of the priest, carried out during his annual term in office[25].

---

[15] Kanellopoulos 2000, 29. 33. 97. For the Katagogion see Kraynak 1991.
[16] Katakis 2002, 327. 520 n. 1684 for the theology of the emperor Julian.
[17] Kanellopoulos 2000, 30–31; Melfi 2007, 145–146.
[18] Pfaff 2018, 418–419.
[19] Kanellopoulos 2000, 31.
[20] IG IV² (cf. p. XXXVI–XXXIX); Peek 1969 and 1972; Melfi 2007, 308–309 no. 619–634 (a new study of the inscriptions is ongoing by Dr A. Sfyroera, University of Athens).
[21] Many of the inscriptions can be accurately dated. Dates inscribed on them use Hadrian's visit in AD 124/125 as the first year of a new era, as it is clearly mentioned on some of them; some scholars have tried to find another starting point or more starting points for a new counting, but their efforts did not prove fruitful (Katakis 2002, 390–391 n. 561–562, with related bibliography).
[22] IG IV² 129–135; Wagman 1995, 41–146. 159–172. 216–217; Galli 2004, 338–343; Melfi 2010b, 319. 321.
[23] Nilsson 1945, 68; Sweetman 2010, 209 with n. 25.
[24] IG IV² 288, the only one with two numerals and two symbols, cf. Pfaff 2018, 403 fig. 6.
[25] Pfaff 2018, esp. 399 for the estimated number of the marked altars, and 417–419 for the date of the project.

2   Altar of the hero Epidauros (3rd c. BC) in front of the Building K with later incised no. OA (71) and the symbol of the hero (© EphAArg; photo author)

Apart from the inscriptions on the bases of votive statuettes and small altars, it should be briefly mentioned that the last emperor honoured with a statue in the Asklepieion was Volusianus (AD 251–253), son of Trebonianus Gallus[26]. The unique dedication to Asklepios Aigeotes in AD 355 recalls the destruction by the troops of the emperor Constantine of the great Sanctuary of Asklepios in Aigai (in Cilicia) 30 years earlier[27]. The last inscription that mentions an accurate date (the year AD 366/367) belongs to an offering to the two very old local goddesses, closely related to the Eleusinian goddesses Demeter and Kore, Damia and Auxesia, the cult of which was revived in the 2nd century[28].

Several sculptures from the sanctuary can be dated from the late 3rd century onwards[29]. The well-known, very expressive head NAM inv. 582 in the so-called Iamblichos or Epidauros type is the only portrait that survives from that period[30]. As it has already been adequately discussed in scholarship, it will not be analyzed here again. We only note that mainly after the invasion of the Heruli in southern Greece in AD 267, portraits of this type (or of this person) have been found also in Athens, Eleusis, Delphi, Isthmia, and even Rome (if the head in the Vatican comes from the city)[31]; the presence of a portrait of this kind is an eloquent testimony of the importance of the Asklepios Sanctuary during this period.

---

[26]  Peek 1972, 43 n. 79; Melfi 2007, 206 n. 609.
[27]  IG IV² 438; Katakis 2002, 390 n. 562; Schörner 2003, 394 n. 647; Melfi 2007, 208 no. 623. For the destruction of the Asklepios Temple in Aigai in AD 326 (Eus. vit. Const. 3, 56) see Ziegler 1994, 207–208.
[28]  Peek 1972, 38–39 n. 66; Melfi 2007, 209 no. 630. At St. Anna Chapel, near the Apollo Maleatas Sanctuary, an altar was found dedicated in AD 307 to Auxesia (i.e. Azosia) by the priest for life of Apollo Maleatas, and the goddesses Azosiai (IG IV² 434; Schörner 2003, 393 n. 645; Melfi 2007, 209 no. 634). For the two deities s. Lambrinudakis 1986.
[29]  Katakis 2002, 194–205. Only the most important and securely dated sculptures are mentioned here.
[30]  Katakis 2002, 100–101 cat. 104 pl. 112; Gehn 2013, 100. 106–108 pl. 25, 10a–b; Gehn 2016, 96 fig. 7, 5–6; Lenaghan 2016, 260; Voutiras 2022, 85. 90–95 no. 6 fig. 7–8.
[31]  Cf. bibliography in the previous note.

3  Statuette of Asklepios NAM 1809 (© National Archaeological Museum; photo Eir. Miari)

The possible presence of a late Roman magistrate in Epidauros is also crucial for the history of the site. A fragment of folds could be a part of an older togate statue[32] that was repaired and re-used later on, a practice commonly attested in the sanctuary in the case of the statue bases[33]. From an inscription, we learn that in the 4th century the *boule* and *demos* of Epidauros were active and sought to ask for the authorisation of the emperor to honour their benefactor Bassos[34].

The offering of votive statuettes continued, although in reduced number. In the case of the statuettes of Athena NAM inv. 274[35] and Asklepios NAM inv. 264[36], the accompanying inscriptions are very eloquent; they were dedicated in AD 304 and 308 by prominent members of the Athenian elite, who were also connected with the Eleusinian mysteries, the cult of Dionysos, and the Neoplatonic philosophical schools[37]. Links between Epidauros and Athens were reinforced via the close theological connection between Demeter and Kore and the local ancient olive-tree deities of Damia and Auxesia, whose cult was revived in the Antonine period and lasted till the end of the 4th century. According to an Attic tradition, Asklepios was also initiated into the Eleusinian mysteries[38].

The most significant sculpture of late antique Epidauros is of course the statuette NAM inv. 1809, of the beardless, young Asklepios in a variant of the well-known Campana type, holding a scroll in his left hand (fig. 3). It is convincingly dated to the second half of the 4th century and attributed to the famous ›school‹ of Aphrodisias by Marianne Bergmann[39]. The high-quality marble is not Greek and most prob-

---

[32] Epidauros Museum inv. 268: Katakis 2002, 113 no. 122 pl. 136 d–e. Cf. Goette 1990, pl. 45; Gehn 2012, *passim*.

[33] Cf. Griesbach 2014. It should be noted that most of the portrait statues found in the sanctuary date to the 1st c. AD, while the most extensive building construction activity took place in the Antonine period (Katakis 2023).

[34] IG IV² 692; Avraméa 1997, 122; Rizakis – Zoumbaki 2001, 170 no. 64; Melfi 2007, 209 no. 632. The base is currently in Venice, which means that its provenance is merely the coastal city of Epidauros and not the sanctuary.

[35] Katakis 2002, 73–75 cat. 70 pl. 88–89 a; Schörner 2003, 342 cat. 446 pl. 75; Stirling 2008, 147–150 fig. 35 right.

[36] Katakis 2002, 23–25 cat. 21 pl. 26–27; Schörner 2003, 145 cat. 442 pl. 73, 2; Stirling 2008, 147–150 fig. 35 left.

[37] Katakis 2002, 201. 390 n. 563. 566; Melfi 2007, 143. For the family of Minoukianos, dedicant of the Athena statuette s. Heath 1996, esp. 67 with n. 12.

[38] Lambrinudakis 1986; Katakis 2002, 266. 459 n. 1124–1126; Konstantinidis 2022, 48–49. For the possible cult of the Eleusinian goddesses in the *skana* s. Melfi 2007, 138–140.

[39] Bergmann 1999, 45. 47. 51 no. 19; 52. 69. 70 pls. 47; 48, 1–3; 49, 1–2; Katakis 2002, 22–23 cat. 20; 217–218. 310–312. 327 pl. 24–25 (where I dated it to the 2nd c. AD; my monograph was in press when the book of M. Bergmann was published; therefore, I could not study thoroughly and incorporate Bergmann's arguments on the date and the workshop of the statuette); Schörner 2003, 90 pl. 73, 2 (in the text and cat. 443 he confused it with the statuette NAM inv. 270 [Katakis 2002, 21–22 cat. 19 pl. 23]); Vorster 2012/2013, 418 n. 109.

ably originates from Asia Minor. A significant number of sculptures in Aphrodisias marble were found in nearby Corinth and Isthmia[40], and the Asklepios statuette probably reached Epidauros via Corinth, the capital city of the Roman province of Achaea and a major harbour. It was probably in the sanctuary that the statuette was set in a new, broader ›plinth‹ with mouldings, made of Pentelic marble.

The statuette was found in the central hall, just after the entrance of the so-called *skana* (*skene* in the Attic dialect), identified as the house of the priests in the Apollo Maleatas Sanctuary, according to late Antonine/early Severan inscriptions carved on either side of the main entrance[41]. Recent excavations have confirmed the continued use of the building until the late 4$^{th}$ century[42]. Besides that of Asklepios, three more statuettes of Aphrodite, Hygieia, and Eros (dated to the 1$^{st}$ and the 2$^{nd}$ c. AD) were also found in the same room[43]. The fact that the larger statuettes were found almost intact confirms that they had been buried under the collapsed walls of the building after a strong earthquake, as in the case of Building K in the Asklepieion discussed below.

In the Sanctuary of Asklepios, two major gatherings of sculptures were unearthed during the late 19$^{th}$ century excavations. In the area between the temple and the Tholos, i.e. the area for the celestial and chthonic cult of the healing god, six life-sized portrait statues were found together with a statue of Athena and only one portrait head, the above-mentioned NAM inv. 582, which is also chronologically the latest find from that area[44]. The fact that all heads and generally the attached parts of the statues are missing is explained by the presence of a rather small limekiln just over the ramp of the Tholos[45].

A somehow different configuration is attested in the nearby so-called Building K, northeast of the Dormitory Stoa, along the road that leads from the Propylaia (in the north) to the Temple of Asklepios (fig. 1 n. 11; fig. 4). Here, in 1886, five statues of gods of the 1$^{st}$ and 2$^{nd}$ centuries AD, approximately 30 votive marbles, and a few bronze statuettes, dating from the Early Hellenistic period up to the 4$^{th}$ century AD, were found, as well as a great number of inscribed votive altars[46].

The preliminary results of the ongoing ›post-excavation‹ confirmed that the Building K was built during the reign of Antoninus Pius by the senator Antoninus Pythodorus, above an early Hellenistic construction (»Hellenistic K«). The function of the latter remains unfortunately obscure, but it must have been important, judging from its robust and carefully constructed limestone foundations, comparable to those of the early Hellenistic Hestiatorion[47]. Building K had multiple

---

[40] Cf. Ridgway 1981, 444–445 with n. 85 pl. 96 a–c; Sturgeon 1987, 189 (results of the isotopic analysis: among them from Aphrodisias or Mylasa and Aphrodisias or Usak); Lattimore 1996, 53–54 cat. 106 pl. 35 e (from Aphrodisias or, less likely, Mylasa).

[41] IG IV$^2$ 293 (AD 183); 400 (AD 206).

[42] Cf. Lambrinoudakis 1989, 49 pl. 34–35 (finds from the drainage system of the cistern of Antoninus dated from the mid-3$^{rd}$ c. to the end of the 4$^{th}$ c. AD); Lambrinoudakis 1992, 51 (»according to the … pottery finds, the south-east Bath complex was used from the 2$^{nd}$ to the 4$^{th}$ c. AD, while human presence continued up to the Byzantine period«).

[43] These are the following statuettes: Aphrodite, Louvre-Naples type (NAM inv. 1811: Katakis 2002, 51–53 cat. 51 pl. 60–61, late 1$^{st}$ c. BC–early 1$^{st}$ c. AD); Hygieia, Hope type (NAM inv. 1810: Katakis 2002, 26–28 cat. 24 pl. 29–30, 2$^{nd}$ c. AD). For the find-spot of the statuettes and the inscribed monuments, mainly altars of the 2$^{nd}$ to the 4$^{th}$ c. AD, which were unearthed in the same place, s. Kavvadias 1900, 179; Katakis 2002, 310–312. The fragmentary figure of an Eros was found near the entrance to the central hall (Epidauros Museum, Storerooms: Katakis 2002, 65–65 cat. 65 pl. 78 d–f, 2$^{nd}$ c. AD [?]).

[44] Katakis 2002, 295–297; Katakis 2023, 59.

[45] The date of the kiln is not known. Kavvadias 1900, 25, associates the existence of the lime kilns with the use of materials from the Asklepieion for the repair of the castles of Nauplion and the building of a mosque in Argos in the late 18$^{th}$ c. In the case of Messene, Tsivikis 2012, 65–66 fig. 7, dates the lime kilns to the Early Byzantine period, as in Olympia, where the lime kilns seem to have been created also in Late Antiquity (Bol 1984, 104).

[46] A short catalogue of the finds in Stais 1886, 79–82; for the sculptures of the Roman period see Katakis 2002, 300. The substantial lack of excavation data (Kavvadias 1900, 157–158) and the finding of the sculptures were the main reasons for initiating the further investigation of Building K (ongoing since 2017).

[47] Kavvadias does not mention this building in his excavation reports; the outline of its masonry is illustrated only in one of his mostly unpublished plans fig. 4; cf. Lembidaki 2003, 160 plan 56.

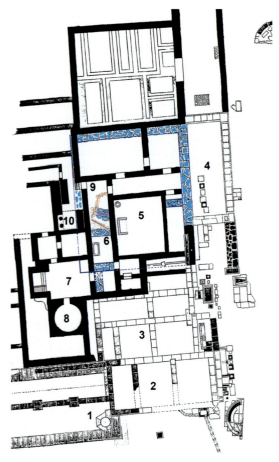

4 Building K. Walls in black: »Roman K«; walls in blue: »Hellenistic K«; 1) Dormitory Stoa with sacred well, 2) »Classical K« (»Asklepios' Bath«), 3) Late classical annex of the »Asklepios' Bath«, 4) Hellenistic Peribolos, 5) Central courtyard of »K« with parts of a water basin, 6) Room with a basin and drainage system closed in late 4th c. AD, 7) Hall with a built basin, 8) Circular room, 9) Staircase to the so-called Crypt, 10) so-called Crypt (© Archaeological Society at Athens [1905] – EphAArg; elaborated by J. Mavrommatidis and the author)

construction phases, not as yet accurately dated. The first phase includes the hall with a basin (in a later period reduced by about ⅓ of its size) and the adjacent circular room at the south-western part of the building (fig. 4 no. 7–8). The same architectural arrangement was implemented in the aforementioned *skana* in the Apollo Maleatas Sanctuary (fig. 1 no. 19), and the Building Φ in the Asklepieion (fig. 1 no. 5), north-east of the Temple of Hygieia, i.e. the Propylon of the early Hellenistic Hestiatorion, which is tentatively identified with the »Temple of the Egyptian Apollo and Asklepios« mentioned by Pausanias 2, 27, 6[48]. Furthermore, three of the original four marble slabs from earlier monuments remain at the western part of the central courtyard of »K«, forming a water basin[49], while another monolithic basin was found in secondary use in the adjacent room to the west (fig. 4 no. 5–6). In this room, parts of the water drainage system were revealed: a channel constructed with limestone belonging to the »Hellenistic K«, and two conduits consisting of clay tubes with mortar all around, placed in the solid Hellenistic layer; one of the latter was somehow connected to the basin in the central courtyard. Water played a very important role in Building K.

Around the end of the 4th century (or even later), according to the pottery and the many lamps found in a level that was probably a filling layer in the room west of the courtyard mentioned above, the western wall was rebuilt or radically repaired without an opening for the Roman ducts, which means they were no longer functional.

At the same time, a staircase was added to the north-western part of this room (fig. 4 no. 9; fig. 5), leading to a kind of crypt with a tripartite arrangement on the west side, erected using parts of two columns of unknown origin (fig. 4 no. 10; fig. 6). A special feature of the wall behind it allows the sun to enter at noon on specific days (fig. 7). Also, the lower parts of four amphoras of a not fully recognizable type were found embedded in the bedrock of this so-called Crypt. The finds, especially the pottery, confirm that the area

---

[48] All three buildings have a room provided with a shallow basin and next to it a circular room with a hollow in the ground, maybe for a *perirrhanterion* in the case of the Building K and the *skana* or a small water basin in a niche in the case of Building Φ: cf. Katakis 2002, 302. 306. 311; Melfi 2007, 116–121 fig. 20 (plan of the *skana*); 140–144 fig. 22 (plan of »Φ«); Trümper 2014, 224–230 fig. 8–10 (plans). For these rooms in the *skana* after restoration works, s. Lambrinoudakis 1992, 44–45 pl. 7–8. The use of these three buildings will be discussed in more detail when the excavation works in Building K are completed; cf., apart from the above, Roux 1961, 302; Galli 2004, 343–345.

[49] In earlier publications, this basin is described as a statue base (Kavvadias 1900, 157), while it is not mentioned in later studies.

was not abandoned before the 6th century. My initial thought was that the Crypt could have been dedicated to the cult of Isis, as a water crypt, reminiscent of the Egyptian nilometer, while the amphoras could have been used as containers for holy water. But, to my knowledge, there are no exact parallels[50]. Just like in the *skana*, the many fragments of lamps found in Building K indicate the nocturnal use of the rooms, which of course cannot help us to identify their function. In any case, it is difficult to believe that these three important buildings in the sanctuary – »K«, »Φ« and part of the *skana* – were dedicated to the cult of Isis, even if we have found her image in front of an altar on one lamp from the *skana* of the 2nd to 3rd century AD[51].

The great perimetric stoa of the 4th century AD incorporated the eastern part of the area of the Building K, mainly the so-called Hellenistic Peribolos (fig. 4), the *krepis* of which became part of the stylobate of the stoa[52], but we do not know yet of other transformations on the form of the building complex[53]. We hope that the progress of our excavation will eluci-

5   Building K; staircase to the so-called Crypt (© EphAArg – NKUA; photo author)

date further the history and function of Building K, as also of its predecessor »Hellenistic K«. What is certain is that the users of Building K, priests or other magistrates of the sanctuary in Late Antiquity, gathered here several statues of gods and many small votive offerings. A potent mid-6th century earthquake destroyed the building and buried these sculptures under the rubble until their rediscovery in 1886.

The gradual process of Christianization in the region of Epidauros is not clear. A five-aisled Christian basilica, with atrium and baptistery and richly decorated with mosaics was erected just outside the temenos in the early 5th century (fig. 1 no. 14)[54]. Pilgrims did not have to enter the pagan sanctuary to reach the basilica; they turned to the east just before the northern monumental, early Hellenistic Propylaia (fig. 1 no. 13). For the construction of the basilica, no recycled material from the main cult buildings of the Asklepios Sanctuary was used, hence the latter must have been

---

[50] The subject is researched in depth in Kleibl 2009, 102–114, and recently Mazurek 2022, 178–183. In the case of the *skana* at the Apollo Sanctuary, the special narrow and deep space used for the water management of the adjacent great cistern sponsored by Antoninus, could serve as a water crypt (Lambrinoudakis 1989, 48–49 pl. 33–35).

[51] Lambrinoudakis 1999, 71–72 fig. 55 (V. Lambrinoudakis); Podvin – Veymiers 2008, 63–64 fig. 2, who note the rarity of the subject; Veymiers 2014, 148–150, who doubts the attribution of the finds in Epidauros to the cult of Isis. For the rather few sculptures and inscriptions referring to Isis in Epidauros, s. Katakis 2002, 91–92 cat. 89 pl. 104 (head of an Isis statuette); 106–107 cat. 114 pl. 119 (doubtful fragments of a statue); 267–268. A sacred law with reference to an »Aphrodiseion«, a common temple for Aphrodite and Isis whose location remains unknown (IG IV² 743; Mazurek 2022, 38 with n. 55), is dated to the 2nd–3rd c. AD.

[52] The enclosure was thoroughly studied by Roux 1961, 246–249 fig. 61 pl. 72, 1, and later on by Lembidaki 2003, 160–166 plan 58 a fig. 67–70. Possible architectural elements from its superstructure were used later on in the early Christian basilica: Lembidaki 2003, 163–165 pls. 57. 58 b fig. 71.

[53] An inscription found in »K« mentions a library (IG IV² 456; Peek 1969, 99 no. 178), although its location remains unknown (cf. Katakis 2002, 302. 502 n. 1505; Melfi 2007, 123–124; Caruso 2014, 68–69. 75).

[54] Kavvadias 1918, 172–185. 190–191 fig. 12–28; Sotiriou 1929, 198–201 fig. 31–32 (late 4th c. AD); Asimakopoulou-Atzaka 1987, 59–61 no. 10 pl. 48–53 (early 5th c. AD).

6   Building K; so-called Crypt (© EphAArg – NKUA; photo author)

7   Building K; the west wall of the so-called Crypt (© EphAArg – NKUA; photo author)

still standing. The question of whether the old sanctuary and the Christian basilica both functioned at the same time cannot be easily answered. We have no evidence of an urban centre in this period, but at the same time the baths (at least the northeast complex) were still in use, and Building K was repaired, while the mosaics of a nearby house (fig. 1 no. 15) date a few years later than the basilica[55]. Therefore, people continued to visit the old sanctuary, despite the prohibitory laws of the emperors of the 4th and 5th centuries. The building of the new basilica was meant to convince people of the healing power of the new Christian saints; we know that the medieval chapel erected in the apse of the basilica was dedicated to Saint John the Baptist, who also had healing abilities[56].

Furthermore, written sources confirm that Epidauros was still not fully Christianized at the end of the 5th century. Soon after the death of Proclus in AD 485, Marinos, his successor as headmaster of the Neoplatonic School in Athens, took refuge in Epidauros[57].

Even if the city of Epidauros is only partially excavated, the architectural study of the theatre has provided us with strong evidence for the existence of a pagan, mystical worship. During Late Antiquity, the theatre was extensively remodelled: the *parodoi* on either side of the 2nd century AD stage building were closed, and access to the *orchestra* was only possible through a staircase in the middle of the *pulpitum*. Furthermore, a cubic

---

[55] It is the so-called House of the Partridge (named after the bird depicted on the mosaic floor of one of its rooms), dated to the 2nd quarter of the 5th c. (Kavvadias 1918, 172–173. 191 figs. 12. 29–35; Asimakopoulou-Atzaka 1987, 61–63 no. 11 pl. 54–55).

[56] Kavvadia-Spondyli 1989/1990.

[57] Katakis 2002, 328. 521 n. 1693. 1694.

8  Theatre of the city of Epidauros, late antique altar in the *orchestra* (© EphAArg – NKUA; photo author)

altar was built at the northern part of the *orchestra*, and beside it a stone bench from the *cavea* was set into the ground and equipped with a metal ring used for tying the animal destined for sacrifice (fig. 8)[58]. It is also evident that the theatre no longer served as the site of dramatic performances or as a place for the city's assembly, but for a mystical cult. We must always keep in mind that we have strong evidence for the mystical character of the cult in the Apollo and Asklepios Sanctuary since the Archaic period in relation to the chthonic cult of Asklepios[59], as well as the above-mentioned cult of Damia and Axesia. This tendency was reinforced in the Roman and Late Roman periods[60].

In any case, the transition from pagan beliefs to Christianity was gradual and smooth, as no traces of violent destruction are evident in the main buildings of the Asklepieion. The statuette of the young Asklepios with a scroll (fig. 3) whose iconography is directly connected to that of Christ, as the well-known statuette in Rome testifies[61], is an infallible testimony to this tranquil transition. We hope that the continuation of the excavations or even post-excavation research in the sanctuary, as well as in the city of Epidauros, will bring to light new evidence regarding this transitional period as it is attested in other sanctuaries[62].

---

[58] Petrounakos 2015, 81–87 figs. 3. 7–8, who suggested a date to the late 3rd or 4th c. AD. Maybe in the same period, many stone benches were also built into the fortifications on the acropolis of the city (Petrounakos 2015, 82–83 fig. 141–151). Recently, in the new publication of the so-called Herulermauer in the sanctuary of Olympia, Völling – Ladstätter 2018, 125–127 and Miller 2018, 138–142 argued that it was built in the 6th c., in the reign of Justinian, and that other fortifications in the Peloponnese, among them that on the hill above the theatre of the city of Epidauros, were erected in the same period.

[59] In 2017, the largest part of a peripteral building with an underground room was excavated by Prof. V. Lambrinoudakis in front of the late classical Tholos. According to the finds, it was built in the late 7th c. BC and demolished in the early 4th c. BC to make room for the lavish Thymele/Tholos. The three labyrinth-like corridors under its cella now played the role of the predecessor underground room (of the extensive bibliography on the Tholos see mainly Roux 1961, 131–200 fig. 29–42 pl. 37–52).

[60] Supra 253 with n. 28 and 254 n. 38. Apart from the already discussed buildings »K«, »Φ« and the *skana*, the so-called Building II at the eastern part of the Asklepieion was also destined for a mystic cult, especially in the Roman period up to the 4th c. AD: Lembidaki 2003, 146–159. 179–187. 210–211 pls. 48–55 fig. 57–66. Cf. also the finds, mainly lamps, from the drainage system of the cistern of Antoninos in the Apollon Maleatas Sanctuary (Lambrinoudakis 1989, 49 pl. 25 a; the final publication of the lamps is forthcoming by S. Vasiadi).

[61] Rome, Museo Nazionale Romano, Palazzo Massimo inv. 61.565: Bergmann 1999, 47–48 no. 8 pls. 40, 1–2; 76, 4; Jensen 2005, 32 and no. 75 fig. 13; Vorster 2012–2013, 418 and n. 104.

[62] Cf. the sanctuary of Olympia, where inscriptions document the presence of athletes even in AD 385, while a Christian basilica was established in the so-called Workshop of Phidias around the middle of the 5th c. outside the fortified area (Sinn 2002; Volling 2018).

## ABBREVIATIONS

EphAArg = Ephorate of Antiquities of Argolis
NKUA = National and Kapodistrian University of Athens

## BIBLIOGRAPHY

| | |
|---|---|
| Aslanidis 2003 | K. Aslanidis, The Roman Odeion at Epidaurus, JRA 16, 2003, 300–311 |
| Asimakopoulou-Atzaka 1987 | P. Asimakopoulou-Atzaka, Σύνταγμα των παλαιοχριστιανικών ψηφιδωτών δαπέδων της Ελλάδος II, Πελοπόννησος-Στερεά Ελλάδα (Thessaloniki 1987) |
| Avraméa 1997 | A. Avraméa, Le Péloponnèse du IVe au VIIIe siècle. Changements et persistances (Paris 1997) |
| Bergmann 1999 | M. Bergmann, Chiragan, Aphrodisias, Konstantinopel. Zur mythologischen Skulptur der Spätantike, Palilia 7 (Wiesbaden 1999) |
| Bilis 2007 | Th. Bilis, Ασκληπιείο Επιδαύρου: Θέρμες ΒΔ1 »Ισείον« (Athens 2007) |
| Bol 1984 | R. Bol, Das Statuenprogramm des Herodes-Atticus-Nymphäums, OF XV (Berlin 1984) |
| Caruso 2014 | A. Caruso, Le biblioteche come centri di cultura nel mondo romano, in: R. Meneghini – R. Rea (eds.), La biblioteca infinita. I luoghi del sapere nel mondo antico. Exhibition catalogue (Rome 2014) 61–81 |
| Defrasse – Lechat 1895 | A. Defrasse – H. Lechat, Épidaure. Restauration et description des principaux monuments du sanctuaire d'Asclépios (Paris 1895) |
| Galli 2004 | M. Galli, ›Creating Religious Identities‹: Paideia e religione nella Seconda Sofistica, in: B. E. Borg (ed.), Paideia: The World of the Second Sophistic (Berlin 2004) 315–356 |
| Gehn 2012 | U. Gehn, Ehrenstatuen in der Spatantike. Chlamydati und Togati (Wiesbaden 2012) |
| Gehn 2013 | U. Gehn, Eine Gruppe attischer Porträts im mittleren und späten 3. Jh. n. Chr. Eine Neubetrachtung, Boreas 36, 2013, 99–118 |
| Gehn 2016 | U. Gehn, Greek Mainland and Islands, in: R. R. R. Smith – B. Ward-Perkins (eds.), The Last Statues of Antiquity (Oxford 2016) 87–97 |
| Ginouvès 1955 | R. Ginouvès, Sur un aspect de l'évolution des bains en Grèce vers le IVe siècle de notre ère, BCH 79, 1955, 135–152 |
| Goette 1990 | H. R. Goette, Studien zu Togadarstellungen, BeitrESkAr 10 (Mainz 1990) |
| Griesbach 2014 | J. Griesbach, Jede(r) ist ersetzbar? Zur Wiederverwendung von Statuenbasen im Asklepios-Heiligtum von Epidauros, in: C. Leypold – M. Mohr – C. Russeberger (eds.), Weiter- und Wiederverwendungen von Weihestatuen in griechischen Heiligtümern. Tagung am Archäologischen Institut der Universität Zürich 21./22.01.2011, Zürcher Archäologische Forschungen 2 (Rahden/Westf. 2014) 55–70 |
| Heath 1996 | M. Heath, The Family of Minucianus, ZPE 113, 1996, 66–70 |
| Holtzmann 1984 | B. Holtzmann, LIMC II (1984) 863–897 s. v. Asklepios |
| Jacobs 2014 | I. Jacobs, Prosperity after Disaster? The Effects of the Gothic invasion in Athens and Corinth, in: I. Jacobs (ed.), Production and Prosperity in the Theodosian Period, Interdisciplinary Studies in Ancient Culture and Religion 14 (Leuven 2014) 69–89 |
| Jensen 2005 | R. M. Jensen, Face to Face. Portraits of the Divine in Early Christianity (Minneapolis 2005) |
| Kanellopoulos 2000 | C. Kanellopoulos, Το υστερορωμαϊκό »τείχος«: περίβολος τεμένους και περιμετρική στοά στο Ασκληπιείο Επιδαύρου (Athens 2000) |
| Katakis 2002 | St. E. Katakis, Επίδαυρος. Τα γλυπτά των ρωμαϊκών χρόνων από το Ιερό του Απόλλωνος Μαλεάτα και του Ασκληπιού, Βιβλιοθήκη της εν Αθήναις Αρχαιολογικής Εταιρείας 223–224 (Athens 2002) |
| Katakis 2023 | St. E. Katakis, Les statues honorifiques dans un sanctuaire hors de la ville: le cas du sanctuaire d'Apollon et d'Asclépios à Épidaure à l'époque romaine, in: V. Gaggasis-Robin – G. Biard – N. de Larquier (eds.), Les milles visages de l'honneur. Actes des IVes rencontres autour de la sculpture romaine (Bordeaux 2023) 49–63 |
| Kavvadia-Spondyli 1989/1990 | A. Kavvadia-Spondyli, Επιβιώσεις στοιχείων της λατρείας του Ασκληπιού στη βυζαντινή λατρεία του Αη-Γιάννη Νηστευτή στην Επίδαυρο, Archaiognosia 6, 1989/1990, 177–181 |

| | |
|---|---|
| Kavvadias 1885 | P. Kavvadias, Ἀγάλματα ἐκ τῶν ἐν Ἐπιδαυρίᾳ ἀνασκαφῶν, AEphem 1885, 41–54 |
| Kavvadias 1899 | P. Kavvadias, Περί τῶν ἐν Ἐπιδαύρῳ ἀνασκαφῶν, Prakt 1899, 103–105 |
| Kavvadias 1900 | P. Kavvadias, Τὸ ἱερὸν τοῦ Ἀσκληπιοῦ ἐν Ἐπιδαύρῳ καὶ ἡ θεραπεία τῶν ἀσθενῶν (Athens 1900) |
| Kavvadias 1918 | P. Kavvadias, Ἀνασκαφαὶ ἐν Ἐπιδαύρῳ (1918 και 1919), AEphem 1918, 172–195 |
| Kleibl 2009 | K. Kleibl, Iseion: Raumgestaltung und Kultpraxis in den Heiligtümern gräco-ägyptischer Götter im Mittelmeerraum (Worms 2009) |
| Konstantinidis 2022 | P. Konstantinidis, Η παρουσία και η λατρεία της Αθηνάς στο Ασκληπιείο και στην πόλη της Επιδαύρου, Athens University Review of Archaeology 5, 2022, 45–73 |
| Kraynak 1991 | L. Kraynak, The *Katagogion* at Epidauros: a revised plan, ANews 16, 1991, 1–8 |
| Lambrinoudakis 1989 | V. Lambrinoudakis, Ιερό Απόλλωνος Μαλεάτα Επιδαύρου, Prakt 1989, 43–56 |
| Lambrinoudakis 1992 | V. Lambrinoudakis, Ιερό Απόλλωνος Μαλεάτα Επιδαύρου, Prakt 1992, 44–52 |
| Lambrinoudakis 1999 | V. Lambrinoudakis (ed.), Το Ασκληπιείο της Επιδαύρου. Η έδρα του θεού γιατρού της αρχαιότητας (Marousi 1999) |
| Lambrinoudakis 2002 | V. Lambrinoudakis, Conservation and Research: New Evidence on a Long-living Cult, The Sanctuary of Apollo Maleatas and Asklepios at Epidauros, in: M. Stamatopoulou – M. Geroulanou (eds.), Excavating Classical Culture. Recent Archaeological Discoveries in Greece, Studies in Classical Archaeology I (Oxford 2002) 213–224 |
| Lambrinoudakis 2013 | V. Lambrinoudakis, Grenzen im Asklepioskult, in: M. Guggisberg (ed.), Genzen in Ritual und Kult der Antike. Internationales Kolloquium Basel 05.–06.11.2009 (Basel 2013) 92–112 |
| Lambrinoudakis 2018 | V. Lambrinoudakis, Anfänge und Entwicklung des Asklepioskultes in Epidauros. Der »Apollonaltar« und die Tholos, in: H. Frielinghaus – T. G. Schattner (eds.), Ad summum templum architecturae. Forschungen zur antiken Architektur im Spannungsfeld der Fragestellungen und Methoden (Möhnesee 2018) 125–138 |
| Lambrinudakis 1986 | LIMC III (1986) 323–324 s. v. Damia et Auxesia (W. Lambrinudakis) |
| Lattimore 1996 | S. Lattimore, Sculpture II. Marble Sculpture 1967–1980, Isthmia 6 (Princeton 1996) |
| Lenaghan 2016 | J. Lenaghan, Cultural Heroes, in: R. R. R. Smith – B. Ward-Perkins, The Last Statues of Antiquity (Oxford 2016) 259–266 |
| Lembidaki 2003 | E. M. Lembidaki, Μικρά ιερά στο Ασκληπιείο Επιδαύρου (PhD thesis, National and Capodistrian University of Athens 2003), <Μικρά ιερά στο Ασκληπιείο Επιδαύρου (didaktorika.gr)> (05.04.2023) |
| Mazurek 2022 | L. A. Mazurek, Isis in Global Empire. Greek Identity through Egyptian Religion in Roman Greece (Cambridge 2022) |
| Melfi 2007 | M. Melfi, I santuari di Asclepio in Grecia I (Rome 2007) |
| Melfi 2010a | M. Melfi, Rebuilding the Myth of Asklepios at the Sanctuary of Epidauros in the Roman Period, in: A. D. Rizakis – Cl. E. Lepenioti (eds.), Roman Peloponnese III. Society, Economy and Culture under the Roman Empire: Continuity and Innovation, Meletemata 63 (Athens 2010) 329–339 |
| Melfi 2010b | M. Melfi, Ritual Spaces and Performances in the Asklepieia of Roman Greece, BSA 105, 2010, 317–338 |
| Miller 2018 | M. Miller, Die sogenannte Herulermauer. Ein Beitrag zur spätantiken Geschichte des Heiligtums, in: Völling 2018, 129–143 |
| Mostratos 2013 | G. Mostratos, Οι αετωματικές συνθέσεις των Πελοποννησιακών ναών του 4$^{ου}$ αιώνα π.Χ. Εικονογραφία, ερμηνεία και αποκατάσταση (PhD Thesis, National and Capodistrian University of Athens 2013), <Οι αετωματικές συνθέσεις των πελοποννησιακών ναών του 4ου αιώνα π.Χ.: εικονογραφία, ερμηνεία και αποκατάσταση (didaktorika.gr)> (05.04.2023) |
| Nilsson 1945 | M. Nilsson, Pagan Divine Service in Late Antiquity, The Harvard Theological Review 38/1, 1945, 63–69 |
| Peek 1969 | W. Peek, Inschriften aus dem Asklepieion von Epidauros, AbhLeipzig 60, 2 (Berlin 1969) |
| Peek 1972 | W. Peek, Neue Inschriften aus dem Asklepieion von Epidauros, AbhLeipzig 63, 5 (Berlin 1972) |

| | |
|---|---|
| Petrounakos 2003 | S. Petrounakos, Ένα νέο λουτρικό συγκρότημα της ύστερης ρωμαϊκής περιόδου στο Ασκληπιείο της Επιδαύρου (unpublished Master dissertation, National and Kapodistrian University of Athens 2003) |
| Petrounakos 2015 | S. Petrounakos, Οι επιγραφές του θεάτρου της πόλης της αρχαίας Επιδαύρου (Athens 2015) |
| Pfaff 2018 | C. A. Pfaff, Late antique Symbols and Numerals in the Asklepieion at Epidauros, Hesperia 87, 2018, 387–428 |
| Podvin – Veymiers 2008 | J.-L. Podvin – R. Veymiers, À propos des lampes corinthiennes à motifs isiaques, in: L. Bricault (dir.), Bibliotheca isiaca I (Bordeaux 2008) 63–68 |
| Reinhardt 2018 | C. Reinhardt, Akroter und Architektur. Figürliche Skulptur auf Dächern griechischer Bauten vom 6. bis zum 4. Jahrhundert v. Chr. (Berlin 2018) |
| Ridgway 1981 | B. S. Ridgway, Sculpture from Corinth, Hesperia 50, 1981, 422–448 |
| Rizakis – Zoumbaki 2001 | A. D. Rizakis – S. Zoumbaki, Roman Peloponnese I. Roman Personal Names in their Social Context, Meletemata 31 (Athens 2001) |
| Roux 1961 | G. Roux, L'architecture de l'Argolide aux IV$^e$ et III$^e$ siècles avant J.-C. (Paris 1961) |
| Schörner 2003 | G. Schörner, Votive im römischen Griechenland. Untersuchungen zur späthellenistischen und kaiserzeitlichen Kunst- und Religionsgeschichte (Wiesbaden 2003) |
| Sinn 2002 | U. Sinn, Ειδωλολάτρες προσκυνητές, αθλητές, αθλητές και χριστιανοί, in: P. Themelis – V. Konti (eds.), Πρωτοβυζαντινή Μεσσήνη και Ολυμπία. Πρακτικά του Διεθνούς Συμποσίου Αθήνα 29–30 Μαΐου 1998 (Athens 2002) 189–194 |
| Sotiriou 1929 | G. A. Sotiriou, Αι παλαιοχριστιανικαί Βασιλικαί της Ελλάδος, AEphem 1929, 161–248 |
| Stais 1886 | V. Stais, Ἀνασκαφαὶ ἐν Ἐπιδαυρίᾳ (1886), Prakt 1886, 79–82 |
| Stirling 2008 | L. M. Stirling, Pagan Statuettes in Late Antique Corinth. Sculpture from the Panayia Domus, Hesperia 7, 2008, 89–161 |
| Sturgeon 1987 | M. C. Sturgeon, Sculpture I. 1952–1967, Isthmia 4 (Princeton 1987) |
| Sweetman 2010 | R. Sweetman, The Christianization of the Peloponnese: The Topography and Function of Late Antique Churches, Journal of Late Antiquity 3/2, 2010, 203–261 |
| Trümper 2014 | M. Trümper, Bathing in the Sanctuaries of Asklepios and Apollo Maleatas at Epidauros, in: A. Avramidou – D. Demetriou (eds.), Approaching the Ancient Artifact. Representation, Narrative, and Function. Festschrift in honor of H. Alan Shapiro (Berlin 2014) 211–231 |
| Tsivikis 2012 | N. Tsivikis, Πού πάνε οι πόλεις όταν εξαφανίζονται; Ο οικισμός της πρώιμης και μέσης βυζαντινής Μεσσήνης, in: T. Kiousopoulou (ed.), Οι Βυζαντινές πόλεις (8$^{ος}$–15$^{ος}$ αιώνας). Προοπτικές της έρευνας και νέες ερμηνευτικές προσεγγίσεις (Rethymno 2012) 47–71 |
| Veymiers 2014 | R. Veymiers, La présence isiaque dans le Péloponnèse. Sur les traces des lieux de culte, RA 2014/1, 143–151 |
| Vitti 2016 | P. Vitti, Building Roman Greece. Innovation in vaulted Construction in the Peloponnese (Rome 2016) |
| Völling 2018 | T. Völling, Olympia in frühbyzantinischer Zeit. Siedlung – Landwirtschaftliches Gerät – Grabfunde – Spolienmauer, OF 34 (Wiesbaden 2018) |
| Völling – Ladstätter 2018 | T. Völling – S. Ladstätter, Die spätantike Spolienmauer in Olympia, in: Völling 2018, 119–127 |
| Vorster 2012/2013 | C. Vorster, Spätantike Bildhauerwerkstätten in Rom. Beobachtungen zur Idealskulptur der nachkonstantinischen Zeit, JdI 127–128, 2012/2013, 393–497 |
| Voutiras 2022 | E. Voutiras, Πορτραίτα διακεκριμένων Αθηναίων του όψιμου τρίτου αιώνα μ.Χ., in: D. Damaskos – P. Karanastassi – Th. Stefanidou-Tiveriou (eds.), Πλαστική στη ρωμαϊκή Ελλάδα: νέα ευρήματα και νέες έρευνες. Διεθνές αρχαιολογικό συνέδριο, Αθήνα 12.–14.12.2019 (Thessaloniki 2022) 85–96 |
| Wagman 1995 | R. Wagman, Inni di Epidauro (Pisa 1995) |
| Ziegler 1994 | R. Ziegler, Aigeai, der Asklepioskult, das Kaiserhaus der Decier und das Christentum, Tyche 9, 1994, 187–212 |

*Stylianos E. Katakis, Associate Professor of Classical Archaeology, National and Kapodistrian University of Athens, Department of History and Archaeology. School of Philosophy, University Campus Zografou, 15784 Athens/Zografou.*
*[e] stylkatakis@arch.uoa.gr*

Panagiotis Konstantinidis

# RELIGIOUS SYNCRETISM IN LATE ROMAN *ACHAEA*

## RECONSIDERING THE IDENTITY OF »ISTHMIA IS 445«

**Abstract**

The study revisits an impressive, but not well-known old find, a larger-than-life seated male figure in the guise of Jupiter (inv. IS 445), found by chance in the area of the so-called Later Stadium of the renowned Panhellenic Sanctuary of Poseidon Isthmios, near Corinth. It is argued that the statue's tentative identification as a seated emperor is not plausible, and the same is true for its dating to the second half of the 2nd century AD. It is argued that its overall style points to a date in the second quarter of the 3rd century AD, while its hybrid iconography points to an identification as either Zeus/Sarapis or Zeus/Helios/Serapis. Its iconographic hybridity is in trend with the prevalent religious syncretism of the period, especially in the eastern part of the Empire.

The over-life-size seated male statue inv. IS 445 is an impressive old chance find, today displayed in the permanent exhibition of the archaeological museum at the Panhellenic Sanctuary of Poseidon at *Isthmia*, near Corinth (fig. 1–5)[1]. According to the official publication and the Isthmia excavations archive, the statue was found after heavy rain in the »gully next to road opposite Fortress and starting line of Later Stadium« (fig. 8). No exact findspot or date is recorded, although it is catalogued among the 1952–1967 finds from the sanctuary in the fourth volume of the Isthmia series[2].

The statue is carved in white, medium grained marble (probably Pentelic). Its head is broken through the lower neck, the right arm through the elbow, both feet below the drapery. The left arm was carved separately and attached to the shoulder by means of a circular dowel (0.043 × 0.036 m, depth ca. 0.07 m). The male figure is depicted seated on a high-backed throne, facing front, wearing a sleeved *chiton* and a thick *himation* draped over the left shoulder and across the lap, where it forms a large bunch-roll. The right arm is placed downwards, resting on the front of the throne (a small part of the hand is preserved on the armrest, fig. 4 b), while the left was raised, probably holding a long scepter. The right foot was placed forward, the left slightly back. The front of the throne's legs is decorated with thunderbolts in low relief (fig. 5). The figure wears long tousled hair falling on the shoulders on either side of the neck (fig. 4 a). No evidence of a beard survives, although Mary Sturgeon suggested its presence based on the relatively wide break at the bottom at mid-neck. The throne belongs to a common Classical type characterized by a high back and legs decorated with palmettes and volutes, also present in Macedonian tombs[3]. At *Isthmia*, a much more simplified version is employed, with simple volutes at the upper corners of the legs and an additional volute upside down near the bottom of the left leg (fig. 5). While in other

---

[1] For an overall presentation of the sanctuary's history (controlled by Corinth): Sturgeon 1987, 1–2; Gebhard 1993. Pausanias' account of the sanctuary: Gebhard 2013.

[2] Sturgeon 1987, 138 cat. 63 (»chance find from the gully next to road opposite Fortress and starting line of Later Stadium«. Dimensions: pres. h. 0.60 m, w. shoulders 0.68 m. Throne: w. front 0.92 m, pres. h. front 0.737 m, th. at right 0.515 m, w. rear 0.74 m, pres. h. rear 1.442 m). 183 (Appendix 1: »East of Sanctuary of Poseidon near Fortress«). The entry in the Isthmia inventory notebook reads: »Found in gully after heavy rain beside road downhill from excavation, across from city walls.«

[3] For the type in general see Richter 1966, 23–28; Stirling 2008, 100 with n. 22–23. The throne of the so-called Westmacott Zeus (n. 28) belongs to the same type.

1–3 Statue of a seated male figure, Isthmia Archaeological Museum inv. IS 445 (P. Konstantinidis; © Hellenic Ministry of Culture and Sports – Hellenic Organization of Cultural Resources Development, Ephorate of Antiquities of Korinthia)

4   Statue of a seated male figure, Isthmia Archaeological Museum inv. IS 445; a) Detail of the break at the neck, b) remnants of the right hand (P. Konstantinidis; © Hellenic Ministry of Culture and Sports – Hellenic Organization of Cultural Resources Development, Ephorate of Antiquities of Korinthia)

5   Statue of a seated male figure, Isthmia Archaeological Museum inv. IS 445, relief thunderbolts on the throne's legs (P. Konstantinidis; © Hellenic Ministry of Culture and Sports – Hellenic Organization of Cultural Resources Development, Ephorate of Antiquities of Korinthia)

examples a rectangular pillar (sometimes with moldings) supports the seat of the chair[4], at *Isthmia* a solid, roughly worked mass of marble is left underneath the seat. Rough-worked surfaces, together with the rough-worked back of the throne (and nape of the figure), were probably not meant to be seen, and traces of bright red color preserved on the sides of the throne could indicate the intention to partially conceal the unfinished surface.

Although expressing reservations due to its iconography (in particular the presence of the *chiton*), Sturgeon tentatively identified the statue as a portrait of an emperor or an imperial magistrate in the guise of Zeus/Jupiter »combining elements from the Italian and Greek traditions«, while, mainly due to the long hair and probable beard, it was dated to the Antonine period.

A more careful look at the style and iconography of the statue, however, leads to quite different conclusions. First of all, a dating to the mid-3rd century AD and not to the late 2nd century AD seems commensurate with its style. The overall treatment of the drapery, with the stiff ›schematic‹ cuts, deep drilled channels and ›manneristic‹ execution finds its best parallels in mid-3rd century AD sculpture[5], especially Attic sculptural production, such as

---

4   Cf. e.g. the Westmacott Zeus (n. 28), and the Asklepios statuette from a domestic shrine in Corinth, Stirling 2008, 97–98 cat. 3a figs. 5–6. 36 (later 2nd c. AD).

5   Cf. the cuts on the drapery of the portrait busts of Gordian III in Berlin (Staatliche Museen inv. Sk 385 [R102], AD 238–241: Wegner et al. 1979, 16–17. 21 pl. 7; Berressem 2018, 358 cat. 13) and Philipp the Arab in Rome

6 Portrait statue of Balbinus, Piraeus Archaeological Museum inv. 278 (D-DAI-ATH-Piraeus 123: K. Kübler; © Hellenic Ministry of Culture and Sports – Hellenic Organization of Cultural Resources Development, Ephorate of Antiquities of Piraeus and Islands)

sarcophagi[6] and portrait sculpture[7]. One of the closest parallels is the portrait statue of the emperor Balbinus in the guise of Zeus from the port of Piraeus (fig. 6)[8]. The identification of the statue as the emperor, owning to its close likeness to his numismatic portraits, is accepted by most scholars and, consequently, the statue is securely dated to AD 238, during the short five-month reign of Balbinus together with Pupienus Maximus (January–May)[9]. Based on the above, a dating to the second quarter of the 3rd century AD (ca. AD 235–250) is most probable for the Isthmia statue.

We now turn to the statue's iconography. As already noted by Mary Sturgeon, the high-backed throne, the raised left arm (probably holding a scepter), and the lowered right arm placed on the throne's armrest are direct reflections of the Pheidian statue of Zeus at *Olympia*[10], which, in turn, inspired the Iuppiter Capitolinus statue in Rome, a subsequent model for imperial representation in the guise of Zeus/Jupiter[11]. Nevertheless, both iconographic types have the chest bare, and, furthermore, up to now, no representation of a Roman emperor in the guise of the god wearing both the *chiton* and the *himation* survives[12]. Emperors are occasionally depicted seated on a throne fully clothed, but they usually wear the toga; in addition, no such example is accompanied by the symbol of the thunderbolt[13]. Furthermore, the identification of the statue as an imperial portrait can be excluded based on its long hair. No emperor of the 3rd century AD is depicted with long, tousled, unbound hair at shoul-

(Musei Vaticani Braccio Nuovo 124 inv. 2216, AD 244–249: Wegner et al. 1979, 32–33. 40 pls. 11 a; 12 a; Berressem 2018, 373–374 cat. 40).

[6] Cf. e.g. Rogge 1995, 135 cat. 22 pl. 51, 1 (2nd quarter of the 3rd c. AD); Katakis 2018, 124–125 cat. 119 pl. 46 (ca. 230 AD).

[7] Cf. the male portrait statue Athens National Museum inv. 3699, found in the riverbed of the *Ilissos*, 3rd c. AD: Theophaneidis 1939–1941, 4 no. 16 fig. 5.

[8] Piraeus Archaeological Museum inv. 278, AD 238: Wiggers – Wegner 1971, 242–243. 248 pls. 56 b; 78 b; Berressem 2018, 357–358 cat. 12; Tulunay 2018, 238–240. 245 fig. 7 c.

[9] Kienast 2011, 193.

[10] Kansteiner et al. 2014 II 221–284 no. 942–1020.

[11] Maderna 1988, 27–49; Papazapheiriou 2004, 36–42.

[12] Emperor assimilation to Zeus/Jupiter: Maderna 1988, 18–55; Karanastasi 1995, 221–226; Papazapheiriou 2004, 32–69. 199–202; Hallett 2005, 166–172.

[13] Cf. the colossal enthroned emperors in porphyry from *Alexandria* (Alexandria, Greco-Roman Museum inv. 5934: L'Orange et al. 1984, 119 pl. 46 a. b) and *Caesarea Crociata* (Caesarea National Park, Israel, without inv.; seated on a throne in grey granite; 2nd/3rd c. AD: L'Orange et al. 1984, 95 pl. 13 d; Fejfer 2008, 169 pl. 22). The British Museum (inv. 1861, 1127.23: Opper 2008, 70 fig. 53; 227 cat. 34. Contra: Fittschen 2014–2015, 217–224), and Louvre (inv. Ma 1121: Fittschen 2021, 22–24 cat. 7m1 [modern copy]) statues mentioned by Sturgeon (Sturgeon 1987, 138 cat. 63 n. 23) have proven not to be portraits of emperors.

der length[14]. The emperors Elagabalus (AD 218–222) and Gallienus (AD 253–268) are depicted in certain portrait types with longer than the military short-styled hair inaugurated by the emperor Caracalla (AD 211–217), but even then, locks are kept short, never reaching the shoulders[15].

Furthermore, despite the statue's findspot in proximity to the sanctuary's Later Stadium, to my knowledge, no other imperial portrait statue has been found in a Greek stadium. Sculptural decoration in Greek stadia was traditionally scarce, and the same continued to be true in imperial times[16]. The best-known examples of free-standing sculpture from a Greek stadium are the 4th century BC statue of Asklepios, the work of the Parian Thrasymedes, in the stadium of neighbouring *Epidauros*[17], and the 2nd century AD herms in the Panathenaic stadium of Athens[18]. The late 2nd century AD monumental arch serving as the entrance to the stadium at Delphi also comprised two niches for statuary in the central pillars, but was never completed[19]. At *Isthmia*, a series of four pre-Hellenistic foundations for bases line the south-western edge of the track in the final phase of the so-called Early Stadium, and two of them could have supported either statues of victors or inscribed decrees related to the conduct of the games (judging from their close association with the stadium). One foundation is much larger than the rest and Π-shaped, and although it might have supported a statue base of a family of victors, as Sturgeon observes, it is more likely that it belonged to a *proedria*[20].

The same is probably true for the so-called Later Stadium of the Isthmian sanctuary[21]. After the earlier stadium had been abandoned, a new stadium was erected in the third quarter of the 4th century BC in a natural hollow some 200 m to the south-east of the Temple of Poseidon (fig. 8). The stadium was rebuilt in the 1st century AD and is mentioned by Pausanias (2, 1, 7) as built of white marble. So far it has only been partially excavated. With the exception of a rectangular base for a small bronze statue placed at the end of the southern starting line[22], no other sculptural decoration has been found, although a small number of sculpture fragments belonging to statuettes and reliefs of different dates come from the area[23].

Based on the above, the statue is more likely to represent a deity. The thunderbolt clearly points to Zeus/Jupiter in his celestial aspect, but the symbol combined with the wearing of the *chiton* together with the *himation* clearly reveals an eastern influence, reflected either in the aspect of the

---

[14] Official 3rd c. AD imperial portraiture: Wiggers – Wegner 1971; Bergmann 1977; Wegner et al. 1979; L'Orange et al. 1984; Fittschen – Zanker 1985; Wood 1986; Berressem 2018.

[15] Elagabalus: Wiggers – Wegner 1971, 146–152; Bergmann 1977, 22–26; Fittschen – Zanker 1985, 114–117 cat. 97–98. Gallienus: Bergmann 1977, 47–59; Wegner et al. 1979, 106–120; Fittschen – Zanker 1985, 134–139 cat. 112–115; Berressem 2018, 192–203 cat. 50–68.

[16] For ancient Greek stadia in general: Zschietzschmann 1960; Romano 1981 (esp. 215 for statues at starting lines); Romano 1993.

[17] Prignitz 2014, 238–239. Statue bases have also been excavated at either end of the *Nemea* stadium starting line (Romano 1981, 77), and similar statues possibly existed at *Halieis* and the Hellenistic *dromos* in Corinth (Romano 1981, 215). In *Olympia*, two small statues of Nemesis were set up on either side of the vaulted passageway to the stadium (Valavanis 2004, 100. 103; Chatzi 2008, 305–306, 2nd c. AD).

[18] Willers 1967, 56–65.

[19] Bommelaer – Laroche 2015, 261–263 fig. 91.

[20] Broneer 1973, 55; Sturgeon 1987, 9; Gebhard – Hemans 1998, 38–39. 43 figs. 10. 15.

[21] Broneer 1973, 55–64. 66 pl. 6. It is also mentioned in IG IV 203, l. 24.

[22] Broneer 1973, 56–57 pl. 26 b (1.065 × 0.81 m, with a shallow cutting in the centre measuring 0.41 × 0.37 m). An analogous statue base is tentatively restored at the other end of the starting line, in the same relative position (Broneer 1973, 58. 60). See also Romano 1981, 77.

[23] It is not always clear if these sculptures were set up in the stadium, its vicinity, or were transported from elsewhere (surface finds). For example, a marble torch flame was excavated amongst the building debris used as filling underneath a passage amongst the seats of the northern part of the stadium (Broneer 1973, 57 pl. 26 e; 60 B5 = Sturgeon 1987, cat. 122). Fragments of sculptures from the Later Stadium: Sturgeon 1987, cat. 35A–C and 37–38 (statue of Leda, Hellenistic); cat. 40 (fragmentary right wing of an early Hellenistic Nike statuette, probably set up in the stadium); cat. 49 (relief of a bearded head, 470–460 BC; surface find); cat. 53 (fragmentary relief of a maenad holding a hare, 2nd c. AD); cat. 54 (Roman fragmentary relief of two legs). For smaller fragments see Sturgeon 1987, 182 (Appendix 1).

god, or, most likely, due to some kind of religious syncretism[24]. Zeus (or Jupiter) is almost never represented in Greece and Asia Minor during the Roman Imperial period wearing both garments. The few representations in media other than sculpture that are interpreted as this god are far from certain, as they lack any specific attributes or symbols pertinent to the god (e.g. the thunderbolt or the eagle) and, hence, could be equally identified as Zeus Ammon, Sarapis or Hades/Pluto[25]. A further handful of more secure identifications (accompanied by the above-mentioned common symbols), depict the god in a different iconographic type, which is not related to the Olympian Zeus and is usually shown in a standing position[26]. To my knowledge, no representation in sculpture of an enthroned Zeus (or Jupiter) in the Pheidian tradition, wearing the *chiton* combined with the *himation* and dating to the Roman Imperial period, survives from mainland Greece. On the contrary, the god is commonly represented wearing the *chiton* and *himation* in the eastern part of the Empire (i.e. Asia Minor, Cyprus, *Syria*, Nabatene, etc.) as e.g. Zeus Anpelites, Chalazios, Hidreus, Kyrios/Baalshamin, Labraundos, Laodikenos, Orkamenes, Stratios, Syrgastes, Thallos, to list but a few examples[27]. A small statuette of Zeus, the so-called Westmacott Zeus, today in the J. Paul Getty Museum in Los Angeles, belongs to the same category[28]. The figure is tentatively identified as a 3rd century AD representation of Zeus deriving »from the Graeco-Roman statues of Sarapis in the Hellenistic tradition«[29], based on the symbol of the eagle on the surviving armrest and the absence of the dog Cerberus.

In 3rd century AD *Isthmia*, although an oriental aspect of Zeus cannot be excluded, it seems however unlikely, as no cult of an oriental Zeus (or Jupiter) is yet documented in literary sources, inscriptions or through votives. In addition, although the cult of Zeus (as Eubouleus and Bouleus) as well as the cult of Iuppiter Capitolinus are attested in Corinth (the latter as expected in a Roman colony)[30], the god is not connected to local Isthmian theology and his cult seems to be overall absent from the sanctuary[31].

On the contrary, the syncretistic deities of Zeus/Sarapis[32] or Zeus/Sarapis/Helios share a similar iconography with the statue, as eloquently displayed in a bronze statuette of the syncretized deity Zeus/Helios/Sarapis, kept today in the British Museum (fig. 7)[33]. The statuette depicts the god seated in a high-backed throne, sporting a long beard, with sun-rays emanating from his tousled long hair, topped by the *modius*. He wears a sleeved *chiton* and *himation* and holds a scepter in his raised left hand. He is accompanied by an eagle on the left, probably balanced by the dog Cerberus on the right (now missing). Similar attributes and, hence, identification could

---

[24] For the meaning and use of the term in general: Van der Ploeg 2018, 37–45.

[25] LIMC VIII (1997) no. 322–323 (silver medallions, 2nd c. AD); no. 421 (gem; Augustan); no. 424 (gem; sometimes interpreted as Sarapis or Zeus Ammon) s. v. Zeus (P. Karanastassi – E. Ralli-Photopoulou).

[26] LIMC VIII (1997) no. 350 (thunderbolt, scepter; 1st/2nd c. AD); no. 353 (eagle, scepter; 2nd/3rd c. AD) s. v. Zeus (P. Karanastassi – E. Ralli-Photopoulou). Also no. 324 (lamp from the Delos synagogue; bust with eagle; Imperial period); no. 357 [?] (gem; standing, scepter, globe). Cf. also LIMC VIII (1997) no. 106 (gem; eagle); no. 110 (cistophoric tetradrachm, *Mylasa*; AD 128–130; eagle, shield, spear) s. v. Zeus/Iuppiter (F. Canciani).

[27] Cf. LIMC VIII (1997) no. 299 (*Cyprus*) s. v. Zeus (P. Karanastassi); LIMC VIII (1997) s. v. Zeus in per. orient. *passim*. Also Tran Tam Tinh 1983, 84.

[28] Inv. 70.AA.124: Vermeule 1975 (Zeus; product of an Asia Minor workshop, exported to Italy); LIMC VIII (1997) 352 no. 305 s. v. Zeus (P. Karanastassi). An alternative identification as Zeus/Sarapis (n. 32) cannot be excluded.

[29] Vermeule 1975, 99.

[30] Zeus Eubouleus/Bouleus: Kent 1966, 13 cat. 42. Iuppiter Capitolinus: Kent 1966, cat. 152. 194–196. Iuppiter Optimus Maximus: Kent 1966, 87 cat. 60. 152. 194–196. 198. Identification of the so-called Temple E as the Capitolium of Corinth: Walbank 1989. See also Evaggelidis 2010, 220–224. 229; Sanders et al. 2018, 30–32.

[31] A statuette of a bearded god was found in a deposit in the residential area of the Imperial period east of the temenos of Poseidon (the so-called East field): Lattimore 1996, 10–11. 57 cat. 4 pl. 4 c–d (probably Poseidon, but Zeus cannot be excluded).

[32] Zeus/Sarapis: Stambaugh 1972, 83–84; Hornbostel 1973, 22 n. 1; 220–232. 310. 318. 343. 353. 377; Tran Tam Tinh 1983, 43. 84–85; Romeo – Portale 1998, 102 (I. Romeo).

[33] Inv. 1772, 0302.172: Walters 1899, cat. 939; Cook 1914, 189 fig. 137; LIMC VII (1994) 689 no. 229 s. v. Sarapis (G. Clerc – J. Leclant).

also be argued for the Isthmia statue. Although the statue's head is not preserved, the presence of the *modius* alone or combined with the sun-rays cannot be excluded, while the eagle could have been combined with the more subtle thunderbolt reliefs on the throne's legs. The animal and the dog Cerberus could have been displayed on separate bases on either side of the statue, partly concealing the rough-worked surfaces painted in red on either side of the throne[34]. In addition, the god would have held a scepter with his raised left arm and, possibly, a phiale (*patera*) in his lowered right hand.

Lastly, it should be noted that an identification as only Zeus/Helios seems unlikely as, on the one hand, like the enthroned Zeus, Helios/Sol is usually depicted bare-chested wearing only the *chlamys* or, alternatively, a sleeved *chiton* (*tunica*) combined with the *chlamys*, while, on the other hand, no shrine of Zeus/Helios is attested in Greece[35].

7   Bronze statuette of Zeus/Sarapis/Helios, London, British Museum inv. 1772, 0302.172 (© The Trustees of the British Museum)

On the contrary, theological assimilation of solar Sarapis[36] to Zeus (Helios/Sol being considered, as we shall see below, as the material form of Zeus) was common in the 2nd and 3rd centuries AD. All around the Empire, frequent dedications to »Zeus the Sun, the mighty Sarapis« or to »Zeus the Sun, Sarapis« appear, and an analogous iconography to the one reflected in the British Museum statuette (fig. 7) develops[37]. More specifically, in Egypt Osirapis/Sarapis was considered as both a god of the upper (celestial deity symbolized by the sun disk) and lower worlds. Its dual aspect was reflected in its iconography, which drew on that of the Greek Hades/Pluton (*chiton* – Cerberus – *modius* – scepter), i.e. the Underworld Zeus (Zeus Chthonios), guardian of fertility and harvest, and that of celestial Zeus (Zeus Hypsistos; eagle – thunderbolt – sunrays), master of the sky[38].

At *Isthmia*, no ancient source mentions a shrine of Sarapis, syncretistic or otherwise, and a terracotta lamp decorated with the figure of Isis is the only votive found in the

---

[34] Cf. the early 4th c. BC cult statue of Cybele from Moschato, near Piraeus, where the lion is displayed on a separate base on the right (Papachristodoulou 1973, 189. 196 fig. 5 pl. 89).

[35] For a dubious exception in *Amorgos* see Cook 1914, 194–195 (under eastern influence [?]). Helios/Sol iconography: LIMC IV (1988) s. v. Sol (C. Letta); LIMC V (1990) Add. s. v. Helios (N. Yalouris – T. Visser-Choitz); Matern 2002.

[36] Sarapis/Helios: Stambaugh 1972, 79–82; Tran Tam Tinh 1983, 43. 85; LIMC VII (1994) 667. 692 s. v. Sarapis (G. Clerc – J. Leclant); Romeo – Portale 1998, 100–101 (I. Romeo).

[37] Zeus/Helios/Serapis: Cook 1914, 188–190; Vidman 1970, 116. 124. 144. 147. 151. 172–173; Stambaugh 1972, 79; Hornbostel 1973, 23 n. 3; 28; Tran Tam Tinh 1983, 48. 50; LIMC V (1990) Add. 1032 nos. 323. 388–391 s. v. Helios (N. Yalouris – T. Visser-Choitz); Veymiers 2003. Cf. also the temple of the god built by Hadrian on *Mons Claudianus* after the suppression of the Jewish Diaspora Revolt of AD 116–117 (Vidman 1970, 116 n. 46; Capponi 2010, 124–125).

[38] Cook 1914, 188–190. 430–437; Hornbostel 1973, 18; Tran Tam Tinh 1983, 85–86; LIMC VII (1994) 666–667 s. v. Sarapis (G. Clerc – J. Leclant); Portale-Romeo 1998, 100–102; Bergmann 2010, 117–119; Capponi 2010, 121–122. 127. The presence of the thunderbolts excludes an identification as Zeus Chthonios/Hades/Pluto (cf. LIMC IV [1988] no. 54 s. v. Hades/Pluto [R. Lindner]). Cf. also Cook 1914, 187 (Zeus/Hades/Helios Sarapis – one). For Zeus and the cult epithet *hypsistos* see also Parker 2017, 124–131.

sanctuary that can be associated with the Egyptian deities in general[39]. Nevertheless, the cult of Isis and Sarapis was popular at Corinth, with at least five temples attested in the city, Acrocorinth and neighboring settlements[40], while the cult of Helios was of particular significance in the sanctuary and especially relevant in the local myth[41].

According to the poet Eumelos (cited by Pausanias 2, 1, 1), the descendants of Helios became the mythic founders of Corinth. Pausanias (2, 1, 6) also describes how Helios and Poseidon vied for the city, with Poseidon getting the Isthmus of Corinth and Helios being awarded with Acrocorinth (later handed over to Aphrodite, the city's tutelary deity; 2, 4, 6)[42]. He also describes an altar to Helios (2, 4, 6) and his statue with those of the Armed Aphrodite and Eros at Acrocorinth (2, 5, 1). Furthermore, two gilded chariots – one carrying Helios' son, Phaethon, the other Helios himself – are mentioned, that stood on top of the arch that marked the starting point of the Lechaion Road, overlooking the Corinthian forum (2, 3, 2)[43]. Lastly, according to Mary Sturgeon, the significance of the god in Roman Corinth, along with Poseidon and Ceres, is also reflected in the Hadrianic decoration of the *scenae frons* of the city's theatre[44]. More specifically, high-relief heads of a Triton and a Nereid (or Aphrodite) project over the *hospitalia*, while busts tentatively identified as Demeter and Poseidon enhance the side pediments of the second storey. A bust of Helios crowns the entire facade in the pediment of the third storey, forming a group of the most important deities in the cult of the Roman city.

In addition, Helios is traditionally closely connected to Poseidon, the principal deity of the Isthmus, in literature and mythology. His daily journey begins and ends at sea, flying over the ocean. At its beginning and on his return, the Hours and the Nereids greet and attend to him. Thetis opens the stable door in the morning, while at night Poseidon is waiting for him at the edge of the ocean and Phosphorus picks up his horses to clean and rest them[45]. The assimilation of Helios to Zeus is also attested in literature, even prior to the Hellenistic period, as both deities are in essence personifications of the heaven/sky[46]. In Euripides (Med. 1258), Helios is referred to as »light born from Zeus«, while in orphic theology he is equated with Zeus, addressed as »immortal Zeus« to accentuate his universality[47]. According to Plutarch, Romans believed that the sun is Jupiter himself in his material form, and in the same way the moon is Juno[48]. In addition, just as the sun metaphorically ›sees‹ everything from the sky, Helios is consistently described in ancient literature as all-seeing, sharing the gift of omniscience with Zeus, and thus he is often invoked as a patron of oaths and referred to as »Zeus's eye«[49]. The identification is also attested in both

---

[39] Isthmia Museum inv. IP 2785: Podvin – Veymiers 2008, 63. 68 fig. 1 with bibliography.

[40] Two sanctuaries of Isis and two of Serapis on the slopes of Acrocorinth and Temple of Isis at *Kenchreai*: Paus. 2, 4, 6. See also Sanders et al. 2018, 74–75 (South Stoa Serapeum). Votive sculpture: Sturgeon 2004, cat. 88 (statuette of Isis from the *cavea* of the theatre; see also p. 205 with n. 28); Milleker 1985 (three heads of Sarapis); Sanders et al. 2018, 74 fig. 57. Frescoes: Sanders et al. 2018, 124 (Buildings 5 and 7 east of the theatre). Coinage: Bricault – Veymiers 2007. Inscriptions: Kent 1966, cat. 57. See also Bookidis 2003, 257–258.

[41] According to Farnell (Farnell 1896, 419) Helios' prominence in Corinth might go back to Mycenaean times, and predate the arrival of Poseidon.

[42] The myth was depicted in a fresco in the so-called Southeast Building of the forum, tentatively identified as a city archive or library (Sanders et al. 2018, 80–81 no. 21).

[43] Matern 2002, 12. 63–65; Sturgeon 2004, 80 n. 109; Sanders et al 2018, 104 no. 35.

[44] Sturgeon 2004, 77–85.

[45] Kakridis 1986, 224 (E. Roussos; also p. 226 for his numerous affairs with various Oceanids); LIMC V (1990) 1005–1007 s. v. Helios (N. Yalouris – T. Visser-Choitz). Cf. also Cook 1914, 333–338 (solar chariot).

[46] Cook 1914, 1–9. 186–730 esp. 186–197; Kakridis 1986, 224 (E. Roussos); LIMC VIII (1997) 310. 312 s. v. Zeus (E. Voutiras).

[47] Cook 1914, 197; Sick 2004, 434–435; Athanassakis – Wolkow 2013, 10. 88.

[48] Plut. qu. R. 77.

[49] Cook 1914, 196–197. Cf. also Kakridis 1986, 227–228 (E. Roussos; Helios »omniscient«, »despot of heaven«, »father of all«, »supreme«).

late antique Egyptian[50] and Mithraic traditions (one supreme god/celestial deity, the creator and controller of the universe)[51].

An increasing significance of the cult of the Sun is also in keeping with the overall 3rd century AD religious climate[52]. At the beginning of the century, the cult of the Syrian sun-god El Gabal (assimilated to the Roman sun god Sol and later on with Sol Invictus, regarded as a solar Zeus or Jupiter), promoted first by the empress Julia Domna and a little later by the emperor Elagabalus, would have resonated with the sanctuary. The god was worshipped in the form of a holy stone, a black conical meteorite (*baetilos*), and was usually depicted accompanied by the eagle of Zeus, symbol of the sky[53]. The importance of the cult of Helios/Sol culminated in the dedication of a large temple to Sol Invictus in Rome by the emperor Aurelian in AD 274, after his victory over Palmyra, establishing the cult as an official religion alongside the traditional Roman cults[54]. From Aurelian to Constantine I, Sol was of supreme importance, until Constantine abandoned Sol in favour of Christianity[55].

Based on the above and the importance of the god in local tradition, it is not surprising that a separate shrine of Helios is attested in the late 2nd century AD inscription IG IV 203, originally set up in the Sanctuary of Palaimon, and today housed in the Museo Lapidario Maffeiano in Verona. The text records the impressive list of buildings erected and repaired at the Isthmian sanctuary by the high priest for life, Publius Licinius Priscus Iuventianus, an official also known from several other inscriptions of the Antonine period found at Corinth and *Isthmia* (his career appears to culminate ca. AD 170–180)[56].

Although the buildings mentioned in the text are grouped together broadly according to their type, new constructions or repairs, their order within these groups seems to indicate geographical proximity (although nothing can be certain without excavation). This is implied by the mention (in the same section as the shrine of Helios) of the Palaimonion together with the *enagisterion* (i.e. the place of the *enagismos* or offering to the dead), two shrines identified through excavation as the two distinct enclosed areas built next to each other immediately south of the precinct of Poseidon's Temple (fig. 8)[57]. Following this logic, the Temple of Helios should be located in the vicinity of the Palaimonion and »the examining chambers« (ll. 12–13: τοὺς ἐνκριτηρί|ους οἴκους), as it is mentioned right after them and before the sacred Glen (an enclosed space tentatively located west of the Temple of Poseidon)[58]. The ἐνκριτήριοι οἴκοι (examining chambers)[59], judging from their name, must have had some connection to the local games and therefore should have been erected in the area of the Later Stadium, where the Panhellenic festival of the *Isthmia* took place. This is also the case for the athletes' and guests' quarters mentioned elsewhere in the text (l.

---

50  Bortolani 2016, 117–150 esp. 128–130. 144–145 (Hymns to Helios, early 4th c. AD).
51  Vidman 1970, 147–151. 173; Sick 2004, 447–461.
52  Cumont 1929, 181–194; Bailey 1932, 246–276; Beaujeu 1955, 410–412; LIMC IV (1988) 593–595 s. v. Sol (C. Letta); Martens 2015, 57 (iconographic hybridity within the religious culture of Roman Greece). The trend towards the establishment of one supreme god starts back in the reign of Commodus with the cult of Iuppiter *summus exsuperantissimus*.
53  LIMC III (1986) s. v. Elagabalos (C. Auge – P. Linant de Bellefonds); LIMC V (1990) 1037 no. 58–60 s. v. Helios in per. orient. (M. Gawlikowski); Matern 2002, 30–35. See also Frey 1989 (religious politics of the emperor); Altmayer 2014, 175–186. The identification of the statue as a representation of Elagabalus wearing oriental clothes (tunic and *chiton*) with the thunderbolt as the equivalent symbol of the eagle of El Gabal, or an imperial emblem, is excluded by the long hair of the figure, its dating and lack of parallels.
54  Sol Invictus: Halsberghe 1972; Matern 2002, 35–46.
55  Bailey 1932, 260; Halsberghe 1972, 155. 169. For the relation of solar imagery to imperial iconography see Bergmann 1998; Bardill 2012, 28–125; Deligiannakis 2017. Serapis and Roman emperors: Takács 1995; Taylor 2004 and Capponi 2010, 124–126 (Hadrian).
56  Geagan 1989; Sturgeon 2015, 162–164. 166–171. 179–180. 182 figs. 10.2; 10.4 (portrait statue in the Palaimonion). Contra: Piérart 1998, 97–100 (the benefactions of Priscus are dated ca. AD 100).
57  Geagan 1989, 358–359; Piérart 1998, 106.
58  Broneer 1973, 113–116.
59  See also Piérart 1998, 99 (»les pièces destinées à l'admission des candidats«).

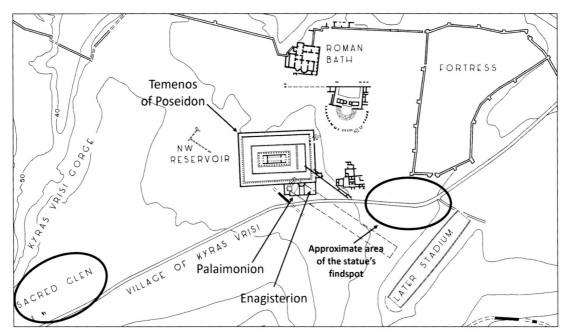

8　Plan of the Sanctuary of Poseidon at *Isthmia* and its environs (Courtesy of the American School of Classical Studies, University of Chicago »Isthmia Excavations«; elaborated by the author)

5: τὰς καταλύσεις; col. B l. 29: τὰς ξενίας[60]), along with a stoa with vaulted rooms and furnishings mentioned next to it (ll. 24–26: καὶ | τὴν στοὰν τὴν πρὸς τῷ σταδίῳ σὺν | τοῖς κεκαμαρωμένοις οἴκοις καὶ προσ | κοσμήμασιν). Consequently, the Temple of Helios was a new construction sponsored by Iuventianus, with a distinct enclosure and a cult statue (ll. 7–8: κατασκεύασεν ὁ αὐτός […]; ll. 13–14: καὶ τοῦ Ἡλίου τὸν ναὸν καὶ τὸ | ἐν αὐτῷ ἄγαλμα καὶ τὸν περίβολον), located in the vicinity of the Palaimonion and the adjuncts of the Stadium, i.e. roughly in the area where the statue was found (fig. 8).

The size and weight of the Isthmia statue indicate that its findspot could not have been far from its original placement[61]. Hence, the possibility should be considered that it represents the syncretistic deity of Zeus/Helios/Sarapis, in some way connected to the shrine of Helios, tentatively located in this area (east of the Palaimonion, in the vicinity of the 6$^{th}$ c. AD Fortress and the Later Stadium). Its identification as the cult statue of the shrine, a syncretistic successor to that of Iuventianus, is an intriguing possibility. At *Isthmia*, a 3$^{rd}$ century AD cult statue of Zeus/Helios/Sarapis would be well in line with the overall contemporary trend of accentuating the importance of the cult of the sun towards an ultimate henotheism, expanding on the well-established local tradition of sun worship on the one hand, and drawing on well-known contemporary theological assimilation traditions between the three gods on the other.

In terms of sculptural production, the statue would probably have been one of the last significant commissions undertaken in the sanctuary, as a considerable decrease in many types of activity is observed from about the middle of the 3$^{rd}$ century AD onwards, declining more sharply after the Herulian invasions of Greece in AD 267/268[62]. The use of Pentelic marble is consistent with the general trend observed in the sanctuary of using Pentelic marble for all good-quality

---

[60]　See also Kent 1966, 119–121 cat. 306, l. 15.
[61]　Conversely to M. Sturgeon's observation, the statue does not seem to be heavily weathered.
[62]　Sturgeon 1987, 2; Gebhard et al. 1998, 446 (activity in the central sanctuary declines abruptly ca. AD 220–240). Nevertheless, dedications of sculpture did not cease, as indicated by the late 3$^{rd}$ c. AD statue inv. IS 2415 (male portrait head; Sturgeon 1987, cat. 85 = Fittschen 2021, 108 cat. 65f pl. 69, 3–5, ca. AD 250–270). Other 3$^{rd}$ c. AD sculpture from the sanctuary: Sturgeon 1987, cat. 84 (bearded male portrait, 2$^{nd}$ quarter of the century); cat. 134 (= Sturgeon 2015, 181–182; inscribed tail shaped object, most likely part of a portrait statue support).

sculpture⁶³. Whether the sculptor worked on the spot or whether the piece was imported ready-made cannot be determined⁶⁴.

To sum up, the over-life size statue IS 445 should be correctly dated to the second quarter of the 3rd century AD and identified, based on its iconography, as a representation of a syncretistic deity, Zeus/Sarapis or Zeus/Helios/Serapis. A separate 2nd century AD shrine of Helios, a deity of local importance, is attested in the sanctuary (although not yet located). The statue could be a representation of Zeus/Helios/Sarapis, in some way connected to the local shrine of Helios, as seems to be indicated by its findspot. Its identification as the 3rd century AD syncretistic cult statue of the Temple of Helios is an intriguing possibility. The prevalent climate of religious syncretism attested in the Empire from the Severan period onwards is consistent with the presence of such a deity in a Panhellenic sanctuary.

## ACKNOWLEDGEMENTS

I would like to thank the director of the University of Chicago excavations at Isthmia Prof. Emerita E. Gebhard and administrator J. Perras for the information provided on the statue's findspot from the Isthmia archives and for permission to use the Isthmia village plan, as well as the Ephorate of Antiquities of Korinthia for permission to study the statue.

## BIBLIOGRAPHY

| | |
|---|---|
| Altmayer 2014 | K. Altmayer, Elagabal. Roms Priesterkaiser und seine Zeit (Nordhausen 2014) |
| Athanassakis – Wolkow 2013 | A. Athanassakis – B. Wolkow, The Orphic Hymns. Translation, Introduction and Notes (Baltimore 2013) |
| Bailey 1932 | C. Bailey, Phases in the Religion of Ancient Rome (Berkeley 1932) |
| Bardill 2012 | J. Bardill, Constantine, Divine Emperor of the Christian Golden Age (Cambridge 2012) |
| Beaujeu 1955 | J. Beaujeu, La religion romaine à l'apogée de l'Empire (Paris 1955) |
| Bergmann 1977 | M. Bergmann, Studien zum römischen Porträt des 3. Jahrhunderts n. Chr. (Bonn 1977) |
| Bergmann 1998 | M. Bergmann, Die Strahlen der Herrscher. Theomorphes Herrscherbild und politische Symbolik im Hellenismus und in der römischen Kaiserzeit (Mainz 1998) |
| Bergmann 2010 | M. Bergmann, Sarapis im 3. Jh. v. Chr., in: G. Weber (ed.), Alexandreia und das ptolemäische Ägypten. Kulturbegegnungen in hellenistischer Zeit (Berlin 2010) 109–135 |
| Berressem 2018 | B. Berressem, Die Repräsentation der Soldatenkaiser. Studien zur kaiserlichen Selbstdarstellung im 3. Jh. n. Chr. (Wiesbaden 2018) |
| Bommelaer – Laroche 2015 | J.-F. Bommelaer – D. Laroche, Guide de Delphes. Le site (Athens 2015) |
| Bookidis 2003 | N. Bookidis, The Sanctuaries of Corinth, in: C. K. Williams – N. Bookidis (eds.), Corinth. The Centenary: 1896–1996, Corinth 20 (Princeton 2003) 247–259 |
| Bortolani 2016 | L. Bortolani, Magical Hymns from Roman Egypt. A Study of Greek and Egyptian Traditions of Divinity (Cambridge 2016) |
| Bricault – Veymiers 2007 | L. Bricault – R. Veymiers, Isis in Corinth. The Numismatic Evidence. City, Image and Religion, in: L. Bricault – M. Versluys – P. Meyboom (eds.), Nile into Tiber. Egypt in the Roman World. Proceedings of the IIIrd International Conference of Isis Studies Leiden 11.–14.05.2005 (Leiden 2007) 392–413 |

---

[63] Sturgeon 1987, 3. 6 (also Appendix 3). Workshop activity at *Isthmia* is indicated by three pieces, all from small scale figures, dated to the period 390–146 BC, which were discarded unfinished: Sturgeon 1987, 5 cat. 22–23. 101. For Attic sculptural production in the Roman Imperial period in brief: Kokkorou-Alevras 2001. For Roman sculpture from Corinth in brief: De Grazia Vanderpool 2003; Sturgeon 2003.

[64] The statue does not seem to fit the criteria set by M. Sturgeon (Sturgeon 1989, 115) for recognizing the products of local Corinthian marble carving workshops. The rather mediocre quality of Pentelic marble used for the statue (micaceous, medium grained) is not necessarily an indication for a local workshop either, as an Athenian sculptor could have worked on the spot in imported lesser grade Pentelic marble.

| | |
|---|---|
| Broneer 1973 | O. Broneer, Isthmia 2. Topography and Architecture (Princeton 1973) |
| Capponi 2010 | L. Capponi, Serapis, Boukoloi and Christians from Hadrian to Marcus Aurelius, in: M. Rizzi (ed.), Hadrian and the Christians (Berlin 2010) 121–139 |
| Chatzi 2008 | G. Chatzi, Το αρχαιολογικό μουσείο Ολυμπίας (Athens 2008) |
| Cook 1914 | A. Cook, Zeus. A Study in Ancient Religion I (Cambridge 1914) |
| Cumont 1929 | F. Cumont, Les religions orientales dans le paganisme romain. Conférences faites au Collège de France en 1905 (Paris 1929) |
| De Grazia Vanderpool 2003 | C. De Grazia Vanderpool, Roman Portraiture. The Many Faces of Corinth, in: C. K. Williams – N. Bookidis (eds.), Corinth. The centenary: 1896–1996, Corinth 20 (Princeton 2003) 369–384 |
| Deligiannakis 2017 | G. Deligiannakis, Helios and the Emperor in the Late Antique Peloponnese, Journal of Late Antiquity 10, 2017, 325–350 |
| Evaggelidis 2010 | V. Evaggelidis, Η Αγορά των πόλεων της Ελλάδας από τη ρωμαϊκή κατάκτηση ως τον 3ο αι. μ.Χ. (Thessaloniki 2010) |
| Farnell 1896 | L. Farnell, The Cults of the Greek States V (Oxford 1896) |
| Fejfer 2008 | J. Fejfer, Roman Portraits in Context (Berlin 2008) |
| Fittschen 2014–2015 | K. Fittschen, Lesefrüchte VI, Boreas 37/38, 2014–2015, 205–224 |
| Fittschen 2021 | K. Fittschen, Privatporträts mit Repliken. Zur Sozialgeschichte römischer Bildnisse der mittleren Kaiserzeit (Wiesbaden 2021) |
| Fittschen – Zanker 1985 | K. Fittschen – P. Zanker, Katalog der römischen Porträts in den Capitolinischen Museen und den anderen kommunalen Sammlungen der Stadt Rom I. Kaiser- und Prinzenbildnisse (Mainz 1985) |
| Frey 1989 | M. Frey, Untersuchungen zur Religion und zur Religionspolitik des Kaisers Elagabal (Stuttgart 1989) |
| Geagan 1989 | D. Geagan, The Isthmian Dossier of P. Licinius Priscus Juventianus, Hesperia 58, 1989, 349–360 |
| Gebhard 1993 | E. Gebhard, The Evolution of a Pan-Hellenic Sanctuary. From Archaeology Towards History at Isthmia, in: N. Marinatos – R. Hägg (eds.), Greek Sanctuaries. New Approaches (London 1993) 123–141 |
| Gebhard 2013 | E. Gebhard, Pausanias at the Isthmian Sanctuary. The Principles Governing his Narrative, in: K. Kissas – W. Niemeier (eds.), The Corinthia and the Northeast Peloponnese. Proceedings of the International Conference Loutraki 26.–29.03.2009 (Munich 2013) 263–274 |
| Gebhard – Hemans 1998 | E. Gebhard – F. Hemans, University of Chicago Excavations at Isthmia II, Hesperia 67, 1998, 1–63 |
| Gebhard et al. 1998 | E. Gebhard – F. Hemans – J. Hayes, University of Chicago Excavations at Isthmia 1989 III, Hesperia 67, 1998, 405–456 |
| Hallett 2005 | C. Hallett, The Roman Nude. Heroic Portrait Statuary 200 B.C. – A.D. 300 (Oxford 2005) |
| Halsberghe 1972 | G. Halsberghe, The Cult of Sol Invictus (Leiden 1972) |
| Hornbostel 1973 | W. Hornbostel, Sarapis. Studien zur Überlieferungsgeschichte, den Erscheinungsformen und Wandlungen der Gestalt eines Gottes (Leiden 1973) |
| Kakridis 1986 | I. Kakridis (ed.), Ελληνική Μυθολογία Β΄ (Athens 1986) |
| Kansteiner et al. 2014 | S. Kansteiner – L. Lehmann – K. Hallof – A. Filges – R. Krumeich – P. Weitmann, Der neue Overbeck. Die antiken Schriftquellen zu den bildenden Künsten der Griechen (Berlin 2014) |
| Karanastasi 1995 | P. Karanastasi, Ζητήματα της εικονογραφίας και της παρουσίας των ρωμαίων αυτοκρατόρων στην Ελλάδα, AEphem 134, 1995, 221–226 |
| Katakis 2018 | S. Katakis, Athens, National Archaeological Museum I. Attic Sarcophagi with Garlands, Erotes and Dionysiac Themes, CSIR Greece I 2 (Athens 2018) |
| Kent 1966 | J. Kent, Corinth 8, 3. The Inscriptions 1926–1950 (Princeton 1966) |
| Kienast 2011 | D. Kienast, Römische Kaisertabelle. Grundzüge einer römischen Kaiserchronologie $^5$(Darmstadt 2011) |

| | |
|---|---|
| Kokkorou-Alevras 2001 | G. Kokkorou-Alevras, Δραστηριότητες των αττικών εργαστηρίων γλυπτικής την εποχή της ρωμαιοκρατίας, in: Καλλίστευμα. Μελέτες προς τιμήν της Όλγας Τζάχου-Αλεξανδρή (Athens 2001) 319–348 |
| Lattimore 1996 | S. Lattimore, Isthmia 6. Sculpture II. Marble Sculpture 1967–1980 (Princeton 1996) |
| L'Orange et al. 1984 | H. L'Orange – R. Unger – M. Wegner, Das spätantike Herrscherbild von Diokletian bis zu den Konstantin-Söhnen 284–361 n. Chr., Das römische Herrscherbild III 4 (Berlin 1984) |
| Maderna 1988 | C. Maderna, Iuppiter, Diomedes und Merkur als Vorbilder für römische Bildnisstatuen. Untersuchungen zum römischen statuarischen Idealporträt (Heidelberg 1988) |
| Martens 2015 | B. A. Martens, Sarapis as Healer in Roman Athens: Reconsidering the Identity of Agora S 1068, in: M. Miles (ed.), Autopsy in Athens. Recent Archaeological Research on Athens and Attica (Oxford 2015) 51–65 |
| Matern 2002 | P. Matern, Helios und Sol. Kulte und Ikonographie des griechischen und römischen Sonnengottes (Istanbul 2002) |
| Milleker 1985 | E. Milleker, Three Heads of Sarapis from Corinth, Hesperia 54, 1985, 121–135 |
| Opper 2008 | T. Opper, Hadrian. Empire and Conflict. Exhibition Catalogue British Museum (London 2008) |
| Papachristodoulou 1973 | C. Papachristodoulou, Άγαλμα και ναός Κυβέλης εν Μοσχάτω Αττικής, AEphem 1973, 189–217 |
| Papazapheiriou 2004 | G. Papazapheiriou, Οι ιδεαλιστικές απεικονίσεις των Ρωμαίων αυτοκρατόρων (PhD University of Thessaloniki 2004) |
| Parker 2017 | R. Parker, Greek Gods Abroad. Names, Natures, and Transformations (Berkeley 2017) |
| Piérart 1998 | M. Piérart, Panthéon et hellénisation dans la colonie romaine de Corinthe. La »redécouverte« du culte de Palaimon à l'Isthme, Kernos 11, 1998, 85–109 |
| Podvin – Veymiers 2008 | J. Podvin – R. Veymiers, A propos des lampes corinthiennes à motifs isiaques, in: L. Bricault (ed.), Bibliotheca Isiaca I (Bordeaux 2008) 63–68 |
| Prignitz 2014 | S. Prignitz, Bauurkunden und Bauprogramm von Epidauros (400–350). Asklepiostempel, Tholos, Kultbild, Brunnenhaus (Munich 2014) |
| Richter 1966 | G. Richter, The Furniture of the Greeks, Etruscans and Romans (London 1966) |
| Rogge 1995 | S. Rogge, Die attischen Sarkophage I. Achill und Hippolytos, Die antiken Sarkophagreliefs IX 1, 1 (Berlin 1995) |
| Romano 1981 | D. Romano, The Stadia of the Peloponnesos (PhD University of Pennsylvania 1981) |
| Romano 1993 | D. Romano, Athletics and Mathematics in Archaic Corinth. The Origins of the Greek Stadion (Philadelphia 1993) |
| Romeo – Portale 1998 | I. Romeo – E. Portale, Gortina 3. Le sculture (Padova 1998) |
| Sanders et al. 2018 | G. Sanders – J. Palinkas – I. Tzonou-Herbst – J. Herbst, Ancient Corinth. Site Guide (Princenton 2018) |
| Sick 2004 | D. Sick, Mit(h)ra(s) and the Myths of the Sun, Numen 51, 2004, 432–467 |
| Stambaugh 1972 | J. Stambaugh, Sarapis Under the Early Ptolemies (Leiden 1972) |
| Stirling 2008 | L. Stirling, Pagan Statuettes in Late Antique Corinth, Hesperia 77, 2008, 89–161 |
| Sturgeon 1987 | M. Sturgeon, Isthmia 4. Sculpture I 1952–1967 (Princeton 1987) |
| Sturgeon 1989 | M. Sturgeon, Sculptures from Corinthia and Isthmia. A Case for a local »Workshop«, in: S. Walker – A. Cameron (eds.), The Greek Renaissance in the Roman Empire. Papers from the 10th British Museum Classical Colloquium (London 1989) 114–121 |
| Sturgeon 2003 | M. Sturgeon, Sculptures at Corinth 1896–1996, in: C. K. Williams – N. Bookidis (eds.), Corinth. The centenary: 1896–1996, Corinth 20 (Princeton 2003) 351–368 |
| Sturgeon 2004 | M. Sturgeon, Corinth 9, 3. Sculpture. The Assemblage from the Theatre (Princeton 2004) |
| Sturgeon 2015 | M. Sturgeon, New Sculptures from the Isthmian Palaimonion, in: E. Gebhard – T. Gregory (eds.), Bridge of the Untiring Sea. The Corinthian Isthmus from Prehistory to Late Antiquity (Princeton 2015) 159–192 |
| Takács 1995 | S. Takács, Isis and Sarapis in the Roman World (Leiden 1995) |
| Taylor 2004 | R. Taylor, Hadrian's Serapeum in Rome, AJA 108, 2004, 223–266 |

| | |
|---|---|
| Theophaneidis 1939–1941 | B. Theophaneidis, Αρχαιολογικά χρονικά. Νέα προσκτήματα Εθνικού Αρχαιολογικού Μουσείου κατά τα έτη 1930, 1931 και 1932, AEphem 1939–1941, 1–23 |
| Tran Tam Tinh 1983 | V. Tran Tam Tinh, Sérapis debout. Corpus des monuments de Sérapis debout et étude iconographique (Leiden 1983) |
| Tulunay 2018 | E. Tulunay, Eine Statue des Balbinus aus Soloi Pompeiopolis in Kilikien. Identifikation und Interpretation, in: M. Aurenhammer (ed.), Sculpture in Roman Asia Minor. Proceedings of the International Conference Selçuk 01.–03.10.2013, SoSchrÖAI 56 (Vienna 2018) 237–245 |
| Valavanis 2004 | P. Valavanis, Games and Sanctuaries in Ancient Greece. Olympia, Delphi, Isthmia, Nemea, Athens (Athens 2004) |
| Van der Ploeg 2018 | G. van der Ploeg, The Impact of the Roman Empire on the Cult of Asclepius (Leiden 2018) |
| Vermeule 1975 | C. Vermeule, The Westmacott Jupiter. An Enthroned Zeus of Late Antique Aspect, GettyMusJ 2, 1975, 99–108 |
| Veymiers 2003 | R. Veymiers, Sérapis et l'aigle. Polysémie d'un iconotype, in: C. Cannuyer – D. Fredericq-Homes – V. Prevost – J. Ries – A. Schoors – J. Verpoorten (eds.), Les lieux de culte en Orient. Jacques Thiry in honorem (Brussels 2003) 265–285 |
| Vidman 1970 | L. Vidman, Isis und Sarapis bei den Griechen und Römern. Epigraphische Studien zur Verbreitung und zu den Trägern des ägyptischen Kultes (Berlin 1970) |
| Walbank 1989 | M. Walbank, Pausanias, Octavia and the Temple E at Corinth, BSA 84, 1989, 361–394 |
| Walters 1899 | H. Walters, Catalogue of the Bronzes in the British Museum. Greek, Roman & Etruscan (London 1899) |
| Wegner et al. 1979 | M. Wegner – J. Bracker – W. Real, Gordianus III bis Carinus, Das römische Herrscherbild III 3 (Berlin 1979) |
| Wiggers – Wegner 1971 | H. Wiggers – M. Wegner, Caracalla, Geta, Plautilla, Macrinus bis Balbinus, Das römische Herrscherbild III 1 (Berlin 1971) |
| Willers 1967 | D. Willers, Zum Hermes Propylaios des Alkamenes, JdI 82, 1967, 37–109 |
| Wood 1986 | S. Wood, Roman Portrait Sculpture 217–260 A.D. The Transformation of an Artistic Tradition (Leiden 1986) |
| Zschietschmann 1960 | W. Zschietschmann, Wettkampf- und Übungsstätten in Griechenland. Stadion – Palästra – Gymnasion. Eine Übersicht (Schorndorf 1960) |

*Panagiotis Konstantinidis, Post-Doctoral Researcher, Institute of Historical Research, National Hellenic Research Foundation, 83 Fotiou Korytsas str., 18545 Piraeus, Greece.*
*[e] panagiotis_konstantinidis@hotmail.com*

Aleksandra Nikoloska

# STATUARY COLLECTIONS FROM THE LATE ANTIQUE RESIDENCES IN *STOBI*

**Abstract**

Further considerations about the statuary found in the context of the late antique residences in *Stobi* are made, particularly those from the so-called Houses of Parthenius and Polycharmos. These statues belong to different periods than the context of their finding, ranging in date from the Hellenistic period up to Roman Imperial times. Some of them might have been locally made, but most of them are imports exhibiting high artistic qualities, all of them serving new purposes as collectables. This study focuses mostly on their possible original position and their reuse in secondary contexts before their final deposit. It also argues whether they are a legacy from the local heritage or imported; their style, dating and provenience are considered, introducing new perspectives, all with the purpose of recognizing the late antique habit of preserving Roman statuary and worship among the local aristocracy.

A number of late antique urban residences of considerable size, located in the prominent central area of *Stobi*, have been excavated between 1920s and 1940s by the National Museum in Belgrade; today they are known as the House of Parthenius, the House of Polycharmos, the House of Peristeria, Domus Fullonica, the Episcopal Residence, etc.[1] They were built or re-built in the 4th century and survived over the next two centuries. All of them have common features such as peristyle courts with columns, paved floors with elaborate mosaics, and large apsidal rooms with niches, demonstrating the life of the provincial aristocracy and the changing society of late antique *Stobi*. Late antique residences were inhabited by influential city aristocrats, men of wealth and prestige, well-educated and well-travelled[2]. In those days *Stobi* was oriented more towards the ruling East, culturally more dominant in the 5th century throughout the Mediterranean. Many of these eastern influences can be observed since such urban residences were predominant in the East and in northern Africa, contrary to the western provinces where we usually find them in the countryside[3].

Among them, the House of Parthenius (fig. 1) stands out in terms of its architectural decor and the statuary found within as the most luxurious house excavated in *Stobi*[4]. Built probably in the mid-4th century and refurbished around the early 5th, it was occupied until the late 6th century. It was given a rather romanticized name – the House of Parthenius, also known as the Theodosian Palace. It is called the House of Parthenius because of the bronze seal bearing that name that was found in one of the rooms, and the name Theodosius refers to the fact that he was visiting *Stobi* in 388 where he issued two decrees (Cod. Theod. 16, 4, 2; 16, 5, 15) and this residence was believed most fit for an emperor[5]. However, a distinction is made between the two in the literature, regarded as separate objects because at the state of their discovery they did not correspond

---

[1] Nestorović 1931; Nestorović 1936; Mano-Zissi 1940; Kitzinger 1946; Wiseman 1973.
[2] Ellis 1991; Sodini 2003, 35–36.
[3] The opened central courtyard is in fact a Greek tradition; mostly we find analogies among late antique houses in Asia Minor. See Özgenel 2007, 262–263.
[4] Petković 1928a; 1928b; 1929; 1930; 1931; also Kitzinger 1946, 124–127; Kolarik 1987, 304; Mikulčić 2003, 170–175; Gerasimovska 2009, 68–75.
[5] This arbitrary assumption of the residence being most suited for Theodosius should be reconsidered. A Christian emperor, defiant on the matter of pagan worship, whose decrees diminished religious activity concerning ›past‹ gods and resulted in the complete banning of pagan worship in 391, would not have been conveniently welcomed

architecturally. The proximity of the two, forming a quadrant insula, could be an argument that at one point they formed a single residential complex since the architecture of city houses changed regularly to suit new spatial requirements of different periods[6].

The earliest publications on the House of Parthenius did not go into great detail considering the precise location and context of the discoveries. Nevertheless, we know that within the three years of the campaign (1927–1930) many statues were discovered in the area of the peristyle and the pool of the house, now all in the Belgrade National Museum[7]: the bronze statuettes of Apollo[8], Lar[9], Fortuna[10], the exquisite bronze satyrs[11], a bronze statue of Venus[12] and another marble torso of Venus with a dolphin[13]. Marble statuary of larger dimensions were also discovered, such as the lower part of a marble Hygeia[14], a front half of the gilded marble head of Serapis[15], a marble statue of Dionysus-Liber with an inscription (fig. 2)[16], a statue of Artemis (fig. 3)[17], also a marble head of Kora[18], and a smaller, marble head of Zeus or Asclepius[19]. Votive reliefs were also unearthed, a marble archaistic one depicting Pan with the nymphs (fig. 4)[20], and a fragmented one of enthroned Cybele flanked with lions (fig. 5)[21].

The statuary found in the context of the House of Parthenius has already been understood as a late antique collection[22]. Petković interpreted and described most of the statues as a single assemblage. He selected the preserved ones and focused on their dating and stylistic features, disregarding the fragmented pieces. In his reports we read that many other sculptural fragments were found in the pool, including fingers, limbs and torsos; we should therefore consider that there were more statues originally deposited here[23]. Although the sculptures discussed were found in

---

in an environment where pagan atmosphere was preserved. For the interpretations of the Theodosian decrees in the late antique context of private space see Baldini Lippolis 2007.

[6] See Özgenel 2007, 249–251. In this study I will refer to the entire complex as a single residential building under the name House of Parthenius.

[7] Since recently, most of the statues are on display at the permanent exhibit. I hereby express my gratitude to the National Museum in Belgrade and the colleagues Bojana Borić Brešković and Deana Ratković for kindly providing our Centre with the latest photographs.

[8] Petković 1937, 24 cat. VI; Grbić 1958, 96; Düll 1977, no. 32 fig. 13; Nikoloska 2015c, 83 fig. 1.

[9] Petković 1937, 24–25 cat. VII; Düll 1977, no. 267 fig. 64; Nikoloska 2015c, 83 fig. 2.

[10] Petković 1937, 25 cat. VIII; Grbić 1958, 96; Düll 1977, no. 250 fig. 63; Nikoloska 2015c, 83 fig. 3.

[11] Bronze satyr playing a flute (Petković 1937, 13–15 cat. II; Grbić 1958, 42–44; Bitrakova Grozdanova 1987, 129–130 pl. 3, 1; Sokolovska 1987, no. 161 pl. 65, 1. 2; Nikoloska 2015c, 83 fig. 6). Bronze satyr dancing (Petković 1937, 16–21 cat. III; Grbić 1958, 42–44; Bitrakova Grozdanova 1987, 130–131 pl. 3, 2; Sokolovska 1987, no. 160 pl. 64, 1. 2; Nikoloska 2015c, 83 fig. 7).

[12] Petković 1937, 21–22 cat. IV; Grbić 1958, 92–93; Düll 1977, no. 11 fig. 12; Nikoloska 2015c, 85 fig. 8.

[13] The statue is now unfortunately lost, according to Deana Ratković from the National Museum in Belgrade, probably destroyed during the war.

[14] Petković 1937, 32 fig. 20; Grbić 1958, 91 no. 50 pl. 61; Düll 1977, no. 195 fig. 53; Sokolovska 1987, no. 186 pl. 71, 4; Nikoloska 2015c, 83 fig. 4.

[15] Petković 1937, 30–31 cat. XI fig. 18; Grbić 1958, 89 pl. 57; Hornbostel 1973, 242 no. 5 fig. 200; Düll 1977, no. 276 fig. 66; Sokolovska 1987, 206–207 no. 196 pl. 75, 1; Bitrakova Grozdanova 1999, 58–67 fig. 1; Mikulčić 2003, 67; Nikoloska 2015b, 261; Nikoloska 2015c, 83 fig. 5.

[16] Saria 1930, 64; Vulić 1933, no. 101; Petković 1937, 22–23 cat. V fig. 8; Grbić 1958, 91–92 pl. 62; Düll 1977, no. 106 fig. 26; Sokolovska 1987, no. 154 pl. 61, 3; Nikoloska 2015a, 88–89 fig. 1; Nikoloska 2105c, 91–92 fig. 9.

[17] Petković 1931, 225; Mano-Zissi 1973, fig. 101; Düll 1977, no. 68 fig. 15; Sokolovska 1987, no. 143 pl. 57, 3.

[18] Petković 1937, 12; Grbić 1958, 37 pl. 23; Mano-Zissi 1973, 93; Mano-Zissi 1981, fig. 4; Sokolovska 1987, no. 142 pl. 57, 2; Nikoloska 2015c, 85 fig. 12.

[19] Grbić 1939, 13; Sokolovska 1987, no. 185 pl. 71, 2. 3.

[20] Petković 1937, 12 cat. I; Grbić 1958, 29–30; Düll 1977, no. 208 fig. 65; Bitrakova Grozdanova 1987, 121–122 pl. 4, 1; Nikoloska 2015c, 85 fig. 10.

[21] Vulić 1931, 239 no. 638; Petković 1937, 26 cat. IX; Düll 1977, no. 282; Sokolovska 1988, no. 10; Vermaseren 1989, no. 315; Nikoloska 2010, 70 fig. 4; Nikoloska 2015c, 85 fig. 11.

[22] Petković 1937. During later years, the sculptures were published in separate catalogues and studies often ordered by category instead of by the archaeological context, which led to some anachronistic mistakes.

[23] Further collaboration with the National Museum in Belgrade with the aim of finding more relatable material will certainly shed more light on the study of the late antique residences of *Stobi*.

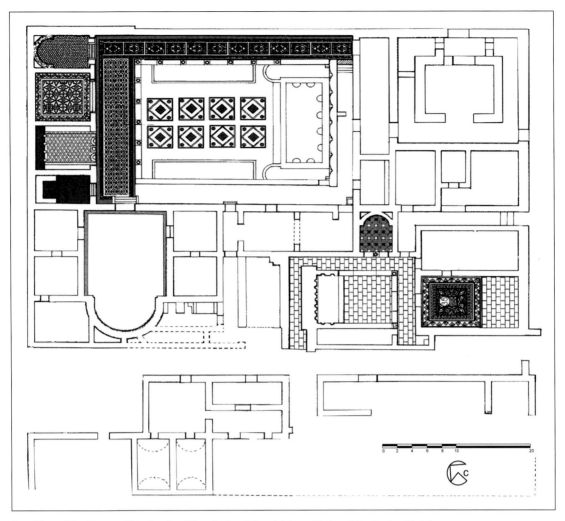

1   Plan of the House of Parthenius (Theodosian Palace) (photo National Institution Stobi)

rather good condition, others were completely broken and reused, most likely as building material. This once luxurious peristyle with a pool seems to have been transformed into a late antique debris receptacle where the sculptures were discarded, that also served as a sort of a quarry for the later population of *Stobi*. Many years later, Stirling (2005), in the course of reviewing other late antique collections from all over the Empire, also included the statuary from the residences in *Stobi*, considering mostly the ones from the House of Parthenius (Theodosian Palace) dividing them into four groups according to their dimensions and possible arrangement, and also discussing their use in worship[24].

Another residence that is considered in this study is the so-called House of Polycharmos (fig. 6) excavated in the period between 1930 and 1933[25]. The name of Polycharmos was applied due to the relations with the Synagogue and the possibility that the peristyle and the *triclinium* are the rooms that he built for himself, as we are informed by his *ex-voto*[26]. Accordingly, the house was built in the 2nd century during the first period of the Synagogue and used even after the 5th century when the Synagogue II was further adapted to serve as a Christian basilica[27]. In this period

---

[24] Stirling 2005, 197–199.
[25] Petković 1932; Petrović 1933/1934; Kitzinger 1946, 129–146. Also Mikulčić 2003, 184–188; Gerasimovska 2009, 69–71.
[26] IStob no. 19.
[27] More on the Jewish community in *Stobi* see Bitrakova Grozdanova 1999, 286–302; Wiseman 2011.

2  Marble statue of Dionysus-Liber (photo National Museum Belgrade)

3  Marble statue of Artemis (photo National Museum Belgrade)

4  Marble relief of Pan with the nymphs (photo National Museum Belgrade)

5  Marble relief of Cybele (photo National Museum Belgrade)

6  The House of Polycharmos (photo National Institution Stobi)

of changed ownership, a mosaic was applied in the *triclinium* of the house. Several statues have been discovered within the context of the House of Polycharmos – an upper part of a Herculaneum woman found in the basin[28], a sculpture of Asclepius (fig. 7)[29], and a relief of Dionysus and his *thiasos* with an inscription found near the peristyle columns[30].

The dating and provenance of any of these sculptures are difficult to determine with certainty. Most of them have been dated differently by different authors, which obliges us to study them further, each with reference to chronological and stylistic analogies, and also by the provenance of the marble, also examining the possibility of a local workshop. Another question that needs addressing is their original position and reuse in a secondary context before their final deposit. Should the statuary found within both the House of Parthenius and the House of Polycharmos be considered as a late antique domestic decor belonging only to a single house, or did some of them belong to other, late antique residences located nearby in *Stobi*? Freestanding statues are movable and can be transported and re-erected from their original setting[31]; nevertheless, it is not very likely that heavy sculptures were moved far from where they were originally displayed. It is more feasible that these particular statues were displayed in the closest connected room to the late antique relocation, before they were deposited in the late antique debris. Since most of the statuary from the House of Parthenius was found within the pool of the courtyard which has architectural features for statuary display, it is very likely that some of these statues were displayed in the chambers of the north courtyard, especially considering the niches, the bases, and the intercolumniation of the peristyle[32]. Similarly, in the House of Polycharmos the large apsidal room with a fountain was, most probably, the one once decorated with the sculptures that were found[33].

It can be easily argued that some of the sculptures were collectables from the local heritage, constituting elements of the religious imagery of contemporary *Stobi* at the time of their making. One statue that can, with some certainty, be treated as a case of local transfer of property from public ownership to private reuse is the one of Dionysus-Liber, the only precisely dated sculpture due to the relevant inscription[34]. It was erected in 119 by a former praetorian L. Dexius Longinus for the health of the emperor, although the epigraphic evidence does not confirm that it was actually erected in *Stobi*. Iconographically, there are similarities with the style of the sculpture of Artemis. Both figures are robustly formed and are not quite proportionate, considering the short legs and the length of the torsos. Also, the execution of the short boots of Artemis, Dionysus and another fragment of a foot with a boot from the sculptural heritage of *Stobi*[35] all have a similar design. According to the style of the sculpting, and to the execution of the details of the clothes, especially the boots, but mostly according to the proportions of the body, these statues can be related to each other, and, based on the inscription, dated to the period of the emperor Trajan. It can be assumed that both are possible local products from the same workshop or master hand, and this could be an argument for the possibility that the workshop was local. For the local worship of Dionysus we learn more from the thiasos relief from the House of Polycharmos, most certainly

---

[28] Petrović 1933/1934, 178; Grbić 1958, 38 pl. 24; Sokolovska 1978, fig. 13; Sokolovska 1987, no. 6 pl. 4, 1; Jevtović 1987, cat. 92; Cambi 1988, cat. 92; Cambi 1989, cat. 134; Bitrakova Grozdanova – Nikoloska 2022, cat. 42 pl. 42.

[29] Wiseman 1973, 79; Düll 1977, 369–370 no. 194 fig. 49; Sokolovska 1981, fig. 5; Sokolovska 1987, no. 183 pl. 70, 4–6.

[30] Δέμονες Ἀντανο[ί]. Vulić 1933, 28 no. 79; Petrović 1933/1934, 179 fig. 13; Robert 1934; Kitzinger 1946, 135; Düll 1977, no. 107 fig. 31; Bitrakova Grozdanova 1999, 164–165; IStob no. 12.

[31] Bartman 1991, 72.

[32] More on their possible arrangement see Nikoloska 2015c, 95–97.

[33] Kitzinger 1946, 135.

[34] *[pr]o [sal(ute) i]mp(eratoris) Tr[aiani Adriani Aug(usti) Libero statu]|[a]m posuit L(ucius) Dex{s}ius Longinus vet[r]|anus ex praet(orio)|imp(eratore) Caes(are) Traiano Adriano Aug(usto) III P(ublio) Dasumio Rustico co(n)s(ulibus) de s|[uis* Διονύσῳ Λ(ούκιος) Δέξιος Λονγεῖνος ἐκ τῶν ἰδίων ἔτους ς ξ σ᾽ (IStob no. 6).

[35] Sokolovska 1987, no. 257 pl. 86, 6.

provincially produced, which also bears an inscription relating him to the enigmatic local Antanoi, confirmed also on an inscription from *Heraclea Lyncestis*[36].

The marble torso of Hygeia seems to be another product of a local provincial workshop. On the right of the body, there is a strut shaped as a tall trunk, which is broken off at the level of the goddess' hip. Simply rendered with a slightly emphasized spine and a bent tail at the end, a long and thick snake is curled around the trunk. This particular iconography of Hygeia is not very common, but if we look into the local artistic portrayals, we find a certain analogy with the relief from nearby Karaslari[37]. Contrary to the usual representations of Hygeia, where the snake is coiling around the arm of the goddess and drinking from a *patera*, now the snake is larger and climbing a tree. Further, in terms of style and craftsmanship we can also compare the sculpture of Hygeia with the one of Artemis Rospigliosi, also found in *Stobi* and now in the Belgrade Museum, according to Sokolovska who published it first in 1987[38]. It resembles the style of carving the drapery, especially the fold ends of the *apoptygma*, the difference being that Artemis is shown in motion, hence the folds are swirling, while Hygeia's ends are in a straight line, indicating steadiness. This could, once more, suggest the possibility of a local workshop. At this point we should also consider the statue of Asclepius from the House of Polycharmos, collected most probably from the city's heritage. Local worship of this divinity has been confirmed in *Stobi* by an inscription excavated in 1970 dated to AD 233[39], according to which statues of Asclepius, Hygeia and Telesphoros were erected. A considerable number of statuettes depicting Asclepius and his companion Hygeia were found at *Stobi*, some of them still unpublished, indicating furthermore the existence of a local sanctuary of the healing deities and therefore a local production of the statuary[40].

Among the statuary collections from both residences, only one honorific statue was found, the relatively well-preserved upper portion of a life-sized large Herculaneum woman from the House of Polycharmos. Based on both the hair treatment and the facial expression, this sculpture is believed to have been made during the Julio-Claudian period when the portraits were idealized according to the Hellenistic models. Like the other Herculaneum woman from *Stobi*[41], this one also belongs to the same period, which is also confirmed by the similarities in manufacture between them. A sole honorific statue of a 1st century Herculaneum woman from a late antique context suggests that it might have been assembled out of purely aesthetic qualities and reverence for its early production, and not necessarily commemorating family relationships with the late antique inhabitants. Maybe these two portraits were produced in a regional or even in a local city workshop, since they do stand out due to their common provincial artistic qualities; nevertheless, this fact is difficult to ascertain without further stone analysis.

On the other hand, the marble torsos of Venus are not likely products of a provincial workshop; it is more likely for them to have been imported for the purpose of the late antique decorative pool arrangement of the House of Parthenius. Statues of Venus, as well as of Dionysus, are part of the traditional decorative repertoire, often seen in late antique residences. Considering the other small scale bronzes, the statuettes of Venus, Apollo, Fortuna and Lar, they reflect a more private aspect of worship, and they were therefore often moved as personal belongings. These kinds of statuettes were mass-produced and highly mobile, and found all over the Empire, so it is hard to speak about them in terms of local heritage or imports. Domestic pagan cult activity in late antique houses is common, and is particularly observed in the minor mythological objects of art, as documented for

---

[36] More on the Antanoi and the interpretations of the inscriptions see IStob, 25–26.
[37] Düll 1977, no. 184 fig. 52.
[38] Sokolovska 1987, no. 144 pl. 57, 4.
[39] IStob, no. 10.
[40] I would like to thank Silvana Blaževska from the National Institution Stobi for her kind collaboration on the statuary material from *Stobi* with results soon to be published, initially presented in 2021 at the Annual Meeting of the Serbian Archaeological Society in Paraćin. A close parallel can be drawn with the shrine of Asclepius at the Athenian Agora where multiple votive statuettes with smaller dimensions have been found (Martens 2018).
[41] Sokolovska 1978, 102 figs. 10. 11; Sokolovska 1981, fig. 1; Sokolovska 1987, no. 7 pl. 5, 1–3; Bitrakova Grozdanova – Nikoloska 2022, cat. 41 pl. 39–41.

7  Marble statue of Asclepius (photo National Institution Stobi)

instance in the Athenian late antique houses from the Agora[42].

Furthermore, the gilded over-life-sized head of Serapis was certainly not produced in *Stobi* on account of its craftsmanship. Dated to the Antonine times, either the middle or the late period, it is an import from *Alexandria* where we encounter similar monumental heads of the god without the characteristic *kalathos*[43]. We might, however, also consider it as evidence of local worship. During the recent excavations in *Stobi*, a temple was unearthed connected to the Egyptian cults[44]. In the direct vicinity of the newly found building, a statue of Isis was discovered[45]. It is of greater dimensions as well, with both statues probably adorning this temple. The statue of Serapis could have been imported during the life of the temple (early 2$^{nd}$–early 5$^{th}$ century)[46], and the broken head later transported to the House of Parthenius as a collectable.

The sculptures that were late antique imports combined for the purpose of the house collection were carefully selected and displayed. Such art collections were very common for late antique residences all over the provinces, assembled from collectible pieces of reused sculpture[47]. There was a competitive market behind it, involving a network of people dealing and distributing all over the Empire. Here, above all, we consider the exceptional bronze satyrs believed by many to be late Hellenistic Pompeian products or made in a bronze workshop in *Alexandria* or *Pergamum*[48]. The bronze satyrs must have been arranged as a sculptural pendant[49], judging by their common craftsmanship, style and character. Moreover, we can perceive the two reliefs as late antique collector's items for the house decor as a sculptural pendant. The one depicting the *thiasos* is part of a group of Neo-Attic Hellenistic copies reproduced from a lost original, made in an archaizing style, and brought here, supposedly in Late Antiquity. Bearing in mind that these particular reliefs were not mass-produced and common to the region of Athens, this possibility is reasonable. It is a similar case with the 3$^{rd}$ century relief of Cybele in a naiskos, which is an

---

[42]  Burkhardt 2016, 136–142.
[43]  Hornbostel 1973, 108; Clerc – Leclant 1994, nos. 83a. 119a.
[44]  Blaževska – Radnjanski 2015.
[45]  Bitrakova Grozdanova 2015, 45–47.
[46]  More on the stratigraphy of the temple see Blaževska – Radnjanski 2015, 229–234.
[47]  Stirling 2005, 165–227; Saradi 2011, 275–280; Sfameni 2012; Jacobs 2016, 108–111.
[48]  Bitrakova Grozdanova 1987, 130–131.
[49]  Bartman 1991, 79–82.

8  Marble head of Dionysus (photo National Museum Belgrade)

iconographical type typical for the Late Classical and Hellenistic periods. The cult of Cybele, judging from the lack of material connected to it, was not worshiped in *Stobi*, so the Cybele relief was also, most probably, imported in Late Antiquity[50]. A relief of such dimensions and grandeur, that would have been a manifestation of a more public form of worship, would not be expected to have been part of the imagery of the earlier city. These two reliefs, similar in both shape and dimensions, might have composed another possible pendant. It is noteworthy that the deities complement each other also in their religious sentiment, both being deemed part of the ›oriental‹ cults, so their possible juxtaposition is even more logical.

Besides the Artemis Rospigliosi mentioned in the discussion of Hygeia, at this point one other sculpture ought to be included: it is documented as being from *Stobi* and is now in the National Museum in Belgrade, unfortunately without an exact record of the context of its discovery. The head of Dionysus (fig. 8)[51] might have been a collectors piece as well. Even though this head was previously identified as belonging to a statue of either a nymph or Apollo, still, it most probably depicted a young Dionysus wearing an ivy wreath, conforming to either the Richelieu or the Woburn Abbey Dionysus type[52]. This god and his *thiasos* was an often-occurring mythological theme among the private collections all over the Empire. This is also the case with the House of Parthenius where Dionysian imagery is noteworthy, including the statue with an inscription, the relief with the *thiasos*, the bronze satyrs, a smaller marble head of a satyr and a torso of the god (reported on by Petković), but also the relief of the Dionysus group from the House of Polycharmos.

In order to round up this contribution and bring together some concluding thoughts, let us first underline that the provincial aristocrats who inhabited these luxurious city residences lived mostly during the times of the triumph of Christianity, which was present and influential relatively early at *Stobi*. This change subsequently brought with it new moral grounds and rules, when numerous Christian basilicas existed contemporarily, as centres of the city's religious life. Authoritative, as the owners of the city residences must have been, their private quarters were also used for official city-related activity. They were allowed to freely exhibit pagan imagery within their own chambers, while Christianity prevailed in the public life of the city. Little Christian material was found in the House of Parthenius, the crosses on the impost capitals in the small peristyle and in the northern apsidal room being the only certain indication of any Christian symbolism. We also should acknowledge that for the élite to continue pagan worship demanded cautiousness, so Christian symbols were sometimes used as a means of precaution[53]. More Christian connotations can be drawn with the House of Polycharmos since after the time of the Synagogue this building

---

[50] The Great Mother did not leave a significant mark in *Stobi* during Roman times. The only evidence consists of terracotta figurines, not great in number, however very frequent in Hellenistic and Early Roman times all over *Macedonia*, Thrace and Asia Minor, found in graves, which speaks only of private worship with a sepulchral aspect (Bitrakova Grozdanova 2015, 36–41; Nikoloska 2015b, 262–264).

[51] Vulić 1941–1948, 44 no. 95; Grbić 1958, 37 pl. 22; Mano-Zissi 1973, 190 fig. 94; Mano-Zissi 1981, fig. 5; Sokolovska 1987, 176 no. 141 pl. 57, 1.

[52] Gasparri 1986, 435.

[53] Caseau 2011, 120.

was connected to a basilica. Nevertheless, besides the Julio-Claudian female portrait, sculptures from the local religious heritage have been preserved.

The inventory from the House of Parthenius contains only mythological statues, images of enthroned divinities, of worship and frenzy, votive reliefs, and even a votive inscription mentioning an altar of Artemis[54], but no portraits or any honorific statuary and none of them contemporary to any of the building phases of the house. It comprises a certain thematic unity of reused mythological statuary from the local heritage, some perhaps even products of a local workshop, as well as imported statues with high artistic value. A collection based on such selection criteria, including a wide range of cultic imagery, demonstrates the preservation of a substantial pagan atmosphere within a private context and represents yet another notable example of the persistence of pagan worship among the higher strata of Roman provincial society in Late Antiquity. The sculptural abundance associated with the House of Parthenius must have made this residence, at one point in its history, a gallery of revered art acquisitions, in addition to displaying opulence and wealth. The owners were, presumably, art collectors, provincial aristocrats with political and social privileges and influence who enjoyed a cultured life. The sculptural finds associated with the House of Polycharmos are not as numerous, yet they also demonstrate a secondary context of display as a collection. They were once part of the local religious heritage, relocated here in Late Antiquity as a secondary display of cultic imagery. We may also consider the sculptures as part of the lush display of power as well as religious orientation that connected the inhabitants with the ways of their ancestors. At least five generations inhabited these residences over nearly two centuries, traditionally preserving and passing on the pagan customs of the city through *paideia*[55], as part of the educational curriculum of the young aristocrats in late antique *Stobi*. The pagan revival, or rather, its preservation in Late Antiquity was common among the urban élite, who seemingly were the last to forget about the ways of the past; the pagan statues of the urban heritage are eloquent testimony of the cultural aspirations and religious practices of this social class.

## BIBLIOGRAPHY

| | |
|---|---|
| Baldini Lippolis 2007 | I. Baldini Lippolis, Private space in late antique cities: Laws and building procedures, in: L. Lavan – L. Özgenel – A. Sarantis (eds.), Housing in Late Antiquity. From Palaces to Shops, Late antique archaeology 3, 2 (Leiden 2007) 197–237 |
| Bartman 1991 | E. Bartman, Sculptural Collecting and Display in the Private Realm, in: E. K. Gazda (ed.), Roman Art in the Private Sphere. New Perspectives on the Architecture and Décor of the Domus, Villa, and Insula (Ann Arbor 1991) 71–88 |
| Bitrakova Grozdanova 1987 | V. Bitrakova Grozdanova, Monuments de l'Époque Hellénistique dans la République Socialiste de Macédoine (Skopje 1987) |
| Bitrakova Grozdanova 1999 | V. Bitrakova Grozdanova, Religion et art dans l'antiquité en Macédoine (Skopje 1999) |
| Bitrakova Grozdanova 2015 | V. Bitrakova Grozdanova, Les cultes orientaux dans la Haute Macédoine, leur survie et leur adoption au temps romain, in: A. Nikoloska – S. Müskens (eds.), Romanising Oriental Gods? Religious transformations in the Balkan provinces in the Roman period. New finds and novel perspectives. Proceedings of the International Symposium Skopje 2013 (Skopje 2015) 35–86 |
| Bitrakova Grozdanova – Nikoloska 2022 | V. Bitrakova Grozdanova – A. Nikoloska (eds.), Sculpture in the round, CSIR North Macedonia I 1 (Skopje 2022) |
| Blaževska – Radnjanski 2015 | S. Blaževska – J. Radnjanski, The tempe of Isis in Stobi, in: A. Nikoloska – S. Müskens (eds.), Romanising Oriental Gods? Religious transformations in the Balkan provinces in the Roman period. New finds and novel perspectives. Proceedings of the International Symposium Skopje 2013 (Skopje 2015) 215–257 |

---

[54] IStob no. 3.
[55] *Paideia* was considered an important part of the daily life of the late Roman aristocracy. See chap. 7 in Stirling 2005.

| | |
|---|---|
| Burkhardt 2016 | N. Burkhardt, The Reuse of Ancient Sculpture in the Urban Spaces of Late Antique Athens, in: T. M. Kristenses – L. Stirling (eds.), The Afterlife of Greek and Roman Sculpture: Late Antique Responses and Practices (Ann Arbor 2016) 118–149 |
| Cambi 1988 | N. Cambi (ed.), Antike Porträts aus Jugoslawien. Eine Ausstellung veranstaltet vom Dezernat Kultur und Freizeit, Museum für Vor- und Frühgeschichte der Stadt Frankfurt am Main, vom 9. Sept. bis 27. Nov. 1988 (Frankfurt a. M. 1988) |
| Cambi 1989 | N. Cambi (ed.), Retrats antics a Iugoslàvia, Fundació Caixa (Barcelona 1989) |
| Caseau 2011 | B. Caseau, Late Antique Paganism: Adaptation under Duress, in: L. Lavan – M. Mulryan (eds.), The Archaeology of Late Antique ›Paganism‹, Late antique archaeology 7 (Leiden 2011) 111–134 |
| Clerc – Leclant 1994 | LIMC VII 1 (1994) 666–692 s. v. Sarapis (G. Clerc – J. Leclant) |
| Düll 1977 | S. Düll, Die Götterkulte Nordmakedoniens in Römischer Zeit (Munich 1977) |
| Ellis 1991 | S. P. Ellis, Power, Architecture, and Décor: How the Late Roman aristocrat appeared to his guests, in: E. K. Gazda (ed.), Roman Art in the Private Sphere. New Perspectives on the Architecture and Décor of the Domus, Villa, and Insula (Ann Arbor 1991) 117–134 |
| Gasparri 1986 | LIMC III 1 (1986) 414–514 s. v. Dionysos (C. Gasparri) |
| Gerasimovska 2009 | D. Gerasimovska, The Role of Habitat in the Culture of Life through Antiquity in the Republic of Macedonia (Skopje 2009) |
| Grbić 1939 | М. Грбић, Античка ситна пластика, Umetnički pregled 2, 1939, 12–15 |
| Grbić 1958 | M. Grbić, Odabrana grčka i rimska plastika u Narodnom muzeju u Beogradu (Belgrade 1958) |
| Hornbostel 1973 | W. Hornbostel, Sarapis: Studien zur Überlieferungsgeschichte, den Erscheinungsformen und Wandlungen der Gestalt eines Gottes, EPRO 32 (Leiden 1973) |
| IStob | S. Babamova, Inscriptiones Stoborum, Studies in the Antiquities of Stobi (Stobi 2012) |
| Jacobs 2016 | I. Jacobs, Old Habits Die Hard. A Group of Mythological Statuettes from Sagalassos and the Afterlife of Sculpture in Asia Minor, in: T. M. Kristenses – L. Stirling (eds.), The Afterlife of Greek and Roman Sculpture: Late Antique Responses and Practices (Ann Arbor 2016) 94–117 |
| Jevtović 1987 | J. Jevtović (ed.), Antički portret u Jugoslaviji, Narodni muzej (Belgrade 1987) |
| Kitzinger 1946 | E. Kitzinger, A Survey of the early Christian town of Stobi, DOP 3, 1946, 81–162 |
| Kolarik 1987 | R. E. Kolarik, Mosaics of the Early Church at Stobi, in: W. Tronzo – I. Lavin (eds.), Studies on art and archaeology in honor of Ernst Kitzinger on his seventy-fifth birthday, DOP 41 (Washington 1987) 295–306 |
| Mano-Zissi 1940 | D. Mano-Zissi, Bemerkungen über die altbyzantinische Stadt von Stobi, in: Atti del V Congresso Internazionale di Studi Bizantini. Roma 20.–26.09.1936. Storia, Filologia, Diritto, Studi bizantini e neoellenici 5 (Rome 1940) 224–237 |
| Mano-Zissi 1973 | D. Mano-Zissi, Stratigraphic Problems and the Urban Development of Stobi, Studies in the Antiquities of Stobi 1, 1973, 185–232 |
| Mano-Zissi 1981 | D. Mano-Zissi, Hellenism and the Orient in Stobi, Studies in the Antiquities of Stobi 3, 1981, 121–132 |
| Martens 2018 | B. Martens, The Statuary of Asklepios from the Athenian Agora, Hesperia 87, 2018, 545–610 |
| Mikulčić 2003 | I. Mikulčić, Stobi, an ancient city (Skopje 2003) |
| Nestorović 1931 | B. N. Nestorović, Iskopavanja u Stobima, Starinar 6, 1931, 109–114 |
| Nestorović 1936 | B. N. Nestorović, Un Palais à Stobi, in: Actes du IVᵉ Congrès International des études Byzantines, Sofia, September 1934 (Sofia 1936) 173–183 |
| Nikoloska 2010 | A. Nikoloska, Genesis, development and prevalence of the iconographical motif Cybele in a Naiscos, Patrimonium 7/8, 2010, 69–80 |
| Nikoloska 2015a | A. Nikoloska, The world of Dionysos on the monuments from the Republic of Macedonia, in: C.-G. Alexandrescu (ed.), Cult and Votive Monuments in the Roman Provinces. Proceedings of the 13th International Colloquium on Roman Provincial Art, Bucharest – Alba Iulia – Constanţa 27.05.–03.06.2013 (within the framework of CSIR) (Cluj Napoca 2015) 87–95 |
| Nikoloska 2015b | A. Nikoloska, Evidence of ›Oriental‹ cults from the territory of the Republic of Macedonia, in: A. Nikoloska – S. Müskens (eds.), Romanising Oriental Gods? Religious |

| | |
|---|---|
| | transformations in the Balkan provinces in the Roman period. New finds and novel perspectives. Proceedings of the International Symposium Skopje 2013 (Skopje 2015) 257–278 |
| Nikoloska 2015c | A. Nikoloska, The ›House of Parthenius‹ revisited, FolA Balkanica 3, 2015, 83–103 |
| Özgenel 2007 | L. Özgenel, Public Use and Privacy in Late Antique Houses in Asia Minor: the Architecture of Spatial Control, in: L. Lavan – L. Özgenel – A. Sarantis (eds.), Housing in Late Antiquity. From Palaces to Shops, Late antique archaeology 3, 2 (Leiden 2007) 239–281 |
| Petković 1928a | V. Petković, Godišnjak Srpske Kraljevske Akademije 37, 1928, 190–191 |
| Petković 1928b | V. Petković, Godišnjak Srpske Kraljevske Akademije 37, 1928, 220–221 |
| Petković 1929 | V. Petković, Godišnjak Srpske Kraljevske Akademije 38, 1929, 231–234 |
| Petković 1930 | V. Petković, Godišnjak Srpske Kraljevske Akademije 39, 1930, 188–191 |
| Petković 1931 | V. Petković, Godišnjak Srpske Kraljevske Akademije 40, 1931, 220–225 |
| Petković 1932 | V. Petković, Godišnjak Srpske Kraljevske Akademije 41, 1932, 208–210 |
| Petković 1937 | V. Petković, Antičke skulpture iz Stobija, Starinar 12, 1937, 12–35 |
| Petrović 1933/1934 | J. Petrović, Stobi 1932, Starinar 8/9, 1933/1934, 169–191 |
| Robert 1934 | L. Robert, Antanoi, REG 47, 1934, 31–36 |
| Saradi 2011 | H. G. Saradi (with the contribution of D. Eliopoulos), in: L. Lavan – M. Mulryan (eds.), Late paganism and Christianisation in Greece. The Archaeology of Late Antique ›Paganism‹, Late antique archaeology 7 (Leiden 2011) 263–309 |
| Saria 1930 | B. Saria, Ein Dionysosvotiv aus dem Konsulatsjahr des P. Dasumius Rusticus, ÖJh 36, 1930, 64–74 |
| Sfameni 2012 | C. Sfameni, Isis, Cybele and other oriental gods in Rome in Late Antiquity: »private« contexts and the role of senatorial aristocracy, in: A. Mastrocinque – C. Giuffre Scibona (eds.), Demeter, Isis, Vesta and Cybele. Studies in Greek and Roman religion in honour of Giulia Sfameni Gasparro, Potsdamer altertumswissenschaftliche Beiträge 36 (Stuttgart 2012) 119–138 |
| Sodini 2003 | J.-P. Sodini, Archaeology and late antique social structures, in: L. Lavan – W. Bowden (eds.), Theory and practice in late antique archaeology, Late antique archaeology 1 (Leiden 2003) 25–56 |
| Sokolovska 1978 | V. Sokolovska, Copies de la Grande et de la Petite Herculanaise en Macédoine, BCH 102, 1978, 77–85 |
| Sokolovska 1981 | V. Sokolovska, Stobi in the Light of Ancient Sculpture, Studies in the Antiquities of Stobi 3, 1981, 95–106 |
| Sokolovska 1987 | V. Sokolovska, Ancient Sculpture in SR Macedonia (Skopje 1987) |
| Sokolovska 1988 | V. Sokolovska, The Images of Cybele in Macedonia, MacActaA 9, 1988, 113–127 |
| Stirling 2005 | L. Stirling, The Learned Collector. Mythological Statuettes and Classical Taste in Late Antique Gaul (Ann Arbor 2005) |
| Vermaseren 1989 | M. J. Vermaseren, Corpus Cultus Cybelae Attidisque VI. Germania, Raetia, Noricum, Pannonia, Dalmatia, Macedonia, Thracia, Moesia, Dacia, Regnum Bospori, Colchis, Scythia et Sarmatia, EPRO 50 (Leiden 1989) |
| Vulić 1931 | N. Vulić, Antički spomenici naše zemlje, Spomenik Srpske Kraljevske Akademije 71 (Belgrade 1931) |
| Vulić 1933 | N. Vulić, Antički spomenici naše zemlje, Spomenik Srpske Kraljevske Akademije 75 (Belgrade 1933) |
| Vulić 1941–1948 | N. Vulić, Antički spomenici naše zemlje, Spomenik Srpske Kraljevske Akademije 98 (Belgrade 1941–1948) |
| Wiseman 1973 | J. R. Wiseman, Stobi. A Guide to Excavations (Belgrade 1973) |
| Wiseman 2011 | J. Wiseman, Jews at Stobi, in: H. G. Jurišić (ed.), Miscellanea Emilio Marin sexagenario dicata (Split 2011) 325–350 |

*Aleksandra Nikoloska, Research Centre for Cultural Heritage »Cvetan Grozdanov«, Macedonian Academy of Sciences and Arts, Boulevard Krste Petkov Misirkov, Skopje 1000, North Macedonia.*
*[e] anikoloska@manu.edu.mk*

# NEUE FUNDE UND FORSCHUNGEN

Jeanine Abdul Massih – Frédéric Alpi – Zeina Fani Alpi

# *CYRRHUS*, PLACE MILITAIRE DE L'ARMÉE ROMAINE EN SYRIE DU NORD

## INDICES ARCHÉOLOGIQUES, ÉPIGRAPHIQUES ET ICONOGRAPHIQUES

**Abstract**
Probably founded in the Hellenistic period, the city of *Cyrrhus*, in northern *Syria*, established on the so-called Nebi Houri site, underwent an important and continuous urban development during the Roman Empire, due to its strategic position in the defense system of its eastern borders. Both archaeology and epigraphy have recently confirmed the military vocation of the city at that time: the apparent remains of a legionary camp to the north and a small series of inscribed and sculpted funerary steles of soldiers attest to its military nature. A fragmentary altar dedicated to Zeus-Helios-Serapis is evidence of the popularity of this syncretic cult among the armies of the Severan period.

L'exploration du site de *Cyrrhus*, situé à 70 km au nord-ouest d'Alep, à la frontière syro-turque, a été conduite par la Mission syro-libanaise créée en 2006, qui succède ainsi à la Mission archéologique française dirigée par Edmond Frézouls de 1952 à 1993[1].

Possible fondation hellénistique de Séleucos Nicator[2], *Kyrrhos* n'apparaît dans les sources qu'en 221 av. J.-C., en concordance avec le toponyme d'un site de Macédoine[3]. Cette ville de taille moyenne, d'environ 60 ha, créée à proximité de la tétrapole constituée par Antioche, Séleucie-de-Piérie, Laodicée-sur-mer et Apamée-de-l'Oronte, se trouve sur un nœud routier de Syrie du nord qui relie la Méditerranée à l'Euphrate, par Antioche et *Zeugma* (Séleucie-de-l'Euphrate et Apamée-de-l'Euphrate), mais également connectant, sur un axe nord-sud, Apamée-de-l'Oronte à la Commagène et à l'Hellespont. Ce dernier a perduré jusqu'à la période romaine et n'a été supplanté qu'à la fin du IIe siècle apr. J.-C. Les vestiges de ces voies et le tracé des routes sont notables à proximité immédiate du site au nord, à l'est et au sud. Divers aménagements du rocher ont été relevés aux abords de la ville, notamment sur la voie allant en Commagène, mais ce sont les célèbres ponts datés du IIe siècle apr. J.-C. qui témoignent encore aujourd'hui de l'importance de la présence romaine dans la cité antique.

C'est en 64 av. J.-C., avec la conquête de l'Orient par Pompée, que *Cyrrhus* et la Cyrrhestique sont incorporés à la province romaine de Syrie. La première mention directe de la ville apparaît à propos de la rencontre de Germanicus et Pison – en 17 ou 18 apr. J.-C. – où l'on signale pour la première fois la légion *X Fretensis* qui tint garnison à *Cyrrhus* jusqu'au Ier siècle (66 apr. J.-C.)[4]. Les Romains s'installèrent ainsi dans les limites de la première ville hellénistique. La porte sud d'origine a été reconstruite et la rue principale nord-sud dotée d'un portique et d'un revêtement de dalles de basalte. Ce pavement et ces rues dallées se poursuivent vers l'extérieur de la ville,

---

[1] Mission de l'Université libanaise (dir. Jeanine Abdul Massih) et de la Direction générale des antiquités et musées de Syrie (dir. Shaker Al-Shbib). La Mission française avait été créée en 1952 par Henri Seyrig, directeur de l'Institut français d'archéologie de Beyrouth, et dirigée par Edmond Frézouls, membre de l'Institut et professeur à l'Université de Strasbourg (Abdul Massih 2012a, 15–76).

[2] *Kyrrhos* devint le chef-lieu de la Cyrrhestique, territoire s'étendant d'est en ouest, de *Gindaros* à l'Euphrate. La ligne *Nicopolis* – *Zeugma* marquait sa frontière nord et la ligne *Beroea* – *Chalcis* sa frontière sud (Frézouls 1977).

[3] Pol. 5, 50, 7 et 57, 4.

[4] Tac. ann. 2, 57.

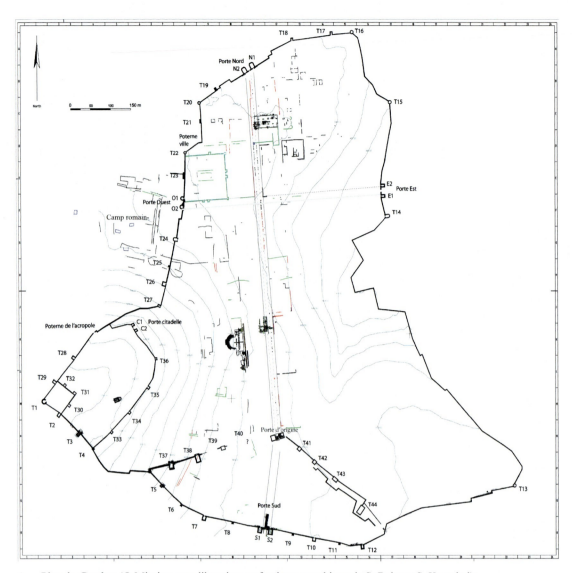

1   Plan de *Cyrrhus* (© Mission syro-libanaise sur fond topographique de S. Baier et S. Knetchel)

entraînant une urbanisation qui se prolonge *extra muros*, notamment au sud et à l'ouest. C'est le long de ces axes de circulation, en adoptant les directions générales du plan orthogonal établi à la fondation de la ville, que se développèrent d'abord les édifices (fig. 1).

Le plus spectaculaire en est le théâtre, monument le mieux conservé de *Cyrrhus*. Il a été construit au pied de la colline de la citadelle, dans la deuxième moitié du IIe siècle. Cet édifice de spectacle, entièrement revêtu de pierre de taille calcaire, occupe deux îlots du plan hippodamien et s'ouvre vers une rue nord-sud à proximité de la rue principale et de la porte occidentale. Deuxième plus grand théâtre de Syrie après celui d'Apamée-de-l'Oronte, son diamètre atteint les 114 m et il devait se développer sur deux étages. Actuellement, seule l'*ima cavea* est préservée et l'orchestre est rempli de blocs chus du mur de scène[5].

Le second monument romain qui a fait l'objet d'une exploration complète et d'un projet de restauration et de réhabilitation par la Mission actuelle est la maison romaine. Découverte de manière fortuite, à la suite d'une fouille clandestine dans le secteur nord-est du site, elle a livré

---

[5]   Dégagé par la Mission française, il a fait l'objet d'une analyse architecturale et d'une étude de la modénature des blocs de l'orchestre. Les résultats de ces travaux et les archives de Frézouls sont présentés dans le volume Cyrrhus I consacré au théâtre (Abdul Massih 2012a).

2   Vue du camp romain à partir de la citadelle (© J. Abdul Massih)

de nombreux pavements de mosaïques. Six pièces ont ainsi été dégagées, dont trois recouvertes de pavements géométriques et une salle centrale décorée d'une mosaïque figurée associée à une bordure à rinceaux[6]. Cet édifice a été daté de la fin du IIe siècle au début du IIIe siècle et témoigne de l'importance de *Cyrrhus* sous les Sévères, comme le corroborent des tétradrachmes frappés à l'effigie de Caracalla (211–217) et de Macrin (avril 217–juin 218)[7].

En termes d'urbanisme, la ville se dote alors de deux nouvelles portes, est et ouest, ainsi que d'une deuxième voie principale, de même direction, perpendiculaire à l'axe nord-sud. Cette rue, avec son pavement de basalte et ses portiques, a été conçue pour desservir les quartiers nord-ouest qui se sont développés à l'extérieur de la ville. L'analyse des vestiges de ce secteur, à travers des prospections archéologiques et topographiques et une documentation photographique aérienne, souligne la présence d'un dispositif de fortification installé dans le vallon, entre la citadelle et le sommet voisin du Golgovan, qui s'ouvrait vers le nord en direction de la Commagène (fig. 2). Cette installation pourrait correspondre dans son plan au camp légionnaire romain rapporté par les sources, qui présentent la ville de *Cyrrhus* comme un centre militaire inclus dans le dispositif mis en œuvre par Rome contre les Parthes. Progressivement, ce camp a été envahi par la nécropole, qui a livré de nombreuses inscriptions et des stèles de soldats. Les voyageurs d'Orient en avaient reconnu plusieurs et la Mission actuelle s'est attachée à compléter au mieux cette documentation.

Outre les épitaphes de soldats romains déjà connues à *Cyrrhus*[8], nous avons pu relever trois stèles fragmentaires, sculptées et inscrites en latin, dont deux inédites à ce jour. À cette série, on ajoutera le fragment d'un autel dédié en grec à Hélios Sérapis, puisqu'il s'agit aussi d'un culte répandu en milieu militaire.

---

[6]   Abdul Massih 2012b.
[7]   Bellinger 1940.
[8]   IGLS 148 (= CIL III 6706). 150 (= CIL III 195). 151 (= CIL III 194). 152 (= CIL III 193). On peut rattacher à ce groupe une stèle inscrite en grec, érigée par une veuve pour son époux défunt, le centurion M. Likinios Proklos (IGLS 149 [= AE 1903, 253 = IGRR III 1004]).

3  Stèle d'Aurélius (photo © F. Alpi)   4  Stèle d'Aurélius (dessin © É. Akiki)

## LA STÈLE DU *SIGNIFER* AURÉLIUS

Dans le cimetière musulman entourant le *ziyaret* du Nebi Houri, où Maundrell avait déjà repéré deux textes latins désormais consignés aux IGLS sous les nos. 150 et 151, nous relevions en effet, dès 1995, au sud du mausolée romain octogonal, un fragment de stèle documenté par la Mission syro-libanaise de *Cyrrhus* en 2010[9] (figs. 3. 4).

Il s'agit d'un bloc calcaire à la surface grise; hauteur totale préservée: 95 cm; largeur: 59 cm, épaisseur: 30 cm.

Un bandeau sert de cadre au monument et une bande/méplat horizontale le divise en délimitant deux registres: le supérieur, conservé entièrement, composé d'un arc avec deux acrotères ébauchés aux angles, abritait le portrait en pied du défunt; l'inférieur, seulement fragmentaire, portait l'inscription latine.

Actuellement acéphale, le portrait du défunt est chaussé de bottines délimitées par des lanières au niveau des chevilles. Il est vêtu d'une tunique courte, avec une ceinture fermée par une boucle circulaire, au-dessous des hanches. Sa chlamyde couvre l'épaule, l'avant-bras et le bras gauches. La main, de ce même côté, désigne le bouclier circulaire posé au sol. Celui-ci était probablement décoré d'une tête de méduse ou de lion, comme le laissent deviner les diverses ébréchures. Un poignard est suspendu au côté gauche du personnage, qui tient de la main droite une hampe décorée de plusieurs ornements, ainsi que l'indiquent tout au long de celle-ci diverses excroissances. Elles laissent penser qu'il s'agit d'une enseigne décorée, selon l'usage légionnaire, par

---

[9] À cette date, les textes signalés par Maundrell au XVIIe s. (Maundrell 1740, 159 et pl. p. 7) semblaient avoir disparu. En 1917, F. Cumont pouvait encore proposer, par autopsie, une relecture de l'inscription CIL III 194 = IGLS 151 (Cumont 1917, no. 339). Le fragment que nous présentons ici paraît avoir échappé au voyageur anglais, comme au savant belge, mais il avait été signalé et photographié en 1993 par F. et O. Harl, Ubi Erat Lupa <http://lupa.at/13190> (13.12.2022), et fut ensuite intégré au catalogue de la thèse de N. Bel (Bel 2021, II, no. 64).

des phalères, des couronnes ou autres récompenses accordées à la troupe. Au sommet, figurait sans doute une main (*manus*) ou une aigle (*aquila*), faisant du personnage figuré un *signifer*[10]. Ce costume militaire avec ceinture à boucle est caractéristique du IIIe siècle[11].

Sur le bandeau qui constitue la ligne de sol de la représentation du défunt, se trouve inscrite l'invocation traditionnelle aux Mânes, suivie, au registre inférieur, d'un fragment d'épitaphe disposé sur deux lignes. Hauteur des lettres: 6 cm.

*D(is) M(anibus) / Aurel(io) Ca/[l]ẹndio .. /- -*

»Aux Dieux Mânes. À Aurélius Calendius …«

Le *nomen* Aurelius se rencontre très souvent dans la troupe au IIIe siècle, notamment à la suite de la »Constitutio Antoniniana« promulguée en 212 par Caracalla (Marcus Aurelius Severus Antoninus) qui, accordant la citoyenneté romaine à tous les habitants libres de l'Empire, contribua à élargir le recrutement militaire à de nouveaux Romains, qui adoptèrent le nom de l'empereur[12]. Passé en *cognomen*, Calendius aurait été la dénomination originale de ce soldat ou d'un ascendant. La brisure de la stèle n'exclut pas absolument une formulation au nominatif et une variante du *cognomen* (Aurelius Calendio).

## LA STÈLE DE L'*AQUILIFER* AURÉLIANUS

Dans le voisinage de la porte nord, une stèle funéraire sculptée, à demi enterrée, a été partiellement dégagée pour mettre au jour la totalité de son inscription (figs. 5. 6). Au registre supérieur, on distingue le relief érodé d'un soldat, dont la partie haute a disparu. Le registre inférieur porte une épitaphe latine sur 11 lignes.

Le bloc de calcaire grisâtre est très érodé dans la moitié haute exposée aux intempéries; hauteur totale préservée et dégagée: 105 cm; largeur: 55 cm; épaisseur: 32 cm.

Un méplat vertical court le long d'un côté de la stèle, sur la droite du personnage représenté, faisant défaut sur le côté opposé. Peut-être le monument a-t-il été mutilé lors d'une réutilisation. Du corps du soldat, qui se tient debout sur ses deux jambes nues, ne restent que la partie inférieure et le bas d'une courte tunique aux multiples plis, ainsi qu'une partie de sa chlamyde qui devait lui couvrir le côté gauche du corps. De la main gauche, comme il est d'usage sur ce type de représentations, il maintient un bouclier rond à *umbo*, posé au sol[13]. De l'autre main, il tenait probablement une aigle, dont ne subsiste que la hampe, car l'inscription précise sa qualité d'*aquilifer*[14]. Ces éléments vestimentaires et militaires nous orientent vers le IIIe siècle.

Préservée de l'érosion, seule la deuxième moitié de l'inscription (l. 7–11) demeure bien lisible. Par autopsie, photographie agrandie à l'ordinateur et estampage, on s'est essayé toutefois à reconstituer l'ensemble du texte, qui suit l'ordonnance habituelle à ce type d'épitaphes. Hauteur des lettres: 4 cm (l. 1–10) et 5 cm (l. 11).

*Aur(e)lia(no) .. ER ... O . / aquilifer(o) le[g](ionis) VII (?) / - - - [vi]x[it] - - - / - - - AM . LXḶ·Ạ·/ - - - ṬM - - - / RIA - - - eius [qui?] / vixit annos XVII[I?] / Ulp(ius) Ulpianus e[x]/ces(sus) aquilif(er) le<g>(ionis) s(upra) [s(cripta)] / fratri et nepot[i] / posuit*

»À Aurélianus … (?), *aquilifer* de la VIIe légion (?), qui a vécu tant d'années – états de service – et à son fils Untel, qui a vécu 16/18 (?) ans, Ulpius Ulpianus, promu lui-même *aquilifer* de la légion désignée plus haut, pour son frère et son neveu, a fait ériger ce monument.«

---

[10] Alföldy 1959, 12; Galinier 2000, 424–425; Alexandrescu 2005, 148–150; Alexandrescu 2010, 150. 207–211. 219 pls. 4–6. 8–9. 17. 23–24.

[11] Bishop – Coulston 2006, 182–184; Coulston 2007, 530–532; Hoss 2011, 29–30. 38–40; Waebens 2015, 61–62. 64–65; Hoss 2017, 96. 102–103; Balty 2018, 36–37.

[12] Le Bohec 2002, 96.

[13] Balty 2018, 34 n. 162: inventaire des parallèles, avec une allusion à cette stèle de *Cyrrhus*.

[14] Alexandrescu 2010, 149. 200. 203–205. 231. 244 pls. 1. 20. 27.

 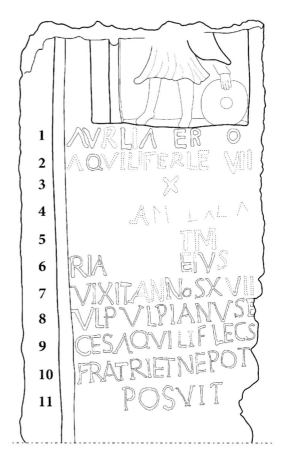

5   Stèle d'Aurélianus (photo © F. Alpi)    6   Stèle d'Aurélianus (dessin © É. Akiki)

Le défunt exerçait la charge insigne de porte-aigle (*aquilifer*) d'une légion qui peut être la *legio VII Claudia*, dont on connaît déjà un *imaginifer*[15] et un simple soldat[16] enterrés à *Cyrrhus*. Ulpius Ulpianus lui aura succédé (l. 9). Il semble avoir été non seulement le frère d'armes mais le propre frère d'Aurélianus. Selon le schéma ordinaire de telles épitaphes, la l. 3 devait indiquer en effet l'âge de celui-ci (*qui vixit*), puis venaient ses états de service (l. 4). Or, l. 7, s'ajoute la mention explicite de l'âge d'un adolescent de 16 ou 17 ans, mort trop jeune pour avoir connu une carrière militaire. L. 6, le génitif possessif *eius* marquait bien un lien de parenté: il s'agissait probablement du fils d'Aurélianus, disparu lui aussi, dont les nom et qualité devaient figurer aux l. 5–6. En fin de texte (l. 10–11), Ulpius Ulpianus indique clairement qu'il a fait ériger la stèle à la double mémoire de son frère et de ce neveu, bien que le relief sommital ne représente que le seul *aquilifer* disparu, avec l'attribut de sa fonction.

## LA STÈLE DE PUBLIUS ULPIUS IULIUS

Un sondage effectué au nord du site par Shaker Al-Shbib, co-directeur syrien de la Mission de *Cyrrhus*, au pied d'un bastion de la muraille byzantine[17], fit apparaître, remployée en pierre de fondation de celle-ci, une autre stèle funéraire de soldat qu'il n'a pas été possible de déplacer ni de mesurer, mais dont la photographie, traitée par ordinateur, autorise une étude du relief fragmentaire et une lecture de l'épitaphe, intégralement conservée quant à elle (fig. 7).

---

[15]   IGLS 150 = CIL III 195.
[16]   IGLS 151 = CIL III 194.
[17]   Al-Shbib 2015, II, 48–49.

Sur le registre supérieur, délimité par un bandeau, figurent les jambes dénudées d'un soldat, d'où l'on peut déduire qu'il portait une tunique courte. Le morceau de hampe qui subsiste à sa droite indique qu'il devait tenir une enseigne (*signum*), une lance (*hasta*)[18], voire une aigle (*aquila*)[19]. Un autel de forme rectangulaire est posé du côté opposé, du type commun en Syrie, composé de trois parties: base, dé et couronnement[20]. Dans un cadre très soigné et mouluré, l'inscription s'étend sur 10 lignes:

*D(is) M(anibus) / P(ublio) Ulp(io) ❦ Iulio ❦ / opt(ioni) le<g>(ionis) XI / Cl(audiae, qui) vixit ann(os) / XL (et) militavit / ann(os) XVIIII, co/h(ors) cl(assica) eius ob / pietatem de / s[ua] p(e)<q>(un)ia / f(aciendum) c(uravit)*

»Aux Dieux Mânes. À Publius Ulpius Iulius, *optio* de la légion *XI Claudia*, qui vécut 40 ans et servit comme soldat 19 années. Sa cohorte navale, par piété, s'est acquittée de la tâche à ses propres frais.«

Le soldat défunt possède le nom gentilice de l'empereur Trajan (Marcus Ulpius Traianus)[21] et, mis en évidence entre deux *hederae*, celui de la dynastie augustéenne (Iulius), indice probable d'une naturalisation plus ancienne[22]. Il appartenait à la légion *XI Claudia*, qui était ordinairement cantonnée en Mésie, le long du Danube, et qui fut engagée sous Trajan lors des guerres de conquête de la Dacie (101–106)[23]. C'est probablement son expérience du combat en milieu fluvial qui l'a fait affecter à la *cohors classica*, »cohorte nautique«, dont les membres se sont cotisés pour ériger ce monument. Il paraît tentant de rapprocher ce texte de l'acclamation lapidaire, découverte à *Cyrrhus* en 1952 par Edmond Frézouls[24], en l'honneur de Q. Marcius Turbo, préfet de la flotte de Misène, qui avait accompagné Trajan avec ses navires jusqu'à Séleucie-de-Piérie en 114 et serait resté quelque temps auprès de l'empereur pour assurer la logistique de sa campagne contre les Parthes (114–117)[25]. Celle-ci comportait

7  Stèle de Publius Ulpius Iulius (photo © Sh. Al-Shbib)

en effet la construction et l'équipement de flottilles fluviales pour la traversée de l'Euphrate et du Tigre. Le cantonnement d'une *cohors classica* à *Cyrrhus*, base arrière où Marcius Turbo se serait établi, s'expliquerait ainsi.

---

[18] Alföldy 1959.
[19] Le Bohec 2002, 51.
[20] Les représentations de soldats faisant une libation sur un autel sont les plus nombreuses à *Nicopolis* d'Égypte. Cf. Waebens 2015, 66–67 fig. 2. À Apamée, des *salariarii* effectuent cette offrande; Balty 2018, 43. 45–46. 54 figs. 42–43. 60.
[21] C'est aussi le cas sur l'épitaphe IGLS 150 et sur la stèle précédente.
[22] Sur les gentilices impériaux: Le Bohec 2002, 94–96.
[23] Pollard – Berry 2012, 178–180.
[24] AE 1955, 225; Yon – Gatier 2009, 10.
[25] Frézouls 1953, en particulier 274–275.

8 Autel de Zeus Hélios Sérapis (photo © F. Alpi)

## L'AUTEL DE ZEUS HÉLIOS SÉRAPIS

Un fragment d'autel inscrit fut inopinément mis au jour en 2010, par suite de l'incendie malveillant d'un bosquet qui le dissimulait, en contre-bas de la porte est. Le document s'inscrit dans le cadre de la présence légionnaire à *Cyrrhus* sous le Haut-Empire (fig. 8).

Il s'agit d'un fragment d'autel de section carrée (50 × 50 cm).

Sous le couronnement richement mouluré se lisent, sur le dé, deux lignes d'une dédicace en grec. Hauteur des lettres: 4 cm (l. 1) et 3 cm (l. 2)

Διὶ Ἡλίῳ Σεράπιδι /καὶ θεοῖς πᾶσι καὶ πάσαις

»À Zeus Hélios Sérapis et à tous les dieux et toutes les déesses.«

D'origine égyptienne, le culte de Sérapis, puis de Zeus Hélios Sérapis, s'est répandu dans tout l'Empire au sein des garnisons légionnaires[26]. Il évolue progressivement vers un syncrétisme universel, comme l'atteste bien ce formulaire englobant toutes les entités divines, masculines et féminines. Sur la partie qui subsiste du tablier, en-dessous de l'inscription, vers la gauche, on distingue la forme d'un bonnet surmonté d'un *apex*, qui s'écarte de l'iconographie connue de Sérapis, ordinairement représenté coiffé d'un *kalathos*[27]. Peut-être s'agit-il plutôt du couvre-chef d'un officiant en train de performer un sacrifice.

La puissance romaine a massivement transformé la ville de *Cyrrhus* dès le Haut-Empire, avec la mise en place d'un urbanisme rigoureux et l'édification de monuments considérables. L'importance stratégique de sa position et, partant, la vocation militaire de la cité, mentionnées dans les sources littéraires, sont à l'origine de ce développement alors ininterrompu et qui reprendra dans la période suivante. Dans le temps, les éléments que nous avons présentés attestent ainsi la continuité de cette présence légionnaire. La stèle d'Ulpius Iulianus, issu de la *legio XI Claudia* et probablement engagé comme membre d'une unité nautique dans la campagne parthique de l'em-

---

[26] Cf. ainsi Vidman 1969, nos. 280. 332. 345 (Asie mineure); 480. 505. 553 (Italie). Outre ces inscriptions, des représentations de Zeus (Jupiter)-Sérapis se rencontrent en Syrie, ainsi à el-Aweinniyé (Kater-Sibbes 1973, no. 441) et à Doura-Europos (Kater-Sibbes 1973, no. 453 et pl. 13).

[27] LIMC VII 1, 666–692 s. v. Sarapis (G. Clerc/J. Leclant); VII 2, 504–518 s. v. Sarapis. Pour Sérapis-Hélios en particulier, LIMC VII 1, 687–689 nos. 212–213; VII 2, 516–518.

pereur Trajan, se rapporte au début du IIe siècle apr. J.-C. Les éléments vestimentaires et les accessoires militaires que montrent les portraits funéraires des deux autres soldats placent ceux-ci au siècle suivant, ce que corrobore l'adoption des gentilices impériaux Aurélius et Aurélianus. Cette chronologie pourra trouver confirmation avec le rapprochement des monuments des nécropoles militaires que réserve la région, ceux d'Apamée-de-l'Oronte[28], de *Zeugma*[29], de Doliché[30] ou encore le cimetière marin de Séleucie-de-Piérie[31]. La popularité dans les armées du culte de Sérapis, associé à Zeus, à Hélios et à d'autres divinités, sensible depuis Commode (180–192), atteint son apogée à l'époque sévérienne (193–235), lorsqu'il devient le dieu protecteur des empereurs, le garant de la prospérité et de la victoire.

## SOURCES LITTÉRAIRES

Tacite, Annales I–II, H. Goelzer (éd. et trad.) (Paris 1938)

Polybe, Histoires V, P. Pédech (éd. et trad.) (Paris 1977)

## BIBLIOGRAPHIE

| | |
|---|---|
| Abdul Massih 2012a | J. Abdul Massih (éd.), Le théâtre de Cyrrhus d'après les archives d'Edmond Frézouls, Cyrrhus 1 (Beyrouth 2012) |
| Abdul Massih 2012b | J. Abdul Massih, La mission archéologique libano-syrienne de Cyrrhus. Bilan des travaux 2006–2011, Comptes rendus des séances de l'Académie des Inscriptions et Belles-Lettres 213, 2012, 303–330 |
| Alexandrescu 2005 | C.-G. Alexandrescu, A Contribution on the Standards of the Roman Army, dans: Zs. Visy (éd.), Limes XIX. Proceedings of the XIX[th] International Congress of Roman Frontier Studies held in Pécs, Hungary, September 2003 (Pécs 2005) 147–156 |
| Alexandrescu 2010 | C.-G. Alexandrescu, Blasmusiker und Standartenträger im römischen Heer: Untersuchungen zur Benennung, Funktion und Ikonographie (Cluj-Napoca 2010) |
| Alföldy 1959 | A. Alföldy, Hasta-Summa Imperii. The Spears as Embodiment of Sovereignity in Rome?, AJA 63, 1959, 1–27 |
| Al-Shbib 2015 | Sh. Al-Shbib, Les fortifications de Cyrrhus – Nabi Houri, de la période hellénistique à la reconstruction par Justinien (Thèse de doctorat Université Paris 1, Paris 2015) |
| Balty 1986 | J.-Ch. Balty, Apamée. Nouvelles données sur l'armée romaine d'Orient et les raids sassanides du milieu du IIIe siècle, Comptes rendus des séances de l'Académie des Inscriptions et Belles-Lettres 187, 1986, 213–242 |
| Balty 1993 | J.-Ch. Balty, Apamée de Syrie. Quartiers d'hiver de la IIe Légion parthique. Monuments funéraires de la nécropole militaire (Bruxelles 1993) |
| Balty 2016 | J.-Ch. Balty, Le *volumen* ou »Schriftrolle« des stèles et cippes militaires dans l'Empire romain: à propos des inscriptions apaméennes de la *Legio II Parthica*, Syria 93, 2016, 83–96 |
| Balty 2018 | J.-Ch. Balty, Cippes, autels funéraires et stèles militaires d'Apamée: typologie des monuments, modèles iconographiques et ateliers, Syria 95, 2018, 15–63 |
| Bel 2021 | N. Bel, La stèle funéraire au Proche-Orient hellénistique et romain: une typologie pour la Syrie du Nord. Art et histoire de l'art (Thèse de doctorat Université Lyon 2, Lyon 2021) |
| Bellinger 1940 | A. R. Bellinger, The Syrian Tetradrachms of Caracalla and Macrinus (New York 1940) |
| Bishop – Coulston 2006 | M. C. Bishop – J. C. N. Coulston, Roman Military Equipment (Oxford 2006) |
| Coulston 2007 | J. Coulston, Art, culture and service. The depiction of soldiers on funerary monuments of the 3rd century AD, dans: L. de Blois – E. Lo Cascio (éds.), The Impact of the Roman |

---

[28] Balty 1986; 1993; 2016; 2018; Speidel 2019, 87–89.
[29] Hartmann – Speidel 2003; Hartman 2013.
[30] En dernier lieu, Facella – Speidel 2011.
[31] IGLS 1155–1182.

| | |
|---|---|
| | Army (200 BC–AD 476): Economic, Social, Political, Religious and Cultural Aspects. Proceedings of the Sixth Workshop of the International Network Impact of Empire in Capri, 29.03.–02.04.2005 (Leiden 2007) 529–561 |
| Cumont 1917 | F. Cumont, Études syriennes (Paris 1917) |
| Facella – Speidel 2011 | M. Facella – M. A. Speidel, From Dacia to Doliche (and back). A New Gravestone for a Roman Soldier, dans: E. Winter (éd.), Von Kummuch nach Telouch. Historische und archäologische Untersuchungen in Kommagene (Bonn 2011) 207–216 |
| Frézouls 1953 | E. Frézouls, Inscription de Cyrrhus relative à Q. Marcius Turbo, Syria 30/3–4, 1953, 247–278 |
| Frézouls 1977 | E. Frézouls, Cyrrhus et la Cyrrhestique jusqu'à la fin du Haut-Empire, dans: ANRW II 8 (Berlin 1977) 164–197 |
| Galinier 2000 | M. Galinier, La représentation iconographique du légionnaire romain, dans: Y. Le Bohec (éd.), Les légions de Rome sous le Haut-Empire II (Lyon 2000) 417–439 |
| Hartmann 2013 | M. Hartmann, Roman Military Installations and New Inscriptions at Zeugma, dans: W. Aylward (éd.), Excavations at Zeugma conducted by Oxford Archaeology 3 (Los Altos 2013) 381–392 |
| Hartmann – Speidel 2003 | M. Hartmann – M. Speidel, The Roman Army at Zeugma: Results of New Research, dans: C. Crowther – R. Nardi (éds.), Zeugma Interim Reports, JRA Suppl. 51 (Portsmouth 2003) 270–297 |
| Hoss 2011 | S. Hoss, The Roman Military Belt, dans: M. L. Nosch – H. Koefoed (éds.), Wearing the Cloak, Dressing the soldier in Roman Times (Oxford 2011) 29–44 |
| Hoss 2017 | S. Hoss, The Roman military belt – a status symbol and object of fashion, dans: T. F. Martin – R. Weech (éds.), Dress and Society. Contributions from Archaeology (Oxford 2017) 94–113 |
| IGLS | L. Jalabert – R. Mouterde (éds.), Inscriptions grecques et latines de la Syrie I, Commagène et Cyrrhestique. N°$^{os}$ 1–256 (Paris 1929) |
| Kater-Sibbes 1973 | G. J. F. Kater-Sibbes, Preliminary catalogue of Sarapis monuments (Leiden 1973) |
| Le Bohec 2022 | Y. Le Bohec, L'armée romaine (Paris 2002) |
| Maundrell 1740 | H. Maundrell, A journey from Aleppo to Jerusalem, at Easter, A.D. 1697 (Oxford 1740) |
| Pollard – Berry 2012 | N. Pollard – J. Berry, The complete Roman Legions (Londres 2012) |
| Speidel 2019 | M. A. Speidel, Roman Solders' Grave Stones in Greater Syria. Thoughts on designs, imports, and impact, dans: M. Blömer – R. Raja (éds.), Funerary Portraiture in Greater Syria (Turnhout 2019) 83–93 |
| Vidman 1969 | L. Vidman (éd.), Sylloge inscriptionum religionis Isiacae et Serapiacae (Berlin 1969) |
| Waebens 2015 | S. Waebens, The representation of Roman soldiers on third-century AD funerary monuments from Nikopolis (Egypt), Revue internationale d'histoire militaire ancienne 1, 2015, 63–77 |
| Yon – Gatier 2009 | J.-B. Yon – P.-L. Gatier (dir.), Choix d'inscriptions grecques et latines de la Syrie (Beyrouth 2099) |

*Jeanine Abdul Massih, Université libanaise, PoBOX 59 Jounieh, Liban.*
*[e] abdulmassih.j@gmail.com*

*Frédéric Alpi, Institut français du Proche-Orient, 31 rue Camille Mouquet, 94220 Charenton-le-Pont, France.*
*[e] frederic.alpi@gmail.com*

*Zeina Fani Alpi, Université libanaise, Institut français du Proche-Orient, BP 11-1279 (Riad El-Solh), Beyrouth, Liban.*
*[e] zf.xyz7@gmail.com*

Lucia Carmen Ardeț – Adrian Ardeț

# STATUE GROUP OF LIBER PATER ACCOMPANIED BY PAN AND PANTHER FROM ROMAN *DACIA*

**Abstract**

Three marble pedestals were discovered at *Tibiscum* in the 1970s: the first pedestal preserves the footprints of Liber Pater, Pan, the panther and a *thyrsos*. On the second, only the footprints of Liber Pater, the panther and a *thyrsos* can be seen. On the third one the traces of the statuary group can no longer be observed, but the inscription can be read: *Deo Liber[o Patri ---] | us Dignu [s ---]*. A special discovery was made in the 1990s at *Apulum* where in a sacred precinct, the meeting place of a Dionysian association, the statuary group of Liber Pater accompanied by Pan and the panther came to light. Following research carried out in March 2020 in the storage depot of the National Museum of Banat in Timișoara, four other fragments were discovered in the box in which that statue base was located, two of them representing a hand holding a *kantharos*. From this *kantharos*, a fragment from the rim and body of the vessel has been preserved. Another fragment is represented by a hand holding a *thyrsos*.

The Roman province of *Dacia* was founded in AD 106 at the end of the two wars between the Dacians and the Romans; it was a senatorial province, governed by a *legatus Augusti pro praetore* consul in Rome with the mandate of governor in the newly conquered province[1].

In late 102, when the first war between the Dacians and the Romans concluded, part of the territory of the Dacian kingdom (today's Banat and Oltenia) was integrated into the Roman Empire, forming part of the province of *Moesia superior*. Until AD 109, the governor of this province was Julius Sabinus. For Roman propaganda, this year represented the inauguration of triumphal monuments throughout the Empire, among which we mention: Trajan's Column in Rome; the Triumphal Arch of Benevento; the inauguration of the *Via Traiana* between Benevento and Rome; and additional roads in *Dacia* through the founding of the new capital, *Colonia Augusta Dacica* inaugurated in honour of emperor Trajan, illustrating the glorious victory of the Romans[2].

Starting with the year 109, the imperial province of *Dacia* had its own governor, D. Terentius Scaurianus as deputy of the emperor (*legatus Augusti pro praetore*), appointed from among the members of the senatorial order; because three legions were stationed in the province (*I Adiutrix, IIII Flavia* and *XIII Gemina*), the governor was of consular rank (*vir consularis*), that is, he came from among the former consuls[3]. He had military and legal powers, which he exercised on behalf of the emperor.

Located at the intersection of the main roads coming from the Danube and heading towards the new capital of the province, the old Dacian fortress *Tibiscum*, mentioned by Ptolemy[4], gives the name to the settlements founded by the Romans after AD 102. First of all, the Romans built two camps on the banks of the Timiș river where the *Palmyreni Sagittarii qui sunt in Dacia Superiore*[5], mentioned in the year 118[6], were stationed, and during the time of Antoninus Pius they appeared in the form of a *vexillatio Palmyrenorum* on the occasion of some works at the Temple

---

[1] Bărbulescu et al. 1998, 51–70.
[2] Petolescu 2010, 161–178.
[3] Piso 1994, 297–331; Piso 1993.
[4] Bogdan-Cătăniciu 1987/1988, 145–162.
[5] Daicoviciu – Groza 1965, 135–139.
[6] IDR I, 8-DiplD VIII, p. 93–97 fig. 22–23.

of Liber Pater[7], *cohors I Sagittariorum*[8] and *cohors I Vindelicorum miliaria c. R*[9]. In the years 159/160 they were organized into a *numerus Palmyrenorum Tibiscensium* as an irregular auxiliary unit that remained until they left the province[10].

After the year 155, *Mauri pedites et equites*[11] were brought to *Dacia*; these formed the *numerus maurorum Tibiscensium* at *Tibiscum*, and stayed until they left the province[12].

A possible military unit identified by the PCH stamp would represent *p(edites) c(ohortis) H(ispanorum)*[13] which is known in the year 114[14].

The settlements in *Tibiscum* were founded by the Romans at the beginning of the 2nd century AD. They obtained the rank of *municipium*[15] at the time of Septimius Severus, being the most important in the western part of the province *Dacia*.

Liber Pater[16] is the epithet used by the Latin poets to indicate Bacchus. Liber and Libera, ancient Italic protector divinities of the field, were celebrated every year on March 17 when *Liberalia* took place. The celebrations occurred both in urban and rural areas. Local residents put on masks, danced, sang, and formed processions. On this occasion, the transition of young males to adulthood was celebrated. After the age of 16, youths wore the virile toga for the first time.

In Roman mythology, Bacchus is the most popular in the provincial environment, and modern historical research through the analysis of the dedications has proven that nothing in the cult of divinities such as Liber and Libera, Silvanus and Diana allows us to attribute a Dacian origin to them[17].

The origin of the Liber and Libera cult is controversial. Liber is the Latinized form of the Greek Dionysos. According to earlier research, Liber and Libera originated from the archaic Latin pantheon. Today, the two deities are believed to be protectors of crops[18]. The rituals associated with them facilitated their equation with the Hellenistic Dionysos, and in the course of time they were transformed into gods of viticulture, primordial gods equated with Ceres.

In Rome, the cult of Ceres is attested on the Aventine[19] starting from 493 BC; here the goddess was worshipped together with Liber and Libera, in a triad. From the beginning the cult spread among commoners and slaves[20]. In the 1st to 2nd centuries AD the wine and grain industry attained the greatest importance in the economy of Rome and the provinces. The worship of the Liber-Dionysos cult is thus widespread[21].

In addition to the economic, social and religious importance, the Liber-Libera cult was also influenced by subjective factors that made it attractive to the imperial cult[22]. During the reign of the emperor Septimius Severus, Liber Pater was joined to the deities of the *Dii Consentes*[23] group. This is one reason for the diffusion of the cult of Liber Pater in wide areas of the Roman Empire,

---

[7] Piso – Benea 1999, 91–107.
[8] Benea 1977, 77–84; Benea 1982, 175; Țentea 2007, 209–218.
[9] Benea 2018, 127–128.
[10] Petolescu 2002, 139–140.
[11] Benea 1985, 150–151.
[12] Petolescu 2002, 135.
[13] Moga 1970, 146.
[14] Benea 2018, 135–137.
[15] Ardeț – Ardeț 2004.
[16] Isler-Kerényi 2010, 27–44.
[17] Nemeti 2005, 187.
[18] Altheim 1938, 125. 268 and *passim*.
[19] Ferrari 2003, 277.
[20] Bodor 1963, 214.
[21] Turcan 2003; Simon 1990, 126–135.
[22] Bodor 1963, 216.
[23] Bărbulescu 1994, 160.

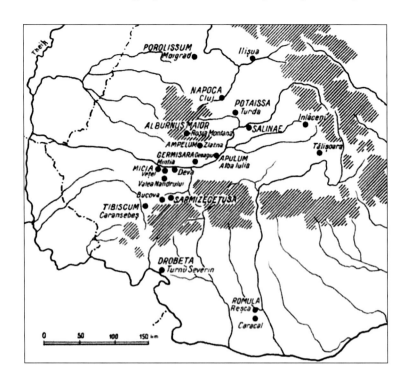

1 Map representing the finds from Roman *Dacia* with direct reference to Liber Pater (after Bodor 1963, 220 fig. 7)

especially in the 2ⁿᵈ century and the first half of the 3ʳᵈ century AD[24]. The greatest dissemination of the cult was in the Danubian provinces, in *Pannonia*, *Dalmatia*, Thrace and the two *Moesia*[25].

In *Dacia* the cult of Liber Pater is attested by numerous discoveries (fig. 1) such as votive inscriptions, building slabs, bas-reliefs, statuettes, statuary groups and temples[26]. The cult was adopted both in the economic and agricultural centres[27] and in camp[28].

A recent reinterpretation of a votive plaque discovered at *Tibiscum* in the 1960s speaks of the construction of a temple dedicated to Liber Pater[29]. It comes from outside the east corner of the castle[30]:

*[L]ibero Patri pr]o sa[l]ute Imp(eratoris) [Ca]e[s(aris) T(iti) Ael(ii)] H[a\driani Antonini Aug(usti)] Pi[i et M(arci) Aurel(ii) Veri] / [Caes(aris) ceterorumq(ue) liberorum] ei[u]s / [ --- le]g(atus) Aug(usti) pr(o) [pr(aetore) / temp]pl[um? --- fecit per uex]illation[em / Pal]myren[or(um) cu?]ra [......]good?[..........] / fru[?gifero].*

»To Liber Pater for the health of the emperor Augustus Titus Aelius Hadrianus Antoninus Augustus.«

The inscription was restored from a collage made of eight fragments. The only information regarding the conditions of the discovery is provided by Marius Moga, who writes in the excavation diary from the 1970s that the discovered fragment »G« was brought to light during excavations carried out outside the castle in the eastern corner[31]. The other fragments were discovered by Doina Benea. Today the inscription is housed at the National Museum of Banat. According to the graphic reconstruction, the fragments represent a votive and building plaque commemorating

---

[24] Bodor 1963, 215–216.
[25] Mayer I Olivé 2017, 517–538.
[26] Bodor 1963, 217–225.
[27] Popescu – Popescu 1995, 227–235; Daicoviciu – Alicu 1981, 63–72; Daicoviciu – Alicu 1984.
[28] Alicu 2004, 327–329; Popescu 2004–2005, 199–220.
[29] Piso – Benea 1999, 91–96 no. 1; AE 1999, 1295; CEpR XIX–XX, 842; Petolescu 2005, 111–112.
[30] IDR III/1, 181 = AE 1999, 1295 = ILD 202 = EDCS-16100181.
[31] IDR III1, 181.

a temple of Liber Pater, erected by the *vexillatio Palmyrenorum* during the reign of the emperor Antoninus Pius and not under Hadrian[32].

Palmyrene troops were brought to *Dacia* by emperor Hadrian during the crisis of 117–118 and a first garrison of archers settled at *Tibiscum*[33], where they made an effort to construct this temple. An important aspect must be mentioned, namely the epithet *fru[gifero]* associated with Liber Pater, like the deity Ceres[34]. After 160 the troops were organized into the *numerus Palmyrenorum Tibiscensium* under Antoninus Pius.

Temples dedicated to Liber Pater are known at *Sarmizegetusa*[35], *Apulum*[36] and *Porolissum*[37], all built in the first half of the 2nd century, and the supposed one from *Tibiscum* is similar to the one from *Porolissum*. The votive plaque is one of the most important finds and is believed to reflect the preferences of the emperor Septimius Severus[38].

A votive altar dedicated to Liber Pater[39] was discovered in Caransebeș, on Traian Doda street, built into a doctor's house; today it is in the Caransebeș Museum. The calcareous stone votive altar has dimensions of 44 ×33 ×15 cm, with letters 2 cm high; the capital is mostly mutilated, while the base is mostly preserved, and has a correctly executed profile.

*Libero Patri / pro salute Mar(ci) / Turrani Dil(---) et / [F]l(avia?) Aeliae Nices / M(arcus) Turran(ius) / Patroclus ex / voto*[40].

»To Liber Pater for the health of Marcus Turranius Dil(---) and Flavia(?) Aelia Nice(s) Marcus Turranius Patroclus from the oath (dedicated the altar).«

The dedicator with the Greek *cognomen* M. Turranius Patroclus dedicates this altar to the god Liber Pater; he was in the service of the rich M. Turranius who had the *cognomen* Dius from the Greek Δίος[41], well known at *Tibiscum* and from the inscription IDR III/1, 145. We meet a C. Iulius Dius, from Asia Minor, in *Dacia* at *Apulum* in the inscription IDR III/5, 20[42]. As for the woman with the *tria nomina*, a Lucia or Flavia Aelia Nice, we also have an analogy at *Tibiscum* on the funerary stela IDR III/1, 159, found in the courtyard of the Capra mansion in the town of Jupa near Caransebeș, alongside other Roman objects[43].

2 Statuette pedestal representing Liber Pater, the panther and Pan from *Tibiscum* (after Traleș 2022)

---

[32] Piso – Benea 1999, 96.
[33] IDR III1, 181; Piso – Benea 1999, 96.
[34] Piso – Benea 1999, 96.
[35] Daicoviciu – Piso 1975, 159–163; Daicoviciu – Piso 1977, 155–159; Daicoviciu – Alicu 1981, 63–72.
[36] Schäfer – Diaconescu 1997, 195–208.
[37] Porolissum 1996, 98–100. 102. 104 fig. 32.
[38] Popescu 2004–2005, 199–220.
[39] IDR III1,141.
[40] IDR III1, 141 = CIL III 1548.
[41] Piso 1983, 110.
[42] Piso 2001, 17–18.
[43] IDR III1, 141. 186.

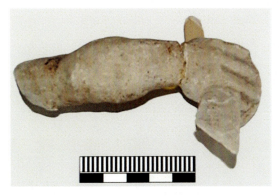

3   Fragment of the statuette representing the forearm from *Tibiscum* (after Traleș 2022)

4   Statuette fragment with forearm and hand holding a *kantharos* bowl from *Tibiscum* (after Traleș 2022)

5   Statuette fragment with hand holding a *thyrsos* from *Tibiscum* (after Traleș 2022)

6   Fragment from the statuette representing the lip and body of the *kantharos* vessel (after Traleș 2022)

At the beginning of the 1970s, during the archaeological research at *Tibiscum*, three marble pedestals were discovered. The first pedestal preserves the traces of Liber Pater, Pan and Pantera (fig. 2). It comes from Marius Moga's excavations at *Tibiscum*. The dimensions of the pedestal are: height 4 cm, length 12.5 cm, width 7 cm.

Following the research carried out in March 2020 in the storage of the Banat National Museum in Timișoara, in the box containing the first pedestal with the traces of Liber Pater, Pan and Pantera, four other fragments were discovered, two of them representing a hand holding a *kantharos* (figs. 3–4). This fragment has forearm and finger dimensions of 22 cm, a forearm thickness of 5 cm and a *patera* diameter of 6.2 cm. From this *kantharos* a fragment of the rim and the body of the vessel have been preserved (fig. 5). Another fragment (fig. 6) represents a hand holding a *thyrsos*, which is 10 cm long and 6 cm wide.

From this statuary group, the marble pedestal[44] (fig. 2) that represented the base of the statuary group of Liber Pater accompanied by the panther, fragments of legs representing Liber Pater, and the panther's left hip, are preserved, as well as a hoof fragment of Pan, the semi-human[45] divinity and the strategist of Dionysos. This is a specific feature of the Asia Minor workshops, which produced such statuettes, so the piece is very likely an import[46].

A statuary group depicting Liber Pater/Dionysos, the god of wine and vegetation, leaning on a *thyrsos* and pouring wine to a panther from a *kantharos*, was discovered at *Apulum* and described in exemplary fashion by Alexandru Diaconescu[47]. The group from *Apulum* is an eclectic product of the Hadrianic era, dated to the 2nd century AD. After describing Liber Pater with his attributes, the strongly flexed left leg, the presence of the god Pan as Dionysos' strategist, Diaconescu calls this type of sculptural representation »Dionysos pantocrator«, a type which was very popular

---

[44]   National Museum of Banat Timișoara inv. 7583.
[45]   Benea 1998, 233–240.
[46]   Diaconescu 2004, 313.
[47]   Diaconescu 2001, 161–167.

7   Pedestal with the traces of Liber Pater, the panther and the place where a *thyrsos* was from *Tibiscum* (after Traleș 2022)

8   Statuette plinth, with inscription representing Liber Pater from *Tibiscum* (after Traleș 2022)

in Italy, where we find the most analogies[48]. The marble from which the *Apulum* group is made comes from the quarry at Afyon, *Phrygia*[49].

The piece at *Tibiscum* is made of a marble similar to that at *Apulum*, of high quality, either imported from other provinces, or it may be a copy made by a competent local artist.

On the second pedestal (fig. 7) only the traces of Liber Pater, a panther and the traces of a *thyrsos*[50] are preserved. It is marked with two grooves[51] and made of high-quality marble with a height of 4 cm, length 12.5 cm, width 7 cm. It was discovered in research in the 1970s without, however, the find spot being more precisely specified.

Liber Pater's lower limbs can be seen, the left leg strongly flexed and the heel detached; on the right are the traces of the panther, and on the left a round impression suggesting probably the location of a *thyrsos* which he usually holds in his left hand.

The third pedestal[52] represents a statuette plinth (fig. 8), with an inscription representing Liber Pater; it was discovered in room no. 2, Building 8 of the *vicus* located near the auxiliary fort, on the first stratigraphic level arrangement[53]. The piece is made of marble with the dimensions of 8 × 16 × 9.5 cm. The left side of the pedestal is preserved. The inscription is carved on the façade[54]:

*Deo Liber[o Patri---] / us Dignu[s---]*, and the panther's paw can be identified in the sculptural elements.

The text is difficult, as the name of the dedicator[55] cannot be read. The first stratigraphic level comes after the demolition of a phase of the edifice probably built after the Marcomannic wars. The plan of Building 8, in the opinion of Ioan Piso, does not support the hypothesis that it could have been a temple of Liber Pater[56].

The marble statue pedestal fragment with an inscription dedicated to Liber Pater[57] joins the other discoveries from Roman *Dacia*, namely from *Ulpia Traiana Sarmizegetusa*, *Apulum*[58] and

---

[48]  Diaconescu 2014, 94.
[49]  Diaconescu 2014, 98.
[50]  Ardeț 2022.
[51]  Ardeț 2022.
[52]  National Museum of Banat Timișoara inv. 28035.
[53]  Piso – Benea 1999, 96–97; Diaconescu 2001, 161–176.
[54]  AE 1999, 1296 = ILD 203 = EDCS-16100182.
[55]  Piso – Benea 1999, 96.
[56]  Piso – Benea 1999, 97.
[57]  Piso – Benea 1999, 97.
[58]  Diaconescu 2001, 161–176.

others. At *Tibiscum*, a votive marble construction plaque[59] was also discovered dedicated to the god Liber Pater for the health of the emperor Titus Aelius Hadrianus Antoninus Augustus.

Considering the presence of the inscription IDR III/1, 181, the pedestal with an inscription dedicated to Liber Pater and the two statuary groups, we assume the existence of a meeting place of a Dionysian association at *Tibiscum*. Usually these statuettes were placed in a niche in the wall of the supposed sanctuary[60].

The *Tibiscum* civil and military population adopted the official religion as well as the mystery cults best represented by votive inscriptions, altars, statuary groups, as well as by votive practices, gifts to the gods. The cult of Liber Pater at *Tibiscum* is well represented and we cannot exclude the existence of a meeting place of a Dionysian association to satisfy the religious needs of this population.

## BIBLIOGRAPHY

| | |
|---|---|
| Altheim 1938 | F. Altheim, A History of Roman Religion (London 1938) |
| Alicu 2004 | D. Alicu, Edifices de culte dédiés à des divinités greco-romaines sur les sites à caractère militaire de la Dacie romaine, in: C. Roman et al. (eds.), Orbis Antiquus. Studia in honorem Ioannis Pisonis (Cluj-Napoca 2004) 327–329 |
| Ardeț – Ardeț 2004 | A. Ardeț – L. C. Ardeț, Tibiscum. Așezările romane (Cluj-Napoca 2004) |
| Ardeț 2022 | L. C. Ardeț, Religious life from Tibiscum (PhD Thesis »Babeș-Bolyai«, Cluj-Napoca 2022) |
| Bărbulescu 1994 | M. Bărbulescu, Potaissa, Studiu monografic (Turda 1994) |
| Bărbulescu et al. 1998 | M. Bărbulescu – D. Deletant – K. Hitchins – Ș. Papacostea – P. Teodor, Istoria României, Ediție revăzută și adăugită 1998, 51–70 |
| Benea 1977 | D. Benea, Câteva precizări cu privire la monumentele epigrafice ale cohortei Sagittariorum la Drobeta, Studii și cercetări de istorie veche și arheologie 27/1, 1977, 77–84 |
| Benea 1982 | D. Benea, Contribuții la cunoașterea unităților militare din castrul roman de la Tibiscum, Studies and Communications of Ancient History Caransebeș 4, 1982, 173–184 |
| Benea 1985 | D. Benea, Numerus Maurorum Tibiscensium. Contribuții la istoria trupelor de mauri din Dacia, Banatica 8, 1985, 139–153 |
| Benea 1998 | D. Benea, Reliefuri sculpturale votive tibisciense (Des reliefs sculpturals votifs tibisciens), Analele Banatului S.N. 6, 1998, 233–240 |
| Benea 2018 | D. Benea, Castrul roman de la Tibiscum (Timișoara 2018) |
| Bodor 1963 | A. Bodor, Der Liber- und Libera-Kult. Ein Beitrag zur Fortdauer der bodenständigen Bevölkerung im römerzeitlichen Dazien, Dacia N. S. 7, 1963, 211–239 |
| Bogdan-Cătăniciu 1987/1988 | I. Bogdan Cătăniciu, Ptolemeu și Provincia Dacia, ActaMusNapoca 24–25, 1987/1988, 145–162 |
| CEpR | C. C. Petolescu, Cronica epigrafică a României, in: Studii și cercetări de istorie veche și arheologie 1981– |
| Daicoviciu – Alicu 1981 | H. Daicoviciu – D. Alicu, Edificii de cult la Ulpia Traiana Sarmizegetusa (II), ActaMusNapoca 18, 1981, 63–72 |
| Daicoviciu – Alicu 1984 | H. Daicoviciu – D. Alicu, Colonia Augusta Dacica Ulpia Traiana (Bucharest 1984) |
| Daicoviciu – Groza 1965 | H. Daicoviciu – L. Groza, Diploma militară de la Tibiscum, ActaMusNapoca 2, 1965, 135–139 |
| Daicoviciu – Piso 1975 | H. Daicoviciu – I. Piso, Sarmizegetusa și războaiele marcomanice, ActaMusNapoca 12, 1975, 159–163 |
| Daicoviciu – Piso 1977 | H. Daicoviciu – I. Piso, Sarmizegetusa et les guerres marcomannes, Revue Roumaine d'Histoire, 1977, 16/1, 155–159 |
| Diaconescu 2001 | A. Diaconescu, A Statue of Liber Pater from Apulum (Alba Iulia), ActaMusNapoca 38/1, 2001, 161–176 |

---

[59] IDR III1, 181; Piso – Benea 1999, 91–96 no. 1; AE 1999, 1295; CEpR XIX–XX, 842; Petolescu 2005, 111–112.
[60] Diaconescu 2014, 78–79.

| | |
|---|---|
| Diaconescu 2004 | A. Diaconescu, Repertoriul statuilor și bazelor de statui din Dacia romană II (Cluj-Napoca 2004) |
| Diaconescu 2014 | A. Diaconescu, Clasicismul în plastica minoră din Dacia Romană (Cluj-Napoca 2014) |
| Ferrari 2003 | A. Ferrari, Dicționar de mitologie Gracă și Romană (Iași 2003) |
| IDR | D. M. Pippidi – I. I. Russu, Inscriptions of Roman Dacia I. Historical and epigraphic introduction. Military diplomas. The waxed tablets (Bucharest 1975) |
| ILD | C. C. Petolescu, Inscripții latine din Dacia I–II (Bucharest 2005–2016) |
| Isler-Kerényi 2010 | C. Isler-Kerényi, The Cult of Liber/Bacchus in the Roman World, in: E. da Rocca (ed.), Il sorriso di Dioniso (Turin 2010) 27–44 |
| Mayer I Olivé 2017 | M. Mayer I Olivé, Aproximación al estudio de la presencia del culto de Liber Pater en las provincias romanas danubianas a través de las inscripciones latinas, Euphrosyne 45, 2017, 517–538 |
| Moga 1970 | M. Moga, Pagus Tibiscensis. În legătură cu teritoriul rural al Ulpiei Traiana, Tibiscus I (Timișoara 1970) 41–51 |
| Nemeti 2005 | S. Nemeti, Sincretismul religios în Dacia romană (Cluj-Napoca 2005) |
| Petolescu 2002 | C. C. Petolescu, Auxilia Daciae (Bucharest 2002) 139–140 |
| Petolescu 2005 | C. C. Petolescu, Inscripții latine din Dacia I–II (Bucharest 2005–2016) |
| Petolescu 2010 | C. C. Petolescu, Dacia. Un mileniu de istorie (Bucharest 2010) |
| Piso 1983 | I. Piso, Epigraphica (XIV), ActaMusNapoca 20, 1983, 103–111 |
| Piso 1993 | I. Piso, Fasti provinciae Daciae I. Die senatorischen Amtsträger (Bonn 1993) |
| Piso 1994 | I. Piso, Eine Parallele zwischen den Praetoria der Statthalter in Carnuntum und in Apulum, CarnuntumJb 1993–1994, 206–208 |
| Piso 2001 | I. Piso, Inscriptions d'Apulum (Inscriptions de la Dacie Romaine) III 5 = Mémoires de l'Académie des Inscriptions et Belles-Lettres 3 (Paris 2001) |
| Piso – Benea 1999 | I. Piso – D. Benea, Epigraphica Tibiscensia, ActaMusNapoca 36/1, 1999, 91–107 |
| Popescu 2004–2005 | M. Popescu, Les troupes de Dacie et les dieux : les temoignages collectifs de piété. Piae memoriae magistri Radu Florescu, Pontica 37–38, 2004–2005, 199–220 |
| Popescu – Popescu 1995 | C. Popescu – M. Popescu, Le culte de Liber Pater en Dacie romaine, Thraco-Dacica 16/1–2, 1995, 227–235 |
| Porolissum 1996 | Porolissum, Res publica municipii Septimii Porolissensium (Bucharest 1996) |
| Schäfer – Diaconescu 1997 | A. Schäfer – A. Diaconescu, Das Liber-Pater-Heiligtum von Apulum (Dakien), in: H. Cancik – J. Rüpke (eds.), Römische Reichsreligion und Provinzialreligion (Tübingen 1997) 195–218 |
| Simon 1990 | E. Simon, Liber Pater (Bacchus), in: E. Simon (ed.), Die Götter der Römer (Munich 1990) 126–135 |
| Traleș 2022 | L. C. Traleș (Ardeț), Religious life from Tibiscum (PhD Thesis »Babeș-Bolyai« University Cluj-Napoca 2022) |
| Turcan 2003 | R. Turcan, Liturgies de l'initiation bachique à l'époque romaine (Liber): documentation littéraire, inscrite et figurée (Paris 2003) |
| Țentea 2007 | O. Țentea, Religia trupelor siriene din provinciile dunărene în timpul Principatului, in: S. Nemeti (ed.), Dacia Felix. Studia Michaeli Bărbulescu oblata (Cluj-Napoca 2007) 209–218 |

*Lucia Carmen Ardeț, National College »Traian Doda« Caransebeș, Str. Ardealului No. 4, Caransebeș, 325400, Romania.*
*[e] ardetcarmen@yahoo.ro*

*Adrian Ardeț, Institute of Banatic Studies »Titu Maiorescu«, Romanian Academy, Timisoara branch, Str. Ardealului No. 4, Caransebeș, 325400, Romania.*
*[e] ardetadrian8@gmail.com*

Georgia Aristodemou

# A POLYPHEMUS GROUP IN CRETE?

## AN OLD FIND RECONSIDERED

**Abstract**
This paper discusses a headless male statue holding a wineskin, from the area of *Knossos*, today at the Archaeological Museum of Heraklion, in Crete (inv. Γ46). It has visible water outlets in order to function as a spout, and possibly decorated a fountain at a private villa of the area. Until today it has been considered to represent a figure of a satyr. The main goal of this paper is to discuss the possibility that this statue may once belonged to a sculptural group of the blinding of Polyphemus. To this end, we highlight its similarities with figures carrying a wineskin from the other known Polyphemus groups (e.g. Sperlonga, Baia, Domus Aurea, Castelgandolfo, *Ephesos*) of the Late Republican and Early Imperial period, that adorned natural or artificial grottoes mostly in imperial grounds. If this argument stands, it will provide us with another Polyphemus group, and will again prove the cultural connectivity between the centre and the peripheries of the Roman Empire on grounds of artistic production.

The sculpture AMH Γ46 depicts a naked male figure (fig. 1–3). It is exhibited at the Archaeological Museum of Heraklion, labelled as a »Satyr figure with a wine sack«. It has not been thoroughly discussed, except in a few references[1]. The inventory of the Archaeological Museum of Heraklion records the area of Knossos as its provenance Κνωσός. Ηγοράσθη (transl. »Knossos, purchased«), probably before 1900, however without further information on its exact find spot or original location[2].

The sculpture is almost 0.50 m high. The head is missing from the beginning of the neck. The legs are broken from the knees. The right arm is bent at the elbow and fully preserved, while the left forearm is missing from just above the elbow. The arm was placed downwards. The figure is standing with its weight on his fixed left leg, whereas the right leg is bent at the knee and was raised as if to step onto something, perhaps a rocky plinth. Minor abrasions are visible on the rear side of the right thigh. The torso is slightly turned leftwards. The entire surface of the sculpture is highly polished. The preserved right hand of the figure supports a wineskin on the elevated thigh of the same side. This wineskin is pierced so as to operate as a water outlet[3]. Two water holes are visible: one that runs through the body of the animal from the neck to the tail, and a second one, located about 1.50 cm to the right. The latter clearly seems to have been executed at a later point in time. The small scale of the sculpture indicates its origin from a small fountain structure, probably within a private residence. The way the figure holds the wineskin, as if trying to carry it by transferring the weight to the right thigh, is compared to a figure known to us by only one drawing in Salomon Reinach's catalogue (fig. 4)[4].

---

[1] Sakelarakis 2005, 143 (reference only); Aristodemou 2012, no. 354 pl. 49, 2.
[2] I express my sincere thanks to the Director of the Museum of Knossos, and the Department of Sculpture Head, Dr. Irini Gallis, for any information they provided and the permission to present the sculpture AMH Γ 46. I am also most grateful to Dr. Anna Kouremenos, for generously providing me with the manuscript of her unpublished PhD on Roman Knossos and to Dr. Sara Paton, for kindly allowing me to reproduce the plan of Villa Dionysos in Knossos from her article (Paton 2022).
[3] Generally, on the motif of the raised leg, Lange 1879, 31–53.
[4] Reinach 1913, no. 73.8 (Monceau-les-Mines, at Chalon sur Saône).

1   Heraklion, Archaeological Museum inv. Γ46; frontal view (photo G. Aristodemou)

A similar (if not identical) marble figure of a satyr holding a wineskin was once included in a Sotheby's catalogue (Lot 24)[5]. He is standing with the weight on his left leg and holding a wineskin with both hands against his thighs. This statue, which is dated to the Late Hellenistic or Early Roman period (presumably in the 1st c. BC), preserves restorations of the 18th century.

Another known example of this motif can be found today at the Thermae Museum in Rome[6]. It dates to the 1st century BC and it repeats the motif, yet here reversed and with slight variations. A standing satyr figure dated to the 1st century BC (Meischner) was found at *Daphne* village (today Harbiye), near Antioch-on-the-Orontes, and is now exhibited at the Antakya Archaeological Museum[7]. In this example, the wineskin rests diagonally over the abdomen and the chest of the figure.

An interesting satyr figure from Naples reproduces the same motif as the Cretan figure, but in reverse body posture (fig. 5). He bends his left arm and supports the wineskin on his left thigh, with the body weight resting on the fixed right leg. However, it differs with regard to the movement of the rest of the body[8].

The similarities between the Knossos statue with figures of satyrs and silenoi depicted as wine-carrying marble statues (of which, however, the greater majority are shown holding the skin over their shoulder or under the arm) are undisputable. A large percentage of these sculptures were often used as fountain figures, with a channel drilled through the wineskin to accommodate a lead pipe that spouts water into a water basin in front of them[9].

The question posed here is whether this Cretan figure depicts another such wineskin-bearing satyr figure – or a figure from an entirely different world.

To address this question we shall turn to a sculptural group closely associated with water and fountain environments, one which narrates a Homeric episode: namely, the sculptural complex of the blinding of Polyphemus by Odysseus and his companions.

---

[5]   Cf. <https://www.sothebys.com/en/auctions/ecatalogue/2014/antiquities-n09236/lot.24.html> (2014, accessed 25.04.2023). In connection with this object, the OeAI refers to its commitment regarding the handling of artefacts of unknown provenance <https://www.oeaw.ac.at/oeai/publikationen/allgemein> (30.11.2023) and expressively points out the problems of the recent art trade in particular. The mention of this object is due to the completion of documentation (note of the editors of the series).

[6]   Museo Nazionale Romano inv. 72. De Lachenal 1981, 344–345 no. 46 (DAI Neg. 76-787), accessed from <https://archive.org/details/museonazionalero0000anto/page/345/mode/1up> (26.04.2023).

[7]   Antakya Archaeological Museum inv. 1371. Vermeule 2001, 99 fig. 14; Meischner 2003, 302–303 pl. 13 (cf. photo accessed from <https://arachne.dainst.org/entity/1060764> [25.04.2023]).

[8]   Neaples, Archaeological Museum, inv. 120383 (?). (cf. Arachne ID: 1932509, accessed from <https://arachne.dainst.org/entity/1932509> (25.04.2023). Similar figure in Kapossy 1969, 30 fig. 17.

[9]   Kapossy 1969, 30–31; Aristodemou 2012, 124–129 (iconography). 217–219 (function).

2   Heraklion, Archaeological Museum inv. Γ46; left side view (photo G. Aristodemou)

3   Heraklion, Archaeological Museum inv. Γ46; right side view (photo G. Aristodemou)

The episode of the blinding of the Cyclops Polyphemus appears from the Hellenistic period in all manner and scales of art. Especially during the Late Republican and Early Imperial period this episode was impressively reproduced in large scale sculpture[10]. Almost all of the early examples of the group originate from luxurious villas and monumental nymphaea, where they decorated the artificially transformed caves, known as *antra Cyclopis*[11]. Even Strabo in his »Geography« (5, 3, 6) makes a reference to these imposing sites. The most complete sculptural group of the episode and the one assumingly closer to the Hellenistic models is considered the one at *antrum Cyclopis*, a now lost grotto at the hillside of *Caelius*, near the Porta Capena of Rome (*Regio II, Caelemontium*) and the so-called Fons Camenarum[12].

---

[10] On the popularity of the Polyphemus episode in the Late Hellenistic and Republican period see Buitron – Cohen 1992; LIMC VI (1992) 954–956 no. 69–137 s. v. Odysseus (O. Touchefeu-Meynier); Himmelmann 1995, 42–43; Alvino 1996, 200–205; Sanzi di Mino 1996. Cf. the Exhibition Catalogues, Andreae – Parisi Presicce 1996 and Andreae 1999a.

[11] On grottoes, Elderkin 1941; Lavagne 1988; Viscogliosi 1996, 252–269. On the appearance of this episode at fountain structures, Aristodemou 2012, 151–153.

[12] Lavagne 1988, 529. 586; Moreno 1994, 392. On the Fons Camenarum, cf. <https://www.digitalaugustanrome.org/records/camenae-camenarum-fons#/map:dag> (2009), s. v. Camenae, Camenarum Fons, Nr. 282 (L. Haselberger – G. Varinlioğlu) (25.04.2023).

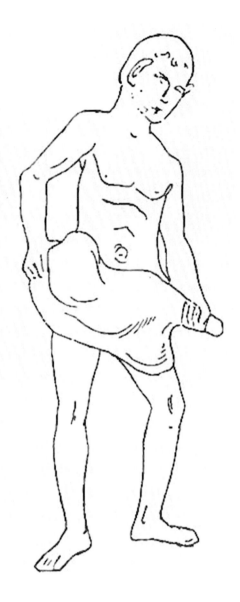

5   Naples, Museo Archeologico Nazionale; satyr figure with wineskin (D-DAI-ROM-7040, with DAI permission)

4   Monceau-les-Mines, Chalon sur Saône; drawing of a satyr figure with a wineskin (after Reinach 1913, no. 73.8)

Next in line is a terracotta group from Colle Ceserano, near Tivoli, which has been dated to the Late Republican period (mid-1st c. BC)[13]. It was found within a colonnaded portico of an elaborate hydraulic complex that might have served the water supply of the nymphaeum of the early 1st century BC *villa rustica*[14].

A second terracotta group, dated also to the second half of the 1st century BC, derives from the villa nymphaeum in Tortoreto near Chieti. It was found along with other terracotta statues, depicting among others Apollo and the Nymphs[15]. Both the Colle Ceserano and the Tortoreto groups have been associated with a Rhodian prototype of the High Hellenistic period, although the fact that they are made of terracotta suggests direct comparisons with examples from Etruscan architectural sculpture and Etruscan urns[16].

---

[13] Tivoli, Magazin de Soprintendenza archeologica del Lazi inv. 38994. 38995.
[14] Andreae – Parisi Presicce 1996, 239 no. 4,3; Alvino 1996, 200–209; Andreae 1999a, 147 fig. 59; 386 no. 59; Ridgway 2002, 70–71 fig. 22; Carrey 2002, 56 n. 31; Granieri 2008, 135 n. 350.
[15] Candeloro 1982–1983, 126–162; Andreae – Parisi Presicce 1996, 244 no. 4, 5; Sanzi di Mino 1996, 210–219; Ridgway 2002, 71–72 fig. 23; Carey 2002, 44–61; Granieri 2008, 135 n. 351.
[16] Andreae – Parisi Presicce 1996, 180–81 nos. 3. 12–16 (terracotta groups from Tortoreto and Colle Cesarano, Etruscan urns); Andreae 1999a, 142–147 nos. 55. 56. 59 with figures; Ridgway 2002, 72.

These two early Italian sculptural groups indicate that the selection of Trojan subjects was, at least at the beginning, not restricted to imperial grounds. In support of this argument, one may refer to the Antikythera shipwreck. Its sculptures are exhibited today at the National Archaeological Museum of Athens and include among them figures from the Homeric realm[17]. Since they are dated to the early 1st century BC, they constitute yet more evidence that wealthy Italians decorated their villas with Trojan subjects prior to the Imperial period – and these wealthy owners may in fact have ordered such sculptural groups from famous sculptural workshops of the East[18].

To continue, early in the Imperial period and onwards, the episode of the blinding of Polyphemus was narrated in large scale sculpture and/or other media now employed at the decoration of imperial establishments. The first in a series of imperial grottoes decorated with the Homeric episodes, and especially the blinding of Polyphemus and the Scylla Group, is Tiberius' grotto at Sperlonga[19]. Scholars agree that the sculptures were placed in the cave some time between AD 4 and 26 and consisted of an entirely original and innovative display providing an emphatic and vivid theatrical background to the guests of this island *triclinium*[20]. Next in line comes the now sunken Triclinium-Nymphaeum at Punta Epitaffio in *Baiae*, located on the coast just to the north of Naples[21]. It has been dated to the mid 40's AD and was part of a villa complex belonging to emperor Claudius. It was an entirely artificial space – in contrast to the Sperlonga natural cave, where the Polyphemus and Odysseus group was placed on a raised platform[22]. Only twenty years after the Baiae grotto display, sometime between AD 64 and 68, another example of this episode appears in an imperial grotto. It is almost an exact replica of the Baiae group, only this time executed not as a free-standing sculptural group but as a mosaic depiction, placed high in the vault of an artificial grotto within the Domus Aurea of Nero in Rome[23]. Almost 30 years later, at the end of the 1st century AD, the Polyphemus group was displayed along with the sculptural complex of Scylla at another grotto-nymphaeum of the villa belonging to the emperor Domitian, at Castelgandolfo, to the north of Rome. Better known as the Baths of Diana, the Bergantino Nymphaeum is located on the western shore of Lake Albano[24]. The circular cave of ca. 17 m diameter clearly recalls the Sperlonga cave, both in form and decoration[25]. A pool is in the middle of the cave, and the floor was completely covered with mosaics, of which a few fragments remain[26]. The sculptures of the Ninfeo Bergantino and in particular the remains of the group illustrating the blinding

---

[17] Vlachogianni 2012, 62–115 on the sculpture from the Antikythera shipwreck, esp. 104 no. 50 (inv. 2773); 106 no. 51 (inv. 5745); 107 no. 52 (inv. 5746); 108 no. 53 (inv. 15488).

[18] Ridgway 2002, 70.

[19] Andreae et al. 1974; Andreae 1994; Cassieri 1996, 18–19. 30–32; Andreae – Parisi Presicce 1996; Andreae 1999a, 177–224; Ridgway 2000, 78–91; Weiss 2000, 111–165; Granieri 2008, 120–122. On the Sperlonga Scylla group, Andreae-Conticello 1987; Andreae 2003.

[20] Carey 2002, 47–48 with bibliography.

[21] Tocco-Sciarelli et al. 1983.

[22] Andreae 1974, 74 no. 1 fig. 22–23; Andreae 1983, 67–71; Lavagne 1988, 515. 573–577; Andreae 1991, 237–265; LIMC VI (1992) 956 no. 86 s. v. Odysseus (O. Touchefeu-Meynier); Zevi 1996; Andreae 1999a, 225–241 with figures; Carey 2002, 48–52; Recently, <http://www.pafleg.it/it/4406/opere/129/ulisse> (2020) and <http://www.pafleg.it/it/4406/opere/118/compagno-di-ulisse-baio> (2020), with bibliography (25.04.2023).

[23] The Domus Aurea does not actually narrate the myth itself, but repeats the existing sculptural group in a different medium. It constitutes the earliest example of a multifigural group adorning a vaulted ceiling imitating a natural cave, Andreae 1974, 76 no. 22 fig. 26–27; Lavagne 1970, 673–721; Lavagne 1988, 583–584; LIMC VI (1992) 955 no. 69 s. v. Odysseus (O. Touchefeu-Meynier); Moreno 1994, 392; Zevi 1996, 320–331; Vassal 2020, 284–285, fig. 2. Perhaps in this manner, Nero wanted to make a visual play and connection with his predecessors Tiberius and Claudius (and their sculptural groups at Sperlonga and *Baiae* respectively), cf. Carey 2002, 53–56 fig. 4–5.

[24] Balland 1967, 421–502, mainly 460–495 (sculptures); Liverani 1996.

[25] Liverani 1989, 71–72; Carey 2002, 58.

[26] Most of the artifacts found in the Nymphaeum during the excavations of Cardinal Giustiniani are preserved and displayed in the Antiquarium of Villa Barberini, while others have been dispersed. Di Gigi er Gigliola – Opera propria, CC BY-SA 3.0, <https://commons.wikimedia.org/w/index.php?curid=29338798> (2013) (25.04.2023).

of Polyphemus and the Scylla episode, published by Paolo Liverani (1989), are inspired by the sculptures from the grotto of Tiberius at Sperlonga[27].

The last example of the use of the blinding of Polyphemus and the Scylla sculptural groups in imperial grounds, comes from Hadrian's Villa at Tivoli[28]. The Polyphemus group consists of Odysseus, his three companions and the colossal figure of Polyphemus, all fragmentarily preserved[29]. It was installed in the grotto *triclinium* sometime between AD 126 and 128[30]. The two Scylla groups framed each end of the Canopus canal displayed on plinths set in the water[31].

Outside of Italy, the episode of the blinding of Polyphemus by Odysseus and his companions has been recognised at least once, at the Fountain of Domitian in *Ephesos*[32]. This group contains nine figures[33]. The fountain has been dated around the end of the 1st century AD, and is the earliest example of the type of the semicircular nymphaeum in Asia Minor. The building and dedicatory inscription record the proconsul Publius Calvisius Ruso Frontinus as the monument's sponsor[34]. Scholarly research has accepted that the sculptural group predates the fountain and that it was transferred there from another monument dated to the mid 1st century BC[35]. The major arguments were, 1) the stylistic similarities that Bernard Andreae detected between the Polyphemus group and the reliefs from the Memmius Monument, dated to 40/30 BC[36], and 2) the clear evidence that the sculptures were converted into fountain figures by being hastily and awkwardly perforated for the insertion of water pipes to function as water spouts[37].

As far as the narration in concerned, both for the Colle Cesarano and the Tortoreto groups, the Homeric episode represented is not, as in the cases of Sperlonga and the Villa Adriana, the actual blinding of Polyphemus, but the moment that precedes it, the offering of the wine cup by Odysseus to the Cyclops. The Ephesian group differs from the previous groups because it includes

---

[27] Today the exhibition of Villa Barberini includes the torso of Polyphemus lying on a rocky ground and the lower part of the body of one of the Greek companions of Odysseus. Polyphemus' figure dates to around AD 90 and takes after a Pergamene prototype of the 2nd c. BC. Liverani 1989, 73–79 with bibliography; Andreae 1999a, 386 no. 71.

[28] On the Digital Villa Adriana project: <http://vwhl.soic.indiana.edu/villa/index.php> (2013) (25.04.2023). On the statuary display project of the Villa Adriana, cf. Raeder 1983. On the Canopus sculptures, cf. Pensabene 2011, 17–32.

[29] Andreae 1974, 81–82; Andreae 1996b, 342–366; Andreae 2000, 77–80; Carey 2002, 58–59; Salza Prina Ricotti 2000, 255. 375 (statues). Recently, with all previous research, bibliography and reconstructions, Granieri 2008, 119–123 figs. 31 a; 41 a; 87; 98–99; 110 a. b; 111.

[30] Carey 2002, 58–59.

[31] On the Scylla Group, cf. Raeder 1983, 302; Andreae 1996b, 342–366; Andreae 1999a, 316–317 with figures of the reconstruction by H. Schroeteler, 392 no. 142. Recently, with all previous bibliography and research, Granieri 2008, 128–133 figs. 98. 99 and Pensabene 2011, 30.

[32] Fleischer 1968–1971, 160–161; Fellmann 1972, 37–57; Andreae 1974, 74–75; LIMC VI (1992) 943–970, mainly 954–955 s. v. Odysseus (O. Touchefeu-Meynier); Andreae 1996a, 205. 240–243; Andreae 1999a, 162–177; Longfellow 2011, 69–70; Aristodemou 2012, 151–154. 269–270 no. 117, 1–9.

[33] Odysseus who offers the wine cup to Polyphemus, a Greek about to give the cup to Odysseus, a second Greek that carries the wineskin. Two more Greeks are supporting the wooden pole, whereas a fifth is sharpening the pole edge. Polyphemus is placed in the center of the composition, and is almost twice as large as the Greek figures. Two more Greeks are lying dead on the ground in front of the Cyclops, cf. Andreae 1977, 1–11; Andreae 1985, 209–211.

[34] Cramme 2001, 143–144.

[35] The discussion regarding the original location of the Polyphemus group, hypothetically from the pediment of a temple dedicated to Dionysus, is long. On this, cf. Andreae 1977, 7–11; Andreae 1982, 69–90; Andreae 1985, 211 fig. 24, 2; Aurenhammer 1990, 175–176; Alvino 1996, 206–207; Andreae – Parisi Presicce 1996, 240–243; Andreae 1999a, 173–177; Granieri 2008, 135–136 fig. 105 a. b; Longfellow 2011, 71–72. Based on stylistic and iconographical criteria, Lenz 1998, 237–248 supported that the Polyphemus group is a combination of two different sculptural groups, one of Homeric and one from the Galatian realm.

[36] Andreae 1977, 9; Andreae 1999a, 171; Andreae 1999b, 531–533. On the Memmius monument, Bammer – Alzinger 1971; Aurenhammer 1990, 74.

[37] Fleischer 1968–1971, 162–163; Aurenhammer 1990, 174. 176 n. 37; Longfellow 2011, 71; Aristodemou 2012, 152.

three deceased Greeks instead of one, as is the case in the groups of Sperlonga, *Baiae*, and Bergantino. Furthermore, in *Ephesos* there is no discretion with regard to the actual act of cannibalism. Polyphemus is depicted seated, and clearly visible on his thigh are the remains of the body of one of Odysseus' companions. On the other hand, in the groups of Tortoreto, Colle Cesarano and *Baiae*, the corpse of Odysseus' companion is intact and does not indicate the act of cannibalism[38]. The scene of the offering of the wine cup to Polyphemus is repeated in Domitian's Fountain, as well as in the groups from Colle Cesarano and *Baiae*[39]. Moreover, the figures of Odysseus offering the wine cup from *Ephesos*, *Baiae* and Sperlonga (as well as from the Antikythera shipwreck) are dressed in a *chiton* and *himation*, thrown over the shoulders so that the figures have freedom of movement[40].

## THE CRETAN FIGURE

Could the statue from Crete be just another satyr figure holding a wineskin and placed as an ornament at a private fountain structure, as was common? It might, since a significant number of satyr and silenoi fountain statues have indeed been found at small-scale fountains decorating the gardens, the atria or the bath complexes of wealthy households[41].

As we have now briefly reviewed, the Homeric episodes and especially the blinding of Polyphemus as a narrative subject acquired great significance in the period between the 1st century BC and the 1st century AD[42]. Should, or could, the statue from Crete be placed within this thematic framework and be seen as a surviving member of a now lost statuary group of the blinding of Polyphemus, in Crete?

For what it is worth, the Cretan figure has similarities with the so-called satyr figure from the *Daphne* village (Antakya Museum inv. 1371) for which Cornelius Vermeule has already suggested that it may indeed belong to the realm of the Homeric heroes[43]. He considered its body position to resemble one of the companions of Odysseus from the group at the Sperlonga cave – especially the figure that carries the wineskin[44].

Additionally, the statue from Crete presents significant similarities with the figure of the Greek that carries the wineskin from the Polyphemus group from Claudius' nymphaeum in *Baiae*, which has been dated to the first half of the 1st century AD[45] (fig. 6). The Baiae complex recalls Hellenistic models of the first half of the 2nd century BC. The statue depicts a companion of Odysseus, probably Baios. The man is portrayed in heroic nudity, with the muscles of his body tense, in the act of advancing together with Odysseus. Baios holds the full wineskin, necessary to make the Cyclops inebriated. Given the presence of a lead channel inside the statue, it is understood that some wine actually may have flowed from the wineskin.

---

[38] On the observation, Longfellow 2011, 69.
[39] Cf. also the example from the Vatican (Museo Chiaramonti no.1901), LIMC VI (1992) 956 no. 87 s. v. Odysseus (O. Touchefeu-Meynier); also, cf. Andreae 1996b, 146–147 fig. 59 (Colle Cesarano Odysseus), 161 fig. 73 (Vatican example) and 128–129 fig. 80 (Baiae Odysseus).
[40] Moreno 1994, 395 fig. 496. 501; Vlachogianni 2012, 106 no. 51.
[41] On silenoi figures from fountains, cf. Aristodemou 2012, nos. 3. 6 (Athens); no. 66 (Sikyon); nos. 73. 74 (Sparta); no. 206 (Lesbos); no. 209 (Rhodes); no. 289 (Antioch-on-the-Orontes); no. 86 (Andrianopolis); no. 354 (Knossos); no. 79 (Thessaloniki); nos. 355. 356 (Kissamos).
[42] Balensiefen 2005.
[43] Vermeule 2001, 99 fig. 14.
[44] He further points out the figure of the Greek companion who brings the wine cup to make the Cyclops drunk, highlighting the fact that it became popular and was often used indipendently in appropriate settings. The importance of the wineskin bearer to the Polyphemus blinding group is emphasized by Andreae 1982, 146–48; Andreae 1994, 69–71.
[45] Baia, Museo archeologico dei Campi Flegrei inv. 222737. Dimensions: height 169 cm; depth 110 cm. Miniero – Zevi 2008, 156–158. Also: <http://www.pafleg.it/it/4406/opere/118/compagno-di-ulisse-baio> (2020) (26.04.2023).

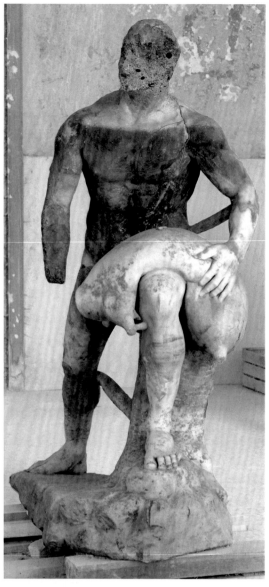

6 Baia, Museo Archeologico dei Campi Flegrei inv. 222737 (D-DAI-ROM-73.1409, with DAI permission)

Based on the similarities in the subject and the body posture with the above figure, one might suggest that the Cretan statue belonged to a similar group, and that it was placed within a fountain niche re-embodying the episode of the blinding of Polyphemus. There is really no reason to believe that such a sculptural group could not exist in Crete, especially when a fine copy of a Scylla figure has already been found at *Eleutherna*[46].

## IN WHAT PREMISES AND FOR WHOM?

The answer to this question can be sought within the framework of the social and political conditions developed in Crete in the period between the 1st century BC and the 1st century AD[47].

Crete had been an important player in the Mediterranean even as early as the 2nd century BC. Located in the middle of the Eastern Mediterranean basin, protected by the *Pax Romana*, and upon the routes of commercial ships traveling between Italy, North Africa, Asia Minor, Greece and the islands it became a significant link in the network of islands and cities that formed the Mediterranean heart of the Roman Empire. Cretans living in the Roman period lived in a far different and more prosperous island than that of their ancestors in the Minoan or Archaic periods. Especially after AD 67, when the island was incorporated into the Empire as part of the joined province of *Creta et Cyrenaica*, and for almost three centuries the inhabitants of the approximately twenty cities that flourished on the island enjoyed a level of prosperity and lifestyle that was comparable to the lifestyle of other prosperous areas of the empire[48].

From the 1st century BC onwards, part of the area between *Knossos* and *Gortyn* was awarded by Octavian to veterans from *Capua* and was known thereafter as the »Capuan lands«, where Italians had been settled and thrived[49]. Crete acquired a cosmopolitan character and for the first time, spectacle monuments (theatres and amphitheatres), hydraulic infrastructural works such as aqueducts, *thermae*, and fountains, as well as private villas adorned with mosaics and equipped with bath systems and elegant nymphaea appeared in numbers[50].

---

[46] On the Scylla from *Eleutherna*, Tegou 2004, 148 no. 3. On Roman *Eleutherna*, Karanastasi 2015.
[47] On the Cretan political situation between 67–27 BC, recently Kouremenos 2018, 44–46. Also previously, Kouremenos 2013, *passim*.
[48] Karanastasi 2012, 433 n. 1, with extended bibliography.
[49] Rigsby 1976, 316–318; Paton 1994, 141–153; Sweetman 2007, 67; Kouremenos 2018, 52.
[50] Karanastasi 2012, 434 n. 3–5. On the Knossos area aqueducts, Kelly 2004 (unpublished PhD Thesis) no. 8, 1–13 fig. 31–33 pl. 13 a–19 c.

The people who enjoyed such a privileged life were members of a socially and economically upper class – both citizens and officials from Rome and the cities of Campania and wealthy Knossians adopting Italian fashions. This elite class, through the possession of wealth, wanted to give an idyllic and luxurious allure to their daily life by adorning their households with high quality sculpture, both local and imported[51].

The statue discussed today originates from *Knossos*, but nothing is known with regard to its original environment. After the foundation of the joint province, and with *Gortyn* becoming the capital of *Creta et Cyrenaica*, at around 27 BC *Knossos* was chosen to be the only colony of the province, named *colonia Julia Nobilis Knossus*. Not much was known from its Augustan foundation until its period of flourishing, in the late 1st and early 2nd centuries AD[52]. Current research has shown that, apart from small scale adaptations between Hellenistic and early Roman *Knossos*, the Roman impact becomes increasingly visible from the mid-1st century AD – correspondingly, Ian F. Sanders underlines the similar absence of major changes in stone sculpture until the late 1st century AD[53]. Wealthy private villas, such as the North House (northwards of the Unexplored Mansion)[54], the so-called Villa Dionysos, the House of the Diamond Frescoes or the Corinthian House appear only by the end of the 1st century AD[55]. From then on and throughout the 2nd century AD, all data point to a vibrant city with economic strength, well-organized urban structure and an architectural armature that facilitated the Knossian stratified society[56].

Of special interest seems to be the so-called Villa Dionysos, located 350 m north-west of the Unexplored Mansion and half a kilometre northwest of the Minoan palace[57] (fig. 7). It was a building designed to impress, developed around a peristyle court with rooms deployed on its three sides. Excavations at the peristyle have brought to light a brick-built fountain that belonged to the so-called Period IV, dated to the middle of the 2nd century AD[58]. The researchers of the villa have come to the conclusion that it was of a semi-public character[59]. The peristyle and its associated halls consisted the public reception area of an elaborately decorated Roman *domus* of the 2nd century AD and the adjacent buildings to the south were probably the private quarters. An elaborate water system including a large cistern was installed in the upper south-west corner of the villa and was connected to the Knossos aqueduct, thus providing the villa with a continuous water supply[60]. Within the same domicile, a large room with a monumental entrance and an impressive mosaic floor with a Dionysiac subject has been recognized as a *triclinium*[61]. This corresponds with Vitruvius' descriptions (5, 11) where the *triclinia* were usually arranged in proximity to the peristyle courts so as to allow the guests a relaxing view of the courtyard filled with fountains, running water and vegetation. The abundance of water in a private estate is of no surprise. The urban elites demonstrated their status and their ability to manipulate the city's water supply by using their private connections to provide their own houses with running water for their ornamental

---

[51] On mythological-idealistic sculpture deriving from private houses from Kissamos, *Eleutherna* and *Knossos*, see Sporn 2018, 273–292. On the local sculptural workshops of Crete and the imported sculpture, Karanastasi 2016. On Roman *Knossos*, Sweetman 2007, 61–81. On houses and identity in Roman *Knossos* and Kissamos, Kouremenos 2013 (unpublished PhD Thesis).
[52] Sweetman 2007, 61–63. 67.
[53] Sanders 1982, 47–51; Sweetman 2007, 67–68.
[54] Lately Kelly-O'Neill 2023, 31–34.
[55] On the Knossos houses, Kouremenos 2013, chap. 3.
[56] Sweetman 2010, 339.
[57] Paton 2022 with all previous bibliography.
[58] The villa destruction began between AD 160–185. Paton 1998, 125 figs. 15, 1; 126; Kouremenos 2013, n. 518; Patton 2022, *passim*.
[59] Cf. villas including bath complexes and with a semi-public character are also known in Macedonia. Characteristic examples are the »House of the Wild Animals« in Philippi (cf. Oulkeroglou 2018, 72–73 no. K 84 plans 97. 105. 106 fig. 158), and the »Eastern Baths« in Dion that are actually part of the so-called Villa Dionysos complex (cf. Bonini 2006, 343–346; Oulkeroglou 2018, 33–34 no. K28 plans 23. 31–33 fig. 38–70).
[60] On the Roman aqueduct associated with the Villa Dionysos, Kelly 2004, 36 no. 8, 13 pl. 74 c and Kelly-O'Neill 2023, 35. The system's life span was from the 2nd until the 4th c. AD.
[61] Kouremenos 2013, 115–117 fig. 68–71.

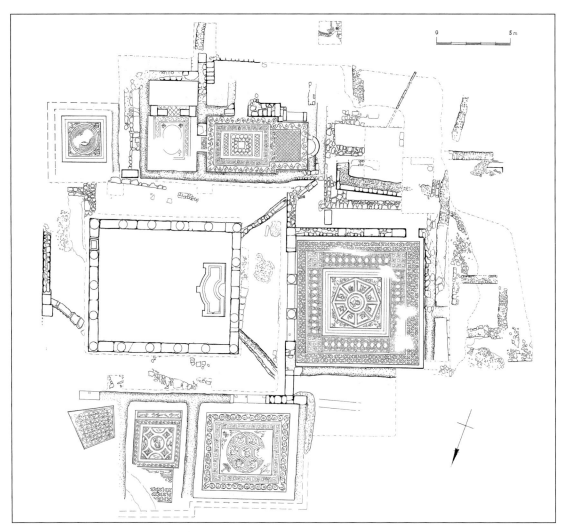

7   *Knossos*, Villa Dionysos. Plan (after Paton 2022, fig.1 [supplementary material])

fountains and pools[62]. The owner of the Villa Dionysos was without doubt an important resident, either a Cretan or a Roman magistrate with powerful connections and a large clientele that one can easily imagine waiting in the columnar entrance, next to the shallow fountain, for the morning *salutatio*.

Since one of the profound expressions of wealth is the possession of high quality sculpture by the local elite, the presence of a sculptural complex depicting a Homeric episode in the idyllic garden environment of the villa would definitely be appropriate[63]. Whether a wealthy Knossian or a Roman magistrate, just like Publius Calvisius Ruso Frontinus in *Ephesos*, such individuals had the means to travel to Rome, or elsewhere in the Mediterranean[64], and see for themselves major works of sculpture and incorporate them into their own wealthy premises.

---

[62] Kouremenos 2013, n. 649–650 citing Wilson 1995; Wilson 1997, 145. 161; Wilson 2011. Lately on Rogers 2018 (esp. chap. 6).

[63] Although publications of Roman sculpture in Crete are inscreasing, still, outside of presentations in conferences it remains rather under-studied. A considerable amount of statuary has been and continues to be discovered in Hierapetra, Kissamos, Heraklion, even though much of the Roman architecture is still not well studied, Sweetmann 2013, 28 n. 104–105; Karanastasi 2012, *passim*.

[64] On the dating of the Sperlonga groups and by extend the dating and the origin of the Hellenistic prototypes, Ridgway 2000, 112–113. 138–142; Ridgway 2002, 72–74 on the significance of the Ephesian group and the possibility of *Ephesos* being the initial production point.

The placement of the Polyphemus group within an apsis, »pays homage to the cavernous setting of the actual myth«[65]. The grotto-like interior would enhance the 3D dimension of the complex, whereas the running water or wine would enhance the overall sensation. Sperlonga, *Baiae*, Castelgandolfo, Nero's Domus Aurea, Villa Adriana and the Fountain of Domitian are quite different spaces. The natural – theatrical like – cave space at Sperlonga, became a more refined semicircular apse at the private *triclinium* at *Baiae*, which in turn was monumentalised in the Domus Aurea (where, however, we have no clear evidence whether it was used as a dining chamber)[66]. What all these spaces do share in common is the emphasis given to the display and exhibition of the sculpture. Placed in these premises the Polyphemus group united the different architectonic forms, became associated with the emperor, and was thereafter used to define a place as imperial. Therefore the display of an acknowledged ›imperial‹ theme at semi-public premises owned by a wealthy individual gives specific meaning to the place and associates the owner with the imperial tradition. This illusionistic aspect of the sculpture gradually evolved into a trophy prize, where the possession and display of such an imposing sculptural complex became the main purpose.

## CONCLUSION

Odysseus, a traveling hero, became a role model for aristocrats who travelled to gather knowledge and experience. And when those wealthy Romans, who had access to the imperial villas of Italy, came to Crete they could associate this statue ensemble with one of the imperial ensembles. The owner of this Cretan *domus* – that could be the Villa Dionysos, or another wealthy villa from the Knossos area[67] – chose to decorate his domestic nymphaeum with the episode of the blinding of Polyphemus on purpose. In this manner, he addressed the particular cultivated audience of those who could see the connection and promote his political or economic ambitions. Through this close network of shared memories and experiences, the owner of such sculpture projected his own wealth, as well as social and educational status.

Admittedly, there is no concrete evidence that the statue AMH Γ 46 actually derives from the Villa Dionysos. What this paper aims to demonstrate is that the statue may well be part of the sculptural group of the blinding of Polyphemus. Furthermore, such a sculptural group may very well have adorned a wealthy Cretan residence between the 1st and the 2nd century AD, proving on the one hand the cultural interconnectivity between the centre and the peripheries of the Roman Empire on grounds of artistic production, and on the other demonstrating Crete's prosperity and dynamics into the new globalized Mediterranean society created within the Roman Empire[68].

## BIBLIOGRAPHY

| | |
|---|---|
| Alvino 1996 | G. Alvino, Il IX libro dell'Odissea: l'offerta della coppa di vino. Il gruppo fitile di colle cesarano e il gruppo scultoreo di Efeso, in: Andreae – Parisi Presicce 1996, 200–209 |
| Andreae 1974 | B. Andreae, Die römischen Repliken der mythologischen Skulpturengruppen von Sperlonga, in: Andreae et al. 1974, 61–105 |
| Andreae 1977 | B. Andreae, Vorschlag für eine Rekonstruktion der Polyphemgruppe von Ephesos, in: U. Hockmann – A. Krug (eds.), Festschrift Frank Brommer (Mainz 1977) 1–11 |
| Andreae 1982 | B. Andreae, Odysseus. Archäologie des europäischen Menschenbildes (Frankfurt 1982) |
| Andreae 1983 | B. Andreae, L'Imperatore Claudio a Baia, in: G. Tocco Sciarelli (ed.), Baia. Il Ninfeo imperiale sommerso di Punta Epitaffio (Naples 1983) 67–71 |

---

[65] Carey 2002, 50.
[66] Viscogliosi 1996, 252–269.
[67] On the wealthy Roman private residences and small bath complexes lining up at the Knossos aqueduct trajectory and probably supplied by it, Kelly – O'Neill 2023, 35–38 and fig. 24.
[68] von Hesberg 2009, 285.

| | |
|---|---|
| Andreae 1985 | B. Andreae, Die Polyphem-Gruppe von Ephesos, in: M. Kandler – S. Karwiese – R. Pillinger (eds.), Lebendige Altertumswissenschaft. Festschrift Hermann Vetters (Vienna 1985) 209–211 |
| Andreae 1991 | B. Andreae, Il Ninfeo di Punta dell'Epitaffio a Baia, in: S. Stucchi – M. Bonanno Aravantinos (eds.), Giornate di studio in onore di Achille Adriani, Roma 26.–27.11.1984, Studi miscellanei 28 (Rome 1991) 237–265 |
| Andreae 1994 | B. Andreae, Praetorium Speluncae. Tiberius und Ovid in Sperlonga (Mainz 1994) |
| Andreae 1996a | B. Andreae, L'immagine di Ulisse nell'arte antica, in: Andreae – Parisi Presicce 1996, 42–71 |
| Andreae 1996b | B. Andreae, I gruppi di Polifemo e di Scilla a Villa Adriana, in: Andreae – Parisi Presicce 1996, 342–366 |
| Andreae 1999a | B. Andreae, Odysseus. Mythos und Erinnerung. Kurze Anleitung. Katalog zur Ausstellung in München 1999/2000 (Mainz 1999) |
| Andreae 1999b | B. Andreae, Ist die Hypothese vom Polyphem-Giebel in Ephesos bereits falsifiziert?, in: H. Friesinger – F. Krinzinger (eds.), 100 Jahre Österreichische Forschungen in Ephesos. Akten des Symposions Wien 1995, AForsch 1 = DenkschrWien 260 (Vienna 1999) 531–533 |
| Andreae 2000 | B. Andreae, Il gruppo di Polifemo di Villa Adriana, in: Adriano Architettura e progetto, Catalogo Mostra Tivoli (Milan 2000) 77–80 |
| Andreae 2003 | B. Andreae, Il gruppo di Scilla di Sperlonga ricomposto, in: G. Fiorentini – M. Caltabiano – A. Calderone (eds.), Archeologia del Mediterraneo. Studi in onore di Ernesto De Miro, Bibliotheca Archaeologica 35 (Rome 2003) 51–60 |
| Andreae et al. 1974 | B. Andreae – B. Conticello – P. C. Bol (eds.), Die Skulpturen von Sperlonga, AntPl 14 (Berlin 1974) |
| Andreae – Conticello 1987 | B. Andreae – B. Conticello (eds.), Skylla und Charybdis. Zur Skylla-Gruppe von Sperlonga, Abhandlungen der Geistes- und Sozialwissenschaftlichen Klasse XIV (Mainz 1987) |
| Andreae – Parisi Presicce 1996 | B. Andreae – C. Parisi Presicce (eds.), Ulisse. Il Mito e la Memoria. Roma, Palazzo delle Esposizioni. Catalogo della Mostra (Rome 1996) |
| Aristodemou 2012 | G. Aristodemou, Ο γλυπτός διάκοσμος νυμφαίων και κρηνών στο ανατολικό τμήμα της Ρωμαϊκής Αυτοκρατορίας (Thessaloniki 2012) |
| Aurenhammer 1990 | M. Aurenhammer, Die Skulpturen von Ephesos, Idealplastik I, FiE 10, 1 (Vienna 1990) |
| Balensiefen 2005 | L. Balensiefen, Polyphem-Grotten und Skylla-Gewässer: Schauplätze der »Odyssee« in römischen Villen, in: A. Luther (ed.), Odyssee-Rezeptionen (Frankfurt/M. 2005) 9–31 |
| Balland 1967 | A. Balland, Une transposition de la grotte de Tibère à Sperlonga; le Ninfeo Bergantino de Castelgandolfo, MEFRA 79/2, 1967, 421–502 |
| Bammer – Alzinger 1971 | A. Bammer – W. Alzinger, Das Monument des C. Memmius, FiE 7 (Vienna 1971) |
| Bonini 2006 | P. Bonini, La casa nella Grecia romana. Forme e funzioni dello spazio privato fra I e VI secolo (Rome 2006) |
| Buitron – Cohen 1992 | D. Buitron – B. Cohen (eds.), The Odyssey and Ancient Art. An Epic in Word and Image (New York 1992) |
| Candeloro 1982–1983 | A. Candeloro, Un gruppo fittile der Tortoretto con rapresentazione di tema omerico, QuadChieti 3, 1982–1983, 126–162 |
| Carey 2002 | S. Carey, A Tradition of Adventures in the Imperial Grotto, GaR 49/1, 2002, 44–61 |
| Cassieri 1996 | N. Cassieri, Il Museo Archaeologico di Sperlonga (Rome 1996) |
| Cramme 2001 | S. Cramme, Die Bedeutung des Euergetismus für die Finanzierung städtischer Aufgaben in der Provinz Asia (PhD Thesis Cologne 2001) |
| De Lachenal 1981 | L. De Lachenal, in: A. Giuliano (ed.), Museo Nazionale Romano, Le Sculture I 2 (Rome 1981) |
| Elderkin 1941 | G. W. Elderkin, The Natural and the Artificial Grotto, Hesperia 10, 1941, 125–137 |
| Fellmann 1972 | B. Fellmann, Die antiken Darstellungen des Polyphemabenteuers (Munich 1972) |
| Fleischer 1968–1971 | R. Fleischer, Späthellenistische Gruppe vom Pollionymphaeum in Ephesos mit dem Polyphemabenteuer des Odysseus, ÖJh 49, 1968–1971, 137–164 |
| Granieri 2008 | F. Granieri, Scavi al Pantanello: proposta per una ricontestualizzazione delle antichità negli ambienti di Villa Adriana (PhD Thesis Università degli Studi di Roma »Tor Vergata«, Rome 2008) |

| | |
|---|---|
| Himmelmann 1995 | N. Himmelmann, Sperlonga: Die homerischen Gruppen und ihre Bildquellen (Nordrhein-Westfälische Akademie der Wissenschaften, Vorträge, G 340 (Opladen 1995) |
| Kapossy 1969 | B. Kapossy, Brunnenfiguren der hellenistischen und römischen Zeit (Zurich 1969) |
| Karanastasi 2012 | P. Karanastasi, Η πλαστική της Κρήτης στην αυτοκρατορική περίοδο, in: Th. Stefanidou-Tiveriou – P. Karanastasi – D. Damaskos (eds.), Κλασική παράδοση και νεωτερικά στοιχεία στην πλαστική της ρωμαϊκής Ελλάδας. Πρακτικά Διεθνούς Συνεδρίου Θεσσαλονίκη, 7–9 Μαΐου 2009 (Thessaloniki 2012) 433–450 |
| Karanastasi 2015 | P. Karanastasi, Νέα στοιχεία για τη ρωμαϊκή Ελεύθερνα, in: P. Karanastasi – A. Tzigounaki – C. Tsigonaki (eds.), Αρχαιολογικό Έργο Κρήτης. Πρακτικά της 3ης Συνάντησης, Ρέθυμνο, 5–8 Δεκεμβρίου 2013, Vol. B: Χανιά – Ρέθυμνο – Λασίθι (Rethymno 2015) 417–428 |
| Karanastasi 2016 | P. Karanastasi, Roman imperial sculpture from Crete: a re-appraisal, in: J. E. Francis – A. Kouremenos (eds.), Roman Crete. New perspectives (Philadelphia 2016) 101–118 |
| Kelly 2004 | A. Kelly, The Roman Aqueducts and Bathhouses of Crete (unpublished PhD Thesis Trinity College, Dublin 2004), <www.tara.tcd.ie/handle/2262/77829> (26.04.2023) |
| Kelly 2023 | A. Kelly – B. O'Neill, The Roman Aqueduct of Knossos, A Model for Nineteenth-Century Aqueduct Design. BSA, First View, 2023, 1–49, DOI:10.1017/S0068245422000156 |
| Kouremenos 2013 | A. Kouremenos, Houses and Identity in Roman Knossos and Kissamos, Crete: A Study in Emulative Acculturatio (Unpublished PhD Thesis University of Oxford 2013) |
| Kouremenos 2018 | A. Kouremenos, In the Heart of the Wine-Dark Sea: Cretan Insularity and Identity in the Roman Period, in: A. Kouremenos (ed.), Insularity and Identity in the Roman Mediterranean (Philadelphia 2018) 41–64 |
| Lange 1879 | K. Lange, Das Motiv des aufgestützen Fusses in der antiken Kunst und dessen statuarische Verwendung durch Lysippos (Lipsia 1879) |
| Lavagne 1970 | H. Lavagne, Le Nymphée au Polyphème de la Domus Aurea, MEFRA 82, 1970, 673–721 |
| Lavagne 1988 | H. Lavagne, Operosa Antra. Recherches sur la grotte à Roma de Sylla à Hadrien (Rome 1988) |
| Lenz 1998 | D. Lenz, Ein Gallier unter den Gefährten des Odysseus. Zur Polyphemgruppe aus dem Pollio-Nymphaeum in Ephesos, IstMitt 48, 1998, 237–248 |
| Liverani 1989 | P. Liverani, L'antiquarium di villa Barberini a Castel Gandolfo. Monumenti, musei e gallerie pontificie, Città del Vaticano (Rome 1989) |
| Liverani 1996 | P. Liverani, L'antro del ciclope a Castelgandolfo: Ninfeo Bergantino, in: Andreae – Parisi Presicce 1996, 332–341 |
| Longfellow 2011 | B. Longfellow, Roman Imperialism and Civic Patronage: Form, Meaning and Ideology in Monumental Fountain Complexes (New York 2011) |
| Meischner 2003 | J. Meischner, Die Skulpturen des Hatay Museums in Antakya, JdI 118, 2003, 285–384 |
| Miniero – Zevi 2008 | P. Miniero – F. Zevi (eds.), Museo Archeologico dei Campi Flegrei 3. Catalogo Generale, literum, Baia, Miseno (Naples 2008) |
| Moreno 1994 | P. Moreno, Scultura Ellenistica I–III (Rome 1994) |
| Oulkeroglou 2018 | A. Oulkeroglou, Οι λουτρικές εγκαταστάσεις στη Μακεδονία κατά τη Ρωμαϊκή αυτοκρατορική και την Πρωτοβυζαντινή περίοδο (Thessaloniki 2018) |
| Paton 1994 | S. Paton, Roman Knossos and the Colonia Julia Nobilis Knossus, in: D. Evely – H. Hughes-Brock – N. Momigliano (eds.), A Labyrinth of History, Papers in Honour of Sinclair Hood (London 1994) 141–153 |
| Paton 1998 | S. Paton, The Villa Dionysos at Knossos and its predecessors, in: W. G. Cavanagh – M. Curtis (eds.), Post-Minoan Crete: Proceedings of the First Colloquium (London 1998) 123–128 |
| Paton 2022 | S. Paton, The so-called Villa Dionysos at Knossos, BSA 117, 2022, 1–41 |
| Pensabene 2011 | P. Pensabene, Arredo statuario del Canopo di Villa Adriana, in: G Ghini, Lazio e Sabina 7. Atti del Convegno. Settimo Incontro di Studi sul Lazio e la Sabina, Roma, 9–11 marzo 2010 (Rome 2011) 17–32. |
| Raeder 1983 | J. Raeder, Die statuarische Ausstattung der Villa Hadriana bei Tivoli (Frankfurt/M. 1983) |
| Reinach 1913 | S. Reinach, Repértoires de la Statuaire Grecque et Romaine IV (Paris 1913) |

| | |
|---|---|
| Ridgway 2000 | B. S. Ridgway, The Sperlonga Sculptures. Current state of Research, in: N. T. De Grummond – B. S. Ridgway (eds.), From Pergamon to Sperlonga: sculpture and context (Berkeley 2000) 78–91 |
| Ridgway 2002 | B. S. Ridgway, Hellenistic Sculpture III: the styles of ca. 100–31 B.C., Wisconsin Studies in Classics (Madison 2002) |
| Rigsby 1976 | K. J. Rigsby, Cnossus and Capua, TransactAmPhilAss 106, 1976, 313–330 |
| Rogers 2018 | D. K. Rogers, Water Culture in Roman Society, BRP (Leiden 2018) |
| Sakelarakis 2005 | I. A. Sakelarakis, Μουσείο Ηρακλείου. Εικονογραφημένος Οδηγός ²(Athens 2005) |
| Salza Prina Ricotti 2000 | E. Salza Prina Ricotti, Villa Adriana. Il sogno di un imperatore (Rome 2000) |
| Sanders 1982 | I. F. Sanders, Roman Crete (Warminister 1982) |
| Sanzi di Mino 1996 | M. R. Sanzi di Mino, L'uomo ricco di Astuzie raccontami o Musa (odissea I.1) il complesso di statue fittili del ninfeo di Tortoreto, in: Andreae – Parisi Presicce 1996, 210–219 |
| Sporn 2018 | K. Sporn, The Cretan Venus. Überlegungen zur Skulpturenausstattung von römischen Privathäusern auf Kreta, in: P. Karanastassi – Th. Stefanidou-Tiveriou – D. Damaskos (eds.), Γλυπτική και κοινωνία στη ρωμαϊκή Ελλάδα: καλλιτεχνικά προϊόντα, κοινωνικές προβολές. Διεθνές συνέδριο Ρέθυμνο, 26–28 Σεπτεμβρίου 2014 (Thessaloniki 2018) 273–292 |
| Sweetman 2007 | R. J. Sweetman, Roman Knossos: The Nature of a Globalized City, AJA 111/1, 2007, 61–81 |
| Sweetman 2010 | R. J. Sweetman, Roman Knossos: Discovering the City through the Evidence of Rescue Excavations, BSA 105, 2010, 339–369 |
| Sweetman 2013 | R. J. Sweetman, The Mosaics of Roman Crete: Art, Archaeology and Social Change (Cambridge 2013) |
| Tegou 2004 | E. Tegou in: N. Ch. Stambolides (ed.), Eleutherna: Polis – Acropolis – Necropolis (translated by A. Doumas), Museum of Cycladic Art (Athens 2004) 148 no. 3 |
| Tocco-Sciarelli et al. 1983 | G. Tocco-Sciarelli et al. (eds.), Baia. Il Ninfeo Imperiale Sommerso di Punta Epitaffio (Naples 1983) |
| Vassal 2020 | V. Vassal, La représentation d'Ulysse et de Polyphème dans la mosaïque romaine. Analyses et comparaisons, JMR 13, 2020, 281–294 |
| Vermeule 2001 | C. Vermeule, The Sculptures of Roman Syria, in: C. Kondoleon (ed.), Antioch. The Lost Ancient City. Exhibition catalogue (Princeton 2001) 95–97 |
| Viscogliosi 1996 | A. Viscogliosi, »Antra Cyclopis«: osservazioni su una tipologia di *coenatio*, in: Andreae – Parisi Presicce 1996, 252–269 |
| Vlachogianni 2012 | E. Vlachogianni, Sculpture: Gods and heroes from the depths of the sea, in: N. Kaltsas – E. Vlachogianni – P. Bouyia (eds.), The Antikythera shipwreck: the ship, the treasures, the mechanism. Exhibition Catalogue (Athens 2012) |
| von Hesberg 2009 | H. von Hesberg, Ρωμαϊκή Αρχιτεκτονική. Transl. P. Papageorghiou (Thessaloniki 2009) |
| Weiss 2000 | H. A. Weiss, Odysseus at Sperlonga: Hellenistic hero or Roman heroic foil?, in: N. T. De Grummond – B. S. Ridgway (eds.), From Pergamon to Sperlonga: sculpture and context (Berkeley 2000) 111–165 |
| Wilson 1995 | A. I. Wilson, Running water and social status in North Africa, in: M. Horton – T. Wiedemann (eds.), North Africa from Antiquity to Islam (Bristol 1995) 52–56 |
| Wilson 1997 | A. I. Wilson, Water Management and Usage in Roman North Africa. A Social and Technological Study (unpublished DPhil Thesis Oxford 1997) |
| Wilson 2011 | A. I. Wilson, City Size and Urbanization in the Roman Empire, in: A. Bowman – A. I. Wilson (eds.), Settlement, Urbanization, and Population (Oxford 2011) 161–195 |
| Zevi 1996 | F. Zevi, Claudio e Nerone: Ulisse a Baia e nella Domus Aurea, in: Andreae – Parisi Presicce 1996, 316–331 |

*Georgia Aristodemou, International Hellenic University, University Centre for International Programmes of Studies, School of Humanities, Social Sciences and Economics, Papapetrou 19 str, 55131 Thessaloniki, Greece.*
*[e] garistodemou@gmail.com; g.aristodemou@ihu.edu.gr*

Fabian Auer

## *AD LIMBVM DIDVCTI* – ENTRÜCKUNGSDARSTELLUNGEN IN DER SEPULKRALKUNST DER DONAUPROVINZEN

### ÜBERLEGUNGEN ZU BILDCHIFFREN UND DEREN URSPRUNG

**Abstract**
Icarus falling from the sky, Ganymede being carried to Olympus by the eagle, and Europa being abducted to Crete by Zeus in the form of a bull – three quite different narratives from the world of Greek myths that have a common theme: all of them are about the rape or abduction of the person in question into a better – or at least different – existence. With the implication that the grave owner, like the mythological figure, reached a better afterlife through death, the myths were also received in the sepulchral art of antiquity in *Noricum*, *Pannonia* and the *Regio Decima*. The aim of this article is to trace the Ganymede and Europa iconography depicted on funerary monuments back to their origins in Graeco-Roman art from the Mediterranean. In doing so, it is possible to recognise variations of the image motifs specific to the study area. Furthermore, various image cyphers could be identified and examined regarding their origins in compositions prior to the establishment of the cypher.

## EINLEITUNG

Ikarus, der vom Himmel stürzt, Ganymed, der vom Zeusadler in den Olymp getragen wird, und die von Zeus in Stiergestalt nach Kreta entführte Europa. Drei recht unterschiedliche Geschichten aus der griechischen Mythenwelt, die ein gemeinsames Thema behandeln: In allen geht es darum, dass die Hauptperson der Handlung unfreiwillig die irdene Sphäre verlässt und in ein anderes – möglicherweise auch besseres – Dasein übergeht. In den Fällen von Ganymed und Europa geschieht dies durch die Entrückung oder Entführung des/der Betroffenen in den Olymp und nach Kreta, während Ikarus verunglückt und stirbt.

In dieser Rolle wurden die Mythen auch in der Sepulkralkunst der Antike rezipiert, um zu implizieren, dass der Grabinhaber/die Grabinhaberin gleich der mythologischen Gestalt durch den Tod in das Nachleben übergegangen ist. Um es in den Worten von Elisabeth Walde auszudrücken: »Solche Themen werden gerne auf Grabsteinen dargestellt, da diese Sagenfiguren ebenso wie der geliebte Verstorbene den Blicken der Hinterbliebenen entzogen wurden. […] Gleichzeitig nähren diese Sagenbilder die Hoffnung, der Verstorbene genieße nun ein glückliches Weiterleben.«[1] Auf Basis dieser Ansicht werden die Bilder von Ikarus, Ganymed und Europa unter dem Überbegriff ›Entrückungsdarstellungen‹ zusammengefasst.

Im Fokus dieses Beitrags stehen die Entrückungsdarstellungen aus *Noricum*, konkret die, die Europa und Ganymed zeigen. Im Sinne einer größeren Datenmenge und besserer Vergleichbarkeit wurden auch Werke aus Pannonien, der *Regio Decima* und darüber hinaus berücksichtigt. Anhand der Steindenkmäler sollen Überlegungen zum Ursprung der Ikonografie gemacht und mögliche Bildchiffren besprochen werden. Die Ikarus-Darstellungen wurden an anderer Stelle bereits detailliert besprochen[2] und sollen daher hier nicht näher behandelt werden.

---

[1] Walde 2005, 123.
[2] s. dazu u. a. Lamm 2016; Verzár-Bass 2008.

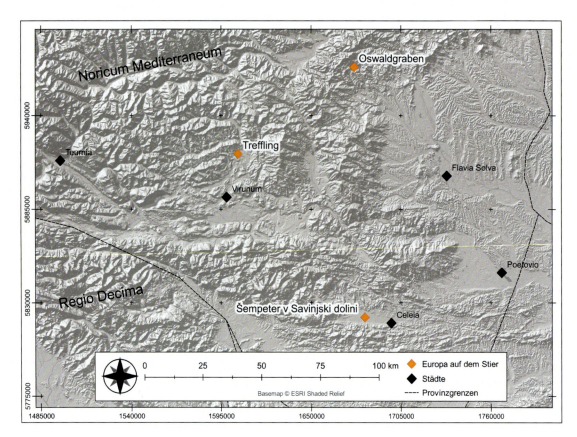

1   Kartierung der Europa-Darstellungen (Grafik F. Auer)

**EUROPA**

Grundlage für die Darstellung der Europa in der bildenden Kunst ist das Narrativ ihres Mythos, wie es bei Ovid festgehalten wurde[3]: Europa, die Tochter König Agenors von Sidon, hielt sich eines Tages an der Küste auf. Dort näherte sich ihr der Gott Zeus in Gestalt eines wunderbaren Stiers. Er zeigte sich Europa gegenüber zutraulich, bis diese sich auf seinen Rücken setzte. Sobald dies geschehen war, schwamm der Stier jedoch ins Meer hinaus und trug die Königstochter auf die ferne Insel Kreta, wo er mit ihr drei Kinder zeugte, darunter den späteren König der Insel, Minos.

Wie bereits aus dieser kürzesten Fassung des Mythos hervorgeht, ist der zentrale Moment der Entrückung oder Entführung mit dem Wegtragen der Europa über das Meer gegeben. Eben dieser Moment der Handlung fand auch Eingang in die Sepulkralkunst der Donauprovinzen. Aus der Provinz *Noricum* sind drei Reliefsteine bekannt, die Europa zeigen: in Treffling, Oswaldgraben bei Kainach sowie auf dem Ennier-Grabmal im Grabbezirk von Šempeter v Savinjski dolini (Abb. 1).

Das Relief aus Treffling besteht aus Marmor und wird 180–220 n. Chr. datiert[4]. Ein von einem floralen Ornament durch einen einfachen Steg getrenntes Bildfeld zeigt Europa als junge Frau im Damensitz auf dem Rücken des Stiers sitzend. Ihr Oberkörper ist entblößt, ihre Beine sind von einem Gewand oder Tuch bedeckt. Ihre beiden Arme sind erhoben und halten das Tuch, welches sich über ihrem Kopf bogenförmig aufbläht. Der Stier ist im kraftvollen Sprung nach links dargestellt.

Das ebenfalls aus Marmor bestehende Relief aus Oswaldgraben bei Kainach (Abb. 2 a) wird als Kassette aus der Decke einer Grabaedicula angesprochen[5]. In einem von kreisförmigen Motiven und Ornamenten umgebenen zentralen Tondo ist der Stier im Sprung nach links dar-

---

[3]   Ov. met. 2, 833–875.
[4]   CSIR Österreich II 6 Nr. 39; lupa.at/2131.
[5]   Hebert 1993, 139; Kremer 2001, 76 Nr. 17b; lupa.at/4642.

2   Europa-Relief aus a) Oswaldgraben bei Kainach (lupa 4642, Foto O. Harl), b) Šempeter v Savinjski dolini (lupa 13329, Foto O. Harl; mit Erlaubnis des Regionalmuseums Celje veröffentlicht)

gestellt. Auf seinem Rücken sitzt Europa, erneut im Damensitz und mit nacktem Oberkörper. Das sich über ihrem Kopf aufbauschende Tuch hält sie mit dem erhobenen linken Arm fest, den rechten Arm hat sie zum Kopf des Stiers ausgestreckt, um sich an seinen Hörnern festzuhalten.

Von den drei südnorischen Europa-Reliefs ist das vom Ennier-Grabmal (Abb. 2 b) aus dem Grabbezirk Šempeter v Savinjski dolini das am besten erhaltene. Es besteht ebenfalls aus Marmor und kann ins 2. Jahrhundert n. Chr. datiert werden[6]. Es zeigt Europa mit entblößtem Oberkörper im Damensitz auf dem Stier sitzend. Dieser springt kraftvoll noch rechts. Europas Beine sind von einem Tuch bedeckt, das sich über ihrem Kopf aufbauscht. Auf diesem Relief hält Europa das Tuch mit der linken Hand an ihrer Hüfte und mit der erhobenen rechten Hand fest. Unter dem Stier deuten eine als Wellen gestaltete Standlinie und ein Delfin das Meer an, in den oberen Zwickeln des Bildfeldes sind zwei Adler abgebildet, die den Bezug zu Zeus herausstreichen.

Die drei norischen Europa-Reliefs folgen klar einem einheitlichem Bildschema der Europa-Ikonografie. Diese Darstellungsweise kann auf Vorbilder aus dem griechischen Mittelmeerraum zurückgeführt werden. Die ältesten bekannten Bilder, die Europa auf dem Stier mit im Wind aufgeblähten Mantel zeigen, sind auf Stateren und kleineren Bronze-Nominalen aus der ägäischen Inselwelt des 5. Jahrhunderts v. Chr. belegt. Das Vorkommen dieses Motivs in der süditalischen Vasenmalerei zeigt auf, wie diese spezifische Ikonografie Eingang in die italische Kunst gehalten hat. Exemplarisch kann ein paestanischer Calyx-Krater des 4./3. Jahrhunderts v. Chr. angeführt werden. Die frühesten Darstellungen der Europa auf dem Stier mit geblähtem Mantel in der römischen Kunst datieren ins 1. Jahrhundert v. Chr. Konkret handelt es sich dabei um ein Mosaik, welches in Kopenhagen aufbewahrt wird, und um ein steinernes Relief aus Padua. Neben diesen frühen Werken ist besonders eine – heute leider verschollene – Wandmalerei zu nennen. Diese stammt aus dem Grab der Nasonii in Rom und datiert in die Mitte des 1. Jahrhunderts n. Chr., womit sie der älteste bekannte Beleg des Europa-Motivs in der römischen Sepulkralkunst ist[7].

---

[6]   Klemenc u. a. 1972, 44 Nr. 243; 53; lupa.at/13329; LIMC IV (1988) 86 Nr. 174 s. v. Europa (M. Robertson).

[7]   Statere: LIMC IV (1988) 82 Nr. 105–110 s. v. Europa (M. Robertson). – Calyx-Krater: LIMC IV (1988) 80 Nr. 74 s. v. Europa (M. Robertson). – Kopenhagen: LIMC IV (1988) 85 Nr. 166 s. v. Europa (M. Robertson). – Padua: LIMC IV (1988) 86 Nr. 170 s. v. Europa (M. Robertson). – Grab der Nasonii: LIMC IV (1988) 83 Nr. 127 s. v. Europa (M. Robertson); Messineo 2000, 50–52. 54 Abb. 54.

Die norischen Reliefs folgen also deutlich einer kanonisierten Darstellungsweise Europas, die sich schon früh etabliert hat. Diese spezifische Ikonografie Europas auf dem Stier kann nicht nur auf eine lange Bildtradition zurückblicken, sondern hat auch den Vorteil, dass die ganze Komposition logisch aufgebaut ist. Der Stier bewegt sich kraftvoll und schnell, wodurch ein Gegenwind entsteht, der Europas Gewand erfasst und fortzureißen droht. Um dies zu verhindern, muss sie es mit einer oder beiden Händen festhalten. Durch diese Verankerung des Gewands folgt, dass es sich aufbauscht.

Wie wichtig dieses Element des im Wind geblähten Mantels in der Europa-Ikonografie ist, wird an einem Kalksteinrelief aus Svishtov[8] in Bulgarien, dem antiken Legionsstandort *Novae* in der Provinz *Moesia inferior*, deutlich. Das Werk zeigt den nach links schreitenden Stier mit Europa im Damensitz auf seinem Rücken. Sie ist voll bekleidet und ihre Arme ruhen auf dem Kopf und dem Rumpf des Stiers. Über ihrem Kopf ist ein bogenförmig aufgebauschtes Tuch dargestellt. Im Gegensatz zu den norischen Reliefs und den Vorbildern aus dem Mittelmeerraum wohnt diesem Werk keinerlei Kraft oder Bewegung inne. Sowohl der Stier als auch die junge Frau sind in absoluter Ruhe dargestellt – es fehlt also in der Komposition die logische Begründung dafür, dass sich das Tuch über Europas Kopf im Wind aufbauscht. Daraus lässt sich erkennen, dass sich das Element des über dem Kopf aufgeblähten Tuchs zu einem charakterisierenden Element der Europa-Ikonografie entwickelt hat und im Sinne der Erkennbarkeit des Motivs unerlässlich wurde – auch, wenn es in der Komposition nicht mehr logisch bedingt war.

## EUROPA ODER NEREIDE?

Ein weiterer Aspekt, den es sich zu diskutieren lohnt, ist, dass sich die Ikonografie der Europa nicht auf sie beschränkt, sondern auch in der Darstellung von Nereiden erkannt werden kann. Diese Wesen aus dem Seethiasos, die als junge Frauen dargestellt werden, findet man wie Europa im Damensitz auf Seegreifen, Hippokampen oder Seestieren sitzend. Sie sind ebenfalls mit nacktem Oberkörper und geblähtem Mantel dargestellt, den sie noch zu halten versuchen. Aus *Noricum* sind fünf solcher Nereiden-Darstellungen bekannt, die – sofern feststellbar – auch aus dem Grabkontext stammen. Zwei kommen vom Seggauberg, eine aus Tschahitsch und eine aus Enns. Die fünfte befindet sich im Giebelfeld des Spectatii-Grabmals in Šempeter[9]. Sofern datierbar, werden sie alle ins 2.–3. Jahrhundert n. Chr. gesetzt. Die Auflistung von weiteren Nereiden-Darstellungen ließe sich beliebig erweitern, doch hier soll nur noch eine dargelegt werden. Auf der Langseite eines stadtrömischen Sarkophags ist ein Relief des Meeresthiasos gezeigt, im Konkreten zwei Tritonen und eine Nereide, die in der besprochenen Ikonografie auf dem Fischleib des linken Tritonen sitzt. Der Sarkophag datiert 170–180 n. Chr.[10].

Wie diese exemplarisch ausgewählten Reliefs zeigen, ist die Ikonografie von Nereiden und Europa derart ident, dass eine Verwandtschaft nicht ausgeschlossen werden kann. Bei den Bildelementen handelt es sich durchwegs um durch die intendierte Aussage des Motivs bedingte Darstellungen: Der im Wind aufgebauschte Mantel soll nichts anderes als schnelle Bewegung vermitteln, und der Damensitz ist funktional. Aufgrund dessen ist es auch nicht möglich definitiv festzustellen, welches Motiv das ursprüngliche war, das von dem anderen nachgeahmt wurde. Die Ikonografie ist hierfür schlicht zu allgemein. Das oben besprochene Europa-Relief aus Svishtov zeigt allerdings, dass sich der im Wind aufbauschende Mantel zu einem charakterisierenden Merkmal von Europa entwickelt hat, sodass er auch dann dargestellt wurde, wenn es die Szene nicht logisch erforderte.

Unter der Annahme, dass Entwicklungen eher vom Allgemeinen (Nereiden auf Seetieren oder Tritonen) ins Spezifische (Europa auf dem Stier) gehen, und nicht andersherum, ist es naheliegender, dass die Nereiden-Ikonografie für Europa übernommen wurde.

---

[8] lupa.at/22290.
[9] Seggauberg: Hainzmann – Pochmarski 1994, 58–59. 230–231. – Tschahitsch: CSIR Österreich II 4 Nr. 364. – Enns: CSIR Österreich III 2 Nr. 76. – Šempeter v Savinjski dolini: Klemenc u. a. 1972, 32 Nr. 114.
[10] Koch 1988, 22–23.

## GANYMED

Ganymed, der Jüngling, der von Zeus in Adlergestalt auf den Olymp entführt wurde, findet sich öfter in der Sepulkralkunst als die oben besprochene Europa. Aus *Noricum* sind drei Werke bekannt, zwei aus Pannonien und nochmals fünf aus der *Regio Decima*. Unter den Ganymed-Darstellungen können drei Typen unterschieden werden: die Ergreifung des Ganymed, die Entführung des Ganymed und die Tränkung des Adlers. Zumeist handelt es sich bei den Werken um Reliefs, lediglich zwei sind unterlebensgroße Statuetten.

Die Ikonografie Ganymeds ist sehr einheitlich und soll daher nicht für jedes Werk einzeln besprochen werden: Er ist immer als junger Mann dargestellt, der lediglich mit einer Chlamys bekleidet ist und eine phrygische Mütze trägt. Als Attribut kann er ein *pedum* in der Hand halten. Diese Darstellungsweise lässt sich bis in die archaische Vasenmalerei zurückverfolgen. In Grabkontexten findet sich das Motiv der Entführung des Ganymed bereits in hellenistischer Zeit, konkret auf süditalischen Grabgefäßen. Was die römische Sepulkralkunst betrifft, war Ganymed ein gängiges Motiv auf Sarkophagen. Da dieser Mythos jedoch nur wenige Protagonisten umfasst, eignet er sich nicht dafür, ganze Sarkophagseiten zu füllen. Daher kommen Ganymed und der Adler hauptsächlich unter den *clipei*, die das Porträt des Grabinhabers/der Grabinhaberin zeigen, oder im zentralen Bildfeld von Riefelsarkophagen vor. Seltener findet sich Ganymed auch auf kaiserzeitlichen Grabmonumenten[11].

## DIE ERGREIFUNG DES GANYMED

Die Hälfte aller bekannten Ganymed-Darstellungen zeigt das Motiv der Ergreifung des Ganymed durch den Adler. Aus *Noricum* ist ein Werk bekannt: Eine Statuette aus dem Umland von *Flavia Solva*, konkret aus St. Veit am Vogau. Zwei weitere sind aus Pannonien bekannt, eine Statuette aus Bilje und ein Relief aus Pécs, dem antiken *Sopianae*. Aus *Aquileia* in der *Regio Decima* stammen zwei Reliefs (Abb. 3 a).

Die Statuette aus St. Veit am Vogau (Abb. 4 a) besteht aus Marmor[12]. Sie zeigt Ganymed in sitzender Pose, sein Körper ist nach hinten geneigt. Er stützt sich auf seinen linken Arm, den rechten hat er von sich gestreckt. Hinter ihm sind die Federn einer Schwinge des Adlers zu erkennen.

Die Ganymed-Statuette aus Bilje besteht ebenfalls aus Marmor[13]. Ganymed ist frontal stehend dargestellt, sein linker Arm hängt neben seinem Körper herab, sein rechter ist vor dem Körper angewinkelt. In seiner rechten Hand hält er ein nicht mehr zu erkennendes Attribut. Hinter dem Jüngling sind die Reste des Adlers zu sehen. Es lassen sich noch die Schwingen und der Nacken ausmachen sowie die Klauen, mit denen er Ganymed an den Schultern packt.

Bei dem Werk aus Pécs handelt es sich um ein marmornes Relief aus der Zeit um 150–200 n. Chr., von dem lediglich der oberste Teil nicht mehr erhalten ist[14]. Ganymed ist stehend dargestellt, in seiner gesenkten linken Hand hält er ein *pedum*, der rechte Arm ist in einem abwehrenden Gestus nach hinten, dem Adler entgegen, erhoben. Sein Kopf ist in Richtung der abwehrenden Hand gewandt. Der Adler erfasst den Jüngling von hinten an der Hüfte.

Das erste der Reliefs aus *Aquileia* (Abb. 4 b) besteht aus Marmor[15]. Der Adler füllt mit seinen gewaltigen Schwingen den gesamten Hintergrund aus. Ganymed ist stürzend dargestellt, nur noch sein rechter Fuß hat Kontakt zum Boden. Er hält den rechten Arm abwehrend nach hinten erhoben, dem Adler entgegen, während der linke im rechten Winkel abgewinkelt ist. Die Stellung sei-

---

[11] Archaische Vasenmalerei: LIMC IV (1988) 157–158 Nr. 57. 60 s. v. Ganymedes (H. Sichtermann). – Süditalische Grabgefäße: Engemann 1973, 18–25. – Römische Sarkophage: Engemann 1973, 18–20; Koch – Sichtermann 1982, 146–147 Nr. 13; Koch – Sichtermann 1975, 30 Nr. 20; ASR XII (1992) 166–167 Nr. 143–144 s. v. Ganymed (H. Sichtermann). – Grabmonumente: Engemann 1973, 20–21.

[12] CSIR Österreich IV 1 Nr. 69; lupa.at/7260.

[13] lupa.at/5701.

[14] LIMC IV (1988) 163 Nr. 183 s. v. Ganymedes (H. Sichtermann); lupa.at/827.

[15] LIMC IV (1988) 163 Nr. 184 s. v. Ganymedes (H. Sichtermann); lupa.at/13988; Scrinari 1972, 185 Nr. 569.

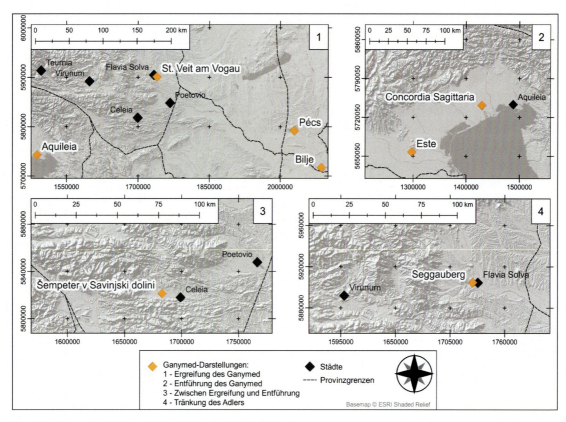

3   Kartierung der Ganymed-Darstellungen (Grafik F. Auer)

nes linken Arms lässt vermuten, dass er in dieser Hand einst ein Attribut, womöglich ein *pedum*, gehalten hat. Der Kopf des jungen Manns ist nach hinten dem Adler zugewandt. An seiner Hüfte sind die Klauen des Adlers zu erkennen.

Das zweite Relief aus *Aquileia* (Abb. 4 c) ist die Schmalseite eines marmornen Sarkophags und kann in die zweite Hälfte des 2. Jahrhunderts n. Chr. datiert werden[16]. Zu sehen ist der Adler, der Ganymed an der Hüfte packt. Vom Jüngling ist lediglich ein schmaler Teil des Oberkörpers und der zur Abwehr erhobene rechte Arm erhalten.

Anhand dieser Steindenkmäler – mit Ausnahme der Statuette aus Bilje – lassen sich die Grundzüge der Ergreifungsikonografie fassen. Ganymed ist durchwegs in der für ihn üblichen Weise dargestellt und wird vom Adler von hinten an der Hüfte gepackt. Ganymed selbst nimmt eine klar abwehrende Haltung ein: Sein Körper lehnt sich vom Adler weg, und er versucht noch, den Vogel mit dem erhobenen rechten Arm abzuwehren. Die Drehung des Kopfes in Richtung des Adlers geht mit dieser Handlung einher.

Mit dieser Ikonografie folgen die norisch-pannonischen und nordostitalischen Ergreifungsszenen eindeutig älteren Vorbildern. Exemplarisch kann ein Mosaik aus *Morgantina* angeführt werden. Dieses datiert in die zweite Hälfte des 3. Jahrhunderts v. Chr. und zeigt – obwohl es stark beschädigt ist – deutlich einen auf die Knie gestürzten Jüngling, der von hinten von einem Adler ergriffen wird und versucht, sich mit erhobener rechter Hand zur Wehr zu setzen. Als weitere Beispiele können ein Mosaik severischer Zeit aus Rom, ein frühkaiserzeitliches Marmorrelief aus Florenz und vier stadtrömische Clipeus-Sarkophage aus dem frühen 3. Jahrhundert n. Chr. genannt werden[17]. Sie alle zeigen dieselbe Ikonografie des auf die Knie gesunkenen Ganymed, der mit erhobenem rechten Arm den Adler abzuwehren versucht. Die Ergreifungsszenen mit Ab-

---

[16] LIMC IV (1988) 163 Nr. 184 s. v. Ganymedes (H. Sichtermann); lupa.at/18272; Gabelmann 1973, 68. 211 Nr. 37; Scrinari 1972, 185 Nr. 570.

[17] Mosaik aus *Morgantina*: LIMC IV (1988) 162 Nr. 170 s. v. Ganymedes (H. Sichtermann). – Mosaik aus Rom: LIMC IV (1988) 162–163 Nr. 173 s. v. Ganymedes (H. Sichtermann). – Relief aus Florenz: LIMC IV (1988) 163

4  Darstellungen der Ergreifung des Ganymed aus a) St. Veit am Vogau (lupa 7260, Foto O. Harl), b) *Aquileia* (Archäologisches Nationalmuseum Aquileia Inv. 355, lupa 13988, Foto O. Harl), c) *Aquileia* (Archäologisches Nationalmuseum Aquileia, lupa 18272, Foto O. Harl. Reliefs aus Aquileia mit Erlaubnis des Kultusministeriums [ITA], Regionaldirektion der Museen von Friaul-Julisch Venetien veröffentlicht)

wehrgestus tragen also eindeutig eine schon früh etablierte Ikonografie weiter, doch lässt sich an den Werken aus *Noricum*, Pannonien und *Aquileia* die Weiterentwicklung zu der Variante mit stehendem Ganymed feststellen.

## DIE ENTFÜHRUNG DES GANYMED

Die Entführung des Ganymed ist weder aus *Noricum* noch aus Pannonien bekannt, sondern lediglich aus der *Regio Decima*, konkret anhand eines Reliefs aus *Concordia Sagittaria* und zweier Reliefs aus Este (Abb. 3 b).

Das Relief aus *Concordia Sagittaria* (Abb. 5 a) besteht aus Kalkstein und wird als Teil der Kassettendecke einer Grabaedicula angesehen[18]. Ein zentrales, rhomboides Bildfeld, welches von Hippokampen und Metopen mit Rosetten umgeben ist, zeigt den Adler in vollem Fluge. Er hält den Jüngling Ganymed vor seinem Körper, dabei liegen die Klauen des Adlers an der Hüfte des jungen Mannes und umfassen auch dessen Arme. Von dem aktiven Widerstand gegen den Adler, wie er in den Ergreifungsszenen gezeigt wird, findet sich keine Spur mehr. Dass diese Entführung gegen den Willen Ganymeds geschieht, wird in diesem Werk nur subtil über die vom Adler festgehaltenen Arme des Ganymed ausgedrückt.

Das erste der Reliefs aus Este besteht aus Trachit[19]. In einem mittigen, rhomboiden Bildfeld, das mit floralen Ornamenten umgeben ist, ist der Adler im Flug zu sehen. In seinen Klauen hält er Ganymed an der Hüfte fest. Dieser hat zusätzlich seinen linken Arm um den Nacken des

---

Nr. 180 s. v. Ganymedes (H. Sichtermann). – Clipeus-Sarkophage: LIMC IV (1988) 163 Nr. 182 s. v. Ganymedes (H. Sichtermann).

[18] LIMC IV (1988) 165 Nr. 225 s. v. Ganymedes (H. Sichtermann); lupa.at/29447.
[19] Compostella 1997, 217–218 Abb. 6; LIMC IV (1988) 165 Nr. 227 s. v. Ganymedes (H. Sichtermann); lupa.at/14623.

5 Darstellungen der Entführung des Ganymed aus a) *Concordia Sagittaria* (Portogruaro, Nationalmuseum Concordia Inv. 220, Foto Nationalmuseum Concordia), b) Este (Nationalmuseum Este Inv. 1468, Foto Nationalmuseum Este. Mit Erlaubnis des Kultusministeriums [ITA], Regionaldirektion der Museen Veneto veröffentlicht)

Adlers gelegt. Sein Blick ist nach links dem Adler entgegen gerichtet. Ganymeds rechter Arm ist auf eine Weise erhoben, die stark an die Abwehrikonografie aus den Ergreifungsszenen erinnert. In diesem Werk fehlt jedoch ein Grund, der diesen abwehrenden Gestus bedingt, schließlich ist der Adler auf der anderen Seite des Jünglings. Zusätzlich steht es in einem deutlichen Gegensatz dazu, dass Ganymed sich mit dem anderen Arm am Adler festhält. Die fehlende logische Begründung des Abwehrgestus in der Komposition lässt erkennen, dass diese Armhaltung als derart typisch für Ganymed angesehen wurde, dass sie unabdinglich war, um das Motiv eindeutig erkennen zu können.

Das letzte Relief, das die Entführungsszene zeigt, stammt ebenfalls aus Este (Abb. 5 b) und kann ins späte 1. bis frühe 2. Jahrhundert n. Chr. datiert werden[20]. Das Motiv ist in ein oktogonales Bildfeld eingefasst. In den Zwickeln sind Delphinpaare dargestellt, darüber eine Metopenreihe mit Rosetten. Das zentrale Bild zeigt den fliegenden Adler, der Ganymed an der Hüfte vor seinem Körper hält. Ganymed streckt seinen rechten Arm locker zur Seite, der linke ist erhoben und in einem zärtlichen Gestus auf den Nacken des Adlers gelegt. Der Kopf des jungen Mannes ist dem Adler zugewandt und leicht nach oben gerichtet. Diese Darstellung der Entführungsszene unterscheidet sich darin von den anderen, dass der gewalttätige Charakter des Mythos gänzlich aus der Komposition gestrichen wurde. Ganymed setzt sich weder zur Wehr, noch muss er vom Adler in seiner Bewegungsfreiheit behindert werden. Vielmehr vermittelt das hier gezeigt Bild eine Zuneigung zwischen Adler und Jüngling. Trotz dieser Entschärfung der Szene lässt sich ein Bezug zu den Ergreifungsszenen erkennen. Die grundlegende Ikonografie des Abwehrgestus – abgewinkelt erhobener Arm und in dessen Richtung gewandter Blick – findet sich auch in diesem Werk, allerdings wurde die vermittelte Aussage des Gestus durch leichte Änderungen umgekehrt.

Wie schon bei den Ergreifungsszenen kann die Ikonografie der Entführungsszenen auf Vorbilder aus dem griechisch-römischen Mittelmeerraum zurückgeführt werden. Die ältesten Darstellungen finden sich auf griechischen Gemmen und Reliefs aus dem 4. Jahrhundert v. Chr. Funde

---

[20] Compostella 1997, 217–218 Abb. 7; LIMC IV (1988) 165 Nr. 226 s. v. Ganymedes (H. Sichtermann).

aus Tarent bezeugen die Ausbreitung des Motivs in den westlichen Mittelmeerraum und nach Italien. Zahllose Werke belegen, dass die Entführungsmotivik Eingang in die römische und in weiterer Folge in die provinzielle Kunst fand, wo sie in unterschiedlichsten Medien bis zumindest ins 3. Jahrhundert n. Chr. rezipiert wurde[21]. Das Resultat daraus war eine Vielzahl an sich in Details unterscheidenden Werken, die die Entführung derart zeigen, dass sich Ganymed widerstandslos wegtragen lässt oder sich sogar am Adler festhält – Grundzüge der Ikonografie, die auch für die Werke aus *Concordia Sagittaria* und Este übernommen wurden.

## ZWISCHEN ERGREIFUNG UND ENTFÜHRUNG

Die Momente der Ergreifung und Entführung des Ganymed folgen im Narrativ des Mythos unmittelbar aufeinander. In der bildenden Kunst sind sie anhand diverser Details voneinander zu unterscheiden – anhand der Art der Interaktion zwischen Ganymed und Adler, der Haltung der Figuren etc. –, allerdings sind die Grenzen nicht immer klar zu trennen. Diese Problematik lässt sich an einem südnorischen Relief gut fassen: dem Ganymed-Relief (Abb. 6) aus dem Grabbezirk von Šempeter v Savinjski dolini (Abb. 3 c).

Bei diesem Werk handelt es sich um ein marmornes Relief, welches Teil des Ennier-Grabmals ist. Es wird ins 2. Jahrhundert n. Chr. datiert[22]. Dargestellt ist Ganymed in stehender Pose. Sein linker Arm hängt entspannt herab, sein rechter ist seitlich ausgestreckt und um den Nacken des Adlers gelegt. Dieser ist hinter dem jungen Mann dargestellt, seine linke Schwinge verschwindet hinter Ganymed, die linke Klaue des Adlers liegt an der Hüfte des Jünglings und die rechte auf dessen Oberschenkel. Die Köpfe von Ganymed und dem Adler sind einander zugewandt. In der linken unteren Ecke des Bildfelds sind Felsen dargestellt, auf denen ein Hund sitzt, der Ganymed nachblickt. Die Füße des Ganymeds haben noch Kontakt zu dem Felsen. Rechts unter Ganymed sind eine Panflöte und ein Bogen, den Ganymed noch an der Sehne hält, abgebildet. Nach oben hin wird das Bildfeld von zwei Bögen abgeschlossen.

Die auf dem Šempeter-Relief dargestellte Szene erfasst exakt den Moment, der zwischen den Ergreifungs- und den Entführungsszenen steht. Dies lässt sich nicht nur kontextual feststellen, sondern auch anhand der Ikonografie, die sich aus Elementen sowohl der Ergreifungs- als auch der Entführungsmotive zusammensetzt. Aus Ersteren wurde das Motiv des von hinten kommenden Adlers, der Ganymed an der Hüfte ergreift, übernommen. Ebenso kann in der Darstellung des Felsen im linken unteren Teil des Bildfelds ein Bezug auf die Ergreifungsszenen festgestellt werden. Die Körperhaltung Ganymeds und die Handlung des Festhaltens an dem Adler stehen hingegen deutlich in Tradition der Entführungsszenen.

Diese Darstellung des spezifischen Moments zwischen Ergreifung und Entführung des Ganymed auf dem Relief aus Šempeter v Savinjski dolini ist – nach jetzigem Kenntnisstand – die einzige ihrer Art.

## DIE TRÄNKUNG DES ADLERS

Die letzte Variante der Ganymed-Darstellungen in den mittleren Donauprovinzen ist die der Tränkung des Adlers. Dieses Motiv kommt lediglich einmal in Form eines Reliefs am Seggauberg bei Leibnitz, nahe dem antiken *Flavia Solva*, vor (Abb. 3, 4; 7).

Das Relief besteht aus Marmor und wird 150–230 n. Chr. datiert[23]. Es zeigt Ganymed nach rechts gewandt auf einem Felsen sitzend. Sein rechter Arm ruht auf seinem Bein, in der Hand

---

[21] Griechische Gemmen und Reliefs: LIMC IV (1988) 163–164 Nr. 193–199 s. v. Ganymedes (H. Sichtermann). – Tarent: LIMC IV (1988) 164 Nr. 200–201. 204–205 s. v. Ganymedes (H. Sichtermann). – Römische und provinzielle Werke: LIMC IV (1988) 164–166 Nr. 206–256 s. v. Ganymedes (H. Sichtermann) mit Ausnahme der Nr. 236, die m. E. zu den Ergreifungsszenen zu setzen ist.
[22] Klemenc u. a. 1972, 54 Nr. 425; 66; lupa.at/13331.
[23] Hainzmann – Pochmarski 1994, 20–21; lupa.at/1259; LIMC IV (1988) 162 Nr. 143 s. v. Ganymedes (H. Sichtermann).

6 Ganymed-Relief aus Šempeter v Savinjski dolini (lupa 13331, Foto O. Harl. Mit Erlaubnis des Regionalmuseums Celje veröffentlicht)

hält er ein Gefäß. Der linke Arm ist nach oben gestreckt und greift nach dem Nacken des Adlers vor ihm. Dieser ist nach links dem Ganymed zugewandt. Die Schwingen sind erhoben, sein rechter Fang liegt am Knie des Ganymed, auf dem linken steht er. Der Adler hat den Kopf über das Gefäß in der Hand des Ganymed gesenkt (Abb. 7).

In den mittleren Donauprovinzen ist kein zweites Steindenkmal bekannt, das diese Szene der Tränkung zeigt. Als Vergleich können zwei Statuen aus der Provinz *Germania inferior* hinzugezogen werden. Eine stammt aus Köln, die zweite aus Bonn[24]. Beide zeigen Ganymed stehend und an eine Säule gelehnt, auf der der Adler sitzt. Diesem streckt Ganymed eine Schüssel entgegen, der sich der Adler zuwendet. Sie zeigen also deutlich dieselbe Szene wie das Seggauberg-Relief. Die Tränkungsszene ist weiters auch auf römischen Riefelsarkophagen abgebildet: auf dem Sarkophag aus dem Cortile del Belvedere und auf dem aus dem Mausoleum bei San Sebastiano. Zudem sind Zeichnungen eines heute verschollenen Sarkophags bekannt, die nochmals dieses Motiv zeigen[25]. Die erhaltenen Sarkophage werden ins 3. Jahrhundert n. Chr. datiert[26] und sind somit jünger als das norische Relief. Sie zeigen Ganymed frei stehend oder auf eine kleine Säule gestützt. Rechts von ihm ist in beiden Fällen der Adler, dem er eine Schale entgegenhält, über die sich der Vogel leicht beugt. Sie sind somit enger mit den Statuen aus der *Germania inferior* verwandt als mit dem norischen Relief. Die Zeichnung des verschollenen Sarkophags zeigt Ganymed am Boden liegend. Der Adler sitzt neben ihm und trinkt aus dem ihm dargebotenen Becher.

Die Vergleiche auf den Sarkophagen stehen kontextual dem Relief aus *Noricum* am nächsten. Umso bemerkenswerter ist daher die Tatsache, dass sie sich deutlich von den norischen Darstellungen unterscheiden. Das Bildmotiv, welches am Seggauberg-Relief dargestellt ist, scheint auf dieser Basis nicht aus der römisch-italischen Sarkophagkunst zu stammen. Die Ursprünge sind daher anderswo zu suchen. Das älteste bekannte Werk, das die Tränkung des Adlers nach Art des Seggauberg-Reliefs zeigt, ist ein späthellenistisches Gipsrelief aus Kabul, das in das 1. Jahrhundert v. Chr. datiert[27] und bereits an anderer Stelle als ursprüngliches Vorbild des norischen Reliefs diskutiert wurde[28]. Aufgrund des großen geografischen und zeitlichen Abstands zwischen dem Kabul-Relief und dem aus der Steiermark ist eine direkte Tradierung der Ikonografie nicht wahrscheinlich, was die Frage aufwirft, über welche Zwischenstufen die Ikonografie von Kabul bis in die Steiermark gelangt ist.

---

[24] Köln: CSIR Deutschland III 2 Nr. 67; lupa.at/15471. – Bonn: CSIR Deutschland III 2 Nr. 68; lupa.at/15657.
[25] Cortile del Belvedere: ASR XII (1992) 166 Nr. 143 s. v. Ganymed (H. Sichtermann); Koch – Sichtermann 1975, 30 Nr. 20; Koch –Sichtermann 1982, 147; Engemann 1973, 19 Taf. 5c. – San Sebastiano: ASR XII (1992) 166–167 Nr. 144 s. v. Ganymed (H. Sichtermann); Koch – Sichtermann 1982, 147. – Verschollener Sarkophag: ASR XII (1992) 167 Nr. 145 s. v. Ganymed (H. Sichtermann); Engemann 1973, 19.
[26] Koch – Sichtermann 1982, 147.
[27] LIMC IV (1988) 161 Nr. 138 s. v. Ganymedes (H. Sichtermann).
[28] Hainzmann – Pochmarski 1994, 20.

7   Darstellung der Tränkung des Adlers vom Seggauberg bei Leibnitz (lupa 1259, Foto O. Harl)

An großformatigen Werken sind lediglich vier weitere, allesamt frühkaiserzeitliche, bekannt, die dasselbe Bildmotiv zeigen: zwei Wandmalereien aus Pompeji und *Stabiae* sowie ein Relief und eine Grabmalbekrönung aus Rom[29]. Das Bildthema der Tränkung des Adlers mit sitzendem Ganymed war demnach zumindest in der italischen Kunst bekannt.

Neben den wenigen großformatigen Werken findet sich die Tränkungsikonografie vor allem in der Kleinkunst vereinzelt auf Tonlampen und Metallwerken[30], vor allem jedoch in der Glyptik. Bereits aus dem 1. Jahrhundert v. Chr. gibt es Gemmen, die die Tränkungsszene in der exakten Ikonografie des Reliefs aus der Steiermark zeigen: Ganymed sitzend mit nach dem Adler ausgestrecktem Arm und den Adler mit leicht erhobenen Schwingen, der mit einer Klaue nach dem Knie des Ganymed greift. Als exemplarische Beispiele können eine Gemme aus dem Kunsthistorischen Museum Wien und eine aus Hannover genannt werden. Diese Ikonografie wurde zumindest bis ins 2. Jahrhundert n. Chr. beibehalten, wie eine Gemme aus Braunschweig zeigt[31].

Die starke Ähnlichkeit dieser Gemmendarstellungen zu beiden Reliefs ist evident und lässt einen Bezug der Bilder aufeinander erkennen. Als Teil von Schmuckstücken waren Gemmen ein leicht zu transportierendes Handelsgut. Zudem werden alle Gemmen mit Tränkungsszene in die Zeitspanne zwischen dem Kabul-Relief (1. Jh. v. Chr.) und dem Seggauberg-Relief (spätes 2. bis frühes 3. Jh. n. Chr.) datiert. Auf dieser Grundlage soll die Möglichkeit vorgeschlagen werden, dass die Ikonografie der Tränkung des Adlers über unterschiedliche Medien tradiert wurde. Die ursprünglichste Darstellung findet sich auf dem ältesten uns bekannten Werk – dem Gipsrelief aus Kabul[32]. Dessen Ikonografie fand Eingang in den Bildschatz der Glyptik und wurde in diesem Medium bis ins 2. Jahrhundert n. Chr. weitergetragen. Das südnorische Relief auf dem Seggauberg wiederum ist den Gemmen selbst in Details derart ähnlich, dass es möglich ist, hierbei von einer großformatigen Ausführung eines aus der Glyptik übernommenen Motivs auszugehen.

## FAZIT ZU DEN ENTRÜCKUNGSDARSTELLUNGEN IN DEN DONAUPROVINZEN

Die Darstellungen der Europa und des Ganymed in *Noricum*, Pannonien und der *Regio Decima* lassen sich allesamt auf Vorbilder aus dem griechisch-römischen Mittelmeerraum zurückführen und zeigen Bildmotive, die teils bis ins 5. Jahrhundert v. Chr. zurückreichen. Die Tradierung der Bildthemen von den griechischen Ursprüngen bis in die kaiserzeitliche provinzielle Kunst ist evident und kann durch die Verwendung von Musterbüchern oder anderen Vorlagen erklärt

---

[29]   Pompeji: LIMC IV (1988) 161 Nr. 139 s. v. Ganymedes (H. Sichtermann). – *Stabiae*: LIMC IV (1988) 162 Nr. 140 s. v. Ganymedes (H. Sichtermann). – Rom: LIMC IV (1988) 162 Nr. 141–142 s. v. Ganymedes (H. Sichtermann).
[30]   LIMC IV (1988) 162 Nr. 165–169 s. v. Ganymedes (H. Sichtermann).
[31]   Wiener Gemme: LIMC IV (1988) 162 Nr. 145 s. v. Ganymedes (H. Sichtermann). – Hannover Gemme: LIMC IV (1988) 162 Nr. 146 s. v. Ganymedes (H. Sichtermann). – Braunschweiger Gemme: LIMC IV (1988) 162 Nr. 154 s. v. Ganymedes (H. Sichtermann).
[32]   Dass sich auch dieses Werk auf ältere Vorbilder bezieht, kann natürlich nicht ausgeschlossen werden.

werden[33]. Besonders interessant ist hierbei das Ganymed-Relief vom Seggauberg bei Leibnitz, anhand dessen eine transmediale Tradierung eines ikonografischen Motivs greifbar wird. *Aquileia* als zu *Noricum* und Pannonien nächstgelegener Umschlagplatz von Waren aus dem gesamten Mittelmeerraum dürfte eine wichtige Rolle in der Verbreitung der Ikonografien gespielt haben[34]. Dies wird innerhalb der Gruppe der Entrückungsdarstellungen besonders anhand der Szenen der Ergreifung und Entführung des Ganymed ersichtlich, die sowohl in den Provinzen als auch um *Aquileia* belegt sind.

Über die Bildung von Chiffren, wie dem aufgeblähten Mantel der Europa oder dem Abwehrgestus des Ganymed, lässt sich zudem eine gewisse Institutionalisierung der jeweiligen Ikonografie feststellen, in der bestimmte Elemente nur noch im Sinne der Erkennbarkeit des Bildes dargestellt wurden, und nicht mehr weil sie durch die Komposition logisch bedingt waren.

## BIBLIOGRAFIE

| | |
|---|---|
| Compostella 1997 | C. Compostella, I Monumenti Funerari di Este e di Padova. Immagini e Committenti, in: M. Mirabella Roberti (Hrsg.), Monumenti Sepolcrali Romani in Aquileia e nella Cisalpina, Antichità Altoadriatiche 43 (Triest 1997) 211–242 |
| Engemann 1973 | J. Engemann, Untersuchungen zur Sepulkralsymbolik der späteren römischen Kaiserzeit, JbAC Ergänzungsband 2 (Münster 1973) |
| Gabelmann 1973 | H. Gabelmann, Die Werkstattgruppen der oberitalischen Sarkophage, BJb Beih. 34 (Bonn 1973) |
| Hainzmann – Pochmarski 1994 | M. Hainzmann – E. Pochmarski, Die römerzeitlichen Inschriften und Reliefs von Schloß Seggau bei Leibnitz, Die römerzeitlichen Steindenkmäler der Steiermark I (Graz 1994) |
| Hebert 1993 | B. Hebert, Römerzeitliche Funde im Oswaldgraben in der Steiermark, FÖ 32, 1993, 139–153 |
| Klemenc u. a. 1972 | J. Klemenc – V. Kolšek – P. Petru, Antične Grobnice v Šempetru = Antike Grabmonumente in Šempeter, Katalogi in monografije 9. Šempeter 2 (Laibach 1972) |
| Koch – Sichtermann 1975 | G. Koch – H. Sichtermann, Griechische Mythen auf römischen Sarkophagen, Bilderhefte des Deutschen Archäologischen Instituts Rom 5/6 (Tübingen 1975) |
| Koch – Sichtermann 1982 | G. Koch – H. Sichtermann, Römische Sarkophage, HdA (München 1982) |
| Koch 1988 | G. Koch, Roman Funerary Sculpture. Catalogue of the Collections (Malibu 1988) |
| Kremer 2001 | G. Kremer, Antike Grabbauten in Noricum. Katalog und Auswertung von Werkstücken als Beitrag zur Rekonstruktion und Typologie, SoSchrÖAI 36 (Wien 2001) |
| Lamm 2016 | S. Lamm, Ikarusdarstellungen in Österreich, in: G. Koiner – U. Lohner-Urban (Hrsg.), »Ich bin dann mal weg«. Festschrift Thuri Lorenz, VIKAGraz 13 (Wien 2016) 113–119 |
| lupa.at | F. und O. Harl, <http://lupa.at> (Bilddatenbank zu antiken Steindenkmälern) |
| Messineo 2000 | G. Messineo, La Tomba dei Nasonii, StA 104, 2000, 1–79 |
| Scrinari 1972 | V. S. M. Scrinari, Museo Archeologico di Aquileia. Catalogo delle Sculture Romane, Cataloghi dei Musei e Galerie d'Italia (Rom 1972) |
| Verzár-Bass 2008 | M. Verzár-Bass, Icarusdarstellungen aus Flavia Solva und das Problem der Vorbilder, in: C. Franek – S. Lamm – T. Neuhauser – B. Porod – K. Zöhrer (Hrsg.), Thiasos. Festschrift Erwin Pochmarski, VIKAGraz 10 (Wien 2008) 1081–1094 |
| Walde 1997 | E. Walde, Der Einfluss griechischer Bildsprache auf die Grabplastik der römischen Provinz Noricum, in: G. Erath – M. Lehner – G. Schwarz (Hrsg.), Komos. Festschrift Thuri Lorenz (Wien 1997) 239–242 |
| Walde 2005 | E. Walde, Im herrlichen Glanze Roms. Die Bilderwelt der Römersteine in Österreich (Innsbruck 2005) |

*Fabian Auer, Universität Innsbruck, Institut für Archäologien, Innrain 52A, 6020 Innsbruck, Österreich.*
*[e] csas9138@student.uibk.ac.at*

---

[33] Walde 2005, 170.
[34] Walde 1997, 241.

Domagoj Bužanić

# EXAMPLES OF ROMAN ORNAMENTAL WATERSPOUTS FROM CROATIA

**Abstract**
As one of the primary forms of water distribution in cities, urban fountains were an integral part of the Roman water supply infrastructure. The report of Sextus Iulius Frontinus, *curator aquarum* of 1st century Rome, reveals that the city in his time had 630 fountains. They are, in essence, a simple reservoir to which water flows from an outlet. From the 1st century onwards, these fountains became increasingly decorated throughout the Empire. Their basic elements, such as the outlet, became more ornamental and often were used as a means of decorating such important urban spaces. Whether as a part of a so-called nymphaeum or even a simple fountain, Roman waterspouts vary in type and motif. Research into these finds in Croatia is almost completely overlooked; therefore the aim of this study is to examine several unpublished or unstudied examples of ornamental Roman waterspouts found in Croatia and compare them to finds from the other parts of the Empire.

## INTRODUCTION

As one of the primary forms of water distribution in cities, urban fountains were an integral part of the Roman water supply infrastructure. In essence, a fountain is a simple reservoir to which water flows from an outlet. From the 1st century AD onwards, fountains became increasingly decorated throughout the Empire. Their basic elements, such as the outlet, became more ornamental and often were used as a means of decorating streets and squares. All of this was done to increase the attractiveness of urban space, propagate imperial propaganda, and strengthen the image of the local elite. Whether as a part of a so-called nymphaeum or even a simple fountain, Roman waterspouts vary in type and motif. Research into these finds in Croatia is almost completely overlooked so the aim of this paper is to examine several examples of ornamental Roman waterspouts found there and compare them to finds from the other parts of the Empire.

The study of historical water supply systems by its very purpose drives researchers in the direction of studying their mere functionality and efficiency, and we often see them exclusively as a tool to meet the basic needs of humans[1]. Because of this, we tend to overlook the other dimensions of water use, namely aesthetics and spirituality, which are themselves often intertwined in execution. In this paper, I will pay closer attention to fountains, and especially to one aspect of their aesthetics, ornamental waterspouts, focusing primarily on those that have been published in Croatia to this day. In Roman times, the territory of Croatia was part of the provinces *Pannonia* and *Dalmatia*, with Istria being a part of the tenth region of Italia[2].

## BRIEF REMARKS ON THE FOUNTAIN AND THE WATERSPOUT

A fountain can be defined today as in ancient times as an architecturally designed object with an outlet from which the water flows and a recipient or basin that receives the water. Throughout history, fountains have been built in many forms, mostly adapting to the environment in which they were built and the needs of the people using it. Water for fountains usually comes from a water source on which the fountain was built or the local aqueduct to which it is connected. Early fountains were mostly built near natural springs or streams, sometimes in caves where the spring

---

[1] The most detailed study of Roman water supply was carried out by Hodge 2002.
[2] For general information about the territory of Croatia in antiquity see Sanader 2007.

was located³. It seems that the earliest documented use of fountains can be traced back to the Bronze Age. Already at this time we can identify the first examples of fountain decoration, which we can also see in the examples of Minoan zoomorphic waterspouts⁴.

With the development of more reliable water supply systems during the Greek, Hellenistic and Roman periods the use of fountains increased. Then, their position and number was no longer as limited as before, with the limit now being almost solely the construction and hydraulic skills of its builders. Over time, fountains became the most important water supply points of many ancient cities. In reality, most of the citizens' households did not have direct access to the water supply network. The importance of public fountains can be seen in the example of *Pompeii*, whose water supply system is best known to us. Only ten per cent of Pompeian households were directly connected to the water supply, and these connections appear to have been more a sign of status than need. It seems that connected private users used the water for their own ornamental fountains rather than immediate household necessity. The importance of these objects is obvious in the fact that houses in *Pompeii* are usually found no more than 50 m away from a public fountain⁵.

As places of distribution of fresh drinking water, and, consequently, a frequent spot in the city, fountains became an increasingly popular tool for state and personal propaganda, as well as urban embellishment. By the 1ˢᵗ century AD, facades of certain fountains became more and more decorated with statues, colonnades, and even gold, which spread as a fashion throughout the Empire⁶. These highly decorated buildings are commonly called nymphaea by researchers. The size and extent of decoration can be seen as well as imagined when looking at the remains of the ornamental fountains such as the one in Roman *Gerasa* in modern-day Jordan.

At this point, we should remind ourselves that Frontinus (aqu. 78), a Roman *curator aquarum* of the 1ˢᵗ century AD, in his survey of water consumption in Rome mentioned city fountains, distinguishing between ornamental ones, which he called *munera* – in the city in his time there were only 39 of those –, and other public fountains, which he calls simply *lacus*, of which there were 591. Thus, we need to bear in mind that the sheer number of standard public fountains meant that the vast majority were far less decorated, or not at all. A fine example of an undecorated fountain from Croatia, and the only one known to us at the moment, was found on the island of Pag, in modern-day Novalja (Roman *Navalia*). It was the sole discharge point of a qanat-like aqueduct, which probably ran in its entirety through the hill overlooking the town⁷.

As I have already mentioned, there are numerous ways in which a fountain could have been decorated – with statues, facades, colonnades, mosaics, precious metals, etc. The waterspouts, on which I am focusing in this paper, are usually counted among the fountain figures, together with other fountain statues, which are used primarily for decoration. Fountain figures can depict gods or mythological beings and heroes, animals and everyday people (genre sculpture), as well as imperial or private portraits⁸. However, figures used as waterspouts are mostly mythological beings and deities somehow connected with water or animals and depictions of everyday life connected to water (genre sculpture)⁹.

In the most basic terms, a waterspout is a sculpture with a visible water outlet. These sculptures can be perforated by the outlet pipe channel or the channel can be located in its base, plinth or statue's support¹⁰. If the outlet perforates the body of the sculpture, it is usually through the

---

³ A good general overview of fountain forms in antiquity is given by Glaser 2000, 413–436.
⁴ Juuti et al. 2015, 2315–2318.
⁵ On the *Pompeii* water supply system see Eschebach 1983; Jansen 2007.
⁶ Glaser 2000, 431–451; Wilson 2008, 306–307.
⁷ For more information on the aqueduct and fountain in *Navalia* see Ilakovac 1982, 251; Ilakovac 2008; Radić Rossi – Zmaić 2009.
⁸ Kapossy 1969, 12–47; Aristodemou 2011, 153.
⁹ Kapossy 1969, 70; Aristodemou 2011, 154.
¹⁰ Kapossy 1969, 10. 57; Kent Hill 1981, 84; Dorl-Klingenschmid 2001, 92. 94; Aristodemou 2011, 150–151. There are instances of reuse of earlier sculptures as new waterspouts by drilling an outlet through them. It seems that

mouth. There are exceptions, as with the rather common depiction of a nymph holding a shell, where the outlet perforates the shell she holds[11].

## EXAMPLES OF ORNAMENTAL ROMAN WATERSPOUTS IN CROATIA

Most of the ornamental waterspouts known to us from the territory of Croatia come from the Roman towns of *Pola* (modern-day Pula), *Iader* (modern-day Zadar) and *Salona* (modern-day Solin). This fact should not surprise us since those were arguably some of the most important Roman colonies on the eastern Adriatic coast, with elaborate water supply systems and rich urban culture.

### Pola

Roman *Pola*, modern-day Pula, is located in the southern part of the Istrian Peninsula, on its west coast. Research done on the water supply of *Pola* show that at the latest from the middle of the 2nd century AD the town was supplied by an aqueduct fed most probably by a local water source located on the town's central hill or beside it. In addition to this, it seems that there were other water sources, primarily an underground aquifer exploited by wells, in the wider area of Pula, but it is not entirely clear at the moment to what extent they were used after the aqueduct was built[12]. From the territory of *Pola*, two ornamental waterspouts are known. Both are reliefs on stone slabs.

A. THE HEAD OF A MEDUSA (FIG. 1)

The first relief depicts the head of a Medusa, with the outlet positioned on its mouth. The waterspout consists of a rectangular marble slab, 50 cm high, 47 cm wide and 13 cm deep, with the head shown in relief. The Medusa is shown in a grotesque manner and with stylized hair and parts of the face. It is a typical provincial piece, with the face carried out with deep/expressive lines (e.g. large almond-shaped eyes), and with only basic features shown. Previous research dated the relief to the 2nd or 3rd century and concluded that the relief did not originally function as a waterspout, but that it was perforated and reused that way[13]. The relief is now kept at the Archaeological Museum in Pula. The form of this waterspout could point to similar reliefs on slabs found on public street fountains of *Pompeii*, which commonly depict faces of humans and gods, as well as monster and animal heads made on stone slabs and installed over fountain

1   A waterspout depicting the head of a Medusa from *Pola* (modern-day Pula) (photo S. Petešić, Archaeological Museum of Istria inv. A-240)

---

   this produces mixed results as the water could be spewed awkwardly from it. See Auinger – Rathmayr 2007; Aristodemou 2011, 152.
[11] Kapossy 1969, 54; Kent Hill 1981, 90–91; Aristodemou 2011, 151.
[12] For more information on the water supply of *Pola* see Gnirs 1924, 131–137; De Franceschi 1934; Fischer 1996, 47–49; Girardi-Jurkić 2003; Krizmanić 2018; Matijašić 2018, 70.
[13] Girardi-Jurkić 1970, 35–36.

2  A waterspout depicting a young woman with a basket from *Pola* (Archaeological Museum of Istria inv. A-438, photo S. Petešić)

4  Statue of a nymph holding a shell from *Iader* (Archaeological Museum in Zadar, photo D. Maršić)

3  Statue of a sleeping nymph from the forum in *Iader* (Archaeological Museum in Zadar, photo O. Harl)

basins[14]. On the other hand, we cannot rule out that it could have been a part of a larger group on a more elaborate ornamental fountain somewhere in *Pola*, but such a fountain has not yet been found.

### B. A YOUNG WOMAN CARRYING A BASKET (FIG. 2)

The second relief is a rectangular limestone slab 88.5 cm high, 37 cm wide and 6.5 (upper part) – 11 (lower part) cm deep. It depicts a young woman carrying a basket on her head with the help of a type of head pillow used for carrying heavy objects, with the water outlet also positioned on her mouth. The woman is shown in full height, holding a dress with one hand and a basket on her head with the other. The relief has similar design features as the previous one, but is carved more skilfully. The relief was dated to the 2nd or 3rd century AD and is today kept in the temple of Augustus and Roma in Pula[15].

## Iader

*Iader*, modern-day Zadar, was located on an elongated peninsula on the Adriatic coast in central Dalmatia. The area of *Iader* was rich in underground water, which was exploited since its founding, but the town's water supply infrastructure was supplemented with two aqueducts supplying it with water from outside springs, one of them located almost 50 km away. Present research suggests one of the aqueducts was built sometime in the 1st century AD, while the other was constructed during the reign of emperor Trajan[16]. From the territory of *Iader*, two ornamental waterspouts are known.

### C. THE SLEEPING NYMPH (FIG. 3)

One waterspout is a figure of a sleeping nymph dated to the end of the 1st or to the early 2nd century AD. It is now kept in the Archaeological Museum in Zadar (inv. A10218). It is 157 cm long and 51 cm high. The water outlet is positioned beneath her left arm, shaped as if running from an amphora. The canal carved beneath the figure, which was obviously meant to fit a pipe, or act as a sort of pipe itself, has an upward angle. This means that the water had to reach the fountain at a certain hydrostatic pressure, creating a spouting effect, and did not just flow freely from the outlet. The statue was discovered during excavations of the Roman forum in *Iader*, and was used secondarily as a cover for the city sewer. The research on the forum concluded that its south side contained a fountain with the mentioned statue and a semi-circular vaulted roof with cassettes, next to which was a public toilet[17].

### D. THE WATER NYMPH WITH A SHELL (FIG. 4)

The second waterspout is a half-naked female figure, of which only the lower half is preserved. The white marble figure, 65 cm high and 27 cm wide, is also kept in the Archaeological Museum in Zadar (inv. A10301) and is dated to the same period – late 1st or early 2nd century AD. In front of her body, a shell can be seen, which today is also not completely preserved[18]. Nevertheless, we can assume with certainty that it is a representation of a nymph holding a shell, a motif that can often be seen on Roman reliefs in Dalmatia and which represents water nymphs[19]. The sculpture

---

[14] Hodge 2002, 306.
[15] Starac 2004, 26; Sanader 2008.
[16] For more information on the aqueducts of *Iader* see Alačević 1898; Jelić 1898; Medini 1969, 55–56; Ilakovac 1982, 147–240; Miletić 2017; Štefanac 2021.
[17] Suić 1981, 218; Giunio 1999, 58–59; Giunio 2005, 213–214; Giunio 2008, 154–156; Cambi 2005, 17–18.
[18] See also Giunio 2008, 156–157.
[19] For examples of nymphs with shells in Dalmatia see Maršić 1997.

5   A marble relief depicting a head serving as a waterspout from *Salona* (photo Archaeological Museum Split)

6   A lead pipe with the point of discharge shaped as a lion's head (Archaeological Museum in Zadar, photo I. Čondić)

is drilled through from the shell to the other side to accommodate a pipe or to serve as a water conduit itself. Here also it seems that the outlet was drilled at an upward angle from back to front, which should again mean that water was spouted from the area of the shell under some pressure. Unfortunately, the exact find spot of this sculpture is unknown, but it can be assumed that it was a part of a public ornamental fountain somewhere in the city.

## Salona

*Salona*, modern-day Solin, was located on the Adriatic coast in southern Dalmatia and was the capital of the province. Its water was supplied by an aqueduct, which was probably built sometime in the 1st century and was fed by the spring of the river Jadro. The same spring also fed the aqueduct supplying the nearby Palace of Diocletian, built at the start of the 4th century[20].

### E. The mask (fig. 5)

From the area of *Salona*, only one ornamental waterspout is currently known, and it is kept in the Archaeological Museum Split (inv. AMS-C-210). It is a marble relief depicting a mask, whose mouth served as a water outlet. The relief appears to be a fragment of a larger slab, which might have depicted the rest of the body. This also might be argued considering the piece itself is only 7.7 cm high, 9.2 cm wide and 7.3 cm deep. However, this cannot be confirmed, and we should not rule out that it was originally simply a smaller waterspout depicting only the head. Its original location is unknown, apart from it originating from the area of *Salona*. At the moment it is widely dated from the 1st to the 4th century AD. In this state where the relief depicts only the head, we might consider it being used in the similar way as the head of a Medusa from *Pola* and the already mentioned *Pompeii* public fountain reliefs. Although the size difference between these is considerable (the waterspout from *Salona* is only 7.7 cm tall), they could be related in form. This, as well as the rough design, could point to an earlier dating of the waterspout, more precisely to the 1st century AD.

---

[20]   For research on the aqueduct of *Salona* see Bulić 1911; Marasović et al. 2017.

## Bobodol

F. The lion's head (fig. 6)

The last waterspout presented in this paper is a lead pipe whose point of discharge is shaped as a lion's head. The waterspout was obviously connected to another pipe, which can be seen on its other side, where a joint had been preserved. The fact that it is *de facto* a pipe makes it unique among the other finds currently known from Croatia. Also, it is the only waterspout known to us which does not originate from an urban centre, but rather a site near the dried-up Lake Bobodol, in the canyon of the river Krka, relatively close to the Roman legionary fortress, and later *municipium*, *Burnum*. Even though it was not found in an urban setting, the site was most probably very frequented, as it is one of the few river crossing points over which a Roman bridge was probably built. Initial reports from the site, which are dated to the 18th and 19th centuries, mentioned architectural fragments which are today interpreted as remains of a nymphaeum[21].

## CONCLUSION

My research has shown that there are six known and published examples so far of Roman ornamental waterspouts from the territory of Croatia. Although this number is relatively small, it seems that they are essentially no different in style and motif than the others known throughout the Empire. The main difference is the level of workmanship. In relation to other waterspouts from Croatia, the water nymphs from *Iader* are exceptional examples and stand out for their beauty. We also have to keep in mind that the study of waterspouts, until now often overlooked, offers new insights into the ways water supply systems worked, and especially shows potential in widening our knowledge with regard to the dating of the aqueducts and their water-related infrastructure.

## BIBLIOGRAPHY

| | |
|---|---|
| Alačević 1898 | G. Alačević, L'Antichissimo Acquedotto di Zara, Bulletino di archeologia e storia dalmata 21, 1898, 1–12 |
| Aristodemou 2011 | G. A. Aristodemou, Sculptured Decoration of Monumental Nymphaea at the Eastern Provinces of the Roman Empire, in: T. Nogales – I. Rodà (eds.), Roma y las provincias. Modelo y difusión I (Rome 2011) 149–160 |
| Auinger – Rathmayr 2007 | J. Auinger – E. Rathmayr, Zur spätantiken Ausstattung der Thermen und Nymphäen in Ephesos, in: A. F. Bauer – C. Witschel (eds.), Statuen in der Spätantike, Spätantike – frühes Christentum – Byzanz. Reihe B, Studien und Perspektiven 23 (Wiesbaden 2007) 237–269 |
| Bulić 1911 | F. Bulić, Trovamenti riguardanti l'acquedotto urbano di Salona, Bullettino di archeologia e storia dalmata 34, 1911, 66–68 |
| Cambi 2005 | N. Cambi, Kiparstvo rimske Dalmacije (Split 2005) |
| De Franceschi 1934 | C. De Franceschi, Il Ninfeo e l'acquedotto di Pola romana, Atti della Società Istriana di Archeologia e Storia Patria 46, 1934, 227–249 |
| Dorl-Klingenschmid 2001 | C. Dorl-Klingenschmid, Prunkbrunnen in kleinasiatischen Städten. Funktion im Kontext, Studien zur antiken Stadt 7 (Munich 2001) |
| Eschebach 1983 | H. Eschebach, Die innerstädtische Gebrauchswasserversorgung dargestellt am Beispiel Pompejis, in: J.-P. Boucher (ed.), Journées d'Études sur les aqueducs romains, Lyon 26.–28.05.1977 (Paris 1983) 81–132 |
| Fischer 1996 | G. Fischer, Das römische Pola. Eine archäologische Stadtgeschichte (Munich 1996) |
| Girardi-Jurkić 1970 | V. Girardi-Jurkić, Meduze na reljefima Arheološkog muzeja Istre u Puli, HistriaA 1/2, 1970, 29–43 |
| Girardi-Jurkić 2003 | V. Girardi-Jurkić, Izvori i vodoopskrba antičke Pule, HistriaAnt 10, 2003, 11–21 |

---

[21] Vrkić 2017, 216–218; B. Ilakovac considered this waterspout to be from an unknown site (Ilakovac 1982, 130–131).

| | |
|---|---|
| Giunio 1999 | K. A. Giunio, Neke bilješke o zadarskom forumu i kapitoliju, HistriaAnt 5, 1999, 55–66 |
| Giunio 2005 | K. A. Giunio, Religion and Myth on Monuments from Zadar and surroundings in the Archaeological Museum in Zadar, in: M. Sanader – A. Rendić-Miočević (eds.), Akti VIII. međunarodnog kolovija o problemima rimskog provincijalnog stvaralaštva (Zagreb 2005) 213–222 |
| Giunio 2008 | K. A. Giunio, Skulpture nimfi iz Jadera, Archaeologia Adriatica 11, 2008, 151–160 |
| Glaser 2000 | F. Glaser, Fountains and Nymphaea, in: Ö. Wikander (ed.), Handbook of Ancient Water Technology (Leiden 2000) 413–451 |
| Gnirs 1924 | A. Gnirs, Beispiele der antiken Wasserversorgung aus dem istrichen Karstlande, in: M. Abramić – V. Hoffiller (eds.), Strena Buliciana (Zagreb 1924) 129–150 |
| Hodge 2002 | A. Trevor Hodge, Roman Aqueducts and Water Supply (Bristol 2002) |
| Ilakovac 1982 | B. Ilakovac, Rimski akvedukti na području sjeverne Dalmacije (Zagreb 1982) |
| Ilakovac 2008 | B. Ilakovac, Roman aqueducts on the Island of Pag, VjesAMuzZagreb 41/3, 2008, 129–166 |
| Jansen 2007 | G. Jansen, The water system: supply and drainage, in: J. J. Dobbins – P. W. Foss (eds.), The World of Pompeii (London 2007) 257–266 |
| Jelić 1898 | L. Jelić, Povijesno-topografske crtice o biogradskom primorju, Vjesnik Hrvatskog arheološkog društva 3, 1898, 33–126 |
| Juuti et al. 2015 | P. S. Juuti – G. P. Antoniou – W. Dragoni – F. El-Gohary – G. De Feo – T. S. Katko – R. P. Rajala – X. Yun Zheng – R. Drusiani – A. N. Angelakis, Short Global History of Fountains, Water 7, 2015, 2314–2348 |
| Kapossy 1969 | B. Kapossy, Brunnenfiguren der hellenistischen und römischen Zeit (Zurich 1969) |
| Kent Hill 1981 | D. Kent Hill, Some sculpture from Roman Domestic Gardens, in: E. B. MacDougall – W. F. Jashemski (eds.), Ancient Roman Gardens (Washington 1981) 81–94 |
| Krizmanić 2018 | A. Krizmanić, Amfiteatar u Puli. Vodoopskrbni sustav, Prostor 26/2, 2018, 218–231 |
| Marasović et al. 2017 | K. Marasović – J. Margeta – S. Perojević – D. Bojanić – M. Katić, The aqueduct of the Roman town Salona – Croatia, Water Science and Technology-Water Supply 17, 2017, 929–939 |
| Maršić 1997 | D. Maršić, Ikonografski tip Nimfa sa školjkama, VjesAMuzZagreb 30–31/1, 1997, 103–124 |
| Matijašić 2018 | R. Matijašić, Water Supply in Roman Istria, in: E. Tamburrino (ed.), Aquam ducere II. Proceedings of the Second International Summer School Water and the City: hydraulic systems in the Roman age, Feltre 24.–28.08.2015 (Seren del Grappa 2018) 67–79 |
| Medini 1969 | J. Medini, Epigrafički podaci o munificencijama i ostalim javnim gradnjama iz antičke Liburnije, Radovi, Razdio historije, arheologije i historije umjetnosti 6/3, 1969, 45–74 |
| Miletić 2017 | Ž. Miletić, Rimski akvedukt Vrana-Zadar, in: B. Došen (ed.), Braća Vranjani i vransko područje tijekom povijesti (Zadar 2017) 39–51 |
| Radić Rossi – Zmaić 2009 | I. Radić Rossi – J. Zmaić, Podzemni antički vodovod u Novalji na otoku Pagu, HistriaAnt 18/2, 2009, 147–166 |
| Sanader 2007 | M. Sanader, Kroatien in der Antike (Mainz on Rhine 2007) |
| Sanader 2008 | M. Sanader, Imago provinciarum (Zagreb 2008) |
| Starac 2004 | A. Starac, Augustov hram (Pula 2004) |
| Štefanac 2021 | B. Štefanac, Podzemna trasa rimskog akvedukta Biba – Jader, Diadora 35, 2021, 153–170 |
| Suić 1981 | M. Suić, Zadar u starom vijeku (Zadar 1981) |
| Vrkić 2017 | Š. Vrkić, Prilog arheološkoj topografiji sela Radučić kod Knina, Diadora 31, 2017, 197–222 |
| Wilson 2008 | A. I. Wilson, Hydraulic Engineering, in: J. P. Oleson (ed.), Handbook of Engineering and Technology in the Classical World (Oxford 2008) 285–318 |

*Domagoj Bužanić, Faculty of Humanities and Social Sciences, University of Zagreb, Ivana Lučića 3, 10000 Zagreb, Croatia.*
*[e] dbuzanic@m.ffzg.hr*

Fulvia Ciliberto – Paola Ventura

# NUOVE SCULTURE FUNERARIE DA *AQUILEIA*

**Abstract**

In 2020, scheduled archaeological surveillance during public works in the centre of *Aquileia* made it possible to recover some elements of funerary monuments that had been reused in a later building. They include the marble lid of a sarcophagus and several limestone fragments, two of which have a figurative scene. The first depicts the stern of a ship, where the oars – guided by a male figure in profile – and the sail can also be recognized: we suggest an intrepretation as a craft scene (navigation or commerce), although the reconstruction of the monument (an *ara* or, more doubtfully, the pediment of a sarcophagus lid) is not definitely ascertained. The second fragment, attributable to a sarcophagus lid with corner acroteria, shows in the only surviving pediment a scene of labour, which could be connected to one of the steps of honey processing – a unique piece that helps to expand the already rich iconographic heritage of *Aquileia*.

Il cospicuo corpus della scultura aquileiese, ad oggi non ancora oggetto di una edizione esaustiva[1], continua ad arricchirsi a seguito di nuovi rinvenimenti.

Nel giugno 2020, due pezzi figurati frammentari sono stati recuperati in occasione di opere pubbliche per l'installazione di alcuni plinti di sostegno della segnaletica stradale lungo la via Iulia Augusta (che ricalca l'asse principale nord-sud dell'impianto urbano)[2]. In particolare, per lo scavo di uno dei pozzetti si è intervenuti all'incrocio ad est con l'attuale via Patriarchi, sita nell'area meridionale della città in prossimità di un quartiere prioritariamente destinato ad edifici commerciali, e lungo la quale precedenti verifiche alle trincee per opere di urbanizzazione avevano restituito un'articolata situazione, includente un tratto di basolato ed una struttura est-ovest collegata ad almeno tre fasi di pilastri nel segmento più occidentale (fig. 1 a. b)[3]. Lo scavo ora condotto, nonostante le dimensioni ridotte (inizialmente 180 × 160 cm), ha evidenziato subito un contesto caratterizzato dal reimpiego di elementi riconducibili a monumenti funerari ad una quota abbastanza superficiale (−50–60 cm dal piano stradale); l'ampliamento del sondaggio (fino ad un'area di 300 × 240 cm) ha permesso di identificare una struttura muraria con andamento nord-sud, costituita alla base da almeno sei blocchi lapidei (dimensioni max 100 × 100 × 40 cm) riutilizzati, superiormente da pietre squadrate (dimensioni medie 20 × 20 cm) alternate a laterizi: si tratterebbe del perimetrale di un fabbricato affacciato sulla strada, databile in epoca post-antica, forse rinascimentale (fig. 2 a. b). Esso si sovrappone – separato da una serie di livelli di abban-

---

[1] Si rimanda alle considerazioni già esposte in Ventura 2017, 141–143, che fotografava la situazione nel 2013, tuttavia non mutata sostanzialmente con il riallestimento del Museo nel 2018: a cinquant'anni dal catalogo Scrinari 1972 (649 monumenti selezionati dalle collezioni, sia dal percorso espositivo che dai depositi), si dispone tuttavia del prezioso sistematico censimento nella banca dati »Ubi Erat Lupa« (<lupa.at>), che annovera oltre 3300 esemplari rinvenuti nella colonia nord-adriatica. Da ultimo si veda Ciliberto 2020, 207–212.

[2] La sorveglianza e le verifiche di approfondimento sono state condotte per conto del Comune di Aquileia dalla società Arxè s.n.c. (Giulio Simeoni) sotto la direzione scientifica della Soprintendenza Archeologia, belle arti e paesaggio del Friuli Venezia Giulia (Paola Ventura), dal 10 al 15 giugno 2020. La posizione nella carreggiata stradale non ha consentito ulteriori allargamenti per una migliore definizione del contesto, per cui non si può escludere la presenza di altri materiali da reimpiego ancora in sito.

[3] Le indagini degli anni '70 sono sostanzialmente inedite ed i dati si basano principalmente sulla documentazione fotografica e grafica dell'Archivio disegni del Museo Archeologico Nazionale di Aquileia, quest'ultima solo parzialmente riportata nella Pianta complessiva della città (Bertacchi 2003), ove però non è accompagnata da una numerazione e legenda e quindi resta priva di descrizione e interpretazione.

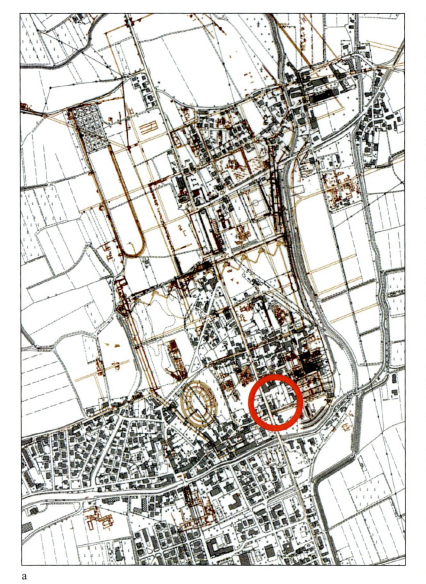

dono – ad un precedente muro con lo stesso orientamento, a sua volta legato a un secondo muro perpendicolare spoliato e ad una preparazione pavimentale, riferibile ad un edificio di età tardo-antica, forse collegabile a quanto in precedenza rilevato in via Patriarchi.

L'epoca recente del riuso non agevola la formulazione di ipotesi sul momento della distruzione e recupero dei pezzi ed avvalora l'impressione di una loro provenienza da bacini anche diversificati. Accanto ai due manufatti decorati su cui ci si soffermerà, si segnala infatti la presenza di altri quattro elementi da reimpiego, solo in un caso riconducibili con certezza ad un originario contesto funerario: si tratta di un ulteriore coperchio di sarcofago (lunghezza 148 × larghezza 20 × altezza 22 cm), forse frammentato longitudinalmente e riadattato proprio per l'inserimento nella muratura, di cui si conserva uno dei due spioventi con copertura a tegoloni e parte di un lato breve, con frontone non decorato, cornice ed acroterio lisci, che spicca per il materiale scelto (marmo, a differenza de-

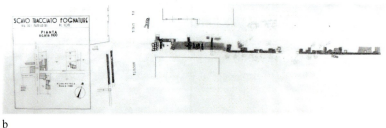

1  a) *Aquileia*. Il sito di rinvenimento con il punto dell'indagine 2020 (da Bertacchi 2003, rielab.), b) *Aquileia*, scavo fognature, via Patriarchi, tratto ovest, 1970 ca. (MAN Aquileia, Archivio disegni, n. 1524)

gli altri reperti tutti in calcare). Erano inoltre presenti una base di colonna (base 56 × 54,5, diametro 53, altezza totale 28 cm), un blocco forse di architrave (95 × 55 × 60 cm) ed un possibile acroterio (35 × 33 × 25 cm), compatibili con, ma non necessariamente riconducibili a, monumenti sepolcrali[4].

---

[4]  Tutti i pezzi sono provvisoriamente conservati nel cortile di Palazzo Meizlik ad Aquileia; non è stato ancora possibile sottoporli a restauro conservativo, che ne agevolerebbe la lettura dei dettagli.

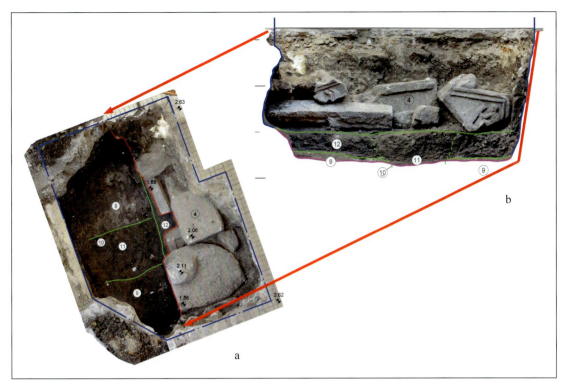

2  *Aquileia*, via Iulia Augusta angolo via Patriarchi, saggio 5: a) ortofotopiano, b) sezione (Arxé s.n.c., Archivio Soprintendenza Archeologia, belle arti e paesaggio del Friuli Venezia Giulia)

Il primo monumento figurato che qui si presenta è risultato immediatamente di agevole lettura per quanto riguarda l'identificazione generica dell'iconografia (personaggio maschile su un'imbarcazione), ma più problematico per il corretto orientamento, e di conseguenza per l'inquadramento tipologico, stante la frammentarietà su tutti i lati (larghezza max. 38, altezza 34, profondità 50 cm).

Esclusa subito la pertinenza ad una stele, in considerazione dello spessore, si è presa quindi in considerazione – anche per la suggestione rappresentata dall'associazione con due coperchi di sarcofago – l'ipotesi che si trattasse della cassa o piuttosto del frontone di un terzo coperchio, decorato con scena di mestiere (come quello trattato di seguito da Fulvia Ciliberto), con l'unico tratto conservato di cornice (semplice listello e gola) corrispondente allo spiovente destro e parte di un acroterio sulla faccia perpendicolare adiacente da questo lato; anche tale soluzione contrasta con il volume pieno, difficilmente compatibile con una cassa – comunque non in questione – ma anche con un coperchio (fig. 3 a).

Ci si è quindi indirizzati verso un'ara, ma sollevava parecchi dubbi l'orientamento con la cornice sul lato superiore, che pur pareva inizialmente avvalorato dal confronto con alcuni esempi di poppa fortemente rimontante e fors'anche con la posizione del personaggio eretto e tendente a chinarsi in avanti[5], ma non altrettanto con un'identificazione coerente degli ulteriori elementi dell'imbarcazione in parte leggibili (fig. 3 b).

---

[5]  In particolare, pur nella diversa tipologia e materiale, due lastre a rilievo marmoree: la prima murata nel Duomo di Salerno (Zimmer 1982, 210–211 n. 160), assegnata al II sec. d.C., mentre non sono avanzate proposte sulla classificazione tipologica; la seconda nei depositi del Museo Archeologico Nazionale di Venezia (lupa 19864), con rappresentazione di Giona, e quindi datata ad epoca paleocristiana. Essa è però meglio identificabile come frammento del lato lungo di un sarcofago, grazie al puntuale confronto con il Sarcofago di Giona del Museo Pio Cristiano, che tuttavia differisce proprio nella configurazione della poppa (Deichmann et al. 1967, 30–32 n. 35; sullo stesso si veda poi Utro et al. 2013, anche con diversi confronti di ulteriori esemplari). Per l'imbarcazione del rilievo di Giona già al Museo Lateranense come fonte per la conoscenza delle imbarcazioni di medie dimensioni

3   *Aquileia*. Frammento di monumento funerario figurato, ipotesi di orientamento: a) frontone con acroterio angolare, b) specchio di ara con cornice superiore, c) specchio di ara con cornice laterale destra (foto P. Ventura)

La presenza dei resti di un alto rilievo sulla faccia perpendicolare a quella figurata (in prima ipotesi assegnati ad un acroterio) ha fatto infine postulare una rotazione di 90°, con la cornice allineata lungo il lato verticale destro dello specchio figurato, sullo spigolo in comune con la seconda faccia sopra detta (fig. 3 c); non è tuttavia al momento possibile discernere quale delle due fosse la fronte e quale un lato dell'ara, entrambe eleggibili per una rappresentazione di mestiere, a cui pare di poter ricondurre, ad ogni modo, la sola scena parzialmente conservata.

Passando ad analizzare ora su quanto rimane di essa, vi si può riconoscere con buona certezza la poppa di un'imbarcazione rivolta verso sinistra (fig. 4): come riportato dagli studi di archeologia navale – basati sulle fonti testuali incrociate con iconografie desunte dalle più svariate tipologie di materiali – questa parte, nelle meglio note navi da trasporto di grandi dimensioni di epoca imperiale, era in forma di collo di cigno ripiegato, ovvero una sua semplificazione a voluta, oppure talvolta appariva configurata a palmetta, come la prua[6]. Nelle navi di medie dimensioni è più frequentemente ricostruibile – anche con il supporto dei dati di imbarcazioni reali – una poppa rialzata e rotonda[7], che ritorna anche in quelle più piccole, sia a vela che a remi, in genere priva di decorazioni[8].

Al di sotto della poppa, obliqui e fra loro paralleli, a bassissimo rilievo, si distinguono i timoni, o timoni-derive, come d'uso in numero di due[9], il sinistro visibile anche davanti alla fiancata, mentre il destro spunta al di sotto della chiglia. Un confronto dove è chiaramente leggibile il doppio timone è offerto dalla nave, priva di equipaggio, riprodotta mediante rilievo piuttosto schiacciato sulla base di una stele da Istra/*Histria* (*Moesia inferior*)[10]. Tuttavia nella maggior parte dei casi viene rappresentato solo quello in primo piano, così nel già citato rilievo di Salerno[11], ed anche in raffigurazioni ben più ricche di particolari: per limitarsi a scene di genere in ambito funerario, si veda il lato destro della nota ara di Naevoleia Tyche da Pompei[12], ovvero l'ancor più spesso richiamato – per questioni di archeologia navale – bassorilievo votivo da Portus nella Collezione

---

del IV sec. d.C. (ma di una tipologia in uso già dal II sec.), cfr. Bonino 2015, 55–57. Sulla forma della poppa, si veda più in dettaglio *infra*.

[6]  Bonino 2015, 47, riferito alle navi annonarie medio-imperiali, meglio conosciute grazie all'ampia casistica.
[7]  Bonino 2015, ad es. 44 e fig. 9 (collo di cigno), 55–57 e fig. 15 (poppa rientrante stilizzata).
[8]  Bonino 2015, 70–73 e fig. 18 (nave *caudicaria*); 77–80 e fig. 21 (barca C di Pisa, a remi e vela, forse da diporto); 81–83 e fig. 22 (barca di Monfalcone, imbarcazione sulla stele ravennate di P. Longidienus – entrambe a remi – e barca raffigurata in un mosaico probabilmente aquileiese, a vela, forse da diporto – quest'ultima la più pertinente).
[9]  Per i due timoni ai lati della poppa, e sul sistema di appoggio alla nave, si veda Bonino 2015, 128–129.
[10] Stele di Theokritos, cfr. lupa 21710.
[11] Cfr. n. 5 e Zimmer 1982, 210–211 n. 160.
[12] Zimmer 1982, 209 n. 157.

Torlonia[13]; ad essi aggiungiamo anche un ulteriore pezzo di provenienza romana nella medesima collezione, interpretato come scena di mestiere da Michel Reddé, e su cui pure a breve si tornerà[14].

I due timoni sembrano immergersi inferiormente in un esiguo resto – nell'angolo inferiore conservato del pezzo – di quella che plausibilmente è interpretabile come la superficie ondosa del mare, resa a maggior rilievo: confronti in questo senso sono offerti da diversi dei monumenti già menzionati, ovvero il rilievo da Salerno ed entrambi i pezzi della Collezione Torlonia[15]. Purtroppo il breve tratto residuo e la stessa ondulazione non consentono di supportare in maniera incontrovertibile l'orientamento, quale sarebbe stato fornito invece da una linea di superficie orizzontale.

4  *Aquileia*. Frammento di monumento funerario figurato: dettaglio della prua, con i timoni e la superficie ondosa del mare (?) (foto P. Ventura)

5  *Aquileia*. Frammento di monumento funerario figurato: dettaglio della vela e del timoniere (foto P. Ventura)

Ci si rivolge quindi all'ultimo elemento riconoscibile dell'attrezzatura di bordo, nella parte superiore/sinistra (fig. 5), riconducibile con buona certezza ad una vela – il che già consente di meglio inquadrare la tipologia dell'imbarcazione, escludendo quindi le barche a remi, ma necessita di una più dettagliata classificazione, fra archeologia navale e confronti iconografici.

Partendo da questi, si torna al citato rilievo con imbarcazione da Roma nella Collezione Torlonia[16] ed al frammento veneziano del Sarcofago di Giona[17], i quali entrambi presentano una vela quadra spiegata e rigonfia per il vento, con il lato inferiore di conseguenza fortemente arcuato, come appare nel nostro pezzo, se orientato verticalmente (fig. 3 c); permane tuttavia qualche dubbio sul significato che assumerebbe in tal caso la fascia ispessita sul margine destro rettilineo, orientato obliquamente, oltre la quale pare di poter ravvisare, con molta incertezza, un ulteriore elemento triangolare allungato.

Se viceversa si riprendesse in considerazione l'ipotesi dell'orientamento obliquo del pezzo (fig. 3 a), la raffigurazione, ancorché con qualche dubbio di scala, potrebbe accostarsi a quella della vela sul rilievo portuense della Collezione Torlonia[18], ove si riconoscono il lato arcuato corrispondente invece a quello verticale della vela quadrata, sormontata dal braccio orizzontale (si veda la fascia rilevata del frammento in questione), a sua volta sovrastato dalla vela di gabbia, a forma appunto di doppio triangolo molto abbassato[19]. A questa soluzione porterebbe anche l'accostamento con la vela della nave sul Sarcofago di Giona del Museo Pio Cristiano[20], sebbene in tal caso il braccio e la vela di gabbia siano inclinati.

---

[13] Casson 1994, 110; Meiggs 1997, tav. 20; Bonino 2015, 44–47; cfr. lupa 32826.

[14] Reddé 1978, 46. Cfr. lupa 31798, ove sono riprese le immagini della Mostra della romanità del 1938.

[15] Per questi aspetti il nostro esemplare si affianca a quelli maggiormente dettagliati, in quanto la raffigurazione del mare consente comunque la lettura di entrambi i timoni, mentre più frequentemente questi ultimi (o in genere solo quello in primo piano) appaiono nella loro interezza quando manca la superficie acquea e la nave è rappresentata quasi ›galleggiasse‹ nel vuoto: si vedano i due timoni nella stele di Theokritos (cfr. *supra* e n. 10) ed i remi in quella di C. Utius, da Spalato, su cui Rinaldi Tufi 1987; lupa 24496.

[16] Cfr. n. 15.

[17] Cfr. n. 5, lupa 19864.

[18] Cfr. n. 13. Anche questo rilievo, tuttavia, non è esente da sproporzioni, come segnalato da Bonino 2015, 46.

[19] Bonino 2015, 123–128 e in particolare fig. 39, A–B.

[20] Cfr. n. 5, Deichmann et al. 1967, 30–32 n. 35; Utro et al. 2013.

Sulla base di quanto esposto, la figura maschile di profilo con le spalle alla poppa (fig. 5) riveste la funzione di timoniere: più frequentemente raffigurato in piedi[21], in questo caso appare seduto[22], come il personaggio con lo stesso ruolo nell'ara di Naevoleia Tyche, il quale per le maggiori dimensioni rispetto agli altri marinai e per l'atteggiamento è stato identificato con il co-dedicatario C. Munatius Faustus, che con la mano sinistra governa il timone, con la destra impartisce ordini all'equipaggio[23]. Nel frammento aquileiese il timoniere sembra parimenti vestito di una tunica, tuttavia senza le pieghe ed il rimbocco visibili su quella dell'omologo pompeiano, probabilmente la mano sinistra regge il timone, mentre la destra, forse sollevata, poteva piuttosto tenere un oggetto non identificabile, di cui si ravvisano poche tracce davanti al petto. Purtroppo l'esecuzione piuttosto corsiva non facilita una più approfondita analisi, ancor più per quanto riguarda il volto e la capigliatura, che appare ad ogni modo piuttosto compatta e rigonfia[24]; è quindi arduo avanzare, su queste basi, una proposta di cronologia.

La datazione sarà piuttosto legata alla corretta individuazione della tipologia monumentale, che potrebbe essere circoscritta alla fine del I – inizi del II secolo d. C. (prima dell'affermarsi delle are monumentali alla metà del secolo), ove fosse confermata la lettura come frammento di ara (fig. 3 c), ma non si può del tutto escludere, per i motivi sopra detti, l'ipotesi del frontone di sarcofago (fig. 3 a), nel qual caso il termine scenderebbe quantomeno alla seconda metà del II secolo d. C., come il pezzo seguente, cui lo accomunerebbe la presenza di scena di genere su frontone, o probabilmente oltre, per l'esecuzione meno accurata.

Pur nell'incertezza della classificazione e della cronologia, nei termini appena descritti, il monumento fornisce un apporto originale al patrimonio scultoreo di Aquileia in genere e più in particolare all'iconografia legata alla navigazione, al momento senza riscontri diretti.

Partendo da quest'ultima, ciascun elemento, singolarmente analizzato (poppa arrotondata, doppio timone-deriva e vela in funzione), assieme alla rappresentazione del timoniere, può forse consentire di avvicinarsi a circoscrivere il tipo di imbarcazione rappresentata. Rilevano a questo proposito soprattutto le dimensioni della figura umana rispetto ad essa, fatto salvo quanto già segnalato sulla frequente indifferenza, in scene simili, alle proporzioni[25] – la quale nel nostro pezzo potrebbe dipendere sia dalla necessità di utilizzare al meglio lo scarso spazio disponibile per la raffigurazione, sia dall'intenzione di dare maggior rilievo al protagonista della scena[26]: è comunque plausibile escludere che possa trattarsi di una nave da trasporto di grande portata (come le annonarie, con lunghezza fino a 40 m e di regola più vele), ciò benché sia stato necessario avvalersi ripetutamente di confronti con questa classe, proprio perché meglio attestata[27]; potremmo tuttavia forse ricadere fra le navi da trasporto di medie dimensioni (entro i 20 m), che presentano gli stessi elementi essenziali che abbiamo ritrovato (vela, doppio timone)[28]. È altrettanto da scartare, all'altro estremo, l'inquadramento fra le barche a remi, di diverse tipologie, utilizzate per piccoli e medi trasporti e per acque interne[29], ed anche delle *naves caudicariae* (che pur in presenza di

---

[21] Ad esempio nel rilievo da Salerno e nel frammento veneziano con Giona, citati a n. 5 e più volte richiamati. Spesso però il timoniere non compare e talvolta a poppa, nelle navi di maggiori dimensioni, sono presenti invece ballatoi o cabine, come nel rilievo portuense della Collezione Torlonia, cfr. n. 13, o in altro rilievo con la stessa provenienza, ora alla Ny Carlsberg Glyptothek, su cui Bonino 2015, 52–55.

[22] Ciò vale sia nell'ipotesi dell'orientamento obliquo (fig. 3 a), che in quella ›verticale‹ (fig. 3 c), nel qual caso la posizione con la schiena reclinata potrebbe giustificarsi con lo sforzo nella manovra, benché piuttosto improprio per un timoniere, mentre sarebbe più naturale per un rematore.

[23] Zimmer 1982, 209 n. 157.

[24] Gli auspicati interventi di pulitura e restauro, cui si faceva inizialmente cenno, potrebbero forse rivelare ulteriori dettagli utili (ivi inclusa l'eventuale presenza di elementi resi mediante cromia), sia per l'interpretazione che per l'inquadramento stilistico e cronologico.

[25] Cfr. *supra* e n. 18: Bonino 2015, 46.

[26] Come per le dimensioni del timoniere maggiori rispetto all'equipaggio sull'ara di Naevoleia Tyche, cfr. *supra* e n. 23 (Zimmer 1982, 209 n. 157).

[27] Bonino 2015, 42–44. 44–55.

[28] Bonino 2015, 44–45. 55–57.

[29] Bonino 2015, 59–70. 74–77. 82–88.

doppio timone e poppa arrotondata, nonché dell'albero, non prevedevano l'uso delle vele, ma il sistema dell'alaggio[30]; ci si dovrà forse orientare nell'ambito di un gruppo di imbarcazioni, che invece erano sospinte (anche) a vela, prevalentemente identificate e ricostruite da fonte archeologica, per le quali non sempre esiste una classificazione standardizzata[31]. Non si può infine trascurare del tutto l'eventualità che la scena possa riferirsi ad una nave da guerra[32], ma non si sono rinvenuti confronti stringenti in questo senso.

Attenendosi quindi alla più probabile assegnazione ad una scena di genere, e specificamente di mestiere[33], pare opportuno rifarsi alla suddivisione di Gerhard Zimmer dei monumenti di tema navale, fra costruzione – dove sono raffigurati prevalentemente strumenti di lavoro, ma in alcuni casi anche imbarcazioni, e risulta allora determinante l'iscrizione[34] – e attività di navigazione, ove è invertito il rapporto fra la rappresentazione di singoli attrezzi di bordo e quella predominante di navi o barche di varia tipologia[35]. Il nuovo pezzo aquileiese andrebbe quindi ad incrementare questa seconda categoria, affiancandosi ad una stele ad edicola, qui inquadrata per la presenza di un'ancora ed un timone[36]; essa integra nel contempo un corpus finora costituito per la maggior parte appunto da stele (unica tipologia registrata per l'ambito cisalpino), un paio di are, accanto ad alcune lastre in origine parte di monumenti maggiori.

*P. Ventura*

Il secondo pezzo, che ha attratto in modo particolare l'attenzione, è un coperchio di sarcofago in calcare, purtroppo molto frammentario, a forma di tetto a due spioventi con acroteri angolari[37] (fig. 6 a–d). Presenta su un solo spiovente un listello molto rilevato lungo il culmine del tetto e del bordo dell'unico frontone conservato (fig. 6 c) e sulla superficie si notano i resti di due larghi tegoloni, coperti nei punti di congiunzione da lunghi coppi ad arco leggermente ribassato. Il secondo spiovente, del quale rimane parte dell'acroterio angolare, è grossolanamente sbozzato a gradina (fig. 6 d).

Il frontone superstite è corniciato su tutti e tre i lati da un listello piatto, che lungo il lato orizzontale si fa più alto, mentre su quelli obliqui è seguito da una gola dritta piuttosto accentuata (fig. 7). Segue, infine, lungo il margine inferiore un profilo piatto obliquo e rientrante (figg. 6 a. b; 7), che in origine certamente correva lungo tutto il bordo inferiore del coperchio, interrotto al centro del lato breve da una bugna a vista non rifinita. Il timpano è decorato a rilievo piuttosto basso (2,5 cm) con una scena figurata di non immediata interpretazione (fig. 7): si vede un uomo con capigliatura corta e riccia (fig. 8 a), seduto di profilo verso sinistra, dal punto di vista dell'osservatore, vestito con una *exomis*. È raffigurato in atto di versare qualcosa da un alto contenitore di forma cilindrica, tenuto rovesciato verticalmente con la mano destra per un lungo manico con attacco sulla base piatta e leggermente ispessita, mentre con la sinistra sembra aiutare a far scendere il contenuto, ben indicato a rilievo, nell'ampio recipiente di forma svasata sottostante (figg. 7. 8 b).

---

[30] Bonino 2015, 70–73; fra queste rientra comunque anche l'imbarcazione sul rilievo di Salerno, cfr. *supra*, n. 5 e Zimmer 1982, 210–211 n. 160.

[31] Bonino 2015, 77–80 e fig. 21 (barca C di Pisa, a remi e vela, forse da diporto); 81–83 e fig. 22, ed in particolare la terza (ricostruita sulla base di un mosaico probabilmente aquileiese, a vela, forse da diporto).

[32] A quest'ambito, ad esempio, va certamente ascritta, sulla base dell'iscrizione, la pure ben nota raffigurazione di una nave sulla stele tergestina di P. Clodius Chrestus, sulla quale Verzár-Bass 1997, 120; lupa 16210.

[33] Residua anche, vista l'incertezza della classificazione del monumento, la possibile interpretazione come scena narrativa di ambito votivo, o pubblico, oppure mitologica, ma nessun indizio soccorre per queste ipotesi.

[34] Zimmer 1982, 143–148 n. 62–69, fra i quali l'esemplare più parlante è la stele ravennate di P. Longidienus (Zimmer 1982, 143–144 n. 62); *Aquileia* contribuisce con una stele altoimperiale, con raffigurazione stilizzata di una nave con timone, accompagnata dalla menzione nell'epigrafe di un *faber navees* (Zimmer 1982, 145–146 n. 64).

[35] Zimmer 1982, 206–211 n. 152–162, numericamente di poco prevalente, sebbene il catalogo non sia esaustivo, si veda anche, ad esempio, la stele dalmata di C. Utius, già richiamata a n. 15 (Rinaldi Tufi 1987).

[36] Zimmer 1982, 206–207 n. 153.

[37] Misure (cm): altezza max. 56, lunghezza max. 100, larghezza max. 70.

6   *Aquileia*. Frammento di coperchio di sarcofago: a) il pezzo al momento del ritrovamento, b) frontone con scena figurata, c) spiovente decorato, d) spiovente inornato (foto P. Ventura)

L'esecuzione, a solo scalpello, è di buon livello e indugia nei dettagli, che forse in origine erano evidenziati dal colore[38].

Il differente stato di lavorazione degli spioventi e la decorazione a tegoloni e coppi, entrambe caratteristiche tipiche della produzione aquileiese[39], confermata anche dal tipo di materiale, permette di identificare il lato decorato con quello principale; pertanto il frontone conservato è il sinistro. Mette invece più in difficoltà la scena figurata sia per la collocazione sia per l'interpretazione del soggetto.

Per quanto riguarda la collocazione, si ricorda che ad Aquileia nei sarcofagi locali le scene figurate sono finora attestate sui lati brevi della cassa; su quello principale di norma si trova una tabella per l'iscrizione, eventualmente affiancata da eroti o da altre figure di carattere funerario, mentre il lato posteriore non è lavorato[40].

Per quanto concerne, invece, il soggetto, il tipo di veste e il gesto dell'uomo orienterebbero verso una scena di mestiere, la cui comprensione dipende chiaramente dalla natura dell'elemento che sta travasando: questo non può essere né un liquido, ad esempio vino, né un solido, ad

---

[38]  Si auspica una prossima accurata pulitura del pezzo che permetta di rendere più evidenti i particolari ed eventuali resti di colore, che potrebbero essere determinanti per la comprensione della scena.

[39]  In generale sulla produzione aquileiese si veda: Gabelmann 1973, 11–90; Ciliberto 2005; Ciliberto 2006; Ciliberto 2007a; Ciliberto 2008a; Ciliberto 2008b; Ciliberto 2013; Ciliberto 2015.

[40]  In generale sulla decorazione dei sarcofagi aquileiesi si veda Gabelmann 1973, 60–78, in particolare per le scene di mestiere p. 71.

7   *Aquileia*. Frammento di coperchio di sarcofago: dettaglio del frontone con scena di mestiere (foto P. Ventura)

esempio cereali o legumi, perché non ci sarebbe bisogno di aiutarne con la mano il travaso; tale osservazione vale anche per una sostanza densa come l'olio. L'unico prodotto che per la sua densità e vischiosità può aver bisogno di essere spinto nel travaso per farlo scorrere è il miele. Pertanto, si propone qui, in via ipotetica, di vedere nella scena il riferimento ad una delle fasi della sua lavorazione e più precisamente quella successiva alla smielatura, cioè la decantazione, in vista della conservazione. Dopo aver estratto il miele dai favi, filtrandolo in modo da liberarlo dalle impurità, costituite da residui di cera o favo, esso viene versato in contenitori utili a farlo decantare per un certo tempo, in modo che si liberi definitivamente da eventuali resti di impurità e dall'aria incorporata durante la smielatura, che risale in superficie[41].

Infruttuoso è stato il tentativo di trovare confronti puntuali per questa scena[42], cosa che conferma una volta di più la mancanza ad oggi di raffigurazioni legate all'apicultura ed alle fasi produttive del miele nell'antichità classica[43]. Per questo motivo il pezzo di *Aquileia*, se correttamente interpretato, risulta molto interessante[44].

Per quanto riguarda la datazione, l'accuratezza nella resa dei dettagli del tetto, che presenta ancora la cornice profilata[45], fa propendere per una proposta di datazione all'interno della seconda metà del II secolo d. C., che appare rafforzata dall'attenta esecuzione anche del rilievo figurato.

---

[41] Sull'apicoltura in generale e in particolare per l'antichità classica la letteratura è ormai ricca; pertanto qui di seguito viene indicata una selezione di testi, che permettono ad ogni modo al lettore interessato di risalire alla bibliografia completa: Crane 1999; Bortolin 2008; Bortolin 2011; Bormetti 2014; Hatjina et al. 2017; Mavrofridis 2018. Per quanto riguarda nello specifico la raccolta e le varie fasi di lavorazione del miele si rimanda a Bortolin 2008, 53–99; Bormetti 2014, 27–30.

[42] Per le raffigurazioni dei mestieri nel mondo romano si rimanda a Reddé 1978; Zimmer 1982; Zimmer 1985; Lefebvre 2017 e alle banche dati online »Ubi Erat Lupa. Bilddatenbank zu antiken Steindenkmälern«, <lupa.at> (31.03.2023), e RBR/Nouvel Espérandieu <https://sculpturo.huma-num.fr/base/> (31.03.2023).

[43] In generale per la documentazione iconografica si veda Bortolin 2008, 13–14. 57–58. 63–65. 101–102. 118 n. 94; 119–124. Una scena di interpretazione non univoca (mitologica o reale [?] Raccolta di miele selvatico o cattura di uno sciame di api per avviare la produzione del miele [?]) è raffigurata su due anfore attiche a figure nere, entrambi variamente datate all'interno della seconda metà del VI sec. a.C.: una da Vulci, oggi al British Museum a Londra (cfr. Crane 1999, 45–46 fig. 7.3a, dove si fa solo cenno al secondo vaso; Bortolin 2008, 58 fig. 20; Kalogirou – Papachristoforou 2017, 73 fig. 9; Beazley Archive Online Databases n. 4330); il secondo nell'Antikenmuseum und Sammlung Ludwig di Basilea (cfr. Kalogirou – Papachristoforou 2017, 73 fig. 10; Beazley Archive Online Databases n. 340559). Per quanto rare, non mancano raffigurazioni del miele stesso nella pittura di nature morte: si veda Ghedini 2016, 37 (un favo pieno di miele e del miele stesso); Bortolin 2008, 24 figg. 4. 5 (contenitore vitreo con carrube o carote in acqua e miele; kantharos con miele o vino mischiato al miele). La rappresentazione di un favo in scultura si trova su una stele da Sillègne (Algeria) della fine del III–inizio IV sec. d.C., per la quale si rimanda a Bortolin 2008, 31 fig. 8. Infine, per le raffigurazioni legate al cibo in generale si veda Ghedini 2016; Rambaldi – Porta 2016, in particolare per l'età romana 57–69.

[44] Potrebbe costituire un'eccezione il rilievo funerario in marmo di Tito Paconio Caledo, datato nella seconda metà del I sec. a.C., che ha scolpita una serie di attività agricole di interpretazione discussa, ma da alcuni riferite all'apicultura. Il pezzo è stato murato, motivo per cui non si è certi della natura del rilievo, forse proveniente da un sarcofago: Città del Vaticano, Musei Vaticani, Gabinetto delle Maschere (inv. n. 808); bibliografia: Zimmer 1982, 70–71; Goette 1990, 111 cat. Ab 110; Spinola 1999, 163–164 cat. 33; Diosono 2007, 11 fig. 5; EDR n. 156621.

[45] Coperchi molto semplici si possono trovare già nella produzione locale di II sec. d.C., ma non sono la regola; mentre con il passare del tempo molti dettagli vengono trascurati. A solo titolo di esempio si veda Ciliberto 2007b, 183–184 n. S50 tav. 50, 172. 173; 185–188 n. 52–54 tav. 51, 175–LII, 177.

a        b

8    *Aquileia.* a) Frontone del coperchio di sarcofago, b) dettagli della scena figurata (foto P. Ventura)

Non si ha alcun elemento per l'identificazione del defunto, probabilmente un produttore, che vendeva forse anche ad ampio raggio e che ha voluto raffigurare l'attività, fonte della sua ricchezza, sul proprio monumento funerario. È un peccato non avere la cassa, dove forse erano rappresentate anche le altre fasi della lavorazione, oltre probabilmente all'epigrafe, usuale sui sarcofagi aquileiesi, che avrebbe rivelato il nome del proprietario.

Per quanto riguarda, infine, l'aspetto del consumo, lo spettro d'uso del miele è amplissimo: ovviamente come dolcificante e per realizzare dolci, ma anche pietanze agrodolci; serviva a conservare altri alimenti, come ad esempio la frutta, per produrre farmaci, unguenti e pozioni, come decotti e tisane, e non da ultimo in ambito sacro e funerario; per non parlare poi dell'impiego – pure molteplice – della cera d'api[46]. Si tratta pertanto di un'attività redditizia, tanto da permettere alla persona di farsi un monumento funerario non poco costoso.

Il miele era certamente prodotto ad *Aquileia* nell'antichità[47], come ancora oggi, anche se non sono noti ritrovamenti archeologici di residui organici dello stesso[48] oppure legati alla sua produzione come ad esempio apiari, attrezzi, contenitori per lo stoccaggio[49], per il trasporto o la vendita[50], oppure arnie, che pur essendo per lo più in materiale deperibile, potevano essere pure in terracotta e che potrebbero anche non essere state riconosciute[51].

*F. Ciliberto*

---

[46] In generale sui molteplici impieghi del miele si rimanda ai seguenti lavori, attraverso i quali è possibile accedere alla bibliografia meno recente: Crane 1999, 481–553; Bortolin 2008, 17–35; Bormetti 2014, 30–43; Balandier c.s.

[47] Purtroppo nelle fonti antiche l'agro aquileiese è citato a proposito del miele solo per ricordare che vi era importato, tra le altre cose, il miele del Norico. A riguardo si veda Bortolin 2008, 48.

[48] Fino ad ora non sono attestati ritrovamenti di resti di miele, che potrebbero provenire soprattutto da contesti funerari. Per i tipi di alimenti rinvenuti finora nelle tombe aquileiesi si veda Giovannini 2016.

[49] Su questi in generale si rimanda a Persano 2014–2015. Si richiama qui un tipo di urceo, considerato come un ›vaso da miele‹, attestato anche ad *Aquileia* (Bortolin 2008, 109 con n. 48 fig. 84), il cui uso come contenitore di miele – almeno per il rinvenimento aquileiese – non è acclarato. Per alcuni contenitori a corpo cilindrico e alto bordo ritrovati ad Altino, la possibilità che servissero come contenitori di miele è largamente ipotetica (cfr. Cipriano – Sandrini 2018), mentre nell'ambito della *X Regio* si hanno solo due attestazioni di contenitori per l'uso e la conservazione del miele, uno di prima età imperiale dall'agro atestino (Bortolin 2008, 107. 109. 118 fig. 82; 177 n. 172), il secondo da Trento, datato alla fine del I–prima metà del II sec. d.C. (Bortolin 2008, 110–111. 177 n. 179), identificati con certezza grazie ai graffiti incisi sulla superficie dei vasi.

[50] A riguardo si veda Bortolin 2008, 119–133.

[51] Per le differenti tipologie di arnie si veda Bortolin 2008, 60–86; Bormetti 2014, 16–24.

# BIBLIOGRAFIA

| | |
|---|---|
| Balandier c.s. | C. Balandier, The divine nectar, a universal panacea? Uses of honey in ancient medicine: comments on Egyptian, Greek and Roman sources, in: Convivium. An International Conference in honour of Prof. Emeritus Demetrios Michaelides on the occasion of his 75th birthday, Nicosia 26.–28.10.2021, in corso di stampa |
| Beazley Archive Online Databases | <https://digital.humanities.ox.ac.uk/project/beazley-archive-online-databases> (31.03.2023) |
| Bertacchi 2003 | L. Bertacchi, Nuova pianta archeologica di Aquileia (Udine 2003) |
| Bonino 2015 | M. Bonino, Navi mercantili e barche di età romana, StA 203 (Roma 2015) |
| Bormetti 2014 | M. Bormetti, Api e miele nel mediterraneo antico, Acme 1, 2014, 7–50 |
| Bortolin 2008 | R. Bortolin, Archeologia del miele, Documenti di archeologia 45 (Mantova 2008) |
| Bortolin 2011 | R. Bortolin, Arnie, miele e api nella Grecia antica, RdA 35, 2011, 149–165 |
| Casson 1994 | L. Casson, Ships and seafaring in ancient times (Londra 1994) |
| Ciliberto 2005 | F. Ciliberto, I sarcofagi aquileiesi: stato della ricerca, novità e prospettive, in: G. Cuscito – M. Verzár Bass (eds.), Aquileia dalle origini alla costituzione del ducato longobardo. La cultura artistica in età romana (II sec. a.C.–III sec. d.C.), Antichità Altoadriatiche 61 (Trieste 2005) 287–304 |
| Ciliberto 2006 | F. Ciliberto, I sarcofagi paleocristiani di Aquileia: stato della ricerca e prospettive, in: G. Cuscito (ed.), Aquileia dalle origini alla costituzione del ducato longobardo. L'arte ad Aquileia dal sec. IV al IX, Antichità Altoadriatiche 62 (Trieste 2006) 501–518 |
| Ciliberto 2007a | F. Ciliberto, Die Sarkophage der Region von Friuli-Venezia Giulia, in: G. Koch (ed.), Akten des Symposiums des Sarkophag-Corpus 2001, Sarkophag-Studien 3 (Magonza 2007) 159–163 |
| Ciliberto 2007b | F. Ciliberto, I sarcofagi, in: M. Verzár-Bass (ed.), Buttrio. La collezione di Francesco di Toppo a Villa Florio, CSIR Italia. Regio X, Friuli-Venezia Giulia III (Roma 2007) 131–189 |
| Ciliberto 2008a | F. Ciliberto, I sarcofagi dell'Italia settentrionale, in: F. Slavazzi – M. Maggi (eds.), La scultura romana dell'Italia settentrionale. Quarant'anni dopo la Mostra di Bologna. Atti del Convegno Internazionale di Studi Pavia 22.–23.09.2005, Flos Italiae. Documenti di Archeologia della Cisalpina romana 8 (Firenze 2008) 153–160 |
| Ciliberto 2008b | F. Ciliberto, Die Anfänge der Sarkophagproduktion Aquileias: kritische Beobachtungen, in: C. Franek – S. Lamm – T. Neuhauser – B. Porod – K. Zöhrer (eds.), Thiasos. Festschrift Erwin Pochmarski, VIKAGraz 10 (Vienna 2008) 117–124 |
| Ciliberto 2013 | F. Ciliberto, La fine della produzione dei sarcofagi aquileiesi: interruzione o trasformazione?, in: N. Cambi – G. Koch (eds.), Funerary Sculpture of the Western Illyricum and Neighbouring Regions of the Roman Empire. Proceedings of the International Scholarly Conference Split 27.–30.09.2009, Biblioteka Knjiga Mediterana 72 (Split 2013) 179–192 |
| Ciliberto 2015 | F. Ciliberto, La produzione dei sarcofagi altoadriatici: status quaestionis, in: F. Rinaldi – A. Vigoni (eds.), Le necropoli della media e tarda età imperiale (III–IV sec. d.C.) a Iulia Concordia e nell'arco altoadriatico. Organizzazione spaziale, aspetti monumentali e strutture sociali. Atti del Convegno di studio Concordia Sagittaria 05.–06.06.2014, L'album 20 (Rubano 2015) 379–388 |
| Ciliberto 2020 | F. Ciliberto, La cultura artistica di Aquileia romana: *status quaestionis*, novità e prospettive, in: G. Cuscito (ed.), 50a settimana. Bilanci e prospettive. Aquileia e le sue musealizzazioni, Antichità Altoadriatiche 93 (Trieste 2020) 207–224 |
| Cipriano – Sandrini 2018 | S. Cipriano – G. M. Sandrini, La produzione altinate di contenitori a corpo cilindrico con alto bordo, ReiCretActa 45, 2018, 273–280 |
| Crane 1999 | E. Crane, The world history of beekeeping and honey hunting (Londra 1999) |
| Cuscito 2016 | G. Cuscito (ed.), L'alimentazione nell'antichità. Atti della XLVI Settimana di Studi Aquileiesi, Aquileia 14.–16.05.2015, Antichità Altoadriatiche 84 (Trieste 2016) |
| Deichmann et al. 1967 | F. W. Deichmann – G. Bovini – H. Brandenburg, Repertorium der christlich-antiken Sarkophage I, Rom und Ostia (Wiesbaden 2007) |
| Diosono 2007 | F. Diosono, *Collegia*. Le associazioni professionali nel mondo romano (Roma 2007) |
| EDR | Epigraphic Database Roma <www.edr-edr.it> |

| | |
|---|---|
| Gabelmann 1973 | H. Gabelmann, Die Werkstattgruppen der oberitalischen Sarkophage (Bonn 1973) |
| Ghedini 2016 | F. Ghedini, Raffigurazioni di cibo nel repertorio ellenistico romano, in: Cuscito 2016, 21–44 |
| Giovannini 2016 | A. Giovannini, »*Parva petunt Manes*« (Ov. Fast. II, 535). Cibo e bevande nelle necropoli di Aquileia, in: Cuscito 2016, 323–349 |
| Goette 1990 | H. R. Goette, Studien zu römischen Togadarstellungen, BeitrESkAr 10 (Magonza 1990) |
| Hatjina et al. 2017 | F. Hatjina – G. Mavrofridis – R. Jones (eds.), Beekeeping in the Mediterranean from antiquity to the present (Nea Moudania 2017) |
| Kalogirou – Papachristoforou 2017 | K. Kalogirou – A. Papachristoforou, The construction of two copies of ancient Greek clay beehives and the control of their colonies' homeostasis, in: Hatjina et al. 2017, 69–78 |
| Lefebvre 2017 | S. Lefebvre (ed.), Iconographie du quotidien dans l'art provincial romain: modèles régionaux. Actes du XIV$^{ème}$ Congrès International d'Art Provincial Romain, Dijon 01.–06.06.2015 (Dijon 2017) |
| lupa | F. Harl – O. Harl, Bilddatenbank zu antiken Steindenkmälern <lupa.at> |
| Mavrofridis 2018 | G. Mavrofridis, Μελισσοκομία στον ελληνορωμαϊκό κόσμο – οι κυψέλες (Beekeeping in the Graeco-Roman World – Beehives), Αρχαιολογία & Τέχνες/Archaeology & Arts 127, 2018, 100–111. |
| Meiggs 1997 | R. Meiggs, Roman Ostia ²(Oxford 1997) |
| Persano 2014–2015 | P. Persano, Vasi ›a colletto‹ come contenitori per miele. Alcune considerazioni, RStLig 80–81, 2014–2015, 113–124 |
| Rambaldi – Porta 2016 | S. Rambaldi – P. Porta, Dalla terra alla mensa attraverso l'arte, fra età romana e il Medioevo, in: Cuscito 2016, 57–84 |
| Reddé 1978 | M. Reddé, Les scènes de métier dans la sculpture funéraire gallo-romaine, Gallia 36, 1978, 43–63 |
| Rinaldi Tufi 1987 | S. Rinaldi Tufi, Stele di un navigatore dalmata, in: Studi per Laura Breglia III, Archeologia e storia, BNumRoma 4, suppl. (Roma 1987) 97–100 |
| Scrinari 1972 | V. Santa Maria Scrinari, Museo Archeologico di Aquileia. Catalogo delle sculture romane, Cataloghi dei Musei e Gallerie d'Italia (Roma 1972) |
| Spinola 1999 | G. Spinola, Il Museo Pio Clementino 2 (Città del Vaticano 1999) |
| Utro et al. 2013 | U. Utro – A. Vella – M. Bernacchi, Il ›Sarcofago di Giona‹, in: Restituzioni 2013. Tesori d'arte restaurati, Sedicesima edizione (Venezia 2013) 136–143 |
| Ventura 2017 | P. Ventura, Le sculture del Museo Archeologico Nazionale di Aquileia: questioni di gestione e di studio, in: L. Sperti (ed.), Scultura di *Iulia Concordia* e Aquileia. Giornata di Studio, Udine 12.04.2013, RdA Suppl. 31 (Roma 2017) 141–154 |
| Verzár-Bass 1997 | M. Verzár-Bass, Monumenti funerari di Trieste, in: M. Mirabella Roberti (ed.), Monumenti sepolcrali romani in Aquileia e nella Cisalpina, Antichità Altoadriatiche 43 (Udine 1997) 117–136 |
| Zimmer 1982 | G. Zimmer, Römische Berufsdarstellungen, AF 12 (Berlino 1982) |
| Zimmer 1985 | G. Zimmer, Römische Handwerker, in: ANRW II 12, 3 (Berlino 1985) 205–228 |

*Fulvia Ciliberto, Università degli Studi del Molise, Dipartimento di Scienze Umanistiche, Sociali e della Formazione, Via Francesco De Sanctis, 86100 Campobasso, Italia.*
*[e] fulvia.ciliberto@unimol.it*

*Paola Ventura, Ministero della Cultura, Soprintendenza Archeologia, belle arti e paesaggio del Friuli Venezia Giulia, Piazza Libertà 7, 34135 Trieste, Italia.*
*[e] paola.ventura@cultura.gov.it*

Chloé Damay

# PRELIMINARY RESEARCH ON OUTPUT FROM ONE OR MORE LIMESTONE SCULPTURE WORKSHOPS IN *THUGGA* (TUNISIA)[1]

**Abstract**
Despite the absence of epigraphic and archeological data, the presence of a workshop producing limestone sculpture in the round in *Thugga* can be surmised from the examination of tool marks, the analysis of techniques used to produce works, and the observation of stylistic similarities. Superseding Punic stelae production, the Imperial period workshop carved the locally-quarried, soft grey-beige limestone with nummulites. The various items in the corpus allow us, given the current state of our knowledge, to situate this activity between the mid-2$^{nd}$ and the 3$^{rd}$ century AD. The subjects treated are extremely varied and cover the repertoire of representations of the elites in the public, private, or funerary sphere and of divinities, from modest stelai to colossal statues in the round.

*Thugga*, in what is now Tunisia, was located in Proconsular Africa southwest of Carthage. It developed into a large and monumental city during the Imperial period with the erection of many public buildings and monuments. Since the end of the 19$^{th}$ century, the site has yielded a rich corpus of statues (including local benefactors, emperors, and mythological statues), running to several hundred sculpted fragments[2]. Some of these statues were made of marble, imported as blocks, as semi-finished or finished statues[3]; however, it is the second type of material used, the local limestone, that currently holds our attention in the context of an investigation into Roman provincial art.

Addressing the subject of the sculpture workshops in *Thugga* remains complex and problematic. In the first place, the absolute silence of the epigraphic sources about the craftsmen, artists, and workshops is regrettable. No *officinae* are mentioned of the kind known in *Carthago*[4], *Cae-*

---

[1] This paper is part of a doctoral study: »La sculpture de Thugga (Dougga): politique et culture d'une ville d'Afrique romaine à l'époque impériale (I$^{er}$–IV$^{e}$ siècles)«, Université Rennes 2 (UMR 6566 CREAAH) and Sorbonne Université, under the joint supervision of Professors M. Denti and E. Rosso, whom I thank for their reviewing.

[2] For the excavations, see Poinssot 1958. More recently, see the publications of archeological excavations in the framework of the Tunisian-French cooperation program titled »Architecture religieuse païenne de Dougga: Déar 1 and Déar 2«. Currently, a program called »Dougga, de l'agglomération numide à la colonie romaine: dynamiques urbaines«, directed by S. Aounallah and V. Brouquier-Reddé, whom I thank, is underway (Aounallah – Brouquier-Reddé 2020). The latter program is supported by the Institut National du Patrimoine (Tunis), the Institut français de Tunis, the CNRS, the ENS (Paris), of the laboratory of excellence TransferS (ENS-Collège de France-PSL, programme Investissements d'avenir ANR-10-IDEX-0001-02 PSL* and ANR-10-LABX-0099), the »PHC Utique«, program of the Ministère français de l'Europe et des Affaires étrangères, the Ministère tunisien de l'Enseignement supérieur, de la Recherche scientifique et de l'Innovation (projet CMCU 19G0405/39269PA) and by a personal mobility subsidy from the Ministère de l'enseignement supérieur de la recherche et de l'innovation (Mesri-2022). This study of sculptures was carried out as part of this project. I wish to thank Y. Maligorne (Centre de recherche bretonne et celtique) for his reviewing. The inventory of the carved fragments has been undertaken since 2017 by A. Riahi (INP, Tunis), K. Ferjani and C. Damay. A. el Fettah, N. Bendhief and the workers of the Dougga Conservancy provided technical support, under the direction of M. A. Chehidi, chief conservator.

[3] According to our estimate, the distribution of the use of marble and limestone is equivalent.

[4] The base of a statuary group has the following inscription: *Ex off(icinae) T(iti) Corn(eli) Saturn(ini)*, Picard 1946, 675.

*sarea*[5], or *Hippo Regius*[6], where workshop marks were engraved on statues or their plinths. At other African sites, plaster casts were revealed during the excavations, as at *Thysdrus*[7], identifying the activity of a workshop with certainty. In *Thugga*, the workshop as a place, as a workroom, remains unknown. We must therefore look for evidence of a workshop in the sense of an institution by studying the sculptures themselves. Technical analysis and the observation of stylistic similarities suggest there was at least one limestone sculpture workshop using the stone from local quarries and whose activity is attested throughout the Imperial period.

## THE NUMIDIAN TRADITION

What information do we have about the sculptural tradition in *Thugga* before the cultural phenomenon called Romanization? In Africa, funerary or votive stelae are well documented for the pre-Roman and Early Imperial periods. In *Thugga*, abundant finds of limestone stelae prove the existence of a local sculptural tradition. The geological signature of the local stone, a nummulitic limestone, is that of a soft grey-beige rock with a very fine yet solid texture. The patterns decorating the stelae are Punic symbols: rosettes, sacrificial scenes, palms, garlands, and the sign of Tanit. Stelae dedicated to Baal, Saturn and Tanit have been found in recent excavations in the Sanctuary of Saturn in *Thugga*[8], and these discoveries have shown that they continued to be produced up until the beginning of the Flavian period.

The inclusion of *Thugga* in the *pertica* of the Roman colony of Carthage during the reign of Augustus and the subsequent addition of a *pagus* of Roman settlers to the urban site disrupted the cultural environment and prompted sculptural production on a larger scale. The limestone provided a way to represent members of the local elite as well as divinities on stelae, but also in larger formats in the round.

## EVIDENCE OF WORKSHOP ACTIVITY DURING THE IMPERIAL PERIOD

A series of *togati* provides the starting point for an analysis of sculpture in the round in *Thugga*. Having come down to us in a fragmentary state and without any precise archaeological context, these seven statues must initially have been about 2 m in height (fig. 1, 1–7)[9].

They were carved in local stone and represent men standing in the contrapposto position. Two ways of using the drill can be seen: the folds of the clothes are invariably heavy on the torso, where smooth-bottomed, sharp-edged drill channels separate the curves. Smooth-edged drill bit channels pass through the folds of the *ima toga*, i.e. around the legs. The surface of the toga has been smoothed with a toothed scraper. All the statues are carved schematically at the back, where the folds of the clothes are evoked by simple edges cut with chisels of various shapes and sizes: two types of flat chisel can be identified – the smaller one outlining the folds – and traces of a point chisel and of a large, toothed chisel are also visible, used for sequences left rough-worked (fig. 2). Stylistic analysis combined with technical analysis dates these statues to the Antonine period, and more specifically to the decades around the middle of the 2nd century[10]. However, the sculptures are not identical in style and must have been made by different sculptors, although there is no basis on which to propose any relative dating. In addition to their identical proportions,

---

[5] A statue representing Venus is signed *ex of(f)icina Murisias*, Gsell 1952, 58 fig. 61.
[6] A sculpture of Minerva presents an engraved plinth *ex officina L. Plotis Clementis*, Marec 1954, 54 fig. 2; Formigé 1955, 131–132.
[7] Ghalia – Terrer 2004, 315.
[8] Aounallah – Brouquier-Reddé 2020, 268 fig. 21.
[9] Dougga. 1: inv. 24-03-26-337; 2: inv. 24-03-26-235; 3: inv. 24-03-26-237; 4: inv. 24-03-26-240; 5: inv. 24-03-26-238; 6: inv. 24-03-26-241; 7: inv. 24-03-26-259.
[10] Damay 2023.

# Preliminary research on output from one or more limestone sculpture workshops in *Thugga* (Tunisia)  357

1   Statues of *togati*, local limestone, Dougga, storerooms (after Damay 2023, fig. 2)

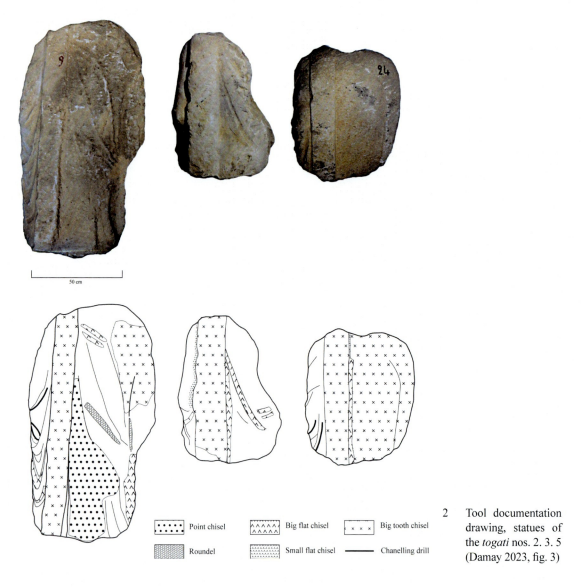

2 Tool documentation drawing, statues of the *togati* nos. 2. 3. 5 (Damay 2023, fig. 3)

the particularly homogeneous plastic and stylistic characteristics of these statues reveal a unity of design prior to their execution that point to them being from one and same workshop.

Certain details of the production of these *togati* are found in other carved examples, highlighting additional technical features. This analysis allows us to reconstruct the organization of different tasks within a workshop, detailing the method and sequence of the sculptural production.

First of all, a roughed-out fragment of a draped leg (fig. 3)[11] clarifies our knowledge of the preparatory work and stone removal techniques: the stonecutter removed material from each side of the ankle and foot by cutting grooves, before freeing the interior with a point chisel[12], thereby producing an outline of the required shape. The surface of the draped part shows traces of another technique, whereby the stone was roughed out with a toothed chisel and evened out to a greater or lesser degree with a flat chisel. Unfortunately this unfinished fragment has come down to us without any precise archaeological context.

A second example, at a more advanced stage in the production process but also testifying to the shaping techniques, is provided by the torso of a male divinity (fig. 4)[13]: the absence of ex-

---

[11] Dougga inv. 24-03-26-339.
[12] For the tool vocabulary, see the digital project for the study of Roman stoneworking: <https://artofmaking.ac.uk/> (14.04.2023) centered on the photographic archive of P. Rockwell.
[13] Dougga inv. 24-03-26-291.

tensive surface treatment means other traces of roughing out can be observed. The original block was roughed out with a small, toothed chisel, the traces of which can still be seen clearly on the right flank. Thereafter, the surface was smoothed with a small, flat chisel. The tool marks run in all directions and cover almost the entire surface. These types of chisel were therefore used to remove surplus stone, to outline the shape of the statue, and even to regularize the surface.

Drills were used extensively for detailing. The drill is well-characterized within the Thugga corpus, as can be seen on the *togati*. However, it is an extremely varied range of chisels that shows a further stage of the sculptural work and attracts our attention: a medium-sized statue of a female deity (fig. 5)[14], dressed in a *peplos*, has preserved traces of a wide range of chisels of different sizes and profiles, much as can be seen on the back of the *togati*. Flat chisels come in two sizes, wide and narrow. Then, there are two types of toothed chisel, a thick and a thin one, with similar sized teeth. Occasionally a roundel (a small round-headed chisel) can be noted, as shown by a slightly concave groove with fine tooth marks indicating that it was toothed. This evidence is not often documented for sculptural work as stonecutters generally used toothed roundels for architecture. The full set of tools is attested on another series of medium-sized limestone sculptures, which are unpublished.

3   Roughed out fragment, inv. 24-03-26-339, Dougga, storerooms (C. Damay © INP – AOROC, CNRS-ENS-PSL)

Finally, the surfaces of the skin or of draped parts were smoothed and flattened with a scraper. As with marble, scraper traces are mostly preserved on the draped parts. Scrapers leave characteristic parallel lines that differ from the criss-cross pattern left by rasps. In *Thugga*, almost all of the limestone statues present scraper marks. The position of the surface striations indicates a single

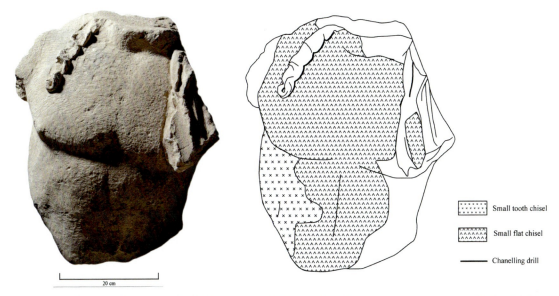

4   Statue of a male deity (torso), local limestone, probably Bacchus, Dougga, storerooms (picture T. Ben Makhad, CAD C. Damay © INP – AOROC, CNRS-ENS-PSL)

---

[14]  Dougga inv. 24-03-26-290.

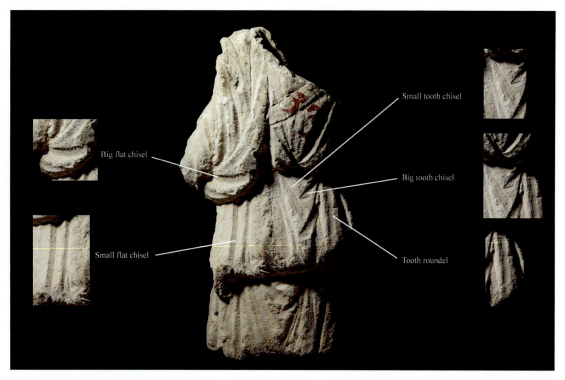

5   Small statue of a female deity, local limestone, Dougga, storerooms (T. Ben Makhad, CAD C. Damay © INP – AOROC, CNRS-ENS-PSL)

type of tool: a flat-edged scraper no more than 4 cm wide. A few examples show work finished with flat chisels of various sizes covering over the tooth chisel traces. Some sequences were left rough-worked, as can be seen on the male torso (fig. 4) with the tooth tool marks on the flank or again on the backs of the *togati* (fig. 2)[15]. This readiness to leave areas rough suggests that these parts of the statue were out of sight and indicates that the »view of the spectator is a crucial factor in many of the sculptor's technical decisions«[16].

Concerning the presence of paint, there are occasional examples that prove that limestone monuments could be painted, as is known from *Thugga*, which provided some examples of rubricature, common in the Roman Empire, as well as painted stelae[17]. The surface of the limestone statues, which is badly damaged and corroded, and sometimes even crystallized, makes it very difficult to read the polychromy. Only two fragments of limestone statues have preserved traces of red paint.

Thus, a detailed analysis of the production of the limestone fragments reveals a certain technical ›signature‹, characterized in particular by the systematic use of a varied range of tools, of which the different flat chisels and toothed chisels are the most evocative. It is therefore the technical treatment, in addition to the homogeneity of the material, and the typology that attest to the existence of a group of individuals sharing the same techniques, within the same production structure. The sculptors, most probably residents, would certainly have been active there in the 2nd century and would have worked the local limestone.

Some of the imperial stelae[18] and reliefs[19] reveal the same technical treatment. The tools are less varied, but their use, coupled with the stylistic choices, is comparable to what is found for the production of the statues.

---

[15] Rockwell 1990 studied the different parameters that determine whether a Roman marble sculpture is finished or not.
[16] Rockwell 1990, 118.
[17] Aounallah – Brouquier-Reddé 2020, 268 fig. 21b and 21e.
[18] Some examples are stelae of Pluto: see Saint-Amans 2004, 322 fig. 48; DÉAR 2, 348.
[19] See for instance the Capitol's pediment, DÉAR 2, 179 fig. 61.

Where was the limestone excavated? The quarries[20] have not yet revealed the precise location of the workshop for cutting the blocks used to make the statues. However, prospecting in the northern outcrop and the analysis of tool marks and blocks left in place have made it possible to identify one sector as a place where the stelae and cippi could have been cut and shaped[21].

## THE PRODUCTION OF THE WORKSHOP: A CHRONOLOGICAL APPROACH

The most homogeneous evidence of this limestone sculpture production, as stated earlier, is clustered around the 2nd century. What can be observed for the other periods?

Annexed to the *pertica* of Carthage, under the reign of Augustus, *Thugga* encompassed a *ciuitas* and a Carthaginian *pagus* whose presence dynamized the municipal *aemulatio* and so contributed to urban monumentalization. The Julio-Claudian period thus saw – as archaeology and epigraphy have clearly shown – the construction of many public buildings in the forum. These constructions were accompanied by the erection of statues, following the model of Roman euergetism. The absence of fragments of limestone sculptures from this period is not significant: the monumental building activity makes it easy to assume the need for a local sculpture workshop.

After the Flavian period, when fewer monuments were built, the urban decoration of *Thugga* continued throughout the 2nd century, especially during the reign of the Antonines. In the same decades that the statues of men in togas were made, the theatre was decorated, in AD 168 or 169. Colossal male and female bodies, uncovered in the excavations of the *frons scaenae* by Louis Carton in the early 20th century[22], show a technical treatment of the stone and stylistic characteristics similar to the *togati* already studied. On the colossal male torso for instance, the drill was used in channels with softened edges to draw folds, delimiting triangular flat areas, a flat chisel outlined some of the folds and a flat scraper was used on the surface. This treatment is similar to the work of the seven *togati*.

Two statues confirm a production of limestone sculpture in *Thugga* in the middle of the 3rd century: a *togatus* of above life size, discovered and preserved in the Place de la Rose-des-Vents, and a broken fragment of a man's leg in a toga[23] can be dated stylistically and technically to the mid-3rd century. Techniques evolved: the drill, for example, was only used to create deep channels with sharp edges, as was common at the time.

The persistence of major construction and decoration projects during the 3rd century in *Thugga* (such as the renovation of the Sanctuary of Fortune, or the construction of several religious monuments) supports this continuity of a local tradition of sculpture in the round. One last piece of evidence is represented by a colossal head[24], found near the theatre, reworked during the 3rd century. The reworked traces are a sure sign of the existence of local workshops, as pointed out by Jean-Charles Balty[25].

To conclude on the subject of chronology, all these limestone works, made over several centuries, characterize different phases of local sculptural production, whether they were sporadic and generated by major building projects or part of a continuous production process. Sculpture thus kept pace with the constant development of the city, making the monumental adornment of the city ever more varied. Even if the exact location of production escapes us, it is possible to trace the output from the same workshop by comparing the technical, plastic and stylistic characteristics of the evidence preserved. At least one group of sculptors worked a stone of excellent quality that was found in abundance in *Thugga*, supplying the city with statues in the round. This output, which in the vast majority of instances related to models from urban workshops, highlighted the

---

[20] Currently the subject of an ongoing archeological study with Y. Maligorne (Centre de recherche bretonne et celtique, France).
[21] Younès 2017, 107 fig. 11.
[22] Carton 1902, 15. 20; Damay 2022.
[23] Dougga, storerooms, inv. 24-03-26-266.
[24] Musée National du Bardo inv. 010326 14. Neri et al. 2021, 2a.
[25] Balty 2019, 231–232.

high level of training of the sculptors, who were creative and learned almost to perfection the know-how of their Roman counterparts (if they were not Roman themselves). This paper focuses on limestone statues in the round, but the other types of output should not be overlooked. Indeed, the large number of marble fragments discovered, carved from imported blocks, as well as the reference to terracotta statues and bronze statues[26] makes it very likely that there were other workshops specializing in other types of production.

## BIBLIOGRAPHY

| | |
|---|---|
| Aounallah – Brouquier-Reddé 2020 | S. Aounallah – V. Brouquier-Reddé (eds.), Dossier: Dougga, la périphérie nord (résultats des campagnes 2017–2019, AntAfr 56, 2020, 175–273 |
| Balty 2019 | J.-C. Balty, Ateliers de sculpture et diffusion de l'image impériale. L'exemple des provinces de la Méditerranée occidentale (Gaule, péninsule Ibérique, Afrique du Nord), in: J.-M. Roddaz – M. Navarro Caballero (eds.), La transmission de l'idéologie impériale dans l'Occident romain, Études 13 (Pessac 2019) 221–246 |
| Carton 1902 | L. Carton, Le théâtre romain de Dougga, Mémoires présentés par divers savants à l'Académie des Inscriptions et Belles-Lettres, 1ère série, tiré-à-part (Paris 1902) |
| Damay 2022 | C. Damay, Un torse masculin au théâtre de Dougga, Chroniques d'archéologie maghrébine 2022, 200–201 |
| Damay 2023 | C. Damay, Un série de togati à Dougga, in: V. Gaggadis-Robin – G. Biard (eds.), Les milles visages de l'honneur. Actes des IIIes Recontres autour de la sculpture romaine à Arles, 11–12 novembre 2019, L'Atelier du sculpteur 3, Ausonius (Bordeaux 2023) 181–188 |
| DÉAR 1 | J.-C. Golvin – M. Khanoussi (eds.) – V. Brouquier-Reddé – N. Hosni – H. Khaldi – K. Karoui – L. Maurin – S. Saint-Amans, Dougga. Études d'architecture religieuse: les sanctuaires des Victoires de Caracalla, de »Pluton« et de Caelestis, Mémoires 12 (Bordeaux 2005) |
| DÉAR 2 | S. Aounallah – J.-C. Golvin (eds.) – H. Ben Romdhane – V. Brouquier-Reddé – M. A. Chehidi – M. Ghaki – M. Khanoussi – L. Maurin – S. Saint-Amans, Dougga. Études d'architecture religieuse 2. Les sanctuaires du forum, du centre de l'agglomération et de la Grande rue courbe, Mémoires 42 (Bordeaux 2016) |
| Formigé 1955 | J. Formigé, Les officines romaines de marbrerie artistique à Carrare, BAntFr 1, 1955, 130–132 |
| Ghalia – Terrer 2004 | T. Ghalia – D. Terrer, Un portrait julio-claudien retrouvé près de Carthage, AntAfr 40/1, 2004, 311–317 |
| Gsell 1952 | S. Gsell, Cherchel, antique Iol-Caesarea (Alger 1952) |
| Marec 1954 | E. Marec, Hippone la Royale: antique »Hippo Regius« (Alger 1954) |
| Neri et al. 2021 | E. Neri – C. Bouvier – L. de Viguorie – A. Brunelle – N. Nasr – F. Béjaoui – F. Baratte – P. Walter, Wax finishing in Roman polychrome statuary: Ganosis on the colossal head from Dougga (Tunisia), Journal of Cultural Heritage 51, 2021, 29–36 |
| Picard 1946 | G. C. Picard, Rapport sur l'archéologie romaine en Tunisie dans le premier semestre 1949, BAParis 1946, 673–689 |
| Poinssot 1958 | C. Poinssot, Les ruines de Dougga (Tunis 1958) |
| Rockwell 1990 | P. Rockwell, Finish and unfinish in the carving of the Sebasteion, in: C. Roueché – K. T. Erim (eds.), Aphrodisias Papers 1: Recent work on architecture and sculpture (Ann Arbor, MI 1990) 101–118 |
| Saint-Amans 2004 | S. Saint-Amans, Topographie religieuse de *Thugga* (Dougga): ville romaine d'Afrique proconsulaire, Scripta Antiqua 9 (Paris 2004) |
| Younès 2017 | A. Younès, Geoarchaeological study of ancient quarriers of Thugga, Marmora 13, 2017, 97–110 |

*Chloé Damay, UMR 6566 CReAAH – Sorbonne Université, 49 rue de Dinan, 29160 Crozon, France.*
*[e] chloedamay@gmail.com*

---

[26] Photographs of the Fonds Poinssot, Institut National d'Histoire de l'Art, Paris.

Zdravko Dimitrov

# NEW STONE MONUMENTS FROM
# *COLONIA ULPIA TRAIANA RATIARIA*

**Abstract**

The ancient city of *Ratiaria* near today's Vidin is the largest archaeological site in north-western Bulgaria. The Roman town has been actively studied in the last ten years. Particularly important discoveries were made in the last two field seasons of 2020–2021, when archaeological excavations of the largest bath complex of the Roman era discovered so far in Bulgaria began – the Roman baths of imperial type in the colony of *Ratiaria*. Among the most interesting finds are the architectural elements that were found in the interior of the baths. These constitute an entire complex of sculptural monuments in the Corinthian order excavated *in situ* on the floor level in the rooms of the eastern wing of the Roman baths.These newest monuments of Roman stone sculpture in Bulgaria are not only huge (the capitals are over 1.00 m high and the bases have a diameter of 1.50 m), but also with magnificent three-dimensional decoration according to the classical versions of the Corinthian order.

The aim of the study is to publish for the first time some impressive stone monuments, especially because Ratiarian architectural elements are not as well known as the inscriptions and grave complexes from this site. These Corinthian details are extremely intriguing due to their huge dimensions and splendid decoration. It is also important to discuss their place in the architectural environment of the cities along the Lower Danubian Limes system of the Roman Empire during the principate.

The Roman town of *Ratiaria* is located on the north-western outskirts of the largest village in north-western Bulgaria – the village of Archar, located on the banks of the Danube (fig. 1). The ruins of the ancient centre are to be found both in the so-called Turkish quarter of the modern village, and also in the fields around it. There are also archaeological complexes under the other neighbourhoods of todays Archar – individual graves, whole vaulted tombs and many finds have been discovered[1].

The site was a huge Roman centre consisting of urban structures, satellite settlements, villas, roads, a large port, necropolises and many other facilities[2]. *Ratiaria* and its surroundings contain the largest archaeological remains in the western part of the Lower Danube from the time of the Roman Empire. Although the city perished completely during the invasions of the Avars and Slavs towards the end of the 6th century AD, its ruins were visible throughout all historical ages to the present day.

In recent years (2013–2022) many new finds have been unearthed during the active archaeological excavations of the Roman colony *Ulpia Ratiaria*[3]. Whole architectural complexes, streets, neighbourhoods of the ancient city and some of the temples were studied, the latter most probably dedicated to the Roman goddess Diana. Beyond doubt, the most serious progress in terms of new excavations was made when the archaeological team began excavating the largest architectural complex of the Roman city – the large *thermae* of *Ratiaria*.

These public baths were studied with aerial photographs as early as 1976, and subsequently the Italian team active at *Ratiaria* in the 1980s published an article on the ancient topography of the

---

[1] Atanasova 1964, 24–28; Atanasova 1969, 87–103; Atanasova 1978, 43–57; Atanasova 1991, 11–19.
[2] Giorgetti 1987, 33–84.
[3] Dimitrov 2015, 28–35.

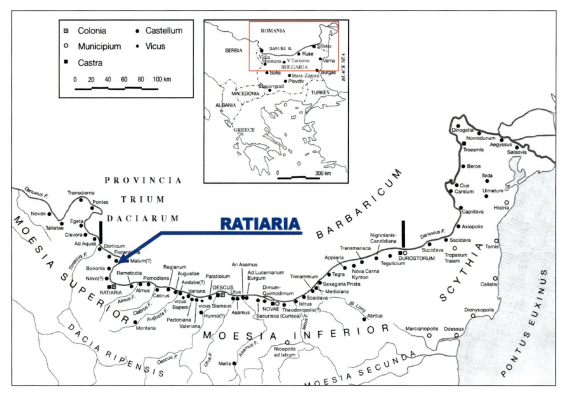

1　Map of the Roman Limes system along the Lower Danube area with the position of *Ratiaria* (after Ivanov 1999, map 1)

city[4]. Although the outline of the *thermae* could be seen on the surface, covering an area of about 100 × 90 m, no archaeological excavations have ever been carried out.

In 2020 and 2021, we worked in the east wing of this architectural complex. We have identified large east-west rooms in the central sector and a number of adjacent smaller ones in the southern sector[5]. The largest room is the central courtyard of the *thermae*, probably the *palaestra*, and in the southern part of the architectural complex there are changing rooms (*apodyteria*), shops aligned along the street from the east around the baths, and probably one of the small *frigidaria*. The architectural structures are astonishing: the walls are built in the *opus mixtum* technique and have an average thickness of 2.20 to 3.50 m, which is greater than the fortification wall of the city. These solid, massive walls suggest the great height of the complex.

The stratigraphy and the construction periods of these Roman *thermae* in *Ratiaria* are very interesting. These baths, designed to resemble the so-called Imperial baths in the capital city of Rome, were probably built in the Severan period (this conclusion was made at the early stage of the excavations), and functioned as public baths until the end of the 4th century AD. After this first period, a large part of the *thermae* was completely redesigned. In the first half of the 5th century AD, an early Christian church was erected in the large courtyard (probably previous *palaestra* of the baths) and the adjoining rooms in the south (fig. 2). This three-nave basilica reused the old solid bath walls for the outer walls of the church and two internal stylobates were constructed from stone blocks brought here from the ruins of the fortress wall. Henceforth, there was an early Christian church inside the former Roman baths.

The church did not last for long. After *Ratiaria* was destroyed by the Huns of Attila (441–444) the citizens of the large late antique centre, the capital city of the province of *Dacia Ripensis*, built

---

[4]　Giorgetti 1987, pl. B.
[5]　Dimitrov et al. 2021, 595–598.

2  Early Christian church built in the ruins of the Roman *thermae* – end of the 4th to the first half of the 5th century AD (photo Z. Dimitrov)

3  New stone monuments found in the complex of the Roman *thermae* – double half-column pilaster elements (photo Z. Dimitrov)

many new small dwellings in the former baths and early Christian church. As living circumstances were extremely difficult in these times of continuous invasions by Huns, Avars and Slavs, the citizens of *Ratiaria* mainly used the old, already devastated large public buildings.

In the remains of these last two periods of the life of the *thermae* – in the 5th and 6th centuries – our team uncovered more than 30 new stone monuments, all architectural elements of the Corinthian order. These numerous newly discovered monuments provide us with knowledge, both in terms of archaeology, i.e. as a new database of the architectural history of the Roman colony and capital city *Ratiaria*, and in terms of analyzing the architectural decoration, i.e. as new details in the Corinthian order in the Lower Danube Limes zone.

Components of the entire order can be found among these elements – bases, columns, capitals, frieze-architraves and cornices. For most of these elements it is complicated to determine their original position in the architectural constructions. We found double half-column bases, double half-column pilasters, half-column capitals (German words of these architectural elements: »Doppelhalbsäulen-Basen«, »Doppelhalbsäulen-Pilaster« and »Halbsäulen-Kapitelle« – fig. 3).

For example, the largest base of the Ionic order was found at the easternmost end of the *thermae* (fig. 4). It is a half-column pilaster architectural element that was the base of the Corinthian-style order. The workmanship of this stone monument is very characteristic for the first half of the 2nd century AD, and especially for the reign of emperor Hadrian and his successors. In *Ratiaria*, we have already obtained new data regarding the building of a temple during the reign of

4   New stone monuments found in the complex of the Roman *thermae* – the largest base element, from a half-column pilaster in Ionic order (photo Z. Dimitrov)

Hadrian. This is the Temple of Diana, which also has decoration in the Corinthian order, but only parts of the interior have been found[6].

This largest Ionic base of the *thermae* in *Ratiaria* measures 1.20 m in height and 1.50 m in diameter. Given these dimensions, the height of the module for the entire order is 0.75 m (radius of the upper surface of the detail). The decorative features of this base show that it was shaped according to the criteria of the Corinthian order. The base consists of a very high and solid plinth, above which one can see the characteristic two *tori*, a *trochilos* between them, and listels finely carved into the stone surface (fig. 4). This piece has a strong outward curvature of the *torus*, as all classical Ionic bases from the Trajanic-Hadrianic era do. This is particularly obvious in the lower *torus*. The stonemason's work is remarkable: the base stands out with its finely polished surfaces, and especially with the perfect lines in the curvatures of the *torus*. The perfect stonemason's work is also apparent in the vertical curvatures of the elements – the *tori*, listels and the *trochilos*, and also when analyzing the overall design of the piece. Its upper surface reveals the form of a perfect circle.

The analysis of this base provides an idea of the architectural decorations and the superb stone-carving in *Ratiaria* in the early 2nd century AD. It is also of foremost importance in answering several key questions, since these fine stone-carving practices were applied so early in the existence of the Roman colony, immediately after it had been founded: where were the workshops, and what is the origin of the raw materials? It seems that serious measures were taken to supply stone material for the construction of large public complexes before the development of the Roman city actually began. The question arises where the stone material was extracted from: local quarries, deliveries from the hinterland of *Moesia*, or marble and limestone which were distributed from elsewhere – along the Danube or from other places.

Indeed, a very important source of information about the architectural monuments in the Roman colony of *Ratiaria* are also other construction elements that were found during the excavations of the *thermae*. Several similar bases from the levels dating to Late Antiquity were found in the centre of the eastern wing. This wing contains small rooms that were built in the second half of the 5th century AD and in the 6th century AD, during and after the Hun and Avar invasions. In this area, distinct layers could be identified – layers with burned small dwellings, constructed in the already abandoned Roman imperial *thermae*. Entire walls, partitioning the old large rooms of the *thermae*, were erected of the huge architectural elements – bases, upper parts of the half-column pilasters, capitals and cornices.

Certain architectural elements, namely a similar base in the same style, were split into parts for better reuse. Particularly interesting is the case of the large base, probably of the same columnar order as the Ionic base described above, which was laid down in its entirety but facing downwards, so that the flat part of the plinth could be used as a floor surface in a newly built small dwelling in the 6th century AD.

The opposite side of the same makeshift dwelling, which the citizens of *Ratiaria* – suffering from continuous barbaric invasions – had to build in the abandoned *thermae*, was made entirely from column elements of the same Corinthian order. The parameters of these columns correspond

---

[6]   Topalilov 2017, 292–296; Topalilov – Bru 2016, 217–222.

5   New stone monuments found in the complex of the Roman *thermae* – part of the group of details in Corinthian order: half-column pilaster capitals (photo Z. Dimitrov)

to the upper diameter of the Ionic base. Obviously, these are architectural fragments from the same row of columns which were dismantled and transferred here. They are all half-column pilaster elements from architectural constructions, as well as the largest Ionic base, shown in figure 4.

The most impressive new stone monuments from *Ratiaria* are a large group of Corinthian capitals, which certainly formed the upper terminus of precisely these half-column pilasters, some of which are also double half-column pilasters (see fig. 5). They are really imposing, not only due to their parameters, but especially due to their wonderful decoration. The capitals were found also in the largest eastern room of the Roman imperial *thermae*. This huge group of Corinthian elements was brought here in Late Antiquity, as were the bases and columns. The capitals do not have the complete set of elements; instead, they consist of only one row of acanthus leaves. Furthermore, the second section is the upper half of the details – where the clearly visible calyx cup, helices and volutes, abacus flowers, visible lips of the kalathos and well-profiled abacus plates are carved.

The workmanship is exceptional. The relief of the leaves is raised, and the acanthus leaves are distinctly separated from the calathos. According to the classifications and examples published by Wolf-Dieter Heilmeyer, Klaus Stefan Freiberger and Jens Rohmann, these Corinthian capitals can be securely dated to the first half of the 2$^{nd}$ century AD[7].

The style of carving is definitely Anatolian. If we search for specific prototypes for these stone monuments, they perfectly replicate the best examples from the western coast of Asia Minor – especially the examples in *Ephesos* and *Pergamon* dating to the reign of emperor Hadrian and a few decades later, until the middle/third quarter of the 2$^{nd}$ century AD, but not later. In the analysis of the decorative schemes of the Corinthian capitals, if the acanthus decoration is considered more closely, then here we should also pay attention to the execution of the helices, volutes and elements in the upper third of the kalathos. According to the form of the acanthus leaf and the style of its execution, these capitals copy without doubt the schemes of the Asia Minor stoneworking schools. However, if we examine in detail the model and execution of the curves of the helices, we will see that they have direct analogies in *Ephesos* in the examples from the residential buildings that have been studied in recent years[8].

In our opinion, this comparison provides direct evidence of the complete copying of the technique of the Ephesian-Pergamene stonemason school on the Lower Danube Limes. The capitals from *Ratiaria* are analogous in pattern to the acanthus leaves, but also in the helices and curves of the volutes of the Asia Minor examples. Moreover, the style of stone carving is completely

---

[7] Heilmeyer 1970, pls. 22. 24–26. 36. 37; Freyberger 1990, pl. 44–49; Rohmann 1998, pls. 45. 46.
[8] Koller 2002, 125–128 pl. 72–79.

similar. These facts lead us to another confirmation of the theory that Asia Minor stone-working groups were involved in the construction of the Roman colonies of *Oescus*, *Ratiaria* and *Sarmizegetusa* along the Lower Danube Limes and the newly-conquered Dacian lands from the era of the emperors Trajan and Hadrian.

In addition to the bases, columns and capitals of the *thermae* in *Ratiaria*, several Corinthian cornices were unearthed. All of them are built into the structure of the early Christian church from the 5th century AD and in the later buildings reusing details from the *thermae*. The best-preserved parts of the cornices are also in the Ionic order. They show simas decorated with palmettes and an Ionic cyma. These elements also provide a large amount of data for analyzing marble production and its distribution in the territory of Upper Moesia.

These new marble monuments from *Ratiaria* are found in three contexts of the archaeological situation on the ground:
1. As reused details in the walls of the Christian basilica in Late Antiquity;
2. As elements (again spolia) in the walls of the late antique buildings from the 6th century AD, into which the earlier rooms of the Roman bath were transformed;
3. As a large group of monuments in the easternmost room of the eastern wing of the *thermae* – probably the changing room (*apodyterium*) from the baths complex, but in the late level from the beginning of Late Antiquity.

The main question here is whether these architectural details are from the decoration of the baths? It is also possible that these details originate from other large public complexes of the Roman colony. There are two considerations that suggest that this might be the case: firstly, the huge parameters and the structural features of the details – most of them are half-column pilaster elements – and secondly, the difference in chronology.

Such massive elements were included in an order that was over 15 m high, and more specifically, between 18 and 20 m. Although the *thermae* were exceedingly tall, a column of this height is not likely to be found in the *palaestra* or somewhere in the interior. The only probable place for such a column is in the main façade of the baths, which has not yet been localized. Another, more likely, possibility is that all of these architectural details were removed from the central square or another huge public complex in *Ratiaria*, which has not yet been archaeologically investigated, and were brought here to be reused at first in the early Christian church from the beginning of the 5th century AD. In fact, the probable location of the forum of *Ratiaria* is just 150–200 m to the north-east of the large Roman *thermae*.

In terms of structure, these half-column pilaster elements would fit perfectly in the peristyle courtyard of a large temple complex or indeed of the entire forum. Such complexes would certainly have been built in *Ratiaria*, as a colony of the Roman Empire, in the early 2nd century AD. A similar situation existed in the Roman colony of *Ulpia Oescus*[9].

After the end of the pagan era in the late 4th century AD – after Theodosius I (379–395) – elements of the destroyed temples might possibly have been transferred to the *thermae* when the three-nave basilica was built. Both pagan temples and public Roman baths were no longer needed by the Christian city, which became one of the largest episcopal centres along the Lower Danube[10]. In terms of the structure and height of the order, these Corinthian details – half-column bases, pilasters and capitals – are perfectly suitable for large temple buildings. For example, from an architectural and structural point of view it is far more conceivable that these details belonged to facades and peristyle porticoes measuring 15–18 m in height, rather than to the interior decorations of the thermal complex.

As noted above, there is also a substantial discrepancy in the chronology. These Corinthian details can definitely be dated to the Hadrianic period or a little later (to the 2nd or 3rd quarter of the 2nd c. AD), but the stratigraphy of the *thermae* shows that they were built about 100 years later, under the Severan dynasty (2nd or 3rd decade of the 3rd c. AD).

---

[9]  Ivanov – Ivanov 1998, 92–104. 142–143 figs. 56–66. 103. 104.
[10] Velkov 1966, 169; Martelli 1980, 65–82.

In conclusion, the great number of magnificent and highly impressive architectural details in the Corinthian order are among the greatest findings during the latest excavations of *Ratiaria*, providing new data on the architectural decoration of the Roman province of *Moesia superior* from the era of the principate. Furthermore, they are also important as architectural elements from the region of the Lower Danube Limes. So the pending question – where are the large-scale architectural details of this Roman colony (very similar to the history of *Ulpia Oescus*) – starts to find an answer.

On the other hand, filling in the gaps in the study of the architectural orders and the architectural decoration of the Lower Danube Limes, this large group of Corinthian elements also raises a number of questions regarding the chronology of the public complexes in the Roman colony of *Ratiaria*, as well as their exact location. Perhaps these monuments are the first evidence for the forum of this huge and flourishing city, as well as for its monumental temples and public building complexes which we have not yet located. We believe that they can be localized during further archaeological excavations.

## BIBLIOGRAPHY

| | |
|---|---|
| Atanasova 1964 | Y. Atanasova, Dva novootkriti skulpturni pametnika ot s. Arčar, Vidinsko, ArcheologijaSof 6/1, 1964, 24–28 |
| Atanasova 1969 | Y. Atanasova, Pogrebenija ot nekropola na Ratiaria, Izvestija na bulgarskite musei 1, 1969, 87–103 |
| Atanasova 1978 | Y. Atanasova, Grobni saorazheniya ot nekropola pri Ratiaria, Izvestija na Museite v Severozapadna Bulgaria 2, 1978, 43–57 |
| Atanasova 1991 | Y. Atanasova, Archeologicheski nahodki ot s. Archar, Vidinsko, Izvestija na Museite v Severozapadna Bulgaria 16, 1991, 11–19 |
| Dimitrov 2015 | Z. Dimitrov, Resumption of regular archaeological excavations in Ratiaria, The European Archaeologist. Newsletter of EAA Members for EAA Members 41, 2015, 28–35 |
| Dimitrov et al. 2021 | Z. Dimitrov – I. Topalilov – I. Tsvetkov, Planned Archaeological Excavations of Ratiaria, in: Archaeological Discoveries and Excavations in 2020 II (Sofia 2021) 595–598 |
| Freyberger 1990 | K. S. Freyberger, Stadtrömische Kapitelle aus der Zeit von Domitian bis Alexander Severus (Mainz 1990) |
| Giorgetti 1987 | D. Giorgetti, Res ad topographiam veteris urbis Ratiariae perinentes. Prolegomeni all' urbanistica della citta romana, Ratiariensia 3–4, 1987, 33–84 |
| Heilmeyer 1970 | W. D. Heilmeyer, Korinthische Normalkapitelle. Studien zur Geschichte der römischen Architekturdekoration, RM Ergh. 16 (Heidelberg 1970) |
| Ivanov – Ivanov 1998 | T. Ivanov – R. Ivanov, Ulpia Oescus 1 (Sofia 1998) |
| Ivanov 1999 | R. Ivanov, Dolnodunavskata otbranitelna sistema mezhdu Dortikum i Durostorum ot Avgust do Mavrikii (Sofia 1999) |
| Koller 2002 | K. Koller, Die Pilasterkapitelle aus dem ›Marmorsaal‹ der Wohneinheit 6. Bemerkungen zu Dekoration und Zeitstellung, in: F. Krinzinger (ed.), Das Hanghaus 2 von Ephesos. Studien zu Baugeschichte und Chronologie, DenkschrWien 302 = AForsch 7 (Vienna 2002) 119–136 |
| Martelli 1980 | F. Martelli, Cultura ecclesiastica ratiarense e lotta politica nel IV secolo, Ratiarenisa 1, 1980, 65–82 |
| Rohmann 1998 | J. Rohmann, Die Kapitellproduktion der römischen Kaiserzeit in Pergamon, PF 10 (Berlin 1998) |
| Topalilov 2017 | I. Topalilov, A new governor of Moesia Superior, ZPE 201, 2017, 292–296 |
| Topalilov – Bru 2016 | I. Topalilov – H. Bru, Chronique de Orient. T. Mummius Sisenna Rutilianus a Ratiaria (Mesie Superieure), DialHistAnc 42/2, 2016, 217–222 |
| Velkov 1966 | V. Velkov, Ratiaria. Eine römische Stadt in Bulgarien, Eirene 5, 1966, 155–175 |

*Zdravko Dimitrov, National Institute of Archaeology and Museum by the Bulgarian Academy of Sciences, Department of Antiquities, Saborna Street 2, 1000 Sofia, Bulgaria.*
*[e] zdravkodimitrov74@gmail.com*

Michael Eisenberg – Arleta Kowalewska

# THE FLOWERS MAUSOLEUM AT HIPPOS OF THE DECAPOLIS

## A FIRST GLANCE INTO ONE OF THE FINEST ROMAN PROVINCIAL ARCHITECTURAL DECORATIONS IN BASALT

**Abstract**
The Flowers Mausoleum is the most elaborately decorated funerary structure of the Saddle Necropolis, the most representative of the three known *necropoleis* of Hippos of the Decapolis. The foundations of the mausoleum, built in the late 1st to early 2nd century AD, have been fully excavated, together with some of its architectural blocks, collapsed during the 363 AD earthquake. The basalt fragments collected until now give evidence of a building composed of five decorative segments, two rectangular and two circular, with a conical roof. The rectangular ground floor was decorated with a particularly interesting Doric frieze of unusually rendered triglyphs and metopes filled with flowers, which give the mausoleum its name. The meticulously sculpted architectural decorations are some of the finest examples executed in basalt, most probably created in a local workshop. The article introduces Hippos' *necropoleis*, and gives a preliminary description of the Flowers Mausoleum, considering the regional parallels as well as Hippos' timeline.

## INTRODUCTION

Antiochia Hippos (Sussita in Aramaic), one of the *poleis* of the Decapolis, is located 2 km east of the shores of the Sea of Galilee, in modern Israel. Situated on Mt. Sussita, which rises to a height of about 350 m above the lake, the city was cut off from its surroundings by three streams and could only be accessed through a topographic formation of a saddle (fig. 1) in the south-east and a winding path in the west[1]. The city's main construction materials were the two local stones: basalt and a soft calcrete/caliche (*nari*)[2].

Antiochia Hippos was founded after the Battle of Paneion (ca. 199 BC), either by Antiochus IV Epiphanes (175–164 BC), or most probably by Antiochus III the Great (222–187 BC)[3]. After Pompey's conquest in 64 BC, the city was incorporated into Provincia Syria. It flourished throughout the Roman period, being the only polis directly next to the Sea of Galilee from the east with a *territorium* expanding to all the southern Golan[4]. As early as mid-4th century AD, Hippos became the seat of a bishopric, and during the Byzantine period at least seven churches were built in the city. During the Early Islamic period, Hippos was replaced as a regional capital by Tiberias, situated on the opposite side of the Sea of Galilee. In AD 749, just at the end of the Umayyad rule, Hippos was destroyed by an earthquake and never resettled[5].

## THE *NECROPOLEIS* OF HIPPOS

Three *necropoleis* served the city of Hippos (fig. 1)[6]. The Southern Necropolis included dozens of burial caves with a few preserved decorative basalt doors and hundreds of pit graves cut in the soft

---

[1] In Hippos, the saddle is the raised area that connects Mt. Sussita with the south-western hills of the Golan Heights.
[2] Shtober-Zisu 2014.
[3] Eisenberg 2014; Eisenberg 2016; Eisenberg 2017a.
[4] Pažout – Eisenberg 2021.
[5] For the historical geography of Hippos, see Dvorjetski 2014. For an updated summary see Eisenberg – Segal 2022.
[6] Eisenberg 2017b, 17–19; Zingboym 2018.

sandy rock and earth, all robbed out and undated[7]. The little-surveyed Eastern Necropolis, located on a small rocky hill, had multiple pit graves with basalt covering slabs. The most prestigious and the best-researched burial ground is the Saddle Necropolis located along Hippos' main approach via the saddle.

The Saddle Necropolis stretched for ca. 150 m from the south, where it met the Roman road (the modern site's parking lot)[8], to the north, where it ended with a ditch cut in the middle of the saddle (a symbolic border between the necropolis and the polis)[9]. It incorporated dozens of limestone and basalt sarcophagi, numerous pit graves cut into the bedrock, burial caves accessed from the slopes, and a few more substantial funerary architectural creations. The location of *necropoleis* along the main roads has parallels not only in Rome, but also locally, most visibly in Tiberias on the western shores of the Sea of Galilee, just opposite Hippos[10].

**Sarcophagi from the Saddle Necropolis**

So far, sarcophagi were identified only in the Saddle Necropolis and only on its eastern side. Most of them are concentrated in a section of the necropolis which begins ca. 13 m north of the Flowers Mausoleum and stretches to the ditch[11]. Most of the sarcophagi were partly or fully inserted into pits cut in the *nari* bedrock, while a few were standing above ground[12]. Most are made of the local *nari*, while some are of the local basalt and some of limestone. The more lavish sarcophagi were surely taken and reused already in antiquity.

Nine sarcophagi were excavated[13]: two of basalt and the rest of *nari* and limestone. Their average dimensions are 2.0 length × 0.65 width × 0.65 m height. Some of the sarcophagi and the pits they were placed in produced a small quantity of diagnostic finds (pottery sherds and two coins), all dated to the Roman period (1st–4th c. AD). Two of the *nari* and limestone examples can be dated by their relief decorations. The first depicts two lion heads that hold rings in their jaws (see below). The second includes reliefs of piers, arches, discs, and an empty *tabula ansata* (S15285). Sarcophagi with these exact set of motifs are very familiar around the Sea of Galilee and are labelled the »Tiberias Group«. The Hippos example is the first found in a non-Jewish context[14].

**Burial caves in the Saddle Necropolis**

Dozens of burial caves were cut into the soft *nari* stone in the western and mainly in the eastern slopes of the Saddle Necropolis. The caves are aligned in rather straight lines along artificially cut rock steps. Unlike the sarcophagi field, which stops at the ditch, the burial caves continue further north-east along the slopes. A survey following a recent fire showed that many of the cave entrances have collapsed and the vast majority of the caves are buried and concealed from the eye.

---

[7] Eisenberg – Staab 2021.

[8] The exact course of the Roman road has not been archaeologically proven, but its presence can be confidently reconstructed based on descriptions of several scholars from the late 19th c., the location of the *necropoleis*, and several milestones (Pažout – Eisenberg 2021).

[9] Eisenberg 2014, 91–96.

[10] In a recent overview, Betzer describes the Northern Necropolis that was built along the main roads leading to the city from north and north-west and sums up the various burials: 378 pit graves, 29 sarcophagi, 14 stone doors (apparently from mausolea), remains of 7 mausolea, 4 ossuaries and a single burial cave (Betzer 2021, 85). See also Stepansky 1999, *84–*96. The bedrock at Tiberias is basalt, which may explain the lack of burial caves in contrast to Hippos.

[11] During his survey, Zingboym counted 31 sarcophagi within the Saddle Necropolis (Zingboym 2018, 40), but many more can be spotted on aerial photographs and during closer field inspection. Zingboym noted mostly limestone sarcophagi, with a few basalt examples, and one marble sarcophagus (reported by Schumacher but long since missing).

[12] The practice of burying sarcophagi (even the decorated ones) in specially cut pits is well attested in the Bekaa Valley (Newson 2015, 359).

[13] For a partial list of the sarcophagi see Eisenberg – Kowalewska 2022, 6–8.

[14] For the typology, see Aviam 2016, 4–10. None of the sarcophagi of the »Tiberias Group« is archaeologically dated, but a 2nd–3rd c. AD dating is proposed (personal communication with Mordechai Aviam).

1   Mt. Sussita and its environs with the three *necropoleis* and the Saddle Necropolis monuments indicated: 1) funerary podia, 2) Lion's Mausoleum, 3) Flowers Mausoleum, 4) Burial Cave A, 5) sarcophagi field, 6) ditch, 7) Burial Cave B; drone view towards north (photo M. Eisenberg)

Two burial caves were almost fully uncovered along the eastern saddle slopes (fig. 1–2). Cave A, located ca. 15 m east and below the Flowers Mausoleum, is poorly preserved, with four niches (*kokhim*) and a hewed stepped entrance corridor. Cave B is located ca. 50 m north-east of the ditch, at the same line as Cave A. Excavations at the cave began in 2022 after an *in situ* inscription in Greek was accidently found just beneath the surface[15]. The inscribed *tabula* was cut above a stepped entrance corridor. The cave is almost fully preserved with three niches, and the excavations produced small finds dated only to the Roman period.

## Funerary podia

A unique series of at least 13 funerary podia was excavated along the eastern side of the saddle road (fig. 1)[16]. All the funerary podia were similar in size (ca. 5.5 × 5 m) and originally reached the height of ca. 3.8 m. They were all built in dry masonry of large, well-made *nari* ashlars with drafted margins and protruding bosses. Their flat tops were designed for the display of freestanding sarcophagi. It seems that they were built by the city itself in the first half of the 1st century AD and sold to its wealthy inhabitants. They probably collapsed in the 363 AD earthquake.

## Mausolea in the Saddle Necropolis

At least two mausolea distinguished the Saddle Necropolis[17]: the Lion's Mausoleum and the Flowers Mausoleum to its north, both fully excavated (fig. 1–2).

---

[15]   The 7–8 lines inscription has not been deciphered yet.
[16]   Eisenberg – Kowalewska 2022.
[17]   The term »mausoleum« tends to be used very loosely, especially in the scholarly literature pertaining to our region, so we want to include a proper definition here, even if somewhat strict: a mausoleum is a decorative funerary construction of more than one storey above ground.

2   Drone's view towards west looking at the Lion's Mausoleum (left), the Flowers Mausoleum (right), and Burial Cave A beneath them (photo M. Eisenberg)

The Lion's Mausoleum, named after a lion sculpture found in the debris, is located 18 m east of the saddle road[18]. What was preserved is the ground floor, covered with a vault and measuring ca. 7.5 × 7.5 m (25 Roman feet). The architectural fragments and two basalt lock boxes indicate that the mausoleum had two more storeys reaching a total estimated height of at least 13 m, including a pine-cone finial above a pyramid-shaped or conical roof. A perimeter wall, measuring ca. 15 × 20 m, surrounded the mausoleum. Based on the small finds and the architectural studies, the mausoleum's construction was dated to the early 2$^{nd}$ century AD (even though some architectural elements are more characteristic of the 1$^{st}$ c. AD) and its destruction to the 363 AD earthquake. The vaulted ground floor may have survived the earthquake as simple burials dated to the 380s were discovered within its plaster floor.

## THE FLOWERS MAUSOLEUM

The Flowers Mausoleum was identified only in 2019, during the excavations of the northern wall of the Lion's Mausoleum perimeter. A concentration of well-dressed basalt architectural fragments was exposed here, and underneath them four walls of the new mausoleum were found. The walls of the mausoleum are now fully exposed, but since many of its decorative fragments are still buried down the slope, it is premature to finalize the report[19]. The building was named after the phenomenal pieces of its decoration – basalt-sculpted reliefs of flowers that filled the metopes.

---

[18]   Eisenberg 2021a.
[19]   The Flowers Mausoleum was excavated during one-day digs in between main seasons with a small volunteer team of Hippos enthusiasts. The excavations at Hippos are directed by A. Kowalewska and M. Eisenberg on behalf of the Zinman Institute of Archaeology, University of Haifa, Israel. Excavations at Susita National Park were carried out under Israel Nature and Parks Authority (NPA) permit number A004-20 and Israel Antiquities Authority license number G-22/2020. The research was partially supported by the Israel Science Foundation (grant 722/17), headed by M. Eisenberg and M. Osband.

3  The Flowers Mausoleum and the perimeter wall of the Lion's Mausoleum at the end of excavations; vertical view from the photogrammetric model (photo and modeling M. Eisenberg)

Nothing worth noting was found inside the structure (only the foundations have survived) or around it, except for a sarcophagus made of *nari*. The eroded sarcophagus (S14948; external dimensions – 2.04 × 0.65 × 0.7 m) was found *in situ* just below surface, 1 m west of the mausoleum. As the sarcophagus is not directly parallel to the mausoleum's western wall, it was probably placed parallel to a path that ran behind the funerary podia. Its long face fronting the path depicts two lion heads holding rings in their jaws (door knockers/pullers), with a simplified garland hanging between them[20]. Most probably, it was placed there after the construction of the mausoleum and can be dated roughly to the 2nd century AD[21].

**Excavations and architectural description**

What has been preserved and excavated of the Flowers Mausoleum is a rectangular frame (5.48 m E-W and 5.4 m N-S, so 15 × 15 regular Roman feet) of basalt foundations, only up to two courses high. No remains of a floor or an entrance were preserved (fig. 3). The two courses of the foundations survived because they were constructed mainly against bedrock. The east-sloping bedrock was somewhat levelled under the walls, but inside them was left unworked, protruding upwards. The whole upper part, filled up with stones and soil, was washed away after the mausoleum's collapse. There are no signs of a wider crepidoma or a podium. There is no hypogeum, which means that the burials were located inside the building. Both the foundations and the superstructure were built of basalt blocks with finely carved outer face. The masonry was seemingly dry, with the spaces between the blocks filled with smaller stones and the blocks arranged as headers and stretchers without a repeated rhythm.

---

[20] Eisenberg – Kowalewska 2022, 6 and fig. 6 b.
[21] Similar lion-head decorations are known from sarcophagi at Jiyeh in the *chora* of Sidon (Gwiazda 2013, 58–60) and at Kedesh (Ovadiah – Mucznik 2011, 537–538). For ›door knockers‹ from Nysa-Scythopolis and additional references of their regional appearance in the funerary world, see Rosenthal-Heginbottom 2022.

4   The Flowers Mausoleum architectural fragment exhibition court on the gravel platform; some of the fragments are partly reconstructed on top of one another (photo M. Eisenberg)

5   The Flowers Mausoleum northern wall and architectural fragments at its foot during excavations; view towards east (photo M. Eisenberg)

A few dozens of the mausoleum's ashlars and some of the architectural fragments were uncovered on the ruined foundations, mainly at the side of them. Many other pieces have tumbled down the steep slope to the east. While some are almost inaccessible, others, which rolled all the way towards the Noa Stream, are occasionally salvaged with the expedition's ATV (e.g. the bumped-up frieze fragment A15426; fig. 6 a). There is a clear correlation between the position of the fragments in the building and the chances of their recovery – there are ten known engaged bases (of 12 that the mausoleum must have had), but only five fragments of capitals.

As of February 2023, there are 84 basalt architectural fragments that are assigned as belonging to the Flowers Mausoleum. Most of them are currently exhibited on a gravel platform to the north of the mausoleum and a few were documented but not yet salvaged from the slopes (fig. 4–6). The recovered fragments are only a small part of the building, yet their variety seemingly represents most of the architectural elements of the mausoleum. The fragments can be sorted into 13 groups (A to M below).

| Group | Architectural fragment | Number of fragments found | Remarks |
|---|---|---|---|
| A. A moulded bottom of the ground floor | – | 2 | |
| B. Engaged Ionic corner columns (0.6 m max width) | Engaged Attic corner column base | 3 | One is only a ¼ preserved |
| | Engaged corner column shaft drum | 4 | Including 1 in the stream |
| | Engaged Ionic corner capital | 3 | One only ½ preserved |
| C. Engaged half-columns (0.37 m diameter) | Engaged Attic half-column base including a plinth | 7 | 0.54 m max. width at the plinth |
| | Engaged half-column shaft drum | 12 | |
| | Engaged Ionic capital | 2 | |
| D. Doric architrave (0.4 m high, 1.3 m long) | | 1 | Complete block bearing a *taenia* with three *regulae* hanging from it but lacking *guttae* |
| E. Doric frieze (0.46 m high) | Metope-triglyph block decorated with a flower | 5 | |
| | Triglyph | 2 | |
| F. Corinthian modillion cornice | – | 10 | |
| G. Plain Doric cornice | – | 5 | |
| H. Rounded Corinthian modillion cornice | – | 4 | Including 1 in the stream |
| I. Rounded base of the tholos | – | 4 | Including 1 in the stream |
| J. Elements of tholos (see M.) | – | – | |
| K. Plain rounded Doric cornice | – | 3 | |
| L. Rounded frieze | – | 5 | A horizontal decorative band probably placed above the upper short part of the tholos and immediately beneath the conical roof |
| M. Elements of tholos and conical roof (not sorted) | – | 12 | Including 3 in the stream |

The quality of most of the architectural elements is very high, although they are sculpted in basalt. The diameters of the columns are very accurate, within the range of 1 cm difference. The quality is especially noticeable in the flower metopes and the engaged Ionic capitals (fig. 6). They are more meticulously worked than any other basalt architectural fragments from the city. Even the Corinthian capitals of the Roman basilica, built at the end of the 1st century AD as the largest roofed structure in Hippos, are of a lesser quality[22].

Due to the limited scope of the present article and its preliminary nature, only the most curious of the architectural elements will be discussed further – the ground floor's Doric frieze.

---

[22] Eisenberg 2021b, 164. 166.

## Flowered metope and triglyph frieze

Five metopes bearing finely sculpted flowers in high relief have been located so far (fig. 6). All the flowers are different in design, and none seems identifiable with the local flora. They are probably imaginative, each flower sculpted in a unique shape. The flowers have six to eight petals, and one has a double row of petals. The sculpted flowers protrude from their designated metope area, partially overhanging the triglyphs. They are sculpted in high relief reaching up to 6–9 cm.

Metopes decorated with rosettes are a frequent phenomenon in the public and private, mainly funerary, architecture in free-standing and cut-rock facades in Judaea, Samaria, and the Decapolis, from Herod the Great's reign (mid-1$^{st}$ c. BC) to the end of the Early Roman period (early 2$^{nd}$ c. AD). However, they are mostly in low relief and carry simple rosettes. In more than a few of these examples a Doric frieze sits above Ionic columns, as in the Flowers Mausoleum[23].

Two blocks of basalt Doric friezes with metopes decorated with high relief flowers are exhibited in the Golan Archaeological Museum in Katzrin. Their exact find-spot is unknown but must be located in the southern Golan. The metopes are similar to the ones from the Flowers Mausoleum, yet not as finely executed.

In Hippos, several fragments of a large *nari* Doric frieze were found in the Hellenistic Compound. Their metopes are decorated with reliefs of discs, rosettes, or an amphora, and on two of the blocks the triglyph is replaced by a tetraglyph. This frieze could have been part of the temple, either of the late 2$^{nd}$ century BC or more likely of the late 1$^{st}$ century BC[24].

The design of the triglyphs from the Flowers Mausoleum is a point of particular interest. Instead of three protruding vertical bands separated by deep grooves, the triglyphs are made of a double sunken band with an inner frame. A ›drop‹ hangs from the cap of each sunken band (fig. 6 a–d)[25]. An exact parallel for this triglyph design has not been found, but in southern Syria there are a few examples of Doric friezes that do not strictly adhere to the classical canon. The Doric entablature was used in the Hauran (Auranitis)[26] in southern Syria primarily during the Early Roman period and H. C. Butler assigned it to the Nabataean influence[27]. These unusual Doric friezes decorated funerary architecture, mainly rock-cut tomb facades. Two examples, from Sweida and Kanawat (both ca. 90 km away from Hippos), are the most relevant. The Tomb of Ḥamrath in Sweida had a square plan (9 × 9 m) and was surmounted by a stepped pyramid with six engaged Doric half-columns set on each side[28]. A bilingual Aramaic-Greek inscription indicates that this tomb was built for a woman named Ḥamrath at the end of the 1$^{st}$ century BC. The architrave has *regulae* but *guttae* are missing, as in the Flowers Mausoleum. Two rather crude basalt frieze blocks from the Hauran have a ›drop‹ hanging from the top of the glyphs, although the glyphs are carved as expected[29]. The blocks come from Kanawat and Sweida but it is unknown to which buildings they belonged.

In general, the design of the Flowers Mausoleum frieze can be classified as a pure case of local provincial imagination of the Hauran area. The artisanship is superb, rendered in basalt as if it were marble, yet the provincial nature is evident due to the unusual details. The lack of datable examples from the Hauran, or elsewhere does not allow the dating to be pinpointed more accurately than to the late 1$^{st}$ century BC and the early 2$^{nd}$ century AD.

---

[23] For the list of the funerary monuments in Judaea, Samaria, and the Decapolis, bearing a Doric frieze, some with metope decorated with rosettes, see Peleg-Barkat 2011, 431–432; Peleg-Barkat 2014, 146–147; Peleg-Barkat – Chachy 2015, 323–324; Raviv – Zissu 2020.

[24] Młynarczyk – Burdajewicz 2005, 48–49 fig. 18; Segal 2014, 144–145 fig. 174.

[25] A photogrammetric model of two metopes and two triglyphs reconstructed on the original architrave is available at <https://dighippos_org/app/3d-explorer/preview.html?models=MjA> (29.03.2023).

[26] The Golan (Gaulanitis) is a western continuation of the basaltic Hauran.

[27] Butler 1903, 316–317. 327.

[28] de Vogüé 1865–1877, 29–31 pl. 1; based mainly on Butler's description following de Vogüé. By Butler's visit the site has already been partly demolished: Butler 1903, 324–327; Dentzer-Feydy 1986, 263–265.

[29] Dentzer-Feydy 1986, 264.

6   Architectural fragments from the Flowers Mausoleum: a) triglyph-metope (A15426), b) triglyph-metope (A14943), c) triglyph-metope (A15361) and triglyph (A15370), d) triglyph-metope (A7173), e) engaged Ionic corner capital (A10900), f) engaged Ionic half-column base (A15425), g) round modillion cornice of the tholos (A14950) (photos M. Eisenberg)

## Assembly marks

Some of the architectural fragments of the Flowers Mausoleum bear assembly marks (fig. 6 f). The marks are single Greek letters, sometimes accompanied by a line. They were most probably used to instruct the placement of the stones within the structure, and they indicate that the fragments were most likely sculpted at the quarry workshop and brought ready for assembly to the construction site[30]. At Hippos and in the rest of the Decapolis, these and other types of masons' marks are dated within the period from the mid-1st to the early 2nd century AD[31]. No marks were noted on the ashlar blocks of the walls. Apparently, there was more freedom in their assembly and the whole project was small enough to work without the need for accounting marks.

## Parallels

The building boom that characterized the Roman Near East from the early 2nd century AD is also noticeable in the funerary architecture. From the mid-1st century AD, regional styles started to evolve, reaching a peak of local monumental expression in the 2nd century, and a noted decline from the mid-3rd century[32].

7  The Tomb of Absalom in Kidron Valley, Jerusalem (photo M. Eisenberg)

Most Roman-period mausolea in Syria were rectangular, some with a pyramid-shaped roof, which apparently was preferred to the conical one[33]. The geographically closest examples to the mausolea from Hippos with conical roofs are found in Judaea and in the Decapolis city of Gerasa.

The Herodium mausoleum, the presumed tomb of Herod the Great, is the earliest, the largest and the most impressive. It was built of limestone. Only the square (9.95 m) podium was partially preserved, while the square structure above it, decorated with Doric pilasters and a Doric frieze, topped with a tholos of 18 monolithic Ionic columns with a conical concave roof are reconstructed from excavated fragments (estimated height: 25 m). The construction of this monument is dated towards the very end of the 1st century BC, and it too bears assembly marks on some of the stones[34].

The closest stylistically to the Flowers Mausoleum is the Tomb of Absalom in the Kidron Valley in Jerusalem (fig. 7). Its construction is dated by most scholars to the first half of the 1st century AD (and certainly before AD 70)[35]. Its raised podium (7.9 m long) with the square ground floor (6.9 m long) is carved

---

[30] Kowalewska – Eisenberg 2020, 90–91 fig. 7 a–c.
[31] Kowalewska – Eisenberg 2019; Kowalewska – Eisenberg 2021. Uscatescu 2022, 8–9.
[32] de Jong 2017, 70–71.
[33] Butler, in his survey of Syria, describes several pyramid-shaped tomb roofs but no conical ones from northern Syria or the Hauran (Butler 1903, 109–110; 1920, 91. 93. 132. 139. 299. 300).
[34] Chachy 2015; Peleg-Barkat – Chachy 2015, 330–333.
[35] Avigad 1954, 127–133; Kloner – Zissu 2007, 243.

from bedrock, while the tholos above it (with a conical concave roof crowned by a flower/acanthus-shaped finial) is built of large, sculpted fragments (total height: 19.7 m). The lower cube is decorated with pilasters at the corners and engaged Ionic columns between them, crowned by an architrave with *regulae* and *guttae* and a Doric frieze of triglyphs and discs in metopes.

The mausoleum at Gerasa (ca. 60 km from Hippos) is constructed in the local *nari*. In 1993, 24 architectural fragments of a mausoleum were documented in the Southern Necropolis. They were first found in 1932, but have since been buried again and some could not be traced[36]. The exact location of the structure is unknown, but the analyses of the fragments allowed a proposed reconstruction and a proposed dating for the mausoleum to the beginning of the 1st century AD[37]. The mausoleum is reconstructed as a circular structure with a diameter of 6.47 m. The ground floor is decorated with engaged Ionic semi-columns with a Doric frieze, while the second storey was designed as a Corinthian portico with a Doric frieze and above it a conical roof, crowned with a finial (total height: 14.37 m)[38]. The frieze blocks were of two sizes, corresponding to the two storeys, and the metopes were decorated with various motifs, among them wreath, rosettes, bird, and grapes. Assembly marks appear in this mausoleum on the Corinthian capitals of the second storey (a single letter in Greek, corresponding to the 12 columns of the portico) and the 23 blocks of the frieze-architrave.

**Chronological framework**

The Flowers Mausoleum belongs to the Roman period history at Hippos, the same as all the other parts of the Saddle Necropolis. Several points are considered below to try and pinpoint the dating.

Spatial correlation to nearby funerary architecture: The nearby Lion's Mausoleum was dated by small finds and architectural fragments to the early 2nd century AD[39]. The Lion's Mausoleum perimeter wall was built directly adjacent to the Flowers Mausoleum, yet it is not aligned with it, which suggests that the two buildings were not planned and constructed at the same time. It seems that the Flowers Mausoleum was erected first, since it is closer to the road; later on the poorer quality perimeter wall of the Lion's Mausoleum was added (consequently removing any floor that might previously have existed on this side of the mausoleum and depriving us of a sealed dating context). The series of the funerary podia, located west of the Flowers Mausoleum, were built in the first half of the 1st century AD[40]. Located directly next to the main road, the podia must be earlier than the Flowers Mausoleum. As for the destruction, the best candidate is the 363 AD earthquake that also toppled all other excavated funerary monuments of the Saddle Necropolis (none of them was rebuilt afterwards). The earthquake would surely have been strong enough to send the upper stones of the mausoleum rolling down to the stream below.

Small finds: The excavations of the Flowers Mausoleum revealed no sealed contexts, neither of the construction stage nor in the destruction layer. No coins were found in the foundations and the small number of sherds recovered from the debris and above bedrock were very small and widely dated, from types typical of the 1st century AD up to types of the 3rd and 4th centuries AD.

Raw materials: All the architectural elements of the Flowers Mausoleum are made of basalt and not of the local *nari* or an imported stone. At Hippos, as well as Gerasa (see above), the use of *nari* for architectural decorative elements seems typical for the late 2nd century BC to the 1st century AD, and more specifically for the early 1st century BC to the early 1st century AD. The use of basalt for fine architectural sculpture characterizes the large public constructions of the end of the 1st and the 2nd century AD (e.g. the Roman basilica).

---

[36] As in Hippos, also in Gerasa the use of *nari* for construction ceases during the 1st c. AD. It was replaced by more durable raw building material, namely limestone (Seigne – Morin 1995, 179).
[37] Seigne – Morin 1995; Seigne 2006.
[38] Seigne 2006, 153–155.
[39] Eisenberg 2021a, 297.
[40] Eisenberg – Kowalewska 2022, 16–18.

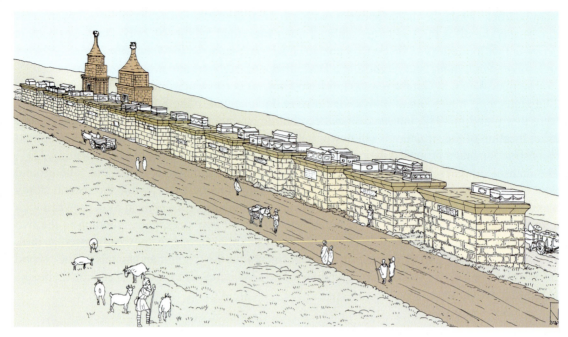

8   An artistic reconstruction of the funerary monuments along the main road in the Saddle Necropolis with the funerary podia series and the two mausolea (Y. Nakas and M. Eisenberg)

Design of the architectural fragments: A preliminary analysis of the design of the Doric architrave and frieze with flowers metopes, the engaged Ionic columns, and the Corinthian modillion cornices (not described) points to the 1st century AD as the preferred date for the mausoleum's construction.

Mason's Marks: The assembly masons' marks noted on some of the stones of the Flowers Mausoleum suggest a dating not later than the early 2nd century AD. Masons' marks are generally known from the Decapolis only in the 1st and 2nd centuries AD[41].

Altogether, the chronological parameters point to the conclusion that the Flowers Mausoleum was constructed somewhere between the late 1st century AD and the early 2nd century AD. The proposed exact destruction date is AD 363, when a strong earthquake hit Hippos and the whole region.

**Suggested reconstruction**

Based on the architectural elements at hand, especially the four different types of cornices, we may reconstruct the mausoleum as a structure composed of five segments: 1) a square ground floor decorated with engaged Ionic columns and Doric frieze with flower metopes, crowned with a Corinthian cornice; 2) a square upper floor with plain cornice; 3) a tholos with a Corinthian cornice; 4) a tholos crowned with a plain cornice; 5) a concave conical roof, probably finished with a finial, which has not yet been found.

Judging by the size of the remaining foundations (5.5 × 5.5 m, that is 15 × 15 Roman feet) and the recovered fragments, and correlating to the larger conical-roof mausolea in nearby regions, the height of the Flowers Mausoleum can be estimated at ca. 14 m[42].

---

[41] For details on marks from Hippos, see Kowalewska – Eisenberg 2019. For a compilation of regional masons' marks, see Kowalewska – Eisenberg 2020.

[42] First square storey – 5 m, second square storey – 2 m, lower part of the tholos – 2 m, upper part of the tholos – 1 m, and a conical roof including a finial – 4 m. The reconstruction of the height of the shorter square storey and mainly the conical roof is only preliminary and requires further analysis.

No clear remains of plaster were found on any of the stones of the Flowers Mausoleum, yet the finds from other basalt pieces at Hippos (most noticeably the Corinthian capitals of the Roman basilica) and the general expectation of colours in Roman architecture suggest that the façades of the mausoleum were fully plastered in white, most probably with additional vivid colours decorating, for example, the flowers. A general artistic proposal of the Saddle Necropolis with its funerary monuments, including a simplified representation of the Flowers Mausoleum, is illustrated in figure 8.

## CONCLUSIONS

The *necropoleis* of Hippos represent a full socioeconomic stratification of burials – from the poorest pit graves to the most lavish mausolea. The ca. 14 m high Flowers Mausoleum was, as far as is known at the current stage of excavations, the most elaborately decorated element of the funerary landscape of the city of Hippos. Its location on the upper part of the saddle, only a few metres from the main road leading to the city gate, made it a prominent mark in the landscape – it advertised not only the family of the deceased buried there but also the splendour of the polis of Hippos throughout the Roman period.

The mausoleum was built at the end of the 1st/early 2nd century AD and destroyed together with the other monuments of the necropolis in the AD 363 earthquake. The choice for this monument was to create a hybrid of all three classical architectural orders – the engaged columns are Ionic, the ground floor frieze is Doric, while some of the cornices have a Corinthian modillion. The unique execution of some parts of these classical orders suggests the work of a local Hippos workshop, which had mastered the art of basalt sculpting close to perfection. It is plausible that the artisans wished to compete with the new trend of exquisitely detailed imports of marble that appeared in the region from the early 2nd century AD and reached Hippos as well. The local workshop was successful in its effort of following the classical canons, but also created an original piece of architectural artistry.

With continued recovery of more architectural fragments, it may one day be possible to partially re-erect one or two of the mausoleum's façades as one of the most impressive examples of ancient funerary monuments preserved in modern Israel from its Roman provincial past.

## ACKNOWLEDGEMENT

We wish to thank all those who keep joining us during Friday dig-days and help us expose the Saddle Necropolis, and to Yana Qedem for her help in conservation. We thank Prof. Arthur Segal for his valuable advice and many discussions. The work is supported logistically by the Zinman Institute of Archaeology at the University of Haifa, and we thank its head, Prof. Adi Erlich, for the continued assistance. The paper was finalized during our stay at the Hanse-Wissenschaftskolleg (HWK), Germany, and we are grateful for this fellowship opportunity. The research has been partly financed by the Israel Science Foundation (grant 722/17).

## BIBLIOGRAPHY

| | |
|---|---|
| Aviam 2016 | M. Aviam, Two Groups of Non-Figurative Jewish Sarcophagi from Galilee, in: A. E. Killebrew – G. Faßbeck (eds.), Viewing Ancient Jewish Art and Archaeology: VeHinnei Rachel. Essays in Honor of Rachel Hachlili, Supplements to the Journal for the Study of Judaism 172 (Leiden 2016) 1–15 |
| Avigad 1954 | N. Avigad, Ancient Monuments in the Kidron Valley (Jerusalem 1954) |
| Betzer 2021 | P. Betzer, The Cemeteries of Tiberias and Hammath during the Roman and Byzantine Periods, Qadmoniot 162, 2021, 85–90 |
| Butler 1903 | H. C. Butler, Part II of the Publications of an American Archaeological Expedition to Syria in 1899–1900: Architecture and other Arts (New York 1903) |

| | |
|---|---|
| Butler 1920 | H. C. Butler, Ancient Architecture in Syria: Division II, Section B: Northern Syria. Publications of the Princeton University Archaeological Expeditions to Syria in 1904–1905 (Leyden 1920) |
| Chachy 2015 | R. Chachy, The Reconstruction of the Mausoleum, in: R. Porat – R. Chachy – Y. Kalman, Herod's Tomb Precinct I, Herodium Final Reports of the 1972–2010 Excavations Directed by Ehud Netzer (Jerusalem 2015) 201–313 |
| de Jong 2017 | L. de Jong, The Archaeology of Death in Roman Syria: Burial, Commemoration, and Empire (Cambridge 2017) |
| de Vogüé 1865–1877 | M. de Vogüé, Syrie Centrale: Architecture civile et religieuse du I$^{er}$ au VII$^e$ siècle (Paris 1865–1877) |
| Dentzer-Feydy 1986 | J. Dentzer-Feydy, Décor architectural et développement du Hauran du 1$^{er}$ s. av. J.-C. au VII$^e$ s. apr. J.-C., in: J.-M. Dentzer (ed.), Hauran 1 (Paris 1986) 261–309 |
| Dvorjetski 2014 | E. Dvorjetski, The Historical Geography of Sussita - Antiochia Hippos-Qal'at el-Husn, in: A. Segal – M. Eisenberg – J. Młynarczyk – M. Burdajewicz – M. Schuler, Hippos-Sussita of the Decapolis: The First Twelve Seasons of Excavations (2000–2011) I (Haifa 2014) 41–63 |
| Eisenberg 2014 | M. Eisenberg, Military Architecture, in: A. Segal – M. Eisenberg – J. Młynarczyk – M. Burdajewicz – M. Schuler, Hippos-Sussita of the Decapolis: The First Twelve Seasons of Excavations (2000–2011) I (Haifa 2014) 86–127 |
| Eisenberg 2016 | M. Eisenberg, Graeco-Roman Poliorketics and the Development of Military Architecture in Antiochia Hippos of the Decapolis as a Test Case, in: S. M. R. Fredriksen – P. P. Schinider – M. Schnelle (eds.), Focus on Fortification. New Research on Fortifications in the Ancient Mediterranean and the Near East, Monograph Series of the Danish Institute at Athens 18 (Oxford 2016) 609–622 |
| Eisenberg 2017a | M. Eisenberg, A Military Portrait of Hippos – from Ptolemaic Fortress to Seleucid Polis, Michmanim 27, 2017, 57–69, 32* (Hebrew with an English abstract) |
| Eisenberg 2017b | M. Eisenberg, The Current State of Research of Antiochia Hippos, Michmanim 27, 2017, 7–24, 29* (Hebrew with an English abstract) |
| Eisenberg 2021a | M. Eisenberg, The Lion's Mausoleum of Hippos of the Decapolis, PEQ 153/4, 2021, 279–303 |
| Eisenberg 2021b | M. Eisenberg, The Basilica of Hippos of the Decapolis and a Corpus of the Regional Basilicae, in: A. Dell'Acqua – O. Peleg-Barkat (eds.), The Basilica in Roman Palestine, Adoption and Adaptation Processes, in Light of Comparanda in Italy and North Africa (Gorgonzola 2021) 153–184 |
| Eisenberg – Kowalewska 2022 | M. Eisenberg – A. Kowalewska, Funerary podia of Hippos of the Decapolis and the phenomenon in the Roman world, JRA 35/1, 2022, 107–138 |
| Eisenberg – Segal 2022 | M. Eisenberg – A. Segal, Town Planning and Architecture of Hippos (Sussita) of the Decapolis in Hellenistic, Roman and Byzantine Periods, in: A. Kevo – I. Majnarić – O. S. Lipar (eds.), MARINOV ZBORNIK. Papers in Honour of Professor Emilio Marin (Zagreb 2022) 342–367 |
| Eisenberg – Staab 2020 | M. Eisenberg – G. Staab, Eusebios' Aedicula Tombstone from Hippos, PEQ 153/1, 2021, 62–69 |
| Gwiazda 2013 | M. Gwiazda, Grave Monuments from Jiyeh (Porphyreon) and the Sepulchral Art of Sidon's Chora, Archeologia 64, 2013, 53–66 |
| Kloner – Zissu 2007 | A. Kloner – B. Zissu, The Necropolis of Jerusalem in the Second Temple Period, Interdisciplinary Studies in Ancient Culture and Religion 8 (Leuven-Dudley, MA 2007) |
| Kowalewska – Eisenberg 2019 | A. Kowalewska – M. Eisenberg, Masons' Marks of Antiochia Hippos, TelAvivJA 46/1, 2019, 108–127 |
| Kowalewska – Eisenberg 2020 | A. Kowalewska – M. Eisenberg, Stonemasons and their Marks in Roman Syria-Palaestina and Arabia, in: S. Vinci – A. Ottati – D. Gorostidi (eds.), La cava e il monumento. Materiali, officinae, sistemi di costruzione e produzione nei cantieri edilizi di età imperiale (Rome 2020) 85–98 |
| Kowalewska – Eisenberg 2021 | A. Kowalewska – M. Eisenberg, Masons' Marks of Antiochia Hippos and Roman Syria-Palaestina, in: M. S. Vinci – A. Ottati (eds.), From the Quarry to the Monument. The Process behind the Process: Design and Organization of the Work in Ancient Architecture (Heidelberg 2021) 57–67 |

| | |
|---|---|
| Młynarczyk – Burdajewicz 2005 | J. Młynarczyk – M. Burdajewicz, North-West Church Complex (NWC), in: A. Segal – J. Młynarczyk – M. Burdajewicz – M. Schuler – M. Eisenberg, Hippos-Sussita – Sixth Season of Excavations, July 2005 (Haifa 2005) 32–50 |
| Newson 2015 | P. Newson, Greco-Roman burial practices in the Bekaa Valley, Lebanon, and its adjacent uplands, Journal of Eastern Mediterranean Archaeology & Heritage Studies 3/4, 2015, 349–371 |
| Ovadiah – Mucznik 2011 | A. Ovadiah – S. Mucznik, The Roman Sarcophagi at Kedesh, Upper Galilee: Iconography, Typology and Significance, Liber Annuus 61, 2011, 531–554 |
| Pažout – Eisenberg 2021 | A. Pažout – M. Eisenberg, The territory of Hippos: Its settlement dynamics and development from the Hellenistic to the Late Roman period as seen through spatial analytical methods, JASc Reports 38, 2021, 103066 |
| Peleg-Barkat 2011 | O. Peleg-Barkat, The Introduction of Classical Architectural Decoration into Cities of the Decapolis: Hippos, Gadara, Gerasa and Scythopolis, ARAM 23, 2011, 425–445 |
| Peleg-Barkat 2014 | O. Peleg-Barkat, Fit for a King: Architectural decor in Judaea and Herod as trendsetter, BASOR 371, 2014, 141–161 |
| Peleg-Barkat – Chachy 2015 | O. Peleg-Barkat – R. Chachy, The Architectural Decoration of the Herodium Mausoleum, in: R. Porat – R. Chachy – Y. Kalman, Herod's Tomb Precinct 1, Herodium, Final Reports of the 1972–2010 Excavations Directed by Ehud Netzer (Jerusalem 2015) 314–348 |
| Raviv – Zissu 2020 | D. Raviv – B. Zissu, Tombs with Decorated Facades in the Judean Countryside, ZDPV 136/2, 2020, 152–175 |
| Rosenthal-Heginbottom 2022 | R. Rosenthal-Heginbottom, Swinging Handles/›Door Knockers‹ from Nysa-Scythopolis, in: W. Atrash – A. Overman – P. Gendelman (eds.), Cities, Monuments and Objects in the Roman and Byzantine Levant: Studies in Honour of Gabi Mazor (Oxford 2022) 59–69 |
| Segal 2014 | A. Segal, Hellenistic Sanctuary, in: A. Segal – M. Eisenberg – J. Młynarczyk – M. Burdajewicz – M. Schuler, Hippos-Sussita of the Decapolis: The First Twelve Seasons of Excavations (2000–2011) I (Haifa 2014) 128–147 |
| Seigne 2006 | J. Seigne, Les monuments funéraires de Gerasa de la Décapole (Jordanie), in: J.-C. Moretti – D. Tardy (eds.), L'architecture funéraire monumentale. La Gaule dans l'empire romain. Actes du colloque oragnisé par l'IRAA du CNRS et le Musée Archéologique Henri-Prades, Lattes 11.–13.10.2001 (Paris 2006) 141–158 |
| Seigne – Morin 1995 | J. Seigne – T. Morin, Preliminary Report on a Mausoleum at the turn of the BC/AD century at Jarash, AAJ 39, 1995, 175–191 |
| Shtober-Zisu 2014 | N. Shtober-Zisu, The Geographical, Geological and Geomorphological Settings of the Sussita Region, in: A. Segal – M. Eisenberg – J. Młynarczyk – M. Burdajewicz – M. Schuler, Hippos-Sussita of the Decapolis: The First Twelve Seasons of Excavations (2000–2011) I (Haifa 2014) 32–39 |
| Stepansky 1999 | Y. Stepansky, Two Mausolea on the Northern Fringes of the Roman-Period Cemetery of Tiberias, 'Atiqot 38, 1999, 73*–90* (Hebrew) |
| Uscatescu 2022 | A. Uscatescu, Assembling Columns. Construction Process through the Mansons' Marks from the Macellum of Gerasa (Jerash, Jordan), Levant 54/3, 2022, 378–405 |
| Zingboym 2018 | O. Zingboym, The Necropoleis, in: M. Eisenberg, Hippos-Sussita of the Decapolis: The First Twelve Seasons of Excavations (2000–2011) II (Haifa 2018) 24–43 |

*Michael Eisenberg, The Zinman Institute of Archaeology, University of Haifa, Haifa, 3498838 Israel.*
*[e] mayzenb@gmail.com*

*Arleta Kowalewska, The Zinman Institute of Archaeology, University of Haifa, Haifa, 3498838 Israel.*
*[e] arleta.kow@gmail.com*

Carlos Fabião – Trinidad Nogales – Nova Barrero – Amílcar Guerra – Joaquim Carvalho – José María Murciano – Rafael Sabio – Catarina Viegas – Sofia Borges – Ricardo Laria Machado – Daniel Moreno – João Aires – Sandro Barradas

# ANFITEATRO DE *AMMAIA (LUSITANIA)*

## NUEVO EJEMPLO DE MODELO PROVINCIAL[1]

**Abstract**
The Roman Amphitheater of *Ammaia (Hispania-Lusitania)* is a new archaeological discovery, an example of a Roman provincial model in the public buildings of spectacles. In this article we analyse different aspects: its discovery, constructive elements and building characteristics, as well as its chronology, use and abandonment. Its model can be included in the provincial examples of *Lusitania*, where five amphitheatres have been documented to date.

## *AMMAIA*

La ciudad romana de *Ammaia*, ubicada en el centro de la provincia de *Lusitania* a 100 km al noroeste de la capital provincial *Augusta Emerita*, es una creación *ex novo* del Principado de Augusto, hacia el cambio de la Era, en la actual comarca de Marvão (Portugal) – CNS 300 del sistema portugués de identificación de patrimonio/ yacimientos arqueológicos[2].

Las ruinas de la ciudad eran bien conocidas desde tiempos de los humanistas, aunque con dudas sobre su nombre[3], estas fueron aclaradas de modo definitivo en 1931, por el hallazgo de un epígrafe de homenaje a Claudio por la *civitas ammaiensis* (IRCP 615) publicado por José Leite de Vasconcelos en 1932[4]. Aunque fue clasificada como Monumento Nacional en 1949 – IPA 00001844, del Sistema portugués de clasificación del Patrimonio Arquitectónico[5] – por encontrarse en terrenos privados pertenecientes a propietarios contrarios a cualquier intervención arqueológica, estuvo fuera del alcance de los investigadores varias décadas. En 1997 el Ingeniero Carlos Melancia, antiguo ministro de la República portuguesa e inversor local en el área del turismo, decidió adquirir los terrenos del yacimiento arqueológico y crear la Fundación Cidade de Ammaia con el objetivo de promover el estudio, conservación y puesta en valor de sus vestigios, gestionando el monumento[6]. Así entró la ciudad romana en el circuito de la investigación[7].

En los primeros años los trabajos se centraron en la puerta sur de la ciudad, en el forum, unas termas públicas y un espacio doméstico que se encontraba bajo una casa rural, hoy convertida en el Museo Monográfico de la ciudad de *Ammaia*[8]. Así se reconoció el perímetro urbano, particularmente su muralla que abarca unas 22 hectáreas, y se identificaron algunos edificios públicos.

---

[1] Trabajo desarrollado en el marco del Proyecto Nacional I+D »Augusta Emerita: Modelo Urbano, Arquitectónico y Decorativo en Lusitania I« (PID2020-114954GB-I00), financiado por el Ministerio de Ciencia e Innovación.
[2] <https://arqueologia.patrimoniocultural.pt/index.php?sid=sitios&subsid=48078> (31.03.2023).
[3] Guerra 1996.
[4] Vasconcelos 1935.
[5] <http://www.monumentos.gov.pt/site/app_pagesuser/SIPA.aspx?id=1844> (31.03.2023).
[6] Pereira 2009.
[7] Guerra 2021, 177–186.
[8] Pereira 2009; Corsi 2014; Guerra 2021.

1   Imagen aérea ideal de la ciudad de *Ammaia* a partir del Proyecto Radio-Past (Reconstrucción 3D: Michael Klein – 7Reasons Medien GmbH, Áustria)

Desde entonces se suponía, por observaciones en superficie, que los edificios lúdicos, teatro y anfiteatro, se ubicarían en la zona Norte, en las afueras del área amurallada[9].

De 2009 a 2013, un gran proyecto internacional de prospecciones no invasivas que abarcó toda el área urbana y suburbana, el proyecto RadioPast, posibilitó un conocimiento detallado de la estructura urbana que, como fundación en área no ocupada previamente, dibuja un modélico ejemplo de ciudad romana al modo vitrubiano, basada en un entramado rectilíneo ortogonal[10]. Estas prospecciones no lograron identificar la presencia de los edificios lúdicos, dando consistencia a la idea de que, si existían, se ubicarían en el área donde siempre se supuso que estarían en las afueras de la ciudad, en la zona Noroeste (fig. 1).

Esta área ha sido en realidad prospectada pero sus resultados no han sido concluyentes. Particularmente, el área donde está el anfiteatro anteriormente había sido considerada como lugar de ubicación del teatro[11]. También había sido identificada con una cantera de extracción pétrea, una observación efectivamente correcta, como se comentará, pero que hizo descartar el lugar como punto de interés para la investigación[12].

En el año 2018 el Museo Nacional de Arte Romano/Fundación de Estudios Romanos de Mérida, en asociación con el Centro de Arqueología de la Universidade de Lisboa (Uniarq), la Fundación Cidade de Ammaia y el apoyo del municipio de Marvão, promovió un proyecto internacional, con un equipo luso-español, que tenía por objetivo la identificación y estudio de los edificios lúdicos de la ciudad romana. Con el apoyo del Ministerio de Cultura, a través de las Ayudas para Proyectos Arqueológicos en el Exterior, se comenzó a explorar la zona noreste del entorno urbano que naturalmente fue elegida como la que potencialmente interesaba al proyecto[13].

---

[9]   Vermeulen et al. 2005; Pereira 2009.
[10]  Corsi 2014; Corsi – Vermeulen 2012.
[11]  Vermeulen et al. 2005; Pereira 2009.
[12]  Corsi 2012, 163; Meyer et al. 2012, 109–110.
[13]  Nogales et al. 2020.

2   Vista general del área intervenida (Archivo MNAR/ZniR Sensing Solutions). Resultados de las prospecciones geomagnéticas (elaboración propia en base a imágenes del Archivo MNAR/ZNiR Sensing Solutions y de la Unidad de Servicio de Métodos no destructivos en Arqueología, IAM, CSIC)

## ANFITEATRO DE AMMAIA: PROSPECCIÓN Y DESCUBRIMIENTO

El equipo científico comenzó en 2018 a plantearse la posibilidad de actuar en un área en la que se observaba una vaguada de forma cóncava, que se encontraba excavada artificialmente en la roca y que en la fotografía aérea de entonces era, si cabe, más evidente mediante la presencia de una densa masa arbórea que la remarcaba aún más.

Durante la campaña de 2019, se decidió realizar dos tipos de intervenciones: una preliminar de prospecciones geofísicas que confirmase la existencia de estructuras arqueológicas y, en base a ella, en otra fase posterior intervenir con excavaciones sistemáticas. Además, la cuenca descrita al estar cubierta por la densa vegetación no permitía a través de las fotografías aéreas disponibles observar la exacta orografía del terreno, por lo que, en una segunda fase, se planteó también la creación de un Modelo Digital del Terreno.

Las prospecciones geomagnéticas fueron llevadas a cabo por Victorino Mayoral Herrera, José Ángel Salgado Carmona y Cristina Charro Lobato, pertenecientes a la Unidad de Servicio de Métodos no destructivos en Arqueología, perteneciente al Instituto de Arqueología-Mérida (CSIC, Junta de Extremadura). La instrumentación usada fue un gradiómetro de flujo modelo Grad601-2 de la casa Bartington.

Los resultados de las prospecciones documentaron de forma clara la presencia de dos líneas paralelas de muros de tendencia circular, que cerraban el otro semicírculo que mostraba el corte en la roca, para formar así una elipse que demostraba que el equipo se encontraba ante la presencia de un anfiteatro (fig. 2).

La decisión para la idoneidad del sondeo fue basada en dos indicios: el principal era que había que intervenir en una zona en la que las prospecciones presentaban unas estructuras que podían ser interpretadas como una posible puerta de acceso monumental, viendo la silueta y la orientación del óvalo, así como su relación con la ciudad. A ello se sumaba un indicio menor, cuál era la presencia en superficie de un gran sillar de grauvaca, que el equipo limpió y documentó en los días de las prospecciones, y que ejemplificaba la presencia en una cota inmediata de restos constructivos, posiblemente derrumbes de la fase de abandono del edificio.

Después de los primeros sondeos que confirmaron la presencia del anfiteatro, sometimos una exitosa candidatura de financiación a la Fundación »La Caixa«, en ámbito del Programa »Promove Regiones Fronterizas 2019«, una financiación que acompañó los trabajos subsecuentes.

3   Vista de la *porta triumphalis*, 2019 (foto N. Barrero)

## EXCAVACIÓN

Una vez identificada la presencia del anfiteatro, se inició la excavación por un sondeo en el área donde se percibía la presencia de una puerta (la *porta triumphalis*) con sus accesos, al parecer, flanqueada por las *carceres*, un modelo bien conocido en edificios similares[14].

El sondeo posibilitó la identificación de un umbral de cuidada construcción en granito, flanqueado por dos paredes que formaban el acceso al interior de la arena, construidas con bloques de grauvaca de color ceniciento bien tallados. La presencia de distintos agujeros en el umbral, unos de formato rectangular junto a los extremos del umbral, y otros circulares de menor talla, en el centro del mismo, evidenciaban la existencia de una puerta de dos hojas, abriendo para el exterior, una vez que el umbral ostentaba un resalte en su cara interna. Los agujeros rectangulares serían las bases de las jambas de madera que sostenían la puerta, mientras que los agujeros menores se destinarían a posibilitar su cierre. El conjunto de agujeros rectangulares, tres, y los menores, nueve, hacen suponer que la puerta tuvo una remodelación que la estrechó, en un posterior momento indeterminado de la existencia del anfiteatro. Por otra parte, los elementos que flanqueaban la entrada son también diversos: del lado Norte, un gran sillar de granito, paralelepipédico, con la cara menor apuntada a la entrada y la mayor a la arena, y del lado Sur un gran boque bien tallado de grauvaca, también paralelepipédico, pero con la cara mayor apuntada a la entrada y la menor a la arena, que son suficientemente dispares para suponer que podrían ser elementos de una misma etapa constructiva. A esta remodelación más tardía estará también asociada la utilización de largas lajas graníticas en el acceso exterior del que se conservan solamente tres elementos de un conjunto que debería ser más numeroso (fig. 3).

Desde la puerta se observaban los arranques de la pared perimetral de la arena construida en una edilicia muy sencilla de bloques de piedras variadas (esquisto, cuarcita, grauvaca y, poco, granito) sin argamasa, solamente unidos por tierra. Así comprobamos que el edificio no usó de *opus caementicium*, como es usual en los típicos anfiteatros de graderío de madera, de los que se conocen ejemplos por todo el Imperio Romano[15].

La excavación no ha sido particularmente rica en materiales. Tres monedas tardías, tres AE4, dos con las dos *victoriae* y otra ilegible, nos dan una cronología de emisión hacia el 342–348 d. C., y fragmentos de un ánfora lusitana del tipo Almagro 51C permitieron determinar que el edificio estaría en uso a finales del siglo IV e incluso durante el siglo V d. C. La presencia de

---

[14]   Golvin 1988.
[15]   Golvin 1988, *passim*.

docena y media de clavos de hierro en la zona de la puerta ha sido muy sugerente para la posible construcción de madera, que el estado actual de la estructura no permite identificar.

A partir de aquí, se trazó un extenso plan de excavación que no se ha concluido. Por un lado, se apuntó a la excavación de las *carceres* que se percibían en la prospección geofísica y, aquí, tuvimos alguna sorpresa. Aunque salían perfectamente definidos los dos compartimentos al Sur de la *porta*, lo que parecía otro compartimiento del lado Norte de esta en realidad no existe. El sondeo de ese lado reveló solamente un potente relleno de cascajo contenido por la pared que delimitaba la arena y la que componía el acceso a la *porta*. Del lado Sur, se descubrieron dos compartimientos con vanos de acceso a la arena con umbrales de granito. Ambos compartimientos sufrirán remodelaciones a lo largo de su utilización, pero es imposible fecharlos con seguridad más allá de una relación de anterioridad/posterioridad que se observa en algunos de sus paramentos constructivos.

Percibimos también que por el lado Sur la *carcer* se apoyaba directamente en la cara externa de la muralla de la ciudad construida con bloques graníticos, conservada sólo al nivel de su base. El granito ha sido la materia prima utilizada mayoritariamente en la edilicia pública de *Ammaia*, extraída y transportada desde las canteras de Pitaranha, como la analítica demostró[16]. Este granito utilizado masivamente en los edificios públicos, incluyendo la muralla, aparece de un modo muy puntual y selectivo en el anfiteatro, un dato curioso, que dirá más sobre la disponibilidad de la inversión en la construcción del edificio que de la efectiva disponibilidad de materias primas pétreas más nobles.

Esta relación entre el edificio lúdico y la muralla de la ciudad, una implantación en las afueras del recinto urbano, que corresponde a la mayoría de los casos documentados de anfiteatros en el Imperio Romano[17], plantea desde luego un problema de diseño del edificio, dado que no sería posible mantener un diseño regular geométrico del contorno exterior del mismo, por anteponerse la muralla. La única explicación que podemos plantear es que habría prevalecido una opción pragmática, al utilizar esa cara exterior de la muralla para apoyar la *cavea*, necesariamente de menor anchura en ese área.

Acompañando la cara exterior de la muralla, identificamos una extensa zanja que segmentó parcialmente las paredes de las *carceres*. No resulta claro si esta zanja es obra de la Tarda Antigüedad o de la Edad Media, relacionada con la defensa de la ciudad, un foso que se asocia a la muralla primigenia que se mantuvo como el principal elemento defensivo, o simplemente es producto de la extracción de piedra de época moderna que se conoce en el sitio, cierto es que se rasgó en un momento en que el anfiteatro estaría sin uso. El relleno de la zanja no ha permitido extraer conclusiones más determinantes.

La pared que delimitaba la arena se construyó en *opus incertum* de bloques de dimensión irregular de cuarcita y esquisto, con prevalencia de la primera. La continuación de la excavación reveló que aproximadamente dos tercios del edificio se apoyaba o en el substrato arcilloso o directamente en las canteras de las que se extrajo el material pétreo utilizado en la construcción. Sólo la parte al Norte de la *porta triumphalis* se hizo sobre base de cascajo, resultante también de las actividades extractivas. La geología local es compleja. Hay un substrato dominante de cuarcita, en el lado Oeste, pero con áreas donde se intercalan esquistos muy blandos y también una importante bancada de grauvaca muy dura, lo que posibilitó la extracción de los bloques paralelepipédicos que conformaron parte del acceso a la *porta triumphalis*.

Estas canteras estuvieron también activas en época moderna, lo que plantea algunos problemas de conocimiento del edificio. Por ejemplo, la bancada de grauvaca, situada en el eje mayor del anfiteatro, alineada con la *porta triumphalis*, era visible desde el inicio, por lo que no sabemos si alguna estructura perteneciente al edificio existía. En otras áreas, rellenos con basura moderna cubrían directamente la roca.

En el proceso de excavación pudimos reconocer una buena parte de la pared del *podium*, que se presenta continua, excepto en el lado Oeste, donde se observa un vano, de acceso a un pequeño

---

[16] Taelman et al. 2012.
[17] Golvin 1988, 408.

espacio construido. El vano de acceso a la arena se encuentra moldurado con canterías y umbral de granito, de cuidada labor. La parte trasera de este espacio era el frente de cantera, sin que se observe acceso por ahí, pues el único acceso sería directamente desde la arena. Tal como sucedió con las *carceres*, este espacio fue amortizado con el cierre del vano por una pared de mampostería. Las jambas de la puerta de conservaban tumbadas en el interior del pequeño compartimento, por lo que sabemos que el vano tendría al menos 1.8 m de alto, dependiendo de otros elementos pétreos o latericios que pudieron componer la altura de las jambas. No se identificó el dintel, que pudo ser de madera o habría desaparecido antes del colapso final del vano.

En estos primeros trabajos percibimos que el relleno de la arena era sencillo, de sedimento limpio, sin apenas materiales arqueológicos, por lo que decidimos removerlo en buena parte con medios mecánicos, naturalmente, siempre bajo supervisión. En el decurso de esos trabajos pudimos también reconocer algunos aspectos importantes del edifico y de su historia. Por un lado, percibimos que la construcción de la arena ha sido compleja, con un relleno antrópico de cascajo muy potente en el lado Este en dirección a la *porta triumphalis* con casi dos metros de potencia, cara a la superficie de la arena en la banda Oeste, donde asienta directamente sobre la roca de base de esquisto una solución arquitectónica relacionada con el sistema de construcción.

Junto a la pared perimetral de la arena, eran muy irregulares los niveles de derrumbe del *podium*, en algunos puntos relativamente potente y en otros casi inexistente, por lo que concluimos que el edifico habría sido objeto de expolio de piedra en su fase de abandono. Afortunadamente, en el Noroeste, encontramos un punto donde el *podium* sufrió un derrumbe súbito y unitario, conservándose los elementos *in situ*. Por la observación de este punto, pudimos concluir que el *podium* mediría unos 3 m de alto.

4   Vista aérea del anfiteatro de *Ammaia*, 2022 (foto J. Carvalho, Fundação Cidade de Ammaia)

## EDILICIA Y ESTRUCTURA MONUMENTAL

Las soluciones arquitectónicas que se aplican al diseño y ejecución del edificio y que se han podido documentar hasta el momento son muy variadas. Se busca una respuesta adaptada a los condicionantes previos orográficos en cada flanco y ceñida a la concepción previa del edificio, que marcaba su ubicación en este punto de la periferia de la ciudad. En este sentido, el diseño de la obra plantea una acomodación a la ladera del macizo esquistoso, modificado en parte por la cantera pre-existente o coetánea a la construcción del anfiteatro, que explota las incursiones de grauvacas. El modelo de implantación del anfiteatro corresponde al llamado tercer tipo de Golvin: en flanco de colina, por lo cual la pendiente se utiliza para apoyar la *cavea*, con otra parte asentada sobre terreno antrópico[18]. Este es el mismo modo adoptado en el anfiteatro de la capital provincial, *Augusta Emerita*, aunque con escala y modos arquitectónicos muy distintos. Ello implica diferentes soluciones constructivas, a la vez que se busca un intento de dar uniformidad al edificio, especialmente al anillo del muro que delimita la arena (figg. 4. 5).

En el flanco oeste, el edificio se adosa a la ladera de esquisto, creando un muro con cara de mampostería de cuarcitas de tamaño mediano y pequeño, que aparece bien careada, trabada a seco. El interior del muro está relleno con cuarcitas y esquistos mezclados con tierras, que se adaptan a la irregularidad del terreno en este punto. Se ha retirado la vegetación en esa zona de ladera y se ha limpiado superficialmente, pero no se observa ningún elemento que permita sugerir hasta el momento la creación de gradas a partir de la excavación de la roca natural. No sabemos tampoco cuál sería el límite del edificio por esa parte. Es posible que una pared rural existente, delimitando un viejo camino ya sin uso, pudiera estar superpuesta al límite del anfiteatro.

Este modelo de mampostería del muro de delimitación de la arena ha sido reconocido en otros puntos de su perímetro, siempre con el mismo formato. Singularmente, también se ha podido documentar el enfoscado que debió recubrir su superficie y dar unidad al conjunto. Estas concentraciones de revoco de cal, que probablemente cubrirían y ennoblecerían estos paramentos, se encuentran documentados en distintos puntos, en ocasiones alcanzando espesores destacados que permite suponer distintas superposiciones del mismo. En algunos puntos se pudieron documentar pequeños restos aún adheridos al muro, lo que confirma dicha solución y también concentraciones de tierras calcáreas en la base del mismo, en algún caso con fragmentos de material constructivo latericio, que sirvieron para igualar la superficie antes de ser estucada.

Más al norte, en el contacto entre los esquistos y los afloramientos grauváquicos, se ha podido documentar una pequeña estancia, abierta a la arena, y monumentalizada mediante umbral y jambas de granito, dos conservadas *in situ* y otras dos derrumbadas. La estancia cierra en su interior con una gran masa pétrea, habilitando un espacio reducido de apenas 3 m cuadrados (fig. 6).

En este mismo flanco, siguiendo un poco más al norte, donde fue identificada la cantera[19], la extracción de grauvaca ofrece un frente de perfiles rectos y planos, a los que el muro se adosa con gran facilidad, creando también un revestimiento constructivo de mampostería bajo los mismos parámetros antes mencionados. Este frente de cantera está en el eje de la *porta triumphalis* y podría ser el lugar donde existiría una tribuna, que no se conserva. En ese área apareció un tambor de columna de granito de 0.5 m de diámetro y 0.6 m de alto, con una concentración de *tegulae*, ambos elementos son posibles indicios de que ahí se podría ubicar alguna construcción destacable del edificio.

Probablemente la dureza del frente de grauvaca limitó el esfuerzo de desbaste en la fase constructiva, lo que motivó una cierta deformación de la elipse que delimita la arena, que pierde regularidad en la zona Oeste.

En el flanco Sur, la orografía del terreno presenta una suave pendiente de orientación noroeste-sureste, hacia la ribera del río Sever. En la zona de contacto entre el frente de ladera y dicha pendiente, se realizaron extracciones de grauvaca, colapsadas al inicio de la excavación por material moderno, lo que permitió hipotetizar sobre una posible cantera moderna en este punto.

---

[18] Golvin 1988, 407.
[19] Meyer et al. 2012, 109.

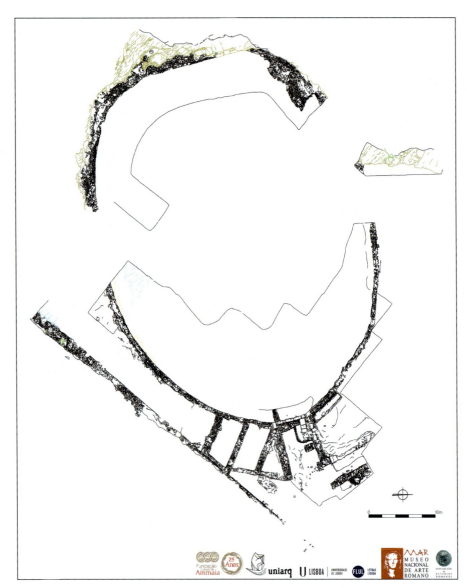

5   Planimetría del anfiteatro de *Ammaia*, 2022 (Fundaçao Cidade de Ammaia/Fundación de Estudios Romanos)

El edifico parece limitado en el exterior por la muralla sobre la que apoya la cerca moderna. El muro que delimita la arena continúa en todo el perímetro con alzados entre 50 hasta 126 cm y anchura en torno a 60–70 cm. El relleno de ambos límites del anillo, parece encontrarse en la roca natural, que por la parte más próxima a la muralla parece tener aportes antrópicos, de tipo arcilloso. Próxima a la muralla, esta superficie permitió escalonar el terreno para apoyar la cimentación del muro.

El muro perimetral delimita una arena de considerables dimensiones: unos 54 m en su eje mayor y 40 m en el menor. A pesar de la deformación comentada, estas cifras nos dan una proporción de 1.35, característica de los anfiteatros excavados en el terreno[20], como es este caso.

En el este del edificio los sondeos realizados frente al interior del umbral de acceso de la *porta triunphalis* permitieron comprobar que tuvo importantes aportes artificiales para subir la cota del terreno en este punto y crear una explanada a nivel en la arena. Los aportes que hasta ahora han sido documentados confirman al menos 1.8 m de espesor. Están conformados por capas sucesivas de arcillas muy compactadas, con pequeños esquistos, que le dan gran solidez.

---

[20]  Golvin 1988, 289.

6 Estancia en el lado oeste del anfiteatro, 2022 (João Aires, Fundação Cidade de Ammaia)

La *porta triumphalis* es un espacio monumentalizado. El corredor de acceso debió ser en rampa, enlosado por piezas de granito de las que quedan tres al interior, en el contacto entre el corredor y el umbral. Una es casi cuadrada (80 × 90 cm) y las otras dos rectangulares (80 × 55 cm). Todas ellas tienen su cara superior biselada. Los muros que marcan dicho corredor de acceso tienen un revestimiento de sillares de grauvaca, bien alineados y careados, mientras que su interior está conformado por un mampuesto de piedras cuarcíticas irregulares, de tamaño pequeño y mediano aplicado en seco. Bajo ellos se documentó otra hilada que se encontraba adelantada y con presencia de cal, y que podría tratarse de una cimentación subterránea. El umbral tiene 4.8 m de longitud y 50 cm de ancho y está configurado por cinco piezas de granito, de distintas proporciones y tamaños (la de mayor tamaño mide 1.2 m de longitud, la más pequeña aproximadamente 50 cm). Las lajas del umbral presentan numerosas perforaciones que deben corresponder con las distintas remodelaciones de las puertas de acceso. En los extremos se rebajan sendas cajas cuadradas de 34 por 15–20 cm aproximadamente, para embutir las jambas que permitirían la movilidad de las hojas de la puerta. Una tercera caja, menor a las descritas, de 20 por 12 cm, se ubica cercana al límite noroccidental. Un gran bloque de granito con una esquina rebajada y otro de grauvaca monumentalizan el acceso y dan muestra, una vez más, de las distintas reformas que sufrió el edificio en su vida de uso. Las puertas, tal y como muestra el resalte de las losas de granito, debieron abrir hacia el interior del corredor. Hasta el momento, éste es el único acceso conocido del anfiteatro, aunque no descartamos la posibilidad de que pueda identificarse otro acceso en el flanco norte, aún poco conocido, debido a la necesidad de mantener la zona de tránsito necesaria para la infraestructura de la excavación.

Al norte del acceso, el anillo murario de la arena está cedido hacia el interior de ésta por la presión ejercida por las tierras desplazadas y acumuladas precipitadamente hacia este punto, dada la inclinación del terreno. Estos aportes, que hoy cubren el área de juegos, están constituidos por arcillas, siendo prácticamente inertes en cuanto a material arqueológico. Los sedimentos acumulados llegaron a colmatar la altura del muro que no era visible en el terreno antes del inicio de la excavación aunque las estructuras se localizaron a escasísima profundidad, apenas 15–20 cm en los puntos mejor conservados. Parte de estos muros cedieron sobre la arena, donde fueron documentados en su fase de derrumbe. Que este flanco del edificio era la salida natural de las correntías producidas por las lluvias se evidencia en el hecho de que se realizaron aperturas de desagüe en el lienzo, que permitieron dicha función, un sistema ya empleado en otras construcciones de la ciudad, como el pórtico del foro. En este lienzo al norte de la puerta, el sondeo al intradós del muro de la arena permitió comprobar los densos rellenos del anillo murario, mediante capas de arcillas muy compactas mezcladas con esquistos de pequeño tamaño.

Al sur de la *porta*, la solución es muy distinta. Se construyen dos estancias pareadas, que crean un triángulo, entre el corredor y el inicio de las mismas. Este espacio triangular, a modo de cuña, de nuevo se colmata con rellenos antrópicos similares a los observados al norte del acceso. Este espacio, que a priori rompe la estructura conocida *cunei* de los anfiteatros, permite que las estancias queden perpendiculares a la muralla. Las estancias presentan mampostería de cuarcita a seco, sin argamasa, carenada en su cara vista al interior de la estancia, con un relleno de cuarcitas y esquistos de pequeño tamaño trabados con tierra. Se emplean piezas de mayor tamaño en la base de los muros, mientras que en el alzado son de mediano y pequeño tamaño. El acceso a dichas estancias se realiza desde el interior de la arena, señalados los umbrales con bloques bien escuadrados de granito de menos de 1 m de longitud. La superficie ocupada por las estancias es de unos 24 m² en el caso de la estancia A y de unos 19 m² en la estancia B. El suelo se conforma con distintas capas de arcilla compactada. Los muros laterales de las estancias se apoyan en la base de la muralla de la ciudad, aunque este punto aún no está contrastado y habrá que esperar a futuras campañas de excavación para completar la información sobre la relación entre ambas estructuras. Se documentan distintas remodelaciones en las estancias, con engrosados y refuerzo de los lienzos, empleando para ello lajas de pizarra e incluso material latericio; quizá fue necesaria esta reparación por la presión ejercida por el terreno en este punto o simplemente por el normal desgaste de un edificio con larga diacronía de uso. También los accesos fueron cegados en un momento posterior al uso lúdico del edificio (fig. 7).

7   Vista aérea de las *carceres*, 2021 (foto J. Ventura)

Suponemos que el graderío del anfiteatro debió completarse con estructura de madera, al modo de otros edificios semejantes conocidos[21]. Sin embargo, no ha podido documentarse hasta el momento ningún elemento estructural que permita reconocer esta construcción lígnea. Es cierto que se han documentado dos decenas de clavos de hierro durante la intervención, pero no son un número suficiente como para argumentar dicha hipótesis. Sin embargo, creemos que una solución constructiva mixta, obras de mampostería y estructura de madera, se debió adaptar fácilmente al terreno y dar una verdadera funcionalidad al edificio. Quizá dicha estructura no fuese fija y se creara un graderío desmontable durante la celebración de los *munera* así como otros tipos de espectáculos públicos que probablemente acogiera. Esto reduciría los problemas de mantenimiento que seguramente generaría una estructura fija de madera.

## CRONOLOGÍA

Ante la ausencia de epigrafía que determine fechas fundacionales, es difícil establecer la cronología de la construcción del anfiteatro. Los mejores datos que tenemos posibilitan proponer un *terminus post quem* para la construcción, en base a los materiales arqueológicos encontrados en estratos anteriores a la construcción en el área del acceso a la *porta triumphalis* y en los rellenos que soportarían el graderío en la zona Nordeste del edificio, y una posible fecha de amortización del edificio, en base a los materiales arqueológicos más recientes documentados.

En estos estratos previos a la construcción del anfiteatro o a lo largo de su edificación, se identificaron fragmentos de terra sigillata itálica, un sello *C.MF* in *planta pedis* (sello OCK 1132), y también algún fragmento de sigillata sudgálica de La Graufesenque y un borde de ánfora del tipo Haltern 70, procedente del valle del Guadalquivir, en el área subyacente al acceso a la arena. El mismo panorama de cerámicas finas se observa en los rellenos que soportaban el graderío en el área Este del edificio. Aquí, junto a algunos escasos fragmentos de terra sigillata itálica, donde merece particular relieve un fragmento de borde de cálix decorada del tipo Conspectus R8, se reconocen también escasos fragmentos de terra sigillata gálica.

Este panorama *post quem*, una vez más, con todas las limitaciones que una observación de este tipo implica, sobretodo en este caso en que no están todavía finalizados los trabajos, admite un abanico cronológico entre los finales de la dinastía Julio-Claudia y la etapa Flavia temprana para la construcción inicial del edificio.

Los restantes materiales arqueológicos, no muy abundantes, apuntan para una larga diacronía de utilización hasta los fines del siglo IV o el V. En este caso, valoramos las monedas encontradas en el área de los rellenos de la arena, particularmente los AE4, pero también los fragmentos de bordes y asas de ánforas lusitanas del tipo Almagro 51C, producidas en los estuarios del Tajo o Sado. Hay fragmentos de ánforas de este tipo procedentes de los derrumbes del área de la *porta*, pero también del relleno de la arena.

Tenemos así un ámbito cronológico comprendido entre mediados del siglo I y fines del siglo IV o V de nuestra Era. En el transcurso de tan larga diacronía el edificio tuvo seguramente muchísimas reconstrucciones/remodelaciones que, de momento, podemos observar, sobre todo en las diferencias en el aparejo constructivo, pero muy difíciles de fechar, más allá de la sencilla consideración de anterioridad y posterioridad.

La amortización final del edificio se hizo cerrando con paredes de albañilería los vanos de acceso a la arena, tanto en las *carceres* junto a la *porta triumphalis* como en el pequeño compartimiento adosado a la cantera. No se excluirá la posibilidad de tener un uso el recinto en época posterior a la amortización, por ejemplo, como aprisco de ganado, pero no tenemos ninguna prueba arqueológica de este supuesto uso, además de la referencia toponímica que sobrevivió hasta hoy, el área del anfiteatro conserva el micro topónimo de *picadero*, quizás la perduración de remota memoria de sus usos pasados.

---

[21] Golvin 1988.

## EL ANFITEATRO DE *AMMAIA* EN EL CONTEXTO DE LOS ANFITEATROS DE *LUSITANIA*

El completo estudio sobre el anfiteatro romano de Golvin vino a cimentar algunos de los parámetros esenciales a la hora de analizar un edificio de estas características; se trata de un patrón diseminado por todo el imperio, pero adaptando sus formas a distintos condicionantes, especialmente topográficos y sociales. Y este aspecto de adaptación territorial es lo que analizamos en los ejemplos lusitanos.

El investigador francés identificaba en el momento de su edición sólo dos anfiteatros en la provincia de *Lusitania*[22] que eran *Augusta Emerita* y *Conimbriga*. Apenas unos años más tarde, en ocasión de la celebración del Bimilenario del anfiteatro de *Augusta Emerita* en 1992, dada la *inauguratio* del emeritense en el año 8 a.C., en la monografía editada por el Museo Nacional de Arte Romano (MNAR) »El Anfiteatro en la Hispania Romana«, ya se recogía la existencia de cinco posibles anfiteatros en *Lusitania*[23], *Augusta Emerita, Conimbriga, Caparra,* Bobadela y Évora (fig. 8).

La iniciativa del MNAR de registrar en un solo Corpus los anfiteatros conocidos se venía a unir al volumen precedente del »Teatro en la Hispania Romana«[24], a los que posteriormente se incorporó »El Circo en Hispania Romana«[25]. La intención era dar a conocer nuevos ejemplos monumentales de los edificios de espectáculos que, en ocasiones, se escapaban a la bibliografía internacional. Muchos de estos edificios eran fruto de trabajos locales, a veces de emergencia urbana, como el ejemplo de algunos circos hispanos y, en consecuencia, eran nuevos hallazgos escasamente conocidos.

Es evidente que en *Hispania*, en el contexto de lo que se podrá denominar arquitectura del espectáculo, los edificios a tal fin conservados se clasifican en los tres grupos de teatros, anfiteatros y circos, siguiendo este orden por su presencia numérica[26], una tónica que se podría extender a las provincias occidentales, pues en Oriente los estadios fueron muy numerosos dada su tradición y versatilidad de uso.

Los anfiteatros lusitanos documentados arqueológicamente en la actualidad son cinco: *Augusta Emerita, Conimbriga, Capera,* Bobadela, y *Ammaia*, objeto de nuestro estudio desde 2018. Hay otros posibles anfiteatros lusitanos que han sido apuntados como hipótesis, pero que precisan de su confirmación constructiva y documental; *Ebora, Aeminium, Vissaium* e *Igaedis*.

En el caso de la ciudad de Évora[27], se han planteado sucesivas hipótesis sobre los edificios de espectáculos, que todavía no poseen evidencia arqueológica. Es cierto que existía la propuesta de un teatro[28], y en los avanzados y útiles trabajos de fotografía aérea[29], se quiso intuir la presencia de recintos públicos como el teatro o anfiteatro; será en el estudio de Correia, donde tome cuerpo la propuesta de un anfiteatro en la ciudad, alineado con el eje mayor del foro, y ›visible‹ en la fosilización urbana en las manzanas colindantes al S. del foro[30]. En su análisis se daban las dimensiones de los ejes de la elipse 80 (E/O) × 65 (N/S) m[31]. Y estas mismas dimensiones y planteamientos sirvieron para incorporarlas al corpus de teatros, anfiteatros y circos hispanos[32]. Los últimos estudios sobre la ciudad de Évora, acompañados por los datos de excavaciones más recientes, ponen en cuestión esta hipótesis, decantándose más por la presencia de un teatro junto al recinto forense

---

[22] Golvin 1988, 275–277 tabl. 26.
[23] Álvarez – Enríquez 1995, *passim*.
[24] Álvarez 1983.
[25] Nogales – Sánchez-Palencia 2001.
[26] Ramallo 2001, 117.
[27] Como último, Carneiro 2021.
[28] Alarção 1983, 112.
[29] Mantas 1986.
[30] Correia 1995, figg. 1. 2.
[31] Correia 1995, 345.
[32] Ramallo 2001, 117.

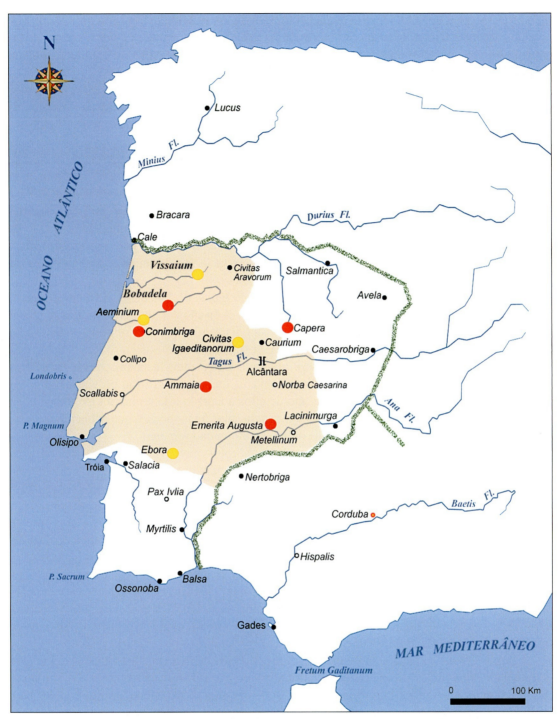

8   Mapa de la *Lusitania* reelaborado a partir de V. G. Mantas (2010), con la localización de los anfiteatros documentados arqueológicamente (rojo) y aquellos edificios posibles (naranja)

que de un anfiteatro[33]. Estaría, pues, el anfiteatro de *Ebora* pendiente de ser ubicado y confirmado por la evidencia arqueológica. Tal vez la arqueología urbana depare novedades en el futuro.

También en su día y a modo de hipótesis, el Prof. J. de Alarção[34] planteaba la existencia de edificios de espectáculos, quizá teatro y anfiteatro, no lejos del foro en la zona alta de la antigua

---

[33] Carneiro 2021, 169–170 fig. 3.
[34] Alarção 2008, 51–57.

*Aeminium*. Nuevos análisis sobre la ciudad confirman la fosilización del trazado urbano con una notable curvatura, teniendo los anchos muros de las antiguas edificaciones tal vez los restos de las potentes cimentaciones que precisaban este tipo de fábricas monumentales[35]. Por el momento, no deja de ser un verosímil planteamiento que debe acreditarse arqueológicamente.

Otras dos nuevas y sugerentes hipótesis son los anfiteatros de *Vissaium* e *Igaedis*, propuestas que ha efectuado P. Carvalho en el reciente »Workshop Internacional Anfiteatros Romanos da Lusitânia«, celebrado en Marvão el 18 y 19 de noviembre de 2022, recogidas en algunas de sus publicaciones más recientes.

En *Vissaium* la hipótesis de ubicación de un anfiteatro se basa en la topografía de la ciudad, en cuyo casco antiguo se aprecia una desviación del trazado rectilíneo *decumanus maximus*, y se dibuja una elipse que se ha fosilizado en el callejero actual[36]. Sus dimensiones serían de unos 85 × 68 m, propias de un anfiteatro de dimensión mediana, cercano al de *Conimbriga*[37]. La construcción de este monumento aprovecharía la colina natural del terreno, uso habitual constructivo en numerosos casos[38]. También señalan sus estudiosos la posición alineada con respecto al forum, siguiendo el cercano ejemplo de Bobadela y, si fuera cierta, de la hipotética propuesta de *Ebora* de Correia[39].

La otra hipótesis planteada es el posible anfiteatro de *Igaedis*[40]. Los datos, de momento escasos, están en proceso de estudio. Los autores relacionan el diseño del hipotético anfiteatro con el de la vecina Bobadela en cuanto a su posible dimensión y trazado. Los futuros trabajos del equipo dirigido por P. C. Carvalho continúan analizando esta sugerente hipótesis.

De confirmarse los hipotéticos casos, *Lusitania* sería la provincia hispana con más anfiteatros registrados, en número de nueve. Lo más interesante es que en el territorio provincial se documentan tipos de anfiteatros diversos, cada uno de ellos adaptado a la realidad topográfica y, en consecuencia, a las necesidades urbanísticas y, sin duda, a los fines sociales que debía realizar este tipo de edificio público, emblemático para cualquier comunidad romana.

Cada uno de los anfiteatros lusitanos responde a conceptos muy diversos, si bien se pueden establecer entre ellos ciertas similitudes, lo que nos invita a reflexionar sobre la organización de una política edilicia provincial relacionada con este tipo monumental de eminente carácter utilitario y social. Los anfiteatros formarían parte de una planificación pública provincial, que debía contar con las *officinae* territoriales especializadas en este tipo de trabajos, lo que se refleja en el empleo de semejantes sistemas constructivos y soluciones edilicias muy próximas. La eficiencia en los proyectos locales, de distinta dimensión, invitaría a contar con aquellos operarios habituados y especializados en la ejecución de estas obras. Al igual que se intuye una innegable cercanía en los proyectos y *officinae* de los teatros provinciales lusitanos[41], los anfiteatros debieron ser también objeto de planificación, con la presencia de estos trabajadores locales especializados y conocedores de los problemas del territorio. Y esta proximidad entre los anfiteatros lusitanos se pone de manifiesto en algunos ejemplos concretos.

La praxis urbana romana aconsejaba ubicar los edificios de espectáculos alejados del núcleo urbano para evitar molestias en el centro de la ciudad, porque este tipo de recintos en época imperial, de carácter muy utilitario, precisaban estar acompañados de dependencias de servicios para las distintas actividades que entrañaban los *munera*[42].

---

[35] Carvalho et al. 2021a, 149.
[36] Carvalho et al. 2021b, 442–444 fig. 3–5.
[37] Ruivo – Correia 2017; Correia 2021.
[38] Golvin 1988, 407 lám. XX, 3.
[39] Correia 1995.
[40] Carvalho et al. 2021c, 400.
[41] Fernandes – Nogales 2018.
[42] Golvin 1988, 408–412.

El anfiteatro de *Ammaia* se ubica extramuros. En *Lusitania* otros anfiteatros ubicados extramuros son el de *Capera*[43] y el de *Conimbriga*[44]. Los tres se asemejan en cuanto a su posición periurbana, estando el de *Conimbriga* literalmente ›adherido‹ a la muralla urbana, que es una de las cuestiones que plantea ciertas dudas en el de *Ammaia*, dada su compleja conexión con los restos de la posible muralla.

El anfiteatro de *Augusta Emerita*, también ›adherido‹ a la muralla, es bien distinto, pues el recinto desde su primera etapa se sitúa intramuros, y su contacto con la muralla fundacional se explica por la posible reforma de ampliación del recinto, a partir del primitivo anfiteatro inaugurado en el año 8 a.C. como atestiguan las inscripciones monumentales de las tribunas[45]. La reforma, en época flavia, acercó el anfiteatro al lienzo de la muralla fundacional; la primitiva fachada del recinto de espectáculos originalmente estaba separada de la muralla, conformando una estructura mixta de fábrica pétrea y madera, muy al uso en época augustea[46].

Desde un punto de vista edilicio los anfiteatros que más se asemejan al de *Ammaia* son los de *Capera* y Bobadela. Los tres monumentos parecen responder a dimensiones muy parecidas, pues se podrían considerar anfiteatros de un tamaño medio, nada que ver con la dimensión que alcanzó el de la capital provincial de *Augusta Emerita*, cuyos ejes de 126.30 × 102.65 m superan en mucho los de los tres mencionados.

El anfiteatro de *Ammaia* posee un emplazamiento singular en un terreno de pendiente natural. El aprovechamiento de las colinas y sus condiciones orográficas era habitual para aligerar los costes y simplificar la tarea constructiva[47].

En *Ammaia* la ladera que va a ocupar el anfiteatro se excava, lo que favorece proveerse del material necesario para su construcción, siguiendo la misma técnica que en el teatro romano de *Metellinum*, *Capera* y Bobadela, se levantan en un espacio menos accidentado.

Un elemento común entre los anfiteatros de *Capera* y Bobadela es su edilicia, muy semejante a la empleada en *Ammaia*: el aparejo del *podium* está efectuado en una fábrica de *opus incertum* de piedra local, que se refuerza en las zonas de acceso y vanos con piezas de granito en *opus quadratum* de cierta regularidad. Las imágenes del *podium* de Bobadela en su excavación[48] son de gran semejanza a lo conservado en *Ammaia* y a lo visible en *Capera*[49].

También para la construcción de la *cavea* se emplea el mismo sistema de muros radiales que conforman cajones con relleno interno, sobre los que presumiblemente se asentarían las estructuras de madera. En *Capera* pueden definirse con toda nitidez[50], en Bobadela las fotos de su excavación también parecen atestiguar este sistema constructivo[51].

Estos aspectos constructivos, definidores de los patrones de los anfiteatros lusitanos de *Capera*, Bobadela y *Ammaia*, nos pueden indicar que los tres recintos fueron diseñados e inspirados por equipos de trabajadores muy próximos, formados en las mismas técnicas y habituados a construcciones de esta envergadura.

En cada lugar mandaba la topografía elegida para el emplazamiento, sin duda determinada por la posición más favorable y el espacio disponible dentro del *terminus*. Tal vez fueran cuadrillas itinerantes que se trasladaran por el territorio provincial para acometer estos encargos, contando en cada puesto con la mano de obra local. Un sistema común para dotar a estos núcleos urbanos, relativamente secundarios, de infraestructuras y servicios acordes a las demandas sociales y las posibilidades de inversión.

---

[43] Cerrillo 1995; Bejarano 2021, 68–70 fig. 6; Bejarano 2022, 80–98.
[44] Correia 1995; Ruivo – Correia 2017, 216.
[45] Nogales 2000, 34–42.
[46] Nogales 2021, 43–45.
[47] Golvin 1988, 407.
[48] Frade – Portas 1995, 369 fig. 4.
[49] Bejarano 2022, 80–88 fig. 11.
[50] Bejarano 2022, 83 fig. 7.
[51] Frade – Portas 1995, 369 foto 1.

Hablamos, por tanto, de modelos provinciales de anfiteatros lusitanos, recintos más utilitarios que artísticos, donde la población local, en este caso de centros comerciales y mineros, pasaba su tiempo de *otium* según las costumbres importadas de Roma desde el siglo I a. C., *panem et circenses*.

## BIBLIOGRAFÍA

| | |
|---|---|
| Alarção 1983 | J. de Alarção, Portugal Romano (Lisboa 1983) |
| Alarção 2008 | J. de Alarção, Coimbra. A montagem do cenário urbano (Coimbra 2008) |
| Álvarez 1983 | J. M. Álvarez Martínez, El Teatro en la Hispania Romana (Badajoz 1983) |
| Álvarez – Enríquez 1995 | J. M. Álvarez Martínez – J. J. Enríquez Navascués, El Anfiteatro en la Hispania Romana (Badajoz 1995) |
| Bejarano 2021 | A. M. Bejarano, *Capera*, en: T. Nogales Basarrate (ed.), Ciudades Romanas de Hispania I, Hispania Antigua, Serie Arqueológica 13 (Mérida-Roma 2021) 63–74 |
| Bejarano 2022 | A. M. Bejarano, El Suburbio Suroriental de Cáparra: el área funeraria y el anfiteatro, Anas 35, 2022, 73–103 |
| Carneiro 2021 | A. Carneiro, *Liberalitas Iulia Ebora*, en: T. Nogales Basarrate (ed.), Ciudades Romanas de Hispania I, Hispania Antigua, Serie Arqueológica 13 (Mérida-Roma 2021) 167–176 |
| Carvalho et al. 2021a | P. C. Carvalho – R. Costeira da Silva – S. Lacerda, *Aeminium*, en: T. Nogales Basarrate (ed.), Ciudades Romanas de Hispania I, Hispania Antigua, Serie Arqueológica 13 (Mérida-Roma 2021) 141–152 |
| Carvalho et al. 2021b | P. C. Carvalho – P. Sobral – J. Perpetuo, *Vissaium*, en: T. Nogales Basarrate (ed.), Ciudades Romanas de Hispania I, Hispania Antigua, Serie Arqueológica 13 (Mérida-Roma 2021) 439–447 |
| Carvalho et al. 2021c | P. C. Carvalho – A. Fernández – A. Redentor, *Igaedis*, en: T. Nogales Basarrate (ed.), Ciudades Romanas de Hispania I, Hispania Antigua, Serie Arqueológica 13 (Mérida-Roma 2021) 393–412 |
| Cerillo 1995 | E. Cerrillo, El anfiteatro de Cáparra, en: Álvarez – Enríquez 1995, 311–326 |
| Correia 1995 | V. H. Correia, O anfiteatro romano de Evora. Noticia de sua identificação, en: Álvarez – Enríquez 1995, 345–348 |
| Correia 2021 | V. H. Correia, *Conimbriga*, en: T. Nogales Basarrate (ed.), Ciudades Romanas de Hispania I, Hispania Antigua, Serie Arqueológica 13 (Mérida-Roma 2021) 125–139 |
| Corsi 2012 | C. Corsi, The Ammaia Project: Integrated Approaches for Studying Roman Towns in Lusitania, en: F. Vermeulen – G.-J. Burgers – S. Keay – C. Corsi (eds.), Urban Landscape Survey in Italy and the Mediterranean (Oxford 2012) 160–169 |
| Corsi 2014 | C. Corsi, Ammaia 2: The Excavation Contexts 1994–2011, Archaeological reports Ghent University 9 (Ghent 2014) |
| Corsi – Vermeulen 2012 | C. Corsi – F. Vermeulen (eds.), Ammaia 1: The Survey. A Romano-Lusitanian townscape revealed, Archaeological reports Ghent University 8 (Ghent 2012) |
| Fernandes – Nogales 2018 | L. Fernandes – T. Nogales Basarrate, Teatro romano de *Olisipo*: programas decorativos teatrales de Lusitania, en: C. Márquez – D. Ojeda (eds.), Escultura romana en Hispania VIII. Homenaje a Luis Baena del Alcázar (Córdoba 2018) 431–456 |
| Frade – Portas 1995 | H. Frade – C. Portas, A Arquitectura do Anfiteatro Romano de Bobadela, en: Álvarez – Enríquez 1995, 349–371 |
| Golvin 1988 | J.-C. Golvin, L'Amphithéâtre Romain. Essai sur le théorisation de sa forme et de ses fonctions (Paris 1988) |
| Guerra 1996 | A. Guerra, *Ammaia*, *Medobriga* e as Ruínas de S. Salvador de Aramenha. Dos Antiquários à Historiografia Actual, A Cidade. Revista cultural de Portalegre, Nova Série 11, 1996, 7–33 |
| Guerra 2021 | A. Guerra, *Ammaia*, en: T. Nogales Basarrate (ed.), Ciudades Romanas de Hispania I, Hispania Antigua, Serie Arqueológica 13 (Mérida-Roma 2021) 177–186 |
| IRCP | J. d'Encarnação, Inscrições romanas do *conuentus Pacensis* (Coimbra 1984) |
| Mantas 1986 | V. G. Mantas, Arqueología urbana e fotografía aérea: Contributo para o estudo do urbanismo antigo de Santarém, Évora e Faro, en: I Encontro Nacional de Arqueología Urbana, Setubal 1985, TrabArq 3 (Lisboa 1986) 13–26 |

| | |
|---|---|
| Mantas 2010 | V. G. Mantas, Ammaia e *Civitas Igaeditanorum*. Dois espaços forenses lusitanos, en: T. Nogales Basarrate (ed.), Ciudad y foro en Lusitania Romana/Cidade e foro na Lusitânia Romana (Mérida 2010) 167–188 |
| Meyer et al. 2012 | C. Meyer – R. Plesnicar – D. Pilz, Extramural magnetic survey, en: Corsi – Vermeulen 2012, 105–114 |
| Nogales 2000 | T. Nogales Basarrate, Espectáculos en Augusta Emerita, Monografías emeritenses 5 (Mérida 2000) |
| Nogales 2021 | T. Nogales Basarrate, Colonia Augusta Emerita, en: T. Nogales Basarrate (ed.), Ciudades Romanas de Hispania I, Hispania Antigua, Serie Arqueológica 13 (Mérida-Roma 2021) 33–61 |
| Nogales – Sánchez-Palencia 2001 | T. Nogales Basarrate – F. J. Sánchez-Palencia, El Circo en Hispania Romana (Madrid 2001) |
| Nogales et al. 2020 | T. Nogales – N. Barrero – J. M. Murciano – R. Sabio – C. Fabião – A. Guerra – J. Carvalho, Lusitania: investigación y proyecto arqueológico en la ciudad romana de *Ammaia*. Primeros resultados y expectativas de futuro, Informes y Trabajos. Excavaciones en el exterior 19, 2020, 16–32 <http://hdl.handle.net/10451/46324> (25.05.2023) |
| Pereira 2009 | S. Pereira, A cidade romana de *Ammaia*: escavações arqueológicas 2000–2006, Número especial de Ibn Maruan 1 (Marvão 2009) |
| Ramallo 2001 | S. F. Ramallo, La arquitectura del espectáculo en Hispania: teatros, anfiteatros y circos, en: T. Nogales Basarrate – A. Castellano, *Ludi Romani*. Espectáculos en Hispania Romana (Mérida 2001) 91–117 |
| Ruivo – Correia 2017 | J. Ruivo – V. H. Correia, Um quarto de século de investigação arqueológica en Conimbriga, en: T. Nogales Basarrate (ed.), Lusitania Romana: del pasado al presente de la investigación (Mérida 2017) 209–232 |
| Taelman et al. 2012 | D. Taelman – F. Vermeulen – M. De Dapper – D. De Paepe, The Stones of Ammaia (Portugal): use and provenance, en: A. Gutiérrez Garcia – P. Lapuente – I. Rodá (eds.), Interdisciplinary Studies on Ancient Stone. Proceedings of the IX Association for the Study of Marbles and other Stones in Antiquity (ASMOSIA) Conference (Tarragona 2009), Documenta 23 (Tarragona 2012) 117–126 |
| Vasconcelos 1935 | J. L. Vasconcelos, Localização da cidade de *Ammaia*, Ethnos 1, 1935, 5–9 – primeramente publicado en: O Século, Lisboa, 29/03/1932 |
| Vermeulen et al. 2005 | F. Vermeulen – M. De Dapper – C. Corsi – S. Deprez, Geoarchaeological Observations on the Roman Town of Ammaia, Internet Archaeology 19, 2005, DOI: 10.11141/ia.19.1 (31.03.2023) |

Sitio de Internet de información sobre el patrimonio arqueológico portugués: <https://www.patrimoniocultural.gov.pt/pt/patrimonio/patrimonio-imovel/patrimonio-arqueologico/endovelico-inventario/> (31.03.2023)

Sitio de Internet sobre el patrimonio arquitectónico portugués: <http://www.monumentos.gov.pt/site/app_pagesuser/Default.aspx> (31.03.2023)

*Carlos Fabião, Faculdade de Letras da Universidade de Lisboa, Alameda da Universidade, 1600-214 Lisboa, Portugal.*
*[e] cfabiao@edu.ulisboa.pt*

*Trinidad Nogales, Museo Nacional de Arte Romano, Calle José Ramón Mélida s/n, 06800 Mérida, España.*
*[e] trinidad.nogales@cultura.gob.es*

*Nova Barrero, Museo Nacional de Arte Romano, Calle José Ramón Mélida s/n, 06800 Mérida, España.*
*[e] nova.barrero@cultura.gob.es*

*Amílcar Guerra, Faculdade de Letras da Universidade de Lisboa, Alameda da Universidade, 1600-214 Lisboa, Portugal.*
*[e] aguerra@campus.ul.pt*

*Joaquim Carvalho, Fundação Cidade de Ammaia, Estrada da Calçadinha nº 4, 7330-318 São Salvador de Aramenha, Marvão, Portugal.*
*[e] jcammaia@hotmail.com*

*José María Murciano, Museo Nacional de Arte Romano, Calle José Ramón Mélida s/n, 06800 Mérida, España.*
*[e] jmaria.murciano@cultura.gob.es*

*Rafael Sabio, Museo Nacional de Arqueología Subacuática de Cartagena, P.º Alfonso XII, 22 , 30202 Cartagena, España.*
*[e] rafael.sabio@cultura.gob.es*

*Catarina Viegas, Faculdade de Letras da Universidade de Lisboa, Alameda da Universidade, 1600-214 Lisboa, Portugal.*
*[e] c.viegas@letras.ulisboa.pt*

*Sofia Borges, Fundação Cidade de Ammaia, Estrada da Calçadinha nº 4, 7330-318 São Salvador de Aramenha, Marvão, Portugal.*
*[e] sbammaia@hotmail.com*

*Ricardo Laria Machado, Fundação Cidade de Ammaia, Estrada da Calçadinha nº 4, 7330-318 São Salvador de Aramenha, Marvão, Portugal.*
*[e] ricardolariamachado@hotmail.com*

*Daniel Moreno, Fundação Cidade de Ammaia, Estrada da Calçadinha nº 4, 7330-318 São Salvador de Aramenha, Marvão, Portugal.*
*[e] danielmoreno.1394@gmail.com*

*João Aires, Fundação Cidade de Ammaia, Estrada da Calçadinha nº 4, 7330-318 São Salvador de Aramenha, Marvão, Portugal.*
*[e] jony_aires@hotmail.com*

*Sandro Barradas, Fundação Cidade de Ammaia, Estrada da Calçadinha nº 4, 7330-318 São Salvador de Aramenha, Marvão, Portugal.*
*[e] sandrobarradas1984@gmail.com*

Sabrina Geiermann – Hannelore Rose

# DAS RÖMERGRAB WEIDEN

## ASPEKTE SEINER PRÄSENTATION VOM 19. BIS IN DAS 21. JAHRHUNDERT

**Abstract**
This article offers an overview of the various aspects of the presentation of the Roman tomb in Cologne-Weiden. Shortly after its discovery in 1843 it was almost filled in again, yet it was finally acquired by the state of Prussia and perfectly reconstructed, protected and made accessible to the public. Over time, there was little new activity and gradually it fell more and more into oblivion, especially as access was difficult. Since 2017 a civic association has been taking care of the monument. The association has set up a space for education and experience in the neighbouring cottage, offers regular opening hours, and has initiated new scientific research. One example is an interdisciplinary research project, which produced a digitised recording of the burial chamber and presented the results in virtual 3D space. In this way, a three-dimensional digital twin was created, offering the possibility to better understand the complex structures as well as its objects and to make them accessible to a broad public.

»Die im Jahre 1843 beim Dorf Weiden, 9 km westlich von Köln zutage gekommene Grabkammer zählt unstreitig zu den bedeutendsten Denkmälern römischer Zeit im ganzen Norden; denn nördlich der Alpen gibt es nichts, das an Vortrefflichkeit der Erhaltung und Vollständigkeit der Ausstattung mit ihr verglichen werden könnte. Um so verwunderlicher ist es, daß dieses Denkmal selbst in Fachkreisen nur wenig bekannt ist.«[1]

Mit dieser Einschätzung beginnt Fritz Fremersdorf 1957 seine Monografie »Das Römergrab in Weiden bei Köln« – und daran hat sich bis heute nur wenig geändert. Doch lohnt es sich ungemein, dieses in vieler Hinsicht außergewöhnliche Denkmal stärker ins Bewusstsein der Forschung zu rücken, was hier insbesondere unter dem Aspekt seiner Präsentation geschehen soll. War diese in der Anfangszeit im wahrsten Sinne des Wortes vorbildlich, folgten danach viele Jahrzehnte, in denen das Denkmal eher wenig beachtet – aber glücklicherweise weitgehend unbeschadet – vor sich hin existierte. Nun aber haben erneut Zeiten des Um- und Aufbruchs begonnen, die das Römergrab aus seinem Dornröschenschlaf geweckt haben. Doch bevor von den Aspekten der Präsentation zu sprechen sein wird, sind zunächst das Monument und seine Entdeckungsgeschichte zu umreißen.

In der ersten Hälfte des 2. Jahrhunderts errichtete sich eine Gutsbesitzerfamilie 8,6 km vor der westlichen Stadtmauer des römischen Köln und unmittelbar an der Fernstraße, die von Köln ausgehend über Aachen nach Innergallien und an die Atlantikküste führte, ein Grabmonument. Dieses bestand aus einem oberirdischen Bau, für dessen Aussehen nur sehr wenige Hinweise vorliegen, und einem Hypogaeum, das wie ein römisches Speisezimmer gestaltet war – allerdings, da es ein Haus für die Ewigkeit sein sollte, in Stein umgesetzt (Abb. 1). Die Möblierung dieser Grabkammer bestand aus drei marmorverkleideten Klinen oder *lecti* in der Rückwand und den Seitenwänden. Diese sind in große Nischen mit gewölbtem Abschluss eingestellt. Am Fußende der seitlichen Klinen steht jeweils ein Sessel; hinzu kommen drei Marmorbüsten. Abgesehen von den drei großen gliedern weitere 29 kleine Nischen in harmonischer Anordnung die Wände. Ein Marmorsarkophag, der sich heute ebenfalls in der unterirdischen Grabkammer befindet, hatte seinen ursprünglichen Standort in der Etage darüber – also im Erdgeschoss –, stürzte jedoch, als im Laufe der Zeit das Gewölbe der Kammer einbrach, nach unten und wurde aus zahlreichen

---
[1] Fremersdorf 1957, 9.

1  Blick in die Grabkammer (Förderverein Römergrab Weiden e. V., Foto A. Thünker DGPh, Bonn)

Fragmenten rekonstruiert[2]. Der Sarkophag ist in das 4. Jahrhundert zu datieren und bildet somit einen guten Indikator für die lange Nutzungsdauer dieser Grablege. Von der oberirdischen Gestaltung des Grabmonumentes haben sich nur sehr wenige Fragmente erhalten, allen voran zwei Säulenbruchstücke aus Sandstein mit tuskanischen Kapitellen[3].

Die Entdeckungsgeschichte des Hypogaeums beginnt im Jahr 1843 und ist »einer anmuthigen Gunst des Zufalls«[4] zu verdanken. Kurz zuvor hatte der »Ackerbürger«[5] Ferdinand Sieger das Grundstück erworben und wollte darauf an einer Stelle unmittelbar an der Aachener Straße ein neues Wirtschaftsgebäudes errichten. Weiden war zu dieser Zeit ein stark landwirtschaftlich geprägtes Straßendorf der Bürgermeisterei Lövenich im Landkreis Köln und lag im Jahr 1843 in der preußischen Rheinprovinz. Bei den Fundamentierungsarbeiten für besagtes Wirtschaftsgebäude stieß Ferdinand Sieger zunächst auf große Steine und dann auf abwärtsführende Stufen, die in mehr als 5 m Tiefe vor einer steinernen Verschlussplatte endeten. Nachdem er die Stufen entfernt und die steinerne Tür zerschlagen hatte, wäre die Unternehmung beinahe schon wieder beendet gewesen, denn »es schien sich nichts vorzufinden, als eine äußerst compacte, zähe Erdmaße, aus Mergel mit untermischten Ziegeln und anderen Steinen«[6], jedoch keine Schätze der Art, wie Herr Sieger sie sich erhofft hatte.

Dennoch verbreitete sich die Kunde von dem ungewöhnlichen Fund rasch, und Bürgermeister Weygold aus dem angrenzenden Üsdorf sowie ein Gutsbesitzer aus Lövenich namens Dapper finanzierten gegen eine vereinbarte Fundteilung eine Ausgrabung unter Aufsicht eines Bergmannes[7]. Diese begann bereits am 10. April 1843. Wichtig für das weitere Schicksal der Grabkammer

---

[2] Sehr wahrscheinlich war er zuvor jedoch schon beraubt und zerschlagen worden.
[3] Horn 2019, 55; Noelke 2008, 449 mit Abb. 15.
[4] Schneider 1843, 5.
[5] Schneider 1843, 5.
[6] Schneider 1843, 6.
[7] Schneider 1843, 6–7; Urlichs 1843, 135.

war, dass es noch im Entdeckungsjahr zwei Publikationen gab, die das Monument bekannt machten. Als Erster, und zwar unmittelbar nach der Auffindung, berichtet davon Sebastian Roderich Schneider in einer kleinen Publikation mit Lithografien, die unter dem Titel »Nachricht über die Entdeckung eines römischen Grabmals« 1843 und dann in einem Neudruck 1913 erschien. Für diese Schrift stellten Weygold und Dapper Schneider wichtige Informationen zur weiteren Erforschung zur Verfügung und ermöglichten – zusammen mit dem Bürgermeister Klein – die Vermessung und Aufnahme der Grabkammer zur Anfertigung der Lithografien. Leider berichtet Schneider jedoch nicht sonderlich detailliert über die Grabung und die Auffindungsumstände der Stücke. Ebenfalls noch 1843 erschien zudem in den »Bonner Jahrbüchern« ein wissenschaftlicher Aufsatz von Ludwig Urlichs, einem Mitbegründer und gleichzeitig dem ersten Chronisten des Vereins von Altertumsfreunden im Rheinlande. Dieser stimmt auf der ersten Seite sogleich einen Abgesang auf das Grabmal von Weiden an: »Indessen darf unser Verein ein so wichtiges Denkmal nicht übergehen, und es ist seine Pflicht, so lange das Grab noch unser genannt werden kann, die bedeutendsten Werke daraus abzubilden und demselben, da mehr dafür zu thun die Beschränktheit der Mittel verbietet, wenigstens einen Abschiedsgruss zuzurufen. Denn dahin ist es gekommen, da trotz dringender Vorstellungen weder Staat noch Provinz sich seiner annehmen, dass das ganze Monument, Steine und Bildwerk, unsere Gegend verlassen und einen gastlicheren Boden suchen werden! Dem Vernehmen nach ist von mehreren Belgiern eine namhafte Summe für die Erlaubniss geboten worden, es abzubrechen und in Belgien wieder aufzubauen!«[8] Dazu kam es dann aber glücklicherweise doch nicht, denn das Königreich Preußen interessierte sich für die Funde. Und im Jahr 1844 gelang es diesem schließlich auf einer Auktion in Köln, das gesamte Ensemble zum Preis von 2300 Talern zu erwerben[9], d. h. nicht nur die Funde, sondern – und dieser Umstand ist nicht hoch genug zu bewerten – auch den betreffenden Teil des Sieger'schen Grundstücks, auf dem sich die Grabkammer befand.

Treibende Kraft in dieser Angelegenheit war Ignaz von Olfers, der Generaldirektor des Königlichen Museums in Berlin, der sich in der preußischen Denkmalpflege, die gerade erst im Entstehen begriffen war, sehr engagierte. Ihm gelang es, König Friedrich Wilhelm IV. davon zu überzeugen, das Projekt zu unterstützen – auch finanziell. Bereits zu diesem Zeitpunkt hatte sich zudem Ernst Friedrich Zwirner, der damalige Baumeister des Kölner Domes, vor Ort eingesetzt und die Interessen des preußischen Staates vertreten. So wurde er im weiteren Verlauf damit beauftragt, die Anlage instand zu setzen, mit einem Schutzbau zu versehen und für das interessierte Publikum zugänglich zu machen (Abb. 2. 3)[10].

Obwohl die Grabkammer selbst wie auch ihre zentralen Objekte wiederholt Gegenstand wissenschaftlicher Bearbeitung waren[11], sind andererseits immer noch viele Forschungsfragen offen.

Der zentrale Punkt für ihre Erhaltung ist in dem großen Interesse zu sehen, das dem Römergrab und seinen Funden gleich bei seiner Entdeckung entgegengebracht wurde[12]. Die kurz darauf realisierten Maßnahmen zu seiner Instandsetzung und Erhaltung sind für die damalige Zeit unerhört und völlig neuartig. Neuartig war erstens, dass man nicht nur an den Funden an sich interessiert war, sondern erkannte, dass der nahezu intakte antike Grabraum nördlich der Alpen eine absolute Ausnahme darstellte und deswegen an Ort und Stelle erhalten werden sollte. Zweitens

---

[8] Urlichs 1843, 134.
[9] Fremersdorf 1957, 11; Noelke 2011, 2. Noelke ist auch zu entnehmen, dass dafür ursprünglich die ungleich höhere Summe von 6000 Talern aufgerufen worden war.
[10] Fremersdorf 1957, 11; Noelke 2011, 2.
[11] Abgesehen von den beiden Publikationen seien hier genannt: Fremersdorf 1957; Sinn 2003, 307; Noelke 2008; Noelke 2011; Noelke 1982 (zu den Büsten) sowie aktuell Horn 2019 und Lee 2021. – Leider konnte Fritz Fremersdorf seine Monografie zum Römergrab nicht in dem Umfang verfassen wie ursprünglich geplant, da seine Aufzeichnungen zu den in Berlin befindlichen Kleinfunden im Zweiten Weltkrieg vernichtet worden waren (Fremersdorf 1957, 9). Dies ist umso bedauerlicher, als auch ebendiese Kleinfunde seit dem Zweiten Weltkrieg als verschollen gelten.
[12] Und dieses Interesse bestand, wie oben gezeigt, sowohl in der Bevölkerung wie auch in wissenschaftlichen Kreisen und nicht zuletzt auf der Ebene von Verwaltung und Politik.

2 Außenansicht von Schutzbau und Chaussee-Aufseher-Häuschen, 2019 (Förderverein Römergrab Weiden e. V., Foto A. Thünker DGPh, Bonn)

wurden die zentralen Steinobjekte – Kalksteinsessel, Büsten und Sarkophag – ebenfalls am Fundort belassen. Lediglich die Kleinfunde wurden in das Königliche Museum in Berlin[13] verbracht, sind allerdings zum allergrößten Teil seit dem Ende des Zweiten Weltkriegs verschollen[14]. Und drittens ist die Maßgabe, die Grabkammer für den Besuch interessierter Bürger herzurichten für die damalige Zeit als bahnbrechend zu bezeichnen. Peter Noelke bezeichnete dieses Konzept und seine Umsetzung zu Recht als »Pioniertat früher Denkmalpflege in Deutschland«[15].

Ernst Friedrich Zwirner restaurierte das Hypogaeum sehr behutsam und respektvoll. Er schloss das eingestürzte Gewölbe und errichtet darüber einen dreischiffigen, quadratischen Schutzbau (Abb. 4), der im Inneren mit seinen Pfeilern, welche über Rundbögen mit Lisenen an den Außenwänden verbunden sind, an eine romanische Kapelle erinnert. In Baumaterial und Ausführung orientierte er sich bewusst an römischen Vorbildern. So ist der Schutzbau aus Feldbrandziegeln gemauert, deren Fugen durch Fugenstrich betont werden, und der Boden erinnert an römische Opus-Sectile-Böden. Zur Beleuchtung des Hypogäums diente eine mittige, kreisförmige Öffnung im rekonstruierten Gewölbe – Elektrizität gab es damals noch nicht –, mit der eine Lichtkuppel in der Decke des Schutzbaus korrespondiert. Das Glas dieser Kuppel liegt nicht bündig auf, sondern lässt bewusst einen Spalt, über den Feuchtigkeit entweichen kann. Der Bau ist somit nicht nur ästhetisch sehr gelungen, er erfüllt auch alle wesentlichen praktischen Kriterien für einen Schutzbau: Er schützt den römischen Bau zuverlässig vor Witterungseinflüssen und sorgt für ausreichende Belüftung, sodass sich keine Moose und Ähnliches bilden. Zudem ist trotz der Verwendung identischer oder ähnlicher Materialien erkennbar, welche Bereiche neuzeitlich ergänzt wurden, etwa indem beim Türgewände die Oberfläche der Sandsteinquader anders behandelt wurde. Und schließlich ermöglicht der Schutzbau ganzjährig die Zugänglichkeit für Besuche. Diese wird über einen zur Straße hin vorgelagerten Eingangsbereich mit einem Giebeldach gewährt, der über der Tür die Inschrift »Römergrab« (Abb. 2) trägt und mittels einiger Treppenstufen den Höhenunterschied von ca. 1,60 m zum heutigen Straßenniveau überwindet.

---

[13] Heute: Antikensammlung der Staatlichen Museen zu Berlin. Dies geschah wohl aus der Überlegung heraus, dass es am Auffindungsort kein Museum gab. Jedenfalls äußert Fremerdorf sein Bedauern, dass sie nicht ins Kölner Wallraf-Richartz-Museum gelangt sind, welches bis zum Bau des Römisch-Germanischen Museums auch römische Funde beherbergte (Fremersdorf 1957, 11).

[14] Schneider 1843, 21–29 zählt diese Funde, sortiert nach Materialien, auf.

[15] Noelke 2011, 3.

3 Schnitt durch die Punktwolke: unten das Hypogaeum, darüber der Zwirner'sche Schutzbau und im Hintergrund das Chaussee-Aufseher-Häuschen (Grafik S. Geiermann scandric 3D Solutions)

Der Aspekt der Zugänglichkeit spielte im ursprünglichen denkmalpflegerischen Konzept eine zentrale Rolle. Um ihn zu gewährleisten, wurde unmittelbar neben dem Schutzbau ein sich in Form und Material harmonisch anfügendes Wohnhaus für einen Chaussee-Aufseher und seine Familie errichtet, zu dessen Aufgaben es gehörte, interessierten Personen den Zugang zum Römergrab zu ermöglichen. Dieses wurde 1912 mit elektrischem Licht ausgestattet.

Und in der Tat besteht dieser Gesamtkomplex aus römischer Grabkammer, Schutzbau und Aufseherhaus bis heute nahezu unverändert und zählt zu den frühesten und herausragenden Zeugnissen staatlicher Denkmalpflege in Deutschland – auch den Zweiten Weltkrieg hat er unbeschadet überstanden. Heute stehen nicht nur die Grabkammer, sondern auch Schutzbau und Chaussee-Aufseher-Häuschen unter Denkmalschutz. Und in der Nachfolge Preußens befindet sich die Liegenschaft seit 1946 im Eigentum des Landes Nordrhein-Westfalen.

In starkem Kontrast zum denkmalpflegerisch vorbildlichen und respektvollen Umgang durch Zwirner steht eine Episode aus dem Jahr 1947, als für die Ausstellung »Römisches Rheinland« auf Schloss Rheydt in Mönchengladbach die drei Büsten, einer der Sessel sowie der Sarkophag zur Verfügung gestellt wurden. Beim Abtransport lösten sich offenbar Teile der restaurierten Par-

4  Innenansicht des Zwirner'schen Schutzbaus. In der Mitte ist die Öffnung im Gewölbe der Grabkammer zu erkennen, im Hintergrund die beiden Tuffsteinsäulen (Förderverein Römergrab Weiden e. V., Foto A. Thünker DGPh, Bonn)

tien, sodass der Sarkophag auseinanderbrach und für die Ausstellung neu zusammengefügt werden musste. Als sich beim Rücktransport zeigte, dass er zu breit für die Tür der Grabkammer war, wurden Teile des linken Türgewändes abgearbeitet, um ihn wieder ins Hypogaeum verbringen zu können[16].

1955 erfolgte dann eine systematische fotografische Dokumentation[17]. Diese zeigt die Funde im Hypogaeum unter ästhetischen Gesichtspunkten angeordnet[18]: Zentral vor der Rückwand steht der Sarkophag, allerdings noch ohne Deckel. Dahinter ist mittig in der großen Nische eine der weiblichen Büsten zu sehen. Rechts und links des Sarkophags sind die – zu dieser Zeit noch nicht als solche identifizierten – Tuffsäulchen aus dem Erdgeschoss mit dem Kapitell nach unten aufgestellt, und vor ihnen lagern an der Seitenwand die – ebenfalls noch nicht sicher als solche identifizierten – pyramidenförmigen Urnenständer. Die Kalksteinsessel sind zentral vor die großen Nischen in den Seitenwänden gerückt und mit der Sitzfläche zur Mitte der Grabkammer ausgerichtet. Und rechts neben der Eingangstür lehnt eine Marmorplatte, die man zeitweilig für den Rest der zerbrochenen Tür hielt[19], welche aber später als Sarkophagdeckel erkannt wurde.

Nachdem Weiden, das bis dahin zur Bürgermeisterei Lövenich im Landkreis Köln gehört hatte, 1975 zusammen mit dieser in die Stadt Köln eingemeindet wurde, oblag die wissenschaftliche Betreuung dem Römisch-Germanischen Museum. Unter seiner Obhut erfolgten in der zweiten Hälfte der 1970er Jahre umfangreiche Restaurierungs- und Dokumentierungsarbeiten. An Letzteren war auch das Rheinische Bildarchiv beteiligt. Hinzu kam eine fotogrammetrische Bauaufnahme durch den Landeskonservator Rheinland[20]. In diesem Zusammenhang wurden die Objekte in der Grabkammer weitgehend so arrangiert, wie sie laut Schneiders Bericht bei der Auffindung angetroffen worden waren – und heute immer noch stehen (Abb. 1): Am Fußende der in die Seitenwände eingelassenen Klinen befinden sich die Korbsessel, und zwar mit dem Rücken zur Eingangswand. Die große Nische der linken Wand überfängt die beiden weiblichen Büsten. Ihnen gegenüber in der Nische der rechten Seitenwand steht die männliche Büste[21].

---

[16] Fremersdorf 1957, 17. Fremersdorf stützt sich dabei auf Aussagen von Frau Otten, deren Mann zu dieser Zeit die Aufgabe des Grabwächters ausgeübt hatte. Bei Noelke 2008, 446 Abb. 7 sind Beschädigungen und Abarbeitungen grafisch dargestellt.

[17] Noelke 2011, 4. – Auf diese Fotos greift Fremersdorf in seiner Publikation von 1957 zurück.

[18] Fremersdorf 1957, Taf. 1.

[19] Fremersdorf 1957, 17.

[20] Noelke 2008, 437 Anm. 1; Noelke 2011, 4.

[21] Die weiblichen Büsten in der Nische sind »an eben diesem Ort in aufrechter Stellung gefunden worden« (Schneider 1843, 15) und befinden sich folglich aller Wahrscheinlichkeit nach an ihrem antiken Aufstellungsort. Die männliche Büste wurde hingegen umgestürzt in der Erdschicht gefunden, mit der die Grabkammer verfüllt war. Doch hält Schneider es für sehr wahrscheinlich, dass diese Büste in der Nische der rechten Wand gestanden hatte (Schneider 1843, 16).

In den rückwärtigen Raumecken befindet sich je ein pyramidenförmiger Stein, in dem eine Urne mit der Öffnung nach unten vorgefunden worden war[22]. Und mangels Alternativen wurde der aus Fragmenten zusammengesetzte Sarkophag mittig vor der Rückwand platziert, jedoch mit etwas Abstand zu dieser.

Während all dieser Jahrzehnte hatte weiterhin der Modus Bestand, den Zugang für die Öffentlichkeit über die im Wärterhaus wohnende Familie zu regeln. Doch irgendwann funktionierte dieses System nicht mehr und fand 2014 sein Ende. Zuvor war das Römergrab jedoch über viele Jahre de facto für Besucher kaum zugänglich und trat im öffentlichen Bewusstsein auch in keiner Weise in Erscheinung[23]. Um diese Missstände zu ändern, gründete sich 2017 der Förderverein Römergrab Weiden e.V.[24] Ziel dieses Trägervereins ist es, die Grabkammer durch regelmäßige Öffnungszeiten wieder zugänglich zu machen und einer breiten Öffentlichkeit in vielfältiger Weise zu vermitteln. Dazu wurde das Wärterhaus in einen Lern- und Erlebnisort umgewandelt und das gesamte Ensemble im Sommer 2019

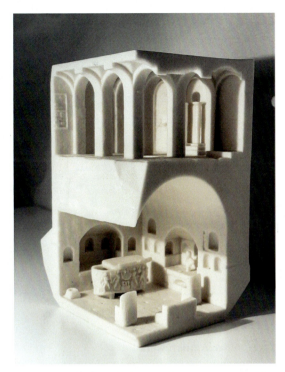

5   Das taktile Modell der Grabkammer wurde im 3D-Druckverfahren hergestellt. Es steht in der Ausstellung im Wärterhaus (Foto S. Geiermann scandric 3D Solutions)

wiedereröffnet. Es verfügt nun über ein nach modernsten Maßstäben eingerichtetes kleines Museum mit Wandprojektionen, Hörstationen und Tastmodell (Abb. 5), das die wesentlichen Informationen zur Grabkammer, ihrem regionalen Umfeld und zum römischen Totenkult vermittelt. Aus dem Schutzbau und der Grabkammer wurden hingegen alle didaktischen Elemente entfernt, sodass diese Räume samt der originalen Ausstattung nun so authentisch wie möglich erfahrbar sind – ein für Deutschland einmaliges Erlebnis.

Gerade an dem Detail, wo die Informationstafeln angebracht wurden, werden die Veränderungen im Umgang mit der Grabkammer und im Verständnis von Präsentation besonders deutlich: Lange Zeit waren sie sowohl in der Grabkammer selbst[25] als auch an den Wänden des Zwirner'schen Schutzbaus montiert. Erst mit der Eröffnung des Lern- und Erlebnisortes 2019 war es möglich, Grabkammer und Schutzbau von jeglichen Informationstafeln zu befreien, sodass jetzt der Ort ganz für sich wirken kann.

Ein nicht unwichtiger Aspekt, um die Bekanntheit des Monumentes bei der Kölner Bevölkerung zu erhöhen, war ferner die Umbenennung der nächstgelegenen Straßenbahnhaltestelle von »Schulstraße« in »Römergrab Weiden«. Zudem wurden erste Forschungsvorhaben initiiert[26]. So startete 2017 am Archäologischen Institut der Universität zu Köln ein interdisziplinäres Forschungsprojekt, dessen Gegenstand die digitale Erfassung antiker Architektur, deren Umwand-

---

[22] Schneider 1843, 12. Allerdings erwähnt Schneider auf S. 11 in die Ecken eingestellt die Säulenstümpfe und erst neben diesen, zur Mitte hin, die pyramidenförmigen Urnenständer.

[23] Danach war der Zugang über die Abteilung Denkmalverwaltung bei der Bezirksregierung Köln geregelt, aber ebenfalls nur in sehr eingeschränktem Maße möglich.

[24] <www.roemergrab.de> (27.10.2022).

[25] Vgl. Sinn 2003, 325 Abb. 14: im Innern der Grabkammer rechts neben der Tür. Dort sind sie auch noch im Schnitt der Punktwolke (Abb. 3) zu erkennen.

[26] Lee 2021.

6 Mit dem terrestrischen Laserscanner wurden die Grabkammer, der Schutzbau, das Wärterhaus sowie das Umfeld dreidimensional vermessen. Insgesamt 51 Standorte wurden für die maßstabsgerechte Erfassung der Architektur benötigt (Foto S. Geiermann scandric 3D Solutions)

lung in ein virtuelles Modell und ihre Präsentation im virtuellen 3D-Raum am Beispiel des Römergrabes Weiden waren[27].

Das gemeinschaftliche Projektziel von Universität und Technischer Hochschule Köln war es, die römische Grabkammer mittels neuester Mess- und Aufnahmemethoden dreidimensional zu erfassen, diese Resultate mit den Erkenntnissen der archäologischen Wissenschaft anzureichern und auf dieser Grundlage das Römergrab zuletzt virtuell begehbar zu machen. Zurzeit wird das Ergebnis dieses Projektes in der »CAVE« des Regionalen Rechenzentrums der Universität zu Köln präsentiert[28].

Auf die verschiedenen Dokumentationsmethoden wird hier nicht eingegangen, vielmehr werden der Mehrwert einer digitalen Vermessung und ihrer Präsentation erläutert. Der dreidimensionale digitale Zwilling, ob mit einem Vermessungsinstrument oder im Structure from Motion-Verfahren erzeugt, bietet die Möglichkeit, komplexe Strukturen oder empfindliche Objekte besser zu verstehen. Er kann nicht die Forschungsarbeiten am eigentlichen Objekt ersetzen, bietet aber die Option, dieses einem breiten Publikum zugänglich zu machen und es aus anderem Blickwinkel zu betrachten. Genau das hat sich der Förderverein zu Nutze gemacht und unter anderem den Gästen des Römergrabes in Zeiten der Schließung die Möglichkeit gegeben, einen virtuellen Rundgang im Internet zu besuchen. Dieser basiert auf den Daten des terrestrischen Laserscanners (Abb. 6) und wurde mit ergänzenden Informationen sowie Fotos ausgestattet.

Zudem ist mittlerweile ein aus hochauflösenden Fotos (Abb. 7) bestehender virtueller Rundgang mittels einer VR-Brille in der Ausstellung im ehemaligen Chaussee-Aufseher-Haus eingerichtet. Diese Tour ermöglicht auch in ihrer Mobilität eingeschränkten Menschen, die römische Grabkammer zu erfahren. Dabei steht der Besucher im Mittelpunkt eines Scannerstandortes und kann sich ähnlich wie bei Google Street View um 360° drehen.

Das taktile Modell (Abb. 5) bietet Personen mit eingeschränkter Sehfähigkeit die Möglichkeit, die Grabkammer zu ertasten. Das gedruckte Modell entstand auf Grundlage der 3D-Punktwolke[29] und wurde von einem Modellbauer nachgearbeitet. Ein aus der Punktwolke und extrem hoch-

---

[27] Deschler-Erb u. a. 2019/2020, 203. s. hierzu auch die Dokumentation auf youtube: <https://youtu.be/WN-hdxS__P8> (27.10.2022).

[28] CAVE – Cave Automatic Virtual Environment bezeichnet einen Raum zur Projektion einer dreidimensionalen Illusionswelt der virtuellen Realität. Es wird z. B. im Flugsimulator eingesetzt: <https://de.wikipedia.org/wiki/Cave_Automatic_Virtual_Environment> (27.10.2022).

[29] Punktwolke bezeichnet in der Geodäsie das Produkt einer Vermessung. Das zu dokumentierende Objekt wird mittels millionenfacher Messung in einer speziellen Software dreidimensional aufgebaut – der digitale Zwilling entsteht.

7    Nach dem eigentlichen Messvorgang des Scanners zeichnete eine integrierte HDR-Kamera 42 Einzelbilder in bis zu elf Belichtungsstufen auf. Das daraus generierte 80-Megapixel-Panorama wurde für die Einfärbung der Messpunktwolke verwendet (Foto S. Geiermann scandric 3D Solutions)

aufgelösten Fotos texturiertes 3D-Modell der Grabkammer und ihrer Einrichtung ermöglichte überdies den Besuchern der archäologischen Landesausstellung Nordrhein-Westfalen 2021/2022 »Roms fließende Grenzen«[30] in Köln einen virtuellen Blick in die Grabkammer.

Als besondere Souvenirs schließlich werden im Museumsshop des Römergrabes die Repliken der drei Porträtbüsten und des Sarkophags angeboten (Abb. 8). Dies ist ein netter Nebeneffekt der gewonnenen Daten, denn mittels 3D-Drucker können Befunde und Funde in allen Genauigkeitsstufen, Größen und Materialien vervielfältigt werden. Alle hier aufgeführten Resultate – vom virtuellen Rundgang bis zum 3D-Print der Objekte – basieren auf den verschiedenen Dokumentationsmethoden der digitalen Vermessung. Diese Verfahren eignen sich somit hervorragend, um Ausstellungen digital und dreidimensional zu konservieren oder schwer zugängliche Denkmäler erlebbar zu machen[31].

Das nächste Projekt des Vereins bildet der Anbau zusätzlicher Räumlichkeiten im rückwärtigen Bereich des Chaussee-Aufseher-Hauses. Denn Schutzbau und Hypogaeum wie auch der Lern- und Erlebnisort lassen aufgrund ihrer geringen Grundflächen nur eine sehr begrenzte Besucherzahl zu. Dies erweist sich im laufenden Betrieb als schwierig. Um auch größeren Gruppen – wie Schulklassen – den Besuch der Grabkammer zu ermöglichen, ist diese Erweiterung dringend erforderlich, denn durch sie ist eine Teilung in Kleingruppen und damit eine bessere Verteilung der Besucher in den verschiedenen Abschnitten möglich. Im Vorfeld und parallel zu den Bauarbeiten fand zudem eine archäologische Untersuchung der Fläche statt. Direkt bei den ersten Sondierungen im April 2022 kamen – neben anderen – römische Funde zutage; vor allem große Fragmente von Dachziegeln. Diese könnten durchaus vom Dach des Grabmals stammen. Weitere römische Funde wurden im Verlauf der Bauarbeiten allerdings nicht angetroffen. Die Eröffnung des Erweiterungsbaus ist für das Jahr 2024 vorgesehen. Welche Funde und Überraschungen in dieser Fläche schlummern, wird sich bald zeigen, denn die Bauarbeiten haben im Jahr 2023 begonnen.

So hat die Grabkammer seit ihrer Entdeckung vor 180 Jahren einige Umbrüche erlebt, und es ist zu hoffen, dass sie durch die Maßnahmen der jüngsten Zeit wieder stärker in das Bewusstsein der Bevölkerung wie auch der Wissenschaft rückt – bestimmt wird es auch nicht der letzte Umbruch gewesen sein. Es ist ein kleines Wunder, dass über diesen langen Zeitraum hinweg

---

[30] Im gleichnamigen Begleitband zur Ausstellung wird die Grabkammer zwar erwähnt (Schmitz 2021, 280–283), es geht dort jedoch nicht um das 3D-Modell und die virtuellen Rekonstruktionen, die in der Ausstellung zu sehen waren.

[31] <https://wadisura.scandric.net/> (27.10.2022).

8 Die Verkleinerungen der römischen Büsten können im Wärterhaus käuflich erworben werden (Foto S. Geiermann scandric 3D Solutions)

die zentralen Ausstattungselemente – Büsten, Sessel, Klinenverkleidung und Sarkophag – *in situ* verblieben sind, denn nur dort, im Zusammenspiel mit der harmonisch gestalteten Grabkammer, können sie ihre volle Wirkung entfalten und den heutigen Menschen einen Einblick in die römische Vergangenheit dieses Ortes gewähren.

## BIBLIOGRAFIE

| | |
|---|---|
| Deschler-Erb u. a. 2019/2020 | E. Deschler-Erb – S. Geiermann – S. Hageneuer – D. Ch. Wilk, Das Römergrab Weiden auf dem Weg in die virtuelle Welt, Kölner und Bonner Archaeologica 9/10, 2019/2020, 203–210 |
| Fremersdorf 1957 | F. Fremersdorf, Das Römergrab in Weiden bei Köln (Köln 1957) |
| Horn 2019 | H. G. Horn – Förderverein Römergrab Weiden e. V. (Hrsg.), Ein »ewiges Haus« – das Römergrab Weiden (Köln 2019) |
| Lee 2021 | D. Lee, STATUS – IMAGE – TOD. Untersuchungen zu den repräsentativen Aspekten in der Grabkammer in Köln-Weiden (unpublizierte Masterarbeit Universität zu Köln 2021) |
| Noelke 1982 | P. Noelke, Zu den Porträts der römischen Grabkammer von Köln Weiden, WissZBerl 31, 1982, 249–252 |
| Noelke 2008 | P. Noelke, Das »Römergrab« in Köln-Weiden und die Grabkammern in den germanischen Provinzen, KölnJb 41, 2008, 437–511 |
| Noelke 2011 | P. Noelke, Das »Römergrab« in Köln-Weiden und Grabkammern im Rheinland, Rheinische Kunststätten 238 (Neuss 2011) |
| Schmitz 2021 | D. Schmitz, Städte der Toten, in: E. Claßen – M. M. Rind – Th. Schürmann – M. Trier (Hrsg.), Roms fließende Grenzen. Archäologische Landesaustellung Nordrhein-Westfalen, Schriften zur Bodendenkmalpflege in Nordrhein-Westfalen 12 (Darmstadt 2021) 272–283 |
| Schneider 1843 | S. R. Schneider, Nachricht über die Entdeckung eines römischen Grabmals in Weiden bei Köln (Köln 1843, Neudruck Köln 1913) |
| Sinn 2003 | F. Sinn, Die Grabkammer in Köln-Weiden. Formen stadtrömischer Privatgräber für den lokalen Grabbrauch, in: P. Noelke – F. Naumann-Steckner – B. Schneider (Hrsg.), Romanisation und Resistenz in Plastik, Architektur und Inschriften der Provinzen des Imperium Romanum. Neue Funde und Forschungen. Akten des VII. internationalen Colloquiums über Probleme des Provinzialrömischen Kunstschaffens Köln 02.–06.05.2001 (Mainz 2003) 307–325 |
| Urlichs 1843 | L. Urlichs, Das römische Grabmal in Weyden bei Cöln, BJb 3, 1843, 134–148 |

*Sabrina Geiermann, Novalisstraße 26, 51147 Köln, Deutschland.*
*[e] sabrina.geiermann@scandric.de*

*Hannelore Rose, Räderscheidtstr. 6, 50935 Köln, Deutschland.*
*[e] hanne.rose@gmx.net*

Emmanouela Gounari

# ROMAN PORTRAITS FROM *PHILIPPI*[1]

**Abstract**
The paper deals with seven portraits found in the Roman colony of *Philippi* in excavations conducted during the last four decades. They were found in the theatre and in the late antique houses and most of them were reused as building material. In the theatre, two male and a female portrait were found, whereas in the houses a female, two male and a child's portrait were unearthed. One of the portraits is dated to the 1st century AD while the rest date to the 2nd century, a period of prosperity for the city. They most probably represent members of the local elite and were probably erected near the place they were found. Their discovery is important because until recently few portraits have been found in the city and the area of *Philippi*, although the Romanization of the city was quite apparent. The fact that they were used as building material may explain what happened to other portraits erected in *Philippi*.

The Roman colony of *Philippi*, founded in 42 BC after the Battle of Philippi[2], was a town that had an obvious Roman character. The dominance of the Latin language, which is proved by the inscriptions[3], confirms the strong western ties as does the presence of Roman institutions[4]. Moreover, the architectural layout of the city centre, where a new forum was erected, and the presence of Roman building types, such as the atrium house[5]. In addition, specific elements in the mosaic pavements[6], such as the circus theme and certain geometric patterns, as well as Roman forms of entertainment[7], reflect a predominant western influence[8].

Despite this ›Romanization‹ of *Philippi*, portraits, a characteristic element of the Roman culture, were a rather rare find until recently. Before the Second World War, a head of Augustus' grandson Gaius Caesar[9], and a bronze portrait of the 4th century emperor Gratian[10] were unearthed in the forum, whereas a portrait of Lucius Verus[11] was found reused as building material in the eastern city-walls. In addition, a portrait of Commodus[12] reused in a Byzantine wall near

---

[1] I would like to thank Dr. Haido Koukouli Chryssanthaki, Director Emeritus of the Ephorate of Antiquities of Kavala and Director of the Excavation of the theatre of Philippi, who assigned me the study of the sculptures of the theatre of Philippi. For the permission to publish the sculptures I would like to thank the current Director of the Ephorate of Antiquities of Kavala, Ms. Stavroula Dadaki. The publication of the sculptures from the University of Thessaloniki excavation is due to my participation in the team of the excavation from 1988–2018, under the direction of the late Professor of Byzantine Archaeology Georgios Gounaris and Professor Emeritus of Byzantine Archaeology Aristoteles Mentzos.
[2] Strab. 7, 331 fr. 41. Collart 1937, 224–227. 240; Brélaz 2018a, 19–27.
[3] For the use of the Latin language see Pilhofer 1995, 118–122; Brélaz 2018a, 85–90; Rizakis 2018, 199–200.
[4] Collart 1937, 259–260, 265 with catalogue of inscriptions referring to magistrates of the colony. See also Pilhofer 2009, for example inscriptions nos. 213. 214. 252. 253m. 257. 718. 743; Rizakis 2016, 176–180; Brélaz 2018a, 119–230 (with previous bibliography).
[5] For the atrium house see Gounari 2021.
[6] For the mosaic pavements see Gounari 2008a; Gounari 2008b.
[7] For gladiatorial games held at the theatre of the city see Brélaz – Rizakis 2003, 160; Pilhofer 2009, inscriptions nos. 87. 142–144. 296. For the transformation of the theatre to an arena see Karadedos – Koukouli Chrysanthaki 2007, 275–280.
[8] Brélaz 2018b, 156–157.
[9] Lapalus 1933, 449–452.
[10] Lapalus 1932, 360–371 pl. 20. There is also a dedicatory inscription for Gratian. Brélaz 2014, 133–134 no. 31.
[11] Chioti 2012, 250–251 cat. 27; Roger 1938, 30 fig. 5.
[12] Ntatsouli-Stavridis 1970, 65. 92 fig. 144; Chioti 2012, 255 cat. 34.

1 Male portrait from the theatre, Philippi Museum inv. Λ2224 (Ephorate of Antiquities of Kavala, photo E. Gounari)

Basilica B and a base for the statues of priestesses of the empress Livia from the forum[13] as well as dedicatory inscriptions found in different places in the city[14] are proof of the existence of more portraits which are now lost. The portraits of Gratian and Lucius Verus are also lost.

During recent decades, excavations brought to light seven new portraits. During the excavations conducted in the 1990s in the theatre before restoration works[15] the local Ephorate of Antiquities found three portraits. In the excavation of the late antique houses east of the Octagon Complex the School of History and Archaeology of the University of Thessaloniki unearthed four. Most of the sculptures were reused as building material; hence, their state of preservation is sometimes poor.

The portraits from the theatre were found near the eastern city wall. They are life-size and depict a woman and two men. The first male portrait (Philippi Museum inv. Λ2224) is fragmentary, as the right part of the head including the ear and part of the face is missing (fig. 1). The hair that is preserved is so damaged that only the general outline of the hairstyle can be discerned. The sculpture represents a youthful, clean-shaven man with short hair that lies close to the head arranged in thick locks that end in a fringe. Over the inner corner of the left eye, fork-shaped locks are observed, and on the left side in front of the ear a lock is turned inwards against the movement of the other locks on the brow. The hairstyle and the form of the face are typical of the Julio-Claudian period. Comparisons can be made with portraits of Tiberius, as for example with a head in Copenhagen[16] or two heads of the emperor in the Vatican Museums[17]. We can also compare it with portraits of Claudius, such as two heads in Copenhagen and another one in Woburn Abbey[18], as well as with portraits of Caligula[19]. Therefore, we can date the portrait from *Philippi* to the 1st century AD, perhaps to the mid-century. It was during the time of Claudius that the first forum of the city was constructed, which means that it was a period of prosperity for *Philippi*[20].

The second male head (Philippi Museum inv. Λ2221) is preserved with part of the neck and represents a mature bearded man with a wreath (fig. 2–3). The neck support suggests that the head was broken from a statue[21]. Part of the nose and the moustache along with part of the lips are broken off, as well as part of the left ear and the locks on the forehead. The man has a long

---

[13] Sève – Weber 1988, 474–479; Brélaz 2014, 276–280 no. 126.
[14] For example Brélaz 2014, 85–104 nos. 5–14; 170–171 no. 55; 176 no. 58 and many others. Brélaz 2018b, 158–161.
[15] For the theatre excavations Karadedos – Koukouli Chrysanthaki 1999, 69–86.
[16] Ny Carlsberg Glyptothek inv. 1445. Johansen 1994, 114–115 cat. 45; Fittschen – Zanker 1985, 11 cat. 10 (Replik 1).
[17] a) Musei Vaticani, Museo Pio Clementino, Sala dei Busti inv. 650. Polacco 1955, 119–120 pl. 15,1; 18,2; Helbig 1963, cat. 179; Fittschen – Zanker 1985, 11–12 cat. 10 (Replik 9). – b) Musei Vaticani, Galleria Chiaramonti 400, inv. 1641. Helbig 1963, cat. 348; Hertel 1982, 254 cat. 95; Andreae 1995, pl. 165–169.
[18] a) Ny Carlsberg Glyptothek inv. 1277. Johansen 1994, 142–143 cat. 59. – b) Ny Carlsberg Glyptothek inv. 1423. Poulsen 1962, 92–93 cat. 58 fig. 96–97; Johansen 1994, 144 cat. 60. – c) Angelicoussis 1992, 56–57 cat. 25.
[19] Head from Constantinople now in Copenhagen, Ny Carlsberg Glyptothek inv. 2687. İnan – Alföldi Rosenbaum 1979, 69 cat. 15; Johansen 1994, 136–137 cat. 56.
[20] Sève – Weber 2012, 12–16.
[21] Smith 2006, 268–269 cat. 170 with no. 1.

2   Male portrait from the theatre, Philippi Museum inv. Λ2221 (Ephorate of Antiquities of Kavala, photo E. Gounari)

3   Male portrait from the theatre, Philippi Museum inv. Λ2221 (Ephorate of Antiquities of Kavala, photo E. Gounari)

rectangular face with a curly full beard, with locks that part in the middle, and a heavy moustache. The hair is curly and better preserved at the sides under the wreath, whereas above the forehead the locks are very damaged. Above the wreath and at the back the locks are schematically worked, an indication that the monument was intended to be seen from the front. The wreath consists of elongated leaves, perhaps laurel, and is tied with a long ribbon that falls on the neck. The drill has been used for the curls of the hair at the sides and for the beard as well as for the rendering of the eyes. The pupils and the tear ducts are drilled, and the irises are incised. The eyelids are thin and heavy and the eyebrows prominent. Two horizontal furrows on the forehead and the nasolabial lines indicate the mature age of the man. The portrait can be compared with both imperial and private portraits. We can compare the hairstyle and especially the part over the forehead, as well as the beard that parts in the middle, with a head in the Archaeological Museum of Thessaloniki that represents Septimius Severus[22]. The forehead, the moustache, and the beard, as well as the eyelids can be also compared with portraits of Pertinax[23], such as a head in *Aquileia*[24], a colossal head in the Vatican Museum[25], or another one from *Ostia* in the same museum[26]. Moreover, there are affinities with private portraits, such as a portrait dated to the beginning of the 3rd century AD that is saved in three copies and according to Klaus Fittschen must represent an important person

---

[22] Despinis et al. 2010, 183–186 cat. 289 (Th. Stefanidou Tiveriou). According to Stefanidou Tiveriou it belongs to the second type of the emperor's portraits.

[23] von Heinze 1977, 160–170.

[24] Aquileia inv. 2624. Santa Maria Scrinari 1972, 67 cat. 198 (according to Scrinari the head represents Antoninus Pius). von Heinze 1977, 165 pl. 81.

[25] Musei Vaticani, Sala Rotonda inv. 258. von Heinze 1977, 163–164 pl. 82, 1.

[26] Musei Vaticani, Sala dei Busti inv. 707. von Heinze 1977, 162 pl. 83, 1.

4  Female portrait from the theatre, Philippi Museum inv. Λ2220 (Ephorate of Antiquities of Kavala, photo E. Gounari)

of that time[27], or another one in Petworth House, dated to the last decade of the 2nd century AD[28]. Consequently, we can date the sculpture to the end of the 2nd or to the beginning of the 3rd century AD. The presence of the laurel wreath is an important feature that could lead to the identification of the subject as perhaps a local priest[29].

The female portrait is in a better condition. It is preserved with the neck that was worked for insertion in a statue (fig. 4). The nose and part of the bun are broken and the hair on top and the back of the head is summarily treated. The head that turns slightly to its right represents a youthful woman with a hairstyle of the Antonine period. The subject has a thin, oval face, small mouth and narrow almond-shaped eyes, with heavy upper eyelids. The irises are incised but the pupils are not drilled. The hair is parted in the centre, swept back in bands of scalloped waves, and gathered in a bun above the neck. The earlobes are uncovered and in front of each ear three corkscrew locks hang down. That hairstyle corresponds to hairstyles worn by empresses of the 2nd century AD. The waves above the forehead are seen in the first type of portraits of Faustina the Younger[30], whereas the hairstyle at the sides and the bun can be compared with portraits of Faustina's daughter Lucilla[31], and the locks in front of the ears with portraits of the Trajanic period[32]. The comparison with the imperial portraits leads to the conclusion that the head from *Philippi* is a private portrait dated in the Antonine period. The existence and the shape of the tenon shows that it was set into a separately worked draped statue body of the Small Herculaneum woman type[33]. The woman represented belonged to the city elite, perhaps either a local benefactress herself or belonging to a family of benefactors. In the latter case, the statue could be part of a group of statues that represented members of the family[34].

Although the portraits from the theatre were not found *in situ* it is possible that they were originally erected in it, since we know that in the theatres of the Empire private statues were not uncommon. On the contrary, in the eastern Empire most of the portraits found in theatres depict members of the local elite[35].

---

[27]  According to Fittschen it must represent an important man of that time. Fittschen et al. 2010, 127–128 cat. 127 pl. 158.
[28]  Raeder 2000, 164–166 cat. 56 pl. 72.
[29]  Research has shown that such wreaths could be worn by emperors, priests, and participants in sacrifices, as well as by poets and victors in music contests. Raeder 2000, 207–208 cat. 77. For the wreath see RE IV 2 (1901) 1636–1643 s. v. corona (O. Fiebiger). DNP 15 (2010) 762–764 s. v. wreath (R. Hurschmann).
[30]  Fittschen 1982, 44.
[31]  Fittschen – Zanker 1985, 24–25 cat. 24 (Centrale Montemartini).
[32]  Fittschen – Zanker 1983, 6–7 cat. 5.
[33]  Despinis et al. 2003, 133–135 cat. 255 (Th. Stefanidou Tiveriou). For the type of the Small Herculaneum woman see: Linfert-Reich 1971, 53–57; Kruse 1975, 68–89; Bieber 1977, 148–162; Despinis et al. 1997, cat. 83 (G. Despinis).
[34]  Gheivanidou 2021, 138–139.
[35]  Gheivanidou 2021, 136–139.

5 Female portrait, University of Thessaloniki excavation, inv. 166/88 (University of Thessaloniki Excavation Archive, photo G. Gounaris)

6 Male portrait, University of Thessaloniki excavation, inv. 1321/2002 (University of Thessaloniki Excavation Archive, photo G. Gounaris)

In the late antique houses excavated by the University of Thessaloniki, a very damaged female head was unearthed in the north-western section of the excavation (fig. 5). Only the back, a small part of the left side of the face and a small part of the neck is preserved. The hair is arranged in parallel ›mellon‹-like sections and ends in a large bun. It can be compared to the hairstyle of Lucilla[36], but also to that of Crispina[37]. The ›mellon‹-like sections are compared to the hairstyle in the first type of Lucilla's portraits[38], whereas the type of bun is similar to that found in the portraits of Crispina[39]. Hence, it can be dated to the late Antonine period, between AD 178 and 190[40]. The combination of elements of different imperial portraits is evidence that the Philippi portrait is not an imperial one.

In the so-called Circus Mosaic Insula[41] two male and a child's portraits were unearthed. The first male life-sized portrait, representing a mature clean-shaven man is preserved with a small part of the neck[42] (fig. 6). Part of the hair above the nape, most of the nose, most of the left ear and part of the right are missing. The face of the man is oval, the chin lightly protruding, the cheekbones prominent and the forehead high. The almond-shaped eyes have irises indicated with an incision and tear ducts indicated with the drill. The vertical wrinkles on the forehead and the representation of bags under the eyes are signs of the subject's age. The hair of the figure lies in a compact mass close to the head. Thin parallel long locks are combed from the crown to the forehead. Over the inner corner of the left eye a fork configuration is formed and another one is formed over

---

[36] Gounari 2021, 240.
[37] Chioti 2012, 167.
[38] Fittschen – Zanker 1985, 24–25 cat. 24 (Fittschen).
[39] Fittschen 1982, 84 pl. 49.
[40] Chioti 2012, 167. 364–365.
[41] The building was named after a pavement representing a circus race scene that decorated the central court. For the building see Gounaris 1995–2000, 323–356. Gounaris 2003, 353–368. For the circus pavement see Gounaris 2008a, 28–33; Gounaris 2008b, 91–104.
[42] Gounaris 2003, 364–365 fig. 11.

7   Male portrait from the University of Thessaloniki excavation, inv. 864/96 (University of Thessaloniki Excavation Archive, photo G. Gounaris)

the right temple. At the back the long S-shaped locks are arranged in a circular pattern and end at the neck, behind and in front of the ears. This hairstyle can be compared to hairstyles in three of Trajan's portrait types. The way the hair is sculpted close to the head, the thin, long, parallel locks and the continuous line on the forehead and the back of the head are compared to portraits of the first type, such as a portrait in the Liebighaus Museum in Frankfurt[43]. The forked configuration over the left eye, the locks in front of the ear and the continuous fringe on the forehead are found in portraits of the second type, the so-called »Bürgerkronentypus«[44], such as on a head from Ostia[45], or another one in Copenhagen[46], whereas the fork configuration over the right temple is found in portraits of the so-called »Opferbildtypus«[47]. Beside the hairstyle, the form of the face with the prominent cheekbones, the indication only of the irises and the absence of the use of the drill for the pupils, the almond-shaped eyes, the bags under the eyes, and the mouth with the thin lips are compared to portraits of Trajan and private portraits of the Trajanic period[48]. Therefore, we must date the portrait found in *Philippi* after AD 110[49], perhaps in the second decade of the 2nd century AD. The affinities with the imperial portraits are not so close; consequently, the portrait is a private one.

The second life-sized male portrait that was found in the building represents a mature bearded man and is preserved with a small part of the neck (fig. 7). Part of the nose is broken and there is damage to different areas of the face, the beard, and the hair. The face was polished, but only a small part of the polish on the right cheek remains. The hair has short locks that are brushed down from the crown of the head and fall in a few distinctive locks over the forehead and the temples. At the back and the sides, the hair is arranged in tiers of thick locks that also cover the upper part of the ears. The beard is thick, and the ends of the large moustache droop downwards into it. The hair is worked mostly with the chisel, with the drill only being used at the sides to separate the locks. The face is square in shape, with a high forehead. The almond-shaped eyes have incised irises and drilled, bean shaped pupils, set under heavy eyelids. The drill was also used to indicate the tear ducts. The eyebrows are plastically rendered and articulated with incised lines. The cheekbones are well defined, and the mouth is unsmiling, with the upper lip covered by the moustache. The naso-labial lines and the wrinkles under the eyes are characteristic of the subject's maturity. The use of the drill for the pupils leads to a date after the time of Hadrian or in the late

---

[43]   Inv. 156. Gros 1940, 73–74. 126 no. 7 pl. 8 a; Bol 1983, 229–232 no. 72.
[44]   Gros 1940, 75–84.
[45]   Musei Vaticani, Museo Pio Clementino, Sala à Croce Greca inv. 232. Lippold 1936, 183–184 no. 581; Gros 1940, 125 cat. 12 pl. 10 a.
[46]   Ny Carlsberg Glyptotek inv. 1578. Gros 1940, 126 cat. 17 pl. 10 b; Jucker 1957, 250–251; Poulsen 1974, II cat. 672; Johansen 1995, cat. 35.
[47]   Gros 1940, 106–111; Fittschen – Zanker 1985, 43 cat. 44.
[48]   For example, a portrait in Ny Carlsberg Glyptotek inv. 724. Poulsen 1974, II, 77–78 no. 51 pl. 84; Johansen 1995, 132 no. 50.
[49]   The »Opferbildtypus« is dated before AD 113, probably around AD 110. Gros 1940, 111; Boschung 1999, 141.

Hadrianic period⁵⁰. We can compare the shape of the face and the beard with that of Antoninus Pius, as for example in a portrait in Museo Capitolino (inv. 446)⁵¹, another portrait in Museo Nazionale Romano (inv. 627)⁵², or a third one in Woburn Abbey (140–160 AD)⁵³. Comparisons can also be made with portraits of Herodes Atticus, such as the one found in Attica, now in the Louvre (MA 1164), dated to AD 160⁵⁴. The heads are similar in the form of the face and the type of beard, and in the lack of use of the drill for the hair and beard. Therefore, we can date the Philippi portrait to the middle of the 2nd century⁵⁵.

Moreover, there are private portraits that share some characteristics with the Philippi head. Two male portraits in the Museo Capitolino, Sala dei Filosofi (inv. 597⁵⁶ and 588⁵⁷), dated to the late Hadrianic period have a similar shape of the face, beard, and moustache. The second can be also compared with regard to the hair and the eyes. We can also find similarities with a private portrait in the Louvre (inv. 461), of unknown origin. Although the drill has been used for the hair and the beard of the Louvre portrait, the shape of the head and the face are similar and the physiognomy of the two men is the same. We can also compare the eyes and eyebrows, the cheeks as well as the slightly protruding high forehead. The Louvre portrait perhaps represents a Greek philosopher that lived in Rome in the 2nd century AD, as it is compared to Greek philosophers' portraits⁵⁸. The type of mature bearded man is generally associated with intellectuals, and scholars believe that portraits of Greek philosophers that were known through their Roman copies inspired Roman artists to create new portraits. Another portrait in Athens National Museum (inv. 388) that represents a *cosmetes*, that is an official responsible for the *ephebes* in the gymnasium⁵⁹, has a hairstyle similar to the Philippi portrait, with a few distinctive locks above the middle of the forehead⁶⁰. That type of hairstyle that shows the beginning of baldness is found in Roman portraits that follow Greek types of intellectuals' portraits; hence, it is a hairstyle that is associated with the type of intellectual man⁶¹. The affinities of the Philippi portrait with representations of philosophers or literati leads to the assumption that the subject could be a local intellectual.

The last portrait found in the same building is a portrait of a boy made of an alloy of bronze (fig. 8). It is partially preserved, as it was broken, and the rest was probably melted down to be reused⁶². Most of the face remains, as well as a small part of the hair above the forehead, part of the left temple and the front part of the neck. Its total height is 18 cm and the height of the face 11.5 cm, that is life size, since it represents a child between two and five years old. The face is round, with soft outline, small chin, and small mouth with full lips. The large almond-shaped eyes have a heavy upper lid, irises indicated with incision and drilled pupils. From the hair, only some locks over the forehead are preserved. The hair was combed from the crown to the front and divided in the middle, a hairstyle common for children. Above the forehead a plaque with three pendent pearls belonged to a jewel that was on the head, beginning from the crown. The tech-

---

[50] The bean shaped eyes appear in the final portraits of Hadrian. Wegner 1956, 16–17 type »Panzer-Paludamentbüste Baie«, pl. 20 type »Paludamentbüste-Vatikan Busti« 238, 25–26 pl. 26.
[51] Fittschen – Zanker 1985, 63–65 cat. 59.
[52] Wegner 1939, 141 pl. 3; Fittschen – Zanker 1985, 65 cat. 59 n. 15a; Giuliano 1987, 277–278 cat. R203.
[53] Angelicoussis 1992, 60–61 no. 34.
[54] De Kersauson 1996, 290–293 cat. 132 (AD 160–162).
[55] Gounari 1997–1998, 395; Chioti 2012, 85. 277–278 cat. 66.
[56] Fittschen – Zanker 2010, 99 cat. 94.
[57] Fittschen – Zanker 2010, 96–97 cat. 91; Stuart Jones 1912, 244 cat. 74, dates the sculpture to the middle of the 3rd c. AD.
[58] De Kersauson 1996, 336–337 cat. 154 (inv. Ma 49).
[59] Liddel – Scott II, 762 s. v. κοσμητής.
[60] Lattanzi 1968, 55–56 no. 22 pl. 22; Ntatsouli-Savridi 1985, 100–101 pl. 151/152; Danguillier 2001, 231 cat. 15 fig. 25–26. The Athens head is dated to the 3rd c. AD.
[61] Danguillier 2001, 68–69.
[62] It was found near the kiln that was installed in the insula in its second phase. According to Georgios Gounaris this was a kiln for the manufacture of the glass that was used in the glass workshop, which was also installed in the north part of the insula (Gounaris 2004, 81–83).

8  Bronze portrait of a child from the University of Thessaloniki excavation (University of Thessaloniki Excavation Archive, photo G. Gounaris)

nical features of the sculpture show that it was manufactured with the lost wax technique[63]. The fact that the eyes were not inlaid suggests a date after the time of Hadrian[64]. Moreover, the rendering of the eyebrows with incisions was common between the time of Hadrian and that of Septimius Severus[65]. The style of the sculpture confirms its dating to the second half of the 2nd century AD. The shape of the face and the physiognomy, with large, open eyes and small mouth are compared to portraits of Commodus as a child, dated to AD 166[66]. The rendering of the locks is similar to the one found in portraits of Polydeukion, Herodes Atticus' student, dated between AD 148–178[67]. Moreover, a bronze portrait found in *Cyprus*, dated around AD 160, can be also compared in the rendering of the eyes as well as in the hairstyle[68]. Consequently, we can date the portrait from *Philippi* around AD 170. The chemical analysis of the alloy[69] is consistent with the date in the second half of the 2nd century[70]. The jewel on the middle of the head is found mostly on portraits of children and has a special meaning[71]. According to scholars, this kind of jewel associated the child wearing it with deities that were mothers themselves, such as Aphrodite or Isis, or were venerated as *kourotrophoi*, such as Artemis, the Nymphs, or even with Dionysos[72]. Those deities protected the child while living and after its death. In the area of Roman *Macedonia*, three portraits with that jewel were found in *Thasos*[73], and two more are in the Archeological Museum of Thessaloniki[74], whereas in *Philippi* such a jewel was found in the Hellenistic tomb excavated in the Octagon complex[75]. Although we do not know where the portrait was erected, we can state that the child's family belonged to the elite of the city, since such jewels were made of precious materials[76].

The portraits presented above from the recent excavations in *Philippi* show that portraits were not rare in the Roman colony. There are finds dated to the 1st century AD, but the majority of them were created in the 2nd century and especially in its second half. The 2nd century was a period of

---

[63] Gounari 2006, 150–153.
[64] Lahusen – Formigli 1993, 670–672; Lahusen – Formigli 2001, 463–464.
[65] Lahusen – Formigli 2001, 464–465.
[66] Fittschen 1999, 55 H1 pl. 84. Commodus »Caesar-type« (Typ Genf).
[67] For example, cf. a portrait from Kiphisia, now in Athens, National Archaeological Museum inv. 4811. Romiopoulou 1997, no. 90; Kaltsas 2001, no. 735.
[68] Kahil 1976, 44–47.
[69] The alloy consists of Cu 71,78 % w/w, Pb 21,83 % w/w, Sn 7,8 % w/w (Tzebrailidou 2008, 95).
[70] Lahusen – Formigli 2001, 194–196 no. 116: statue of Hadrian from Israel (Pb 22 %, Sn 7,6 %); 240–243 no. 148: statue of Septimius Severus in Copenhagen and in art commerce (torso Cu 69,6 %, Pb 21,3 %, Sn 7,9 %; head Cu 76 %, Pb 20,6 %, Sn 0,5 %). Faltermeier 1976, 49–50: head from Soloi, Cyprus (Cu 69,69 %, Pb 20,39 %, Sn 9,65 %).
[71] Gonzenbach 1969, 904. See also Rolley 1968, 204–219.
[72] Gonzenbach 1969, 912. See also Hahl 1960, 9–49.
[73] Gonzenbach 1969, 943 cat. 23–25. See also Trillmich 1976, 13–14.
[74] Inv. MΘ 1021 and MΘ 1052. Despinis et al. 2003, no. 258 and no. 278.
[75] Kavala, Archaeological Museum inv. 577. Rolley 1968, 218 no. 29; Gonzenbach 1969, 941 no. 20.
[76] Gounari 2006, 159–160.

prosperity for the city, as the building of the second phase of the Roman forum and other buildings attest[77]. During that period, the city as well as the inhabitants had the means to commission portraits. Some of them were probably erected as honorary monuments in the forum, the theatre, or other public places, but others were probably displayed in the home or at the tomb of the depicted person. The portraits found in the theatre were probably erected in that building. The subjects were members of the local elite, and their presence in the theatre could be associated with donations they had made for the building or for performances[78]. One of them depicted probably a local priest[79]. Those found in the houses were probably erected in a domestic context. It is possible, however, that they were originally set up in the forum or at another public place.

The marble from the island of Thasos that was used shows that portraits were commissioned either to workshops in Thasos or to artisans that had come from the island and worked in the city using marble from their place of origin. The workshop that manufactured the bronze portrait cannot be traced so far.

All the marble portraits found in the excavations were reused as building material in late antique or Byzantine walls, and the bronze image was destroyed to be melted down. That recycling of the material is the reason why few portraits have been found in the city, though as the finds reveal there must once have existed many more, as in any other city of the Roman Empire.

## BIBLIOGRAPHY

| | |
|---|---|
| Andreae 1995 | B. Andreae (ed.), Bildkatalog der Skulpturen des Vatikanischen Museums I 1, Museo Chiaramonti (Berlin 1995) |
| Angelicoussis 1992 | E. Angelicoussis, The Woburn Abbey Collection of Classical Antiquities (Mainz 1992) |
| Bieber 1977 | M. Bieber, Ancient Copies (New York 1977) |
| Bol 1983 | P. C. Bol, Bildwerke aus Stein und aus Stuck von archaischer Zeit bis zur Spätantike, Liebieghaus – Museum alter Plastik. Antike Bildwerke I (Melsung 1983) |
| Boschung 1999 | D. Boschung, Die Bildnisse des Trajan, in: E. Schallmayer (ed.), Traian in Germanien Traian im Reich, Bericht des dritten Saalburgkolloquiums 1998 (Bad Homburg 1999) 137–144 |
| Brélaz 2014 | C. Brélaz, Corpus des Incriptions grecques et latines de Philippes II 1. La vie publique de la colonie (Athens 2014) |
| Brélaz 2018a | C. Brélaz, Philippes, colonie romaine d'Orient. Recherches d'histoire institutionnelle et sociale, BCH suppl. 59 (Athens 2018) |
| Brélaz 2018b | C. Brélaz, First-Century Philippi: Contextualizing Paul's Visit, in: J. R. Harisson – L. L. Welborn (eds.), The First Urban Churches 4. Roman Philippi (Atlanta 2018) 153–188 |
| Brélaz – Rizakis 2003 | C. Brélaz – A. Rizakis, Le fonctionnement des institutions et le déroulement des carrières dans la colonie de Philippes, CahGlotz 14, 2003 (2005), 155–165 |
| Chioti 2012 | E. Chioti, Αυτοκρατορικά και ιδιωτικά πορτρέτα της εποχής των Αντωνίνων στην Ελλάδα (doctoral thesis Aristotle University of Thessaloniki 2012) |
| Collart 1937 | P. Collart, Philippes. Ville de Macédoine depuis ses origines jusqu'à la fin de l'époque romaine (Paris 1937) |
| Danguillier 2001 | C. Danguillier, Typologische Untersuchungen zur Dichter- und Denkerikonographie in römischen Darstellungen von der mittleren Kaiserzeit bis in die Spätantike (Oxford 2001) |
| De Kersauson 1996 | K. de Kersauson, Musée du Louvre: Catalogue des portraits romains II. De l'année de la guerre civile (68–69 après J.-C.) à la fin de l'Empire (Paris 1996) |
| Despinis et al. 1997 | G. Despinis – Th. Stefanidou Tiveriou – E. Voutiras (eds.), Κατάλογος Γλυπτών Αρχαιολογικού Μουσείου Θεσσαλονίκης I (Thessaloniki 1997) |

---

[77] Sève 2016, 148–149.
[78] Gheivanidou 2021, 130.
[79] Statues depicting priests were numerous in the theatres of the Eastern Empire. Gheivanidou 2021, 136.

| | |
|---|---|
| Despinis et al. 2003 | G. Despinis – Th. Stefanidou Tiveriou – E. Voutiras (eds.), Κατάλογος Γλυπτών Αρχαιολογικού Μουσείου Θεσσαλονίκης II (Thessaloniki 2003) |
| Despinis et al. 2010 | G. Despinis – Th. Stefanidou Tiveriou – E. Voutiras (eds.), Κατάλογος Γλυπτών Αρχαιολογικού Μουσείου Θεσσαλονίκης III (Thessaloniki 2010) |
| Faltermeier 1976 | K. Faltermeier, Tête de bronze de Soloi (Chypre). Rückformung eines eingedrückten Bronzekopfes in den ursprünglichen Zustand, AntK 19, 1976, 49–50 |
| Fittschen 1982 | K. Fittschen, Die Bildnistypen der Faustina minor und die Fecunditas Augustae (Göttingen 1982) |
| Fittschen 1999 | K. Fittschen, Prinzenbildnisse antoninischer Zeit (Mainz 1999) |
| Fittschen – Zanker 1983 | K. Fittschen – P. Zanker, Katalog der römischen Porträts in den Capitolinischen Museen und den anderen kommunalen Sammlungen der Stadt Rom III: Kaiserinnen- und Prinzessinnenbildnisse, Frauenporträts (Mainz 1983) |
| Fittschen – Zanker 1985 | K. Fittschen – P. Zanker, Katalog der römischen Porträts in den Capitolinischen Museen und den anderen kommunalen Sammlungen der Stadt Rom I: Kaiser und Prinzenbildnisse (Mainz 1985) |
| Fittschen et al. 2010 | K. Fittschen – P. Zanker – P. Cain, Katalog der römischen Porträts in den Capitolinischen Museen und den anderen kommunalen Sammlungen der Stadt Rom II: Die männlichen Privatporträts (Berlin 2010) |
| Gheivanidou 2021 | M. Gheivanidou, Εικονιστικοί ανδριάντες στα θέατρα των ρωμαϊκών ανατολικών επαρχιών (Thessaloniki 2021) |
| Giuliano 1987 | A. Giuliano (ed.), Museo Nazionale Romano. Le Sculture I 9, 2, Magazzini. I ritratti (Rome 1987) |
| Gonzenbach 1969 | V. von Gonzenbach, Der griechisch-römische Scheitelschmuck und die Funde aus Thasos, BCH 93, 1969, 885–945 |
| Gounari 1997–98 | E. Gounari, Κεφαλή γενειοφόρου ανδρός από τους Φιλίππους (864/96), Makedonika 31, 1997–98, 391–403 |
| Gounari 2006 | E. Gounari, Χάλκινο παιδικό πορτρέτο από τους Φιλίππους, Egnatia 10, 2006, 145–161 |
| Gounari 2008a | E. Gounari, The Roman Mosaics from Philippi: Evidence of the Presence of Romans in the City. XVII International Conference of Classical Archaeology, Rome 2008, Bolletino di Archaeologia online I, 2010, volume speciale, 27–38, <https://bollettinodiarcheologiaonline.beniculturali.it/wp-content/uploads/2010/01/3_GOUNARI.pdf> (29.03.2023) |
| Gounari 2008b | E. Gounari, Τα ψηφιδωτά της νησίδας του Ιπποδρόμου στους Φιλίππους, Egnatia12, 2008, 87–123 |
| Gounari 2021 | E. Gounari, Φίλιπποι. Η οικία της τέταρτης οικοδομικής νησίδας ανατολικά του forum (Thessaloniki 2021) |
| Gounaris 1995–2000 | G. Gounaris, Πανεπιστημιακή ανασκαφή Φιλίππων 1997–2000. Ψηφιδωτό δάπεδο με παράσταση αρματοδρομίας και άλλα ευρήματα, Egnatia 5, 1995–2000, 323–356 |
| Gounaris 2003 | G. Gounaris, Πανεπιστημιακή ανασκαφή Φιλίππων 2000–2002, Egnatia 7, 2003, 353–368 |
| Gounaris 2004 | G. Gounaris, Εγκαταστάσεις υαλοποιίας και υαλουργίας στους Φιλίππους, in: Αρχαιολογικά τεκμήρια βιοτεχνικών εγκαταστάσεων κατά τη βυζαντινή εποχή $5^{ος}$–$15^{ος}$ αιώνας. Ειδικό θέμα του 22$^{ου}$ Συμποσίου Βυζαντινής και Μεταβυζαντινής Αρχαιολογίας και Τέχνης, Αθήνα 17–19 Μαΐου 2002 (Athens 2004) 73–87 |
| Gros 1940 | W. H. Gross, Bildnisse Traians, Das römische Herrscherbild II 2 (Berlin 1940) |
| Hahl 1960 | L. Hahl, Zur Erklärung der niedergermanischen Matronendenkmäler, BJb 160, 1969, 9–49 |
| Helbig 1963 | W. Helbig, Führer durch die öffentlichen Sammlungen klassischer Altertümer in Rom $^4$(Tübingen 1963–72) |
| Hertel 1982 | E. D. Hertel, Untersuchungen zu Stil und Chronologie des Kaiser- und Prinzenporträts von Augustus bis Claudius (doctoral thesis University of Bonn 1982) |
| İnan – Alföldi Rosenbaum 1979 | J. İnan – E. Alföldi-Rosenbaum, Römische und frühbyzantinische Porträtplastik aus der Turkei. Neue Funde (Mainz 1979) |
| Johansen 1994 | F. Johansen, Roman Portraits: Catalogue Ny Carlsberg Glyptotek I (Copenhagen 1994) |

| | |
|---|---|
| Johansen 1995 | F. Johansen, Roman Portraits: Catalogue Ny Carlsberg Glyptotek II (Copenhagen 1995) |
| Jucker 1957 | H. Jucker, Nachtrag zu W. H. Gross, Bildnisse Trajans, Berlin 1940, AJA 61, 1957, 250–253 |
| Kahil 1976 | L. Kahil, Tête de bronze de Soloi (Chypre), AntK 19, 1976, 41–47 |
| Kaltsas 2001 | N. Kaltsas, Εθνικό Αρχαιολογικό Μουσείο. Τα Γλυπτά (Athens 2001) |
| Karadedos – Koukouli Chryssanthaki 1999 | G. Karadedos – Ch. Koukouli Chryssanthaki, Ανασκαφικές έρευνες στο θέατρο των Φιλίππων, AErgoMak 13, 1999, 69–86 |
| Karadedos – Koukouli Chryssanthaki 2007 | G. Karadedos – Ch. Koukouli Chryssanthaki, From the Greek Theatre to the Roman Arena: The Theatres at Philippi, Thasos and Maroneia, in: A. Ioakonidou (ed.), Thrace in the Greco-Roman World, Proceedings of the 10th International Congress of Thracology, Komotini – Alexandroupolis 18.–23.10.2005 (Athens 2007) 273–290 |
| Kruse 1975 | H.-J. Kruse, Römische weibliche Gewandstatuen des zweiten Jahrhunderts n. Chr. (Göttingen 1975) |
| Lahusen – Formigli 1993 | G. Lahusen – E. Formigli, Der Augustus von Meroë und die Augen der römischen Bronzenbildnisse, AA 1993, 655–674 |
| Lahusen – Formigli 2001 | G. Lahusen – E. Formigli, Römische Bildnisse aus Bronze, Kunst und Technik (Munich 2001) |
| Lapalus 1932 | E. Lapalus, Tête de bronze de Philippes, BCH 56, 1932, 360–371 |
| Lapalus 1933 | E. Lapalus, Sculptures de Philippes, BCH 57, 1933, 449–452 |
| Liddel – Scott 1915 | H. G. Liddel – R. Scott, Μέγα Λεξικό της Ελληνικής Γλώσσης (Athens 1915) |
| Linfert-Reich 1971 | I. Linfert-Reich, Musen- und Dichterinnenfiguren des vierten und frühen dritten Jahrhunderts (Cologne 1971) |
| Lippold 1936 | G. Lippold, Die Skulpturen des Vatikanischen Museums III (Berlin 1936) |
| Ntatsouli-Stavridis 1970 | A. Ntatsouli-Stavridis, Untersuchungen zu den Kaiserporträts in Griechenland. Augustus bis Caracalla (Berlin 1970) |
| Ntatsouli-Stavridis 1985 | A. Ntatsouli-Stavridis, Ρωμαϊκά πορτραίτα στο Εθνικό Αρχαιολογικό Μουσείο της Αθήνας (Athens 1985) |
| Pilhofer 1995 | P. Pilhofer, Philippi I. Die erste christliche Gemeinde Europas (Tübingen 1995) |
| Pilhofer 2009 | P. Pilhofer, Philippi II. Katalog der Inschriften von Philippi ²(Tübingen 2009) |
| Polacco 1955 | L. Polacco, Il volto di Tiberio (Rome 1955) |
| Poulsen 1962 | V. Poulsen, Les Portraits Romains I. République et dynastie julienne (Copenhagen 1962) |
| Poulsen 1974 | V. Poulsen, Les Portraits Romains II (Copenhagen 1974) |
| Raeder 2000 | J. Raeder, Die antiken Skulpturen in Petworth House (West Sussex) (Mainz 2000) |
| Rizakis 2016 | A.D. Rizakis, Société, institutions, cultes, in J. Fournier (ed.), Philippes, de la préhistoire à Byzance, BCH suppl. 55 (Athens 2016) 175–197 |
| Rizakis 2018 | A. D. Rizakis, Formes d'acculturation dans un contexte colonial: l'exemple de Philippes, colonie romaine en Macédoine orientale, in: L. Maksimović – M. Ricl (eds.), ΤΗ ΠΡΟΣΦΙΛΕΣΤΑΤΗ ΚΑΙ ΠΑΝΤΑ ΑΡΙΣΤΗ ΜΑΚΕΔΟΝΙΑΡΧΙΣΣΗ. Students and Colleagues for Professor Fanoula Papazoglou, International Conference Belgrade 17.–18.10.2017 (Belgrade 2018) 189–207 |
| Roger 1938 | J. Roger, L'enceinte basse de Philippes, BCH 62, 1938, 20–41 |
| Rolley 1968 | C. Rolley, Les cultes égyptiens à Thasos. A propos de quelques documents nouveaux, BCH 92, 1968, 187–219 |
| Romiopoulou 1997 | A. Romiopoulou, Ελληνορωμαϊκά Γλυπτά του Εθνικού Αρχαιολογικού Μουσείου (Athens 1997) |
| Santa Maria Scrinari 1972 | V. Santa Maria Scrinari, Museo Archeologico di Aquileia, Catalogo delle sculture romane (Rome 1972) |
| Sève 2016 | M. Sève, Urbanisme, architecture et territoire, in: J. Fournier (ed.), Philippes, de la Préhistoire à Byzance (Athens 2016) 130–150 |
| Sève – Weber 1988 | M. Sève – P. Weber, Un monument honorifique au forum de Philippes, BCH 112, 1988, 467–479 |
| Sève – Weber 2012 | M. Sève – P. Weber, Guide du forum de Philippes (Athens 2012) |

| | |
|---|---|
| Smith 2006 | R. R. R. Smith, Roman Portrait Statuary from Aphrodisias (Mainz 2006) |
| Stuart Jones 1912 | H. Stuart Jones, A Catalogue of the Sculptures preserved in the Municipal Collections of Rome: The Sculptures of the Museo Capitolino (Oxford 1912) |
| Trillmich 1976 | W. Trillmich, Das Torlonia Mädchen. Zur Herkunft und Entstehung des kaiserzeitlichen Frauenporträts, AbhGöttingen 99 (Göttingen 1976) |
| Tzebrailidou 2008 | G. Tzebrailidou, Χάλκινο παιδικό πορτρέτο από τους Φιλίππους, αρχαιομετρική προσέγγιση (diploma thesis Aristotle University of Thessaloniki 2008) |
| von Heinze 1977 | H. von Heinze, Studien zu den Porträts des 3. Jahrhunderts n. Chr. 8. Die Kaiser der Krisenjahre 193–197 n. Chr., RM 84, 1977, 159–180 |
| Wegner 1939 | M. Wegner, Die Herrscherbildnisse in antoninischer Zeit, Das römische Herrscherbild IV (Berlin 1939) |
| Wegner 1956 | M. Wegner, Hadrian: Plotina, Marciana, Matidia, Sabina. Das römische Herrscherbild II 3 (Berlin 1956) |

*Emmanouela Gounari, School of History and Archaeology, Aristotle University of Thessaloniki, Proxenou Koromila 49 Street, 54622 Thessaloniki, Greece.*
*[e] emma@hist.auth.gr*

Jochen Griesbach

# »ÜBER GELD SPRICHT MAN NICHT!«?

## UNTERSCHIEDE IN DER ZURSCHAUSTELLUNG VON REICHTUM UND STATUS IN RÖMISCHEN GRABDENKMÄLERN ITALIENS UND DER NORDWESTPROVINZEN

*Assem habeas, assem valeas*
(Trimalchio in: Petron. 77)

**Abstract**

In the sepulchral imagery of the north(-west) provinces, the explicit display of wealth in the form of money seems to have been unproblematic. Piles of coins are encountered there in the so-called payment scenes or inside money bags carried by the central family members as a sign of their business acumen. Such examples are particularly common in *Gallia Belgica* and the neighbouring regions, where there is also a disproportionate number of representations of trade and crafts. In the tombs of Roman Italy, on the other hand, the reproduction of coins is usually avoided. Only a small number of sarcophagi, which were probably not displayed in public, are an exception. The paper explores the reasons for this phenomenon by incorporating insights from monetary theory (sociology). What seems essential here is that the two geographical areas were configured differently in social terms and therefore allowed for different discourses on values.

## EINLEITUNG: ZUM AMBIVALENTEN VERHÄLTNIS VON GELD UND ÖFFENTLICHKEIT IN DER GEGENWART

»Über Geld spricht man nicht!«[1] – Dieser von den Medien regelmäßig aufgegriffene Leitsatz unserer Tage kann in der deutschen Gesellschaft laut jüngeren Umfragen eine Mehrheit von über 60 % für sich verbuchen, und zwar weitgehend unabhängig von Geschlecht und Bildungsstand[2]. Je nach Perspektive gilt das Reden über Vermögensverhältnisse als unanständig oder ehrenrührig. Dabei ist durchaus fragwürdig, ob das Tabu rein moralisch begründet ist, im Sinne anstößiger Prahlerei, oder psychologisch tiefer wurzelt. Denn das generelle Unbehagen scheint vor allem daraus zu resultieren, dass Geldsummen in unserer ökonomisch geprägten Welt die gewohnte Messeinheit bilden, in der Werte, und zwar nicht nur materielle, arithmetisch miteinander verglichen werden können[3]. So droht das Gehalt als monetärer Ausdruck von Leistung[4] unter Umständen zur Messlatte des persönlichen Eigenwerts innerhalb eines Rankings zu werden, wie unter anderem der Medientheoretiker Marshal McLuhan in seiner Analyse der wirtschaftlichen und symbolischen

---

[1] Nach den Einsichten der Geldtheorie muss diese Maxime geradezu paradox anmuten, sind doch Geld und Sprache (Schrift) längst als ontologische Verwandte entlarvt: Simmel 1989, 136–138; Luhmann 2001, 33–36; Brodbeck 2016, 325–331; vgl. Krämer 2016, 162–164. – Für die Bereitstellung des Bildmaterials zu diesem Beitrag danke ich Daria Lanzuolo, Camilla Colombi, Ellen Riemer, Philipp Groß, Anja Klöckner und Ute Kelp.

[2] Laut einer von der Postbank 2014 beim Meinungsforschungsinstitut Emnid in Auftrag gegebenen Umfrage: <https://www.postbank.de/unternehmen/medien/postbank-pressedienst/umfrage/tabuthema-geld.html> (02.02.2023, 18:53); s. dazu auch die Online-Ausgabe der Frankfurter Allgemeinen Zeitung vom 08.08.2015: <https://www.faz.net/aktuell/finanzen/meine-finanzen/ueber-geld-spricht-man-nicht-tabuthema-unter-deutschen-13738804html> (02.02.2023, 19:02).

[3] Zur Objektivierungsfunktion von Geld in Relation zum subjektiven Wertempfinden s. Simmel 1989, 23–54.

[4] Zu Geld als Mittel der Geltung s. Gerloff 1952, 124–129.

Funktionen von Geld sehr klar erkannt hat[5]. Wer möchte sich schon gerne in Geld aufwiegen lassen, wenn eigentlich der Grundsatz der Gleichheit gelten soll[6]? Die geläufige Vorstellung von öffentlicher Anerkennung ist offenbar nach wie vor eher romantischer Natur: Wertschätzung wird in unserer Gesellschaft idealiter mit vorbildlichen Eigenschaften, Fähigkeiten und von uneigennützigen Motiven geleitetem Engagement verknüpft, während Geld von derlei Werten abstrahiert und sich damit tendenziell in eine konträre Position begibt[7], vorzugsweise sogar mit niederen Beweggründen assoziiert wird[8]. Geld kann zwar auch beim Generieren ›wahrer Werte‹ eine nicht unerhebliche Rolle spielen, wird aber in den Medien nur selten visuell in den Vordergrund gestellt, wenn man von den Überreichungen überdimensionierter Checks zu Charity-Zwecken absieht.

Wenn es um andere als uns selbst geht, sind wir hinsichtlich der Offenlegung von Vermögenswerten weniger zimperlich. Von Politik und Wirtschaft wird seit Jahren mehr Transparenz der Bezüge und Geldflüsse gefordert[9]. Hier besteht die Befürchtung, dass die demokratischen Volksvertretungen nicht immer nach bestem Wissen und Gewissen handeln, sondern durch gezielte geldwerte Offerten von Lobbyisten in ihren Handlungen und Entscheidungen korrumpierbar sind. Aber auch jenseits der Politik gibt es in unserer Gesellschaft ein reges Interesse daran, wie ›die Reichen‹ ihr Geld ausgeben. Von der Klatschpresse über Hochglanzmagazine bis hin zu beliebten Fernsehformaten lebt eine ganze Unterhaltungsindustrie nicht zuletzt davon, mittels tagesaktueller Observation des Jet-Set ihr Publikum regelmäßig durch kathartische Gefühlswellen von Neid und Empörung einerseits sowie verspottender Distanzierung andererseits zu jagen[10]. In der medialen Öffentlichkeit bewegt sich die Aufmerksamkeit für das Geld demnach gegenwärtig irgendwo zwischen den Polen Aufklärung und Voyeurismus.

So oder so: Die Zurschaustellung von Reichtum ist (und war) stets ein Thema, das die Gemüter erregt, weil sie unmittelbar und in vielfältiger Weise an den Kosmos kollektiver wie individueller Wertvorstellungen rührt[11].

## EINE FRAGE DES *DECOR*: STIMMEN ZUR MACHT DES GELDES UND ZUR ZURSCHAUSTELLUNG VON REICHTUM IN RÖMISCHEN SCHRIFTQUELLEN

Für die römische Kultur gilt das nicht minder, zumal das individuelle Vermögen aufgrund des Census einen wesentlichen Faktor für die Verortung des Einzelnen innerhalb der Gesellschaftspyramide darstellte[12]. Aber mindestens ebenso wichtig war die Abstammung. Insofern täuscht sich Horaz ein wenig, wenn er dem Geld förmlich alles zutraut[13]. Wie andere römische Literaten be-

---

[5] McLuhan 1964, 143–144 exemplifiziert diesen Zusammenhang – inspiriert durch Elias Canetti – mit den psychologischen Auswirkungen der Inflation nach dem I. Weltkrieg auf das Selbstwertgefühl der Deutschen.

[6] Zu Geld als Grundlage sozialer Hierarchien und Klassenbildung s. Gerloff 1952, 129–135; zum Problem der Anerkennung Hénaff 2009, 593–604 bes. 595.

[7] Zum grundsätzlichen Konflikt zwischen Geld und Wahrheit s. Hénaff 2009, 12–24.

[8] Die Geldtheorie geht davon aus, dass die Geldwirtschaft das menschliche Denken über Werte nachhaltig unter ihre Kontrolle gebracht und Kategorien wie Gier, Geiz, Verschwendung, aber auch Zynismus und Blasiertheit erst prominent gemacht hat: Simmel 1989, 310–337; Gerloff 1952, 236–254; Krämer 2016, 158. 167–168; Brodbeck 2016, bes. 334.

[9] Institutionalisiert finden solche Bestrebungen Rückhalt etwa in Organisationen wie dem Dachverband Transparency International e.V. mit Sitz in Berlin, gegründet 1993.

[10] Stellvertretend sei hier das besonders populäre, seit 2011 ausgestrahlte ›Reality-TV‹-Format »Die Geissens – Eine schrecklich glamouröse Familie« genannt: s. Wikipedia s. v. Die Geissens.

[11] DNP IV (2012) 892–893 s. v. Geldtheorie (S. von Reden); RAC IX (1976) 899–901 s. v. Geld (R. Bogaert). Einen kurzen Überblick zur Geschichte der Geldkritik von der Antike bis in die Moderne liefert Weber 1979; eine exemplarische Bildgeschichte zu Reichtum und Armut in der Neuzeit bietet Holten 2016.

[12] Alföldy 2011, 33–35.

[13] Hor. epist. 1, 6, 36–38: *Scilicet uxorem cum dote fidemque et amicos | et* genus *et formam regina* Pecunia *donat | ac bene nummatum decorat Suadela Venusque.* Q. Horatius Flaccus (65–8 v. Chr.) stammt aus Venusia in Apulien, ist libertiner Herkunft und hat es früh bis zum *tribunus militum* gebracht, eine Anstellung als Privatsekretär des Augustus schlug er aus: PIR IV (1952–56) Nr. 198; DNP V (1998) s. v. Horatius 7 (B. Kytzler). – Ähnlich äußert sich Cicero in Verr. 1, 4. M. Tullius Cicero (106–43 v. Chr.) stammt aus *Arpinum* im Süden Latiums, sein Vater war Ritter, doch stieg er selbst als *homo novus* zum Senator (cos. 63 v. Chr.) auf; zu seinem eigenen Umgang mit

schwört er die geradezu universelle Weisheit, dass Geld und Reichtum (alleine) nicht glücklich machen und es im Leben auf andere Werte ankomme wie Freundschaft, Bildung und Familie[14]. Ein Philosoph wie Seneca, der in seinen Schriften den Materialismus seiner Zeit regelmäßig anprangert[15], sah sich daher ob seines umfänglichen Besitzes[16] leicht öffentlichen Vorwürfen ausgesetzt, etwa durch seinen Standesgenossen P. Suillius Rufus[17]. In der Schrift »De vita beata« an seinen Bruder Gallio rechtfertigt Seneca seinen Reichtum damit, dass er ihm durch Arbeit und Taten zugekommen sei und nicht etwa durch Gier[18]. Beruft er sich damit auf allgemein anerkannte Wertvorstellungen, erweist sich der Tonfall seiner Selbstbetrachtung an anderer Stelle nicht frei von Arroganz: »Reichtum dient dem Weisen, den Toren beherrscht er«[19]. Den Verdacht einer doppelzüngigen Einstellung zum Besitz wurde er jedenfalls nicht mehr los[20]. Mehr Gespür für die Auffassung des römischen Durchschnittsbürgers darf man dem Dichter Martial zutrauen, obgleich auch er entgegen den eigenen Beteuerungen nicht gerade mittellos war[21]. In seinen Epigrammen spricht er beständig über Geld, wobei Reiche im Wesentlichen aus zwei Gründen Spott verdienen: namentlich diejenigen, die in Wirklichkeit nur so tun, als seien sie vermögend[22], und solche, die ihren Reichtum nicht zur Freigebigkeit einsetzen, sondern dem Geiz frönen[23]. Allerdings tadelt auch er gern die Verschwendung und Ausgaben, die sich nicht lohnen[24], und stimmt damit letztlich ein in den althergebrachten Chor der *luxuria*-Kritik[25]. Die Zurschaustellung von Reichtum ist Martial aber nicht grundsätzlich ein Dorn im Auge; nur wer außer Geld überhaupt kein anderes Gesprächsthema mehr kennt, der ist ihm zuwider[26]. Es geht also letztlich um die Angemessenheit, den *decor*; darum, wer wieviel in welchem Kontext über Geld oder andere Symbole des Reichtums spricht.

Dass die Frage des Dekorum im Herzen der römischen Welt in hohem Maße vom gesellschaftlichen Status der Betroffenen abhängig war, machen zwei Beispiele deutlich, die zum ausgewählten Gegenstand der Analyse überleiten, der Zurschaustellung von Reichtum auf Grabmälern. Als auf Dauer angelegte, repräsentative Monumente waren sie dazu prädestiniert, Wertvorstellungen kondensiert und personalisiert zum Ausdruck zu bringen. In einer bekannten Passage aus Petrons »Satyricon« malt sich der neureiche Gastgeber Trimalchio beim Bankett sein üppig bemessenes Grabmal unter anderem so aus[27]: Er möchte darauf in der Toga praetexta auf einem Tribunal

---

Geld s. Scheuermann 2015. – Zum psychologischen Verhältnis von Macht und Geld s. jüngst Gloy 2020, 161–191; zu den Grenzen der Geldmacht s. Krämer 2016, 170.

[14] s. z. B. Ter. Ad. 216; Cic. Lael. 54; Sall. Catil. 11, 3; Hor. carm. 4, 9, 45–46; Mart. 5, 42; vgl. Hdt. 1, 30, 4–5.
[15] Sen. epist. 123, 7.
[16] Mratschek-Halfmann 1993, 307–308 Nr. 128.
[17] Tac. ann. 13, 42.
[18] Sen. dial. 7, 21–23. – Dabei bestand bereits in der Antike ein Bewusstsein dafür, dass die Gier nach Geld im Grunde unstillbar ist, weil dem Prinzip der Geldvermehrung theoretisch keine Grenzen gesetzt sind: Graßl 2019, bes. 65 mit Verweis auf Dion Chrys. 4, 93; vgl. Weber 1979, 29.
[19] Sen. dial. 7, 26, 1: »*Quid ergo inter me stultum et te sapientem interest, si uterque habere volumus?*« *Plurimum: divitiae enim apud sapientem virum in servitute sunt, apud stultum in imperio.* Martial würde darauf kontern: *Semper pauper eris, si pauper es, Aemiliane. | Dantur opes nullis nunc nisi divitibus* (5, 81); s. auch Hor. epist. 1, 10, 47: *Imperat aut servit collecta pecunia cuique.* Vermeintlich erhaben über die Verlockungen des Reichtums trivialisiert Sen. epist. 18, 7–8 die Erfahrung der Armut. – Fundamentale Zweifel am herkömmlich hergestellten Zusammenhang zwischen Reichtum und Areté gehen im Wesentlichen auf die klassische Zeit zurück, haben aber auch vereinzelte Vorläufer: Schriefl 2013, bes. 265–276.
[20] Tac. ann. 14, 52–54.
[21] M. Valerius Martialis stammt aus Bilbilis (Tarraconensis), hatte möglicherweise keltiberische Wurzeln und wurde wohl erst durch die Flavier in den Ritterstand erhoben: PIR VIII 2 (2015) Nr. 123. Zu seiner angeblichen Mittellosigkeit: Mart. 1, 76; 2, 30. 46; 4, 77; 5, 39. 59. 62; 6, 5; 7, 16; 9, 22; 11, 3; zu seinem tatsächlich vorhandenen Vermögen: 3, 41; 5, 19; zu seinem Landgut bei *Nomentum*: 2, 38; 6, 43; 7, 31. 93; 8, 61; 9, 60; 10, 92. 94; 11, 18; 12, 57; 13, 119; s. auch 4, 79.
[22] s. z. B. Mart. 2, 29. 57; 5, 8. 14. 23. 35. 38; 6, 77. 94; 11, 59.
[23] s. z. B. Mart. 1, 43. 99. 103; 2, 46; 3, 26; 4, 26. 51. 85; 5, 32. 82; 9, 59; 10, 15; 12, 13. 53. 81.
[24] s. z. B. Mart. 2, 63; 3, 58; 5, 25; 10, 30.
[25] Zum Kampfbegriff der *luxuria* und der mit ihr verbundenen Doppelmoral s. Henig 2001; Weeber 2007.
[26] Mart. 4, 37.
[27] Petron. 71, 3.

sitzend wiedergegeben werden, mit fünf goldenen Fingerringen und einem Säckchen Gold in der Hand, aus dem er Münzen an die Volksmenge verteilt. Dabei beruft er sich auf eine von ihm gestiftete öffentliche Verkostung, bei der alle Anwesenden je zwei Denare erhalten hätten. Schließlich kommt er in der Grabinschrift, die er seinem anwesenden Architekten förmlich diktiert, erneut aufs Geld zu sprechen:

C. POMPEIUS TRIMALCHIO MAECENATIANUS HIC REQUIESCIT.
HUIC SEVIRATUS ABSENTI DECRETUS EST.
CUM POSSET IN OMNIBUS DECURIIS ROMAE ESSE, TAMEN NOLUIT.
PIUS, FORTIS, FIDELIS, EX PARVO CREVIT.
SESTERTIUM RELIQUIT TRECENTIES;
NEC UMQUAM PHILOSOPHUM AUDIVIT.
VALE ET TU

Bis auf das des Augustalen hätte er alle anderen an ihn herangetragenen Ämter ausgeschlagen, sei dafür aber imstande gewesen, seinen Erben 30 Millionen zu hinterlassen[28]. Aus dem Genre der Erzählung geht unzweifelhaft hervor, dass Petron, Berater Neros in Fragen der *elegantia*[29], hier sämtliche Register zieht, um sich und seine Leserschaft aus aristokratischer Sicht über das soziale Milieu der reichen Freigelassenen und deren eklatanten Mangel an Dekorum zu amüsieren[30].

Bar jeder Fiktion kommt die zugrundeliegende elitäre Haltung dagegen in einem der Briefe Plinius d. J. an seinen Standesgenossen T. Iunius Montanus[31] zum Ausdruck[32]. Dort ereifert sich der Autor über die kürzlich von ihm an der Via Tiburtina entdeckte Grabinschrift des M. Antonius Pallas, eines Freigelassenen, der als Finanzverwalter unter Kaiser Claudius zu großem Einfluss und Reichtum gelangt war[33]. In der wörtlich zitierten Grabinschrift geht Pallas darauf ein, dass der Senat ihm den Rang eines Prätoren verliehen und 15 Millionen Sesterzen angeboten habe; er wiederum habe sich mit der Ehre begnügt und auf das Geld verzichtet.

Plinius nimmt in diesem Zusammenhang nicht so sehr Anstoß an den Ehrungen an sich, die er gleichwohl nicht gutheißt (*mimica et inepta*), sondern an der Tatsache, dass sich Pallas als Vorbild des Maßhaltens (*moderationis exemplum*) geriert[34]. In Plinius' Augen wird hier der *decor* mit seinen eigenen Mitteln verletzt: Schlimm genug, dass ein reicher Freigelassener erwartungsgemäß mit seinem Grabmal protzt; aber dass er sich angesichts seiner Herkunft (*furcifer*) in der Inschrift erdreistet, seine Erhebung in den Adel und seinen ›edelmütigen‹ Verzicht auf sehr viel Geld herauszustellen, bedeutet für den geborenen Aristokraten nicht nur einen klaren Verstoß gegen die Regeln des guten Geschmacks, sondern eine Überschreitung der libertinen Standesgrenzen, die dem Emporkömmling unter gar keinen Umständen zusteht[35].

---

[28] Die als Grabschmuck vorgesehenen Segelschiffe lassen erahnen, dass dieses Vermögen aus einem im Fernhandel tätigen Unternehmen erwachsen ist, spielen aber vielleicht auch auf die Lex Claudia von 218 v. Chr. an; s. dazu El Beheiri 2001; Bringmann 2003.

[29] T. Petronius Niger »Arbiter« (14–66 n. Chr.) aus *Cumae* war römischer Senator (cos. 60 n. Chr. [?]): PIR VI (1998) Nr. 294.

[30] Bezeichnenderweise assoziiert Dion Chrys. 4, 96 den Charakter des Geldgierigen phänotypisch nicht mit einem Vertreter der Oberschicht, sondern mit einem Sklaven: s. Graßl 2019, 67. Dion Cocceianus von Prusa (ca. 40–120 n. Chr.), Redner und Philosoph, war ein enger Freund des Kaisers Trajan: DNP III (1997) s. v. Dion I 3 (M. Weißenberger).

[31] PIR IV (1952–1956) Nr. 781 (*cos. suff.* 81 n. Chr.).

[32] Plin. epist. 7, 29, 1. C. Plinius Caecilius Secundus (61–115 n. Chr. [?]) stammt aus *Novum Comum* (Como) und war römischer Senator (*cos. suff.* 100 n. Chr. [?]): PIR VI (1998) Nr. 490.

[33] Suet. Claud. 28; Mratschek-Halfmann 1993, 305–306 Nr. 122.

[34] Plin. epist. 7, 29, 3.

[35] Ähnlich entsetzt und angewidert äußert sich Tac. ann. 12, 53 über den Sachverhalt, auch er ein Senator: DNP XI (2001) s. v. Tacitus 1 (E. Flaig). Auch die Rechtsgelehrten der römischen Kaiserzeit befassten sich mit der standesgemäßen Angemessenheit des Grabaufwands: Schrumpf 2006, 229 Anm. 566; vgl. von Hesberg 1992, 11.

»Über Geld spricht man nicht!«? Unterschiede in der Zurschaustellung von Reichtum und Status 431

1   Reliefblock von einem Grabbau mit Geldabrechnung, gefunden in Neumagen, 1. Hälfte 3. Jh. n. Chr., RLM Trier Inv. 739 (Foto Th. Zühmer)

## »MAN ZEIGT, WAS MAN HAT«: GELD AUF GRABDENKMÄLERN DER NORDWESTPROVINZEN

Wenn Geld also auch innerhalb der römischen Gesellschaft *expressis verbis* ein sensibles Thema mit hohem Konfliktpotenzial war, so verdient seine Darstellung im Medium der Bilder in jedem Fall erhöhte Aufmerksamkeit[36]. Für unseren Zusammenhang ist diesbezüglich das konzentrierte Vorkommen solcher Bilder auf Grabdenkmälern von Interesse, in denen Geld ›gehäuft‹ in Szene gesetzt wird, wie es vor allem für die nordwestlichen Provinzen und dort insbesondere für das Gebiet der *Gallia Belgica* zwischen Maas und Mosel konstatiert werden kann. Die ausführlichsten Bilder dieser Art stammen von Grabbauten des Trierer Umlandes, weshalb sie hier exemplarisch eingehender betrachtet werden sollen: Ein Reliefblock aus Neumagen[37] (Abb. 1) zeigt in der Mitte des Bildes eine Tischplatte, auf der ein großer Haufen Münzen verteilt liegt. Rechts streicht ein Mann mit der Hand über diesen Haufen, offenbar um das Geld zur besseren Ansicht auf dem Tisch zu verteilen. Ihm zugewandt hält ein anderer, ganz ähnlich aussehender Mann eine der Münzen zwischen Daumen und Zeigefinger, wie um deren Echtheit zu prüfen[38]. Ein dritter, dicht hinter dem Tisch stehender Mann schaut hingegen in die entgegengesetzte Richtung und macht einen Zeigegestus mit der rechten Hand, entweder auf den Mann hinter ihm oder auf die Vorgänge am Tisch weisend; wahrscheinlich spricht er mit einer Person, die links in dem fehlenden Teil des Reliefs zu ergänzen ist und aufgeklappt vor sich ein ähnliches Konvolut von Schrifttafeln hält, wie es vor ihr auf dem Tisch liegt[39]. Daneben ist ein Körbchen mit kleineren Rundlingen zu erkennen, wahrscheinlich auch Münzen, also Klein- und damit wohl am ehesten Wechselgeld. Von den Männern im Vordergrund unterscheiden sich vier weitere Männer im Hintergrund nicht nur durch ihre Bärte und die größere Vielfalt an Frisuren. Augenscheinlich sind sie älter, ihre Gesichter wirken expressiver, gleichsam vom Leben gezeichnet; der Mann in der Mitte hält das Haupt nach vorne gebeugt, als ächze er vor Anstrengung. Im Gegensatz zu der Gruppe am Tisch haben die Mäntel der Älteren alle Kapuzen, eine gebräuchliche Chiffre dafür, dass sie eine längere Weg-

---

[36] Geld wird bei der Interpretation von ›Alltagsbildern‹ oft vorschnell als harmloser Gegenstand der Lebensrealität verkannt, übt aber assoziativ starke Reize aus und wird folglich kaum beiläufig in die Bilder gesetzt, sondern markiert zumeist Hierarchien und/oder auch Wertkonflikte. In der attischen Vasenmalerei etwa ersetzen Geldsäcke ab ca. 500 v. Chr. zunehmend die gegenständlichen Geschenke bei Szenen der sog. Liebeswerbung und erhöhen dadurch den Aspekt der Käuflichkeit der Liebe: s. Meyer 1988, bes. 103–123.

[37] von Massow 1932, 215–216 Kat. 303 Taf. 59; Baltzer 1983, 49–50. 98 Kat. 28 Abb. 61; Langner 2001, 339 Abb. 24; Birley 2012, 21 Abb. oben.

[38] Vgl. von Massow 1932, 215; Drinkwater 1981, 217–218.

[39] Baltzer 1983, 49; Klöckner – Stark 2017, 98 Abb. 1.

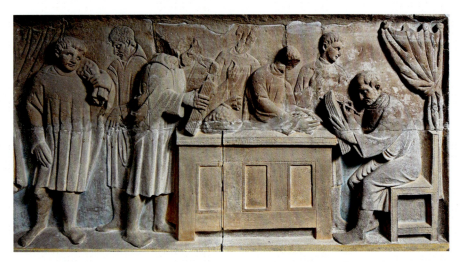

2   Reliefblock vom sog. Zirkusdenkmal mit Geldabrechnung, gefunden in Neumagen, 1. Hälfte 3. Jh. n. Chr., RLM Trier Inv. 994. 10014b–d <https://arachne.dainst.org/entity/6910595>, Foto Th. Zühmer)

strecke über Land hinter sich haben[40]. Die beiden Männer rechts weisen je einen breiten Riemen auf, der von der Schulter schräg über den Körper geführt ist. Vermutlich führen sie Taschen mit sich; der Bildzusammenhang legt nahe: Taschen voller Geld! Dass es sich tatsächlich so verhält, wissen wir dank besser erhaltener Bildszenen übereinstimmenden Sujets. Ein unwesentlich größerer Reliefblock, der vom sog. Zirkusdenkmal aus Neumagen stammt (Abb. 2)[41], komplettiert für uns die Szenerie: Hier erfahren wir, dass die abschließende Figur ein sitzender Mann sein muss, der ein Tafelwerk aufgeschlagen vor sich hält und mit einem Stilus Eintragungen vornimmt; seine Stirn ist gefurcht, der Blick fixiert, das Schreiben verlangt ihm alle Konzentration ab. Haltung und Tätigkeit sowie die Barttracht und die etwas feiner gefältelte Gewandung verraten uns, dass er in diesem Bild die entscheidende Autoritätsperson sein muss. Vorhänge zeigen an, dass sich die Szene in einem separierten Innenraum abspielt. Durch die Komposition und die bereits benannten Details wird folgender Ablauf der Handlung suggeriert: Männer, müde vom langen Schleppen, bringen säckeweise Geld in ein Haus, wo es von der Dienerschaft in Empfang genommen, geprüft und gezählt wird[42]. Der Schreiber hält das Ergebnis zum Zwecke der Dokumentation fest. Das Geld verbleibt danach im Haus, denn die Tische erweisen sich bei näherer Betrachtung häufig als mächtige, abschließbare Truhen, bilden also nicht nur eine Unterlage, sondern zugleich den Tresor[43].

Die Taxonomie archäologischer Bildbetrachtung zählt solche Darstellungen zu den sog. Alltagsszenen, genauer zu den Wiedergaben von Berufen. In dieser Sparte werden sie herkömmlich mit Margot Baltzer als ›Kontorszenen‹ oder ›Zahlungsszenen‹ angesprochen[44]. Wie Martin Langner in seiner eingehenden Analyse zu den Darstellungen von Handel und Handwerk auf gallorömischen Grabmälern zu Recht bemerkt hat, kann die Bezeichnung Kontor jedoch zu Missverständnissen führen, wenn man sich darunter ein spezifisches Büro oder gar eine eigene Profession vorstellt[45]. Außerdem handelt es sich bei den Zählenden auch nicht um Beamte, wie in Analogie

---

[40] Klöckner – Stark 2017, 100.
[41] von Massow 1932, 145–148 Kat. 182 Abb. 93 Taf. 29 unten (vgl. oben links); Baltzer 1983, 50–58. 98 Nr. 29 Abb. 62; Klöckner – Stark 2017, 101–102 Abb. 5. – Von diesem Denkmal stammt auch eine weitere, schlechter erhaltene ›Kontorszene‹, die auf der gegenüberliegenden Langseite angebracht war: Klöckner – Stark 2017, 101–102 Abb. 3. 4; zum Grabmal s. auch Numrich 1997, 110–113.
[42] Aus der Betonung der Anstrengung geht im Grunde unmissverständlich hervor, dass das Geld gebracht und nicht mitgenommen wird; s. dagegen Drinkwater 1981, 218. 224; Langner 2001, 340–342.
[43] Langner 2001, 339 Abb. 23.
[44] Baltzer 1983, 46–60.
[45] Langner 2001, 337.

zu römischen Staatsreliefs angenommen wurde[46]. Vielmehr lassen die Bilder dort, wo ihr ikonologischer Kontext besser zu greifen ist, klar erkennen, dass wir es in aller Regel mit Geldgeschäften zu tun haben, die einen Teil des Handels mit Ländereien oder Waren ausmachen[47]. Unverkennbar ist das der Fall am Pfeilergrabmal der Secundinier in Igel, wo eine solche ›Kontorszene‹ sogar zweimal vorhanden ist: Auf dem Sockel der südlichen Vorderseite des Grabbaus (Abb. 3 a. b), gleich unterhalb der zentralen Wiedergabe der Grabherren, wird links im Relief Geld gezählt und notiert, während rechts eine große Stoffbahn ausgebreitet und begutachtet wird. Getrennt voneinander wiederholen sich diese Vorgänge im Attikageschoss, wo die Textilien auf der Südseite für den Verkauf verhandelt und auf der Ostseite kassiert werden[48]. Weitere über den Bau verteilte Reliefs zeigen, wie die Tuche zu Ballen verschnürt und auf allen möglichen Wegen – per Schiff, mit dem Wagen oder mit Mauleseln – zu den Abnehmern transportiert werden sowie Klienten, die Abgaben in Form von Naturalien leisten[49]. Es handelt sich hier also um Bilder, die den reichen Ertrag der weitläufigen Geschäfte sinnfällig machen[50], auf dem der Wohlstand der Secundinier beruhte[51]. Dieser ermöglichte ihnen einen gehobenen Lebensstil, wie aus dem Fries über dem Bild der Grabherren hervorgeht, wo die Männer mit ihren Frauen tafeln, während in den Nachbarräumen Sklaven Speisen und Getränke vorbereiten[52]. In der Zusammenschau wird demnach deutlich, dass die einzelnen Bildszenen des Grabmals inhaltlich aufeinander abgestimmt sind und sich zu einer Gesamtaussage verdichten lassen, in deren Zentrum der gesellschaftliche Status der Familie steht[53]. Anja Klöckner hat jüngst aufgezeigt, mit welchen subtilen Bildmitteln die Rezipienten der Igeler Säule zu einer solchen Synthese regelrecht hingeleitet wurden, etwa durch das wiederkehrende Element des Wassers nicht nur in den Schifffahrts-, sondern auch in den mythologischen Szenen, die hier nicht weiter berücksichtigt werden können[54]. Wurde früher vor allem der Unterschied zwischen mythologischen und lebensweltlichen Darstellungen hinsichtlich ihrer Bildsprache betont, indem man bei Letzteren ihren ›Realismus‹ in den Vordergrund stellte, überwiegt inzwischen in der Forschung die Einsicht, dass auch die sog. Alltagsszenen als Konstrukte im Dienste zielgerichteter Mitteilungsabsichten zu begreifen sind und nicht etwa retrospektive, aus naiver Erzählfreude resultierende ›Momentaufnahmen‹ aus dem Leben der Verstorbenen präsentieren[55]. Die vielbeschworene Detailtreue der Realien erweist sich vielmehr als völlig zweckgebunden, nämlich die ökonomische Tüchtigkeit der Grabherrn in allen Belangen zu unterstreichen. In

---

[46] Baltzer 1983, bes. 48–49.
[47] Die Bilder selbst geben kaum konkreten Aufschluss darüber, aus welchen Quellen das Geld stammt. Vielmehr erweisen sie sich als kontextabhängig, sodass es kaum sinnvoll erscheint, die ›Zahlungsszenen‹ als Bildtypus in ihrem Gehalt auf ganz bestimmte Geschäfte zu verengen: vgl. Drinkwater 1981, 216. In manchen Fällen kommen auch Darlehen oder ähnliche Geldgeschäfte in Frage (s. Drinkwater 1981, 218–223; Langner 2001, 342), aber der Sinn der Szenen bleibt stets der, dass der Grabinhaber daran erheblich verdient.
[48] Zahn 1982, 9 Abb. 5; 19–20 Abb. 16. 17.
[49] Zahn 1982, 22 Abb. 19; 24 Abb. 22; 25–26 Abb. 25. 30; 28–31 Abb. 28. 29; vgl. Colling – Zeippen 2009, 59 Abb. unten; 165 Abb. oben (*Ara Lunae* – Arlon); s. auch Ritter 2002, 169 Abb. 10 (Sarkophagdeckel Trier). Drinkwater 1981, 225–226 schlägt alternativ vor, dass die mitgebrachten Lebensmittel keine Abgaben, sondern lediglich die Versorgung des Hauses mit den Erträgen der eigenen Ländereien meinen. Die Darstellungsabsicht ändert sich dadurch freilich kaum, da so oder so das reiche Auskommen der Secundinii zur Schau getragen wird.
[50] Geld als Medium macht Kapital in abstrakter Form konkurrenzlos gegenständlich erfahrbar: vgl. Krämer 2016, 157–158. Dieses Vorzeigen oder Evident-Machen korrespondiert zum grundsätzlichen Habitus vieler öffentlicher Bildwerke in den Provinzen: s. Hölscher 2012.
[51] Drinkwater 1981, 223–224 betont m. E. zu Recht das Großunternehmen der Secundinier, da die Reliefbilder keineswegs auf einen Familienbetrieb hindeuten, der sich auf das eigene Haus beschränkt.
[52] Ritter 2002/2003, 150 Abb. 2–3.
[53] Vgl. Klöckner – Stark 2017, 103–105 Abb. 6–8, die in ihrer Analyse des sog. Elternpaarpfeilers aus Neumagen (Numrich 1997, 114–117) zu einem übereinstimmenden Ergebnis gelangen. Dieses Grabmal enthält ebenfalls eine Zahlungsszene, wenn auch stark verkürzt und ohne deutliche Hervorhebung des Geldes wie bei den oben besprochenen Neumagener Grabreliefs mit ›Kontorszenen‹. Möglicherweise spielt es eine Rolle, dass hier anscheinend der Grabherr selbst die Einnahmen registriert und nicht sein Verwalter.
[54] Klöckner 2020.
[55] s. dazu Ritter 2002/2003, bes. 166–168.

3   Igeler Säule, Relief mit Geldabrechnungsszene vom Sockel der Südseite, 1. Drittel 3. Jh. n. Chr. (a: Projekt Grabdenkmäler aus Augusta Treverorum, GU Frankfurt, Foto K.-U. Mahler; b: Umzeichnung aus: Zahn 1982, 8 Abb. 5)

unserem Zusammenhang wird Reichtum durch die Wiedergabe von Geld somit nicht einfach bloß explizit gemacht. Der Gelderwerb ist eingebettet in eine Reihe von notwendigen Voraussetzungen. So ist er nicht zuletzt das Resultat exakter Buchführung und präziser Kalkulation, wie Martin Langner bestechend herausgestellt hat[56]. Er erfordert erhebliche Kompetenzen im Rechnen und Schreiben; darüber hinaus Sorgfalt in der Produktion und im Umgang mit den Waren, eine ausgeklügelte Logistik und Einsicht in die Bedürfnisse der Kunden. Der Reichtum ist nicht einfach da, sondern er ist verdient und seine Zurschaustellung wird dadurch leistungsorientiert legitimiert.

Bemerkenswert ist nun, dass die besagten ›Kontor-‹ und ›Zahlungsszenen‹ nicht nur auf großen Grabbauten gang und gäbe sind, die schon an und für sich einen gewissen Reichtum signalisieren, sondern auch auf Grabmälern mittlerer und kleiner Größe, wobei die Szenen der geringeren Bildfläche gemäß auf das Wesentliche reduziert sind. Der Nischengrabstein eines Sagum-Herstel-

[56] Langner 2001, 342–343.

4   Nischengrabstein eines Textilhändlers aus Arlon, 1. Hälfte 3. Jh. n. Chr., Musée Archéologique d'Arlon Inv. GR/S 047 (aus: Deru 2010, 74 Abb. 67)

lers aus Arlon etwa (Abb. 4)[57] zeigt auf der einen Nebenseite den Geschäftsinhaber einmal beim Verkaufsgespräch mit Kunden aus dem militärischen Umfeld, die auf komfortablen Sitzmöbeln das Warenangebot vorgeführt bekommen, einmal im Register darunter bei der Abrechnung. Auf der gegenüberliegenden Schmalseite korrespondieren dazu zwei Transportszenen mit Fuhrwerk, während die Hauptansichtsseite auch hier die Familie der Grabmalsetzer in reicher provinzialer Bürgertracht präsentiert[58]. Auf einem kleinen Grabpfeiler in Metz ist die ›Kontorszene‹ sogar in den Mittelpunkt gerückt[59]; der Haufen Geld vor dem *dominus* ist so groß, dass die Münzen bald von der Truhe zu rutschen drohen. Nach Hannelore Rose sind auf den Nebenseiten Bedienstete zu sehen, die analog zu den ausführlicheren Wiedergaben weitere Geldsäcke herbeibringen[60]. Ähnlich verhält es sich auf einem noch kleineren Grabstein in Arlon (Abb. 5)[61], dessen Vorderseite die vertraute Abrechnungsszene wiedergibt, während auf den Nebenseiten der Tuchhandel lediglich durch aufgehängte Vorhänge evoziert wird, über denen sich heute nur noch schemenhaft kleine Büsten abzeichnen[62], die eventuell auf das übliche Präsentieren der Ware verweisen sollten[63]. Mit seinem überdimensionierten Aufsatz eines Pinienzapfens erinnert das Grabmal an den typischen Firstschmuck großer Grabbauten[64]. Der Anspruch seiner Auftraggeber, als besonders geschäftstüchtig angesehen zu werden, war also nicht weniger ausgeprägt als bei Großunternehmern wie den Secundinii. Und Vergleichbares dürfte generell für die überaus zahlreichen Berufsdarstellungen auf Grabdenkmälern in den Nordwestprovinzen gelten, wobei sich ihre Verbreitung im Gebiet der Treverer und Mediomatriker, also vor allem an der Wasserstraße Mosel, aber auch im

---

[57] Baltzer 1983, 99 Kat. 34 Abb. 66; Lefèbvre 1990, 73–75 Nr. 49; Freigang 1997, 410 Kat. Trev 80 Taf. 25; Langner 2001, 329–331. 339 Abb. 15; Deru 2010, 70 Abb. 67; Langner 2020, 22 Abb. 4.
[58] Vgl. Freigang 1997, 421 Kat. Med 167 Taf. 37.
[59] Baltzer 1983, 100 Kat. 41 Abb. 69; Langner 2001, 339 Abb. 22.
[60] Rose 2007, 153–154 Abb. 2–4; Rose 2020, 123 Abb. 7.
[61] Esp. 4098; Baltzer 1983, 99 Kat. 35; Rose 2007, 155–156 Abb. 5.
[62] s. allerdings die eher kommemorativ eingesetzten Vorhänge auf den Nebenseiten eines anderen Grabsteins aus Arlon: Colling – Zeippen 2009, 120–121 Nr. 71.
[63] Zu ähnlichen ›Verkürzungen‹ der Tuchszene s. Drexel 1920, 93–94 Abb. 6; Rose 2007, 158–159 Abb. 9–11.
[64] Vgl. z. B. Kempchen 1995, 7–8 (Bierbach); Kremer 2009a, 99. 213 Nr. 82 (Bartringen [?]); Henz – Klöckner 2009, 69–70 Abb. 3 (Wareswald); s. auch Numrich 1997, Kat. 45. 50; Colling – Zeippen 2009, 125–126 Nr. 78. 79.

Einzugsgebiet der Rhône auffällig verdichtet[65]. Gleichwohl sind ›Kontor-‹ oder ›Zahlungsszenen‹ nicht nur in der *Gallia Belgica*, wo sie besonders zahlreich vertreten sind[66], sondern auch aus den benachbarten gallischen und germanischen Provinzen sowie in Rätien und auf dem Balkan überliefert[67]. Weitere affine Motive ließen sich einbeziehen – so das Vorzeigen von in Schatullen aufbewahrtem Schmuck –, die eine ähnliche Verbreitung erahnen lassen[68].

## STATUSSYMBOLE UND STÄNDEGESELLSCHAFT: DIE BILDERWELT DER GRABDENKMÄLER IN ITALIEN

Blickt man nun zum Vergleich auf Berufsdarstellungen auf Grabmälern in Rom und Italien, so ergeben sich gerade im Hinblick auf die Thematisierung von monetären Einnahmen als Chiffre für wirtschaftlichen Erfolg und durch Arbeit verdienten Wohlstand einige, m. E. signifikante Unterschiede. In seiner einschlägigen Monografie über die römischen Berufsdarstellungen in Italien verweist Gerhard Zimmer auf die *arca*, die Geldtruhe als Kennzeichen gut laufender Geschäfte[69]. Unter den knapp 200 Denkmälern in seinem Katalog, darunter die weitaus größte Gruppe aus sepulkralen Kontexten, sind es lediglich zwei, die Geldtruhen zeigen[70]: zum einen ein recht schlichter Grabbau von 3 m Höhe in Bolsena, auf dessen Fassade zwei Bäckerkollegen, ein Freigeborener und ein Freigelassener, die Kasse neben anderen Gegenständen ihres Metiers im Relief aufreihen ließen[71]; zum anderen die über 2,50 m hohe Grabstele des P. Longidienus (Abb. 6)[72], eines auf den Schiffsbau spezialisierten Freigelassenen in Ravenna, der die Geldtruhe ganz unten und sehr klein, aber gleichsam mit einem Augenzwinkern ins Bild gesetzt hat, indem sein bildliches Alter Ego sie bei der Bearbeitung der Schiffsspante als Trittstufe nutzt, um zu dem aufgedockten Boot emporzusteigen. Während das Registrieren von Einnahmen und der Abschluss von Geschäften mit zahlungskräftigen Kunden bei den Berufsdarstellungen durchaus eine Rolle spielt[73], bleibt das explizite Ins-Bild-Setzen von Geld auf den Denkmälern bezeichnenderweise aus.

Anders verhält es sich bei den ›Kontorszenen‹ auf Sarkophagen stadtrömischer Produktion: Sie stellen die Geldkisten meist prononciert in den Vordergrund, Geld liegt darauf entweder unmittelbar sichtbar oder in Säcken[74]. Allerdings sind diese Szenen selbst in der Regel eher zu-

---

[65] s. die Verbreitungskarte bei Langner 2001, 303 Abb. 3; s. außerdem Freigang 1997, 421 Kat. Med. 168; S. 426 Kat. Med 183 Taf. 40; S. 431–432 Kat. Med 197 Taf. 41; Langner 2020, 22 Abb. 5. In letzter Konsequenz reichte auch der Geldbeutel als Zeichen für sich, ohne dass herleitende Bilder hinzutraten: s. z. B. Freigang 1997, 310. 418 Kat. Trev 140 Taf. 34; S. 420 Kat. Med 158. Etwas dezenter, aber nicht weniger symbolträchtig sind die Codices aus mehreren Schreibtäfelchen in den Händen der Grabherren: Freigang 1997, 310; ausführlich stehen sie im Vordergrund in der ›Zahlungsszene‹ auf dem Neumagener Elternpaarpfeiler: Stark 2020, 66–67 Abb. 4. 5.

[66] Baltzer 1983, Kat. 18–22. 28–41; s. ferner (nach Langner 2001, 337 Anm. 163): Esp. 4102. 4161 (?). 4183 (?). 5098 (?). 7236 (?)

[67] Baltzer 1983, Kat. 23. 42–50; Bakker 1985; Gairhos – Schneider-Kerl 2020, 205 Abb. 9; s. ferner (nach Langner 2001, 337 Anm. 163): Esp. 2778 (?). 2835 (?). 3198 (?). 3200 (beide Paris). 3444 (?). 3638 (?). CSIR Deutschland I 1 (1973) 25–26 Kat. 26 Taf. 10; Neu 1989, 348–351 Abb. 141. 142. Deschler-Erb – Agricola 2021, 118.

[68] Lefèbvre 1990, 48 Nr. 22; Freigang 1997, 314. 316 Kat. Trev 83, 1 VS Taf. 25; Boppert 2001a, 106 Kat. 87 Taf. 60; Boppert 2001b; Langner 2003, 194–196 Abb. 4. 8. 9; s. auch Klöckner – Stark 2019. Einen Nachklang erlebte das Motiv im berühmten Deckengemälde der spätantiken Domus unter dem Trierer Dom: Weber 2000, 24 Abb. 15. – Das abgeschwächte Pendant bilden die Parfumfläschchen, die auf Grabsteinen von Paaren oft als Accessoire des weiblichen Luxus dem männlichen Attribut der Schreibtäfelchen gegenüberstehen: s. z. B. Lefèbvre 1990, 56 Nr. 27; S. 74 Nr. 49; Rose 2007, 174–175 Abb. 31; s. allg. Freigang 1997, 314–315. Sie können als Abbreviatur für die ausführliche Szene aufwendiger Damentoilette auf dem Neumagener Elternpaarpfeiler verstanden werden: Drexel 1920, 98–99 Abb. 9; Freigang 1997, 326–327; Stark 2020, 64–66 Abb. 2. 3; vgl. Colling – Zeippen 2009, 165 Abb. unten.

[69] Zimmer 1982, 69.

[70] Allerdings sind ›Kontorszenen‹ bei ihm bewusst außer Acht gelassen worden: Zimmer 1982, 2. Baltzer 1983, 57–58 verweist auf zwei Sarkophagreliefs aus Aquileia (Kat. 51 Abb. 83) und Ravenna.

[71] Zimmer 1982, 118–119 Kat. 30.

[72] Zimmer 1982, 143–144 Kat. 62; Petersen 2015, 226–227 Abb. 11.6.

[73] Baltzer 1983, 97–98 Kat. 24–26; Zimmer 1981, Kat. 2. 177. 179. 193.

[74] Baltzer 1983, 102 Kat. 53. 54. 56. 57; Amedick 1991, 113–114 Kat. 88. 134. 172. 251. 259.

»Über Geld spricht man nicht!«? Unterschiede in der Zurschaustellung von Reichtum und Status  437

6   Grabstele des Schiffsbauers P. Longidienus aus *Classis*, Beginn 1. Jh. n. Chr., Ravenna, San Vitale, Museo Nazionale Inv. 7 (D-DAI-ROM-4672)

5   Grabstein aus Arlon mit Abrechnung auf der Vorderseite, 1. Hälfte 3. Jh. n. Chr., La Cour d'Or, Musées de Metz Inv. 75.38.70 (iDAI.objects/Arachne: 90125,00_FA-Fitt-4045-07)

7   Fragment eines Riefelsarkophags mit Darstellung eines Geldwechslers, Beginn 3. Jh. n. Chr., Rom, Pal. Salviati (D-DAI-ROM-4657)

rückhaltend auf den Deckeln oder Nebenseiten der Sarkophage angebracht. Lediglich auf einem Riefelsarkophag aus der Sammlung Salviati (Abb. 7)[75] befindet sich die ›Kontorszene‹ mit der aus Neumagen vertrauten Prüfung der Münzen prominent und ohne weitere erzählerische Einbettung unter dem inzwischen verlorenen Porträtmedaillon im Zentrum der Vorderseite, weshalb hier über den Berufsstand eines Bankiers (*argentarius*) spekuliert wird[76]. Geldsäcke spielen ferner bei Sarkophagen eine Rolle, die aufwendige Reisen oder Preisgelder bei Wettkämpfen thematisieren[77]. Für unseren Zusammenhang ist jedoch entscheidend, dass die Bilder auf den Sarkophagen dereinst im Vergleich zu den bisher behandelten Grabdenkmälern lediglich einen sehr überschaubaren Rezipientenkreis angesprochen haben, der nur bedingt als öffentlich bezeichnet werden kann, vielmehr im engsten Kreis von Familie, Freunden und Bekannten anzusiedeln ist[78].

---

[75] Baltzer 1983, 102 Kat. 55 Abb. 87.
[76] Amedick 1991, 156 Kat. 214 Taf. 111, 1–3.
[77] Wagenfahrten mit Reisebörsen und kostbarem Hausrat: Amedick 1991, 50. 108; Preisgelder: Amedick 1991, 92. 116.
[78] Zanker – Ewald 2004, 31–33; Meinecke 2014, 16–20. 34–37. 62–71.

## BILDERRÄUME UND WERTEWELTEN

Bleibt also abschließend die Frage, wie der unterschiedliche Umgang mit Geld als Formel der Bildsprache am Grab in den Nordwestprovinzen und in Italien erklärt werden kann. Dabei ist zunächst zu betonen, dass die Zurschaustellung von Reichtum den römischen Grabmälern in Italien ja alles andere als fremd ist. Implizit ist sie zumindest allen aufwendigen Grabarchitekturen naturgemäß zu eigen. Im Bildrepertoire der Grabbauten wird dort aber in der Regel auf andere Mittel zurückgegriffen, um sich innerhalb der Gesellschaft zu profilieren[79]. Adelige aus dem Senatoren- und Ritterstand verweisen bevorzugt auf allgemeine, für die *res publica* relevante Errungenschaften oder bringen ohne Umschweife Amtsinsignien oder andere Symbole ihres aristokratischen Standings zum Einsatz[80]. Ganz im Sinne der eingangs zitierten Ansicht des Plinius definieren sie ihren Status exklusiv, zelebrieren sich gegenüber den Anderen als unerreichbare Elite.

Für die wohlhabende Mittelschicht boten sich verschiedene Wege an, darauf zu reagieren: Der Selfmademan Eurysaces inszeniert sich mit seinem ungewöhnlichen Grabbau aus der Übergangszeit von der späten Republik zum frühen Prinzipat durchaus vergleichbar zu den Provinzialen[81]. Trotz Abrechnungsszene setzt er allerdings mehr auf die Komplexität seines Handwerks und die Vielzahl an Arbeitskräften, die für ihn tätig sind, als auf die unmittelbare Wirkung des Geldes; daneben betont er durch die Toga den erreichten Bürgerstatus und rühmt sich inschriftlich, nicht nur Großunternehmer, sondern auch Amtsdiener der Ädilen gewesen zu sein[82]. Es kann allerdings kaum ein Zufall sein, dass wir in Rom in der Folgezeit keine direkten Nachahmer finden[83].

Im munizipalen Kontext Italiens betonen vermögende Freigelassene wie etwa C. Munatius Faustus, der Gatte der Naevolaeia Tyche, in Pompeji[84] und C. Lusius Storax in *Teate Marrucinorum* (Chieti)[85] vor allem ihre Munifizenz sowie die Ämter, die ihrem gesellschaftlichen Status zugänglich waren, und priorisieren diese Statussymbole vor gleichwohl auch vorhandenen Bildern, die den Ursprung ihres Vermögens andeuten; im Falle des Faustus wohl der Fernhandel zur See[86]. Dadurch setzen sie sich freilich auch von den unteren Schichten stärker ab. Es hat somit den Anschein, dass die repräsentativen Strategien solcher Grabbauten der räumlichen Nähe zu den Kreisen der Aristokratie, die vor allem in Italien sesshaft waren, insbesondere, was die Herausstellung von Ämtern betrifft, Rechnung trugen. Die Zurschaustellung von persönlichem Reichtum spielte auch hier – analog zu Trimalchios fiktiver Wohltätigkeit – eine große Rolle, allerdings nur so weit, wie die Grenzen des *decor* gewahrt blieben.

In den Nordwestprovinzen ist der vorherrschende Eindruck ein völlig anderer[87]: Zwar gibt es auch hier erhebliche Unterschiede im Aufwand der Grabdenkmäler, aber die zugehörige Bilderwelt erweist sich als deutlich homogener. Das gilt nicht nur für die hier betrachteten Monumente mit Darstellungen aus dem Berufsleben, sondern ließe sich auch an anderen Beispielen aufzeigen wie etwa den Reitergrabsteinen[88], die den großen Grabbauten mit Reliefs von Reiterschlachten[89] motivisch denkbar nahestehen. Viele andere Motive wie etwa dionysische oder Bankettszenen

---

[79] von Hesberg 1992, 235–237.
[80] Schäfer 1989, 233–410; Feraudi-Gruénais 2005; Spalthoff 2010, bes. 111. 113–118 Kat. 2. 3. 5. 11. 20. 21. 23. 25. 26. 28. 31. 33. 35. 37. 40. 42. 44. 45. 47. 49–54. 60. 62. 63. 65–67. 68–70. 74. 75. 77. 81. 84. 86–88. 92. 103–105. 109. 110. 112. 116. 118. 119. 122. 130. 133. 135. 136. 140. 141–145. 149–151. 153. 154. 156. 161. 163. 166. 170. 171.173. 175. 178. 182. M15; Borg 2019, 1–76.
[81] Ciancio Rossetto 1973; Zimmer 1982, 21–24. 106–109 Kat. 18.
[82] CIL I² 1203–1205.
[83] Petersen 2006, 84–120; Stewart 2008, 64–65; Silver 2009.
[84] Kockel 1983, 100–109.
[85] Bianchi Bandinelli u. a. 1963/1964; Flecker 2015, 205–209 Kat. A 27; Petersen 2015, 219–220 Abb. 11.3.
[86] Vgl. oben Anm. 28.
[87] Anders von Hesberg 1992, 211–213, der die Unterschiede zeitlich vor dem Hintergrund eines allgemeinen Mentalitätswandels im Sinne des bürgerlichen ›Rückzugs ins Private‹ begreift.
[88] Schleiermacher 1984.
[89] Gabelmann 1973; Andrikopoulou-Strack 1986, Taf. 25 c; Colling – Zeippen 2009, 69–70 Nr. 29; S. 72 Nr. 31; S. 76 Nr. 35; Kremer 2009a, 79–85; Scholz 2012, 99–100 Abb. 70. 71; Tabaczek 2019.

kommen hinzu⁹⁰. Es besteht also eine generell große Anschlussfähigkeit, die selbst in den Denkmalformen wie in einzelnen Ornamenten und isolierten Bildmotiven zum Ausdruck kommt⁹¹. Daher lässt sich m. E. die Grabrepräsentation der Nordwestprovinzen im Kontrast zu der in Italien als inklusiv bezeichnen⁹². Dass Geld in dieser durchaus leistungsorientierten Bilderwelt offenbar keinen Anstoß erregte, ergibt sich dadurch, dass von diesem Medium auf symbolischer Ebene ebenfalls eine inklusive (und interaktive) Botschaft ausging⁹³. Zweifelsohne hängt Reichtum maßgeblich davon ab, wie viel Ertrag die Geschäfte abwerfen: Besitz ist exklusiv, das wesentliche Merkmal des Geldes ist seine Quantität⁹⁴. Aber Geld als Tauschmittel und Wertspeicher schließt alle Waren und Dienstleistungen ein und macht sie übersetz- und übertragbar⁹⁵. In der Wertewelt des Handels schafft Geld – nicht zuletzt auch über die kulturellen Unterschiede innerhalb der provinzialen Bevölkerung hinweg⁹⁶ – soziale Beziehungen⁹⁷, Teilhabe und theoretisch unbegrenzte Wachstumsmöglichkeiten. Seine Früchte standen grundsätzlich jedem offen, nicht nur den von Geburt an Privilegierten⁹⁸. Außer Frage steht, dass auch hier in den Bildern klare Hierarchien zwischen Herrschaft und Sklaven, Gläubigern und Schuldnern formuliert werden⁹⁹. Aber in den Bildprogrammen der Grabmäler werden umgekehrt keine Standesgrenzen gezogen, die den gesellschaftlichen Aufstieg per se aussichtslos erscheinen lassen.

In den Regionen der Nordwestprovinzen, die im Fokus der hier geäußerten Überlegungen stehen, scheinen vielmehr die skizzierten Qualitäten des Handels und Geldverkehrs so dominant gewesen zu sein, dass sie einen bemerkenswert großen Anteil an der sepulkralen Bilderwelt gewonnen haben¹⁰⁰. Damit korrespondiert auch, dass die munizipale Amtselite und ritterliche Würdenträger in den Grabmälern des Trierer Raums, aber auch weit darüber hinaus – zumindest nach dem 1. Jahrhundert n. Chr. – quantitativ keine nennenswerte Rolle spielten, wie jüngst Jean

---

⁹⁰ Die Denkmäler ähneln einander trotz denkbar unterschiedlicher Dimensionen erheblich: Langner 2001, 302 Abb. 1. 2; Kremer 2020, 34 Abb. 6. – Zu Bankettszenen s. z. B. Drexel 1920, 97. 126 Abb. 13 (integriert in den Alkestis-Mythos auf einem Sarkophag in Köln); Selzer 1988, 56 Abb. 38; Lefèbvre 1990, 78–79 Nr. 54; Freigang 1997, 323–325; Ritter 2002/2003, bes. 153 Anm. 7; S. 155 Abb. 5; S. 167; Rose 2020, 124 Abb. 9; s. auch Andrikopoulou-Strack 1986, Taf. 7. 21; Stewart 2008, 157 Abb. 38. 39. – Zu dionysischen Tänzern und Tänzerinnen s. z. B. Precht 1975, 52–54 Abb. 13 Taf. 14; Andrikopoulou-Strack 1986, Taf. 28 a. 29 a; Lefèbvre 1990, 39–41 Nr. 16; S. 41–45 Nr. 19; S. 48 Nr. 22; S. 53 Nr. 24; S. 56 Nr. 27; Colling – Zeippen 2009, 128 Nr. 82; Ditsch 2009, 94 Abb. 3; Kremer 2009a, 87–91; Kremer 2020, 32 Abb. 4; s. allgemein Freigang 1997, 350.

⁹¹ Bemerkenswert erscheinen in dieser Hinsicht etwa kleine Grabsteine aus den Nekropolen von Metz, die als Hauptbild die ubiquitären Akanthusblätter oder Rankenmotive tragen und mitunter die großen Grabbauten explizit als Architekturen *en miniature* zitieren: s. z. B. Rose 2020, 120 Abb. 4. 5; iDAI.objects: Nr. 1116001. 1116002. 1116009. 1116012. 1116013 (<https://arachne.dainst.org> [04.12.2023]); vgl. Selzer 1988, 55 Abb. 37; Scholz 2012, 180–182 Abb. 142–144; S. 431–432 Abb. 362. 364.

⁹² Ähnlich Freigang 1997, 382–383.

⁹³ Krämer 2016, 155–157. – Die Wertsachen waren einst farblich hervorgehoben: Delferrière – Edme 2020, bes. 175 Abb. 1; S. 185 Abb. 9 b.

⁹⁴ Simmel 1989, 338–371. – Freigang 1997, 368 betont daher, dass es den Auftraggebern der aufwendigen Grabmäler beim Hervorheben ihres Reichtums vornehmlich um soziale Distinktion gegangen sei; auf bildlich-symbolischer Ebene wäre diese Strategie dann allerdings tendenziell gescheitert, da die kleinen Grabmäler, wenn auch verkürzt, dieselben Motive zeigen.

⁹⁵ Simmel 1989, 55–92; Hénaff 2009, 505–508; Krämer 2016, 159–162. Luhmann 1994, 232 geht sogar so weit, eine strukturelle Analogie zwischen Geld und Sinn zu erkennen; vgl. Simmel 1989, 136.

⁹⁶ Zur Problematik des Begriffs kultureller Identität im gallorömischen Raum s. jüngst Langner 2020. – Die prominente Wiedergabe einer Abrechnungsszene bzw. eines Sacks voller Münzen (oder Schmuck [?]) auf einem Mausoleum in Saintes (Aquitanien) führt zu der Vermutung, dass eine direkte Beziehung zu den Treverern bestanden haben muss, doch ist das auch nicht zwingend zu fordern: Bouet 2015, 121–122 Abb. 11; s. auch S. 86 Abb. 74.

⁹⁷ Gerloff 1952, 122–124. – Zur Bedeutung der Münzprägung für die ›Romanisierung‹ s. jüngst Wigg-Wolf 2019, bes. 21; vgl. zur Wirkung der Monetarisierung Italiens in der späten Republik: Maschek 2018, 223–224.

⁹⁸ Bis in die Moderne wird dieser Aspekt der sozialen Nivellierung freilich mit Argumenten der Ästhetik kritisiert: Simmel 1989, 541 bringt das beispielsweise auf die Formel, dass Geld die »Vornehmheit« eliminiere.

⁹⁹ Vgl. Drexel 1920, 97. 99–102, der in den Darstellungen, angelehnt an Hettner 1881, 446–447 eine bewusste Herabwürdigung der Landbevölkerung sieht; s. dagegen überzeugend Drinkwater 1981, 216–217.

¹⁰⁰ Langner 2001, 305–306 gelangt in seiner Kalkulation zu etwa 25 % Anteil der Berufsdarstellungen unter den gallorömischen Grabmälern allgemein.

8 Grabstein des Blussus und der Menimane aus Mainz, Mitte 1. Jh. n. Chr., Landesmuseum Mainz Inv. S 146 (© GDKE_Landesmuseum Mainz, U. Rudischer)

Krier und Markus Scholz noch einmal festgestellt haben[101]. Die Abweichungen im sepulkralen Kommunikationsverhalten zu Italien lassen sich daher auf die spezifischen Charakteristika der Sozialstruktur in diesem Teil des Imperium Romanum zurückführen.

Letztlich spiegelt sich das ideologisch positive Image des Geldes auch in zahllosen Votivdenkmälern für Merkur, die den Gott stets mit einem prall gefüllten Sack voller Münzen wiedergeben, während er in Rom und Mittelitalien mit deutlich abwechslungsreicheren Attributen versehen wird[102]. Die wenigsten Zeitgenossen werden also angesichts des berühmten Grabsteins des Schiffseigners Blussus und seiner Frau Menimane (Abb. 8)[103] in Mainz die Nase gerümpft haben, wenn sie den ostentativ ins Bild gesetzten Sack mit Geld in seiner Linken wahrnahmen[104]. Vielmehr stand bei den gewiss nicht wenigen Menschen, die seine Werte- und Bilderwelt und damit seine Präferenzen der Sinnstiftung teilten, ein Gedanke im Vordergrund: Der Blussus und seine Familie, die haben es zu etwas gebracht! Und wer weiß: Vielleicht würde ihnen der ein oder andere Angehörige des Reichsadels, wie etwa der Dichter Ovid, trotz unterschwelliger Überheblichkeit sogar beipflichten[105]?

---

[101] Krier 2020; Scholz 2020. Vgl. Drinkwater 1981, 230–231, der m. E. allerdings etwas vorschnell davon ausgeht, dass die gallischen Händler und Unternehmer über keinen nennenswerten Grundbesitz verfügt hätten. So lassen sich Szenen wie etwa die der Jagd auf dem Elternpaarpfeiler aus Neumagen (s. Drexel 1920, 98 Abb. 8; Klöckner – Stark 2017, 107 Abb. 6; Stark 2020, 69 Abb. 9; s. außerdem Freigang 1997, 325–326; von Hesberg 2009, 182–184 Abb. 4. 5) durchaus als Anspielung auf ausgedehnte Ländereien verstehen, während die privaten Wagenfahrten den Aspekt wohlhabender Muße mit weitreichender Mobilität verknüpfen (vgl. oben Anm. 15 und 77): Freigang 1997, 329. – Freilich gibt es in dieser Region auch vereinzelt aristokratische Denkmäler, die sich einer anderen Formen- und Bildsprache bedienen, s. z. B. Deru 2010, 81 Abb. 75 (Kenotaph für die *principes iuventutis* C. und L. Caesar in Reims). Aber auch der Grabbau des *flamen Augusti* in Mersch scheint nicht aus dem üblichen Dekorrepertoire auszubrechen: Kremer 2009b.

[102] LIMC VI (1992) 500–554 s. v. Mercurius (E. Simon – G. Bauchhenß); Flecker 2021; Dorka Moreno u. a. 2021, 8 Abb. 8. Anders als Freigang 1997, 310 vermutet, ist der Geldbeutel aber gewiss nicht als symbolträchtiges Zeichen von den Darstellungen des Gottes auf die Bürger übertragen worden, sondern hat seinen bleibenden Bezugspunkt hier wie dort in der Lebenswelt.

[103] Selzer 1988, 95–98 Abb. 60; S. 168–169 Nr. 110; vgl. S. 167 Nr. 108.

[104] Ganz anders als die archäologische Forschung, die sich die Sichtweise der römischen Eliten lange Zeit mehr oder weniger bewusst zu eigen gemacht hat: s. Drexel 1920, 108, der mit Nachdruck von »Parvenukunst« als gleichsam zeitloser Kategorie spricht. – Freigang 1997, 372 erkennt zwar in den Bildideen der Region grundsätzlich »schöpferische Energie« am Werk, bescheinigt den Gallo-Römern dann aber doch bloß eine »konservative Grundhaltung«, indem sie entgegen der weiteren Entwicklung in Italien an der »Sepulkralkultur der sozialen Aufsteiger« im Stile eines Eurysaces festgehalten hätten. Das lässt sich allerdings nur behaupten, wenn die formalen und ikonografischen Anleihen der provinziellen Denkmäler an italische Vorbilder in traditioneller Einseitigkeit als pure Imitationen und nicht im Sinne der kreativen Aneignung ausgelegt werden; s. dagegen Maschek 2017; Dorka Moreno u. a. 2021.

[105] Ov. ars 2, 276: *Dummodo sit dives, barbarus ipse placet*. – P. Ovidius Naso (43 v.–17 [?] n. Chr.) war ritterlichen Standes und stammte aus *Sulmo*/Italien: PIR V 3 (1987) Nr. 180.

# BIBLIOGRAFIE

| | |
|---|---|
| Alföldy 2011 | G. Alföldy, Römische Sozialgeschichte ⁴(Stuttgart 2011) |
| Amedick 1991 | R. Amedick, Die Sarkophage mit Darstellungen aus dem Menschenleben, IV. Vita privata, ASR I 4 (Berlin 1991) |
| Andrikopoulou-Strack 1986 | J.-N. Andrikopoulou-Strack, Grabbauten des 1. Jahrhunderts n. Chr. im Rheingebiet (Bonn 1986) |
| Bakker 1985 | L. Bakker, Weinverkauf und Kontorszene auf dem Grabmal des Pompeianius Silvinus aus Augsburg, in: Die Römer in Schwaben. Jubiläumsausstellung »2000 Jahre Augsburg«. Ausstellungskatalog Augsburg 1985 (München 1985) 129–130 |
| Baltzer 1983 | M. Baltzer, Die Alltagsdarstellungen der treverischen Grabdenkmäler, TrZ 46, 1983, 7–151 |
| Bianchi Bandinelli u. a. 1963/1964 | R. Bianchi Bandinelli – M. Torelli – F. Coarelli – A. Giuliano, Il Monumento Teatino di C. Lusius Storax al Museo di Chieti, in: R. Bianchi Bandinelli (Hrsg.), Sculture municipali dell'area sabellica tra l'età di Cesare e quella di Nerone, StMisc 10 (Rom 1963/1964) 57–99 |
| Binsfeld u. a. 2020 | A. Binsfeld – A. Klöckner – G. Kremer – M. Reuter – M. Scholz (Hrsg.), Stadt – Land – Fluss. Grabdenkmäler der Treverer in lokaler und überegionaler Perspektive. Akten der internationalen Konferenz Neumagen/Trier 25.–27.10.2018, TrZ Beih. 37 (Trier 2020) |
| Birley 2012 | A. Birley, Das Landleben in der römischen Kunst, in: V. Rupp – H. Birley (Hrsg.), Landleben im römischen Deutschland (Stuttgart 2012) 16–22 |
| Boppert 2001a | W. Boppert, Römische Steindenkmäler aus dem Landkreis Bad Kreuznach, CSIR Deutschland II 9 (Mainz 2001) |
| Boppert 2001b | W. Boppert, Die Dame mit dem Schmuckkästchen. Zu einem Bildthema auf einem Grabsteinfragment aus Bad Kreuznach, in: T. A. S. M. Panhuysen (Hrsg.). Akten des 5. Internationalen Kolloquiums über das provinzialrömische Kunstschaffen im Rahmen des CSIR, Maastricht 29.05.–01.06.1997 (Maastricht 2001) 43–61 |
| Borg 2019 | B. Borg, Roman Tombs and the Art of Commemoration. Contextual Approachs to Funerary Customs in the Second Century CE (Cambridge 2019) |
| Boschung 2009 | D. Boschung (Hrsg.), Grabbauten des 2. und 3. Jahrhunderts in den gallischen und germanischen Provinzen. Akten des Internationalen Kolloquiums Köln 22.–23.02.2007 (Wiesbaden 2009) |
| Bouet 2015 | A. Bouet, Aquitanien in römischer Zeit (Darmstadt 2015) |
| Bringmann 2003 | K. Bringmann, Zur Überlieferung und zum Entstehungsgrund der lex Claudia de nave senatoris, Klio 85/2, 2003, 312–321 |
| Brodbeck 2016 | K.-H. Brodbeck, Geldtheorie im interdisziplinären Kontext, in: K.-H. Brodbeck – S. Graupe (Hrsg.), Geld! Welches Geld? Geld als Denkform. Symposium Bernkastel-Kues 08.–10.05.2015 (Marburg 2016) 295–341 |
| Ciancio Rossetto 1973 | P. Ciancio Rossetto, Il sepolcro del fornaio Marco Virgilio Eurisace a Porta Maggiore (Rom 1973) |
| Colling – Zeippen 2009 | D. Colling – L. Zeippen, La période gallo-romaine, in: L. Lejeune (Hrsg.), Le Musée Archéologique Luxembourgeois Arlon (Arlon 2009) 51–205 |
| Delferrière – Edme 2020 | N. Delferrière – A.-L. Edme, L'emploi de la couleur sur les monuments funéraires de Gaule romaine, in: Binsfeld u. a. 2020, 175–186 |
| Deschler-Erb – Agricola 2021 | E. Deschler-Erb – C. Agricola, Germania inferior. Die zivile Verwaltungsstruktur einer Provinz Roms, in: E. Claßen u. a. (Hrsg.), Roms fließende Grenzen. Ausstellungskatalog Detmold u. a. 2021/22 (Darmstadt 2021) 119–125. |
| Deru 2010 | X. Deru, Die Römer an Maas und Mosel (Mainz 2010) |
| Ditsch 2009 | S. Ditsch, Römische Grabbauten des 2. und 3. Jh. n. Chr. aus der Pfalz, in: Boschung 2009, 89–107 |
| Dorka Moreno u. a. 2021 | M. Dorka Moreno – J. Griesbach – J. Lipps, »You are all individuals!« Towards a phenomenology of sculpture production in the Roman provinces, in: J. Lipps – M. Dorka Moreno – J. Griesbach (Hrsg.), Aneignungsprozesse antiker Statuenschemata in den römischen Provinzen. Kolloquium Tübingen 15.–17.11.2018 (Wiesbaden 2021) 1–19 |
| Drexel 1920 | F. Drexel, Die Bilder der Igeler Säule, RM 35, 1920, 83–142 |

| | |
|---|---|
| Drinkwater 1981 | J. F. Drinkwater, Money-rents and food-renders in Gallic funerary reliefs, in: A. King – M. Henig (Hrsg.), The Roman West in the Third Century. Contributions from Archaeology and History (Oxford 1981) 216–225 |
| El Beheiri 2001 | N. El Beheiri, Die Lex Claudia de nave senatorum, RDroitsAnt, 48, 2001, 57–63 |
| Esp. | É. Espérandieu u. a., Recueil général des bas-reliefs, statues et bustes de la Gaule romaine I–XVI (Paris 1907–1981) |
| Feraudi-Gruénais 2005 | F. Feraudi-Gruénais, Für die Ewigkeit? Die Gestaltung von senatorischen Grablegen Roms und ihr Kontext, in: W. Eck – M. Heil (Hrsg.), Senatores populi Romani. Realität und mediale Präsentation einer Führungsschicht (Stuttgart 2005) 137–168 |
| Flecker 2015 | M. Flecker, Römische Gladiatorenbilder. Studien zu den Gladiatorenreliefs der späten Republik und der Kaiserzeit aus Italien (Wiesbaden 2015) |
| Flecker 2021 | M. Flecker, Glück, Fruchtbarkeit und Wohlstand. Weihesteine für Mercur, in: J. Lipps – J. Osnabrügge – S. Ardeleanu – C. Witschel (Hrsg.), Die römischen Steindenkmäler in den Reiss-Engelhorn-Museen Mannheim (Mannheim 2021) 472–511 |
| Freigang 1997 | Y. Freigang, Die Grabmäler der gallo-römischen Kultur im Moselland, JbRGZM 44, 1997, 277–440 |
| Gabelmann 1973 | H. Gabelmann, Römische Grabmonumente mit Reiterkampfszenen im Rheingebiet, BJb 173, 1973, 132–200 |
| Gairhos – Schneider-Kerl 2020 | S. Gairhos – S. Schneider-Kerl, Grabdenkmäler aus der rätischen Provinzhauptstadt Aelia Augusta/Augsburg. Merkmale, Einflüsse, Überlieferung, in: Binsfeld u. a. 2020, 197–206 |
| Gerloff 1952 | W. Gerloff, Geld und Gesellschaft (Frankfurt a. M. 1952) |
| Gloy 2020 | K. Gloy, Macht und Gewalt. Politik, Wissen, Psychologie, Geld, Netzwerke (Würzburg 2020) |
| Graßl 2019 | H. Graßl, Geldgier im Diskurs der späten Republik und frühen Kaiserzeit, in: C. Bachhiesel – M. Handy – P. Mauritsch – W. Petermandl (Hrsg.), Gier, Korruption und Machtmissbrauch in der Antike (Wien 2019) 57–70 |
| Hénaff 2009 | M. Hénaff, Der Preis der Wahrheit. Gabe, Geld und Philosophie (Frankfurt a. M. 2009) |
| Henig 2001 | M. Henig, Luxuria and Decorum. Changing values in Public and Private Live, in: L. Golden (Hrsg.), Raising the Eyebrow. John Onians and World Art Studies (London 2001) 133–151 |
| Henz – Klöckner 2009 | K.-P. Henz – A. Klöckner, Die Grabmäler im Wareswald bei Tholey, in: Boschung 2009, 69–88 |
| Hettner 1881 | F. Hettner, Die Neumagener Monumente, RhMusPhil 36, 1881, 435–462 |
| Hölscher 2012 | T. Hölscher, »Präsentativer Stil« im System der römischen Kunst, in: F. De Angelis – J.-A. Dickmann – F. Pirson – R. von den Hoff (Hrsg.), Kunst von unten? Stil und Gesellschaft in der antiken Welt von der »arte plebea« bis heute. Internationales Kolloquium anlässlich des 70. Geburtstages von Paul Zanker, Rom, Villa Massimo 08.–09.06.2007 (Wiesbaden 2012) 27–58 |
| Holten 2016 | J. Holten (Hrsg.), Gutes böses Geld: Eine Bildgeschichte der Ökonomie. Ausstellungskatalog Baden-Baden 2016 (Bielefeld 2016) |
| Kempchen 1995 | M. Kempchen, Mythologische Themen in der Grabskulptur. Germania Inferior, Germania Superior, Gallia Belgica und Raetia (Münster 1995) |
| Klöckner 2020 | A. Klöckner, Quelle, Fluss, Meer. Rezeptionslenkung durch Bezugsrahmen und Varianzstrategien am Beispiel des Secundiniergrabmals von Igel, in: Binsfeld u. a. 2020, 73–81 |
| Klöckner – Stark 2017 | A. Klöckner – M. Stark, Bildsprache und Semantik der sog. Kontorszenen auf den Grabmonumenten der *Civitas Treverorum*, in: S. Lefebvre (Hrsg.), Iconographie du quotidien dans l'art provincial romain: modèles régionaux. Actes du XIVe Congrès international d'art provincial romain Dijon 01.–06.06.2015 (Dijon 2017) 97–108 |
| Klöckner – Stark 2019 | A. Klöckner – M. Stark, Der Stifter und sein Schmuck. Männer mit Fingerringen auf Grabdenkmälern der Nordwest- und Donauprovinzen, in: Porod – Scherrer 2019, 236–249 |
| Kockel 1983 | V. Kockel, Die Grabbauten vor dem Herkulaner Tor in Pompeji (Mainz 1983) |
| Krämer 2016 | S. Krämer, Medialität, Performativität und Sprachförmigkeit des Geldes. Drei Dimensionen über das Geld als Denkform zu reflektieren, in: K.-H. Brodbeck – S. Graupe (Hrsg.), Geld! Welches Geld? Geld als Denkform. Symposium Bernkastel-Kues 08.–10.05.2015 (Marburg 2016) 153–172 |

| | |
|---|---|
| Kremer 2009a | G. Kremer, Das frühkaiserzeitliche Mausoleum von Bartringen, Luxemburg (Luxemburg 2009) |
| Kremer 2009b | G. Kremer, Der Grabbau eines *flamen* aus Mersch und die kaiserzeitlichen Grabbauten des Mosel- und Rheingebietes, in: Boschung 2009, 109–135 |
| Kremer 2020 | G. Kremer, Grabbauten des westlichen Treverergebiets. Neue Forschungsfragen und -ergebnisse, in: Binsfeld u. a. 2020, 27–36 |
| Krier 2020 | J. Krier, Die einheimische Führungsschicht in den Grabdenkmälern und Grabinschriften des Treverergebiets: Das 1. Jh. n. Chr. – und danach?, in: Binsfeld u. a. 2020, 37–48 |
| Langner 2001 | M. Langner, Szenen aus Handwerk und Handel auf gallo-römischen Grabmälern, JdI 116, 2001, 299–356 |
| Langner 2003 | M. Langner, Attribute auf gallo-römischen Grabreliefs als Ausdruck einer gesteigerten Wertschätzung materieller Güter, in: P. Noelke (Hrsg.), Romanisation und Resistenz in Plastik, Architektur und Inschriften der Provinzen des Imperium Romanum. Neue Funde und Forschungen. Akten des VII. Internationalen Colloquiums über Probleme des provinzialrömischen Kunstschaffens Köln 02.–06.05.2001 (Mainz 2003) 191–202 |
| Langner 2020 | M. Langner, Die Konstruktion einer gallo-römischen Identität, in: Binsfeld u. a. 2020, 13–26 |
| Lefèbvre 1990 | L. Lefèbvre, Le Musée Luxembourgeois Arlon (Brüssel 1990) |
| Luhmann 1994 | N. Luhmann, Geld als Kommunikationsmedium: Über symbolische und diabolische Generalisierungen, in: N. Luhmann, Die Wirtschaft der Gesellschaft (Frankfurt a. M. 1994) |
| Luhmann 2001 | N. Luhmann, Einführende Bemerkungen zu einer Theorie symbolisch generalisierter Kommunikationsmedien, in: N. Luhmann, Aufsätze und Reden (Stuttgart 2001) 31–75 |
| Maschek 2017 | D. Maschek, Transfer, Rezeption, Adaption. Archäologische Erklärungsmodelle zur Verbreitung römischer Steinarchitektur zwischen Struktur und Prozess, in: J. Lipps (Hrsg.), Transfer und Transformation römischer Architektur in den Nordwestprovinzen. Kolloquium Tübingen 06.–07.11.2015 (Rahden 2017) 35–45 |
| Maschek 2018 | D. Maschek, Die römischen Bürgerkriege. Archäologie und Geschichte einer Krisenzeit (Darmstadt 2018) |
| McLuhan 1964 | M. McLuhan, Money. The Poor Man's Credit Card, in: M. McLuhan, Understandig Media: The Extensions of Man (London 1964) 131–144 |
| Meinecke 2014 | K. Meinecke, Sarcophagum posuit. Römische Steinsarkophage im Kontext (Ruhpolding 2014) |
| Meyer 1988 | M. Meyer, Männer mit Geld. Zu einer rotfigurigen Vase mit ›Alltagsszene‹, JdI 103, 1988, 87–125 |
| Mratschek-Halfmann 1993 | S. Mratschek-Halfmann, Divites et praepotentes. Reichtum und soziale Stellung in der Literatur der Prinzipatszeit (Stuttgart 1993) |
| Neu 1989 | S. Neu, Römische Reliefs vom Kölner Rheinufer, KölnJb 22, 1989, 241–364 |
| Numrich 1997 | B. Numrich, Die Architektur der römischen Grabdenkmäler aus Neumagen. Beiträge zur Chronologie und Typologie, TrZ Beih. 22 (Trier 1997) |
| Petersen 2006 | L. H. Petersen, The Freedman in Roman Art and Art History (Cambridge 2006) |
| Petersen 2015 | L. H. Petersen, »Arte Plebea« and Non-elite Roman Art, in: B. Borg (Hrsg.), A Companion to Roman Art (Oxford 2015) 214–230 |
| Porod – Scherrer 2019 | B. Porod – P. Scherrer (Hrsg.), Der Stifter und sein Monument. Gesellschaft – Ikonographie – Chronologie. Akten des 15. Internationalen Kolloquiums zum Provinzialrömischen Kunstschaffen Graz 14.–20.06.2017 (Graz 2019) |
| Precht 1975 | G. Precht, Das Grabmal des L. Poblicius (Köln 1975) |
| Ritter 2002/2003 | S. Ritter, Zur Bildsprache römischer ›Alltagsszenen‹: Die Mahl- und Küchenreliefs am Pfeilergrabmal von Igel, BJb 202/203, 2002/2003, 149–170 |
| Rose 2007 | H. Rose, Vom Ruhm des Berufs. Darstellungen von Händlern und Handwerkern auf römischen Grabreliefs in Metz, in: F. Hölscher – T. Hölscher (Hrsg.), Römische Bilderwelten. Von der Wirklichkeit zum Bild und zurück. Kolloquium der Gerda Henkel Stiftung am DAI Rom 15.–17.03.2004 (Heidelberg 2007) 145–179 |
| Rose 2020 | H. Rose, Wer will fleißige Handwerker sehen … Ein Überblick über die reliefverzierten Grabmäler von Metz unter ikonographischen Gesichtspunkten, in: Binsfeld u. a. 2020, 117–127 |

| | |
|---|---|
| Schäfer 1989 | T. Schäfer, Imperii insignia. Sella curulis und fasces. Zur Repräsentation römischer Magistrate (Mainz 1989) |
| Scheuermann 2015 | E. S. Scheuermann, Cicero und das Geld (Frankfurt a. M. 2015) |
| Schleiermacher 1984 | M. Schleiermacher, Römische Reitergrabsteine. Die kaiserzeitlichen Reliefs des triumphierenden Reiters (Bonn 1984) |
| Scholz 2012 | M. Scholz, Grabbauten des 1.–3. Jahrhunderts in den nördlichen Grenzprovinzen des Römischen Reiches (Mainz 2012) |
| Scholz 2020 | M. Scholz, Zur Repräsentation munizipaler Magistrate und Würdenträger in Monumentinschriften in Augusta Treverorum/Trier und in anderen civitas-Metropolen Ostgalliens, in: Binsfeld u. a. 2020, 49–58 |
| Schriefl 2013 | A. Schriefl, Platons Kritik an Geld und Reichtum (Berlin 2013) |
| Schrumpf 2006 | S. Schrumpf, Bestattung und Bestattungswesen im römischen Reich. Ablauf, soziale Dimension und ökonomische Bedeutung der Totenfürsorge im lateinischen Westen (Göttingen 2006) |
| Selzer 1988 | W. Selzer, Römische Steindenkmäler. Mainz in römischer Zeit. Katalog zur Sammlung in der Steinhalle (Mainz 1988) |
| Silver 2009 | M. Silver, Glimpses of Vertical Integration/Disintegration in Ancient Rome, AncSoc 39, 2009, 171–184 |
| Simmel 1989 | G. Simmel, Philosophie des Geldes (Neudruck Frankfurt a. M. 1989) |
| Spalthoff 2010 | B. H. Spalthoff, Repräsentationsformen des römischen Ritterstandes (Rahden 2010) |
| Stark 2020 | M. Stark, Blick- und Betrachterführung auf den Grabdenkmälern der *Gallia Belgica*, in: Binsfeld u. a. 2020, 63–72 |
| Stewart 2008 | P. Stewart, The Social History of Art (Cambridge 2008) |
| Tabaczek 2019 | M. Tabaczek, Ein Relief mit Reiterkampf aus Neumagen, in: Porod – Scherrer 2019, 414–422 |
| von Hesberg 1992 | H. von Hesberg, Römische Grabbauten (Darmstadt 1992) |
| von Hesberg 2009 | H. von Hesberg, Grabbauten des 2. und 3. Jhs. n. Chr. in Köln, in: Boschung 2009, 167–187 |
| von Massow 1932 | A. von Massow, Die Grabmäler von Neumagen, Römische Grabmäler des Mosellandes und der angrenzenden Gebiete II (Berlin 1932) |
| Weber 1979 | W. Weber, Geld, Glaube, Gesellschaft (Opladen 1979) |
| Weber 2000 | W. Weber, Constantinische Deckengemälde aus dem römischen Palast unter dem Dom ⁴(Trier 2000) |
| Weeber 2007 | K.-W. Weeber, Luxuria, das »süße Gift«, in: R. Aßkamp – M. Brouwer – J. Christiansen – H. Kenzler – L. Wamser (Hrsg.), Luxus und Dekadenz. Römisches Leben am Golf von Neapel. Ausstellungskatalog Haltern am See u. a. (Mainz 2007) 3–15 |
| Wigg-Wolf 2019 | D. Wigg-Wolf, Geld eint, Geld trennt – einige Grundgedanken, in: T. G. Schattner – D. Vieweger – D. Wigg-Wolf (Hrsg.), Kontinuität und Diskontinuität. Prozesse der Romanisierung (Rahden 2019) 13–28 |
| Zahn 1982 | E. Zahn, Die Igeler Säule in Igel bei Trier ⁵(Neuss 1982) |
| Zanker – Ewald 2004 | P. Zanker – B. Ewald, Mit Mythen leben. Die Bilderwelt der römischen Sarkophage (München 2004) |
| Zimmer 1982 | G. Zimmer, Römische Berufsdarstellungen (Berlin 1982) |

*Jochen Griesbach, Martin von Wagner Museum der Universität Würzburg, Residenzplatz 2a, 97070 Würzburg, Deutschland.*
*[e] jochen.griesbach@uni-wuerzburg.de*

Tibor Grüll – Nándor Agócs – János Jusztinger – Ernő Szabó

# THE ICONOGRAPHIC MOTIF OF BOOK-SCROLLS ON FUNERARY RELIEFS IN *NORICUM*

**Abstract**

Our article is dedicated to the questions that arise when analyzing the book-scrolls depicted on the funerary monuments of the Danube provinces (*Raetia, Noricum, Pannonia, Moesia, Dacia*) and *Dalmatia*. Among the provinces of the Danube region, most book-scroll depictions are known in *Pannonia* (250–300 examples); Noricum also has over 200 monuments with book-scrolls, while in the other provinces the number of book-scroll depictions barely reaches 50. After a brief introduction to the scroll-in-hand database, we will analyse similarities and differences between individual provinces and regions and their possible causes. Our research shows that we have to treat the so-called *librarius* reliefs from *Noricum* differently from the Pannonian book-scroll depictions. At the same time, deciphering their meaning is perhaps even more difficult than with the other depictions of book-scrolls. We are probably not dealing with the religious ideas of the Celtic natives, but with Italic influence.

In August 2021, with the support of the National Research, Development, and Innovation Office (NRDI) of Hungary, we established the »Scroll-in-Hand Research Group« at the Department of Ancient History at the University of Pécs[1]. Our aim was to clarify, to the best of our knowledge, the possible meanings of the relatively large number of ›scroll-in-hand‹ iconographic motifs in the Roman provinces along the Danube and also to create a database, as complete as possible, of the writing materials and writing instruments depicted on such artefacts in the territory of the Roman Empire, which can serve as a tool for future research.

In the course of our research, we relied heavily on the findings of Austrian and Hungarian »Altertumswissenschaft« to date, especially on the volumes of the CSIR »Corpus Signorum Imperii Romani«, and the epigraphic corpuses (e.g. ILLPRON »Inscriptionum lapidariarum Latinarum provinciae Norici«; RISt »Die römerzeitlichen Inschriften der Steiermark«), but the ever-expanding online database of »Ubi Erat Lupa« was also of great use to us. Austrian researchers, such as Erna Diez, Manfred Hainzmann, Gerhard Grabher, Christoph Öllerer, and Elisabeth Walde, among many others, have published a number of inspiring studies in the past decades which have enriched our knowledge with valuable observations[2].

Why build a database? Above all, to be able to provide specific numbers and proportions. To date, we have processed 245 tombstones from *Noricum* based on the Lupa-website and the CSIR volumes, on which a total of 287 writing tools and instruments have been identified. The statistical distribution of these depictions is:

- scrolls: 174 (60 %)
  - closed scrolls (one-column): 118
  - closed scrolls (two-columns): 25
  - open scrolls: 31

---

[1] NKFIH, K 135317. Members of the research team are Tibor Grüll (Ph.D. habil. D.Sc.), full professor, head of department, team leader (Department of Ancient History, University of Pécs); János Jusztinger (Ph.D.) assistant professor, head of department (Department of Roman Law, University of Pécs); Nándor Agócs (Ph.D.) assistant professor (Department of History, ELTE Berzsenyi Dániel Teacher Training Centre); and Ernő Szabó (Ph.D. candidate) assistant research fellow (Department of Ancient History, University of Pécs), <https://scrollinhand.hu> (30.03.2023).

[2] Brein 1973; Grabher 1991; Hainzmann 1991; Walde 1997; Öllerer 2001; Kremer 2004; Walde 2005, 66–70.

- writing tablets: 37 (14 %)
- one-eared tablets: 9 (3 %)
- polyptych hanging from a strip (*codex ansatus*): 8 (2 %)
- containers for books (*capsa*): 18 (7 %)
- *stili*: 41 (14 %)

It is also relevant to our research that 114 scroll-in-hand depictions (46 %) display the gesture of pointing to them in some way (»Ein-« or »Zweifingergestus«). Unfortunately, only 57 reliefs (23 %) have been connected to inscriptions, but for the most part, they did little to further the interpretations of the images. In any case, one thing was clear at the outset of our endeavour: the common scroll-in-hand depictions on the funerary monuments – that is, when a man is holding a rolled-up scroll in his left hand – must be separated from the research on the so-called *librarius*-reliefs, which are specific to the province of *Noricum*. There are 89 such reliefs in our database. Thus, our article will also consist of two parts: the first part deals with the scroll-in-hand iconographic motif, and the second with the depictions of *librarii*. Without wanting to spoil the conclusion, by the end of the study, it will also be clear that certain scroll-in-hand depictions are related to the so-called *librarius*-reliefs.

## THE »SCROLL-IN-HAND« MOTIF

As for the closed scrolls mostly held in the left hands of men (to a lesser extent of boys and rarely of women), it would be a mistake to think that this iconographic motif is prevalent only in *Noricum* and *Pannonia*, although it is comparatively common in these two provinces. We can find funerary reliefs depicting men holding a scroll in their left hand – which we have to separate from the oratorial gesture seen in the statues – in Britain, Gaul, *Achaia, Africa, Asia, Syria*, and even Egypt[3]. All this is important because we seem to be dealing with an iconographic motif that is widespread throughout the Empire; but the interpretation of this motif raises many questions. In fact, the research to date has been much more about asking questions than providing answers.

To our knowledge, there is only one exception: the French-Belgian scholar Jean-Charles Balty showed in a 2016 publication that on the tombstones made by the soldiers of the *legio II Parthica* stationed in *Syria* at the beginning of the 3rd century, the depiction of rolled-up scrolls in the left hands of the deceased soldiers can be linked to testaments or inheritance[4]. This had previously been suggested by others based on analyses of specific tombstones[5], but Balty's research was

---

[3] It is typical that the scroll depictions found on tombstones from these areas are evaluated on an *ad hoc* basis by researchers, e.g. 1) at Sion/Sous-le-Scex (*Raetia*), a scroll in the left hand of a cavalry officer, which according to Devijver is a marching order or promotion document, or, possibly, symbolically refers to education (Devijver 1987, 366–367); 2) at Carthage (*Africa proconsularis*, 2nd–3rd c. AD) a boy wearing a *bulla* holds a scroll (*rotulus*) in his left hand, which is »not only a sign of erudition, it also echoes portraits of Roman emperors and magistrates which also display the attribute, thereby emphasizing the ›Romanitas‹ of the boy displayed« (Yale University Art Gallery; Varner 1990); 3) at *Arados* (*Syria-Phoenicia* 2nd–3rd c. AD) there is a funerary relief of a ship-owner, on which »Die Schrift- oder Buchrolle darf als geläufiges Motiv bei Reliefs in sepulkralem Zusammenhang angesehen werden, das entweder den Bildungsanspruch des Verstorbenen symbolisiert oder eine Urkunde (Testament, Bürgerrecht) darstellen soll« (Schmidts 2010, 253); 4a) at *Nikopolis* (*Aegyptus*, AD 188/189) there is a funerary relief depicting an ex-soldier called Ares, who holds in his left hand a double-columned closed scroll which has been interpreted as a *diploma militaris* by the research (Łajtar 2002, 46; Waebens 2012, 326); 4b) at the necropolis of *Terenouthis* (Kom Abou Billou, *Aegyptus*) there is a series of Roman grave-stelae from the 3rd c. AD, e.g. of Hermene and Atilion, in a semi-recumbent position, with a scroll in their left hand, surrounded by Egyptian symbols (Abd el-Al et al. 1985).

[4] Balty 2016, 88.

[5] See e.g. Bauchhenß 1978, 24; Parra 1979, 131. There is no scholarly consensus about the meaning of the scroll depicted on military gravestones, but for some interpretations see Bingen 2003, 67 (scroll contains the will of the deceased soldier); Schmidt 2003, 38–39 (scroll could be produced as evidence of the *honesta missio* or *immunitas* of the deceased soldier); Speidel 2012, 4 n. 18 (scroll may indicate that the deceased soldier had held a position involving administrative tasks); Waebens 2015, 66 n. 29 (scroll which is also shown on civilian gravestones often with an *anulus aureus* was meant to present the deceased as »Roman«; for a similar observation see also Carrié 1992, 132).

compelling, because he investigated almost one hundred funerary monuments of Roman soldiers stationed at *Apameia* (*Syria*). On these grave monuments, the scroll-in-hand motif is linked to the mention of »heir« (*heres*) or »made out of will« (*ex testamento fecit*) in the inscription; however, when we find the term »made out of his money« (*sua pecunia fecit*) or »[died] with no will« (*intestatus*) in the epitaph, there is no scroll depicted in the hand of the deceased soldier. The scroll is therefore easily identifiable with the document of transfer of the *bona castrensia et domestica* received by the heir; or, possibly, with a document recording the ownership and exact description of the tomb, the text of which has survived on an inscription as well (*testamentum Lingonum*)[6]. But to what extent can this solution be applied to the funerary reliefs of *Noricum*?

When we examine funerary monuments of a province – that is, not a single military unit – our first trivial observation is that the scroll-in-hand motif is not limited to monuments depicting soldiers. Although we can draw certain conclusions about the owners of tombstones based on their gestures, clothing, jewellery, etc., the most reliable source is the funerary inscription itself.

## People holding scrolls

Data on the people holding scrolls could be extracted from the epitaphs, but unfortunately there are not many of them, only 57 pieces (23 %); on the other hand, these inscriptions are not very informative either. They do not reveal much, for example, about the social circumstances and occupations of the owners. 236 people holding scrolls are male (96 %), and only seven boys and one woman occur. Analysis of the names revealed that there were Roman citizens among them: e.g. P(ublius) Alb(ius) Calandinus and his wife Silvia Ursula[7] and M(arcus) Mog(etius) Valentinus Vibi *f(ilius)* and his wife Mog(etia) Iustina[8]. In both cases, the wives wear Celtic clothing typical in *Noricum*, so it can be assumed that they belonged to the indigenous population[9]. A monument from the Severan era was erected for Iunianus Burrani *f(ilius)* and his wife Sucella Ucconis *f(ilia)*, who may have had peregrine status (i.e., the tomb was built before AD 212)[10]. A tombstone from the Antonine era in today's Slovenia was erected by Iulia Calandina to her husband, Sacronius Verinus, who died at the age of 50 and was a veteran armourer at the *legio II Italica: vet(eranus) leg(ionis) II Ital(icae) custos armor(um)*[11]. Another tombstone was made for Lucco *Suri filius* and his wife Dubna[12], and it is interesting that the man shows the »Zweifingergestus«, with his palms upside down in front of his wife. Given their names, they are probably *peregrini* of Celtic origin. On these, too, the man holds a scroll in his left hand, which he points to with two fingers of his right hand. An example is Candidus, who is referred to in the text of the inscription as *Q(uinti) Morsi Potentis Titiani ser(vus)*[13].

Depictions in which both father and son hold a scroll in their left hand may be important for the interpretation of the scroll-in-hand iconographic motif. A funerary monument from the border between Slovenia and Austria (Straß/Styria) dated to the middle of the 3rd century shows four figures. Fortunately, we are able to identify the individuals on the basis of the epitaph: two adult sons on either side of the image field, Cassius Ingenuus and Cassius Restutianus, with their parents in the middle, the mother, Cassia Quarta, from the left, and the father, Claudius Restutus, from the right. The right hand of the husband and wife are clasped together (*dextrarum iunctio*), and she rests her left hand on her husband's shoulder; the husband's left hand holds a closed roll, his fingers show a »horn-gesture« (*cornu*), and a signet ring can be seen on his little finger. There

---

[6] CIL XIII, 5708 = ILS 8379 = FIRA I, 118 = FIRA III, 49 = AE 2003, 108; cf. Le Bohec 1991.
[7] CIL III 5407 = lupa 1403.
[8] CIL III 5455 = lupa 1424.
[9] One of the additional tasks of the research would be to examine the clothes, to see if they also reveal something about the identity of their owner, cf. the research of the Rhine-Mosel region from a similar point of view (Rothe 2009).
[10] CIL III 5463 = lupa 1402.
[11] CIL III 5106 = lupa 3599.
[12] CIL III 5368 = lupa 1248.
[13] CIL III 5699 = lupa 1229.

is also a rolled-up scroll in the left hand of the boy to his left, but the boy is not making any gesture and is not wearing a signet ring[14]. Even more interesting is a very elaborate but uninscribed depiction of a family. Two minor children are depicted in front of their parents: the son stands in front of his mother and the daughter in front of her father. The father holds a closed scroll in his left hand, and his right hand rests on his daughter's shoulder; his son also holds a scroll, at which the index finger of his right hand is pointing[15]. But why is this gesture only being made by the minor child? In a medallion portrait found at *Flavia Solva*, there is also a scroll in the hands of a father and his minor son, at which, however, both are pointing[16]; in another grave, a father and a minor son are also holding a scroll, but in the boy's right hand we find a fruit[17]. Naturally, the explanation of depictions such as the late 3rd century tombstone in *Celeia*, which has a *stilus* and a *polyptichon* in the hands of a young boy, is not difficult, as the writing tools here clearly refer to the child's schooling[18] (fig. 1).

So far, no one has noted the obvious fact that on the funerary reliefs of *Noricum* we see 124 depictions of male and female figures – not necessarily married couples – together (51 %), but if we subtract the 89 *librarius*-reliefs from the total, this proportion increases to 80 %. Nevertheless, the *dextrarum iunctio* gesture is found in only 23 reliefs (18 % of the tombstones depicting couples), and only 18 inscriptions contain the term *coniunx* (spouse)[19]. We observed that the right-hand-clasp gesture occurs in *Pannonia superior* only along with the scroll, which is also characteristic of *Noricum*. This fact may even suggest that the scroll-in-hand motif could be interpreted as a marriage contract as well.

## Types of scrolls and their possible meanings

A scroll held in the left hand of a man is usually referred to in the secondary literature as *volumen*, which means papyrus scroll. A standard size papyrus scroll is approximately 700 cm long and 22–25 cm high, meaning it extended far below and above the hand of an adult man. In contrast, many depictions show narrower scrolls, which are called *rotuli*. The *rotulus* was a narrower and shorter strip of papyrus on which the text was written in a single long column and was therefore read vertically. These scrolls usually contained legal texts, e.g. testaments[20]. Among the depictions of scrolls, we find both a narrow *rotulus* (lupa 593) and a wide *volumen* (lupa 1394) rolled up in two columns; as well as both a *rotulus* (lupa 3614. 4628) and a *volumen* (lupa 1486) rolled up in a single column (fig. 2). Of course, it is not always possible to determine whether the stonemason accurately depicted the scrolls, as sometimes he carved only a slab or a stick. Moreover, the writing materials depicted on the reliefs are not always scrolls in the technical sense, but merely folded sheets of papyrus.

Attempts to interpret the scrolls so far range on a wide scale. In his classic work »Mousikos aner: Étude sur les scènes de la vie intellectuelle figurant sur les monuments funéraires romains« published in 1938, Henri-Irénée Marrou placed the scroll depictions in the context of the Greek

---

[14] CIL III 5357 = lupa 1355.
[15] Kremer 2001, cat. I 88 = lupa 4613.
[16] Pochmarski 2011, no. 10 = lupa 1350.
[17] CIL III 5463 = lupa 1402.
[18] CIL III 5246 = lupa 3118. The writing tablet is interpreted as a widely used symbol of education (Meyer 2004); and, of course, a symbol of the intellectual work of the *scribae* (Hartmann 2020).
[19] For the interpretation of the *dextrarum iunctio* gesture see Reekmans 1958; Walter 1979; Stupperich 1983; Davies 1985; Larsson Lovén 2010.
[20] In the Ptolemaic, Byzantine, Coptic, and Early Western Medieval period the *charta transversa* (script parallel to the width) was popular. Primarily legal texts were written on it, but from the early Middle Ages certain liturgical texts were also written on such scrolls (Daly 1973). Among them only a few wills have been found so far: in 1986 there were 132, mostly from the 4th to 7th c. (Bagnall 1986). Legal papyri written on *rotuli* from the area of the Middle-Euphrates: P. Euphr. 11. pap. 16.9 × 17.2 cm which is a contract of sale of a ship; P. Euphr. 13. pap. 10.5 × 15.5 cm which is a receipt; P. Euphr. 15. parchment *rotulus* 23 × 23.3 cm which is a donation document of the *ius liberorum* (Feissel – Gascou 2000).

1 Tombstone in *Celeia* with *stilus* and *polyptichon* in the hands of a young boy. Celje – Pokrajinski Muzej inv. L 82, lupa 3118 (drawn by N. Agócs)

2 Depiction of *rotulus* and *volumen*. Stambach/Grafendorf bei Hartberg, private property, lupa 4628 (drawn by N. Agócs)

ideal of *paideia*. »The scrolls« – he writes – »are related to the things of the spirit.«[21] According to Jean-Michel Carrié, the scroll is »the cultural object par excellence, the main mediator of education until the appearance of the codex«[22], and the scrolls placed in the hands of the soldiers show the efforts of the Antonine era to present the Roman military as defenders of civilization. More down-to-earth researchers examined some monuments and gave a different – less high-sounding – explanation: on a stele at Split, C. Publicius Romanus, *decurio* of the *colonia Narona*, can be seen holding a scroll, which is, obviously, »a symbol of official power«[23]. The scroll on the relief of Ser. Ennius Fuscus and his wife has been interpreted as »nuptial agreement«[24], but on the stele of P. Romanius Modestus *libertus* at Bonn it was explained as a »document of manumission«[25]. In the case of soldiers, it has already been proposed that the scroll is nothing more than an »enrolment-list«[26], »Truppenstammrolle«[27], or a document of discharge[28].

In our view, the relative iconographic stability of the scroll-in-hand motif throughout the Roman Empire tends to point to a legal interpretation of the scrolls. As we have seen, many scholars have suggested that the *rotulus* or *volumen* are documents of some legal nature: contracts, deeds

---

[21] »Lié aux choses de l'esprit«, Marrou 1938, 192.
[22] Carrié 1992, 167.
[23] Rinaldi Tufi 1971, 99–100.
[24] Rinaldi Tufi 1971, 102.
[25] Bauchhenß 1978, 15.
[26] »Matricule d'enrôlement«, Carrié 1992, 167.
[27] Hainzmann 1996, 61. 64.
[28] Łajtar 2002, 46.

of possession, bequests[29], grants of civil rights, documents of discharge, etc. – or in other words, not literary works or the text of the *laudatio funebris*. Research to date mostly attributed this interpretation to depictions of scrolls on an *ad hoc* basis: if the relief depicted a married couple, the scroll represented a marriage contract; if a soldier was seen on the relief, this was a document of discharge; if the inscription spoke of a freedman (*libertus*), it was, of course, a deed of manumission. Our research on the scroll-in-hand motif in *Pannonia* has revealed on several occasions that the holder of the scroll was a *peregrinus*, which means that the scroll cannot be interpreted as a civil rights-granting document[30]. This would not make much sense after AD 212 anyway. In our view, it is worth considering the possibility that the closed scroll held in the left hand is in most cases a document indicating the possession of a tomb.

**Gestures connected to scrolls**

According to our database, almost half (46 %) of the scroll depictions in *Noricum* are connected to pointing gestures[31]. In other words, the two things, gesture and scroll, belong together. As is known, the index finger (»Einfingergestus«) or middle and index finger (»Zweifingergestus«) of the right hand point towards the scroll held in the left hand, and in the largest percentage of cases, they also touch the scroll.

- »Zweifingergestus«: 46 (56 %)
  - pointing towards the scroll: 9
  - touching the scroll: 37
- »Einfingergestus«: 36 (44 %)
  - pointing towards the scroll: 5
  - touching the scroll: 31

Manfred Hainzmann and Gerhard Grabher interpret this as a gesture related to an oath (»Schwurgestus«)[32]. But the oath is not necessarily connected to an object; two or three fingers point toward the sky or the heart[33]. In contrast, the gesture we are discussing is deictic: it points towards the scroll as an object and even makes physical contact with it[34]. In addition, a signet ring was observed 22 times on the little finger of the left hand holding the scroll, which also indicates that the nature of this document could be legal. In 2003, Thomas Richter devoted a complete monograph to the issue of »Zweifingergestus«. We agree with what Richter writes about the funerary reliefs in *Noricum*: »It can be assumed principally that only one interpretation of the gesture-scroll motif can be correct, and then it is also consistently valid. This is borne out by the fundamental fact that image motifs must be clear in order to be comprehensible in general.«[35] Put

---

[29] See the so-called Testamentum Relief from the Trajanic period (Rome, Museo Capitolino): the *testator* lies on a keel, leaning on his elbow, holding a half-open scroll in his left hand, at his feet is a slave-boy with an *abacus*, behind him is a portrait of a shield on the wall, his wife is sitting on a chair at the head of the bed (D'Ambra 1995).

[30] *Peregrini* depicted with scrolls: lupa 2855 = TRHR 116; lupa 632 = CIL III 11302; lupa 3827 = TRHR 42; lupa 3120 = RIU 689, 3273 = RIU 733; lupa 802 = RIU 690; scroll in the hand of a Roman knight: lupa 8817 = CIL III 3985; scroll in the hand of a senatorial woman: lupa 3803 = CIL III 10852.

[31] We found a few funerary monuments where the »Ein-« or »Zweifingergestus« is not connected to scrolls, e.g. lupa 861 = CIL III 4994; lupa 3594 = CIL III 5218; lupa 2882 = Pochmarski 2011, no. 5.

[32] Hainzmann 1991, 128–132; Grabher 1991, 46–48.

[33] Hainzmann here refers to the well-known cult object of Iupiter Sabazius as an example, but the gesture shown on these votive objects (the thumb, index and middle fingers are extended, while the ring and little fingers are folded into the palm) is the so-called *benedictio Latina* (Lane 1980; Berndt 2018).

[34] On the funerary relief of the soldier Servius Ennius Fuscus and his wife at Split (CIL III 9782 = lupa 24430), the man's left hand shows the usual scroll depiction, but the right hand shows a three-fingered greeting gesture up above his neck.

[35] »Grundsätzlich ist davon auszugehen, daß nur eine Deutung für das Motiv Gestus-Buchrolle zutreffend sein kann und dann auch durchgehend Gültigkeit hat. Dafür spricht das grundlegende Faktum, daß Bildmotive eindeutig sein sollten, um allgemein verständlich zu sein.« (Richter 2003, 90).

simply, the scroll motif and the gestures associated with it must have a single meaning. Richter then cites two interpretations: Elisabeth Walde interprets the scroll as a sign of discretionary power, official authority, and the like[36]; while Manfred Hainzmann »sees a reference to the occupation in the rotulus«[37]. Richter, however, sees the scroll depictions in the context of Roman education, culture, and rhetoric, and he lumps together the murals, mosaics, and sculptures unearthed in any part of the Roman Empire – which we think is methodologically wrong[38].

But there is also a different, fundamentally legal interpretation of the »Ein«- and »Zweifingergestus« that fits perfectly with the explanation according to which the scrolls depicted in the left hand of the deceased are legal documents. As late as the 2nd century AD, the Roman lawyer Sextus Pedius asserts that, for the contract of *stipulatio* to be valid, the subject matter of the obligation can with equal validity be indicated by words or by the gesture of pointing with the finger[39]. As Anthony Corbeill writes, »Gestures viewed as a manifestation of formality, by contrast, are thought to have a real and essential effect on the proceedings within which they are enacted. Without the formality, the legal process or decision has no validity.«[40].

## THE *LIBRARIUS*-RELIEFS

In the Lupa-database, 89 reliefs have been classified as *librarius*-reliefs. We are going to examine these depictions in the remainder of this study. First, we consider the type of monument on which these paired depictions usually appear[41]. They most often can be found on large funerary monuments composed of several building blocks: at the bottom there is a rectangular pedestal (often with mythological scenes on it); above it, one finds a rectangular middle part with a field inscribed on the frontal side, and on its two narrower sides there is usually a depiction of a male servant and a maid: the former is the *librarius*, the latter perhaps a dresser. The top of the monument was sometimes decorated with medallion portraits depicting the owners of the monument. Within the province of *Noricum*, these reliefs are clearly concentrated in and around *Virunum*, and they occur less frequently in the towns along the Danube. Their dating ranges widely, roughly to the Antonine-Severan era (the 2nd and 3rd c.).

Of the monuments containing *librarius*-reliefs, only 19 have inscriptions (21 %), and they are rarely associated with slaves, as the inscriptions refer to the owners and/or builders of the tombs. Of the former, only four held official positions (*aedilis* [2]; *aedilicius*; *servus vilicus vectigalis Illyrici*); three were military personnel (*veteranus legionis*; *veteranus ex praetorio*; *optio legionis*); and two named the status of the deceased (*servus; libertus*). Officers usually had clerical servants, and these are perhaps not exceptional for a veteran and an *optio* either. But from these seven cases we cannot draw far-reaching conclusions. Furthermore, the fact that only one-fifth of the reliefs have inscriptions is mainly due to the fact that these depictions have mostly been preserved for us as *spolia*[42].

Depictions of servants are rather formal: on the left of the central part of the funerary monument is the maidservant with a jug, a chest, a *mappa*, and in each case with a mirror; while on the right hand side one finds the depiction of the *librarius*. We can observe a greater variety in the latter. At first glance, two basic types can be distinguished: those of the reader (41 = 46 %) and

---

[36] Walde 1997, 244.
[37] Hainzmann 1991, 144–146.
[38] After all this, it is no wonder that he also rejects M. Hainzmann' oath theory, saying that »representations should always be understood as a reference to rhetorical or other types of training«, which is a typical case of circular reasoning: Richter 2003, 92.
[39] Paul. Dig. 12, 1, 6: *Certum est, cuius species vel quantitas, quae in obligatione versatur, aut nomine suo aut ea demonstratione quae nominis vice fungitur qualis quantaque sit ostenditur. nam et pedius libro primo de stipulationibus nihil referre ait, proprio nomine res appelletur an digito ostendatur an vocabulis quibusdam demonstretur: quatenus mutua vice fungantur, quae tantundem praestent.*
[40] Corbeill 2005, 158.
[41] Pochmarski 1994; Kremer 2001.
[42] Wagner 2001.

the writer (30 = 33 %), while on 18 reliefs (21 %) we do not find either of these activities (fig. 3). We should also mention here the writing tools and materials depicted on the *librarius*-reliefs:

- writing tablets (*diptycha* and *polypticha*): 45 = 43 %
- open scrolls: 29 = 28 %
- cylindrical bookcases (*capsa*): 16 = 16 %
- tablets hanging from a strip (*codex ansatus*): 8 = 7 %
- one-eared writing tablets: 7 = 6 %

Our database revealed that 59 % of the scenes depicting *reading* contained scrolls, and 41 % had writing tablets; while 87 % of the reliefs that showed *writing* depicted writing tablets, and only 13 % had depictions of papyrus scrolls. Thus, in the case of reading, the use of the two basic writing materials is relatively balanced: although for the most part, scrolls were used as indications of reading, writing tablets were also used intensively for this purpose. In the case of writing, however, this ratio is much less balanced: writing tablets were mostly used for this purpose, and the use of scrolls constitutes only a negligible percentage. The latter may be due to the fact that while writing tablets were used for everyday activities and economic records, writing on scrolls may also have been related to literary activity, in which obviously very few people engaged. Of course, we caution against drawing conclusions concerning the level of literacy in 2nd to 3rd century *Noricum* on the basis of these data. It is by no means certain that the *librarius*-reliefs depict real persons, and are not just decorative motifs intended to embellish the magnificent tombs of the wealthy deceased, exactly as we read about Trimalchio's tomb in Petronius's famous novel, on which, among other things, servants were carved in fictitious situations[43].

However, the clerks called *librarii* belonged to the bureaucratic apparatus of a city or province[44]. *Librarii* can also be found in the provincial administration of *Noricum*: the deceased husband of Nammonia Materiu, Gaius Sempronius Secundinus, was a *decurio* of the *municipium* of *Solva*; while his son, Gaius Sempronius Secundinus (who died at the age of 19), served as a *librarius consularis*[45]. But the veteran Titus Flavius Campestrinus, and his 20-year-old deceased son Iulius Exoratus were also *librarii consulares*[46] (*Ovilava*/Wels, AD 235–285). Of course, the *librarii* were also important administrators of the legions stationed in *Noricum*, see a *li[br(arius) leg(ionis)] II Ital(icae) [p(iae) f(idelis)]* from *Virunum*[47] (*Virunum*/Steindorf, AD 211–235). Besides these *librarii* may also have served the richer aristocratic families. As Benjamin Hartmann writes in his 2020 monograph on the *scribae* that »[a]ristocratic households had long made use of *librarii* for a wide range of clerical and secretarial duties, above all the transcription and copying of texts«[48]. However, all this does not help much in the interpretation of the *librarius*-reliefs, since – as we mentioned above – only a fifth of the reliefs have inscriptions, and these do not reveal much about the owners of the tombs either.

Assuming that the *librarius*-reliefs served as ornaments for monumental tombs, which may have belonged not only to members of the municipal decurionate but also, according to the inscriptions, to persons of slave or freedman status, we cannot insist on the interpretation that these depictions reflected the official authority of the tomb owner. On the funerary monuments

---

[43] Petr. Sat. 71, 11: *Ad dexteram meam pones statuam Fortunatae meae columbam tenentem, et catellam cingulo alligatam ducat, et cicaronem meum, et amphoras copiose gypsatas, ne effluant vinum. Et unam licet fractam sculpas, et super eam puerum plorantem.* – Ancient novels usually refer to fictitious inscriptions in situations where the realization of the novel requires this from a literary point of view (»Beglaubigungsapparat«), see e.g. Liddel – Low 2013.

[44] For the range of clerical work exercised by *librarii* see Haines-Eitzen 2000, 30–31.

[45] CIL III 5435 = lupa 1450, Straßgang, AD 180–220; about the administration of the province *Noricum* see Alföldy 1974, 159–165; Wedenig 1995. – In *Pannonia*, the decurions/magistrates of larger cities undertook the duty of *scriba* in smaller cities as *summa honoraria* (see Mócsy 1964).

[46] CIL III 5631 = lupa 579.

[47] AE 2004, 1096.

[48] Hartmann 2020, 44–45.

3   *Librarius* writing on a scroll, Maria Saal, Propstei, lupa 964 (drawn by N. Agócs)

of *Pannonia* and *Noricum* it was customary to depict male and female servants, especially in the scenes of the funeral feasts[49]. The maids seen on »Totenmahlszenen« are indeed very similar to maidservants depicted on *librarius*-reliefs. According to some interpretations, the female servants are sacrificial assistants: the *mappa* held in their hands or on their shoulders is a sacrificial tablecloth; the jar (*urceus*) is an offering; and the box is an *acerra* for storing incense – so perhaps the female servants of the *librarius*-reliefs are also sacrificial servants[50]? The suggestion is legitimate, but in the hands of the male servants on the »Totenmahlreliefs« we can see the same sacrificial instruments (*urceus, patera, mappa*)[51], and we never find writing instruments with them. In addition, there are no signs of a funerary feast on the *librarius*-reliefs in *Noricum*.

Herbert Graßl has traced depictions of *librarii* straight back to Celtic traditions. The 1st century BC, the Greek historian Diodorus Siculus claimed that the Celts threw letters at the funeral pyres of their relatives in the belief that they would read them in the afterlife (5, 28, 6). Based on this text, Graßl argues that the *librarii* of *Noricum* »maintain communication between the living and the dead with letters«, and the writings in their hands are signs of continuous communication between the »underworld« and the »upper world«[52]. However, firstly, only 33 % of *librarius*-reliefs show writing activity, while the other 67 % show reading; and, secondly, it is not at all certain that the owners of the tombs were of Celtic descent. We may introduce a more distant example, just for the sake of comparison: we now know that the famous *matres/matronae* depictions, equally popular among the Gallic and Germanic tribes, were introduced by Roman settlers in the 1st century AD. Moreover, an interesting transformation can be observed on these reliefs in the 2nd and 3rd centuries: instead of the fruit-basket, an open papyrus-scroll appears in the lap of some *matronae*. This transformation does not imply an increasing Gallic or Germanic influence. On the contrary, it refers to the wider spread of Graeco-Roman customs, namely, the cult of the goddesses of destiny (Moirae, Camenae, Carmenta)[53].

In the scholarship on the scroll-in-hand motif, the ›realistic‹ or ›symbolic‹ approaches have prevailed so far, most often in disagreement with each other. But could the ancient men separate these two forms of meaning? The ›realistic‹ meaning of the servant depictions placed in the tombs of the wealthy inhabitants of *Noricum* obviously included the neatness, beauty, and wealth of the wife of the owner of the monument (»Grabherrin«), to which the objects held by the maid-

---

[49]  Diez 1959–1961; Gáspár 2016, 84–94.
[50]  For the female servants see Walde 2001.
[51]  E.g. lupa 7805 (Stuttgart, Württembergisches Landesmuseum), where the male servant standing by the *kline* of the deceased holds in his right hand a jug, and – according to the editors of <lupa.at> – in his left hand there is a towel (*mappa*); however, we should consider the possibility that he is holding a scroll in his left hand. On the relief lupa 15354 (*Histria, Moesia inferior*) the male servant clearly hold a *mappa* slung over his left shoulder.
[52]  Graßl 1989, 34–37.
[53]  On this process of Romanisation see Grüll 2021.

servant referred; while the social and economic status, occupation, and education of the owner of the monument (»Grabherr«) may have been indicated by the writing tools and materials held in the hands of the *librarius*-servant. At the same time, the servants may have conveyed ›symbolic‹ meaning as well, as they were depicted on funerary monuments. It is not a question that the objects in the hands of the maidservant may have evoked the sacrifice for the deceased; the real mystery is how to interpret writing or reading *librarii* in this context. It has already been suggested that the *librarius* may be related to the scroll-in-hand depiction of the tomb owner, although there is little evidence of this. On the other hand, if we accept this presumption, it would follow that the *librarius* is preoccupied with a will, or inheritance, or the ownership of the funeral monument.

## BIBLIOGRAPHY

| | |
|---|---|
| Abd el-Al et al. 1985 | A. Abd el-Al – J. C. Grenier – G. Wagner, Stèles funéraires de Kom Abu Bellou, Mémoire 55 (Paris 1985) |
| Alföldy 1974 | G. Alföldy, Noricum (London 1974) |
| Bagnall 1986 | R. Bagnall, Two Byzantine legal papyri in a private collection, in: R. S. Bagnall – W. V. Harris (eds.), Studies in Roman Law: In Memory of A. Arthur Schiller, Columbia Studies in the Classical Tradition 13 (Leiden 1986) |
| Balty 2016 | J.-C. Balty, Le volumen ou »Schriftrolle« des stèles et cippes militaires dans l'Empire romain: à propos des inscriptions apaméennes de la legio II Parthica, Syria 93, 2016, 84–95 |
| Bauchhenß 1978 | G. Bauchhenß, Germania Inferior. Bonn und Umgebung. Militärische Grabdenkmäler, CSIR Deutschland III 1 (Bonn 1978) |
| Berndt 2018 | S. Berndt, The hand gesture and symbols of Sabazios, Opuscula 11, 2018, 151–168 |
| Bingen 2003 | J. Bingen, Miles armorum custos (CIL III Suppl. 14138², Alexandrie), in: P. DeFosse (ed.), Hommages à Carl Deroux III. Histoire et épigraphie, Droit, Coll. Latomus 270 (Brussels 2003) 67–73 |
| Brein 1973 | F. Brein, Bücher auf Grabsteinen, RÖ 1, 1973, 1–6 |
| Carrié 1992 | J.-M. Carrié, Le soldat, in: A. Giardina (ed.), L'homme romain (Paris 1992) 127–172 |
| Corbeill 2005 | A. P. Corbeill, Gesture in early Roman law: empty form or essential formalities?, in: D. L. Cairns (ed.), Body language in the Greek and Roman worlds (Swansea 2005) 157–174 |
| D'Ambra 1995 | E. D'Ambra, Mourning and the Making of Ancestors in the Testamentum Relief, AJA 99/4, 1995, 667–681 |
| Daly 1973 | L. W. Daly, Rotuli: Liturgy Rolls and Formal Documents, GrRomByzSt 14/3, 1973, 333–338 |
| Davies 1985 | G. Davies, The significance of the handshake motif in classical funerary art, AJA 89/4, 1985, 627–640 |
| Devijver 1987 | H. Devijver, L'iconographie de la stèle funéraire de T. Exomnius Mansuetus, praefectus cohortis, Vallesia 42, 1987, 363–367 |
| Diez 1959–1961 | E. Diez, Zur Darstellung des Totenopfers auf norischen Grabsteinen, SchildStei 9, 1959–1961, 47–57 |
| Feissel – Gascou 2000 | D. Feissel – J. Gascou, Documents d'archives romains inédits du Moyen Euphrate (IIIᵉ s. après J.-C.), JSav 2/1, 2000, 157–208 |
| FIRA | F. Riccobono – V. Arangio Ruiz (eds.), Fontes iuris Romani anteiustiniani I–III ²(Floence 1940–1943) |
| Gáspár 2016 | D. Gáspár, Pannoniai síremlékek I–III. Római kori halottkultusz a mai Magyarország területén [Grave monuments in Pannonia. Ancient Roman cult of the dead on the territory of present-day Hungary] (Budapest 2016) |
| Grabher 1991 | G. Grabher, Die Schriftrolle auf römischen Grabsteinen in Österreich. Bürgerrechtsdekret und Schwurgestus, in: M. Hainzmann – D. Kramer – E. Pochmarski (eds.), Akten des 1. internationalen Colloquiums über Probleme des Provinzialrömischen Kunstschaffens Graz 27.–30.04.1989, Teil II, Mitteilungen der Archäologischen Gesellschaft Steiermark 5, 1991, 42–56 |
| Graßl 1989 | H. Graßl, Beiträge zum keltischen Brauchtum in Noricum, in: J. Grabmeyer – E. Polte (eds.), Die Kultur der Kelten 1. St. Veiter Historikergespräche 16.–18.06.1988 (St. Veit an der Glan 1989) 29–37 |

| | |
|---|---|
| Grüll 2021 | T. Grüll, ›The Book of Fate‹: A distinctive representation of Matronae/Parcae and the spread of literacy in the Northern provinces of the Roman Empire, in: Religion in the Roman Empire VII 3 (Tübingen 2021) 403–429 |
| Haines-Eitzen 2000 | K. Haines-Eitzen, Guardians of Letters. Literacy, Power, and the Transmitters of Early Christian Literature (Oxford 2000) |
| Hainzmann 1991 | M. Hainzmann, Schriftrolle und Schwurgestus. Neue Beobachtungen zu einem alten Bildmotiv, in: M. Hainzmann – D. Kramer – E. Pochmarski (eds.), Akten des 1. internationalen Colloquiums über Probleme des Provinzialrömischen Kunstschaffens Graz 27.–30.04.1989, Teil II, Mitteilungen der Archäologischen Gesellschaft Steiermark 5, 1991, 120–146 |
| Hainzmann 1996 | M. Hainzmann, Publius Flavoleius Cordus aus Mainz, ein Angehöriger des militärischen Verwaltungsdienstes?, in: G. Bauchhenß (ed.), Akten des 3. internationalen Kolloquiums über Probleme des provinzialrömischen Kunstschaffens Bonn 21.–24.04.1993, BJb Beih. 512 (Bonn 1996) 59–65 |
| Hartmann 2020 | B. Hartmann, The Scribes of Rome. A Cultural and Social History of the Scribae (Cambridge 2020) |
| ILS | H. Dessau (ed.), Inscriptiones Latinae Selectae (Berlin 1892–1916) |
| Kremer 2001 | G. Kremer, Antike Grabbauten in Noricum. Katalog und Auswertung von Werkstücken als Beitrag zur Rekonstruktion und Typologie, SoSchrÖAI 36 (Vienna 2001) |
| Kremer 2004 | G. Kremer, Die norisch-pannonischen Grabbauten als Ausdruck kultureller Identität?, in: A. Schmidt-Colinet (ed.), Lokale Identitäten in Randgebieten des römischen Reiches. Akten des internationalen Symposiums Wiener Neustadt 24.–26.04.2003, WForsch 7 (Vienna 2004) 147–159 |
| Łajtar 2002 | A. Łajtar, A tombstone for the soldier Ares (Egypt, late Antonine period), JJurP 32, 2002, 45–48 |
| Lane 1980 | E. Lane, Towards a Definition of the Iconography of Sabazius, Numen 27/1, 1980, 9–33 |
| Larsson Lovén 2010 | L. Larsson Lovén, Coniugal concordia: marriage and marital ideals on Roman funerary monuments, in: L. Larsson Lovén – A. Strömberg (eds.), Ancient marriage in myth and reality (Newcastle upon Tyne 2010) 204–220 |
| Le Bohec 1991 | Y. Le Bohec, Le testament du Lingon, Collection du Centre d'études romaines et gallo-romaines: nouvelle série 9 (Lyon 1991) |
| Liddel – Low 2013 | P. Liddel – P. Low (eds.), Inscriptions and their uses in Greek and Latin literature (Oxford 2013) |
| lupa | F. und O. Harl, <lupa.at> (Bilddatenbank zu antiken Steindenkmälern) |
| Marrou 1938 | H. I. Marrou, Μουσικὸς ἀνήρ. Étude sur les scènes de la vie intellectuelle figurant sur les monuments funéraires romains (Grenoble 1938) |
| Meyer 2004 | E. A. Meyer, Legitimacy and law in the Roman world: tabulae in Roman belief and practice (Cambridge 2004) |
| Mócsy 1964 | A. Mócsy, Scribák a pannóniai kisvárosokban, AErt 91, 1964, 16–17 |
| Öllerer 2001 | C. Öllerer, Die Darstellung von Schreibgerät auf norischen Librarierreliefs, in: F. W. Leitner (ed.), Carinthia Romana und die römische Welt. Festschrift Gernot Piccottini (Klagenfurt 2001) 249–262 |
| Parra 1979 | M. C. Parra, Una stele di Roma ritrovata a Livorno, in: G. Camporeale – M. Martelli – E. Paribeni – M. Cristofani – G. Maetzke (eds.), Studi per Enrico Fiumi (Pisa 1979) 121–139 |
| Pochmarski 1994 | E. Pochmarski, Grabsitten und Grabformen in Noricum, Archäologische Gesellschaft Steiermark, Nachrichtenblatt 1, 1994, 35–60 |
| Pochmarski 2011 | E. Pochmarski, Die Porträtmedaillons und Porträtnischen des Stadtgebietes von Flavia Solva, CSIR Österreich IV 2 (Vienna 2011) |
| Reekmans 1958 | L Reekmans, La »dextrarum iunctio« dans l'iconographie romaine et paléochrétienne (Rome 1958) |
| Richter 2003 | T. Richter, Der Zweifingergestus in der römischen Kunst, Frankfurter Archäologische Schriften 2 (Möhnesee 2003) |
| Rinaldi Tufi 1971 | S. Rinaldi Tufi, Stele funerarie con ritratti di età romana nel Museo archeologico di Spalato. Saggio di una tipologia strutturale, MemLinc 8/16/3, 1971, 87–167 |
| RIU | L. Barkóczi – A. Mócsy et al. (eds.), Die römischen Inschriften Ungarns (Budapest 1972–) |

| | |
|---|---|
| Rothe 2009 | U. Rothe, Dress and Cultural Identity in the Rhine-Moselle Region of the Roman Empire, BARIntSer 2038 (Oxford 2009) |
| Schmidt 2003 | S. Schmidt, Grabreliefs im Griechisch-Römischen Museum von Alexandria, ADAIK, Ägyptologische Reihe 17 (Berlin 2003) |
| Schmidts 2010 | T. Schmidts, Aurelius Theogeiton: Ein Schiffseigner aus dem syrischen Arados auf Italienfahrt, AKorrBl 40/2, 2010, 251–263 |
| Speidel 2012 | M. A. Speidel, Dressed for the occasion. Clothes and context in the Roman army, in: M. A. Speidel, Heer und Herrschaft im römischen Reich der hohen Kaiserzeit, MAVORS 16 (Stuttgart 2012) 235–248 |
| Stupperich 1983 | R. Stupperich, Zur dextrarum iunctio auf frühen römischen Grabreliefs, Boreas 6, 1983, 143–150 |
| TRHR | P. Kovács, Tituli Romani in Hungaria reperti. Supplementum (Budapest 2005) |
| Varner 1990 | E. R. Varner, Two portrait stelae and the Romanization of North Africa, YaleUnivB 1990, 10–19 |
| Waebens 2012 | S. Waebens, Ares: Brother, Commander, Deity or Son? A New Interpretation of the Ares Tombstone, ChronEg 87, 2012, 322–339 |
| Waebens 2015 | S. Waebens, The Representation of Roman Soldiers on Third-Century AD Funerary Monuments from Nikopolis (Egypt), Revue Internationale d'Histoire Militaire Ancienne 1, 2015, 63–77 |
| Wagner 2001 | J. Wagner, Zur ostentativen Wiederverwendung römerzeitlicher Spolien in mittelalterlichen und frühneuzeitlichen Kirchenbauten der Steiermark. Bannung, Exorzismus und humanistische Intentionen im Spiegel einer Interpretatio christiana, FÖ 40, 2001, 345–479 |
| Walde 1997 | E. Walde, Noch einmal zur Buchrolle, in: B. Djurić – I. Lazar (eds.), Akten des IV. Internationalen Kolloquiums über Probleme des provinzialrömischen Kunstschaffens Celje 08.–12.05.1995, Situla 36 (Ljubljana 1997) 243–246 |
| Walde 2001 | E. Walde, Die Dienerinnen auf den römischen Grabreliefs in der Provinz Noricum, in: T. Panhuysen (ed.), Typologie, Ikonographie und soziale Hintergründe der provinzialen Grabdenkmäler und Wege der ikonographischen Einwirkung. Akten des Interntionalen Kolloquiums über das provinzialrömische Kunstschaffen Maastricht 29.05.–01.06.1997 (Maastricht 2001) 235–243 |
| Walde 2005 | E. Walde, Im herrlichen Glanze Roms. Die Bilderwelt der Römersteine in Österreich (Innsbruck 2005) |
| Walter 1979 | C. Walter, The dextrarum junctio of Lepcis Magna in relationship to the iconography of marriage, AntAfr 14/1, 1979, 271–283 |
| Wedenig 1997 | R. Wedenig, Epigraphische Quellen zur städtischen Administration in Noricum (Klagenfurt 1997) |

*Tibor Grüll, Department of Ancient History, University of Pécs, Rókus utca 2, 7624 Pécs, Hungary.*
*[e] grull.tibor@pte.hu*

*Nándor Agócs, Department of History, ELTE Berzsenyi Dániel Teacher Training Centre, Károlyi Gáspár tér 4, 9700 Szombathely, Hungary.*
*[e] agocs.nandor@sek.elte.hu*

*János Jusztinger, Department of Roman Law, University of Pécs, 48-as tér 1, 7622 Pécs, Hungary.*
*[e] jusztinger.janos@ajk.pte.hu*

*Ernő Szabó, Department of Ancient History, University of Pécs, Rókus utca 2, 7624 Pécs, Hungary.*
*[e] szabo.erno@pte.hu*

CRAIG A. HARVEY

# A MARBLE STATUE FRAGMENT OF VICTORIA/NIKE FROM HUMAYMA, JORDAN (NABATAEAN *HAWARA*, ROMAN *HAUARRA*)

**Abstract**

This contribution presents a small fragment of carved white marble found at the site of Humayma (Nabataean *Hawara*/Roman *Hauarra*), in what is now southern Jordan. Uncovered during excavation of the site's Abbasid family's *qasr* in 1993, this fragment is the first and thus far only known example of marble figural sculpture from Humayma. It is therefore a significant addition to the limited corpus of marble sculpture in this part of the Roman Empire and contributes greatly to our understanding of the sculptural landscape of the site itself. Although poorly preserved, enough of the carved drapery survives to identify the depicted figure as a gliding Victoria/Nike. This fragment's discovery in a secondary context prevents a firm understanding of its original use and display. Regional comparanda, however, suggest that this statue, which likely dates to the first three centuries AD, may have been part of a public display at a sanctuary or may have stood within the Roman fort on site.

## INTRODUCTION

Located on the south-eastern frontier of the Roman Empire, in the deserts of southern Jordan, the archaeological site of Humayma may seem an unlikely place to find marble sculpture, yet during excavation of the site's Islamic *qasr* in 1993, archaeologists unexpectedly uncovered a fragment of white marble, which was quickly recognized as coming from a torso of a statue that likely stood approximately 60 cm in height. Despite the findspot of this fragment, the carved folds of a belted *apoptygma* convincingly date this sculpture to the Roman Imperial period. While excavation of the Byzantine churches at Humayma has produced a considerable quantity of ecclesiastical marble, this fragment is the first and thus far only fragment of a marble statue to be found at this site. Although uncovered during the 1993 excavation season, this marble sculpture has been briefly referenced only once previously in publication[1]. It is described and presented here for the first time.

## THE ARCHAEOLOGICAL SITE OF HUMAYMA

The site of Humayma (Nabataean *Hawara*, Roman *Hauarra*) is located in the north-west corner of the Hisma desert in present-day southern Jordan, approximately 55 km northeast of Aqaba and 45 km south of *Petra* (fig. 1). Although evidence for habitation in the vicinity of the site dates back to the Paleolithic period, the Nabataean settlement of *Hawara* was established in the late 1st century BC[2]. Situated along the King's Highway, the town served as an important stop on the trade route between the Nabataean capital at *Petra* and the port of *Aila* (modern Aqaba) on the Red Sea. Despite the aridity of the Hisma desert, the settlement flourished thanks to a complex water catchment and storage system that included no less than five reservoirs, 57 cisterns, three

---

[1] Schick et al. 2013, 449.
[2] For an overview of the history and development of Humayma, see Oleson 2010, 50–62.

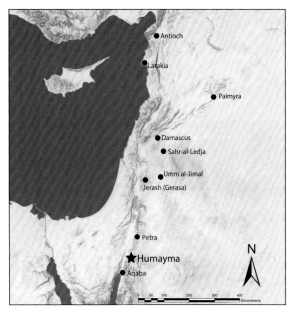

1  Map showing the location of Humayma (C. A. Harvey)

dams or barrier walls, and a two-branched 27 km long aqueduct[3].

Shortly after the Roman annexation of the Nabataean kingdom in AD 106, the town (then known as *Hauarra*) became home to an auxiliary fort situated on a low rise to the north-east of the Nabataean settlement[4]. This fort, one of the first in the newly organized *Provincia Arabia*, was designed for a garrison of about 500 soldiers and their mounts, likely composed of a mix of auxiliary soldiers and detachments from the *legio III Cyrenaica*. Between the military fort and the settlement, a small cluster of mudbrick and stone structures (including the extramural garrison baths) developed, possibly to service the needs of the troops and their extended community. The strategic location of *Hauarra* at the nexus of trade and communication routes between *Petra*, *Aila*, and *Hegra* further south ensured its continued relevance as a military site and distribution hub. Although the fort appears to have been briefly abandoned in the late 3rd century AD, it was re-garrisoned between the early and late 4th century. *Hauarra* retained its importance throughout the reorganization of the region into the province of *Palaestina Salutaris* (*Palaestina Tertia*) and into late Roman and Byzantine periods, as evidenced by its mention in the »Notitia Dignitatum«, »Peutinger Table«, and the »Beer Sheva Edict« as well as the construction of five churches in the 6th and 7th centuries[5].

In the Early Islamic period, the site was renamed Humayma, and in the early 8th century it was bought by the Abbasid family, who established their home there with the construction of a *qasr* and adjacent mosque on the eastern edge of the town[6]. This family would shortly thereafter go on to overthrow the Umayyad Caliphate and establish their own caliphate with their seat of power at Baghdad.

## HISTORY OF EXCAVATION AND DISCOVERY OF THE MARBLE FRAGMENT

Since 1986, the Humayma Excavation Project has conducted a series of surveys and excavations in and around the settlement, revealing its history and development. This archaeological investigation has focused primarily on the site's water system, Byzantine churches, Roman fort, extramural settlement, and Islamic *qasr*. The marble fragment presented here was uncovered in the Abbasid family *qasr* on the eastern edge of the settlement (fig. 2)[7]. Excavation of this 8th-century residence and its associated mosque was carried out between 1992 and 2002 under the direction of Dr. Rebecca M. Foote.

On June 12th, 1993, during the initial surface cleaning of Square 79 in the south-eastern corner of the *qasr* (Field F103), excavators uncovered a fragment of carved marble in the tumble just south of an interior wall (Wall 02)[8]. As this fragment was a surface find, there was little archaeo-

---

[3] Oleson 2010, 63–171.
[4] Oleson 2009; 2019; Oleson et al., in press.
[5] For discussion of the site's mention in the »Notitia Dignitatum« (or. 34, 25) and the »Beer Sheva Edict« (fr. 2, line 2), see: Oleson 2010, 54–55.
[6] Foote 2007.
[7] It was registered with the number 1993.0198.01.
[8] As recorded on the daily sheet for F103.79, on June 12, 1993. For the preliminary report of this excavation, which does not mention the marble fragment, see Oleson et al. 1995, 343–349.

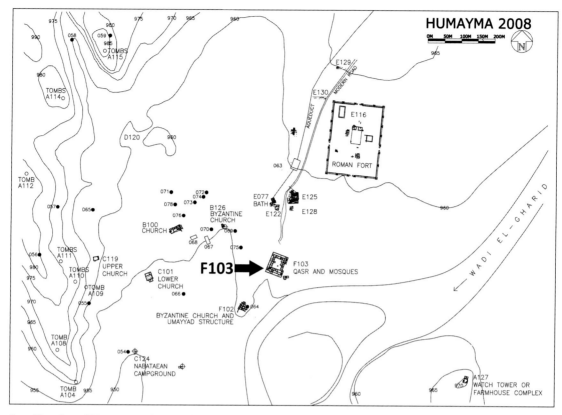

2   Site plan of Humayma, showing the location of the *qasr* and the findspot of the marble fragment (Area F103) (courtesy of M. B. Reeves)

logical context to help date and identify it, but inspection of the object's surfaces noted finely carved »Hellenistic-looking drapery«. The excavators identified the fragment as part of a marble statue dating to the Roman Imperial period, recorded its measurements, and photographed the piece before it was sent to storage. No samples were taken for provenance research, nor was the marble fragment available for subsequent study by the author.

This statue fragment is the first and thus far only marble sculpture found at Humayma. The site has, however, produced numerous examples of ecclesiastical marble, including chancel screens, colonettes, and other decorative elements, from its excavated churches and other structures[9]. One such marble chancel screen fragment was found in close proximity to the marble sculpture presented here (1993.0128.01), and a total of 17 fragments of marble were found throughout the Abbasid family's manor house (F103)[10].

## DESCRIPTION AND IDENTIFICATION OF THE MARBLE FRAGMENT

The small fragment of carved white marble has maximum preserved dimensions of 14 cm, by 9 cm, by 9 cm and weighs 1360 g. Although poorly preserved, the front and back surfaces display the finely carved folds of a belted *apoptygma* over the abdomen of a female figure (figs. 3. 4). The drapery on the front appears to cling tightly to the centre of the abdomen, while the sickle-shaped lateral folds of the *apoptygma* are blown back to the sides, where much of the girded drapery appears collected above the waist. On the back, the hem of the *apoptygma* is rendered with blousing folds. Below, the *peplos* hangs down over the backside of the figure. The fineness of the carving on both the front and back of the fragment suggests that this piece belongs to a statue in the round (rather than a sarcophagus) and likely one designed to be seen from all directions, as opposed

---

[9]   See Schick et al. 2013, 449–485.
[10]  Schick et al. 2013, 480–483.

3   Front of marble statue fragment from Humayma, showing the sickle-shaped folds of the *apoptygma* (1993.0198.01) (courtesy of J. P. Oleson)

4   Back of the marble statue fragment from Humayma, showing the hem of the belted *apoptygma* (1993.0198.01) (courtesy of J. P. Oleson)

to being placed in a niche or against a wall. Although the inaccessibility of the fragment prevented a detailed assessment of its carving technique, it appears to be carved with linear detail in the recesses across its front, while the marble itself appears to be of medium grain without any discernible geological bedding planes or flaws. Based on the proportions and size of this fragment, it is estimated that the entire statue would have once stood approximately 60 cm in height.

The sickle-shaped lateral folds of the *apoptygma* and the clinging of the garment to the abdomen in the fragment are closely paralleled in the drapery of the gliding Victoriae/Nikai that formed a conspicuously common iconographic type in the Hauran region of southern *Syria* (fig. 5)[11]. Primarily sculpted in basalt, these statues were locally produced and fall into two clear categories[12]. The first type, the so-called Amazonen-Typus (Amazon type), portrays the goddess in a *peplos* fastened with a broach, with her right breast exposed in similar fashion to depictions of Amazons. The second type, the so-called Heraklesknoten-Typus (Heracles knot type), depicts the goddess in a *peplos*, the *apoptygma* of which is tied under the covered breasts with a belt that is held with a symmetrical Heracles knot.

In both schemes, the goddess is rendered with the fabric of the *apoptygma* pressed against the abdomen by a headwind that causes the garment to ripple out in curved folds that frame the abdominal area as an oval. Better preserved examples of these sculpted Victoriae/Nikai reveal the winged deity holding a cornucopia or palm fronds in her lowered hand and a crown in her raised and outstretched hand, thereby rendering her in the act of crowning a god or mortal. The use of these Victoriae/Nikai to frame sculptural groups resulted in laterally inverted copies, with some examples portrayed with a raised right arm, and other with a raised left arm. In seemingly all cases, one leg is extended to portray a forward movement that is also seen in the flowing folds of the *apoptygma*, and either sandals or closed shoes appear on the feet. While some of these statues rest on simple square or rectangular plinths, many of the figures are depicted atop full or hemispherical globes, an iconographic representation that took inspiration from Roman models[13].

All the known examples of these Victoriae/Nikai are presumed to date to the first three centuries AD and are likely to have come from sanctuaries where they were set up as separate votive offerings or as part of larger cultic or triumphal monuments[14]. One such large-scale display was

---

[11] Linant de Bellefonds 1997; Dentzer – Weber 2009, 60–64; Töpfer 2015, 9–13; Töpfer 2021, 238–240.
[12] Dentzer – Weber 2009, 60–64.
[13] Töpfer 2015, 11–13.
[14] Töpfer 2015, 10.

5 Basalt statues of Victoria/Nike from the Hauran. Left: Victoria/Nike from Souweida, in guise of an Amazon. Damascus Museum. Right: Statue of Victoria/Nike with Heracles knot in the garden of the Damascus Museum (courtesy of K. M. Töpfer)

found in the Sanctuary of Sahr-al-Ledja, in southern Syria, the reconstruction of which comprises two figures of Victoria/Nike on high pillars flanking a sculptural group of riders and a central mounted figure that may have been a local ruler[15]. On the back of this monument, two divine carriages driven by gods are similarly flanked by Victoriae/Nikai on high pillars. A comparable sculptural display featuring carved Victoriae/Nikai also existed at Umm al-Jimal, in present-day northern Jordan, where it was constructed in the 1st or 2nd century AD and possibly destroyed by Zenobia's forces in the later 3rd century[16].

While particularly common in the basalt statues of the Hauran, this sculptural formula also appears on a 2nd- to 3rd-century AD marble statue of a gliding Victoria/Nike from Latakia (ancient *Laodikeia ad Mare*) on the Syrian coast, which is now in the Kunsthistorisches Museum in Vienna (fig. 6). Like the fragment of marble found at Humayma, the oval-shaped lower abdomen of this figure is framed by the sickle-shaped folds of the *apoptygma*, and its size (38 cm tall, with a recon-

---

[15] Dentzer – Weber 2009, 23–88 fig. 120.
[16] Weber-Karyotakis – al-Khdair 2018.

6   Marble figurine of a gliding Victoria/Nike from Latakia (ancient *Laodikeia ad Mare*), Kunsthistorisches Museum, Vienna (KHM Vienna)

structed height of about 1 m) is also analogous to the presumed height of the Humayma example. The drapery on the Latakia Victoria/Nike, however, appears less finely finished than that of the Humayma piece[17]. Significantly, the statue from Latakia demonstrates the extension of this iconographic scheme to white marble sculpture.

The popularity of Victoria/Nike extended across the Roman East and appears in a broad array of artistic media[18]. In *Nabataea* and Roman *Arabia*, in which *Hawara/Hauarra* was located, depictions of these winged deities appear on relief sculpture from *Petra*[19] and Khirbet et-Tannur[20], wall paintings at Mampsis[21], and even on Nabataean coins[22]. This iconography may have been used as royal propaganda to celebrate a military victory, much in the same way as their Roman antecedents[23]. Alternatively, the Syrian practice of depicting Victoriae/Nikai with cornucopiae suggests that the popularity of these figures may have partly resulted from their association with ideas of protection and fortune, through syncretism with Tyche and Gad/Gadde[24].

Unsurprisingly, depictions of Victoria/Nike commonly appear in military contexts of the Roman East. Recently, a fragmentary limestone sculpture of Victoria/Nike was found at the Roman legionary base at *Legio*[25]. Further away, at *Dura-Europos*, excavators uncovered a painting of a gliding Victoria/Nike on a plastered pillar in the *frigidarium* of Bath F3[26], while a another depiction was found on a wooden panel of a shrine in the site's Palmyrene Gate[27]. Also from *Dura-Europos* comes the remarkable painted *scutum*, adorned with two Victoriae/Nikai flanking a central eagle[28]. Other examples of this deity's representation on Roman military equipment in the eastern Empire include those found on a late Roman shield

---

[17] Weber 2015, 580–581 suggests the Latakia statue may have a training piece of a local sculptor working with imported marble.
[18] Linant de Bellefonds 1997.
[19] McKenzie 1990, 142 pl. 80; Schmid 2009, 329.
[20] Glueck 1965, 430–450 pl. 179–185. 188–189; McKenzie et al. 2013, 78–87 fig. 139–157.
[21] Negev 1988, 154–156 photos 153. 154.
[22] Hoover 2006, 114–115.
[23] Hoover 2006, 114; Schmid 2009, 329–330.
[24] Töpfer 2015, 13–16.
[25] Fischer et al. 2022.
[26] Brown 1936a, 63–67 pl. 41, 1.
[27] Rostovtzeff – Baur 1931, 181–193 pl. 1.
[28] Brown 1936b, 459–460 pls. 25. 25 A.

cover, purportedly found in Egypt[29], and the one seen on the 3rd-century painted *vexillum* also found in Egypt[30].

While the fragment of sculpture presented here is the first marble statue found at Humayma, it is not the first Victoria/Nike from the site[31]. Excavation in the Roman fort uncovered the remains of wall paintings which may depict representations of this winged deity[32]. A fragmentary figural scene depicts what appears to be a triumphal scene with a likely Victoria/Nike placing a laurel crown on a figure's head, while a separate fragmentary depiction of a larger figure from the fort's *praetorium* may also represent a Victoria/Nike, similar to those seen at Mampsis[33].

Although fragmentary and poorly preserved, the piece of marble sculpture found at Humayma likely comes from a statue of a Victoria/Nike. The presence of sickle-shaped folds of drapery that frame the abdomen of the figure closely parallel the renderings of Victoriae/Nikai found elsewhere in the Roman East. Furthermore, the placement of *Hawara/Hauarra* within the Nabataean heartland and the site's military character after the Roman annexation of this territory in AD 106 further support this identification, given the popularity of this deity in Nabataean art and the Roman military community.

If not a depiction of a Victoria/Nike, the carved drapery on this fragment bears some resemblance to the tucked and girded *chiton* found on statues of the goddess Artemis, and marble sculptures of this goddess have been found at several sites in Roman *Arabia* and the neighbouring regions. Examples include those uncovered at *Gerasa*[34], *Abila*[35], *Pella*[36], the Sanctuary of Pan at *Caesarea Philippi*[37], and at *Petra* where a life-sized bronze statue of the goddess was fortuitously found in a wadi after a flash flood[38]. While these regional finds, combined with the wide-spread veneration of Artemis in the Roman East and her syncretization with local goddesses like Atargatis within Nabataean society[39], raise the possibility that the Humayma fragment belongs to a statue of Artemis, the details of the preserved drapery suggest an identification as a gliding Victoria/Nike is much more likely.

Assigning a date to the sculptural fragment is complicated both by its discovery as a surface find and its poor preservation. If its identification as a gliding Victoria/Nike is correct, the cited comparanda suggest a date ranging from the 1st to 3rd century AD. It may be possible to refine this date range by identifying the location of the statue's original placement, but the site of its display remains uncertain.

## LOCATION OF DISPLAY ON SITE

The marble fragment's discovery among wall tumble in the Abbasid family's *qasr* suggests that it was reused for wall construction, and it is unlikely that the statue was ever displayed in this structure. Although excavation under the *qasr* uncovered the remains of an earlier building dating to the Nabataean or Roman period[40], there is no evidence that the statue was displayed in this earlier structure either. Instead, it is likely that this fragment was carried to the *qasr* for reuse, as was done with the numerous fragments of ecclesiastical marble found throughout the building[41].

---

[29] Goethert 1996, 119–124 figs. 198. 203–204.
[30] Rostovtzeff 1942, pl. 4.
[31] Harvey, forthcoming.
[32] Harvey, in press.
[33] Negev 1988, 154–156 photos 153. 154.
[34] Weber 2002, 485–486; Lichtenberger – Raja 2015, 493 fig. 12.
[35] Mare 1997; Weber 2002, 465.
[36] Weber 2002, 483.
[37] Friedland 2012, 110–113.
[38] Weber 2002, 525.
[39] Kampen 2003; Ovadiah – Mucznik 2012, 520–533.
[40] Oleson et al. 2003, 59–60.
[41] Schick et al. 2013, 480–483.

At present, there is no clear candidate for the location of the statue's original installation, and it is entirely possible that its place of display has not yet been excavated. According to Töpfer, most of the basalt statues of Victoria/Nike found in the Hauran were likely set up in sanctuaries as votive offerings comprising single statues or larger compositions[42]. The only sanctuary thus far excavated at Humayma is the community shrine in Field E125, which is located east of the garrison baths and south-west of the fort[43]. This small sanctuary was not large enough to have held a monumental composition such as those found in the Hauran, but it is possible that a single votive statue of a gliding Victoria/Nike could have been erected along the processional way leading to the shrine.

If not at this small shrine, it is possible that the sculpture was displayed in a larger temple or sanctuary on site. The discovery of numerous architectural cut stone blocks at Humayma (including Nabataean capitals, column drums, bases, and moldings) point towards the existence of a monumental public structure, most probably a temple, that was dismantled sometime in the Roman or Byzantine period[44]. There is not enough evidence to suggest that a cultic or triumphal sculptural display like those found at sanctuaries in the Hauran was ever erected at Humayma. If, however, the Humayma Victoria/Nike was set up at a larger temple or sanctuary at the site, this statue may have been placed atop a stone pillar similar to those found at Umm al-Jimal and elsewhere in the Hauran[45].

Another possible location for the statue's display at Humayma is an enigmatic stone platform (in Field E121), which is located approximately 100 m west of the military fort and close to the *Via Nova Traiana*[46]. The north and east edges of this platform measure almost exactly ten Roman feet, suggesting that its construction dates to the Roman period, which corresponds to the likely date range of the marble sculpture. Although the use of this platform remains unclear, it may have functioned as a base for a sculptural display set up along the northern approach to the settlement.[47]

If not displayed publicly, the gliding Victoria/Nike statue may have once adorned a private residence. Similarly sized marble statues have been found in domestic spaces in *Petra*, such as those recovered on the summit of Umm al-Biyara[48]. Two marble statues of Aphrodite were also uncovered in an elite residence on Petra's North Ridge, although these were likely deposited in a dump long after the abandonment of the complex[49]. Few domestic spaces have been investigated at Humayma, but of those which have been excavated, the most likely location for the display of the marble Victoria/Nike is the *praetorium* (the commander's residence) of the Roman military fort. This elite domestic space featured a central courtyard with a fountain and interior rooms richly decorated with bright wall paintings and complex mosaics[50]. An imported marble sculpture would have aligned with the decorative scheme of the residence, and the image of a Victoria/Nike would have similarly been appropriate for decorating the *praetorium* of a Roman fort.

Another option for display in the fort at Humayma is in the *principia* (the headquarters building). Excavation of this structure uncovered several examples of statue bases on which statues such as the one presented here may have stood[51]. Statuary was a common feature of the *principia*[52], and statues and altars to Victoria have been found in the *principia* of forts across the Empire[53]. The fragmentary limestone statue of Victoria/Nike found at *Legio*, for example, is thought

---

[42] Töpfer 2015, 10.
[43] Reeves 2019.
[44] Oleson 2013, 214; Schick et al. 2013, 497–501.
[45] Weber-Karyotakis – al-Khdair 2018, 217–219 fig. 6–8.
[46] Reeves et al. 2009, 241–246 fig. 21; Babbitt 2009, 52–94.
[47] Babbitt 2009, 72–74; Reeves 2016, 172–173 fig. 9.
[48] Schmid – Bienkowski 2012, 258–259 figs. 13. 15; Schmid et al. 2012, 81–83 figs. 11. 13.
[49] Parker – Perry 2019, 719 fig. 25.
[50] Oleson – Reeves, in press; Harvey, in press; Harvey, forthcoming; Klapecki – Oleson, in press.
[51] de Bruijn – Oleson, forthcoming.
[52] Johnson 1983, 111–114.
[53] Sarnowski 1989, tab. 4–5.

to have come from the *principia* of the site's Roman fort[54]. Display in the *principia* is thus one further possibility for the original placement of this marble Victory/Nike statue at Humayma.

## SOURCE OF THE MARBLE

The absence of marble quarries in the Roman Near East necessitated the importation of white marble statues to the region, either as unfinished blocks of stone or in a semi-finished or fully finished state[55]. Unfortunately, no isotopic analysis was conducted on the statue fragment from Humayma, and thus it is not possible to identify the source of the marble. Despite this lack of analysis, provenance studies conducted on several samples of ecclesiastical marble found at Humayma suggested that these architectural fragments were imported from the quarries at *Prokonnesos*, *Thasos*, and *Naxos*[56]. Similar investigations of white marble veneer uncovered from structures in *Petra* have likewise determined that this material came from quarries in Greece, Asia Minor, and Italy, including *Thasos*, *Naxos*, *Paros*, Penteli, *Prokonnesos*, *Dokimeion*, and Carrara[57]. White marble statues uncovered in the Decapolis cities of *Gerasa*[58], *Gadara*[59], and *Philadelphia*[60] were similarly sourced from quarries in Greece and Asia Minor, and this near complete reliance on Greek and western Anatolian quarries (with the possible use of the Italian quarry at Carrara) is true for white marble sculpture more generally throughout the Roman East[61]. Thus, although the statue fragment found at Humayma was not analyzed, regional comparanda and other imported marble found at the site strongly suggest that it was sourced from quarries in the Aegean or Asia Minor. The difficulty and cost of importing marble sculpture to this inland site no doubt contributed to the paucity of marble sculpture at *Hawara*/*Hauarra*.

## CONCLUSION

As the only known marble sculpture thus far uncovered at Humayma, the fragment presented here represents a significant contribution to our understanding of sculptural display at the site and is an important addition to the limited corpus of white marble sculpture from *Nabataea* and the Roman Province of *Arabia*. Despite its small size and poor preservation, the marble fragment still preserves enough of its carved drapery to allow recognition of the sickle-shaped curves of a belted *apoptygma* framing the abdomen that characterize gliding Victoriae/Nikai found in the Hauran region. The identification of the Humayma sculpture as a similar Victoria/Nike is supported by this deity's popularity in Nabataean art and the military character of the site after Roman annexation in AD 106.

The discovery of this marble statue fragment as a surface find prevents a clear understanding of where and how it was displayed on site. It may have once stood alone or formed part of a monumental sculptural group of cultic or triumphal character erected on a Roman-period stone platform on the northern edge of town or at a temple which was disassembled later in the site's history. Alternatively, it may have adorned a building in the Roman fort, such as the *praetorium* or *principia*. Most likely, however, the original place of its display has not yet been uncovered, and thus it is difficult to assess how it was viewed or appeared in ancient *Hawara*/*Hauarra*.

Despite these uncertainties, the presence of this imported marble sculpture speaks to the prosperity and status of the settlement. *Hawara* was the largest Nabataean settlement in the northern Hisma and was located strategically along the important trade route between *Petra* and *Aila*, on

---

[54] Fischer et al. 2022, 230.
[55] For general discussions on the importation of marble sculpture to the Roman Near East, see Fischer 1998, 245–265; Friedland 2012, 21–34.
[56] Schick et al. 2013, 485–492.
[57] Abu-Jaber et al. 2012; Al-Bashaireh – Bedal 2017.
[58] Friedland 2003, 415–417; Al-Bashaireh – Weber-Karyotakis 2021.
[59] Al-Bashaireh et al. 2019, 356–360; Al-Bashaireh 2022.
[60] Friedland – Tykot 2012.
[61] Fischer 1998, 245–258; Friedland 2012, 21–24.

the Red Sea. The significance of the site increased after annexation and the establishment of the Roman fort next to the settlement. It should be no surprise, therefore, that a resident or group thereof had the funds to commission, import, and erect this statue. While there is not enough evidence to suggest that this marble statue belongs to the same tradition of erecting chariot sculptural groups seen in the Hauran to the north, the similar rendering of this Victoria/Nike to those in the Hauran reflects the connectivity of the site and the awareness of its inhabitants to the artistic visual language of the wider region. The regional popularity of this statue type as well as the scale and technique of the Humayma sculpture may suggest that this statue was a product of a coastal or regional workshop in the Roman East, rather than an import from Greece or Asia Minor. The poor preservation of the fragment, however, severely limits any attempt at identifying the place of its fabrication. While much remains unknown about this marble statue, it has provided new insight into the sculptural landscape of Humayma, and its existence hints at the possibility that other marble figural sculptures once existed at *Hawara/Hauarra* and have yet to be uncovered.

## ACKNOWLEDGMENTS

This publication would not have been possible without the support of many people. First and foremost, I am thankful to Rebecca M. Foote for permission to study and publish this marble fragment. I also wish to thank John P. Oleson and M. Barbara Reeves for their support of this project and to Ian W. N. Jones for his assistance with the excavation reports of the Abbasid *qasr*. I am extremely grateful to Thomas M. Weber-Karyotakis for generously sharing his expertise and helping to identify this sculpture and to Mark Abbe for his helpful comments on an earlier draft. I am also grateful to Kai Michael Töpfer, the Kunsthistorisches Museum Vienna, and the Humayma Excavation Project for permission to use the included images. Finally, I wish to thank the organizers of the 17th International Colloquium on Roman Provincial Art in Vienna/Carnuntum for their support of this research.

## BIBLIOGRAPHY

| | |
|---|---|
| Abu-Jaber et al. 2012 | N. Abu-Jaber – Z. al-Saad – A. Shiyyab – P. Degryse, Provenance of white marbles from the Nabatean sites of Qasr al Bint and the colonnaded street baths at Petra, Jordan, Mediterranean Archaeology and Archaeometry 12/1, 2012, 21–29 |
| Al-Bashaireh 2022 | K. Al-Bashaireh, Quarry origin determination of marble statues from Umm Qeis Antiquities Museum, Gadara, Jordan by multi-analytical techniques, JASc Reports 41, 2022, 103305, DOI: 10.1016/j.jasrep.2021.103305 (29.03.2023) |
| Al-Bashaireh – Bedal 2017 | K. Al-Bashaireh – L.-A. Bedal, Provenance of white and colored marbles from the Petra garden and pool complex, Petra, South Jordan, Archaeological and Anthropological Sciences 9/5, 2017, 817–829, DOI: 10.1007/s12520-015-0305-9 (05.05.2023) |
| Al-Bashaireh – Weber-Karyotakis 2021 | K. Al-Bashaireh – T. M. Weber-Karyotakis, The muses and other statues of the Eastern Roman Baths of Gerasa, Jordan (2018 Campaign): Form and provenance, JASc Reports 36, 2021, 102862, DOI: 10.1016/j.jasrep.2021.102862 (05.05.2023) |
| Babbitt 2009 | I. Babbitt, Second to Fourth Century Structures from Hawara's Vicus: Interim Report on Field E121 at Humayma (M.A. thesis Queen's University, Kingston 2009) |
| Brown 1936a | F. E. Brown, Block F3, in: M. I. Rostovtzeff – A. R. Bellinger – C. Hopkins – C. B. Welles (eds.), Excavations at Dura-Europos. Preliminary Report of the Sixth Season of Work October 1932–March 1933 (New Haven 1936) 49–83 |
| Brown 1936b | F. E. Brown, Arms and Armor, in: M. I. Rostovtzeff – A. R. Bellinger – C. Hopkins – C. B. Welles (eds.), Excavations at Dura-Europos. Preliminary Report of the Sixth Season of Work October 1932–March 1933 (New Haven 1936) 439–466 |
| de Bruijn – Oleson, in press | E. de Bruijn – J. P. Oleson, *Principia* and Parade Ground (Area G), in: Oleson et al., in press |
| Dentzer – Weber 2009 | J.-M. Dentzer – T. M. Weber, Hauran 4. Sahr al-Ledja II: Un sanctuaire du désert basaltique à l'époque romaine (Beirut 2009) |
| Fischer 1998 | M. Fischer, Marble Studies: Roman Palestine and the Marble Trade, XeniaKonst 40 (Constance 1998) |

| | |
|---|---|
| Fischer et al. 2022 | M. Fischer – M. J. Adams – N. Lect Ben Ami – Y. Tepper, A Fragmentary Sculpture of Victoria from the Legionary Base at Legio, IEJ 72/2, 2022, 219–235 |
| Foote 2007 | R. M. Foote, From residence to revolutionary headquarters: The early Islamic qasr and mosque complex at al-Humayma and its 8th-century context, in: T. E. Levy – P. M. M. Daviau – R. W. Younker – M. Shaer (eds.), Crossing Jordan. North American Contributions to the Archaeology of Jordan (London 2007) 457–465 |
| Friedland 2003 | E. A. Friedland, The Roman marble sculptures from the North Hall of the East Baths at Gerasa, AJA 107/3, 2003, 413–448 |
| Friedland 2012 | E. A. Friedland, The Roman Marble Sculptures from the Sanctuary of Pan at Caesarea Philippi/Panias (Israel) (Boston 2012) |
| Friedland – Tykot 2012 | E. A. Friedland – R. H. Tykot, Quarry origins, commission, and import of marble sculptures from the Roman theater in Philadelphia/Amman, Jordan, in: A. Gutiérrez Garcia-M. – L. Lapuente – I. Rodà (eds.), Interdisciplinary Studies on Ancient Stone. Proceedings of the IX Association for the Study of Marbles and Other Stones in Antiquity (ASMOSIA) Conference, Tarragona 2009 (Tarragona 2012) 52–60 |
| Glueck 1965 | N. Glueck, Deities and Dolphins: The story of the Nabataeans (New York 1965) |
| Goethert 1996 | K. P. Goethert, Neue römische Prunkschilde, in: M. Junkelmann (ed.), Reiter wie Statuen aus Erz (Mainz 1996) 115–126 |
| Harvey, forthcoming | C. A. Harvey, The Goddess of Victory at Humayma and in Nabataean Art, Studies in the History and Archaeology of Jordan 15, forthcoming |
| Harvey, in press | C. A. Harvey, Painted Plaster, in: Oleson et al., in press |
| Hoover 2006 | O. D. Hoover, A reassessment of Nabataean lead coinage in light of new discoveries, NumChron 166, 2006, 105–119 |
| Johnson 1983 | A. Johnson, Roman Forts of the 1st and 2nd Centuries AD in Britain and the German Provinces (London 1983) |
| Kampen 2003 | J. Kampen, The Cult of Artemis and the Essenes in Syro-Palestine, Dead Sea Discoveries 10/2, 2003, 205–22 |
| Klapecki – Oleson, in press | D. Klapecki – J. P. Oleson, *Praetorium* Mosaics, in: Oleson et al., in press |
| Lichtenberger – Raja 2015 | A. Lichtenberger – R. Raja, New archaeological research in the Northwest quarter of Jerash and its implications for the urban development of Roman Gerasa, AJA 119/4, 2015, 483–500 |
| Linant de Bellefonds 1997 | LIMC VIII suppl. (1997) 879–888 s. v. Nike (in Peripheria Orientali) (P. Linant de Bellefonds) |
| McKenzie 1990 | J. S. McKenzie, The Architecture of Petra (Oxford 1990) |
| McKenzie et al. 2013 | J. S. McKenzie – J. A. Greene – A. T. Reyes – C. S. Alexander – D. G. Barrett – B. Gilmour – J. F. Healey – M. O'Hea – N. Schibille – S. G. Schmid – W. Wetterstrom – S. W. Kansa, The Nabataean Temple at Khirbet et-Tannur, Jordan. Final Report on Nelson Glueck's 1937 Excavation, AASOR 68 (Boston 2013) |
| Mare 1997 | W. H. Mare, The Artemis Statue Excavated at Abila of the Decapolis in 1994, AAJ 41, 1997, 277–281 |
| Negev 1988 | A. Negev, The architecture of Mampsis Final Report 1. The Middle and Late Nabatean Periods, Qedem 26 (Jerusalem 1988) |
| Oleson 2009 | J. P. Oleson, Trajan's Engineers and the Roman Fort at al-Humayma (Ancient Hawara, Jordan), Studies in the History and Archaeology of Jordan 10, 2009, 535–547 |
| Oleson 2010 | J. P. Oleson, Humayma Excavation Project, 1. Resources, History, and the Water-Supply System (Boston 2010) |
| Oleson 2013 | J. P. Oleson, Field B100: Byzantine Church and Early Islamic House, in: J. P. Oleson – R. Schick, Humayma Excavation Project 2. Nabatean Campground and Necropolis, Byzantine Churches, and Early Islamic Domestic Structures (Boston 2013) 161–219 |
| Oleson 2019 | J. P. Oleson, The Trajanic Auxiliary Fort at Ḥawara (Modern Ḥumayma), Jordan, Studies in the History and Archaeology of Jordan 13, 2019, 395–406 |
| Oleson et al. 1995 | J. P. Oleson – K. ʿAmr – R. M. Foote – R. Schick, Preliminary Report of the Humayma Excavation Project, 1993, AAJ 39, 1995, 317–354 |

| | |
|---|---|
| Oleson et al. 2003 | J. P. Oleson – G. S. Barker – E. De Bruijn – R. M. Foote – J. Logan – M. B. Reeves – A. N. Sherwood, Preliminary Report of the Humayma Excavation Project, 2000, 2002, AAJ 47, 2003, 37–64 |
| Oleson et al., in press | J. P. Oleson – E. De Bruijn – M. B. Reeves – A. N. Sherwood – C. A. Harvey – Y. Gerber – M. Nikolic, Humayma Excavation Project 3. The Roman Fort, in press |
| Oleson – Reeves, in press | J. P. Oleson – M. B. Reeves, *Praetorium* (Area I), in: Oleson et al., in press |
| Ovadiah – Mucznik 2012 | A. Ovadiah – S. Mucznik, Apollo and Artemis in the Decapolis, Liber Annuus 62, 2012, 515–534 |
| Parker – Perry 2019 | S. T. Parker – M. A. Perry, Petra North Ridge Project. The 2016 Season, AAJ 60, 2019, 709–721 |
| Reeves 2016 | M. B. Reeves, Humayma's notched peak. A focus of Nabataean and Roman veneration and civic identity, ArabAEpigr 27/2, 2016, 166–175 |
| Reeves 2019 | M. B. Reeves, A Nabataean and Roman shrine with civic and military gods at Humayma, Jordan, ArabAEpigr 30/1, 2019, 134–155 |
| Reeves et al. 2009 | M. B. Reeves – I. Babbitt – K. Cummer – B. V. Karas – B. Seymour – A. Shelton, Preliminary Report on Excavations in the Nabataean Town and Roman Vicus at Humayma (Ancient Hawara), 2008, AAJ 53, 2009, 229–263 |
| Rostovtzeff 1942 | M. Rostovtzeff, *Vexillum* and Victory, JRS 32, 1942, 92–106 |
| Rostovtzeff – Baur 1931 | M. I. Rostovtzeff – P. V. C. Baur, Victory on a Painted Panel, in: M. I. Rostovtzeff – P. V. C. Baur (eds.), Excavations at Dura-Europos. Preliminary Report of the Second Season of Work, 1928–1929 (New Haven 1931) 181–193 |
| Sarnowski 1989 | T. Sarnowski, Zur Statuenausstattung römischer Stabsgebäude, BJb 189, 1989, 97–120 |
| Schick et al. 2013 | R. Schick – J. P. Oleson – K. Al-Bashaireh – D. Graf – N. Herz – G. D. Rowe, Ecclesiastical Marble, Inscriptions, and Miscellaneous Stone Finds, in: J. P. Oleson – R. Schick, Humayma Excavation Project 2. Nabatean Campground and Necropolis, Byzantine Churches, and Early Islamic Domestic Structures (Boston 2013) 449–513 |
| Schmid 2009 | S. G. Schmid, Nabataean royal propaganda: a response to Herod and Augustus?, in: D. M. Jacobson – N. Kokkinos (eds.), Herod and Augustus. Papers Presented at the IJS Conference 21.–23.06.2005, University College London (Leiden 2009) 325–360 |
| Schmid – Bienkowski 2012 | S. G. Schmid – P. Bienkowski, Eine nabatäische Königsresidenz auf Umm al-Biyara, in: Petra – Wunder in der Wüste. Auf den Spuren von J. L. Burckhardt alias Scheich Ibrahim. Ausstellung Antikenmuseum Basel und Sammlung Ludwig 23.10.2012–17.03.2013 (Basel 2012) 252–261 |
| Schmid et al. 2012 | S. G. Schmid – P. Bienkowski – Z. T. Fiema – B. Kolb, The Palaces of the Nabataean Kings at Petra, in: L. Nehmé – L. Wadeson (eds.), The Nabataeans in Focus. Current Archaeological Research at Petra, Supplement to the Proceedings of the Seminar for Arabian Studies 42 (Oxford 2012) 73–98 |
| Töpfer 2015 | K. M. Töpfer, The goddess of victory in Greek and Roman art, in: N. Gutschow – K. Weiler (eds.), Spirits in Transcultural Skies. Auspicious and Protective Spirits in Artefacts and Architecture Between East and West (Heidelberg 2015) 1–18 |
| Töpfer 2021 | K. M. Töpfer, Götterstatuen in der Provinz Syria, in: J. Lipps – M. Dorka Moreno – J. Griesbach (eds.), Appropriation Processes of Statue Schemata in the Roman Provinces, Material Appropriation Processes in Antiquity I (Wiesbaden 2021) 231–244 |
| Weber 2002 | T. M. Weber, Gadara – Umm Qēs 1. Gadara Decapolitana: Untersuchungen zur Topographie, Geschichte, Architektur und der bildenden Kunst einer »Polis Hellenis« im Ostjordanland (Wiesbaden 2002) |
| Weber 2015 | T. M. Weber, Near East, in: E. A. Friedland – M. G. Sobocinski – E. K. Gazda (eds.), The Oxford Handbook of Roman sculpture (Oxford 2015) 569–586 |
| Weber-Karyotakis – al-Khdair 2018 | T. M. Weber-Karyotakis – M. H. S. al-Khdair, An Arab Chariot Monument at Umm al-Jimāl, PEQ 150/3, 2018, 214–235 |

*Craig A. Harvey, University of Alberta, Department of History, Classics, and Religion, 2-25 HM Tory Building, Edmonton, Alberta, Canada, T6G 2H4.*
*[e] caharvey@ualberta.ca*

Melissa Kays

# MONUMENTS OF AURELIA PAULINA AND HER PORTRAYAL OF SOCIAL CHANGE IN ROMAN ASIA MINOR[1]

**Abstract**
Few women embody life during a period of social transition more than Aurelia Paulina of *Perge* in Asia Minor, a wealthy, non-senatorial woman, who was originally from *Syria*. Holding a unique position as an elite woman in the city at a time of a Syrian empress, Aurelia Paulina was well-placed to take advantage of fortuitous circumstances. A benefactress during the late 2nd and early 3rd centuries AD, Aurelia Paulina donated a decorated nymphaeum which highlighted the links between herself, the gods, and the imperial family. Aurelia Paulina represented both her ethnic background and her cultural identity while aligning herself with the most powerful family in the Roman Empire. The building inscription highlights her as the sole benefactor of the fountain structure indicating a potential shift in attitudes towards elite female power and influence. This paper analyzes the assertion of power communicated by Aurelia Paulina's monuments and the unique dress choices conveying her Syrian ethnic identity.

## BACKGROUND

In researching elite benefactresses in the Roman Empire, one would be hard pressed to underestimate the contributions made by Aurelia Paulina in *Perge*, Anatolia. A native of *Syria*, Aurelia Paulina moved to *Perge* in the late 2nd century AD and was granted citizenship by emperor Commodus[2]. Embracing her new surroundings and identity, Aurelia Paulina took on roles as priestess of Artemis Pergaia, as well as priestess of the imperial cult[3]. Artemis Pergaia was the tutelary deity of *Perge*, and appears frequently in statuary depictions and inscriptions in Aurelia Paulina's structure and in numerous others. Aurelia Paulina's most notable donation to the city of *Perge* came in the form of a nymphaeum in the courtyard outside the city gates, built between AD 198 and 211[4]. Mimicking Plancia Magna, another notable local benefactress of the early second century who donated an extraordinary gate complex complete with status niches, Aurelia Paulina chose the *scaenae frons* design for the nymphaeum, filling her niches with intentionally chosen figures[5].

## FEMALE BENEFACTION

Of course, women were not always able to commission massive gate complexes and fountains. This evolution of financial and social power grew over time, and was often reserved for the most elite and dynamic women who held connections with the political elites and historically were established within their local communities. There was no set path which every ancient benefactress followed, but there were hurdles which had to be overcome.

Emily Hemelrijk is a leading expert in the examination of women's roles in elite benefaction, having compiled extensive research and data to determine trends within the Latin West[6]. During

---

[1] This paper is part of the doctoral research project, »Exploring the social mobility and influence of women in Roman public life from the 1st to the 3rd c. AD«, University of York, under the supervision of Maureen Carroll, whom I thank for her support and feedback. All drawings are my own.
[2] McManus (web).
[3] Longfellow 2014/2015.
[4] Longfellow 2011.
[5] McManus (web).
[6] Hemelrijk 2004; Hemelrijk 2015; Hemelrijk – Woolf 2013.

the 1st to 3rd centuries AD, female benefaction surged to new heights as women were encountering new legal and financial freedoms[7]. In researching elite female benefaction, archaeologists are able to gain information regarding a woman's wealth, status, and position within the local and broader societies along with her motivation to give public donations[8]. Women could also be found as patrons of festivals and games, but these leave behind less concrete evidence, and thus are not the focus of the expenditures in this paper[9].

When it comes to the basic motivation for elite benefaction, and particularly benefaction by elite women, scholars have suggested a variety of interpretations. Diana Ng, for example, suggests two potential explanations, contrasting the desire to be commemorated with the societal pressure felt by the elite during the outpouring of public giving[10]. Some benefactresses may have been seeking imperial favour or continuing family tradition, though we must bear in mind that this explanation rescinds some of the agency of these elite women through placing their motivation on relatives who were likely men[11].

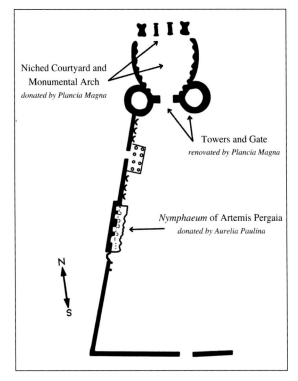

1   *Perge* gate and nymphaeum complexes (illustration by author, after B. F. McManus, VRoma Project)

Whether it was used to appeal for political influence or was decreed by local powers, benefaction led to increased independence and opportunities for elite women[12]. There were varying opinions on the practice though, as the emperor Antoninus Pius did not hesitate to celebrate structural donations while frowning upon the less fundamental public festivals[13]. Though the emperor may have preferred building donations, the non-elite public were to benefit regardless of the form of the donation. This elucidates why statues honoring benefactors were set up across Roman cities, as the non-elite citizens hoped to garner favor and hopefully benefit from additional donations[14]. These honorary statues provide excellent evidence for researchers about dress and the virtues and values of the benefactresses whom other women were hoping to emulate.

## BENEFACTRESSES IN *PERGE*

Before addressing Aurelia Paulina's nymphaeum and her statue (which was thought to have been placed centrally on the structure, below the relief pediment), it would be worthwhile to provide a brief background on the earlier benefactress Plancia Magna and the similarities Aurelia Paulina shared with her predecessor. Plancia Magna, an Italian native of senatorial status due to her family's prominence in Asia Minor and Rome, was an active benefactress earlier in the 2nd century

---

[7]   McCullough 2015, 10.
[8]   Hemelrijk 2004, 217–219. 234–235.
[9]   Ng 2015, 102; Zuiderhoek 2009, 86.
[10]  Ng 2015, 102.
[11]  Hemelrijk 2004, 217–218; Meyers 2012, 145; Ng 2015, 101.
[12]  Pobjoy 2000, 79; Zuiderhoek 2009, 120–121.
[13]  Ng 2015, 103.
[14]  Hemelrijk – Woolf 2013, 483; Ng 2015, 104.

AD, 80–90 years prior to Aurelia Paulina, donating a monumental gate complex which permitted entrance to the southern side of the city of *Perge* (fig. 1)[15].

While Aurelia Paulina's inscriptions are purely in Greek, Plancia Magna chose to inscribe her gate complex in both Greek and Latin[16]. This potentially indicates that during Plancia Magna's era of benefaction, it was seen as beneficial to link oneself to the Roman Empire through utilizing the Latin language in inscriptions, while utilizing *Perge*'s native Greek to be inclusive for local community members. Perhaps by the time that Aurelia Paulina was an active community member in *Perge*, there was less of an expectation to include Latin in local inscriptions. It is worth noting the inscription choices made by Plancia Magna, as they are unique in wording structure, and unseen in other statue bases commissioned by women. Rather than allowing herself to be defined by her relationship to her male relatives, Plancia Magna switches roles and names her father and brother by their relationship to her[17]. This centres Plancia Magna within the conversation, and subtly highlights her dominant role in the family and in the community.

κτίστ]ης
Μ.] Π[λ]άνκιος Οὐᾶρος
πα]τὴρ Πλανκίας Μάγνης
Περγαῖος[18]

»The Founder, Marcus Plancius Varus, father of Plancia Magna. A Pergean«[19].

κτίστης
Γ. Πλάνκιος Οὐᾶρος
ἀδελφὸς
Πλανκίας Μάγνης
Περγαῖος[20]

»The Founder, Gaius Plancius Varus, brother of Plancia Magna. A Pergean«[21].

In terms of dress of their respective statues, Plancia Magna follows the standard Large Herculaneum style, which makes the later Aurelia Paulina's dress choices even more interesting[22]. The Large Herculaneum statue type was defined by a dropped hip, an arm across her chest grasping the mantle fabric, and was most often found veiled[23]. This style was popularized in the eastern Roman Empire and, according to Jane Fejfer, was used to symbolize marriage and motherhood (fig. 2)[24]. Christiane Vorster provides a contrasting view and states that the type is reminiscent of male statue types which were used to emphasize a strong education and self-assuredness[25].

Both of these women were connected to elite family members, as Plancia Magna's father was M. Plancius Varus, and was distinguished as a founder of the city of *Perge* along with her brother C. Plancius Varus[26]. Plancia Magna's marriage to Roman senator C. Iulius Cornutus Tertullus would have sealed the deal in creating a powerful legacy within *Perge*[27]. Aurelia Paulina found

---

[15] Gatzke 2020, 385. 390; McManus (web).
[16] McManus (web).
[17] Boatwright 1991, 255.
[18] I.Perge 108.
[19] Translated by Gatzke 2020, 387.
[20] I.Perge 109.
[21] Translated by Gatzke 2020, 388.
[22] Fejfer 2008, 367.
[23] Long 2014, 82–83.
[24] Fejfer 2008, 342
[25] Vorster 2008, 120.
[26] Gatzke 2020, 387.
[27] Gatzke 2020, 390.

2  Plancia Magna and Aurelia Paulina, comparison (illustration by author)

herself in *Perge* following her marriage to Aquilus from *Sillyon*, who was also very wealthy and involved in the priesthood of the imperial cult in *Perge*[28]. These slight differences surely shaped their views and decisions when it came to donating the *Perge* gate complex and nearby nymphaeum.

Though there are plenty of instances where Plancia Magna and Aurelia Paulina differ, there are notable similarities between the two women as well. Spatially, it is worth noting that Plancia Magna's gate complex stands very close to Aurelia Paulina's nymphaeum (see fig. 1). The inspiration from the earlier benefactress is clear and the connection between the two structures could not be missed. Longfellow addresses similar fountains, and concludes that the placement of new water features near to earlier benefactions emphasized historical relevance while creating a contrast to the previous patron(s)[29]. Aurelia Paulina's decision to construct the nymphaeum in the *scaenae frons* design takes a direct note from Plancia Magna's book, as the gate complex also utilizes this format. In terms of the roles the women held in *Perge*, both of the benefactresses were also priestesses of Artemis and the imperial cult[30]. In fact, they both linked themselves to the reigning empress in their donations. Plancia Magna depicts herself in a nearly identical manner to the statue of the empress Sabina, wife of Hadrian, in her gate complex, while Aurelia Paulina creates links with the empress Julia Domna, wife of Septimius Severus, throughout the fountain complex.

## MOTIVATION

Following the background on earlier benefactress Plancia Magna, one is able to better understand Aurelia Paulina's direct motivations and connections within the city of *Perge* and throughout the larger Roman Empire by inspecting the statues and inscriptions in the monumental fountain complex. One of the best places to gain an understanding of her motivations is through the study of the inscriptions found on the nymphaeum. The inscription below is particularly championed, as it is one of the few examples where historians can determine that Aurelia Paulina was granted citizenship during her lifetime:

---

[28] McManus (web).
[29] Longfellow 2012, 133.
[30] McManus (web).

»Aurelia Paulina, priestess for life under asylum-granting
Artemis Pergaia, daughter of Apellas the son of Dionysus and
Aelia Tertulla, formerly the priestess of the imperial cult in the city
of Sillyum alongside her deceased husband Aquilius the son of
Kidramuas, was presented with Roman citizenship by
Commodus. She built and inaugurated this hydreion and all its
ornamentation at her own expense.«[31]

The following inscription was used to create links to the city of *Perge* through honouring their tutelary deity. It reveals that Aurelia Paulina dedicated the fountain structure to the goddess Artemis Pergaia and the presiding imperial family, which was led by Septimius Severus, his wife Julia Domna, and their two sons. The link to the imperial family was similarly included in order to elevate Aurelia Paulina's rank in the eyes of other local and distant elites. This kind of strategic dedication was common, as it meant that the apparent selfless giving of funds for a monumental building could yield benefits for the benefactor in a number of ways.

θεᾶι Ἀρτέμιδι Περγαίᾳ
ἀσύλωι· καὶ
Αὐτοκράτορσι Καίσαρσι
Λ. Σεπτιμίωι Σεουήρωι Περ-
τίνακι Σεβαστῶι · καὶ Μάρκῳ
Αὐρ. Ἀντωνίνωι Σεβ. ⟦[καὶ]⟧
⟦[Π. Σεπτιμίωι Γέται Καίσαρι]⟧
καὶ Ἰουλίᾳ Δόμνῃ · Σεβ.
μητρὶ Κάστρων
καὶ τῶι σύμπαντι οἴκωι
τῶν Σεβαστῶν
καὶ τῆι γλυκυτάτῃ πατρίδι[32]

»To the goddess Artemis Pergaia
and the Emperors Caesars Lucius Septimius Severus Pertinax Augustus
and Marcus Aurelius Antoninus Augustus
and [Publius Septimius Geta Caesar]
and Julia Domna Augusta, mother of the Camps
and to the entire house of the Augusti
and to the sweetest fatherland.«[33]

As much of this behaviour fits the standard expectations for elite benefactresses, one may wonder what was unique about Aurelia Paulina's actions. This is where the statue of Aurelia Paulina found in the nymphaeum plays a major role in understanding her access to social power and elite connections. Archaeologists have been examining this self-representation in her fountain complex since its discovery in 1968, and have commented on the benefactress' choice of dress[34]. While Plancia Magna (who donated between AD 119 and 122), chose to depict herself in the traditional garb of a Roman matron, appearing respectable and virtuous, Aurelia Paulina went against this standard Roman depiction in favour of non-traditional and non-Roman garments. A number of questions arise from this choice of dress, which this paper hopes to address in new ways.

---

[31] Translation by Longfellow 2011, 186.
[32] I.Perge 196.
[33] Translation by Longfellow 2011, 168.
[34] Aristodemou 2013.

## DRESS AS A SYMBOL

Currently the research on understanding dress as a nonverbal communication of identity, status, and motivation is led by researchers such as Maureen Carroll, Ursula Rothe, and Jane Fejfer. The status of ›others‹ in the Roman Empire is examined through a variety of methods, not limited to dress representation, ancient texts, inscriptions, or community groups[35]. Before discussing the items of dress chosen by the benefactress Aurelia Paulina, it is worthwhile to investigate what dress could indicate for a woman of status in the Roman Empire. We discuss later how each choice made by the benefactress would have been intentional, and how this would have been true for many Romans at the time. Dress was crucial to defining oneself as an individual in cities where there were already plenty of unique identities[36]. Beyond categorizing oneself as a singular entity, dress would also provide the opportunity to establish a connection to a group. This could be a religious, ethnic, or communal group, and even the smallest accessory could be used to formulate connections and motivations within the local society[37].

During the expansion of the Roman Empire, communities on the fringe of the Empire were forced to reckon with how to retain their cultural identities while making lifestyle adjustments to display their newfound Roman identities as well. Facing loss of their culture, Roman ›others‹ strived to innovate and realign with their ethnic origins to preserve their history and identities. Often depicted as inferior and barbaric to the Roman citizens, the indigenous peoples were battling on multiple fronts to be both heard and seen[38].

In a way, the non-native Romans were seen, but often in untoward positions. If the Roman values were humbleness and virtuosity (at least for Roman women), then witnessing a prisoner or captive in indigenous dress would have emphasized a notion of otherness[39]. While Romans were taught not to display self-indulgent decadence, the traditional Persian dress was luxurious, threatening the morals of the Empire[40]. As time progressed, these views became less relevant as the non-Roman conquered peoples were increasingly integrated into Roman society.

An example of attitudes toward the integration of foreigners in the Roman Empire is depicted by Jane Fejfer's analysis of the ever changing status of the Roman toga. Fejfer explains that the clothing was used to emphasize citizenship, an exclusive status reserved for free Roman citizens[41]. Over the first two decades AD, Roman citizenship was estimated to have grown from 6 million to potentially 60 million people, diluting the need for a pride in this no longer exclusive status[42]. As the toga became a mainstream article of clothing due to the increase in Roman citizenship, high-ranking officials sought to find new means to separate themselves out as elite members of society, and invented a new banded toga which is found sparsely within statue depictions[43]. This evolution indicates that while foreigners were increasingly integrated into Roman society through gaining Roman citizenship, there were lasting prejudices that led native Romans to separate themselves out from the masses.

While Ursula Rothe agrees that this narrative was true during the Roman Imperial period, she points out that the toga actually began as the default garment for all Romans (men, women, and children), and it was not until the late Republic that draping pieces such as the *stola* (smock, for married women) and the *palla* (women's cloak) came into use and the toga took on masculine attributes[44]. This is important to keep in mind, as researchers continue to interpret the ways that the symbolism around the toga changed over time.

---

[35] Carroll 2020, 169.
[36] Carroll 2020, 169.
[37] Carroll 2020, 169.
[38] Carroll 2020, 171.
[39] Carroll 2020, 175.
[40] Carroll 2020, 175.
[41] Fejfer 2008, 190.
[42] Fejfer 2008, 190.
[43] Fejfer 2008, 192.
[44] Rothe 2019, 37–41. 163–164.

When it comes to gendered differences within ethnic dress display in the Empire, men tended to display Roman military uniforms on their funerary monuments, reflecting their contribution to the Empire[45]. As women did not hold these military roles, they were able to be more creative in deciding which cultural identity they wanted to display on monuments erected before and after their deaths. Maureen Carroll emphasizes the importance of women's roles in carrying on the traditional values communicated by indigenous dress throughout the Roman Empire[46]. Ursula Rothe shares examples from further afield in the Roman Empire (Africa and Asia) which suggest that men were more in touch with the westernizing world, while women would often be found occupying domestic spaces[47]. Due to men and women's existence in these separate spaces, it was expected that women would continue indigenous traditions in the private spaces and perhaps branch out when in public[48]. Rothe debates whether it was women's choice to ›protect‹ their heritage and culture, or if there was an expectation placed upon them to uphold traditional values during waves of Romanization[49].

A really interesting point is made by David Noy, who discusses the impact of indigenous Romans (particularly freedpeople) assimilating Roman dress in funerary contexts in the city of Rome[50]. While the focus of the current paper is not on either freedpeople or funerary reliefs, a relevant point that Noy makes is that those who sought to display themselves as Romans rather than ›others‹ through the dress on their reliefs lost their native identities and became invisible as foreigners in the Roman Empire[51]. With this knowledge in mind, we can even better appreciate examples such as Aurelia Paulina's, as her iconography aids in analyzing the impact of Roman expansion on peripheral regions. Of course, Aurelia Paulina held a social status where her foreign origins would not render her shameful of her background, whereas freedpersons may have associated their ethnic origin with their slave status, leading to a very clear understanding of their motivations for blending into Roman society.

Depictions such as Aurelia Paulina's aid in the understanding of how identity politics evolved between the 1st to 3rd centuries AD. Since Syrian natives were often looked down upon for their non-Roman traditions, evidence of indigenous people holding steadfast in celebrating their traditions and identity indicates a progression in attitudes toward others in the Roman world. Aurelia Paulina is an example of this in the way that she displays Syrian clothing, jewelry, and symbols alongside Greek inscriptions and also celebrates the imperial family.

## ANALYSIS OF AURELIA PAULINA'S STATUE

### Description of the statue

To begin the analysis of Aurelia Paulina's dress, it would be beneficial to describe the chosen garb without making comparisons to similarly ranked local women. This allows for a non-biased understanding of the dress which Aurelia Paulina chose in which to depict herself. Following this outline, some comparisons will be drawn to aid in interpreting the proposed motivations for Aurelia Paulina's dress choices.

Aurelia Paulina's statue displays a heavy fabric tunic which falls to the floor, barely revealing simple footwear. This base layer is covered by a stole which is situated around Aurelia Paulina's shoulders, and then supported by placement over her forearms, creating a dignified display of draped fabrics. There is no evidence of her bodily shape, suggesting that Aurelia Paulina sought to be seen as youthful but chaste in this depiction. There is a fabric piece which consists of a

---

[45] Carroll 2020, 172.
[46] Carroll 2020, 172.
[47] Rothe 2009, 70–71.
[48] Rothe 2009, 70–71; Schoss 1996.
[49] Rothe 2009, 71.
[50] Noy 2000.
[51] Noy 2000, 157.

3   Statue of Aurelia Paulina (illustration by author)

belt which is placed on Aurelia Paulina's waist, and a vertical segment of fabric which appears to have a fringed threading at the bottom. She dons a head covering, accessorized with at least one band above her forehead. The layers of the head covering continue past her shoulders, and extend to knee length at the rear of the statue. There are cracks within the statue which briefly interrupt the garment, but the folds of the fabric are consistent on both sides of the crack to ensure that viewers can confidently determine that this garment is made up of one piece of material. Her facial features are youthful but serious; the representation is of Aurelia Paulina in younger years.

The jewelry worn in this statue is large and varied, extending to cover most of her chest (fig. 3). A number of unique beads are used to make up each strand on Aurelia Paulina's necklace, and it appears that there is a rope-like necklace falling at the bottom of the layered jewelry. This rope piece could potentially be separate from the jewelry entirely, and part of the fabric of her apparel. There is a unique shell necklace which falls to Aurelia Paulina's waist, lying upon the piece of fabric mentioned above.

Each of the items described above were very intentionally chosen. The nymphaeum was strategically placed near to one of the main entrances to the city of *Perge*, and thus would have received a great deal of attention from citizens of *Perge* as well as any visitors entering the city from this direction. With this exposure in mind, Aurelia Paulina would have utilized the opportunity to elevate her social standing, make connections with her local elite neighbors, and display herself and her familial links in a manner which commanded respect and honor.

## Tunic

The first piece to investigate on this statue of Aurelia Paulina is the tunic worn by the benefactress. It does not appear to be anything out of the ordinary, as it is floor-length and appears to be a single piece of fabric. There is a break in the statue which could lead to interpretations of a break in the tunic, or an additional layering technique, but upon further examination the fabric does appear to be in one piece. It is worth noting that this style does not closely match Palmyrene statues of women, as they often have another layer which is fastened on the shoulder[52]. It could be said that Aurelia Paulina's tunic is reflective of the Roman style, but it is also possible to interpret the layering in other ways once the smaller friezes from Aurelia Paulina's nymphaeum are discussed.

## Fringed fabric

The next piece of Aurelia Paulina's garb to be discussed is the fabric which lies beneath the shell pendant discussed above. This fabric appears to be cinched around Aurelia Paulina's waist, with a singular section falling to the benefactress' knees. At first glance, this accessory does not appear to be an important accessory, but there is a detail of this fabric which requires further analysis. At the bottom of this band of fabric, there is a clear fringe, which could be used to link the benefactress again to her Syrian roots. Syrian portraiture often displayed fringed fabric and it would not be a surprise that Aurelia Paulina chose to connect to her cultural beginnings in this way. In the illustration of the relief from *Palmyra*, the fringe can be found on the ends of the sleeves near the wrists of the woman on the right (fig. 4). If this was the intention behind the fringed piece, it would provide conclusive evidence that Aurelia Paulina was aware of the significance of using Syrian dress for her statue and that it was intentionally chosen.

---

[52]   Heyn 2010, 638.

4　Palmyrene funerary relief displaying fringed sleeve (illustration by author, depicting Palmyrene funerary relief)

## Head covering

When analyzing her head covering, one may make note of the bands around her head which could be symbols of virtue and chastity if they are supposed to represent the *infulae* worn by the Vestal Virgins[53]. There is no visibility into Aurelia Paulina's hairstyle, which suggests that this section of the statue was not meant to draw attention, potentially adding to the idea that Aurelia Paulina sought to be seen as respectable and chaste.

Elaine Fantham discusses *infulae* in her paper »Covering the Head at Rome: Ritual and Gender«, addressing the expectations around head coverings for both men and women in pagan Rome[54]. Fantham discusses how priestesses outside of the city of Rome were less politicized, and thus were occasionally able to lead religious acts without the typical head coverings[55]. Further into this paper, Fantham outlines cases where women seen without a head covering could be considered ostentatious and attention-seeking, noting a particular instance where Sulpicius Gallus called for a divorce after he heard of his wife walking about in public without her head covered[56]. In defining *vittae* headbands, Fantham concludes that *vittae* carried a moral protection similar to a young boy's *bulla*, which corresponds with Aurelia Paulina's desire to portray herself as chaste and morally pure[57]. If *vittae* were to convey morality, the ritualistic *infulae* would be a step beyond this as they were likely uncommonly used as accessories and more often used to adorn valued altars and tombs (reflecting Greek ritual use of the similar *stemmata*)[58]. It seems logical that the Vestal Virgins would don these ceremonial ribbons as headbands, as representatives of chastity and devotion.

An interesting point is made by Michele George, who points out that freedwomen sporting *vittae* valued the headband as a symbol of their new free status and discordant with their previously enslaved positions[59]. At this point in time, the 1st century AD, the empress Livia had discontinued her usage of the *vittae* and it's likely that elite benefactresses like Aurelia Paulina would have followed her example, reinforcing the thought that the bands on her statue must be more sacred and ritualistic than the standard *vittae*, and were presumably *infulae*[60].

---

[53] Fantham 2009.
[54] Fantham 2009.
[55] Fantham 2009, 159.
[56] Fantham 2009, 160.
[57] Fantham 2009, 163.
[58] Fantham 2009, 163.
[59] George 2005, 44. 49–50.
[60] Fantham 2009, 168.

It is possible that Aurelia Paulina is wearing the woolen *vittae* around her head, but this would mean that she missed an opportunity to convey a message, which seems unlikely. Fantham's work researching the ancient authors' usage of these two terms denotes that wearing *vittae* was so common that it would not be mentioned as anything notable within texts while *infulae* indicated ritual significance[61]. As Aurelia Paulina's statue was a central and symbolic piece of her benefaction, it seems highly improbable that she would choose a standard and common headpiece. Similarly ranked benefactresses within the region such as Plancia Magna are depicted without a head covering, so it would seem that Aurelia Paulina chose to depict herself with her head concealed to convey a point.

## Jewelry

The next major section of Aurelia Paulina's statue that deserves detailed analysis is the jewelry donned by the benefactress. This portion of the paper will review the heavy jewelry which lays on Paulina's chest (fig. 3), and will save a focus on the shell pendant for later examination. We first can compare Aurelia Paulina's jewelry with the jewelry, or lack of jewelry, shown in Plancia Magna's statue (fig. 2). Since she would have had similar motivations to Aurelia Paulina, Plancia Magna's statue is an excellent source of comparison in this study.

5   Palmyrene funerary relief (photo The Metropolitan Museum of Art)

These similarities only make it more interesting when one views their statue depictions next to each other, as Plancia Magna opted for a very traditional Roman representation. There is no similarity in terms of jewelry between these women, which leads one to question where Aurelia Paulina received the inspiration for the ornamentation which covers much of her upper chest. This can be answered by looking at examples of elite women from *Syria* (Aurelia Paulina's birthplace).

After establishing that Aurelia Paulina's jewelry is not representative of typical Roman women's jewelry in statuary depictions, we must look elsewhere to find comparable accessories. Much of the evidence of Syrian dress is found in *Palmyra*, due to the wealth of this region, but we must appreciate that these examples are not representative of all of *Syria*. In looking at the Palmyrene funerary relief, which is held in the Metropolitan Museum of Art in New York, one may recognise the luxurious and chunky jewelry worn by the women (fig. 5). Though their necklaces seem to be worn as one piece, the variety and intricate geometric shapes seem to match the stacked necklaces worn by Aurelia Paulina.

## Shell pendant

While most of the jewelry shown on this statue can be compared to the jewelry on Syrian statues, there is one piece which stands out from the rest. The shell pendant which falls to Aurelia

---

[61]   Fantham 2009, 164.

Paulina's waist is spatially separate from the rest of the jewelry, highlighting it as an individual symbol. While there is a trend of crescent-shaped amulets found on Syrian statues, the shell worn by Aurelia Paulina is significantly different from these in shape and design[62]. It has been suggested that the shell is utilized to create a link to Artemis Pergaia, the tutelary deity of *Perge*[63]. Fejfer notes that Artemis Pergaia is known to don shell pendants, and this conclusion has been cited by a number of additional researchers[64].

In preparation for this paper, the conclusion linking the shell pendant and Artemis Pergaia worked perfectly when trying to understand the symbolism highlighted by Aurelia Paulina. Upon further research, it seemed quite difficult to find depictions of Artemis Pergaia with any kind of shell symbols. Artemis could be found with a quiver and bow, moon, or various animals, but it is Aphrodite who is known to have been linked with a scalloped shell[65]. This was unanticipated, as Aphrodite had not been a major part of the conversation around Aurelia Paulina's shell pendant previously, but upon further research into Aphrodite (and her Egyptian counterpart Isis) in Asia Minor, the connection between the goddess and Aurelia Paulina is not as far-reaching as one may think. Aphrodite is in fact featured within the very nymphaeum which Aurelia Paulina commissioned. Additionally, as mentioned above, Aurelia Paulina sought to link herself with the empress Julia Domna, who was worshiped in Asia Minor as both Artemis or Aphrodite[66].

If we are to believe that this pendant links Aurelia Paulina and Aphrodite, then there is work to be done in understanding her motivations. It is possible that Aphrodite or Isis had a larger impact on the elite women of *Perge* than previously thought. This will be investigated further in the coming years of my research, as I hope to uncover previously unnoticed links between the goddess and Aurelia Paulina.

It is worth noting that there was also the goddess Atargatis who was prominent in North Syria and is mentioned by Andreas Schmidt-Colinet[67]. Atargatis is linked to the sea, vegetation, and fertility while being associated with symbols such as the crescent moon, lion, and various sea life[68]. The Yale-French Excavations at a sanctuary in *Dura-Europos* (present-day Syria) in the early 1930s unearthed a temple dedicated to the goddess Atargatis, revealing that she had been worshiped as Artemis Azzanathkona. This would explain the similarities between the goddesses Artemis and Atargatis, though does not exactly clarify the shell pendant worn by Aurelia Paulina[69]. Archaeologists in *Palmyra* are often quick to link sea creatures to the goddess Atargatis, but there does not seem to be evidence of shell jewelry being associated with a connection to Atargatis. Because of this absence of the shell necklace link, which is present in depictions of Aphrodite from the Rock Sanctuary near *Sagalassos*, the author feels that there is stronger evidence that Aurelia Paulina was symbolizing a connection with Aphrodite rather than any other suggested goddess by wearing the shell pendant.

**Fringed fabric**

The next piece of Aurelia Paulina's garb to be discussed is the fabric which lies beneath the shell pendant discussed above. This fabric appears to be cinched around Aurelia Paulina's waist, with a singular section falling to the benefactress' knees. At first glance, this accessory does not appear to be important, but there is a detail of this fabric which requires further analysis. At the bottom of this band of fabric, there is a clear fringe, which could be used to link the benefactress again to her Syrian roots. Syrian portraiture often displayed fringed fabric and it would not be a surprise

---

[62] Tatiana 2021.
[63] Fejfer 2008, 362.
[64] Fejfer 2008, 362.
[65] Bąkowska-Czerner – Czerner 2021.
[66] Aristodemou 2013, 2.
[67] Schmidt-Colinet 1991.
[68] Rostovtzeff 1933, 58.
[69] Rostovtzeff 1933, 58.

that Aurelia Paulina chose to connect to her cultural beginnings in this way. In figure 4 from *Palmyra*, the fringe can be found on the ends of the sleeves near the wrists of the woman on the right. If this was the intention behind the fringed piece, it would provide conclusive evidence that Aurelia Paulina was aware of the significance of using Syrian dress for her statue and that it was intentionally chosen.

**Frieze depictions**

While this paper focuses primarily on the large statue of Aurelia Paulina found centrally in her monumental fountain complex, it is worth noting the smaller friezes of the benefactress accompanied by gods and goddesses found elsewhere in the nymphaeum. Small details which do not feature in the large statue can be explored in a different way, which may lead to more conclusive analysis.

As one can see from the smaller frieze drawings (fig. 6), Aurelia Paulina's dress choices slightly differ throughout the nymphaeum. In the drawing on the left, Aurelia Paulina is shown wearing two tunic layers, and the cloak is more visible than on the main statue. She holds a bouquet of leaves in her right hand, and an orb shaped item in her left hand. The shell pendant is visible, but it is placed higher on her body, and does not compete with the larger necklaces present on the main statue depiction. The frieze drawing on the right also shows two layers of clothing on Aurelia Paulina's body,

6   Depictions of Aurelia Paulina found on reliefs at the nymphaeum (illustrations by author)

though the cloak is difficult to determine due to the poor condition of this part of the relief. The shell pendant is visible again, matching the larger statue in placement on the benefactress' waist. There is the fabric piece which falls to Aurelia Paulina's knees, which was not visible on the frieze depiction on the left. All depictions that we have of Aurelia Paulina show her head covered, and two of them show the band of fabric around her forehead clearly.

While it is worthwhile noting what pieces are present on the frieze depictions, it is fascinating to see which items did not appear on all three images of Aurelia Paulina. It seems as though she dramatically emphasizes her Syrian jewelry in the large statue, but it is not present in the smaller depictions. The piece of fabric which cinches her waist and falls to her lower body is present in two of the depictions, but not the third – why would that be? Is it possible that the statues were carved by different artists and they left details off or were given varying instructions? This seems unlikely knowing that the building commission was quite large for the region. The differences in the tunic are also worth noting: why would Aurelia Paulina choose to be dressed in different ways throughout the fountain complex? It seems as though if she were trying to convey the strength of major relationships, she would not have herself depicted haphazardly throughout the nymphaeum.

Researchers can conclude from these three depictions that the most important symbols are the shell pendant and head covering. There are no other symbols which are on all three images which stand out as clearly as these two do. The head covering is partially a piece of the standard garb, so conveys less symbolism, but it is worth noting that Aurelia Paulina was consistent in being depicted with her head covered. This makes the shell pendant the most important and symbolic piece. There is much to be uncovered about the shell pendant, but in understanding the current literature, it is essential that the link between the shell pendant and Artemis Pergaia is removed in order to expose more information and conclusions about the connections between the shell pendant and Aphrodite or potentially the Near Eastern goddess Atargatis.

## CONCLUSIONS

Aurelia Paulina was a woman born in *Syria* without Roman citizenship, but she utilized her newly acquired citizenship under Commodus to draw connections between Rome and the outer provinces. She links herself to the Roman Empire directly through explicitly mentioning her citizenship in inscriptions, her roles as a priestess of Artemis and the imperial cult, and her honoring of the imperial family with the donation of the nymphaeum in their name. Aurelia Paulina's Syrian roots shine through when one takes the clothing, jewelry trends and fringed fabric featured on her statue into account. Finally, she created a beautiful and intentional connection with both regions when creating links with Julia Domna, another native Syrian who rose to prominence as empress of the Roman Empire. While the shell pendant remains somewhat a mystery in a few ways, there is evidence of shell pendants on statues from sites in *Syria* as well as Roman Egypt which demonstrates that this accessory cannot be attributed to one region, again indicating that it could be seen as a symbol of unity in the Roman Empire.

In terms of dress, the statue of Aurelia Paulina provides fascinating insight for culture in the eastern Roman Empire. Though she emphasizes her newly granted citizenship within inscriptions at the nymphaeum she donated, she links herself to her homeland through clothing and jewelry. Inspired by her ethnic connection to the Syrian empress Julia Domna and by the benefaction by earlier *Perge* benefactress Plancia Magna, Aurelia Paulina sought to carve out a unique and powerful name for herself and her heritage in the new Roman setting. These signs of converging cultures lead to further questions around the acceptance of foreigners within the Roman world, the impact of conveying ethnic origins publicly, and the effect that the expansion of the Empire had on acceptance and individuality within the central and the more marginal regions of the Roman world.

## BIBLIOGRAPHY

| | |
|---|---|
| Aristodemou 2013 | G. Aristodemou, Perge (Antiquity), Nymphaeum of Septimius Severus, Encyclopaedia of the Hellenic World, Asia Minor, 2013, <http://www.ehw.gr/l.aspx?id=9243> (02.04.2023) |
| Bąkowska-Czerner – Czerner 2021 | G. Bąkowska-Czerner – R. Czerner, The Shell Motif in the Culture and Architecture of the Ancient Town of Marina el-Alamein in Egypt, EtTrav 34, 2021, 71–91 |
| Boatwright 1991 | M. Boatwright, Plancia Magna of Perge, and the Roles and Status of Women in Roman Asia Minor, in: S. Pomeroy (ed.), Women's History and Ancient History (Chapel Hill 1991) 249–272 |
| Carroll 2020 | M. Carroll, Invisible foreigners at Rome? Identities in dress behaviour in the imperial Capital, in: S. de Blaauw – E. Enß – P. Linscheid (eds.), Contextus. Festschrift Sabine Schrenk (Münster 2020) |
| Fantham 2009 | E. Fantham, Covering the Head at Rome: Ritual and Gender, in: J. Edmondson – A. Keith (eds.), Roman Dress and the Fabrics of Roman Culture (Toronto 2009) 158–171 |
| Fejfer 2008 | J. Fejfer, Roman Portraits in Context (Berlin 2008) |
| Gatzke 2020 | A. F. Gatzke, The gate complex of Plancia Magna in Perge: A case study in reading bilingual space, ClQ 70/1, 2020, 385–396, DOI: 10.1017/S0009838820000324 |
| George 2005 | M. George, The Roman Family in the Empire (Oxford 2005), DOI: 10.1093/acprof:oso/9780199268412.001.0001 |
| Hemelrijk 2004 | E. Hemelrijk, Patronage of Cities: the Role of Women, in: L. de Ligt – E. Hemelrijk – H. Singor (eds.), Roman Rule and Civic Life. Local and Regional Perspectives (Leiden 2004) 415–427 |
| Hemelrijk 2015 | E. Hemelrijk, Hidden lives, public personae: women and civic life in the Roman West (Oxford 2015) |
| Hemelrijk – Woolf 2013 | E. Hemelrijk – G. Woolf, Women and the Roman City in the Latin West (Leiden 2013) |

| | |
|---|---|
| Heyn 2010 | M. K. Heyn, Gesture and Identity in the Funerary Art of Palmyra, AJA 114/4, 2010, 631–661, DOI: 10.3764/aja.114.4.631 |
| I.Perge | S. Şahin, Die Inschriften von Perge I: Vorrömische Zeit, frühe und hohe Kaiserzeit, IK 54 (Bonn 1999) |
| | S. Şahin, Die Inschriften von Perge II: Historische Texte aus dem 3. Jhdt. n. Chr. – Grabtexte aus den 1.–3. Jahrhunderten der römischen Kaiserzeit – Fragmente, IK 61 (Bonn 2004) |
| Long 2014 | T. E. Long, Great grand mothers: the female portrait sculpture of Aphrodisias: origins and meaning (Ph.D. diss. University of Nottingham 2014) |
| Longfellow 2011 | B. Longfellow, Roman imperialism and civic patronage: form, meaning, and ideology in monumental fountain complexes (Cambridge 2011) |
| Longfellow 2012 | B. Longfellow, Romans in Greek Sanctuaries, AJA 116/1, 2012, 133–155, DOI: 10.3764/aja.116.1.0133 |
| Longfellow 2014/2015 | B. Longfellow, Female Patrons and Honorific Statues in Pompeii, MemAmAc 59, 2014/2015, 81–101, <http://www.jstor.org/stable/44981973> (02.04.2023) |
| McCullough 2015 | K. McCullough, The inclusion and negotiation of the appropriate female presence in public: Thamugadi and Cuicul (University of North Carolina 2015) |
| McManus (web) | B. McManus, Plancia Magna, Aurelia Paulina, and Regilla: Civic Donors, <http://vroma.org/vromans/bmcmanus/women_civicdonors.html> (02.04.2023) |
| Meyers 2012 | R. Meyers, Reconsidering Opportunities for Female Benefactors in the Roman Empire: Julia Antonia Eurydice and the Gerontikon at Nysa, AntCl 81, 2012, 145–159, DOI: 10.2307/antiqclassi.81.145 |
| Ng 2015 | D. Ng, Commemoration and Élite Benefaction of Buildings and Spectacles in the Roman World, JRS 105, 2015, 101–123, DOI: 10.1017/S0075435815000441 |
| Noy 2000 | D. Noy, Foreigners at Rome: citizens and strangers (London 2000) |
| Pobjoy 2000 | M. Pobjoy, Building Inscriptions in Republican Italy: Euergetism, Responsibility, and Civic Virtue, BICS 44, 2000, 77–92, DOI: 10.1111/j.2041-5370.2000.tb01939.x |
| Rostovtzeff 1933 | M. Rostovtzeff, Hadad and Atargatis at Palmyra, AJA 37, 1933, 58–63 |
| Rothe 2009 | U. Rothe, Dress and cultural identity in the Rhine-Moselle Region of the Roman Empire, BARIntSer 2038 (Oxford 2009) |
| Rothe 2019 | U. Rothe, The Toga and Roman Identity (London 2019) |
| Schmidt-Colinet 1991 | A. Schmidt-Colinet, Eine severische Priesterin aus Syrien in Perge, IstMitt 41, 1991, 439–445 |
| Schoss 1996 | J. Schoss, Dressed to »Shine«: Work, Leisure, and Style in Malindi, Kenya, in: H. Hendrickson (ed.), Clothing and Difference. Embodied Identities in Colonial and Post-Colonial Africa (London 1996) 157–188, DOI: 10.1515/9780822396376-009 |
| Tatiana 2021 | M. Tatiana, Priestess of Aphrodite? Shell/crescent motif on sculptures. Isis/Aphrodite/Tyche/Artemis, 2021, <http://colorsandstones.eu/2020/11/04/priestess-of-aphrodite-shell-motif-on-sculptures> (02.04.2023) |
| Vorster 2008 | C. Vorster, The Large and Small Herculaneum Women Sculptures, in: J. Daehner (ed.), The Herculaneum Women. History, Context, Identities (California 2008) 59–84 |
| Zuiderhoek 2009 | A. Zuiderhoek, The Politics of Munificence in the Roman Empire. Citizens, Elites and Benefactors in Asia Minor (Cambridge 2009), DOI: 10.1017/CBO9780511576508 |

*Melissa Kays, University of York, King's Manor, Exhibition Square, York, Y01 7EP, Great Britain.*
*[e] kays.melissa@york.ac.uk*

Ute Kelp – Anja Klöckner

# DAS GROSSE WEINSCHIFF AUS NEUMAGEN

## NEUE ÜBERLEGUNGEN ZU REKONSTRUKTION UND BEDEUTUNG

**Abstract**
The so-called Great Wine Ship from Neumagen, dating from around AD 200, is one of the best-known Treveran monuments and is received far into popular culture as a supposedly typical example of a funerary monument in the Moselle region. In the process, it is often overlooked that its present form in the Rheinisches Landesmuseum Trier is a reconstruction and that its original form can by no means be regarded as certain. In our contribution, we would like to take up recent studies by Karl-Uwe Mahler and Lothar Schwinden and critically examine the preserved inventory and the additions made. We will evaluate 3D scans carried out within the scope of a recent BMBF-funded project on Roman grave monuments in Trier and, on this basis, present new considerations on the original shape of the Neumagen wine ship. Finally, based on this example, the group of ship-shaped funerary monuments as a whole will be examined and analyzed with regard to their significance for the Treveran sepulchral culture.

Das um 200 n. Chr. entstandene sog. Große Weinschiff aus Neumagen gehört zu den bekanntesten kaiserzeitlichen Sepulkraldenkmälern des Treverergebietes (Abb. 1)[1]. Zusammengesetzt aus zwei anpassenden Sandsteinblöcken zeigt es einen Schiffsrumpf, der mit vier großen Fässern beladen ist. Davor sind die Oberkörper der Besatzung zu sehen. Auf jeder Seite sind je sechs Ruderer wiedergegeben. In der rechten Seitenansicht ist die ausgearbeitete linke Schiffsseite mit 22 Riemen noch gut zu erkennen. Im Bug und im Heck sind je zwei Personen platziert, wobei Letztere jeweils ein Steuerruder führen.

Diese rundplastische Schiffsdarstellung ist Teil einer kleinen Gruppe gleichartiger Sandsteinskulpturen. Nach gegenwärtigem Stand umfasst diese Gruppe sechs Blöcke von vier Ruderschiffen[2], die ehemals zu großformatigen Grabmonumenten gehörten. Bei allen vier Beispielen ist eine Seite besser ausgearbeitet und diente anscheinend als Hauptansichtsseite. Die Ruderer blicken jeweils in Fahrtrichtung.

Die Blöcke waren als Spolien in dem spätantiken Kastell von Neumagen verbaut oder im direkten Umfeld der Kastellmauern gefunden worden, ebenso wie zahlreiche andere Teile monumentaler Grabdenkmäler[3]. Die Neumagener Weinschiffe kamen mit dem Großteil der übrigen Funde in das 1889 fertiggestellte Provinzialmuseum, das heutige Rheinische Landesmuseum Trier (RLM)[4].

Bis weit in die Populärkultur hinein wird seitdem gerade das Große Weinschiff als typisches Beispiel für die Grabdenkmäler des Moselraums verstanden. In Neumagen hat man sogar einen Nachbau angefertigt, eine vermeintlich authentische Kopie, die für Flussfahrten vor Ort gebucht werden kann[5]. Dabei gerät allerdings oft aus dem Blick, dass das Große Weinschiff in seiner musealen Präsentation stark ergänzt ist und damit die Authentizität der Überlieferung keineswegs als

---

[1] RLM Trier Inv. 767; Maße: B 63 × H 111 × T 281 cm. Espérandieu 1915, 386–388 Kat. 5193; von Massow 1932, 203–206 Kat. 287a.
[2] Bockius 2001, 148; vgl. Schwinden 2019, 29–30. Eine Diskussion der genauen Anzahl der Schiffe führt an dieser Stelle zu weit; dazu ausführlicher Klöckner u. a., in Druckvorbereitung.
[3] von Massow 1932, 13–28 Taf. 69 und Beil. Lageplan.
[4] Zum Provinzialmuseum, seit 1934 Rheinisches Landesmuseum, s. Merten 2002; Merten 2009, 218.
[5] Zur Stella Noviomagi s. Eiben 2009.

gesichert gelten kann. Sowohl in der öffentlichen Wahrnehmung als auch in der Forschung wird häufig nicht unterschieden zwischen originalen und ergänzten Teilen.

Im Folgenden werden wir zunächst den erhaltenen Bestand des Großen Weinschiffs und die vorgenommenen Ergänzungen kritisch überprüfen[6]. Vorab stellen wir die einzelnen Fragmente vor, die mit diesem und den anderen Neumagener Schiffsmonumenten verbunden wurden. Anhand von bislang unerschlossenen Archivaufnahmen werden wir die wichtigsten Stadien der Rekonstruktion nachverfolgen[7]. Auf der Basis der von uns durchgeführten 3D-Scans des Großen Weinschiffs möchten wir schließlich einige Überlegungen zu seiner ursprünglichen Gestalt anstellen.

## FUNDSITUATION IN NEUMAGEN: FRAGMENTE VON SCHIFFSMONUMENTEN

Von einem Teil der als Spolien in Neumagen verbauten Fragmente und Blöcke sind die Fundstellen bekannt (Abb. 2), während für andere nur die allgemeine Fundortangabe »Neumagen« existiert. Die beiden Blöcke des Großen Weinschiffs kamen nach mündlicher Überlieferung 1878 im Grundstück der Familie Thomas neben der Bürgermeisterei zu Tage (Abb. 2, a)[8].

Als 1884 auf einem Grundstück des damaligen Lehrers Seibert ein bärtiger Kopf gefunden wurde (Abb. 1; 2, b1–2), wies man diesen den beiden Blöcken zu[9]. Auf dem von Wilhelm von Massow publizierten Lageplan der Fundstellen kommen dafür zwei Parzellen in Frage: nahe Turm D oder, etwas näher an der Fundstelle der Schiffsrumpf-Fragmente, zwischen den Türmen K und L der spätantiken Kastellmauer.

Siegfried Loeschcke schrieb 1927 ein weiteres Fragment dem Monument zu. Es handelt sich um den Kopf eines Ketos (Abb. 1; 2, c), der beim Bau eines Wasserleitungsgrabens in der Nähe des Bürgermeisteramtes und der Kirche gefunden worden war und 1905 als Geschenk des damaligen Neumagener Bürgermeisters Molz ins Trierer Museum gelangte[10].

Bei einem Fragment mit der unteren Hälfte eines bärtigen Kopfes, das 1885 auf der Ostseite des Kastells, südlich von Haus Nr. 123 (ehem. Kesselstatt) gefunden wurde (Abb. 2, d), erwog von Massow ebenfalls eine Verbindung mit dem Großen Weinschiff[11].

Von den Fragmenten ohne dokumentierte Fundstelle werden ein 1884 entdecktes Volutenfragment[12] sowie zwei weitere Bruchstücke bärtiger Köpfe nur allgemein mit den Schiffsmonumenten in Verbindung gebracht[13]. Zwei andere Fragmente ohne bekannten Fundort wies Elvira Fölzer im Jahr 1911 konkret dem Großen Weinschiff zu: einen sog. Knauf mit Volute[14] (Abb. 3 a)

---

[6] Die Untersuchungen erfolgten im Rahmen der umfassenden Neubearbeitung der kaiserzeitlichen Grabdenkmäler der *civitas Treverorum* durch zwei Kooperationsprojekte. Unser an der GU Frankfurt angesiedeltes DFG-Projekt »Römische Grabdenkmäler aus Augusta Treverorum im überregionalen Vergleich: mediale Strategien sozialer Repräsentation« im Verbund mit dem RLM Trier und der Hochschule Mainz, s. <https://www.uni-frankfurt. de/65008064/Trier_Grabdenkmäler> (22.03.23), wurde abgestimmt mit dem österreichisch-luxemburgischen Kooperationsprojekt »Grabbauten des westlichen Trevererbietes im interregionalen Kontext« unter der Leitung von Gabrielle Kremer und Andrea Binsfeld; s. Binsfeld u. a. 2020, 9–10. Das Vorhaben wird seit Ende 2022 fortgesetzt durch unser neues DFG-Projekt »Römische Grabdenkmäler des Trevererbietes im Kontext«, s. <https://www.uni-frankfurt.de/128552583/Trier_Grabdenkmäler_im_Kontext> (22.03.23).

[7] Die Archivaufnahmen konnten wir in Zusammenarbeit mit dem RLM Trier, der Hochschule Mainz und dem Deutschen Archäologischen Institut im Rahmen eines vom Bundesministerium für Bildung und Forschung (BMBF) geförderten Digitalisierungsprojektes auswerten; s. <https://www.uni-frankfurt.de/72384901/Grabdenkmäler_digital> (22.03.23). Die Ergebnisse sind demnächst unter <https://arachne.dainst.org/search?q=TrierGlasplatten> online zugänglich.

[8] von Massow 1932, 203–205 Kat. 287a1+a2 Abb. 123 Taf. 54.

[9] Fölzer 1911, 236–237 Abb. 1; von Massow 1932, 206 Kat. 287a3 Abb. 124; Mahler 2019.

[10] von Massow 1932, 206 Kat. 287a5 Taf. 56; Loeschcke 1927, 107–108. 116 Abb. 10 a–c.

[11] von Massow 1932, 222 Kat. 327 Taf. 62. Allerdings ist der Kopf kleiner dimensioniert als die potenziell in Frage kommenden Fehlstellen am Großen Weinschiff. Laut von Massow spricht außerdem »die Steinäderung« gegen eine Zugehörigkeit.

[12] von Massow 1932, 232 Kat. 407 Taf. 56.

[13] von Massow 1932, 222–223 Kat. 329–330 Taf. 56.

[14] von Massow 1932, 206 Kat. 287a6 Abb. 126 Taf. 56; Loeschcke 1927, 115 Abb. 9 a–c.

1 Neumagen, Großes Weinschiff in der Teilrekonstruktion im RLM Trier Inv. 767 a) rechte Seitenansicht, b) linke Seitenansicht (Fotos Th. Zühmer, RLM Trier)

und einen weiteren Tierkopf[15] (Abb. 1; 3 b). Ein zweiter, gleichartiger Tierkopf (Abb. 2, e) wurde erst 1965 fotografisch dokumentiert[16]. Er war vermauert in der Gärtnerei Krebs südlich des nördlichen Kastelltores und ist heute verschollen[17].

Zeitgleich mit dem Großen Weinschiff wurden zwei Blöcke eines in Größe und Ausführung vergleichbaren Schiffmonuments[18] (Abb. 2, f. g) ebenfalls auf dem Grundstück der Familie Thomas gefunden. Die Person im Heck dieses Schiffs firmiert aufgrund ihres angeheitert wirkenden Gesichtsausdrucks nicht nur in der Forschungsliteratur als »lustiger« oder »fröhlicher Steuermann«[19]. Diesem Schiff, genauer dem zweiten Ruderer von vorn auf der Innenseite, ordnet von Massow das Fragment eines weiteren bärtigen Kopfes zu[20].

Zwei Blöcke von zwei weiteren, kleineren Schiffen waren in deutlichem Abstand voneinander in der Kastellmauer verbaut (Abb. 2, h. i). Das Vorderteil eines Schiffsrumpfes (Schiff 3)[21] kam 1885 im südlichen Abschnitt der Mauer östlich von Turm G auf der Grenze zwischen den Grundstücken Leib und Schmidt zu Tage, der hintere Block (Schiff 4)[22] 1884 auf der Westseite zwischen den Türmen B und C, auf dem Grundstück des Lehrers Seibert. Beide stammen ursprünglich aufgrund ihrer Abmessungen sowie der übereinstimmenden Ausarbeitung von ein und demselben Gesamtmonument. Wegen der Bruchfläche von Schiff 3 ist es aber wenig plausibel,

---

[15] Fölzer 1911, 237–239 Abb. 1–2; von Massow 1932, 206 Kat. 287a4 Taf. 56; Weidner 2009 (»Drachenkopf«).
[16] RLM Trier, Glasplattennegativ RD 1965-6; s. o. Anm. 7.
[17] Numrich 1997, 152.
[18] von Massow 1932, 206 Kat. 287b1+b2 Abb. 127–128 Taf. 55.
[19] Erstmals von Hettner 1903, 16 verwendet; in diesem Sinne schon Hettner 1881, 456. Kritisch gegenüber derartigen Deutungen des Mienenspiels Bockius 2008, 39–40.
[20] von Massow 1932, 207 Kat. 287b3 Taf. 56.
[21] von Massow 1932, 207–209 Kat. 288a Taf. 56.
[22] von Massow 1932, 209 Kat. 288b Taf. 56.

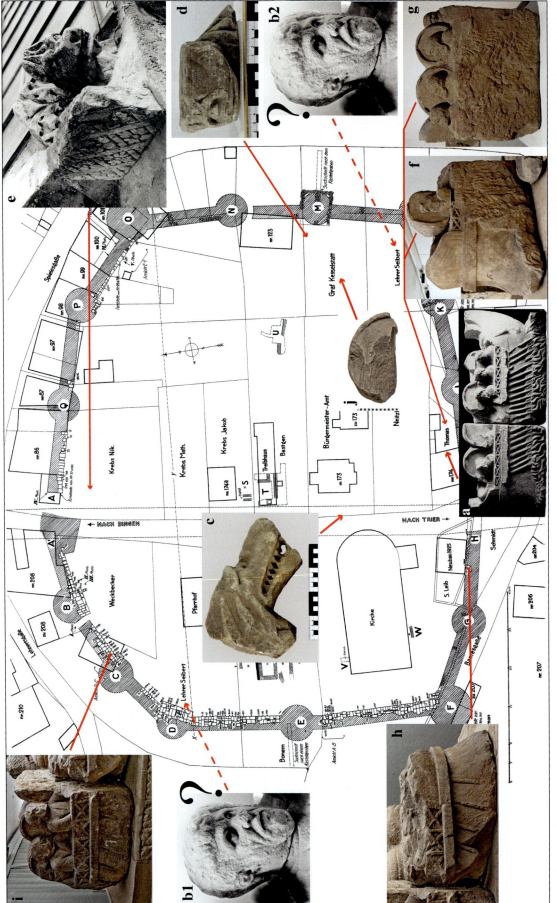

2 Neumagen, Plan des spätantiken Kastells mit bekannten Fundstellen von Schiffsfragmenten: a) Großes Weinschiff (Inv. 767), b) bärtiger Kopf (Inv. 9941), c) Ketos-Kopf (Inv. 1905,108), d) untere Hälfte eines bärtigen Kopfes (Inv. 11593), e) verschollener großer Tierkopf, verbaut in der Gärtnerei Krebs (o. Inv.), f) Bug von Schiff 2 (Inv. 768), g) Heck von Schiff 2 mit ›fröhlichem Steuermann‹ (Inv. 768), h) Bug von Schiff 3 (Inv. 11075), i) Heck von Schiff 4 (Inv. 9931), j) Fassfragment (Inv. 11613) (U. Kelp, GU Frankfurt, auf Grundlage von Massow 1932, Beil. Lageplan; Fotos: a) Loeschcke 1927, 113 Abb. 2; b) RLM Trier, GNeg B 875; c–d) K.-U. Mahler; e) RLM Trier, GNeg RD 1965-6; f–j) Th. Zühmer, RLM Trier)

Das Große Weinschiff aus Neumagen. Neue Überlegungen zu Rekonstruktion und Bedeutung    487

3   Neumagen, Fragmente von Schiffsprotomen im RLM in Trier: a) großer Tierkopf in Vorderansicht, Inv. NN 211, b) Knauf mit Volute, rechte Seitenansicht, Inv. NN 210 (Projekt Grabdenkmäler aus Augusta Treverorum, GU Frankfurt, a) DE-TRI-RLM-0735-21; b) DE-TRI-RLM-948-13; Fotos K.-U. Mahler)

dass beide Blöcke zusammengehören. Es handelt sich höchstwahrscheinlich um die Reste von zwei verschiedenen Schiffen[23].

Diesen Schiffen weist von Massow ein Fassfragment ohne bekannte Fundstelle zu[24]. Im Rahmen des DFG-Projekts wurde ein zweites, bislang nicht dokumentiertes Fassfragment aufgespürt (Abb. 2, j)[25]. Aufgrund des gleichen Fassdurchmessers können beide Fragmente zur Ladung im stark beschädigten Vorderteil von Schiff 3 gehören[26]. Unbekannt ist ferner die Fundstelle eines Aufsatzes in Form eines Amphorenstapels[27] (Abb. 4), der ebenfalls mit einem Schiffsmonument in Verbindung gebracht wird.

Die vier Neumagener Schiffe sind also nur bruchstückhaft überliefert. Bei einigen der vor Ort gefundenen Fragmente ist zudem unklar, ob sie zu einem der Schiffe gehören und wenn ja, zu welchem.

## REKONSTRUKTIONEN UND MUSEALE PRÄSENTATION DES GROSSEN WEINSCHIFFS

### Die Zeit bis zum Ersten Weltkrieg

Unter dem Gründungsdirektor Felix Hettner wurden mit der Eröffnung des Trierer Museums die Neumagener Schiffe in der Dauerausstellung präsentiert[28]. Das einzige Foto des Großen Weinschiffs im Originalzustand von 1878 findet sich im illustrierten Museumsführer Hettners

---

[23]   Aufgrund der übereinstimmenden Ansichtsseiten müssen allerdings die Schiffe 3 und 4 ursprünglich beide auf derselben Seite des Gesamtmonuments gestanden haben.
[24]   von Massow 1932, 209 Kat. 288c Taf. 56.
[25]   RLM Trier Inv. 11613. Schwinden 2019, 29–30 Abb. 5b. Die dort zusätzlich angeführten Fassfragmente sind verschollen: von Massow 1932, 232 Kat. 403 (auf der genannten Taf. 62 nicht abgebildet). 256 Kat. 481 (ohne Fundort, ohne Abb.).
[26]   Nach Schwinden 2019, 30, habe Hettner das Stück »im Südosten der Burg« 1885 dokumentiert und als Zuweisung den »Vorderteil des Schiffes mit fröhlichem Steuermann« in Betracht gezogen. Im Inventarbuch findet sich noch der Zusatz: »…, da wo das kleine, spätere Thürmchen stand (Kesselstadtsches [Kesselstatt] Terrain)«. Wir danken Sabine Faust für diese Zusatzinformation.
[27]   von Massow 1932, 209–211 Kat. 289a–d Abb. 129 Taf. 56. 57. Weitere Fragmente von Amphoren und Fässern befinden sich im MNHA Luxemburg; sie werden von Gabrielle Kremer, der wir für den Hinweis danken, bearbeitet.
[28]   Die Erstaufstellung im Museum ist auf keiner der bekannten Aufnahmen festgehalten. Zu Hettner s. Merten 2002; <https://sempub.ub.uni-heidelberg.de/propylaeum_vitae/de/wisski/navigate/3378/view> (03.03.23).

(Abb. 5, b)²⁹. Hettner selbst hatte dieses als eines der ersten Neumagener Monumente zunächst in einer Zeichnung von Alexander Rüdell publiziert³⁰. In der von ihm als Skizze bezeichneten ersten Teilrekonstruktion ist dem zurückgewandten Oberkörper vorn im Bug ein rundplastischer bärtiger Kopf aufgesetzt (Abb. 5, a)³¹. Obwohl nicht explizit erwähnt, wird damit der ebenfalls aus Neumagen stammende, aber nicht im Zusammenhang mit den Rumpfblöcken gefundene bärtige Kopf³² gemeint sein.

4   Neumagen, Amphorenstapel im RLM Trier Inv. 968+969 (RLM Trier, GNeg B 1905)

Im Museum fanden die Fragmente schließlich ihren Platz in dem großen, hohen Saal C des 1906 eröffneten Erweiterungsbaus³³. Der Museumstechniker Wilhelm Jovy erstellte zeichnerische Rekonstruktionen³⁴, die dann auch am Objekt umgesetzt wurden. Für die Nachverfolgung dieser und weiterer Rekonstruktionsschritte sind die bislang weitgehend unbekannten Glasplattennegative des RLM Trier von großem Wert (Abb. 5). Schon auf den ersten nach 1906 bzw. um 1908 entstandenen Aufnahmen³⁵ (Abb. 5, c. d) ist das Große Weinschiff weitgehend ergänzt. An der Vorderseite hatte man einen kurzen Rammsporn angesetzt. Außerdem wurden Fehlstellen an den Köpfen, den Fässern, der Reling, dem Riemenkasten und den Riemen gefüllt. Das Steuerruder, die Kajüte und die Steven vervollständigte man in Anlehnung an Flusskähne wie jenen auf dem Secundiniergrabmal³⁶, wobei im Achtersteven der Knauf mit Volute als Protome Verwendung fand.

Den bärtigen Kopf hatte man nun im Heck aufmontiert, obwohl es keine übereinstimmenden Ansatzflächen gab. Mit dieser inzwischen widerlegten Rekonstruktion wollte man anscheinend eine Analogie zu dem gefälligen ›fröhlichen Steuermann‹ des zweiten Schiffes schaffen³⁷. Versuchsweise hatte man außerdem im Bug noch eine Kopie dieses Kopfes angebracht. Dieses Prinzip musealer Präsentation ist bei den treverischen Grabdenkmälern mehrfach zu beobachten: Originale Teile werden reproduziert und dazu genutzt, den fragmentarischen Bestand an verschiedenen Stellen zu vervollständigen. Dass einzelne Ergänzungen an ein und demselben Monument gedoppelt, zum Teil sogar mehrfach wiederholt wurden, hat man anscheinend nicht als problematisch empfunden.

Wesentliche Fortschritte ergaben sich durch die Forschungen Elvira Fölzers, die ab Sommer 1907 wissenschaftliche Hilfsarbeiterin und einzige Assistentin am Trierer Museum war. Sie befasste sich unter anderem mit den Neumagener Grabdenkmälern und der Rekonstruktion des Großen Weinschiffs. In ihrer Ergänzung der Steven weist sie mit formalen und stilistischen Argumenten die Voluten-Protome dem Vorsteven und den großen Tierkopf dem Achtersteven

---

²⁹   Hettner 1903, 15 Abb. oben; s. auch Loeschcke 1927, 113 Abb. 2.
³⁰   Hettner 1881 mit Taf. 36, 1; s. auch Merten 2002, 229 Abb. 5.
³¹   Hettner 1881 mit Taf. 36, 2 (Zeichnung: A. Rüdell).
³²   s. o. Anm. 9.
³³   Entworfen von Carl Hocheder. Zur Museumssituation s. Merten 2016, 94.
³⁴   s. Fölzer 1911, 236 Abb. 1.
³⁵   RLM Trier, Glasplattennegativ C 533; s. o. Anm. 7. Dazu: Mahler 2019, 50–51 Abb. 8.
³⁶   Zu den Schiffen auf dem Secundiniergrabmal s. Dragendorff – Krüger 1924, 4. 46–49 Abb. 27–28 Taf. 16–17.
³⁷   Mahler 2019.

zu (Abb. 5, e)³⁸. Umgesetzt wurden ihre Vorschläge wieder von dem bereits genannten Museumstechniker Jovy, der die Protomen mit Originalfragmenten ergänzte. Er verwendete für die Verbindungen Gips, wodurch diese reversibel waren³⁹. Eine historische Aufnahme⁴⁰ zeigt, dass der kurze, eher stumpfe Rammsporn zunächst beibehalten wurde. Publiziert hat Fölzer dann aber eine Version (Abb. 5, f), in der ein längerer, spitz zulaufender Rammsporn am Bug als Ergänzung zu sehen ist. Bezeichnenderweise fällt dies mit ihrer Neuinterpretation des Großen Weinschiffs als Kriegsschiff zusammen. Inspiriert ist diese Ergänzung durch Darstellungen von Transportschiffen der römischen Kriegsflotte auf der Traianssäule⁴¹. Da bei keinem der erhaltenen Schiffsfragmente der Sporn erhalten ist, lässt sich aus dem Befund kein Argument für die Bestimmung des Schiffstyps gewinnen. Die Diskussion, ob ursprünglich ein Transport- oder Kriegsschiff dargestellt war, wird bis heute kontrovers geführt⁴².

**Die Zeit seit dem Ersten Weltkrieg**

Nach Kriegsschäden im Ersten Weltkrieg⁴³ konnte das Museumsgebäude erst 1922 wiederhergestellt werden. Die wohl 1924 entstandenen Aufnahmen⁴⁴ zeigen die schon weit fortgeschrittenen Arbeiten. Am Großen Weinschiff hatte man alle Ergänzungen einschließlich der Kopie des bärtigen Kopfes im Bug abgenommen (Abb. 5, g. h). Nur der originale, aber hier nicht zugehörige bärtige Kopf blieb im Heck montiert. In diesen Zeitraum fiel die systematische Bearbeitung der Neumagener Grabmalfragmente durch Wilhelm von Massow, deren Publikation allerdings erst mit einiger Verzögerung erfolgte⁴⁵.

Zeitgleich beschäftigte sich auch Siegfried Loeschcke als Abteilungsdirektor des Museums mit der Rekonstruktion des Großen Weinschiffs⁴⁶. Auf ihn geht die – aufgrund erheblicher ikonografischer und stilistischer Unterschiede fragliche – Ergänzung des Ketoskopfes im Vorsteven zurück (Abb. 2, c; 5, i. k). Der Kopf war offensichtlich ein Magazinfund⁴⁷.

Auf den Glasplattennegativen ist im Zuge dieser Rekonstruktionsversuche erstmals dokumentiert, wie neben der bis heute im RLM Trier präsentierten Variante mit zwei Tierkopfprotomen verschiedene Ergänzungen am Objekt getestet wurden (Abb. 5, i. k). Dafür verband der Museumsmodelleur P. Welter die Protomen jeweils im Abguss mit dem Schiffsrumpf. Unter anderem wurde der Ketoskopf im Vorsteven mit dem Volutenknauf im Achtersteven kombiniert⁴⁸ (Abb. 5, i). Loeschcke favorisierte dann die Fassung mit zwei Tierkopfprotomen⁴⁹ (Abb. 5, j). Als wichtigste Parallele für diesen Schiffstyp galt ein Goldmedaillon des Constantius Chlorus von 296 n. Chr.,

---

³⁸ Fölzer 1911. Zu E. Fölzer s. Merten 2013; <https://sempub.ub.uni-heidelberg.de/propylaeum_vitae/de/ wisski/navigate/3232/view> (03.03.23).

³⁹ Mahler 2019, 50. Sichtbar auf einigen Aufnahmen im RLM Trier: RLM Trier, Glasplattennegative C 854 + D 109.

⁴⁰ RLM Trier, Glasplattennegativ B 171; s. o. Anm. 7.

⁴¹ Fölzer 1911, bes. 236 Abb. 1; 242 mit Anm. 7. Zur Traianssäule z. B. Coarelli 1999, 93 Taf. 49; 138 Taf. 94.

⁴² Zum Forschungsstand s. zuletzt Schwinden 2019, der überzeugend für eine zivile Funktion der Schiffe argumentiert. Die von der Traianssäule abgeleitete Rekonstruktion einer Flussbireme bleibt auch für den mit Bezug zum Großen Weinschiff rekonstruierten Schiffstyp relevant, s. Bockius 2001, 147–157; Bockius 2008. Das auf dem Bug eindeutig auszumachende Auge bietet keinen typologischen Anhaltspunkt; es ist sowohl bei Transport- als auch bei Kriegsschiffen bezogen.

⁴³ s. z. B. RLM Trier, Glasplattennegativ C 2848; s. o. Anm. 7.

⁴⁴ RLM Trier, Glasplattennegativ D 1895; s. o. Anm. 7.

⁴⁵ von Massow 1932. Zum Autor s. Merten 2003; Merten 2016; <https://sempub.ub.uni-heidelberg.de/propylaeum_ vitae/de/ wisski/navigate/67317/view> (03.03.23). Vorher waren Hettners Überlegungen zu den Grabdenkmälern posthum erschienen (Hettner 1903). Hans Dragendorff und Emil Krüger hatten die Katalogarbeit zugunsten der Publikation des Secundiniergrabmals zurückgestellt (Dragendorff – Krüger 1924). Hierzu s. demnächst Klöckner, im Druck.

⁴⁶ Loeschcke 1927. Zum Autor s. Hebben 2002, 132–136; <https://sempub.ub.uni-heidelberg.de/propylaeum_vitae / de/wisski/navigate/3057/view> (03.03.23).

⁴⁷ Loeschcke 1927, 107; s. o. Anm. 10.

⁴⁸ RLM Trier, Glasplattennegativ C 3869; s. o. Anm. 7.

⁴⁹ RLM Trier, Glasplattennegativ C 3870; s. o. Anm. 7.

490  Ute Kelp – Anja Klöckner

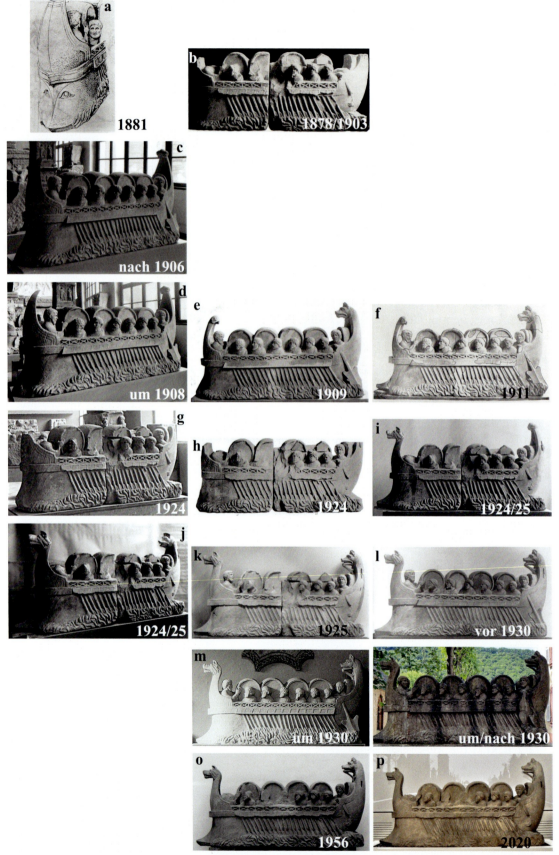

5  Bildunterschrift s. nachfolgende Seite

das aus dem Hortfund von Beaurains nahe Arras stammte und in Trier geprägt worden war[50]. Schließlich erhielt der Tierkopf im Achtersteven, dem Vorschlag Fölzers folgend, in einer Aufnahme von 1925 (Abb. 5, k)[51] einen Bart[52]. Das nicht anpassende Original des bärtigen Kopfes im Heck wurde beibehalten und die anderen drei Büsten in Bug und Heck wurden mit Kopien dieses Kopfes vervollständigt. Zuletzt wurden die Fehlstellen analog zu vorangegangenen Rekonstruktionen ebenfalls ergänzt[53] (Abb. 5, l). Von dieser Fassung mit maximalen Ergänzungen gelangte ein Abguss als Exponat in das ehemalige Trierer Weinmuseum (Abb. 5, m)[54].

Ein Abguss dieser Vollrekonstruktion wurde auch in Neumagen vor der Apsis der St. Peterskapelle an der Römerstraße aufgestellt (Abb. 5, n). In zentraler Lage vor dem Nordtor des spätantiken Kastells stand das Große Weinschiff (Schiff 1) fortan buchstäblich als Flaggschiff der römischen Antike. Wie eingangs beschrieben (Abb. 2), lag die tatsächliche Fundstelle der Rumpfblöcke aber deutlich weiter südlich[55]. Ein Abguss des Heckblocks von Schiff 2 mit dem ebenfalls sehr populären ›fröhlichen Steuermann‹ dagegen wird bis heute an der Stelle präsentiert, wo die Schiffe 1 und 2 am südlichen Rand des Kastellrunds gefunden worden waren. In diesem Fall wird lediglich ein Block und damit nur die Hälfte des bekannten Bestandes gezeigt. Neben der Dislozierung vom Fundort gehört außer dem Wunsch nach möglichst vollständiger Rekonstruktion auch die selektive Wahrnehmung des Objekts zu den charakteristischen Modi der Rezeption römischer Grabdenkmäler.

Im RLM Trier hat man am Original die Replikate des bärtigen Kopfes und einige andere Ergänzungen noch vor 1956 wieder abgenommen (Abb. 5, o)[56], die Tierprotomen aber beibehalten[57]. Im Zuge dessen wurde der bärtige Kopf im Heck mittels einer festen Masse mit dem erhaltenen Befund verbunden. Außerdem hat man die zugewiesenen Tierprotomen zunächst in dem gleichen Material kopiert und anschließend irreversibel auf dem Schiffsrumpf befestigt. Seitdem ist der Forschungsstand Loeschckes im wahrsten Sinne zementiert (Abb. 1; 5, p).

5 Übersicht über die (Teil-)Rekonstruktionen des Großen Weinschiffs im RLM Trier: a) Originalzustand von 1878, b) rekonstruierende Skizze des Bugs von 1881, c) Aufstellung in Saal C nach 1906, d) Aufstellung in Saal C um 1908, gleicher Zustand, e) Rekonstruktion von 1909, f) Rekonstruktion von Jovy/Fölzer 1911, g) Aufstellung in Saal C im Jahr 1924, h) Seitenansicht im gleichen Zustand, i) zusätzlich Ergänzung eines spitzen Rammsporns und der Stevenprotomen, j) großer Tierkopf im Achtersteven, k) erweiterte Teilrekonstruktion von 1925, l) Vollrekonstruktion nach Loeschcke, m) Kopie dieser Vollrekonstruktion in der Aufstellung im Weinmuseum in Trier, um 1930, n) Kopie dieser Vollrekonstruktion in Neumagen, um/nach 1930, o) Teilrekonstruktion von 1956, p) gegenwärtiger unveränderter Zustand (Zusammenstellung U. Kelp, GU Frankfurt; a) nach Hettner 1903, 15 Abb. oben; b) nach Hettner 1881, Taf. 36, 2, Zeichnung A. Rüdell; c) RLM Trier, GNeg A 27; d) RLM Trier, GNeg C 533; e) RLM Trier, GNeg B 171; f) nach Fölzer 1911, 236 Abb. 1; g) RLM Trier, GNeg D 1895; h) nach von Massow 1932, Taf. 54; i) RLM Trier, GNeg C 3869; j) RLM Trier, GNeg C 3870; k) RLM Trier, GNeg B 592; l) RLM Trier, GNeg B 594; m) RLM Trier, GNeg C 7117; n) Foto U. Kelp, GU Frankfurt; o) RLM Trier, GNeg RD-1956-47; p) Foto Th. Zühmer, RLM Trier)

---

[50] Loeschcke 1927, 108. 118 Abb. 13; Bastien – Metzger 1977, 94–95 Kat. 218 mit Farbtaf. nach S. 157 (Museum von Arras); Bockius 2007, 12 Abb. 4 (Cabinet de Médailles, Paris); RIC VI 2, 167 Nr. 34.
[51] RLM Trier, Glasplattennegativ B 592; s. o. Anm. 7.
[52] Hierzu s. u. mit Anm. 78.
[53] RLM Trier, Glasplattennegativ B 594; s. o. Anm. 7.
[54] Das Weinmuseum in Trier wurde 1927 eröffnet, aber schon 1939 nach Ausbruch des Zweiten Weltkriegs wieder geschlossen: Deckers 2018, 94–95.
[55] Noch die moderne »Lauschtour«, eine Touristik-App mit Audioguide, führt an die Fundplätze von Grabdenkmälern um und in der Kastellmauer mit entsprechenden Abgüssen bekannter Fragmente: <https://www.bernkastel.de/regionen/ferienland-bernkastel-kues/moselort-neumagen-dhron-inmitten-der-weinkulturlandschaft/lauschtour-in-neumagen-dhron/> (03.03.23).
[56] RLM Trier, Glasplattennegativ RD 1956-47; s. o. Anm. 7.
[57] Mahler 2019, 52.

# DAS GROSSE WEINSCHIFF – REKONSTRUKTION, DEKONSTRUKTION UND NEUBEWERTUNG

## Wilhelm von Massow und seine unterschätzten Erkenntnisse

Am Großen Weinschiff lässt sich exemplarisch nachvollziehen, wie museale Präsentation und wissenschaftliche Bearbeitung zum Teil unverbunden nebeneinander herlaufen, zum Teil sogar in Widerspruch zueinander geraten. Die Rekonstruktion Loeschckes wird bis heute kaum hinterfragt. Grundlegende Erkenntnisse von Massows werden hingegen vernachlässigt. Das beste Beispiel dafür ist der bärtige Kopf. Von Massow hatte bereits überzeugend herausgearbeitet, dass dieser Kopf nicht zum Steuermann im Heck, sondern nur zu der zurückgewandten Hauptfigur im Bug des Schiffes gehören kann. Karl-Uwe Mahler hat das jüngst nochmals detailliert begründet[58]. Die erste publizierte Rekonstruktionszeichnung von Rüdell (Abb. 5, b) lässt vermuten, dass schon Hettner nach Auffindung der Stücke den bärtigen Kopf an dieser Stelle platzierte[59].

Aufgrund der irreversiblen Restaurierung ist das zentrale Argument von Massows, wonach die Bruchfläche bei der Figur im Heck nicht anpasse, heute nicht mehr nachprüfbar. Der Übergang zwischen Kopf und Körper ist komplett retuschiert. Immerhin lässt sich aber mit Hilfe der historischen Aufnahmen die heute unzugängliche Bruchfläche wenigstens annäherungsweise abschätzen[60]. Einen weiteren Hinweis liefert die Gestaltung des Kopfes mit seinen Asymmetrien und nicht fertig ausgearbeiteten Partien, was besonders gut an den Augen und an der Ausarbeitung der Ohrmuschel abzulesen ist. Dies spricht dafür, dass die rechte und nicht die linke Seite zur Ansicht bestimmt war und dass der Kopf deswegen an der genau entgegengesetzten Stelle im Bug positioniert gewesen sein muss[61].

Außerdem zweifelte von Massow bereits an der zwingenden Zugehörigkeit des Ketoskopfes zum Großen Weinschiff. Er erwog, diesen stattdessen einem der kleineren Schiffe (Schiff 3–4) zuzuweisen[62]. Einerseits bestehen formale Ähnlichkeiten zu den großen Tierköpfen, wie vor allem die lang gezogene Schnauze mit gefletschten Zähnen, die plastisch ausgearbeiteten Augen, die spitzen Ohren und die Mähne. Andererseits gibt es aber auch eindeutige stilistische und motivische Differenzen. Die lang gezogene, hoch gewölbte Schnauze mit ausgearbeiteten Nasenlöchern des Ketos unterscheidet sich von den kompakten Schnauzen der großen Tierköpfe, die an dem heute verschollenen Exemplar besser erhalten ist (Abb. 1; 2, e). Zudem sind die gefletschten Zähne beim Ketoskopf dreieckig, bei den großen Tierköpfen viereckig. Vorn an der Schnauze sind bei Ersterem je drei Reißzähne und bei den Letzteren je zwei Reißzähne dargestellt. Grundlegend anders ist auch die Gestaltung der Mähne, die beim Ketoskopf stark stilisiert ist, während bei den großen Tierköpfen Haarbüschel angegeben sind. Außerdem trägt das Ketos ein schmales Halsband, das bei Letzteren fehlt.

Wie vor ihm schon Fölzer zog von Massow auch den Knauf mit Volute als Protome des Vorstevens in Betracht[63]. Zwar existieren keine originalen Anschlussflächen, da sowohl der Knauf als auch der Steven an der Unter- bzw. Oberseite gebrochen sind. Aber eine sich verjüngende Höhlung im Inneren des Knauffragments passt zur konkav ausgearbeiteten Steveninnenseite im Bug[64]. Dieser Knauf weist an seiner Oberseite ein originales Dübelloch auf. Bei allen Rekonstruktionen, die dieses Fragment verwenden, wurde die Ausrichtung des Dübellochs allerdings bislang nicht berücksichtigt. Wenn man diesen Befund aber ernst nimmt, müsste der Knauf erheblich

---

[58] von Massow 1932, 204–206 Kat. 287a3 Abb. 124. Hierzu Mahler 2019, aufbauend auf den Ergebnissen des BMBF-Projektes (s. o. Anm. 7).
[59] s. o. Anm. 32.
[60] Loeschcke 1927, Abb. 2; Mahler 2019, 49 Abb. 7.
[61] Mahler 2019, 47.
[62] von Massow 1932, 204–206 Kat. 287a5 Taf. 56.
[63] Fölzer 1911; von Massow 1932, 204–205. Mit abweichender Deutung Loeschcke 1927, 106–107.
[64] Fölzer 1911, 239; Loeschcke 1927, 115 Abb. 9; von Massow 1932, 204. 206 Abb. 126.

stärker nach innen geneigt gewesen sein[65]. Einzelbeobachtungen können als zusätzliche Indizien gewertet werden. So finden die beiden aufeinander zulaufenden Kerblinien am unteren Rand des Knauffragments eine mögliche Fortsetzung auf dem Schiffsrumpf.

Voluten gehören in der römischen Ikonografie bei Schiffsdarstellungen zu den gängigen Protomen[66]; etwa auf einem Relief aus *Flavia Solva*, das Teil eines Grabbaus severischer Zeit war und dem Großen Weinschiff damit zeitlich nahesteht[67]. Während großformatige rundplastische Vergleiche für die Neumagener Schiffe insgesamt fehlen und auch die Anzahl entsprechender Reliefs[68] überschaubar bleibt, existieren zahlreiche Münzdarstellungen[69]. Auch Mosaiken wie der Schiffskatalog aus *Althiburos*[70] zeigen, dass sich Vorsteven mit Volutenprotomen bei verschiedenen Schiffstypen finden. Unabhängig von der Bestimmung des Schifftyps und seiner Funktion ist also auch ein Volutenabschluss im Vorsteven vorstellbar[71].

### 3D-Modellierung mit Originalfragmenten

Als weitgehend gesichert galt bisher die Rekonstruktion des großen Tierkopfes als Protome des Achterstevens[72]. Durch die erhaltene Anschlussfläche mit Dübellöchern, einem in der Mitte und zwei an den Seiten, war die Ausgangssituation deutlich günstiger als bei dem Vorsteven. Als wir jedoch auf der Grundlage von 3D-Scans aller Originalteile die Teilrekonstruktion im RLM Trier überprüfen wollten, stießen wir gerade beim Achtersteven auf unerwartet große Schwierigkeiten (Abb. 6).

Die plastischer ausgearbeitete linke Seite des Tierkopfes, gut sichtbar an der Ausführung der Mähne und des sich deutlich vorwölbenden Augenlids, war ein gewichtiges Argument für seine Zuweisung zum Achtersteven; schließlich sind auch alle anderen Teile des Schiffes auf der linken Seite entsprechend gestaltet. Die genaue Ausrichtung des Kopfes ist aber nicht nur wegen der abgestoßenen Schnauze und dem schräg gebrochenen Hals, sondern auch aufgrund seiner Asymmetrien uneindeutig. Jovy hatte beobachtet, dass die Krümmung des Tiernackens in der Außenkontur des Hinterschiffes eine Entsprechung findet. Fölzer lässt deswegen in ihrer Anstückung die Biegung des Schiffshinterteils organisch in den Nacken übergehen[73]. Da der Bruch an genau dieser Stelle jedoch inzwischen durch die Restaurierung überdeckt wird, ist der Grad der Krümmung heute nicht mehr eindeutig zu bestimmen. Darüber hinaus lässt sich ein Anschluss nur dadurch herstellen, dass man den Halsdurchmesser beträchtlich erhöht. Dieser Aspekt wurde in den bisherigen Rekonstruktionen jedoch vernachlässigt. Im 3D-Modell ist die Diskrepanz als deutlicher Knick zu erkennen (Abb. 6, Detail). Auch für den Neigungsgrad des Kopfes fehlen

---

[65] Die zuvor realisierte Rekonstruktion des Knaufs mit Volute im Vorsteven sah von Massow als erhebliches ästhetisches Problem an: »Freilich ist es nicht zu leugnen, daß die seinerzeit vorgenommene Anpassung dieses Bruchstücks einfach unerträglich wirkte.« (von Massow 1932, 204).

[66] Zu Schiffsdarstellungen Pekáry 1999; Navis II+III Datenbanken; Feraudi-Gruenais 2017 (Grabbereich), <https://doi.org/10.11588/data/OOC0ZI> (23.03.23); s. auch Wandfresko in *Pompeii*: Haug – Hoffmann 2022, 303 Abb. 175 (100–40 v. Chr.); Reliefs Neapel, NM, insbesondere zwei Friesfragmente aus Pozzuoli: Pozzi 1989, 116–117 Kat. 102. 103 (1. Jh. n. Chr.); Bockius 2007, 58 Abb. 60.

[67] Kremer 2001, 216–217 Kat. 138 Abb. 128; <lupa.at/1264> (03.03.23).

[68] z. B. Magna Mater-Altar aus Rom: Höckmann 1985, 117 Abb. 102 (1. Jh. n. Chr.); spätantoninischer Portonaccio-Sarkophag in Rom: Reinsberg 2006, 217–218 Kat. 85 Taf. 26, 7; Meinecke 2014, 344–345 Kat. B82, 1.

[69] z. B. Schaaff 2003, 8 Kat. 61g Taf. 53 (Antoninian des Postumus, 259–268 n. Chr.); 10 Kat. 71a Taf. 60 (Denar des Carausius, 286–293 n. Chr.).

[70] Mosaik aus dem Atrium einer Peristylvilla, Tunis, Bardo Nationalmuseum: Duval 1989; Schwinden 2019, 33. s. auch das Odysseus-Mosaik aus Sta. Vitória do Ameixial, Lissabon, Archäologisches Nationalmuseum: Chaves 1938, 53 Abb. 12 (268–330 n. Chr.).

[71] Grundsätzlich spricht nichts dagegen, dass ein Ketoskopf als Protome diente, s. etwa den bronzenen Nadelkopf aus Alttrier: Dövener 2008, 64 Abb. 14; Schwinden 2019, 35 Abb. 12. Wir danken Frau Dövener für den Hinweis auf dieses Stück.

[72] Fölzer 1911; Loeschcke 1927, 105–106; von Massow 1932, 204 Abb. 124.

[73] Fölzer 1911, 238.

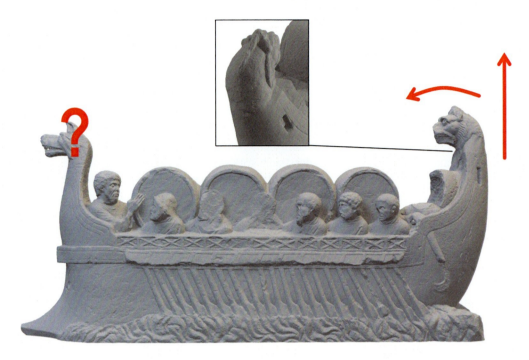

6 Neumagen, 3D-Scan der Teilrekonstruktion des Großen Weinschiffs im RLM Trier; ergänzt ist der Kopf der Person im Bug; rot markiert sind unklare Teile der Rekonstruktion; mit Detail des Achterstevens (3D-Scans: L. Raddatz, i3 mainz; Bearbeitung: U. Kelp, GU Frankfurt)

konkrete Anhaltspunkte. Der Rest eines Dübellochs im Hals ist nur bedingt eine Hilfe[74], zumal das Gegenstück im Schiffskörper durch die irreversible Rekonstruktion nicht mehr zugänglich ist.

Fölzer und Loeschcke nahmen eine Ansatzspur neben dem Auflager auf dem Kajütendach für die Rekonstruktion eines Kinnbartes in Anspruch[75]. Deswegen konnten sie den Hals nicht allzu lang ausführen. Ein solcher Kinnbart ist als Motiv mehrfach bezeugt. Eine formal ähnliche Parallele findet sich jedoch nur ein einziges Mal auf einem Altar aus Neumagen[76]. Zudem deutet der angesprochene Ansatz u. E. nicht zwingend auf einen Kinnbart hin. Aus diesem Grund ziehen wir eine Verlängerung des Halses in Betracht. Dadurch kann der erhaltene Tierkopf wesentlich besser auf das Heck ausgerichtet werden. Außerdem müssen die Seiten nicht erheblich verdickt werden, sondern gehen organisch in den Kopf über. Um wie viel länger der Hals sein müsste, dafür fehlen konkrete Anhaltspunkte. Ebensowenig kann ausgeschlossen werden, dass der Kopf stärker nach vorn geneigt war.

Die bisherige Rekonstruktion beider Steven des Großen Weinschiffs ist also in ihrer jetzigen Form in Frage zu stellen und muss neu bewertet werden (Abb. 6).

## ZUR REKONSTRUKTION DES GESAMTMONUMENTS

Während der Wunsch nach Vervollständigung des Großen Weinschiffs (Schiff 1) seit seiner Auffindung zu immer neuen Entwürfen führte, fand die Frage nach dem Aussehen des Gesamtmonuments deutlich weniger Aufmerksamkeit. Man ging stets davon aus, dass Schiff 1 und 2 als Gegenstücke gearbeitet waren und gemeinsam ein Grabmonument schmückten[77].

---

[74] Fölzer 1911, 238 Abb. 3.
[75] Loeschcke 1927, 105–106. 114–115 Abb. 5–8, setzt die von Fölzer 1911, 239 mit Abb. 4, angeregte Ergänzung um: »Der leere Raum zwischen Kajütendach und dem zu ihm parallel laufenden Unterkiefer wird durch [eine Bartflosse] belebt und der Tierkopf selber scheint nicht mehr so hoch über das Schiff emporzuragen; ein stärkeres Schließen der Komposition wird erreicht.« Er empfand also einen längeren Hals als ästhetisches Problem.
[76] von Massow 1932, 117–119 Kat. 169a Taf. 21 (Fölzer 1911, 239 Abb. 4 = Loeschcke 1927, 114 Abb. 5). Kinnbärte werden zumeist locker herabhängend dargestellt, z. B. von Massow 1932, 175 Kat. 186c Taf. 40. 41.
[77] von Massow 1932, 203: »Das besser erhaltene Schiff a zeigt an seiner rechten, das Schiff b an seiner linken Seite in der unteren Hälfte eine Anschlußfläche und beidemal ist hier in der oberen Hälfte die Ausführung vernachlässigt. Mit diesen Seiten saßen die Schiffe also gemeinsam an einem Denkmal an«.

Das Große Weinschiff aus Neumagen. Neue Überlegungen zu Rekonstruktion und Bedeutung 495

7   Neumagen, sog. Circusmonument in der pasticcioartigen Teilrekonstruktion mit Schiffblöcken und Amphorenstapel im RLM Trier (Foto: Th. Zühmer, RLM Trier)

Bereits Hettner schlug vor, dass die beiden Schiffe (Schiff 1–2) auf den Risaliten des sog. Circusdenkmals gestanden hätten, und illustrierte dies mit einer Zeichnung[78]. Allerdings stellte von Massow klar, dass die Schiffe zu schmal seien und dass speziell die Länge des Großen Weinschiffs nicht mit den Marken auf der Oberseite des Risalitgesimses vereinbart werden könne, was Hettners Rekonstruktion den Boden entzog[79]. Emil Krüger verband die Schiffe 1 und 2 mit dem ebenfalls aus Neumagen stammenden Aufsatz in Form einer Amphorenpyramide. In seinem Modell kombiniert er diese Elemente hypothetisch mit einem Sockel, der keine konkrete Vorlage besitzt, aber anscheinend vom Circusdenkmal inspiriert wurde[80].

Im Museum wird die Amphorenpyramide heute, wie von Hettner vorgeschlagen, auf dem Circusdenkmal präsentiert (Abb. 7). Zu Seiten der Pyramide stehen allerdings der Bug von Schiff 2 sowie die beiden Blöcke der deutlich kleineren Schiffe 3 und 4. In ihrer jetzigen Form stellt diese Installation also ein Pasticcio dar.

Über die bisherigen Vorschläge hinaus gibt es allerdings noch weitere Möglichkeiten für die Rekonstruktion des Gesamtmonuments. Bislang ging man meist davon aus, dass die Schiffe, in welcher Kombination auch immer, den eigentlichen Gegenstand der Darstellung und den Hauptbestandteil eines Monuments gebildet haben. Es wäre jedoch auch in Betracht zu ziehen, dass die Schiffe als rundplastische Elemente in ein wesentlich größeres, mehrstöckiges Denkmal integriert waren; in formaler Hinsicht etwa den Tierfiguren von Duppach[81] ähnlich. Als solche vollplastischen Elemente hätten sie die vordere Ansichtsseite des Monuments verstärkt, vor allem

---

[78]   Hettner 1903, 13. Wieder abgebildet bei von Massow 1932, 153 Abb. 103.
[79]   von Massow 1932, 207. 210 Abb. 131.
[80]   RLM Trier, Glasplattennegativ B 883; s. o. Anm. 7. s. auch von Massow 1932, 209–211 Kat. 289 Abb. 129. 130 (Modell) Taf. 57. Zum Aufbau der Pyramide vgl. den Negotiatorpfeiler: von Massow 1932, 127–132 Kat. 179a4 Taf. 25. Dass es sich bei der Verbindung der Schiffe 1 und 2 mit der Amphorenpyramide um einen auf Jovy zurückgehenden Vorschlag Krügers handelt, erwähnt von Massow 1932, 210–211. Kritisch bereits Numrich 1997, 111–112. Ein verwandtes, in der Gestaltung des Sockels leicht abgewandeltes Modell bei Bockius 2008, 38 Abb. 2.
[81]   Solche Rahmungen erfolgen auch in deutlich kleinerem Format, quasi in einer ›Schrumpfversion‹; s. z. B. ein heute verschollenes Fragment aus der Slg. Binsfeld (Kontorszene, flankiert von zwei anscheinend weitgehend

8   *Belginum*, Amphorenfragmente des Typs Dressel 20 in der Ausstellung »20 Jahre Archäologiepark Belginum. Lebendige Geschichte« im Archäologiepark Belginum (Foto: U. Kelp, GU Frankfurt)

aber eine rahmende Funktion besessen und dazu gedient, unterschiedliche Facetten aus dem für die Grabrepräsentation wichtigen Themenspektrum abzurufen. Sie wären also nicht der primäre Darstellungsgegenstand, sondern ergänzten die durch die Porträts der Grabinhaber, die Inschrift und den übrigen Bildschmuck evozierten Inhalte im Hinblick auf Transport, Flussschifffahrt und Handel.

Schließlich soll noch ein Blick auf die Typologie der Amphoren geworfen werden, die bislang als Behälter für den Transport von Wein verstanden wurden. Um den Gefäßkörper herum ist ein geflochtener Stoß- und Bruchschutz dargestellt, was eine genaue Beschreibung der Form erschwert. Es handelt sich aber auf jeden Fall um bauchige Amphoren, bei denen die Schulter nahtlos in den Hals übergeht und bei denen die Henkel nach oben ausgezogen sind. Dies erinnert sehr an die charakteristischen Amphoren im Typus Dressel 20, die im Treverergebiet durchaus verbreitet waren[82] (Abb. 8). Allerdings dienten solche Gefäße nicht zum Export von mosselländischem Wein, sondern hauptsächlich zum Import von Olivenöl[83]. Auch regionale Amphorenformen kommen als Vergleiche in Frage. Diese wurden zum Transport verschiedener Güter verwendet und sind nicht mit spezifischen Produkten zu verbinden[84]. Ob es sich bei dem Grabaufsatz aus Neumagen also tatsächlich um einen Stapel von Weinamphoren handelt, ist keineswegs sicher. Die gleiche Frage könnte man natürlich auch für die Fässer auf den Neumagener Schiffen stellen, die bis heute meist unhinterfragt als Weinschiffe gelten[85].

## FAZIT

Die von uns vorgenommenen 3D-Rekonstruktionen der Neumagener Monumente führten im Falle des Großen Weinschiffs zur Dekonstruktion jenes zementierten Forschungsstandes, dessen Entstehungsgeschichte wir hier anhand der auf den historischen Aufnahmen dokumentierten Restaurierungsgeschichte nachzeichnen konnten.

Folgendes bleibt festzuhalten (s. Abb. 6): Der bärtige Männerkopf gehört auf der Ansichtsseite zu der Person im Bug. Die Tierprotome im Achtersteven muss einen längeren, eventuell stärker gebogenen Hals gehabt haben. Im Vorsteven ist eine Protome in Form einer Volute nicht auszuschließen; diese muss stärker nach innen gebogen rekonstruiert werden. Bei der Forschungsdiskussion um die Deutung des Großen Weinschiffs als Kriegs- oder Transportschiff ist stärker zu gewichten, was tatsächlich antikem Bestand entspricht. Für die Rekonstruktion des Gesamtmonuments sind über die bisherigen, vor allem implizit vermittelten Vorstellungen hinaus noch weitere Varianten in Betracht zu ziehen. Die populäre Verbindung der Schiffe mit dem für die Moselregion typischen Wein kann nicht als gesichert gelten.

Auf einen konkreten Gegenvorschlag für die Rekonstruktion von Schiff und Gesamtmonument verzichten wir bewusst, solange keine bislang unbekannten, zugehörigen Fragmente auftauchen.

---

vollplastisch gearbeiteten Fässern, die wiederum als Träger der Grabinschrift *D(is) M(anibus)* fungieren): Espérandieu 1913, 315–316 Kat. 4161.

[82]   Martin-Kilcher 1994, Abb. 9–10.
[83]   So weisen z. B. Amphorenfragmente im Typ Dressel 20 aus *Belginum* noch Rückstände von Olivenöl auf, s. Schrickel 2015. Für wichtige Anregungen danken wir Isabel Rodà de Llanza und Rosemaria Cordie.
[84]   Hanut 2001, Abb. 2, 4; 5, 3. Den Hinweis verdanken wir Sascha Schmitz.
[85]   Barzen 1954/1956; Schwinden 2019, 40–41.

Es besteht die Gefahr, dass solche Rekonstruktionen als visuelle Konstrukte eine Eigendynamik entwickeln. Deswegen halten wir es für sinnvoller, zunächst gesicherte Details zusammenzutragen und auf diese Weise ein Spektrum an Möglichkeiten aufzuzeigen. Damit wollen wir zum einen den Blick für die weiter bestehenden Unsicherheiten schärfen, andererseits aber auch eine neue Grundlage für eine weitergehende Beschäftigung mit dem Thema schaffen.

## BIBLIOGRAFIE

| | |
|---|---|
| Barzen 1954/1956 | R. M. Barzen, Die Neumagener Weinschiffe, TrZ 24/26, 1956/1958, 231–234 |
| Bastien – Metzger 1977 | P. Bastien – C. Metzger, Le trésor de Beaurains, dit d'Arras (Wetteren 1977) |
| Binsfeld u. a. 2020 | A. Binsfeld – A. Klöckner – G. Kremer – M. Reuter – M. Scholz – U. Kelp (Hrsg.), Stadt – Land – Fluss. Grabdenkmäler der Treverer in lokaler und überregionaler Perspektive. Akten der Int. Konferenz 25.–27.10.2018 in Neumagen und Trier, TrZ Beih. 37 (Wiesbaden 2020) |
| Bockius 2001 | R. Bockius, Antike Schiffahrt. Boote und Schiffe der Römerzeit zwischen Tiber und Rhein, in: H.-P. Kuhnen (Hrsg.), Abgetaucht, aufgetaucht. Flussfundstücke, aus der Geschichte, mit ihrer Geschichte (Trier 2001) 119–157 |
| Bockius 2007 | R. Bockius, Schifffahrt und Schiffbau in der Antike, AiD Sonderh. (Stuttgart 2007) |
| Bockius 2008 | R. Bockius, Römische Kriegsschiffe auf der Mosel? Schiffsarchäologisch-historische Betrachtungen zum »Neumagener Weinschiff«, FuAusgrTrier 40, 2008, 37–49 |
| Chaves 1938 | L. Chaves, Estudos lusitano-romanos I. A »Villa« de Santa-Vitória do Ameixial (Concelho de Estremoz). Escavações em 1915–1916, APort 30, 1938, 14–117 |
| Coarelli 1999 | F. Coarelli, La colonna Traiana (Rom 1999) |
| Deckers 2018 | D. Deckers, Im Zeichen des Traubenadlers. Eine Geschichte des deutschen Weins ²(Frankfurt 2018) |
| Dragendorff – Krüger 1924 | H. Dragendorff – E. Krüger, Römische Grabmäler des Mosellandes und der angrenzenden Gebiete I. Das Grabmal von Igel (Trier 1924) |
| Dövener 2008 | F. Dövener, Neues zum römischen Vicus von Altrier, Empreintes 1, 2008, 59–64 |
| Duval 1989 | P. M. Duval, La forme des navires romains d'après la mosaïque d'Althiburus, in: P. M. Duval, Travaux sur la Gaule (1946–1986) (Rom 1989) 819–846 |
| Eiben 2009 | H. G. Eiben, Das Neumagener Weinschiff. Eine Erfolgsgeschichte (Trier 2009) |
| Espérandieu 1913 | É. Espérandieu, Belgique I. Recueil général des bas-reliefs de la Gaule Romaine V (Paris 1913) |
| Espérandieu 1915 | É. Espérandieu, Belgique II. Recueil général des bas-reliefs de la Gaule Romaine VI (Paris 1915) |
| Feraudi-Gruénais 2017 | F. Feraudi-Gruénais, ... ubique naufragium ... ? Aspekte und Bedeutungen von Schiffsdarstellungen im Grab. I. Zentralität versus Peripheralität in den Bilddiskursen der römischen Zeugnisse, in: H. Frielinghaus – Th. Schmidts – V. Tsamkda (Hrsg.), Schiffe und ihr Kontext. Darstellungen, Modelle, Bestandteile – von der Bronzezeit bis zum Ende des Byzantinischen Reiches (Mainz 2017) 63–78 |
| Fölzer 1911 | E. Fölzer, Ein Neumagener Schiff, neu ergänzt, BJb 120, 1911, 236–250 |
| Hanut 2001 | F. Hanut, Amphores et Cruches-Amphores regionals de Gaule Belgique et de Germanie Inferieure, in: M. Tuffreau-Libre (Hrsg.), La céramique en Gaule et en Bretagne romaines. Commerce, contacts et romanisation (Berck-sur-Mer 2001) 19–38 |
| Haug – Hoffmann 2022 | A. Haug – A. Hoffmann (Hrsg.), Die neuen Bilder des Augustus. Macht und Medien im antiken Rom, Ausstellung Hamburg (München 2022) |
| Hebben 2002 | C. Hebben, Ein Museum unter dem Hakenkreuz. Das Rheinische Landesmuseum Trier im Spannungsfeld von Ideologie und Wissenschaft 1933–1945, in: H.-P. Kuhnen (Hrsg.), Propaganda. Macht. Geschichte. Archäologie an Rhein und Mosel im Dienst des Nationalsozialismus (Trier 2002) 93–138 |
| Hettner 1881 | F. Hettner, Die Neumagener Monumente, RhM 36, 1881, 435–462 |
| Hettner 1903 | F. Hettner, Illustrierter Führer durch das Provinzialmuseum in Trier (Trier 1903) |
| Höckmann 1985 | O. Höckmann, Antike Seefahrt (München 1985) |
| Klöckner, im Druck | A. Klöckner, Hans Dragendorff und die römischen Grabdenkmäler des Mosellandes, in: K. Hofmann u. a. (Hrsg.), Mehr als nur Scherben. Hans Dragendorff als Forscher und Wissenschaftsorganisator (Frankfurt, im Druck) |

| | |
|---|---|
| Klöckner u. a., in Druckvorbereitung | A. Klöckner – M. Reuter – M. Scholz (Hrsg.), Römische Grabdenkmäler aus Augusta Treverorum im überregionalen Vergleich. Mediale Strategien sozialer Repräsentation, Trierer Grabungen und Forschungen (Wiesbaden, in Druckvorbereitung) |
| Kremer 2001 | G. Kremer, Antike Grabbauten in Noricum. Katalog und Auswertung von Werkstücken als Beitrag zur Rekonstruktion und Typologie, SoSchrÖAI 36 (Wien 2001) |
| Loeschcke 1927 | S. Loeschcke, Der zweite Tierkopf zum Neumagener Moselschiff, TrZ 2, 1927, 104–120 |
| Mahler 2019 | K.-U. Mahler, Wo saß der ›ernste Steuermann‹ des Neumagener Weinschiffs tatsächlich?, FuAusgrTrier 51, 2019, 46–53 |
| Martin-Kilcher 1994 | S. Martin-Kilcher, Verbreitungskarten römischer Amphoren und Absatzgebiete importierter Lebensmittel, MBAH 13, 1994, 95–121 |
| Meinecke 2014 | K. Meinecke, Sarcophagum posuit. Römische Steinsarkophage im Kontext (Ruhpolding 2014) |
| Merten 2002 | J. Merten, Felix Hettner (1851–1902), das Provinzialmuseum zu Trier und die Archäologie Westdeutschlands, TrZ 65, 2002, 215–283 |
| Merten 2003 | J. Merten, Wilhelm v. Massow (1891–1949) – ein Altertumsforscher im Spiegel seines Nachlasses, Neues Trierisches Jahrbuch 2003, 169–177 |
| Merten 2009 | J. Merten, Kurze Geschichte des Rheinischen Landesmuseums Trier, in: Rheinisches Landesmuseum Trier (Hrsg.), Fundstücke. Von der Urgeschichte bis zur Neuzeit (Trier 2009) 218–225 |
| Merten 2013 | J. Merten, Elvira Fölzer (1868). Zum sozialen und beruflichen Umfeld einer frühen Trierer Archäologin, in: J. E. Fries – D. Gutsmiedl-Schümann (Hrsg.), Ausgräberinnen, Forscherinnen, Pionierinnen. Ausgewählte Porträts früher Archäologinnen im Kontext ihrer Zeit (Münster 2013) 119–139 |
| Merten 2016 | J. Merten, Wilhelm v. Massow und die »Grabmäler von Neumagen«, FuAusgrTrier 48, 2016, 93–107 |
| Numrich 1997 | B. Numrich, Die Architektur der römischen Grabdenkmäler aus Neumagen. Beiträge zur Chronologie und Typologie (Trier 1997) |
| Pekáry 1999 | I. Pekáry, Repertorium der hellenistischen und römischen Schiffsdarstellungen (Münster 1999) |
| Pozzi 1989 | E. Pozzi, Le collezioni del Museo Nazionale di Napoli. La scultura greco-romana, le sculture antiche della collezione Farnese, le collezioni monetali, le oreficerie, la collezione glittica (Rom 1989) |
| Reinsberg 2006 | C. Reinsberg, Die Sarkophage mit Darstellungen aus dem Menschenleben, Die antiken Sarkophagreliefs, Vita Romana I 3 (Berlin 2006) |
| Schaaff 2003 | U. Schaaff, Münzen der römischen Kaiserzeit mit Schiffsdarstellungen im Römisch-Germanischen Zentralmuseum (Mainz 2003) |
| Schrickel 2015 | M. Schrickel, Spanisches Olivenöl für Belginum – Amphoren aus dem Tal des Guadalquivir, in: R. Cordie (Hrsg.), VorGESCHICHTEn an der Hunsrückhöhenstraße. Straßen und Wege verbinden. Ausstellung Belginum (Morbach 2015) 19–20 |
| Schwinden 2019 | L. Schwinden, Die Weinschiffe der römischen Grabmäler von Neumagen, FuAusgrTrier 51, 2019, 27–45 |
| von Massow 1932 | W. von Massow, Die Grabmäler von Neumagen (Berlin 1932) |
| Weidner 2009 | M. K. N. Weidner, Kat. 50 Grabmalaufsatz [Inv. 767] Neumagen, in: Rheinisches Landesmuseum Trier (Hrsg.), Fundstücke. Von der Urgeschichte bis zur Neuzeit, Ausstellungskatalog Trier (Stuttgart 2009) 110–111 |

*Ute Kelp, Goethe-Universität Frankfurt, Institut für Archäologische Wissenschaften, Campus Westend, Hausfach 7, Norbert-Wollheim-Platz 1, 60323 Frankfurt, Deutschland.*
*[e] kelp@em.uni-frankfurt.de*

*Anja Klöckner, Goethe-Universität Frankfurt, Institut für Archäologische Wissenschaften, Campus Westend, Hausfach 7, Norbert-Wollheim-Platz 1, 60323 Frankfurt, Deutschland.*
*[e] kloeckner@em.uni-frankfurt.de*

Martin Kemkes

# NEUE STATUENFRAGMENTE AUS DEM WESTKASTELL VON ÖHRINGEN AM OBERGERMANISCHEN LIMES

**Abstract**
In 2020 and 2022, numerous statue parts were found during excavations in the Western Fort of Öhringen in the inner fort ditch. Four monuments are presented here. In the case of the Genius head (no. 1), the carefully removed laurel wreath is particularly striking. The statue no. 2 carries a cornucopia and a shoulder mantle, which is unusual for Genius representations. The statues of Victoria and Mars (nos. 3 and 4), which are very similar, especially on the backs, were probably used to decorate the fort gates. They show the deities in the common types of representation of Victoria striding forward on a globe and Mars Ultor, which were used without exception on stone monuments from military find contexts along the Upper German-Raetian Limes. By comparison with dated monuments from Öhringen and the surrounding area, the erection of the two statues could have taken place in the years AD 231–232. After their destruction by a Germanic raid, they were probably disposed of as building rubble by the local Roman remnant population or the soldiers still stationed here.

Der Kastellstandort Öhringen liegt etwa in der Mitte des rund 80 km langen, schnurgeraden Verlaufs des südlichen Obergermanischen Limes im heutigen Baden-Württemberg. Wahrscheinlich verlief hier in der Antike eine wichtige West-Ost-Verbindung von Rhein und Neckar über die Hohenloher Ebene nach Osten zu den germanischen Siedlungsgebieten am Main und im heutigen Thüringen. Aus diesem Grunde errichteten die Römer am Ort ab der Mitte des 2. Jahrhunderts n. Chr. zwei etwa 2 ha große Kastelle, in denen unterschiedliche Hilfstruppen, wahrscheinlich zeitweise auch Legionssoldaten stationiert waren[1]. Während das sog. Rendel- oder Ostkastell nur wenige Meter von der eigentlichen Limeslinie und einem hier zu vermutenden Limesübergang entfernt liegt, befindet sind das sog. Bürg- oder Westkastell etwa 1200 m weiter westlich. Der zugehörige Kastellvicus lag um die und auch zwischen den beiden Anlagen, wobei allerdings nur wenige Befunde unter der heutigen modernen Bebauung untersucht werden konnten[2]. Zwei wichtige Fundstellen römischer Steindenkmäler sollen hier besonders genannt werden: 1861 wurde beim Bau der Eisenbahnlinie an der Otto-Meister-Straße eine Grube entdeckt, in der mindestens zwölf Steindenkmäler, Inschriften und Fragmente von Weihesteinen, verlocht worden waren, sodass in der Nähe ein Kultbezirk vermutet werden kann[3]. Ein sehr ähnlicher Befund kam 1961 in der Haller-Straße zu Tage, wo ebenfalls in einer Grube acht Statuenfragmente und Weihealtäre entdeckt wurden[4].

Das ca. 2,1 ha große Westkastell (Abb. 1) wurde bereits 1892/1893 durch die Reichslimeskommission in seinen Umrissen erfasst. 1911 konnten beim Bau des Bezirkskrankenhauses Teile des Stabsgebäudes untersucht werden, wobei vor allem die spektakuläre Verfüllung eines Brunnens Aufsehen erregte. In diesem fanden sich die architektonischen Reste eines Nymphäums sowie mehrere Weihesteine aus den Jahren 186, 231 und 241 n. Chr., die anlässlich der Errichtung und späteren Renovierung einer Wasserleitung aufgestellt worden waren[5]. Wegen der damaligen, aus

---

[1] Allgemein zum römischen Öhringen: Roth – Thiel 2016.
[2] Roth – Thiel 2016, 58–69.
[3] Haug – Sixt 1914, 613–621; von Herzog 1929, 26–28.
[4] Nesselhauf – Strocka 1967.
[5] Haug – Sixt 1914, 624–631; Kemkes 2016.

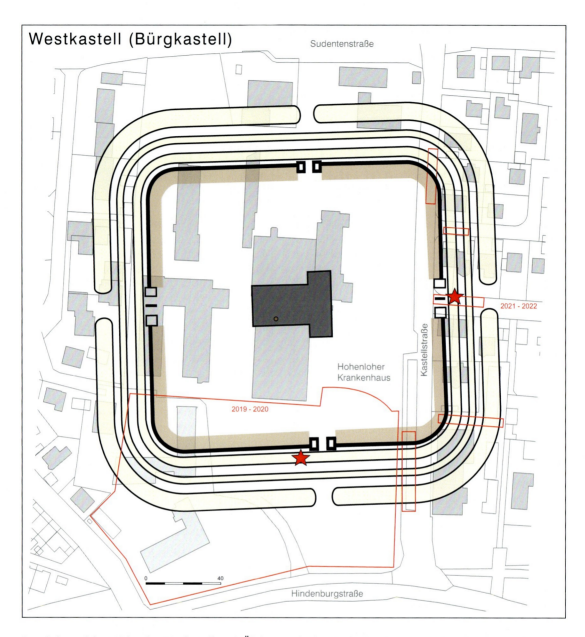

1   Schematisierter Plan des Westkastells von Öhringen mit Eintragung der Grabungsflächen und den Fundorten der Victoria- und Marsstatuen. Die dunkelgraue Fläche im Zentrum markiert die Position des Stabsgebäudes mit dem 1911 ausgegrabenen Brunnen (© Landesamt für Denkmalpflege Baden-Württemberg im Regierungspräsidium Stuttgart, K. Kortüm)

heutiger Sicht unzureichenden Dokumentation des Befundes konnte leider nicht geklärt werden, wann und aus welchem Anlass die aufwendige Verlochung der Steindenkmäler in dem Brunnen erfolgte[6]. Nach weiteren Ausgrabungen zwischen 1959–1970 wurde 1980 als vorerst letzte Maßnahme das nördliche Kastelltor näher untersucht[7]. Mit über 30 Denkmälern aus mindestens drei verschiedenen Kultplätzen, im Westkastell sowie an der Haller- und der Otto-Meister Straße, ist Öhringen einer der Kastellstandorte mit den meisten bekannten Steindenkmälern am Obergermanischen Limes. Sie geben einen zwar zufälligen, aber dennoch vertieften Einblick in die sakrale Infrastruktur eines Militärstandortes am Limes am Ende des 2. und in der ersten Hälfte des

---

[6]  Kemkes 2016, 92–93. – Die Frage wird am Ende des Beitrags noch einmal aufgegriffen.
[7]  Schönberger 1972; Planck 1980.

3. Jahrhunderts n. Chr. Die hier vorzustellenden Neufunde ergänzen dieses Bild in erfreulicher Weise, werfen aber zugleich viele Fragen auf, die im Rahmen dieses Beitrags nicht ausführlich behandelt werden können. Im Folgenden werden auch nur die wichtigsten Neufunde vorgestellt und eingeordnet[8].

## DER BEFUND

Durch die geplante Erweiterung des Bezirkskrankenhauses, dessen bisheriges Gebäude genau im Zentrum des ehemaligen Westkastells liegt, wurde in den Jahren 2019–2020 eine Ausgrabung notwendig[9]. Die 1,54 ha große Fläche umfasste die Südostecke des Kastells mit seiner kompletten Umwehrung, bestehend aus der Kastellmauer, den drei vorgelagerten Gräben und dem Südtor mit einfacher Durchfahrt. Die Kastellmauer östlich des Tores war auf mehreren Metern Länge umgestürzt und in den inneren Kastellgraben gerutscht. Der etwa 2 m tiefe innere Graben war im oberen Teil mit Bauschutt verfüllt. In diesem fanden sich verstreut über mehrere Meter zahlreiche große bis sehr kleine Skulpturenfragmente von etwa 13 verschiedenen Denkmälern, die allerdings nicht im Verbund lagen, sondern zusammen mit anderen Architekturteilen hier wohl als Schutt entsorgt worden waren[10].

Im Frühjahr 2022 wurde zudem bei Kabelarbeiten vor dem Osttor, der *porta praetoria*, ebenfalls im Bereich des inneren Kastellgrabens, völlig überraschend eine Marsstatue gefunden. Durch den kleinteiligen Ausschnitt der Grabung waren weitere Aussagen zum Befund an dieser Stelle nicht möglich. Die vier interessantesten Steindenkmäler werden im Folgenden kurz vorgestellt und interpretiert.

### 1. Kopf einer Geniusstatue, Material Sandstein, Höhe 19,5 cm (Abb. 2 a–c)

Beschreibung: Der Kopf ist wenige Zentimeter unter dem Kinn abgebrochen. Die Nase und das gesamte Kinn einschließlich der Mundpartie wurden abgeschlagen. Bereits vor der endgültigen Zerstörung der Figur wurde der ursprünglich vorhandene Lorbeerkranz zusammen mit dem wahrscheinlich sichtbaren Haaransatz über der Stirn sorgfältig abgearbeitet. Erhalten haben sich nur der Knoten des Kranzes im Nacken mit dem ersten Blatt auf der linken Seite sowie die zentrale Stirnblüte. Um den Kopf herum ist die etwa 6 cm breite, sorgfältig abgearbeitete Fläche gut zu erkennen. Es fehlen jegliche Hinweise darauf, wie etwa Dübellöcher, dass hier anstelle des ursprünglichen Kranzes eventuell ein Haarschmuck aus Bronze oder Holz montiert gewesen sein könnte. Eine Zugehörigkeit des Kopfes zur Statue Nr. 2 ist wegen des andersfarbigen Sandsteins und auch wegen des Größenunterschieds auszuschließen.

Deutung: Dass der leicht unterlebensgroße Kopf ursprünglich zu einer etwa 150 cm großen Geniusstatue gehörte, steht außer Frage[11]. Das gelockte Haar und der Lorbeerkranz mit zentraler Stirnblüte finden sich häufig bei vergleichbaren Genius-Darstellungen. Parallelen in der direkten Umgebung sind unter anderem aus Altrip, Ladenburg, Murrhardt und Osterburken in unterschiedlicher Qualität und Größe bekannt[12]. Die sorgfältige Entfernung des Lorbeerkranzes gibt dagegen

---

[8] Zwei weitere Publikationen sind kürzlich erschienen oder sind in Vorbereitung: A. Brosend – M. Kemkes, Victoria. Der römische Sieg und seine göttlichen Garanten, Schriftenreihe des Limesmuseums Aalen 65 (Oppenheim am Rhein 2023); M. Kemkes, It's all just Propaganda? Victoria and Mars. Representations and Inscriptions on the Upper German-Raetian Limes, in: Proceedings of the 25th International Congress of Roman Frontier Studies (Nijmegen 2022).

[9] Kortüm u. a. 2020.

[10] Von diesen Fragmenten werden hier im Folgenden zunächst nur drei Denkmäler vorgestellt. Eine Gesamtpublikation der Ausgrabung ist in Vorbereitung.

[11] Gegen eine Deutung als Apollo spricht neben der markanten Stirnblüte der fehlende Ansatz der auf die Schulter herabfallenden Haare, vgl. Künzl 2010, 511–512.

[12] Datenbank Ubi Erat Lupa: Altrip Nr. 25540; Ladenburg Nr. 25599; Murrhardt Nr. 7620; Osterburken Nr. 25660. – Ein Geniuskopf mit Eichenkranz und Stirnblüte aus Wimpfen Nr. 7343, <http://www.lupa.at> (02.01.2023).

2 a–c  Kopf eines Genius vom Westkastell Öhringen, Archäologisches Landesmuseum Baden-Württemberg (Archäologisches Landesmuseum Baden-Württemberg, M. Hoffmann)

Rätsel auf. Ein Ersatz durch einen Kranz aus Bronze oder Holz nach einer möglichen Beschädigung erscheint nicht zuletzt wegen fehlender Befestigungslöcher unwahrscheinlich. Die erhaltene, nun markant hervorstehende Stirnblüte spricht wohl auch gegen eine wie auch immer geartete Umwidmung des Kopfes oder der Statue. So bleibt zunächst nur die Feststellung, dass der Figur des Genius bereits vor ihrer endgültigen Zerstörung ein wichtiges Attribut genommen wurde. Bedenkt man die Bedeutung des Lorbeerkranzes in der römischen Religion und als Siegessymbol der Kaiser und damit des gesamten Reiches sowie die Rolle und die Beliebtheit der Genien als Schutzgötter von militärischen wie zivilen Personengruppen und Örtlichkeiten, so erstaunt dieser Befund[13]. Eine schlüssige Erklärung kann an dieser Stelle noch nicht gegeben werden.

Wo die Geniusstatue ursprünglich gestanden hat, bleibt aufgrund des Befundes ebenfalls offen. Eine Aufstellung im militärischen Kontext, also innerhalb des Kastells, ist ebenso denkbar wie die Zuordnung zu einem zivilen Heiligtum im Kastellvicus.

### 2. Statue eines Genius, Material Sandstein, Höhe 75 cm (Abb. 3 a. b)

Beschreibung: Die Statue war bereits bei der Auffindung in mehrere Teile zerbrochen. Nicht erhalten sind der Kopf, der rechte Arm unterhalb des Schulteransatzes, das rechte Bein unterhalb des Oberschenkels sowie der obere Teil des Füllhorns in der Linken. Dazu kommen zahlreiche Beschädigungen wie am rechten Oberschenkel, der linken Hand sowie vor allem am linken Unterschenkel. Trotz dieses fragmentarischen Zustandes ist die Figur noch gut zu erkennen. Sie zeigt einen jugendlich nackten Mann mit rechtem Standbein und leicht vorgestelltem linken Spielbein. Der erhaltene linke Fuß ist nackt. Der rechte Arm war ursprünglich gesenkt und hielt wahrscheinlich eine Opferschale über einem Altar. Über der linken Schulter liegt ein faltenreicher Mantel, der in einem Bogen über den linken Unterarm geführt wird und in einer breiten Stoffbahn bis fast auf den Boden reicht. In der linken Armbeuge ist der untere Teil eines Füllhorns zu erkennen. Der Schaft des Horns ist im unteren Drittel mit nach außen weisenden Blättern verziert. Oberhalb davon weist das Füllhorn eine Mittelrille auf, was eventuell auf ein zweiteiliges Füllhorn schließen lässt, wie es auch von anderen Genius-Darstellungen aus Öhringen sowie aus dem benachbarten Kastellplatz Mainhardt bekannt ist[14].

---

[13] Vgl. Kunckel 1974, bes. 53–64; Mattern 2001, 18–22.
[14] Nesselhauf – Strocka 1967, Taf. 35, 2. 3. – Vgl. auch die Weihung an den Genius beneficiariorum aus Altrip: Datenbank Ubi Erat Lupa, Nr. 25540, <http://www.lupa.at> (02.01.2023); Kunckel 1974, C I 2 Taf. 68.

3 a. b    Statue eines Genius vom Westkastell Öhringen, Archäologisches Landesmuseum Baden-Württemberg (Archäologisches Landesmuseum Baden-Württemberg, M. Hoffmann)

Die Figur steht auf einer etwa 10 cm hohen Standplatte. Aus Stabilitätsgründen wurde die linke Körperhälfte einschließlich des weit herunterhängenden Schultermantels auf der Rückseite nicht plastisch ausgearbeitet. Dagegen steht das rechte Bein annähernd frei im Raum, was dann wohl auch für den rechten Arm und den zugehörigen Altar anzunehmen ist.

Deutung: Die Interpretation als Genius ist aufgrund des Füllhorns in der Linken in Kombination mit der gesamten Haltung der Figur zunächst naheliegend. Dagegen spricht allerdings der stoffreiche Schultermantel, da die bekannten Genien grundsätzlich in der Toga oder mit einem Hüftmantel dargestellt werden. Die zahlreichen Beispiele aus Obergermanien belegen dies eindeutig[15]. Der statuarische Typus eines nackten, jüngeren Mannes mit Schultermantel und gesenktem rechten Arm ist dagegen beinahe kanonisch bei Darstellungen des Gottes Merkur zu finden, der allerdings in der Linken den *caduceus* und in der Rechten zumeist einen Geldbeutel trägt[16].

Eine direkt vergleichbare Darstellung eines Genius mit Schultermantel ist allerdings, nicht weit entfernt von Öhringen, aus Wiesloch, Kr. Heidelberg, bekannt[17]. Das kleine, 30,5 cm hohe Relief zeigt einen nackten Genius mit Schultermantel und Füllhorn, der an einem Altar opfert. Die zugehörige Inschrift identifiziert ihn als Genius des Mars Cenabetius. Die bekannten Weihungen an einen Genius Martis oder an Mars Cenabetius stammen aus der Westpfalz und dem mittleren Neckarraum[18]. Neben dem Relief aus Wiesloch ist nur noch ein heute verschollenes Relief aus Neuenstadt am Kocher bekannt, das allerdings nach einer Zeichnung von 1667 mit einem den ganzen Körper bedeckenden togaähnlichen Gewand dargestellt ist[19]. Eine vermeintlich typische Darstellung eines lokalen Genius Martis mit Schultermantel und damit eine entsprechende Interpretation der Öhringer Statue ist somit auszuschließen. Die für einen Genius ungewöhnliche Bekleidung ist wohl eher ein Hinweis auf die flexible Verwendung ikonografischer Details, die hin-

---

[15] s. o. Anm. 13.
[16] Hupe 1997, 70.
[17] Wiegels 1992, 392–398.
[18] Wiegels 1992, Abb. 11. 12.
[19] Haug – Sixt 1914, 551–552, mit Hinweis auf eine Abbilddung bei Carl Schott, Physica curiosa (1667) 1330.

sichtlich der dargestellten Gottheit für die galloromische Bevölkerung in der Limesregion nicht überbewertet werden sollte. Eine gewisse Bedeutung könnte dagegen in der dargestellten Nacktheit liegen, da auch andere Geniusstatuen, zum Beispiel aus Bad Wimpfen, Bietigheim, Stuttgart oder Wiesbaden den Hüftmantel nur knapp über oder sogar unterhalb der Genitalien tragen[20]. Der ursprüngliche Aufstellungskontext der Statue bleibt wie schon bei Nr. 1 unklar.

### 3. Statue der Victoria, Material Sandstein, Höhe 82 cm (Abb. 4 a. c)

Beschreibung: Die Statue war bei der Auffindung in mehrere Teile zerbrochen, wobei ein kompletter vertikaler Riss die Figur in einen vorderen und einen hinteren Teil zerschneidet. Nicht erhalten sind Hals und Kopf, beide Arme ab oberhalb des Ellenbogens sowie die Füße. Damit fehlen auch die wahrscheinlich vorhandenen Attribute, in der erhobenen Linken ein Kranz sowie in der gesenkten Rechten ein Palmzweig, der über eine noch in Resten vorhandene Stütze an den linken Oberarm angelehnt war. Da die Füße fehlen, bleibt zudem unklar, ob die Göttin auf einem Globus stand. Nur fragmentarisch erhalten sind die beiden Flügel, die wie ein Schirm den Oberkörper einrahmen.

Die Göttin ist in bewegter, nach vorn drängender Haltung dargestellt, wobei das rechte Bein leicht vorgestellt und im Knie angewinkelt ist. Sie trägt ein in der Taille gegürtetes und auf den Schultern geheftetes stoffreiches Obergewand, das durch die Bewegung stark nach hinten weht und an den Vorderseiten der Beine eng anliegt.

Besonders auffällig ist die extreme Frontalität der Figur, wobei der Steinmetz bereits die Seiten nur noch wenig ausarbeitete und auf der Rückseite völlig auf eine Modellierung verzichtete. Dieser Umstand weist darauf hin, dass die Statue ursprünglich wahrscheinlich in einer Nische stand, die dem Betrachter keinen Blick von der Seite erlaubte. Ergänzt man Kopf und Füße sowie eventuell eine Weltkugel, so wird die Statue eine ursprüngliche Größe von etwa 140–150 cm gehabt haben. In der Größe und vor allem in der Behandlung der Rückseite zeigt sich eine große Übereinstimmung mit der Marsstatue (Nr. 4), sodass beide wahrscheinlich zur selben Zeit von derselben Werkstatt gefertigt wurden.

Deutung: Die Ansprache der Statue als Darstellung der römischen Siegesgöttin Victoria steht außer Frage. Ebenso eindeutig kann sie dem weit verbreiteten Typus der »voranschreitenden Victoria mit Kranz und Palmzweig« zugeordnet werden, hier im Folgenden als Typus A bezeichnet[21]. Dieser Typus zeigt die Göttin in der Regel auf einem Globus stehend oder diesen nur mit einem Fuß berührend. In der großen Variationsbreite der Darstellungen in den Nordwestprovinzen steht oder schreitet die Göttin aber auch häufig direkt auf dem Boden, ohne dass darin eine inhaltliche Differenzierung gesehen werden muss.

Eindeutig ist dagegen die klare Abgrenzung zum weit verbreiteten zweiten Typus der Victoria mit einem großen Siegesschild in der Linken, hier im Folgenden als Typus B bezeichnet[22]. Auch bei diesem finden sich zahlreiche Modifikationen, wobei der Schild entweder nur gehalten oder mit dem Sieg des Kaisers, der Victoria Augusta, beschrieben wird. Variabel ist zudem die Kleidung der Göttin sowie das Standmotiv, wobei der linke Fuß auf einem Globus oder auch nur erhöht auf einem Felsen stehend dargestellt wird.

Die Herleitung und Entwicklung beider Typen aus der griechisch/hellenistischen und in der römischen Kunst wurde bereits umfassend behandelt und muss hier nicht wiederholt werden. Hinzuweisen ist jedoch darauf, dass der Typus A von Augustus nach seinem Sieg in *Actium* 31 v. Chr. mit der Aufstellung einer aus Tarent stammenden Statue in der Curia im Jahr 29 v. Chr. gezielt als Motiv

---

[20] Datenbank Ubi Erat Lupa: Bad Wimpfen Nr. 7896; Bietigheim Nr. 7309, 7459, <http://www.lupa.at> (02.01.2023); Stuttgart und Wiesbaden: Kunckel 1974, C I 114 und C I 122–124, Taf. 85. 89. – Mündlicher Hinweis von Peter Noelke, dass auch andere Gottheiten des späten 2. und 3. Jhs. n. Chr. häufiger mit entblößten Köperteilen dargestellt werden.

[21] Hölscher 1967, 6–47.

[22] Hölscher 1967, 98–131 bes. 122–126 Typus 3 (Brescia).

4 a. c  Statue der Victoria vom Westkastell Öhringen, Archäologisches Landesmuseum Baden-Württemberg (Archäologisches Landesmuseum Baden-Württemberg, M. Hoffmann)

in die offizielle römische Siegespropaganda eingeführt wurde. Diese Statue stellte dabei nicht die generelle Sieghaftigkeit des Kaisers als Eigenschaft dar, sondern sie zeigt die Siegesgöttin selbst, die ihm und damit dem gesamten römischen Volk in der Schlacht von *Actium* zum Sieg verholfen hat. Mit der gleichen Intention wird dieser Typus auch von den nachfolgenden Kaisern zumeist dann verwendet, insbesondere in der Münzprägung, wenn ein spezieller militärischer Sieg propagandistisch herausgestellt werden sollte. Eine Änderung hin zu einer deutlich flexibleren Verwendung scheint erst ab der Mitte des 3. Jahrhunderts n. Chr. stattgefunden zu haben[23].

Die Victoria-Darstellungen des Typus B, basierend auf dem klassisch-griechischen Original einer Statue der Aphrodite[24], wurden dagegen in der gesamten Kaiserzeit wesentlich flexibler eingesetzt. Als bedeutsame Vertreter gelten die Bronzestatue der Victoria aus Brescia oder die zentrale Reliefdarstellung auf der Traianssäule in Rom[25].

Betrachtet man die Verbreitung der Darstellungstypen A und B unter den Steindenkmälern der beiden Provinzen *Germania superior* und *Raetia* so ergeben sich interessante Einblicke und Auffälligkeiten (Tab. 1)[26].

Tabelle 1 Steindenkmäler mit Victoria-Darstellungen in den Provinzen *Germania superior* (N = 54) und *Raetia* (N = 5) – davon 27 Darstellungen auf Jupitergigantensäulen

| Darstellungstypen | Militärischer Kontext | | Ziviler Kontext | | Kontext unklar |
|---|---|---|---|---|---|
| | *Germania superior* | *Raetia* | *Germania superior* | *Raetia* | *Germania superior* |
| Victoria Typus A: mit Palmzweig und Kranz, bewegtem Gewand, zum Teil auf Globus stehend | 8 | 2 | 20 | 2 | 4 |
| Victoria Typus B: mit Siegesschild, linker Fuß zum Teil auf Globus | – | – | 16 | – | 2 |
| Sonstige oder unklare Darstellungen | 2 | 1 | 4 | – | – |

Von den insgesamt 59 Victoria-Darstellungen stammen 54 aus Obergermanien und nur fünf aus Raetien. Der Bildtypus A ist insgesamt doppelt so häufig vertreten, während sechs Denkmäler individuell abweichende Darstellungen zeigen und hier nicht näher betrachtet werden sollen[27]. Vergleicht man die Beispiele getrennt nach ihren zivilen oder militärischen Befund- und Fundumständen, so fällt sofort der hohe Anteil der zivilen Kontexte auf, der vor allem durch die 27 Reliefdarstellungen auf Teilen der Jupitergigantensäulen bedingt ist, die in Obergermanien weit verbreitet waren. Beide Darstellungstypen liegen dabei in etwa gleich häufig vor[28].

In den militärischen Kontexten der Limeskastelle finden sich dagegen ausschließlich Darstellungen vom Typus A (Abb. 5) und keine Darstellungen des Typus B[29]. Das gleiche Bild

---

[23] Hölscher 1967, 17–22. – Die zahlreichen Beispiele aus verschiedenen Materialgruppen zeigen dabei vielfältige Abweichungen im Detail bei Haltung und Kleidung der Victoria, ohne dass sich daran ein Bedeutungswandel ablesen ließe.

[24] Bekannt durch die römische Replik der sog. Venus von Capua: Delivorrias u. a. 1984, 71–72 Nr. 627.

[25] Victoria von Brescia: Salcuni – Formigli 2011, 5–34. – Traianssäule: Lehmann-Hartleben 1926, Szene LXXVIII.

[26] Auf Einzelnachweise wird hier aus Platzgründen verzichtet. Eine Liste der Denkmäler wird an anderer Stelle vorgelegt.

[27] Dazu gehören u. a. die nahezu unbekleidete Victoria auf der Seitenfläche des Augsburger Siegesaltars: Bakker 1993, Abb. 3; die fliegende Victoria auf einem Relief aus Ladenburg, gefunden bei der *porta praetoria* des dortigen Kastells: Wiegels 2000, 117–118; und die Pfeilerreliefs aus Augst und Mainz, auf denen Victoria mit beiden Händen einen Schild mit zentralem Bildnis über dem Kopf hält: Bossert-Radtke 1992, 57–60; Frenz 1992, 64–65.

[28] Bauchhenß – Noelke 1981, 51–55.

[29] Bei den in Tab. 1 gelisteten Darstellungen im Typus B mit unklarem Kontext handelt es sich um ein Relief mit Mars und Victoria ohne Fundort im Landesmuseum Württemberg: Datenbank Ubi Erat Lupa, Nr. 7833 <http://

5  Relief mit Victoria (Typus A), Höhe 48 cm, vom Kleinkastell Robern am Odenwaldlimes, Gemeinde Fahrenbach, Neckar-Odenwald-Kreis (Archäologisches Landesmuseum Baden-Württemberg, O. Harl [Ubi erat lupa])

ergibt sich, wenn man die Victoria-Darstellungen auf Waffenteilen in die Betrachtung einbezieht. Die Beispiele insbesondere auf Teilen der sog. Paradewaffen und auf den Schwertern zeigen ein eindeutiges Bild[30]. Wenn auch mit geringen Abweichungen in den ikonografischen Details, finden sich hier ausschließlich Darstellungen vom Typus A, während die Victoria mit dem Siegesschild nicht nachzuweisen ist. Angesichts dieses klaren Befundes lässt sich sagen, dass die von Augustus in die römische Siegespropaganda eingeführte Darstellung der Victoria auf dem Globus mit Kranz und Palmzweig als Symbol für den tatsächlich errungenen militärischen Sieg ihre Wirkung und Bedeutung in den folgenden rund 200 Jahren nicht verändert hat und auch von den Soldaten am Limes, bezogen auf ihren täglichen militärischen Einsatz, genau in diesem Sinne verstanden wurde. Die Öhringer Statue kann somit problemlos in diese Reihe der »Victorien mit militärischem Kontext« eingefügt werden. Der Darstellungstypus B, die Victoria mit dem Siegesschild (Abb. 7), war dagegen angesichts der vielen Beispiele aus zivilen Kontexten auch entlang des Limes wesentlich allgemeiner verbreitet. Ihre Interpretation als Symbol der allgemeinen Sieghaftigkeit der römischen Zivilisation schuf dabei auch Spielraum für eine Verbindung mit einheimisch-keltischen Vorstellungen, wobei Victoria und Mars mit keltischen Götterpaaren gleichgesetzt wurden. Eine ausführliche Betrachtung zu diesem Themenkreis erfolgt an anderer Stelle[31].

## 4. Statue des Mars, Material Sandstein, Höhe 100 cm (Abb. 6 a. c)

Beschreibung: Auch die bei Kabelarbeiten vor der *porta praetoria* des Westkastells entdeckte Marsstatue war bei ihrer Auffindung in mehrere Teile zerbrochen. Nicht erhalten haben sich der Kopf des Mars und der Kopf der Gans an seiner rechten Seite sowie der rechte Arm von der Mitte des Oberarms abwärts. In der rechten Hand hielt Mars wohl eine heute verlorene Lanze. Die linke Hand fehlt ebenso wie der rechte Rand des auf dem Boden stehenden Schildes. Das Schwert auf der linken Seite ist stark beschädigt, wobei hier wegen der eigentlich geschützten

---

www.lupa.at> (02.01.2023); sowie die Victoriastatue mit Siegesschild vom Heiligtum an der Schneidershecke: Kemkes – Willburger 2004, 81–83; Noelke 2012, 479–480 mit vollständiger Literaturliste. – Eine erneute Diskussion der Statuengruppe mit Mars (s. u. bei Nr. 4), Salus und Victoria kann hier nicht erfolgen. Die früher schon diskutierte Zweiphasigkeit der Gruppe und die, wie hier aufgezeigt, offensichtlich eher in zivilen Kontexten übliche Darstellung der Victoria mit dem Siegesschild, sollte allerdings zu weiteren Überlegungen anregen.

[30] Eine vollständige Liste der einzelnen Objekte kann hier nicht gegeben werden. Vgl. Schamper 2015, 101–102 und 129 mit 33 Darstellungen auf Paraderüstungsteilen. – Miks 2007, 140–147 und 269–270 mit 20 Beispielen von Buntmetallinkrustationen auf Schwertklingen und Verzierungen der Schwertscheiden vom Typ Pompeji in Durchbruchtechnik. Als Ausnahme ist die Verzierung der Schwertscheide aus Mainz zu nennen, wo Victoria einen Schild an einer Palme befestigt, Miks 2007, 663 A 467.

[31] s. o. Anm. 8.

6 a. c  Statue des Mars vom Westkastell Öhringen, Archäologisches Landesmuseum Baden-Württemberg (Archäologisches Landesmuseum Baden-Württemberg, M. Hoffmann)

Lage zwischen Körper und Arm eine bewusste Beschädigung bei der Zerstörung der Statue angenommen werden kann.

Der Kriegsgott ist in voller Bewaffnung dargestellt. Er trägt geschlossene Schuhe und glatte Beinschienen. Der Muskelpanzer ist am Halsansatz, an den Oberarmen sowie am unteren Rand mit jeweils zwei Reihen blattförmiger *pteryges* mit Mittelrippe verziert. Die *pteryges* an den Oberarmen sind in ungewöhnlicher Weise mit den Spitzen zum Hals orientiert. Sie liegen also auf dem Panzerblech auf und zeigen nicht wie eigentlich üblich über dessen Rand nach außen[32]. Am unteren Rand des Panzers sind zudem langrechteckige Panzerlaschen angebracht, unter denen der Saum einer Tunika noch zu erkennen ist. Von der rechten Schulter aus verläuft ein Schwertriemen (*balteus*) quer über den Brustpanzer und dient als Aufhängung des links am Körper anliegenden Langschwertes (*spatha*). Besonders auffällig sind die detailliert gearbeiteten Riemenbeschläge, die *balteus*-Schließe und der blattförmige Anhänger, sowie die Schwertteile mit Griff und Ortband, auch wenn diese stark beschädigt sind. Die Einzelteile entsprechen dabei sehr genau den am Limes verbreiteten Militaria aus dem 2./3. Jahrhundert n. Chr.[33].

Auf der linken Schulter liegt ein Mantel, der um den Unterarm geschlagen ist und hinter dem Schild nach unten fällt. Der ovale Schild, dessen Innenseite mit der Schildfessel zum Betrachter zeigt, rahmt den Unterkörper und fungiert gleichzeitig als statische Stütze der ansonsten frei stehenden Beine. Rechts neben dem Kriegsgott steht eine Gans mit gewölbter Brust und angedeuteten Flügeln, die anhand der Füße eindeutig identifiziert werden kann. Die Details des Gefieders waren wohl ursprünglich aufgemalt.

Wie schon die Statue der Victoria, so ist auch die Marsstatue extrem auf Frontalansicht ausgearbeitet, während die Rückseite nur sehr grob modelliert wurde. Auch die Marsstatue wird deshalb wohl in einer Nische oder vor einer Wand gestanden haben. Die große Ähnlichkeit in der Bearbeitung spricht zudem für eine Gleichzeitigkeit beider Figuren.

Deutung: Auch wenn der behelmte Kopf fehlt, so besteht kein Zweifel, dass der Kriegsgott hier in Anlehnung an den Typus des Mars Ultor wiedergegeben ist. Darstellungen des Mars mit Helm und Panzer (Typus A) finden sich auch in Obergermanien und Raetien in großer Zahl, von der Großplastik bis hin zu kleinen Bronzestatuetten[34]. In deutlich geringerer Anzahl sind Darstellungen des jugendlich nackten Mars mit Helm und Lanze (Typus B) verbreitet[35]. Besonders auffällig ist dabei die Verteilung der beiden Typen in den militärischen wie auch zivilen Fundkontexten der beiden Provinzen (Tab. 2)[36].

Während in der Steinplastik mit militärischem Kontext der Typus des Mars Ultor ausschließlich vorkommt, sind beide Typen im zivilen Bereich, besonders bei den zahlreichen Jupitergigantensäulen, häufig zu finden. Besonders enge Parallelen zur Öhringer Statue bietet die Marsstatue von dem Heiligtum bei der Schneidershecke (Abb. 7), die allerdings mit erhaltenen 162 cm deutlich größer ist[37].

Die Dominanz des Typus A bei den militärischen Kontexten am Limes erstaunt angesichts seiner Herleitung und der engen Verbindung zur kaiserlichen Propaganda nicht. Bemerkenswert ist aber, dass sich diese Dominanz bei den Verzierungen der privaten Militaria nicht beobachten lässt. Insbesondere die Dekorationen der Paradewaffen zeigen beide Darstellungstypen in

---

[32] Womöglich waren dem Steinmetz solche Darstellungen im Original nicht klar geläufig. Vgl. die Marsstatuen von der Schneidershecke, aus Trier und Vindonissa mit jeweils einer *pteryges*-Reihe an den Oberarmen: Noelke 2012, 406–407 Abb. 16. 17; 479–483 Kat. 12. 21. 29.

[33] Runde *balteus*-Schließen mit erhöhtem Mittelteil: Oldenstein 1976, 226–234 Taf. 85. 86; Vergleichsfunde aus den Moorfunden von Vimose und Thorsberg: Miks 2007, 287–288 Abb. 65. – Herzförmige, teilweise durchbrochene Anhänger am Schwertriemen: Oldenstein 1976, 127–132 Taf. 31. 33. – Schwertgriff: Oldenstein 1976, 89–95 Taf. 11, 32; Miks 2007, 170–171. – Rundes Dosenortband: Oldenstein 110–123 Taf. 22–24; Miks 2007, 345–367 bes. 364–366.

[34] Noelke 2012, 431–451.

[35] Zur Herleitung und Genese der beiden Darstellungstypen: Simon – Bauchhenß 1984.

[36] Auch hier muss aus Platzgründen auf Einzelnachweise verzichtet werden, s. o. Anm. 26.

[37] Kemkes – Willburger 2004, 81–83; Noelke 2012, 479–480 mit vollständiger Literaturliste.

7   Statuengruppe mit Mars, Salus und Victoria (Typus B), Höhen 164, 114 und 112 cm, Heiligtum an der Schneiderhecke, Gemeinde Mudau-Schlossau, Neckar-Odenwald-Kreis (Archäologisches Landesmuseum Baden-Württemberg, O. Harl [Ubi erat lupa])

Tabelle 2  Steindenkmäler mit Mars-Darstellungen in den Provinzen *Germania superior* (N = 70) und *Raetia* (N = 7) – davon 40 Darstellungen auf Jupitergigantensäulen

| Darstellungstypen | Militärischer Kontext | | Ziviler Kontext | | Kontext unklar |
|---|---|---|---|---|---|
| | *Germania superior* | *Raetia* | *Germania superior* | *Raetia* | *Germania superior* und *Raetia* |
| Mars Typus A: bärtiger oder unbärtiger Kopf mit Helm, Panzer, Schild, Schwert, Lanze und Beinschienen | 11 | 4 | 26 | 2 | 3 |
| Mars Typus B: nackt mit Helm und Lanze | – | – | 13 | – | 2 |
| Sonstige oder unklare Darstellungen | – | – | 12 | 1 | 3 |

ähnlicher Anzahl[38]. Anders als dies bei Victoria zu beobachten war, spielte ein spezifischer Darstellungstyp des Mars für die Soldaten anscheinend keine große Rolle. Auffällig ist jedoch, dass der gepanzerte Mars sowohl auf den Steindenkmälern mit militärischem Kontext als auch auf den Paradewaffen immer jugendlich, ohne Bart dargestellt wurde. Er erscheint dadurch noch als

---

[38] Schamper 2015, 94–96 und 102–103 mit 19 Beispielen des gepanzerten, bartlosen Mars und 16 Beispielen des jugendlich nackten Mars. – Miks 2007, 140–147 und 269–271 mit zwölf Beispielen von Buntmetallinkrustationen auf Schwertklingen und mehreren Verzierungen der Schwertscheiden vom Typ Pompeji.

kämpfender und nicht als bereits endgültig siegreicher Gott, was sicher der aktuellen, realen Situation der Soldaten und der Einheiten am Limes eher entsprach[39].

Als Besonderheit der Öhringer Statue erscheint auf den ersten Blick auch die Darstellung der Gans als Begleittier. Die möglichen germanischen und keltischen Bezüge dieser Kombination wurden schon an anderer Stelle ausführlich diskutiert, wobei in meinen Augen die Argumente überwiegen, die für einen Bezug zu den keltischen Marsvorstellungen als Stammes- und Heilgott sprechen[40]. Ergänzend soll hier auf die Darstellung des Mars mit Gans auf einem medizinischen Bronzekästchen aus Heidelberg[41] und auf die wohl stark beschädigte Gans neben dem linken Bein der Marsstatue von der Schneidershecke hingewiesen werden[42]. Zusammen mit der Öhringer Statue liegen somit 31 Darstellungen des Mars mit einer Gans als Begleittier vor, die alle aus den Nord- und Nordwestprovinzen des Reiches stammen, während Beispiele aus dem Mittelmeerraum oder aus Italien bisher fehlen[43]. Allein dieser Umstand spricht hier wohl sicher für den Einfluss keltischer Religionsvorstellungen.

## DIE STATUEN DES MARS UND DER VICTORIA ALS SCHMUCK DER KASTELLTORE

Der Fundort der beiden Statuen direkt vor dem Süd- und Osttor des Westkastells und die deutliche Ausarbeitung nur der Frontseiten spricht dafür, dass beide Figuren in einer Nische im architektonischen Kontext der Kastelltore oder direkt vor einer Mauer gestanden haben. Zu der Frage, wie die Aufstellungsorte gestaltet waren und wo sie an den Toren zu rekonstruieren sind, gibt es nach den Befunden keine weiteren Hinweise. Einen möglichen optischen Vergleich bietet eine Inschrift aus dem Kastell Risingham/GB nördlich des Hadrianswalls (Abb. 8), bei der links und rechts Victoria und Mars in einer durch Halbsäulen gerahmten Rundbogennische zu sehen sind, wobei die Darstellungstypen den Öhringer Statuen entsprechen[44]. Bei der ursprünglichen Größe der Statuen von ca. 140–150 cm müsste eine solche Nische eine Gesamthöhe von ca. 180 cm aufweisen.

Sucht man nach vergleichbaren Denkmälern und Befunden, so lassen sich zwar mehrere Victoria- und Mars-Darstellungen auflisten, die an oder bei den Kastelltoren gefunden wurden, von denen aber nur drei direkte Hinweise zur ursprünglichen Aufstellung liefern. Das Marsrelief von der *porta praetoria* des Kastells Holzhausen besitzt auf den Nebenseiten viereckige, 4,5 × 2,5 cm große Löcher mit Resten von Bleiverguss, die als Klammerlöcher genutzt wurden, und über die das Relief wohl an der Wand des Kastelltors befestigt wurde[45]. Vor der *porta principalis dextra* des Kastells Miltenberg-Altstadt wurde eine 232 cm hohe Säule mit einer Weiheinschrift an Victoria perpetua gefunden, auf der wahrscheinlich eine Victoriastatue gestanden hat[46]. Im Befund war auch der zugehörige würfelförmige Sockel mit einer runden Vertiefung erhalten, die zur Verankerung des Säulenfußes diente. Die Fundlage beider Teile lässt vermuten, dass die Säule westlich der Toröffnung direkt vor der Front des Torturmes auf der Berme aufgestellt war. Ähnlich wie

---

[39] Bei fünf von neun Steindenkmälern mit Mars-Darstellungen aus militärischem Kontext sind die bartlosen Köpfe erhalten: Bauinschriften vom Odenwaldlimes aus Oberscheidental, Trienz und Zwing: Kemkes – Willburger 2004, 78–79 Abb. 89. 91. 92; Marsstatue aus Eining: S. 72 Abb. 78; Mars auf der Nebenseite des Augsburger Siegesaltars: Bakker 1993, 372 Abb. 2.

[40] Mattern 1994. – Denkmäler mit eindeutig keltischen Bezügen: Statuenbasis für Lenus Mars aus Caerwent/GB Mattern 1994, 114 Nr. 16; Weiherelief für Mars aus Holzhausen, gestiftet von der *cohors Treverorum* S. 116 Nr. 23 und Mattern 1999, Nr. 84; Kultblech aus Hagenbach Mattern 1994, 116–117 Nr. 26; Kästchenbleche aus Nijmegen/NL und Bonn, die wahrscheinlich zu medizinischen Besteckkästchen gehörten, Mattern 1994, 115 Nr. 19. 21. 22.

[41] Hensen 2007.

[42] Noelke 2012, 479.

[43] Mattern 1994, 119–120 Verbreitungskarte.

[44] Phillips 1977, Nr. 215 Taf. 55.

[45] Stoll 1992, 456 Nr. III 6,2; Mattern 1999, Nr. 84.

[46] Beckmann 1975; Stoll 1992, 391 Nr. III 3,1; Steidl 2008, 201 Abb. 206. 207.

8   Weiheinschrift aus dem Kastell Risingham an die Numinibus Augustorum, gesetzt von der *cohors IIII Gallorum equitata*. Links und rechts der Inschrift sind Victoria (Typus A) und Mars (Typus A) in einer Rundbogennische dargestellt (<https://romaninscriptionsofbritain.org/inscriptions/1227>, Foto: Museum of Archaeology and Anthropology Cambridge)

bei den Statuen aus Öhringen ist auch die Rückseite der Säule nicht geglättet. Fragmente einer zweiten Säule mit einer identisch beginnenden Inschrift wurden bereits 1875 im Kastellbad gefunden. Ob diese vom selben Tor stammen und eventuell eine Marsstatue trugen, bleibt unklar[47]. Bei den Ausgrabungen auf der Saalburg wurde vor dem Mittelpfeiler der *porta praetoria* ein quadratisches Fundament ausgegraben, bei dem sich Teile einer Marsstatue, zwei Unterschenkel mit Beinschienen und ein Armfragment von etwa halber Lebensgröße fanden[48].

Diese Vergleichsfunde legen nahe, dass auch in Öhringen die Statuen an den Außenseiten der Tore angebracht waren. Für die Victoriastatue am Südtor kommen dabei wegen der einfachen Durchfahrt nur die Front der Tortürme, wie in Miltenberg, oder eine Position oberhalb der Durchfahrt in einer Art Schaufassade zwischen den Türmen in Frage. Die Marsstatue könnte dagegen auch, wie auf der Saalburg, vor der Spina des Doppeltors gestanden haben. Eine Aufstellung über den Durchfahrten würde den erhaltenen Bauinschriften mit seitlichen Götterdarstellungen entsprechen, wie sie sich aus mehreren Limeskastellen erhalten haben[49]. Figürliche Dekorationen von Torfassaden zwischen den Türmen finden sich auch bei einer Architekturfibel aus London oder dem pannonischen Tonmodell aus Tokod/Ungarn, wobei hier eher keine militärischen Torbauten gemeint sind[50].

Eine Anbringung der Statuen weit über den Köpfen der das Tor passierenden Soldaten gäbe den Figuren allerdings einen stark repräsentativen Charakter und würde sie, in Ergänzung der Bau- und Ehreninschriften, als Bestandteil einer von offizieller Seite gesteuerten Bildpropaganda definieren. Einer anderen Intention entspräche dagegen eine Positionierung der Statuen in Sichthöhe der Soldaten, sei es vor der Front der Tortürme oder vielleicht sogar im Tordurchgang, was

---

[47] Vgl. die Marsstatue aus dem Kastellvicus von Miltenberg: Mattern 2005, Nr. 209; Noelke 2012, 480 Nr. 14.
[48] Stoll 1992, 498–499 Nr. 47 III 1,1; Mattern 2001, Nr. 73–75; Noelke 2012, 481 Nr. 18. 19. Nach Noelke gehören die Beine wegen der unterschiedlichen Größe nicht zu einer Statue.
[49] Bauinschriften vom Odenwaldlimes aus Oberscheidental, Trienz und Zwing: s. o. Anm. 39; Inschriftenplatte mit Victoria aus Stuttgart-Bad Cannstatt: Haug – Sixt 1914, 381 Nr. 260.
[50] Flügel – Obmann 2013, Abb. 13. 25.

einen direkteren Kontakt der Soldaten mit ihren Kriegs- und Siegesgottheiten oder direkte kultische Handlungen in Form von Opfergaben in einer als kleines Heiligtum gedachten Wandnische erlauben würde. Wenn die Soldaten nach einer Patrouille oder einem militärischen Einsatz in ihr Kastell zurückkehrten und von Mars und Victoria an den Toren begrüßt wurden, werden solche Darstellungen ihre identitätsstiftende Wirkung sicher nicht verfehlt haben. Auch wenn keine gesicherte Rekonstruktion möglich ist, so ist eine ebenerdige Positionierung der Statuen neben oder zwischen den Tordurchfahrten wohl am wahrscheinlichsten.

## ZUM MÖGLICHEN ZEITPUNKT DER AUFSTELLUNG UND ZERSTÖRUNG DER STATUEN

Zur möglichen Datierung ihrer Aufstellung und Zerstörung geben die Statuen aus sich heraus zunächst keine Hinweise. Zieht man jedoch die weiteren Steindenkmäler aus Öhringen heran, so lassen sich einige Indizien zusammenstellen. Aus den einleitend erwähnten Sammelfunden in der Otto-Meister- und Hallerstraße liegen drei Statuenweihungen an Minerva, Diana und Hercules vor, die in das Jahr 232 n. Chr. und auf den 13. Dezember 232 n. Chr. datiert sind[51]. Die Renovierung der Wasserleitung in das Westkastell kann durch einen Weihealtar zudem auf den 23. Juli 231 n. Chr. datiert werden[52]. Auch in anderen Orten der Provinz *Germania superior* finden sich datierte Denkmäler aus diesen Jahren[53]. Als wichtiger Vergleichsfund kann hier auch nochmals die Victoriainschrift aus Miltenberg angeführt werden, die zwischen 231 und 234 n. Chr. zu datieren ist[54]. Demnach ist davon auszugehen, dass in diesen Jahren am Ende der Regierungszeit des Severus Alexander diverse Maßnahmen stattgefunden haben, die in einem direkten oder indirekten Zusammenhang mit den Spannungen mit den Germanen im Vorfeld des Limes und den Feldzügen gegen die Sassaniden im Osten standen[55].

Die belegte Renovierung der Wasserleitung des Westkastells im Sommer 231 n. Chr. war dabei vielleicht nicht die einzige (Aus-)Baumaßnahme im Öhringer Westkastell, sodass durchaus auch die beiden Statuen in diesem Jahr entstanden oder aufgestellt worden sein könnten. Ein stilistischer Vergleich der Victoria- und Marsstatue mit den Statuen der Minerva, der Diana und des Hercules von den beiden anderen Öhringer Kultplätzen schließt eine solche Gleichzeitigkeit jedenfalls nicht aus[56]. Ob mit diesen Ausbaumaßnahmen die Soldaten ein stückweit ›beruhigt‹ und die Leistungsfähigkeit und Siegesgewissheit der römischen Armee zur Schau gestellt werden sollten, oder ob sich hierin als Reaktion auf die heraufziehenden Krisen auch ein allgemeines Schutzbedürfnis artikulierte, bleibt freilich Spekulation.

Angesichts der großen Zahl der im römischen Öhringen quasi als Bauschutt entsorgten Steindenkmäler stellt sich abschließend die Frage, wer zu welchem Zeitpunkt hierfür verantwortlich war. Ein bei der Ausgrabung im Westkastell 2019/2020 am unteren Rand des eingefüllten Bauschutts im inneren Graben gefundenes Tierskelett konnte durch eine $^{14}$C-Analyse in die Jahre

---

[51] s. o. Anm. 3 und 4.
[52] s. o. Anm. 5.
[53] CIL XIII 6592: Weiheinschrift für Fortuna aus dem Kastellbad von Walldürn vom 13.8.232 n. Chr.; CIL XIII 6749 und 7212; Eck 1985, 92–93: Weiheinschriften aus Mainz und Gonsenheim aus dem Jahr 231 n. Chr.; CIL XIII 6669: Weihung an Bonus Eventus in Mainz von zwei *quaestores* aus Rottenburg am Neckar aus dem Jahr 231 n. Chr.; angefügt sei hier auch die von J. Lipps auf der Wiener Tagung vorgestellte Salusstaue aus Mainz aus dem Jahr 232 n. Chr.
[54] s. o. Anm. 46. – Ebenfalls aus Miltenberg stammt die Weihung eines Beneficiariers an die *Concordia beneficiariorum Germaniae superioris* vom 23.12.231 n. Chr.: CIL XIII 11771; Mattern 2005, Nr. 251.
[55] So hat die *legio I Minervia* aus Bonn im Jahr 231 n. Chr., nach einer Weiheinschrift an Iuppiter, Mars Propugnatoris und Victoria, wohl einen ersten Feldzug gegen die Germanen rechts des Rheins unternommen: CIL XIII 8017; Eck 1985, 213.
[56] Nesselhauf – Strocka 1967, 119–130.

zwischen 241–370 n. Chr. datiert werden⁵⁷. Damit ist eine mittelalterliche oder neuzeitliche Datierung dieser ›Aufräumarbeiten‹ sicher auszuschließen. Gleiches gilt aber wohl auch für eine Datierung in die ›Nachlimeszeit‹ des späten 3. und 4. Jahrhunderts n. Chr., da aus diesen Jahrzehnten keine größeren Siedlungsspuren in Öhringen erhalten sind, die solche umfänglichen Maßnahmen rechtfertigen würden⁵⁸. So erscheint es zum jetzigen Zeitpunkt eher wahrscheinlich, dass die Beseitigung des Zerstörungsschutts nach einem oder mehreren germanischen Überfällen noch vor der endgültigen Aufgabe des Limes durch eine noch ansässige römische Bevölkerung oder hier noch stationierte Soldaten erfolgte. Einen wichtigen Hinweis für römische Instandsetzungsmaßnahmen liefert ein weiterer Weihestein aus dem Westkastell, der eine letzte Renovierung der Wasserleitung für das Jahr 241 n. Chr. belegt⁵⁹. Die Verlochung dieser Weiheinschrift zusammen mit den zerstörten Überresten des Nymphaeums im Brunnen des Stabsgebäude bietet dabei einen möglichen *terminus post quem* für die umfangreichen Aufräumarbeiten im gesamten Siedlungsareal. Dazu gehörten dann womöglich auch die Verfüllung des inneren Kastellgrabens mit den hier behandelten Statuenteilen und weiterem Bauschutt sowie der Gruben in der Otto-Meister- und Hallerstraße mit den dortigen Denkmälern zweier Kultplätze. Ob die Zerstörung der Denkmäler durch germanische Plünderer bereits mit dem Überfall 233 n. Chr. oder späteren Angriffen und Unruhen in Verbindung steht, kann dagegen nicht gesagt werden. Hinweise auf Zerstörungen und Verlochungen von Steindenkmälern in Brunnen und Gruben liegen aber auch aus vielen anderen Orten im rechtsrheinischen Obergermanien für die Jahrzehnte nach 240 n. Chr. vor, wobei auch dort der Eindruck überwiegt, dass es sich bis auf wenige Ausnahmen um Aufräumarbeiten durch die vor Ort lebende Bevölkerung handelt⁶⁰.

Es bleibt festzustellen, dass zu diesem Zeitpunkt die Funktion solcher Götterstatuen und Weihealtäre, selbst solche für die römischen Kriegs- und Siegesgottheiten Mars und Victoria und die Genien, als sichtbare Zeichen des göttlichen Schutzes der vor Ort lebenden Soldaten und Zivilisten, für die noch hier lebende Restbevölkerung keine Rolle mehr spielte. Sie scheinen angesichts der Katastrophe ihre Wirkmächtigkeit verloren zu haben und konnten deshalb ersatzlos entsorgt werden. Sie wurden, wie von Peter Noelke treffend beschrieben, nicht mehr mit *pietas*, sondern mit *neglegentia* behandelt⁶¹.

## BIBLIOGRAFIE

| | |
|---|---|
| Bakker 1993 | L. Bakker, Raetien unter Postumus – das Siegesdenkmal einer Juthungenschlacht im Jahr 260 n. Chr. in Augsburg, Germania 71/2, 1993, 369–386 |
| Bauchhenß – Noelke 1981 | G. Bauchhenß – P. Noelke, Die Iupitersäulen in den germanischen Provinzen, BJb Beih. 41 (Köln 1981) |
| Beckmann 1975 | B. Beckmann, Eine neue Inschrift vom Miltenberger Altstadtkastell, AKorrBl 5, 1975, 307–312 |
| Bossert-Radtke 1992 | C. Bossert-Radtke, Die figürlichen Rundskulpturen und Reliefs aus Augst und Kaiseraugst, FiA 16 = CSIR Schweiz Band III (Augst 1992) |
| Delivorrias u. a. 1984 | LIMC II (1984) 2–151 s. v. Aphrodite (A. Delivorrias – G. Berger-Doer – A. Kossatz-Deissmann) |
| Eck 1985 | W. Eck, Die Statthalter der germanischen Provinzen vom 1.–3. Jahrhundert, Epigraphische Studien 14 (Bonn 1985) |

---

⁵⁷ Ich danke dem Landesamt für Denkmalpflege Baden-Württemberg im Regierungspräsidium Stuttgart, dieses Ergebnis hier vorab publizieren zu können. Die Analyse wurde im Curt-Engelhorn-Zentrum Archäometrie GmbH in Mannheim durch S. Lindauer durchgeführt, Berichtsdatum: 14.10.2021.
⁵⁸ Vgl. Kortüm 2016 zu einer kleinen frühalamannischen Ansiedlung aus dem 4./5. Jh. n. Chr. am östlichen Rand der ehemaligen römischen Zivilsiedlung.
⁵⁹ Haug – Sixt 1914, 627–628; Kemkes – Willburger 2004, 34–38; Kemkes 2016, 85. 92–93.
⁶⁰ Noelke 2006 mit zahlreichen Beispielen.
⁶¹ Noelke 2006, 338.

| | |
|---|---|
| Flügel – Obmann 2013 | C. Flügel – J. Obmann, Visualisierung römischer Kastelltore: Das Beispiel der porta principalis dextra des Alenkastells Celeusum/Pförring, in: Römische Wehrbauten. Befund und Rekonstruktion, Schriftenreihe des Bayerischen Landesamtes für Denkmalpflege 7 (München 2013) 12–27 |
| Frenz 1992 | H. G. Frenz, Bauplastik und Portraits aus Mainz und Umgebung, CSIR Deutschland II 7 (Mainz 1992) |
| Haug – Sixt 1914 | F. Haug – G. Sixt, Die römischen Inschriften und Bildwerke Württembergs ²(Stuttgart 1914) 624–633 |
| Hensen 2007 | A. Hensen, Ein römisches Salbenreibkästchen aus Heidelberg, in: E. G. Jung (Hrsg.), Kleine Kulturgeschichte der Haut (Darmstadt 2007) 95–97 |
| von Herzog 1929 | E. von Herzog, Die Kastelle bei Öhringen, Der Obergermanisch-Raetische Limes des Römerreiches (ORL) Abt. B Bd. 42 (Berlin 1929) |
| Hölscher 1967 | T. Hölscher, Victoria Romana. Archäologische Untersuchungen zur Geschichte und Wesensart der römischen Siegesgöttin von den Anfängen bis zum Ende des 3. Jhs. n. Chr. (Mainz 1967) |
| Hupe 1997 | J. Hupe, Studien zum Gott Merkur im römischen Gallien und Germanien, TrZ 60, 1997, 53–227 |
| Kemkes 2016 | M. Kemkes, Der Brunnen hat es in sich! Ein Nymphaeum im Bürgkastell, in: Roth – Thiel 2016, 80–95 |
| Kemkes – Willburger 2004 | M. Kemkes – N. Willburger, Der Soldat und die Götter. Römische Religion am Limes, Schriften des Limesmuseums Aalen 56 (Stuttgart 2004) |
| Kortüm 2016 | K. Kortüm, Eine Untersuchung am sogenannten Limesübergang im Ohrntal, in: Roth – Thiel 2016, 56–57 |
| Kortüm u. a. 2020 | K. Kortüm – R. Keller – S. Högner, Im Zeichen der Victoria – Neue Erkenntnisse zum Bürgkastell in Öhringen, AAusgrBadWürt 2020, 174–180 |
| Künzl 2010 | E. Künzl, Die Zwölfgötter von Rohrdorf. Ein Heiligtum im Saltus Sumelocennensis von Marcus Aurelius bis Caracalla, FuBerBadWürt 31, 2010, 449–560 |
| Kunckel 1974 | H. Kunckel, Der römische Genius (Heidelberg 1974) |
| Lehmann-Hartleben 1926 | K. Lehmann-Hartleben, Die Trajanssäule. Ein römisches Kunstwerk zu Beginn der Spätantike (Berlin 1926) |
| Mattern 1994 | M. Mattern, Die Gans auf den Denkmälern des Mars, in: Ch. M. Ternes (Hrsg.), Roman religion in Gallia Belgica and the Germaniae. Actes des quatrième recontres scientifiques de Luxembourg, BAntLux 22, 1993, 94–120 |
| Mattern 1999 | M. Mattern, Die römischen Steindenkmäler des Stadtgebiets von Wiesbaden und der Limesstrecke zwischen Marienfels und Zugmantel, CSIR Deutschland II 11 (Mainz 1999) |
| Mattern 2001 | M. Mattern, Römische Steindenkmäler vom Taunus- und Wetteraulimes mit Hinterland zwischen Heftrich und Großkrotzenburg, CSIR Deutschland II 12 (Mainz 2001) |
| Mattern 2005 | M. Mattern, Römische Steindenkmäler aus Hessen südlich des Mains sowie vom bayerischen Teil des Mainlimes, CSIR Deutschland II 13 (Mainz 2005) |
| Miks 2007 | Ch. Miks, Studien zur römischen Schwertbewaffnung in der Kaiserzeit, Kölner Studien zur Archäologie der römischen Provinzen 8 (Rahden/Westf. 2007) |
| Nesselhauf – Strocka 1967 | H. Nesselhauf – V. M. Strocka, Weihedenkmäler aus Öhringen, FuBerSchwab N. F. 18/1, 1967, 112–131 |
| Noelke 2006 | P. Noelke, Bildersturm und Wiederverwendung am Beispiel der Iuppitersäulen in den germanischen Provinzen des Imperium Romanum, BerRGK 87, 2006, 273–386 |
| Noelke 2012 | P. Noelke, Kaiser, Mars oder Offizier? Eine Kölner Panzerstatue und die Gattung der Ehrenstatuen in den nördlichen Grenzprovinzen des Imperium Romanum, JbRGZM 59, 2012, 391–512 |
| Oldenstein 1976 | J. Oldenstein, Zur Ausrüstung römischer Auxiliareinheiten. Studien zu Beschlägen und Zierrat an der Ausrüstung der römischen Auxiliareinheiten des obergermanisch-raetischen Limesgebietes aus dem zweiten und dritten Jahrhundert n. Chr., BerRGK 57, 1976, 49–284 |
| Phillips 1977 | E. J. Phillips, CSIR Great Britain I 1. Corbridge. Hadrian's Wall East of the North Tyne (Oxford 1977) |

| | |
|---|---|
| Planck 1980 | D. Planck, Grabungen im Bürgkastell von Öhringen, Hohenlohekreis, AAusgrBadWürt 1980, 91–94 |
| Roth – Thiel 2016 | S. Roth – A. Thiel, Vicus Aurelianus. Das römische Öhringen, Archäologische Informationen aus Baden-Württemberg 74 (Stuttgart 2016) |
| Salcuni – Formigli 2011 | A. Salcuni – E. Formigli, Grandi bronzi romani dall'Italia settentrionale. Brescia, Cividate Camuno e Verona (Bonn 2011) |
| Schamper 2015 | J. Schamper, Studien zu Paraderüstungsteilen und anderen verzierten Waffen in der römischen Kaiserzeit, Kölner Studien zur Archäologie der römischen Provinzen 12 (Rahden/Westf. 2015) |
| Schönberger 1972 | H. Schönberger, Das Römerkastell Öhringen-West (Bürgkastell), BerRGK 53, 1972, 233–296 |
| Simon – Bauchhenß 1984 | LIMC II 1 (1984) 505–580 s. v. Ares/Mars (E. Simon – G. Bauchhenß) |
| Steidl 2008 | B. Steidl, Welterbe Limes – Roms Grenze am Main (Obernburg a. Main 2008) |
| Stoll 1992 | O. Stoll, Die Skulpturenausstattung römischer Militäranlagen an Rhein und Donau. Der Obergermanisch-Rätische Limes (St. Katharinen 1992) |
| Wiegels 1992 | R. Wiegels, Adnotationes Epigraphicae – Inschriftliches aus Baden-Württemberg, FuBerBadWürt 17/1, 1992, 379–404 |
| Wiegels 2000 | R. Wiegels, Lopodunum 2. Inschriften und Kultdenkmäler aus dem römischen Ladenburg am Neckar, FBerBadWürt 59 (Stuttgart 2000) |

*Martin Kemkes, Archäologisches Landesmuseum Baden-Württemberg, Zentrales Fundarchiv Rastatt, Lützowerstraße 10, 76437 Rastatt, Deutschland.*
*[e] kemkes@rastatt.alm-bw.de*

Pierre-Antoine Lamy – Christine Louvion
avec la collaboration de Marie-Laure Florent-Michel et Charlie Mairel

# SOUS L'ŒIL DE JUNON

## NOUVEAU REGARD SUR LE PROGRAMME DÉCORATIF DU SECOND FORUM DE *BAGACUM* (BAVAY, NORD)

**Abstract**
Findings of sculptured stones in the Bavay forum date from the 18th century to the most recent excavations. Amongst them are two capitals with divine busts, depicting Jupiter and Juno. Because of the importance of the capitals and their good state of preservation, this article outlines the first results by highlighting 19 of them. This smaller corpus already allows us to shed new light on the monumental decoration of the forum. By returning to the original context of these blocks, and then by proposing a series of morphological, stylistic and iconographic observations, we attribute them more precisely to the second phase of the forum, at the very end of the 2nd century AD. The cross-linking of architectural and archaeological data also permits us to situate the capitals with busts in the pronaos of the temple. It strengthens the presence of the divine couple, Jupiter in particular, in the heart of the Nervian *caput civitatis*.

Les collections lapidaires du musée du Forum antique de Bavay comprennent plus de 1640 blocs sculptés et éléments de construction. Ils ne constituent cependant qu'un maigre témoignage des ornements de la parure monumentale de la capitale de la cité des Nerviens au Haut Empire[1]. À l'exception de quelques spécimens mis au jour lors des fouilles des dernières décennies, la majorité des blocs architectoniques sont des découvertes anciennes, mal documentées ou dépourvues de contexte.

L'inventaire des collections est actuellement en cours, mais parmi les blocs de grand gabarit se distinguent d'ores et déjà une vingtaine de chapiteaux ou fragments de chapiteaux à feuillage possédant des caractéristiques stylistiques et une métrologie suffisamment homogènes pour être attribués à un même monument.

Les découvertes de lapidaire sur le forum s'étalent du XVIIIe siècle, l'époque des Oratoriens, jusqu'aux fouilles les plus récentes (2020–2021 par le Service archéologie et patrimoine du Département du Nord). Parmi les mises au jour les plus anciennes se distinguent deux chapiteaux à bustes humains dans lesquels on a rapidement reconnu Jupiter et Junon. Cependant, leur attribution au programme décoratif du forum – et à plus forte raison à l'une de ses deux phases, soit du Ier siècle apr. J.-C., soit de la fin du IIe siècle – n'a que peu été discutée jusqu'à présent. Elle n'est pas en effet évidente, dans la mesure où la majorité des blocs collectés ont été en remploi dans la fortification tardive (fin IIIe – début IVe siècle).

Notre étude en cours du lapidaire du Forum antique de Bavay s'est d'abord attachée aux chapiteaux, dont 76 sont inscrits à l'inventaire, mais dont nous avons sélectionné 19 chapiteaux corinthiens. Ce corpus plus restreint, et en majorité en meilleur état de conservation, nous permet déjà d'apporter un nouvel éclairage sur la parure monumentale du forum. En revenant au contexte d'origine de ces blocs, puis en proposant une série d'observations morphologiques, stylistiques

---

[1] Nous remercions à cette occasion Sébastien Cormier, qui a réalisé l'inventaire de la grande majorité des blocs des réserves du musée. Nous remercions aussi James Harris (Corinium Museum) pour son aimable reproduction du chapiteau de Cirencester, ainsi que Mathieu Ribolet (UMR 6298 Artehis) pour les discussions fructueuses que nous avons pu avoir au sujet du chapiteau de Junon.

et iconographiques, nous proposons plus précisément de les attribuer au temple du forum, dans une phase de reconstruction de l'ensemble monumental qui intervient à la fin du IIe siècle apr. J.-C. Mais auparavant, une recontextualisation du monument et de ses découvertes permettra au lecteur de percevoir les contours généraux de l'histoire du forum de *Bagacum Nerviorum*.

## *BAGACUM NERVIORUM*: LA VILLE ET LE FORUM

Bavay est aujourd'hui une petite ville de l'extrême nord de la France, à quelques kilomètres de la frontière belge, en zone rurale à l'écart des grands réseaux actuels de communication fluviale et routière. Depuis sa fondation à la période augustéenne jusqu'à la fin du IIIe siècle, *Bagacum Nerviorum* est le chef-lieu de la *civitas* des Nerviens. La ville, créée *ex nihilo,* doit sa prospérité au cours des deux premiers siècles de notre ère à sa situation au croisement de voies d'un intérêt stratégique et économique majeur conduisant vers la Bretagne et la Germanie (fig. 1).

Les nombreux vestiges rencontrés au gré des découvertes fortuites ou des opérations archéologiques permettent d'ébaucher la trame urbaine et d'estimer qu'elle s'étend sur environ 180 ha[2], ce qui correspond à la superficie de la ville au début du XXe siècle. En dépit des nombreuses découvertes ponctuelles révélant tous les éléments du confort urbain (hypocaustes, mosaïques, aqueduc …), l'habitat antique, masqué par la ville actuelle, reste encore très mal connu. Des indices d'activités artisanales variées (atelier de potiers, boucherie, métallurgie, travail du cuir, travail du marbre …) ont été signalés partout dans la ville. Ainsi qu'on peut s'y attendre, des nécropoles se trouvent en bordure de la ville. Il s'agit principalement de tombes en fosse, mais des stèles en pierre bleue surmontées d'ovoïdes signalent les tombes privilégiées et quelques monuments sculptés ont également dû marquer les sépultures les plus riches[3].

Si la connaissance de la ville antique reste encore très lacunaire, un des monuments clefs de la parure monumentale, le forum, est aujourd'hui bien documenté. Il a en effet concentré l'attention des amateurs d'antiquités puis des fouilleurs depuis plus de deux siècles[4]. Il s'étend sur 26 000 m², se classant ainsi parmi les plus grands forums des provinces de l'Empire. Il est également l'un des rares à être presque entièrement dégagé. Il s'inscrit dans la série bien connue des forums en trois parties disposées selon un axe longitudinal, un type de plan qui s'est imposé dans les provinces durant les Ier et IIe siècles et qu'on retrouve notamment à Augst, Avenches, Nyon, Saint-Bertrand-de-Comminges et Paris[5]. Au centre s'étend une vaste place publique d'environ 100 m par 60 m, bordée de portiques abritant des pièces probablement à vocation administrative. Le côté est fermé par une basilique. À l'ouest, l'ensemble est dominé par l'aire sacrée: une place de 49 m par 59 m, entourée sur trois côtés de portiques. À la périphérie s'alignent des boutiques ouvrant sur la rue. Le forum de Bavay présente la particularité d'avoir été ceinturé par une double enceinte durant l'Antiquité tardive, le transformant alors en réduit défensif de 2,5 ha à la fin du IIIe siècle, puis de 5 ha environ au début du siècle suivant. Cette muraille fut longtemps l'unique vestige visible, marquant la topographie du petit bourg. Comme d'autres enceintes tardives, elle a employé dans ses fondations et son soubassement des blocs de grand appareil issus du démantèlement des monuments de la ville[6]. À l'intérieur de l'espace défendu, de nouvelles constructions sont également élevées à l'aide de blocs récupérés. Ce sont ces remplois qui ont permis la conservation de la majorité des sculptures architecturales. Celles-ci sont peu nombreuses, car durant le Moyen-Âge, voire dès la fin de l'Antiquité, ces matériaux ont été à nouveau récupérés.

Après de grands dégagements qui visaient avant tout la connaissance de son architecture dans les années 1940–1950, les fouilles menées selon la méthode stratigraphique depuis la fin des

---

[2] La cartographie des vestiges recensés depuis plus d'un siècle permet de circonscrire assez précisément les contours du noyau urbain et des faubourgs qui s'étirent le long des voies.
[3] Delmaire et al. 2011; Höet-Van Cauwenberghe – Louvion 2017.
[4] Delmaire et al. 2011.
[5] Gros 1996, 220.
[6] Louvion 2019.

Sous l'œil de Junon. Nouveau regard sur le programme décoratif du second forum de *Bagacum* 519

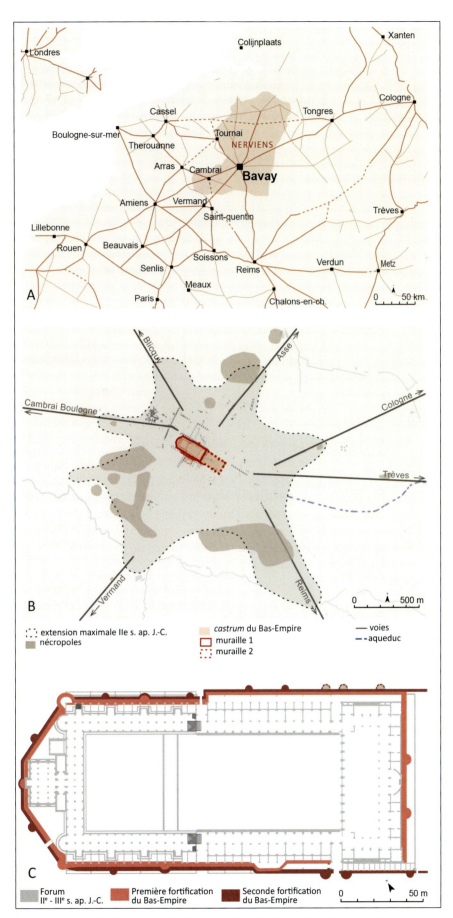

1  a) Bavay, capitale de la cité des Nerviens, b) de la ville du Haut Empire au *castrum*, c) le dernier état du forum et la fortification du Bas-Empire (C. Louvion)

années 1960 ont affiné la compréhension de l'évolution du centre monumental et ont permis de proposer un phasage chronologique fondé sur la nature des matériaux mis en œuvre et sur l'étude du mobilier[7]. Deux états ont été distingués, principalement par des techniques de construction différentes. Au premier état, les murs en petit appareil de moellons de calcaire bleu et de grès vert sont liés par un mortier jaune; tandis qu'au second état, des arases de briques alternent avec des moellons liés par un mortier de tuileau rose. Dans ces deux états, le monument conserve la même emprise, bien que la totalité des élévations ait été reconstruite.

**La première phase du forum**

La construction du premier forum débute vers le milieu du I$^{er}$ siècle apr. J.-C. L'édification des bâtiments est totalement achevée à la fin du siècle. Sans nous attarder sur le détail du plan, soulignons que de part et d'autre de la place, face à la basilique à trois nefs de plan canonique, s'élevait le temple, isolé au milieu de l'aire sacrée. Nous ne connaissons que son massif de fondation d'environ 32 m par 22 m$^8$. L'aire sacrée est entourée par un triple portique supporté par un cryptoportique; à l'arrière de sa branche occidentale se greffe une grande salle quadrangulaire, dont la fonction, à cet état, reste énigmatique. À défaut d'identification, on dénomme ce bâtiment »édifice occidental«. Comme les trois branches du portique, cette grande salle est élevée sur un cryptoportique.

On ne connaît de la sculpture ornementale de cet état que de très petits fragments découverts dans des remblais ou dans le blocage des maçonneries du second état de construction.

**La deuxième phase du forum**

À la suite d'un incendie, le premier forum est entièrement détruit; ce qu'il en reste est méthodiquement démonté. La reconstruction entreprise dans la foulée conserve ses dispositions générales et son emprise originelle. De part et d'autre de l'esplanade, les portiques et les salles sont bâties en profitant partiellement des fondations antérieures. Mais la basilique de plan canonique est remplacée par une cour entourée par un triple portique abritant un système complexe de pièces. Cette situation singulière trahit probablement une impossibilité de mener le projet de reconstruction à son terme.

Une autre transformation majeure intervient sur l'aire sacrée: le temple n'occupe plus le centre de l'espace. Un dallage continu recouvre l'ancienne fondation. Selon toute vraisemblance, le nouveau temple s'élève à l'arrière de la branche occidentale du portique, à la place de l'édifice occidental. En sous-sol, la structure des cryptoportiques est renforcée par des voûtes d'arêtes, imposant la construction de nouveaux supports.

La datation de l'incendie, et partant, le terminus pour la reconstruction du second forum, reposent sur un important dépôt de terre sigillée comportant 168 estampilles correspondant, selon Geoff Dannell, aux années autour de 185. On dispose également dans une couche de destruction d'un denier de Commode émis en 192. Les briques des élévations ont fait l'objet d'une analyse archéo-magnétique datant leur cuisson dans l'intervalle de 190 à 230[9].

## LE DÉCOR ARCHITECTONIQUE DU FORUM

**Des Oratoriens au musée, en passant par Douai**

Les découvertes de blocs décorés sur le forum sont loin d'être uniquement le fruit des mises au jour récentes. En réalité, elles datent même, pour une partie de la série A, que nous présentons

---

[7] Hanoune – Muller 1996; Thollard 1997; Thollard – Denimal 1998; Deru et al. 2019.
[8] Thollard 1997, 119.
[9] Deru et al. 2019.

2   Les blocs découverts au XVIIIe siècle, disposés dans le jardin des Oratoriens; aquarelle d'Antoine Niveleau, 1830 (de: Niveleau 1830, Bl. de l'Institut de France Ms 3799–3800)

plus bas, de l'Ancien Régime. Dans la partie orientale du site actuel s'installe, au XVIIe siècle, un couvent appartenant à la congrégation des Oratoriens. En 1716, c'est sur cette emprise – et donc celle du forum – qu'est exhumée une inscription commémorant le passage de Tibère à *Bagacum* en 4 apr. J.-C.[10], inscription malheureusement détruite depuis. Au cours du même siècle, si ce n'est dans la même décennie, parmi d'autres éléments, on retiendra surtout la découverte d'au moins quatre chapiteaux[11] réalisés dans un style comparable, dont deux chapiteaux à buste, l'un féminin et l'autre masculin (décrits plus bas). Deux faits sont à noter: d'une part le contexte présumé de mise au jour de ces blocs, puisque la propriété de la congrégation, circonscrite par les vestiges de la muraille du Bas-Empire, s'étendait sur toute la longueur du forum. Le collège et les bâtiments conventuels s'élevaient sur la basilique; dans les jardins, en plus du mobilier régulièrement mis au jour, le dallage en pierre bleue de l'aire sacrée et de l'esplanade ainsi que nombre de murs avaient déjà été observés, donnant lieu à des interprétations fantasques[12]. D'autre part, il faut noter l'intérêt que portent les religieux à ces découvertes qui, bien qu'elles ne donnent pas lieu à de véritables fouilles, sont sujet au moins à une mise en scène dont témoigne une aquarelle du XIXe siècle (fig. 2). Précisons toutefois qu'il n'est pas possible d'identifier précisément chaque bloc qu'elle représente, tant son auteur a adopté une approche picturale de ce qui s'offrait à son regard.

Au tournant du siècle suivant, on suppose qu'une partie au moins des blocs des Oratoriens passe sous la propriété d'Augustin Carlier, curé de Bavay et amateur éclairé. Sa collection est partiellement acquise par la ville de Douai en 1833, pour venir enrichir le petit musée local[13] – la ville de Bavay elle-même n'ayant pas de musée en propre avant 1906. Le 11 août 1944, un bombardement sur la ville touche durement le musée, et de nombreuses pièces sont irrémédia-

---

[10] CIL XIII 3570; premières mentions: Delewarde 1718, 31; Caylus 1756, 400.

[11] Masse 1731, 7; Delmaire et al. 2011, 99. On pourrait en dénombrer au moins 8, sur la base du dépôt du Service archéologique de la Ville de Douai: Forum antique de Bavay inv. DA 718. 723. 724c. 724g. 725d. 725g. 727. À ces 7 blocs doit être ajouté le chapiteau à buste de Jupiter, détruit en 1944.

[12] D'abord identifiés au palais d'un roi mythique, les vestiges ont ensuite été interprétés comme ceux d'un cirque ou de thermes. Delmaire et al. 2011, 100; Beirnaert-Mary 2018, 184–186.

[13] Demolon – Labourdette 2013, 72–75.

blement perdues: si le chapiteau dit de Junon subit des éclats – notamment une crosse totalement détruite –, il ne reste rien de l'autre chapiteau, à figure masculine. Entre 1976 et 1994, la ville de Douai met en dépôt au musée de Bavay huit chapiteaux, dont les quatre certainement attribués à l'époque des Oratoriens.

## Des contextes de découverte incertains

Les découvertes de blocs architectoniques au cours du XXe siècle n'ont pas forcément été mieux documentées qu'aux siècles précédents. Il faut le plus souvent faire appel aux photographies de fouille ou d'ambiance pour tenter d'identifier les trouvailles, qui ont rarement fait l'objet de mention dans les comptes-rendus ou les rapports, sauf lorsqu'il s'agissait de blocs portant des inscriptions. On trouvera en Annexe 1 un tableau récapitulatif des blocs mentionnés ci-après et ayant fait l'objet de notre étude.

Des fragments de chapiteaux ont été exhumés lors des grands dégagements entrepris après les bombardements de 1940 (2014.0.188, 201.0.1160) ou ceux réalisés dans les années 1980 (201.0.183). Ils proviennent de niveaux recouvrant la place de l'aire sacrée ou du comblement des cryptoportiques. Dans les rares secteurs épargnés par les pillages postérieurs à l'Antiquité, les fondations et le soubassement des enceintes du Bas-Empire ont livré des blocs sculptés plus ou moins mutilés par leur remploi, mais on ne peut préciser si des chapiteaux des ensembles que nous considérons ici en sont issus.

Même si la provenance de certaines pièces reste incertaine, il est assuré que la majeure partie du lot étudié a été exhumée dans des parcelles où s'élevait le forum. Certes, la construction des enceintes tardives autour du forum a fait converger vers le site des matériaux récupérés sur les constructions les plus diverses de la ville et des nécropoles, mais nous soutenons que les éléments étudiés appartiennent bien au décor du forum, comme nous allons le développer par la suite.

## Les chapiteaux à buste

Parmi les découvertes des religieux, un chapiteau à buste féminin attire d'abord l'attention[14]. Il s'agit plus précisément du sommet d'un chapiteau engagé[15]. Avec lui, un chapiteau à buste masculin a également été mis au jour, vraisemblablement Jupiter, qui fut malheureusement détruit dans le bombardement du musée de Douai en 1944 (fig. 3).

Le chapiteau conservé est en calcaire tendre, d'un type qu'on ne retrouve pas localement. Il mesure en l'état 51,5 cm de haut, pour une largeur de 62 cm et une profondeur de 64,5 cm. Le buste féminin est haut de 41 cm, large de 27 cm et profond de 17,5 cm. Souvenir du bombardement, la crosse droite est entièrement arrachée. L'absence du nez est cependant ancienne, car on observe son négatif déjà sur les clichés d'archive; il était vraisemblablement rapporté, à en juger par la mortaise subsistante. Le style est corinthien, avec un décor d'une file de feuilles obliques soutenue par des crosses à »Fiederblatt«. Les crosses et les hélices, supposées derrière le buste, sont dissimulées par des calices à lobes d'acanthe découpés en cinq digitations lancéolées autour d'un fort creusement. Pour atteindre le chapiteau complet, on doit restituer un second bloc inférieur avec deux couronnes d'acanthes, au-dessus d'un astragale. La déesse Junon est reconnaissable à son voile – insigne des femmes mariées – et surtout à son sceptre. Celui-ci indique son rang supérieur et pourrait même figurer un coucou, quoique très lacunaire, à son extrémité. L'expression est travaillée dans le sens d'une extrême sévérité: légèrement penchée, le buste domine le spectateur et lui jette un regard tenant de la *fulgor oculorum*.

---

[14] Delewarde 1718, 31–32. 42–43; Masse 1731, 25–28 (transcription L. Lemaire, 1912); Caylus 1756, 400; De Bast 1813, 11. 18. 20; Niveleau 1830, 82–83; Derbigny 1837/1838, 457; Bollard-Raineau – Louvion 2012, 17–29; Beirnaert-Mary 2015; Fellague 2017, 134; Beirnaert-Mary 2018.

[15] Comme pour de nombreux blocs sculptés de cette série, il s'agit d'un dépôt du Service archéologique de la Ville de Douai: Forum antique de Bavay inv. DA 724C.

3   Proposition de restitution des chapiteaux à bustes de Junon (mutilé) et Jupiter (disparu), sur double couronne d'acanthes (DAO M.-L. Florent et P.-A. Lamy, 2022)

Pour ce qui concerne le chapiteau de Jupiter, il est documenté par les photos d'avant-guerre du Musée de Douai, qui permettent de saisir les contours généraux de la figure humaine. Nous choisissons, plutôt que de reproduire ces photos d'archive, d'en proposer un dessin de restitution (fig. 3). Le dieu porte une barbe bifide, dont les boucles en coquilles remontent sur la mâchoire en deux rangées. La moustache bien fournie suggère une bouche esquissant une moue. Les cheveux sont également bouclés, avec la frange frontale relevée. Les oreilles ne sont pas apparentes et l'arrière de la tête est relativement lisse – sans pour autant que l'on puisse conclure à un bonnet. L'expression paraît sévère, à en juger par les sourcils plutôt froncés et le regard suggéré par le percement des pupilles, dans une exécution très semblable au regard de Junon. Pour le reste du corps, on croit reconnaître une tunique à col en V épais, bien que le vêtement semble épouser le corps à la manière d'une cuirasse. On le croirait d'autant que l'épaule gauche est recouverte d'un manteau dont émerge un sceptre, au milieu des plissés plus ou moins ondulés.

Un examen même rapide du décor et des parties figurées de ces deux chapiteaux amène à affirmer qu'ils étaient conçus comme une paire. Jupiter seul aurait pu être reconnaissable à son sceptre, avec prudence, mais dans ce contexte d'association avec la déesse, il y a peu de doute sur l'identification du couple divin.

Les premiers éléments de style que l'on relève – enroulements des mèches, yeux percés au regard très appuyé, coiffure féminine pouvant évoquer la mode tardo-antonine – amènent à proposer très largement une datation au moins dans la seconde moitié du IIe siècle apr. J.-C.

**Trois ensembles de chapiteaux**

Exception faite du chapiteau perdu de Jupiter, le Forum antique de Bavay conserve au moins 19 blocs issus de chapiteaux corinthiens que l'on peut désormais mettre en série. Il sont tous engagés; 6 sont des chapiteaux d'angle et un seul est complet, car tous les autres représentent soit la partie basse – de l'astragale à la première ou deuxième couronne de la corbeille, selon l'état de conservation –, soit la partie haute, du sommet du caulicole à l'abaque (Annexe 1). La catégorisation qui suit repose sur des critères de style d'exécution des décors, mais ne doit pas masquer que la composition d'ensemble de leurs décors est similaire dans les trois catégories. À partir des blocs et fragments disponibles, selon leur état de conservation, on peut ainsi décrire sommairement la composition-type, de bas en haut:

- astragale à perles et pirouettes, plus ou moins écrasées
- première couronne d'acanthes molles avec folioles affrontées à cinq digitations; même nombre pour les feuilles, bien distinctes par une triple nervure axiale

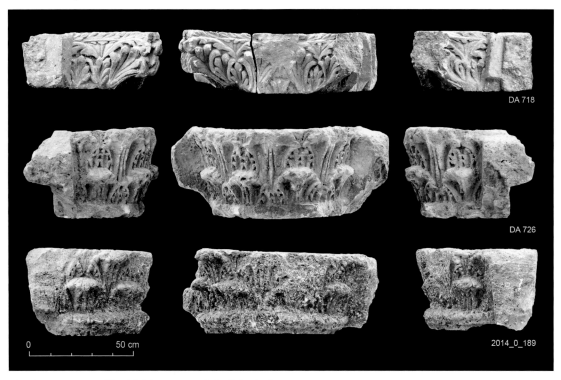

4   Le sous-ensemble A1 (photogrammétrie C. Mairel)

- deuxième couronne avec disposition alternée mais identique
- partie supérieure avec des calices composés des mêmes feuilles que celles des corbeilles, enroulées en faible relief à leur extrémité; à noter le calathos décoré d'une feuille à retombée très peu saillante; feuilles qui recouvrent complètement les crosses et les hélices
- abaque décoré d'un motif d'épis affrontés de part et d'autre du bourgeon axial.

Ensemble A

Avant la prise en compte des arguments métrologiques, cette première série nous est apparue pertinente par l'approche stylistique des décors (figs. 4. 5). Malgré de petites différences de traitement selon les blocs et selon les faces, on observe globalement:
- lobes creusés en ogives et découpe en douceur des digitations, épaisses – presque boudinées – et bien distinctes les unes des autres par des rainures appuyées
- émergeant des calices et dans le calathos, entre les feuilles de la deuxième rangée: des tiges et retombées de folioles plus rapidement exécutées, et en faible relief par rapport aux parties inférieures; on verrait là une nécessité de remplissage de l'espace de même qu'une approche en plusieurs plans.

Au sein de cette première série, regroupée pour les arguments que nous venons de voir, il faut cependant distinguer au moins deux sous-groupes.

On peut théoriquement reconstituer deux chapiteaux complets, par arguments métrologiques: les parties supérieures DA 718 et DA 723 peuvent tout à fait couronner les parties inférieures DA 726 et DA 719, ou inversement. De mêmes dimensions à quelques centimètres près – selon la qualité de conservation –, ces blocs associés forment des chapiteaux à trois rangées d'acanthes et de 72 à 75 cm de hauteur[16]. C'est la proportion que nous retrouvons pour le chapiteau complet DA 727, haut de 74 cm. Deux autres blocs de sections inférieures – 2014.0.189 et bloc sans nu-

---

[16] Les différences observables sur les estimations, très larges, des dimensions des lits d'attente et de pose ne nous paraissent pas suffisantes pour invalider cette hypothèse.

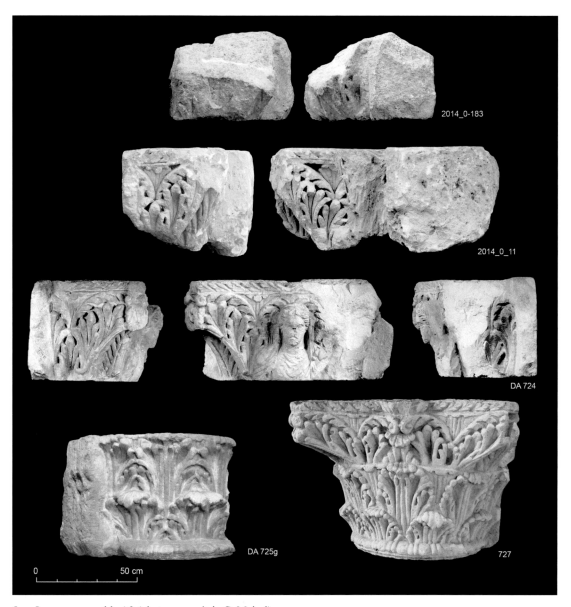

5  Le sous-ensemble A2 (photogrammétrie C. Mairel)

méro – correspondent à cette proportion, mais n'ont pas leur équivalent pour la partie supérieure. Par commodité, on désignera ce sous-ensemble par A.1.

En effet, le troisième bloc restant, DA 725G, relève d'un autre module. Il comprend deux rangées d'acanthes inférieures, est haut de 59 cm, avec des rangées de 26 et 25 cm de hauteur, soit un module de 150 % environ par rapport aux chapiteaux précédents. Répondent à cela deux parties supérieures: le bloc 2014.0.11 et le chapiteau de Junon, DA 724. En associant ces deux sections, on restitue un chapiteau d'environ 110 cm de haut. On désigne ce second sous-ensemble comme A.2.

Ces associations ne sont pas possibles en l'état pour les autres blocs de ce premier ensemble, au vu des difficultés liées à leur conservation ou à la prise de mesures suffisamment précises.

Ensemble B

L'ensemble B reprend le même schéma global que l'ensemble A. Il s'en distingue toutefois, déjà par le style d'exécution (fig. 6), qu'on pourrait résumer par une approche en surface et très graphique, contrairement à un travail en plans et en profondeur comme vu précédemment, ce qui n'est pas sans évoquer la manière d'aborder un chapiteau de placage. Dans le détail, on relèvera

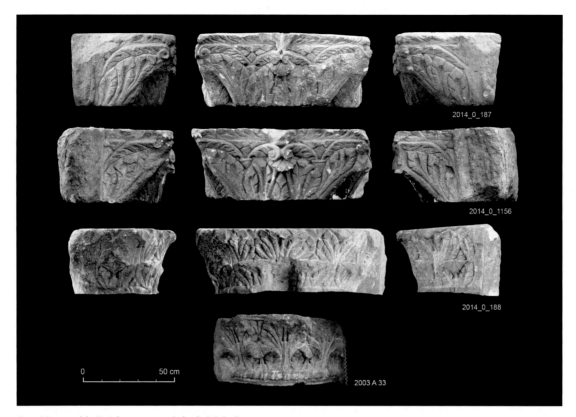

6  L'ensemble B (photogrammétrie C. Mairel)

la découpe des feuilles plutôt que leur travail en modelé ainsi que les digitations légèrement pointues. Répondent à cette description:
- les blocs inférieurs 2003 A 33, 2014.0.188 et 2014.0.1160
- les blocs supérieurs 2014.0.42, 2014.0.187 et 2014.0.1156.

À noter pour ces trois derniers blocs la présence, sur le lit d'attente, de cadres servant de repères pour la taille et/ou pour l'ajustement des blocs supérieurs. Aucune observation comparable n'a été faite sur les autres ensembles.

Pour ce qui est du module de cet ensemble B, les associations des blocs inférieurs et supérieurs restituent des hauteurs totales comprises entre 72 cm au minimum et 77 cm au maximum, ce qui ne manque pas de rappeler les proportions du sous-ensemble A.1, hauteur totale comme hauteurs respectives des tores, rangées d'acanthes, voire jusqu'au réglet.

## Ensemble C

Le bloc 2014.0.43, certainement retaillé à partir d'un bloc de partie supérieure – on reconnaît le calice découpé en palme – se distingue des ensembles précédents par le traitement des digitations, effilées à la pointe, et par l'absence de décor du calathos. Ces caractéristiques pourraient rattacher le chapiteau dont il est issu à une variante sur le modèle-type décrit en préambule. Son état de conservation ne permet pas de suggérer son module et on s'en tiendra à le voir comme un cas unique, dans l'état actuel des connaissances sur la collection lapidaire.

## LA PARURE DU SECOND TEMPLE?

### Datation des ensembles

Les comparaisons stylistiques et iconographiques entre la série A et ce qui est actuellement connu du corpus gallo-romain ne sont pas très nombreuses, et force est de constater qu'aucun parallèle direct à l'échelle de la *civitas* des Nerviens ne nous est apparu pertinent. On notera justement la faible représentation des chapiteaux à buste en série et engagés dans le nord-est des Gaules, alors que la majorité correspond à des colonnes libres, supportant parfois un groupe statuaire[17]. La nature du corpus des chapiteaux étudiés ici exclut cette possibilité et fait entrevoir la décoration d'un édifice complet.

Nous suggérons d'insérer l'ensemble A dans un cadre typologique bien représenté à l'échelle des provinces occidentales et dont un représentant, peut-être parmi les plus anciens, pourrait être le chapiteau J219 du Musée de Sens (Yonne)[18]: on retrouve l'agencement des couronnes d'acanthe, avec notamment le creusement en ogive des folioles, bien découpées et à cinq digitations, ainsi que la triple nervure. L'état de conservation de ce chapiteau ne permet pas d'observer la partie supérieure, notamment le traitement du calice. L'horizon chronologique est au moins dans la deuxième moitié du IIe siècle de notre ère, si l'on met en relation l'ensemble A avec les découvertes du Vieil-Evreux, plus précisément le chapiteau no. 32, publié par Véronique Brunet-Gaston[19]. C'est la même approche du creusement des folioles qu'on observe pour un chapiteau découvert dans la rue Liffol-le-Grand à Grand (Vosges), étudié par Yvan Maligorne, bien qu'il s'agisse dans ce cas d'un chapiteau composite[20]. Mêmes observations d'ensemble enfin pour le type A des IIe et IIIe siècles, développé par Dominique Tardy pour Saintes (Charente-Maritime)[21]. Mais on trouve également des parallèles à l'ensemble A de Bavay en dehors des provinces gauloises. La typologie de Heinz Kähler, bien qu'assez ancienne, nous permet de l'insérer largement dans le type D des IIe et IIIe siècles apr. J.-C.: d'abord par un degré de foisonnement végétal supérieur au type C, mais aussi par le creusement très appuyé en cuillère – ou en ogive – des folioles. L'ensemble bavaisien trouve alors des équivalents à Trèves[22], mais aussi dans un exemplaire de Wiesbaden, où l'on retrouve une conception comparable de la partie supérieure – crosses et abaque en particulier[23].

Dans la catégorie des chapiteaux à buste, on pense en premier lieu à la colonne de Merten (Moselle), support d'un Jupiter à l'anguipède et dont le chapiteau comporte les bustes des quatre saisons[24]. Les deux couronnes d'acanthe y sont encore similaires à l'ensemble A et aux parallèles que nous venons de citer. On pourrait aussi, très prudemment, voir un lien dans le travail des figures humaines, au moins par la recherche d'expressivité et le fort creusement de la bouche, avec ses commissures basses; mais le modelé de la colonne de Merten accuse un travail en rondeur, là où le couple divin de Bavay a été traité avec une approche nettement plus linéaire et découpée – drapés et chevelure en particulier. La meilleure comparaison, qui permet de lier le décor végétal et la représentation humaine, demeure celle que l'on peut établir avec un chapiteau corinthien à quatre bustes, provenant de Cirencester (Gloucestershire, Angleterre), daté de la fin du IIe siècle et début du IIIe siècle apr. J.-C.[25] (fig. 7). Les rapprochements s'imposent déjà pour les

---

[17] En particulier des groupes du type Jupiter à l'anguipède: Noelke 2006.
[18] Haut. 62 cm; diam. 58 cm; Musée de Sens inv. J219; lupa 27721. À rattacher probablement au type C de Kähler.
[19] Musée d'Art, Histoire et Archéologie d'Evreux inv. 11610; Brunet-Gaston 1997, 109–110. 118–19 no. 32 pl. 2. L'auteure regroupe dans le même horizon des IIe–IIIe s. également les chapiteaux nos. 29 et 30, mais le parallèle le plus évident nous paraît être avec le no. 32.
[20] Maligorne 2016, 108 fig. 13.
[21] Tardy 1989, 73–76 fig. 37–38.
[22] Kähler 1939, pl. 3, D1; pl. 4, D9.
[23] Kähler 1939, pl. 4, D21 = O4.
[24] Reis 2012 (avec bibliographie); Metz, Musée de la Cour d'Or inv. 2012.0.126; Espérandieu no. 4425; lupa 31731.
[25] Calcaire oolitique, haut. 1,06 m, diam. inf. 0,59 m/sup. 1,02 m. Corinium Museum inv. A348. Henig 1993, 8–9 no. 18 pl. 5-6-7 (avec bibliographie); von Mercklin 1962, 178–179 no. 431 fig. 834–837.

7   Chapiteau à quatre divinités de Cirencester (Gloucestershire, Angleterre), fin II<sup>e</sup>–début III<sup>e</sup> siècle apr. J.-C.; Corinium Museum inv. A348 (Henig 1993, 8–9 no. 18 pl. 5-6-7, cliché J. Harris, Corinium Museum)

couronnes inférieures lorsqu'on les compare aux blocs DA 725d et 725g, avec non seulement un agencement global très similaire, mais aussi la manière de traiter les digitations dans l'épaisseur. On relève aussi des similitudes sur le traitement du visage: yeux grands ouverts et bien cernés, bouche esquissant une moue, aux commissures percées d'un coup de trépan. Sans qu'il s'agisse nécessairement du travail d'un même atelier, ces points nous amènent à suggérer une proximité chronologique entre le chapiteau de Cirencester et les deux chapiteaux à buste de Bavay.

De cette mise en série, nous pouvons déduire le rattachement de l'ensemble A à la seconde phase du forum, en proposant une datation pour leur réalisation au plus tôt dans les années 190 de notre ère, si ce n'est au démarrage du siècle suivant. Nous rappelions plus haut en effet les arguments de datation pour cette phase que sont le denier de Commode de 192 et l'important lot de céramiques fournissant le *terminus* de 185, présents dans les couches de destruction, ainsi que l'intervalle 190–230 de cuisson des briques. En suivant ce raisonnement, le programme décoratif de cette phase serait un cas fiable de réalisation du début de la dynastie sévérienne. Reste à déterminer l'emplacement, et donc par déduction la fonction de ce programme.

**Une proposition de restitution**

Une restitution architecturale du forum a été proposée sous la forme de maquette numérique dans le cadre du projet »Cyberforum« en 2004. Ce projet visait à doter le musée d'un outil de médiation permettant de présenter une synthèse des données architecturales connues du second forum. Un conseil scientifique a suivi et validé cette restitution, à laquelle des modifications ont été régulièrement apportées au gré des campagnes de fouille ou de restauration. Le modèle numérique, qui combine l'existant et la restitution, a été conçu avec les logiciels AutoCAD et AutoCAD

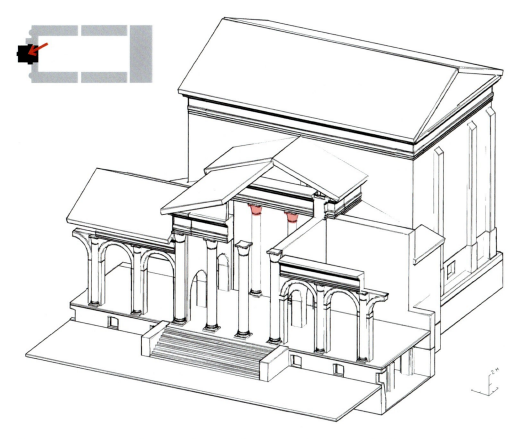

8   Proposition de restitution du pronaos du temple du forum sévérien, au centre de la branche occidentale du portique de l'aire sacrée et hypothèse de localisation des chapiteaux à buste de Jupiter et Junon (C. Louvion)

map 3D. Il est constitué d'un assemblage d'unités construites en volumes (murs, supports, arcs, voûtes, sols, toiture sauf charpentes) à la façon d'un modèle d'informations architecturales[26].

Le plan du dernier état de construction du forum ne pose pas de problème majeur. En revanche, pour la restitution des élévations, à défaut d'argument *in situ*, on s'est appuyé sur la collection de chapiteaux de colonnes engagées dont il est ici question. On avait admis que toutes ces pièces découvertes sur le forum présentaient des caractéristiques suffisamment homogènes pour supposer qu'elles appartenaient à un même monument, ce qui semble confirmer les prémisses de l'étude que nous livrons ici.

En raison de leur iconographie particulière, les chapiteaux à buste ont trouvé logiquement leur place dans le temple que l'on situe, pour cet état de construction, dans le grand édifice rectangulaire greffé au milieu de la branche occidentale du portique de l'aire sacrée (fig. 8). La hauteur du chapiteau à buste de Junon et le diamètre supérieur de sa colonne avaient été estimés respectivement à 112 cm et 109 cm par Eugen von Mercklin[27], des dimensions quasiment identiques à celles que nous pouvons déduire de l'association des blocs du sous-ensemble A2 (110 cm). Si le diamètre inférieur de la colonne équivaut à la hauteur du chapiteau, et si la hauteur de la colonne vaut dix fois cette mesure[28], on peut proposer environ 11 m pour les colonnes du pronaos.

On a supposé que les autres chapiteaux engagés appartenaient aux portiques de l'aire sacrée ou de l'esplanade. En se fondant sur un chapiteau complet (DA 727), haut de 74 cm, et des hauteurs comprises entre 72 et 77 cm pour les éléments associés au sein des sous-ensembles A1 et B, une

---

[26] Deru et al. 2019.
[27] von Mercklin 1962, 107.
[28] Gros 2001, 497.

| ensemble | no. d'inv. | localisation | type | hauteur (en cm) | largeur | profondeur | diam. restitué lit de pose | diam. restitué lit d'attente | hauteur tore | hauteur rangée acanthes 1 | hauteur rangée acanthes 2 | hauteur rangée acanthes 3 | hauteur réglet |
|---|---|---|---|---|---|---|---|---|---|---|---|---|---|
| A.1 | DA 719 | Réserves | chapiteau engagé (inf.) | 43 | NM | 57 | env. 75 | env. 90 | 9 | 15 | 19 | – | – |
| A.1 | DA 726 | Réserves | chapiteau engagé (inf.) | 43 | 101 | 59 | 52 | 70 | NM | NM | – | – | – |
| A.1 | 2014.0.189 | Réserves | chapiteau engagé (inf.) | 42 | 95 | 52 | 66 | 90 | 11 | 16 | 15 | – | – |
| A.1 | sans no. | Réserves | chapiteau, quart (inf.) | 44,5 | 60 | 60 | NM | NM | 10 | 18 | 16,5 | – | – |
| A.1 | DA 723 | Réserves | chapiteau engagé (sup.) | 32 | 89 | 42 | NM | NM | – | – | – | NM | NM |
| A.1 | DA 718 | Réserves | chapiteau engagé (sup.) | 29 | 87 | 59 | 66 | env. 100 | – | – | – | 16 | env. 4 |
| A.2 | DA 725 G | Musée – salle 1 | chapiteau d'angle (inf.) | 59 | 68 | 72 | 96 | 120 | 8 | 26 | 25 | – | – |
| A.2 | 2014.0.11 | Réserves | chapiteau d'angle (sup.) | 52 | 111 | 60 | NM | env. 90 | – | – | 24 | 17 | NM |
| A.2 | DA 724 | Musée – salle 1 | chapiteau engagé (sup.) à buste de Junon | 52 | 103 | 62 | 76 | – | – | – | – | – | 6 |
| A.1 (?) | DA 721 | détruit, anciennement à Douai | chapiteau engagé (sup.) à buste de Jupiter | – | – | – | – | – | – | – | – | – | – |
| A | B13 | Réserves | chapiteau d'angle (mutilé) | 44 | 67 | 42 | NM | – | – | 24 | – | – | – |
| A (?) | DA 722 | non retrouvé, anciennement à Douai | chapiteau engagé (inf.) | NM | NM | NM | NM | NM | NM | NM | NM | NM | NM |
| A2 | 2014.0.183 | Réserves | chapiteau engagé (sup.) | 42 | 62 | 58 | env. 60 (?) | NM | – | – | – | NM | NM |
| A | DA 727 | Musée – salle 1 | chapiteau engagé (complet) | 74 | 106 | 53 | 66 | NM | 9 | 16 | 23 | 23 | 6 |
| B | 2003 A 33 | Musée – salle 1 | chapiteau d'angle (inf.) | 38 | 54 | 58 | 66 | 84 | 9 | 15 | 16 | – | – |
| B | 2014.0.188 | Réserves | chapiteau d'angle (inf.) | 35 | 105 | 57 | NM | env. 80 | 9 | 15 | 17 | – | – |
| B | 2014.0.1160 | Réserves | chapiteau d'angle (inf.) | NM | NM | NM | NM | NM | NM | NM | NM | – | – |
| B | 2014.0.1156 | Réserves | chapiteau engagé (sup.) | 39 | 97 | 60 | 64 | env. 80 | – | – | – | 18 | 6 |
| B | 2014.0.187 | Réserves | chapiteau engagé (sup.) | 39 | 96 | 58 | NM | NM | – | – | – | 19 | 6 |
| B | 2014.0.42 | Réserves | chapiteau engagé (sup.) | 37 | 58 | 52 (restitué) | NM | NM | – | – | – | NM | NM |
| C | 2014.0.43 | Réserves | chapiteau de pilastre (mutilé) | 39 (d'origine) | 45 | 49 | NM | retaillé sur 5 cm env. de haut | – | – | 19 | – | – |

hauteur de 7,40 m a été restituée pour les colonnes engagées et les pilastres des portiques. Un argument métrologique susceptible de corroborer cette hypothèse se trouve dans les piliers maçonnés du portique de l'esplanade. Ceux-ci présentent sur leurs faces externes des tablettes devant supporter les bases des demi-colonnes; ces tablettes mesuraient 0,55 m de profondeur et 1,20 m de large. Sur leurs faces internes, sont adossés des pilastres larges de 0,74 m.

En conséquence de ces observations, il nous paraît pertinent de maintenir l'association des chapiteaux à bustes de Junon et Jupiter avec le temple de ce second forum. En effet, on s'attend aux proportions les plus hautes pour le pronaos, aux plus basses pour les portiques; l'inverse n'est pas envisageable. Mais nous souscrivons également à l'observation d'Yvan Maligorne concernant le choix de l'iconographie en lien avec la destination du monument, une dialectique qu'il a particulièrement mis en lumière pour Vienne (Isère)[29], sans toutefois en déduire prématurément que le temple poliade serait bien dédié à Jupiter et Junon.

**La place des divinités**

Il s'agit bien de procéder par étapes analytiques, et cette première considération de la présence de Jupiter et Junon, au moins dans la parure monumentale du second forum de *Bagacum*, vient de fait exclure la possibilité d'un troisième chapiteau à buste, de Minerve cette fois-ci, afin de réunir les membres de la triade capitoline. En effet, on ne s'explique pas comment une colonnade axée et par multiple de 2 viendrait intercaler une troisième figure sans rompre la symétrie.

Cette faible probabilité du culte de la triade capitoline sur le forum de *Bagacum* est d'ailleurs renforcée par la vision d'ensemble des cités de Gaule Belgique, où globalement les attestations de la triade se rencontrent peu hors des colonies[30], ce que n'est pas, sauf preuve du contraire, la capitale des Nerviens[31]. Cette considération d'ensemble est précisée par les données de la thèse d'Audrey Ferlut[32]. Celle-ci relève, pour la Belgique et les deux Germanies, la présence de Junon sur 193 reliefs et 161 inscriptions, dont 157 reliefs et 142 inscriptions pour la seule Germanie Supérieure, ce qui doit pondérer l'interprétation. Sur le total des inscriptions, 80 % lui donnent l'épiclèse *Regina* – qu'on retrouve avec le sceptre du chapiteau de Bavay – et 84 % l'associent à Jupiter Optimus Maximus. Pour Minerve, sur 43 inscriptions recensées dans les mêmes provinces – et avec la même prééminence de la Germanie Supérieure –, seules 7 l'associent à Jupiter et Junon, tandis que 50 % des 209 reliefs dénombrés l'associent à Junon, mais surtout sur les pierres à quatre divinités. L'auteure conclut donc, à partir de cette répartition, à une faible représentation de la triade capitoline dans les trois provinces citées[33]. Plus récemment encore, le recensement de Florian Blanchard est parvenu à une conclusion similaire, mais étendue à toutes les provinces de Gaule romaine[34]. Cependant, il relève un fait important: la raréfaction progressive de Minerve au profit du seul couple Jupiter – Junon, dans les Germanies et les Champs Décumates à partir du milieu du IIe siècle de notre ère et essentiellement en contexte militaire[35]. Ce n'est certes pas le cas du Forum de Bavay, du moins pas encore. Mais cette mise en perspective de l'ensemble de la Gaule du Nord-Est nous semble un argument supplémentaire pour rejeter l'hypothèse d'une présence de la triade sur le forum, à tout le moins dans son décor architectonique.

---

[29] Maligorne 2016, 323.
[30] Raepsaet-Charlier 2009, 328; Blanchard 2014, 182.
[31] Plin. nat. 4, 106.
[32] Ferlut 2011, 142–150.
[33] Ferlut 2011, 150.
[34] Blanchard 2014. Voir également sur le sujet de Jupiter: Blanchard 2015.
[35] Blanchard 2014, 187–192.

## CONCLUSION

À nouveau, on doit rappeler que cette étude partielle constitue le démarrage d'un programme plus large d'inventaire analytique du lapidaire conservé au Forum antique de Bavay, dont une partie reste même à inventorier, du fait notamment des opérations d'archéologie préventive les plus récentes. Nous considérons cependant avoir avancé sur deux sujets importants pour l'histoire du forum de la capitale des Nerviens.

D'une part, nous avons identifié ici les chapiteaux relatifs à la deuxième phase du centre monumental, avec deux ensembles principaux. Ceux-ci relevant de deux modules distincts, nous les associons au pronaos du temple, pour le plus grand, et au portique – peut-être plus précisément celui de l'*area sacra* – pour le plus petit.

D'autre part, nous avons lié les figures de Jupiter et de Junon à cette parure monumentale. Si nous soulignons l'improbabilité de la présence de Minerve au temple du forum, nous croyons nécessaire de rappeler l'importance de Jupiter Optimus Maximus en renvoyant à un autel qui lui est dédié, enfoui vraisemblablement après la fin du Ier siècle apr. J.-C. dans un édifice rectangulaire juste au sud du forum[36].

## BIBLIOGRAPHIE

| | |
|---|---|
| Beirnaert-Mary 2015 | V. Beirnaert-Mary, Les enjeux des débuts de l'archéologie locale dans le nord de la France à Bavay (Master 2 Université Lille III Charles-de-Gaulle 2015) |
| Beirnaert-Mary 2018 | V. Beirnaert-Mary (dir.), Curieux antiquaires: les débuts de l'archéologie à Bavay aux XVIIIe et XIXe siècles. Catalogue d'exposition Forum antique de Bavay 07.02.–27.08.2019 (Gand 2018) |
| Blanchard 2014 | F. Blanchard, La triade capitoline, ses lieux de culte et ses divinités en Gaule romaine, dans: R. Bedon (dir.), Confinia. Confins et périphéries dans l'Occident romain. Actes du colloque de Limoges, octobre 2012, Caesarodunum 44–46 (Limoges 2014) 157–192 |
| Blanchard 2015 | F. Blanchard, Jupiter dans les Gaules et les Germanies. Du Capitole au cavalier à l'anguipède (Rennes 2015) |
| Bollard-Raineau – Louvion 2012 | I. Bollard-Raineau – C. Louvion, Les décors du forum de Bavay (Nord) sous l'Empire: bilan des découvertes et pistes de réflexion sur la hiérarchisation des espaces, dans: J. Boislève – K. Jardel – G. Tendron (dir.), Décor des édifices publics, civils et religieux en Gaule durant l'Antiquité, Ier–IVe siècle, peinture, mosaïque, stuc et décor architectoniques. Actes du colloque de Caen 07.–08.04.2011 (Caen 2012) 17–29 |
| Brunet-Gaston 1997 | V. Brunet-Gaston, Étude préliminaire du lapidaire architectural gallo-romain d'Evreux (27). Catalogue raisonné, Revue Archéologique de l'Ouest 14/1, 1997, 103–124 |
| Byhet 2003 | T. Byhet, Fouilles sur le forum de Bavay (1993–1998) IV. Un sanctuaire de carrefour au sud du forum?, Revue du Nord – Archéologie de la Picardie et du Nord de la France 353/5, 2003, 209–228 |
| Caylus 1756 | A.-C. Caylus (de), Recueil d'antiquités égyptiennes, étrusques, grecques et romaines II (Paris 1756) |
| De Bast 1813 | M. J. De Bast, Second supplément au recueil d'antiquités Romaines et Gauloises, contenant la description de l'ancienne ville de Bavai et Famars: suivi de remarques historiques et critiques sur les prétendus Forestiers de Flandre, sur les Missi Dominici, sur quelques nouvelles découvertes d'anciens monuments de la période romaine faites dans la Flandre proprement dite et sur plusieurs points intéressants du moyen-âge (Gand 1813) |
| Delewarde 1718 | M. Delewarde, Histoire générale du Hainau par le R. P. M. Delewarde (Mons 1718) |
| Delmaire et al. 2011 | R. Delmaire – J.-C. Carmelez – F. Loridant – C. Louvion, Carte archéologique de la Gaule, Le Nord, Bavay 59/2 (Paris 2011) |

---

[36] Forum antique de Bavay inv. 2014.0.1143. AE 1999, 1079; Thollard 1996, 87; Van Andringa 2002, fig. 12; Byhet 2003; Delmaire et al. 2011, 187.

| | |
|---|---|
| Demolon – Labourdette 2013 | P. Demolon – A. Labourdette, Bavay dans les collections de Douai, dans: Collectif, Collections antiques de Bavay conservées dans d'autres institutions. Catalogue d'exposition Forum antique de Bavay 31.01.–27.08.2013 (Mons 2013) 72–99 |
| Derbigny 1837/1838 | H. Derbigny, Voyage archéologique à Bavai – 1833, Mémoires de la Société centrale d'agriculture, sciences et arts du Département du Nord séant à Douai 7/2, 1837/1838, s. p. |
| Deru et al. 2019 | X. Deru – C. Louvion – G. Dannell – E. Gommaere – Ph. Lanos, Les techniques de construction du second forum de Bavay (Nord). Utilisation, origine et datation des matériaux en terre cuite, Gallia 76/2, 2019, 45–82 |
| Fellague 2017 | D. Fellague, Nouvelle interprétation sur deux sculptures de Périgueux. Des fragments de chapiteaux figurés plutôt que des portraits funéraires?, Aquitania 33, 2017, 123–131 |
| Ferlut 2011 | A. Ferlut, Le culte des divinités féminines en Gaule Belgique et dans les Germanies sous le Haut-Empire romain (Diss. Université Paris IV Sorbonne 2011) |
| Gros 1996 | P. Gros, L'architecture romaine: du début du III$^e$ siècle av. J.-C. à la fin du Haut-Empire I. Les monuments publics (Paris 1996) |
| Gros 2001 | P. Gros, L'architecture romaine: du début du III$^e$ siècle av. J.-C. à la fin du Haut-Empire II. Maisons, palais, villas et tombeaux (Paris 2001) |
| Hanoune – Muller 1996 | R. Hanoune – A. Muller, Recherches archéologiques à Bavay, XIX–XXIII (Basilique civile, 1995–1996), Revue du Nord – Archéologie de la Picardie et du Nord de la France 318, 1996, 97–136 |
| Henig 1993 | M. Henig, Roman Sculpture from the Cotswold Region, with Devon and Cornwall (Oxford 1993) |
| Höet-Van Cauwenberghe – Louvion 2017 | C. Höet-Van Cauwenberghe – C. Louvion, Les monument funéraires des Nerviens: épitaphes sur marbre noir et examen des supports de mémoire, Revue du Nord-Archéologie de la Picardie et du Nord de la France 423, 2017, 9-38 |
| Kähler 1939 | H. Kähler, Die römischen Kapitelle des Rheingebietes (Berlin 1939) |
| Louvion 2019 | C. Louvion, Les enceintes de l'Antiquité tardive de Bavay, synthèse des connaissances, dans: D. Bayard D. – J.-P. Fourdrin (éds.), Villes et fortifications de l'Antiquité tardive dans le Nord de la Gaule, Revue du Nord hors-série Art et archéologie 26, 2019, 251–270 |
| lupa | F. und O. Harl, <lupa.at> (Bilddatenbank zu antiken Steindenkmälern) |
| Maligorne 2016 | Y. Maligorne, Présence de l'élément divin dans les ordres architecturaux des monuments gaulois, dans: R. Bedon – H. Mavéraud-Tardiveau (éds.), Présence des divinités et des cultes dans les villes et les agglomérations secondaires de la Gaule romaine et des régions voisines. Actes du colloque de Limoges 2014, Caesarodunum 47–48 (Limoges 2016) 315–333 |
| Masse 1731 | C. Masse, Mémoire sur la ville de Bavay dans le pays d'Hainaut, Service historique de la Défense, CHA Vincennes, Gr 1 Vh 2215, transcription L. Lemaire, 1912 (s.l. 1731) |
| Niveleau 1830 | A. Niveleau, Bavay ancien et nouveau, ouvrage composé d'un recueil de dessins des antiquités trouvées dans son territoire depuis 1824 jusque fin de 1829 avec un texte explicatif à chaque feuille. Précédé d'une introduction sur cette ancienne capitale des Nerviens et sur les galeries souterraines d'Houdain et de Bellignies. Par Antoine Niveleau, architecte de la ville de Valenciennes, ancien élève et médailliste de l'école spéciale d'architecture de Paris, Bibliothèque et archives de l'Institut de France, Ms 3799–3800, Paris 1830 |
| Noelke 2006 | P. Noelke, Bildersturm und Wiederverwendung am Beispiel der Iuppitersäulen in den germanischen Provinzen des Imperium Romanum, BerRGK 87, 2006, 275–386 |
| Raepsaet-Charlier 2009 | M.-T. Raepsaet-Charlier, La Gaule Belgique d'Auguste à Commode. Perspectives historiques, dans: Y. Le Bohec (éd.), Rome et les provinces de l'Occident de 197 av. J.-C. à 192 ap. J.-C. (Nantes 2009) |
| Reis 2012 | A. Reis, Les colonnes à Jupiter de Merten (Moselle) et de Grand (Vosges): histoire de la découverte, contexte archéologique et fiabilité d'une reconstitution du XIX$^e$ s., RAE 61, 2012, 359–369 |
| Tardy 1989 | D. Tardy, Le décor architectonique de Saintes antique. Les chapiteaux et bases, Aquitania suppl. 5 (Paris 1989) |
| Thollard 1997 | P. Thollard, Les fouilles sur le forum de Bavay (1993–1997). Aire sacrée, cryptoportique et terrasse sud, Revue du Nord – Archéologie de la Picardie et du Nord de la France 79, 1997, 65–140 |

| | |
|---|---|
| Thollard – Denimal 1998 | P. Thollard – C. Denimal, Fouilles sur le forum de Bavay 1993–1998 II: le Bas-Empire, Revue du Nord – Archéologie de la Picardie et du Nord de la France 80, 1998, 153–221 |
| Van Andringa 2002 | W. Van Andringa, La religion en Gaule romaine. Piété et politique (I$^{er}$–III$^e$ siècle apr. J.-C.) (Paris 2002) |
| von Mercklin 1962 | E. von Mercklin, Antike Figuralkapitelle (Berlin 1962) |

*Pierre-Antoine Lamy, directeur du Forum antique de Bavay, Musée archéologique du Département du Nord, chercheur associé UMR 6298 Artehis, 2 allée Chanoine Biévelet, 59570 Bavay, France.*
*[e] pierreantoine.lamy@lenord.fr*

*Christine Louvion, archéologue au Service archéologie et patrimoine du Département du Nord, 2 rue Saint-Bernard, 59000 Lille, France.*
*[e] christine.louvion@lenord.fr*

*Marie-Laure Florent-Michel, Service recherche et conservation, Forum antique de Bavay, 2 allée Chanoine Biévelet, 59570 Bavay, France.*
*[e] marielaure.florent@lenord.fr*

*Charlie Mairel, archéologue au Service archéologie et patrimoine du Département du Nord, Chercheur associé laboratoire UMR 5138 ArAr, 2 rue Saint-Bernard, 59000 Lille, France.*
*[e] charlie.mairel@lenord.fr*

Katja Lembke

# STONE MONUMENTS OF ROMAN EGYPT AS MONUMENTS OF STATE

**Abstract**
Unlike other provinces of the Imperium Romanum, Egypt shows great perseverance on the part of local priests and officials, who adhered to dynastic traditions both stylistically and iconographically. Thus, the absent pharaoh/emperor was continuously present on temple reliefs and stelae until the 4$^{th}$ century in order to guarantee the ritual. For this reason, the *damnatio memoriae* was also only incompletely implemented in Egypt. While the Ptolemies needed the clergy to secure their rule, the image of the Roman pharaoh served cult continuity and the Egyptian priests' raison d'être. Between 30 BC and the 5$^{th}$ century AD, the quantitative and qualitative focus of the monuments related to the state lies at the beginning of Roman rule. Geographically, they are concentrated in *Alexandria* and Upper Egypt. The radical break that the new Roman rule brought is evident in both the Roman and Egyptian contexts, as will be shown with a few examples.

Egypt and Rome had a special relationship in antiquity. It was initially determined by a rejection of the Ptolemies, which became clear even after the conquest of *Alexandria*: Octavian insisted on visiting only the tomb of Alexander because »he wanted to see a king, not some corpses«[1]. As the last major Hellenistic empire, Egypt was incorporated into the Imperium Romanum in 30 BC and also received a special status as the private property of the ruler. In addition, the Graeco-Roman tradition was confronted with an extremely canonized high culture, which had changed during the three hundred years of Ptolemaic rule, but whose core remained as clericalism.

Even in Roman times, continuity is evident in temple construction. Numerous temples were rebuilt and expanded, such as those at Dendera, Kom Ombo or Philae, as well as several temples on the southern border in Lower Nubia, including *Hiera Sykaminos* and Kalabscha. The image program also corresponds iconographically and stylistically to traditional Egyptian models like the temple of Kom Ombo. Octavian, the later Augustus, and his successors appear in countless temple reliefs as sacrificing pharaohs in front of local gods. In this way, the emperors assumed the role of ritualists who ensure the celestial order (»maat«), but without personally carrying it out. Although the scenes do not differ from their predecessors, their meaning is different: the Ptolemies depended on the religious legitimacy of the clergy, while the clergy was no longer important to the Roman rulers. Now it was not the rulers but the priests who were interested in the continuity of royal sacrifices in order to preserve their own religious tradition in a multicultural society. This is the reason why the Roman emperors, unlike the Ptolemies, did not plan and carry out new large-scale projects.

How do the stone monuments fit into this development? How did Roman emperors in the succession of the pharaohs represent themselves in Egypt? And how did the Roman state represent itself within a culture of over 3,000 years? Which style, iconography or stone material was used for ›monuments of state‹? Imported marble, local limestone or dark hard stone from Upper Egypt?[2]

---

[1] Cass. Dio 51, 16, 5; Suet. Aug. 18.
[2] This article is part of a larger publication on Roman state monuments in Egypt, written by the author as a contribution to a project on Roman state monuments in the Imperium Romanum under the direction of T. Hölscher.

It is not the place here to present all the statues of the emperors in Roman style, since they usually served mainly for representation in sanctuaries or in public places[3]. In principle, however, it can be stated that – as in other parts of the Empire – most of the sculptures represent Augustus and his family, including the famous marble portraits of the emperor (fig. 1), Livia and Tiberius said to have been found at *Arsinoe*[4]. The Egyptian type made of hard stone was largely abandoned; exceptions are a colossal statue from the Serapeum at Karnak, which probably represents Augustus (fig. 2)[5], and five sculptures of Caracalla[6]. In addition, Egyptian dark hard stone was used for statues in Graeco-Roman style, as is the case with a porphyry bust of a tetrarch from Benha[7] (fig. 3). In this article, I will focus on the monuments related to the imperial cult.

Archaeological evidence of three Kaisareia or Sebasteia has been found so far: the Serapeum of *Alexandria*, a temple on Philae island, and a cult building at Thebes. Further imperial cult buildings are only documented in papyri.

The oldest and largest imperial cult temple in Egypt was located in *Alexandria*[8]. Already Cleopatra VII began its construction as a heroon for Iulius Caesar, and it was rededicated before completion to a cult building for Marc Antony. Under Augustus the building received the designation ›Serapeum‹. Philo, an influential Jewish philosopher and theologian of the 1st century AD, left a detailed description of the Alexandrian sanctuary. However, there is hardly any archaeological information about the temple itself. Nothing remains today of its rich furnishings, mentioned as »votive offerings, surrounded by paintings and statues of silver and gold«. According to Philo's description, it was a complex in the Graeco-Roman building tradition[9]. Marble statues of Marcus Aurelius (fig. 4)[10] and Septimius Severus (fig. 5)[11], as well as a marble base with a dedication to Caracalla[12] were most presumably erected

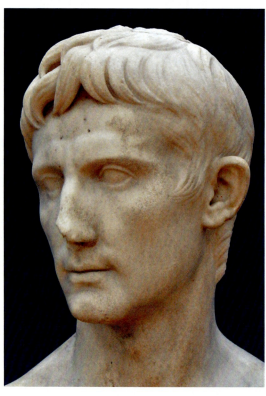

1   Portrait from Augustus said to be from *Arsinoe*, Copenhagen NCG, I.N. 1443 (Jona Lendering; CC BY-SA 3.0: <https://vici.org/image.php?id=13573> [22.04.2023])

---

[3]   Brophy 2015; in summary: Borg 2012, 614–615. Cf. also the destruction of statues of »Caesar« at *Syene*, on Elephantine and on Philae island reported by Strabo (17, 2, 54). On the head of Augustus in *Meroe* as a negative state monument cf. most recently: Matić 2014; Brophy 2016, 161–162 no. 96.

[4]   Copenhagen NCG, I.N. 1443 (Augustus) (fig. 1), I.N. 1444 (Livia), and I.N. 1445 (Tiberius). For their original location cf. di Santi 2017 with further literature.

[5]   Cairo CG 701 (Brophy 2015, 135 no. 65 fig., with further literature).

[6]   Alexandria, Graeco-Roman Museum 3233 (Brophy 2015, 104 no. 26 fig.); Cairo CG 702 (Brophy 2015, 105 no. 27 fig.); Giza Antiquities Storeroom (Brophy 2015, 110 no. 32 fig.); Cairo CG 703 = JE 31621 (Brophy 2015, 124 no. 47 fig.); Philadelphia, University of Pennsylvania Museum of Art and Archaeology E 976 (Brophy 2015, 132–133 no. 60 fig.).

[7]   Cairo CG 7257 (recently: Boschung 2020, 256–257 fig. 160).

[8]   Cf. recently: McKenzie 2007, 177–178 fig. 304; Pfeiffer 2010, 237–241.

[9]   Phil. leg. 149–151; on the excavations in the area cf. Empereur 2017, esp. 1–11.

[10]  Alexandria, Graeco-Roman Museum 3520 (here fig. 4); London, BM 1906 (Brophy 2015, 65. 153–155 no. 89–90).

[11]  Alexandria, Graeco-Roman Museum 3608 (fig. 5) (Brophy 2015, 65. 154–155 no. 91); location unknown (Seif El-Din 2009).

[12]  Alexandria, Graeco-Roman Museum 204 (Brophy 2015, 65. 160 no. 95).

2 Statue from the Sebasteion at Karnak probably representing Augustus: detail of the head, Cairo, Egyptian Museum CG 701 (D. Johannes in: Grimm 1975, pl. 15)

3 Porphyry bust of a tetrarch from Benha/*Athribis*, Cairo CG 7257 (F. Guidetti, <https://www.pinterest.de/fabioguidetti83/antichit%C3%A0/> [22.04.2023])

4 Marble statue of Marcus Aurelius, Alexandria, Graeco-Roman Museum 3520 (Savvopoulos – Bianchi 2012, 39 fig.)

5 Marble statue of Septimius Severus, Alexandria, Graeco-Roman Museum 3608 (A. Pelle, DossAParis 374, 2016, 41 fig., courtesy of CEAlex/CNRS, T. Faucher)

6   »Cleopatra's Needle« at the embankment of the river Thames in London (photo K. Lembke)

7   »Cleopatra's Needle« in New York's Central Park (photo K. Lembke)

8   Vatican obelisk in St. Peter's Square (photo K. Westphalen)

9   New York Obelisk (»Cleopatra's Needle«) in Alexandria around 1870 (photograph attributed to Francis Frith, New York, MMA 2004.217 <https://www.metmuseum.org/art/collection/search/285424> [22.04.2023])

on the occasion of the emperors' visits to Egypt[13]. These are the only remains from this area in the Graeco-Roman style. Furthermore, three obelisks originate from the Alexandrian Serapeum: the so-called Cleopatra's Needles, today in London (fig. 6) and New York (fig. 7)[14], and the obelisk in St. Peter's Square in Rome (fig. 8)[15]. »Cleopatra's Needles« date from the time of Thutmose III (1479–1425 BC) and originally stood at *Heliopolis* near today's Cairo airport; the Vatican obelisk is uninscribed. According to its former dedicatory inscription on the base reconstructed by Géza Alföldy, the *praefectus fabrum* C. Cornelius Gallus erected the Vatican obelisk in *Alexandria* in 30/29 BC, while the *praefectus Aegypti* Publius Rubrius Barbarus was responsible for the erection of the New York obelisk in 13/12 BC (fig. 9)[16]; the same can be assumed for the twin in London. The appointment of Augustus as *pontifex maximus* possibly was the reason for their installation, intended to symbolise the supremacy of the new ruler of Egypt[17]. These three obelisks demonstrate that within a Graeco-Roman sanctuary, described by Philo »with galleries (*stoai*), libraries, rooms, sacred groves, gateways (*propylaioi*), wide plazas (and) open courtyards«, Egyptian elements had also been installed.

The following fate of the Vatican obelisk (fig. 8) also shows an important change in the culture of remembrance. In AD 37, it was brought to Rome and erected in the Circus Gai near its present location. Through this relocation, the Egyptian state monument became a Roman city monument. Moreover, the first sign of victory over Egypt in *Alexandria* was transformed into a decorative

---

[13] Cf. also another marble plate from a pedestal found at *Alexandria* with an inscription in honour of Caracalla, Iulia Domna and *divus* Severus (Alexandria, Graeco-Roman Museum 410: Łukaszewicz 2021, 107–112 figs. 11 and 12). The inscription is dated AD 11 March 216, i.e. during the second visit of Caracalla in Egypt.

[14] For the original location see Arnaud 2002, 177–190; McKenzie 2007, fig. 304. Recent (popular science) publication: Brier 2016.

[15] Alföldy 1990.

[16] McKenzie 2007, fig. 302.

[17] Herklotz 2007, 223.

10  Roman podium temple on Philae island (I. Rémih, CC BY-SA 3.0, <https://commons.wikimedia.org/w/index.php?curid=7223540> [22.04.2023])

element of a circus. A good sixty years after the conquest of Egypt, the memory of the victory had apparently become secondary.

The cases of the sanctuaries at Philae and Karnak are different: both were Roman podium temples, a type of construction that was otherwise unusual in Egypt. As a counterpart to the cult building in *Alexandria* at the shore of the Mediterranean, a podium temple was built on the southern border on Philae island (fig. 10)[18]. The dedication from 13/12 BC is contemporary with the inscription on the New York obelisk and names the *praefectus Aegypti* Publius Rubrius Barbarus. The building was dedicated to Augustus as *soter* and *euergetes*. Like the building type of the podium temple, the architectural design in Doric-Corinthian mixed style is highly unusual for Upper Egypt and refers to a commission from *Alexandria*.

Nothing has been preserved of the cult statues, but an earlier trilingual stela from the year 29 BC was found near the temple (figs. 11. 12)[19]. The background was an uprising in Thebes, which Cornelius Gallus as *praefectus Aegypti* put down. He is the same person who erected the Vatican obelisk in *Alexandria* a few months before. After securing the southern border, he had the stela erected as a sign of victory.

Below a winged sun disk, a horseman appears in the picture field, sprinting to the right. Under the forelegs of the horse, an enemy falls to the ground. Beside and below are hieroglyphic texts, followed by a Latin and a Greek translation. The Latin text is unusual, since this language was hardly used in Roman Egypt apart from testimonies of the military. Moreover, it names Cornelius Gallus in the nominative case, so that the rider is undoubtedly meant to be the prefect, not Octavian. Similar to the inscription of the obelisk in *Alexandria*, Cornelius Gallus shows himself in picture and text as an active participant, although he was not allowed to celebrate a triumph.

For the Egyptians, the figure of the victor on the chariot was associated with the pharaoh. Greek viewers, on the other hand, knew fighting horsemen from private gravestones since the

---

[18] See recently: McKenzie 2007, 166–168 fig. 286–289; Pfeiffer 2010, 241–242.
[19] Hoffmann et al. 2009.

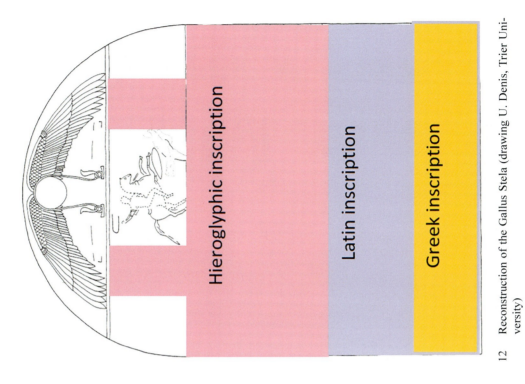

12 Reconstruction of the Gallus Stela (drawing U. Denis, Trier University)

11 The Gallus Stela (Lyons 1896, pl. 51)

13  Virtual reconstruction of the Roman podium temple in front of Karnak's first pylon (virtual reconstruction J. Köster, courtesy S. Pfeiffer)

Classical period[20], although the iconography of power had changed considerably since Alexander the Great, as shown, for example, by the Alexander mosaic or the so-called Alexander Sarcophagus[21]. The victor on horseback was part of the iconography of power in Hellenism[22]. At the beginning of the Principate, equestrian monuments were erected in the East only for Agrippa, Augustus' son-in-law and guarantor for the continued existence of the *gens Iulia*[23].

Cassius Dio later on described Agrippa as the opposite of Cornelius Gallus: while Agrippa supported Octavian, the later Augustus, in every way instead of being envious[24], the author calls Gallus' attitude presumptuous, disrespectful and reprehensible[25]. His hubris was also expressed in the erection of the stela, because even before the establishment of the Principate, every victory was monopolized by Octavian. Cornelius Gallus, however, who imitates Alexander clearly competes with Octavian. As a result, the latter terminated his friendship, putting an end to his political career. A flood of accusations finally led to Cornelius Gallus taking his own life in 27/26 BC.

A third building for the imperial cult, also dating from the Augustan period, is attested at Thebes in front of the Karnak temple (fig. 13)[26]. With its Graeco-Roman architecture in Corinthian order, it stood out like a foreign body in front of the first pylon of the Egyptian Amun Sanctuary. It is probably related to the renewal of the *dromos* after the Roman conquest. At the *dromos*, a statue

---

[20] E.g. the Stela of Dexileos (recently: Hurwit 2007, 35–60 with further literature).
[21] For the Mosaic of Alexander cf. recently Ehrhardt 2009; Cohen 2010, 162–170. For the so-called Sarcophagus of Alexander cf. recently Corfù 2014, with further literature.
[22] Siedentopf 1968, 13–14. 19.
[23] On the honours for Agrippa in general, cf. Rödel-Braune 2015, 175–188. 551–578 E263–299. Equestrian statues: *Oropos,* Amphiareion (p. 558–559 E272); Athens, entrance to the Acropolis (p. 554–556). In both cases, these are dedications of the *demos*. The pillar in Athens possibly previously bore statues of Marcus Antonius and Cleopatra (Plut. Ant. 60, 6; Cass. Dio 50, 15, 2).
[24] Cass. Dio 53, 23, 3–4.
[25] Cass. Dio 53, 23, 5.
[26] Pfeiffer 2017, 303–328.

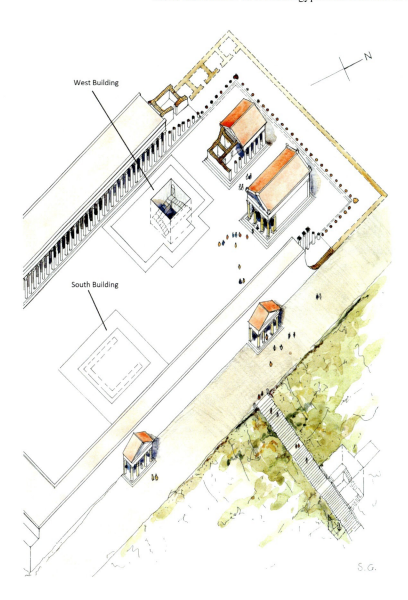

14 Reconstruction of the Serapeum at *Alexandria* (drawing S. Gibson, McKenzie 2007, 189 fig. 324)

of Amenhotep, son of Hapu, dating to the mid-14th century BC was adapted as »Caesar Imperator, Son of God, Zeus Eleutherios, Augustus« during the reign of the first *princeps*[27]. Furthermore, a colossal statue probably representing Augustus as pharaoh was erected at the site[28]. Among the furnishing of the imperial cult temple, the bases of an emperor's gallery with originally 13 statues have been preserved. The two oldest are assigned to Augustus, a further two to Claudius, with the youngest to Titus. At least three pedestals, which probably originally stood at the *dromos*, have been reused several times. Apparently, the building was transformed from a temple of Augustus to a general imperial cult building in late Flavian or later times. As the imprints on the bases show, statues of Egyptian and Graeco-Roman type stood side by side on an equal footing.

A ruler cult, which was probably already installed under Ptolemy III (246–222 BC) can finally be postulated in the so-called South Building of the Serapeum at *Alexandria* (fig. 14)[29]. An altar, whose ornaments refer to the Augustan period, can be associated with the Roman imperial cult

---

[27] Cairo CG 1199; cf. Wildung, 1977, 107–108 fig. 63; Klotz 2012, 232–235.
[28] See above n. 5.
[29] Sabottka 2008, 238–241.

15   Fragments of an altar found in the Serapeum of *Alexandria* (Wace 1943/1944, pl. 7)

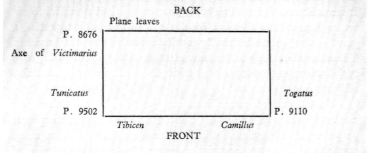

16   Reconstruction of the altar found in the Serapeum of *Alexandria* (Wace 1943/1944, fig. p. 91)

(figs. 15. 16)[30]. The place of its discovery »from the debris on the great rock trench in the southern side of the Ptolemaic enclosure«, however, offers only an approximate clue. Material, style and iconography point to a Roman cult. According to A. J. B. Wace's reconstruction, a *tibicen* and a sacrificial servant were depicted on the front, both facing left, a *togatus* on the right side, who was clearly larger than the sacrificial servant, as well as a *tunicatus* (facing left) and a *victimarius* with an axe (facing right) on the left side. The central sacrificial act was probably represented on the left side, while the main side showed a procession. The altar is supposedly made of Pentelic marble, like the stylistically and thematically similar altar of C. Manlius[31].

If the representations referred to an animal sacrifice – as the axe suggests – this would be highly unusual in the context of the Serapeum, because sacred animals were not sacrificed according to Egyptian conception, but were mummified and buried after their natural death. The galleries of the Serapeum, parts of which already date back to Ptolemy III, probably served as an animal necropolis, which speaks for an Egyptian cult in the sanctuary. The so-called West Building was probably built in Egyptian style, the so-called South Building in the Greek tradition (fig. 14), just as the cults for the Egyptian Osiris-Apis and the Macedonian ruler were different. The early imperial altar in the Serapeum, on the other hand, represented the new Roman cult and clearly commemorated the associated rituals (figs. 15. 16). Because of its material and the high quality of the imported piece, the altar may have been consecrated on the occasion of the introduction of the Roman imperial cult in *Alexandria*.

---

[30]   Wace 1943/1944.
[31]   Torelli 1982, 16–20.

Whether the ruler cult was continued in the following period remains unclear due to the lack of evidence. However, the fact that Caracalla lived in the Serapeum during his stay in AD 215 points to a close connection between the emperor and the sanctuary that still existed at that time[32].

What are the results of this short overview of Roman stone monuments connected to the imperial cult? Obviously, the quantitative and qualitative focus of the monuments related to the state lies at the beginning of Roman rule. Geographically, the monuments are concentrated in *Alexandria* and Upper Egypt. Finally, the radical break represented by the new Roman rule is evident in both the Graeco-Roman and the Egyptian contexts.

## BIBLIOGRAPHY

| | |
|---|---|
| Alföldy 1990 | G. Alföldy, Der Obelisk auf dem Petersplatz in Rom, Sitzungsberichte der Heidelberger Akademie der Wissenschaften, philosophisch-historische Klasse 1990, 2 (Heidelberg 1990) |
| Arnaud 2002 | J.-L. Arnaud, Sources et méthodes de restitution. Les obélisques et le Césaréum d'Alexandrie, in: J.-Y. Empereur (ed.), Alexandrina 2 (Cairo 2002) 177–190 |
| Borg 2012 | B. Borg, Portraits, in: C. Riggs (ed.), The Oxford Handbook of Roman Egypt (Oxford 2012) 613–629 |
| Boschung 2020 | D. Boschung, Art and efficacy. Case Studies from Classical Archaeology, Morphomata 44 (Cologne 2020) |
| Brier 2016 | B. Brier, Cleopatra's Needles: The Lost Obelisks of Egypt (London 2016) |
| Brophy 2015 | E. Brophy, Royal Statues in Egypt 300 BC–AD 220. Context and Function (Oxford 2015) |
| Cohen 2010 | A. Cohen, Art in the Era of Alexander the Great: Paradigms of Manhood and their Cultural Traditions (Cambridge 2010) |
| Corfù 2014 | N. A. Corfù, Zur Zeitstellung und Deutung des Alexandersarkophags aus Sidon, NumAntCl 43, 2014, 149–167 |
| di Santi 2017 | A. di Santi, From Egypt to Copenhagen. The Provenance of the Portraits of Augustus, Livia, and Tiberius at the Ny Carlsberg Glyptotek, AnalRom 42, 2017, 33–46 |
| Ehrhardt 2009 | W. Ehrhardt, The Alexander Mosaic or: How Authentic does a Historical Illustration have to Be? (Regensburg 2009) |
| Empereur 2017 | J.-Y. Empereur (ed.), Alexandrie, Césaréum. Les fouilles du cinéma Majestic, Études Alexandrines 38 (Alexandria 2017) |
| Grimm 1975 | G. Grimm, Kunst der Ptolemäer- und Römerzeit im Ägyptischen Museum Kairo (Mainz 1975) |
| Herklotz 2007 | F. Herklotz, Prinzeps und Pharao. Der Kult des Augustus in Ägypten (Frankfurt/M. 2007) |
| Hoffmann et al. 2009 | F. Hoffmann – M. Minas-Nerpel – S. Pfeiffer, Die dreisprachige Stele des C. Cornelius Gallus, ArchPF Beih. 9 (Berlin 2009) |
| Hurwit 2007 | J. M. Hurwit, The Problem with Dexileos: Heroic and Other Nudities in Greek Art, AJA 111, 2007, 35–60 |
| Klotz 2012 | D. Klotz, Caesar in the City of Amun. Egyptian Temple Construction and Theology in Roman Thebes, Monographies Reine Élisabeth 15 (Turnhout 2012) |
| Łukaszewicz 2021 | A. Łukaszewicz, Caracalla in Egypt A.D. 215–216 (Warsaw 2021) |
| Lyons 1896 | H. G. Lyons, A report on the island and temples of Philae (London 1896) |
| Matić 2014 | U. Matić, Headhunting on the Roman Frontier. (Dis)respect, Mockery, Magic and the Head of Augustus from Meroe, in: M. Janković – V. D. Mihajlović – S. Babić (eds.), The Edges of the Roman World (Cambridge 2014) 117–134 |
| McKenzie 2007 | J. McKenzie, The Architecture of Alexandria 300 BC–AD 700 (New Haven 2007) |
| Pfeiffer 2010 | S. Pfeiffer, Der römische Kaiser und das Land am Nil. Kaiserverehrung und Kaiserkult in Alexandria und Ägypten von Augustus bis Caracalla (30 v. Chr.–217 n. Chr.), Historia 212 (Stuttgart 2010) |

---

[32] Cass. Dio 78, 23, 2. For the visit of Caracalla in Egypt in AD 215/216 see Łukaszewicz 2021.

| | |
|---|---|
| Pfeiffer 2017 | S. Pfeiffer, Die griechischen Inschriften im Podiumtempel von Karnak und der Kaiserkult in Ägypten, CahKarnak 16, 2017, 303–328 |
| Rödel-Braune 2015 | C. Rödel-Braune, Im Osten nichts Neues? Stiftungen und Ehrungen römischer Magistrate im Osten des Römischen Reiches vom Ende des 3. Jahrhunderts v. Chr. bis zum Ende der augusteischen Zeit (Heidelberg 2015) |
| Sabottka 2008 | M. Sabottka, Das Serapeum in Alexandria. Untersuchungen zur Architektur und Baugeschichte des Heiligtums von der frühen ptolemäischen Zeit bis zur Zerstörung 391 n. Chr., Études Alexandrines 15 (Cairo 2008) |
| Savvopoulos – Bianchi 2012 | K. Savvopoulos – R. S. Bianchi, Alexandrian sculpture in the Graeco-Roman Museum (Alexandria 2012) |
| Seif El-Din 2009 | M. Seif El-Din, Une statue cuirassée d'Alexandrie, in: J.-Y. Empereur (ed.), Alexandrina 3, Études Alexandrines 18 (Cairo 2009) 119–133 |
| Siedentopf 1968 | H. B. Siedentopf, Das hellenistische Reiterdenkmal (Waldsassen 1968) |
| Torelli 1982 | M. Torelli, Typology and Structure of Roman Historical Reliefs (Ann Arbor, MI 1982) |
| Wace 1943/1944 | A. J. B. Wace, An Altar from the Serapeum, BArchAlex 36, 1943/44, 83–97 |
| Wildung 1977 | D. Wildung, Egyptian Saints. Deification in Pharaonic Egypt (New York 1977) |

*Katja Lembke, Landesmuseum Hannover, Willy-Brandt-Allee 5, 30169 Hannover, Germany.*
*[e] katja.lembke@landesmuseum-hannover.de*

Ana Zora Maspoli – Örni Akeret – Cornelia Alder –
Debora Brunner – Sabine Deschler-Erb – Claudia Gerling –
Natalie Schmocker – Ulrich Stockinger

# *HIC SITAE SUNT*

## INTERDISZIPLINÄRE AUSWERTUNG DER FRÜHKAISERZEITLICHEN GRÄBER DER MAXSIMILA CASSIA UND HEUPROSINIS IM GRÄBERFELD BRUGG/REMIGERSTEIG IN *VINDONISSA*

**Abstract**

In 2012/2013, a hitherto unknown Roman cemetery was discovered unexpectedly on the slope of the Bruggerberg (CH) outside the civilian settlement of the legionary camp in *Vindonissa*. Nine 4th century inhumations and about 150 early imperial burials (mostly cremations) were uncovered. In addition to the exceptionally good preservation of some of the graves, two stelae found *in situ* provide a unique starting point for research. Two of the best-preserved burials and their shared burial monument and stela were analyzed in an interdisciplinary research project at the University of Basel. The project covered archaeological, epigraphic and iconographic, archeozoological and archaeobotanical, anthropological approaches as well as Sr-Isotope analysis. This unique set of sources and methods provide insights into ancient lifeways and burial practices. The findings are an illustrative showcase of artistic and creative appropriation processes.

## EINLEITUNG

Das Gräberfeld Brugg/Remigersteig befand sich nordwestlich des Legionslagers *Vindonissa* an jener Straße, die vom Legionslager *Vindonissa* und der umliegenden Siedlung Richtung *Augusta Raurica* führte. Das Gräberfeld wurde 2012 entdeckt und bis April 2013 ausgegraben und dokumentiert[1]. Es umfasst etwa 150 frühkaiserzeitliche sowie 9 spätantike Bestattungen[2].

Das Gräberfeld wurde bereits in der Antike durch einen Hangrutsch verschüttet, was zu einer überdurchschnittlich guten Erhaltung der Befunde (und Funde) führte. So konnten mehrere Grabbauten, Grabhügel und oberirdische Grabmarkierungen nachgewiesen werden[3]. Besonders exzeptionell ist ein Rundgrabmonument, zu dem eine Grabstele gehörte, die sich – auf ihre Bildseite gestürzt – noch *in situ* vor dem Grabbau befand. Im Grabmonument wurden zwei Gräber angetroffen, bei denen es sich um die Bestattungen der beiden auf der Grabstele dargestellten und namentlich genannten Verstorbenen handelt: Maxsimila Cassia und Heuprosinis.

Die beiden Gräber waren 2021 Gegenstand einer interdisziplinären Pilotstudie an der Universität Basel[4]. Dabei waren folgende Disziplinen involviert: Archäoanthropologie, Archäobotanik, Archäologie, Archäozoologie, Epigrafik und Isotopenanalytik.

## RUNDGRABBAU UND GRABHÜGEL

Die zwei Gräber waren von einem runden Grabhügel bedeckt, der mit einem gemauerten Rundgrabmonument überbaut wurde (Abb. 1). Grabhügel gab es in vorrömischer Zeit vielerorts[5],

---

[1] Trumm – Huber 2014; Trumm u. a. 2013.
[2] Baerlocher 2017.
[3] Trumm – Huber 2014, 27–28; Trumm u. a. 2013, 17.
[4] Förderung durch den Forschungsfonds der Universität Basel.
[5] Allgemein s. Schwarz 2002, 77–78. Als regionales Beispiel s. die hallstattzeitlichen Gräber von Unterlunkhofen in Lüscher 1993.

Rundbauten über Tumuli sind hingegen ein mediterraner Monumenttyp und treten erst in römischer Zeit auf[6]; bereits die tarquinischen Könige wurden so bestattet und schließlich kam es zu einer Renaissance in spätrepublikanisch/augusteischer Zeit[7]. Diese Renaissance lässt sich zeitlich verzögert auch in den Nordwestprovinzen fassen[8].

Tumuli[9] sind im Gebiet der Provinz *Germania superior* sehr selten nachgewiesen, was insbesondere für den Süden der Provinz gilt, wo sich der Fundort *Vindonissa* befindet. Auffällig ist, dass sich im Raum nördlich von *Mogontiacum* eine Konzentration von Rundgrabbauten fassen lässt[10]. Eine der wenigen Ausnahmen mit mehreren Belegen von Grabhügeln im Süden der Provinz ist das Gräberfeld am Keltenweg in *Petinesca*, das in das ausgehende 1. Jahrhundert n. Chr. datiert wird[11]. Vor den Toren von *Augusta Raurica* an der Straße nach *Vindonissa* wurde ein singuläres Rundgrabmonument dokumentiert, das in flavischer Zeit errichtet worden war[12].

Die frühesten datierbaren Rundgrabmonumente im Gebiet der Provinz *Germania superior* setzen ab claudischer Zeit ein[13]. Somit dürfte das Grabmonument der Maxsimila und Heuprosinis zu den allerfrühesten Exemplaren in dieser Region gehören. Umso bemerkenswerter ist darum, dass das Rundgrabmonument keine einfache Imitation der spätrepublikanischen/augusteischen Vorbilder[14] darstellt: Die Gesamtkomposition mit der hochformatig stehenden, in das Monument eingepassten Grabstele ist ihrerseits eine provinzialrömische Neuschöpfung, die wohl ihrem Kontext entsprang und für diesen angepasst wurde. Die italischen Rundgrabmonumente weisen auch

1   Rundgrabmonument mit den beiden Bestattungen von Maxsimila Cassia und Heuprosinis (Foto Kantonsarchäologie Aargau, © Kanton Aargau)

---

[6]   Scholz 2012, 7.
[7]   Schwarz 2002, 72–74; Scholz 2012, 7–9.
[8]   Schwarz 2002, 99–106; Scholz 2012, 9–11.
[9]   Definition nach Scholz 2012, 7: Grabhügel, die von einer Ringmauer eingefasst werden, und Grabhügel.
[10]  Scholz 2012, 40.
[11]  Bacher 2006, 75.
[12]  Schaub 1992, 101.
[13]  Scholz 2012, 40.
[14]  Zusammenfassend s. Schwarz 2002, 72–74.

Inschriften und Bildfelder auf, aber keine in den Bau integrierten Grabstelen mit Bildfeldern. Bei den italischen Monumenten wurden die Inschriften in quer liegenden, längsrechteckigen Feldern angebracht[15].

Rundmonumente mit integrierten Stelen sind eine provinzialrömische Eigenart, die auch in *Carnuntum* belegt ist[16]. Das besterhaltene Beispiel ist das Grabmonument des Florus, das aus der zweiten Hälfte des 1. Jahrhunderts n. Chr. stammt, also etwa gleichzeitig oder etwas später als das Monument in *Vindonissa* errichtet wurde[17].

## GRABSTELE

Vor dem Rundgrabmonument lag auf ihrer Vorderseite eine Grabstele in Versturzlage. Sie stand ursprünglich auf einem Sockel (Abb. 1), der in der Ringmauer des Grabmonumentes angebracht worden war. Die Grabstele war bis auf einige kleinere Beschädigungen im Bild- und Inschriftenfeld vollständig erhalten geblieben (Abb. 2).

*A. Z. Maspoli*

### Inschrift

Die Inschrift (s. unten und Abb. 2) berichtet, dass diese Grabstele von Lucius Atilius für eine Frau und ein Mädchen, Maxsimila Cassia und Heuprosinis, errichtet wurde[18]. Maxsimila war die Tochter eines Lucius, aus *Bononia* und im Alter von 40 Jahren verstorben. Heuprosinis war Sklavin des Lucius Atilius und zum Zeitpunkt ihres Todes zehn Jahre alt.

*Maxsimila (!) ° | Cassia ° L(uci) ° f(ilia) ° Bon|onie(n)sis ° an̂n(orum) ° XL ° | Heuprosinis (!) ° an|⁵n(orum) ° X ° L(uci) ° Atili ° ancil(la) ° | h(ic) ° sitae ° sun̂t | L(ucius) ° Atilius ° contub(ernali) | suae ° posuit °*

»Maxsimila Cassia, Tochter des Lucius, von *Bononia* (Bologna), 40 Jahre alt, (und) Heuprosinis, 10 Jahre alt, Sklavin des Lucius Atilius, sind hier bestattet. Lucius Atilius setzte (den Grabstein) für seine Lebensgefährtin.«

Bemerkenswert ist, dass Lucius Atilius in der Inschrift Maxsimila als seine *contubernalis*, also als Lebensgefährtin, bezeichnet und nicht als Ehefrau[19]. Dies könnte bedeuten, dass die beiden nicht verheiratet sein konnten. Möglicherweise war Lucius Atilius, obwohl es nicht genannt ist, im aktiven Militärdienst in *Vindonissa* und durfte nicht heiraten[20].

*N. Schmocker – U. Stockinger*

### BILDFELD

Das Bildfeld (Abb. 2) zeigt in einer Bogennische mit muschelförmigem Abschluss auf der linken Seite eine sitzende Frau und rechts daneben ein stehendes Kind jeweils in einem Untergewand und Mantel (ohne Fibeln)[21]. Die sitzende große Frauenfigur und die stehende kleine

---

[15] Schwarz 2002, 60–62 Taf. 2.
[16] Kandler 1997, 71–72.
[17] Kandler 1997, 71–73 Abb. 2–5.
[18] Trumm u. a. 2013, 31. Wir behalten die ungewöhnliche Orthografie der Namen der Bestatteten bei – insbesondere die latinisierte Form des griechischen Namens Εὐφροσύνη entspricht nicht der geläufigen Schreibweise.
[19] Trumm u. a. 2013, 31.
[20] Trumm u. a. 2013, 31. Vgl. einführend dazu Phang 2001.
[21] Trumm u. a. 2013, 31.

2   Grabstele der Maxsimila und Heuprosinis (Foto Kantonsarchäologie Aargau, © Kanton Aargau)

Figur reichen einander die rechte Hand. Über der Muschelbogennische findet sich auf beiden Seiten eine Rosette.

Die Mischung regionaler Eigenheiten mit Elementen, die klar in mediterraner Tradition stehen, ist auffallend: Steinerne Grabstelen zu errichten ist für den Untersuchungsraum in der Latènezeit nicht üblich. Einzelne Gestaltungselemente der Grabstele wie die Bogennische mit Muschelabschluss[22] und die beiden Rosetten[23] weisen grundsätzlich in den mediterranen Raum und sind auch in den Provinzen sehr geläufig. Allerdings ist die Orientierung der Muschel sehr ungewöhnlich. Üblicherweise befindet sich das Schloss der Muschel oben über und nicht hinter dem Kopf der dargestellten Person[24]. Ein Beispiel, das in der Ausführung (nicht aber der Orientierung) der Muschel sehr gut mit der Grabstele der Maxsimila vergleichbar ist, ist die Grabstele eines Mannes aus *Mogontiacum*[25]. Es ist nicht auszuschließen, dass die Orientierung der Muschel einfach ein Fehler des Steinmetzen war. Zu bedenken ist diesbezüglich jedoch der optische Effekt der falschen Orientierung der Muschel, der die Augen des Betrachters fast zwingt, sich auf das Gesicht von Maxsimila zu konzentrieren. Es kommt durchaus in Frage, dass dieser Effekt für den Steinmetz und/oder L. Atilius wichtiger war als die ›richtige‹ Orientierung der Muschel.

Frontal dargestellte, sitzende Ganzfiguren sind auf (ober-)italischen Grabstelen die absolute Ausnahme[26], während sie in *Mogontiacum* mehrfach nachgewiesen sind[27]. Prominentestes Beispiel dafür ist die Grabstele der Menimane und des Blussus. Das Motiv der frontal dargestellten Sitzfiguren ist sehr auffällig und scheint eine lokale Eigenheit zu sein, die im mediterranen Raum nicht für die Darstellung von Privatpersonen auf Grabstelen üblich war[28]. In den Provinzen sowie im italischen Raum waren frontale Sitz-

---

[22]   s. z. B. Pflug 1989, 59.
[23]   Pflug 1989, 113–115.
[24]   Eines der wenigen Beispiele mit ebenfalls verkehrter Muschel ist die Grabstele des Tiberius Claudius Satto aus *Aquincum:* <http://lupa.at/2705?query=646314288> (13.02.2023).
[25]   Boppert 1992, 63–65 Kat. 6.
[26]   Boppert 1992, 30–34.
[27]   Boppert 1992, 24–29.
[28]   s. Pflug 1989, 106 Taf. 46,1 mit einer Ausnahme aus Mailand.

figuren hingegen durchaus für die Darstellungen von Gottheiten geläufig[29]. Entsprechend findet sich für das Motiv der frontal sitzenden, weiblichen Ganzfigur auch in *Vindonissa* eine Parallele in Form einer kleinen Plastik. Diese wird als sitzende Muttergottheit mit Schoßhündchen interpretiert[30].

Die Geste der *dextrarum iunctio,* also der verbundenen Hände, findet sich am häufigsten bei Darstellungen von Ehepaaren und wird dann als Symbol für Liebe und Ehe gelesen[31]. In bildlichen Darstellungen von Erwachsenen gemeinsam mit Kindern ist das Motiv der *dextrarum iunctio* im Vergleich zu anderen Arten von Körperkontakt sehr selten, und eine viel geläufigere Geste wäre beispielsweise die auf der Schulter abgelegte Hand[32]. In dieser Konstellation – d. h. zwischen Kindern und Erwachsenen – wird die *dextrarum iunctio* als Symbol der Liebe und Verbundenheit interpretiert, normalerweise zwischen Eltern und ihren Kindern[33]. L. Atilius ließ also einen Grabstein für seine Partnerin und seine Sklavin anfertigen, was in vielerlei Hinsicht außergewöhnlich ist: Üblicherweise werden Frauen zusammen mit ihrem Ehemann dargestellt, was hier nicht zutrifft. Oft werden Frauen auf Grabstelen mit ihren Kindern abgebildet, was ebenfalls nicht der Fall ist. Außer in den Donauprovinzen wird körperlicher Kontakt grundsätzlich nur selten auf Grabsteinen dargestellt – ganz besonders selten in den germanischen Provinzen[34]. Aus diesem Grund ist davon auszugehen, dass die Grabstele eine Anfertigung auf ausdrücklichen Wunsch war und kein Grabstein ›von der Stange‹.

## GRABAUSSTATTUNG

### Objekte

Die archäologischen Artefakte des Grabes von Maxsimila sind für ein provinzialrömisches Grab unauffällig: Das Fundmaterial claudischer Zeit fügt sich in den Rahmen des Fundspektrums in *Vindonissa*. Grundsätzlich wäre die Menge an Beifunden für ein Grab im italischen Raum oder in mediterraner Tradition zu umfangreich[35], da neben den klassischen Gegenständen wie Lampe, Münze und Unguentarium eine Reihe weiterer Objekte im Grab deponiert wurden (Abb. 3). Im Grab der Heuprosinis fanden sich nur zwei Keramikgefäße, die als Urne oder deren Abdeckung dienten (Abb. 4).

*A. Z. Maspoli*

### Tierknochenfunde

Bei den Tierknochen wird das Artspektrum in beiden Bestattungen dominiert von Schwein und Huhn, wobei die Menge an Tierknochen in beiden Gräbern verhältnismäßig groß ist und es sich fast ausschließlich um verbrannte Knochen handelt. Schweine sind grundsätzlich häufig in gallorömischen Nekropolen nachweisbar und Geflügel begegnet dort ebenfalls regelmäßig[36]. Ein hoher Anteil an Schwein- und Geflügelknochen kann als Indiz für eine höhere soziale Stellung

---

[29] Boppert 1992, 24–45.
[30] Bossert 1999, 17–18 Taf. 6 Kat. 4. Ebenfalls als Muttergottheit interpretiert wird ein Relief aus *Lousonna*, das eine auf einem Thron sitzende Frau zeigt, neben der ein Füllhorn steht (Neukom 2002, Kat. 53). s auch eine als thronende Iuno interpretierte Statue (Bossert-Neukom 2004, 18 Kat. 2) und ein Relief mit thronenden weiblichen Gottheiten (Bossert-Neukom 2004, 2527 Kat. 16) aus *Genava*.
[31] Pflug 1989, 105 mit weiterführender Literatur in Anm. 642.
[32] Mander 2012, 115 Tab. 16.
[33] Mander 2012, 116–117 mit weiterführender Literatur in Anm. 136.
[34] Mander 2012, 115 Tab. 17.
[35] Witteyer – Fasold 1995, 37–38.
[36] s. z. B. Veszeli 2000, 172–173; Baerlocher u. a. 2012, 39–40.

3　Grabausstattung im Grab der Maxsimila (Foto Kantonsarchäologie Aargau, © Kanton Aargau)

4　Grabausstattung im Grab der Heuprosinis (Foto Kantonsarchäologie Aargau, © Kanton Aargau)

gelesen werden[37]. Singvögel sind in den beiden Gräbern nicht nachgewiesen, was insofern von Bedeutung ist, als Singvögel in der Küche mediterraner Tradition beliebt waren und als Nachweis einer hohen sozialen Stellung gelesen werden[38].

Grundsätzlich steht ein hoher Anteil an Fleischbeigaben wohl in latènezeitlicher und nicht in mediterraner Tradition[39].

Auffällig ist jedenfalls die Altersverteilung der Schweineknochen aus dem Grab der Maxsimila, da ein sehr hoher Anteil an fötalen/neonaten Individuen nachgewiesen werden konnte. In den augusteisch-tiberischen Gräbern von Windisch/Vision Mitte westlich des Legionslagers *Vindonissa* wurde die Frage in den Raum gestellt, ob eine übereinstimmende Altersverteilung mit mediterranen Praktiken (Opfern einer trächtigen Sau) erklärt werden kann[40].

*D. Brunner – S. Deschler-Erb*


**Pflanzenfunde**

Das Beigeben von pflanzlichen Speisen war bereits in vorrömischer Zeit üblich und kommt sowohl im italischen Raum als auch im Raum der späteren Provinzen vor[41]. Bei den Kulturpflanzen in den Gräbern von Maxsimila und Heuprosinis sind Hülsenfrüchte (Ackerbohne, Erbse, Linse) dominant, gefolgt von Obst (besonders Birne). Getreide wurde hingegen kaum beigegeben. Auch in anderen Gräbern in *Vindonissa* sind Hülsenfrüchte die häufigste nachgewiesene Nahrungspflanzengruppe[42]. Währenddem die Hülsenfrucht- und Getreidearten nördlich der Alpen schon lange in Kultur waren, handelt es sich beim Kulturobst um eine römerzeitliche Neuerung[43].

Möglicherweise wurde die Ackerbohne im Verlauf des 1. Jahrhunderts n. Chr. durch die Linse als beliebteste Hülsenfrucht abgelöst[44]. In den Gräbern von Maxsimila und Heuprosinis, die in die Mitte des 1. Jahrhunderts n. Chr. datiert werden können, übertreffen Linsen die Ackerbohnen zahlenmäßig um etwa ein Drittel; da Letztere aber deutlich größer sind, bilden sie in diesen Gräbern bezüglich Gewicht die wichtigste botanische Grabbeigabe.

*Ö. Akeret*


**LEICHENBRÄNDE**

Bei beiden Gräbern handelt es sich um Brandschüttungsgräber mit Urnen. Beide Gräber enthielten verhältnismäßig umfangreiche anthropologische Überreste. Dies erlaubte es, die beiden Bestattungen mit den auf der Grabstele genannten und dargestellten Personen Maxsimila und Heuprosinis zu identifizieren. Im Fall von Maxsimila war der Leichenbrand repräsentativ, im Fall von Heuprosinis nur annähernd, was jedoch in beiden Fällen für eine sorgfältige Auslese und Überführung der Knochen und des Brandschuttes vom Platz der Verbrennung zu den Gräbern spricht. Die inschriftlich überlieferten Sterbealter von Maxsimila und Heuprosinis konnten anhand der Sterbealter-Bestimmung der anthropologischen Funde bestätigt werden. Für Maxsimila konnte außerdem ihr biologisches Geschlecht bestimmt werden.

*C. Alder*

---

[37] Veszeli 2000, 172; Baerlocher u. a. 2012, 40.
[38] Baerlocher u. a. 2012, 40.
[39] Zur Problematik des für eine entsprechende Aussage unzureichenden Forschungsstandes s. auch Baerlocher u. a. 2012, 51. Bemerkenswerterweise spielen Tierknochen in den spätlatènezeitlichen Brandgräbern von Regensdorf Gubrist keine große Rolle. s. dazu Deschler-Erb 2019, 138.
[40] Baerlocher u. a. 2012, 41–42.
[41] Baerlocher u. a. 2012, 42; Vandorpe 2019, 58.
[42] Petrucci-Bavaud u. a. 2000, 153; Baerlocher u. a. 2012, 42–46.
[43] Meylan Krause u. a. 2002, 234.
[44] Baerlocher u. a. 2012, 45–46. 51.

## ISOTOPENANALYSE

Von beiden Personen wurden jeweils ein Zahn, ein Felsenbein (*pars petrosa*) und eine Rippe beprobt und für Strontiumisotopenanalysen herangezogen, um Einblicke in die Aufenthaltsorte zu unterschiedlichen Lebensabschnitten zu erhalten[45]. Um das für *Vindonissa* typische Strontiumisotopensignal zu definieren, wurden zudem mehrere Bodenproben untersucht. Dabei zeigte sich, dass für definitive Aussagen eine noch breiter abgestützte Basis für das ortstypische Isotopensignal nötig sein wird. Nach aktuellem Stand lässt sich festhalten, dass alle menschlichen Proben der ortstypischen Isotopensignatur entsprechen. Es darf daher als wahrscheinlich gelten, dass Heuprosinis in *Vindonissa* oder einem Ort mit gleicher Isotopensignatur gelebt hat. Dies gilt auch für Maxsimila, wobei sie möglicherweise in ihrem letzten Lebensjahrzehnt an einem anderen Ort gelebt haben könnte. Das an der Rippe ermittelte Strontiumisotopenverhältnis liegt am äußersten Rand der für *Vindonissa* typischen Isotopensignatur und in einem Bereich, der auch für *Bononia*[46] charakteristisch ist (und ebenso für viele andere Regionen in Mittel- und Südeuropa). Es wäre möglich, dass Maxsimila eine gewisse Zeit (im letzten Lebensjahrzehnt) in *Bononia* (oder einem Ort mit identischer Signatur) gelebt hat. Die Ergebnisse der Strontiumisotopenanalysen lassen vermuten, dass sich die Origo-Angabe *Bononia* auf der Grabstele auf die Herkunft der Familie der Cassier beziehen dürfte[47] und nicht auf die Herkunft der Einzelperson Maxsimila[48].

*C. Gerling*

## INTERPRETATION

### Was geschah während Maxsimilas Lebenszeit in Vindonissa?

Maxsimila wurde um 40/50 n. Chr. begraben, und da sie im Alter von 40 Jahren verstorben ist, muss sie um die Zeitenwende bis etwa 10 n. Chr. geboren worden sein. Derzeit lässt sich (noch) nicht mit Sicherheit sagen, wo sie geboren wurde – möglicherweise in *Vindonissa* oder einem Ort mit identischer Isotopensignatur. Darum soll an dieser Stelle kurz skizziert werden, was in dieser Zeit in *Vindonissa* und allgemein in der Region geschah. Um 15 v. Chr. wurde unter Kaiser Augustus der Alpenfeldzug durchgeführt[49], und spätestens ab diesem Zeitpunkt beginnt die militärische Kontrolle von *Vindonissa* durch Rom[50]. Die Interpretation der vorlagerzeitlichen Bebauung von *Vindonissa* ist erst in Ausschnitten bekannt und besteht aus einem jüngeren militärisch geprägten Teil innerhalb der Befestigung (ab LTD2a), der einen älteren zivil geprägten Teil davor ablöst (frühes 1. Jh. n. Chr.)[51]. Ab 14/17 n. Chr. war die *legio XIII Gemina* in *Vindonissa* stationiert[52]. Wenn Maxsimila also in *Vindonissa* geboren wurde, würde das bedeuten, dass ihre Geburt jedenfalls vor die Errichtung des frühesten Legionslagers fällt, in die Vorlagerzeit. In diesem Rahmen drängt sich die Frage auf, wer Maxsimilas Eltern waren und was sie in *Vindonissa* machten.

### In welcher Beziehung standen Maxsimila und Heuprosinis zueinander?

In der Inschrift wird Maxsimila Cassia als Tochter eines Lucius (Cassius) sowie als Lebensgefährtin von L. Atilius bezeichnet; Heuprosinis war eine Sklavin von L. Atilius. Da der Grabstein von

---

[45] z. B. Hillson 1996; Hedges u. a. 2007; Snoeck u. a. 2015.
[46] Milella u. a. 2019.
[47] Zur Definition von Origo s. Giovannini 2004, 192–196 (freundl. Mitteilung M. Aberson).
[48] Es ist einschränkend anzumerken, dass die etwas weitere Umgebung von Bologna (Cavazzuti u. a. 2019) auch ähnliche Sr-Isotopenverhältnisse wie die Proben aufweist und eine Herkunft aus der weiteren Umgebung von *Bononia* nicht ausgeschlossen werden kann.
[49] Martin-Kilcher 2015, 271–276.
[50] <https://hls-dhs-dss.ch/de/articles/012287/2015-04-22/#HFrFChzeitvonVindonissa> (08.02.2023).
[51] Flück 2022, 18. 99–100; Hagendorn u. a. 2003, 103–113.
[52] Zusammenstellung von Literatur zum Gründungsjahr von *Vindonissa* s. Flück 2022, 113 Anm. 385.

L. Atilius errichtet wurde, werden seine Beziehungen zu den Verstorbenen beleuchtet und nicht die Beziehung der beiden dargestellten Personen zueinander. Während die Inschrift bezüglich der Beziehung der beiden zueinander keine weiteren Informationen liefert, geben der archäologische Befund und das Bildfeld der Grabstele einige Indizien dazu:

Maxsimila und Heuprosinis wurden in einem gemeinsamen Grabbau bestattet, und für sie wurde eine gemeinsame Grabstele errichtet, auf der sie beide sowohl bildlich dargestellt als auch in der Inschrift genannt wurden. In diesem großzügig dimensionierten Rundgrabbau wäre genug Platz für zwei oder noch mehr Bestattungen. Es ist darum bemerkenswert, dass die Gräber direkt nebeneinander angelegt wurden, sodass die beiden Urnen in direktem physischen Kontakt standen. Auch auf der Grabstele sind das Mädchen und die Frau nicht nur eng nebeneinander dargestellt, was dort eventuell mit dem begrenzten Platz auf dem Bildfeld hätte erklärt werden können, ihre Verbindung wird zusätzlich durch das – abgesehen von Ehegatten- und Eltern-Kind-Beziehungen – sehr seltene Motiv der *dextrarium iunctio* explizit zum Ausdruck gebracht. Es stehen verschiedene Szenarien zur Debatte, wie diese Indizien gelesen werden können. Standen sich Maxsimila und Heuprosinis schon zu Lebzeiten nahe und bildeten zusammen mit L. Atilius eine Art antike Patchworkfamilie, oder erlitten sie ein gemeinsames Schicksal und standen einander darüber, zumindest aus der Sicht von L. Atilius, nahe? Eine abschließende Antwort auf diese Fragen lässt sich derzeit nicht geben.

**Appropriationsprozesse**

Eine zentrale Rolle für das Verständnis dessen, was in *Vindonissa* im 1. Jahrhundert n. Chr. nach der Eroberung durch Rom vorging, spielen sog. Appropriationsprozesse – also künstlerische und kreative Aneignungsprozesse[53]. Der Grabbau der Maxsimila und Heuprosinis steht als rundes steinernes Grabmonument in mediterraner Genealogie[54]. Im Gegensatz zum Grabmonument ist die Umsetzung der Gesamtkomposition von Grabbau mit Grabstele eine provinzialrömische Neuschöpfung. Hier lässt sich ein Aneignungsprozess fassen, im Zuge dessen verschiedene Gestaltungsvarianten neu kombiniert wurden.

Steinerne Grabstelen und das Inschriftenformular gehen ebenfalls auf mediterrane Traditionen zurück, während die Herleitung des Bildfeldes komplexer ist: Die beiden Rosetten stehen in mediterraner Genealogie und grundsätzlich lässt sich das auch für die Muschelbogennische festhalten, wenngleich ihre unübliche Orientierung schon deutlich anzeigt, dass die Bedeutung dieses Bildelementes zumindest dem Gestalter der Grabstele nicht (selbst-)verständlich war. Es ist zu diskutieren, ob dies einfach ein Fehler des Steinmetzen/Auftraggebers war, oder aber, ob dahinter ein Appropriationsprozess stand, der eine neuartige und auf den Zielkontext abgestimmte Verwendung von Bildelementen ermöglichte.

Das Motiv frontal dargestellter sitzender Ganzfiguren wurde möglicherweise aus dem Norden der späteren Provinz *Germania superior* für die Grabstele aus *Vindonissa* übernommen. Es ist von einer sehr gezielten Auswahl des Motivs auszugehen, da dieses im Süden der späteren Provinz *Germania superior* nicht geläufig war[55]. Hinter der Umnutzung des Motivs der sitzenden Ganzfigur für eine Privatperson auf Grabreliefs könnte ebenfalls ein Appropriationsprozess gestanden haben, der eine Übertragung dieses Motivs auch auf Grabstelen von Privatpersonen erlaubte.

*Vindonissa* war ein wichtiger Knotenpunkt im Netzwerk der Provinz *Belgica* und später *Germania superior*[56]. Wir können schon in der Latènezeit eine zunehmende Vernetzung von

---

[53] Lipps u. a. 2021, bes. 4–9 sowie zahlreiche Beispiele im selben Band.
[54] Zu Rundgräbern in Italien s. Schwarz 2002; Scholz 2012, 7–11.
[55] Keine Parallelen finden sich in Bossert 1998 (*Aventicum*); Bossert 2002 (*Colonia Iulia Equestris*); Bossert-Radtke 1992 (*Augusta Raurica*) und Bossert – Neukom 2004 (*Gallia Narbonensis: Colonia Iulia Vienna: Genava, Vallis Poenina, Raetia, Italia*).
[56] <https://hls-dhs-dss.ch/de/articles/012287/2015-04-22/#HSpE4tkeltischeSiedlung> (08.02.2023).

*Vindonissa* mit dem Mittelmeerraum fassen[57]. Die Interkonnektivität nimmt dann in römischer Zeit noch einmal stark zu[58]. Eine der Kernfragen für das Verständnis einer frühkaiserzeitlichen Fundstelle wie *Vindonissa* ist, was in der materiellen Kultur passiert, wenn latènezeitliche und mediterrane Traditionen aufeinandertreffen. Die vorgelegten Befunde zeigen eindrücklich, dass es nicht nur zu einer wechselseitigen (und auf keinen Fall nur einseitigen) Beeinflussung kam, sondern vor allem zu Neuschöpfungen, die überhaupt erst in einem so stark vernetzten Umfeld möglich waren.

*A. Z. Maspoli – Ö. Akeret – C. Alder –*
*D. Brunner – S. Deschler-Erb – C. Gerling –*
*N. Schmocker – U. Stockinger*

## BIBLIOGRAFIE

| | |
|---|---|
| Bacher 2006 | R. Bacher, Das Gräberfeld von Petinesca, Petinesca 3 (Bern 2006) |
| Boppert 1992 | W. Boppert, Zivile Grabsteine aus Mainz und Umgebung, CSIR Germania Superior II 6 (Mainz 1992) |
| Bossert 1998 | M. Bossert, Die figürlichen Reliefs von Aventicum, CSIR Schweiz I 1, Cahiers d'archéologie romande 69 (Lausanne 1998) |
| Bossert 1999 | M. Bossert, Die figürlichen Skulpturen des Legionslagers von Vindonissa, CSIR Schweiz I 5, VGesVind 16 (Brugg 1999) |
| Bossert 2002 | M. Bossert, Die figürlichen Skulpturen von Colonia Iulia Equestris, CSIR Schweiz I 4, Cahiers d'archéologie romande 92 (Lausanne 2002) |
| Bossert-Radtke 1992 | C. Bossert-Radtke, Die figürlichen Rundskulpturen und Reliefs aus Augst und Kaiseraugst, CSIR Schweiz 3, FiA 16 (Bern 1992) |
| Bossert – Neukom 2004 | M. Bossert – C. Neukom, CSIR Schweiz 2: Gallia Narbonensis: Colonia Iulia Vienna: Genava. Vallis Poenina – Raetia – Italia, Antiqua 36 (Basel 2004) |
| Baerlocher 2017 | J. Baerlocher, Jenseits der Aare. Die spätantiken Gräber der Grabung Brugg-Remigersteig 2012–2013 (Bru.012.2), JberProVindon 2017, 19–44 |
| Baerlocher u. a. 2012 | J. Baerlocher – Ö. Akeret – A. Cueni – S. Deschler-Erb – P.-A. Schwarz, Prächtige Bestattung fern der Heimat. Interdisziplinäre Auswertung der frührömischen Gräber der Grabung Windisch-»Vision Mitte« 2006–2009, JberProVindon 2012, 29–55 |
| Cavazzuti u. a. 2019 | C. Cavazzuti – R. Skeates – A. R. Millard – G. Nowell – J. Peterkin – M. Bernabò Brea – A. Cardarelli – L. Salzani, Flows of people in villages and large centres in Bronze Age Italy through strontium and oxygen isotopes, PLOS ONE 14,1, 2019: e0209693, DOI: 10.1371/journal.pone.0209693 (29.03.2023) |
| Deschler-Erb 2019 | S. Deschler-Erb, Archäozoologische Untersuchungen zu den Tierknochen aus den spätlatènezeitlichen Brandgräbern und »Deponierungen«, in: B. Horisberger, Keltische und römische Eliten im zürcherischen Furttal, Monographien der Kantonsarchäologie Zürich 53 (Zürich 2019) 134–139 |
| Flück 2022 | M. Flück, Zu Gast bei Offizieren in Vindonissa, VGesVind 26 (Brugg 2022) |
| Flück – Lippe 2002 | M. Flück – Th. Lippe, Fundmaterial aus dem Kontext der spätlatènezeitlichen Befestigung, in: Flück 2022, 69–78 |
| Flutsch u. a. 2002 | L. Flutsch – U. Niffeler – F. Rossi (Hrsg.), Römische Zeit: Bäder – Reben – Legionen. Die Schweiz vom Paläolithikum bis zum frühen Mittelalter 5 (Basel 2002) |
| Giovannini 2004 | A. Giovannini, Die Tabula Heracleensis, Chiron 34, 2004, 187–204 |
| Hagendorn u. a. 2003 | A. Hagendorn – H. W. Doppler – A. Huber – H. H. Plogmann – St. Jacomet – Ch. Meyer-Freuler – B. Pfäffli – J. Schibler, Zur Frühzeit von Vindonissa. Auswertung der Holzbauten der Grabung Windisch-Breite 1996–1998, VGesVind 18 (Brugg 2003) |

---

[57] s. z. B. Flück – Lippe 2022, 69. 71–72. 75.
[58] s. z. B. Flück 2022, 247.

| | |
|---|---|
| Hedges u. a. 2007 | R. E. M. Hedges – J. G. Clement – D. L. Thomas – T. C. O'Connell, Collagen Turnover in the Adult Femoral Mid-Shaft: Modeled from Anthropogenic Radiocarbon Tracer Measurements, American Journal of Physical Anthropology 133, 2007, 808–816, DOI: 10.1002/ajpa.20598 (29.03.2023) |
| Hillson 1996 | S. Hillson, Dental Anthropology (Cambridge 1996) |
| Hintermann 2000 | D. Hintermann, Der Südfriedhof von Vindonissa. Archäologische und naturwissenschaftliche Untersuchungen im römerzeitlichen Gräberfeld Windisch-Dägerli, VGesVind 17 (Brugg 2000) |
| Kandler 1997 | M. Kandler, Römische Rundgräber (*tumuli*) in Carnuntum, in: M. Kandler (Hrsg.), Das Auxiliarkastell Carnuntum 2. Forschungen seit 1988, SoSchrÖAI 30 (Wien 1997) 69–88 |
| Lipps u. a. 2021 | J. Lipps – M. Dorka Moreno – J. Griesbach (Hrsg.), Appropriation processes of statue schemata in the Roman provinces = Aneignungsprozesse antiker Statuenschemata in den römischen Provinzen, Material Appropriation Processes in Antiquity 1 (Wiesbaden 2021) |
| Lüscher 1993 | G. Lüscher, Unterlunkhofen und die hallstattzeitliche Grabkeramik in der Schweiz, Antiqua 24 (Basel 1993) |
| Mander 2012 | J. Mander, Portraits of children on Roman funerary monuments (Cambridge 2012) |
| Martin-Kilcher 2015 | S. Martin-Kilcher, Archäologische Spuren der römischen Okkupation zwischen Alpen und Hochrhein und die städtische Besiedlung der *civitas Helvetiorum* im 1. Jh. v. Chr., in: G. A. Lehmann – R. Wiegels (Hrsg.), »Über die Alpen und über den Rhein …«. Beiträge zu den Anfängen und zum Verlauf der römischen Expansion nach Mitteleuropa, AbhGöttingen N. F. 37 (Berlin 2015) 235–281 |
| Meylan Krause u. a. 2002 | M.-F. Meylan Krause – S. Jacomet – J. Schibler, Essen und Trinken, in: Flutsch u. a. 2002, 231–242 |
| Milella u. a. 2019 | M. Milella – C. Gerling – Th. Doppler – Th. Kuhn – M. Cooper – V. Mariotti – M. G. Belcastro – M. S. Ponce de León – Ch. P. E. Zollikofer, Different in death. Different in life? Diet and mobility correlates of irregular burials in a Roman necropolis from Bologna (Northern Italy, 1st–4th century CE), JASc Reports 27, 2019, 101926, DOI: 10.1016/j.jasrep.2019.101926 (29.03.2023) |
| Petrucci-Bavaud u. a. 2000 | M. Petrucci-Bavaud – A. Schlumbaum – S. Jacomet, Bestimmung der botanischen Makroreste, in: Hintermann 2000, 151–168 |
| Pflug 1989 | H. Pflug, Römische Porträtstelen in Oberitalien. Untersuchungen zur Chronologie, Typologie und Ikonographie (Mainz 1989) |
| Phang 2001 | S. E. Phang, The Marriage of Roman Soldiers (13 B.C. – A.D. 235). Law and Family in the Imperial Army, Columbia Studies in the Classical Tradition 24 (Leiden 2001) |
| Schaub 1992 | M. Schaub, Zur Baugeschichte und Situation des Grabmonumentes beim Augster Osttor (Grabung 1991.52), JberAugst 13, 1992, 77–102 |
| Scholz 2012 | M. Scholz, Grabbauten in den nördlichen Grenzprovinzen des Römischen Reiches zwischen Britannien und dem Schwarzen Meer, 1.–3. Jahrhundert n. Chr., Monographien RGZM 103 (Mainz 2012) |
| Schwarz 2002 | M. Schwarz, Tumulat Italia tellus: Gestaltung, Chronologie und Bedeutung der römischen Rundgräber in Italien, Internationale Archäologie 72 (Rahden/Westfalen 2002) |
| Snoeck u. a. 2015 | Ch. Snoeck – J. Lee-Thorp – R. Schulting – J. de Jong – W. Debouge – N. Mattielli, Calcined bone provides a reliable substrate for strontium isotope ratios as shown by an enrichment experiment, Rapid Communication in Mass Spectrometry 29, 2015, 107114, DOI: 10.1002/rcm.7078 |
| Trumm u. a. 2013 | J. Trumm – R. Fellmann – R. Frei-Stolba – Th. Kahlau, Bestattet und begraben. Ein neu entdecktes römisches Gräberfeld in Vindonissa, ASchw 36/4, 2013, 26–33 |
| Trumm – Huber 2014 | J. Trumm – H. Huber, Hundertfacher Tod am Bruggerberg, Brugger Neujahrsblätter 124, 2014, 16–21 |
| Vandorpe 2019 | P. Vandorpe, Pflanzliche Beigaben in Brandbestattungen der römischen Schweiz, JbSchwUrgesch 102, 2019, 57–76 |
| Veszeli 2000 | M. Veszeli, Bestimmung der Tierknochen, in: Hintermann 2000, 169–178 |

Witteyer – Fasold 1995    M. Witteyer – P. Fasold, Des Lichtes beraubt: Totenehrung in der römischen Gräberstraße von Mainz-Weisenau. Katalog zur Ausstellung 08.09.–19.11.1995 Frankfurt (Wiesbaden 1995)

*Ana Zora Maspoli, Universität Basel, Fachbereich Ur- und Frühgeschichtliche und Provinzialrömische Archäologie, Petersgraben 51, 4051 Basel, Schweiz.*
*[e] ana.maspoli@unibas.ch*

*Örni Akeret, Universität Basel, Integrative Prähistorische und Naturwissenschaftliche Archäologie (IPNA) & Vindonissa-Professur, Spalenring 145, 4055 Basel, Schweiz.*
*[e] oerni.akeret@unibas.ch*

*Cornelia Alder, Universität Basel, Integrative Prähistorische und Naturwissenschaftliche Archäologie (IPNA), Spalenring 145, 4055 Basel, Schweiz.*
*[e] cornelia.alder@unibas.ch*

*Debora Brunner, Universität Basel, Integrative Prähistorische und Naturwissenschaftliche Archäologie (IPNA), Spalenring 145, 4055 Basel, Schweiz.*
*[e] debora.brunner@stud.unibas.ch*

*Sabine Deschler-Erb, Universität Basel, Integrative Prähistorische und Naturwissenschaftliche Archäologie (IPNA) & Vindonissa-Professur, Spalenring 145, 4055 Basel, Schweiz.*
*[e] sabine.deschler@unibas.ch*

*Claudia Gerling, Universität Basel, Integrative Prähistorische und Naturwissenschaftliche Archäologie (IPNA), Spalenring 145, 4055 Basel, Schweiz.*
*[e] claudia.gerling@unibas.ch*

*Natalie Schmocker, Universität Zürich, Historisches Seminar, Karl Schmid-Strasse 4, 8006 Zürich, Schweiz.*
*[e] natalie.schmocker@uzh.ch*

*Ulrich Stockinger, Universität Basel, Fachbereich Ur- und Frühgeschichtliche und Provinzialrömische Archäologie, Petersgraben 51, 4051 Basel, Schweiz.*
*[e] ulrich.stockinger@unibas.ch*

Sorin Nemeti

# THE DANUBIAN RIDERS

## ART, MYTH AND RITUAL OF A REGIONAL CULT

**Abstract**
The stone and lead reliefs of the Danubian Rider Gods are the iconographical illustrations of several stages of adaptation of a local myth and the rituals of a local cult to the structure and exigencies of an evolved mystery cult. The myth is explained by means of a figurative narration that contains mythical episodes involving gods and mythical figures. Several scenes recount the ritual passages of the worshippers in the process of learning the cult postulates (sacrifices, ritual *occultationes*, masked rituals, communal ritual meals, etc.), meanwhile the plethora of animal and utilitarian symbols indicate a speculation born in the reflections about the myth, associated rituals and, maybe, a soteriological proposal of the cult. Because the only monuments that illustrate the cult are votive reliefs and *philacteria*, the only way to analyze the cultic data is the method of contextualized symbolism in a comparative way. The main reference is the Mithraic religious structure, but one must take into account all the general knowledge about the so-called mystery cults from the time of the Principate.

The popularity of the local gods conventionally called Danubian Riders in the Danubian provinces is a well-known fact[1]. The reliefs depicting these twin gods contain a series of symbols borrowed from the iconographies of other cults (such as the cults of the Thracian Rider, the Dioscuri, Mithras, or even the Great Gods from Samothrake). The tree with a coiled snake[2] (fig. 1), the egg-shaped vessel flanked by two snakes (fig. 2)[3], the *principia vitae* (the lion, the krater, the snake and the rooster [fig. 3], interpreted as symbols of the four elements, fire, water, earth and air)[4] and the ram sacrifice (fig. 3)[5] are merely iconographical borrowings, given the popularity of cults of the Thracian Rider, the Dioscuri and Mithras in the Balkan-Danubian provinces of the Roman Empire.

But these are not the only symbols borrowed by the Danubian Riders from the iconographies of other gods. The whole iconographic structure seems to be strongly influenced by the various mystery cults[6] (the banquet, the sacrifice of the ram, the *occultatio* scene, the *neophites* in front of a temple, etc.)[7]. In the secondary registers of these reliefs, many individual symbols illustrating cult objects (three-legged table, candelabra, daggers, lamps), various vessels (cups, krater, kantharos, rhyton), food (fish, bread, fruits), and associated animals (bull, ram, rooster, raven, serpents, dog, dolphin) are displayed[8].

---

[1] Antonescu 1889; Tudor 1937; Will 1955; Tudor 1969; Tudor 1976; Zotović 1978; Oppermann 1981; LIMC VI 1 (1992) 1078–1081 s. v. Heros Equitans (I. Popović); Ertl 1996; Tatcheva 2000; Nemeti – Nemeti 2011, 247–261; Nemeti 2015, 129–138; Nemeti 2019.

[2] Dimitrova 2002, 213–214 (on 33 of the 340 monuments with inscriptions published in CCET, a symbol borrowed from Greek art, not evolved from a native tradition); Oppermann 2006, 299–300.

[3] Nikoloska 2015, 259–260 fig. 2–5.

[4] Cumont 1899, 100–103; Cumont 1913, 117–118.

[5] For the prominence of ram sacrifice in the Samothracian cult and in Lemnos see Bremmer 2014, 26. 41; sacrifice of Mount Pelion in Thessaly: Burkert 1983, 113–116.

[6] Burkert 1987, 1–11; Bremmer 2014; Belayche – Massa 2021, 1–37.

[7] Tudor 1976, 232–262.

[8] Tudor 1976, 262–276.

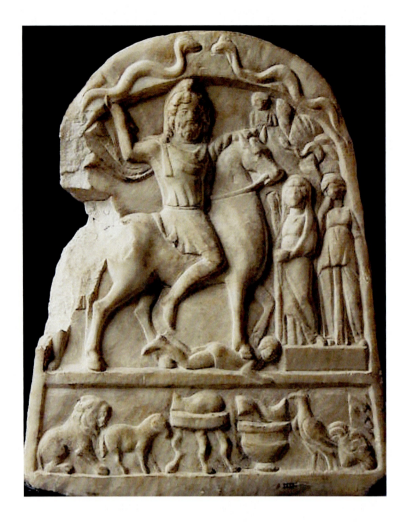

1 Votive relief from Alba Iulia-*Apulum* (lupa 17455, photo O. Harl)

2 Votive relief from Sarmizegetusa-*Ulpia Traiana Sarmizegetusa* (photo S. Nemeti)

3  Tablet from *Pannonia*, Collection of the National History Museum of Transylvania (photo S. Odenie)

Some of these symbols are isolated and only appear on a few of the monuments illustrating this cult of the twin Rider gods, but others are solid components of a structured iconography, passing from one variant of monuments to another. What is behind this artistic collage? Can we take into account a main mythological background (a central myth) and some associated rituals (inspired, of course by the common ritual practice of the time)?

Applying Clifford Geertz's »thick description« method[9], Richard Gordon analyzed, in 1980, the structure of the Mithraic grades in connection to the generalized »encyclopedic knowledge« of the Greek and Roman world, the sum of knowledge in the area where the cult of Mithras appeared and developed. The author noted how much the structure of the hierarchy of grades owes to the popular Greco-Roman culture, the encyclopedia of that era[10].

Using the same methods, we will try to answer the following questions: where does the simple iconographical influence end and where does the theological and ritual copying begin? Did the cult of these three Danubian gods evolve from the local cult of the Thracian Rider, an iconographical pastiche of various cults popular in the area in the time of the Principate (like the cults of the Dioscuri, of the Great Gods, or of Mithras)? Are there also victorious gods (trampling an enemy under the hooves of the horse) like Mithras, *invictus*, offering an *exemplum* for the worshippers grouped in an initiatic structure? How different are the ›Danubian mysteries‹ from other known mysteries of the time?

---

[9]  Geertz 1973, 3–30.
[10] Gordon 1996, 19–99.

## THE LOCAL ROOTS: THE MODEL OF THE THRACIAN HERO-RIDER

The distinction between the Danubian Riders and other Rider Gods can be easily made because of the presence of the man under the hooves of the horse, as well as the presence of the two main animal symbols, the fish and the ram[11]. There is a class of monuments of the Thracian Rider trampling a fallen enemy (fig. 4) in the area of *Philippi*, where the god is called Dominus Rincaleus[12]. Many riding figures trampling human enemies are attested in ancient iconography, starting with the victorious emperor, and including the funerary stelae of the Roman soldiers from the Rhine and the Danube, the Holy Riders as Solomon, trampling the demoness Lilith, and so on[13]. But the immediate model for the Danubian Riders is the local Hero-Rider, presented in epiphany (Kazarow class A), hunting (Kazarow class B) or returning from a hunt (Kazarow class C) (fig. 5). Over 3,000 reliefs depicting these repetitive scenes are found in the Balkan-Danubian area[14].

The model for the reliefs with one Danubian Rider (Tudor class A) is clearly inspired by the reliefs of the Thracian Hero-Rider. The Danubian Rider wears a Phrygian costume, is associated with a goddess and one or more attendants, and holds a spear in a striking position[15]. Many reliefs preserve the form of the round-top stele, a very popular model in the area south of the Danube[16]. The reliefs that are directly related to the Hero-Rider preserve some elements which are unusual for the Danubian Riders compositions, namely the animal accompanying the horseman as a hunter, the dog and the lion[17]. Another remaining symbol, without any connection to the new iconography, is the tree encircled by a snake, found in several cases in *Dacia* and in *Moesia*[18].

## THE CLASSICAL INPUT: THE GRECO-ROMAN GODS AND ALLEGORICAL FIGURES

The main classical reference for the Danubian Riders are the Dioscuri and their sister Helen. The main model for the iconography of the reliefs with two Riders is taken from the images of Helen between Castor and Pollux, very popular in northern Greece and in the Balkan area (the heraldic scheme with the two Rider Gods flanking the central goddess)[19]. On the single Rider reliefs (Tudor class A), the Rider is always wearing a Phrygian cap, like the Thracian Hero-Rider, while when there are two Riders and a goddess (Tudor class B), sometimes both riders are bare-headed[20]. Astral symbolism is often associated with the Dioscuri: the two divine twins are symbolized by two stars[21]. The busts of Sol and Luna associated with stars are common elements on the votive monuments dedicated to Mithras, Dolichenus and to other gods, setting the celestial context of the figurative narration[22], but when two stars are depicted on the reliefs of the Danubian Riders, one can interpret them as symbols for the twin gods[23]. A symbolic depiction of a triad, Helen and the Dioscuri, could be the so-called symbolic triad, namely a krater or an egg-shaped vessel flanked

---

[11] Will 1955, 118. 120 (»le Héros est un chasseur ...«, »les Cavaliers danubiens ... sont des dieux guerriers et combattants; le motif du vaincu prostré sous les sabots l'indique clairement«); Tudor 1976, 58–59; Popović 1992, 1079.
[12] LIMC VI 1 (1992) nos. 621. 621bis s. v. Heros Equitans (H. Koukouli-Chrysanthaki).
[13] Benoit 1954, 49–86; Will 1955, 93–103; Perdrizet 1922, 7–16.
[14] Kazarow 1938; LIMC VI 1 (1992) 1019–1081 s. v. Heros Equitans (A. Cermanović-Kuzmanović, H. Koukouli-Chrysanthaki, V. Machaira, M. Oppermann, P. A. Pantos, I. Popović); Opperman 2006.
[15] Tudor 1969, nos. 9. 11.15. 19. 22. 29. 55. 120. 183. 188. 189. 194.
[16] Will 1955, 25–29.
[17] Tudor 1969, nos. 118. 154. 182 (dog); 18. 27. 49. 59. 64. 77. 79. 80. 85. 87. 104. 118. 122. 153. 154. 181. 184 (lion); Opermann 2006, 305–309.
[18] Tudor 1969, nos. 1. 41. 64. 79. 90; Dimitrova 2002, 213–214; Oppermann 2006, 299–300.
[19] Chapouthier 1935, 21–21 nos. 1–62; LIMC III 1 (1986) 577–580. 593 nos. 123–160 s. v. Dioskouroi (A. Hermary).
[20] Tudor 1976, 110–111; Tudor 1969, nos. 34. 48. 83. 113. 114. 127. 132. 133. 135.
[21] LIMC III 1 (1986) 587–588 nos. 232–249 s. v. Dioskouroi (A. Hermary).
[22] Will 1955, 272–300.
[23] Tudor 1969, nos. 37. 41. 57. 72. 75. 79. 83. 113. 120. 127. 132. 133. 135. 140. 153. 174. 189. 191–193. 197. 199.

4   Votive relief from Gilău (Cluj county), Collection of the National History Museum of Transylvania (photo S. Odenie)

5   Votive relief from Alba Iulia-*Apulum*, Collection of the National History Museum of Transylvania (photo S. Odenie)

by two rearing snakes²⁴ (fig. 2). The symbols appear often on the class A monuments with a single Rider and a goddess, reminding that three divine individuals are involved in the central myth²⁵. The symbol of the vessel flanked by two snakes appears in North Macedonia on a Dionysiac stela from *Heracleia*, but also as an independent motif on several monuments²⁶.

Several Greco-Roman gods are secondary characters playing the attendant role in the Danubian Riders compositions. They can be recognized thanks to their attributes, costumes or gestures, and their iconographies following the artistic canon. A goddess wearing the *chiton* and *himation* makes a clear gesture of placing her right hand on her mouth (lips), thus suggesting silence (in the style of the Alexandrine god Harpocrates). The goddess is shown in the main field, in the attendants' row or next to the main goddess, but also in the lower register among ritual scenes or cult objects²⁷. The gesture is associated with Nemesis, mainly on magical gems, where the epigraphic legend ensures the identity of the goddess (fig. 6)²⁸.

6  Magical gem, Kunsthistorisches Musem Vienna (<cbd.mfab.hu> [30.04.2023], no. CBd-2430)

Another popular Greco-Roman goddess is Victoria/Nike, depicted with the common traits of this allegorical character. She is winged, wearing the *chiton* and *himation*, and stands upright behind the Riders, placing a crown on their heads²⁹.

An attendant dressed in military attire (with cuirass and helmet), holding a spear and a shield is generally identified with the god Mars/Ares³⁰.

The last character borrowed from the classical repertoire is Sol quadrigatus on the Pannonian lead plaques (type Ertl B1-2) (fig. 3). A bust of Sol with radiate crown is a constant presence on the upper corners of the reliefs, together with a bust of Luna. In this position they are the luminaries, Sun and Moon, an astral setting in a figurative language. But on several Pannonian lead plaques, Sol is to be found in the upper register, in a quadriga, holding a globe and a whip³¹.

With the exception of the Dioscuri and Helen, which served as models for the main scene, all other Greco-Roman gods (Mars and Sol) or allegorical characters (Nemesis and Victoria) play secondary roles, enhancing some ideas generated by the scene that involves the main protagonists. Nemesis, as an attendant of the goddess, is Fate, but she could also suggest secrecy or even revenge. Mars/Ares as an attendant underlines the warlike character of the main scene, where a human is trampled by the Rider, meanwhile Victoria/Nike rewards the Hero-Rider by crowning

---

²⁴  Will 1955, 320–325.
²⁵  Nemeti – Nemeti 2011, 253–254; Nemeti 2012, 181.
²⁶  Nikoloska 2015, 259–260 fig. 2–5.
²⁷  Tudor 1969, nos. 1. 3. 7. 9. 10. 16–18. 25. 29. 32. 33. 47. 48. 50. 55. 57–59. 62. 64. 71–73. 75. 79. 81. 83. 95. 99. 100. 106. 108. 110. 112. 118–120. 125. 127. 132. 133. 135. 137. 160. 162. 173. 175. 177. 182–184. 189. 190. 194. 195. 198. 199; LIMC VI 1 (1992) 752 nos. 200–203; 767 nos. 295–296 s. v. Nemesis (P. Karanastassi – F. Rausa).
²⁸  Mouterde 1931, 27–29 no. 11; The Campbell Bonner Magical Gems Database (cbd.mfab.hu), nos. CBd-487; CBd-1308; CBd-2430; CBd-3057; CBd-3651.
²⁹  Tudor 1969, nos. 27. 47. 48. 50. 59. 75. 77. 83. 97. 149. 199; LIMC VIII 1 (1997) 249–251 nos. 151–183 s. v. Victoria (R. Vollkommer).
³⁰  Tudor 1969, nos. 9. 14. 34. 55. 81. 112. 125. 127. 132. 133. 135. 150. 193. 199.
³¹  Tudor 1969, nos. 37. 75. 83. 127. 132. 133. 135. 199; Tóth 2003, 467–480.

him. Sol, from above, patronizes the events as lord and master of the Universe. The Greco-Roman characters are, in fact, tools to explain the ideas in a language of instruction, which is familiar to the inhabitants of the Greco-Roman world, and also terms for the translation of the messages implying fate, war, victory and, possibly, revenge.

## THE RITUAL CONTEXT OF THE *MYSTERIA*: MITHRAS, THE GREAT GODS AND OTHERS

When attempting to read the images on the Danubian Riders reliefs, the viewer is in the same position as Jules Toutain, when he wrote the legend of Mithras starting from the figurative story in the votive and sacral art[32]. There is no written text from antiquity regarding the cult and the myth of the gods called the Danubian Riders. Two different classes of texts were taken into account: those related to the Hero-Rider (the so-called Thracian Rider)[33] and the complex bulk of textual data about the Cabirian religion (Cabiri, Dioscuri, Corybantes, Theoi Megaloi and other smaller *mysteria* from Greece)[34]. These written texts could have served as an explanatory legend of the pseudo-narrative reliefs that show a goddess and two riders trampling human characters.

One scene that occurs exclusively in the lower registers of the stone reliefs (type B2a, variant I) is that of »the preparation of the *criobolium*«. It is a scene that predates the sacrifice: a character wearing a Phrygian cap extends his right hand towards an altar and with his left hand pulls a ram by its horns towards the altar[35]. In all the cases where this character appears, there is a ram's head on the *mensa Delphica* in the same register[36] (fig. 7).

On the lead tablets, the sacrifice of the ram is explicitly depicted in the lower register: a decapitated ram, hanging from a tree with three branches, is about to be skinned by a man. Next to that scene, usually a male character wearing a ram-head mask is depicted[37]. Sometimes a vessel is at the foot of the tree, and it is destined to receive the ram's blood[38].

The scene called *occultatio/ostentatio*, the concealment and revelation of the initiate, features in the lower registers of the stone reliefs[39]. Two bearded men, wearing Phrygian caps, flank a kneeling character holding an animal skin – identified as the skin of the sacrificed ram – in front of him[40]. The interpretation of the scene as an *occultatio* (the simulation of a ritual, a liturgical death) and an *ostentatio* (the rebirth as a spiritually regenerated initiate) was first formulated by Mihovil Abramić and Michael Rostovtseff, and accepted by Dumitru Tudor[41]. The initiate is covered by the mystagogues with the skin of the sacrificed animal, simulating a ritual death (*occultatio*). The ram's skin is then taken off and the initiate is ›revealed‹, reborn, to the assistance (*ostentatio*)[42].

Other episodes of this ritual setting imply two or three naked male characters in front of an edifice (temple [?]) or standing next to the participants at the banquet[43].

---

[32] Toutain 1909, 228–245.
[33] LIMC VI 1 (1992) 1019–1020 s. v. Heros Equitans (literary sources for Heros) (A. Cermanović Kuzmanović – H. Koukoli Chrysanthaki – V. Machaira – M. Oppermann – P. Pantos – I. Popović).
[34] Antonescu 1899, 81–216.
[35] Tudor 1969, nos. 9. 29. 55. 118; Nemeti – Nemeti 2011, 255–256.
[36] Tudor 1969, nos. 9. 14. 16. 29. 55. 118. 203.
[37] Tudor 1969, nos. 57. 111. 120. 125–127. 132. 133. 135. 137. 146. 155. 157. 162. 173. 194. 195, etc.
[38] Tudor 1969, no. 135.
[39] Nemeti – Nemeti 2011, 256.
[40] Tudor 1969, nos. 3. 18. 23. 25. 27. 28. 32. 47. 50. 59. 62. 63. 76. 82. 84. 95. 100. 118. 122. 154. 161. 182. 184.
[41] Rostovtseff 1923, 396–397; Tudor 1976, 243–245.
[42] Another possible interpretation of the scene is the identification of the sacrifice with the animal victim, following the interpretation of W. Burkert of a passage from Heraclides (Herakl. 2, 8) about the sacrifice of rams and sheep at the cave of Cheiron on Mount Pelion in Thessaly. After the sacrifice, every man put on the skin of the sacrificed animal and thus the procession climbed the mountain to the cave of Cheiron and the shrine of Zeus Aktaios: Burkert 1983, 113.
[43] Tudor 1969, nos. 34. 81. 127. 132. 133. 135. 179. 197.

7 Gem from Turda-*Potaissa* (after Antonescu 1889)

The banquet scene on the Pannonian lead plaques shows an entirely classical arrangement: in the middle, there is a circular table, and a plate with a fish on it. Two or three young naked men approach the table from the right. At the table, there are three figures, a female character in the center flanked by two men[44]. The quasi-omnipresent symbols, the tripod with a fish or a ram's head upon it, shown in various registers, allude to this banquet as a simplified version of it[45].

Various ritual episodes correspond to the canonical development of the rituals in ancient polytheistic cults: the preparation of the ram's sacrifice, the sacrifice of the ram hanging from a tree, the manipulation of parts of the sacrificed animal in rituals (ram's skin in initiatory rituals, ram's head as a mask for the initiated of some degree, ram's blood collected in a vessel), the preparation of the meal/banquet for the initiates, and, finally the banquet itself. One can see here a standard scenario that was embraced by the ancient cults and understood by worshippers as *teletai* or *mysteria*[46]. It is difficult to say if the criobolium copies the well-known taurobolic ritual[47] or the better known banquet of the Mithras worshippers[48]. The worshippers of the Danubian Riders followed in fact a common ritual structure when they translated their religious data into a common religious language of the era by ›hellenizing‹ their local cult.

---

[44] Tudor 1969, nos. 127. 132. 133. 135. 195.
[45] Tudor 1976, 208–216.
[46] Burkert 1987, 89–114; Alvar 2008, 205–364.
[47] Alvar 2008, 261–276.
[48] Kane 1975, 313–351.

## FROM *MYSTERIA* TO MYSTERIOSOPHY: THE SYMBOLISM OF THE CULTIC OBJECTS

Another dimension illustrated by the stone reliefs, lead plates or magic gemstones with the depiction of the Danubian Riders is that of mystic speculation. Guided by *horror vacui*, the artisans filled the relief fields with various animals or objects, intended as explanatory symbols and borrowed from various cults. One of the most significant borrowings is the symbolic group snake – krater – lion – rooster[49]. The group snake – krater – lion is common on the Mithraic reliefs from Gaul, Germany, and Central Europe. Franz Cumont, in his allegorical-symbolic interpretation, concludes that the three symbols represented earth, water and fire[50].

Many animals are depicted on the Danubian Riders monuments, but the most frequent of them are the fish and the ram[51], apart from the horse, the mandatory counterpart of the Rider. Very popular symbols were also the lion[52], the snakes[53] and the rooster[54]. Other birds were present in the field as well, such as the eagle[55], the raven[56] and, rarely, the peacock[57]. Moreover, the bull[58], the dog[59], a poorly-rendered quadruped[60], and the dolphin[61] also occur. Many cultic or utilitarian objects are also depicted, filling the entire sculptural field, sometimes doubled or tripled. Vessels and containers are the krater[62] and the kantharos[63], cups (two or three)[64], the rhyton[65], rarely an amphora[66], a patera[67] or an oinochoe[68]. Among the cultic objects one can include altars[69], candelabra[70], lamps[71], daggers[72], a sword[73], and various masks (of the ram, of humans and of the lion)[74]. As symbols of the banquet, dishes of different food, such as apples, fruits, breads, etc.[75], are depicted as well.

Every symbol has a special meaning in a given context[76], and it is very difficult to explain that chaotic assemblage of animals and objects. The fish sometimes replaces the human fallen under

---

[49] Tudor 1969, nos. 127. 132. 133. 135; Tudor 1976, 227–231.
[50] Cumont 1899, 100–103; Cumont 1913, 117–118.
[51] Tudor 1976, 208–216.
[52] Tudor 1969, nos. 1. 32. 34. 37. 41. 42. 47. 55. 57. 62. 65. 66. 71. 72. 75. 78. 81. 83. 86. 88. 104. 118. 120. 126. 152. 153. 160. 173. 190–192. 194. 199.
[53] Tudor 1969, nos. 1. 4. 7. 9–11. 15. 16. 19. 22. 23. 27–29. 34. 37–39. 42. 45–47. 50. 55. 66. 71. 75. 80. 86. 100. 105. 108. 113. 137. 140. 150. 155. 156. 173. 182. 183. 189. 193.
[54] Tudor 1969, nos. 1. 11. 18. 20. 25–27. 29. 34. 42. 48. 50. 55. 57. 58. 62. 66. 71. 75. 76. 78. 80. 82. 83. 86. 95. 113. 114. 118–120. 122. 125–127. 132. 133. 135. 137. 140. 148. 153. 157. 160. 162. 173. 176. 181–184. 191. 194. 195. 199.
[55] Tudor 1969, nos. 3. 4. 8. 18. 19. 34. 37. 48. 56. 64. 72. 75. 81. 83. 97. 99. 106. 112. 182. 190. 191. 193. 199.
[56] Tudor 1969, nos. 37. 41. 42. 75. 120. 126. 174. 181. 190. 193. 197. 199.
[57] Tudor 1969, nos. 44. 72.
[58] Tudor 1969, nos. 3. 29. 32. 37. 42. 72. 75. 88. 100. 174. 182.
[59] Tudor 1969, nos. 23. 34. 72. 152. 181.
[60] Tudor 1969, nos. 18. 28. 56. 58. 63. 73. 81. 118. 119. 122. 161. 192. 193.
[61] Tudor 1969, nos. 14. 34. 72. 133.
[62] Tudor 1969, nos. 1. 7. 11. 24. 25. 27. 31. 37. 41. 45. 59. 64–66. 72. 75. 80. 82. 100. 104. 106. 113. 114. 118. 122. 133. 137. 154–156. 174. 181. 190. 194. 199.
[63] Tudor 1969, nos. 34. 42. 44. 48. 83. 87. 108. 110. 111. 126. 127. 132. 135. 137. 140. 153. 162.
[64] Tudor 1969, nos. 7. 42. 98. 148. 162. 191. 193. 198.
[65] Tudor 1969, nos. 3. 9. 16. 29. 45. 47.
[66] Tudor 1969, nos. 41. 42. 48. 55. 57. 120. 173. 194. 199.
[67] Tudor 1969, nos. 22. 45. 55.
[68] Tudor 1969, no. 125.
[69] Tudor 1969, nos. 9. 14. 16. 20. 26. 29. 34. 42. 50. 55. 56. 66. 83. 85. 86. 91. 104. 154. 176. 179. 182.
[70] Tudor 1969, nos. 2. 34. 48. 57. 72. 73. 75. 77. 78. 81. 120. 125. 126. 135. 137. 154. 155. 162. 175.
[71] Tudor 1969, nos. 7. 26. 34. 37. 41. 42. 55. 71–73. 75. 77. 81. 83. 106. 113. 120. 125. 135. 137. 155. 157. 161. 162. 174. 175.
[72] Tudor 1969, nos. 34. 37. 47. 48. 62. 71. 75. 83. 137. 173. 191.
[73] Tudor 1969, no. 55.
[74] Tudor 1969, nos. 9. 45. 46. 97. 100. 174.
[75] Tudor 1969, nos. 42. 55. 59. 64. 71. 73. 77. 81. 104. 125. 137. 173. 191.
[76] Eliade 1994, 11–26; Durand 1999, 13–24.

the hooves of the horse on Pannonian lead plates[77], and the snakes and the vessel – the symbolic triad – replace the anthropomorphic triad, that is the goddess and the two Riders[78]. The ram is clearly the sacrificed animal[79], and the ram's mask indicates a grade of initiation, like the lion or raven masks on the contemporary Mithraic reliefs[80]. Cultic and daily use objects could indicate, at least, sequences of an elaborate ritual. All these symbols suggest certain speculative ideas developed around an initiatory ritual inspired by the mystic vulgate of the era. In the absence of any textual source, it is impossible to try to rebuild the hierarchy of the initiation grades, as Tudor has done, stipulating the existence of the Aries, Miles and Leo initiates[81].

## ASPECTS OF THE MYTH: RETURN TO THE LOCAL ROOTS

The key scene of the Danubian Riders cult is the one in the central register, as is the case of Mithras sacrificing the bull, which is the key scene in Mithraism[82]. One can infer the primary meaning of this obscure local myth: two divine warriors defeat their enemies and are received by a goddess, who has their horses fed and awaits them behind a *mensa Delphica* with a fish placed on it[83]. A similar mythical story can be read on the reliefs depicting the Balkan-Danubian god Hero-Rider/Thracian Rider, with the difference that in the latter case the rider is exclusively a hunter and his victims are hunted wild animals[84].

A ›fisherman‹ is represented near the *mensa:* a seated character who catches a fish with a fishing rod. Two acolytes wearing Phrygian caps walk towards the ›anthropomorphic triad‹, either each holding a fish, or one holding a fish and the other an altar. The tripod with a fish upon it is always present in front of the goddess or somewhere in the field. At the banquet, on the table, there is a plate with a fish. Sometimes, a large fish replaces one of the human characters fallen under the hooves of the horse (fig. 3). The reconstructed succession of sequences in the myth illustrated by these images would thus be: a secondary character catches a fish (the scene of the ›fisherman‹) (fig. 7), the sacrificial victim is presented to the divine triad (the fish and the altar held by the acolytes) and it ends up as a dish of the sacred banquet (the fish placed on the *mensa Delphica* in front of the goddess, the fish on the banquet table in

8   Votive relief from Jupa-*Tibiscum*, Caransebeș Museum (photo A. Ardeț)

---

[77] Tudor 1969, nos. 127. 132. 133; Nemeti – Nemeti 2011, 254.
[78] Will 1955, 320–325; Nemeti – Nemeti 2011, 253–254; Nemeti 2012, 181.
[79] Nemeti – Nemeti 2011, 255–257.
[80] Vermaseren 1960, no. 1896 fig. 491.
[81] Tudor 1979, 249–255.
[82] Mastrocinque 2017, 35–39.
[83] Nemeti – Nemeti 2011, 253–255.
[84] Oppermann 2006, 7–75.

front of the triad)[85] (fig. 8). The large fish under the hooves of the horse establishes an allegorical synonymy in the mythical language between the fish caught by the fisherman and the fish presented to the goddess, as well as the human character trampled by the Rider.

## BRIEF CONCLUSION

The stone and lead reliefs of the Danubian Rider gods are the iconographical illustrations of several stages of adaptation of a local myth and the rituals of a local cult to the structure and exigencies of an evolved mystery cult. The myth is explained by means of a figurative narration that contains mythical episodes involving gods and mythical figures. Several scenes recount the ritual passages of the worshippers in the process of learning the cult postulates (sacrifices, ritual *occultationes*, masked rituals, communal ritual meals, etc.), meanwhile the plethora of animal and utilitarian symbols indicate a speculation born in the reflections about the myth, associated rituals and, maybe, a soteriological proposal of the cult. Because the only monuments that illustrate the cult are votive reliefs and *philacteria*, the only way to analyze the cultic data is the method of contextualized symbolism in a comparative way. The main reference is the Mithraic religious structure, but one must take into account all the general knowledge about the so-called mystery cults from the time of the Principate.

## BIBLIOGRAPHY

| Alvar 2008 | J. Alvar, Romanising Oriental Gods. Myth, salvation and Ethics in the Cult of Cybele, Isis and Mithras (Leiden 2008) |
|---|---|
| Antonescu 1889 | T. Antonescu, Cultul Cabirilor în Dacia. Studiu arheologic și mythologic asupra unor monumente antice, în mare parte inedite și descoperite în regiunile Istrului (Bucharest 1889) |
| Belayche – Massa 2021 | N. Belayche – F. Massa, Mystery Cults and Visual Language in Graeco-Roman Antiquity: An Introduction, in: N. Belayche – F. Massa (eds.), Mystery Cults and Visual Representation in Graeco-Roman Antiquity (Leiden 2021) 1–37 |
| Benoit 1954 | F. Benoit, L'héroïsation équestre (Aix-en-Provence 1954) |
| Bremmer 2014 | J. N. Bremmer, Initiation into the Mysteries of the Ancient World (Berlin 2014) |
| Burkert 1983 | W. Burkert, *Homo necans,* the Anthropology of Ancient Greek Sacrificial Ritual and Myth (Berkeley 1983) |
| Burkert 1987 | W. Burkert, Ancient Mystery Cults (Cambridge 1987) |
| Chapouthier 1935 | F. Chapouthier, Les Dioscures au service d'une déesse (Paris 1935) |
| Cumont 1899 | F. Cumont, Textes et monuments figurés relatifs aux mystères de Mithra I (Brussels 1899) |
| Cumont 1913 | F. Cumont, Les mystères de Mithra (Brussels 1913) |
| Dimitrova 2002 | N. Dimitrova, Inscriptions and Iconography in the Monuments of Thracian Rider, Hesperia, 71/2, 2002, 209–229 |
| Durand 1999 | G. Durand, Aventurile imaginii. Imaginația simbolică. Imaginarul (Bucharest 1999) |
| Eliade 1994 | M. Eliade, Imagini și simboluri. Eseu despre simbolismul magico-religios (Bucharest 1994) |
| Ertl 1996 | R. F. Ertl, Donaureiter Bleivotivtafeln. Versuch einer Typologie (Petronell 1996) |
| Geertz 1973 | C. Geertz, The Interpretation of Cultures. Selected Essays (New York 1973) |
| Gordon 1996 | R. Gordon, Reality, Evocation and Boundary in the Mysteries of Mithras, in: R. Gordon, Image and Value in the Graeco-Roman World, Studies in Mithraism and Religious Art (Aldershot 1996) 19–99 |
| Hubert – Mauss 1964 | H. Hubert – M. Mauss, Sacrifice: its Nature and Function (Chicago 1964) |

---

[85] Nemeti – Nemeti 2011, 255.

| | |
|---|---|
| Kane 1975 | J. P. Kane, The Mithraic cult meal in its Greek and Roman environment, in: J. R. Hinnells (ed.), Mithraic Studies. Proceedings of the First International Congress of Mithraic Studies II (Manchester 1975) 313–351 |
| Kazarow 1938 | G. Kazarow, Die Denkmäler des thrakischen Reitergottes in Bulgarien (Budapest 1938) |
| Mastrocinque 2017 | A. Mastrocinque, The mysteries of Mithras. A different account (Tübingen 2017) |
| Mouterde 1931 | R. Mouterde, La glaive de Dardanos. Objets et inscriptions magiques de Syrie, Mel-Beyrouth 15, 1930–1931, 51–137 |
| Nemeti 2012 | S. Nemeti, Dialoguri păgâne. Formule votive și limbaj figurat în Dacia romană (Iași 2012) |
| Nemeti 2015 | S. Nemeti, I rilievi dei Cavalieri Danubiani. Spunti per l'interpretazione diacronica delle varianti regionali, in: C.-G. Alexandrescu (ed.), Cult and Votive Monuments. Proceedings of the 13$^{th}$ International Colloquium on Roman Provincial Art Bucarest – Alba Iulia – Constanța 27.05.–03.06.2013 (Bucharest 2015) 129–138 |
| Nemeti 2019 | S. Nemeti, Le syncrétisme religieux en Dacie romaine (Cluj-Napoca 2019) |
| Nemeti – Nemeti 2011 | S. Nemeti – I. Nemeti, Il pesce e l'ariete: festeggiando con i Cavalieri Danubiani, ARYS. Antiguedad, Religiones y Sociedades 9, 2011, 247–261 |
| Nikoloska 2015 | A. Nikoloska, Evidence of »Oriental« Cults from the Republic of Macedonia, in: A. Nikoloska – S. Müskens (eds.), Romanising Oriental Gods? Religious Transformations in the Balkan provinces in the Roman Period. New Finds and Novel Perspectives. Proceedings of the International Symposium Skopje 18.–21.09.2013 (Skopje 2015) 257–278 |
| Oppermann 1981 | M. Oppermann, Thrakische und Danubische Reitergötter und ihre Beziehungen zu orientalischen Kulten, in: M. J. Vermaseren (ed.), Die orientalische Religionen im Römerreich (Leiden 1981) 510–536 |
| Oppermann 2006 | M. Oppermann, Der Thrakische Reiter des Ostbalkanraumes im Spannungsfeld von Graecitas, Romanitas und lokalen Traditionen (Langenweissbach 2006) |
| Perdrizet 1922 | P. Perdrizet, Negotium perambulans in tenebris. Études de démonologie gréco-orientale (Paris 1922) |
| Popović 1992 | I. Popović, Les Cavaliers Danubiens, in: LIMC VI 1 (1992) 1078–1081 s. v. Heros Equitans |
| Rostovtseff 1923 | M. Rostovtseff, Une tablette votive thraco-mithriaque du Louvre, MemAcInscr XIII 2, 1923, 385–415 |
| Tatcheva 2000 | M. Tacheva, Le syncrétisme religieux dans les provinces balkaniques de l'Empire romain. Les réliefs des soi-disants Cavaliers Danubiens, ŽivaAnt 50, 2000, 231–245 |
| Tóth 2003 | I. Tóth, Sol Invictus Illyricus I. Problematik des sogenannten donauländischen Reitergottes, in: A. Szabó – E. Tóth (eds.), Pannonia provincialia et archaeologia Eugenio Fitz octogenario dedicata (Budapest 2003) 467–480 |
| Toutain 1909 | J. Toutain, La légende de Mithra étudiée surtout dans les bas-reliefs mithriaques, in: J. Toutain, Études de mythologie et d'histoire des religions antiques (Paris 1909) 228–245 |
| Tudor 1937 | D. Tudor, I Cavalieri danubiani, EphemDac 7, 1937, 189–356 |
| Tudor 1969 | D. Tudor, Corpus monumentorum religionis Equitum Danuvinorum I. The Monuments (Leiden 1969) |
| Tudor 1976 | D. Tudor, Corpus monumentorum religionis Equitum Danuvinorum II. The Analysis and Interpretation of the Monuments (Leiden 1976) |
| Vermaseren 1960 | M. J. Vermaseren, Corpus Inscriptionum et Monumentorum Religionis Mithriacae II (Den Haag 1960) |
| Will 1955 | E. Will, Le relief cultuel gréco-romain. Contribution à l'histoire de l'art de l'Empire romain (Paris 1955) |
| Zotović 1978 | Lj. Zotović, Les éléments orientaux dans le culte des Cavaliers Danubiens et quelques aspects nouveaux de ce culte, in: M. B. De Boer – T. A. Edrige (eds.), Hommages à Maarten J. Vermaseren III (Leiden 1978) 1351–1378 |

*Sorin Nemeti, Babeș-Bolyai University Cluj-Napoca, 1 Melodiei Street, G27, Cluj-Napoca, Romania.*
*[e] sorin.nemeti@ubbcluj.ro*

Christine Ruppert – Gabrielle Kremer – Andrea Binsfeld

# GRABBAUTEN DES 1. JAHRHUNDERTS IN DER WESTLICHEN *CIVITAS TREVERORUM*

**Abstract**

In the framework of the project on the tomb buildings of western *civitas Treverorum*, architectual elements from at least four multi-storeyed tombs of the 1st century from *Orolaunum vicus*/Arlon (B) were identified and analyzed applying methods of architectural research. Supplementary proposals for individual storeys with rectangular, polygonal, or circular groundplan could be made, although not for the overall design of the monuments. In the case of the so-called Amazon Monument, the original erection in the necropolis »Hochgericht«, attested after the Early Imperial period, could be ascertained by means of the fitting of fragments found *in situ* to building elements with secondary find spot. Architectural elements and groundplans of 40 additional monumental grave buildings are known from the remaining area of the western *civitas Treverorum*, and are typologically classified. The majority of the early tomb buildings in this region are associated with large villa sites. The relief decoration of the monuments includes, typically, military and mythological themes.

## FRÜHKAISERZEITLICHE GRABBAUTEN IN ARLON UND IM ÜBRIGEN WESTLICHEN TREVERERGEBIET

Ein wesentlicher Bestandteil des Forschungsprojekts zu den Grabbauten des westlichen Treverergebietes[1] war die Rekonstruktion der frühkaiserzeitlichen, mehrstöckigen Grabdenkmäler aus *Orolaunum vicus*/Arlon[2]. Diese außergewöhnlichen Monumente haben in der Vergangenheit wenig Beachtung erfahren, da sie nur in Form einzelner, meist isolierter Bauteile erhalten sind[3]. Um die Anzahl und Form dieser Grabbauten rekonstruieren zu können, wurden die relevanten Architekturteile innerhalb des erhaltenen Materials nun identifiziert und bauforscherisch aufgearbeitet. Eine wesentliche Herausforderung bestand darin, die einzelnen Bauteile den jeweiligen Monumenten und die rekonstruierten Monumente ihrem Aufstellungsort zuzuordnen, da aufgrund der sekundären Wiederverwendung der Blöcke der originale Kontext verloren ist. Um dieser Ausgangslage zu begegnen, wurde eine Kombination traditioneller Methoden der Bauforschung (Bauaufnahme, Analyse der bautechnischen Bearbeitungsspuren) mit neueren digitalen Methoden (GIS-Kartierungen, 3D-Scans) angewandt. Diese Vorgangsweise erlaubt es, die sekundären Fundumstände in großen Teilen zu rekonstruieren und Zusammenhänge zwischen einzelnen Ensembles von Bauteilen herzustellen. So konnten Erkenntnisse zu den Vorgängen auf der spätantiken Baustelle gewonnen und – im Fall des sog. Amazonenmonumentes (Abb. 1) – der Aufstellungsort und der komplette Lebenszyklus des Monumentes rekonstruiert werden.

Die Analyse der Bauteile und deren Zuordnung zu einzelnen Stockwerken mehrstöckiger Mausoleen führte zu dem Ergebnis, dass es insgesamt mindestens vier derartige Denkmäler der frühen Kaiserzeit in Arlon gegeben hat (Abb. 2). Derzeit erlauben die erhaltenen Blöcke Ergänzungsvorschläge für einzelne Stockwerke, nicht jedoch für den Gesamtaufbau der Monumente. Dabei konnten sowohl Stockwerke mit rechteckigem als auch solche mit kreisförmigem und polygonalem Querschnitt erschlossen werden. Ein kleineres und in seinem Aufbau sehr originel-

---

[1] »Grabbauten des westlichen Treverergebietes im interregionalen Kontext. Vernetzte Auswertung einer gesellschaftsgeschichtlich relevanten Fundgattung«, Joint Project FWF/FNR I 2269-G25 (G. Kremer, A. Binsfeld).

[2] Ruppert 2020 (Universität Luxemburg – TU Berlin, Betreuerinnen: A. Binsfeld, Th. Schulz-Brize, verteidigt am 17. November 2020). s. auch Ruppert 2018; Kremer – Ruppert 2019; Ruppert – Binsfeld 2020.

[3] Mariën 1945; Lefèbvre 1990; Hannick 2009. s. z. B. in Gabelmann 1973; Andrikopoulou-Strack 1986; Numrich 1997; Kremer 2009.

1   Rekonstruktionsvorschlag des sog. Amazonenmonumentes aus Arlon, Obergeschoss (Zeichnung C. Ruppert)

les Denkmal aus Arlon besaß einen hexagonalen Querschnitt. Die frühen Grabbauten aus Arlon stehen damit in der Tradition der hellenistischen mehrstöckigen Mausoleen, die auch in den nordwestlichen Provinzen des Römischen Reiches bereits zahlreich dokumentiert sind[4].

Über die Ensembles von Bauteilen aus Arlon erhalten wir erstmals einen Überblick über Grabbauformen des 1. Jahrhunderts in einem *vicus* des westlichen Trevererogebietes. Nur sporadisch sind vergleichbare Monumente auch in anderen Bereichen dieses Gebietes bekannt geworden (Abb. 3). Mit Ausnahme des Grabbaus von Bartringen, für den aus 109 Einzelteilen ein Rekonstruktionsvorschlag erstellt wurde[5], können diese allerdings nicht in ihrem Gesamtaufbau erfasst werden. Ihre Zeitstellung und ihre Zuordnung zu einem repräsentativen Grabbau erschließt sich hauptsächlich aufgrund der Bauornamentik[6], der figürlichen Darstellungen und der technischen Zurichtung der Blöcke[7] sowie bis zu einem gewissen Grad auch aus dem verwendeten Steinmaterial[8].

---

[4]   s. z. B. Moretti – Tardy 2006; Kremer 2009, 113–127; Scholz 2012, 93–159.
[5]   Kremer 2009.
[6]   Kremer, in Druckvorbereitung.
[7]   Dazu ausführlich Ruppert 2020.
[8]   Kremer u. a. 2023.

2   Hypothetische Rekonstruktion von vier Mausoleen aus Arlon (Zeichnung C. Ruppert)

Neben den mehrstöckigen Mausoleen gehören in diesem Zeitraum die monumentalen Rundgräber mit architektonisch gegliedertem und teilweise reliefdekorierten Tambour und Tumulusaufschüttung zu den gängigen Grabbautypen im untersuchten Gebiet[9].

Insgesamt konnten Architekturteile und Grundrisse von 40 monumentalen Grabdenkmälern in der westlichen *civitas Treverorum* registriert und großteils untersucht werden.

## AUFSTELLUNGSORT DER GRABDENKMÄLER

Für das teilweise rekonstruierbare sog. Amazonenmonument aus Arlon gelang die gesicherte Bestimmung des ursprünglichen Aufstellungsortes in der ab der frühen Kaiserzeit belegten Nekropole auf dem Plateau »Hochgericht«, am südlichen Rand der antiken Siedlung von Arlon[10]. Die Zuordnung kann sich auf Fragmente aus den in den 1970er Jahren erfolgten Funden an diesem Standort stützen, die an Bauteile mit sekundärem Fundort aus der spätantiken Befestigung von Arlon anpassen. Durch die genaue Analyse der an sich unscheinbaren, nach dem Abriss, dem Abtransport und der Wiederverwertung des Monumentes am Aufstellungsort zurückgebliebenen Fragmente konnte so ein wichtiger Nachweis zweifelsfrei erbracht werden. Eine Aufstellung auch der übrigen frühkaiserzeitlichen Monumente in diesem Bereich erscheint naheliegend und kann zum Teil über die Verortung der Spolien im Bauzusammenhang der spätantiken Befestigung plausibel argumentiert, aber nicht nachgewiesen werden[11]. Für den Standort des sog. Amazonenmonu-

---

[9]   Vgl. z. B. Castorio – Maligorne 2007; Krier 2007; Scholz 2012, 7–92; Krier 2020.
[10]  Ruppert 2020. Zur Nekropole s. u. a. Fairon 2005; Ruppert 2018; Henrotay 2018.
[11]  Dazu *in extenso* Ruppert 2020.

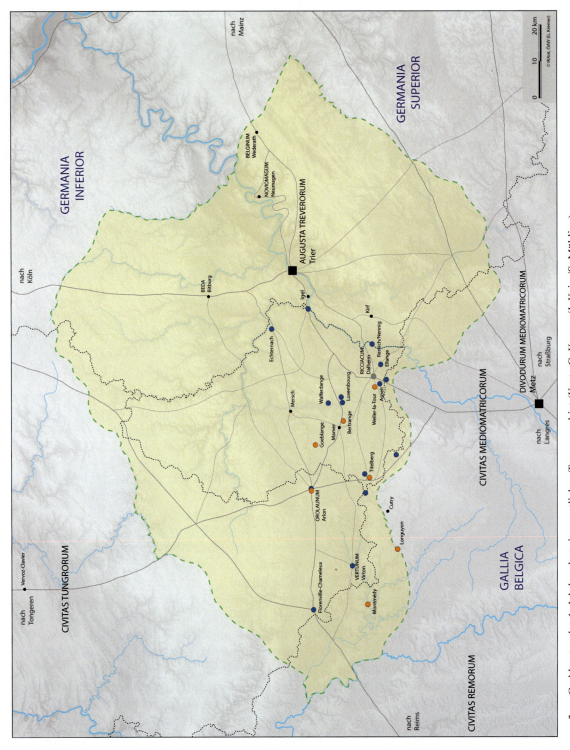

3   Grabbauten des 1. Jahrhunderts im westlichen Treverergebiet (Karte G. Kremer/J. Krier/S. Mühling)

mentes dürften sowohl die erhöhte und weithin sichtbare Lage der Nekropole auf einem Plateau als auch deren Nähe zum übergeordneten Straßennetz ausschlaggebend gewesen sein[12].

Außerhalb der *vici* von *Orolaunum*/Arlon (Belgien) und *Ricciacum*/Dalheim (Luxemburg) steht die Mehrzahl der Grabbauten des 1. Jahrhunderts im westlichen Treverergebiet im Zusammenhang mit großen Villenanlagen, so unter anderem in Bartringen[13], Goeblingen-»Miécher«[14], Walferdingen/Helmsingen[15] oder Echternach[16] (alle Luxemburg). Soweit sich das noch erschließen lässt, waren die Monumente Bestandteil des repräsentativen Konzeptes dieser Anlagen[17].

## BILDTHEMEN

Charakteristisch für die verwendeten Bildthemen sind militärische und mythologische Szenen. Sie unterscheiden sich in der Bildauswahl kaum von denjenigen des Rheingebietes. Im Vordergrund stehen ›militärische‹ Inhalte, allen voran die (Reiter-)Kampfszenen zwischen römischen Soldaten und ihren barbarischen Gegnern. Sie waren an den Sockelgeschossen mehrstöckiger Grabbauten angebracht, wie die Beispiele aus Arlon und Bartringen nahelegen[18] (Abb. 4).

Daneben ist auch eine Reihe mythologischer Figuren vertreten. Es handelt sich vor allem um Darstellungen von Amazonen, Mänaden und Attisfiguren. So ist auf der Außenwand des polygonalen Geschosses des vermutlich dreistöckigen sog. Amazonenmonumentes aus Arlon eine einzelne Amazone dargestellt (Abb. 5). Sie ist aus dem Kontext der Kampfgruppe herausgelöst und als Einzelfigur auf ein Podest gerückt. Der Kopf der Amazone ist weggebrochen, ansonsten ist die Figur aber fast vollständig erhalten. Sie trägt einen langen, gegürteten Chiton, der über der Brust gekreuzt ist und die Brüste frei lässt. In der rechten Hand hält sie eine Doppelaxt, mit der linken trägt sie einen Schild[19]. Einzelne Amazonen sind eher selten auf Grabdenkmälern abgebildet. Daher ist es bemerkenswert, dass man die beste Parallele zur Arloner Amazone in Trier findet. Es handelt sich um ein Grabmonument mit der Darstellung von Perseus und Andromeda auf der Vorderseite und einer einzeln dargestellten Amazone auf der Nebenseite. Eine Deutung als Amazone kommt auch für eine Reliefdarstellung des Monumentes in Bartringen in Betracht[20]. Erhalten sind auf diesem Block noch der Kopf und die Schulter einer weiblichen Figur, während der Körper in Rückenansicht dargestellt ist. Die Bartringer Parallele ist für Arlon vor allem wegen der architektonischen Einbindung interessant, da der Reliefblock ebenfalls zu einer durch Halbsäulen gegliederten Tambourwand gehörte. Wegen der Häufigkeit der Mänadendarstellungen auf frühkaiserzeitlichen Grabbauten in Südgallien sowie im Rhein- und Moselgebiet wurde jedoch bislang der Interpretation als Mänade der Vorzug gegeben[21]. Wie die Amazone wird auch die Mänade als einzelne Tänzerin dargestellt, die aus dem dionysischen Thiasos herausgelöst ist[22].

Auf einem kleinen sechseckigen Grabbau aus Arlon wird das zentrale Relief mit den Porträts der Verstorbenen vermutlich von zwei Attisfiguren flankiert[23] (Abb. 6). Der Trauergestus der rech-

---

[12] Vgl. z. B. Gualandi 2016.
[13] J. Krier in: Kremer 2009, 13–30.
[14] Krier 2007; Krier – Henrich 2011, 213–214.
[15] Krier 2000; Krier – Henrich 2011, 214; Krier 2020, 38.
[16] Metzler u. a. 1981, 304–312; Krier 1999; Krier – Henrich 2011, 214–215; Krier 2020, 41.
[17] Zur Lage der Grabbauten im Kontext großer Villenanlagen: Krier – Henrich 2011.
[18] Gabelmann 1973; Krier – Reinert 1993; Kremer 2009, bes. 79–86.
[19] Zur Darstellung der Amazone auf dem Arloner Monument und weiteren Parallelen vgl. Ruppert – Binsfeld 2020, 105–115. Ausführlich dazu: Ruppert 2020, 83–92 Kat. 06; vgl. auch Ruppert 2018, 179–183; Kremer 2009, 87–91 Abb. 82 Kat. 70; Lefèbvre 1981, 49–50.
[20] Kremer 2009, 87–91, 203–205 Kat. 70.
[21] Vgl. Andrikopoulou-Strack 1986, 115–121.
[22] Zum Vorbild und zur Entwicklung der einzelnen Tänzerin, die aus dem dionysischen Thiasos herausgelöst ist, vgl. Bauchhenß 1976, 170–171.
[23] IAL GR/S018; Ruppert 2020, 156–159 Kat. 83; Henrotay – Warzée 2012, 11 Abb. 12; Hannick 2009, 108, Kat. 54; Lefèbvre 1990, 48. 53 Kat. 23; Andrikopoulou-Strack 1986, 45; Mariën 1945, 100–104 Abb. 42; Lefèbvre 1975,

4 Sockelreliefs mit Reiterkampfszenen aus Arlon im Musée Archéologique d'Arlon Inv. GR/S 3 (oben) und Bartringen im MNHA Luxembourg (unten) (Fotos C. Ruppert, G. Kremer)

ten Figur legt eine Interpretation als Attis oder als Orientale nahe, wobei allerdings nur die linke Figur den für Attis typischen gegürteten Chiton trägt. Für die Interpretation dieses Monumentes und seiner Reliefs stellen sich nun mehrere Fragen. Umstritten ist einerseits die Identifizierung der beiden Figuren. Handelt es sich tatsächlich um Attisdarstellungen, oder haben wir es eher mit Orientalen, Hirten oder auch kriegsgefangenen Barbaren zu tun[24]? Alice Landskron kommt als Fazit dieser Diskussion zu dem Schluss, dass die Ikonografie des stützenden und trauernden Orientalen mit der des Attis verschmilzt[25]. Eine eindeutige Entscheidung wird durch den fragmentarischen Zustand der Darstellungen erschwert. Die Attisfiguren werden im Rahmen der Triumphalikonografie als gefangene und besiegte östliche Barbaren interpretiert. Für eine Zuordnung der Attisfiguren zur Triumphalsymbolik spricht, dass sie häufig für die Nebenseiten von Soldatengrabsteinen gewählt wurden[26].

Der starke Bezug zum Militär zeigt sich auch in der Kombination der Motive von Mänaden, Attiden und Amazonen. Offenbar gehören sie zu einem gemeinsamen Bildrepertoire[27]. So können Amazone und Attis als Ausdruck der militärischen Tüchtigkeit des Verstorbenen, seiner *virtus* und Sieghaftigkeit gelten. Amazonen, Attiden und Mänaden können aber auch für das Fremde und Andersartige, für die Begegnung mit Tod und Trauer sowie die Hoffnung auf Auferstehung

---

40–43 Nr. 18.

[24] Vgl. dazu Bauchhenß 1997, 43–51; Dexheimer 2001, 107–115; Landskron 2005, 121–130; Cambi 2001, 511–520.

[25] Landskron 2005, 128.

[26] Beispiele für die Kombination von Soldatengrabsteinen und Attis- bzw. Orientalenfiguren – z. B. aus Bonn, Andernach, Bingerbrück sowie Koblenz und Umgebung – führt Bauchhenß 1997 an: s. vor allem die Tab. 50–51; Boppert 2005, Nr. 47. 49; Bauchhenß 1978, Nr. 2. 3. 27; Cambi 2001, 511–515; Dexheimer 2001, 107–115.

[27] Kombination Attis – Amazone: Bauchhenß 1978, Nr. 2. 3. 5; Bauchhenß 1975, 86–88 Taf. 31; Kombination Attis/Amazone – dionysische Themen: Boppert 1992, Nr. 4 Taf. 9; Nr. 6 Taf. 10; Boppert 2001, Nr. 140; Coquelet 2019, 187–212; Schnitzler 2017, 196–197 Abb. 2 und 3; Kempchen 1995, 18–20; Vermaseren 1966, 41–59.

5   Amazonenrelief aus Arlon im Musée Archéologique d'Arlon Inv. IAL GR/S 144, IAL GR/S 152 (Foto C. Weber)

6   Teil eines sechseckigen Grabbaus aus Arlon im Musée Archéologique d'Arlon Inv. IAL GR/S 00018, mit Darstellungen des Attis oder von Orientalen zu beiden Seiten des/der Verstorbenen (Foto C. Weber)

und Erlösung stehen[28]. Szenen aus der griechischen und römischen Mythologie waren zudem Zeichen eines Traditions- und Bildungsbewusstseins sowie der ›Romanisierung‹ einer provinzialen Oberschicht. Sie setzen die neue Identität der ersten Generationen von Provinzbewohnern unter römischer Herrschaft ins Bild. Diese Bilder orientieren sich zwar an griechisch-römischen Vorbildern, werden aber – wie die Beispiele für einzelne Amazonen im Treverergebiet zeigen – von den Rezipienten kreativ adaptiert[29].

## GRABINHABER

Aussagen über die Auftraggeber und Besitzer der monumentalen Grabbauten des 1. Jahrhunderts aus dem westlichen Treverergebiet sind nahezu ausschließlich auf die Beurteilung des architektonischen Erscheinungsbildes der Denkmäler sowie des verwendeten Bilddekors angewiesen. Nur wenig Aufschluss lässt sich aus den spärlichen und sehr fragmentarisch erhaltenen Grabinschriften gewinnen[30]. Von besonderer Bedeutung wäre daher die gesellschaftshistorische Auswertung der archäologischen Kontexte, so solche vorhanden sind. Für die Grabbauten im Zusammenhang mit Villenanlagen ist dabei die Frage nach den Anfängen und nach der Nutzungskontinuität der

---

[28] Russenberger 2015, 96–141. 190–193; Nikoloska 2013, 507–526; Cambi 2001, 511–515; Kempchen 1995, 136–137. Zum Sinngehalt mythologischer Bilder auf Grabbauten in *Noricum* und Pannonien und den mit ihnen verbundenen Wertvorstellungen vgl. Kremer 2006, 47–52; Tabaczek 2011, 223–231; Andrikopoulou-Strack 1986, 113 Anm. 449 mit weiterer Literatur. Henner von Hesberg spricht von einer »poétisation« des Grabmals: von Hesberg 2006, 38.

[29] Zu ähnlichen Ergebnissen führte auch die ikonografische Analyse der mythologischen Szenen auf römerzeitlichen Grabbauten in *Noricum*: s. Kremer 2006, 47.

[30] Krier 2020. Vgl. Scholz 2020; Reuter 2020.

Anlagen während und nach dem Gallischen Krieg von Belang, wie sich etwa am Beispiel der Villen von Goeblingen-»Miécher« oder Bartringen zeigen lässt[31].

Die Errichtung von mehrstöckigen Mausoleen im periurbanen Umfeld des *Orolaunum vicus* wirft hingegen Fragen der Siedlungsentwicklung auf, die aufgrund der derzeitigen Forschungslage noch nicht zufriedenstellend beantwortet werden können[32].

Dass es sich bei den hier behandelten Monumenten um Denkmäler einer gesellschaftlichen und wirtschaftlichen Elite handelt, steht allein wegen des notwendigen finanziellen Aufwandes für ihre Errichtung außer Frage. Die häufige Darstellung von Reiterkampfszenen (Abb. 4) und Waffenfriesen lässt eventuell Rückschlüsse auf militärische Laufbahnen der Bestatteten oder zumindest ihre eindeutige Positionierung auf prorömischer Seite in der Anfangsphase der ›Romanisierung‹ zu. Für gesicherte Aussagen über ihre ethnische Herkunft und ihre mutmaßlichen zivilen Karrieren im gallorömischen Umfeld fehlt es derzeit jedoch bis auf wenige Ausnahmen noch an Belegen[33].

## BIBLIOGRAFIE

| | |
|---|---|
| Andrikopoulou-Strack 1986 | J.-N. Andrikopoulou-Strack, Grabbauten des 1. Jahrhunderts n. Chr. im Rheingebiet. Untersuchungen zu Chronologie und Typologie, BJb Beih. 43 (Köln 1986) |
| Bauchhenß 1975 | G. Bauchhenß, Römische Grabmäler aus den Randgebieten des Neuwieder Beckens, JbRGZM 22, 1975, 81–95 |
| Bauchhenß 1976 | G. Bauchhenß, Zu zwei Grabsteinen der cohors VIII Breucorum in Bonn, BJb 176, 1976, 165–178 |
| Bauchhenß 1997 | G. Bauchhenß, Barbaren oder Attis?, in: B. Djurić – I. Lazar (Hrsg.), Akten des IV. Internationalen Kolloquiums über Probleme des provinzialrömischen Kunstschaffens Celje 08.–12.05.1995 (Laibach 1997) 43–51 |
| Bauchhenß 1978 | G. Bauchhenß, Germania Inferior, Bonn und Umgebung. Militärische Grabdenkmäler, CSIR Deutschland III 1 (Bonn 1978) |
| Binsfeld u. a. 2020 | A. Binsfeld – A. Klöckner – G. Kremer – M. Reuter – M. Scholz (Hrsg.), Stadt – Land – Fluss. Grabdenkmäler der Treverer in lokaler undd überregionaler Perspektive. Akten der Internationalen Konferenz in Neumagen und Trier, 25.–27.10.2018, TrZ Beih. 37 (Trier 2020) |
| Boppert 1992 | W. Boppert, Zivile Grabsteine aus Mainz und Umgebung, CSIR Deutschland II 6 (Mainz 1992) |
| Boppert 2001 | W. Boppert, Römische Steindenkmäler aus dem Landkreis Bad Kreuznach, CSIR Deutschland II 9 (Mainz 2001) |
| Boppert 2005 | W. Boppert, Römische Steindenkmäler aus dem Landkreis Mainz-Bingen, CSIR Deutschland II 14 (Mainz 2005) |
| Cambi 2001 | N. Cambi, Attis or someone else on funerary monuments from Dalmatia?, in: P. Noelke u. a. (Hrsg.), Romanisation und Resistenz in Plastik, Architektur und Inschriften der Provinzen des Imperium Romanum. Neue Funde und Forschungen. Akten des VII. Internationalen Colloquiums über Probleme des Provinzialrömischen Kunstschaffens Köln 02.–06.05.2001 (Mainz 2001) 511–520 |
| Castorio – Maligorne 2007 | J.-N. Castorio – Y. Maligorne, Une tombe monumentale d'époque tibérienne à Nasium (cité des Leuques), Études lorraines d'Antiquité Nationale 4 (Paris 2007) |
| Castorio – Maligorne 2016 | J.-N. Castorio – Y. Maligorne (Hrsg.), Mausolées et grands domaines ruraux à l'époque romaine dans le nord-est de la Gaule, Scripta antiqua 90 (Bordeaux 2016) |
| Coquelet 2019 | C. Coquelet, Le mausolée de Vervoz (Belgique) dans la cité des Tongres, entre agglomération routière et *villa*, Gallia 76/1, 2019, 187–212 |
| Dexheimer 2001 | D. Dexheimer, Zur Deutung von Attisfiguren auf Grabaltären Oberitaliens, in: T. Panhuysen (Hrsg.), Die Maastrichter Akten des 5. Internationalen Kolloquiums über das provinzialrömische Kunstschaffen, im Rahmen des CSIR. Typologie, Ikonographie und |

---

[31] Dazu Kremer 2009, 127–129; Krier 2020.
[32] Dazu Ruppert 2020; Krier 2020, 39.
[33] Zusammenfassend s. Kremer 2016 (mit weiterer Literatur); Krier 2020.

| | soziale Hintergründe der provinzialen Grabdenkmäler und Wege der ikonographischen Einwirkung, Maastricht 29.05.–01.06.1997 (Maastricht 2001) 107–115 |
|---|---|
| Espérandieu VI | É. Espérandieu, Recueil général des bas-reliefs, statues et bustes de la Gaule Romaine VI. Suppléments (suite) (Paris 1915) |
| Fairon 2005 | G. Fairon, Contribution à l'étude de l'Arlon romain. Les découvertes faites en 1979–80 lors de l'implantation du Fonds des Bâtiments Scolaires à la rue de Sesselich, Les cahiers du Groupe de Recherches Aériennes du Sud Belge 38 (Waltzing 2005) |
| Gabelmann 1973 | H. Gabelmann, Römische Grabmonumente mit Reiterkampfszenen im Rheingebiet, BJb 173, 1973, 132–200 |
| Gualandi 2016 | S. Gualandi, Périurbains ou ruraux: critères d'implantation de quelques mausolées lingons, in: Castorio – Maligorne 2016, 65–74 |
| Hannick 2009 | P. Hannick (Hrsg.), Le Musée archéologique luxembourgeois d'Arlon (Arlon 2009) |
| Henrotay 2018 | D. Henrotay, Réexamen du contexte archéologique de la nécropole du Hochgericht, Signa 7, 2018, 127–130 |
| Henrotay – Warzée 2012 | D. Henrotay – G. Warzée, Arlon la gallo-romaine, Carnets du Patrimoine 98 (Namur 2012) |
| Kempchen 1995 | M. Kempchen, Mythologische Themen in der Grabskulptur. Germania Inferior, Germania Superior, Gallia Belgica und Raetia (Münster 1995) |
| Kremer 2006 | G. Kremer, Mythologie und Grabarchitektur am Beispiel der römerzeitlichen Grabbauten in Noricum und Pannonien, in: M. Kokole – B. Murovec – M. Šašel Kos – M. Talbot (Hrsg.), Mediterranean Myths from Classical Antiquity to the Eighteenth Century (Laibach 2006) 37–52 |
| Kremer 2009 | G. Kremer, Das frühkaiserzeitliche Mausoleum von Bartringen (Luxemburg). Mit einem Beitrag von J. Krier, Dossiers d'archéologie du Musée national d'histoire et d'art 12 (Luxemburg 2009) |
| Kremer 2016 | G. Kremer, Monuments funéraires de la cité des Trévires occidentale: réflexions sur les commanditaires, in: Castorio – Maligorne 2016, 75–92 |
| Kremer, in Druckvorbereitung | G. Kremer, Monuments funéraires de la civitas Treverorum occidentale: le décor architectural, in: Actes du colloque »Le décor d'architecture dans les cités du Centre-Est: une école régionale?«, Sens 14.–15.10.2021 (vorläufiger Titel), in Druckvorbereitung |
| Kremer – Ruppert 2019 | G. Kremer – Ch. Ruppert, Les monuments funéraires de la civitas Treverorum (partie occidentale), Annales de l'Institut archéologique du Luxembourg 148, 2017 (2019) 29–41 |
| Kremer u. a. 2023 | G. Kremer – R. Dreesen – E. Goemaere, Les monuments funéraires gallo-romains et l'emploi de la pierre dans la région occidentale de la Civitas Treverorum, in: M. Piavaux – C. Moulis – M. Macaux – L. Verslype (Hrsg.), Pierre à pierre II. Économie de la pierre dans la vallée de la Meuse et dans les régions limitrophes (I$^{er}$ siècle avant J.-C. – VIII$^{e}$ siècle). Actes du colloque international Namur – Dinant 06.–08.12.2018, Études et Documents, Archéologie 45 (Namur 2022) 149–161 |
| Krier 1999 | J. Krier, Von Epternus zu Willibrord. Die Vor- und Frühgeschichte der Abtei Echternach aus archäologischer Sicht, in: M. C. Ferrari – J. Schroeder – H. Trauffler (Hrsg.), Die Abtei Echternach 698–1998 (Luxemburg 1999) 29–46 |
| Krier 2000 | J. Krier, Romains et Francs à Helmsange, in: 150 Joer Gemeng Walfer 1851–2000 II (Walferdingen 2000) 334–343 |
| Krier 2007 | J. Krier, Ein neuer Grabrundbau des 1. Jahrhunderts n. Chr. in Goeblingen (Luxemburg), in: E. Walde – B. Kainrath (Hrsg.), Die Selbstdarstellung der römischen Gesellschaft in den Provinzen im Spiegel der Steindenkmäler. Akten des IX. Internationalen Kolloquiums über Probleme des Provinzialrömischen Kunstschaffens, IKARUS 2 (Innsbruck 2007) 159–171 |
| Krier 2020 | J. Krier, Die einheimische Führungsschicht in den Grabdenkmälern und Grabinschriften des Treverergebiets: Das 1. Jh. n. Chr. – und danach?, in: Binsfeld u. a. 2020, 37–48 |
| Krier – Henrich 2011 | J. Krier – P. Henrich, Monumental funerary structures of the 1$^{st}$ to 3$^{rd}$ centuries associated with Roman villas in the area of the Treveri, in: N. Roymans – T. Derks (Hrsg.), Villa Landscapes in the Roman North. Economy, Culture and Lifestyles, Amsterdam Archaeological Studies 17 (Amsterdam 2011) 211–234 |
| Krier – Reinert 1993 | J. Krier – F. Reinert, Das Reitergrab von Hellingen. Die Treverer und das römische Militär in der frühen Kaiserzeit (Luxemburg 1993) |
| Landskron 2005 | A. Landskron, Attis, Parther und andere Barbaren. Ein Beitrag zum Verständnis von Orientalendarstellungen auf Grabsteinen der nördlichen Provinzen, in: M. Sanader |

| | (Hrsg.), Religion und Mythos als Anregung für die provinzialrömische Plastik. Akten des VIII. Internationalen Kolloquiums über Probleme des provinzialrömischen Kunstschaffens Zagreb 05.–08.05.2003 (Zagreb 2005) 121–130 |
|---|---|
| Lefèbvre 1975 | L. Lefèbvre, Les sculptures gallo-romaines du Musée d'Arlon, Bulletin trimestriel de l'Institut Archéologique du Luxembourg 51, 1975 |
| Lefèbvre 1981 | L. Lefèbvre, Les sculptures gallo-romaines découvertes dans le sous-sol de la Breck à Arlon, Bulletin trimestriel de l'Institut Archéologique du Luxembourg 57, 1981, 34–54 |
| Lefèbvre 1990 | L. Lefèbvre, Le Musée Luxembourgeois Arlon (Brüssel 1990) |
| Mariën 1945 | M. E. Mariën, Les monuments funéraires de l'Arlon romain, Annales de l'Institut Archéologique du Luxembourg 76, 1945 |
| Metzler u. a. 1981 | J. Metzler – J. Zimmer – L. Bakker, Ausgrabungen in Echternach (Luxemburg 1981) |
| Moretti – Tardy 2006 | J.-Ch. Moretti – D. Tardy (Hrsg.), L'architecture funéraire monumentale: la Gaule dans l'Empire romain. Actes du colloque organisé par l'IRAA du CNRS et le musée archéologique Henri-Prades à Lattes 11.–13.10.2001 (Paris 2006) |
| Nikoloska 2013 | A. Nikoloska, The Sepulchral Character of the Cult of Cybele and Attis on the Monuments from the Republic of Croatia, in: N. Cambi – G. Koch (Hrsg.), Funerary Sculpture of the Western Illyricum and Neighbouring Regions of the Roman Empire. Proceedings of the International Scholarly Conference in Split 27.–30.09.2009 (Split 2013) 507–527 |
| Numrich 1997 | B. Numrich, Die Architektur der römischen Grabdenkmäler aus Neumagen. Beiträge zur Chronologie und Typologie (Trier 1997) |
| Ruppert 2018 | Ch. Ruppert, Tombeaux monumentaux d'Arlon/Orolaunum vicus, Signa 7, 2018, 179–183 |
| Ruppert 2020 | Ch. Ruppert, Die frühkaiserzeitliche Grabarchitektur aus *Orolaunum vicus*/Arlon. Rekonstruktion und Kontextualisierung der Grabbauten einer ruralen Elite (Diss. Université du Luxembourg 2020) |
| Ruppert – Binsfeld 2020 | Ch. Ruppert – A. Binsfeld, Das Amazonenmonument. Ein frühkaiserzeitliches Mausoleum aus Arlon, in: Binsfeld u. a. 2020, 105–115 |
| Russenberger 2015 | Ch. Russenberger, Der Tod und die Mädchen. Amazonen auf römischen Sarkophagen (Berlin 2015) |
| Schnitzler 2017 | B. Schnitzler, Un mausolée poul l'éternité, in: B. Schnitzler – P. Flotté (Hrsg.), Vivre à Koenigshoffen à l'époque romaine. Un quartier civil de Strasbourg-Argentorate du I$^{er}$–IV$^e$ siècle après J.-C. (Straßburg 2017) 196–197 |
| Scholz 2012 | M. Scholz, Grabbauten in den nördlichen Grenzprovinzen des römischen Reiches zwischen Britannien und dem Schwarzen Meer, 1.–3. Jh. n. Chr., Monographien RGZM 103 (Mainz 2012) |
| Scholz 2020 | M. Scholz, Zur Repräsentation munizipaler Magistrate und Würdenträger in Monumentinschriften in *Augusta Treverorum*/Trier und in anderen *civitas*-Metropolen Ostgalliens, in: Binsfeld u. a. 2020, 49–58 |
| Reuter 2020 | M. Reuter, Zu den Inschriften römischer Grabdenkmäler im Moselgebiet, in: Binsfeld u. a. 2020, 59–61 |
| Tabaczek 2011 | M. Tabaczek, Mythologische Themen an Grabdenkmälern der Gallia Belgica, in: T. Nogales Basarrate – I. Rodà (Hrsg.), Roma y las provincias. Modelo y difusion (Rom 2011) 223–231 |
| Vermaseren 1966 | M. J. Vermaseren, The Legend of Attis in Greek and Roman Art (Leiden 1966) |
| von Hesberg 2006 | H. von Hesberg, Les modèles des édifices funéraires en Italie: leur message et leur réception, in: Moretti – Tardy 2006, 11–39 |

*Christine Ruppert*
*[e] ruppert_christine@web.de*

*Gabrielle Kremer, Österreichisches Archäologisches Institut, Österreichische Akademie der Wissenschaften, Dominikanerbastei 16, 1010 Wien, Österreich.*
*[e] gabrielle.kremer@oeaw.ac.at*

*Andrea Binsfeld, Institut d'Histoire, Université du Luxembourg, 11, Porte des Sciences, 4366 Esch-sur-Alzette (Belval), Luxemburg.*
*[e] andrea.binsfeld@uni.lu*

Mirjana Sanader

# EINE SKULPTUR DES APOLLO KITHARODOS AUS DALMATIEN[1]

**Abstract**
The collection of the Archaeological Museum in Split preserves a fragmented sculpture of a seated Apollo Kitharodos (AMS-55156). Stone statues depicting the seated Apollo Kitharodos, wearing a *chiton*, are rare in the Roman provinces, which was the inspiration to carry out an iconographic and comparative study to get as detailed information as possible for the sculptural reconstruction.

Die Sammlung des Archäologischen Museums in Split bewahrt eine teilweise erhaltene, sitzende männliche Statue (AMS-55156)[2]. Trotz der starken Fragmentierung der Statue ist zu erkennen, dass es sich um Apollo Kitharodos handelt (Abb. 1 a–c).

Statuen des sitzenden, mit einem Hüftmantel bekleideten Apollo Kitharodos sind in den römischen Provinzen eher selten, was uns veranlasste, eine ikonografische und komparative Untersuchung dieser Statue vorzunehmen, um eine möglichst detaillierte Rekonstruktion ihres ehemaligen Erscheinungsbildes zu gewinnen und ihren ursprünglichen Aufstellungskontext zu ermitteln.

## ZEUGNISSE DES APOLLO-KULTES IN KROATIEN

Zu Zeiten des Römischen Reiches befanden sich auf dem Gebiet des heutigen Kroatiens Teile zweier römischer Provinzen – Dalmatien und Pannonien – sowie einer der elf italischen Regionen, nämlich der *regio X*. Insofern ist es nicht überraschend, dass auch in Kroatien zahlreiche Inschriften, Statuen und Statuetten, Reliefs und andere Denkmäler erhalten sind, die von der Existenz römischer Kulte zeugen. Sie belegen, dass nach dem am häufigsten verehrten Jupiter die Verehrung für Silvanus und Liber sowie Diana und Venus folgte[3].

In viel geringerem Umfang wurde Apollo verehrt, unter anderem als Sonnengott, als Heilgott, oder als Gott der Orakel und Weissagung wie auch der Künste[4]. Sein Kult ist in Kroatien bislang durch nur sieben Altäre und eine Statue dokumentiert. Drei Altäre und eine schöne Marmorskulptur des Gottes wurden in *Aquae Iasae* gefunden[5], zwei Altäre stammen aus Bribir (EDCS-59500041; EDCS-10000825), einer kam in *Salona* (EDCS-10101756) und einer in Jader (EDCS-28400154) zu Tage. Diesen Belegen können wir nun die salonitanische Apollo-Skulptur an die Seite stellen (lupa 24979) sowie einen bisher nicht veröffentlichten Altar aus *Salona*, auf den wir im Zuge der Recherche zu diesem Beitrag gestoßen sind (lupa 24861). Darüber hinaus sind römische Gemmen mit Apollo-Darstellungen, unter ihnen auch solche als Apollo Kitharodos, in

---

[1] Diese Arbeit wurde von der Kroatischen Wissenschaftsstiftung durch das Forschungsprojekt »Razumijevanje rimskih granica: primjer istočnog Jadrana« (IP-2018-01-4934) finanziert.
[2] Ich danke Frau Dr. Zrinka Buljević für das Angebot zur Veröffentlichung dieses interessanten Denkmals.
[3] Sanader 2008, 157–186; Cvetko 2022.
[4] Bilić 2011, 45–64.
[5] Kušan Špalj 2017, 280–281. 285–286. 288; Cvetko 2022, Nr. 777.

a

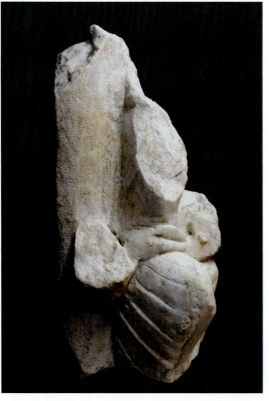

b

c

1 a–c  Skulptur des Apollo Kitharodos aus *Salona*, Archäologisches Museum in Split (Fotos T. Seser)

kroatischen Museen zu finden[6] wie auch unter den antiken Gemmen aus Dalmatien, die Arthur Evans nach Oxford brachte[7].

Nur am Rande sind hier zwei schöne Marmorskulpturen und ein Marmorkopf des Apollo im Archäologischen Museum in Zagreb zu erwähnen: Bei ihnen handelt es sich um Denkmäler aus der Nugent-Sammlung, die in der überwiegenden Mehrheit aus Minturno stammen[8] und daher für die Verehrung des Apollo in Kroatien nicht von Bedeutung sind.

## DER HEUTIGE ZUSTAND DES SALONITANISCHEN APOLLO

Die Marmorstatue, die wir hier besprechen, ist dreiansichtig: sie konnte frontal und von der Seite betrachtet werden kann; ihre Rückseite war nicht zu sehen. Damit ähnelt sie auf den ersten Blick einem aus der Fläche heraustretenden Objekt, eigentlich einem Hochrelief. Bekleidet ist die Figur des sitzenden Apollo nur mit einem Hüftmantel, der den gesamten Unterkörper verhüllt, am Rücken hochgezogen ist und vorn am Körper in einem Schulterbausch endet, der mit einer Fibel (Knoten [?]) zusammengehalten wird. Auf dem linken Oberschenkel des Gottes ruht ein nur teilweise erhaltenes Saiteninstrument, das er mit der linken, im Ellenbogen angewinkelten und nach vorn geführten Hand hält. Ein Tragegurt über der rechten Schulter und dem Oberkörper hält die Kithara (in deren Saiten die linke Hand greifen sollte). Die Figur sitzt auf einem gegabelten Baumstamm (Lorbeerbaum [?]). Der Kopf, die rechte Schulter und der rechte Arm, Teile des linken Unterarmes sowie das rechte Knie sind abgebrochen, wie dies auch für die beiden Füße der Fall ist, sofern diese überhaupt dargestellt waren. Die erhaltene Höhe der Statue beträgt 49 cm.

## KURZER EXKURS ZU KITHARA UND LYRA

Bevor wir mit der Analyse des Denkmals fortfahren, widmen wir uns kurz dem Saitenmusikinstrument, das an Apollos linkem Oberschenkel ruht. Das Wissen über antike Musikinstrumente beruht vor allem auf drei Quellen: erstens auf den literarischen Beschreibungen, wie den »Hymnis Homerici« (Hymnos an Hermes 4), Pausanias (2, 19, 7; 5, 14, 8; 8, 17, 5; 9, 5, 8; 9, 30, 1), Philostratos (imag. 1, 10. 26), Pseudo-Hyginus (astr. 2, 7), Ovid (met. 2, 679 f.) und Pseudo-Apollodorus (bibliotheca 3, 113); zweitens auf bildlichen Darstellungen, vor allem der Vasenmalerei, den Skulpturen und Fresken; und drittens, seltener, auf archäologischen Zeugnissen, d. h. Überresten von Musikinstrumenten[9]. Beurteilt man anhand der bildlichen Belege richtig, so waren Lyra und Kithara neben dem Aulos die bevorzugten Musikinstrumente[10].

Anders als die Musikwissenschaft hat sich die Archäologie bislang für antike Musik und antike Instrumente weniger interessiert[11]. Dies könnte erklären, warum in der archäologischen Literatur bei der Verwendung der Begriffe Lyra und Kithara eine gewisse Widersprüchlichkeit und auch Austauschbarkeit herrscht. Nicht selten kommt es vor, dass bei der Beschreibung einer Apollo-Darstellung das Saiteninstrument in seinen Händen einmal als Kithara und ein andermal als Lyra bezeichnet wird[12]. Grund dürfte sein, dass zur Formentwicklung dieser beiden Instru-

---

[6] Nardelli 2002, 207 Nr. 5; Kaić 2013.
[7] Hoey Middleton 1991, Nr. 40. 41. 43–48.
[8] Karković Takalić – Rabar 2019, 53–92.
[9] Die ältesten Lyren wurden aus Schildkrötenpanzern hergestellt. Fragmente solcher Lyren sind im British Museum London (Inv. 1816.6-10.501), im Archäologischen Museum von Argos (Inv. A 56), im Museo Archeologico Nazionale di Locri (Tomb 1143) und im Museo Provinciale Lecce (Inv. 3935) aufbewahrt. Roberts 1981, 303–312. s. auch Maas – Snyder 1989.
[10] Altgriechische Musiker spielten auch noch andere antike Saiteninstrumente, z. B. Phorminx und Barbitos: Sachs 1943.
[11] Eine der Ausnahmen ist die Forschungsgruppe Antike Musik am Österreichischen Archäologischen Institut Wien <https://www.oeaw.ac.at/oeai/forschung/altertumswissenschaften/antike-musik> (02.11.2023) mit dem neuen »Journal of Music Archaeology« <https://jma.vlg.oeaw.ac.at/> (04.12.2023).
[12] Šoštarić 2018, 663–674.

mente noch keine allgemein gültigen Ergebnisse und Kenntnisse vorliegen. So gibt es noch keine zufriedenstellenden Antworten auf die Frage, wie diese Instrumente konstruiert waren und wie sie gespielt wurden[13]. Beide Instrumente waren einander in vielerlei Hinsicht sehr ähnlich, ihr wesentlicher Unterschied, so John G. Landels, bestand darin, dass Resonanzkörper und Rahmen der Kithara aus einem Material – Holz – gefertigt waren, während der Resonanzkörper der Lyra aus Schildpatt und Tierhaut bestand, in den hölzerne Arme eingefügt waren[14]. Vermutet wird auch, dass die Kithara hinsichtlich der Erzeugung von Tönen komplexer als die Lyra war, weshalb sie vor allem von professionellen Musikern, den *kitharodes*, gespielt wurde[15]. Angenommen wird zudem, dass Lyra und Kithara nicht nur mit den Fingerspitzen, sondern auch mit einem festen Plektrum aus trockenem Leder, das in der rechten Hand mit ausgestrecktem Ellbogen und nach innen gebogener Handfläche gehalten wurde, gespielt werden konnten[16]. Mit den Fingerspitzen der linken Hand wurden die Saiten gedrückt, um die durch das Plektrum erzeugten Töne zu steuern und der Kithara die gewünschten Töne zu entlocken.

## APOLLO IN ROM

Apollo, treuer Begleiter der ersten griechischen Kolonisten der *Magna Graecia*, wurde im 6. Jahrhundert v. Chr. während der Herrschaft der etruskischen Könige in Rom heimisch. In der Folge wurde er in das römische Pantheon integriert – mit allen seinen griechischen Eigenschaften und Vorstellungen, zumal kein römisches Äquivalent existierte[17]. Erika Simon formulierte: »… neben seinen Funktionen als Gott der Sybyllen und der Lustration, der die Stadt von Seuchen und das Heer von Blutschuld befreite, wurde Apollo für die Römer während der Republik auch zum Gott der Musen, ja sogar, den Dionysos ›ersetzend‹, zum Theatergott«[18]. Verehrt wurde Apollo in einem Tempel am Marsfeld, der, wie Plinius (nat. 36, 35) überliefert, überladen mit Votivdenkmälern war, darunter auch eine Apollon Kitharodos-Statue des Timarchides aus Athen. Diese heute verschollene Statue scheint als Vorbild für vielen Kopien gedient zu haben, unter ihnen auch der sog. Apollo von Kyrene, der heute im British Museum aufbewahrt wird[19].

Die Regierungszeit des Augustus, der sich Apollo besonders verbunden fühlte, steht für eine neue Ära der Verehrung des Gottes. Alles begann, als Augustus im Jahre 36 v. Chr., damals noch als Octavian, der – wenn wir Sueton (Aug. 72, 1) vertrauen können – bis dahin am Forum Romanum gewohnt hatte, ein Grundstück am Palatin erwarb, um sich hier eine neue Residenz zu errichten. Laut Vergil (Aen. 8, 704 f.) wurde dieses Verhältnis besonders nach Octavians Sieg über Antonius in *Actium* am 2. September 31 v. Chr. augenscheinlich. In Folge dieses Sieges ließ der erste römische Kaiser aus Dankbarkeit einen neuen prächtigen Tempel ebenfalls am Palatin und eng verbunden mit seinem Wohnhaus anlegen, in den er sogar die sibyllinischen Bücher aus dem kapitolinischen Jupiter-Tempel verbringen ließ[20]. Man hat den Apollo-Tempel am Palatin auch Actius, Actiacus oder Navalis genannt, was an den Sieg über Antonius erinnerte, aber auch Rhamnusius, was an das Nemesion in *Rhamnus* in Attika erinnerte, woher die in dem Tempel aufgestellte Kultstatue des Gottes stammte[21]. Als Besonderheit gilt zu vermerken, dass das Kultbild den musischen Apollo in Gestalt des lang gewandeten Kitharoden darstellte.

---

[13] A. Bélis versuchte, eine Lyra zu rekonstruieren: Bélis 1989, 203–216. P. Kurfürst hat etwas später griechische Kitharen, die man zwischen 650–450 v. Chr. spielte, untersucht: Kurfürst 1992, 7–13.

[14] Landels 1999. Landels unterscheidet auch zwei Formen von Kithara, und zwar eine ältere mit abgerundetem und eine jüngere mit flachem Boden.

[15] Es gab auch eine sog. thrakische Kithara, die eine virtuosere Technik als Lyra und Kithara ermöglichte. s. Kárpáti 2012, 221–246 bes. 232.

[16] Thurn 1998, 411–434; Landels 1999, 47–68.

[17] Laut E. Simon hatte Veiovis einige Merkmale von Apollos Wesen: Simon 1990, 210.

[18] All diese Funktionen kann man in dem Tempel am Marsfeld und dem Theater daneben erkennen.

[19] Hill 1962, 126.

[20] Jucker 1982, 82–100; Carettoni 1988, 263–267.

[21] Hill 1962, 129.

## ÜBER DIE IKONOGRAFIE DES APOLLO KITHARODOS

Unzählige Darstellungen des Apollo sind erhalten geblieben, darunter viele, die ihn stehend oder auch sitzend mit einem Saitenmusikinstrument zeigen[22]. Die Darstellung des Instruments offenbart nicht nur Apollo als Beschützer der Künste, sondern erinnert auch an die Legende von den Zwistigkeiten mit Hermes und daran, wie er in den Besitz des Instruments gelangte[23]. Der Typ des sitzenden, Kithara spielenden Apollo erscheint in der Vasenmalerei ab dem 6. Jahrhundert v. Chr.[24]. Auf diesen Bildern hält er die Kithara immer in der linken und das Plektron in der rechten Hand, wie es auch bei den erhaltenen Statuen der Fall ist[25].

Apollo, der mit dem Saiteninstrument dargestellt ist, wird als Apollo Kitharodos oder als Kitharode bezeichnet[26]. Martin Flashar unterscheidet – von den ersten griechischen Skulpturen bis zur klassizistischen Strömung des 1. Jahrhunderts bzw. den augusteischen Schöpfungen – basierend auf Haltung und Art der Kleidung unterschiedliche Typen von Kitharoden-Darstellungen[27], so etwa stehende von sitzenden Kitharoden, wobei aber beide Typen lang gewandet, im Hüftmantel, mit Himation oder nackt dargestellt werden können.

An dieser Stelle soll noch einmal an die zahlreichen Darstellungen professioneller Kithara spielender Musiker insbesondere auf griechischen Vasen erinnert werden. Da diese Musiker grundsätzlich formelle und festliche Gewänder tragen, sind sie aber leicht von Apollo zu unterscheiden, zumal der Gott meist in Chiton und Himation gehüllt oder völlig nackt dargestellt wird[28].

## SCHLUSSFOLGERUNG

Wie bereits betont, sind mehrere sitzende Statuen des ein Saitenmusikinstrument spielenden Apollo erhalten geblieben[29]. Diese stammen laut Martin Flashar vor allem aus römischen oder östlichen Werkstätten[30]. Wie wir feststellen konnten, sind Statuen des sitzenden Apollo Kitharodos in den römischen Provinzen selten zu finden. Uns ist nur eine Statue eines sitzenden Apollo Kitharodos bekannt. Sie wurde in Bonn gefunden[31] und ist wie der Apollo aus *Salona* nur dreiansichtig gearbeitet (60 × 40 × 50 cm; 66 cm mit Plinthe)[32]. Den seltenen Statuen des sitzenden musizierenden Apollo stehen zahlreiche Reliefdarstellungen gegenüber, die in vielen römischen Provinzen verbreitet waren[33].

Obwohl alle Darstellungen des sitzenden Apollo Kitharodos auf den ersten Blick einander ähneln, lassen sich gewisse Unterschiede feststellen, nicht nur in der Darstellung des Instruments, sondern auch in der Art der Kleidung und in Bezug auf den Sitz. Zumeist sitzt der Gott auf dem Omphalos oder auf einem Felsen, der mit seinem Mantel bedeckt sein kann. Er kann aber auch auf einem Hocker, Stuhl oder Thron platziert sein oder stehend neben einem Altar oder Dreifuss dar-

---

[22] Jucker 1982, 82–100.
[23] Der Hymnus an Hermes 4 erzählt detailliert, wie Hermes seine Wiege verlässt, um die Rinder Apollos zu rauben, nachdem er den Panzer einer Schildkröte zur Lyra verarbeitet hatte. s. auch Schenck zu Schweinsberg 2017.
[24] Flashar 1992.
[25] Kárpáti 2012, 231.
[26] Für diese Arbeit wurde vor allem auf den umfassenden Beitrag im LIMC und die Monografie von M. Flashar zurückgegriffen: Simon 1984; Palagia 1984, 183–203; Flashar 1992.
[27] Dabei hatte M. Flashar die Schwierigkeit, dass nur sehr wenige Originalwerke erhalten sind. Daher führte er sowohl die Beispiele kaiserzeitlicher Kopien als auch kleinere Werke an, wie Votivreliefs oder Münzbildnisse: Flashar 1992, 10.
[28] Ercoles 2014, 95–110; Beazley 1922, 70–98.
[29] Palagia 1984, 183–203; Simon 1984, 363–446.
[30] Flashar 1992, 143–157. 173–181.
[31] Ich möchte Herrn Prof. Dr. Peter Noelke danken, der mich auf die Bonner Statue hingewiesen hat, sowie dem geschätzten Kollegen Dr. Hans-H. von Prittwitz und Graffon für den Artikel, den er mir zusandte.
[32] von Prittwitz und Graffon 2019, 120–122.
[33] Palagia 1984, 183–203.

2 Mosaik mit Büste des Apollo aus *Salona*, Archäologisches Museum in Split (Foto T. Seser)

gestellt werden. Bei unserer Skulptur aus *Salona* sitzt Apollo auf einem gegabelten Baumstamm (Lorbeerbaum [?]), wofür wir keine Analogie finden konnten. Die besten Vergleichsbeispiele fanden wir auf einem rotfigurigen Skyphos aus dem Archäologischen Museum Palermo, der den Gott in einem Busch sitzend zeigt, sowie auf einem Amethystring in Hannover, auf dem Apollo Kithara spielend auf einem Ast sitzend dargestellt ist[34].

Bevor wir uns abschließend der Frage widmen, wo die Figur des musizierenden Apollo im antiken *Salona* gestanden haben könnte, soll erwähnt werden, dass in *Salona* nur ein einziger Apollo-Altar, errichtet von einem gewissen Caius Iulius Numida, gefunden wurde. Das führt zu der Annahme, dass der Apollo-Kult in *Salona* bekannt, aber nicht weit verbreitet war. Obwohl die Fundumstände unserer Statue nicht bekannt sind, ist davon auszugehen, dass sie nicht Teil eines Sakralbaus war, sondern in profanem Umfeld anzusiedeln ist, zumal ihre Rückseite nicht zur Ansicht bestimmt war. Wie für die Apollo-Statue aus Bonn vermuten wir auch für jene aus *Salona*, dass sie ursprünglich im Garten einer Stadtvilla stand[35]. Unter den Statuen, mit denen römische Villen geschmückt wurden, war offensichtlich auch Platz für einen musizierenden Apollo[36].

Zurzeit ist nur eine Stadtvilla in *Salona*, und zwar der sog. Gouverneurspalast, näher bekannt[37]. Sein Grundriss wie auch die Ausstattung mit Bodenmosaiken belegen den direkten Bezug zu einer typischen römischen Peristylvilla. Unter den erhaltenen Mosaiken zeigt eines im zentralen Medaillon die Büste des Apollo (Abb. 2)[38]. Der Gedanke, unsere Statue und das Mosaikemblem miteinander zu einem Ausstattungsprogramm für eine Villa zu verbinden, ist attraktiv, jedoch bislang ohne ausreichende Beweise. Man kann abschließend nur festhalten, dass die Statue des

---

[34] Simon 1984, 402 Nr. 259.
[35] Zu den Austattungsprogrammen römischer Villen s. Neudecker 1988.
[36] Jones Roccos 2002, 273–293.
[37] Bulić 1924/1925, 88–89; Matulić 1995, 155–162; Jeličić Radonić 2019, 1. 313–329.
[38] Medrer 2003, 109 Taf. 46, 1.

musizierenden Apollo aus *Salona* nicht als Kultobjekt aufgestellt war, sondern als Vermittlerin des kultivierten Geschmacks ihrer Besitzer.

Da die antike Stadt *Salona* bisher bei Weitem nicht zur Gänze ausgegraben und erforscht ist, sollte man mit Spannung in die Zukunft blicken – nicht nur in Bezug auf eventuelle weitere Zeugnisse der Apollo-Verehrung in der einstigen Metropole der Provinz Dalmatien, sondern auch aus der prinzipiellen Erwartung heraus, dass künftige Forschungen generell neue wichtige Erkenntnisse über die Stadt, ihre Kultur, Religion und Wirtschaft an den Tag bringen werden. Dass dies möglich ist, zeigte sich während der Abfassung dieses Beitrags: Eine Tageszeitung berichtete, dass im Ostteil der Stadt, in unmittelbarer Nähe der salonitanischen Stadtmauer, ein prunkvolles römisches Wohnhaus ausgegraben worden war[39]. Dabei handelt es sich um ein monumentales Gebäude mit Peristyl, einem Brunnen in dessen Mitte und umliegenden, mit Mosaikböden ausgestatteten Räumlichkeiten, einige davon mit Exedren. Vorläufig wurde die Villa im Zustand des 2.–7. Jahrhunderts erfasst, und zwar vom klassischen römischen Wohnbau mit Thermen samt Badewannen und Wasserbecken bis hin zum spätantik umgebauten Wohnhaus mit Hypokausten und christlich geprägten Mosaiken.

## BIBLIOGRAFIE

| | |
|---|---|
| Beazley 1922 | J. D. Beazley, Citharoedus, JHS 42/1, 1922, 70–98 |
| Bélis 1989 | A. Bélis, Reconstruction d'une lyre antique, Cahiers de musiques traditionnelles 2, 1989, 203–216 |
| Bilić 2011 | T. Bilić, Numizmatički dokazi Apolonovog solarnog karaktera, VjesAMuzZagreb 44, 2011, 45–64 |
| Bulić 1924/1925 | F. Bulić, Il mosaico nel Paetorium del luogotenente della Dalmazia a Salona, VjesDal 67–68, 1924/25, 88–89 |
| Carettoni 1988 | G. Carettoni, Die Bauten des Augustus auf dem Palatin, in: Kaiser Augustus und die verlorene Republik. Eine Ausstellung im Martin-Gropius-Bau, Berlin 07.06.–14.08.1988 (Frankfurt am Main 1988) 263–267 |
| Cvetko 2022 | M. Cvetko, Rimski zavjetni žrtvenici s područja Hrvatske (Zagreb 2022) |
| Ercoles 2014 | M. Ercoles, Dressing the Citharode. A chapter in Greek musical and cultic imagery, Greek and Roman Textiles and Dress. An Interdisciplinary Anthology (Oxford 2014) 95–110 |
| Flashar 1992 | M. Flashar, Apollon Kitharodos. Statuarische Typen des musischen Apollon (Köln 1992) |
| Hill 1962 | P. V. Hill, The temples and statues of Apollo in Rome, NumChron 2, 1962, 125–142 |
| Hoey Middleton 1991 | S. Hoey Middleton, Engraved Gems from Dalmatia (Oxford 1991) |
| Jeličić Radonić 2019 | J. Jeličić Radonić, Namjesnikova palača u Saloni, Prilozi povijesti umjetnosti u Dalmaciji 44/1, 2019, 313–329 |
| Jones Roccos 2002 | L. Jones Roccos, The Citharode Apollo in Villa Contexts: A Roman Theme with Variations, MemAmAc 1, 2002, 273–293 |
| Jucker 1982 | H. Jucker, Apollo Palatinus und Apollo Actius auf augusteischen Münzen, MusHelv 39/1, 1982, 82–100 |
| Kaić 2013 | I. Kaić, Rimski svijet u malome. Geme kao svjedočanstva svakodnevnog života (doktorska disertacija, FF Zagreb 2013) |
| Karković Takalić – Rabar 2019 | P. Karković Takalić – K. Rabar, Potječe li kasnoantički portret muškarca iz Tarsatike? Još jednom o pitanju provenijencije rimskih spomenika iz fundusa Pomorskoga i povijesnoga muzeja Hrvatskog primorja Rijeka i zbirke Lavala Nugenta, Histria 9, 2019, 53–92 |
| Kárpáti 2012 | A. Kárpáti, A Satyr-Chorus with Thracian Kithara: Toward an Iconography of the Fifth-Century New Music Debate, Phoenix 66/3–4, 2012, 221–246 |

---

[39] <https://slobodnadalmacija.hr/kultura/arhitektura/otkriveni-su-mozda-i-najvrjedniji-nalazi-stare-salone-svih-vremena-i-sto-sad-hocemo-li-i-njih-po-nasem-starom-obicaju-zatrpati-1160908> (17.01.2023).

| | |
|---|---|
| Kurfürst 1992 | P. Kurfürst, The ancient Greek kithara, Studia minora Facultatis Philosophicae Universitatis Brunensis 92, 1992, 7–13 |
| Kušan Špalj 2017 | D. Kušan Špalj, Aquae Iasae – nova otkrića u rimskom svetištu – s posebnim osvrtom na kultove Apolonia, Eskulapa i Serapisa, VjesAMuzZagreb 50, 2017, 255–308 |
| Landels 1999 | G. Landels, Music in ancient Greece and Rome (London 1999) |
| lupa | F. und O. Harl, <lupa.at> (Bilddatenbank zu antiken Steindenkmälern) |
| Maas – Snyder 1989 | M. Maas – J. M. Snyder, Stringed Instruments of Ancient Greece (New Haven 1989) |
| Matulić 1995 | B. Matulić, Prilog proučavanju nastanka, razvoja i trajanja salonitanske škole-radionice mozaika, Opuscula archaeologica 18, 1995, 155–162 |
| Medrer 2003 | J. Medrer, Podni mozaici u Hrvatskoj od 1. do 6. stoljeća (Zagreb 2003) |
| Nardelli 2002 | B. Nardelli, Gemmen, Longae Salonae I–II (Split 2002) |
| Neudecker 1988 | R. Neudecker, Die Skulpturenausstattung römischer Villen in Italien (Mainz 1988) |
| Palagia 1984 | LIMC II 1 (1984) 183–203 s. v. Apollon/Apollo (O. Palagia) |
| von Prittwitz und Graffon 2019 | H.-H. von Prittwitz und Graffon, Ein »tief gesunkener« Gott und seine Begleitung, Archäologie im Rheinland 2019, 120–122 |
| Roberts 1981 | H. Roberts, Reconstructing the Greek Tortoise-Shell Lyre, WorldA 12/3, 1981, 303–312 |
| Sachs 1943 | C. Sachs, The History of Musical Instruments (New York 1943) |
| Sanader 2008 | M. Sanader, O antičkom kultu u Hrvatskoj, VjesDal 101, 2008, 157–186 |
| Schenck zu Schweinsberg 2017 | J.-M. Schenck zu Schweinsberg, Der pseudohomerische Hermes-Hymnus: ein interpretierender Kommentar (Heidelberg 2017) |
| Simon 1984 | LIMC II 1 (1984) 363–446 s. v. Apollon/Apollo (E. Simon) |
| Simon 1990 | E. Simon, Die Götter der Römer (München 1990) |
| Šoštarić 2018 | L. Šoštarić, Terminološki problemi u standardizaciji naziva instrumenata antičke Grčke, Rasprave: Časopis Instituta za hrvatski jezik i jezikoslovlje 44/2, 2018, 663–674 |
| Thurn 1998 | N. Thurn, Die siebensaitige Lyra, Mnemosyne 51/4, 1998, 411–434 |

*Mirjana Sanader, Odsjek za arheologiji, Filozofskog fakulteta u Zagrebu, Ivana Lučića 3, 10000 Zagreb, Kroatien.*
*[e] msanader@ffzg.hr*

Alfred Schäfer

# ZWEI GEBÄLKBLÖCKE MIT RÖMISCHEM OPFERZUG

**Abstract**
During the construction of the north-south extension of the urban train system of Cologne, two limestone blocks dating to the Roman period were discovered in the vicinity of the station Heumarkt/Pipinstrasse. They had been re-used as building material in a mediaeval foundation wall. Originally, the two blocks fitted together seamlessly. The first of them, a rectangular architrave block, carried the second one, a frieze depicting a Roman sacrificial procession. The shape of the blocks allows for the reconstruction of a small, circular temple building without a separate cella, whose exterior entablature formed a dodecagon. The interior face of the entablature, however, has a circular shape. This monopteros-style temple is the first of its kind to be documented in the Roman city of *Colonia Claudia Ara Agrippinensium* (CCAA). A local comparison exists in the Sanctuary of the Matronae in Pesch in the Eifel mountain range, where a monopteros with a polygonal entablature was found.

Bei archäologischen Ausgrabungen im Bereich der Haltestelle Heumarkt/Pipinstraße im Stadtzentrum von Köln entdeckte man in mittelalterlichen Mauerfundamenten zwei römische Kalksteinblöcke[1]. Aufgrund ihrer Wiederverwendung in einem anderen baulichen Zusammenhang sind sie als Spolien anzusprechen[2]. Ursprünglich gehörten die antiken Werksteine passgenau zusammen. Es handelt sich um einen langrechteckigen Architravblock und einen darüberliegenden Friesblock mit einer figürlichen Darstellung.

Der Architravblock (RGM Inv. 2004.022.224-281) besteht aus Kalkstein. Die erhaltene Länge beträgt 91 cm, die Breite 33 cm und die Höhe 33 cm (Abb. 1). Die Vorderseite wird durch drei waagerechte Streifen gegliedert, die von unten nach oben an Höhe zunehmen. Die sorgfältig geglätteten Faszien werden durch rahmende Ornamentleisten akzentuiert. Auf ein unteres Kordelband folgt ein Perlstab mit lang gezogenen Perlen. Als oberer horizontaler Abschluss dient ein vorkragender Blattstab, der in späterer Zeit größtenteils abgeschlagen wurde. Allein die unteren Blattspitzen sind erhalten. Oberhalb des Blattstabes setzt auf einem schmalen Streifen ein figürliches Relief an, das seine Fortsetzung auf dem darüberliegenden Friesblock finden sollte. Zu erkennen sind von links nach rechts zwei Klauen eines Rindes sowie die unteren Beinpartien von zwei menschlichen Figuren. Der Reliefgrund ist uneben gestaltet und nicht so fein geglättet wie die drei Faszien.

Von den beiden Schmalseiten ist allein die rechte mit ihrer antiken Oberfläche größtenteils erhalten. Anhand der rillenförmigen Bearbeitungsspuren erkennt man die Führung des Spitzeisens von rechts oben nach links unten. Die aufgeraute Stoßfläche ist nur zur Vorderseite hin geglättet. Der Anathyrosesaum ist kaum zu sehen, aber eindeutig mit der Hand zu ertasten. Der Werkstein besitzt einen Gehrungswinkel von 75°, der sich aus der erhaltenen Vorderseite und der originalen rechten Schmalseite zusammensetzt. Die linke Nebenseite ist stark bestoßen, sodass

---
[1] Für die fotografische Dokumentation im Römisch-Germanischen Museum der Stadt Köln habe ich A. Wegner (Rheinisches Bildarchiv) zu danken. Das sfm-Modell fertigten C. Maas und O. Steinert an. Für Hinweise zur architektonischen Ausstattung und zu den Skulpturen des Matronenheiligtums bei Pesch danke ich G. Hartke, M. Schmauder und Ch. Röser (LVR-Landesmuseum Bonn) sowie P. Noelke. J. Vogel fotografierte die Iuppiterstatue in Bonn. Fruchtbare Diskussionen zur Rekonstruktion des neuerschlossenen Monopteros aus dem römischen Köln führte ich mit S. Helas (RWTH Aachen) und E. Traeder (Humboldt-Universität zu Berlin). Weiterführende Hinweise gaben dankenswerterweise F. Dövener, A. Klöckner, G. Kremer und J. Lipps.

[2] Fundbericht 2004.022 Stelle 224–281 und 244–272; Frasheri 2012, 160; Oenbrink 2012, 164–165.

1   Architravblock RGM Inv. 2004.022.224-281, Ansichten nach sfm-Modell (RGM, C. Maas/O. Steinert)

2   Architravblock RGM Inv. 2004.022.224-281 und Friesblock RGM Inv. 2004.022.244-272, Rückseiten nach sfm-Modell (RGM, C. Maas/O. Steinert)

die ursprüngliche Länge des Architravblocks nicht abzumessen ist. Ein Teil der linken hinteren Seitenfläche wurde sekundär grob abgearbeitet.

Wie die rechte Nebenseite ist auch die Unterseite des Dreifaszienarchitravs eine originale Seite mit Werkspuren römischer Steinbearbeitung. Auf der Unterseite liegt allerdings nicht wie bei der rechten seitlichen Stoßfläche ein Anathyrosesaum vor, was für die Rekonstruktion der tragenden Architektur bedeutsam ist. Im Grad ihrer Aufrauung kommt die Unterseite der gleichmäßig gekrümmten Innenseite nahe (Abb. 2 oben). Die Oberseite des Architravblocks weist einen guten Erhaltungszustand auf. Sie wurde durchgehend sehr fein geglättet, um als Auflagefläche für den Friesblock zu dienen.

3  Friesblock RGM Inv. 2004.022.244-272, Ansichten nach sfm-Modell (RGM, C. Maas/O. Steinert)

## BESCHREIBUNG DES FRIESBLOCKS

Der Friesblock (RGM Inv. 2004.022.244-272) besteht aus Kalkstein. Die erhaltene Länge beträgt 106 cm, die Breite 33 cm und die Höhe 35 cm (Abb. 3). Das figürliche Relief an der Vorderseite ist bestoßen oder in großen Teilen intentionell abgearbeitet. Trotz des beeinträchtigten Erhaltungszustandes erlauben die überlieferten Konturen eine Rekonstruktion der Bilderzählung. Links ist im Flachrelief ein kapitaler Stier wiedergegeben, der von einer männlichen Gestalt an den Hörnern geführt wird. Der Dargestellte ist mit einem Schurz bekleidet und hält in seiner Linken eine Axt für die spätere Tötung des Stieres. Erhalten ist allein der lange Stiel, nicht der Kopf der Axt. Der Dargestellte ist als Opferdiener, genauer als Opferschlächter (*victimarius*) gekennzeichnet[3]. Bei der zweiten Relieffigur handelt es sich um eine frontal stehende, männliche Gestalt in der Tunika. Dieser Kultdiener hält in der rechten Hand wahrscheinlich eine Kanne mit einem Tuch (*mappa*) für die rituelle Handwaschung und in der linken Hand eine Schale für den Opferguss. Die Bewegungsrichtung des Opferzuges geht nach rechts.

Von den beiden Schmalseiten ist nur die rechte mit ihrer antiken Oberfläche bis auf wenige randliche Bestoßungen erhalten. Charakteristisch sind rillenförmige Bearbeitungsspuren, die zur Vorderseite hin etwas geglättet sind. Vergleichbar ist der Anathyrosesaum der rechten Stoßfläche des Architravblocks. Der Werkstein besitzt einen Gehrungswinkel von 75°, der sich aus der erhaltenen Vorderseite und der originalen rechten Schmalseite zusammensetzt. Die linke Schmalseite ist hingegen stark bestoßen, sodass die ursprüngliche Länge des Friesblocks nicht abzumessen ist. Ein Teil der hinteren linken Seitenfläche wurde sekundär grob abgearbeitet. Es handelt sich von der Position und von der handwerklichen Bearbeitung her um die gleiche Abarbeitung wie am Architravblock. Damit liegt eine nachträgliche Umarbeitung beider Gebälkblöcke vor. Die

---

[3]  Vgl. Fless 1995, 15–19. 70–78.

Unterseite des Friesblocks hat man wie die Oberseite des Dreifaszienarchitravs gleichmäßig fein geglättet.

Auch die Oberseite des Friesblocks wurde als glatt gearbeitete Auflagerfläche vorbereitet. An ihrem äußeren rechten Rand befindet sich eine lineare Einkerbung, die auf eine vertikale Kante an der Außenseite des Friesblocks zuläuft[4]. Hier liegt eindeutig eine Ecke vor, die im stumpfen Winkel abknickt. Im mittleren Bereich der Friesoberseite befindet sich ein längliches Stemmloch, das später mit einem ziegelsplitthaltigen Zementmörtel verstrichen wurde. Es diente ursprünglich dazu, die aufliegende Geisonplatte mit einem Stemmeisen an die vorgesehene Position zu rücken. Am äußeren linken Rand der Friesoberseite sind Reste des Bleivergusses einer Verklammerung zu erkennen. Nach der Position des einstigen Klammerlochs zu urteilen, geht die Verklammerung mit der nachträglichen Abarbeitung des Friesblocks einher. In einer späteren Nutzungsphase wiederum, als man bereits die Eisenklammer herausgenommen hatte, verstrich man das Klammerloch mit Schamottmörtel.

Die Innenseite des Friesblocks ist wie die Innenseite des Architravblocks gleichmäßig gekrümmt. Auf der originalen Oberfläche ist die Bearbeitungsrichtung zu erkennen (Abb. 2 unten).

## STILISTISCHE DATIERUNG DER BAUORNAMENTIK

Die zeitliche Einordnung beruht auf der Bauornamentik des Architravs. So sind der Perlstab mit den lang gezogenen Perlen und der durch tiefe Bohrungen akzentuierte Blattstab sehr ungewöhnlich für das frühe 1. Jahrhundert n. Chr.[5]. Ein Architravblock aus Lyon, der in flavische Zeit datiert wird, weist einen Perlstab mit kleineren Einzelelementen auf[6]. Lang gezogene Perlen sind an einem Dreifaszienarchitrav des Hafentempels in Xanten belegt. Nach der jüngsten Auswertung der Architekturglieder des Hafentempels wird auf eine Errichtung in der ersten Hälfte des 2. Jahrhunderts n. Chr. geschlossen, wobei der Datierungsschwerpunkt in hadrianischer Zeit bis zur Mitte des 2. Jahrhunderts liegt[7]. Aufgrund der vergleichenden Analyse ist für die beiden Kölner Gebälkblöcke ein Datierungsrahmen vom Ende des 1. bis in die Mitte des 2. Jahrhunderts n. Chr. wahrscheinlich.

## REKONSTRUKTION DES GEBÄLKS

Für eine Rekonstruktion der Gebälkzone können nur die hier vorgestellten, einzig erhaltenen Bauglieder herangezogen werden. An erster Stelle ist festzuhalten, dass der Architrav- und der Friesblock passgenau zusammengehören. Dafür sprechen die Formate der Kalksteinblöcke in Verbindung mit dem figürlichen Dekor, der auf beide Vorderseiten übergreift (Abb. 4). Der vorkragende Blattstab des Dreifaszienarchitravs bildet gewissermaßen die Standleiste für die Teilnehmer des Opferzuges, die auf dem darüberliegenden Friesblock ab Höhe der Kniegelenke im Relief wiedergegeben werden. Dass die beiden Gebälkblöcke einzeln gearbeitet wurden, um sie später zusammenzufügen, wird durch die sorgfältige Ausarbeitung der betreffenden Lagerflächen nahegelegt. Die Oberseite des Dreifaszienarchitravs und die Unterseite des Friesblocks sind fein geglättet und offensichtlich als Lagerflächen für einander bestimmt[8]. Architrav- und Friesblock sind leicht zueinander versetzt, wie die erhaltenen rechten Nebenseiten belegen (Abb. 5).

Die geraden Vorderseiten der beiden Werksteine sprechen für ein nach außen polygonales, und die gekrümmten Innenseiten für ein nach innen rundes Gebälk (Abb. 6). Da die erhaltenen Nebenseiten und die geraden Vorderseiten des Architrav- und Friesblocks jeweils einen Gehrungswinkel

---

[4] Schäfer 2021, 352 Abb. 6.
[5] Vgl. Leon 1971, 87–208. – Zur Licht-Schatten-Wirkung des Blattstabes vgl. Schörner 1995, 167 Kat. 194.
[6] Fellague 2009, 42.
[7] Oenbrink 2022, 191 Taf. 26, I273 und I278.
[8] Eine etwaige nachträgliche Durchtrennung der Frieszone hätte zu einem erheblichen Substanzverlust des figürlichen Aufbaus geführt.

4   Kalksteinblöcke mit der Darstellung eines römischen Opferzuges, gefunden in der Baugrube der Haltestelle Heumarkt/Pipinstraße der Nord-Süd Stadtbahn Köln (Rheinisches Bildarchiv RBA-Nr. d031791_01/02, Foto A. Wegner)

5   Seitliche Ansicht des römischen Architrav- und Friesblocks aus der Baugrube der Haltestelle Heumarkt/Pipinstraße in Köln (Rheinisches Bildarchiv RBA-Nr. d031791_01/02, Foto A. Wegner)

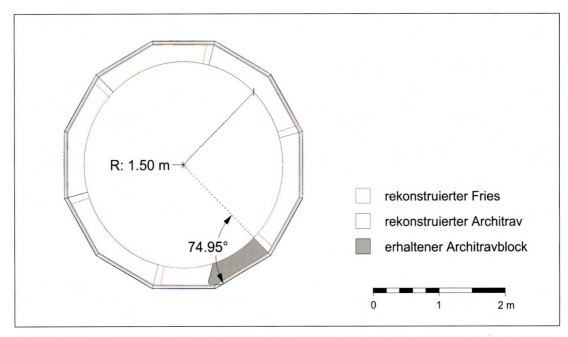

6  Rekonstruierte Aufsicht des polygonalen Gebälks eines römischen Rundbaus aus dem Stadtzentrum des römischen Köln (zeichnerische Rekonstruktion: E. Träder nach Vorgaben A. Schäfer)

von 75 Grad bilden, ergibt sich für die Außenansicht des Gebälks zwingend ein regelmäßiges Zwölfeck, um den inneren Kreis zu schließen[9]. Die erhaltene lineare Einkerbung auf der Oberseite des Friesblocks stellt in diesem Zusammenhang wahrscheinlich eine Konstruktionslinie dar, die durch den Mittelpunkt des Zwölfecks führt.

Es erschließt sich ein regelmäßiges Zwölfeck (Dodekagon), dessen innere Rundung einen Radius von 1,50 m hat. Architrav- und Friesblöcke waren sehr wahrscheinlich leicht zueinander verdreht, wie die rechten Nebenseiten der erhaltenen Werksteine belegen.

## ARCHITEKTUR- UND BILDERSPRACHE

Die überlieferte Bauornamentik legt nahe, dass für den ursprünglichen Bau kleinteilige dekorative Elemente charakteristisch waren. Mit hoher Wahrscheinlichkeit ist der erhaltene Ausschnitt eines Opferzuges Teil einer weitaus umfangreicheren Bilderzählung gewesen. Zum umlaufenden Bildfries könnte unter anderem ein unblutiges Voropfer am Altar gehört haben. Als Vergleich für einen derartigen Bildentwurf ist der figürliche Fries auf einem Gebälkblock domitianischer Zeit zu nennen, der sich heute im Musée gallo-romain in Lyon (Inv. 2000.0.318) befindet[10].

Sakrale Bildchiffren, wie Bukranien und Opferbinden, sind mitunter auch an polygonalen Grab- oder Ehrenmonumenten wie beispielsweise in *Ephesos* belegt[11]. Ein ausführlicher Bildzyklus eines religiösen Opferfestes ist hingegen nicht für die genannten Bautypen charakteristisch. Den hier erschlossenen Bilderzyklus eines religiösen Festes mit Opferzug wird man am ehesten einer sakralen Schmuckarchitektur in römischer Bautradition zuweisen wollen[12].

---

[9]  Zum Auflagern von Gebälkquadern mit versetztem Gehrungsstoß s. Precht 1975, 34–35.
[10] Maligorne 2011, 237 Abb. 1.
[11] Quatember – Scheibelreiter-Gail 2017, 301–302; Ruppert 2018, 181.
[12] Eher unwahrscheinlich ist die Rekonstruktion eines polygonalen Umgangstempels mit turmhoher Cella, da dieser wie im *vicus* von Dahlheim eher für eine provinzialrömische Architektursprache steht; vgl. Krier 2022, 4–5.

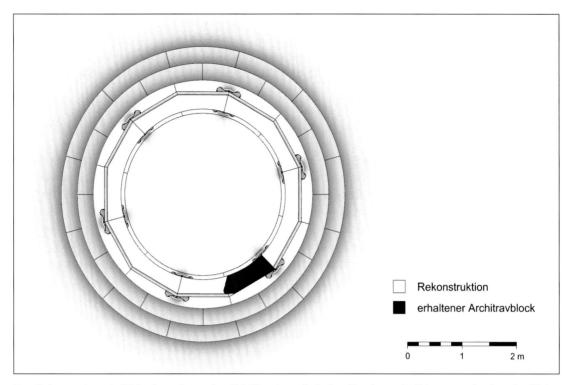

7  Rekonstruierte Aufsicht des polygonalen Gebälks eines römischen Rundtempels (Monopteros) mit sechs Säulen (zeichnerische Rekonstruktion: E. Träder nach Vorgaben A. Schäfer)

## REKONSTRUKTION DES ARCHITEKTONISCHEN AUFBAUS

Auf welchem Unterbau ruhte das erschlossene polygonale Gebälk? Die Oberseite des Architravblocks und die Unterseite des Friesblocks hat man sorgsam auf der Baustelle vor dem Versatz geglättet. Sie wurden als Auflagerflächen angefertigt. Die Unterseite des Dreifaszienarchitravs weist demgegenüber deutliche Werkspuren römischer Steinbearbeitung auf, die im Grad ihrer Aufrauung der gekrümmten Innenseite desselben Blocks weitgehend entspricht. Zudem besitzt die Architravunterseite keinen Anathyrosesaum wie die originale rechte Stoßfläche. Diese Steinbearbeitung legt nahe, dass unter dem Architravblock ursprünglich kein Kalksteinquader saß. Nicht ein geschlossener Wandaufbau, sondern eine offene, von Säulen getragene Sakralarchitektur ist anzunehmen. Dass an den originalen Nebenseiten der Werksteine keine Dübel- und Klammerlöcher vorliegen, spricht nicht gegen diese Deutung. Nicht an jedem Werkstein eines römischen Gebälks dürfen Dübel- oder Klammerlöcher erwartet werden[13].

Aufgrund des erschlossenen Innendurchmessers des Gebäudes von 3 m ist m. E. die Rekonstruktion eines kleinen, offenen Rundbaus ohne Cella am wahrscheinlichsten. Zwei Optionen sind zu prüfen. Unter den zwölf Ecken des Gebälks könnte theoretisch jeweils eine Säule gestanden haben, sodass sich eine enge Säulenstellung ergäbe[14]. Wahrscheinlicher sind jedoch sechs Säulen, da die linke Seite des Architravblocks bereits als Stoßfuge ausgebildet hätte sein müssen, wenn die Fuge oberhalb des Kapitells zu liegen kommen sollte (Abb. 7). Offensichtlich ist diese ist aber sekundär abgeschlagen worden.

Folgt man der vorliegenden Argumentation, so erschließt sich anhand des zusammengehörigen römischen Architrav- und Friesblocks aus Köln ein bestimmter Typus des antiken Rundbaus. Es handelt sich um einen kreisrunden Tempel ohne Cella, dessen Gebälk von Säulen getragen wurde. In seiner römischen Architekturgeschichte spricht Vitruv einen solchen Bautyp als Mo-

---

[13] Lipps 2011, 63–64. 76.
[14] Schäfer 2021, 353–355.

596                                      *Alfred Schäfer*

nopteros an¹⁵. Nach der literarischen Beschreibung erhoben sich die Säulen auf einem erhöhten Unterbau (Tribunal). Als Bekrönung der Säulen möchte man korinthische Kapitelle annehmen, da in der römischen Innenstadt von Köln tuskanische Kapitelle vor allem für straßenbegleitende Laubengänge und Peristylhöfe von Häusern charakteristisch waren und ionische Kapitelle eine Ausnahmeerscheinung gewesen wären.

## EIN MONOPTEROS IM UMLAND DER *CCAA*

Als Vergleiche zu dem neu erschlossenen Monopteros aus dem römischen Stadtzentrum von Köln können zahlreiche kleine Rundtempel auf öffentlichen Platzanlagen und in Heiligtümern der mediterranen Welt angeführt werden, beispielsweise auf der Agora von Korinth, am Marcellustheater und Tiberufer in Rom, auf dem Forum triangulare von Pompeji, im Poseidonheiligtum von *Isthmia*, auf der Akropolis von Athen oder in Baalbek¹⁶. Aus regionalspezifischer Perspektive bietet sich eine Gegenüberstellung mit einem Monopteros aus dem Umland der *CCAA* an.

In der Nordeifel bei Pesch liegt ein Matronenheiligtum, das zu den besterhaltenen römischen Tempelanlagen in Nordrhein-Westfalen gehört¹⁷. Es befindet sich auf einer Anhöhe über dem Zusammenfluss von Wespelbach und Hornbach. Innerhalb des weiträumigen Tempelkomplexes wurde im ersten Drittel des 3. Jahrhunderts n. Chr. ein sechseckiger Monopteros aus gelbem Sandstein errichtet¹⁸. Für seine Architektur sind sechs Säulen mit Schuppenverzierung und ein polygonales Gebälk charakteristisch¹⁹. Möglicherweise diente der Sechseckbau zur Aufstellung einer lebensgroßen, stehenden Iuppiterstatue aus dem gleichen Steinmaterial (Abb. 8 a. b)²⁰. Aufgrund der Fundlage ist die räumliche Zuweisung der Statuenfragmente zwar nicht gesichert, aufgrund des gleichen Steinmaterials besteht für diese These des Ausgräbers aber eine gewisse Wahrscheinlichkeit. Stilistisch ist die Iuppiterstatue mit ihrer überbetonten Muskulatur in die Jahre um 230 n. Chr. zu datieren und ordnet sich damit gut in die severische Datierung des Monopteros ein, die über Fundmünzen vorgenommen wurde²¹. Durch die zeitliche Übereinstimmung gewinnt die These der Zusammengehörigkeit von Sechsecktempel und Iuppiterstatue an Wahrscheinlichkeit. In jedem Fall ist die rundplastische Skulptur von ihrer handwerklichen Bearbeitung her auf Mehransichtigkeit angelegt. Inhaltlich ist die Statue des höchsten Gottes Iuppiter gut mit der Ikonografie der Schuppensäulen zu verbinden, die man von frei stehenden Iuppiter-Säulen kennt²². Ob das Götterbild als Kultstatue oder Weihestatue anzusprechen ist, hängt letztlich davon ab, ob zum baulichen Aufstellungskontext ein Opferaltar gehörte. Bisher konnte ein solcher nicht zweifelsfrei nachgewiesen werden.

Überzeugend hat Hans Lehner die exzeptionelle Form des sechsseitigen Monopteros herausgestellt, die ihm von keinem anderen Rundtempel mit frei stehenden Säulen bekannt war²³. Der neu erschlossene Monopteros aus dem römischen Köln mit seinem nach außen polygonalen und nach innen runden Gebälk kann nun dem Tempelchen bei Pesch zur Seite gestellt werden. Gegenüber dem Bau aus dem Umland der *CCAA*, der mit seinen Schuppensäulen offenbar einer provinzialrömischen Architektursprache verpflichtet ist, reiht sich das Kölner Monument zumindest nach dem Zeugnis der beiden erhaltenen Architekturglieder in die Überlieferung anderer

---

¹⁵ Zum Bautypus des Monopteros: Vitr. 4, 8, 1; Trunk 1991, 20; Quatember – Scheibelreiter-Gail 2017, 292–303.
¹⁶ Schäfer 2021, 359–363.
¹⁷ Lehner 1919; Biller 2010, 198–240.
¹⁸ Lehner 1919, 85–86. 90. 108. 116. 144–146. 162.
¹⁹ Vgl. das Architravfragment im LVR-Landesmuseum Bonn Inv. 24992; Höhe 28 cm, erh. Breite 19 cm.
²⁰ Bonn, LVR-Landesmuseum Inv. 25069. – Lehner 1917, Taf. 3, 2; Lehner 1919, 86; Horn 1972, 78 Taf. 12, 2; Noelke 1981, 281; Biller 2010, 209 Nr. 1, 238.
²¹ Lehner 1919, 108. 162. – Auf die Gruppe stehender und sitzender Götter mit wie aufgepumpt wirkender Muskulatur hat mich P. Noelke freundlicherweise aufmerksam gemacht; Noelke 1990, 118 Abb. 25; Kemkes – Willburger 2004, 41 Abb. 35.
²² Noelke 1981.
²³ Lehner 1919, 146.

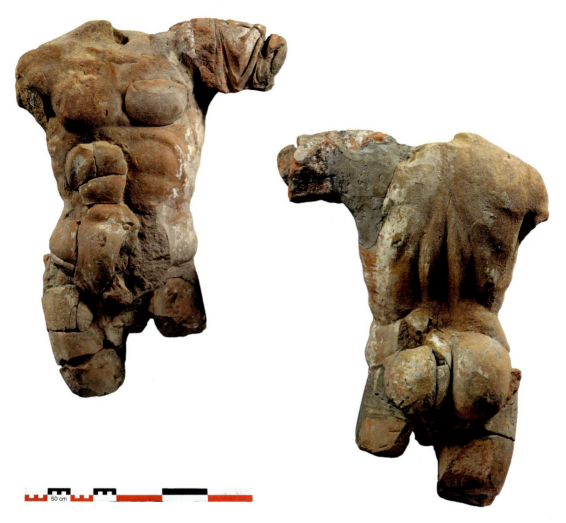

8 a. b  Torso einer Iuppiterstatue aus gelbem Sandstein, gefunden im Matronenheiligtum bei Pesch, Bonn LVR-Landesmuseum Inv. 25069 (Bonn, LVR-Landesmuseum, Foto J. Vogel)

bedeutender Städte und Heiligtümer des mediterranen Raumes ein, in denen die schmuckvolle Architektur eines Monopteros überliefert ist.

## AUSBLICK: FARBFASSUNGEN VON ARCHITEKTUR UND SKULPTUR

Eine Betrachtung der überlieferten Elemente der beiden vorgestellten Sakralbauten aus dem Stadtzentrum und Umland der *CCAA* erhält eine neue Perspektive, wenn man die originale Oberfläche der Iuppiterstatue aus dem Matronenheiligtum bei Pesch in die Diskussion einbezieht. Der Torso (LVR-Landesmuseum Inv. 25069) besteht aus gelbem Sandstein und ist 81 cm hoch erhalten. Der Werkstein ist an vielen Stellen wahrscheinlich durch Hitzeeinwirkung oder Feuer rötlich verfärbt[24]. Aschereste in den Faltenwürfen deuten des Weiteren auf Feuer hin. Hiebspuren, die auf eine mutwillige Zerstörung zurückgehen, können ebenfalls identifiziert werden. Ob die Zerstörung vor oder nach dem Feuer stattgefunden hat, konnte noch nicht eindeutig geklärt werden. Trotz der intentionellen Zerschlagung der Iuppiterstatue ist die originale Oberfläche an vielen Stellen erhalten geblieben. In den Falten des Umhangs befinden sich rötliche, aufgemalte

---

[24] Nach freundlicher Auskunft von H.-G. Hartke konnte die durch Hitzeeinwirkung verursachte Farbveränderung auch an anderen römischen Sandsteinmonumenten im LVR-Landesmuseum Bonn beobachtet werden.

Schattierungen auf weißem Grund. Farbspuren in Weiß sind eindeutig als dünne Kalkschicht zu identifizieren, da punktuell aufgetragene Zitronensäure stark aufschäumte[25]. Eine umfassende restauratorische und archäologische Analyse, die abschließend mit einer behutsamen Erneuerung der rezenten Ergänzungen und Ausbesserungen des Torsos einherginge, drängt sich geradezu auf[26]. Zu untersuchen ist, ob die Skulptur gleichmäßig mit einer weißen Kalkschicht als Grundlage für eine antike Farbfassung überzogen worden ist. Bereits bei der ersten Sichtung des Torsos wurde deutlich, dass der dünne Kalkauftrag als integrativer Bestandteil der Farbkonzeption zu werten ist. Welches Spektrum an Farbpigmenten kann mit Hilfe von verschiedenen technischen und naturwissenschaftlichen Analysen noch erfasst werden?

Nach einer kursorischen Sichtung der Altarfragmente aus dem Tempelbezirk bei Pesch sind farbige Fassungsreste am Ort nicht selten[27]. So findet sich auf einem Weihealtar für die Matronae Vacallinehae nicht nur eine Bemalung auf der Vorder-, sondern auch an den Nebenseiten[28]. Letztere zeigten jeweils auf dem glatten, weiß grundierten Bildfeld einen in grüner Farbe wiedergegebenen Baum mit gelben Blüten, der durch rote Umrisslinien konturiert worden ist. Das Aussehen dieser Bäume entspricht den zahlreichen Weihealtären im Rheinland, deren Reliefdarstellungen als Lorbeerbäumchen identifiziert werden konnten. Nach dem Zeugnis einiger Architekturglieder im Römisch-Germanischen Museum der Stadt Köln dürften auch öffentliche Sakralbauten und private Grabdenkmäler der *CCAA* in der Regel ein farbliche Fassung erhalten haben[29]. Mit Blick auf die bisher nicht umfänglich untersuchte Polychromie römischer Architektur des römischen Köln eröffnen sich für die hier vorgestellten Gebälkblöcke gänzlich neue Bewertungsmöglichkeiten.

Die Vorder- und Rückseiten der beiden passgenau füreinander zugerichteten Gebälkblöcke aus dem Stadtzentrum des römischen Köln eigneten sich aufgrund ihrer Aufrauung sehr gut für eine vor der Bemalung gleichmäßig aufgetragene Schicht von Kalziumkarbonat ($CaCO_3$) aus gelöschtem Kalk. Da die Unterseite des Architravs annähernd der aufgerauten Rückseite entspricht, ist auch hier der Überzug mit einer Kalkschicht nicht auszuschließen. Die freie Unteransicht zwischen den rekonstruierten Kapitellen könnte demnach durchaus eine Bemalung, in diesem Fall am ehesten das Motiv einer Soffitte, aufgewiesen haben. Raue Steinoberflächen wie an der Architravunterseite und den Rückseiten beider Gebälkblöcke aus dem Bereich der U-Bahnhaltestelle Heumarkt in Köln waren jedenfalls für eine Farbfassung nicht nachteilig, sondern boten einem grundierenden Kalküberzug besonders gut Halt.

## BAULICHE UMNUTZUNGEN IN SPÄTANTIKE UND MITTELALTER

Wie lange der römische Monopteros in Köln als Sakralbau Bestand hatte, kann nicht sicher beantwortet werden. Die Verklammerung des erhaltenen Friesblocks geht mit einer sekundären Abarbeitung der Seitenfläche einher, sodass von einer Umnutzung auszugehen ist. In einer späteren Bauphase wiederum, als man bereits die Eisenklammer herausgenommen hatte, verstrich man das Klammerloch mit ziegelsplitthaltigem, sehr hartem Mörtel. Vermutlich handelt es sich um römischen Schamottmörtel, der für eine grundlegende bauliche Veränderung in der Spätantike sprechen könnte. Es stellt sich die Frage, ob die Kalksteinblöcke des Monopteros wie andere kaiserzeitliche Bauglieder in der konstantinischen Brückenrampe oder der spätantiken Befestigung der Rheinvorstadt der *Colonia Agrippina* systematisch verbaut wurden[30]. Später wurden die beiden Gebälkblöcke als Spolien in der mittelalterlichen Innenstadt von Köln wiederverwendet.

---

[25] Hinweis H.-G. Hartke, LVR-Landesmuseum Bonn.
[26] Verf. plant zu diesem Thema eine ausführlichere Studie.
[27] Reis 2010/2011.
[28] Reis 2010/2011, 140–141 mit Abb.
[29] So weist beispielsweise ein korinthisches Kapitell aus der Grabung am Offenbachplatz Überreste einer farblichen Fassung auf; Römisch-Germanisches Museum Fundbericht 2012.022 Sonderfund 167.
[30] Vgl. Dodt – Schäfer 2019.

# BIBLIOGRAFIE

| | |
|---|---|
| Biller 2010 | F. Biller, Kultische Zentren und Matronenverehrung in der südlichen Germania inferior, Osnabrücker Forschungen zu Altertum und Antike Rezeption 13 (Rahden/Westfalen 2010) |
| Dodt – Schäfer 2019 | M. Dodt – A. Schäfer, Der Kölner Hafen in der Römerzeit, in: M. Mirschenz – R. Gerlach – J. Bemmann (Hrsg.), Der Rhein als europäische Verkehrsachse III, Bonner Beiträge zur Vor- und Frühgeschichtlichen Archäologie 22 (Bonn 2019) 153–176 |
| Fellague 2009 | D. Fellague, Les édifices religieux, in: L'Archéo-Thema Lyon capitale de la Gaule romaine, Revue d'archéologie et d'histoire 1 mars-avril 2009, 40–42 |
| Fless 1995 | F. Fless, Opferdiener und Kultmusiker auf stadtrömischen historischen Reliefs. Untersuchungen zur Ikonographie, Funktion und Benennung (Mainz 1995) |
| Frasheri 2012 | G. Frasheri, Ausgrabungen im Bereich der Haltestelle Heumarkt in Köln, 2004–2009. Ergebnisse der archäologischen Untersuchungen im Rahmen des Baus der Nord-Süd-Bahn (Köln 2012) |
| Horn 1972 | H. G. Horn, Ein römischer Bronzeadler, JbRGZM 19, 1972, 63–82 |
| Kemkes – Willburger 2004 | M. Kemkes – N. Willburger, Der Soldat und die Götter. Römische Religion am Limes, Schriften des Limesmuseums Aalen 56 (Esslingen 2004) |
| Krier 2022 | J. Krier, Der römische Vicus in Dahlheim ²(Luxemburg 2022) |
| Lehner 1917 | H. Lehner, Das Provinzialmuseum in Bonn. Abbildungen seiner wichtigsten Denkmäler II. Die römischen und fränkischen Skulpturen (Bonn 1917) |
| Lehner 1919 | H. Lehner, Der Tempelbezirk der Matronae Vacallinehae bei Pesch, BJb 125, 1919, 74–162 |
| Leon 1971 | Ch. F. Leon, Die Bauornamentik des Trajansforums und ihre Stellung in der früh- und mittelkaiserzeitlichen Architekturdekoration Roms, Publikationen des Österreichischen Kulturinstituts in Rom 4 (Wien 1971) |
| Lipps 2011 | J. Lipps, Die Basilica Aemilia am Forum Romanum. Der kaiserzeitliche Bau und seine Ornamentik, Palilia 24 (Wiesbaden 2011) |
| Maligorne 2011 | Y. Maligorne, Le bloc d'entablement de Beaujeu (Rhône), Gallia 68/2, 2011, 237–247 |
| Noelke 1981 | P. Noelke, Die Iupitersäulen und -pfeiler in der römischen Provinz Germania inferior, BJb Beih. 41 (Bonn 1981) |
| Noelke 1990 | P. Noelke, Ara et aedicula. Zwei Gattungen von Votivdenkmälern in den germanischen Provinzen, BJb 190, 1990, 79–124 |
| Oenbrink 2012 | W. Oenbrink, Ein Stieropfer für die Götter, in: M. Trier – F. Naumann-Steckner (Hrsg.), Köln im Spiegel der U-Bahn-Archäologie (Köln 2012) 164–165 |
| Oenbrink 2022 | W. Oenbrink, Der Hafentempel auf Insula 37 der Colonia Ulpia Traiana, Xanten. Tempelbau und Temenos des coloniazeitlichen Heiligtums. Architektur, Baudekor, Skulptur, Xantener Berichte 37 (Oppenheim 2022) |
| Precht 1975 | G. Precht, Das Grabmal des Lucius Poblicius. Rekonstruktion und Aufbau (Köln 1975) |
| Quatember – Scheibelreiter-Gail 2017 | U. Quatember – V. Scheibelreiter-Gail, T. Flavius Damianus und der Grabbau seiner Familie, ÖJh 86, 2017, 221–355 |
| Reis 2010/2011 | A. Reis, Ein farbiger Weihaltar aus dem Matronenheiligtum bei Pesch, BJb 210, 2010/2011, 139–147 |
| Ruppert 2018 | Ch. Ruppert, Tombeaux monumentaux d'Arlon/*Orolaunum vicus*, Signa 7, 2018, 179–183 |
| Schäfer 2021 | A. Schäfer, Monopteros. Der erste römische Rundtempel mit offener Säulenhalle in Köln, KölnJb 54, 2021, 347–370 |
| Schörner 1995 | G. Schörner, Römische Rankenfriese. Untersuchungen zur Baudekoration der späten Republik und der frühen und mittleren Kaiserzeit im Westen des Imperium Romanum (Mainz 1995) |
| Trunk 1991 | M. Trunk, Römische Tempel in den Rhein- und westlichen Donauprovinzen, FiA 14 (Augst 1991) |

*Alfred Schäfer, Römisch-Germanisches Museum der Stadt Köln/Archäologische Bodendenkmalpflege, Cäcilienstraße 46, 50667 Köln, Deutschland.*
*[e] alfred.schaefer@stadt-koeln.de*

Astrid Schmölzer

# GODDESSES OF *GERMANIA INFERIOR*

## INVESTIGATIONS INTO THE ICONOGRAPHY OF THE RHINELAND MATRONAE

**Abstract**
The following paper summarizes the analysis of the iconography of the so-called Rhineland Matronae, which are to be found mainly in the area around modern-day Cologne (*Colonia Claudia Ara Agrippinensium*). The 433 stone objects showing depictions of the goddesses, and symbols and motifs linked with their stone dedications, provide a data basis to investigate the iconographic elements given Mediterranean impacts and models. Referring to the depictions, the Rhineland Matronae evolved as a Roman concept, which was established and used in the period from AD 150 to 250/260. Local elements are the clothing of the goddesses and the inscribed bynames that have been analyzed as Germanic or Celtic. The completed study guarantees a profound material basis for further studies on the evolution of provincial deities depicted in Roman imagery.

## INTRODUCTION

Different stone dedications to the so-called Matronae or Matres are widespread throughout the Roman Empire. In the province of *Germania inferior*, however, they occupy a special place, since there they make up the bulk of the preserved dedicatory inscriptions, meaning that they are well known and studied. In this, iconographic analysis was mostly a by-product.

Even though most of the material discussed here has been known for several decades, often centuries, the investigation with a clear focus on iconography represents a central research desideratum. In contrast to the extensive efforts at epigraphic and linguistic explanatory models, this is a new examination of the material, more than 80 years after the very first detailed discussion of the iconography of the Matronae by Lothar Hahl[1].

The first interest of the project was the comprehensive compilation of known stone altar material with representations of the deities or relief decoration. With the collected project data on more than 400 objects[2] – with and without inscriptions – a new material basis exists, including some unpublished fragments. Therefore, not only the depiction of deities but also the symbols and motifs linked with their stone dedications can be analyzed in the view of Mediterranean impacts and models. Depictions of multi-numbered female deities in the north-western provinces as well as images of classical Greek and Roman goddesses and portraits of Roman empresses serve as examples to compare the evolution of attributes and attached symbols.

The Rhineland Matronae are notable not only because of their schematic representation as a trinity but also because of their very short era of existence; most stone altars depicting the goddesses are dated between AD 150 and 250, with rare examples before that period. The way of dedicating a votive stone was abandoned in the later 3rd century AD. This did not mean, however, that the worship of the Matronae ceased[3].

---

[1] Hahl 1937a; Hahl 1937b; Hahl – Clairmont-von Gonzenbach 1960.
[2] The dataset excluded scenes of burial context (e.g. the portraits of a woman on a sarcophagus found at Cologne, see Galsterer – Galsterer 2010, 382–383 no. 462) and ritual scenes in connection with other deities than the Matronae (e.g. the base of a Jupiter column showing a woman in local clothing next to her husband during the sacrifice, see Galsterer – Galsterer 2010, 111 no. 104), which serve as comparative examples. See Schmölzer 2023, 48–53.
[3] For a summary of the historical evolution of the province of *Germania inferior* and the ethnically and socio-culturally heterogeneous population see Wiegels et al. 2007, 31; Spickermann 2008a, 11–13; Herz 1989, 214–216.

## RESEARCH OVERVIEW

In *Germania inferior*, the Matronae and Matres are named in a total of 835 inscriptional dedications as recipients either alone or in conjunction with other deities[4]. The naming of the goddesses as Matronae used in the present study mainly follows the numerically most frequent designation of the goddesses in the inscriptions as Matronae. Other designations that occur, in addition to Matres, include e.g. Deae and Iunones[5].

The evidence of the Rhineland Matronae is widespread, especially in the south-eastern part of the province of *Germania inferior*. So far, it has been largely processed according to epigraphic, historical, and linguistic aspects[6]. However, an exact archaeological analysis of the iconography of the deities has not been undertaken.

The first collection of so-called mother deities was compiled by Jan de Wal as early as 1846[7]. In 1937, Lothar Hahl attempted a comprehensive treatment of the sculpture of the Roman provinces counting the monuments of the Matronae among the most striking pictorial evidence of *Germania inferior*[8]. Harald von Petrikovits provided a comprehensive synopsis of the distribution of similar deities. Among other things, he initiated a new orientation in the research discussion with his reflections on the trinity of the Matronae[9].

Hahl sees the stone dedications as an adequate reflection of local beliefs. According to him, the attributes of Greco-Roman deities were transferred to the Matronae for better recognition. Likewise, their worship was carried out according to the genuine Roman procedure, which can be reconstructed[10]. On questions of cult and ritual practices, inscribed venerations of Matronae and Matres are known from Rome, northern Italy, Gaul, and Germania, but also Britain. The pictorial representations, if available and assignable, differ from province to province, although they also retain certain elements throughout, such as the generally multi-numbered representation (usually as a trinity)[11]. In general, the Matronae are described as a local or regional cult, whose inscriptional and iconographic evidence are the only clues to the cult practice that took place[12].

A mythical narrative concerning the deities is missing[13]; related to *Germania inferior* only a few known Matronae sanctuaries provide further insights. These are also located in south-eastern *Germania inferior*, except for the temple at *Colonia Ulpia Traiana* (*CUT*/Xanten), consecrated to the Aufaniae[14].

---

[4] Spickermann 2010, 129.

[5] Different groups of Matronae can be distinguished because of their bynames. It is important to recognize the fact that e.g. the group of the Aufaniae can be called Matronae, Matres or Deae. They cannot be distinguished in their depictions either. See Schmölzer 2022 for more information on this.

[6] For linguistic analyses on Celtic theonymes see e.g. Gutenbrunner 1937; Delamarre 2001; Spickermann – de Bernardo Stempel 2005; Delamarre 2009; Delamarre 2013; Hofeneder – de Bernardo Stempel 2013; de Bernardo Stempel 2014; de Bernardo Stempel 2021. For epigraphic and interpretative approaches of the inscriptions see especially the publications of the FERCAN-project; last published workshop papers Matijević 2016.

[7] de Wal 1846.

[8] Hahl 1937b, 48–49.

[9] von Petrikovits 1987.

[10] Hahl 1937a, 256. For sacrificial scenes, also especially in combination with the Matronae cult, see further Huet 2008; Huet 2017; Noelke 2011; Noelke 2013; Bauchhenß 2012; Noelke 1998; Herz 2003.

[11] Schmölzer 2023, 100–105.

[12] Woolf 2003, 133–134.

[13] E. Bickel (Bickel 1938, 164) treated a passage of the excurse on *Gallia* by Ammianus Marcellinus (15, 9, 8) as a hint to the Matronae; furthermore, he names a passage by Poseidonius as another proof but gives no exact quotation. It can be doubted that Ammianus meant holy women or goddesses similar to the Matronae and the comment of Poseidonius could not be found, despite a thorough search. Overall, the arguments of Bickel seem forced and, because of missing quotations, not comprehensible.

[14] For a summary of the various locations see Schmölzer 2023, 77–96, and the literature cited there. For Xanten see especially Schmölzer 2023, 94–96.

The research on the Matronae in the province of *Germania inferior* reached a peak with a colloquium in the 1980s[15]. There, Heinz Günter Horn provided an overview of depicted monuments located in the area of the Ubii, who settled in the south-east around *Colonia Claudia Ara Agrippinensium* (*CCAA*/Cologne), while Edgar C. Polomé gave an overview of mother deities and their similarities in Western Europe[16].

More recent efforts, which are not only dedicated to the research questions surrounding the Matronae dedications, are for example the investigations of the F.E.R.C.AN-project on the province of *Germania inferior*, investigating Celtic divine names in Roman inscriptions with epigraphic approaches but also providing the archaeological documentation of the objects[17].

For the archaeological analysis, the find reports of the early 19th and 20th centuries also proved very useful, which were largely ignored in the research literature (presumably also due to the non-archaeological research questions). The number of recent publications[18] shows once more that interest in the discussion of the Rhineland Matronae remains.

## THE ICONOGRAPHY OF THE RHINELAND MATRONAE

In total, a number of 433 stone objects have been analyzed according to their decorative reliefs, showing the deities or naming them in the inscription. The 433 objects in total were found in 53 locations; only four objects could not be traced back to their exact find spots. The majority of objects have been found in the south-eastern part of the province – as aforementioned –, mostly in the region around *CCAA* (see fig. 1), where also most of the sanctuaries ascribed to the Matronae are located (see above).

The focus on pictorial representations meant a consideration of the material from a completely different perspective and concerning a different characteristic, namely the presence of depictions. Some inscriptions had therefore to be excluded, while the material base expanded when including those fragments that had previously received little attention due to their lack of inscriptions (see fig. 2)[19]. The compilation made according to these principles now offers a broad and trend-setting starting point for working out classical influences and models.

The votive stones from the province of *Germania inferior* are generally characterized by their richness of images. Besides the extensive images of deities, the reliefs on the altar sides are to be considered an important element of the visual language of the cult. In addition to laurel trees,

---

[15] Bauchhenß 1987. The associated pictorial index, called Index MWG (= Index epigraphischer Zeugnisse mehrzahliger weiblicher Gottheiten in den lateinischen Provinzen des Römischen Reiches) is consistently referred to in the published papers of the colloquium and currently still in progress. In addition to the pictorial material, it should also have included a considerable number of distribution and overview maps as well as a well-researched bibliography (see Rüger 1987).

[16] Horn 1987; Polomé 1987.

[17] For the online available database on the edited inscriptions see <https://gams.uni-graz.at/context:fercan> (10.11.2022). The research questions are meanwhile being extended to a follow-up project on the province of *Germania superior*.

[18] Further research on the matron cult is provided e.g. by the dissertations of V. Burns (Burns 1994) and A. G. Garman (Garman 2008), who has particularly elaborated on the differences between the Matronae and Matres. The analysis by P. A. Shaw (Shaw 2011) looks primarily at the deities Hreda and Eostre, which occur in Britain. He draws on the Matronae in *Germania inferior* for comparisons. Raepsaet-Charlier 2015, 207–209 provides a concise literature overview including some of the newest works, e.g. Derks 1998; Spickermann 2008b; Eck – Koßmann 2009; Noelke 2013; Huet 2017. Raepsaet-Charlier 2019 studied the Matronae as an essential part of the pantheon of the provincial capital *CCAA*. The most recent work on the stone monuments of the Reiss-Engelhorn museums at Mannheim, including the so-called Mannheimer Matronenaltäre has been accomplished by Bauchhenß 2021. Ferlut 2022 provided the newest overview on the cult of female deities in both Germanic provinces and *Gallia Belgica*.

[19] A very large amount of head and body fragments of Matronae altars has been found at sanctuaries like Abenden or especially at Pesch. Most of them were documented during a museum stay in 2018. See Schmölzer 2023, cat. 1–25 (Abenden) and cat. 312–384 (Pesch).

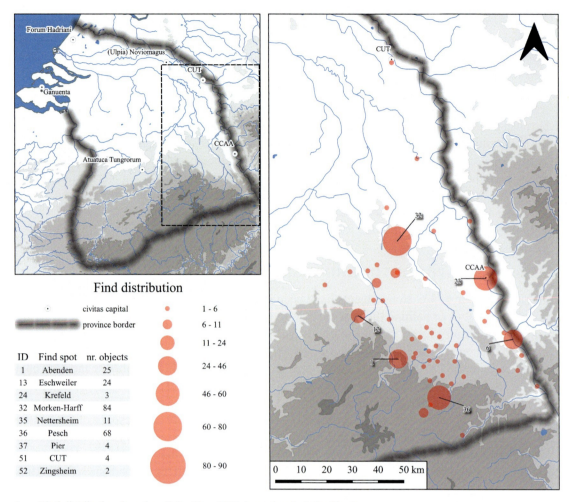

1   Find distribution, based on Schmölzer 2023 (mapping A. Schmölzer)

which are the most common motif, the relief motifs include horns of plenty, representations of ritualistic meals, sacrificial servants, and tendril motifs of various forms. These were also evaluated for a final interpretation of the function of the cult.

First, using the iconographic method, the existing images were analyzed and compared with each other to distinguish types, and in a second step further compared with existing depictions of female (so-called mother) deities in the provinces. The method of comparison was also used to clarify points of contact with classical impacts. Attributes as well as decorative relief motifs point to classical Mediterranean deities and further to portraits of Roman empresses (also very often depicted with divine attributes and symbols)[20].

For visualizing the data concerning iconographic types or diffusion and documented combinations of certain motifs, distributional mapping with QGIS and statistic analysis with R have been used. The software is free to use and both provide an extensive toolbox when handling archaeological data of this kind. The resulting advantage of using digital tools is a compatible dataset that allows for extensions and is open to further investigations.

The main representation known from the Rhineland Matronae (»niederrheinischer Typus«)[21] shows them as a trinity. The goddesses wear floor-length dresses and cloaks of equal length over them, held together at the breast by a large fibula or brooch. The voluminous bonnet is the most

---

[20]   For the images of Roman empresses see e.g. Smith 1994; Alexandridis 2004; Portale 2013 as well as Wrede 1981 for an analysis of depictions of deified private individuals.
[21]   As defined by Ihm 1887, 45.

2 Matching fragments (head and body) of a Matrona, found at the sanctuary of Pesch (presumably part of an aedicula altar; Schmölzer 2023, cat. 358; photo A. Schmölzer)

characteristic feature of both goddesses at the sides. In contrast, the middle goddess usually wears her shoulder-long, wavy hair open. Furthermore, she is very often portrayed as slightly smaller than her companions are (see fig. 3). The main fact about the representations in the Roman province of *Germania inferior* is that the trinity is conspicuous by the middle goddess. Even though wearing the same cloak and dress, she is depicted without a bonnet and thus visually distinguished from the other two. In some cases, a parietal band, as worn especially by children and young women, adorns her shoulder-length, open hair[22].

The clothing also referred to as »Ubian« is – next to the Matronae's Celtic or Germanic bynames known through the inscriptions – a local element[23]. In their hands, the goddesses usually hold flowers, ears of corn, or baskets of fruit. Other items are caskets and in rare cases bread loaves and fruit without a container. One case even shows the middle goddess with the *caduceus*[24].

The Matronae also wear jewellery – mostly necklaces or neck rings with a *lunula* pendant. Pins for fastening the bonnet can be found at some Matronae heads. This element forms one part of the head jewellery (see fig. 2, on the left cheek of the Matrona), next to the already mentioned parietal band worn by the middle goddess. Another part of the jewellery is the fibula or brooch which serves to close the cloak[25].

This schematic type of depiction is rarely deviated from; only one stone altar is known showing the middle goddess standing between the other two who are seated (see fig. 4). Another rare form of depiction shows the Matronae as portrait busts in medallions or growing out of leaves[26].

When looking for examples for comparison in the north-west provinces, trinities of female deities as well as female divine pairs are widespread and well-researched[27]. Also individually depicted goddesses like Dea Nehalennia, who is located on today's coast of Zeeland (a modern district in the Netherlands) show similarities[28].

---

[22] Hahl – Clairmont-von Gonzenbach 1960, 27–34.

[23] Schmölzer 2023, 48–53. Wild 1968 was the first to summarize the elements of women's dress in the region around *Colonia Claudia Ara Agrippinensium*, also known as the settlement area of the Ubii. The most recent investigations on women's dress in this region has been conducted by U. Rothe, see Rothe 2005 and Rothe 2009.

[24] Schmölzer 2023, cat. 301.

[25] Schmölzer 2023, 29–32.

[26] Schmölzer 2023, 35–38. The iconographic analysis was focused on the stone monuments. Concerning terracotta figurines depicting Matronae, see Schauerte 1985; Gonzenbach 1986; Gonzenbach 1995.

[27] See Schauerte 1987 on depictions of mother deities, and Bauchhenß 2014 on female divine pairs in the north-west provinces as well as further literature cited there.

[28] For an overview of Nehalennia see Hondius-Crone 1955; Spickermann 2009; Stuart – Bogaers 2001; Stuart 2013; Derks 2015.

3   Aedicula of the »Vettius-Stein«, found at the Bonn Minster (Schmölzer 2023, cat. 40; photo A. Schmölzer)

Next to the search and argumentation on Mediterranean comparisons and impacts, the collection of data provides a well-established analysis of details such as jewellery, clothing or gestures of the deities. Furthermore, the related motifs and symbols were collected to round out the picture of a functional interpretation of the goddesses.

As mentioned before, the altar sides show motifs of laurel trees, horns of plenty, various combinations of floral elements, desks with ritual meals on them, male and female servants for various tasks of sacrifice as well as divine attributes like the *caduceus*, etc. Also, animals (goats and different kinds of birds) are shown in nature and arcadian landscape motifs as well as in their role as a sacrifice. On rare occasions, even the dedicants themselves and different deities (Hercules or Venus) are depicted[29].

The collage of various attributes and the polyvalence caused by them can be found in the concept of Michael Lipka's »iconographic foci«. He states that there is an infinite number of visual forms of divine concepts, but that Roman culture works in very selective ways – by the term »iconographic foci« the evolution of certain imagery types of different deities (meaning that certain forms of expression were used repeatedly) is understood[30]. This is true for deities in the Roman provinces as a part of Roman provincial religion[31] as well. Consequently, the definition of the concept must be extended.

Resulting of Lipka's statements, only the most popular deities received an iconographic focus. The worship of Roman deities was therefore limited to a certain number of variations of a potentially bigger pool of possible depictions[32]. Especially the Imperial period is furthermore marked by the interaction of various iconographic foci, meaning the exchange of attributes or the acceptance

---

[29] Schmölzer 2023, 62–63. Preliminary work concerning various side motifs was carried out by Bauchhenß 2005; Noelke 2011; Bauchhenß 2013; Noelke 2013.
[30] Lipka 2009, 88–89.
[31] The term »Provinzialreligion« (Roman provincial religion) is defined according to Rüpke 1997, 20–21.
[32] Lipka 2009, 91. The Matronae might be popular deities, if according to Raepsaet-Charlier 2015, 213–214, speaking of a local Pantheon, of which the Matronae have been an important part.

of attributes originally known from the Greek area[33]. Engaged with the iconographic focus also a ritual focus could be transferred from one deity to another; moreover, two or more deities could also have been combined and worshipped together[34]. As an example, the existence of pairs of one male and a female deity, following the concept of *parhedros* can be applied here (e.g. Mercurius and Rosmerta)[35].

According to Günther Schauerte, the majority of the stone evidence of individually depicted goddesses, which can be used for a comparison with the Matronae, are mainly depicted enthroned and with classical clothing (*tunica* and *palla*). As attributes, they hold fruits in baskets or other vessels, sometimes only loosely on their laps. The cornucopia and the *patera* also appear frequently. Sometimes there is a wheel leaning against the throne, which places the goddess in the realm of Fortuna/Tyche. Dogs, sacrificial servants, children, or erotes appear as supporting figures. Sometimes, there are no attributes at all[36].

4  Aedicula altar dedicated to the Matronae Vesuniahenae, found at Vettweiß (Schmölzer 2023, cat. 409; photo archive of CIL XIII-project)

The general conclusion of the analysis includes the origins of the pictorial themes from the Classical-Roman area as well as the local elements as an example of the Romanization process. According to this, the Matronae of *Germania inferior* is a Roman construct that takes up and carries forward local elements with the help of Roman media and imagery.

## THE MATRONAE AS MOTHER GODDESSES

While the known multi-numbered goddesses in the north-west provinces are interpreted as a group of protecting and nurturing deities, also involved with childcare and therefore summarized under the umbrella term of mother deities, the striking feature of biological motherhood – nursing a child or babies and toddlers as accompanying figures – are missing with the Rhineland Matronae. Nonetheless, they were counted as mother deities, not least because of their honorary title *matronae* or *matres*, meaning »mother«. A *matrona* can also be the female head of the Roman household, next to the *pater familias*, describing a married woman and mother. She has to guard her family, children and the slaves, and she is also the keeper of the house keys[37].

Although the nurturing and protecting character is indicated by the term »Mother Goddesses«, it is certainly misleading, because it is used as an umbrella term combining breastfeeding goddesses, so-called *nutrices*, as well as goddesses such as Fortuna/Tyche, Ceres/Demeter or Magna

---

[33] Lipka 2009, 95. Lipka is especially referring to syncretistic deities, e.g. Isis. Also, our polyvalent examples fit into this setting. The high number of votive altars with depictions speak in favour of this repeatedly used expression.
[34] Lipka 2009, 109.
[35] Rüger 1983. Mercurius Gebrinius was thought to be a *parhedros* of the Matronae Aufaniae at Bonn, where a large number of votive stones for both have been found under the minster of Bonn. As Gerhard Bauchhenß states, the findings hint toward Mercurius having been worshipped in his temple (as mentioned in the epigraphic record (Bauchhenß 2015, 157), and not being just a part of a collectively worshipped group of deities. See Rüger 1983 on the discussion of Mercurius being a ›husband‹ (or *parhedros*) of the Aufaniae.
[36] Schauerte 1987, 61–65.
[37] RE XIV 2 (1930) 2300–2305 s. v. Matrona 3 (H. Schroff).

Mater/Kybele, who are not only protectors but each has a certain functional area and partly even their feasts as well as different clienteles. Therefore, the term needs a clear definition when used for the description of the Matronae and Nehalennia – as well as for all the goddesses mentioned above. The term »Mother Goddess(es)« is commonly used for female deities, most of them within a protecting and nurturing functional range.

However, there is no contrary term like »father deities« – although there are deities which may be called like that, e.g. Dis Pater, Zeus/Iuppiter, Mars, etc.[38]. And what about the rare cases where a male deity takes on maternal duties, such as Zeus in various cases?

Florence Pasche Guignard and Giulia Pedrucci include approaches of maternal theory in their analysis of religious practices and depictions of deities in antique polytheistic religious systems. With theoretical input from the so-called mother studies (a field which emerged in the last two decades from gender and women's studies), they form a concept for analyzing the history of parenting and the representation of maternal figures (which can be male as well as female) inside religious studies. They consider and define maternity as a cultural practice, not a biological function, which leads to a much wider definition. Therefore, the use of the term »mother« is neither limited to aspects of nurturing and caregiving nor reduced to biological features like pregnancy, birth or lactation[39].

## CONCLUSION

After collecting and cataloguing the existing material bearing images of the deities or combined relief motifs, the iconography has been fully analyzed. The study shifted the focus from epigraphic-based working processes to an analysis relying on images of deities and relief motifs showing symbols regularly combined with them.

The work process began with the application of classical archaeological methods such as the iconographic method and the method of comparison. In addition to describing, analyzing and comparing the iconography, the data has been visualized with the help of mappings, carried out and created with QGIS, and of statistical evaluation, carried out with R. The digital tools provided not only help with visualization issues but also made it possible to create a dataset that is now ready for further use.

Referring to their depictions, the Rhineland Matronae are a Roman concept. The concept was established and employed in the period of AD 150 to 250/260. Local elements are the clothing of the goddesses and the inscribed bynames that have been analyzed as Germanic or Celtic.

Further research needs to be carried out on the still unprocessed museum complexes with fragments that can be assigned to matronae altars. This task alone may fill further catalogues.

Frank Biller's definition of the Ubian settlement region as a »religious landscape« proves that the area was lastingly shaped by the places of worship, the religious content and cult practices in both the private and public spheres. The cult of the Matronae was certainly firmly entrenched in public life and the consciousness of the population[40].

Archaeological findings like the structures at Nettersheim[41] raise questions about what we know about pre-Roman cult traditions. The question of the veneration of the Matronae as ancestresses in the pre-Roman era is supported by identifying divine ancestresses in connection with the sepulchral cult, e.g. based on the relief ornament of a fragmented tombstone from Beller (Ahrweiler)[42].

---

[38] E.g. Cato, de agr. 141, 2, naming »Mars Pater«; not to mention »Dis Pater« as the old name form of Iuppiter, see RE V 1 (1903) 478–479 s. v. Diespiter (G. Wissowa) and RE X 1 (1918) 1126–1144 s. v. Iuppiter (C. O. Thulin).
[39] Pasche Guignard – Pedrucci 2018, 405–410.
[40] Biller 2010, 324–327. The religious landscape, as defined by Wiegels 2006, 38, is an important area of human thought, feeling, and action. In addition to ideas and basic contents such as forms, places, objects of cultic practice, modes of organization, and social or political references must also be taken into consideration. Starting from the religious testimonies, a partial landscape is obtained with the underlying criteria.
[41] Forrest 2013.
[42] Martin-Kilcher 2014, 583–610. See also Herz 2003, 146–147 on the interpretation of the Matronae as female ancestors.

As a follow-up question, the Roman manner of dealing with religious structures and influences of their conquered regions has to be analyzed. We know for certain that the Roman expansion worked differently in each occupied region and newly established province. The next step would be to compare the building and designing of Roman concepts with local deities of whatever shape and task area. Approaches like Romanization, syncretism, etc. provide an orientation on how to describe the existing material.

In the area of Roman provincial art, the Matronae altars form one large complex. The accomplished study guarantees a profound material basis for further studies on the evolution of provincial deities depicted in Roman imagery.

**ACKNOWLEDGEMENT**

I would like to thank Susanne Willers (LVR LandesMuseum Bonn) for the permission to publish the objects illustrated here (figs. 2. 3) as well as Wolfgang Spickermann for the access to the photo archive of the CIL XIII-project (fig. 4).

**BIBLIOGRAPHY**

| | |
|---|---|
| Alexandridis 2004 | A. Alexandridis, Die Frauen des römischen Kaiserhauses. Eine Untersuchung ihrer bildlichen Darstellung von Livia bis Iulia Domna (Mainz on Rhine 2004) |
| Bauchhenß 1987 | G. Bauchhenß (ed.), Matronen und verwandte Gottheiten. Ergebnisse eines Kolloquiums, Beih. BJb 44 (Cologne 1987) |
| Bauchhenß 2005 | G. Bauchhenß, Ziegen, Vögel, Baum und Schlange. Zu den Rückseiten zweier Matronenaltäre vom Bonner Münster, in: W. Spickermann – R. Wiegels (eds.), Keltische Götter im Römischen Reich. Akten des 4. Internationalen Workshops »Fontes Epigraphici Religionis Celticae Antiquae« (F.E.R.C.AN.) vom 04.–06.10.2002 an der Universität Osnabrück, Osnabrücker Forschungen zu Altertum und Antike-Rezeption 9 (Möhnesee 2005) 149–163 |
| Bauchhenß 2012 | G. Bauchhenß, Neues zu bekannten Funden: Mahlrelief und Weihaltäre, in: J. Kunow (ed.), 25 Jahre Archäologie im Rheinland 1987–2011 (Stuttgart 2012) 115–117 |
| Bauchhenß 2013 | G. Bauchhenß, Füllhörner und andere Nebenseitenmotive, in: A. Hofeneder – P. de Bernardo Stempel (eds.), Théonymie celtique, cultes, *interpretatio*. Workshop F.E.R.C.AN., Paris 24.–26.05.2010, MPK 79 (Vienna 2013) 145–155 |
| Bauchhenß 2014 | G. Bauchhenß, Doppelgöttinnen in den römischen Nordwestprovinzen, AnzWien 148, 2014, 127–148 |
| Bauchhenß 2015 | G. Bauchhenß, Die Weihealtäre aus Bonn, in: A. W. Busch – A. Schäfer (eds.), Römische Weihealtäre im Kontext. Internationale Tagung Köln 03.–05.12.2009 (Friedberg 2015) 155–178 |
| Bauchhenß 2021 | G. Bauchhenß, Weihedenkmäler. Die ›Mannheimer Matronenaltäre‹, in: J. Lipps – S. Ardeleanu – J. Osnabrügge – C. Witschel (eds.), Die römischen Steindenkmäler in den Reiss-Engelhorn-Museen Mannheim. Mit Beiträgen von G. Bauchhenß, C. Berthold, M. Flecker, R. Gordon, J. Griesbach, A. Hensen, P. Noelke, S. Traunmüller sowie Materialansprachen von J. Zöldföldi, Mannheimer Geschichtsblätter Sonderveröffentlichung 14 (Mannheim 2021) 440–463 |
| Bickel 1938 | E. Bickel, Zu Ammians Exkurs über Gallien, in: H. von Petrikovits – A. Steeger (eds.), Festschrift August Oxé (Darmstadt 1938) 164–169 |
| Biller 2010 | F. Biller, Kultische Zentren und Matronenverehrung in der südlichen Germania inferior, Osnabrücker Forschungen zu Altertum und Antike-Rezeption 13 (Rahden 2010) |
| Burns 1994 | V. Burns, Romanization and acculturation: The Rhineland *matronae* (Ann Arbor, MI 1994) |
| de Bernardo Stempel 2014 | P. de Bernardo Stempel, Keltische Äquivalente klassischer Epitheta und andere sprachliche und nicht-sprachliche Phänomene im Rahmen der sogenannten ›interpretatio Romana‹, Zeitschrift für celtische Philologie 61, 2014, 7–48 |
| de Bernardo Stempel 2021 | P. de Bernardo Stempel, Muttergöttinnen und ihre Votivformulare. Eine sprachhistorische Studie, Indogermanische Bibliothek. 3. Reihe, Untersuchungen (Heidelberg 2021) |

| | |
|---|---|
| Delamarre 2001 | X. Delamarre, Dictionnaire de la langue gauloise. Une approche linguistique du viex-celtique continental, Collection des Hespérides (Paris 2001) |
| Delamarre 2009 | X. Delamarre, ›Octocannae Matres‹ et le thème ›aucto-, octo-‹ (celtique ›*ougtu-› ōχtu-‹), Studia Celtica Fennica 5, 2009, 21–25 |
| Delamarre 2013 | X. Delamarre, La structuration verticale de l'espace chez les anciens Celtes et les déesses rhénanes Matronae Andrusteihae, in: A. Hofeneder – P. de Bernardo Stempel (eds.), Théonymie celtique, cultes, *interpretatio*. Workshop F.E.R.C.AN., Paris 24.–26.05.2010, MPK 79 (Vienna 2013) 97–100 |
| Derks 1998 | T. Derks, Gods, Temples and Ritual Practices. The Transformation of Religious Ideas and Values in Roman Gaul, Amsterdam Archaeological Studies 2 (Amsterdam 1998) |
| Derks 2015 | T. Derks, Die Weihealtäre aus den Nehalennia-Heiligtümern und verwandten ländlichen Tempelbezirken in Niedergermanien, in: A. W. Busch – A. Schäfer (eds.), Römische Weihealtäre im Kontext. Internationale Tagung Köln 03.–05.12.2009 (Friedberg 2015) 199–219 |
| de Wal 1846 | J. de Wal, De moedergodinnen. Eene oudheidkundig-mythologische verhandeling (Leiden 1846) |
| Eck – Koßmann 2009 | W. Eck – D. Koßmann, Votivaltäre in den Matronenheiligtümern in Niedergermanien. Ein Reflex der städtischen und ländlichen Gesellschaften einer römischen Provinzstadt, in: C. Auffarth (ed.), Religion auf dem Lande. Entstehung und Veränderung von Sakrallandschaften unter römischer Herrschaft, Potsdamer altertumswissenschaftliche Beiträge 28 (Stuttgart 2009) 73–102 |
| Forrest 2013 | M.-C. Forrest, Neues zum Heiligtum der aufanischen Matronen bei Nettersheim, BJb 213, 2013, 135–164 |
| Ferlut 2022 | A. Ferlut, Le culte des divinités féminines en Gaul Belgique et dans les Germanies sous le-Haut-Empire romain (Bordeaux 2022) |
| Galsterer – Galsterer 2010 | B. Galsterer – H. Galsterer, Die römischen Steininschriften aus Köln ²(Mainz 2010) |
| Garman 2008 | A. G. Garman, The cult of the Matronae in the Roman Rhineland. A historical evaluation of the archaeological evidence, Hors serie (Lewiston 2008) |
| Gonzenbach 1986 | V. Gonzenbach, Die römischen Terracotten in der Schweiz. Untersuchungen zu Zeitstellung, Typologie und Ursprung der mittelgallischen Tonstatuetten. Katalog und Tafeln B (Tübingen 1986) |
| Gonzenbach 1995 | V. Gonzenbach, Die römischen Terracotten in der Schweiz. Untersuchungen zu Zeitstellung, Typologie und Ursprung der mittelgallischen Tonstatuetten. Textteil A (Tübingen 1995) |
| Gutenbrunner 1937 | S. Gutenbrunner, Neue Zeugnisse zur Sprache der Ubier, Zeitschrift für Mundartforschung 13/2, 1937, 65–77 |
| Hahl 1937a | L. Hahl, Zur Matronenverehrung in Niedergermanien, Germania 21/4, 1937, 253–264 |
| Hahl 1937b | L. Hahl, Zur Stilentwicklung der provinzialrömischen Plastik in Germanien und Gallien (Darmstadt 1937) |
| Hahl – Clairmont-von Gonzenbach 1960 | L. Hahl – V. Clairmont-von Gonzenbach, Zur Erklärung der niedergermanischen Matronendenkmäler, BJb 160, 1960, 9–49 |
| Herz 1989 | P. Herz, Einheimische Kulte und ethnische Strukturen. Methodische Überlegungen am Beispiel der Provinzen Germania Inferior, Germania Superior und Belgica, in: H. E. Herzig – R. Frei-Stolba (eds.), Labor omnibus unus. Festschrift Gerold Walser, Historia Einzelschriften 60 (Stuttgart 1989) 206–218 |
| Herz 2003 | P. Herz, Matronenkult und kultische Mahlzeiten, in: P. Noelke – F. Naumann-Steckner – B. Schneider (eds.), Romanisation und Resistenz in Plastik, Architektur und Inschriften der Provinzen des Imperium Romanum. Neue Funde und Forschungen. Akten des VII. Internationalen Colloquiums über Probleme des Provinzialrömischen Kunstschaffens Köln 02.–06.05.2001 (Mainz on Rhine 2003) 139–148 |
| Hofeneder – de Bernardo Stempel 2013 | A. Hofeneder – P. de Bernardo Stempel (eds.), Théonymie celtique, cultes, *interpretatio* – Keltische Theonymie, Kulte, *interpretatio*. Workshop F.E.R.C.AN., Paris 24.–26.05.2010, MPK 79 (Vienna 2013) |
| Hondius-Crone 1955 | A. Hondius-Crone, The temple of Nehalennia at Domburg (Amsterdam 1955) |
| Horn 1987 | H. G. Horn, Bilddenkmäler des Matronenkultes im Ubiergebiet, in: Bauchhenß 1987, 31–54 |

| | |
|---|---|
| Huet 2008 | V. Huet, Les images de sacrifice en Gaule romaine, in: S. Lepetz – W. van Andringa (eds.), Archéologie du sacrifice animal en Gaule romaine. Rituels et pratiques alimentaires, Archéologie des plantes et des animaux 2 (Montagnac 2008) 43–74 |
| Huet 2017 | V. Huet, Roman Sacrificial Reliefs in Rome, Italy, and Gaul. Reconstructing Archaeological Evidence?, in: J. W. Knust – C. Moser (eds.), Ritual matters. Material residues of ancient religions (Ann Arbor, MI 2017) 11–32 |
| Ihm 1887 | M. Ihm, Der Mütter- oder Matronenkultus und seine Denkmäler, Jahrbücher des Vereins von Alterthumsfreunden im Rheinlande 83, 1887, 1–200 |
| Lipka 2009 | M. Lipka, Roman Gods. A Conceptual Approach, Religions in the Graeco-Roman World 167 (Leiden 2009) |
| Martin-Kilcher 2014 | S. Martin-Kilcher, Nachbarinnen. Matronen auf einem frühkaiserzeitlichen Grabstein in der Gegend von Ahrweiler, AMosel 9, 2014, 583–610 |
| Matijević 2016 | K. Matijević (ed.), Kelto-römische Gottheiten und ihre Verehrer. Akten des 14. F.E.R.C.A.N-Workshops, Trier 12.–14.10.2015, Pharos 39 (Rahden/Westf. 2016) |
| Noelke 1998 | P. Noelke, Grabreliefs mit Mahldarstellung in den germanisch-gallischen Provinzen – soziale und religiöse Aspekte, in: P. Fasold – T. Fischer – H. von Hesberg – M. Witteyer (eds.), Bestattungssitte und kulturelle Identität. Grabanlagen und Grabbeigaben der frühen römischen Kaiserzeit in Italien und den Nordwest-Provinzen. Kolloquium Xanten 16.–18.02.1995, Xantener Berichte 7 (Köln 1998) 399–418 |
| Noelke 2011 | P. Noelke, Weihaltäre mit Opferdarstellungen und -bezügen in der Germania Inferior und den übrigen Nordwestprovinzen des Imperium Romanum, JbRGZM 58/2, 2011, 467–590 |
| Noelke 2013 | P. Noelke, Niedergermanische Weihealtäre mit Opferthematik, Archäologie im Rheinland 2012, 2013, 152–156 |
| Pasche Guignard – Pedrucci 2018 | F. Pasche Guignard – G. Pedrucci, Motherhood(s) and Polytheisms. Epistemological and Methodological Reflections on the Study of Religions, Gender and Women, Numen 65, 2018, 405–435 |
| von Petrikovits 1987 | H. von Petrikovits, Matronen und verwandte Gottheiten. Zusammenfassende Bemerkungen, in: Bauchhenß 1987, 241–254 |
| Polomé 1987 | E. C. Polomé, Muttergottheiten im alten Westeuropa, in: Bauchhenß 1987, 201–212 |
| Portale 2013 | E. C. Portale, *Augustae*, Matrons, Goddesses: Imperial women in the sacred space, in: M. Galli (ed.), Roman power and Greek sanctuaries. Forms of interaction and communication, Tripodes. Scuola Archeologica Italiana di Atene 14 (Athens 2013) 205–243 |
| Raepsaet-Charlier 2015 | M.-T. Raepsaet-Charlier, Cultes et territoire, Mères et Matrones, dieux «celtiques»: quelques aspects de la religion dans les provinces romaines de Gaule et de Germanie à la lumière de travaux récents, AntCl 84, 2015, 173–226 |
| Raepsaet-Charlier 2019 | M.-T. Raepsaet-Charlier, Les Matrones ubiennes et la colonie agrippienne, in: F. Fontana – E. Murgia (eds.), Sacrum Facere. Atti del V Seminario di Archeologia del Sacro. Sacra peregrina. La gestione della pluralità religiosa nel mondo antico (Trieste 2019) 167–191 |
| Rothe 2005 | U. Rothe, Kleidung und Romanisierung: Der Raum Rhein/Mosel, in: G. Schörner (ed.), Romanisierung – Romanisation. Theoretische Modelle und praktische Fallbeispiele, BARIntSer 1427 (Oxford 2005) 169–179 |
| Rothe 2009 | U. Rothe, Dress and cultural identity in the Rhine-Moselle region of the Roman Empire, BARIntSer 2038 (Oxford 2009) |
| Rüger 1983 | C. B. Rüger, A Husband for the Mother Goddess. Some Observations on the Matronae Aufaniae, in: B. Hartley – J. Wacher (eds.), Rome and her Northern Provinces. Papers presented to Sheppard Frere in honour of his retirement from the Chair of the Archaeology of the Roman Empire, University of Oxford, 1983 (Gloucester 1983) 210–221 |
| Rüger 1987 | C. B. Rüger, Beobachtungen zu den epigraphischen Belegen der Muttergottheiten in den lateinischen Provinzen des Imperium Romanum, in: Bauchhenß 1987, 1–30 |
| Rüpke 1997 | J. Rüpke, Römische Religion und ›Reichsreligion‹: Begriffsgeschichtliche und methodische Bemerkungen, in: H. Cancik – J. Rüpke (eds.), Römische Reichsreligion und Provinzialreligion (Tübingen 1997) 3–23 |
| Schauerte 1985 | G. Schauerte, Terrakotten mütterlicher Gottheiten. Formen und Werkstätten rheinischer und gallischer Tonstatuetten der römischen Kaiserzeit, BJb Beih. 45 (Cologne 1985) |

| | |
|---|---|
| Schauerte 1987 | G. Schauerte, Darstellungen mütterlicher Gottheiten in den römischen Nordwestprovinzen, in: Bauchhenß 1987, 55–102 |
| Schmölzer 2022 | A. Schmölzer, Erkennbar in Bild und Schrift? Auf der Suche nach ikonographischen Markern für die Ehrenbezeichnungen der niedergermanischen Matronen, in: G. Koiner – M. Lehner – E. Trinkl (eds.), Akten des 18. Österreichischen Archäologietages am Institut für Antike der Universität Graz, VIKAGraz 18 (Vienna 2022) 243–251 |
| Schmölzer 2023 | A. Schmölzer, Göttinnen der Germania Inferior. Neue archäologische Untersuchungen zur Ikonographie der Matronen, Xantener Berichte 40 (Oppenheim 2023) |
| Shaw 2011 | P. A. Shaw, Pagan Goddesses in the Early Germanic World. Eostre, Hreda and the Cult of Matrons, Studies in Early Medieval History (London 2011) |
| Smith 1994 | A. Smith, Queens and Empresses as Goddesses: The Public Role of the Personal Tyche in the Graeco-Roman World, YaleUnivB 1994, 86–105 |
| Spickermann 2008a | W. Spickermann, Germania Inferior. Religionsgeschichte des römischen Germanien II, Religion der römischen Provinzen III (Tübingen 2008) |
| Spickermann 2008b | W. Spickermann, Romanisierung und Romanisation am Beispiel der Epigraphik der germanischen Provinzen Roms, in: R. Häussler (ed.), Romanisation et épigraphie. Études interdisciplinaires sur l'acculturation et l'identité dans L'Empire Romain, Archéologie et histoire romaine 17 (Montagnac 2008) 307–320 |
| Spickermann 2009 | W. Spickermann, Matronen und Nehalennia. Die Verbreitung von mütterlichen Gottheiten in der Germania Inferior, in: E. Olshausen – V. Sauer (eds.), Die Landschaft und die Religion. Stuttgarter Kolloquium zur Historischen Geographie des Altertums 9, 2005, Geographica Historia 26 (Stuttgart 2009) 353–373 |
| Spickermann 2010 | W. Spickermann, Religion an der Nordseeküste: Dea Nehalennia, in: K. Ruffing – A. Becker – G. Rasbach (eds.), Kontaktzone Lahn. Studien zum Kulturkontakt zwischen Römern und germanischen Stämmen, Philippika 38 (Wiesbaden 2010) 125–135 |
| Spickermann – de Bernardo Stempel 2005 | W. Spickermann – P. de Bernardo Stempel, Keltische Götter in der Germania Inferior mit einem sprachwissenschaftlichen Kommentar von Patrizia de Bernardo Stempel, in: W. Spickermann – R. Wiegels (eds.), Keltische Götter im Römischen Reich. Akten des 4. Internationalen Workshops »Fontes Epigraphici Religionis Celticae Antiquae« (F.E.R.C.AN.) 04.–06.10.2002 an der Universität Osnabrück, Osnabrücker Forschungen zu Altertum und Antike-Rezeption 9 (Möhnesee 2005) 125–148 |
| Stuart 2013 | P. Stuart, Nehalennia van Domburg. Geschiedenis van de stenen Monumenten (Utrecht 2013) |
| Stuart – Bogaers 2001 | P. Stuart – J. E. Bogaers, Nehalennia. Römische Steindenkmäler aus der Oosterschelde bei Colijnsplaat, Collections of the National Museum of Antiquities at Leiden 11 (Leiden 2001) |
| Wiegels 2006 | R. Wiegels, Zentralität – Kulturraum – Landschaft: Zur Tauglichkeit von Begriffen und Ordnungskriterien bei der Erfassung religiöser Phänomene im Imperium Romanum, in: H. Cancik – A. Schäfer – W. Spickermann (eds.), Zentralität und Religion. Zur Formierung urbaner Zentren im Imperium Romanum, Studien und Texte zu Antike und Christentum 39 (Tübingen 2006) 21–46 |
| Wiegels et al. 2007 | R. Wiegels – W. Spickermann – F. Biller, Stadt und Hinterland: Religiöse Landschaften im südlichen Niedergermanien, in: J. Rüpke (ed.), Antike Religionsgeschichte in räumlicher Perspektive. Abschlussbericht zum Schwerpunktprogramm 1080 der Deutschen Forschungsgemeinschaft »Römische Reichsreligion und Provinzialreligion« (Tübingen 2007) 31–36 |
| Wild 1968 | J. P. Wild, Die Frauentracht der Ubier, Germania 46, 1968, 67–73 |
| Woolf 2003 | G. Woolf, Local Cult in Imperial Context: The *Matronae* revisited, in: P. Noelke – F. Naumann-Steckner – B. Schneider (eds.), Romanisation und Resistenz in Plastik, Architektur und Inschriften der Provinzen des Imperium Romanum. Neue Funde und Forschungen. Akten des VII. Internationalen Colloquiums über Probleme des Provinzialrömischen Kunstschaffens Köln 02.–06.05.2001 (Mainz on Rhine 2003) 131–138 |
| Wrede 1981 | H. Wrede, Consecratio in formam deorum. Vergöttlichte Privatpersonen in der römischen Kaiserzeit (Mainz 1981) |

*Astrid Schmölzer, Professur für Archäologie der Römischen Provinzen, Otto-Friedrich Universität Bamberg, Am Kranen 14, 02.14, 96047 Bamberg, Deutschland.*
*[e] astrid.schmoelzer@uni-bamberg.de*

Kathrin Schuchter

# DIE ENTHAUPTUNG MEDUSAS AUF NORISCHEN UND PANNONISCHEN GRABRELIEFS

## ÜBERLEGUNGEN ZU MUSTERBÜCHERN, WERKSTÄTTEN UND BILDSCHEMATA

**Abstract**
On funerary monuments from *Noricum* and *Pannonia*, Perseus is most frequently shown in the act of killing Medusa, with a recurring image scheme in all four known reliefs taking up the mythological theme. Perseus, depicted in heroic nudity except for his waving *chlamys* and Phrygian cap, cuts off Medusa's head, who has already collapsed to her knees. In three of them, his patron goddess Athena helps him to accomplish the task by holding a shield as a mirror, as the hero has to avert his gaze from the Gorgon to avoid being turned into stone. The aim of this paper is to show to what extent the image scheme can be traced back in the Greco-Roman cultural sphere and how it was implemented on the reliefs in *Noricum* and *Pannonia*. In this respect, the question of pattern books is raised and basic considerations on different workshops are made. Other compositional influences, especially in regard to representations of the bull-killing Mithras, are also discussed.

Mythologische Bilder als Bestandteile römischer Grabbauten stellen im norisch-pannonischen Raum keine Seltenheit dar. Obwohl keine Sicherheit bezüglich der Bedeutung dieser Szenen für die Menschen der Antike besteht – insbesondere in Hinblick auf die tatsächliche Kenntnis der Mythen oder individuelle Präferenzen der Grabinhaber und -inhaberinnen für ausgewählte Motive – wird heute davon ausgegangen, dass den Bildern wohl überwiegend symbolischer Charakter innewohnte. Mythologische Szenen aus dem Sagenkreis um Heroen wie Herakles oder Theseus, die oftmals bei der Bewältigung scheinbar unmöglicher Aufgaben gezeigt werden, konnten mitunter als Symbol für die Überwindung des Todes gesehen werden oder auch der Heroisierung der Verstorbenen im übertragenen Sinne gedient haben[1].

Ähnlich verhält es sich bei Reliefdarstellungen, die Perseus bei der Tötung Medusas zeigen und deshalb gerne als mythologische Szenen auf Grabbauten verwendet wurden. Zwar wird Perseus auch allein stehend ohne mythologischen Rahmen oder bei der Rettung der schönen Andromeda gezeigt, die Enthauptungsszene überwiegt jedoch unter den derzeit bekannten Darstellungen der Provinzen *Noricum* und *Pannonia* (Abb. 1). Gleich vier provinziale Reliefs (Abb. 2) zeigen die Szene, wobei die Bildwerke auffallend starke Gemeinsamkeiten in ihrer ikonografischen Ausführung aufweisen. Auf allen Darstellungen ist Perseus als jugendlicher Heros abgebildet, der mit abgewandtem Kopf der bereits in die Knie gegangenen Gorgone das Haupt abschneidet. Seine Schutzgöttin Athena hilft ihm auf drei der

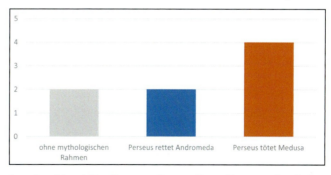

1  Anzahl und Verteilung von Perseus-Darstellungen auf norischen und pannonischen Grabreliefs (n = 8) (Grafik K. Schuchter)

---

[1] Walde 2005, 96; Zanker – Ewald 2004.

2     1) FO: Pécs (Kom. Baranya, HU), Ungarisches Nationalmuseum (Budapest, HU); 2) FO: Budapest (Kom. Budapest, HU), Ungarisches Nationalmuseum (Budapest, HU); 3) FO: Kainach bei Voitsberg (Steiermark, AT), Universalmuseum Joanneum (Graz, AT); 4) FO: Neumarkt im Tauchental (Burgenland, AT), Pfarrkirche Neumarkt (Burgenland, AT) (Fotos K. Schuchter)

Steindenkmäler bei der Bewältigung seiner Aufgabe, indem sie einen Rundschild vor ihren Körper hält – erst durch Perseus' Blick in den spiegelnden Schild kann er das versteinernde Antlitz Medusas betrachten. Obwohl die Ausformungen sich in ihrer Qualität durch die Details der Darstellungen unterscheiden und formale Teilaspekte individuelle Abwandlungen erfahren haben, lassen sie ein einheitliches Bildschema erkennen.

## DAS BILDSCHEMA

Dass dieses Darstellungsschema bereits seit mehreren Jahrhunderten im griechisch-römischen Kulturkreis verbreitet war und dabei nicht auf ein Medium beschränkt blieb, zeigen die vorhandenen materiellen Zeugnisse. Am Anfang einer längeren Reihe an Bildwerken steht das Fragment eines Reliefrhytons aus Ruvo di Puglia[2] (Abb. 3), das bereits mehrfach Aufmerksamkeit in der Literatur erfahren hat[3]. Obwohl die genaue Datierung des Gefäßes umstritten ist, gilt eine Einordnung in das dritte Viertel des 4. Jahrhunderts v. Chr. als wahrscheinlich. Die Vorderseite des Rhytons zeigt Perseus bis auf die phrygische Mütze und die wehende Chlamys im Rücken in heroischer Nacktheit, während er mit der linken Hand Medusa am Haar gepackt hält, um ihr das Haupt abzuschneiden[4]. Medusa ist geflügelt und mit einer sich hinter ihr windenden Schlange

---

[2]    CVA Bonn (3) Taf. 45, 4. 5; LIMC VII (1994) 339 Nr. 118 s. v. Perseus (J. Ch. Balty).
[3]    Loeschke 1893, 3; Sieveking 1922; Schauenburg 1960, 24–29. 134.
[4]    Vgl. das etwa zeitgleiche Motiv auf einem apulisch rotfigurigen Volutenkrater, der die Opferung der Trojaner bei der Bestattung des Patroklos zeigt (LIMC I [1981] 108 Nr. 487 Taf. 108 s. v. Achilleus [A. Kossatz-Deißmann]). Zu ähnlichen Übereinstimmungen aus der unteritalischen Vasenmalerei mit norischen Grabreliefs vgl. Walde 2005, 172–173.

dargestellt⁵. Mit der Rechten versucht sie, Perseus am Unterarm zurückzuhalten – die Linke greift nach oben hin aus. Das Gewand ist ihr dabei bereits bis auf die Hüften hinabgerutscht und entblößt ihren nackten Oberkörper. Um der versteinernden Wirkung ihres Blickes zu entgehen, schaut Perseus zurück. Aufgrund des fragmentarischen Erhaltungszustandes kann nicht mehr festgestellt werden, ob auch Athena als Teil der Szene zu rekonstruieren ist, und wie sie in einem solchen Fall dargestellt war. Besonders in Hinblick auf die mögliche Verwendung des Spiegelmotivs wäre dies jedoch von Interesse.

Grundsätzlich kann die gleiche Komposition (mit Vorsicht in Bezug auf die Darstellungsweise Athenas) bis etwa an den Anfang des 3. Jahrhunderts n. Chr. sowohl in Toreutik, Glyptik und Numismatik als auch in der Wandmalerei nachverfolgt werden⁶. In Einzelfällen wird lediglich das Spiegelmotiv aus Platzgründen weggelassen oder in stark reduzierter Form gezeigt (etwa durch einen nur halb angedeuteten Schild, der am Rand des Bildfeldes zu erahnen ist). Auch die Einbettung des Geschehens in einen landschaftlichen Rahmen kommt vor. Da das Bildschema in Hinblick auf

3  Fragment eines Reliefrhytons, FO: Ruvo di Puglia (Prov. Bari, IT), Akademisches Kunstmuseum (Bonn, DE) (© Akademisches Kunstmuseum Bonn)

die beiden Protagonisten des Mythos stets konstant bleibt, stellt sich in weiterer Folge die Frage nach einem gemeinsamen Vorbild der Darstellungen. Für das Rhyton, welches das früheste fassbare materielle Zeugnis bildet und somit einem ursprünglichen Werk zeitlich am nächsten stünde, wird grundsätzlich die Fertigung nach einem Tarentiner Metallwerk oder -gefäß angenommen⁷. Da toreutische Werke oftmals großformatige (groß-)griechische Gemälde zum Vorbild hatten, kann ein solcher Überlieferungszweig auch in diesem Fall nicht ausgeschlossen werden⁸. Ein Metallwerk könnte dabei die Mittlerrolle zwischen einem Werk aus dem Bereich der Malerei und dem Rhyton übernommen haben⁹.

---

⁵  Schlange und Flügel gelten als frühe Attribute Medusas, verschwinden jedoch mit fortschreitender Vermenschlichung der Gorgone (Payne 1931, 80–87; Loeschke 1894, 14).

⁶  Toreutik: Silberpatera aus Lameira Larga Ende 1.–Mitte 2. Jh. n. Chr. (LIMC VII [1994] 340 Nr. 135 s. v. Perseus [J. Ch. Balty]); Barata 2018, 58. Bronzeoinochoe aus Thorey (LIMC VII [1994] 340 Nr. 134 Taf. 295 s. v. Perseus [J. Ch. Balty]); Bonnamour 1969, 288–291. Glyptik: Glaspaste (Loeschke 1893, 10); Numismatik: Prägungen Caracallas aus *Sebaste Galatiae*, 198–217 n. Chr. (LIMC VII [1994] 340 Nr. 136 s. v. Perseus [J. Ch. Balty]); Barclay 1906, 375. Wandmalerei: Wandgemälde aus *Herculaneum* (LIMC VII [1994] 340 Nr. 130 s. v. Perseus [J. Ch. Balty]).

⁷  Zur Diskussion hierzu vgl. Schauenburg 1960, 29.

⁸  Lippold 1951, 71.

⁹  Schauenburg 1960, 28–29.

## DIE PROVINZIALEN RELIEFS

Mit einer ungefähren Datierung in antoninische bis spätseverische Zeit gehören die vier genannten provinzialen Reliefs zu den jüngsten Darstellungen des Bildschemas. Trotz der zeitlichen Differenz ist aber auch hier ein eindeutiger Bezug zu der spätestens hellenistischen Komposition fassbar.

Am deutlichsten tritt dieser Bezug in einem Relief aus Pécs[10], dem antiken *Sopianae*, zutage (Abb. 2, 1), das sich heute im Ungarischen Nationalmuseum befindet. Gemeinsam mit drei weiteren Marmorelementen mit mythologischen Szenen konnte es zu einem Sarkophag rekonstruiert werden, der wahrscheinlich im dritten Viertel des 2. Jahrhunderts n. Chr. gefertigt worden war. Es wird vermutet, dass es sich aufgrund stilistischer Merkmale um ein importiertes Werk aus Celje-*Celeia* handelt[11]. Dargestellt ist in einem einfachen profilierten Rahmen Perseus mit phrygischer Mütze sowie wehender Chlamys in seinem Rücken. Der Heros ist nach rechts gewandt und packt mit der linken Hand das Haupt der Medusa – mit der rechten hält er der Gorgone ein Schwert an den Hals. Die vor ihm in die Knie Gesunkene, die mit einem herabgerutschten Gewand um Hüfte und Schulter abgebildet ist, versucht Perseus, mit je einer Hand an dessen Arm und Schwertspitze zurückzuhalten und blickt ihn direkt an. Der Heros jedoch hat seinen Kopf nach hinten zu Athena gewandt. Die Göttin ist in einem Peplos mit Helm gezeigt und hält in den Händen einen Rundschild vor ihrem Körper, um Perseus das Spiegelbild Medusas zu zeigen[12].

In einer in der Figurenkonstellation abgeänderten Form begegnet das Schema des Reliefs aus Pécs in einem Reliefblock aus dem Gebiet um Budapest[13], dem antiken *Aquincum* (Abb. 2, 2). Er ist ebenfalls im Ungarischen Nationalmuseum ausgestellt. Der Eckstein eines Grabbaus kann auf die Zeit zwischen 180 und 230 n. Chr. datiert werden und zeigt auf einer seiner Seiten die Enthauptungsszene in einem einfachen profilierten Rahmen, dessen obere Leiste als Bogen mit Volutenenden geformt ist[14]. Perseus und Medusa sind in beinahe identischer Weise abgebildet wie im vorigen Beispiel, wobei sich als einziger Unterschied das verringerte Raumangebot zwischen den beiden Gestalten nennen lässt. Dies führt zu einer beinahe senkrechten Position von Perseus' linker Hand, mit der er Medusa am Haar gepackt hält, und auch der rechte Arm der Gorgone verschwindet hinter dem Helden. Da das Relief stark erodiert ist, kann über die Blickrichtung der Figuren keine Angabe mehr gemacht werden, jedoch haben beide den Kopf leicht zurückgewandt[15]. Am auffälligsten ist allerdings das Fehlen Athenas in der linken Bildhälfte. Zwar ist das mythologische Thema auch ohne die Göttin klar erkennbar, jedoch wird Perseus' Blick nach hinten ohne das Vorhandensein eines Spiegels überflüssig. Es darf daher angenommen werden, dass auf dem Vorbild des Reliefs die Gestalt Athenas abgebildet war und aus Platzmangel, der durch die architektonische Form des Eckblockes bedingt war, weggelassen werden musste. In Hinblick auf die ansonsten beinahe deckungsgleiche Wiedergabe der beiden vorhandenen Figuren – besonders was Perseus' Haltung und die Gestik Medusas anbelangt – kann das Relief aus Pécs als weitere Darstellung dieser Szene angenommen werden. Für eine Einpassung in den vorhandenen Rahmen musste zusätzlich nur noch der Freiraum zwischen den beiden Hauptfiguren angepasst bzw. die Szene gestaucht werden.

Eine weitere verwandte Abbildung, die allerdings stärker von den ungarischen Reliefs abweicht, ist aus Kainach bei Voitsberg[16] bekannt und wird im Universalmuseum Joanneum in Graz verwahrt (Abb. 2, 3). Das Relief wird grob in das 2. Jahrhundert n. Chr. datiert, muss aber aus

---

[10] LIMC VII (1994) 340 Nr. 132a Taf. 293 s. v. Perseus (J. Ch. Balty); lupa 827.
[11] Koch – Sichtermann 1982, 328.
[12] Nagy 1971, 129–130; Koch – Sichtermann 1982, 327–328.
[13] LIMC VII (1994) 340 Nr. 131 s. v. Perseus (J. Ch. Balty); lupa 2984.
[14] Die linke Nebenseite zeigt nicht, wie M. Nagy behauptet, Athena (Nagy 2007, 66), sondern eine männliche (?) Figur mit Spiegel.
[15] Nagy 2007, 65.
[16] lupa 1241; Hebert 1994, 146.

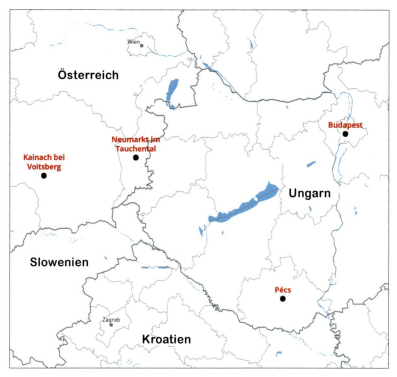

4    Geografische Verteilung der Fundorte (Grafik K. Schuchter)

relativchronologischer Sicht später als das Relief aus Pécs eingeordnet werden. Auch hier handelt es sich um ein Bauteil vom Sockelgeschoss eines Grabbaus[17]. Eine zweifach profilierte Leiste rahmt die stark verwaschene Szene, die im Wesentlichen eine spiegelverkehrte Darstellung der bekannten Enthauptungsszene zeigt. In der Mitte steht Perseus, vom Betrachter aus nach links gewandt, in Ausfallstellung mit schematisch dargestellter wehender Chlamys im Rücken. Als Kopfbedeckung ist trotz des schlechten Erhaltungszustandes eine phrygische Mütze auszumachen. Links vor ihm kniet die halbnackte Medusa, deren Gewand nach unten geglitten ist, und streckt ihre linke Hand nach dem Helden aus. Perseus aber hält ihren Kopf und hat mit der Rechten bereits sein Sichelschwert gezogen, das über dem Haupt der Gorgone abgebildet ist. Der Blick beider Figuren ist auf Athena gerichtet, die mit langem Chiton und Helm bekleidet auf der rechten Seite steht. Auch sie hat ihr Gesicht von Medusa und der grausamen Szene abgewandt und hält einen kleinen Rundschild vor dem Körper. Die rechte Hand ist vor dem Schild gezeigt, während die linke dahinter verschwindet[18].

Bei dem verwendeten Vorbild dürfte es sich wiederum um das Relief aus Pécs handeln, da die Szene im Wesentlichen seitenverkehrt wiedergegeben ist, das Grundschema allerdings gleich bleibt. Anzumerken ist, dass zwar auch Athena gespiegelt ist, jedoch den Kopf abgewandt hat. Diese abweichende Übertragung kann einerseits der individuellen Ausführung des Bildhauers geschuldet sein, andererseits aber auch auf persönliche Wünsche der Grabinhaber/-innen zurückgehen. Beide Erklärungsmöglichkeiten könnten auch auf die neu eingeführten Attribute zutreffen, die im Relief nun als selbstständige Gestaltungselemente hervortreten, so beispielsweise das Sichelschwert. Doch wird die Diskrepanz in der Qualität der Ausführung dort deutlich, wo sich der Bildhauer weiter am Vorbild orientierte: Medusas Unterleib versinkt im Boden, Perseus' Mantel fehlt die Plastizität, und Athenas Helm bleibt schemenhaft angedeutet.

---

[17]  Kremer 2001, 239.
[18]  Modrijan – Weber 1965, 106–107.

Das letzte der provinzialen Reliefs, jenes aus Neumarkt im Tauchental[19] (Abb. 2, 4), ist im Vorraum der dortigen Pfarrkirche eingemauert und weist eine größere mittige Fehlstelle auf. Auffallend ist, dass zwar auch hier wieder klar das Schema des Rhytonfragments nachvollziehbar ist, allerdings freier mit der Gestaltung der Nebenfiguren umgegangen wurde. Allein Perseus ist in gewohnter Ausfallstellung mit phrygischer Mütze und wehender Chlamys gezeigt. Sein Schwert setzt er der vor ihm knienden Medusa an die Kehle, während er mit der Linken ihr Haar fasst – die leere Scheide ist noch unter seiner Achsel zu erkennen. Medusa hingegen ist vollkommen nackt und ohne heruntergerutschtes Gewand dargestellt. Sie fasst mit beiden Händen die Waffe und blickt erstmals nicht zum Heros zurück, sondern dreht ihm vollständig den Rücken zu. Obwohl Perseus dadurch nicht direkt Medusas versteinerndem Blick ausgesetzt ist, schaut er zu Athena zurück, die in unüblicher Weise hinter einem Felsmassiv oder einer Mauer hervorblickt und den Rundschild mit beiden Armen vor ihren Körper hält[20]. Durch die abweichende Gestaltung der Göttin wird im Übrigen ein nicht unwesentliches Problem gelöst, das mit der bildlichen Umsetzung des Mythos zusammenhängt: Hält die stehende Athena nämlich den Schild vor ihrem Körper, ist Perseus' Blick zu weit nach oben gerichtet, um das Spiegelbild darin zu erblicken (eine weitere Drehung des Kopfes würde zu unästhetischen Verzerrungen führen und wäre als Relief nur schwer ausführbar). Indem die Göttin in erhöhter Position dargestellt wird, kann auch Perseus Medusa im Schild betrachten. Zusätzlich wird dem Geschehen eine räumliche Tiefe gegeben und die Szene in eine spezifische Umgebung eingebettet – diese Tendenzen konnten auch schon in Glyptik, Toreutik und Wandmalerei in Bezug auf das Rhyton aus Ruvo festgestellt werden.

## VON MUSTERBÜCHERN UND WERKSTÄTTEN

Weshalb aber orientieren sich die Szenen aus Pécs, Budapest und Kainach bei Voitsberg stärker am klassischen Typus als das letztgenannte Grabrelief aus Neumarkt im Tauchental? Bedenkt man, dass das am qualitätvollsten gearbeitete Relief aus Pécs womöglich Teil eines aus Celje-*Celeia* importierten Sarkophags war[21], so kann eine Verbindung zur Hafenstadt *Aquileia* eine solche Entwicklung begünstigt haben. Denn durch die weitreichenden Kontakte der Stadt mit dem Osten wurden häufig prominente mythologische Bildvorlagen aus dem griechischen Raum übernommen[22]. Darunter könnte sich auch das Vorbild des Perseus-Typus der norischen und pannonischen Reliefs befunden haben. Wie eine Kartierung der Fundorte der genannten Beispiele zeigt (Abb. 4), fand das beliebte klassische Schema über das Relief aus Pécs in weiterer Folge großflächige Verbreitung im norischen und pannonischen Raum.

Wie die Weitergabe dieses Bildmotivs jedoch im Konkreten vonstatten ging, darüber kann keine eindeutige Aussage getroffen werden. Für viele mythologische Motive[23] – auch was die Wiederholung und Übernahme mythologischer Szenen von stadtrömischen Sarkophagen betrifft – wird die Verwendung von Musterbüchern, Gipsabgüssen oder sonstigen Vorlagen vorgeschlagen[24]. Vor allem erstgenannte Möglichkeit suggeriert nach heutigem Verständnis Sammlungen von Zeichnungen oder Motiven, die besonders gelungene Werke abbildeten, um diese als Grundlage weiterer Arbeiten nutzen zu können[25]. Unklar ist hingegen, wie ein solches Musterbuch in römischer Zeit ausgesehen haben könnte und wie man sich die Anwendung eines solchen vorstellen kann. Womöglich befanden sich in derartigen Zusammenstellungen Abbildungen wie das Relief aus Pécs oder zumindest solche desselben Bildschemas, welches dann für die Herstel-

---

[19] LIMC VII (1994) 340 Nr. 132b Taf. 294 s. v. Perseus (J. Ch. Balty); lupa 442.
[20] Ubl 1974, 19–61; Hekler 1937, 77–80.
[21] Koch – Sichtermann 1982, 327–328.
[22] Walde 1997, 241.
[23] Auf norischen Grabbauten beispielsweise die sog. Anschleichgruppe mit Satyr und Mänade; Darstellungen um Ikarus mit den Moiren, die Flucht Iphigenies von Tauris sowie Achill auf Skyros (Walde 2005, 108. 125. 132. 154).
[24] Walde 2005, 170.
[25] <https://www.dwds.de/wb/Musterbuch> (05.10.2022).

lung der Bilder aus Budapest und Kainach bei Voitsberg verwendet wurde. Abweichungen in den Details zwischen den drei Bildwerken wären in einem solchen Fall durch die Gestaltung durch verschiedene Werkstätten begründet. Dies konnte sowohl rein gestaltungstechnische oder architektonische Gründe im Sinne des vorhandenen Platzes haben (z. B. beim Relief aus Budapest), der individuellen Ausführung des Bildhauers oder den persönlichen Wünschen der Grabinhaber und -inhaberinnen (z. B. das Relief aus Kainach bei Voitsberg) geschuldet gewesen sein.

## ÄHNLICHE BILDSCHEMATA

Etwas anders verhält es sich mit der Szene aus Neumarkt im Tauchental. Obwohl auch hier das klassische Bildmotiv vertreten ist, erscheinen vor allem die Figuren der Medusa und der Athena in stark abgewandelter Form. Mit hoher Wahrscheinlichkeit spiegelt das Neumarkter Relief also auch andere Einflüsse wider.

Als Beispiel kommt hierbei die Darstellung der Stiertötung auf Mithras-Reliefs in Frage, deren Ähnlichkeit mit den provinzialen Perseus-Reliefs bereits von anderen Autorinnen und Autoren angemerkt wurde[26]. Diese waren am häufigsten in den Mithräen anzutreffen – sei es in Form eines einzelnen großformatigen Gemäldes oder als Relief, das den Mittelpunkt der Kultstätte bildete. Auch kleinformatigere Darstellungen kommen vor, deren Ausmaße 50 × 50 cm meist nicht überschreiten. Vor allem die letztgenannte Gruppe kleineren Formats ist für unsere Betrachtungen von besonderem Interesse, da diese Reliefs überwiegend in den Donauprovinzen anzutreffen sind und den provinzialen Grabreliefs in ihren Ausmaßen am meisten ähneln[27]. Dies macht sich vor allem in der Komposition des Neumarkter Reliefs bemerkbar. Nicht nur entspricht die Positionierung Athenas in der linken oberen Ecke jener der Büsten von Sol oder Luna, sondern auch die Felswand, hinter der die Göttin dargestellt ist, ähnelt der oftmals felsigen Rahmung der Tauroktonie. Auch die bei genauerer Betrachtung abweichende Proportionierung der Medusa sowie von Perseus' Unterkörper kann durch eine solche Übernahme erklärt werden, da für deren Gestaltung kein Vorbild entsprechender Körper(-partien) auf Kultreliefs gegeben war. Ebenso ähnelt der stimmiger proportionierte Oberkörper des Perseus jenem des Mithras. Die Mäntel beider Gestalten sind weit aufgebauscht, wobei der des Stiertöters häufiger für die Einbringung von Himmelsmotiven (z. B. Sternen) besonders voluminös abgebildet wurde[28].

## FAZIT

Zusammenfassend betrachtet zeigt sich, dass die Darstellung der Enthauptung Medusas auf den vier behandelten norischen und pannonischen Grabreliefs auf eine lange ikonografische Tradition zurückgeführt werden kann. Die Verwendung altbekannter Schemata, die vermutlich über Musterbücher oder sonstige Vorlagen in die Bilderwelt provinzialer Grabbauten Einzug fand, war jedoch nicht zwingend gleichbedeutend mit strikter Übernahme der Abbildungen. Insbesondere die Unterschiede zwischen den Reliefs verdeutlichen, wie Werkstätten und deren Bildhauer Szenen individuell abwandeln konnten oder auch mussten – sei es architektonischen oder technischen Gründen geschuldet oder den Wünschen der einzelnen Grabinhaber/-innen. Auch Einflüsse anderer Denkmälergattungen, wie am Beispiel der Tauroktonie gezeigt wurde, sind dabei nicht auszuschließen.

---

[26] Saxl 1931, 14 Anm. 1; Will 1947, 60–76. Beide Autoren gehen aufgrund der Ähnlichkeiten zwischen den Perseus-Darstellungen, vor allem in Bezug auf das Bonner Rhyton, und den Darstellungen des stiertötenden Mithras von einem gemeinsamen Ursprung beider Typen aus (zusammenfassend Schauenberg 1960, 134–135). Mir scheint hinsichtlich der langen ikonografischen Tradition des Perseus-Typus und einer gewissen Neuschöpfung des Mithras-Typus im 1. Jh. n. Chr. eher wahrscheinlich, dass das Bildschema der Enthauptung Medusas auf das der Stiertötung eingewirkt hat – zumindest die Darstellung des Heros betreffend.

[27] Käppel u. a. 2006; Clauss 1990, 65.

[28] Vgl. hierzu die Darstellung auf dem Fresko aus dem Mithräum von Marino (Vermaseren 1982).

## BIBLIOGRAFIE

| | |
|---|---|
| Barata 2018 | F. Barata, O Tesouro Romano de Lameira Larga, Ebvrobriga 9, 2018, 53–60 |
| Barclay 1906 | H. Barclay, A Catalogue of Greek Coins in the British Museum. Phrygia (London 1906) |
| Bonnamour 1969 | L. Bonnamour, Découvertes gallo-romaines dans la Saône en aval de Chalon à Thorey, RA 1969, 287–300 |
| Clauss 1990 | M. Clauss, Mithras. Kult und Mysterien (München 1990) |
| Hebert 1994 | B. Hebert, Römerzeitliche Funde im Oswaldgraben in der Steiermark, FÖ 32, 1994, 139–154 |
| Hekler 1937 | A. Hekler, Róma i kőemlékek Kethelyen (Sopron), AErt 50, 1937, 77–80 |
| Käppel u. a. 2006 | L. Käppel – B. Bäbler – L.-M. Günther, Perseus, in: H. Cancik – H. Schneider – M. Landfester (Hrsg.), Der Neue Pauly, 2006, DOI:10.1163/1574-9347_dnp_e915230 (16.11.2020) |
| Koch – Sichtermann 1982 | G. Koch – H. Sichtermann, Römische Sarkophage, HdA (München 1982) |
| Kremer 2001 | G. Kremer, Antike Grabbauten in Noricum. Katalog und Auswertung von Werkstücken als Beitrag zur Rekonstruktion und Typologie, SoSchrÖAI 36 (Wien 2001) |
| Lippold 1951 | G. Lippold, Antike Gemäldekopien, AbhMünchen 33 (München 1951) |
| Loeschke 1893 | G. Loeschke, Die Enthauptung der Medusa. Ein Beitrag zur Geschichte der griechischen Malerei. Festschrift Heinrich von Brunn (Bonn 1893) |
| lupa | F. und O. Harl, <lupa.at> (Bilddatenbank zu antiken Steindenkmälern) |
| Modrijan – Weber 1965 | W. Modrijan – E. Weber, Die Römersteinsammlung im Eggenberger Schlosspark, SchildStei 12 (Graz 1965) |
| Nagy 1971 | T. Nagy, Kőfaragás és Szobrászat Aquincumban, BudReg 22, 1971, 103–156 |
| Nagy 2007 | M. Nagy, Lapidárium. A Magyar Nemzeti Múzeum régészeti Kiállításának Vezetője. Római Kőtár (Budapest 2007) |
| Payne 1931 | H. Payne, Necrocorinthia. A Study of Corinthian Art in the Archaic Period (Oxford 1931) |
| Saxl 1931 | F. Saxl, Mithras. Typengeschichtliche Untersuchungen (Berlin 1931) |
| Schauenburg 1960 | K. Schauenburg, Perseus in der Kunst des Altertums, Antiquitas III 1 (Bonn 1960) |
| Sieveking 1922 | J. Sieveking, Ein großgriechisches Tonmodell für toreutische Arbeit, MüJb 12, 1922, 117–129 |
| Ubl 1974 | H. Ubl, Die Römerzeit des Bezirkes Oberwart, in: A. Schmeller-Kitt, Die Kunstdenkmäler des politischen Bezirkes Oberwart, Österreichische Kunsttopographie 40 (Wien 1974) 19–61 |
| Vermaseren 1982 | M. J. Vermaseren, The Mithraeum at Marino, Mithriaca 3 (Leiden 1982) |
| Walde 1997 | E. Walde, Der Einfluss griechischer Bildsprache auf die Grabplastik der römischen Provinz Noricum, in: G. Erath – M. Lehner – G. Schwarz (Hrsg.), Komos. Festschrift Thuri Lorenz (Wien 1997) 239–242 |
| Walde 2005 | E. Walde, Im herrlichen Glanze Roms. Die Bilderwelt der Römersteine in Österreich (Innsbruck 2005) |
| Will 1947 | E. Will, La décollation de Méduse, RA 1947, 60–76 |
| Zanker – Ewald 2004 | P. Zanker – B. C. Ewald, Mit Mythen leben. Die Bilderwelt der römischen Sarkophage (München 2004) |

*Kathrin Schuchter, Universität Innsbruck, Institut für Archäologien, Innrain 52A, 6020 Innsbruck, Österreich.*
*[e] Kathrin.Schuchter@gmx.at*

Nedjma Serradj-Remili – Leila Benchernine

# STÈLES INÉDITES DE LA NUMIDIE ET DE LA MAURÉTANIE CÉSARIENNE ET NOUVELLE LECTURE

**Abstract**
The most popular form of ancient North African art is relief sculpture, essentially that of votive and funerary stelae. The Roman period marks the transformation of the stelae that are often composed of superimposed registers representing real portraits. Important discoveries have been made over the years in the different provinces of North Africa. Some of these monuments have never been published, and in some cases not even inventoried. In our paper, we present both votive and funerary stelae which have been discovered in the Numidian and Mauretanian cities located in Algeria a few years ago, trying to emphasize the local characteristics specific to these provinces. We will also re-examine some votive and funerary monuments of the African provinces using an iconographic analysis, in the context of an analogical study in order to rectify and complete previous incomplete studies.

Le plus populaire des arts antiques nord africains est sans doute la sculpture en relief, principalement sur les stèles votives et funéraires.

Depuis le siècle dernier, des découvertes ont eu lieu à travers tout le territoire de l'Algérie actuelle, souvent signalées dans les périodiques spécialisés en archéologie. Quelquefois certains de ces monuments n'ont pas fait l'objet d'une publication. Ils sont parfois juste cités sans aucune étude ni descriptif, principalement dans les comptes rendus de fouilles. C'est vers le milieu du XXᵉ siècle que les stèles, même anépigraphes, commencèrent à susciter des études académiques. Parmi elles, soulignons celle de Marcel Leglay[1], qui publia sa thèse de doctorat en 1961–1966 sur le culte du dieu Saturne. Deux tomes y sont consacrés aux monuments figuratifs dans les provinces africaines (Algérie et Tunisie actuelles). Pourtant, il reste aujourd'hui encore des stèles qui nécessitent soit une relecture, soit une étude approfondie, sans parler de celles qui ont été découvertes ces dernières années et qui restent encore non publiées.

## NUMIDIE

### Djemila-*Cuicul*[2]

1. Stèle funéraire inscrite (fig. 1 a)

H. 2,05 m; l. 0,64 m; épaisseur 0,23 m. Calcaire.
La stèle a été fortuitement découverte dans un terrain agricole en 2016, dans la banlieue ouest des ruines de Djemila antique-*Cuicul*. Elle se trouve actuellement dans le jardin lapidaire du musée de Djemila.

La stèle en calcaire à sommet triangulaire est composée de trois registres superposés, séparés par des bandeaux inscrits. Dans le registre supérieur se trouve un couple debout entre deux colonnes à chapiteaux corinthiens. L'homme, à droite, est vêtu d'une tunique et d'une toge dont le *balteus* et le bord du *sinus* présentent une ligne continue; il tient dans sa main gauche un *volumen* et touche avec sa main droite le bord du *sinus* de la toge. La femme, à gauche, tient dans sa main

---

[1] Leglay 1961; Leglay 1966a; Leglay 1966b.
[2] Voir Gsell 1911, feuille 16 no. 233.

gauche un objet indistinct, tandis que l'autre main est ramenée vers son abdomen. Elle porte une ample et longue tunique à *colpos* et à manches courtes. Un manteau est posé sur les deux épaules, laissant le bras et la poitrine à découvert. Le tout est maintenu par son bras gauche plié. Ce drapé pourrait être une imitation maladroite du type »Loggia dei Lanzi« à Florence[3]. Au-dessous se trouve une inscription latine martelée.

Le registre médian représente deux hommes dont la posture et le costume sont identiques au personnage masculin du registre supérieur. Leur vêtement peut être qualifié de *toga contabulata* qui apparaît à la fin du IIe siècle apr. J.-C.

Le registre inférieur est occupé par un couple debout: l'homme, à droite, est vêtu de la même toge que les autres personnages masculins. La femme, quant à elle, est drapée différemment que la première; son manteau lui enveloppe les deux épaules et elle tient de sa main droite un pan du bord supérieur qu'elle pose sur le poignet de la main gauche pour qu'il tombe en plis ondulés. Ce drapé est très fréquent sur les stèles de la région de Beni Fouda, qui se trouve à une quinzaine de kilomètres. Ceci nous laisse envisager que notre stèle provient peut-être du même atelier, vu la proximité des deux villes.

La stèle de *Cuicul* se rapproche beaucoup d'une autre stèle, qui fut probablement découverte au même endroit[4], mais à un siècle d'intervalle. La composition architecturale et l'iconographie sont presque identiques.

La toge proche du type *toga contabulata* fait dater notre monument entre la fin du IIe et le IIIe siècle apr. J.-C.

2. STÈLE FUNÉRAIRE ANÉPIGRAPHE (FIG. 1 B)

H. 1,10 m; l. 0,48 m; épaisseur 0,25 m. Calcaire.
Le lieu exact de découverte est inconnu, la stèle est conservée au musée de Djemila. Elle est rectangulaire à sommet arrondi; son extrémité inférieure est brisée et la tête du personnage martelée.

La partie supérieure du monument est décorée d'un croissant (pointes vers le haut). Au-dessous se trouve une guirlande en forme de croissant munie d'un nœud à chaque extrémité.

Au-dessous, dans une niche cintrée et entre deux colonnes à chapiteaux corinthiens, se trouve une femme debout tenant entre ses deux mains un objet sphérique. Son visage est joufflu, ses cheveux sont agencés en mèches ondulées et crantés de part et d'autre d'une raie médiane, puis réunis à l'arrière en haut chignon aux mèches également ondulées. C'est l'une des coiffures de Faustine la Jeune, épouse de Marc Aurèle, qu'on pourrait classer dans le type 8 de la liste typologique établie par Klaus Fittschen[5].

La défunte est élégamment vêtue d'une tunique probablement longue, serrée à l'aide d'une cordelette nouée sous les seins. Elle est drapée dans un manteau posé sur les deux épaules et lui couvrant la partie inférieure laissant, toutefois, libres la poitrine et l'abdomen. Le cou est orné d'un collier à médaillon central.

La stèle est de bonne facture, l'artisan a excellé dans le cisèlement de la guirlande et a respecté les proportions du corps. Les plis des vêtements sont finement travaillés et les cheveux élégamment coiffés. Nous pouvons rapprocher cette image de celle d'une stèle de *Zarai* (voir fig. 7 a) datant de la même période, c'est-à-dire du milieu ou du troisième quart du IIe siècle apr. J.-C., aussi bien dans la façon dont a été drapé le corps, que dans la finesse des plis, jusqu'au collier à médaillon.

---

[3] Ce type tire son origine de quatre statues d'impératrices après leur divinisation. Il s'agit de Livia, Plotina, Matidia et Marciana. Elles furent réalisées sous le règne d'Hadrien. Voir Bieber 1977, pl. 126.
[4] Ballu 1914, no. 18.
[5] Fittschen 1982, 55–59 pl. 24–34.

1 a  Stèle funéraire inscrite de Djemila-*Cuicul* no. 1 (photo L. Benchernine)

1 b  Stèle funéraire anépigraphe de Djemila-*Cuicul* no. 2 (photo L. Benchernine)

1 c  Stèle funéraire anépigraphe de Djemila-*Cuicul* no. 3 (photo L. Benchernine)

3. Stèle probablement funéraire (fig. 1 c)

H. 0,65 m; l. 0,58 m. Calcaire.
La stèle est un bas-relief découvert fortuitement le 22 juillet 1995 près d'une rivière à Djemila. Elle est conservée dans le jardin lapidaire du site archéologique.

Elle comporte deux colonnes à chapiteaux doriques supportant un fronton vide. Au-dessous, une femme debout sur une estrade tient dans sa main gauche pliée vers la poitrine un objet qui pourrait être une quenouille et de l'autre main une bourse ou un vase (?). Sa bouche est petite et ses yeux sont tirés en amandes sous une arcade sourcilière saillante. Son visage est rond et charmant et les cheveux sont coiffés en trois bandeaux de mèches alignées, séparés par une raie médiane et dirigés vers l'arrière.

La défunte est vêtue d'une longue tunique qui lui arrive aux pieds avec des manches de trois-quarts. Une ceinture la serre sous la poitrine, provoquant ainsi deux séries de plis venant des deux épaules et convergeant au milieu de la poitrine.

Un manteau entoure le bas du corps à partir du haut du flanc gauche, puis descend vers le bas de la hanche en un bandeau enroulé sur lui-même. Le reste du vêtement descend jusqu'en bas des jambes en deux séries de plis curvilignes.

La stèle est d'une bonne facture, même si les plis des vêtements ne semblent pas naturels, le visage, en revanche, est charmant et bien soigné. Quant à l'objet que la dame tient dans sa main gauche, nous pouvons le rapprocher de quelques stèles de Palmyre sur lesquelles les femmes tiennent un attribut qui serait, d'après Jean-Baptiste Yon, une quenouille, un fuseau ou une clé valorisant le rôle de la femme comme gardienne du foyer[6]. Dans le cas des deux premières hypothèses, la bourse que la défunte tient dans sa main droite contiendrait peut-être de la laine. A noter, que cette bourse est identique à celle du personnage masculin d'une stèle de *Cuicul*[7] et de celle de *Zarai* (fig. 7 a). Son costume est également très proche de celui que portent d'autres femmes sur des stèles de *Cuicul*[8].

Cette stèle remonterait d'après le type de coiffure au IIIe siècle apr. J.-C.

D'après l'étude des trois stèles précédentes, comme dans la grande majorité des reliefs de *Cuicul*, nous constatons que les personnages représentés sont très imprégnés de la culture romaine. Nous le percevons dans les éléments décoratifs architecturaux comme les colonnes, la présence des *volumina*, les vêtements et la coiffure des personnages ainsi que les noms romanisés (pour les stèles inscrites).

## MAURÉTANIE CÉSARIENNE

### Hammam Guergour-*Ad Savam municipium*

4. Stèle probablement funéraire (fig. 2)

De provenance inconnue, la stèle n'a été mentionnée que dans une liste manuscrite d'objets conservés dans la maison d'un particulier. Cette liste accompagne un rapport préliminaire manuscrit des fouilles effectuées par Roger Guery en 1964 à Hammam Guergour conservé aux archives de l'office OGEBC[9]. La stèle aurait été découverte en juin 1964, puis déposée à la villa du sous-préfet avec d'autres objets lapidaires. Le lieu de conservation actuel du monument est malheureusement inconnu.

---

[6] Yon 2019, 189 no. 1.
[7] Leglay 1966a, pl. 34, 6.
[8] Leglay 1966a, pl. 33, 4. 5.
[9] Voir Dossier Hammam Guergour-wilaya de Sétif dans les archives de l'Office de Gestion et d'Exploitation des Biens Culturels OGEBC, Alger.

2  Stèle funéraire (?) de Hammam Guergour-*Ad Savam municipium* no. 4 (photo L. Benchernine)

C'est une stèle en grès à sommet triangulaire, dont le bord inférieur et le côté gauche sont brisés. Dans une niche se trouve une femme voilée debout, tenant dans sa main droite une bourse et dans sa main gauche une sorte de baguette. Le corps est frontal, le visage large semble serein et digne d'une défunte au repos. Le front est étroit, les yeux en amandes sont surmontés d'une fine arcade sourcilière, le nez est long et la bouche aux lèvres bien dessinées semble esquisser un sourire. Elle est coiffée à la façon la plus en vogue au IIIe siècle apr. J.-C.; ses cheveux sont séparés de part et d'autre d'une raie médiane, puis ils sont tirés vers l'arrière en dégageant les tempes. Le manteau est drapé à la romaine, il ne couvre pas le bras droit et ne descend pas de la tête. Le voile apparaît comme une pièce indépendante posée sur la tête et les deux pans se chevauchent sur la poitrine, puis sont jetés de chaque côté sur les épaules. Il peut s'agir d'un choix de l'artisan et de la cliente, mais cela peut aussi être dû à une incompréhension de l'artisan du voile romain, qui devrait envelopper le corps entier.

Il nous semble que l'artisan a essayé d'être soigneux dans son travail, mais le matériau utilisé (grès) ne l'a pas beaucoup avantagé. Concernant les objets que tient la défunte, nous proposons d'y voir une quenouille dirigée vers le bas dans la main gauche et une bourse (de laine [?]) dans la main droite.

Il est important de noter que la gorge de cygne visible sur le rampant du fronton se retrouve surtout auprès des stèles de *Cuicul*[10].

Ce bas-relief est de loin le plus soigné parmi ceux qui ont été découverts dans la région de Guergour[11] et le mieux conservé de la région.

**Tigzirt-*Iomnium*[12]**

5. Stèle votive (fig. 3 a)

H. 0,58 m; l. 0,32 m. Calcaire.
La stèle est probablement dédiée au dieu suprême Saturne Africain. Elle aurait été trouvée à Tigzirt ou à Taksebt[13] et se trouve actuellement encastrée dans le mur d'une maison. Elle se compose de deux registres superposés. Le premier registre est un fronton triangulaire contenant probablement deux oiseaux se faisant face, surmontés d'un croissant lunaire (pointe vers le haut) comme c'est le cas sur une autre stèle votive[14] de la même région. L'oiseau à gauche est moins

---

[10] Benseddik – Lochin 2005, 278 fig. 4; Leglay 1966a, 213 no. 8 pl. 33, 3.
[11] Des photos de ces bas-reliefs se trouvent dans le dossier Hammam Guergour aux archives de l'OGEBC, Alger. Malheureusement, leur état très dégradé et la qualité des prises de vues ne nous permettent pas de les étudier.
[12] Voir Gsell 1911, feuille 6 no. 87.
[13] Le lieu exact est inconnu, mais les stèles qui se trouvent actuellement dans la ville de Tigzirt ont été découvertes dans ces deux sites antiques.
[14] Gavault 1897, 125 fig. 23 no. 8.

3 a   Stèle votive de Tigzirt-*Iomnium* no. 5 (photo N. Serradj)

3 b   Stèle votive de Tigzirt-*Iomnium* no. 6 (photo N. Serradj)

soigné, il apparait collé au fronton et la queue n'a pas été représentée. Le registre inférieur comporte deux niches, dont la première est rectangulaire à bords plats. Dans cette niche est creusée une autre niche à sommet arrondi et au cadre mouluré. Au milieu, une femme se tient debout dans une position frontale, son pied gauche étant représenté de face alors que le pied droit est de profil. Elle tient dans sa main droite une lourde grappe de raisin et dans la main gauche un objet arrondi, peut-être un gâteau. Son visage est large et allongé, les yeux sont représentés sous forme de deux points dans deux creux, surmontés des arcades sourcilières. Le nez est large, la bouche entrouverte est dessinée par deux traits épais. Les cheveux sont coiffés à la mode du IIIe siècle apr. J.-C. Des mèches parallèles assez épaisses sont tirées vers l'arrière sur la totalité du crâne, en dégageant les tempes comme dans les portraits de Plautille, femme de Caracalla. Elle est vêtue d'une tunique étroite s'arrêtant au-dessus des chevilles; les plis apparents sur son torse sont fins et verticaux alors que ceux du bas sont épais et verticaux. Le corps de la fidèle est disproportionné, la tête est lourde et allongée, le bras droit est exagérément long, au point que la grappe de raisin touche le sol.

6. Stèle votive (fig. 3 b)

H. 0,61 m; l. 0,36 m. Calcaire.

La stèle est encastrée dans le mur de la même maison que la stèle précédente. Elle provient probablement du même endroit, vu la ressemblance évidente entre les deux monuments. La stèle, composée de deux registres superposés, est brisée au milieu et recollée à l'aide d'un ciment blanc. Le registre supérieur est un fronton triangulaire abritant un croissant (pointes vers le haut) surmonté d'une rosace et accosté de deux autres rosaces plus petites sur les deux côtés.

Le deuxième registre est une niche rectangulaire dans laquelle se trouve un personnage debout, pied gauche de face et pied droit de profil. Il tient dans sa main gauche un oiseau et dans sa main droite une grappe de raisin. Son visage est ovale, les traits sont rudimentaires, les yeux en amandes sont proéminents sous une arcade sourcilière marquée. Les cheveux sont tirés en épaisses mèches parallèles vers l'arrière. En tenant compte de la coiffure, on pourrait dire que le personnage est une femme coiffée comme la dame de la stèle précédente selon la mode du IIIe siècle apr. J.-C. Mais le costume semble masculin, car il s'agit d'une tunique étroite aux plis rectilignes descendant jusqu'aux chevilles. Le drapé par-dessus est plutôt proche d'une toge médiocrement présentée, le repli arrondi sur l'abdomen devrait représenter le *sinus*, mais les autres composantes de la toge sont absentes. La forme de la stèle, l'iconographie et surtout l'image du dédicant sont semblables à celle d'une autre stèle votive de la région[15].

Comme une grande partie des stèles de la région, l'exécution des deux monuments est d'une qualité médiocre, due sans doute au manque d'habileté des artisans locaux. La forme de ces deux stèles (jamais publiées auparavant) est inspirée, comme beaucoup d'autres monuments de la région, du modèle punique à sommet triangulaire. En effet, *Iomnium* fut d'abord un comptoir punique avant de devenir un municipe romain. Le croissant lunaire qui se trouve dans le fronton ainsi que le pied de profil sont également un héritage punique. En revanche, les vêtements des personnages ont des caractères proches du modèle romain, même si le drapé n'est pas identique. Beaucoup d'hommes portent la toge tandis que les femmes sont en tunique et manteau, mais à dimensions réduites : la tunique est droite, pas assez longue, et le manteau souvent réduit en un châle étroit.

4 Stèle votive de Taouarga-*Tigisi* no. 7 (photo N. Serradj)

**Taouarga-*Tigisi*[16]**

7. Stèle probablement votive (fig. 4)

H. 1,42 m; l. 0,62 m; épaisseur 0,11 m. Calcaire
De style néo-punique, la stèle probablement dédiée au grand dieu Saturne fut trouvée en 1988 dans la localité de Taouarga, à proximité de la ville de Dellys (antique *Russuccuru*) et se trouve actuellement au musée de la ville[17]. Elle se compose de deux registres superposés, le registre supérieur étant rectangulaire et comportant un croissant et une rosace.

Le registre inférieur présente deux personnages debout dans une position frontale. Ils se tiennent par la main et tiennent chacun une pomme de pin de l'autre main. Les visages sont allongés, les yeux sont à peine creusés et le nez droit est positionné très haut entre les yeux. Ce sont des traits qui relèvent des caractéristiques numido-puniques. Les deux personnages sont habillés pareillement, une longue tunique aux plis rectilignes arrivant aux chevilles et par-dessus un manteau représenté par une série de quatre gros plis allant d'une épaule à l'autre en s'arrondissant jusqu'en bas du ventre,

---

[15] Orfali 1989, pl. 9, 1.
[16] Gsell 1911, feuille 6 no. 27.
[17] Musée de l'Office de Gestion et d'Exploitation des Biens Culturels, OGEBC, Antenne de Dellys.

laissant le torse découvert. La coiffure du personnage de droite porte un renflement sur les deux tempes, rappelant la coiffure du berger représenté sur la stèle-menhir de *Sigus*[18]. Il s'agit sans doute d'une coiffure autochtone (numide/libyque).

Le style de sculpture se rapproche des stèles à tradition numide (pré romaine) de la région d'Ain Nechma, mais date de l'époque romaine (IIe s. apr. J.-C.). La stèle de *Tigisi* est sans doute plus ancienne, puisqu'elle porte une inscription néo-punique gravée juste au-dessous des personnages.

### Sour el Ghozlane-*Auzia*

La provenance de deux stèles dédiées au dieu Saturne reste inconnue; elles ont été déposées avec d'autres vestiges lapidaires dans le parc automobile de la mairie où elles se trouvent d'après le quotidien arabophone »El Khabar« depuis 1996, après avoir séjourné dans un autre endroit de la ville[19]. Elles sont d'une qualité moyenne et d'une exécution grossière, mais ne sont pas dépourvues d'éléments iconographiques intéressants.

8. Stèle votive anépigraphe (fig. 5)

H. 1,88 m; l. 0,83 m. Calcaire.
La stèle dédiée au dieu Saturne est légèrement abimée, la tête d'un des personnages fut martelée.

Le monument se compose de trois registres superposés. Dans le registre supérieur se trouve le dieu Saturne drapé et allongé sur le côté. Il s'appuie avec son coude sur les pattes d'un lion situé à droite; derrière lui apparaît la tête d'un bélier. La scène de ce registre est très proche de celle d'une autre stèle trouvée dans la ville de Sour El Djouab, antique *Rapidum* (fig. 8).

Le registre médian présente deux femmes debout de face, chacune tenant dans sa main droite un oiseau et dans la main gauche une grappe de raisin. Leur costume se compose d'une longue tunique à manches longues et d'un manteau drapé à la romaine; il s'agit probablement de la *palla*. La coiffure est également typiquement romaine: les cheveux sont séparés de part et d'autre d'une raie médiane, puis ramenés vers l'arrière au-dessus des oreilles, et enfin remontés jusqu'au sommet de la tête. Elle est proche de la coiffure arborée par Salonina, la seconde épouse de l'empereur Gallien[20]. A noter, cependant, des différences avec la dame d'*Auzia* dans

5  Stèle votive de Sour El Ghozlane-*Auzia* no. 8 (photo L. Benchernine)

---

[18] Daho-Kitouni – Filah 2008, 98.
[19] Article signé M.B. dans le Journal »El Khabar«, daté de novembre 1997.
[20] Se référer à l'effigie de Salonina sur des pièces de monnaie: Bergmann 1977, 89 pl. monnaie 1 figs. 11. 12.

l'absence des boucles autour du front et des cheveux remontés au-dessus des oreilles au lieu de toucher la nuque.

Le registre inférieur présente deux hommes imberbes tenant chacun un *volumen* dans la main gauche. La tête de l'homme à gauche est ceinte d'une couronne de fleurs. Les deux personnages sont vêtus d'une tunique et d'une toge de type *contabulata*. Cette stèle est l'une des rares représentations qui reflètent fidèlement cette mode en vogue à la fin du IIe et au IIIe siècle apr. J.-C. dans la région, surtout si l'on considère le personnage de gauche, qui porte la *contabulata* haute.

Le monument remonte au troisième quart du IIIe siècle apr. J.-C. d'après le type de la toge et la coiffure féminine.

### 9. Stèle votive anépigraphe (fig. 6 a)

H. 0,65 m; l. 0,54 m. Calcaire.

La stèle est probablement dédiée au dieu Saturne, vu la présence de deux béliers. Elle est très abimée, il ne reste plus que deux registres. Le sommet a disparu et les visages des personnages sont mutilés.

Dans une niche rectangulaire se trouvent trois personnages debout de face. Celui de droite est un homme vêtu d'une tunique et d'une toge; il tient dans sa main gauche un vase. Celui du milieu est une femme vêtue de deux tuniques plissées et superposées; celle de dessous est longue arrivant aux pieds et celle de dessus s'arrête au-dessous des genoux et une ceinture est nouée sous les seins. Le personnage situé à gauche tient un objet indéfini dans la main gauche. Il est vêtu d'une tunique lisse qui lui arrive aux chevilles et d'un manteau qui lui enveloppe les deux épaules et tombe en deux pans sur les deux côtés jusqu'en bas.

Au-dessous sont représentés deux béliers qui s'affrontent.

Il semblerait que l'homme soit vêtu du costume du citoyen romain, alors que la femme n'est pas drapée dans une *palla*, comme le veut la tradition romaine, mais porte deux tuniques superposées. Le tout est serré sous les seins à l'aide d'une épaisse ceinture dont un pendant est empoigné par la main gauche. Ce modèle était probablement apprécié dans la région, car nous le retrouvons ailleurs, dans deux autres stèles d'*Auzia* (fig. 6 b. c) dont les photos apparaissent dans une thèse non publiée et soutenue à l'université d'Aix en Provence[21]. Nous pensons qu'il s'agit peut-être d'un costume local propre à la région.

## RELECTURE

### Zraia-*Zaraï*[22]

### 10. Stèle votive dédiée à Saturne (fig. 7 a)

H. 1,57 m[23]; l. 0,66 m. Calcaire.

La stèle est exposée dans un petit jardin («jardin de Baral«) près de la citadelle de la ville de Sétif. D'après Léon Renier[24], elle aurait été découverte à quelques mètres des ruines de l'antique *Zaraï* (ville située sur le limes séparant la Numidie de la Maurétanie) avant 1855, date de sa première publication. Par la suite, elle fut probablement transférée à Sétif par Paul Massiera en 1959 (selon les archives de l'OGEBC), avec d'autres inscriptions citées dans un rapport de mission daté de 1959[25].

---

[21] Orfali 1989, pls. 47, 3; 49, 3; 50, 1.
[22] Gsell 1911, feuille 26 no. 69.
[23] La hauteur à l'origine était de 1,95 m d'après CIL VIII 4512.
[24] Renier 1855.
[25] Nous avons retrouvé le rapport de la mission faite par P. Massiera en 1959 dans le dossier »Zaraï«, OGEBC, Alger.

6 a  Stèle votive de Sour El Ghozlane-*Auzia* no. 9 (photo L. Benchernine)

6 b  Stèle funéraire d'*Auzia* pour comparaison du vêtement féminin (photo L. Benchernine)

6 c  Stèle funéraire d'*Auzia* pour comparaison du vêtement féminin (photo L. Benchernine)

Le texte épigraphique de cette stèle fut publié[26]. L'aspect iconographique a été évoqué d'abord par Alexandre Poulle[27], puis brièvement repris par Marcel Leglay[28] et plus récemment cité par Alain Cadotte[29], aucun d'eux n'ayant vu le monument. Peu après la présentation de cette stèle, pour la première fois lors du colloque à *Carnuntum*, elle fut publiée en Algérie[30] dans un article qui propose un lien entre le culte de Saturne et d'autres divinités, notamment Cybèle.

---

[26] CIL VIII 4512.
[27] Poulle 1873/1874, no. 78.
[28] Leglay 1966a, 66 no. 1.
[29] Cadotte 2007, 41.
[30] Bouder – Annane 2022, 888–902.

7 a  Stèle votive dédiée à Saturne Africain de Zraia-*Zarai* no. 10 (photo L. Benchernine)

7 b  Stèle votive de Kherbet Medjouba-*Novar* pour comparaison (photo L. Benchernine)

La stèle se compose de quatre registres superposés, séparés par des bandeaux inscrits, dont le registre inférieur se trouve aujourd'hui entièrement recouvert par la végétation. Le registre supérieur sculpté en fronton abrite le buste du dieu barbu et voilé; sur les deux rampants se trouvent deux sphinx (ou leurs féminins [?]) dont il ne subsiste que quelques traces.

Le registre suivant est occupé par une tête de lion entourée de part et d'autre de deux Dioscures nus accompagnés de leurs chevaux. Leurs têtes sont surmontées d'un couvre-chef orné d'une croix, qui semble être un bonnet différent du bonnet phrygien habituel. Ceci lui a valu la désignation de *corona muralis* dans le CIL[31], prudemment cité par Marcel Leglay[32], qui est plutôt en faveur d'un bonnet phrygien. Cadotte, quant à lui, juge qu'il est impossible d'affirmer que ce sont des bonnets phrygiens sans examen de la pierre[33]. L'identification du CIL a été dernièrement reprise par Bouder et Annane, qui comparent la coiffe des jumeaux avec la couronne tourelée

---

[31] CIL VIII 4512.
[32] Leglay 1966a, 66 no. 1.
[33] Cadotte 2007, 41.

(*turrita*) que porte Cybèle. Leur hypothèse est argumentée par la présence du lion, attribut animalier habituel de la divinité.

Dans notre relecture iconographique, nous proposons de voir plutôt un couvre-chef qui se rapproche plus d'un casque à cimier (*pilos* [?]) grossièrement sculpté par un artisan local et orné d'un astre/étoile à quatre branches, qui apparaît quelquefois au-dessus de la tête des Dioscures, avec[34] ou sans[35] bonnet. La présence de ces deux astres sur un bonnet conique en Afrique est attestée sur un sarcophage dit »sarcophage des époux«, trouvé à *Tipasa* de Maurétanie[36]. Elle faisait allusion aux deux étoiles qui, pendant la tempête menaçant les Argonautes, brillèrent sur leurs têtes et sauvèrent du naufrage le navire de ces hardis navigateurs en le remettant sur le droit chemin[37].

Sachant que Saturne Africain préside au cours des astres et se présente comme le dieu du ciel[38], il est concevable qu'on ait voulu reconstituer le monde céleste, dans lequel il réside en ornant le bonnet des deux Dioscures d'un astre à quatre branches. Ceci est d'autant plus probable que vers la fin du IIe siècle, les cavaliers jumeaux apparaissent aux cotés de Saturne Africain en tant qu'assesseurs, qui personnifient les deux hémisphères célestes, lui conférant ainsi un caractère cosmique et éternel[39]. Ainsi, le dieu Saturne semble apparaître sur la stèle de *Zarai* comme le dieu *cosmocrator* avec le lion comme roi des animaux séparant les Dioscures, ce qui accentue encore davantage ce trait, car c'est l'emblème de l'ardeur solaire qui fait référence à Saturne, dieu de la lumière. Le lion est fréquemment représenté sur les stèles à Saturne en Afrique du Nord, particulièrement en Numidie et en Maurétanie, comme le souligne Leglay[40], qui associe l'animal directement au dieu africain dont il est le compagnon, la monture et le substitut. Leglay nous rappelle aussi que le roi des animaux apparaît aux cotés de Saturne Africain dès le début du IIe siècle, bien avant l'expansion en Afrique des cultes mithriaque et métroaque, et qu'il n'a donc pas pu être apporté en Afrique suite à l'introduction des cultes de Mithra et de Cybèle sous l'Empire, comme le pense Jules Toutain[41]. La stèle de *Zarai* s'inscrit parfaitement dans ce contexte chronologique, puisqu'elle est datée de 149 apr. J-.C.

Un bandeau inscrit sépare ce registre du suivant: *Deo [Do]mi[no] Saturno Aug(usto) sac(rum)*.

Le troisième registre présente un couple de fidèles debout, séparés par un autel. L'homme est vêtu d'une tunique et d'une toge du Haut-Empire et la femme est élégamment habillée à la mode romaine d'une tunique et d'un manteau finement plissé. Son cou est orné d'un collier à médaillon central. Au-dessous se trouve une bande horizontale inscrite: *C(aius) Iulius Rufinus sacerdo[s]*.

Le registre inférieur, brisé à son extrémité[42], présente à gauche un victimaire en longue tunique, tirant vers lui un taureau par les cornes.

*Saturni [fec(it) et dedic(avit)]*

Un autre bandeau inscrit ferme le cadre du registre inférieur: *Orfito et Pri[sco[43] co(n)s(ulibus)]*.

Cette stèle est d'une bonne facture et elle ressemble dans sa composition à une autre stèle dédiée au dieu Saturne, trouvée dans le site de Kherbet Medjouba-*Novar*[44]. Les acrotères en forme de sphinx furent fréquemment utilisés dans la région de Beni Fouda[45] (voir à titre d'exemple

---

[34] Gury 1986, no. 124.
[35] Gury 1986, no. 126.
[36] Papier 1893, 109 n. 7.
[37] Papier 1893, 109 n. 7.
[38] Leglay 1966b, 228.
[39] Cadotte 2007, 41.
[40] Leglay 1961, 139.
[41] Toutain 1894, 44–46.
[42] Voir photo Bouder – Annane 2022, 889 fig. 2.
[43] C'est grâce à la mention des deux consuls Orfitus et Priscus que la stèle de *Zarai* a été datée de l'année provinciale 110 = 149 apr. J.-C.
[44] Février 1970, 377–378 no. 70; Poulle 1890/1891, 383 no. 76.
[45] On peut également comparer avec une stèle de Henchir El Ksar-*MOPT* de la même région au musée du Louvre (DAGER no. d'inv. MA 1999) et dont un dessin a été publié dans Delamare 1850, pl. 94, 3; ainsi qu'avec une stèle de Béni Fouda, cf. Février 1970, 383–384 no. 77.

fig. 7 b), ce qui nous incite à voir la jambe et probablement un peu de la tête d'un sphinx (ou sphinge [?]) dans la partie de l'acrotère encore visible.

Le monument de *Zarai* se rapproche également, de par son style de sculpture et le drapé du personnage féminin, de la stèle funéraire de *Cuicul* abordée au début (fig. 2). Il est donc évident que la stèle de *Zarai*, unique dans son genre dans le site de découverte, s'inscrit dans une composition architecturale et iconographique commune aux stèles de la région, qui allait de *Cuicul* à *Sitifis* en passant par *Novar* et *Mopt*. Cette comparaison s'impose notamment pour la scène du deuxième registre (à partir du haut)[46]. Par ailleurs, le vase ou la bourse (?) que la fidèle tient dans sa main est identique à ce que l'on retrouve sur la stèle de Dejmila (fig. 1 c).

Ces similitudes frappantes et le fait que *Zarai* n'ait donné aucune autre stèle comparable, nous laissent perplexes et nous poussent à envisager la possibilité que ce monument votif ait été sculpté dans un atelier de la région sétifienne, distante de 70 km seulement du site de l'antique *Zarai*.

### Sour el Djouab-*Rapidum*[47]

Pendant la préparation de son catalogue sur les monuments liés au culte du Dieu Saturne, Marcel Leglay n'a pas pu voir toutes les stèles mentionnées dans son ouvrage. Il recevait souvent du courrier comportant des informations sur des sculptures trouvées: parfois il s'agissait juste d'un croquis, d'une description ou d'une photo du monument.

Il semble qu'il n'ait pas eu l'occasion de voir de ses propres yeux les stèles trouvées à Sour Djouab, antique *Rapidum,* ni même leurs photos, et qu'il se soit donc basé sur les écrits d'André Ballu, dont l'interprétation était parfois approximative. Citons parmi ces monuments:

11. STÈLE VOTIVE[48] (FIG. 8)

H. 0,88 m; l. 0,55m; épaisseur 0,11 m. Calcaire.
La stèle est composée de trois registres; la partie supérieure est brisée et recollée avec du ciment. La date et le lieu de découverte sont inconnus; la stèle fut évoquée la première fois par Albert Ballu, qui l'attribua au culte de Cérès, croyant voir, au sommet, la déesse assise sur un trône accompagnée d'une tête de vache surmontée d'un disque[49]. Quant à Leglay, il a douté de cette identification, se demandant s'il n'agissait pas plutôt du dieu Saturne assis sur son trône et accompagné d'un bucrane ou de *Caelestis*[50].

Nous avons eu l'opportunité de voir ce bas-relief, qui se trouvait, il y a une quinzaine

8  Stèle votive dédiée à Saturne Africain de Sour El Djouab-*Rapidum* no. 11 (photo L. Benchernine)

---

[46] Voir une stèle de Djemila: Leglay 1953, 63–64 no. 42 pl. 4, 4; Leglay 1966a, 229–230 no. 36 pl. 34, 6. Une stèle de *Novar* avec le lion en train de dévorer une antilope: Février 1970, 377–378 no. 70.
[47] Gsell 1911, feuille 14 no. 90.
[48] Photo non publiée jusqu'à ce jour.
[49] Ballu 1914, 273 no. 1.
[50] Leglay 1966a, 311 no. 3.

d'années, dans une salle de la mairie de Sour El Djouab et nous avons constaté que Leglay avait en partie raison. Il s'agit bien du dieu Saturne, sauf qu'il n'est pas assis, mais allongé sur son côté gauche, portant un objet dans sa main gauche qui pourrait être un rayon de miel. Derrière lui et au milieu du registre se trouve un bélier à laine frisée et à l'angle gauche une harpé. Ces deux éléments ne sont pas mentionnés par les deux auteurs dans leurs écrits respectifs. La scène est très proche de celle du registre supérieur de la stèle d'*Auzia* abordée plus haut, il manque juste le lion (fig. 5).

Quant au registre central, il est destiné à la scène de sacrifice. Ballu le décrit comme suit:
»Au centre un autel à degrés surmonté d'une pierre pointue. A droite, prêtre sacrifiant un bélier; à gauche, une femme s'avançant vers l'autel avec une offrande«[51]. En réalité, l'autel est une pierre rectangulaire, à laquelle on accédait par un escalier à trois marches, tandis que la forme pointue est une flamme, comme le pensait Leglay[52]. En effet, à droite, un homme pousse un bélier cornu vers l'autel et à gauche, le victimaire lève avec ses mains une hache comme s'il attendait l'arrivée de l'animal à sacrifier.

Ce qui reste du registre inférieur est la tête d'une femme dans une niche cintrée, élégamment coiffée avec trois rangées de boucles étagées, dites »en marteau«[53].

La raison qui amena Ballu à voir dans le bas-relief de *Rapidum* un *ex-voto* en l'honneur de Cérès est sans doute la richesse de sculptures liées à cette déesse dans la région.

### Tigzirt-*Iomnium*[54]

Il s'agit d'une nouvelle lecture d'un groupe de stèles trouvées en remploi dans la basilique d'*Iomnium*, actuelle Tigzirt, en Maurétanie Césarienne. Certaines de ces stèles sont malheureusement perdues, mais elles ont été reproduites sous forme de dessins dans l'ouvrage de Pierre Gavault publié en 1897. Marcel Leglay[55] considéra la majorité des stèles dans la basilique d'*Iomnium*, publiés par Gavault[56], comme étant des *ex-voto*. Il en identifia une comme une stèle à Cérès, et considéra le reste comme des monuments dédiés au dieu Saturne. Ces derniers sont probablement liés au culte des *Cereres*, car ils présentent des femmes levant des objets vers le haut avec une ou deux mains levées tenant des objets. Ce sont peut-être des dévotes brandissant une torche – ou même deux torches à la fois – vers le haut. D'ailleurs, il existe des stèles découvertes dans la même ville, sur lesquelles on voit clairement que ces femmes tiennent des torches[57].

Selon nous, il s'agit soit d'une mauvaise reproduction de cet attribut, dessiné en forme de trident, soit d'une des représentations très rares d'épis de blé, comme c'est le cas chez une dévote de Sidi Mediouni en Proconsulaire[58].

### CONCLUSION

En conclusion, nous dirons que nous sommes redevables au 17e colloque sur l'art provincial romain, qui nous a donné l'occasion de présenter devant d'éminents spécialistes de la sculpture et de l'iconographie du monde romain quelques reliefs votifs et funéraires inédits, découverts ces dernières années en Algérie. Nous avons également pu reprendre certaines identifications et inter-

---

[51] Ballu 1914, 273 no. 1.
[52] Leglay 1966a, 311 no. 3.
[53] De Kersauson 1996, 115.
[54] Nous n'avons malheureusement pas pu reproduire les figures de cette relecture faute de place, nous renvoyons donc à la planche publiée par Gavault 1897, fig. 15.
[55] Leglay 1966a, 302.
[56] Gavault 1897, 87 fig. 15.
[57] Benseddik 2017, 190 fig. 149.
[58] Benseddik 2017, fig. 147.

prétations nécessitant une profonde relecture analytique de quelques stèles déjà publiées et nous avons ainsi relevé les points suivants:
- Certaines stèles sont typiquement romaines dans leur architecture et leur contenu. Nous les retrouvons davantage dans les grandes villes très romanisées comme Djemila-*Cuicul*.
- Les caractéristiques d'africanité cohabitent avec les spécificités romaines dans beaucoup de stèles provenant des petites agglomérations, comme celle de Hammam Guergour-*Ad Savam Municipium*, où nous notons que le drapé reste dans sa forme générale romain, mais comporte tout de même des touches locales.
- Les traits autochtones se retrouvent particulièrement dans les petites cités, principalement les municipes en Maurétanie Césarienne, comme Sour el Djouab-*Rapidum* ou dans les villes qui connurent une présence préromaine comme Tigzirt-*Iomnium* et Sour El Ghozlane-*Auzia*.
- La sculpture en bas-relief liée au Cereres (Cérès et sa fille Proserpine) est attestée en force dans la plupart des provinces africaines. Pour ce qui est du territoire de l'Algérie actuelle, nous la retrouvons surtout en Maurétanie Césarienne, dans les villes d'*Iomnium*, *Rapidum* et *Auzia*. A rappeler que les fidèles africains qualifièrent les Cereres de *Punicia* et parfois de *Maurusia*, et Tertullien[59] fait même référence à la Ceres Africana.

## BIBLIOGRAPHIE

| | |
|---|---|
| Ballu 1914 | A. Ballu, Rapports sur les fouilles exécutées en 1913 par le service des monuments historiques de l'Algérie, Bulletin du Comité des Travaux Historiques, 1914, 270–329 |
| Benseddik – Lochin 2005 | N. Benseddik – C. Lochin, Saturne et ses fidèles: à propos de stèles de Cuicul, Mopth… et Sitifis, dans: C. Briand Ponsard (éd.), Identités et culture dans l'Algérie antique. Colloque international Rouen avril 2003 (Rouen 2005) 261–292 |
| Benseddik 2017 | N. Benseddik, Femmes en Afrique ancienne (Bordeaux 2017) |
| Bergmann 1977 | M. Bergmann, Studien zum römischen Porträt des 3. Jahrhunderts n. Chr. (Bonn 1977) |
| Bieber 1977 | M. Bieber, Ancient copies. Contribution to the history of Greek and Roman art (New York 1977) |
| Bouder – Annane 2022 | A. Bouder – S. Annane, La redécouverte d'une stèle de Zarai exposée dans le jardin Barral à Sétif. Relecture iconographique et nouveau témoignage du culte de Cybèle, Revue des recherches historiques ASJP 6/1, 2022, 887–902 |
| Cadotte 2007 | A. Cadotte, La romanisation des dieux: L'interpretatio romana en Afrique du Nord sous le haut empire (Boston 2007) |
| Daho-Kitouni – Filah 2008 | K. Daho-Kitouni – M. Filah, L'Algérie aux temps des royaumes numides, Musée National Cirta (Constantine 2008) |
| Delamare 1850 | A. H. A. Delamare, Exploration scientifique de l'Algérie pendant les années 1840, 1841, 1842, 1843, 1844 et 1845. Archéologie (Paris 1850) |
| Février 1970 | P. A. Février, Inscriptions de Sétif et de la région, BAAlger 4, 1970, 319–410 |
| Fittschen 1982 | K. Fittschen, Dis Bildnistypen der Faustina minor und die Fecunditas Augustae (Göttingen 1982) |
| Gavault 1897 | P. Gavault, Etudes sur les ruines Romaines de Tigzirt (Paris 1897) |
| Gsell 1911 | S. Gsell, Atlas archéologique de l'Algérie (Paris 1911) |
| Gury 1986 | F. Gury in: LIMC III 1 (1986) 567–635; III 2, 456–503 s. v. Dioskouroi |
| de Kersauson 1996 | K. de Kersauson, Musée du Louvre. Catalogue des portraits romains II. De l'année de la guerre civile (68–69 apr. J.-C) à la fin de l'empire (Paris 1996) |
| Leglay 1953 | M. Leglay, Les stèles à Saturne de Djemila-Cuicul, LibycaBServAnt 1, 1953, 37–86 |
| Leglay 1961 | M. Leglay, Saturne Africain. Monuments I (Paris 1961) |
| Leglay 1966a | M. Leglay, Saturne Africain. Monuments. Numidie-Maurétanies II (Paris 1966) |
| Leglay 1966b | M. Leglay, Saturne Africain. Histoire (Paris 1966) |

---

[59] Tert. nat. 2, 8, 4–5 (trad. E. A. de Genoude) (Paris 1852).

| | |
|---|---|
| Orfali 1989 | M. K. Orfali, Inventaire des sculptures funéraires votives de la Maurétanie Césarienne (Thèse de doctorat Université de Provence Aix en Provence 1989) |
| Papier 1893 | A. Papier, Description de deux sarcophages à Tipasa, Bulletin de l'Académie d'Hippone 26, 1893, 105–110 |
| Poulle 1873/1874 | A. Poulle, Inscriptions diverses de la Mauritanie Sétifienne et de la Numidie, Rec-Constantine 16, 1873–1874, 363–459 |
| Poulle 1890/1891 | A. Poulle, Inscriptions diverses de la Numidie et de la Mauritanie Sétifienne, Rec-Constantine 26, 1890–1891, 305–422 |
| Renier 1855 | L. Renier, Inscriptions romaines de l'Algérie (Paris 1855) |
| Toutain 1894 | J. Toutain, De Saturni dei in Africa romana cultu (Paris 1894) |
| Yon 2019 | J.-B. Yon, Femmes de Palmyre, dans: S. Lalanne (éd.), Femmes grecques de l'Orient romain, DialHistAnc suppl. 18 (Besançon 2019) 183–203 |

*Nedjma Serradj, Université Alger 2, Institut d'archéologie, Djamel Eddine El Afghani, Bouzareah, Algérie.*
*[e] nedjma.serradj@univ-alger2.dz*

*Leila Benchernine, Université Alger 2, Institut d'archéologie, Djamel Eddine El Afghani, Bouzareah, Algérie.*
*[e] tafssout@hotmail.com*

Nirvana Silnović

# A NEW LION STATUETTE FROM THE MITHRAEUM IN JAJCE[1]

**Abstract**

A lion statuette was found during construction work around the Mithraeum in Jajce in 2012. It is exhibited inside the Mithraeum, close to the rock-cut tauroctony relief; however, its original purpose was somewhat different. The statuette shows a recumbent lion on a roughly trimmed plinth, with his head slightly turned to the left. A roundish object is placed between the lion's forelegs, which, based on the comparative examples, can be identified as an animal head. The statuette was probably set up at the entrance to the sanctuary, where the water basin was presumably installed as well. The statuette was most likely part of the original furnishings of the Mithraeum and can be dated to the same time – late 3$^{rd}$/early 4$^{th}$ century AD.

## INTRODUCTION

The Mithraeum in Jajce (Bosnia and Herzegovina) is the best-preserved Mithraic temple from the Roman province of *Dalmatia* and the only surviving Roman temple from the territory of Jajce[2]. The temple was accidentally discovered during construction work in 1931, on the wetland area called Bare (»swamp«), on the left bank of the river Pliva[3]. It was built on the western periphery of the Roman settlement, some 200 m from the medieval hilltop fortress[4].

Roman Jajce, whose ancient name remains unknown, was the most important settlement in the Vrbas river valley[5]. It commanded a geographically strategic position at the place where the only crossing over a deep Vrbas river canyon is possible. The settlement lay on the intersection of important water and land routes connecting the coastal centres (the capital *Salona*) with large inner Pannonian cities (*Servitium, Mursa, Siscia,* and *Sirmium*)[6]. Moreover, Jajce was closely associated with the mining region in the Japra Valley, and a nearby route connected *Salona* with *Argentaria*, an area rich in silver ore[7]. Due to its exceptional strategic position, a customs station is presumed to have existed here[8].

The Mithraeum (7 × 4.5 m) has a trapezoidal ground plan and is of a rock-temple type: its western part uses the natural marl rock which carries the tauroctony relief, while the remaining parts of the temple were built using the irregular, roughly processed marlstone blocks (fig. 1)[9]. The walls

---

[1] I am immensely grateful to Dr. Gabrielle Kremer for her invaluable comments and suggestions which helped improve the quality of this paper.
[2] Only five other Mithraea have been discovered in *Dalmatia*: Oltari, *Arupium* (only the rock-cut tauroctony remains), Rajanov grič, *Arupium* (only the rock-cut tauroctony remains), Konjic (overgrown by the forest), Močići, *Epidaurum* (rock-cut tauroctony and part of the cave are preserved), and Sv. Juraj, *Epidaurum* (rock-cut tauroctony taken out from the rock, church and cemetery built at the site), see Silnović 2022.
[3] Sergejevski 1937, 11–18.
[4] The medieval city was built on top of the Roman settlement, and its topography is only partially known. See Pašalić 1960, 22–23; Basler 1963/1964, 43–45; Bojanovski 1988, 294; Škegro 2002, 9–16.
[5] For a different opinion see Basler 1963/1964, 43. 45, who thought Jajce served only as a refuge for the population of the nearby *municipium* in Šipovo. It has been recently suggested that Jajce should be identified as Roman *Sapua*, however, this requires further confirmation, see Mesihović 2009, 171–185.
[6] Pašalić 1960, 22–23; Bojanovski 1974, 199–202; Bojanovski 1988, 296–297.
[7] Basler 1977, 121–171; Bojanovski 1983, 119–130; Imamović 1985, 31–52; Glicksman 2018, 272–273.
[8] Bojanovski 1988, 292. 296. Bojanovski believed that there was a smaller fortress here as well, controlling the river crossing, along with the observation post and a toll station.
[9] The natural rock was partially used for the southern wall as well.

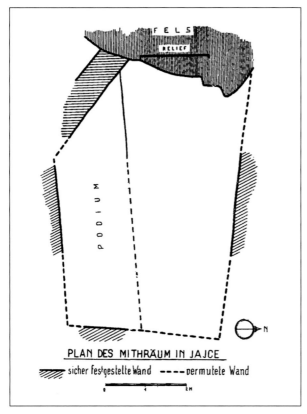

1 Groundplan of the Mithraeum in Jajce (Sergejevski 1937, 12, plan 2)

were constructed without foundations, indicating a light roof construction (possibly a wicker roof). The floor (2.80 m below the current floor level) was made of beaten earth and sand. The entrance was probably located on the south-western corner of the building, where D. Sergejevski discovered two steps[10].

Only the remains of the left podium are preserved (width 1.80 m), and no traces of the right one have been found. It is not possible to determine the exact location of the north wall as well, as the stone blocks were not found in their original position[11]. The Mithraeum was discovered in a poorly preserved state due to its exposure to water and tufa deposition, which ultimately caused the collapse of the building.

The rock-cut tauroctony relief, the largest Mithraic cult image from the province of *Dalmatia* (1.68 × 1.5 m), is placed inside the shallow niche topped with a gable that is decorated with palmettes (fig. 2)[12]. Two stairs lead to the ledge below the relief (height 1 m). Small triangular niches are inserted above the figures of torchbearers and were probably used for placing lamps. The statue of Cautopates was found on the podium, together with three small altars[13]. Another three altars (all anepigraphic) were found in front of the cult image[14]. Sergejevski also made note of several small finds discovered in front of the cult image[15].

According to some reports, the most valuable finds were taken from the site before the authorities were informed of the Mithraeum's discovery[16]. Only seventy years after Sergejevski's excavation report, one of these objects resurfaced from a private collection. It is the bronze *askos*, dated to the 1st century AD, and believed to have been imported from a southern Italian workshop[17]. Recently, another monument appeared, which seems to have belonged to the original furnishing of the temple: the statuette of a lion[18]. This statuette is discussed here for the first time,

---

[10] A limestone stepping stone was found as well, not *in situ*, but in the north-east corner of the cella: Sergejevski 1937, 13.

[11] Sergejevski 1937, 13.

[12] Unfortunately, the relief has suffered from sintering and some parts of the figures are missing: Mithras' right hand and parts of his tunic and hat, part of the bull's head and parts of its body, as well as the snake's head.

[13] Two are anepigraphic, and the third one contains the partially preserved dedication *Inv[icto ---?]*; ILJug 1619; AE 1983, 0741; Epigraphic Database Heidelberg (EDH) 033920.

[14] Sergejevski 1937, 14 nos. 1–3.

[15] Sergejevski 1937, 16–17.

[16] Domić Kunić 2001, 39–40.

[17] Domić Kunić 2001, 39–102.

[18] The statuette was discussed in my unpublished doctoral dissertation, see Silnović 2022, 151 no. 18. I would like to thank Dragan Glavaš from the Agency for Cultural-Historical and Natural Heritage and Development of the tourist potential of the city of Jajce for allowing me to publish the statuette and for providing me with the necessary information.

2   The tauroctony and the altar arrangement, Mithraeum in Jajce (photo N. Silnović 2019)

and besides its description, the potential function and placement inside the Mithraeum will be analyzed as well. Finally, a possible dating of the statuette will be proposed.

## LION STATUETTE: FUNCTION AND MEANING

A lion statuette (max. 5 × 45 × max. 15 cm) was found during the construction of a protective structure built around the Mithraeum in 2012 at a depth of 3 m (fig. 3 a–c)[19]. It is exhibited inside the Mithraeum, placed in front of the cult image (fig. 2). The statuette is made of local limestone and shows a recumbent lion on a roughly trimmed plinth, with his head slightly turned to the left. The statuette is badly worn, with some parts missing (left ear, upper part of the lion's mouth and nose, and front part of the plinth), and several recent scratches can be observed on the front and rear part of the lion's body. The overall surface treatment is rough and the lion's body has been rendered clumsily, without much attention given to the anatomical details.

The upper part of the lion's head is covered with the thick strands of the mane, which takes the form of shallow curls on the lion's neck. The preserved right ear is small and round. The eyes have been rendered as shallow round recesses (the left one seems more worn out). The mouth is wide open, with a slightly protruding tongue. A small tail ends in thick curls on the rear of the statuette. A roundish object is placed between the lion's forelegs. Due to its bad state of preservation, the object is hard to identify. However, several analogous examples of lion statuettes from other Mithraea might help to identify it, as well as to determine its original function.

Geographically closest comparative example is a lion statuette from Mithraeum II in *Poetovio* (in use from the beginning of the 3rd to mid-4th c. AD), showing a recumbent lion with an animal's

---

[19]   No further information about the exact find spot or other relevant details were available when this text was written.

3 a–c  Lion statuette from the Mithraeum in Jajce (photo N. Silnović 2019)

head under its front left paw (height 39 × width 37 cm)[20]. The sculpture stood next to the water basin, which was installed on a column to the left of the entrance to the sanctuary[21]. Water basins were part of the regular furnishing of many Mithraea, and were usually set up next to the entrance to the cella, where worshippers washed their hands before entering the sanctuary[22].

Furthermore, the Mithraeum II was built around a water source found in the middle of the central aisle. M. Abramić mentioned bronze coins found as offerings inside the water source, while an altar dedicated to the eternal source (*fons perennis*) stood next to it, thus indicating the importance of water for the cult of Mithras[23]. In many cases, including Jajce, Mithraea were built close to water sources, streams, or rivers[24]. Water had not only a practical role in the cult, in which it was used for various ritual purposes, but it had an important symbolical meaning as well.

---

[20] Abramić 1925, 68–69. I would like to thank Aleksandra Nestorović from the Regional Museum Ptuj – Ormož for the photograph of the statuette (inv. RL 133 MI2).
[21] Abramić 1925, 68; Vomer Gojkovič 2001, 106; lupa 9407.
[22] Clauss 2012, 74.
[23] Abramić 1925, 68 no. 56; CIL III 15184[24]; lupa 9402; EDH 071858.
[24] Sergejevski 1937, 12.

Among the famous deeds of Mithras was the so-called water miracle, in which the god forced a dead rock to produce water, usually depicted on reliefs with an image of Mithras aiming a bow at a rock face[25]. The aforementioned dedication to the eternal source, which seems to have been particularly spread in the Danubian provinces, as well as other imagery (e.g. representations of Oceanus or water vessels), attests to the centrality of water for the cult.

Further important analogies are the two lion sculptures from *Carnuntum*. The first statuette (20.5 × 35.5 × max. 17.2 cm), dated to the beginning or mid-2$^{nd}$ century AD, was found in the so-called Mithraeum I[26]. It shows a recumbent lion holding a bull's skull between its front paws. It has an opening in the head area (diameter 3 cm), interpreted as the smoke or fire channel[27]. Presumably, it was used for incense burning during the initiation rituals of the fourth grade, which is that of the lion. Its exact find spot inside the Mithraeum is unfortunately unknown, but it must have been installed somewhere inside the sanctuary, closer to the main altar where these rites would have taken place.

The second lion statuette (64 × 107 × 57 cm) belonged to the inventory of the so-called Mithraeum III and is dated to the end of the 2$^{nd}$ or beginning of the 3$^{rd}$ century AD[28]. It similarly represents a recumbent lion with a bull's skull placed between its forelegs. The statue was found in front of the right-side podium, set up in connection to the water basin, which stood on the opposite side of the central aisle[29].

Apart from these three, geographically relatively closely associated examples, a lion statuette from the Mithraeum in Les Bolards (Nuits-Saint-Georges, Côte-d'Or), should be mentioned as well (breadth of the base 55 cm)[30]. It is dated to the 3$^{rd}$ century AD and depicts a recumbent lion holding an object between its forelegs[31]. However, instead of an animal head/skull, there is an inverted urn with flowing water set between the animal's paws. The statuette was erected near the entrance to the sanctuary, where the water basin stood as well. The Mithraeum in Les Bolards was built next to an important religious complex associated with a healing water source, with which the water urn was probably symbolically associated as well[32].

The lion from Jajce shows the greatest similarities with the statuettes from *Poetovio* and *Carnuntum* (especially the one from Mithraeum III) and the object held between the lion's forelegs can thus be identified as a head/skull of an animal. All sculptures are of comparable size and show a similarly recumbent lion. The lion statuette from Les Bolards is only distinguished by the attribute placed between the lion's forelegs, and it should be included in this group as well. Furthermore, the lion's body is shown in almost all examples: the head is turned to the animal's left side, indicating this was their viewing side. The only exception is the statuette from *Poetovio*, on which the lion turns its head to the right side.

Unfortunately, it is not possible to identify exactly the animal whose head the lion from Jajce holds. The head is also unrecognizable on the statuette from *Poetovio*: Abramić made no concrete identification, while M. J. Vermaseren, whose entry is based on Abramić's description, identified the head as belonging to a swine[33]. The statue is today badly worn and it is impossible to make a judgment whether the head belongs to a swine or to some other animal. Fortunately, the animal, i.e. the bull, can be recognized on the two statuettes from *Carnuntum*. Since all statuettes belong to the same type and probably share the same function (except the one from Mithraeum I in *Car-*

---

[25] Clauss 2012, 72–74. See also Kremer 2005, 433–440.
[26] Kremer 2012, 66–67 nos. 85. 330–331. 384–385.
[27] The opening widens on the rear side into an almost rectangular recess, see Kremer 2012, 67.
[28] Kremer 2012, 66 nos. 84. 332–334.
[29] Kremer 2012, 333 fig. 15.
[30] Mouraire 1997, 261–278; Bricault – Roy 2021, 258–259.
[31] Mouraire 1997, 261–278.
[32] Several Mithraea in *Gallia* were associated with water and healing sanctuaries, see Roy 2013, 360–378.
[33] CIMRM 1535.

*nuntum*), it would be logical to assume they all contained a bull's head. However, this remains hypothetical.

Thus, all this enables a conjecture concerning the function of the lion statuette from Jajce. It was probably installed near the entrance to the sanctuary where it accompanied the water basin as in the previously discussed examples. Although Sergejevski could not surely determine whether the Mithraeum had an anteroom or not, recent research has shown how in most cases these rooms were constructed of less solid materials, such as wood or half-timbering[34]. Such structures are more prone to decay and were rarely detected by the early excavators. Certainly, the constant exposure to water in the case of the Mithraeum in Jajce did not help preserve it either. Since the Mithraeum was built without foundations, and possibly covered only with a light wicker roof, it is reasonable to assume that putting additional weight onto such a construction was not intended by the builders. Moreover, the building material was readily available, since Jajce is surrounded by dense forests.

It is inside this presumed anteroom that the lion statuette (and the supposed water basin) would have been installed, probably on the right side of the entrance to the cella. Such an arrangement corresponds to the orientation of the lion's head, which means it was to be viewed from its left side, with its head oriented towards the sanctuary. If we accept Sergejevski's suggestion that the entrance to the Mithraeum was located on the south-western corner of the building, such a placement of the statuette would also be in accordance with the imagined movement path of the worshipper. Once inside the anteroom, he would turn to the right and proceed towards the entrance to the cella, making a stop at this place to wash his hands at the basin.

A similar arrangement might have existed at another Mithraeum in *Dalmatia* as well. Two votive stone blocks from *Raetinium* (Golubić, near Bihać), were found secondarily used as building material in one of the private houses in Golubić[35]. They bear dedications *Fonti* and *Leoni* and probably come from the same sanctuary[36]. The one with the dedication *Fonti*, according to C. Patsch, could have carried a water container, the other one a lion statuette, probably installed at the entrance to the cella[37]. As it is not possible to identify with certainty the original purpose of these two blocks, Patsch's interpretation is only one possibility. The two postaments could have been arranged in front of the podia (similarly to *Carnuntum* III), or even as a part of the altar arrangement[38].

There are other types of lion sculptures set up in connection with water basins besides the recumbent one described above. For example, the lion statuettes from the Mithraea I and II in *Nida*-Heddernheim show lions sitting on their hind legs, with an opening running from the mouth to the back of the statuette, which supposedly communicated with water basins in the respective Mithraea[39]. Moreover, lions of various size and purposes had their place in many Mithraea[40]. Besides sculptures and dedications to lions, they appear as a part of functional furnishings[41], small

---

[34] Sergejevski 1937, 13. The Mithraea in Riegel and Wiesloch, as well as Mithraeum I in Stockstadt had wooden anterooms, see Hensen 2017, 391.
[35] Tomaschek 1882, 496; Radimsky 1893, 57 figs. 38. 39.
[36] *Fonti*: CIL III 13276ᵇ; ILJug 0216b; EDH 033259; lupa 23787. *Leoni*: CIL III 10042, 13276ᵃ; ILJug 0216a; EDH 033256; lupa 23787.
[37] Patsch 1897, 654–656.
[38] Silnović, in press.
[39] Huld-Zetsche 1986, 59 no. 15; 67 no. 26.
[40] See, for example, large lion statues from the Mithraeum in Königshoffen, Forrer 1915, 40–42 pl. 13; or a lion statue from Mithraeum I in Stockstadt, CIMRM 1191.
[41] Lion's head and paws decorated *trapezophores* from Mithraeum II in *Poetovio*, see Abramić 1925, 70. They were installed against the side podia and were used during the communal dining.

objects[42], or as a decoration on vases and cult utensils. They also appear as a part of the lion-krater-snake triad, particularly on reliefs in the Germanic and Danubian provinces[43].

Lion (*leo*), as mentioned earlier, was the name of the fourth grade of initiation. It is the most frequently attested grade in the epigraphic sources after the highest grade of the Father (*pater*)[44]. In *Dalmatia*, where not a single epigraphic evidence of any of the seven grades exists, at least two are shown on the reverse of the double-sided relief from Konjic: raven and lion, recognisable through the animal masks worn by the two attendees flanking the scene of Mithras' and Sol's shared meal.

The initiation into this grade marked a significant shift in the status of the worshipper, as with this grade one became a full member of the cult[45]. The elaborate rituals associated with this grade included processions, during which acclamations were repeatedly recited. These rites were also intended for the purification of space by fire and incense burning, as mentioned in connection to the lion statuette from Mithraeum I in *Carnuntum*. Furthermore, members of this grade had their hands purified by honey or liquid fire[46].

The specific arrangement of the lion statuette with the bull's head/skull (if this identification is accepted for the animal heads on the statuettes from Jajce and *Poetovio*), linked with the water basin at the entrances to the sanctuaries, was certainly not accidental. Since the lion's grade held such an important place in the initiatory path of an individual worshipper, marking the transition to proper membership in the cult, its placement as a guardian of the entry to the cella is not surprising. Symbolically, it marked the boundary between the space of the uninitiated and the actual sanctuary, where only initiated members were allowed.

In the cases described, the lions are depicted as having defeated the animal (bull), holding their heads/skulls between their paws as trophies[47]. The image can be taken as an allusion to the grand victory of Mithras, who defeated and sacrificed the bull, which he then ate together with Sol[48]. This narrative was depicted, in greater or lesser detail, on the tauroctony images that were placed at the rear of each Mithraeum. More importantly, these glorious events were ritually commemorated at each gathering in the form of a shared meal, the most important ritual celebrated in Mithraea[49]. Therefore, the representation of a lion with a bull's head seems like an appropriate and probably first image to welcome worshippers entering the sanctuary.

The bull's head otherwise appears seldom as an iconographical motif in the cult of Mithras. A rare instance is the group of statues from *Dacia*, on which the bull's head appears as an attribute of Cautes[50]. On these statues, Cautes holds the bull's head in his left arm, while Cautopates holds the scorpion[51]. Another part of the bull's body, his (pelvic or thoracic) limb, was a symbol associated with the third grade of initiation, the Soldier (*miles*)[52].

---

[42] E.g. a bronze lion from the Mithraeum in Martigny, holding a globe under its paw, see Wiblé 1995, 14 fig. 26.
[43] Also attested in *Dalmatia*, on a reverse of a tauroctony relief from Konjic (lupa 22318) and on the reverse of a tauroctony relief from Proložac Donji, see Gudelj 2006.
[44] Bricault – Roy 2021, 375.
[45] Gordon 1980, 32–33; Bricault-Roy 2021, 375.
[46] Gordon 1980, 24.
[47] Similar lion statues are also found in the sepulchral context, see, e.g. two lion statues from *Carnuntum* (lupa 28037. 28065) or the lion statue from *Poetovio* (lupa 9427). Due to their striking similarities, it is almost impossible to determine their original purpose (sepulchral or Mithraic) without a firm archaeological context.
[48] Note how the previously mentioned lion-krater-snake triad is usually placed below the sacrificed bull on the scene of the joint supper eaten by Mithras and Sol.
[49] Dirven 2015, 41–42.
[50] Hinnells 1976, 43–45; Szabó 2015, 237–247.
[51] According to Beck and Gordon, these represent the zodiacal signs of *Taurus* and *Scorpio*, symbolizing the seasons of spring and autumn. See Beck 1977, 3–4; Gordon 1976, 152–153.
[52] Chalupa – Glomb 2013, 9–32.

## DATE OF THE MITHRAEUM AND OF THE LION STATUETTE

The date of the statuette is hard to determine based on its stylistic criteria, as it is badly worn. However, presuming that it was part of the original inventory of the Mithraeum, it could have been installed at the same time when the Mithraeum was built and furnished; alternatively, it could have been installed slightly later, perhaps as a votive gift.

Based on the early date of the *askos* and of some of the coins found in the Mithraeum, A. Domić Kunić proposed its early date in the 2$^{nd}$ century AD[53]. However, since both coins and *askos* lack any stratigraphic context, they cannot be used for dating the temple[54]. Some small finds discovered in front of the cult image, including a red clay »Firmalampe« and a fragment of another »Firmalampe«, are dated to the 4$^{th}$ century AD[55].

The stylistic features of the cult image seem to point to the later date as well. These are especially observable on the busts of Sol and Luna which bear the features of the portraits from the Tetrarchic period, i.e. late 3$^{rd}$/early 4$^{th}$ century AD. Their faces are rounded, with large, almond-shaped eyes and stiff facial expressions lacking any sign of individuality. Sol has short hair with broad locks, while Luna's hair is parted in the middle and falls to her shoulders in gentle waves; a wide braid turns from the back of her head forward, ending in a characteristic bun on the top of her head, details which are all characteristic for portraits from the Tetrarchic period in *Dalmatia*[56].

Since the rock on which the tauroctony relief is carved was incorporated into the architectural construction of the Mithraeum, it seems logical to assume they were made at the same time. As mentioned earlier, the lion statuette, probably a part of its original inventory, was set up either when the Mithraeum was built or slightly later and should be dated roughly to the same period – that is, the late 3$^{rd}$ or the early 4$^{th}$ century AD[57].

## BIBLIOGRAPHY

| | |
|---|---|
| Abramić 1925 | M. Abramić, Poetovio. Führer durch die Denkmäler der römischen Stadt (Vienna 1925) |
| Basler 1963/1964 | Đ. Basler, Manji nalazi iz starije prošlosti Jajca [Smaller finds from the older past of Jajce], Zbornik krajiških muzeja 2, 1963/1964, 40–49 |
| Basler 1977 | Đ. Basler, Rimski metalurški pogon i naselje u dolini Japre [Roman metallurgy and settlement in Japra valley], GlasSarajevo 30/31, 1977, 121–216 |
| Beck 1977 | R. Beck, Cautes and Cautopates: Some Astronomical Considerations, JMithrSt 2, 1977, 1–17 |
| Bojanovski 1974 | I. Bojanovski, Dolabelin sistem cesta u rimskoj provinciji Dalmaciji [Dolabella's road network in the Roman province of Dalmatia] (Sarajevo 1974) |
| Bojanovski 1983 | I. Bojanovski, O rimskom rudarstvu i metalurgiji u sjeverozapadnoj Bosni. Rimska feraria u Starom Majdan u na Sani [On Roman mining and metallurgy in northwestern Bosnia. Roman *ferraria* in Stari Majdan in Sana], Zbornik arheološkog društva BiH I, 1983, 119–130 |
| Bojanovski 1988 | I. Bojanovski, Bosna i Hercegovina u antičko doba [Bosnie et Herzegovine à l'époque antique] (Sarajevo 1988) |
| Bricault – Roy 2001 | L. Bricault – P. Roy (eds.), Les cultes de Mithra dans l'Empire romain, Amphi 7 (Toulouse 2021) |

---

[53] Domić Kunić 2001, 53.
[54] The *askos* is made of durable material and could have survived for a longer period, thus ending up in the Mithraeum, probably as a votive gift.
[55] Sergejevski 1937, 17.
[56] They can be compared to the portraits of the emperor Diocletian and his wife Prisca on the frieze in Diocletian's Mausoleum, Split; also compare Luna's hairstyle with the one on a female portrait from Konjic, dated to the Tetrarchic period as well, in Cambi 2000, cat. 128–129, and cat. 127; lupa 30484.
[57] Sergejsvski also argued for the early 4$^{th}$ c. AD as a construction date of the Mithraeum, which is the time when the settlement had its floruit as well, see Sergejevski 1937, 17; Basler 1963/1964, 45.

| | |
|---|---|
| Cambi 2000 | N. Cambi, Imago Animi. Antički portret u Hrvatskoj [Imago Animi. Ancient portrait in Croatia] (Split 2000) |
| Chalupa – Glomb 2013 | A. Chalupa – T. Glomb, The Third Symbol of the Miles Grade on the Floor Mosaic of the Felicissimus Mithraeum in Ostia: A New Interpretation, Religio 21, 2013, 9–32 |
| CIMRM | M. J. Vermaseren, Corpus Inscriptionum et Monumentorum Religionis I. II (The Hague 1956. 1960) |
| Clauss 2012 | M. Clauss, Mithras. Kult und Mysterium (Darmstadt 2012) |
| Dirven 2015 | L. Dirven, The Mithraeum as tableau vivant. A Preliminary Study of Ritual Performance and Emotional Involvement in Ancient Mystery Cults, Religion in the Roman Empire 1/1, 2015, 20–50 |
| Domić Kunić 2001 | A. Domić Kunić, *Askos* iz mitreja u Jajcu (Uz poseban osvrt na mitraizam kao na imitaciju kršćanstva) [An *askos* from a Mithraeum in Jajce with special reference on Mithraism as an imitation of Christianity], ARadRaspr 13, 2001, 39–102 |
| Forrer 1915 | R. Forrer, Das Mithra-Heiligtum von Königshofen bei Strassburg (Stuttgart 1915) |
| Glicksman 2018 | K. Glicksman, Metal Mining in Roman Dalmatia, Opvscvla Archaeologica 39/40, 2018, 261–283 |
| Gordon 1976 | R. Gordon, The Sacred Geography of a Mithraeum. The Example of Sette Sfere, JMithrSt 1/2, 1976, 119–165 |
| Gordon 1980 | R. Gordon, Reality, evocation and boundary in the Mysteries of Mithras, JMithrSt 3/1–2, 1980, 19–99 |
| Gudelj 2006 | Lj. Gudelj, Od svetišta Mitre do crkve Sv. Mihovila. Rezultati istraživanja kod crkve Sv. Mihovila u Prološcu Donjem-Postranju (1986–1997. godine) [From the sanctuary of Mithras to the church of St. Michael. Results of the research at the church of St. Michael in Proložac Donji-Postranje (1986–1997)], Katalozi i monografije 16 (Split 2006) |
| Hensen 2017 | A. Hensen, *Templa et spelaea Mithrae*. Unity and Diversity in the Topography, Architecture and Design of Sanctuaries in the cult of Mithras, in: S. Nagel – J. F. Quack – C. Witschel (eds.), Entangled Worlds. Religious Confluences between East and West in the Roman Empire (Tübingen 2017) 384–412 |
| Hinnells 1976 | J. R. Hinnells, The Iconography of Cautes and Cautopates, JMithrSt 1, 1976, 36–67 |
| Huld-Zetsche 1986 | I. Huld-Zetsche, Mithras in Nida-Heddernheim: Gesamtkatalog, Archäologische Reihe 6 (Frankfurt 1986) |
| Imamović 1985 | E. Imamović, Rimske rudarske ceste na području Bosne i Hercegovine [Roman mining roads on the territory of Bosnia and Herzegovina], Prilozi 21, 1985, 31–52 |
| Kremer 2005 | G. Kremer, Ein Bogenschütze aus Carnuntum, in: B. Brandt – V. Gassner – S. Ladstätter (eds.), Synergia. Festschrift Friedrich Krinzinger (Vienna 2005) I 433–440 |
| Kremer 2012 | G. Kremer, Götterdarstellungen, Kult- und Weihedenkmäler aus Carnuntum. Mit Beiträgen von C. Gugl, C. Uhlir, M. Unterwurzacher, CSIR Österreich, Carnuntum Suppl. 1 (Vienna 2012) |
| lupa | F. und O. Harl, <lupa.at> (Bilddatenbank zu antiken Steindenkmälern) |
| Mesihović 2009 | S. Mesihović, Prilozi antičkoj topografiji Bosne i Hercegovine – dva toponima sa šireg jajačkog područja [Contribution to the ancient topography of Bosnia and Herzegovina – two toponyms from the wider Jajce area], Godišnjak Bošnjačke kulturne zajednice ›Preporod‹ 9, 2009, 171–185 |
| Mouraire 1997 | D. Mouraire, La statuaire du *mithraeum* des Bolards à Nuits-Saint-Georges (Côte-d'Or): nouvelles observations, RAE 48, 1997, 261–278 |
| Pašalić 1960 | E. Pašalić, Antička naselja i komunikacije u Bosni i Hercegovini [Ancient settlements and roads in Bosnia and Herzegovina] (Sarajevo 1960) |
| Patsch 1897 | C. Patsch, Mithraeum u Konjicu [Mithraeum in Konjic], GlasSarajevo 4, 1897, 629–656 |
| Radimsky 1893 | V. Radimsky, Nekropola na Jezerinama u Pritoci kod Bišća [Necropolis in Jezerine in Pritoka near Bišće], GlasSarajevo 5, 1893, 37–92 |
| Roy 2013 | P. Roy, Mithra et l'Apollon celtique en Gaule, StMatStorRel 79/2, 2013, 360–378 |
| Sergejevski 1937 | D. Sergejevski, Das Mithräum von Jajce, GlasSarajevo 49, 1937, 11–18 |
| Silnović 2022 | N. Silnović, *Invicto Mithraea spelaeum fecit*: Typology and Topography of Mithraic Temples in the Roman Province of Dalmatia (Doctoral dissertation Budapest 2022) |

| | |
|---|---|
| Silnović in press | N. Silnović, Evidence of a Specific Form of Worshipping Mithras in the Roman Province of Dalmatia and the Role of the Portorium in the Local Spread of the Cult, in: Cs. Szabó – C. Gugl (eds.), Sanctuaries in the Danubian provinces. Interdisciplinary dialogue in archaeology and religion (in press) |
| Szabó 2015 | Cs. Szabó, Notes on a new Cautes statue from Apulum (Jud. Alba/RO), AKorrBl 45/2, 2015, 237–247 |
| Škegro 2002 | A. Škegro, Jajačko područje u prapovijesti i antici [Area of Jajce in prehistory and antiquity], in: D. Lovrenović (ed.), Jajce 1386–1996. Zbornik radova sa znanstvenog simpozija u povodu 600. obljetnice spomena imena grada Jajca 05.–07.12.1996 (Jajce 2002) 9–16 |
| Tomaschek 1882 | W. Tomaschek, Archäologische Funde in der bosnischen Krajina, SBWien 99, 1882, 466–474 |
| Vomer Gojkovič 2001 | M. Vomer Gojkovič, Petovionski mitreji [Poetovian mithraea], in: M. Vomer Gojkovič (ed.), Ptuj im römischen Reich. Mithraskult und seine Zeit. Internationales Symposium Ptuj 11.–15.10.1999, Archaeologia Poetoviensis 2 (Ptuj 2001) 105–133 |
| Wiblé 1995 | F. Wiblé, Les petits objets du mithraeum de Martigny/Forum Claudii Vallensium, in: M. Martens – G. De Boer (eds.), Roman Mithraism. The Evidence of the Small Finds (Brussels 2004) 135–146 |

*Nirvana Silnović, Austrian Archaeological Institute, Austrian Academy of Sciences, Dominikanerbastei 16, 1010 Vienna, Austria.*
*[e] nirvana.silnovic@oeaw.ac.at*

Katarina Šmid

# THE CURIOUS BUST, FOUND IN THE THIRD MITHRAEUM IN *POETOVIO, PANNONIA SUPERIOR*

**Abstract**

In the adjoining room of the third Poetovian Mithraeum, a female bust dressed in a *peplos* was found. Her head is adorned by a poorly preserved wreath, which is decorated with one round object. Due to the lack of clearly distinguishable attributes, the interpretation appeared to be challenging. First, Mihovil Abramić interpreted it as the Great Mother, later Erna Diez drew attention to the locally widespread cult of the Nutrices and concluded that the bust instead represents Dea Nutrix. However, quite uncommon for both is the headgear, whose preserved features conform to the attributes of some divinities, although due to the state of preservation it is impossible to identify with certainty the round object and therefore to identify the goddess with certainty. Based on the garment and find spot of the bust, Luna, an ever-present deity in the Mithraic religion, probably associated with one of her syncretistic evocations, seems one plausible choice.

In 1913, the third Poetovian Mithraeum in Zgornji Breg, Ptuj (German »Ober-Rann, Pettau«) was discovered by Viktor Skrabar[1]. In its north-eastern adjoining room (11 × 6 m), the female bust (Ptuj Ormož Regional Museum inv. RL 301; fig. 1 a–c), dressed in a *peplos*, was found[2]. The Mithraeum was built in the first half of the 3rd century and enlarged during the reign of Gallienus (259–268), when the anteroom in front of the earliest anteroom and extensions to the eastern and western sides were added, while the former anteroom was incorporated into the cella (cf. fig. 2)[3]. The whole complex was situated within the district of the urban villas, which were abandoned before the end of the 4th century[4].

The bust represents a woman dressed in a Greek *peplos*, attached to her shoulders. In her hair she wears a wreath – in some places, vestiges of the leaves are still visible –, which is decorated with one round object, maybe a medallion or a rosette, just above her forehead. Her pupils are not modelled, and the reverse is unworked, which points to a location within a niche or against the wall. Two bases of columns, a relief with the Nutrices (Ptuj Ormož Regional Museum inv. RL 320; lupa 9367), a relief with a sea dragon (Ptuj Ormož Regional Museum inv. RL 321; lupa 22311), a statuette of Icarus (lupa 22312), a Corinthian capital (lupa 22313), another capital with leaf ornament (lupa 22314) and the stele of a woman (lupa 3774) come from the same place of discovery[5].

Emil Reisch first referred to the bust as a female deity and interpreted the room as a cult room for Magna Mater[6]. Later on, Mihovil Abramić – due to the findspot in the assumed Metroon, and the appearance of the bust – interpreted her as the Great Mother[7]. Since two bases of columns[8] were also found in the same room, Abramić concluded that they originally could have formed the

---

[1] Reisch 1913, 101–105. On the Mithraeum: Abramić 1925, 172–193; Selem 1980, 125–140 no. 85–109; Diez 1993, 251–254; Horvat et al. 2003, 178; Vomer Gojkovič 2014; Vomer Gojkovič 2021, 169–170.
[2] Abramić 1925, 190 no. 252; Diez 1993; lupa 10849.
[3] Diez 1993, 251; Vomer Gojkovič 2014, 12; Walsh 2019, 110–111 no. D.5.
[4] Vomer Gojkovič 2014, 4–6; Preložnik – Nestorović 2018, 279–281.
[5] Cf. Abramić 1925, 190–191.
[6] Reisch 1913, 104.
[7] Abramić 1925, 174.
[8] Cf. Ertel 2001, 171.

aedicula in which the statue was placed[9]. His remarks were accepted also by some other scholars, although with some reservation due to the lack of attributes[10].

Abramić's thesis was questioned by Erna Diez. She stressed several shortcomings regarding this interpretation: the lack of any certain attributes associated with Magna Mater, and her dress and headgear, which do not find analogies in her iconography[11]. Diez pointed out that the extension of the Mithraeum was carried out under the auspices of the Dacian legions stationed there at the time, namely the *legio V Macedonica* and the *legio XIII Gemina*, nicknamed *Gallienae*, whose soldiers dedicated five marble altars in the 3rd Poetovian Mithraeum[12]. She pointed out that it would be rather unusual that the military would erect the cult building for the mother goddess Cybele directly near the Mithraeum, which was only accessible to men, as both mystery cults differ substantially from each other[13].

As in the provinces, especially in the frontier regions, several dedications to not only Roman state cults, but also to local, autochthonous deities, like Epona, Nutrix and especially the Matrones, were found in Mithraea[14], and since the pre-Roman cult of the Nutrices was widespread in *Poetovio* and its *ager* (in fact three dedications were unearthed near the Mithraeum)[15], Diez concluded that the bust could represent Dea Nutrix rather than Magna Mater. Accordingly, she also interpreted the room where the bust was found as the shrine dedicated to the Nutrices. In a similar fashion to the worshippers of the Mithras cult, also the adherents of the Nutrices cult, who pray for the safeguarding of their children, belonged to all social classes. Diez dated the statue to the third quarter of the 3rd century, in the Gallienic era, and considered it as the product of one of the Poetovian workshops[16]. However, she also admitted some drawbacks to her thesis, such as the lack of attributes, for example the baby in her arms and the dress that differs from other representations of Nutrices[17].

The cult of the Nutrices was without doubt one of the most, if not the most popular cult in *Poetovio*. It is most likely of pre-Roman, Celtic origin and distinctive for *Poetovio* with its *ager*[18]. The Nutrices are associated with divine nurses; they were protective deities of the family and are represented in a more or less uniform attitude[19]. Although their number is not strictly defined, to conclude from the numerous preserved relief depictions in Ptuj, they were at least two and may have been – in comparison to Celtic Matres – a trinity[20]. Most of the monuments are dated to the 2nd century, and subsequently the cult declined along with the other pagan cults in *Poetovio*; none of the known monuments is dated to the end of the 3rd century[21].

Although the bust is somewhat deteriorated on the surface, some particular features are still visible. One of them is her attire. She is dressed in the *peplos*, which is a typical Greek garment. Although it was already regarded as old-fashioned by the Classical period, and was therefore worn primarily on certain ritual occasions[22], it remained the dress of several divinities.

---

[9] Abramić 1925, 190 no. 252.
[10] Vermaseren 1960, 192–193 no. 1578; Swoboda 1969, 202 no. 11; Selem 1980, 126. 201 no. 7; Lazar 1998, 101 no. 185; Vomer Gojkovič 2014, 16.
[11] Diez 1993, 254–255.
[12] On the altars: Ragolič 2015, 326–331.
[13] Diez 1993, 255.
[14] Cf. Diez 1993, 255–256; Clauss 2000, 157–158; Siemers-Klenner 2020, 158–159.
[15] Cf. AIJ 325, 329–330; Šašel Kos 1999, 166–168 no. 25–27; Jerala 2009, 77.
[16] Diez 1993, 255–259.
[17] Diez 1993, 259.
[18] On the cult of Nutrices see lately Šašel Kos 1999, 153–192; Šašel Kos 2016, 168–171 with the cited literature.
[19] On their iconography: Šašel Kos 2016, 168–169.
[20] Šašel Kos 2016, 168–169.
[21] Šašel Kos 2016, 172.
[22] Lee 2005, 59–60; Davies 2021, 60.

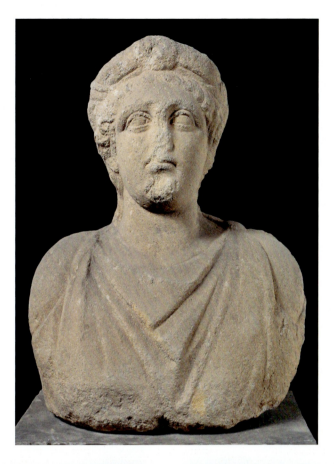

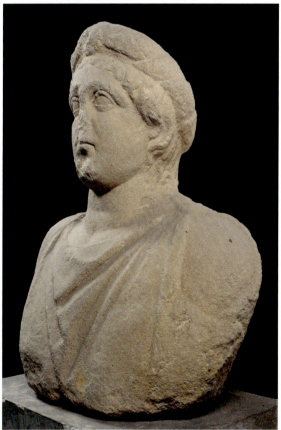

1 a–c  Female bust, 3rd Poetovian Mithraeum (© Pokrajinski muzej Ptuj – Ormož, photo B. Farić)

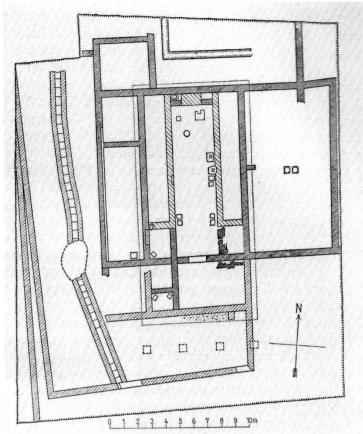

122. Grundriß des sogenannten dritten Mithräums und seiner Zubauten am Ober-Rann. Die dichten Straffen ▓▓▓ bezeichnen den älteren Bau, die gesperrten ▓▓▓ seine Erweiterungen. ▓▓▓ Innenmauern der Bankette und des sogenannten Altars im alten, ▓▓▓ im erweiterten Bau. Die punktierte Linie gibt den Umriß des modernen Schutzbaues.

2   Groundplan of the 3rd Poetovian Mithraeum with its extensions (after Abramić 1925)

The only distinctive attribute of the bust is the wreath, adorned by a round, convex object. It has been identified as a gem[23], an ornament in the shape of a rosette[24], or a gem with a figure in the middle[25]. Probably due to the headgear, Maarten J. Vermaseren suggested that the bust »might equally [like Cybele] be that of a priestess«[26].

Wreaths bearing medallions or gems have been preserved in the highest number in *Palmyra*[27] and were, just like the bands with the busts (»Büstenkronen«) from Asia Minor, often superficially understood as insignia of the priestly service of the Eastern deities[28], although only a scant number of inscriptions are preserved, and the busts in the medallions have in most cases not been preserved in such a condition that would enable their identification[29].

Thus, due to its place of discovery and the old-fashioned *peplos* worn by goddesses, it is more likely that the female bust represents a deity, rather than a mortal priestess or a well-off deceased.

---

[23] Abramić 1925, 190 no. 252; Vermaseren 1989.
[24] Diez 1993, 254.
[25] Selem 1980, 201 no. 7.
[26] Vermaseren 1989, 35 no. 112.
[27] Cf. Rumscheid 2000, 93–94.
[28] Robert 1930, 264–265; Février 1931, 156; Ingholt 1934, 35; Rumscheid 2000, 93.
[29] Cf. Rumscheid 2000, 52. 59. The wreath bearing the bust of the deity in the medallion was, however, not worn only by priests, but in all likelihood also by persons who performed some function within the cult. In some cases, the wreath is embellished by the head of Medusa and therefore has apotropaic meaning or is a medallion adorned with military emblems (Rumscheid 2000, 110).

It is quite common and far from unusual that – according to several votive inscriptions and images – many other deities were also venerated in Mithraic communities[30].

*Poetovio*, where the bust was found, was the administrative seat of the *publicum portorii Illyrici* since the reign of emperor Hadrian[31]. It was without doubt a cosmopolitan town with a very vibrant religious life, including several Eastern cults, cultivated especially by the newcomers[32]. Soon after the Roman occupation, several military camps were located in the town[33], and military units dedicated a vast number of monuments, not only to Graeco-Roman gods but also to deities of oriental[34] or local origin[35], some of which were found within or nearby Mithraea. Therefore, it seems quite likely that it was the military, presumably of the *legio V Macedonica* or *legio XIII Gemina*, who dedicated the bust in question.

As an omnipresent female deity in the Mithraic religion, who is occasionally dressed in the *peplos*[36], the goddess Luna has also to be considered. She occurs in the main cult reliefs with the tauroctony in the upper right corner, in juxtaposition with Sol on the left. She is commonly represented in the shape of a bust[37] and is also a key planetary divinity in the Mithraic hierarchy, as the tutelary planet of the grade Perses[38]. Furthermore, she can easily be assimilated with other divinities. Among her various attributes is also the wreath, which could be an allusion to her authority over vegetation and fertility[39], and her syncretistic evocations are recalled also in Mithraea[40]. Her main attribute, the crescent, is usually rising above her head or is located behind her. The Poetovian bust, however, has no hole on the top of the wreath to which that symbol could have been hypothetically attached.

Somewhat unusual is the crescent represented as an attribute of a deity, interpreted as Diana or Diana(-Nemesis [?]) on a stele from *Gallia Belgica* (Luxembourg, Musée national d'histoire et d'art Luxembourg inv. 2009-63/546; fig. 3)[41]. It is placed on the top of her head and, a large star is carved within its semicircle. Taking into consideration the round object embellishing the wreath of the Poetovian bust in question, its convexity and uneven surface, it is quite feasible that it could represent a crescent with a star in the middle.

Ever since the Imperial period, with a climax in Late Antiquity, the planetary goddess Luna has been easily merged with other divinities, especially with Diana; nevertheless it has to be emphasised that Diana's typical costume, the short *chiton* of the huntress, was in general only seldom applied to her[42]. The syncretistic goddess Luna-Nemesis[43] with the crescent above her forehead

---

[30] Diez 1993, 255–256; Clauss 2000, 155–167.
[31] Šašel Kos 2020, 225; on *publicum portorii Illyrici* see esp. Dobó 1940, 186–194; Pavan 1955, 459–467; Dobó 1968, 180–188; Ørsted 1985, 251–347; Mišić 2013, 291–294.
[32] See Horvat et al. 2002, 158–159; Jerala 2009, 65–84; Jerala 2011, 77–82; Mišić 2013, 295–393; Šašel Kos 2020, 317–320.
[33] Horvat et al. 2003, 156–157.
[34] Cf. Cumont 1911, 22–26; Birley 1978, 1516–1523.
[35] Cf. Hingley 2012, 751.
[36] Cf. for example a votive niche in London (British Museum inv. 2162; Gury 1994, 707 no. 2), a statue in the Vatican (Musei Vaticani Braccio Nuovo inv. 2268; Gury 1994, 709 no. 33).
[37] Cf. Beck 2007, 197–199; Boschung 2021, 134–136.
[38] Clauss 2000, 136; Chalupa 2008, 187.
[39] Gury 1994, 714.
[40] Cf. the mosaic in the Mithraeum in *Ostia* (Mitreo delle Sette Sfere [II, VIII, 6]), in which she holds an arrow and maybe a pomegranate (Gordon 1976, 120–146), or the fresco with the tauroctony in the Mithraeum in Santa Maria Capua Vetere, in which she wears a diadem with an oval gem rising above the front (Vermaseren 1971, 8–10). In the upper part of the eastern wall of the latter, the large fresco of Luna, being carried away by her *biga*, is a unique representation in Mithraic art, whereas the motif is also exceptional for being a separate painting within a Mithraeum (Vermaseren 1971, 14–16).
[41] Dövener 2011, 110; Kremer 2015, 267–268. On the assimilation of both goddesses in the Imperial era see Hornum 1993, 66–67. 71–72. 80–81.
[42] Gury 1994, 714.
[43] Gugl 2001, 41.

3  Diana(-Nemesis [?]), Luxembourg, Musée national d'histoire et d'art inv. 2009-63/546 (© MNHA/INRA Luxembourg, photo T. Lucas)

4  Female bust, immured in the St. Stephen parish church, Spodnja Polskava (photo F. Lazarini)

is only firmly attested in the visual arts[44] in the statue from *Carnuntum* (Bad Deutsch-Altenburg, Archäologisches Museum Carnuntinum inv. 28, 3772)[45], in a relief from *Virunum* (Klagenfurt, kärnten.museum inv. VA99/79)[46], and, with a question mark, in the figure in Spodnja Polskava in Styria (built into the parish church of St. Stephen; fig. 4)[47].

As Nemesis is also easily assimilated to other divinities and personifications, her identification is in many cases complicated or even impossible[48]. The goddess is dressed either in a *chiton* or a *peplos*[49], and although *peplos*-wearing Nemesis was more diffused in the Danubian regions in the provincial coinage during the late 2nd and early 3rd centuries AD, she is also attested in sculpture[50]. Her cult, however, was not highly popular in *Poetovio*, as to my knowledge only one badly damaged votive altar attesting to her veneration has been unearthed here so far; it was found in a secondary location in the walls between the marketplace (then Tyrš Square) and the parish church of St. George (Ptuj Ormož Regional Museum)[51].

Although a clearly identified sculpture in the round of Luna has not yet been found in a Mithraic context, it has been recently suggested that one of the statues from the Mithraeum in *Augusta Emerita* in the province of *Lusitania*, which was previously interpreted as Isis, could represent

---

[44]  There is some more epigraphic evidence. Cf. for example an altar from *castra Divitia* (Köln, Römisch-Germanisches Museum inv. 55,311; Hornum 1993, 189–190 no. 65), an altar from *Bonnonia* (Bonn, immured in the monastery church, Hornum 1993, 189 no. 64), an altar from *Carnuntum* (Bad Deutsch-Altenburg, AMC inv. CAR-S 320; Hornum 1993, 157–158 no. 8; lupa 13710) or an altar from *Aquincum* (Budapest, Magyar Nemzeti Múzeum inv. 190.1880.1; Hornum 1993, 214–215 no. 114; lupa 10027).

[45]  Kremer 2012, 32–33 no. 14; Kremer 2015, 259–265; lupa 4925.

[46]  Gugl 2001, 35–37; Gugl – Jernej 2003, 377–378; Kremer 2015, 267–270; lupa 11253.

[47]  Pahič 1977, 55; lupa 5308.

[48]  Rausa 1992, 768–769; cf. Kremer 2015, 265–277.

[49]  Rausa 1992, 769–770.

[50]  Aristodemou 2016, 194.

[51]  AIJ 323; Saria 1933, 126–127; Kolšek 1968, 278; Selem 1980, 265 no. 2; Jerala 2009, 140 no. VIII; Mišić 2013, 361–362.

5   Seasons, altar in the Mithraeum in Inveresk (© National Museums Scotland)

Luna instead, even though it is without any distinctive iconographic characteristics[52]. Bearing in mind the possible identification of the round object on the wreath of the Poetovian bust as a medallion, perhaps with the addition of the crescent and the star (although on a much smaller scale than in other cases), as well as the *peplos* and the find spot, an identification with Luna rather than Luna-Nemesis cannot be totally excluded.

Particularly intriguing is the headgear, which matches with attributes of certain divinities, of whom some are associated with the Mithraic religion or whose dedications were at least found in Mithraea. Observing the distinctive features of the wreath (traces of the lancets, especially on the left side, the convexity and uneven surface of the round object), these traits could perhaps speak in favour of the stalks-wreath with a rosette, which is an attribute of the personification of the summer, sometimes also represented in the guise of Hora and, just as the other Seasons, often shown in the form of a bust[53].

The interconnectedness of the Seasons and the Mithraic religion is not unprecedented[54]. In the capital of *Pannonia superior*, in *Carnuntum*, all the Seasons are attested in the altar dedicated by Magnius Heracla to Deo Invicto in the 3rd Mithraeum (Bad Deutsch-Altenburg, AMC inv. 303)[55]. However, the Seasons on that altar are represented as nude male figures and therefore differ completely from the Poetovian bust.

As is attested by the altar dedicated to Sol from the Mithraeum in Inveresk, about 8 km east of Edinburgh, Horae in the form of busts were also not unknown in a Mithraic context. The altar is dated around AD 140, and the busts of the four Seasons in the guise of Horae adorn its top[56]. Remarkably, the headgear of the personification of Summer is quite similar to the Poetovian bust; nevertheless, they differ in their dress, as the personification of Inveresk wears an off-the-shoulder dress, exposing her right breast (cf. fig. 5).

However, to my knowledge, all depictions of Seasons in Mithraea are represented in relief and never as free-standing busts. Whereas all four are carved and not merely one, there is a slight

---

[52]   Romero Mayorga 2018, 197; Nogales Basarrate – Romero Mayorga 2021, 261.
[53]   Cf. Abad Casal 1990, 523–527 no. 116–162.
[54]   Abad Casal 1990, 537; Hunter et al. 2016, 154; Hunter 2021, 268; Kremer 2021, 251–256.
[55]   Krüger 1970, 19–20 no. 181; Stiglitz 1977, 607; Jobst 1992, 34–35 no. 12; Kremer 2012, 177–179 no. 350; Kremer 2021, 253; lupa 8916.
[56]   Hunter et al. 2016, 126–133; Hunter 2021, 266–268.

possibility that the other three personifications have not been preserved. Although they are more often wearing off-the-shoulder dresses, *peploi* or tunics were not uncommon in their iconography as well[57]. Nevertheless, the representation in the form of a free-standing bust would be unique in Mithraic iconography, and there is also no hint at all as to why they would be so emphasized in the context of the 3rd Mithraeum.

The room where the bust was found was considered a shrine, either dedicated to Cybele or to the Nutrices, whereas later Christine Ertel recognized it rather as the adjoining assembly room, which is positioned in a similar location to the assembly place of the 1st Poetovian Mithraeum[58]. She assumed that the bases were found in their original site and that they did not flank the aedicula with the bust, as concluded by Abramić and repeated by Diez, but were instead bases of the columns that supported the vaulted ceiling, in a similar fashion to the pillars from the assembly room of the 1st Mithraeum. Also, due to their diameter, one of the two capitals could belong to the columns of the assembly room[59]. Hence, the bust would have been located in the assembly room, either in the niche or against the wall.

*Summa summarum*, I have encountered the same difficulties as Abramić and Diez years before, that is, in addition to the lack of attributes, the lack of comparable visual depictions makes a secure identification problematic. None of the plausible interpretations can be firmly confirmed and, on that account, the proper identification of the bust must remain open. In my opinion, due to the old-fashioned garment, the find spot in the adjoining room of the cult room of the Mithraeum, and the possible explanation of the round object as the crescent with the star, the interpretation as Luna, probably associated with one of her syncretistic evocations, seems the most credible conclusion so far. On the other hand, the preserved traits of the headgear apparently match the attributes of several divinities, or even Eastern priests, and it may be that it was designed as a polysemic attribute, meant to evoke different meanings and symbolism to initiates, but remaining unclear to others[60].

Nevertheless, since the late 2nd century AD, the number of polyvalent, hybrid deities increased in the provinces[61], and in a cosmopolitan town like *Poetovio*, the vivid religious life was attested by the profusion of various deities, also syncretistic ones, praised by the newcomers. Perhaps one of them – an adherent of the Mithras cult as well – venerated the divinity whose appearance merged with the portrayals in his home town or province presumably located in the East, and her proper identity has consequently been concealed[62].

## BIBLIOGRAPHY

| | |
|---|---|
| Abad Casal 1990 | L. Abad Casal, in: LIMC V 1 (1990) 510–538 s. v. Horae no. 1–226 |
| Abramić 1925 | M. Abramić, Poetovio. Führer durch die Denkmäler der römischen Stadt (Vienna 1925) |
| AIJ | V. Hoffiller – B. Saria, Antike Inschriften aus Jugoslawien 1. Noricum und Pannonia Superior (Zagreb 1938) |
| Aristodemou 2016 | G. Aristodemou, Nemesis' Cult and the Arena Spectacles. Evidence from the Black Sea Region, in: M. Manōledakēs (ed.), The Black Sea in the Light of New Archaeological Data and Theoretical Approaches. Proceedings of the 2nd International Workshop on the Black Sea in Antiquity Thessaloniki 18.–20.09.2015 (Oxford 2016) 181–204 |

---

[57] Abad Casal 1990, 537. Cf. Abad Casal 1990, 529–530. 532–533 nos. 187. 193. 222.
[58] Cf. Abramić 1925, 23 fig. 4.
[59] Ertel 2001, 171–172.
[60] Cf. Elsner 1995, 220. In that case, it could function in a similar manner as the individual objects which are arranged on the votive altars without any precise programme, but which are intended to evoke the Mithraic imagery and ritual practice to the initiates (cf. Gordon 1998, 232–236. 258).
[61] Latte 1960, 334–336; Kremer 2015, 282.
[62] For helpful suggestions regarding the interpretation of the bust, I express my gratitude to Claudina Romero Mayorga, PhD.

| | |
|---|---|
| Beck 2007 | R. Beck, The Religion of the Mithras Cult in the Roman Empire. Mysteries of the Unconquered Sun (Oxford 2007) |
| Birley 1978 | E. Birley, The Religion of the Roman Army: 1895–1977, in: ANRW II 16, 2 (Berlin 1978) 1506–1541 |
| Boschung 2021 | D. Boschung, L'image d'un culte. La tauroctonie, in: L. Bricault – R. Veymiers – N. Amoroso (eds.), Le mystère Mithra. Plongée au Coeur d'un culte Romain (Mariemont 2021) 133–141 |
| Chalupa 2008 | A. Chalupa, Seven Mithraic Grades. An Initiatory or Priestly Hierarchy?, Religio 16/ 2, 2008, 177–201 |
| Clauss 2000 | M. Clauss, The Roman Cult of Mithras. The God and his Mysteries (Edinburgh 2000) |
| Cumont 1911 | F. Cumont, The Oriental Religions in Roman Paganism (Chicago 1911) |
| Davies 2021 | G. Davies, Clothing in Marble and Bronze. The Representation of Dress in Greek and Roman Sculpture, in: A. J. Batten – K. Olson (eds.), Dress in Mediterranean Antiquity. Greeks, Romans, Jews, Christians (London 2021) 53–65 |
| Diez 1993 | E. Diez, Magna Mater oder Nutrix?, in: B. Lamut (ed.), Ptujski arheološki zbornik. Ob 100-letnici muzeja in Muzejskega društva (Ptuj 1993) 251–162 |
| Dobó 1940 | Á Dobó, Publicum portorium illyrici. Documenti e commentario (Budapest 1940) |
| Dobó 1968 | Á Dobó, Die Verwaltung der römischen Provinz Pannonien von Augustus bis Diocletianus. Die provinziale Verwaltung (Budapest 1968) |
| Dövener 2011 | F. Dövener, Tabula rasa … ab in den Brunnen!, in: Unter unseren Füßen. Archäologie in Luxemburg / Sous nos pieds. Archéologie au Luxembourg 1995–2010 (Luxemburg 2011) 109–113 |
| Elsner 1995 | J. Elsner, Art and the Roman Viewer. The Transformation of Art from the Pagan World to Christianity, Cambridge Studies in New Art History and Criticism (Cambridge 1995) |
| Ertel 2001 | C. Ertel, Zur Architektur der Mithräen von Poetovio, in: M. Vomer Gojkovič – N. Kolar (eds.), Ptuj in the Roman Empire. Mithraism and its Era. International Scientific Symposium Ptuj 11.–15.10.1999, Archaeologia Poetovionensis 2 (Ptuj 2001) 167–178 |
| Février 1931 | J. G. Février, La religion des Palmyréniens (Paris 1931) |
| Gordon 1976 | R. L. Gordon, The Sacred Geography of a Mithraeum. The Example of Sette Sfere, JMithrSt 1, 1976, 119–165 |
| Gordon 1998 | R. Gordon, Viewing Mithraic Art: The Altar from Burginatium (Kalkar), Germania Inferior, Arys 1, 1998, 227–258 |
| Gugl 2001 | C. Gugl, Zwei Nemesis-Votivreliefs aus dem Amphitheater von Virunum, ÖJh 70, 2001, 35–49 |
| Gugl – Jernej 2003 | C. Gugl – R. Jernej, Nemesis in Virunum. Entdeckung zweier Nemesis-Votivreliefs im Amphitheater von Virunum, AW 34/4, 2003, 375–380 |
| Gury 1994 | F. Gury, in: LIMC VII 1 (Zurich 1994) 706–715 s. v. Selene, Luna no. 1–80 |
| Hingley 2012 | R. Hingley, Rome. Imperial and Local Tradition, in: The Oxford Handbook of Ritual and Religion (Oxford 2012) 745–757 |
| Hornum 1993 | M. B. Hornum, Nemesis, the Roman State and the Games, Religions in the Graeco-Roman World 117 (Leiden 1993) |
| Horvat et al. 2003 | J. Horvat et al., Poetovio. Development and Topography, in: M. Šašel Kos – P. Scherrer (eds.), The Autonomous Towns of Noricum and Pannonia. Pannonia, Situla 41 (Ljubljana 2003) 153–189 |
| Hunter 2021 | F. Hunter, Le mithréum d'Inveresk et ses autels, in: L. Bricault – R. Veymiers – N. Amoroso (eds.), Le mystère Mithra. Plongée au Coeur d'un culte Romain (Mariemont 2021) 263–269 |
| Hunter et al. 2016 | F. Hunter et al., Mithras in Scotland. A Mithraeum at Inveresk (East Lothian), Britannia 47, 2016, 119–168 |
| Ingholt 1934 | H. Ingholt, Palmyrene Sculpture in Beirut, Berytus 1, 1934, 32–43 |
| Jerala 2009 | M. Jerala, Poskus rekonstrukcije svetišča Kabirov na Panorami in topografija kultov v Petovioni (abstract: An Attempt of a Reconstruction of a Cabeiri Temple at Panorama and the Topography of Cults in Poetoviona) (Dipl. University of Ljubljana 2009) |
| Jerala 2011 | M. Jerala, The Topography of Ritual Monuments in Poetovio, in: I. Lazar (ed.), Religion in Public and Private Sphere. Acta of the 4th International Colloquium The Autonomous |

| | |
|---|---|
| | Towns of Noricum and Pannonia Celje 22.–25.09.2008, Annales Mediterranei (Koper 2011) 75–86 |
| Jobst 1992 | H. Jobst, Die römischen Mithrasmysterien, in: W. Jobst (ed.), Carnuntum. Das Erbe Roms an der Donau. Katalog Archäologisches Museum Carnuntum in Bad Deutsch-Altenburg (Vienna 1992) 31–57 |
| Kolšek 1968 | V. Kolšek, Pregled antičnih kultov na slovenskem ozemlju (Summary: Übersicht über die antiken Kulte im slowenischen Gebiet), AVes 19, 1968, 273–286 |
| Kremer 2012 | G. Kremer, Götterdarstellungen, Kult- und Weihedenkmäler aus Carnuntum. Mit Beiträgen von Ch. Gugl, Ch. Uhlir, M. Unterwurzacher, CSIR Carnuntum Suppl. 1 (Vienna 2012) |
| Kremer 2015 | G. Kremer, Synkretistische Neukompositionen von Götterbildern im norisch-pannonischen Raum, in: D. Boschung – A. Schäfer (eds.), Römische Götterbilder der Mittleren und Späten Kaiserzeit, Morphomata 22 (Paderborn 2015) 259–285 |
| Kremer 2021 | G. Kremer, Les mithréums de Carnuntum, in: L. Bricault – R. Veymiers – N. Amoroso (eds.), Le mystère Mithra. Plongée au Coeur d'un culte Romain (Mariemont 2021) 251–256 |
| Krüger 1970 | M.-L. Krüger, Die Reliefs des Stadtgebietes von Carnuntum 1. Teil: Die figürlichen Reliefs, CSIR Österreich I 3 (Vienna 1970) |
| Latte 1960 | K. Latte, Römische Religionsgeschichte (Munich 1960) |
| Lazar 1998 | I. Lazar, in: J. Fitz (ed.), Religions and Cults in Pannonia (Székesfehérvár 1998) |
| Lee 2005 | M. Lee, Constru(ct)ing Gender in the Feminine Greek Peplos, in: L. Cleland – M. Harlow – L. Llewelyn-Jones (eds.), The Clothed Body in the Ancient World (Oxford 2005) 55–64 |
| lupa | F. und O. Harl, <lupa.at> (Bilddatenbank zu antiken Steindenkmälern) |
| Mišić 2013 | B. Mišić, Cults and Religious Integration in the Roman Cities of the Drava Valley (Southern Pannonia) (Diss. Royal Holloway, University of London 2013) |
| Nogales Basarrate – Romero Mayorga 2021 | T. Nogales Basarrate – C. Romero Mayorga, Le mithréum d'*Augusta Emerita* et ses sculptures, in: L. Bricault – R. Veymiers – N. Amoroso (eds.), Le mystère Mithra. Plongée au Coeur d'un culte Romain (Mariemont 2021) 257–262 |
| Ørsted 1985 | P. Ørsted, Roman Imperial Economy and Romanization. A Study in Roman Imperial Administration and the Public Lease System in the Danubian Provinces from the First to the Third Century A.D. (Copenhagen 1985) |
| Pahič 1977 | S. Pahič, Seznam rimskih kamnov v Podravju in Pomurju (Summary: Verzeichnis der Römersteine im slowenischen Drauland), AVes 28, 1977, 13–73 |
| Pavan 1955 | M. Pavan, La provincia romana della Pannonia superior (Rome 1955) |
| Preložnik – Nestorović 2018 | A. Preložnik – A. Nestorović, Between Metropolis and Wilderness. The Topography of Mithraea in Ager Poetoviensis, ActaAntHung 58, 2018, 275–290 |
| Ragolič 2015 | A. Ragolič, Die Zeit des Kaisers Galliens und die Rolle des Heeres in Poetovio, in: J. Istenič et al. (eds.), Evidence of the Roman Army in Slovenia, Katalogi in monografije 41 (Ljubljana 2015) 317–340 |
| Rausa 1992 | F. Rausa, in: LIMC VI 1 (Zürich 1992) 762–770 s. v. Nemesis no. 221–309 |
| Reisch 1913 | E. Reisch, Poetovio, ÖJh 16, 1913, Beibl. 100–105 |
| Robert 1930 | L. Robert, Nouvelles remarques sur l'édit d'Ériza, BCH 54, 1930, 262–267 |
| Romero Mayorga 2018 | C. Romero Mayorga, Mithraic Iconography in Hispania. Reinterpretation of the Catalogue and New Findings, ActaAntHung 58, 2018, 171–197 |
| Rumscheid 2000 | J. Rumscheid, Kranz und Krone. Zu Insignien, Siegespreisen und Ehrenzeichen der römischen Kaiserzeit, IstForsch 43 (Tübingen 2000) |
| Saria 1933 | B. Saria, Nova raziskovanja po stari Poetoviji (Summary: Neue Untersuchungen auf dem Gebiet von Poetovio), Časopis za zgodovino in narodopisje 2–4, 1933, 119–129 |
| Šašel Kos 1999 | M. Šašel Kos, Pre-Roman Divinities of the Eastern Alps and Adriatic, Situla 38 (Ljubljana 1999) |
| Šašel Kos 2016 | M. Šašel Kos, Nutrices, the most Popular Goddesses at Poetovio, in: M. Lehner – B. Schrettle (eds.), Zentralort und Tempelberg. Siedlungs- und Kultentwicklung am Frauenberg bei Leibnitz im Vergleich. Akten des Kolloquiums im Schloss Seggau 04.–05.05.2015 (Vienna 2016) 167–174 |

| | |
|---|---|
| Šašel Kos 2020 | M. Šašel Kos, V srcu rimskega imperija. Zgodovina slovenskega prostora v antiki do vlade Maksimina Tračana, Zbirka Zgodovinskega časopisa 51 (Ljubljana 2020) |
| Selem 1980 | P. Selem, Les Religions Orientales dans la Pannonie Romaine. Partie en Yugoslavie, EPRO 85 (Leiden 1980) |
| Siemers-Klenner 2020 | I. Siemers-Klenner, Archäologie des Mithraskultes. Architektur und Kultpraxis am Beispiel der Tempel von Güglingen, Kreis Heilbronn, FBerBadWürt 16 (Wiesbaden 2020) |
| Stiglitz 1977 | H. Stiglitz, Die Zivilstadt Carnuntum, in: ANRW II 6 (Berlin 1977) 585–625 |
| Swoboda 1969 | R. M. Swoboda, Denkmäler des Mater-Magna-Kultes in Slowenien und Istrien, BJb 169, 1969, 195–207 |
| Vermaseren 1960 | M. J. Vermaseren, Corpus inscriptionum et monumentorum religionis Mithriacae II (The Hague 1960) |
| Vermaseren 1971 | M. J. Vermaseren, The Mithraeum at S. Maria Capua Vetera, Mithraica I (Leiden 1971) |
| Vermaseren 1989 | M. J. Vermaseren, Corpus cultus Cybelae Attidisque (CCCA) VI. Germania, Raetia, Noricum, Pannonia, Dalmatia, Macedonia, Thracia, Moesia, Dacia, Regnum Bospori, Colchis, Scythia et Sarmatia (Leiden 1989) |
| Vomer Gojkovič 2014 | M. Vomer Gojkovič, Tretji petovionski mitrej/Third Mithraeum in Poetovio (Ptuj 2014) |
| Vomer Gojkovič 2021 | M. Vomer Gojkovič, Les mithréums de Poetovio, in: L. Bricault – R. Veymiers – N. Amoroso (eds.), Le mystère Mithra. Plongée au Coeur d'un culte Romain (Mariemont 2021) 163–170 |
| Walsh 2019 | D. Walsh, The Cult of Mithras in the Late Antiquity. Development, Decline and Demise ca. A.D. 270–430, Late Antique Archaeology Suppl. 2 (Leiden 2019) |

*Katarina Šmid, University of Primorska, Faculty of Humanities, Department of Archaeology and Heritage, Institute of Archaeology and Heritage, Titov trg 5, 6000 Koper, Slovenia.*
*[e] katarina.smid@fhs.upr.si*

Jakob Unterhinninghofen

# GRABALTÄRE MIT MEERWESENDEKOR AUS DEM TREVERERGEBIET

## UNTERSUCHUNGEN ZU CHRONOLOGIE, TYPOLOGIE UND IKONOGRAFIE

**Abstract**
The article deals with the results of a study conducted as part of the DFG research project »Römische Grabdenkmäler aus *Augusta Treverorum* im überregionalen Vergleich«. The aim is to provide an answer to the question of which chronological, iconographic, and typological criteria distinguish funeral altars from the Treveri region from examples in Rome and northern Italy. This article examines altars with decoration of sea creatures, which were re-used as spolia in a Roman castle in Neumagen. The results of the study show that the monument form not only appears in the Moselle region later than in Rome and northern Italy, but also that characteristic forms are developed here not only in formal terms, but also in the choice, combination, and design of the pictorial elements. This pictorial language, created in the provincial area, is characterized both thematically and visually by a special differentiation.

Unter den Grabdenkmälern der *civitas Treverorum* stellen die Grabaltäre in verschiedener Hinsicht eine besondere Gruppe dar. Sie treten nicht nur zeitlich später als ihre Vergleichsstücke aus dem italischen Raum auf, sondern unterscheiden sich von diesen ebenfalls durch ihre ausschließlich querrechteckigen Dimensionen. Gleichfalls lässt sich bei ihnen eine abweichende Verwendung bei der Auswahl des Bildschmucks beobachten[1]. So ist eine Gruppe treverischer Altäre mit umlaufenden Relieffriesen versehen, die Darstellungen von Meerwesen zeigen[2]. Meerwesen finden sich auch auf italischen Grabaltären als Verzierungselement, jedoch hier lediglich kleinformatig oder als Teil einer Einzelszene.

Im vorliegenden Text sollen die konkreten chronologischen, typologischen sowie ikonografischen Unterschiede und Gemeinsamkeiten zwischen Grabaltären mit Meerwesendekor aus dem Treverergebiet und Rom sowie Oberitalien herausgearbeitet werden. Darauf aufbauend wird analysiert, ob trotz der signifikanten Unterschiede mögliche Einflüsse aus dem italischen Raum festgestellt werden können. Lassen sich formelle Einwirkungen erfassen? Welche Unterschiede und Gemeinsamkeiten bestehen im Kompositionsarrangement des Meerwesendekors? Sind inhaltliche Parallelen in der Bildthematik bezüglich Meerwesen erkennbar? Wurde im Trevererland ein eigenständiges Bildrepertoire entwickelt?

---

[1] Für die Bedeutung sowie die historische, typologische und ikonografische Entwicklung von Grabaltären im italischen Raum s. u. a. Altmann 1905; Boschung 1987.

[2] Die Thematik von Meerwesen in der römischen Sepulkralkunst erfüllte mutmaßlich die beiden Funktionen der Trauerhilfe und der Repräsentation. Die Meerwesen auf einem Grabmal könnten als Einzelwesen oder als Teil des Meerthiasos, als Sinnbild für ein glückliches Leben im Diesseits verstanden werden. Durch die Interaktion zwischen Nereiden und Seewesen entsteht eine erotisch verspielte Stimmung, die als freudiger und sorgloser Zustand zu Lebzeiten im Diesseits oder als Erwartung und Versinnbildlichung des Glücks im Jenseits interpretiert werden könnte. Zanker – Ewald 2004, 121–124. Zusätzlich können Meerwesen sowohl im Hinblick auf die Erwartung des Jenseits als auch als sichere Führer dorthin gedeutet werden. Andreae 1963, 133–162. Neben der Trauerhilfe kann auch ein zusätzlicher ästhetischer Wert nicht ausgeschlossen werden. Rumpf 1939, 130–131.

Meerwesen sind in der Sepulkralkunst der *civitas Treverorum* ein bekanntes Bildmotiv und werden auf verschiedenen Grabdenkmaltypen abgebildet. Beispielshalber zeigen zwei der vier Stufen auf der Nord- und Westseite des heute noch *in situ* in Igel bei Trier stehenden Grabpfeilers der Secundinier verschiedene Szenen mit Seewesen. Auf dem Fries der zweiten Stufe kämpfen Tritonen gegen unterschiedliche Meermischwesen, auf jenem der vierten Stufe reiten Eroten auf Delfinen[3]. Auch der Fries unterhalb des Giebels des sog. Iphigenienpfeilers stellt einen Triton dar, der sich gegen Meerwesen zur Wehr setzt[4].

Die Gattung der treverischen Grabaltäre umfasst insgesamt 21 Exemplare und bildet eine überschaubare Gruppe. Die Bruchstücke von 17 der 21 Altäre wurden in Neumagen-*Noviomagus Treverorum*, einer Ortschaft, die ca. 29 km Mosel aufwärts von Trier-*Augusta Treverorum* entfernt liegt, zusammen mit anderen Spolien innerhalb spätantiker Kastellmauern verbaut gefunden[5]. Fünf der 17 Stücke sind mit einem Meerwesendekor versehen[6].

Nach Wilhelm von Massow, der im Jahr 1932 als Erster die Neumagener Grabdenkmäler publizierte, kam die Gattung des Grabaltars um 120 n. Chr. auf. Als früheste Beispiele führt er die sog. Altäre 1, 3 und 455 an und begründet dies mit stilistischen Argumenten sowie mit dem Material aus Kalkstein[7]. Als jüngstes Exemplar nennt von Massow eine von ihm um 235 n. Chr. datierte Altarcorona mit Büsten in den Voluten und einem Okeanoshaupt in der Mitte[8].

Vier der fünf Grabaltäre mit Meerwesendekor sind laut Bernhard Numrich, der im Jahr 1997 die Chronologie einzelner Grabmäler aus der *civitas Treverorum* in typologisch-architektonischer sowie ornamentaler Hinsicht neu bewertete, zeitlich zwischen ca. 160 und 185 n. Chr. anzusetzen[9].

## TREVERISCHE GRABALTÄRE MIT MEERWESENDEKOR

Von den fünf Grabaltären sind die Reste von drei Altarkörpern und zwei Bekrönungen erhalten geblieben. Sie bestehen allesamt aus lokalem Sandstein und waren ursprünglich aus mehreren Blöcken zusammengesetzt. Die drei Altarkörper sind oben mit einem umlaufenden, gerahmten Reliefband dekoriert. Die Fragmente erlauben es zudem, oberhalb der Friese ein umlaufendes Blattgesims und bei einem Altar zusätzlich dazu ein Wickelband zu rekonstruieren. Über das Erscheinungsbild der restlichen Altarkörperflächen kann aufgrund des bruchstückhaften Erhaltungszustandes keine Aussage getroffen werden. Gleichwohl ist für die jeweiligen Frontseiten ein eventuell vegetabil gerahmtes Inschriftenfeld, ähnlich wie beim ebenfalls in Neumagen-*Noviomagus Treverorum* entdeckten Grabaltar des Kaufmanns P. Capitonius anzunehmen[10].

Die Bekrönungen sind jeweils rechteckige Blöcke, deren Volutenausläufer sowohl auf der Vorder- als auch auf der Rückseite ausgeschmückt sind. Insofern vorhanden weisen die Seiten der Volutenpolster eine Verzierung mit einem Schuppenmuster und Wickelbändern auf. In Kombination mit den umlaufenden Relieffriesen an den oberen Altarkörpern spricht dies dafür, dass die Stücke in ihrem ursprünglichen Aufstellungskontext für Rundansicht konzipiert wurden.

---

[3] Klöckner 2020, 73–76 Abb. 1–2.

[4] von Massow 1932, 57–58 Taf. 8.

[5] Die Frage, ob die Altäre ursprünglich vor dem Moselvicus oder vor den Toren Triers standen, kann in diesem Zusammenhang nicht geklärt werden. Zum möglichen Aufstellungsort der Neumagener Grabdenkmäler s. zuletzt Henrich 2016, 325–343.

[6] von Massow 1932.

[7] von Massow verweist auf die Beobachtungen Felix Hettners, dass die Neumagener Grabdenkmäler vor der Mitte des 2. Jhs. n. Chr. aus gelblich grauem Jurakalk und danach aus hellgrauem Sandstein hergestellt wurden. von Massow 1932, 280–285.

[8] von Massow 1932, 120–121 Nr. 171. 285 Taf. 20 (Rheinisches Landesmuseum Trier Inv. 1619).

[9] Der sog. kleine Tritonenaltar (Altar 167), die Altäre 168a und b sowie der sog. monumentale Altar (Altar 169). Numrich 1997, 133.

[10] von Massow 1932, 39–41 Nr. 2 Abb. 20–21 Taf. 2–3 (Rheinisches Landesmuseum Trier Inv. 114; 10 891; 772).

1 Teilrekonstruierter Fries und Bekrönung der Rückseite des sog. kleinen Tritonenaltars, RLM Trier Inv. 10 030, 831 (Foto Th. Zühmer)

Die Überreste der Altäre sind heute im Rheinischen Landesmuseum Trier ausgestellt. Die verlorenen Teile der Bildfriese und Altarcoronae wurden im Rahmen von Restaurationsarbeiten plastisch ergänzt. Die dabei rekonstruierten Friesteile basieren inhaltlich und kompositorisch auf den erhaltenen Reliefs.

Im Folgenden sollen die fünf in den Kastellmauern zutage gekommenen Grabaltäre kurz beschrieben werden.

Auf dem großflächig erhaltenen Relieffries an der Rückseite des um 160 n. Chr. datierten sog. kleinen Tritonenaltars[11] wird in antithetischer Zusammensetzung ein nach rechts blickender, bartloser Triton gezeigt, der zwei ihn rahmende Meerlöwen an einem Halfterband führt. Von der rückwärtigen Altarcorona sind die mit Medusenhäuptern geschmückten Volutenausläufer sowie Fische in den Zwickeln gesichert. Zudem ist im Zentrum ein von Fischen gerahmtes Okeanoshaupt innerhalb eines Dreiecks zu erkennen (Abb. 1). Das Friesband der ebenfalls größtenteils gesicherten rechten Nebenseite stellt erneut eine antithetische Anordnung dar. Es wird ein Triton abgebildet, der sich nach links blickend mit einer Muschel und einem erhobenen Mantel gegen von beiden Seiten heranschwimmende Delfine wehrt (Abb. 2). Die Vorderseite gibt einen bartlosen Meerkentauren mit ausgestreckten Armen wieder, unter dessen Fischschwanz eine Muschel liegt. Anhand der Ergänzung ergibt sich ein antithetisches Meerkentaurenpaar mit einer geöffneten Muschel im Zentrum.

Über dem Reliefband haben sich die Reste eines umlaufenden Blattgesimses erhalten. Die Bekrönung wird analog zur besser erhaltenen Rückseite rekonstruiert, also mit Gorgonenhäuptern in den Stirnseiten der Voluten, Fischen in den Zwickeln und einem von einem Dreieck eingefassten Okeanoshaupt (Abb. 1. 2 oben). Von der linken Nebenseite hat sich lediglich ein nach rechts schwimmender Meerpanther erhalten. Als Gegenstück zur gegenüberliegenden Nebenseite werden hier ein antithetischer Meerpanther und im Zentrum ein sich zur Wehr setzender Triton beigefügt. Beide Seiten der Volutenbekrönung sind mit Schuppenmuster und Wickelbändern in der Mitte geschmückt.

Von der Frontseite des zeitlich ebenfalls um 160 n. Chr. eingeordneten sog. Altars 168 haben sich lediglich die Schwanzspitze eines Meerkentauren und ein aufwärts schwimmender Delfin erhalten. Wieder werden hier ein Delfin und zwei Meerkentauren, die eine Muschel halten, zu einer antithetischen Komposition ergänzt.

Der Schmuck der Altarcorona setzt sich aus Medusenhäuptern in den Stirnseiten der Voluten und in den Zwickeln aus Fischen und Trompetenschnecken zusammen. Komplettiert wird die

---

[11] Maße ohne Gesims: H 1,20–1,50 (rekonstruiert) × B 1,79 × T 1,20 m. von Massow 1932, 112 Nr. 167 Abb. 61–65 Taf. 19 (Rheinisches Landesmusuem Trier Inv. 10 044; 10 030; 831); Numrich 1997, 133.

2   Teilrekonstruierter Fries und Bekrönung der rechten Nebenseite des sog. kleinen Tritonenaltars, RLM Trier Inv. 10 044, 10 030 (Foto Th. Zühmer)

3   Teilrekonstruierter Fries und Bekrönung der rechten Nebenseite des sog. Altars 168, RLM Trier Inv. 10 012 (Foto Th. Zühmer)

4   Fries der teilrekonstruierten Vorderseite des sog. monumentalen Altars, RLM Trier Inv. 778 (Foto Th. Zühmer)

Verzierung von einem durch ein Dreieck eingefassten Okeanoshaupt[12]. Auf der fast vollständig erhaltenen rechten Nebenseite reitet ein Silen mit einem Kranz in seiner Linken und einem Blütenkranz im Haar auf einem Meeresel. Er hebt den rechten Arm und hält zwei Finger hoch. Der Silen folgt einer auf einem Seepanther sitzenden Nereide, die links einen Thyrsosstab schultert und ebenfalls den rechten Arm hebt sowie zwei Finger hochhält. Hierbei ist die Bildkomposition nicht als antithetische, sondern als fortlaufende Szene wiedergegeben[13] (Abb. 3). Das Friesband der Grabaltarrückseite gibt auf der linken Seite einen bartlosen und auf der rechten Seite einen bärtigen Triton wieder, die jeweils ein Ruder schultern und zu einem Seestier blicken, den sie an einem Halfterband führen. In diesem Fall ist erneut kein antithetisches Arrangement gegeben, sondern die Gruppe wird gespiegelt abgebildet.

Über dem Relieffries haben sich Reste eines umlaufenden Blattgesimses und eines Wickelbandes erhalten. Oberhalb des Wickelbandes schließt die identisch zur Vorderseite ausgestaltete Altarcorona an.

Der Fries der linke Nebenseite hat anscheinend die gleiche Bildkomposition wie sein gegenüberliegendes Pendant wiedergegeben. Es hat sich ein in allen Einzelheiten korrespondierender Oberkörper eines Silens, der hier anstatt auf einem Meeresel auf einem Hippocampus reitet, sowie der Fischschwanz eines voraus schwimmenden Wesens erhalten. Dies lässt vermuten, dass hier ebenfalls ein Zug von Silen und Nereide als fortlaufende Darstellung abgebildet war. Die Voluten des Altars sind, ebenso wie bei dem weiter oben besprochenen sog. kleinen Tritonenaltar, seitlich mit einem Schuppenmuster und einem Wickelband in der Mitte dekoriert[14].

Von der Vorderseite des um 185 n. Chr. datierten sog. monumentalen Altars[15] haben sich lediglich der Schwanz eines nach rechts schwimmendem Meerwesens und ein nach rechts blickender bärtiger Triton mit ausgestreckten Armen sowie die Reste der von ihm gehaltenen Muschel erhalten. Ergänzt werden eine Muschel und in antithetischer Komposition ein bärtiger Triton sowie zwei Meerwesen, genauer gesagt Hippocampi (Abb. 4). Der Fries der linken Nebenseite zeigt im Zentrum den Vorderlauf eines Tieres und rechts davon eine Nereide. Die Meernymphe reitet auf einem Meereber und hält mit ihrer linken Hand einen Thyrsosstab. Eine leichte Dynamik verleiht der Szene ein Eros, der den Meereber an einem Halfterband führt. Basierend auf der rechten Nebenseite des sog. Altars 168 (Abb. 3) wird an dieser Stelle ein auf einem Meerwesen sitzender und zwei Finger hebender Silen mit Kranz in der Hand ergänzt. Im Unterschied zur Vorderseite handelt es sich hierbei um eine fortlaufende Szene und um keine antithetische Komposition. Auf der vollständig vorhandenen, aber stark beschädigten Rückseite setzt sich ein Triton mit einer Keule, ein anderer mit einer Muschel gegen jeweils von rechts heranschwimmende Meerhunde zur Wehr. Getrennt werden die beiden Gruppen durch einen Delfin in der Mitte. Die Darstellungsweise der beiden Kampfgruppen ist in diesem Fall weder in antithetischer noch in fortlaufender, sondern in gereihter Anordnung wiedergegeben. Die rechte Nebenseite bildet in der Mitte einen bartlosen Triton ab, der sich mit einer Keule in der Rechten und dem Mantel in der Linken gegen einen

---

[12] Die heute im Museum aufsitzende, aus zwei Quadern bestehende (Maße H 0,48 × B 0,91 × T 1,35 m und H 0,47 × B 1,07 × T 1,335 m) Bekrönung 168a wurde gemeinsam mit einem der beiden Blöcke des Altarkörpers 168 gefunden. Eine Zugehörigkeit erscheint aufgrund der Maße naheliegend. Allerdings wurde unweit des Blocks ebenfalls ein Fragment einer in allen Einzelheiten übereinstimmenden Altarcorona dokumentiert (168b), auf die weiter unten eingegangen werden soll. von Massow 1932, 112–113 Nr. 168a Abb. 66–68 Taf. 20–21 (Rheinisches Landesmuseum Trier Inv. 769).

[13] von Massow interpretiert die erhobenen Finger bei Silen- und Nereidendarstellungen als Morra-Spiel, bei dem das Gegenüber erraten muss, wie viele Finger der Mitspieler hochhält. von Massow 1932, 115.

[14] Maße mit Gesims: H 1,50–1,80 (rekonstruiert) × B 1,94 × T 1,34 m. von Massow 1932, 114–117 Nr. 168c Abb. 66–68 Taf. 19–20 (Rheinisches Landesmuseum Trier Inv. 835; 10 012; 26; 28; 58; 158); Numrich 1997, 133; Scholz 2012, 250 Anm. 855.

[15] Maße ohne Gesims: H 2,50 (rekonstruiert) × B 2,98 × T 2,30 m. von Massow 1932, 117–120 Nr. 169 Abb. 69–70 Taf. 21 (Rheinisches Landesmuseum Trier Inv. 777; 832; 833; 778; 11 240; 30; 33); Numrich 1997, 133; Scholz 2012, 250 Anm. 855.

von rechts heranschwimmenden Meerhund mit Flossengurt wehrt. Ergänzt wird ein antithetischer Meerhund mit Flossengurt.

Anhand der oberhalb des Frieses der rechten Nebenseite erhaltenen Reste kann zudem ein umlaufendes Blattgesims rekonstruiert werden. Oberhalb des Gesimses wird zusätzlich ein Wickelband nachgestaltet. Die Altarcorona ist heute verloren.

Eine der beiden zutage gekommenen Bekrönungen[16] schließt optisch, stilistisch und chronologisch an die Altarcoronae des sog. kleinen Tritonenaltars und des Altars 168 an (Abb. 1. 2. 3 oben). Entsprechend wird sie mit Medusenhäuptern in den schuppenbedeckten Volutenausläufern und Fischen in den Zwickeln neben einem Dreieck mit Okeanoshaupt rekonstruiert.

Die zweite Altarcorona[17] zeigt in der Mitte ein Okeanoshaupt, aus dessen Bart links und rechts je ein Delfin heraus schwimmt. In den Stirnseiten der Voluten sind männliche Büsten mit einer von einem Gewand bedeckten Schulter abgebildet, die jeweils einen Stab mit Knotenabsätzen schräg vor sich halten. Die Rück- und Nebenseiten der Bekrönung sind heute verloren. Wilhelm von Massow datiert das Stück um 235 n. Chr.

Zusammenfassend bleibt festzuhalten, dass die umlaufenden Relieffriese an den Altarkörpern ausnahmslos in querrechteckigem Format ausgestaltet sind. Ob die treverischen Grabaltäre mit Meerwesendekor in Gänze querrechteckige Ausmaße aufwiesen, kann aufgrund des fragmentarischen Fundzustandes nicht abschließend geklärt werden, erscheint jedoch aufgrund des starken Größengefälles zwischen Breite und Tiefe schlüssig.

Die auf Basis des Formats der dokumentierten Bruchstücke rekonstruierten Altarhöhen betragen ca. 1,5–2,5 m, was nicht dafürspricht, dass auf den Grabaltären einst Opferhandlungen stattfanden.

Wie die rau belassenen Oberflächen und Klammerlöcher auf den schuppenbedeckten Voluten einzelner Bekrönungen zeigen, schloss sich ursprünglich noch eine Abdeckplatte oder ein aufgehender oberer Abschluss von unbekannter Ausgestaltung an[18]. Auch dies spricht dagegen, dass auf den Altären Opfergaben abgelegt oder Brandopfer abgehalten wurden.

Trotz der bruchstückhaften Überlieferung der Relieffriese lassen sich Muster hinsichtlich der Bildthematik und des Kompositionsarrangements erkennen. So setzt sich der Reliefschmuck aller Altarkörper aus drei Themen- und Kompositionsbestandteilen zusammen:

1. Aus Meerwesen mit gehaltenem Mittelmotiv. Kompositionell antithetisch.
2. Tritonen, die sich gegen Meerwesen wehren oder diese bändigen. Kompositionell sowohl antithetisch als auch gereiht oder gespiegelt.
3. Ausschnitte aus dem Meerthiasos, konkret eine auf Meerwesen reitende Nereide, die von einem Silen und in einem Fall zusätzlich von einem Eros begleitet wird. Kompositionell als fortlaufendes Bildfeld konzipiert.

Die Bekrönungen zeigen primär einen von einem Dreieck eingefassten und von Fischen oder Delfinen, in einem Fall auch zusätzlich von Trompetenschnecken gerahmten Okeanoskopf. Me-

---

[16] Erhaltene Maße: H 0,47 × B 1,05 × T 0,18 m. Das Bruchstück 168b kam gemeinsam mit einem Friesblöcken des Altars 168 und der in allen Einzelheiten übereinstimmenden und in den Maßen nur unwesentlich kleineren Bekrönung 168a zutage. Welcher der beiden oberen Abschlüsse einst den Altar 168 zierte, kann nicht abschließend beantwortet werden. von Massow 1932, 113–114 Nr. 168b Taf. 19 (Rheinisches Landesmuseum Trier Inv. 771).

[17] Zwei Quader mit den erhaltenen Maßen H 0,33 × B 1,21 × T 0,32 m bzw. H 0,28 × B 1,07 × 0,32 m. von Massow gibt an, dass der Altarcorona wahrscheinlich zwei Steinquader mit einem Stieropfer zuzuordnen sind. von Massow 1932, 120–121 Nr. 171 Taf. 20 (Rheinisches Landesmuseum Trier Inv. 1619; 214–215). Das Bruchstück wird heute teilrekonstruiert im RLM Trier auf dem sog. monumentalen Altar (Altar 169) aufsitzend präsentiert.

[18] von Massow 1932, 117 Abb. 66. Schuppenbedeckte Pyramiden sind als aufgehende Bekrönungen für eine Vielzahl treverischer Grabdenkmäler belegt. Den oberen Abschluss bildet hierbei zumeist ein Pinienzapfen, der sich einzeln, aber auch, wie beim Pfeilergrabmal der Secundinier in Igel, in Kombination mit der Darstellung einer mythologischen Szene oder Ähnlichem präsentieren kann. Dass auch Grabaltäre mit einer schuppenbedeckten Pyramide abschlossen, erscheint aufgrund der Verbreitungsdichte von Pyramidenaufsätzen im Sepulkralbereich der *civitas Treverorum* naheliegend. Auch die rau belassenen Oberflächen, Wolfslöcher und schuppenbedeckten Voluten einiger Altäre sind starke Indizien für eine derartig ausgestaltete Altarcorona.

dusenhäupter und andere Köpfe füllen die seitlich abschließenden Voluten. Die Ober- und Nebenseiten sind mit Schuppenmuster und Wickelbändern verziert.

## STADTRÖMISCHE UND OBERITALISCHE GRABALTÄRE MIT MEERWESENDEKOR

Nach dem Blick auf die Grabaltäre mit Meerwesendekor aus der *civitas Treverorum* sollen diese im Folgenden exemplarischen Vergleichsstücken aus Rom und Oberitalien gegenübergestellt werden.

Um den Blickwinkel auf die Nachbarprovinzen der *Gallia Belgica* zu erweitern, wurden im Zuge der Recherche auch Grabaltäre aus den restlichen gallischen und den Donauprovinzen systematisch gesichtet; hierdurch ergaben sich jedoch keine weiterführenden Erkenntnisse. Parallelen zum Treverergebiet sind bei drei Bekrönungen und zwei Altarkörpern aus der benachbarten Provinz *Germania superior* zu erkennen[19]. Um den Rahmen dieses Textes nicht zu sprengen, soll auf diese im Folgenden nur am Rande eingegangen werden.

Der Vergleich mit Rom wird angestellt, da der Reichshauptstadt auch in puncto Grabdenkmäler oftmals ohne zu hinterfragen eine Vorbildfunktion für die Provinzen zugesprochen wird. Oberitalien kam laut Hanns Gabelmann bei der Genese der Grabmäler in den Nordwestprovinzen eine wichtige Vermittlerrolle zu[20]. Durch den Vergleich soll systematisch überprüft werden, ob sich eine stadtrömische Vorbildfunktion oder eine oberitalische Vermittlerrolle auch bei der Gruppe der treverischen Grabaltäre mit Meerwesendekor erkennen lässt.

Aus Rom sind insgesamt knapp 1000 Grabaltäre überliefert. Die Gattung kam in spätaugusteischer Zeit auf. Nach einem Höhepunkt in flavischer Zeit ging die Produktion stark zurück. Für das 2., 3. und 4. Jahrhundert n. Chr. sind kaum noch Altäre belegt[21]. Der erste Grabaltar mit Meerwesendekor wurde in tiberischer Zeit aufgestellt. Der Großteil der insgesamt 36 Stücke (32 Altarkörper, 4 Altarbekrönungen) ist flavisch zu datieren. Danach ging die Anzahl stark zurück, und die beiden letzten bekannten Beispiele wurden Ende des 2. Jahrhunderts n. Chr. aufgestellt[22].

Für Oberitalien sind *in toto* 297 Grabaltäre dokumentiert[23]. Die frühsten Exemplare in den dortigen Nekropolen datieren spättiberisch. Im Unterschied zu Rom ist für die Gattung in Oberitalien lediglich eine Laufzeit bis in antoninische Zeit nachweisbar. Die insgesamt neun mit Meerwesen

---

[19] Die drei zwischen der 2. Hälfte des 2. und Anfang des 3. Jhs. n. Chr. datierten Altarbekrönungen zeigen im Zentrum schwimmende Meerwesen, die von *pulvini* mit Medusenhäuptern in den Stirnseiten gerahmt werden. Das auf den Altarcoronae des Trevererlandes omnipräsente Okeanoshaupt fehlt hier. Ditsch 2011, 326–329. 354–355. Zwei Fragmente eines antoninisch datierten und mit H 3,40 × B 1,90 m rekonstruierten Altarkörpers zeigen auf einer Langseite ein mit Ranken und Blattrosetten gerahmtes Bildfeld. Vom Bildfeld ist lediglich der Fischleib eines Tritons dokumentiert, der nach links schwimmt. Davor sind die Köpfe von zwei schräg nach unten schwimmenden Fischen zu erkennen. Von der gegenüberliegenden Langseite hat sich lediglich ein Bruchstück der Rankenrahmung erhalten. Willer 2005, 205 Nr. 215 Taf. 39, 1–2. Ein Fragment mit den erhaltenen Maßen von H 0,84 × B 1,20 × T 0,73 m, das zeitlich dem 3. Viertel des 2. Jhs. n. Chr. zugehörig ist, zeigt auf einer Langseite einen Triton, der ein nach rechts fortschwimmendes Meerwesen in die Flucht schlägt. Eine Schmalseite gibt die Rückansicht eines Tritons wieder, der mit seiner Rechten die Zügel eines Meerwesens hält und um dessen linken Arm ein Mantel flattert. Willer 2005, 125 Nr. 36 Taf. 2, 3; 3, 1. Wehrhafte Tritonen, die mit Seewesen kämpfen, werden somit ebenfalls auf Grabaltären in der *Germania superior* wiedergegeben. Die vermehrt im Treverergebiet auftretende Darstellung von auf Seewesen reitenden Nereiden, die von einem Silen oder auch Eros begleitet werden, fehlt hier hingegen gänzlich.

[20] Laut Gabelmann knüpfen die Grabbauten des 1. Jhs. n. Chr. aus den Nordwestprovinzen an oberitalische Traditionen an. Gabelmann 1987, 291–294.

[21] Boschung 1987 fasst die stadtrömischen Grabaltäre zusammen.

[22] Boschung 1987, 110 Nr. 888. 889 Taf. 48.

[23] Dexheimer 1998. Als weitere Quelle wurde bei der Recherche der 1972 publizierte »Museo archeologico nazionale di Aquileia: catalogo delle sculture romane« von V. Santa Maria Scrinari genutzt.

5   Vorderseite eines stadtrömischen Grabaltars, Nuovo Museo Gregoriano Profano Lapidario Vaticano Inv. 9305 (Vatikanische Museen)

verzierten Altäre (sechs Altarkörper und drei Bekrönungen[24]) datieren zwischen dem dritten Viertel des 1. und dem zweiten Viertel des 2. Jahrhunderts n. Chr.[25].

Bei dem Vergleich mit den chronologischen Eckdaten des Trevererlandes zeigen sich signifikante Unterschiede. Hier kamen Grabaltäre deutlich später auf, nämlich erst um 120 n. Chr. Zu dieser Zeit war der Produktionshöhepunkt in Stadtrom und Oberitalien überschritten und die Gattung lief dort bereits aus. Die treverischen Grabaltäre mit Meerwesendekor sind für etwa zwei Generationen belegt, zwischen ca. 160–235 n. Chr. Sie setzten also erst kurz nach dem spätesten Vergleichsexemplar aus Oberitalien ein und liefen wenige Jahrzehnte länger als die letzten Beispiele aus Rom. Die Analyse bestätigt neben chronologischen Differenzen ebenfalls, dass Meerwesendekor auf Grabaltären der *civitas Treverorum* eine größere Rolle spielt als in den beiden Vergleichsregionen. Während knapp 24 % der Altäre aus dem Treverland eine Verzierung mit Meerwesen aufweisen, sind es in Oberitalien lediglich 3 %[26], in Stadtrom sogar nur ca. 0,4 %.

Die folgenden typologischen und ikonografischen Vergleiche aus Stadtrom und Oberitalien sind repräsentativ für ihre Gruppe und zeigen die jeweils typische Verwendung von Meerwesendekor in dieser Gattung.

Die Vorderseite eines neronisch datierten und mit nachantiker Inschrift versehenen Altars[27] zeigt oberhalb des Sockels als Einzelszene eine Nereide und zwei Eroten, die auf einem Hippocampus reiten. Gerahmt wird die Darstellung von Sphingen. Den Dekor der Vorderseite komplettieren oberhalb der Meerwesen ein von Schwänen eingefasstes Medusenhaupt und eine Girlande, die von Widderköpfen gehalten wird. Der Giebelschmuck setzt sich aus Muscheln und Eroten in den Stirnseiten sowie im Zentrum aus einem von Schilden gerahmten Panzer zusammen (Abb. 5). Die linke Nebenseite zeigt in der oberen Bildzone zwei streitende Vögel und unterhalb hiervon die Lupa Romana. Rechts wird ein zwei Vögel fütternder Knabe sowie im unteren Bereich die Hindin mit Telephos abgebildet. Der Schmuck der Rückseite setzt sich aus zwei Reihern sowie einem Lorbeerbaum mit Vögeln zusammen.

Auf der Vorderseite des spätflavisch datierten Grabaltars für A. Albius Graptus[28] halten zwei antithetische Tritonen eine Muschel, in der die Göttin Venus unbekleidet zwischen zwei Eroten

---

[24]   Zusätzlich sind für Oberitalien 14 pyramidale Dächer von Grabaltären mit Meerwesendekor (13 Exemplare mit Delfinen, ein Stück mit einem Triton verziert) dokumentiert. Scrinari 1972, 135–140 Nr. 387. 392–401. 403. 407; Dexheimer 1998, 100 Kat. 59. Für die treverischen Grabaltäre sind pyramidenförmige Abschlüsse nur vermutet, aber archäologisch nicht nachgewiesen. Aus diesem Grund werden die 14 oberitalischen Dächer im Folgenden ausgeklammert.

[25]   Dexheimer 1998, 80. 89. 95–100.

[26]   Nicht inbegriffen sind die 14 pyramidalen Dächer.

[27]   Erhaltene Maße: H 1,17 × B 0,74 × T 0,49 m. Boschung 1987, 100 Nr. 704 Taf. 26 (Vatikan, Vatikanische Museen, Nuovo Museo Gregoriano Profano Lapidario Inv. 9305).

[28]   Erhaltene Maße: H 0,71 × B 0,42 × T 0,29 m. Boschung 1987, 103 Nr. 763 Taf. 31 (Rom, Musei Capitolini, Museo Nuovo Inv. 2101).

6   Vorderseite des Grabaltars für A. Albius Graptus, Musei Capitolini Rom Inv. 2101 (DAI Rom)

7   Grabaltar des L. Cantius Fructus, Museo Archeologico Aquileia Inv. 52823 (Gab. Fot. Naz., E 62657)

kauert und nach rechts blickt. Oberhalb hiervon stehen zwei ebenfalls antithetisch angeordnete Eroten jeweils auf einem Delfin und halten ein Inschriftenfeld. Der obere Abschluss ist als Rundgiebel konzipiert und mit Blüten in den Volutenausläufern und einem Hasen, der aus einem Fruchtkorb frisst, dekoriert (Abb. 6). Beide Nebenseiten geben je einen Greif wieder, der auf einer Basis sitzt, an deren hinteren Kanten brennende Fackeln zu erkennen sind. Die Rückseite weist keinen Dekor auf.

Als oberitalisches Beispiel soll der im dritten Viertel des 1. Jahrhunderts n. Chr. erschaffene Grabaltar des L. Cantius Fructus[29] vorgebracht werden. Die Vorderseite wird gänzlich von einem gerahmten Inschriftenfeld eingenommen. Beide Nebenseiten sind mit ungerahmten Reliefbildfeldern versehen. Sie zeigen je als Einzelszene einen Eros, der auf einem Ketos reitet und diesen mittels Zügeln unter Kontrolle hält. Die Reliefausarbeitungen unterhalb des Meerungeheuers deuten Wellen an und verorten die Szene auf ein Gewässer (Abb. 7). Die Rückseite weist keinen Schmuck auf. Der obere Abschluss des Altars ist heute verloren.

## DIE PRODUKTIONSZENTREN IM VERGLEICH

Ein Blick auf Grabaltäre mit Meerwesendekor aus Rom und Oberitalien offenbart augenscheinliche Divergenzen in der Typologie, der Ikonografie und der Verwendung des Dekors. Einer dieser offenkundigen Unterschiede ist in puncto Höhe zu attestieren. Die Höhen der Altäre aus dem Treverergebiet werden zwischen 1,5 und 2,5 m rekonstruiert. Die Vergleichsstücke aus Rom sind nachweislich überwiegend 1 m, die aus Oberitalien mehrheitlich zwischen ca. 1 und 1,5 m hoch[30].

---

[29]   Erh. Maße: H 1,16 × B 0,67 × T 0,70 m. Dexheimer 1998, 98–99 Kat. 56 (Aquileia, Museo Archeologico Inv. 52823).

[30]   In beiden Untersuchungsgebieten fallen einzelne Grabaltäre hinsichtlich größerer Ausmaße auf. In Rom ist der hadrianisch datierte Altar des T. Statilius Aper mit 1,89 m bedeutend höher als die restlichen Stücke. Boschung

Ablageflächen für Opfergaben oder andere Vorrichtungen, welche die Anbringung einer Opferschale implizieren, sind bei keinem stadtrömischen Vergleichsstück dokumentiert[31]. Gleiches gilt für Oberitalien. Überdies zeugen die hier vermehrt anzutreffenden pyramidalen Abschlüsse davon, dass Grabaltäre auch in dieser Region keine Nebenfunktion als Opferfläche hatten.

Der Grabaltar wurde somit in den drei Untersuchungsgebieten als reiner Marker oder Inschriftenträger genutzt[32] und nicht mit der Intention geschaffen, zusätzlich als Ablageort für Opfergaben zu fungieren.

So sehr die Primärfunktionen der Altäre übereinstimmen, umso differenzierter stellt es sich bei den Formaten der Bildfelder dar. Die Friesbänder der treverischen Stücke zeichnen sich gänzlich durch querrechteckige, die stadtrömischen und oberitalischen Bildfelder indes durch hochrechteckige Formate aus. Dieser Umstand wird, durch den längs umlaufenden Bildfries bei den Beispielen aus der *civitas Treverorum* noch unterstrichen.

Auch zeigen die Beispiele aus Rom und Oberitalien exemplarisch wesentliche Unterschiede in Bezug auf Stellenwert und Positionierung des Meerwesendekors.

Im Treverergebiet sind Seewesen jeweils in umlaufenden Relieffriesen, also auf allen vier Seiten präsent[33]. In Stadtrom sind sie ausschließlich kleinformatig und gemeinsam mit anderen Dekorationselementen wie Girlanden, Medusenköpfen oder Ecksphingen dargestellt und finden sich zumeist lediglich auf einer Seite wieder. Infolgedessen finden Meerwesen auf stadtrömischen Grabaltären nicht als alleiniges und somit exponiertes Verzierungselement, sondern lediglich als Teil von unterschiedlichen Schmuckkomponenten Verwendung.

In Oberitalien werden Seewesen zwar großformatig und als Teil einer Einzelszene ohne weiteren Schmuck wiedergegeben, sind jedoch lediglich auf den Nebenseiten vorzufinden. Der Hauptfokus lag in diesem geografischen Raum stets auf einem großflächigen Inschriftenfeld, das die Altarvorderseite ziert (Abb. 7).

In Stadtrom sind Meerwesen auf den Frontseiten von vier[34], in Oberitalien auf drei Bekrönungen[35] abgebildet. Sie alle sitzen auf Altarkörpern auf, welche keinen Meerwesendekor aufweisen. Bei der Positionierungsanalyse des Dekors fällt auf, dass die Grabaltäre Roms und Oberitaliens Seewesen entweder auf dem Körper oder den rechteckigen Blöcken unterhalb eines separat gearbeiteten oberen Abschlusses abbilden, während die Vergleichsstücke der *civitas Treverorum* simultan Verzierungen auf dem Körper und der Altarcorona aufweisen. Auch sind vier der fünf

---

1987, 87 Nr. 326 Taf. 9 (Rom, Musei Capitolini Inv. 209). In Oberitalien setzen sich drei zwischen dem 3. Viertel des 1. Jhs. n. Chr. und trajanischer Zeit datierte Altäre mit Höhen von 2,39 und 2,74 sowie 8 m deutlich vom Rest ab. Dexheimer 1998, 90–91 Kat. 40; 95–96 Kat. 50; 89–90 Kat. 39.

[31] Generell sind Vorrichtungen für Opfergaben auf stadtrömischen Grabaltären sehr unüblich.

[32] In Rom und Oberitalien vereinzelt zusätzlich als Aufbewahrungsort für Urnen.

[33] Da keine Klarheit über die restliche Ausgestaltung der Altarkörper herrscht, muss offenbleiben, ob sich die Reliefs und somit die Seewesen dekorativ von weiteren Verzierungen abhoben.

[34] Spätflavischer Rundgiebel mit zwei Ketoi, die eine Muschel mit zwei Porträtbüsten rahmen. Boschung 1987, 116 Nr. 994 Taf. 61 (Vatikan, Vatikanische Museen Belvedere Inv. 1042). – Hadrianischer Rundgiebel mit zwei Delfinen zwischen einer Muschel, in der ein Porträt wiedergegeben wird. Boschung 1987, 88 Nr. 341 (Florenz, Uffizien Inv. 947). – Hadrianischer Rundgiebel. In der Giebelmitte werden eine Muschel mit einer Frauenbüste und in den Zwickeln zwei Delfine dargestellt. Boschung 1987, 87 Nr. 326 Taf. 9 (Rom, Musei Capitolini Inv. 209). – Um 130–160 n. Chr. datierter Rundgiebel mit einem vorgeblendeten Seegreif in der Mitte. Boschung 1987, 89 Nr. 390 Taf. 11 (Rom, Museo Nazionale Inv. 15 585).

[35] Bekrönung aus dem Ende 1./Anfang des 2. Jhs. n. Chr. mit Medusenköpfen in den Stirnseiten. Dazwischen ein von zwei Vögeln gerahmtes Deckelgefäß und Delfine in den Zwickeln. Dexheimer 1998, 95–96 Kat. 50 (Aquileia, Museo Archeologico Inv. 1072). – Trajanisch datierter rechteckiger Block mit *pulvini* als seitliche Begrenzung, unter denen je eine Opferschale flankiert von Bukranien veranschaulicht wird. Unten: Kantharos zwischen zwei Greifen. Darüber Lorbeerzweig, dessen Enden die Zwickel des Giebels ausfüllen. In den Zwickeln zur Seite schwimmende Delfine. Dexheimer 1998, 90–91 Kat. 40 (Aquileia, Museo Archeologico Inv. 1049). – Rechteckiger Block, mit Blüten gefüllte *pulvini* als seitliche Begrenzung aus dem 2. Viertel des 2. Jhs. n. Chr. Auf der Focusschranke der Bekrönung sind zwei Delfine abgebildet. Dexheimer 1998, 80–81 Kat. 21 (Pola, Arheoloski Muzej Istre Inv. 475).

Bekrönungen auf Vorder- und Rückseite zugleich mit Seewesen ausgeschmückt, während sich der Dekor in Rom und Oberitalien ausschließlich auf die Vorderseite beschränkt.

Auf den Bekrönungen aller drei Untersuchungsgebiete dominieren Darstellungen von Delfinen. Das im Treverland vorherrschende Okeanoshaupt ist hingegen auf keiner Altarcorona eines stadtrömischen oder oberitalischen Grabaltars wiedergegeben.

Nicht nur in der Positionierungs-, sondern auch in der Bildkomposition sind essenzielle Unterschiede festzustellen.

In Rom werden Seewesen stets in heiterem Miteinander gezeigt. Ein häufiges Motiv sind auf Meerwesen reitende Nereiden, die von Eroten und Delfinen begleitet werden. Es herrscht eine gelöste Grundstimmung. Während die Tritonen auf dem stadtrömischen Exemplar die von Eroten umgebene Venus rahmen, sind sie im Treverergebiet primär in Verbindung mit Meerwesen zu sehen, gegen die sie sich unter Zuhilfenahme von unterschiedlichen Objekten zur Wehr setzen oder per Halfterband unter Kontrolle halten müssen. Es herrscht eine angespannte Stimmung.

In Oberitalien werden Meerwesen ebenfalls gebändigt, jedoch geschieht dies durch auf Meerwesen reitende und diese per Zügel unter Kontrolle haltende Eroten (Abb. 7) und nicht wie im Treverland durch Tritonen (Abb. 1. 2), wodurch eine heitere Atmosphäre geschaffen wird.

Neben Darstellungen heiteren Kontextes sind Bildelemente erotischer Konnotation, wie die auf Seewesen reitenden Nereiden sowohl in Rom als auch in der *civitas Treverorum* belegt.

Im Unterschied zu Rom werden die Nereiden im Treverergebiet von einem Silen begleitet und rufen beim Betrachter durch den geschulterten Thyrsosstab eindeutige Assoziationen mit der dionysischen Sphäre hervor (Abb. 4).

Ferner ist in puncto Kompositionsarrangement zu beobachten, dass stadtrömische Grabaltäre stets auf Meerwesen reitende Nereiden als Einzelszene veranschaulichen, während sie im Trevererland als Teil einer fortlaufenden Szene abgebildet werden. Die Nereiden werden in Rom von auf dem gleichen Meerwesen sitzenden Eroten begleitet (Abb. 5), während die Vergleichsstücke einen Zug aus auf separaten Seewesen sitzender Nereide und Silen zeigen (Abb. 4). Die antithetisch angeordneten Tritonen an den Ecken der Frontseite des Altars für A. Albius Graptus lassen hingegen eine kompositorische Parallele erkennen (Abb. 6). Die Singularität der Darstellung und die Tatsache, dass die meisten stadtrömischen Grabaltäre an den Ecken antithetisch angeordnete Wesen wie Sphingen, Greifen oder Victorien aufweisen, lassen eine direkte bildliche und kompositorische Beeinflussung auf das Treverergebiet unrealistisch erscheinen.

Gleiches gilt für die oberitalischen Altäre und die Abbildung von Eroten, die auf Meerwesen reiten. Freilich kommt dieses Motiv auch in der treverischen Sepulkralkunst zur Anwendung[36], als Dekor auf Grabaltären ist es allerdings nicht bezeugt.

Insgesamt bleibt festzuhalten, dass die treverischen Altäre mit Meerwesendekor markante Unterschiede zu Rom und Oberitalien aufweisen. Hinsichtlich der Ausformung, Komposition und Verwendung des Dekors hat anscheinend keine direkte Beeinflussung durch stadtrömische und oberitalische Grabaltäre stattgefunden. Motivische Bezüge zu stadtrömischen Monumenten lassen sich aber finden, wenn man eine andere Gattung in den Blick nimmt: die Sarkophage.

Um 110–120 n. Chr. fand in Rom ein sich rasch vollziehender Wechsel von der Brand- zur Körperbestattung statt[37]. Sarkophage mit Meerwesendekor erfreuen sich hier bereits Mitte des 2. Jahrhunderts n. Chr. einer großen Beliebtheit. In der *civitas Treverorum* war die Körperbestattung zu diesem Zeitpunkt zwar bekannt und wurde praktiziert, Sarkophage als Bestattungsart kamen hier jedoch erst ab etwa der zweiten Hälfte des 3. Jahrhunderts n. Chr. auf[38].

---

[36] Beispielsweise auf zwei Seiten der vierten Stufe des Grabpfeilers der Secundinier in Igel. Klöckner 2020, 74–75 Abb. 2.

[37] R. Neudecker – M. Lesky – H. G. Niemeyer – A. Oepen, Sarkophag, in: Der Neue Pauly, Herausgegeben von: H. Cancik – H. Schneider (Antike), M. Landfester (Rezeptions- und Wissenschaftsgeschichte), DOI: 10.1163/1574-9347_dnp_e1101550 (13.09.2022).

[38] Zum Beispiel ein ca. 270 n. Chr. datierter, reliefierter Sarkophag aus der sog. Albanagruft. Cüppers 1984, 209 Abb. 94–95 (Trier, *in situ* Albanagruft unter der Quirinuskapelle).

8   Fries der Vorderseite eines stadtrömischen Sarkophags mit Meerwesendekor, Museo dell'Opera del Duomo Siena, Inv. nicht angegeben (Zanker – Ewald 2004, 122–124 Abb. 103)

Betrachtet man die beiden unterschiedlichen Gattungen, so fallen dekorative und bildkompositorische Gemeinsamkeiten, aber auch offenkundige Unterschiede auf. Wie bei den treverischen Grabaltären befindet sich auch bei stadtrömischen Sarkophagen unterhalb der Bekrönung, genauer gesagt des Deckels, ein längs verlaufender Relieffries mit fortlaufenden Szenen. Jedoch läuft das Reliefband nicht ringsum, wie es bei den Altären der Fall ist, sondern beschränkt sich in der Regel ausschließlich auf die Frontseiten. Die Neben- und Rückseiten sind zumeist mit großflächigeren und nicht als Relief ausgearbeiteten Einzeldarstellungen verziert oder bleiben leer.

Nichtsdestotrotz lassen sich gestalterische Analogien im Bereich der Bekrönung erkennen. Zahlreiche stadtrömische Sarkophagdeckel sind mit schwimmendem Meeresgetier dekoriert[39], während vier der fünf treverischen Altäre zwar auch Fische oder Delfine, gleichwohl aber keine Meermischwesen in den Zwickeln zeigen.

Okeanoshäupter sind als Verzierungselement ebenfalls auf verschiedenen Sarkophagen der Reichshauptstadt vorzufinden. Vorrangig finden sie dekorativ im Zentrum des Sarkophagkörpers als Teil des Reliefschmucks Verwendung[40]. Darstellungen im Bereich des Deckels sind unüblich und werden, wenn überhaupt, dann auch im Zentrum des Deckels abgebildet, allerdings niemals von einem Dreieck eingefasst[41].

Der sog. Meerthiasos mit Bezügen zur dionysischen Sphäre ist ein in Stadtrom häufig auf Sarkophagen verbildlichtes Thema, so auch auf einem ins späte 2. Jahrhundert n. Chr. datierten Exemplar[42]. Das Mittelmotiv setzt sich aus antithetischen Nereiden zusammen, die eine Muschel mit dem Bildnis der Bestatteten präsentieren. Sie blicken jeweils zu einem bartlosen Meerkentauren, auf dessen Leib sie sitzen. Unterhalb der Muschel stehen drei Eroten. Das Mittelmotiv wird von weiteren Nereiden gerahmt, die auf bärtigen Meerkentauren und Meermischwesen reiten oder mit diesen in unterschiedlichen, ausschließlich heiteren und durch Umarmung erotisch konnotierten Interaktionen stehen (Abb. 8).

In der *civitas Treverorum* wird der Meerthiasos nicht in seiner ganzen Fülle, sondern lediglich als kleiner Ausschnitt in Form einer auf einem Meermischwesen reitenden, von einem Silen

---

[39] Beispielhaft soll an dieser Stelle ein um die Mitte des 2. Jhs. n. Chr. datierter Sarkophag angeführt werden. Neben Meerwesendekor auf dem Friesband des Körpers sind auf der Vorderseite des Deckels in antithetischer Komposition zwischen einem Inschriftenfeld ein auf Wasser schwimmender Meerlöwe, ein Meerhund sowie ein Hippocampus und ein Meerwidder abgebildet. Rumpf 1939, Taf. 45 (Rom, Palazzo Corsini Inv. 608).

[40] Okeanosmasken werden auf den Körpern stadtrömischer Sarkophage sowohl großflächig als Mittelmotiv und gerahmt von Meerwesen als auch am unteren Abschluss des Frieses als Beischmuck reproduziert. z. B. Rumpf 1939, 13 Kat. 36 Taf. 13 (Ostia, Museo Ostiense, Inv. nicht angegeben) und Zanker – Ewald 2004, 61 Abb. 231 (Rom, Palazzo di Conservatori, Inv. nicht angegeben).

[41] Exemplarisch hierfür zu nennen ist die Frontseite eines um 120–130 n. Chr. datierten Deckels, der mit einem von schwimmenden Meermischwesen und Delfinen gerahmten Okeanoshaupt versehen ist. Zanker – Ewald 2004, 248 Abb. 220 (Rom, Villa Albani Inv. 131).

[42] Zanker – Ewald 2004, 122–124 Abb. 103 (Siena, Museo dell'Opera del Duomo, Inv. nicht angegeben).

sowie in einem Fall zusätzlich von einem Eros begleiteten Nereide wiedergegeben (Abb. 3). Die Interaktion findet im Unterschied zu Rom nicht über körperliche Nähe oder Gesten wie einer Umarmung oder dem Anschmiegen statt, sondern die Funktion der Meerwesen beschränkt sich hier rein auf den Nutzen als Reittier. Erotische Konnotation besteht somit ausschließlich über nackte Nereiden und nicht über ihre Interaktionen mit anderen Meerwesen.

Ferner bleibt festzuhalten, dass antithetisch gestaltete Mittelmotive mit einer gehaltenen Muschel ebenfalls ein gängiges Bildelement auf stadtrömischen Sarkophagen mit Meerwesenfries darstellen. Gleichwohl werden sie stets in den Meerthiasos eingebettet und stellen nicht das alleinige Bildmotiv einer Seite dar.

Auf treverischen Grabaltären gängige Bildkompositionen, wie ein mit einer Nereide Morra spielender Silen und vor allem sich gegen Meerwesen zur Wehr setzende Tritonen finden sich auf keinem stadtrömischen Sarkophag wieder. Überhaupt sind keine anderen Motive von stadtrömischen Sarkophagen, etwa mythologische Szenen, auf Altären des Trevererlandes zu identifizieren[43].

Es geht also bei den Grabaltären in der *civitas Treverorum* nicht um eine 1:1-Angleichung an stadtrömische Vorbilder, gleich ob sie derselben oder wie bei Sarkophagen einer anderen Gattung angehören, sondern um die selektive Übernahme einzelner Bild- und Gestaltungselemente.

## ZUSAMMENFASSUNG

Die treverischen Grabaltäre mit Meerwesendekor wurden zwischen ca. 160 und 235 n. Chr. aufgestellt. Die Altarkörper sind mit einem oben umlaufenden Relieffries und die Altarcorona mit einem von Fischen und Delfinen, in einem Fall zusätzlich von Trompetenschnecken gerahmtem Okeanoshaupt geschmückt.

Bei dem Vergleich mit stadtrömischen und oberitalischen Grabaltären zeigt sich, dass die Beispiele aus dem Treverergebiet erstmals aufkamen, als die Gattung in Rom und Oberitalien bereits auslief. Außerdem bestehen fundamentale Unterschiede hinsichtlich des Formats sowie der Dekorausgestaltung. So weisen die Altäre beider Vergleichsgebiete ausschließlich hochrechteckige Ausmaße auf. Zwar kann durch den fragmentarischen Erhaltungszustand das Format der treverischen Grabaltäre nicht abschließend geklärt werden, das Größengefälle zwischen den Lang- und Schmalseiten spricht indes für querrechteckige Dimensionen.

Meerwesendekor findet sich in der *civitas Treverorum* auf allen vier Altarkörperseiten, bei ihren Pendants aus Rom und Oberitalien lediglich auf einer, maximal auf zwei Seiten wieder. Während die stadtrömischen und oberitalischen Vergleichsstücke, bis auf eine Ausnahme in Form von antithetisch angeordneten Tritonen, ausschließlich Einzeldarstellungen von Meerwesen oder auf Meerwesen reitende Protagonisten zeigen, sind die Reliefs der Altäre des Treverergebietes stets mit antithetisch angeordneten, gespiegelten, gereihten oder fortlaufenden Szenen dekoriert.

Durch ihre Verzierung mit querformatigen Relieffriesen erinnern die treverischen Grabaltäre überdies in einigen Punkten an stadtrömische Sarkophage. Direkte typologische und kompositionelle Bezüge gibt es nicht, aber einzelne ikonografische Elemente werden aufgegriffen.

Die Grabaltäre im Treverergebiet haben also ein ganz eigenständiges Formen- und Bildrepertoire entwickelt. Es entstand eine singuläre und neben dieser Region nur vereinzelt in der benachbarten Provinz *Germania superior* verbreitete Form des Grabaltars, welche sich durch anspruchsvolle Gestaltung und hohe Spezifika auszeichnet. Einmal mehr zeigt sich, dass die Metropole Rom zwar eine hohe Strahlkraft besaß, aber nicht alle Impulse vom Zentrum ausgehen mussten. In den Provinzen bestanden der Wille sowie das Potenzial zu innovativen und individuellen Entwicklungen.

---

[43] Diese Feststellung korrespondiert mit der Tatsache, dass mythologische Darstellungen auf Grabdenkmälern in diesem Raum des Imperium Romanum eher selten sind. Klöckner 2020, 75.

## BIBLIOGRAFIE

| | |
|---|---|
| Boschung 1987 | D. Boschung, Antike Grabaltäre aus den Nekropolen Roms, Acta Bernensia 10 (Bern 1987) |
| Cüppers 1984 | H. Cüppers, Trier. Kaiserresidenz und Bischofssitz (Trier 1984) |
| Dexheimer 1998 | D. Dexheimer, Oberitalische Grabaltäre. Ein Beitrag zur Sepulkralkunst der römischen Kaiserzeit, BARIntSer 741 (Oxford 1998) |
| Ditsch 2011 | S. Ditsch, DIS MANIBUS. Die römischen Grabdenkmäler aus der Pfalz (Heidelberg 2011) |
| Gabelmann 1987 | H. Gabelmann, Römische Grabbauten der Nordprovinzen im 2. und 3. Jh., in: H. von Hesberg – P. Zanker (Hrsg.), Römische Gräberstraßen: Selbstdarstellung – Status – Standard. Kolloquium München 28.–30.10.1985 (München 1987) 291–308 |
| Henrich 2016 | P. Henrich, Überlegungen zum ursprünglichen Standort der »Neumagener Grabdenkmäler«, AKorrBl 46/3, 2016, 325–336 |
| Klöckner 2020 | A. Klöckner, Quelle, Fluss und Meer. Rezeptionslenkung durch Bezugsrahmen und Varianzstrategien am Beispiel des Secundiniergrabmals von Igel, in: A. Binsfeld – A. Klöckner – G. Kremer – M. Reuter – M. Scholz (Hrsg.), Stadt – Land – Fluss. Grabdenkmäler der Treverer in lokaler und überregionaler Perspektive. Akten der Internationalen Konferenz in Neumagen und Trier 25.–27.10.2018, TrZ Beih. 37 (Trier 2020) 73–83 |
| Numrich 1997 | B. Numrich, Die Architektur der römischen Grabdenkmäler aus Neumagen. Beiträge zur Chronologie und Typologie, TrZ Beih. 22 (Trier 1997) |
| Rumpf 1939 | A. Rumpf, Die Meerwesen auf den antiken Sarkophagreliefs, ASR V 1 (Berlin 1939) |
| Scholz 2012 | M. Scholz, Grabbauten des 1.–3. Jahrhunderts in den nördlichen Grenzprovinzen des Römischen Reiches I (Mainz 2012) |
| Schulz 2017 | J. Schulz, Meerwesen auf römischen Sarkophagen. Ikonographie und Bedeutung (Diss. Universität zu Köln 2017) |
| Scrinari 1972 | V. S. Scrinari, Museo archeologico nazionale di Aquileia: catalogo delle sculture romane (Rom 1972) |
| von Hesberg 1992 | H. von Hesberg, Römische Grabbauten (Darmstadt 1992) |
| von Massow 1932 | W. von Massow, Die Grabmäler von Neumagen. Römische Grabmäler des Mossellandes und der angrenzenden Gebiete II (Berlin 1932) |
| Willer 2005 | S. Willer, Römische Grabbauten des 2. und 3. Jahrhunderts nach Christus im Rheingebiet, BJb Beih. 56 (Mainz 2005) |
| Zanker – Ewald 2004 | P. Zanker – B. C. Ewald, Mit Mythen leben. Die Bilderwelt der römischen Sarkophage (München 2004) |

*Jakob Unterhinninghofen, Institut für Archäologische Wissenschaften Abt. II, Goethe-Universität Frankfurt, Norbert-Wollheim-Platz 1, Fach 7, 60629 Frankfurt am Main, Deutschland.*
*[e] unterhinninghofen@em.uni-frankfurt.de*